October 20–22, 2014
Rochester, NY, USA

I0036679

**Association for
Computing Machinery**

Advancing Computing as a Science & Profession

ASSETS'14

Proceedings of the The 16th International ACM SIGACCESS Conference on
Computers & Accessibility

Sponsored by:
ACM SIGACCESS

Supported by:
**National Science Foundation, Microsoft Research,
Rochester Institute of Technology & University of Rochester**

**Association for
Computing Machinery**

Advancing Computing as a Science & Profession

The Association for Computing Machinery
2 Penn Plaza, Suite 701
New York, New York 10121-0701

Notice to Past Authors of ACM-Published Articles
ACM intends to create a complete electronic archive of all articles and/or other material previously published by ACM. If you have written a work that has been previously published by ACM in any journal or conference proceedings prior to 1978, or any SIG Newsletter at any time, and you do NOT want this work to appear in the ACM Digital Library, please inform permissions@acm.org, stating the title of the work, the author(s), and where and when published.

ISBN: 978-1-4503-2720-6 (Digital)

ISBN: 978-1-4503-3380-1 (Print)

Additional copies may be ordered prepaid from:

ACM Order Department
PO Box 30777
New York, NY 10087-0777, USA

Phone: 1-800-342-6626 (USA and Canada)
+1-212-626-0500 (Global)
Fax: +1-212-944-1318
E-mail: acmhelp@acm.org
Hours of Operation: 8:30 am – 4:30 pm ET

Printed in the USA

ASSETS 2014 General Chair's Welcome

It is my pleasure to welcome you to ASSETS 2014, the Sixteenth International ACM SIGACCESS Conference on Computers and Accessibility, in Rochester, New York, USA, one of America's first boomtowns that rose to prominence as the site of many flour mills located on the Genesee River. The Rochester area is home to corporations such as Kodak, Bausch & Lomb and Xerox that conduct extensive research and manufacturing in the fields of industrial and consumer products. It is also home to academic and research institutions that conduct transformative medical and technological research, including University of Rochester and Rochester Institute of Technology as well as its National Technical Institute for the Deaf.

We are proud to continue the tradition of the ASSETS conference being the premier forum for presenting innovative research on mainstream and specialized assistive technologies, accessible computing, and assistive applications of computer, network, and information technologies. Our Program Chair, John Richards, and our Posters and Demo Chair, Adam Sporka, have assembled an impressive program, which also introduces new ways of presenting work in accessible computing, including the text entry challenge chaired by Torsten Felzer and the captioning challenge chaired for the second year by Raja Kushalnagar.

As a highlight of our conference program, we are delighted to have Professor Vicki Hanson, who is the 2014 winner of the ACM SIGACCESS Award for Outstanding Contribution to Computing and Accessibility, to present our keynote.

I am pleased to continue the tradition of the ASSETS conference as a welcoming venue for student researchers. I would like to thank Eelke Folmer for chairing our Student Research Competition (SRC) this year, with event sponsorship from Microsoft Research. In addition, I would like to thank Heidi Feng and Claude Chapdelaine for their work in chairing the Doctoral Consortium event for Ph.D. students this year, with generous support from the National Science Foundation.

There are many individuals who contributed to the success of ASSETS 2014. I would like to thank the other members of our organizing committee for their contributions to making the ASSETS 2014 conference a reality: Jeff Bigham (Treasurer and Registration Chair) for work on the conference budget and registration system, Harriet Fell (Mentoring Chair) for continuing the ASSETS tradition of supporting new members of the community, Stephanie Ludi (Local Arrangements Chair) for organizing the reception events and local preparations, Barbara Morris (Logistics Chair) for her work in ensuring the on-site conference details are executed flawlessly, Raja Kushalnagar (Accessibility Chair) for ensuring that ASSETS continues to be a model of how an accessible conference should be run, Hugo Nicolau (Web Chair) for designing and maintaining our informative and accessible website, and Kyle Montague (Publicity Chair) for engaging in a variety of media to spread the word and build excitement for ASSETS 2014. I'm also grateful for the guidance of our steering committee for the conference (Kathy McCoy, Matt Huenerfauth, Clayton Lewis, Andrew Sears, and Shari Trewin), for their valuable advice during the planning of ASSETS 2014.

Finally, I would like to thank University of Rochester and the Golisano College of Computing and Information Sciences of Rochester Institute of Technology for partnering with us in hosting the conference receptions, as well as to the National Technical Institute for the Deaf that kindly lent us their beautiful Rosita Hall for our conference reception.

Welcome to Rochester New York and to ASSETS 2014!

Sri Kurniawan
ASSETS'14 General Chair
University of California Santa Cruz, USA

ASSETS 2014 Program Chair's Welcome

I am pleased to introduce the technical program of ASSETS 2014, the Sixteenth International ACM SIGACCESS Conference on Computers and Accessibility. Our call for participation generated an outstanding set of technical paper, poster, demo, experience report, and text entry challenge submissions. A number of submissions for the ACM Student Research Competition and doctoral consortium were also received. The overall technical program is strong and balanced thanks to the efforts of the many area chairs who solicited and evaluated this work.

I especially thank our program committee, 51 senior members of our community who, along with 5 advanced doctoral students, carefully read the 106 submitted full technical papers from 20 countries and collectively produced 318 reviews. Of these submissions, 28 papers were selected for inclusion in this year's program for an overall technical paper acceptance rate of 26%. The posters and demos committee reviewed another 25 demo submissions choosing 18 for acceptance, and 56 poster submissions, choosing 28 for acceptance. I would also like to acknowledge the five members of the best paper committee who were given the difficult task of evaluating the most highly rated technical papers, selecting both a best paper and best student paper to be announced in the closing session.

This year's program is organized as follows. We begin Day 1 with a keynote presentation by this year's winner of the ACM SIGACCESS Award for Outstanding Contributions to Computing and Accessibility. This is followed by our first paper session examining independent navigation by blind users and technology to reduce social isolation. Our second paper session addresses accessibility-promoting practices and tools and will be followed by our first poster and demo session. We will then move to the campus of the Rochester Institute of Technology for demos, a special poster session featuring the work of participants in both the student research competition and the doctoral consortium, and our first of two receptions hosted by the Golisano College of Computing and Information Sciences and the National Institute for the Deaf at RIT.

Day 2 begins with a paper session on information access, examining efficient ways for blind users to navigate text and understand graphics. A second paper session on objects and interfaces looks at the use of 3D interfaces, the use of 3D printing in special education environments, and the first of two TACCESS presentations. TACCESS presentations are new this year and allow conference participants to hear directly from an author of work recently published in ACM's *Transactions on Accessible Computing*. Following this, we will hear presentations by this year's Student Research Competition finalists (finalists chosen on the basis of their poster presentations the previous evening). We will then conduct our SIGACCESS business meeting, hear about work in support of accessible interaction (including our second TACCESS presentation), and have our second poster and demo session. Following a reception at the Strong Museum of Play we will return to the conference hotel where people can participate in accumulating data for the text entry challenge.

Our final day begins with a look at applications and games for use by several target populations followed by a second paper session on issues of communication and website use. Our final paper session explores mobility issues and will be followed by the closing session featuring announcements of the winners of the student research competition, the text entry challenge, the captioning challenge, the best paper, and the best student paper.

I am confident you will find this year's program both valuable and memorable and join Sri in welcoming you to Rochester!

John Richards
ASSETS'14 Program Chair
IBM Watson Group, USA

Table of Contents

Keynote Address

Session: Independence
Session Chair: Kathy McCoy *(University of Delaware)*

Session: Practices and Tools
Session Chair: Faustina Hwang *(University of Reading)*

Session: Information Access
Session Chair: Shari Trewin *(IBM T.J. Watson Research Center)*

Session: Objects and Interfaces
Session Chair: Heidi Feng *(Towson University)*

Session: Interaction
Session Chair: Tiago Guerreiro *(University of Lisbon)*

Session: Applications and Games
Session Chair: Raja Kushalnagar *(National Technical Institute for the Deaf at Rochester Institute of Technology)*

Session: Communication
Session Chair: Matt Huenerfauth *(Rochester Institute of Technology)*

Session: Mobility

Session Chair: Jeffrey Bigham *(Carnegie Mellon University)*

Poster Abstracts

Demonstration Abstracts

Student Research Competition Abstracts

Text Entry Challenge Abstracts

ASSETS 2014 Conference Organization

General Chair: Sri Kurniawan *(University of California Santa Cruz, USA)*

Program Chair: John Richards *(IBM Watson Group, USA)*

Treasurer & Registration Chair: Jeff Bigham *(Carnegie Mellon University, USA)*

Poster & Demo Chair: Adam Sporka *(Czech Technical University in Prague, Czech Republic)*

Doctoral Consortium Chairs: Jinjuan Heidi Feng *(Towson University, USA)*
Claude Chapdelaine *(CRIM, Canada)*

Student Research Competition Chair: Eelke Folmer *(University of Nevada Reno, USA)*

Mentoring Chair: Harriet Fell *(Northeastern University, USA)*

Local Arrangements Chair: Stephanie Ludi *(Rochester Institute of Technology, USA)*

Logistics Chair: Barbara Morris *(University of Maryland Baltimore County, USA)*

Accessibility Chair: Raja Kushalnagar *(Rochester Institute of Technology, USA)*

Captioning Challenge Chair: Raja Kushalnagar *(Rochester Institute of Technology, USA)*

Text Entry Challenge Chair: Torsten Felzer *(Technical University Darmstadt, Germany)*

Web Chair: Hugo Nicolau *(Rochester Institute of Technology, USA)*

Publicity Chair: Kyle Montague *(University of Dundee, UK)*

Steering Committee Chair: Andrew Sears *(Rochester Institute of Technology, USA)*

Steering Committee: Matt Huenerfauth *(Rochester Institute of Technology, USA)*
Clayton Lewis *(University of Colorado Boulder, USA)*
Kathy McCoy *(University of Delaware, USA)*
Shari Trewin *(IBM T.J. Watson Research Center, USA)*

Program Committee:
* Best Paper Committee
Julio Abascal *(University of the Basque Country EHU, Spain)*
Armando Barreto *(Florida International University, USA)*
Jeffrey Bigham *(Carnegie Mellon University, USA)*
Giorgio Brajnik *(University of Udine, Italy)*
Anna Cavender *(Google, USA)*
Elliot Cole *(Institute for Cognitive Prosthestics, USA)*
James Coughlan *(Smith-Kettlewell Eye Research Institute, USA)*
Lynn Coventry *(Northumbria University, UK)*

Program Committee (continued):

Student Reviewers: Kyle Rector *(University of Washington, USA)*
Luz Rello *(Universitat Pompeu Fabra, Spain)*
Shiri Azenkot *(University of Washington)*
Jessica Tran *(University of Washington)*
Kristen Shinohara *(University of Washington)*

ASSETS 2014 Sponsors & Supporters

Sponsor: SIG ACCESS

Special Interest Group on Accessible Computing

Doctoral Consortium Supporter: NSF

Student Research Competition Supporter: Microsoft Research

Partners: R·I·T UNIVERSITY *of* ROCHESTER

Computing for Humans

Vicki L. Hanson [1]

Golisano College of Computing and Information Sciences
Rochester Institute of Technology
20 Lomb Memorial Drive
Rochester, NY USA 14623
vlh@acm.org

ABSTRACT

In his editorial on *Computing for Humans*, Vardi [1] discusses computing as being an "instrument of the human mind," having the primary goal to enhance what we as humans are able to do. Nowhere is such a computing goal more evident than in the field of accessibility where we seek to create devices and software to serve people with extreme needs. In creating novel accessibility tools, research has advanced the state of the art in many areas from design of environmental spaces, to physical interfaces, to software aspects of computing.

There are several cross-cutting issues that accessibility research can address. For example, there are issues of language and communication. Communication is fundamental to being human. People who have hearing loss, aphasia, cerebral palsy, autism, or dyslexia are among those who experience communication difficulties. How can we drive computing forward to provide solutions for these communication problems? Mobility and independence are other important issues. People with visual impairments, cognitive disability, or physical impairment often face difficulties in independent navigation. How can technology help?

The needs of users can and should inform the agenda for new research in areas such as augmented memory, physical interactions, and human communication.

Categories and Subject Descriptors

H.1.2 [**Information systems**]: User/Machine Systems – *Human information processing;* K.4.2 [**Computers and Society**] Social issues – *Assistive technologies for persons with disabilities.*

General Terms

Design, Experimentation, Human Factors.

Keywords

Accessibility.

Short Biography

Vicki Hanson is a Distinguished Professor at RIT within the HCI and Accessibility research groups. She also is Chair of Inclusive Technologies at the University of Dundee where she leads multiple efforts related to inclusion of older adults and individuals with disabilities. From 1986 – 2009 she was a Research Staff Member and Manager at IBM's T. J. Watson Research Center in New York, founding the Accessibility Research Group in 2000.

She received her PhD and M.A. in Cognitive Psychology from the University of Oregon, and a B.A. in Psychology from the University of Colorado. Her work on accessibility stemmed from language and educational access questions and over the years has grown to include development efforts to support the aging population and people with diverse abilities. For these efforts she has been recognized both by industry and academic honors, including and IBM Corporate Award, the Wolfson Research Merit Award from the Royal Society, and the Social Impact Award from ACM SIGCHI.

She currently serves as the ACM Vice President and as a member of the ACM-W Europe Executive Committee. She is Past Chair of SIGACCESS and was Co-Founder and Editor-in-Chief of *ACM Transitions on Accessible Computing.* She serves on Fellows Committees for ACM and the Royal Society of Edinburgh and has been active in conference organizing and program committees for ASSETS, CHI, and several other ACM conferences

She is a Fellow of the ACM, a Chartered Fellow of the British Computer Society, and a Fellow of the Royal Society of Edinburgh.

Acknowledgements

Work to be discussed in this talk was supported by RCUK grants EP/G066091/1 "RCUK Hub: Inclusion in the Digital Economy" and EP/K037293/1 "BESiDE – The Built Environment for Social Inclusion in the Digital Economy." The talk will also draw on discussions held during the Dagstuhl Seminar on "Augmenting Human Memory" (Dagstuhl, Germany, September 1 – 5, 2014).

Reference

[1] Vardi, M. 2011. Computing for humans. *Comm. of ACM, 54(12).* 5.

[1] Also School of Computing, University of Dundee, Dundee, Scotland DD1 4HN

The Blind Driver Challenge: Steering using Haptic Cues

Burkay Sucu and Eelke Folmer

Computer Science & Engineering - University of Nevada

{bsucu, efolmer}@cse.unr.edu

ABSTRACT

Loss of vision significantly impairs mobility, with blind individuals often relying on sighted individuals or public transportation to get around. Self-driving vehicles could significantly improve the mobility of blind people, but current legislation often requires a legal driver to be present in the vehicle who can take over in case of a malfunction. To enable blind people to eventually use a self-driving car independently, we present a steering interface that allows for steering a vehicle using haptic cues. User studies with six blind and sighted subjects identify what accuracy is required and possible using our interface to steer a vehicle on a track using a simulator. We investigate whether driving experience affects haptic steering performance and perform a qualitative study into the usability of our haptic steering interface.

Categories and Subject Descriptors

H.5.2 [**HCI**]: User Interfaces—*Haptic I/O*

Keywords

Haptics; Visual Impairment; Mobility; Steering.

1. INTRODUCTION

Reduced mobility and subsequent loss of independence severely reduces the quality of life for blind individuals and often leads to social isolation, depression, limited access to education, and fewer employment opportunities [14, 23]. Though various outdoor [28, 29] and indoor navigation systems [13, 17] have been developed, mobility is significantly constrained as these systems only support walking. To travel larger distances blind users often rely upon public transportation. Though public transportation is widely available in urban areas, in rural areas access may be limited. Blind individuals may also experience significant barriers due to a lack of accessible information pertaining schedules and announcements of stops [19]. Though more expensive, cars are considered a more usable form of transportation as they are not constrained to a fixed route and schedule.

Figure 1: A blind subject steering a vehicle in our simulator. Haptic actuators are placed on top of the hands that indicate either to steer to the left or right.

In 2004, the Jernigan Research Institute posed the National Federation of the Blind's *"Blind Driver Challenge"* [11], which challenged researchers and innovators to develop interface technologies that can empower blind people to drive a car independently as to increase their mobility. In recent years, several autonomous vehicles have been developed [10, 27], most notably, Google's driverless car. In recent trials, autonomous vehicles have successfully been used by blind people to get groceries or food [6]. The blind driver challenge, however, aims to be more ambitious by including a role for a blind individual as a pilot beyond being a passenger who just provides a destination. This challenge aims to spur innovation by enabling a blind driver to make informed driving decisions, such as steering and maintaining speed, using a nonvisual interface that can convey real-time information about the environment [11]. There is another important reason to investigate how blind people can drive a vehicle: current legislation doesn't allow blind people to use autonomous vehicles independently. Laws in both California and Florida require a licensed driver to be in the vehicle to take over control in case of a malfunction [1].

This paper makes the following contributions: (1) we improve a haptic steering interface developed in prior research [30] such to enable blind individuals to independently steer a vehicle on a track; (2) a comparative study with sighted and blind subjects identifies what accuracy is required for steering and what accuracy can be achieved with our haptic steering interface; and (3) we investigate whether prior driving experience affects steering performance.

2. RELATED WORK

As part of the blind driver challenge [11] a team from Virginia Tech modified an autonomous vehicle developed for DARPA's Urban Challenge [15] to allow for a blind user to drive this vehicle [21]. This system relies on an autonomous vehicle capable of determining its position on the road using GPS and a map of the environment with drivable roads. How much to steer is indicated using audio provided using a headset, e.g., sonification using frequency indicates the direction and magnitude of a turn. A modified massage chair provides haptic feedback to indicate speeding up or slowing down using a series of vibrotactors. A recent video shows their interface has been refined to convey steering cues using haptic feedback provided to the hands using an array of vibrotactors implemented in haptic gloves [7]. Beyond a number of public demonstrations, no results on the accuracy or usability of their interface are presented. This approach has a number of limitations: (1) several states, such as California, ban the use of headsets that cover both ears while driving [3]; (2) audio provided using a speaker may be annoying for passengers to hear; and (3) haptic gloves are expensive to construct as these generally are not commercially available [31]. Haptic gloves also require the driver to be tethered using cables, which may not be desirable when the driver needs to exit the vehicle quickly, i.e., in case of an emergency.

In recent years there has been increasing interest in improving automotive safety using haptic interfaces. For example, lane keeping [18] or lane changing [26] systems are commercially available where haptic cues warn the driver of impeding danger. Haptic feedback has some desirable properties over other modalities in that it is private and doesn't distract any passengers. Haptic feedback provided through a seat [21] or a belt may be impeded by the driver's clothes, as receptors in a driver's hips and back are not sensitive enough to distinguish complex stimuli [22]. Hands are very sensitive to haptic feedback due to an abundance of tactile receptors in the fingertips [8]. Haptic feedback provided through a steering wheel allows for robust and efficient communication of rich tactile information [24] as the driver is always holding it. Receiving feedback from the steering wheel itself may be more intuitive, as it may allow the driver to control the wheel using an associated physical mapping [24].

A number of haptic steering wheels have been developed. Enriquez et al. [16] was one of the first to implement a tactile display in a vehicle context. Different types of warnings are conveyed through pulsations of varying frequencies on the driver's hands by embedding inflatable pads in the steering wheel. User studies show a significant decrease in response time and demonstrate the feasibility of using frequency to convey different warnings. Griffiths and Gillespie [20] developed a driving simulator where the steering wheel is both held by the driver and motorized for automatic control. The motion of the steering wheel is a response to the sum of forces acting from the human grasp, from the automatic control motor, and from the steering linkage. Feeling the actions of the wheel, the driver can either comply with it or override it by applying more force. User studies show significant increase in the user's lane keeping ability while decreasing the visual demand and reaction time. Kern et al. [24] present a steering wheel with six integrated vibrotactors to convey navigation information to the driver. Spatial cues on the wheel indicate to turn left or right. User studies

Figure 2: Virginia Tech's solution for the NFB Blind driving challenge: steering cues are provided through a headset and haptic gloves.

evaluated the effectiveness of supplemental directional information in different modalities (audio/tactile) and found that haptic feedback impedes driving performance, with no significant effect for the other modalities. They further explored using dynamic patterns for conveying the steering direction, by sequentially activating vibrotactors in the direction the wheel needs to be turned. Qualitative results are reported with users preferring audio over haptic feedback. The "haptic steering wheel" [22] embeds 32 linear vibrotactors in a steering wheel, which allows for communicating information regardless of where the drivers hold their hands and further allows for displaying tactile illusions, such as sensory saltation. Spatial and temporal patterns (clockwise/counter-clock wise activation) are used to indicate whether to steer left or right, as well as to convey various types of alerts. User studies evaluate the user's ability to distinguish different spatial encodings, stimulus times and tactile illusions. Kim et al. present a haptic steering wheel with 20 vibrotactors [25]. Turning directions are indicated using clockwise or counterclockwise activation of vibrotactors. User studies evaluate multimodal feedback for younger and elderly drivers and found significant improvement in performance for haptic feedback.

Previous Work. Glare significantly diminishes visual perception, and is a significant cause of traffic accidents. Existing haptic steering interfaces only communicate warnings or high level navigation instructions. In previous research [30] we developed a haptic steering interface that enables safe steering when visibility is temporarily blocked. Our interface consists of a vibrotactor implemented on the left and the right side of a steering wheel that conveys how far the steering wheel needs to be turned; a value that we calculate a priori for a given curve. Three user studies with 12 sighted subjects were performed, the first study tried to develop a better understanding of driving using visual feedback, the second study evaluates steering using haptic cues (no visual feedback) with two different haptic encoding mechanisms. A third study evaluates the supplemental effect of haptic feedback when used in conjunction with visual feedback. Studies demonstrated this steering interface to safely steer a vehicle through curves up to 45°. We also demonstrated that a driver's lane keeping ability is improved when this interface is used in conjunction with visual feedback.

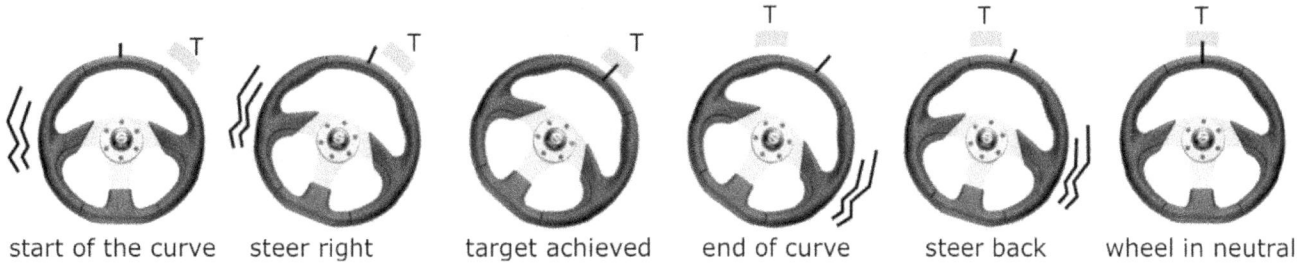

start of the curve   steer right   target achieved   end of curve   steer back   wheel in neutral

Figure 3: Information to steer the vehicle is conveyed using vibrotactors integrated in the left and right of the steering wheel. Similar to rumble strips, drivers steer away from a cue felt in either hand, in order to find a dead-band window that indicates the target orientation of the wheel, which changes as the car drives through the curve.

3. STEERING INTERFACE DESIGN

Similar to the existing solution for the NFB driving challenge [21], we aim for our haptic steering interface to allow for steering a vehicle on a racetrack. We only focus on the steering task rather controlling the speed of a vehicle, as steering is considered the most challenging part of driving a vehicle [30]. Though cruise control can be used to automatically maintain speed, a steering task must always be performed by a human driver (in most US states). Allowing blind drivers to adjust speed also makes it challenging to compare the performance of our steering interface between subjects. We therefore solve the steering problem independently from controlling a vehicle's speed.

Our steering interface extends the interface we developed in prior research [30]. This interface aims to allow for safe steering when the driver is temporarily limited, e.g., due to glare. This interface is inspired by how rumble strips or Bott's dots work. These raised markers or notches in the road provide a tactile sensation to a driver when they drift from their lane and when a haptic feedback is felt, intuitively drivers steer away from the side of the vehicle the tactile sensations are felt from. This interface exploits this natural mapping by integrating a vibrotactor in the left and the right side of a steering wheel. A preliminary study with steering using visual feedback found a linear relationship between the radius (r) of a curve and how far the steering wheel needs to be turned (T) [30]. For a given curvature we calculate (T) and when the driver enters the curve either vibrotactor is activated and the driver steers away from the side the vibrations are felt from until the haptic feedback stops and T is achieved (see Figure 3). When the driver approaches the end of the curve the target orientation of the wheel is reset to center and haptic feedback is provided accordingly. Because it is challenging to hold the wheel exactly at T, a dead-band window of w is defined around the target position, in which no vibrotactile feedback is felt and this minimizes drivers oscillating between turning the wheel left or right. Using a larger w reduces oscillations but reduces the accuracy of steering through the curve. This interface has been evaluated using a simulator to steer through curves using a fixed speed without visual feedback. Different types of haptic feedback provision were explored with a simple on/off encoding yielding a significantly better performance than using frequency modulation to convey how far to turn the wheel.

A limitation of this interface is that it only approximates the target orientation of the wheel for a given curve, but doesn't try to correct for the actual position of the vehicle on

the road. If the driver steers too early or too late or doesn't hold the wheel exactly at T, the car's position will follow the shape of the curve, but not follow the lane's median as it will deviate. Small lane deviations may be acceptable when the driver is only temporarily blinded and the driver can correct their position on the road when visibility returns. For letting a blind person steer a vehicle, small deviations will accumulate and rapidly grow unbounded, with the car eventually leaving the track. A self-correction mechanism could help a blind driver steer the car back to the median of the track after a deviation occurs due to steering through a curve. In theory, this may allow a blind driver to safely steer a car around the track.

3.1 Self-Correction Mechanism

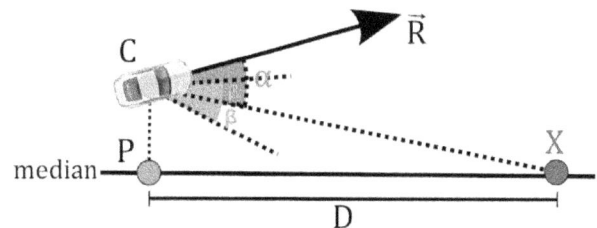

Figure 4: Calculating the car's target position T on the median, α is outside the window around $\vec{R}$ and a haptic steering cue is provided.

A self-correction mechanism was implemented as follows. We first calculate the target position X of the vehicle on the track's median (see Figure 4). The current position of the car is point C, and the orientation of the car is vector $\vec{R}$. Point P is the projection of C on the median of the track. After finding P, the target position X is found by adding a distance D on the median. When X or P are on a curve, D is the length of the arc between P and X. To keep calculations simple, we constrain the shape of our track to one that includes $180°$ circular curves. Then the angle α between $\vec{R}$ and $\overrightarrow{CX}$ is calculated. Haptic cues need to be provided such that the driver will change the current direction of the vehicle $\vec{R}$ to $\overrightarrow{CX}$. To avoid small oscillations, a dead-band window of size β is implemented around $\overrightarrow{CX}$ (see Figure 4). Having a window with a fixed size in terms of angles enables the car come and stay closer to the median and prevents crossing over the median to the other side, since the radius of the target window gets smaller as the car gets closer to the median (see Figure 5).

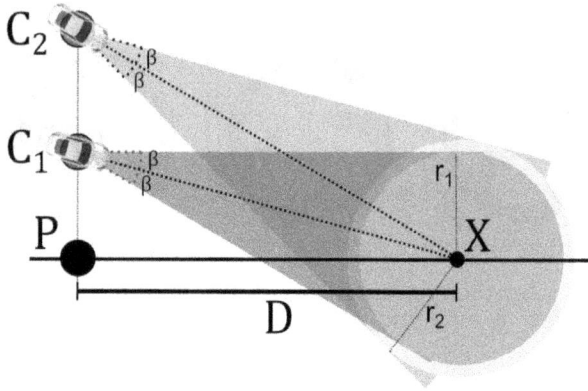

Figure 5: The Dead-band window as a circular target, whose radius changes depending on the distance of the car from the median.

Figure 7: Screenshot of the simulator we developed that shows the third person perspective on the vehicle.

The way haptic feedback is provided is significantly different from the haptic steering interface we developed in prior work [30] as the haptic feedback provision only considers the rotation of the steering wheel and not the actual position of the vehicle on the road. This interface specifically aims to avoid oscillations, where our improved interface relaxes this constraint, and we anticipate this will allow a blind driver to more closely follow the median. If $\vec{R}$ is outside the window, i.e. $\alpha > \beta$, haptic feedback is provided. We calculate |LX| i.e, the distance from the front left corner of the car to point X and |RX| i.e., the distance from the front right corner of the car to point X. If |LX| < |RX|, we activate the right vibrotactor and otherwise the left vibrotactor. Similar to our prior interface [30] a simple on/off encoding was used as this yielded a better performance than using haptic feedback modulation.

4. STEERING USING VISUAL FEEDBACK

We first conducted a user study with sighted subjects steering a vehicle on a track using visual information. This establishes a baseline which can be used to compare the performance of our haptic steering interface with.

4.1 Instrumentation

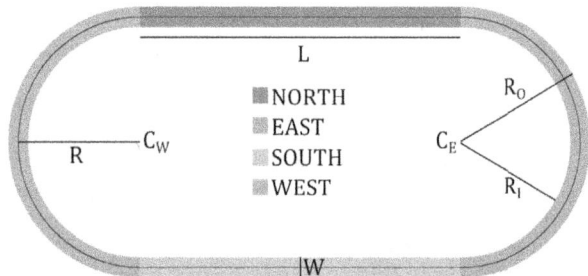

Figure 6: Layout of the Bristol Motor Speedway Track

We created a simulator by modifying an open source driving simulator created in Microsoft XNA [5]. Drivers see a vehicle from a 3rd person perspective on a track (see Figure 7). We use this view as opposed to an overhead view as this view yields a significantly better driving performance [9]. We implemented the Bristol Motor Speedway [2], as shown in Figure 6. This track was chosen due to its relatively small size. We did not include any banking or speeding zones and used a fixed track width. Instead of using elliptic arcs, we used circular arcs, to avoid complex calculations for our self-correction mechanism. The four different segments of the track are illustrated with four different colors in the figure and henceforth the name of each cardinal direction is used to indicate each segment. Our track needs three parameters to be formed: (1) the length of the straight section L; (2) the width of the road W; and (3) the radius (R) of the circular sections East and West. To make it similar to the Bristol Motor Speedway, the parameters, L, W, and R, are assigned the values 200m, 6.1m, and 75m, respectively. The resulting track is 871m measured from its median, slightly longer than the 858m Bristol track. Barriers are placed in the inner and outer edge of the track.

For our user study, we use a constant speed to allow for a performance comparison between subjects. For a curve radius of 75m the department of transportation recommends a speed of 48km/h [4] but since our simulator doesn't take friction into account, we set the speed of the car in the simulator to 50km/h. This value was also chosen because this requires approximately 17 seconds of steering input from the driver, while steering through the circular sections. This is long enough to evaluate the effectiveness of our haptic steering interface. For input, we used a simulator grade racing wheel, the Logitech G27 Racing Wheel, with an 28 cm diameter (see Figure 8) that was attached to a desk. Every 10ms, we log the position of the car and the position of the steering wheel. Drivers don't control the speed of the vehicle but start the vehicle by pressing the gas pedal peripheral once with their foot which will cause the car to immediately drive at the target speed. To indicate whether car is moving or waiting for a subject to push the gas pedal, an engine sound is used. We use a short audio file that is played in a loop, and which does not convey any information about the performance of steering.

4.2 Participants

We recruited six sighted individuals (3 females, average age 31.3, SD=12.5). All were right handed and none reported any non-correctable impairments in perception or

6

Table 1: Steering using visual feedback (stdev)

DIRECTION	PART	AVG DEVIATION (M)	AVG CRASHES
Clockwise	Curves	.58 (.08)	0 (0)
	Straights	.62 (.15)	0 (0)
	Combined	.60 (.11)	0 (0)
Counter Clockwise	Curves	.61 (.05)	0 (0)
	Straights	.69 (.13)	0 (0)
	Combined	.65 (.06)	0 (0)
All	Curves	.60 (.06)	0 (0)
	Straights	.66 (.13)	0 (0)
	Combined	.63 (.08)	0 (0)

motor control. On average, participating subjects had 12.3 years (SD= 13.3) of driving experience.

4.3 Procedure

Subjects were invited into our lab and seated in front of the steering wheel with the pedals placed under their feet. A 27" display was used to show the simulator in fullscreen mode. Subjects were asked to drive on the median of the track, but we did not render any stripes to indicate the median. Subjects were allowed to try a few laps for practice as to minimize any learning effects and when they felt comfortable enough, the trial would start. The start of the track is located in the middle of the north section. The car is positioned in the middle of the start line, facing east or west. Initially the car stops and as soon as the driver hits the gas pedal once, it accelerates to 50 km/h. After 4 laps, the car is stopped and teleported to the start position but facing in the opposite direction from which it started. When the car hits the barrier, a crash sound is played and the car stops and turns to the target point calculated in the last frame before the crash. When car is stopped due to a crash or when changing directions after first 4 laps are completed, the driver is required to hit the gas pedal again to get the car going. Subjects completed 8 laps; which included 4 clockwise and 4 counter-clockwise laps. The order of direction was randomized between subjects. It took ±10 minutes to complete the trial.

4.4 Results

For every single trial, we calculated the standard deviation of the vehicle from the median of the track, for the curve, the straight part as well as the complete track, split up by clockwise and counterclockwise laps. Table 1 shows the result of this experiment. In addition to the standard deviation, we also list the average number of crashes per subject. We achieve an overall average standard deviation from the median of .63 meters (SD=.08). For an α of .05, there was no difference in standard deviation between curves and straights ($t_{10} = 1.027$, $p = .33$) and between clockwise and counterclockwise laps ($t_{10} = .978$, $p = .35$). None of the sighted subjects crashed.

5. STEERING USING HAPTIC CUES

A second user study with blind and sighted users focused on analyzing the performance and accuracy of our steering interface and to determine whether prior driving experience of sighted users would lead to a difference in performance. A brief qualitative study was performed with blind users to understand the usability and usefulness of our steering interface and to collect suggestions for improvements.

5.1 Instrumentation

We used the same steering wheel and setup as for our first experiment. For haptic feedback provision, we used a commercially available wireless motion-sensing controller (Sony Playstation Move), which has an integrated vibrotactor that allows for frequency modulation with a perceivable range of 91 to 275Hz. Similar to our prior interface [30] a controller was attached to each side of the steering wheel using tape. Preliminary trials with using this setup showed that it was sometimes difficult for users to interpret which vibrotactor was active due to resonation problems. Tactile resonance may be avoided by modifying the steering wheel and embedding vibrotactors in each side using a proper amount of insulation. We ended up with an alternative solution that mitigates the resonance problem by mounting the Sony Move controllers to the back of the subjects' hands using straps. The simulator communicates with the Sony Move controllers using a Bluetooth connection. When connected, the Move controllers LED light up using a different color as to distinguish each controller, but this does not convey any other visual information. For the self-correction mechanism a number of parameters, such as D, β were determined experimentally. For D, we experimented with different values of D and found that a tradeoff needs to be made between requiring very fast responses from the driver (as it will steer quickly to the median) versus significantly increasing the average deviation from the median (as it takes longer for the car to reach the median). We ended up choosing a value (15.9m) based on how far the car travels in 1 second (13.9m) plus some small offset (2m) to accommodate for the length of the car and use the center of the car as its position. Using a number of preliminary trials with different values, a value of 6° for β was found to yield the smallest average deviation. Because there is a small delay before each vibrotactor is activated, haptic cues are provided 380ms ahead of when the user must steer in order to accommodate this delay. This value was determined experimentally. We use a simple on/off cue with haptic feedback provided at a frequency (275Hz) that the human skin is most sensitive to. Every 10ms, we log the position of the car on the track, the position of the steering wheel and when a vibrotactor is active.

5.2 Participants

A between subject study was performed with sighted and blind subjects to test whether there was a difference in performance due to driving experience. We recruited six sighted individuals (2 females, average age 26.3, SD=2.0). All were right handed and none reported any non-correctable impairments in perception or motor control. On average, participating subjects had 5.8 years (SD=3.8) of driving experience. Our second group of subjects included blind individuals recruited through a local chapter of the National Federation of the Blind. An inclusion criterion for our study was being blind with no prior driving experience. We recruited six subjects (2 females, average age 46.0, SD=12.5). Five subjects were totally blind with one being legally blind. All were right handed with no impairments in tactile perception or motor control. None of the blind subjects had any driving experience or had used a driving simulator before.

Figure 8: Haptic feedback is provided using Sony Playstation Move controllers to indicate in which direction to steer. The controllers are attached to the back of the driver's hands to avoid tactile resonance problems.

5.3 Procedure

Subjects were invited into our lab and seated in front of the steering wheel and the pedals of the racing wheel kit were placed under their feet. A Sony Move controller is attached to each backhand using their fabric straps (see Figure 1). The display was turned 180° and was only visible to an observer who was present during the trial. Prior to the trial, we explained to subjects how to interpret the haptic feedback, e.g., feel a cue on your left turn right, and we gave feedback on their performance during the familiarization phase. We encouraged subjects to steer using small turns and immediately steering back to neutral as not to oversteer. Both subject groups were allowed to try a number of laps for practice as to minimize any learning effects and when they felt comfortable enough, the trials would start. Subjects completed a total of 8 laps; which included 4 clockwise and 4 counter-clockwise laps. The order of direction was randomized between subjects.

5.4 Results

The standard deviation from the track's median was calculated and reported in the same way as for our first study. Table 2 and Table 3 shows the results for the sighted and blind subjects, respectively. In addition to the standard deviation, we also list the average number of crashes per subject. For the sighted subjects, one subject crashed three times, one subject twice, one subject once and three subjects did not crash. Crashes seemed uniformly distributed over the laps, with 83% of crashes occurring in curves. Two blind subjects crashed twice, and three subjects only once and one didn't crash. 57% of crashes occurred in the first lap and 71% were in curves. Only a single crash occurred in the last three laps. For the standard deviation, no significant difference (sighted/blind) between the curves and the straight parts ($p = 0.173/.454$) and between directions ($p = .269/.077$) was detected. For the average number of crashes, no significant difference (sighted/blind) between the curves and the straight parts ($p = .128/.383$) and between directions ($p = .173/.705$) was detected. Because of these results our analysis focuses on the combined standard deviation and the average number of crashes for the whole track.

Table 2: Results for 6 sighted subjects (stdev)

DIRECTION	PART	AVG DEVIATION (M)	AVG CRASHES
Clockwise	Curves	.82 (.15)	.33 (.47)
	Straights	.88 (.13)	0 (0)
	Combined	.85 (.13)	.33 (.47)
Counter Clockwise	Curves	.87 (.20)	.50 (.50)
	Straights	1.04 (.22)	.17 (.37)
	Combined	.96 (.19)	.66 (.75)
All	Curves	.85 (.17)	.83 (.90)
	Straights	.99 (.16)	.17 (.37)
	Combined	.91 (.16)	1.00 (1.15)

Table 3: Results for 6 blind subjects (stdev)

DIRECTION	PART	AVG DEVIATION (M)	AVG CRASHES
Clockwise	Curves	.88 (.13)	.17 (.37)
	Straights	.96 (.15)	.33 (.47)
	Combined	.92 (.13)	.50 (.76)
Counter Clockwise	Curves	1.04 (.25)	.67 (.74)
	Straights	1.12 (.15)	0 (0)
	Combined	1.08 (.15)	.67 (.75)
All	Curves	.97 (.17)	.83 (.69)
	Straights	1.04 (.14)	.33 (.47)
	Combined	1.01 (.12)	1.16 (.69)

A one-way MANOVA found no statistically significant difference in steering performance (standard deviation, crashes) between sighted and blind subjects ($F_{2,9} = .616$, $p = .562$, Wilk's $\lambda = .880$, partial $\varepsilon^2 = .120$). There was homogeneity of variances, as assessed by Levene's Test ($p > .05$). A statically significant difference in standard deviation ($t_{10} = 4.433$, $p = .0013$) was found between blind subjects and sighted subjects driving using visual feedback, e.g., the results from our first study.

We also analyzed reaction time between both groups of subjects, e.g., the time between when a haptic cue was provided and when the driver started to turn the steering wheel or adjust the direction in which it was turned. Using the log files, we calculated an average response time of 269 milliseconds (SD=52) for blind and 350 ms (SD=50) for sighted subjects. There was a statistically significant difference between these response times ($t_{10} = 2.734$, $p = .021$).

5.5 Qualitative Results

Qualitative experiences from blind subjects were collected after the trial using non-directed interviews. The usability and effectiveness of our haptic steering interface was evaluated using a 5-point Likert scale that ranged from 1 (strongly disagree) to 5 (strongly agree). All subjects expressed that they really enjoyed using the driving simulator (M=4.83, SD=.41) with three of them stating that this was the first time they had ever driven a simulator. Five subjects found that our haptic steering interface was easy to learn to use (M=4.50, SD=1.89) with one subject stating that the haptic interface by itself was difficult to learn to use, but that the verbal instructions were essential in learning how to use it. All subjects agreed that our interface allows for accurately steering a vehicle on a track (M=4.67, SD=0.52). All subjects agreed that the haptic mapping used to convey steering directions was intuitive and comfortable (M=5.00, SD=.00), though one subject noted that an inverse mapping could also have been used. Another subject stated that using a stronger vibration could probably improve performance. All subjects thought our interface could eventually be used for steering a real vehicle (M=4.67, SD=0.52), but two subjects admitted they were unsure how to answer this question, as they had never driven a vehicle.

Open-ended questions were used to collect suggestions for improvements, which included (# of subjects that made this comment): (a) Allow for controlling the speed of the car and shifting gears (3); (b) Support driving in more realistic (non-track) environments, e.g., a city (3); (c) Use frequency modulation to indicate how far to steer (1); (d) Add opponents to race against (2); (e) Add more tracks with more difficult curves that include hairpins and chicanes (2); and (f) Verbally announce the lap time or a score (2). The last three suggestions seem to imply that we turn the driving simulator into a racing game, in which two subjects were very interested in.

6. DISCUSSION

Comparison. We are unable to make a performance comparison between our approach and the existing solution for the Blind driver challenge [21] as no quantitative results on the accuracy of their steering interface are reported. However, public demonstrations have demonstrated it to be effective in a real vehicle [7]. Our previous haptic steering interface [30] achieved an average standard deviation of 2.97m (SD=1.720) for a 180° curve. Our improved interface achieves an average standard deviation of .97m (SD=.17), which demonstrates that a self-correction mechanism significantly reduces deviation. Our first study with sighted drivers steering using visual feedback yields an average standard deviation of .63m (SD=.08) which was significantly lower than the average standard deviation achieved using haptic feedback. Sighted drivers that drove using visual feedback did not crash at all, where blind drivers mostly crashed in the first laps (only 1 crash in the last 3 laps) and this number could further decrease when blind drivers become more proficient with our interface over time. Given that in the US lanes have an average width of 3.7m and that cars have an average width of 1.83m, we believe the standard deviation achieved with our haptic steering interface would allow for safe driving. Regular roads rarely involve 180° curves and steering through smaller curvatures should reduce deviation [30].

Limitations. Our haptic steering interface was tested in a simulator and not in a real vehicle. However, for designing a suitable interface, a simulator has a number of benefits as it allows for accurately measuring the position of the vehicle on the track and we don't have to worry about serious consequences when a driver crashes their vehicle. Because we were interested in testing whether prior driving experience would affect haptic steering performance, subject recruitment was restricted to recruiting blind subjects without any driving experience, which we found were difficult to recruit. Our study did not involve controlling the speed of the vehicle or detecting obstacles. Driving a vehicle on a track without any obstacles is a task where an autonomous vehicle most likely can outperform a human driver, but currently humans are better at driving a vehicle in traffic. As we only focus on steering performance, one could argue that our solution merely has a blind driver rely instructions from the computer to the steering wheel, which to an extent is true. Nevertheless a usable and effective steering interface with a study that presents quantitative data is an important step towards letting blind people drive vehicles independently, where in future work the presence of other traffic will be conveyed using non-visual means.

Differences. We detected a significant difference in response time to haptic cues between sighted and blind drivers, which confirms the observation that blind individuals have a greater sensitivity to haptic feedback, due to the so called plasticity effect [12]. No significant difference in haptic steering performance between sighted and blind users was found, which seems to support our claim that prior driving experience has no effect on using our steering interface. However, because steering using haptic feedback is significantly different from steering using visual feedback, it could be that there are no transfer effects between these modalities. Alternatively, prior driving experience does affect haptic steering performance but this effect is neutralized by that blind drivers responded faster to haptic steering cues. It is difficult to answer this question, as individuals that are blind that have recent (< 5 years) driving experience may not have developed a greater proficiency to haptic feedback as cross-modal plasticity typically takes years to develop [12]. User studies with blind drivers with recent driving experience may or may not show a significant improvement in steering performance when compared to blind drivers without prior driving experience.

7. FUTURE WORK

Integration. We will focus on integrating and evaluating our haptic steering interface in an autonomous vehicle and in more realistic driving environments, but this requires solving a number of problems. Currently our interface enables a blind driver to steer using small oscillations, which helps the vehicle stay close to the median. To an outsider however, the vehicle looks like it is swerving and the driver may appear inebriated, which may be socially undesirable.

Current legislation requires a legal driver to be present in the vehicle who can take over in case of a malfunction [1]. If an autonomous vehicle breaks down, we may not be able to rely on its sensors to determine the vehicles position and other traffic. To allow a blind driver to drive their car to a service point, we can imagine our haptic steering interface to evolve into a rudimentary backup system that uses its own set of sensors. A benefit of our system is that it is relatively low cost to install as vibrotactors do not need to be embedded in the steering wheel but external vibrotactors, i.e., such as those available in motion sensing controllers could be used that can be worn by a blind driver. An approximate orientation of the steering wheel can also be found using the controllers' internal gyroscopes, which avoids having to fully integrate our system with the car's system.

Racing Game. The suggestions posed by two blind subjects to develop our simulator into a fully-fledged racing game is something that we will consider for future research, especially considering that very few games are accessible to blind gamers [32]. In addition to adding different tracks, adding controls for speed and allowing the driver to shift gears, (multiplayer) opponents could be added, but this would require conveying much more information than steering information alone.

8. CONCLUSION

The development of a vehicle that can be driven independently by blind users has great potential to significantly increase their mobility and quality of life. Current legislation, however, requires a licensed driver to be present in the vehicle to take over control in case of a malfunction. This paper presents a haptic steering interface that lets blind people steer a vehicle using haptic cues. Our work innovates over existing work, in that we identify what accuracy is required –and possible– for steering using a haptic interface. We identify that prior driving experience does not affect the performance of haptic steering with no difference in performance found between sighted and blind subjects. Blind drivers respond faster to haptic cues than sighted drivers. Results of this research could eventually allow for blind people to use autonomous vehicles independently.

9. REFERENCES

[1] Automated driving: Legislative and regulatory action, http://cyberlaw.stanford.edu/wiki/index.php/Automated_Driving:_Legislative_and_Regulatory_Action.

[2] Bristol motor speedway. http://www.bristolmotorspeedway.com/.

[3] Department of Motor Vehicle vc section 27400 wearing of headsets or earplugs, http://www.dmv.ca.gov/pubs/vctop/d12/vc27400.htm.

[4] Department of Transportation, roadway design manual, http://www.state.nj.us/transportation/eng/documents/RDM/sec4.shtm.

[5] Driving simulator in XNA, http://www.codeproject.com/Articles/29323/Driving-Simulation-in-XNA, access date: 4-6-2012.

[6] Google self-driving car test: Steve Mahan, http://www.youtube.com/watch?v=cdgQpa1pUUE.

[7] National federation of the blind's blind driving challenge: http://www.youtube.com/watch?v=Z2ciYRB2roA.

[8] Bach-y Rita, P., and Kercel, S. Sensory substitution and the human-machine interface. *Trends in Cognitive Sciences* 7:12 (2003), 541–546.

[9] Bateman, S., Doucette, A., Xiao, R., Gutwin, C., Mandryk, R. L., and Cockburn, A. Effects of view, input device, and track width on video game driving. In *Proc of GI '11*, 207–214.

[10] Baldwin, I., and Newman, P. Laser-only road-vehicle localization with dual 2d push-broom lidars and 3d priors. In *Proc. of IROS'12*, 2490–2497.

[11] National Federation of the Blind: The blind driver challenge, http://www.blinddriverchallenge.org.

[12] Cohen, L. G., Celnik, P., Pascual-Leone, A., Corwell, B., Falz, L., Dambrosia, J., Honda, M., Sadato, N., Gerloff, C., Catalá, M. D., and Hallett, M. Functional relevance of cross-modal plasticity in blind humans. *Nature* 389, (1997), 180–3.

[13] Coughlan, J., and Manduchi, R. A mobile phone wayfinding system for visually impaired users. In *Proc of AAATE'09* .

[14] Crewe, J. M., Morlet, N., Morgan, W. H., Spilsbury, K., Mukhtar, A., Clark, A., Ng, J. Q., Crowley, M., and Semmens, J. B. Quality of life of the most severely vision impaired. *Clin Experiment Ophthalmol* (Nov 2010).

[15] Darpa urban challenge, http://archive.darpa.mil/grandchallenge/.

[16] Enriquez, M., Afonin, O., Yager, B., and Maclean, K. A pneumatic tactile alerting system for the driving environment. In *Proc. of PUI '01*, 1–7.

[17] Fallah, N., Apostolopoulos, I., Bekris, K., and Folmer, E. The user as a sensor: navigating users with visual impairments in indoor spaces using tactile landmarks. In *Proc. of CHI '12*, 425–432.

[18] Ford lane keeping system, http://media.ford.com/article_display.cfm?article_id=35776.

[19] Golledge, R., Costanzo, C. M., and Marston, J. Public transit use by non-driving disabled persons: The case of the blind and vision impaired. Institute of Transportation Studies, Research Reports (1996).

[20] Griffiths, P., and Gillespie, R. Shared control between human and machine: haptic display of automation during manual control of vehicle heading. In *Proc. of HAPTICS'04*, 358 – 366.

[21] Hong, D., Kimmel, S., Boehling, R., Camoriano, N., Cardwell, W., Jannaman, G., Purcell, A., Ross, D., and Russel, E. Development of a semi-autonomous vehicle operable by the visually-impaired. In *Proc. of MFI'08*, 539 –544.

[22] Hwang, S., and hee Ryu, J. The haptic steering wheel: Vibro-tactile based navigation for the driving environment. In *Proc. of PERCOM'10*, 660 –665.

[23] Kempen, G. I. J. M., Ballemans, J., Ranchor, A. V., van Rens, G. H. M. B., and Zijlstra, G. A. R. The impact of low vision on activities of daily living. *Qual Life Res* (2011).

[24] Kern, D., Marshall, P., Hornecker, E., Rogers, Y., and Schmidt, A. Enhancing navigation information with tactile output embedded into the steering wheel. In *Pervasive Computing'09*, 42–58.

[25] Kim, S., Hong, J.-H., Li, K., Forlizzi, J., and Dey, A. Route guidance modality for elder driver navigation. In *Pervasive Computing'12*, 179–196.

[26] Smartmicro's lane change assist system. http://www.smartmicro.de/index.php/en/automotive-radar/lane-change-assist.

[27] Levinson, J., and Thrun, S. Robust vehicle localization in urban environments using probabilistic maps. In *Proc. of ICRA'10*, 4372–4378.

[28] Loomis, J. M., Golledge, R. G., and Klatzky, R. L. Navigation system for the blind: Auditory display modes and guidance. vol. 7, (1998), 193–203.

[29] Ross, D. A., and Lightman, A. Talking braille: a wireless ubiquitous computing network for orientation and wayfinding. In *Proc. of ASSETS'05*, 98–105.

[30] Sucu, B., and Folmer, E. Haptic interface for non-visual steering. In *Proc. of IUI '13*, 427–434.

[31] Yuan, B., and Folmer, E. Blind hero: enabling guitar hero for the visually impaired. In *Proc. of ASSETS'08*, 169–176.

[32] Yuan, B., Folmer, E., and Harris, Jr., F. C. Game accessibility: a survey. *Universal Access in the Information Society 10* (2011), 81–100.

Where's My Bus Stop? Supporting Independence of Blind Transit Riders with StopInfo

Megan Campbell, Cynthia Bennett, Caitlin Bonnar, and Alan Borning
Department of Computer Science & Engineering
University of Washington
Seattle, Washington 98195
{meganca,bennec3,cbonnar,borning}@cs.washington.edu

ABSTRACT

Locating bus stops, particularly in unfamiliar areas, can present challenges to people who are blind or low vision. At the same time, new information technology such as smart phones and mobile devices have enabled them to undertake a much greater range of activities with increased independence. We focus on the intersection of these issues. We developed and deployed StopInfo, a system for public transit riders that provides very detailed information about bus stops with the goal of helping riders find and verify bus stop locations. We augmented internal information from a major transit agency in the Seattle area with information entered by the community, primarily as they waited at these stops. Additionally, we conducted a five week field study with six blind and low vision participants to gauge usage patterns and determine values related to independent travel. We found that StopInfo was received positively and is generally usable. Furthermore, the system supports tenets of independence; participants took public transit trips that they might not have attempted otherwise. Lastly, an audit of bus stops in three Seattle neighborhoods found that information from both the transit agency and the community was accurate.

Categories and Subject Descriptors

K.4.2 [**Computers and Society**]: Social Issues—*Assistive technologies for persons with disabilities*; H.5.2 [**Information Interfaces and Presentation**]: User Interfaces—*User-centered design*

General Terms

Design; Experimentation; Human Factors

Keywords

Public transit; tools for blind and low vision riders; accessible transit stops; community-sourcing; crowdsourcing

1. INTRODUCTION

Public transit plays a key role in the lives of many blind and low vision people by providing access to employment, education, shopping, medical services, friends and family, and recreation. However, significant barriers to its use still abound [1]. Consequently, blind and low vision people often resort to other means of travel such as taxis, paratransit, or rides from others, particularly for unfamiliar routes and destinations [14]. This can be more expensive, less convenient, involve imposing on others, and result in less independence.

One specific challenge for blind and low vision bus riders is locating and verifying bus stop locations, particularly in new or unfamiliar areas [1]. They often search for physical landmarks such as the bus shelter, benches, or transit sign as a cue that they have reached the stop, but the design and location of the stop relative to the intersection are frequently quite variable.

We present StopInfo, which builds upon a widely-used transit application called OneBusAway[1] to provide very detailed information about transit stops, tailored to the needs of blind and low vision riders. We collaborated with King County Metro, a local transit agency in the Puget Sound region, to seed StopInfo's information with their internal data on bus stops. We then constructed an interface that allows the community to verify this data, or add additional information not found in Metro's database.

We present results from a five week deployment of StopInfo to six blind and low vision participants. We also demonstrate how collaborating with a local transit agency and the community produces accurate information through a StopInfo information audit of three Seattle neighborhoods' bus stops.

We investigated the following research questions:

1. Was StopInfo usable, and was the information helpful to blind and low vision transit riders?

2. Did our participants attempt public transit trips with StopInfo that they would not have otherwise?

3. Did our participants feel confident traveling to unfamiliar destinations with StopInfo?

4. Did StopInfo use contribute to our participants' feeling of safety while traveling?

5. Was the aggregate of information from the transit agency and the community accurate?

---

[1]http://onebusaway.org

Our key findings include a successful deployment where StopInfo was usable and helpful. We determined that independence was an important value for blind and low vision transit riders, confirming prior work [1]. StopInfo supported independence by providing information helpful to attempting previously unattainable and unfamiliar trips. However, StopInfo did not affect feelings of confidence traveling and safety in public. This could indicate that blind and low vision people similar to our sample employ tools and strategies to maintain active lifestyles, but are encouraged by new tools like StopInfo, which fill current wayfinding information gaps. Overall, we found that the information disseminated by StopInfo was highly accurate (97.3%) for key fields such as the stop position relative to the intersection, with lower accuracy for more ambiguous fields.

2. RELATED WORK

Prior Work. This work builds upon prior work performed by our group, in which *independence* and *safety* were identified as two key values for visually impaired transit riders [1]. Azenkot et al. investigated the efficacy of providing information about bus stops through a system they developed called GoBraille, which allows blind and deaf-blind riders to access information about bus stops through a wireless Braille display connected to a smartphone. Our work differs in that we utilize the built-in accessibility features on the iPhone such as VoiceOver, and integrate it in to a mainstream transit application used by the general population of public transit riders. By doing so, we enable collection of bus stop information from transit riders already at bus stops, and allow for the dynamic creation of new information categories that can be filled in by the public. Another important difference is that we have deployed a working system that is actually used by blind riders for day-to-day transportation needs. We report the experiences of a small number of participants from our field study, but the system is ready for widespread use. Prasain [19] describes a prototype version of the StopInfo system, called StopFinder, consisting of a standalone iPhone app and sample data for a stop for user testing. The system was well received by the blind community, encouraging us to pursue the work reported here. In 2013, Hara et al. developed a way for crowd workers like those on Mechanical Turk to use pictures of stops on Google Street View to label features of bus stops with 82.5% accuracy [14]. However, accuracy was reliant on the quality of the picture on Google Street View; stops were occasionally obscured by a moving car or pedestrians. StopInfo differs in that it collects stop information within an application that riders often check while waiting at the stop.

Navigation and wayfinding. Research on navigation and wayfinding for blind travelers is extensive. Some of the research has been translated into practice by orientation and mobility professionals, commonly referred to as O&M instructors. O&M instructors teach blind travelers skills including how to use a white cane or dog guide, how to find their way from one point to another, how to cross streets safely, and how to use public transportation. More recently, interest in technology-based wayfinding solutions, such as using GPS services for location and mapping services for finding directions, has increased substantially. It is clear that technology is a lucrative navigation tool for blind people and has room for expansion. Within the HCI and accessibility literature, Quiñones et al. [21] present the results

of a needs-finding study for navigation by visually impaired people, emphasizing issues arising from changes in the environment and other breakdowns. Guentert [11] describes a train station navigation assistant for blind travelers that provides detailed information on navigating complex stations. Banovic et al. [2] examine how visually impaired people learn about and navigate their environments, noting that they not only satisfy their immediate needs but also learn information that may enable future opportunities. Yang et al. [29] describe Talking Points 3, a mobile location-aware system that seeks to make the environment more legible to blind and visually impaired users by representing important features such as paths, landmarks, and functional elements, to support spatial awareness beyond procedural wayfinding. The StopInfo research contributes to the work on supporting wayfinding in two respects: first, by investigating the role of very detailed information about transit stops themselves; and second, by deploying a practical system that can be used on a daily basis by blind and low vision riders, allowing us to investigate use under real conditions.

Geowikis. A system that provides detailed transit stop information can be viewed as a specialized geowiki. Literature on geowikis includes OpenStreetMap[2], which is certainly the largest geowiki. Haklay [13] provides an assessment of the success of OpenStreetMap, both in terms of accuracy and coverage, in comparison with Ordnance Survey datasets in the United Kingdom. Another notable geowiki is Cyclopath for bicyclists [18, 20, 24], which also includes route-finding capabilities. Other research projects have utilized crowdsourcing of geographical data to improve pedestrian route-finding, such as Guy and Truong's work on intersection geometry using Google Street View [12], and Völkel and Weber's work on pedestrian path ratings for different mobility impairments that are derived from user-driven annotations within their system, RouteCheckr [25]. The commercial application BlindSquare[3] also harnesses crowdsourced information from FourSquare[4] and OpenStreetMap to provide information about nearby businesses and other locations for blind travelers. In this work, we concentrate on providing a free system with geographical information optimized for blind and low vision riders.

3. A VALUE SENSITIVE APPROACH

Much of our research is ultimately motivated by attempting to better support certain human values such as independence, safety, equity, participation, respect, and community. To approach these value questions, we employ value sensitive design [10], a principled, systematic approach to the consideration of human values in the design of information technology. The primary features of value sensitive design are: consideration of both direct and indirect stakeholders (that is, the users of technology and those affected by the technology even though they do not use it); a tripartite methodology, consisting of conceptual, empirical, and technical investigations, iteratively and integratively applied; and an interactional theory to the value implications of technology.

In the work reported here, we focus on one key set of direct stakeholders: the blind and low vision users of the tools. An investigation of the full range of stakeholders and their val-

---

[2]http://openstreetmap.org
[3]http://www.blindsquare.com
[4]http://www.foursquare.com

ues is planned for future work. (The other direct stakeholders are the riders who enter or verify information. Key indirect stakeholders include bus and train drivers, other passengers, family and friends of the users of the tools, passersby at the transit stop, and orientation & mobility trainers.) In prior work on transit traveler information systems for blind and low vision riders [1], we found through interviews that *independence* was a central value for these riders, and to a lesser extent *safety*. In our interviews and field work, one of our goals has thus been to investigate whether this is still the case in this project, and also what other values might be important. In other prior value sensitive design work [3, 4], the researchers found it valuable to draw a distinction among stakeholder values, explicitly supported values, and designer values — an important designer value for us is avoiding paternalism toward people with disabilities.

4. SYSTEM DESCRIPTION

Front-end application. We chose to build StopInfo on an existing transit traveler information system called OneBusAway [6, 7, 8, 9, 26, 27], which is a set of tools that provide real-time arrival predictions and other transit information, such as where bus stops are located on a map and which stops are traversed by a particular route. OneBusAway builds on the work of Dan Dailey and others on real-time transit information systems, such as MyBus and BusView [16], and has been widely adopted in the Puget Sound region, used by over 100,000 unique transit riders each week. The system is freely available as an application on the iOS, Android, and Windows Phone platforms, and also via SMS, interactive voice response, and the Web. Research on OneBusAway has found a number of significant benefits, including increased or greatly increased satisfaction with public transit for 92% of survey respondents, increased feelings of safety for some (particularly while waiting at night), and decreased wait time at the stop [27]. One of the goals of our research group is to make these benefits available to as wide a range of people as possible, and we have devoted significant attention to ensuring that the apps, in particular the iOS app, provide adequate accessibility.

We decided to integrate StopInfo with OneBusAway on iOS for a number of reasons. First, OneBusAway is already used by a large number of people, and many check the application from their smartphones while waiting at bus stops. This enables us to leverage a large existing userbase by directly allowing the community to enter information for the stop as they wait. Secondly, the OneBusAway iOS application is already heavily used by members of the blind, low vision, and deaf-blind communities in the greater Seattle region who use and rely on public transit, and has been developed and tested to remain accessible to this community. Finally, StopInfo is a natural extension of OneBusAway, and can also be useful to the general population of transit riders. It includes relevant information such as how well-lit a stop is at night, which has safety implications, and whether a stop may be closed.

We integrated StopInfo with OneBusAway iOS by placing an info button with the accessibility label "About This Stop" next to the name of the stop on the details view for that stop (Figure 1). We also inserted a table cell underneath that stop's arrival times with the text label "About This Stop" in case the button was not discovered. Tapping or double tapping on the button or table cell brings up StopInfo as

an integrated web view within the application, and is also accessible through Apple's VoiceOver screen reader. When a user accesses StopInfo, they are presented with a text list of the stop features. An asterisk indicates that the information still needs verification. Below the list of stop information there are links to add or verify information, report a stop closure, learn what each field means, learn more about the study, and to optionally log in with an existing Facebook or Google account.

Information categories and collection. To seed StopInfo with basic information, King County Metro provided our research team with the database used to record bus stop details for its 8,000 stops in the Seattle area. Based on feedback from interviews with blind and low vision transit riders in prior work [14], we prioritized information about stop location, bus sign type, presence of a schedule holder, and the number of shelters at a stop. Interviews also suggested that the number of benches and the presence of trash cans were helpful for identifying the stop, which was information that Metro did not collect. Our research group additionally chose to include information about the bus sign placement, orientation and position of bus shelters, and the overall stop lighting. These latter two types of information were provided only by community-sourced information.

StopInfo uses a voting system to determine verification of a field. Each information submission, including the original information from the Metro database, counts as one vote. A feature is verified when two requirements were met: it has at least three votes, and the votes have a supermajority of 75% for one value. This means that information is considered verified only when at least two users have submitted agreement with the original Metro value, or three users reach a supermajority consensus on a field not provided by Metro. A disagreeing vote cast after a field has reached verification status will cause it to be marked as unverified again if it takes the voting percentage below the 75% threshold. Users can submit information for any field except the distance (in feet) of the stop from the intersection. Finally, we allow users to submit free-form comments when logged into the system with their Facebook or Google account.

5. METHODS

Our principal evaluation of the StopInfo prototype consisted of a five week field study with blind and low vision participants. Additionally, we measured the rate of user participation in verifying and adding stop information, and assessed the accuracy of the information provided.

5.1 Field Study

Participants. We recruited six participants, four female, from King County through email lists of local blindness organizations. Their ages ranged from 31 to 62, with a median of 45.5 years. Three participants were totally blind; the remainder had varying degrees of usable vision. Four participants reported living in suburbs of Seattle and two live in urban centers. Four participants use public transportation at least once a day and two participants reported traveling on the bus a few times each week. Reasons for using public transportation included traveling to work, appointments, errands, and recreational activities.

We required that participants use their own iPhones for the study and that they use public transportation often enough to report on at least ten such experiences during

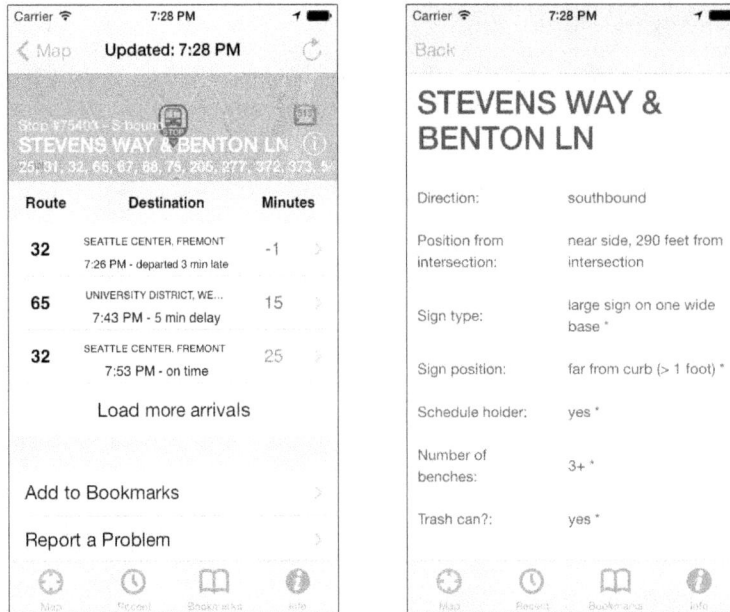

Figure 1: (left) The stop details screen in OneBusAway. StopInfo can be accessed through the info button next to the title. (right) The StopInfo view and associated information for the specified stop. An asterisk next to a field means that information has not yet been verified by three or more people. If no information exists for a particular field, we do not display it. Both screens were also tested extensively for accessibility using VoiceOver.

the study period. We verified (median of 4 out of 5) that participants were comfortable using their iPhones.

Procedure. Participants met for an introductory interview at the University of Washington. They answered questions about demographics and their public transportation use. We then asked about important underlying values to traveling as a blind person, such as independence and safety, using a value-oriented semi-structured interview [15]. We also asked how they find unfamiliar and familiar bus stops. We trained them to use OneBusAway and StopInfo, and oriented them to the web form on which they would report their travel experiences during the field period.

The web form was a quick questionnaire, accessible at any time. The questions asked about the trip, the buses they rode, and included items gauging the familiarity with the trip and their confidence. We also inquired what features of StopInfo they used. We checked in with each participant once a week to answer questions and to update them on their progress. We asked participants to submit 10 forms but incentivized up to 20 forms.

After five weeks, participants met us for an exit interview where we asked for feedback about StopInfo and gauged their overall usage of each StopInfo feature. Participants were compensated for their time and activities, with a maximum compensation of $100.

During all phases of the study, participants rated several values on a 5 point Likert scale. For example, to assess independence, we asked "How important is it to you to travel independently?" with the choices of "not at all important" (1), "somewhat unimportant" (2), "neither important nor unimportant" (3), "somewhat important" (4), and "very important" (5).

Web Forms. Our participants submitted a total of 76 forms during the field study. Participant submissions ranged from six to 20 forms with a median of 12 forms. Participants used StopInfo during 42 (55.26%) of the travel experiences. StopInfo use by individual participants ranged from 0 uses to 13 uses with a median of 6.5 uses. The percent of trips during which participants used StopInfo varied from 0% to 100% with a median of use during 67.5% of total trips submitted.

We recruited a sample that was already savvy at traveling independently and using their smartphones. We recognize that this may not reflect the general population of people who are blind or low vision, but we wanted to evaluate StopInfo and incorporate use patterns into future work that concentrates on how StopInfo can encourage people who do not use public transportation often. We evaluated StopInfo usage patterns according to three themes: usability, independence, and safety. We computed how important certain values were to participants on 5-point Likert scales during the introductory and exit interviews. From the web forms, we computed frequencies of StopInfo use, trip familiarity, and confidence during trips. Qualitative comments extracted from the interviews and web forms reinforce our findings.

5.2 Rider-Contributed Stop Information

User Participation. We obtained the number of user submissions to the system from the app database. One form submission corresponds to one row of data, containing at least 1 and up to 11 fields. From queries, we determined the total number of information submissions, the number of distinct users as indicated by the ID of the device they used to access the service, and the number of bus stops for which information was provided.

Stop Audits. In addition to computing the amount of information submitted, we assessed its accuracy by performing an audit of a sample of bus stops. The primary goal of this audit was to evaluate user submissions, but the data from the transit agency was also considered. We selected three areas in Seattle to audit, focusing on locations with a range of population densities, a high demand for public transit, and a relatively high amount of user feedback from StopInfo. For each survey area we determined which stops users had provided at least one piece of information for. We then walked each survey area on foot, carrying a smartphone with GPS to navigate between bus stops and to ensure that no bus stops with user-submitted data were missed. At each stop we recorded values for every major field for which StopInfo allows information submission: stop position, sign type, sign position, number of benches, number of shelters, orientation and placement of shelters, and presence of trashcans. Because we performed these surveys during the day, and because it was not as relevant to our study, stop lighting was not recorded. Shelter orientation and placement were omitted because these fields received very few information submissions (6 in total, only 1 within survey areas). In total, 38 stops were surveyed. These audit values were later compared with the original Metro data provided, the user-submitted information, and the combined amalgamate data to determine the overall accuracy.

6. RESULTS

In this section, we first present the results from our field study according to the themes of usability, independence, and safety. We follow with results of participation rates for adding or verifying stop information.

6.1 Field Study

StopInfo Usability. StopInfo was usable and the information presented was helpful to our participants. P4 noted that *"StopInfo is great because you know exactly where the stop is."* All participants said they would continue using StopInfo after the study.

The most helpful information categories had median ratings of 5; these included the position of the stop relative to intersection, name of bus stop (e.g., "3rd Ave. and Pine St."), and the position of the sign relative to the curb. Interestingly, P2 described how she appropriated this information to assist her in wayfinding *after* a bus ride: "When I got off the bus, it was helpful to know the bus stop was at the far side of the intersection."

One source of confusion was our use of terms for stop position relative to the nearest intersection. These terms are standard in the transit industry, but not among the general public, such as "near side" (i.e., a stop before an intersection). P1 didn't understand the concept until a researcher *"explained it better."* P4 said we should *"put [the definition] in Help."* Further confusion arose from bus stops at transit centers since our information fields were biased toward bus stops along streets. The relative position and distance from the intersection were not applicable in this case, but these fields remained on the information view, and did not provide any information specific to the transit center, such as the position of each bay. P3 felt this was the only "inaccurate" information in StopInfo.

Independence. Consistent with prior work [1, 14], all participants were very interested in being independent, and rated it a 5 in terms of how important it is to them while traveling. However, their interest in whether others perceived them as independent varied ($Mdn = 4$). This can be explained by some participants citing disinterest in others' opinions. Participants were also very interested in knowing way finding information ahead of time ($Mdn = 5$).

Data from the web forms indicates that StopInfo supports tenets of independence. On 29 (38.16%) of the web forms, participants indicated the trip was one in which they would not normally attempt on public transportation. StopInfo was consulted during 26 (89.66%) of those trips.

We also computed StopInfo use based on each participant's level of familiarity with each trip. An odds ratio shows that during the 12 trips rated at the 1 and 2 familiarity levels, participants were twice (2.04 times) as likely to consult StopInfo when compared to StopInfo use during the 60 trips rated at the 4 and 5 familiarity levels. We omitted the trips rated as neutral (3). These usage patterns answer affirmatively our research question as to whether participants would attempt more unfamiliar trips on public transportation with the given information about bus stops through StopInfo. An unexpected finding was that StopInfo is consulted a high percentage (80% to 100%) of the time until the highest familiarity level (5), where usage drops to 28.57%.

We further broke down StopInfo use compared to the total number of trips taken by participant, shown in Figure 2. Half of the participants found StopInfo useful during all trips. P5 appreciated the option to confirm information, saying, *"I mainly used StopInfo to verify what I already knew."* P3 and P5 found StopInfo especially useful during unfamiliar travel, while P6 liked the system but did not find instances in her daily life that warranted its use.

StopInfo supports independence by providing information previously inaccessible on the go. Furthermore, it could make the difference between a user attempting a trip and staying home, and for confident travelers, can provide confirming information during unfamiliar trips.

During the interviews, we inquired about confidence during trips without access to travel tools. This resulted in a neutral response ($Mdn = 3$), contrasting with a higher ($Mdn = 4$) confidence level given attempting unfamiliar travel with tools. P1 explained, *"I would be very uncomfortable, I wouldn't go"* in response to traveling unfamiliar routes without tools, while P2 mentioned, *"I wouldn't feel confident at all."* However, we found no relationship between trip familiarity level ($R^2 = .34$) and confidence during submitted trips, and no relationship between StopInfo use and confidence during submitted trips ($R^2 = .17$). Many factors can influence confidence, but our sample had problem solving skills and knew about a variety of travel tools prior to the study. Consistent with prior work [14], the most popular strategies (with the number of of the participants who employ them) include consulting OneBusAway (6), searching for characteristic bus stop landmarks (6), using other navigation apps (5), consulting transit agency's online trip planners (4), and asking passersby for assistance (3). For example, P5 said, *"I know how to use my resources,"* and P6 commented that, *"The things that hold me back tend to be information."* Our sample had great skills, but needed more information, which StopInfo provided for the unfamiliar trips attempted during the study.

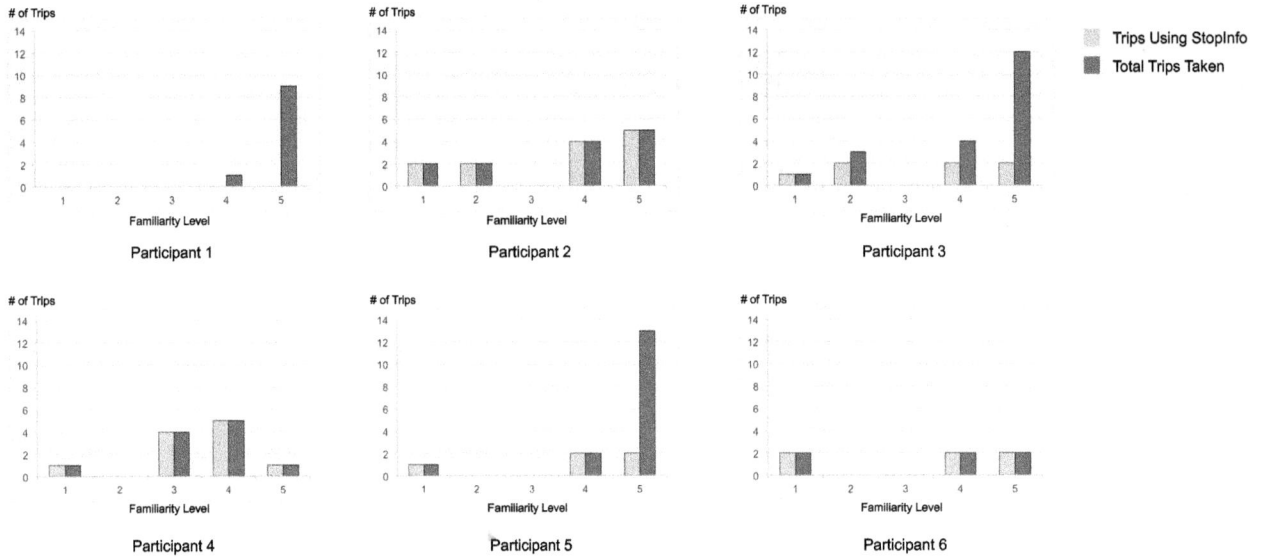

Figure 2: The number of trips (y-axis) taken per familiarity level (x-axis, where 1="very unfamiliar," 5="very familiar") for each participant. The light blue bar (left) indicates transit trips taken while using StopInfo. The dark blue bar (right) indicates the total number of transit trips taken for that familiarity level.

We also noticed that participants considered using their tools and asking for assistance as tenets of independence. P1 stated, *"I'm not afraid to talk to people,"* and P2 defined independence as *"having a balance"* between doing things on her own and asking for help. However, themes of wayfinding information gaps abounded with comments such as P3's: *"I just hope that I'm on the right street and at the right stop."* This sheds light on future research questions to explore designs that fill information gaps and become part of the standard repertoire of tools available.

Safety. Participants felt fairly safe traveling ($Mdn = 4$). Similarly, most participants were unconcerned about using a smartphone in public ($Mdn = 4$). We wanted to make sure StopInfo did not negatively impact feelings of safety, and all participants reported no change in safety traveling or security using a smartphone after the study. In fact, P5 believed the added information presented benefits that outweighed the potential risk of using his smartphone more often in public. *"There was more to take advantage of with the added app and information."* Consistent with prior work [11], safety seemed to have minimal importance to our sample.

In summary, StopInfo is a usable system that provides very detailed information about bus stops on the go. It promotes tenets of independence by positively influencing unfamiliar travel using public transportation. Future work can concentrate on fixing usability issues such as inaccurate transit center information and incorporating StopInfo to work seamlessly with other wayfinding solutions.

6.2 Bus Stop Information Submissions

Reliable information is a key component of making the system usable. We were primarily interested in two things: the information accuracy in aggregate, which combined both Metro data and user-submitted data, and the accuracy of users alone, which will influence future work in improving

the interface and determining thresholds for information verification.

Quantity of information. StopInfo received a high number of information submissions immediately after launch, diminishing after the first two weeks to a slower but steady rate of typically 5-10 submissions per day. In the three months following public deployment, 467 users made 870 information submissions for 576 unique bus stops out of a total 8481 stops covered by StopInfo. User-provided information covers less than 7% of stops, concentrated heavily in high-traffic areas.

Quality of information. We evaluated information accuracy by comparing the audit data to the data provided by Metro and submitted by users, as well as to the aggregate data actually displayed on StopInfo. Because the fields were categoric measures, percentage agreement was used with an exact match qualifying as agreement, similar to Rundle et al. [22].

For each stop, StopInfo displays a minimum of four fields: stop position, sign type, schedule holder, and the number of shelters. This data was provided by Metro and is present for all stops. All additional fields are user-submitted data only. For the information in aggregate, we found that stop position and number of shelters were both highly accurate, correct more than 90% of the time in both cases. Sign type, schedule holder presence, and sign position were the three least accurate fields.

Participants in the field study identified stop position (relative to intersection) and sign position (relative to curb) as two of the most important pieces of information. Though stop position is very accurate, sign position was the least accurate field in aggregate, possibly due to ambiguity. The sign position field in StopInfo presents two options, "close to curb (<1 foot)" and "far from curb (> 1 foot)". The distance may be difficult for users to gauge, or users interpreted "close" more loosely, despite the measurement given.

Landmark Type	Percent of Data Assessed as Accurate			
	Metro	User	Aggregate	Verified (N)
Stop position	97.4%	77.9%	97.3%	100.0% (9)
Sign type	68.4%	71.2%	65.8%	87.5% (8)
Sign position	N/A	56.5%	55.2%	100.0% (2)
Schedule holder	73.7%	46.0%	57.9%	37.5% (8)
Number of shelters	92.1%	92.9%	94.7%	100.0% (13)
Number of benches	N/A	91.1%	93.3%	100.0% (7)
Trash can?	N/A	78.6%	75.0%	100.0% (6)

Table 1: Data Accuracy. "Metro" is data from the transit agency, "User" is data contributed by a single user, "Aggregate" is the aggregate rating displayed by the system, and "Verified" includes only those ratings marked as verified ("N" is the number of such ratings).

The sign type and schedule holder fields have relatively lower accuracy, 65.8% and 57.9% respectively. We identified three likely sources of this error from this audit. Firstly, Metro is in the process of replacing old signs. During the audit, 4 bus signs in the audit area were replaced with signs of different type. While the ultimate goal of StopInfo is for users to provide updated information on such changes, it is unknown yet how quickly they will do so. Secondly, both sign and schedule holder fields map poorly from the original Metro database into StopInfo. The Metro definitions of signs do not perfectly fit into the categories chosen by the research team, and we may need to consider revising categories. Thirdly, there is ambiguity in the intent of the information. We originally intended the schedule holder field to indicate an extra or protruding attachment to a bus stop pole that could be physically felt; based on submissions to StopInfo, users seemed to instead be using the schedule holder field to indicate any bus schedule at the stop, even those otherwise integrated into the pole or sign.

While only about a quarter of bus stops in the audit area had verified information, we found that information marked as verified was highly accurate, 100% in nearly every category except the schedule holder category, due to the ambiguity already explained. The one error in a verified sign type arose from a sign installed after the information submissions were made.

7. CONCLUSIONS AND FUTURE WORK

Our initial deployment saw many entries for bus stops in the Puget Sound area. However, our goals for this work are not only to deploy and field test a research prototype, but also to work in cooperation with the transit agency to transition it to long-term operational use so that it can become a valuable resource for all transit riders in their daily commutes. This will require encouraging continuing participation over time to keep information up to date. In addition, we would like to collect information for as many stops as possible in the region, not just a cluster of stops in the same area (such as downtown). In future work, we plan to investigate this as a question of incentivizing participation [17, 23].

Another application for this work involves the incorporation of the data collected through StopInfo into a trip planner or navigational aid such as BlindSquare or CrossingGuard [12]. Since the most important information to our participants included the stop's position relative to the intersection and the sign's position from the curb, a natural extension would be to utilize a traveler's GPS location to help determine proximity to the bus stop sign or other stop features. Since position relative to intersection was confusing to participants, finding better ways to explain and present that field is crucial. Community-sourced information could expand to include geotags of these features in order to gain precise location data if the navigator is using a GPS-enabled tool. Incorporation of other geowiki data, such as that in OpenStreetMap, can help with planning routes from the traveler's starting point all the way to their destination. Ideally, the presentation of this route-finding information will be integrated with the app itself.

Earlier results from investigating the impacts of OneBusAway [8] included the unexpected finding that 78% of OneBusAway users reported that they were more likely to walk to a different stop as a result of having the application, estimating that they walked an average of 6.9 more blocks/week than before using OneBusAway ($\sigma = 8.2$). The most common reason for doing so was to find a faster route to their destinations, but exercise was also a frequently given reason. We want to investigate whether we can provide similar benefits for blind and low vision riders (both to allow them to find faster routes, and for exercise — the latter being particularly relevant given reported problems this group faces in getting enough exercise [5, 28]). We anticipate two components to this: first, providing good wayfinding information for users to walk between stops, again conveniently presented in context using the app; and second, perhaps providing self-tracking and social incentive tools that allow users to track their progress toward goals, either individually or as part of a self-selected group.

There are multiple possibilities for expanding the system. One is to include information relevant to additional groups of users. We have already collected some additional information on stop closures (of interest to all riders), and whether the stop is well lit at night (relevant to safety). Investigating the results of providing this information is left for future research. Another direction will be to include information tailored for riders with mobility impairments, beyond the current simple "wheelchair accessible" indication in the transit agency database. Finally, OneBusAway is now operational in other regions beyond Puget Sound, including Atlanta, New York City, and Tampa, with experimental deployments elsewhere. A number of other agencies have expressed keen interest in deploying StopInfo in their regions as well, which should both be of practical benefit to riders there, as well as provide research opportunities for cross-region comparison.

In conclusion, we deployed StopInfo as a response to an information gap identified in prior work. The field study showed that the system is generally usable and helpful. Furthermore, we learned that the information can influence spontaneous and unfamiliar travel. This supports independence which is of paramount importance to our sample. The study itself encouraged our participants; for example, P5 concluded that *"[StopInfo] has made me want to do more independent cane travel,"* and P4 echoed with *"This [field study] gets me out of the house."*

8. ACKNOWLEDGEMENTS

Many thanks to the six participants in the field study, to the OneBusAway users who contributed stop information, to Aengus McMillin for helping with the integration of StopInfo with OneBusAway and improving the overall accessibility of the iPhone app, to Melony Joyce and Matthew Weidner at King County Metro for their assistance with the Metro data and support, to Robin Gold for advice on the statistical analysis, and to all the participants in the Mobile Accessibility research group at UW. This research was funded in part by the National Science Foundation under Grants CNS-1042260 and IIS-1116051.

9. REFERENCES

[1] Shiri Azenkot, Sanjana Prasain, Alan Borning, Emily Fortuna, Richard Ladner, and Jacob Wobbrock. Enhancing independence and safety for blind and deaf-blind public transit riders. In *CHI '11*, pages 3247–3256, 2011.

[2] Nikola Banovic, Rachel L. Franz, Khai N. Truong, Jennifer Mankoff, and Anind K. Dey. Uncovering information needs for independent spatial learning for users who are visually impaired. In *ASSETS '13*, pages 24:1–24:8, 2013.

[3] Alan Borning, Batya Friedman, Janet Davis, and Peyina Lin. Informing public deliberation: Value sensitive design of indicators for a large-scale urban simulation. In *ECSCW*, September 2005.

[4] Alan Borning and Michael Muller. Next steps for value sensitive design. In *CHI '12*, pages 1125–1134, 2012.

[5] Michele Capella-McDonnall. The need for health promotion for adults who are visually impaired. *Journal of Visual Impairment & Blindness*, 101(3), March 2007.

[6] Brian Ferris. *OneBusAway: Improving the Usability of Public Transit*. PhD thesis, Dept. of Computer Science & Engineering, University of Washington, 2011.

[7] Brian Ferris, Kari Watkins, and Alan Borning. Location-aware tools for improving public transit usability. *IEEE Pervasive Computing*, 9(1):13–19, Jan–Mar 2010.

[8] Brian Ferris, Kari Watkins, and Alan Borning. OneBusAway: Results from providing real-time arrival information for public transit. In *CHI '10*, pages 1807–1816, 2010.

[9] Brian Ferris, Kari Watkins, and Alan Borning. OneBusAway: Behavioral and satisfaction changes resulting from providing real-time arrival information for public transit. In *Proceedings of the 2011 Transportation Research Board Annual Meeting*, January 2011.

[10] Batya Friedman, Peter H. Kahn Jr., and Alan Borning. Value sensitive design and information systems: Three case studies. In *Human-Computer Interaction and Management Information Systems: Foundations*. M.E. Sharpe, 2006.

[11] Markus Guentert. Improving public transit accessibility for blind riders: A train station navigation assistant. In *ASSETS '11*, pages 317–318, 2011.

[12] Richard Guy and Khai Truong. CrossingGuard: Exploring information content in navigation aids for visually impaired pedestrians. In *CHI '12*, pages 405–414, 2012.

[13] Mordechai Haklay. How good is volunteered geographic information? A comparative study of OpenStreetMap and ordnance survey datasets. *Environment and Planning B*, 37:682–703, 2010.

[14] Kotaro Hara, Shiri Azenkot, Megan Campbell, Cynthia L. Bennett, Vicki Le, Sean Pannella, Robert Moore, Kelly Minckler, Rochelle H. Ng, and Jon E. Froehlich. Improving public transit accessibility for blind riders by crowdsourcing bus stop landmark locations with Google Street View. In *ASSETS '13*, pages 16:1–16:8, 2013.

[15] Peter Kahn. *The Human Relationship with Nature: Development and Culture*, chapter 5: Structural-developmental Methods, pages 77–93. MIT Press, 1999.

[16] S. D. Maclean and Daniel Dailey. Wireless internet access to real-time transit information. *Journal of the Transportation Research Board*, 1791, 2002.

[17] Oded Nov. What motivates wikipedians? *Commun. ACM*, 50(11):60–64, November 2007.

[18] Katherine Panciera, Reid Priedhorsky, Thomas Erickson, and Loren Terveen. Lurking? Cyclopaths?: A quantitative lifecycle analysis of user behavior in a geowiki. In *CHI '10*, pages 1917–1926, 2010.

[19] Sanjana Prasain. Stopfinder: Improving the experience of blind public transit riders with crowdsourcing. In *ASSETS '11*, pages 323–324, 2011.

[20] Reid Priedhorsky, Benjamin Jordan, and Loren Terveen. How a personalized geowiki can help bicyclists share information more effectively. In *WikiSym '07*, pages 93–98, 2007.

[21] Pablo-Alejandro Quiñones, Tammy Greene, Rayoung Yang, and Mark Newman. Supporting visually impaired navigation: A needs-finding study. In *CHI Extended Abstracts '11*, pages 1645–1650, 2011.

[22] Andrew Rundle, Michael Bader, Catherine Richards, Kathryn Neckerman, and Julien Teitler. Using google street view to audit neighborhood environments. *American Journal of Preventive Medicine*, 40(1):94–100, 2011.

[23] Daniel Schultheiss, Anja Blieske, Anja Solf, and Saskia Staeudtner. How to encourage the crowd? a study about user typologies and motivations on crowdsourcing platforms. In *Proc. 2013 IEEE/ACM 6th Int'l Conf on Utility and Cloud Computing*, pages 506–509, 2013.

[24] Fernando Torre, S. Andrew Sheppard, Reid Priedhorsky, and Loren Terveen. bumpy, caution with merging: An exploration of tagging in a geowiki. In *GROUP '10*, pages 155–164, 2010.

[25] Thorsten Völkel and Gerhard Weber. RouteCheckr: Personalized multicriteria routing for mobility impaired pedestrians. In *ASSETS '08*, pages 185–192, 2008.

[26] Kari Watkins. *Using Technology to Revolutionize Public Transportation*. PhD thesis, Dept. of Civil & Environmental Engineering, University of Washington, 2011.

[27] Kari Watkins, Brian Ferris, Alan Borning, G. Scott Rutherford, and David Layton. Where is my bus? Impact of mobile real time information on the perceived and actual wait time of transit riders. *Transportation Research Part A: Policy and Practice*, 45(8), October 2011.

[28] Evette Weil, Melissa Wachterman, Ellen P. McCarthy, Roger B. Davis, Bonnie O'Day, Lisa I. Iezzoni, and Christina C. Wee. Obesity among adults with disabling conditions. *Journal of the American Medical Association*, 288(10), Sept 11 2002.

[29] Rayoung Yang, Sangmi Park, Sonali R. Mishra, Zhenan Hong, Clint Newsom, Hyeon Joo, Erik Hofer, and Mark W. Newman. Supporting spatial awareness and independent wayfinding for pedestrians with visual impairments. In *ASSETS '11*, pages 27–34, 2011.

Headlock: a Wearable Navigation Aid that Helps Blind Cane Users Traverse Large Open Spaces

Alexander Fiannaca, Ilias Apostolopoulous, Eelke Folmer

Computer Science & Engineering - University of Nevada
{fiannaca, ilapost, efolmer}@cse.unr.edu

ABSTRACT

Traversing large open spaces is a challenging task for blind cane users, as such spaces are often devoid of tactile features that can be followed. Consequently, in such spaces cane users may veer from their intended paths. Wearable devices have great potential for assistive applications for users who are blind as they typically feature a camera and support hands and eye free interaction. We present HEADLOCK, a navigation aid for an optical head-mounted display that helps blind users traverse large open spaces by letting them lock onto a salient landmark across the space, such as a door, and then providing audio feedback to guide the user towards the landmark. A user study with 8 blind users evaluated the usability and effectiveness of two types of audio feedback (sonification and text-to-speech) for guiding a user across an open space to a doorway. Qualitative results are reported, which may inform the design of assistive wearable technology for users who are blind.

Categories and Subject Descriptors

K.4.2 [**Social Issues**]: Assistive technology

Keywords

Wearable computing; visual impairment; head-mounted display; veering; mobility; navigation; sonification

1. INTRODUCTION

Vision plays a dominant role in spatial perception [7], the human ability to sense the size, shape, movement, and orientation of objects or people in space. Spatial perception is an essential skill for efficiently navigating spaces, i.e., navigating without running into obstacles or veering from an intended path. Navigating spaces is quite a challenge for users who are blind as they largely have to rely on their hands and ears for spatial perception. Though the haptic modality is largely redundant with the visual modality [22], spatial perception using the tactile sense is significantly slower. Where

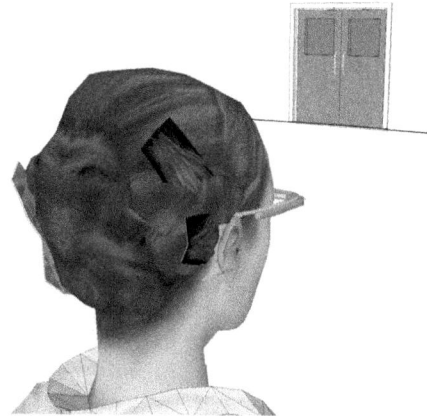

Figure 1: A blind cane user scans the open space to detect the presence of a door using Google Glass. Audio cues then guide the blind cane user towards the door while minimizing veering.

vision can identify objects at a distance, the sensing range of the hands is limited by the length of a user's arm. This range can only be extended through the use of a cane, at the cost of only being able to perceive depth information from a single point. Hands can distinguish shapes and textures, such as Braille, but they cannot sense color, which is an important feature for recognizing objects [19], such as doors. Though a small number of blind people are capable of echolocation by tapping their cane or making clicking noises with their mouths, environments generally don't contain many persistent sound sources that can be used for spatial perception. Consequently, blind people often rely on sighted people to describe spaces for them or to help them navigate spaces. This dependency on others reduces their mobility [15].

Computer vision has been explored to offer various types of assistive perceptual functionality to blind users (see [18] for an overview). Because smartphones feature cameras, various assistive navigation apps have been developed that can help read signs [26] or detect the presence and orientation of crosswalks [11]. Various smartphone based indoor navigation systems [5, 23] have been explored. Though smartphones use is increasing among blind users [3], for navigation the use of smartphones is subject to various challenges: (1) People who are blind may find it challenging to aim a camera independently [12]; (2) existing apps only correctly identify objects that are up close but not far away [10]; and (3) because users typically hold a cane in one hand, holding a smartphone in the other impedes their ability to open doors, recognize landmarks and press buttons [5].

Once only the focus of academic research labs, wearable computing has garnered significant public interest [6]. Of specific interest are Optical Head-mounted Displays (OHMD), such as Google Glass [1]. Because OHMDs typically feature a camera and support hands and eyes free interaction, it has been argued that this platform has great potential for assistive applications for users who are blind [6]. This paper makes the following contributions:

1. We present HEADLOCK, a large open space navigation aid for a soon-to-be commercially available OHMD (Google Glass).

2. We identify what type of audio feedback is most effective and usable to minimize veering; and

3. We report qualitative experiences of people who are blind using HEADLOCK.

2. RELATED WORK

Wearables. One of the earliest wearable navigation systems was that of Ertan et. al. (1998) [4], in which navigation directions in the form of haptic feedback are conveyed through an array of vibrational motors sewn into a vest worn by a blind user. This system requires installing infrared transceivers in a space for localizing the user. Hub et. al. (2003) [9] presents a system that provides navigational instructions through a cane augmented with a stereo camera, a simple keypad, and a speaker. This system relies on wireless local area network (WLAN) localization, which takes advantage of the fact that many indoor locations already have wireless access points. The augmented cane detects objects and retrieves information regarding these objects from a 3D world model. Marston et. al. (2007) [20] present a wearable navigation aid utilizing a GPS antenna and laptop to provide navigational guidance through haptic and audio feedback. Ross and Blasch [24] evaluated three different wearable interfaces for visually impaired users including sonification, speech, and haptic feedback to minimize veering when crossing a street. The interfaces were evaluated with 15 elderly visually impaired users and no significant difference in accuracy was found, though the haptic tapping interface was found to be most usable. Unfortunately, each of these approaches has a reliance on either a priori knowledge in the form of maps or requires prohibitively expensive instrumentation of environments with beacons [5]. Several wearable systems require the user to carry expensive sensors and supporting computing equipment in a backpack, which may impede their mobility, as blind users already carry several assistive devices with them, such as a cane or a braille reader.

Smartphone Apps. Computer vision could be a better technology for developing assistive navigation aids because it is the natural technological parallel of the human vision system which normally handles wayfinding (and thereby navigation) problems [18]. Computer vision based approaches don't rely on installed beacons for localization, but instead take advantage of preexisting visual features in spaces for localization. In recent years, mobile devices such as smartphones have advanced significantly in computational capabilities and available internal sensors, such that smartphones are currently considered one of the biggest assistive devices since the introduction of Braille [3]. Various apps are available that offer functionality to recognize currency, faces, or street signs. A few apps offer functionality related to navigation. The Crosswatch smartphone application [11] identifies crosswalks from a camera phone image and conveys their location and orientation using speech. A similar application performs real-time sign recognition [26] to locate signs and conveys what is on the sign using speech. Manduchi (2012) [17] presents a mobile computer vision system designed to detect and guide users towards artificial landmarks (i.e. fiducials). While this system requires the installation of a set of artificial landmarks, Manduchi argues that this system may detect natural landmarks, such as, elevator buttons or signs. This approach only senses landmarks up to a maximum distance of 3.5 meters. VizWiz::LocateIt [2] allows blind users to take a picture of a scene (e.g. a picture of a shelf of different cereals in a grocery store) using their smartphone and then sends users feedback guiding them towards a nearby target (e.g. a box of Wheaties on the shelf). This approach employed both sonification and text-to-speech (TTS) interfaces to guide users towards objects. User studies with blind users found the sonification and TTS feedback useful for finding objects. Smartphone based approaches are subject to a number of limitations. It is a challenge for blind people to aim a camera independently [12]. Smartphones have a limited field of view (FOV), which makes it easy to miss objects that are close by [17]. If an object is not visible to the camera and the user doesn't have a notion where the object could be, searching for an object may be a slow and cumbersome task [17]. For target finding using a smartphone a user study found that users would prefer wearing the camera over holding the camera in their hand [17]. Assistive smartphone apps typically require their users to hold the smartphone close to an object or person to avoid poorly focused photos and having to solve hard image segmentation problems [2]. Though these apps help understand what something is, they don't convey where something is [10]. Probably the most important limitation of current smartphones is that they are unable to acquire depth information, which could be useful for recognizing objects and landmarks during navigation.

Previous Work. The authors developed an indoor navigation system called NAVATAR [5]. This system is minimal in terms of installation cost, such to enable large scale implementation, as it only relies on an annotated 2D map and relies on dead-reckoning localization using sensors available in smartphones. To improve localization accuracy NAVATAR requires blind users to confirm the presence of anticipated tactile landmarks along a provided path. This approach offloads the computationally hard-to-solve problem of recognizing landmarks to a cognizant agent, which seamlessly integrates with how blind users already navigate familiar spaces. User studies with six blind users in a university environment found a localization accuracy of 1.85 m. GIST [16] is a wearable gestural interface that allows blind individuals to sense color, distance and the presence of humans using different hand gestures, where spatial information is provided depending on where the user's arm is pointed. GIST uses a commercially available depth sensor (Kinect) that the user wears on their chest with a small tablet carried in a backpack. Though GIST is somewhat bulky in design, a user study with 8 blind users demonstrated the feasibility of GIST to perform spatial interaction tasks, including discovering and navigating towards objects and persons of interest.

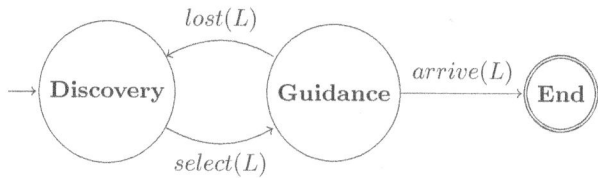

Figure 2: Finite State Machine describing the different modes and transitions between modes with landmark L.

3. DESIGN OF HEADLOCK

When navigating a new space, blind people rely on their spatial image in working memory [13] to memorize salient tactile landmarks they encounter (i.e., doors, hallway intersections, water coolers, stairs, floor transitions, etc.) and which helps them build a cognitive map of the space [14]. This cognitive map is essential for navigation as blind individuals rely on the identification of anticipated tactile landmarks [25] along their path to determine their current location (e.g. *follow the wall on my right until there is a water-cooler*). Williams et. al. (2013) [27] note that this navigation can be challenging for blind users when in large open indoor spaces. Within this context, our previous research [5, 16] identified two problems:

- **Veering.** Traversing large open spaces is a challenge for cane users, as either there aren't any tactile features to be followed or the distance between landmarks is large, which cause users to veer from their intended path (see Fig 3:a).

- **Handsfree.** Because cane users already use one hand to hold a cane, it is desirable to leave the other hand free to allow for identification of landmarks (doors, elevators, railings) and to allow for interaction with the environment (e.g., open doors, press a button, hold handrail).

To address these issues, we developed HEADLOCK, a navigation app for optical head-mounted displays (OHMD). A benefit of using an OHMD is that the camera is closely aligned with the user's field of view (FOV), giving the user an accurate indication of the direction in which the camera is aimed, which helps with orientation. Users don't have to carry heavy supporting computing equipment as OHMDs are lightweight, and only have to be tethered to a smartphone. OHMDs are non-obtrusive, which is important, as a recent study shows blind users prefer "small, easily accessible, and discreet" forms of wearables [6].

Approach. HEADLOCK allows users to remotely sense the presence of a landmark, and then lock onto this landmark to efficiently navigate towards it while minimizing veering. Similar to Manduchi [17], HEADLOCK distinguishes a *discovery* and a *guidance* mode.

Discovery. Computer vision is employed to parse the video stream from the OHMD's camera allowing users to scan a space by moving their head horizontally in order to detect salient landmarks (see Fig 3:b). Particular landmarks may have a known size, which allows HEADLOCK to also acquire an estimate of the distance to the landmark. Once the desired landmark has been found, the user instructs HEADLOCK to lock onto this landmark, at which point HEADLOCK transitions to the guidance phase (see Fig 2).

Guidance. The goal of the guidance mode is to provide feedback so that the user navigates efficiently to the

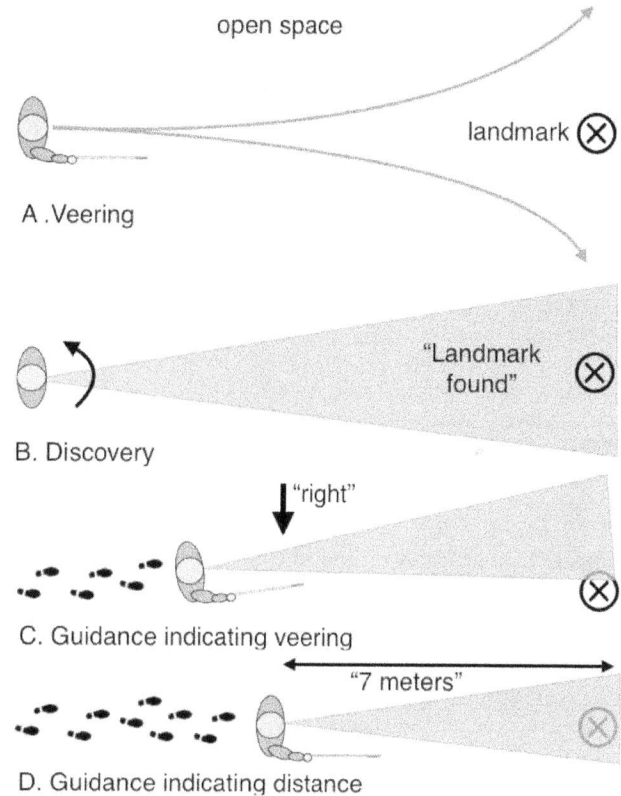

Figure 3: (a) Without any tactile features to follow in an open space, cane users may to veer from their intended path towards a landmark. (b) Users scan the space for landmarks and select one as their target. (c) Audio feedback is provided to correct for veering during the user's navigation towards the landmark. (d) Updated distance information is provided while approaching the landmark.

landmark. To detect veering, we track the position of the landmark relative to the center of the camera's FOV. When it diverges from the center by a certain threshold, feedback is provided to indicate the direction and magnitude of the error allowing the user to correct their course (see Fig 3:c). In the case HEADLOCK loses visual track of the target landmark, we inform the user of this event and indicate the direction in which the user should turn to bring the landmark back into view. The discovery mode is automatically restarted, allowing for a landmark to be relocated quickly (see Fig 2). To convey progress, distance information is provided while the user navigates towards the landmark (see Fig 3:d). Upon reaching a landmark, the navigation task is considered complete and feedback is provided accordingly.

Research. A challenge that needs to be investigated is what type of feedback most efficiently allows a cane user to navigate to a landmark. Because OHMDs are typically not capable of providing haptic feedback, we explore two different types of audio feedback for efficiently guiding users towards a landmark: text-to-speech (TTS) and sonification. TTS takes advantage of the intuitiveness and rich vocabulary offered by human language, where sonification may be harder to learn but can convey multidimensional data efficiently and has previously been explored for guiding users towards objects [2].

4. IMPLEMENTATION

To understand what type of audio feedback is most effective and usable, we implemented HEADLOCK for one specific type of landmark: doorways. Doorways are typically used in the cognitive mapping of spaces by blind individuals [14] as they often have various subtle but distinguishable tactile features (e.g. direction it opens, type of door handle, sound it makes, etc.). Large open spaces often feature doorways, and a reasonable navigation scenario could include crossing large open spaces with the end goal of finding a particular doorway (e.g crossing a foyer to find the elevator door). Since one of the objectives of HEADLOCK is to facilitate navigation of unknown spaces, rather than navigating towards a particular door, a doorway is a useful ubiquitous landmark that is present in many indoor spaces. Doorways are also a useful landmarks for HEADLOCK as they are relatively easy to detect due to their uniform color and shape (within the context of a single building).

Instrumentation. We use Google Glass [1] as our OHMD. Glass is a wearable voice-controlled Android 4.0.3 device that resembles a pair of glasses and only weighs 50 grams. Glass has various sensors including a camera (54.8° x 42.5° FOV), a microphone, and 3-axis accelerometer among others. Users interact with Glass using both natural language voice commands and the touchpad located on the frame. Audio is either provided through a bone conduction transducer or through an external headphone. The 5 megapixel camera on Glass is located on the right side of the frame. A user wearing Google Glass has a natural understanding of the direction in which the camera is aimed based on how their head is oriented.

Door Detection. HEADLOCK was implemented in Java using the Android Development Toolkit targeting Android 4.0.3. The door detection algorithm is a simple OpenCV-based blob detector which searches for blobs within the HSV color range of the doors in our test building. The algorithm processes frames with a scaled-down video resolution of 240x160 at 30 FPS providing HEADLOCK with bounding boxes for all recognized doors. This decreased resolution is utilized in order to achieve a reasonable performance on Glass without overheating the device. Preliminary trials showed that doors could be accurately detected at this resolution up to 12 meters away.

4.1 Discovery

HEADLOCK provides feedback every 2,000 ms indicating whether or not a door has been detected. In the sonification mode, we designed an audio icon consisting of three high pitch beeps to indicate a door and three low pitch beeps if no door is visible. In the TTS mode, the feedback consists of the TTS phrases *"Door found"* or *"No door found"*. Upon receiving feedback indicating the presence of a door, users select the door by tapping on the Google Glass touch pad.

4.2 Guidance

Guidance output is generated using a veering metric (v) and a distance-to-landmark metric (d). The veering metric simply measures the distance from the closest edge of the tracked door to the middle of the field of view:

$$v(x_l, x_r) = max\left(\frac{r_x}{2} - x_r, x_l - \frac{r_x}{2}\right)$$

where x_l and x_r are the X coordinates of the left and right edges (respectively) of the door's bounding box, and r_x is

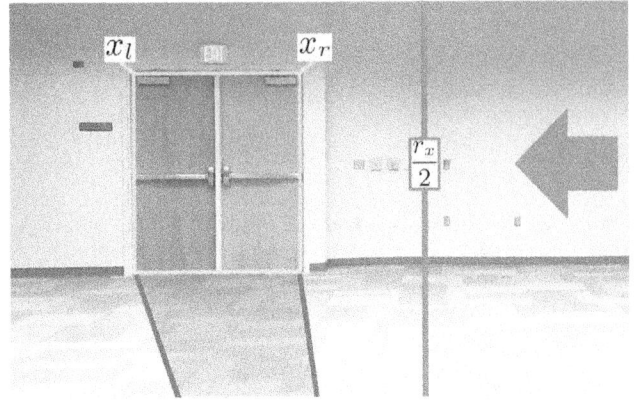

Figure 4: Feedback is based on the position of the middle of the field of view (red vertical line in this cropped image) relative to the nearest edge of the bounding box surrounding the target landmark (green box). In this case, HEADLOCK would indicate for the user to go left toward the blue target orientation.

a constant representing the X resolution of the input image (see Fig 4). The distance metric approximates the percentage of the navigation task the user has completed:

$$d(x_l, x_r) = 0.67 \log\left(100\frac{(x_r - x_l) - w_i}{r_x - w_i} + 4\right) - 0.27$$

where w_i is a constant value set for each tracked door representing its width in pixels when first observed. This equation was determined experimentally to represent a relative measure of the approximate distance traveled during the navigation task based on the observed width of the door. This metric could easily be replaced with a related true distance approximation rather than a relative distance approximation, but this would require a priori knowledge of the actual width of the observed door. Since a goal of the HEADLOCK application is to limit the amount of required a priori knowledge, a relative distance metric was chosen.

Sonification Feedback. Since the data being conveyed to the user is quantitative data representing X (veering) and Z (progress) values, it is well suited to being conveyed as an auditory graph [21]. For the auditory graph sonification scheme employed by HEADLOCK, pulse delay (the length of the silent period between each beep) was chosen to indicate changes in X-axis veering data:

$$p_s(x_l, x_r) = \begin{cases} 200 + 800v(x_l, x_r) & : x_l > 0.5r_x, x_r < 0.5r_x \\ 0 & : x_l \leq 0.5r_x \leq x_r \end{cases}$$

When a user veers (first case), $p_s(x_l, x_r)$ varies the delay between beeps linearly from 200 ms to 1000 ms with respect to $v(x_l, x_r)$, indicating the magnitude of veering to the user. When the user isn't veering (second case), $p_s(x_l, x_r)$ returns a constant value of zero (a continuous tone, no beeping). In auditory graphs, frequency is often used as an analog for changes in Y-axis data [21]. In the case of HEADLOCK, this corresponds with the Z-axis data:

$$f(x_l, x_r) = \begin{cases} 1710 & : x_l > 0.5r_x, x_r < 0.5r_x \\ 130 + 920d(x_l, x_r) & : x_l \leq 0.5r_x \leq x_r \end{cases}$$

All pitches set by $F(x_l, x_r)$ were chosen experimentally and verified to be within the frequency range of human hearing [8]. When the user is veering off course (first case), $f(x_l, x_r)$ sets the output pitch to the constant value of 1710 Hz. Due to the fact that a single high pitch beep is utilized for all veering feedback, users must perceive the direction of their veering by listening to the change in pulse delay over several time steps. In the case that the user is not veering (second case), $f(x_l, x_r)$ varies the pitch of the feedback tone linearly from 130 Hz to 1050 Hz with respect to $d(x_l, x_r)$. This frequency range is significantly lower than the frequency chosen for veering feedback, making it easy for users to distinguish between veering and non-veering feedback pitches.

TTS Feedback. The TTS feedback scheme can be described in terms of pulse delay, $p_t(x_l, x_r)$, and a TTS readable version of the distance-to-landmark metric, $d_{out}(x_l, x_r)$. The only difference between $p_t(x_l, x_r)$ and $p_s(x_l, x_r)$ is in the second case:

$$p_t(x_l, x_r) = \begin{cases} 200 + 800v(x_l, x_r) & : x_l > 0.5r_x, x_r < 0.5r_x \\ 2000 & : x_l \leq 0.5r_x \leq x_r \end{cases}$$

The 2000 ms pulse delay in the second case reduces the feedback redundancy that would be present if there were continuous TTS feedback similar to the continuous sonification feedback described for the second case of $p_s(x_l, x_r)$. Note that, rather than beeps, the system either generates the synthetic speech *"Left"* or *"Right"* in the first case of $p_t(x_l, x_r)$, and *"Straight"* in the second case, indicating the direction the user needs to move in order to proceed to the target landmark. In the second case, the system also generates a speech version of the distance-to-landmark metric $d_{out}(x_l, x_r) = 100 \times d(x_l, x_r)$ indicating the users progress towards the door.

Error & Task Completion. In the case that the door moves outside of the camera's FOV, the user is provided with TTS feedback (during both TTS and sonification modes) indicating the direction which they must turn in order to bring the door back into the FOV, and the discovery phase is automatically restarted. The navigation task is considered complete when the ratio of the perceived width of the door (in pixels) to the X resolution of the image exceeds 70% (i.e. when the door fills 70% of the field of view). This value was determined experimentally. This assumes that the doorway is somewhat large and near the eye level of the user upon completion of the guidance phase. Regardless of the feedback mode, HEADLOCK plays the same "success" sound effect to signal to a user that they have completed their navigation task.

5. EVALUATION

We performed a quantitative evaluation to determine what type of audio feedback was most effective and a qualitative evaluation to assess the usability and utility of HEADLOCK.

Participants. Eight blind participants were recruited from the local chapter of the National Federation of the Blind (3 Female, average age 44.1, SD = 11.1). Five participants were totally blind and three participants were legally blind with a small amount of residual light perception. The legally blind participants wore a blindfold during the user studies in order to ensure that their performance was not unduly affected by their ability to perceive small amounts of light. None had any self-reported impairments in mobil-ity or hearing. All participants were right-handed and used canes for navigation.

Instrumentation. HEADLOCK was implemented on Google Glass as previously described. Ground truth to measure veering was gathered using a commercially available beacon based localization system (Hagisonic StarGazer) that offers a localization accuracy of ±2 cm. The StarGazer camera was worn on a subject's back using a belt with supporting computing equipment (Windows Surface Tablet) in a backpack. Experiments were performed in a large open space (a conference room ≈ 10 X 12 m) on the UNR campus that was instrumented with ceiling tags required for the StarGazer system. The room had a single double door on the south wall (see Fig 4). During the user study, the left door was covered with green paper to ensure that HEADLOCK only recognized the right door.

5.1 Procedure

The user study was organized into four parts:

1. An unaided navigation task without HEADLOCK.
2. A HEADLOCK tutorial.
3. Trials with the first and second feedback modes.
4. A survey eliciting qualitative feedback.

All participants were randomly divided into two groups (A and B). For group A, the first feedback mode was sonification and the second was TTS, while group B had TTS first and sonification second. This counterbalancing ensured that the results of the study were not biased towards one feedback mode due to interference effects.

Unaided Navigation. To establish a baseline for comparison between navigating with and without HEADLOCK, subjects first performed an unaided navigation task. Subjects were taken into the conference room, positioned on one end of the room, 10 meters from the door, and asked to locate the door on the other side of the room. In a real-world scenario, it is unlikely that blind people who are faced with the task of having to cross a large open space would initially be oriented in the exact direction they needed to move unless they enlisted the aid of a sighted individual. Therefore, subjects were positioned facing the correct side of the room, but were not oriented in the exact direction to the target doorway. Subjects used their cane for navigation. Qualitative observations of the manner in which users accomplished this goal were recorded. Additionally, users were asked several open-ended questions regarding how they typically deal with similar navigation scenarios.

Tutorial. The tutorial familiarizes users with Glass and the usage of HEADLOCK . Prior to each trial with a specific feedback mode, users were instructed on how the mode for that trial worked. Subjects were allowed to ask questions regarding the operation of the HEADLOCK interface. After the tutorial, subjects could try HEADLOCK until they felt comfortable using it.

Feedback Trials. To begin each trial, subjects were guided by a sighted observer to five randomly selected points in the room before being guided to the starting location on the north end of the room. The point of this process was to disorient the subjects, ensuring that they did not start the discovery phase of HEADLOCK with an a priori understanding of where the target doorway was located. Users started in the same position as in the unaided navigation task, 10

User	Discovery (s)		Guidance (s)		Veering (o)	
#	Son	TTS	Son	TTS	Son	TTS
1	14.75	8.65	29.50	16.62	12.84	7.42
2	13.43	12.60	38.46	21.02	28.74	13.77
3	25.81	14.65	28.86	18.82	16.43	25.19
4	21.00	12.52	29.95	31.86	6.06	10.39
5	20.30	14.96	23.52	20.94	10.95	11.49
6	14.95	9.79	35.74	19.08	29.00	15.03
7	16.97	17.52	31.61	14.25	7.89	8.07
8	43.56	11.98	*76.84**	*60.29**	20.95	28.02
Mean	21.34	12.83	31.09	20.37	16.61	14.92
σ	9.86	2.86	4.87	5.60	8.89	7.69

Table 1: **Feedback trial results values averaged across each user's 6 sonification trials and 6 TTS trials (* indicates outliers).**

meters away from the door. The starting position was the same for all subjects and trials. They were positioned facing either the east, or west side of the room (randomly selected), while the target doorway was located on the south wall of the room, ensuring that the user would have to scan the room in order to discover the doorway. The HEADLOCK application was then started by the observer and the user was instructed to discover the doorway and then follow the guidance to navigate to it. The time required for the user to complete each phase was recorded. Each user completed six trials (three trials starting with the user facing east and three with the user facing west) for each of the two feedback modes.

5.2 Results

Unaided Navigation. All subjects were observed to follow very similar strategies to find the doorway located on the opposite side of the conference room. Each user began their task by setting out in the general direction of the doorway, using their canes to sense landmarks (e.g. walls). Several subjects veered significantly and found the east wall first, while the remainder of the subjects veered less significantly and found the south wall first. After finding a wall, all subjects followed the wall until they detected the doorway with their cane. One subject commented that wall following was her default strategy for finding a particular store in a mall. Three subjects commented that when faced with situations such as this, they use both sounds (e.g. echoes off of walls and sounds from air vents) and smells (e.g. the scent of the food court in a mall) to help orient themselves in large open spaces.

Feedback Trials. Table 1 lists the average results for each user over the six trials. In order to understand the efficiency of the sonification mode as compared to the TTS mode, the average time required to complete the discovery and guidance phases for each mode was calculated for each user, and the averages were compared using a one-way ANOVA. A Grubbs' test found the average times for one subject to be a statistically significant outlier for TTS ($Z = 2.38, N = 8, p < .05$) as well as sonification ($Z = 2.32, N = 8, p < .05$). It is interesting to note that this subject was the only subject to report no previous experience with mobile technologies, possibly explaining the user's slower performance. It was found that TTS required $12.83\,$s for discovery (39.9% faster than sonification) and $20.37\,$s for guidance (34.5% faster than sonification). Both of these re-

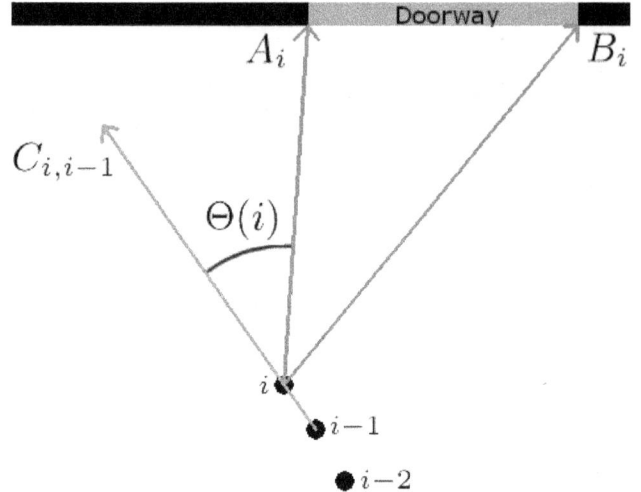

Figure 5: **The veering cost function sums the measure of veering at each point along a user's path weighted by the magnitude of $C_{i,i-1}$.**

sults were found to be statistically significant ($\boldsymbol{F}_{1,14} = 5.496$, $p < 0.05$ and $\boldsymbol{F}_{1,2} = 14.608$, $p < 0.005$ respectively). Next, since HEADLOCK was designed to prevent blind subjects from veering during navigation, veering was analyzed across all subjects' navigation paths for each feedback mode. In order to measure veering, two gradients were defined at every point along each user's path: the vectors between the every point and the points of the left and right sides of the doorway (labeled as vectors A_i and B_i for point i in Figure 5 respectively). The current trajectory at every point of the subjects' navigation path was calculated as the vector between point i and point $i-1$ (labeled vector $C_{i,i-1}$ in Figure 5). These vectors were then used to calculate the subjects' degree of veering, $\Theta(i)$, at each point along their paths. If $C_{i,i-1}$ was angled between A_i and B_i ($\angle AC < \angle AB$ and $\angle BC < \angle AB$), the section of the path between point i and $i - 1$ did not exhibit veering (i.e. $\Theta(i) = 0$). On the other hand, if $C_{i,i-1}$ was angled outside of the region between A_i and B_i, then the degree of veering was accounted for as the angle between $C_{i,i-1}$ and the closest of either A_i or B_i (i.e. $\Theta(i) = min(\angle BC, \angle AC)$). This measurement of veering was used to create a cost function assigning a value to each path, representing the average veering which occurred along each path P:

$$Cost_{veer}(P) = \frac{\sum_{i=1}^{n} \|C_{i,i-1}\| \, \Theta(i)}{\sum_{i=1}^{n} \|C_{i,i-1}\|}$$

The cost of all paths were calculated and averaged for each feedback mode for each user. These average cost values were compared between feedback modes with a one-way ANOVA. No significant difference in veering was found between feedback modes ($\boldsymbol{F}_{1,14} = 0.164$, $p > 0.05$).

Qualitative Feedback. After the feedback trials, nondirected interviews with open-ended questions were used to collect qualitative experiences as to understand the usability of HEADLOCK and to identify areas for improvement.

The usability and effectiveness of the app was evaluated using a 5-point Likert scale that ranged from 1 (strongly disagree) to 5 (strongly agree). Users agreed that HEAD-LOCK allowed them to navigate effectively to a doorway (M = 3.94, SD = 0.63). Additionally, users expressed neutral feelings that the system would minimize the chances they would become lost (M = 3.50, SD = 1.12) but users liked the system overall (M = 4.00, SD = 0.83). With respect to the feedback modes, users expressed neutral feelings about the sonification mode being easy to understand (M = 3.75, SD = 1.48) in addition to neutral feelings about the sonification feedback being insufficient for navigating towards doorways (M = 2.50, SD = 1.58). The TTS feedback was found to be easy to understand (M = 4.31, SD = 0.97) and sufficient to navigate towards a doorway (M = 4.19, SD = 1.27). There was no significant difference in rankings between feedback types (p > 0.05). Users agreed that HEADLOCK would allow them to navigate large open spaces more independently (M = 3.88, SD = 0.93).

In terms of general suggestions for improvement, two users suggested that HEADLOCK should include obstacle detection as a feature. Two users suggested that the pulse delay for TTS feedback should be adjustable to allow for users to receive feedback more or less frequently based on personal taste. This was reflected in another user who said that sonification feedback felt too precise and therefore said the precision should be adjustable. Finally, two users commented that the physical interface of Google Glass should be made more accessible by adding bumps to the touchpad so that users can more easily determine where to tap the touchpad for interactions.

6. DISCUSSION & FUTURE WORK

Our study demonstrated the feasibility of HEADLOCK and allowed us to identify the following research issues.

Feedback Tradeoffs. TTS allows for more efficient navigation to doors than when using sonification though no significant difference in the degree of veering was found. Subjects expressed a preference for TTS (non significant). From our analysis it appears that the sonification feedback during veering often caused subjects to pause in order to find the correct direction to the door. Using TTS, subjects were observed to correct their course while continuing to navigate to the door leading to more efficient navigation with respect to time (see Figure 6). This could be explained that the sonification feedback was harder to interpret and more difficult to learn than using TTS. Several subjects indicated that they found following the increasing pitch of sonification to be less obtrusive than receiving TTS distance updates. Determining the direction in which to turn to correct for veering is easier with TTS than with sonification, as users have to figure out the direction of veering error, where TTS immediately conveys this (e.g. *"Left"* vs. *"Right"*). Based on these results, it seems feasible to explore a hybrid feedback approach where we convey veering error using TTS and distance to the landmark using sonification. Pitch could also be used in conjunction with TTS feedback to convey the magnitude of the veering error (e.g. a high pitch *"Right"* indicating a large turn to the right). Future user studies will evaluate how this feedback will affect HEADLOCK 's efficiency.

Head-Mounted Displays. Subjects were very excited to use Glass. Several subjects stated they found it hard to

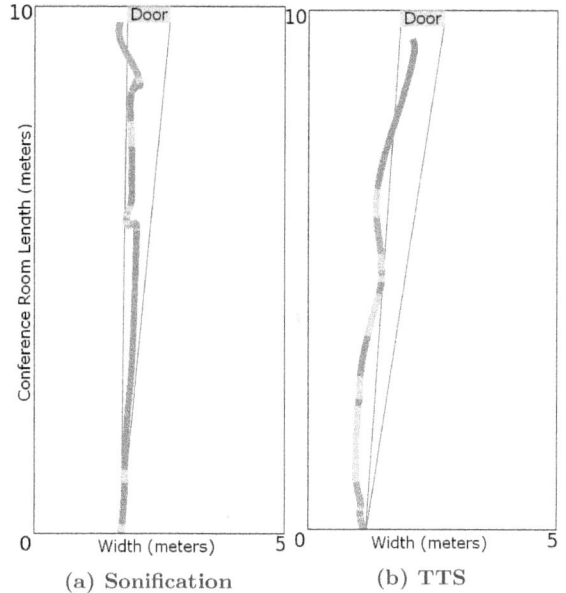

(a) Sonification   (b) TTS

Figure 6: Example traces of paths for both feedback modes. The path is marked as green when $\Theta(i) = 0$, yellow when $\Theta(i) < 10$, and red when $\Theta(i) > 10$. The blue lines represent the vectors A_0 and B_0 (see Figure 5).

imagine that Glass was a fully functioning wearable computer due to its light weight and small size. One minor accessibility issue with the use of Glass was identified. Because all subjects used their cane in their right hand for navigation, they had to temporarily place the cane in their left hand to be able to select the landmark with their right hand using the touchpad. To allow for more efficient interaction with Glass while navigating the touchpad should be on the left side. Voice recognition could be used to enable hands-free input, but we did not implement this as for this study we wanted our input to be most robust as voice recognition may be difficult to use in noisy environments. No subjects expressed any difficulty in hearing the feedback from Glass's bone conduction speaker, which is good as this type of speaker can be used in noisy environments.

Obstacle Detection. Two subjects expressed that obstacle detection should be a feature of HEADLOCK . Due to the position and direction the camera is pointing it may be difficult to implement ground level obstacle detection on an OHMD that has the fidelity, accuracy and reliability of a cane. However, OHMDs may be better suited for over-head obstacle detection due to the camera position, which would address a current limitation of a cane.

Limitations. Our study was limited in that only doors were used as landmarks. We did not evaluate whether OHMDs are a better platform than smartphones for navigation aids. We did not evaluate the maximum distance at which a landmark can be identified nor how distance affects a cane user's ability to efficiently navigate to a landmark. We plan to investigate these issues in future research.

Landmark Detection. Future work will focus on expanding the set of landmarks that can be recognized, which could include signs, staircases or large windows. The environment in which our user study was conducted only had single door but HEADLOCK should allow its users to make a selection from multiple landmarks that are visible. Hallways in airports or schools often feature pattern or lines, which could also be detected and be used for following without cane users having to follow a wall instead. We plan to merge the open space navigation benefits of HEADLOCK with the high level indoor navigation features of NAVATAR [5].

7. CONCLUSION

We present HEADLOCK: a navigation aid specifically developed for optical head-mounted displays, such as Google Glass. Traversing large open spaces has been identified as a navigation challenge for cane users. HEADLOCK addresses this issue, by letting cane users remotely identify and select landmarks, such as a door. Audio feedback then efficiently guides a user to this landmark. A user study with 8 blind users evaluated the usability and effectiveness of two types of audio feedback, i.e. sonification and TTS. Results found TTS to be most effective, though no difference in veering was observed. Qualitative feedback was aggregated to inform the future development of HEADLOCK.

8. ACKNOWLEDGMENTS

This work is supported by a Google Faculty Research Award.

9. REFERENCES

[1] Google glass, http://www.google.com/glass/start/.
[2] J. Bigham, C. Jayant, A. Miller, B. White, and T. Yeh. Vizwiz::locateit - enabling blind people to locate objects in their environment. In *Proc. of CVPRW'10*, pages 65–72.
[3] N. Bilton. New York Times blog. disruptions: Visually impaired turn to smartphones to see their world, http://bits.blogs.nytimes.com/2013/09/29/disruptions-guided-by-touch-screens-blind-turn-to-smartphones-for-sight/.
[4] S. Ertan, C. Lee, A. Willets, H. Tan, and A. Pentland. A wearable haptic navigation guidance system. In *Proc. of ISWC'98*, pages 164–165.
[5] N. Fallah, I. Apostolopoulos, K. Bekris, and E. Folmer. The user as a sensor: navigating users with visual impairments in indoor spaces using tactile landmarks. In *Proc. of CHI '12*, pages 425–432
[6] H. Ye, M. Malu, U. Oh, and L. Findlater. Current and future mobile and wearable device use by people with visual impairments. In *Proc. of CHI '14*. To Appear.
[7] T. Ghirardelli and A. Scharine. Helmet-mounted displays: Sensation, perception and cognition issues. *Army Aeromedical Research Lab*, pages 599–618, 2009.
[8] H. E. Heffner and R. S. Heffner. Hearing ranges of laboratory animals. *JAALAS*, 46(1):20–22, 2007.
[9] A. Hub, J. Diepstraten, and T. Ertl. Design and development of an indoor navigation and object identification system for the blind. In *Proc. of ASSETS '04*, pages 147–152.
[10] A. Israr, O. Bau, S.-C. Kim, and I. Poupyrev. Tactile feedback on flat surfaces for the visually impaired. In *Proc. of CHI EA '12*, pages 1571–1576.
[11] V. Ivanchenko, J. Coughlan, and H. Shen. Crosswatch: a camera phone system for orienting visually impaired pedestrians at traffic intersections. *Proc. of CHPSN'08*, 5105:1122–1128.

[12] C. Jayant, H. Ji, S. White, and J. P. Bigham. Supporting blind photography. In *Proc. of ASSETS '11*, pages 203–210.
[13] S. Lacey, R. Lawson, J. Loomis, R. Klatzky, and N. Giudice, *Representing 3D Space in Working Memory: Spatial Images from Vision, Hearing, Touch, and Language*, pp. 131–155. 2013.
[14] A. A. Kalia, G. E. Legge, and N. A. Giudice. Learning building layouts with non-geometric visual information: the effects of visual impairment and age. *Perception*, 37(11):1677–1699, 2008.
[15] G. Kempen, J. Ballemans, A. Ranchor, G. van Rens, and G. Zijlstra. The impact of low vision on activities of daily living, symptoms of depression, feelings of anxiety and social support in community-living older adults seeking vision rehabilitation services. *Qual Life Res*, Nov 2011.
[16] V. Khambadkar and E. Folmer. GIST: a gestural interface for remote nonvisual spatial perception. In *Proc. of UIST '13*, pages 301–310.
[17] R. Manduchi. Mobile vision as assistive technology for the blind: An experimental study. In *Proc. of ICCHP '13*, 2012. pages 9–16.
[18] R. Manduchi and J. Coughlan. (computer) vision without sight. *Commun. ACM*, 55(1):96–104, Jan. 2012.
[19] D. Mapelli and M. Behrmann. The role of color in object recognition: Evidence from visual agnosia. *Neurocase*, 3(4):237–247, 1997.
[20] J. R. Marston, J. M. Loomis, R. L. Klatzky, and R. G. Golledge Nonvisual Route Following with Guidance from a Simple Haptic or Auditory Display. *JVIB*, 101(4):203-211, 2007.
[21] M. A. Nees and B. N. Walker. Listener, task, and auditory graph: Toward a conceptual model of auditory graph comprehension. In *Proc. of ICAD'07*, pages 266–273.
[22] F. N. Newell, A. T. Woods, M. Mernagh, and H. H. Bülthoff. Visual, haptic and crossmodal recognition of scenes. *Exp. Brain Res.*, 161:233–242, 2005.
[23] T. H. Riehle, S. M. Anderson, P. A. Lichter, W. E. Whalen, and N. A. Giudice. Indoor inertial waypoint navigation for the blind. In *Proc. of EMBC '13*, pages 5187–5190
[24] D. A. Ross and B. B. Blasch. Development of a wearable computer orientation system. *Personal Ubiquitous Comput.*, 6(1):49–63, 2002.
[25] B. J. Stankiewicz and A. A. Kalia, "Acquisition of structural versus object landmark knowledge," *J Exp Psychol Hum Percept Perform*, vol. 33, pages 378–390, Apr 2007.
[26] H. Shen and J. Coughlan. Towards a real-time system for finding and reading signs for visually impaired users. In *Proc. of ICCHP '12*, pages 41–47.
[27] M. A. Williams, A. Hurst, and S. K. Kane "Pray Before You Step out": Describing Personal and Situational Blind Navigation Behaviors. In *Proc. of ASSETS '13*. 28:1–28:8.

Technology to Reduce Social Isolation and Loneliness

Ron Baecker
Technologies for Aging
Gracefully Lab (TAGlab)
University of Toronto
ron@taglab.ca

Kate Sellen
Faculty of Design
OCAD University
ksellen@faculty.ocadu.ca

Sarah Crosskey
Faculty of Design
OCAD University
sc12xh@student.ocadu.ca

Veronique Boscart
CIHR/Schlegel Chair in Seniors Care
Conestoga College
vboscart@conestogac.on.ca

Barbara Barbosa Neves
TAGlab
University of Toronto
barbara@taglab.ca

ABSTRACT

Large numbers of individuals, many of them senior citizens, live in social isolation. This typically leads to loneliness, depression, and vulnerability, and subsequently to other negative health consequences. We report on research focused on understanding the communication needs of people in environments associated with social isolation and loneliness, and how technology facilitates social connection. Our work consists of successive iterations of field studies and technology prototype design, deployment, and analysis. Particular attention is paid to seniors in retirement communities and in long-term care settings (nursing homes). We present design implications for technology to enable seniors' social connections, the "InTouch" prototype that satisfies most of the implications, and a report on one older adult's experience of InTouch.

Categories and Subject Descriptors

H.5.2; K.4.2.

General Terms

Design; experimentation; human factors.

Keywords

Social isolation; loneliness; communications technology; chronic pain; long-term care; seniors; field studies; prototypes.

1. INTRODUCTION

Large numbers of adults live in relative degrees of social isolation. Many, but not all, are senior citizens, who we define as individuals 65 years of age and over. Some seniors live alone, some with a partner or others. Their limited social ties, often caused by geographic relocation or by the death of family and friends, can lead to isolation. Some seniors are lonely at home, or when hospitalized in rehabilitation facilities for weeks, months, or even years. They may suffer from chronic pain, and may have physical or cognitive challenges to mobility or communication. Many perceive themselves as being lonely. Being isolated often results in depression or significant vulnerability (6).

We became interested in this problem through a personal experience — observing two years of the increasing isolation of a close relative in a rehabilitation facility as she declined physically and cognitively. We imagined the hospital TV on her wall as a vehicle to bring in video updates from her children. This seemed especially salient as it became more and more difficult, both physically and emotionally, for family and friends to visit.

In 2009, we began field research and envisioning, prototyping, and testing novel technology to enable communications and support for socially isolated individuals. This paper reviews progress towards the development of the requirements for such technology, beginning with an elaboration of the problem's importance and a survey of relevant previous research. We then focus on the design process — what we have learned from potential users in a variety of relevant settings through observations, interviews, focus groups, and deployment of early prototypes. Then follows an enumeration of design implications synthesized from the studies, a description of the system we are testing in a field trial, and a report on the experiences of the first significant pilot user.

2. SIGNIFICANCE

We define isolation as a lack of quantity and quality of social contacts (4). In this paper, we speak primarily of *social* isolation, but acknowledge that social isolation can be caused *physically*, through distance or disability, or *emotionally*, through unsustainable friendships, social stigmas, or traumatic events. Isolation may lead to feelings of loneliness (7), which largely depends on whether isolation is freely chosen, since voluntary isolation may be associated with positive feelings (4).

A recent meta-analysis of the literature asserts that 10 to 43% of homebound older adults are isolated (30). Even more striking, Perissinotto et al. (31) report on a longitudinal cohort study of 1600 participants and find that 43% are lonely. Similarly, AARP (1) reports on a U.S.-wide representative sample of 3000 adults ages 45 or older and finds that 35% of older adults suffer from chronic loneliness.

There is clear and compelling evidence that social isolation is associated with negative health outcomes (13, 24). Isolation is closely linked to depression, each building on the other (3). In seniors, a limited social network is associated with poor health outcomes in measures such as daily activities, incontinence, vision impairment, and subjective health rating (24).

Social isolation is significantly associated with increased mortality (18, 39). Conversely, robust social networks are associated with reduced mortality among men living with cardiovascular disease (21). In the case of an emergency, any social contact is associated with increased survival rates (22).

Our research has engaged with different groups of individuals where isolation is often a factor in health outcomes. We have carried out an iterative set of mutually reinforcing field studies and prototype development. This work is significant because it has allowed us to make design choices based on an expanding qualitative understanding of social isolation, and the role of interactive systems in potentially alleviating that isolation.

3. RELATED WORK

Interest in technology for social connectedness was sparked early in this millennium, as illustrated by the seminal early papers by Mynatt et al. (28) on digital family portraits and by Hindus et al. (17) on social communication devices for the home. Our technology development is closest in spirit to the design of "communication appliances for intimate social networks" proposed by MacKay, Riche, and LaBrune (26), and typified by their work on "markerClocks" (33). Our field studies complement work on seniors and computers and communication (12), emailing (34), and computer-mediated communication (36).

The last decade has seen the continued expansion of this area of research, as documented in the recent edited volume entitled "Connecting Families" (29). Neustaedter, Harrison, and Sellen (29) stress that technology to support domestic communication differs profoundly from traditional media spaces (16) designed for the workplace. The former focuses on connection for its own sake, and not as a means towards an instrumental goal such as project coordination or document editing.

Although more recent work focuses on supporting video communications, Schatorje and Markopoulos (36) document the value of asynchronous audio messaging. Cao (9) asserts that families trying to bridge time zone differences value synchronous communication the most. Other investigators working in a number of domains, such as Inkpen (19), describe how various mixtures of synchronous and asynchronous communications are used in combination. Judge et al. (20) describe the use of always-on video linking between two or three sites, including a mixture of private and public media spaces. Blythe et al. (5) and Lindley (23) describe the use of technologies for cross-generational messaging.

Tsai and Tsai (41) show that only 3 months of 5 minutes per week of videoconferencing interaction with family alleviated depressive symptoms and loneliness for nursing home residents, as compared to a control group, over a period of a year. Seelye et al. (37) show that tele-operated robotic-controlled videoconferencing is perceived by independently living, cognitively healthy older adults as enhancing their well-being and physical health, social connectedness, and ability to live at home. Additionally, the concept of creating comfort and the role of communication in hospice care is explored in Ferguson et al. (14).

Our work differs from these studies in its focus on a large variety of groups of individuals in isolation, groups who differ in age, health conditions, and where they live; and in our exploration of asynchronous communications as the starting point for design.

4. FIRST STUDIES AND PROTOTYPE DEPLOYMENTS

Many, but not all, isolated individuals are senior citizens; we chose to work in successive studies with contrasting groups, including:

1) Home dwelling seniors suffering from chronic pain;
2) Older people in medium- or long-term hospitalization;
3) Seniors who live in long-term care residences;
4) Seniors who live in retirement residences, and
5) Seniors living at home and receiving health care services.

We began with individuals living at home with chronic pain. More ubiquitous than commonly perceived, chronic pain affects 10-20% of North American adults (15). Pain interferes with appointments, social outings, and regular communications, and often leads to social isolation.

We began our explorations into the design of systems to alleviate isolation by approaching the problem on two fronts. We wanted to build first prototypes that were robust so that these could be deployed in the field. We also wanted to better understand social isolation by speaking with potential users before, during, and after deployments. We took a grounded theory approach to the design and analysis of each successive deployment and engagement with users. We used a combination of observations, interviews, focus groups, and diary studies, depending on the size of the study. Researchers took written notes during the observations. In the case of interviews and focus groups, dialogue was audio recorded and fully transcribed and then analyzed using thematic analysis informed by a grounded theory approach (40).

All studies presented in this paper were carried out with appropriate ethics approvals. This paper presents each study briefly (details of study design and results can be found elsewhere) and then follows with a discussion of our findings and implications for design.

4.1 Interview Study of Individuals at Home Struggling with Chronic Pain

This first interview study aimed at exploring the use of media to prevent isolation by seniors with chronic pain. During 2010, we interviewed 27 seniors who had experienced chronic pain for three months of more. Semi-structured interviews included questions related to background and demographics; social network structure and media use; interaction challenges; use of mass communication modalities; and the roles of loved ones and caregivers.

Three themes emerged from this data: setting the stage for interaction, managing others' expectations, and revealing and concealing pain (3). Participants indicated that participating in social activities required tactics to avoid or minimize possible disruptions that could be caused by their chronic pain. If such disruptions did occur, as was often the case, they sought to mitigate negative impressions that could result. To do so, there were times that they revealed and other times that they tried to conceal the pain. Because it seemed risky and threatening for such individuals to repeatedly arrange times for real-time chat, this study supports an asynchronous communications approach.

4.2 Families in Touch Prototype

Our first prototype was called Families in Touch (FIT), based in part on unpublished undergraduate thesis research (23). During 2009, the student observed three seniors with differing degrees of isolation and loneliness. During conversations with the participants she noticed their tendency to touch pictures of their relatives. She believed that it was a way to reconnect with their family members and treasured memories.

Figure 1. FIT using photo of family and tactile interaction

Her design solution (Figure 1) consisted of a wooden picture frame incorporating a touch screen display surrounded by LEDs as new message indicators, and asynchronous messaging capability leveraging tactile interaction. When the senior touches the frame, a family member may receive an email to indicate that their relative was thinking of them, and access a web site to respond with a video message. The video was then transmitted to the frame, and the LEDs' glow invited the senior to touch the frame, their touch commencing the video playback. The design focused on creating an asynchronous, unobtrusive communication tool with a simple interface and tactile user experience.

In 2010, we deployed FIT for 2 weeks with three participants from the interview study, one of whom lived alone, the other two being a caregiving daughter and her mother. Participants appreciated the asynchronous communications, and developed their own patterns of viewing. Participants and family members really liked FIT and had no difficulty using it, but wanted to be able to send messages, possibly even video recordings, to family members, and not just the "I'm thinking of you" message conveyed by touching the screen.

4.3 Diary Study and Next Prototype — Ringo

To further inform our next design, we then in 2011 carried out a 2-week diary study of daily communication patterns and needs of 11 older adults with chronic pain (11). Participants were asked to record situations where they had social contact (224 situations in total), and situations where they desired social contact (a total of 106). Roughly 60% of the contacts were made by phone, 20% face-to-face, and 20% using a computer. Communication was initiated to catch up, to obtain practical information, to give or receive support about health issues, and for social and holiday purposes. Social contact was initiated for both functional and emotional reasons.

Based on insights derived thus far, we next designed a system (called Ringo) using a 7" Samsung Galaxy Tab (Android) tablet in place of both the picture frame and the enclosed picture. The system supported message sending and easy media uploading to a web site, asynchronously through a touch interface. Messages could be chosen from a set of standard messages: "Missing you", "Not feeling well today", "Change of plans", and "Need information". Media could be text, photos, or videos.

Ringo was deployed with three seniors and their families for 2 weeks each. Each person had been part of the diary study. Results were mixed. In one case, photos and videos were sent most days by family members and viewed and appreciated by the senior. A way to send back different sets of messages, such as "Got it!" was desired. The second senior already used frequent email exchange with family and friends, and did not adopt Ringo. The third senior made use of Ringo, but was limited by technical issues encountered by family members. Another de-motivating factor was that this project was a 2-week test and the technology would then be removed.

4.4 Interview Study with Individuals in a Complex Continuing Care (CCC) Hospital

The objective of the next study (2012-13) was to take what had been learnt previously and engage with a diverse set of potential users who might have a greater variety of issues resulting in social isolation. We designed a study on communication patterns and preferences of older adults residing in a complex care facility. Due to their age and the nature of their medical conditions, many seniors reside in these facilities for a considerable amount of time (years), and are often socially isolated and lonely.

Semi-structured interviews were conducted with 11 seniors who had resided in the facility between three months and 13 years. Diagnoses often included more than one condition including: paraplegia, multiple sclerosis, cerebral palsy, diabetes, hypertension, and chronic obstructive pulmonary disease.

We documented how various participants used face-to-face interaction, Skype, email, Facebook, the telephone, letters, cards, and gifts to maintain intimate relationships (6). We discovered barriers to accessing communication technologies, especially the lack of infrastructure, and the absence of support for learning and use of communication technology.

We can see that a nuanced account of communication needs and the role of technology must consider the diversity of the population of seniors and the settings in which they reside. Hence we turned our attention to seniors living in a variety of settings.

4.5 Interview and Observational Studies of Seniors' Retirement, Long-term Care, and Home Health Care

The objective of the next and last "needs analysis" study was to understand communication patterns with seniors in a range of settings, including long-term care, retirement residences, and the home setting where nursing care was being received on a regular basis. Many older adults in these settings receive care and reside in these settings for a considerable amount of time, again raising concerns about the potential for social isolation and loneliness. Included in these settings were seniors with a broad range of impairments to hearing, vision, mobility, and speech. We also included seniors who were based in rural settings as well as urban centers.

Semi-structured interviews were conducted during 2013-14 with 16 older adults residing in long-term care, retirement, and home care settings. Interview topics were developed based in part on our previous studies; making use of a review of the current HCI research on technology, social connections, and families (29); and adding a few topics from the social science and medicine literature (8, 32) that are relevant to retirement and long-term care.

Eight female and eight male participants ranged between 65 and 90 years of age, with lengths of stay, or receipt of home care, between three months and thirteen years. Diagnoses often included more than one condition including diabetes, hypertension, and heart disease.

We documented how various participants use technology to maintain and control communication specifically in acute situations or when reflecting or tired. We also looked at patterns of communication and interpersonal engagement independent of technology. Themes emerging from a qualitative analysis of the interviews and described in full elsewhere (38) show a range of technology use and communication patterns.

We spoke to some who actively manage contact and communication with family, friends, and providers, such as taxi services, clothing stores, and banks, through technology ("tech-savvy"). Technology is perceived as a tool to manage and adapt to changing circumstances and loss of capabilities.

We also spoke to some who displayed active "social" communication styles and activity patterns. This included sharing memories through pictures, postcards, and conversation, as well as heavy use of the cellphone, mainly through incoming calls from family, at specific designated times. Alternative media formats including video and voice recordings were also described as being desirable and valuable, although tools to create and share such media were not evident.

At the other extreme were those passive in their interpersonal communications and in their use and non-use of technology. This "resigned" style appears often in more acute settings such as long-term care, where loss of capabilities makes use of a cellphone difficult (in particular remembering numbers or using small keypads), and where family are perceived as "busy, unreachable, and not to be disturbed". What we found expressed by participants was a fear of further loss of contact with family that could result from new attempts to connect (i.e., with a new device), and little interest and motivation in learning to use something new. This confirmed findings from our previous studies regarding the need for extra supports for learning and use of technology in institutional settings.

A number of other themes emerged from the data that support the need for communication technologies for story telling and remembering, connecting between generations, and checking-in and maintaining lightweight forms of social interaction. While many participants described using a phone kept close to the body as their main communication device for routine, social, and acute communication needs, there was also recognition that with further loss of capability (hearing, dexterity etc.), this technology would no longer support their needs.

We also observed that photos, letters, and other highly valued tangible objects were referenced by participants in telling stories about people who were meaningful to them, but that considerable work was necessary to protect these objects from deterioration, and maintain orderly proximity to these objects. Different strategies for keeping these objects close and available were used, for instance, taping pictures to specific walls, balancing letters and photos on walking devices, and using notebooks to house letters and photos. Access and manipulation of these objects, however, was challenging for those with limitations to dexterity and mobility such as result from stroke, arthritis, and tremor.

Additional findings point to the prevalence of the phone as the currently preferred communication tool. There is a critical role of family in introducing and maintaining technology beyond the phone for seniors, especially those in institutional settings or with mobility restrictions. These findings were common across all three settings.

5. IMPLICATIONS FOR DESIGN

Themes and connections between themes were used to uncover design implications. Some implications confirmed observations from our previous studies, but there were also new insights.

Particularly important is the difference in style and attitudes towards technology and communication with family and friends. Tech-savvy groups are likely only to use something new if it enables independence and activity beyond the tools they have discovered for themselves, as they may already be well served by

existing technology. Resigned individuals are difficult to reach; their adoption of any technology for communication would need to be facilitated by family and/or staff. Many of these individuals are also fearful of or not interested in computers, or feel that they cannot master high-tech. For example, we found numerous cases of regular mobile devices having been discarded in trash bins. Hence our first three design implications:

Design Implication 1: Avoid traditional computing aesthetics (screens, keyboards, grey, black, and office plastic) and conventions. Design appliances, not computer interfaces. Support compelling concepts and metaphors from real life, such as a "wave."

Design Implication 2: Support expressions of personhood through alternate interaction techniques and tangible interfaces based on real-world objects and practices. Specifically, natural objects may be a good source of design inspiration, given that seniors relate well to animals and plants, and use tangible objects on their persons as emotional supports — letters, pictures, cards, small stuffed animals.

Design Implication 3: Leverage pictures of family to engage seniors. We have seen this idea in many of the studies and locations summarized above.

For the resigned group in particular, light forms of short social engagement, akin to a wave or a smile across the street, may be beneficial as a first step to relieving a sense of resignation and a possible state of social isolation.

For all groups, the family and caregivers play an important role in the adoption of technology. Additionally, it is important to respect existing patterns of communication, e.g., telephones, cell phones, and social media. These insights support the next two design implications:

Design Implication 4: Do not disrupt social ties with existing family or new friends; leverage emergent social activity in place e.g. sharing stories between seniors as well as remote connections with family and friends.

Design Implication 5: Respect existing uses of devices such as smartphones and patterns of family communication, e.g., email and social media.

Our studies support the appropriateness of asynchronous communication in particular to allow seniors and families to manage interaction patterns, to deal with seniors' concerns, and to respect the unpredictability of availability for conversation. Yet, we respect work such as Cao (9), which asserts that families trying to bridge time zone differences value synchronous communication the most, and manage to achieve this by adopting routines for ensuring availability.

Design Implication 6: Support and emphasize asynchronous but also provide opportunities for synchronous communication.

Our various studies also suggest other attributes of ideal communication appliances.

Design Implication 7: Provide multiple possibilities for communication including video, photos, and audio, but do not require seniors to type.

Design Implication 8: Use tactile interaction that accounts for such issues as arthritis or tremor.

Perhaps because our studies were done in Toronto, but we suspect more generally applicable, we encountered many language challenges due to a diverse urban population.

Design Implication 9: Be non-language specific. Make use of icons as much as possible.

Finally, we saw in several settings the need to design systems and infrastructure as well as appliances, and to realize that appliances in seniors' residences and care centers may need to be shared.

Design Implication 10: Design with a realistic understanding of the availability of technology infrastructure, maintenance, and assistance, which is likely to be low in nursing homes.

Design Implication 11: Support an institutional context with sufficient administration and privacy settings. Especially where rooms are shared or use of a device/appliance needs to be facilitated by the staff.

6. INTOUCH SYSTEM DESIGN

We used the design implications from the research described above in the design of our next iteration, InTouch (working name) — an application designed for seniors to connect with family and friends. In particular, we support the ability to send a 'wave' (a pre-set message), the interface is non-language specific, it supports asynchronous capabilities, and it integrates with existing common forms of communication, such as email and use of a smartphone by family members.

InTouch is currently built for use on an Android device, providing users with the option to use a 10" tablet or a 7" tablet. Support of a mobile phone would not be difficult, although screen size does pose a challenge. Users are encouraged to think of the tablet as a communicating digital picture frame. Family members can communicate with the senior via email from laptops or mobile phones as long as they have an email account.

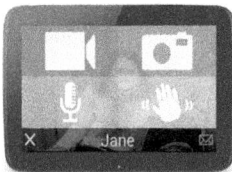

Figure 2. InTouch application key functions.
Going clockwise from the lower right, there is a wave, an audio message, a video message, and a photo message.

InTouch can send and receive photos, videos, audio messages, and waves (see Figures 2 and 3). A wave is a standard message sent to a family member to let them know that the senior is thinking of them (checking-in), and can be responded to by the family members through their email client by sending text, a photo, a voice message, or a video message.

Figure 3. A senior preparing to shoot a video with InTouch.
Icons at the bottom, from left to right are: exit; use the flash; switch from front to back camera, or vice versa; and start the camera rolling.

InTouch also supports reviewing of past messages for memory, storytelling, and sharing with others within the environment (see Figure 4). Choice of a specific communication from a particular

family member is done by touch and gestures on the tablet; no file system or naming method is required.

Figure 4. InTouch review of text and photo messages

InTouch has implemented several security features, for example, a senior can only receive messages from contacts that are pre-set.

To accommodate for seniors in care facilities, who may not have their own device, the senior can log into their account just by tapping on the device with an NFC tag (designed but not yet implemented). The tag could be embedded into an identity wristband, keychain charm or necklace.

Depending on the senior's (dis)abilities and preferences, certain functionalities can be disabled (designed, not yet implemented). For example, a person who experiences tremors may have difficulty hitting the targets, so targets could be adjustable.

The current implementation satisfies all design implications but #2 and #6. It needs to be improved in terms of #8. We are working with care staff to implement design implications #s 9 and 10.

7. PILOT DEPLOYMENT

We now report on the pilot deployment to understand how InTouch is being used to evaluate its impact on the perceived quality of life of potentially socially isolated and lonely seniors. The pilot study was conducted with Ms. J, a lady in her late 70s who resides at a retirement residence with her husband, and Ms. J's daughter who lives nearby. While Ms. J has strong family ties, she often feels left out and frustrated because many of her family members are geographically dispersed and she is not included in the family online communication. Ms. J connects with her family via a landline telephone and in-person, but her family primarily communicates online; sharing personal news and photos on social media platforms and discussing news articles and plans for family gatherings via email. Despite having never used a computing device, Ms. J's 'social' disposition and the support of her daughter made exploring InTouch as a communication tool an exciting opportunity.

The pilot study was conducted over a seven-week period, between Ms. J and ten of her family members, her daughter being the primary contact. The study involved three phases: pre-deployment (introduction to InTouch), deployment (use of InTouch, interaction analysis, usability and accessibility testing), and post-deployment (interviews with senior and family member). Data collection included interviews, observations, and data logging and was analyzed using thematic analysis.

The analysis of the pilot study data revealed that the use of InTouch had reduced Ms. J's frustration and feelings of being left out and improved her overall confidence and quality of life. She was able to keep up to date on family news and remarked that using InTouch felt like, "the whole world is coming into my room" and "It [InTouch] is special. They [family] haven't forgotten me." She was relieved at how easy InTouch was to learn and use. The main communication screen (Figure 2) was particularly appealing to Ms. J, "It's right in front of you, large and comfortable; easy to use." The design to create a minimalistic interface was effective in keeping the interaction clear and simple as Ms. J noted, "There are so few things to push you can't go that far wrong. It's not that complex."

In terms of the messaging functionality, Ms. J began learning InTouch by exploring the 'wave' and audio messages. She found the wave "for beginners is excellent," a technology icebreaker that was "gratifying because it is instant." The audio messaging was also appealing because sending a verbal message takes less time than writing, and it is not as intrusive or disruptive as calling someone on the phone because it is sent asynchronously. Ms. J added that her hand and ear get tired using the telephone, whereas InTouch is quick to send and receive messages and can be used with a stand for support. The video and photo messages were introduced to Ms. J in the initial meeting, but she was not using them even after seven weeks and a second demo. She said she wanted to become proficient with the 'wave' and audio messages first. She regarded this as a positive aspect, "I'll never get tired of it [InTouch] because I can learn new things and they are within reach."

While Ms. J had an overall positive experience using InTouch, the pilot study revealed four key areas that require further consideration: (1) the physical form factor of the InTouch device, (2) the refinement of the interaction and software design, (3) improvement on the participating family member's experiences, and (4) the importance of considering intergenerational differences.

The most challenging part of using InTouch for Ms. J was an accessibility barrier presented by the device form factor: a seven-inch Android tablet. The smooth, flush, 'invisible' external buttons were not only difficult to locate, but they were difficult to depress. To make the location of the power button more prominent a piece of tape was added, however Ms. J still found it difficult to depress the button and determine if the device was on or "asleep." Learning the appropriate duration and pressure required to turn the device and off and to put it to sleep and to wake it up was not intuitive or easy to quantify. There were at least two times during the pilot where the tablet was not used because Ms. J was unable to turn it on.

Charging the device with a micro-USB also proved difficult, but manageable, which was attributed to the small size of the connector and the specific orientation required. The device itself was difficult to hold due to the limited physical abilities of Ms. J who has arthritis in her hands. Replacing or augmenting the external buttons with more prominent, customized ones and designing a stand to hold and automatically charge the device are possible solutions that we are exploring.

The second major consideration is the refinement of the interaction and software design. The tactile nature of the device, while novel and fun, was especially difficult for Ms. J to use with her arthritic hands, which had little to no sensation in her fingertips. She had to touch the screen multiple times before it registered her touch. Haptic feedback and sensitizing her fingers to the necessary amount of pressure and contact were insufficient her situation. Swiping through the contacts and scrolling through messages were also hard to execute, so tapping the screen was preferred even though it was not always successful. Consideration of multi-modal inputs, such as speech, gesture, tangible objects, or eye tracking should be considered to increase accessibility.

Several refinements to the software design were suggested: (a) Supporting the ability to delete old or read messages. Having a lot of messages to scroll through is physically difficult and overwhelming. The challenge is doing this in a way that does not add needless complexity. (b) Touching the 'x' to exit a window was too abstract and difficult to learn. When Ms. J wanted to exit the message screen (Figure 2) she would send a wave instead of tapping the 'x' in the lower left corner because the 'x' symbol did not resonate with her mental model. She said that using an arrow to indicate moving back to the previous screen would have been more intuitive. (c) The digital video recorder icon was not recognizable at first – a reel of film would have been more intuitive.

A third, and critical, consideration is the need to improve the experience of InTouch message recipients. Ms. J's daughter explained that the wave "by the forth or fifth time gets annoying more than anything else" and "there's nothing to respond to." She suggested being able to personalize the 'wave' message with a simple line of text to be more engaging. The daughter expressed that the audio messages were "superficial . . . You don't get into a deep meaningful conversation. There's no actual discourse. Writing gives you pause to think about what you want to say." The daughter also noted the disadvantage of not being able to quickly scan an audio message to reference the original message when writing a response email. These observations raise real design challenges, because we will never require our senior users to type, but speech recognition technologies may enable an answer.

While InTouch offered lightweight communication for Ms. J, it was heavyweight for her daughter, who has become a "Facebook interpreter." This involves relaying messages and photos from Facebook, which requires tedious copying, pasting, and sending. For the daughter, the communication with her mother via InTouch became less personal; however, she added that this did not replace the frequency of their more personal phone conversations. We are of course considering how InTouch should interact with social media such as Facebook.

The fourth and final point is the importance of addressing intergenerational differences. Discussing communication expectations and styles, etiquette for online communication, and technical jargon is critical to ensuring the sustainability of this deployment. Ms. J checked the device only once every couple days and would sit down for an hour or so and reply to messages as if she "was replying to a letter," whereas her family was constantly checking their smart devices and responding to messages within 24 hours. From Ms. J's perspective her family was very responsive and sent frequent messages, but the perceived delay in her responses eventually resulted in family reaching out less frequently or not at all. The etiquette and expectation that one will respond to a digital message within a 24-48 hour time frame is one that should be discussed before the deployment to prevent misunderstandings. Likewise, the differences and preferences in communication styles should be expressed and respected.

Another intergenerational gap identified was the use of technical jargon when talking about the device. Reducing technical jargon and providing a glossary for terms like "swiping" and putting the tablet in "sleep mode" can empower the senior to be on the same level and support their transition in integrating new technology into their personal life.

The pilot study with Ms. J and her daughter demonstrated that InTouch increases the senior's feelings of connectedness and confidence, and that the device is relatively easy to learn and use. Further consideration needs to be given to the overall form factor of the device, the interaction and software design, the experience of message recipients, and the expectations of all stakeholders.

8. DISCUSSION

We have conducted several sets of observations, interviews, focus groups, and deployment studies to understand the communication patterns and needs of older individuals in a number of settings. Despite this variety of population and study contexts, some insights emerge that are useful in guiding current and future designs in the form of the design implications and new understandings that we believe to be useful.

The research described in this paper started with one metaphor as a design strategy: the picture frame, as in (10) and (28). This metaphor seemed to be a good choice given that our research pinpoints tangible forms of communication as being compelling for seniors.

The application's current design relies heavily, but not exclusively, on an understanding of common mobile device form factors (the cell phone or tablet), building on the everyday concept of a picture frame with its own specific meaning and use. We are now also designing and developing a version of InTouch to provide multi-modal input/output with an alternative display option — a flat screen TV controlled by a cell phone masquerading as an augmented TV remote control. Our research suggests that other metaphors may also be useful, for example, devices such as smart watches and display media such as photo albums.

The results of the qualitative studies undertaken with residents in several institutional settings provide new insights into the use of existing communication technology, communication patterns, and social connection. One outcome of our research is the identification of three distinctive styles — Tech-savvy, Social, and Resigned. These styles imply quite different needs and behaviors. There are several opportunities for further research and exploration to develop a richer understanding of each of these groups, and particularly the 'resigned' style that implies greater potential for social isolation.

Our work confirms the importance of mechanisms by which seniors can 'check-in' with family and friends, this serving both a social and practical purpose. As we mention earlier, some recent HCI work on social connection (36) stresses the value of asynchronous audio messaging. Our research highlights the different styles among the seniors we interviewed in terms of the messaging modalities they most appreciate. Some styles prefer synchronous video and perceive this as special, and others view audio communication by phone as useful for managing communication or being 'just enough.' As in (9), we too heard seniors mention routinized communication patterns and mechanisms for coordinating connections, but the issue of physical distance was not present in participants' responses. Instead, participants mentioned that having a busy family was a major factor in connecting, indicating that further research might be needed on the concept of distance (both far and medium), as well as incorporating existing understandings of social distance (27) from the sociology literature.

9. SUMMARY, CONCLUSIONS, FUTURE WORK

Social isolation typically leads to loneliness, depression and vulnerability, and often causes negative health consequences. It is significantly prevalent in subpopulations of senior citizens. We have reported on the evolution and outcomes to date of an iterative research project that elicits the communication needs and patterns of people in environments often associated with social isolation, and the role that technology plays in facilitating social connection. The work has included successive iterations of field studies and technology prototyping, deployment, and evaluation, with significant emphasis on seniors in retirement communities and in long-term health care (nursing homes). We have developed an understanding of the context and diversity of needs of isolated seniors, a number of design implications for technology that can facilitate social connection for isolated seniors, and a prototype that satisfies most of these.

We deployed InTouch this summer in a six-week field trial in a long-term care facility with 5 participants. Preliminary results suggest that the standard usability and accessibility designs and implementations have to be adjusted to better serve the needs of frail older adults. In January, we will be starting a two-month field trial with 12-24 seniors in a retirement residence that provides graceful movement as one gets older from independent living to assisted living to long-term care.

In terms of technology, there remain many opportunities and challenges including supporting synchronous communication gracefully, providing an always-on video and audio connection (20, 33), integrating with social media; enabling new varieties of display media such as large-screen TVs, family albums, smart watches, and wall displays; exploring multi-modal input, including voice; and imagining and prototyping tangible interaction modalities.

Our most recent work also suggests other design research directions including understanding the role of social distance, and the distinction between light and heavyweight communication for seniors (e.g., wave versus video message).

10. LIMITATIONS

The voice of family members has not been fully researched and incorporated yet, nor have we looked carefully at how best to engage staff without increasing their care burden. We plan to address these limitations.

11. ACKNOWLEDGMENTS

Significant contributors to this work included Chris Arnold, Spencer Beacock, Garry Beirne, Yichen Dang, Jessica David, Rachel Franz, Garry Ing, Michael Lenaghan, Elaine Macaranas, Mags Ngo, Thariq Shihipar, Ian Stewart-Binks, and Steve Tsourounis. We are grateful for financial support to Revera Inc., Google Research, NSERC, GRAND, OCE, and CC.

12. REFERENCES

1. AARP (2010). Loneliness Among Older Adults: A National Survey of Adults 45+, Sept. 2010.

2. Anderson, D. N. (2001). Treating depression in old age: the reasons to be positive. *Age & Ageing 30*, 13-17.

3. Benjamin, A., Birnholtz, J., Baecker, R.M., and Gromala, D. (2012). Impression Management Work: How Seniors With Chronic Pain Address Disruptions in Their Interactions. *Proc. ACM CSCW 2012, 799-808.*

4. Biordi, D. L., & Nicholson, N. R. (2102). Social Isolation. *Chronic Illness 8e, 97.*

5. Blythe, M., Wright, P., Bowers, J., Boucher, A., Jarvis, N., Reynolds, P., & Gaver, B. (2010). Age and experience: Ludic engagement in a residential care setting. *Proc. DIS 2010*, 161-170.

6. Boscart, V., Spence, M., Campigotto, R., Sellen, K., Birnholtz, J., and Baecker. R.. (2014). Social Isolation, Loneliness, and Communication Needs of Older Patients in Complex Care Settings, submitted to *Quality of Life Research.*

7. Cacioppo, J.T. & Patrick, W. (2008). *Loneliness: Human nature and the need for social connection.* Norton, NY.

8. Cannuscio C, Block J, Kawachi I. (2003). Social capital and successful aging: The role of senior housing. *Ann. Int. Med.* 139; 5; 2; 395-399.

9. Cao, X. (2013). Connecting Families across Time Zones. In Neustaedter C, Harrison S, Sellen A. (Eds.), *Connecting Families.* (127-140). Springer.

10. Dadlani, P., Sinitsyn, A., Fontijn, W., & Markopolous, P. (2010, January 6). Aurama: caregiver awareness for living independently with an augmented picture frame display. *AI & Society, 25 (2),* 233-245.

11. David, J. (2013). Communications Technology for Seniors with Chronic Pain, Unpublished M.Sc. thesis, Dept. of Computer Science, Univ. of Toronto.

12. Dickinson, A. & Hill, R.L. (2007). Keeping in touch: Talking to older people about computers and communication. *Educational Gerontology* 33:8, 613-630.

13. Edelbrock, D., Buys, L., Creasey, H., & Broe, G. A. (2001). Social support, social networks and social isolation; The Sydney older persons study. *Australasian Journal on Ageing, 20*(3).

14. Ferguson, R.D., Massimi, M., Crist, E., & Moffatt, K. (2104, to appear). Craving, Creating, and Constructing Comfort: Insight and Opportunities for Technology in Hospice, *Proc. CSCW.*

15. Gatchel, R.J., Pen, Y.B., Peters, M.L., Fuchs, P.N., & Turk, D.C. (2007). The Biopsychosocial Approach to Chronic Pain: Scientific Advances and Future Directions, *Psychological Bulletin 133(4),* 581-624.

16. Harrison, S. (2009). *Media Space: 20+ years of mediated life.* New York: Springer.

17. Hindus, D., Mainwaring, S. D., Leduc, N., Hagström, A. E., & Bayley, O. (2001). Casablanca: designing social communication devices for the home. *Proc CHI 2001,* 325-332.

18. House, J. S., Landis, K. R., & Umberson, D. (1988). Social relationships and health. *Science* 241, 540–545.

19. Inkpen, K. M. (2013). Kids & Video: Playing with Friends at a Distance. In Neustaedter C, Harrison S, Sellen A. (Eds.), *Connecting Families.* (95-123). Springer.

20. Judge, T. K., Neustaedter, C., & Harrison, S. (2013). Inter-Family Messaging with Domestic Media Spaces. In Neustaedter C, Harrison S, Sellen A. (Eds.), Connecting Families. (149-157). Springer.

21. Kawachi, I. et al. (1996). A Prospective Study of Social Networks in Relation to Total Mortality and Cardiovascular Disease in Men in the USA. *Journal of Epidemiology and Community Health.* 50(3): 245-251.

22. Klinenberg, E. (2002) *Heat wave: a social autopsy of disaster in Chicago.* University of Chicago Press.

23. Lindley, S.E. (2012). Shades of lightweight: Supporting cross-generational communication through home messaging. *Universal Access in the Information Society* 11:1, 31-43.

24. Litwin, H. (1998). Social network type and health status in a national sample of elderly Israelis. *Social Science and Medicine.* 46(4-5):599-609.

25. Macaranas, E. (2010). Memories in Touch, Unpublished B.A. thesis, OCAD University.

26. Mackay, W., Riche, Y., & LaBrune, J-B. (2005). Communication appliances: Shared awareness for intimate social networks. *CHI Workshop on Awareness Systems: Known results, theory, concepts and future challenges.*

27. Matthews, J.L. & Matlock, T. (2011). Understanding the link between spatial distance and social distance. *Social Psychology, 42,* 185-192.

28. Mynatt, E.D., Rowan, J., Craighill, S., & Jacobs, A. (2001). Digital family portraits: supporting peace of mind for extended family members. *Proc CHI 2001,* 333-340.

29. Neustaedter C, Harrison S, Sellen A. (Eds.). (2013). *Connecting Families.* Springer.

30. Nicholson, N.R. (2012). A Review of Social Isolation: An Important but Underassessed Condition in Older Adults, *J. Primary Prevent 33*: 137-152.

31. Perissinotto, C.M., Cenzer, I.S., & Covinsky, K.E. (2012). Loneliness in Older Persons: A Predictor of Functional Decline and Death, *Arch Intern Med. 172*(14): 1078-1084

32. Pollack CE, von dem Knesebeck O. (2004). Social capital and health among the aged: comparisons between the US & Germany. *Health Place* 10:4, 383-391.

33. Riche, Y., & Mackay, W. (2010). PeerCare: supporting awareness of rhythms and routines for better aging in place. *Computer Supported Cooperative Work (CSCW), 19*(1), 73-104.

34. Sayago, S. & Blat, J. (2010). Telling the story of older people e-mailing: An ethnographical study. *Int. J. Human-Computer Studies* 68, 105-120.

35. Sayago, S., Sloan, D., & Blat, J. (2011). Everyday use of computer-mediated communication tools and its evolution over time: An ethnographical study with older people. *Interacting with Computers* 23, 543-554.

36. Schatorjé, R., & Markopoulos, P. (2013). Intra-Family Messaging with Family Circles. In Neustaedter C, Harrison S, Sellen A. (Eds.), *Connecting Families.* (57-74). Springer.

37. Seelye, A.M., Wild, K.V., Larimer, N., Maxwell, S., Kearns, P., & Kaye, J.A. (2012). Reactions to a remote-controlled video-communication robot in seniors' homes: a pilot study of feasibility and acceptance. *Telemed J. E Health* 18(10), 755-9.

38. Sellen, K., Crosskey, S., Beacock, S., Arnold, C., and Baecker, R. (in preparation). Exploring communication patterns and technology use among seniors receiving care.

39. Steptoe, A., Shankar, A., Demakakos, P., & Wardle, J. (2013). Social isolation, loneliness, and all- cause mortality in older men and women. *Proceedings of the National Academy of Sciences, 110(5),* 5795-5801.

40. Strauss, A., & Corbin, J. Basics of Qualitative Research: Techniques and Procedures for Developing Grounded Theory. Sage, 2008

41. Tsai, H-H and Tsai, Y-F (2011). Changes in Depressive Symptoms, Social Support, and Loneliness Over 1 Year After a Minimum 3-Month Videoconference Program for Older Nursing Home Residents. *Telemed J. E Health* 13(4).

A Large User Pool for Accessibility Research with Representative Users

Marianne Dee[1]
mdee@computing.dundee.ac.uk

Vicki L. Hanson [1, 2]
vlh@acm.org

[1]School of Computing
University of Dundee
Dundee, Scotland DD1 4HN

[2]Golisano College of Computing and Information Sciences
Rochester Institute of Technology
20 Lomb Memorial Drive
Rochester, NY USA 14623

ABSTRACT

A critical element of accessibility research is the exploration and evaluation of ideas with representative users. However, it is often difficult to recruit these users, particularly in a timely manner. In this paper we report on the establishment of a large user pool created to facilitate accessibility research through recruiting sizeable numbers of older adults potentially interested in taking part in research studies about technology. Lessons learned from creating and maintaining this pool of individuals are reported.

Categories and Subject Descriptors

H.1.2 [**Information systems**]: User/Machine Systems – *Human information processing;* K.4.2 [**Computers and Society**] Social issues – *Assistive technologies for persons with disabilities.*

General Terms

Design, Experimentation, Human Factors.

Keywords

Research Participation; User Studies.

1. INTRODUCTION

In the work to be described in this paper, we discuss a 5-year centre that was created in the UK for research directed at the development of inclusive technologies. The focus throughout the centre was primarily on inclusion of older adults, but our research group was also interested in technology development for disabled people. To facilitate evaluation by representative users, we established a large pool of potential participants, comprised of people who were willing to be invited to take part in research on technology.

When developing technologies designed to address the needs of older or disabled users, good practice requires that individuals representative of the target users be involved in the development and evaluation of the technology [30]. Data collected from non-representative users, even if temporarily impaired to simulate disability (such as blindfolding sighted people during their participation in a research study), does not necessarily produce results that are indicative of how representative users will react under the same conditions [10] 0.

However, finding representative users is not always easy as these individuals are often difficult to reach through standard means of participant recruitment. The challenges of finding and recruiting the population sample required is time consuming, at the very least. This is apparent when looking at accessibility studies in particular where the recruitment problem has led to procedural practices such as repeatedly using the same research participants across related studies, simulating impairment using able-bodied participants, testing with proxy users, and employing inappropriate statistical methods to deal with small Ns [30]. The implications for the research outcomes of some of these procedures can be the production of a bespoke system not suited for the target population at large, or worse, the development of a system that does not work at all for the target population.

To avoid these pitfalls, our approach with our centre was to grow a pool of people in advance of research requirements, representing a diverse cross section of older adults with a variety of physical and cognitive abilities. We developed a bank of potentially willing people and created a legacy of established relationships with relevant groups and organisations that would ensure a more streamlined and speedier route to recruitment for a range of accessibility studies.

As will be discussed, the ability to set up and maintain this participant pool was the result of a long-term commitment to accessibility research. It is also the result of specific considerations to recruitment and retention of the participants. The pool was managed so that individual participants were not over-used, thus avoiding contamination from previous research participation. This paper will focus on these management methods, providing information needed by others who wish to similarly establish a user pool.

2. RELATED WORK

To our knowledge there are no other large-scale user pools that exist to serve the requirements of researchers in (HCI) Human-Computer Interaction-based accessibility work. Nowhere in the literature was there evidence of a similar pool, managed to ensure individuals were not over-used and that the sample fit both the research design and the different research methods employed for user engagement across a range of multidisciplinary research studies.

The accessibility literature often publishes on the challenges of recruiting participants, and has looked for new and creative ways of obtaining participants, such as online testing [3] [29]. As indicated, however, we know of no reported case of larger user pools available to a team of accessibility researchers.

Pools of participants do commonly exist, however. For example, pools recruit participants either from a discrete population such as university subject departments (e.g., psychology departments), associations and clubs, and university staff and students. Pools of participants also commonly exist for medical and clinical research. These may be panels recruited by marketing / survey companies who are able to get large numbers of participants, typically for survey research (see, for example, [1]). Often pools for medical and clinical research are self-selected in response to recruitment based on medical records detail [33]. In medical research, time can be critical, with slow patient enrolment a major factor in delays, leading to the database approach to recruiting research participants [33]. In these clinical studies, a pool often evolves by centralising resources (in a database) for recruitment across a number of health centres to reduce costs and ensure more universal processes, protocols and systems [5]. In medical circles they may be in a home, a clinic, a ward, or part of a medical practice where the research interests of the practice or the response of gatekeepers influences the likelihood of inclusion in a research study. Many existing pools advertise each study to all of their members, often online. Inclusion is based on the first volunteers who fit the criteria. As screening is done by each individual researcher, there is no monitoring of participation rates. This can result in experienced participants regularly taking part.

The needs for testing in accessibility research are very different to testing in clinical trials. Use of technology and cognitive testing requires users, who have not been through the same or similar tests previously. The rationale for the existence of our user pool was motivated by the ability to include appropriate research participants, thus providing confidence in the usefulness of the results for the target population.

3. SiDE USER POOL

We describe here the SiDE User Pool. SiDE (Social Inclusion in the Digital Economy) is a multi-year multidisciplinary research effort involving the University of Dundee and Newcastle University[1]. SiDE's remit is to address issues of inclusion for older adults and disabled users in the world of rapidly changing technologies and services. It involves research themes including Accessibility, Connected Home and Community, Creative Industries, Transport, Design, Business, with the User Pool cutting across these themes. To better understand the users' experiences and obstacles faced in trying to access digital information and services, user-centred or participatory research and design underpins all of SiDE's research.

The goals of establishing a User Pool were threefold: to provide ready access to researchers as needed for their work across the multiple project themes; to have background information on participants readily available to researchers; and to provide a group of target users who would be available to interact with

[1] www.side.ac.uk

researchers throughout all phases of work, from defining suitable research projects, providing early input on prototypes, and evaluating project success. The extent to which these goals were achieved will be discussed in this paper.

A unique feature at the School of Computing at the University of Dundee is the User Centre. We have previously reported on this Centre [11], which serves both as a training centre for older adults who wish to develop computer skills and as an educational mechanism for HCI students at the School who benefit from user feedback on projects they develop. It is not unusual for undergraduates to find that the software they developed, that seemed so easy for them to use, is entirely unusable by others. As User Centre members have participated in large numbers of research project evaluations over the years, they have developed a great deal of experience and are invaluable in terms of providing students with feedback. However with respect to the types of SiDE research projects undertaken, this experience makes them often too familiar with SiDE research goals to be naïve participants in research studies.

3.1 Recruitment Strategies

Accessibility researchers have long developed relationships with local community groups or self-help groups as a means of participant recruitment. Consistent with this, our main strategy was to identify key organisations and the senior managers within those organisations. In Scotland, the Local Authority has the greatest links into and across local communities. Meetings were initiated with those Dundee City Council managers who were most likely to direct us to a wide variety of older adults. This yielded an extensive range of contacts in community work, public libraries, adult and community education, community health, sports disability etc. All of these organisations and groups help identify likely participants, advertise our research and agreed to respond to future calls for help. The influence of their managers was central to their continued cooperation.

We also discovered that national organisations proved as important for local recruitment, reaching people through their newsletters and mailing lists as well as linking us directly to various active groups such as local support groups affiliated to the national organisation.

We targeted *age-related* advocacy groups such as pensioners' forums. As women outnumber men in the over 65's, we had to actively recruit older men, who are less likely to volunteer [4] [21]. We also targeted *disability-related* organisations and umbrella groups such as the local society for the blind and visually-impaired as well as a skills centre for people with disabilities. As research with the SiDE User Pool participants was likely to be looking at issues of accessibility, we actively sought out places where we could recruit a variety of people with low mobility, vision, or motor skills. Thus, the pool primarily comprised older adults, with an over-sampling of individuals who had a disability.

Talking to people directly was particularly important given the research focus. Recruiting high numbers of people excluded from, or with low confidence in, using technology is a difficult task. An important assurance for them was that all they were agreeing to was a willingness to listen to the research proposal and only then decide if they would take part. This was more easily achieved in face-to-face discussion with this population.

Marketing strategies included local media advertising, distributing flyers, leaflets and posters, online registration through a website, telephone access and paper registration with a freepost address.

In addition, 'give-aways' were used to increase community awareness of the SiDE User Pool. These included free pens, note pads, and key fobs with trolley coins that were given out at events. Participants were universally delighted to receive 'freebies' with good pens 'always useful' and the key fobs the most desirable item with this population.

3.2 SiDE User Pool Composition

Information about participant numbers for the SiDE User Pool is shown in Table 1. The initial objective at the University of Dundee was for a SiDE User Pool of about 800 – 900 older adults aged 65 and older. Between 2009 and 2012 a pool of over 800 individuals was established. In 2013, an update of participant details was conducted to clarify continuing commitment, correct contact details and any inevitable changes in availability / health for this group of older individuals. At the time of writing, the current number of involved individuals is 702 representing several counties throughout Scotland, with outliers across other regions of the UK. Since the end of 2012, a proactive recruitment drive ceased, as the number of participants is sufficient for User Pool demands. However, the SiDE User Pool is not static and recruitment now focuses on new requirements for specific studies using the relationships and partnerships already established, as well as developing new ones.

Table 1. SiDE User Pool Membership Numbers

	Number
Peak membership (Fall 2012)	817
Total membership (2010 – 2014)	863
Current membership (Spring 2014)	702
Withdrew (2010 – 2014)	159
Participated in 1 or more research studies	694
Participated in 1 or more studies at the university	498

Recruitment to the pool targeted people aged 65 plus, although age is not always the key factor. Younger people have been recruited for comparison studies and people with specific physical or medical conditions have actively been recruited for accessibility projects regardless of age. So at any one time the SiDE User Pool may have 15-20 % of members aged 64 or less.

The SiDE User Pool also includes partnerships with national and local advocacy groups representing people on age, health and issue-based topics such as Parkinson's UK; Celebrate Age Network and RNIB. Our outreach ensures robust user inclusion and has resulted in links into the community. During the initial recruitment years, 30 relevant organizations were recruited.

In terms of being representative of the population, the pool fell short of including any genuine representation of the oldest old, people living in sheltered housing or care homes, older adults with very high support needs or older adults from minority ethnic communities. The socio-economic background was likely to favour those with high school qualifications and the balance of the recruitment for the pool in the latter two years was entirely driven by the current research studies at the time. Enough community relationships were established to allow new recruitment targets if there proved to be a demand for them.

3.3 SiDE User Pool Characteristics

At the outset, one of our goals was to have data on background characteristics of the research participants. With this in mind we collaborated with the CREATE team at the University of Miami Miller School of Medicine [7]. Given a shared goal of interest in cognitive abilities of older adults in relation to technology, we used their cognitive and abilities test batteries to record background information on 188 of our participants. The goal was sharing of data between the two sites, with the potential for joint research that would come from a common base. It should be noted, however, that some of the test items from the CREATE battery had to be adapted for the UK, in particular cultural references and language. Together with data gathered through the recruitment process we had a snapshot of characters of the SiDE User Pool, providing similar data from the CREATE sample population. It is important to realise that these data are exactly as indicated -- a snapshot in time. Several of the cognitive tests in the battery require updating after a couple of years to be accurate measures. As some of the SiDE participants were tested at the very beginning of the SiDE User Pool and others were tested later, not all the data in the database accurately reflect the current state of participants in the User Pool. This is true for data collected at the recruitment stage; however, whenever studies take place information is updated.

3.4 Participant Selection for Studies

Between 2010 and 2012 when the most substantial part of the SiDE User Pool was established, only the manager of the pool had access to personal details. This was a direct response to the keenly expressed concerns of the target population worrying about cold calls from strangers and anxious about their privacy and security.

A single point of contact (SPOC) for User Pool participants and partner organisations was an advantage as the alternative for SiDE would have been dozens of researchers approaching the same organisations throughout similar time frames and most likely using the same enthusiastic individuals. A SPOC made life easier for participants coming to the university as they knew a name or that it was a study involving older or disabled people and were directed to the manager upon arrival. Many older people from the local community are unfamiliar with a university setting and nervous of visiting an academic department – especially where the expertise is something highly technical. Making every effort to meet them and make them feel at ease is important, and a backup person to catch late or lost people is helpful. If the participant is uneasy at the outset, confidence can be undermined and their ability to relax in the experiment affected.

The manager identified candidates fitting the researchers' study design and participant information by searching the SiDE User Pool database contact details. The manager then phoned candidates to explain the study and determine if they matched the research study inclusion criteria. These conversations were both functional and social, but most importantly the conversations ensured the potential participants fully understood the nature of their participation. The 1:1 connection, including polite social conversation, was reassuring and counteracted the 'cold call' effect, resulting in more older adults willing to listen and to positively consider taking part. It is a key factor in the retention of participants in the SiDE User Pool over the past five years resulting in the very low accretion compared to other research pools [28].

Preparation for participant testing takes a significant investment of resources and time that can be underestimated by researchers. With older adults in particular, preparation starts at the selection stage in order to clarify needs in terms of participant access to the university. Maps, car parking vouchers, one-way systems, bus stop locations, building access, location of doors, lifts and seats for waiting, are all important when inviting older or disabled participants to an unfamiliar place. Confirming time, date and place of the agreed study with older adults, via their preferred communication method, offers a prudent safety net, always bearing in mind the vagaries of postal services. Careful scheduling to ensure enough experiment time, and avoid keeping other participants waiting, is a challenge when participant skills may vary and effect timings. With a wide range of people taking part there can be significant differences in the time taken to complete a study. Scheduling multiple participants on the same day can result in participant queues.

Once in the building, the research study environment is important for people unfamiliar with lab or academic space. Offering a non-threatening, quiet setting with no interruptions, a jug of water, a choice of seating and good turning space are all worthy of consideration.

All of this is important to ensure that the participants feel they are part of a professionally managed research study and they can trust the process and the organisation the researcher represents. If the participants feel uncomfortable, unsafe, disrespected or foolish they not only withdraw their cooperation, but they also give negative feedback to others in their community. We have found, in general, that the university brand is a good one (through feedback from participants when we speak to them) and people trust its reputation for serious study. This is only true, however, if they have a safe and interesting experience when they participate in the research.

3.5 Maintaining the User Pool

The hardest task is keeping the User Pool participants up to date with developments as well as feeling like they are still part of a group throughout the life of the project. To this end, the SiDE User Pool have been kept informed of news, developments, and activities through a printed newsletter posted to all members; a website; email correspondence, and individual phone calls where appropriate. Any major changes are disseminated through both print and electronic communication, for example, from 2013 we moved from only allowing the manager access to the SiDE User Pool, to allowing SiDE researchers to recruit participants from the pool. However, we consulted with SiDE User Pool members first, allowing people to withdraw if they were not happy with this new approach to recruitment.

4. EXAMPLES OF SiDE RESEARCH

During the first 3 years, more than 30 individual researchers made use of the pool for a range of studies using a variety of research designs and methodologies. To date, 694 members of the SiDE User Pool have taken part in at least one research study.

Table 2 gives some examples of the work to which they contributed. To give a sense of the breadth of this research, we discuss here a sampling of the studies conducted. The first is a reporting of a one-day workshop held for all SiDE researchers. This effort hasn't been previously reported. In addition, we give examples of other studies from published research.

A one-day *SiDE workshop* was convened to give early input from users to the broad discipline based group of SiDE researchers. To provide feedback from users representing different views, we assembled four user groups:

1. Older adults who had no interest in technology
2. Older adults who were willing to use technology, but it had to be very relevant to their lives to bother with it
3. Older adults who like technology
4. Technology transfer specialists

The first three groups were from the SiDE User Pool. The 4th group was specifically assembled for the day. Throughout the day, representatives from the SiDE research areas pitched potential research ideas to each group of 6 – 8 participants. This was done on a revolving basis so that the research groups moved from one user group to another, getting feedback on their research ideas from each group.

The eye-opening aspect of the day was user group #1, the no interest in technology group. It is common for technologists to be enamoured of technology and its potential to enrich lives. This vision, however, may not be shared by target users. Many researchers were surprised to meet a group of representative users who could not see the value in the ideas pitched.

Table 2. A listing of sample research studies conducted with the SiDE User Pool

Research Method	*Example studies - references*
SiDE Workshop	Unpublished (2011)
Focus Groups	[14] [20] [27]
Co-Design Workshops	[25]
Questionnaires / Surveys	[16] [35] [23] [32]
Interview	[8] [9]
Eye tracking	[15] [34]
Experimental studies	[2] [6] [16] [22] [32]

The SiDE User Pool has been used for a large number of *focus groups*. These studies helped inform work on topics as diverse as in-vehicle systems for older drivers [14], social networking for older adults [27], and older adults' technology use and conversational support systems when engaging with BBC radio discussions [20].

Co-design workshops have been conducted in connection with the BESiDE project that aims to examine how the built environment contributes to the health and well-being of care home residents [19]. In preparation for data collection about activity in these homes, co-design workshops were conducted with SiDE User Pool members [25]. These workshops provided early input about acceptably wearable devices for older adults in preparation for going into care homes; results of these workshops with SiDE participants (all community-dwelling older adults) were then used to conduct co-design workshops with care home residents.

Questionnaires and surveys have been a popular method for getting information from large samples of users. Throughout the first few years of the SiDE User Pool several surveys were distributed both online and in print (with a freepost envelope). Some responses were obtained solely online, but the print versions produced the greatest number of responses. Sample surveys included questions about options for use of mobile phones as memory aids for older adults [23] and support for online health information searches [33]. Response rates to these surveys varied. Initially we had 60% response rates, but this decreased after a couple of years. Comments suggested lack of enthusiasm related to the repetition of questions across the various studies.

While direct interaction with participants was a more common methodology for the User Pool than questionnaires, on occasion when participants came to the university to take part in research studies a questionnaire was used as an element of the study too. For example, SiDE User Pool participants were asked questions about the acceptability of Open Source software as used by older adults [17] and about technology adoption for this population [36].

Individual interviews were often conducted with SiDE User Pool members in conjunction with other studies. In a few cases, however, interviews were the main research method. In one case, older adults provided online interviews about their experiences with technology[2] [9]. More recently, research in connection with the BESiDE project used interviews with visitors to care homes to help understand aspects of the built environment that facilitate social interactions in these homes [8].

The SiDE user studies were not the first to use *eye tracking* with older adults. There hasn't however, been a lot of work with this method for this population. While the method presents challenges for use with older adults, research was conducted with SiDE User Pool members that examined their eye movements when looking at website information in a variety of web information seeking tasks. These studies found differences, for example, in how older and younger adults enter search terms and develop strategies when using search engines [15] [34].

Experimental studies were the most common methodology used with SiDE User Pool participants and were also the most time demanding for the manager. Examples of studies with User Pool members included research with disabled users on cross-platform adaptations for users with visual and mobility disability [22], new television interactive controls for older adults [2], user interface designs to facilitate information seeking by older adults [6], computer input adaptations for older adults [16], and information cues for online health seeking by older adults [32].

5. LESSONS LEARNED
Our experiences with the SiDE User Pool resulted in several lessons learned that might be useful for others contemplating developing and maintaining a user pool, at this or other scale.

5.1 Participation Rationale: Reciprocity
An insight from recruiting over 800 people, and talking to almost 500, is hearing a range of expressed reasons why people took part. No one was 'in it for the money' and although many were delighted to receive a £10 gift voucher, many were reluctant to receive any reward as they felt that 'taking part' was a gift from them.

Recognizing the importance of reciprocity in relationships especially with older adults and people with disabilities is important for an equal relationship. Reciprocity is a norm that underpins social relationships [12] [18] [24] and is one reason why user pool participants need to believe that their knowledge and input is worth listening to; they generally genuinely want to 'give something back' as part of increasing their feeling of autonomy. The importance of autonomy and dignity is a significant aspect of reciprocity and can be undermined if they

feel patronised or if the research study seems disorganized, does not make sense to them, their values or their understanding of where it fits into improving, in some way, the real world as they understand it.

In some cases taking part was a form of 'self-help' with participants reporting their engagement with research as furthering and advancing knowledge. If they don't personally benefit they might help others who will. SiDE User Pool members reported being excited to hear about research of relevance to their situation and an opportunity to share issues they have with digital devices when dealing with low vision or another disability.

5.2 User Pool Manager and Researchers
The success of the SiDE User Pool was enhanced by the ability to have a full time person to manage the pool for the first three years. We recognise, however, that the ability to hire a full-time person for this role is generally not possible. We present the following information about the manager role and interactions, however, as suggestions for best practices in recruiting and testing research participants, particularly in accessibility studies.

The manager was of a similar age with user pool members, having empathy with them through comparable life experiences and shared cultural reference points. This was an advantage given the nature of SiDE research into rapidly changing digital technologies which many of the potential participants were uncomfortable or nervous about. Liking people, good communication skills, unafraid to go out to forge links, meet, talk and persuade groups, organisations and individuals to take part was also important.

The responsibilities of this role included SiDE User Pool recruitment, database management (making sure all participant contact details, characteristics, and study activities were updated and correct in the database), enrolling people for research studies, complying with research needs, typically meeting and greeting participants who took part in studies at the university, and running some of the studies.

The following observations are borne out of the years of working with researchers who, although fully signed up to user-centred research, may not yet have their antennae or emotional intelligence finely tuned to the centrality of the user as a person in the research process. The best of researchers can be focused on the 'thing' they are testing and the participant is the route to an outcome with the 'thing'. Understanding the importance of user experience and involvement is not the same as having the time to empathise with the user's perspective. It begins before the study and follows through and after it and the best intentioned of researchers are inevitably focussed on their research especially when working within tight time constraints.

5.3 Recruitment to the SiDE User Pool
We found that in working with older adults, in particular, on research into digital inclusion, face-to-face recruitment proved to be most effective in recruiting *suitable* participants. Initial recruitment strategies using posters and newspaper advertising resulted in high numbers of volunteers but many did not fit the explicit criteria cited for many of our research studies [13]. Travelling into different neighbourhoods and talking to groups from various local communities expanded the range of gender and socio economic backgrounds within the pool. As the User Pool grew, suitable people were more likely to be found from that larger pool and through the data gathering sessions (such as with the CREATE battery) where the manager could identify participant characteristics, visually and through conversation. However, it has remained the case throughout, that further

---

[2] http://talesoftechnology.co.uk/

recruitment is always needed to get participants with specific disability, age, and technical ability. Established relationships with relevant organisations are the route to easing this process.

5.4 Request Protocols and Processes

Researcher requests for participants from the SiDE User Pool were initiated through a user request form. Information describing the experiment, planned methodologies, recording equipment, numbers and the participants' characteristics, together with a copy of their participant information, consent and ethical approval forms were required. The form also required a jargon-free briefing of the planned study for the manager to use when calling potential participants to both ensure that they understood what they were signing up for and that the manager did not influence the participants' behaviour or attitude when joining the study. Student researchers required sign-off by their supervisor. The completed request form was followed up by a discussion with the User Pool Manager to clarify specific information.

This simple process smoothed the way for the manager, through a series of information steps, to more easily get the right people in a timely fashion. For example, requests were often received to send out an email questionnaire to the whole research pool; when queried this usually needed refining to exclude some participants based on certain characteristics. Preparation, planning and organisation are important, as the process always takes longer than expected and the unexpected will happen. Once working with participants, researchers may learn that the original plans demand a rethink of:

- the research design to ensure the data gathered is valid and the activity is doable by the chosen participants;

- direct recruiting is inappropriate and a slower process is needed: via a warden, a carer or relative to ensure full consent;

- rethinking the participant profile e.g., aged over 65 with a hand tremor and/or visual impairment and experienced using touchscreen technology may be too specific.

The time frame needs to be fluid enough to deal with many such unexpected factors. This also raises the issue of sensitivity when applying a strict health criteria and age range to the potential participants. More arrangements are needed in such cases, e.g., when disabled parking is too far from the entrance and university level clearance is needed to park closer. It takes more time but personally speaking with university personnel, local groups and/or phone screening, when recruiting from 'rare' populations worked best, resulting in higher recruitment numbers, more precise fits for studies and successful support from university bureaucracy.

All of these lessons were dealt with more easily with a full time recruitment manager as lead contact or to provide a safety net.

5.5 SiDE User Pool as a Resource for Others

Not surprisingly, there have been requests over the years from other organisations to have access to the SiDE User Pool. As a UK Research Councils (RCUK) funded research effort, we did work to address requests by other RCUK research.

At one point, there was consideration of whether it would make sense to provide the SiDE User Pool as a consultancy service to industry that needed user input. This was attempted one time. While experiences with other companies would undoubtedly vary, the participants' experiences with the industry researchers led us to abandon the idea of a consultancy. As a valued resource, there was a need to treat participants with a high level of respect. As it was not possible to control the participant experience in consultancy as well as was possible with our SiDE researchers, the idea of consultancy was not pursued beyond the original trial.

6. MEETING OUR ORIGINAL GOALS

At the outset of this paper (Section 3), we mentioned that our initial goals for the SiDE User Pool were to provide ready access for researchers to appropriate study participants, to have background information available to identify likely participants, and to develop a group of participants who could interact with researchers throughout all phases of a research study. How well did we succeed at these goals?

Goal 1: Providing researchers with ready access to participants. In this respect, the SiDE User Pool was a very big success. To date, 694 members of the User Pool have participated in 32 studies involving 58 activities. This work was conducted by SiDE researchers at the University of Dundee and Newcastle University, as well as by collaborators from the Universities of Aberdeen and Glasgow. In many cases, researchers were able to begin testing within days of having received ethical approval. The large variety of study types undertaken (as shown in Table 2) attests to the suitability of the SiDE User Pool members for a variety of research.

Goal 2: *Providing researchers with background information about participants.* By and large, this goal was also met. Information such as age was readily available to researchers and in many cases results of cognitive tests and disability issues were used to pre-screen participants for studies. In some cases, however, researchers had specific requirements or needed tests not administered, so had to do these as part of their experimental protocol.

Goal 3: Providing researchers with representative user input throughout all stages of their research. In this goal, the SiDE User Pool was less successful. The original plan was to create a participant group that would help formulate research strategy, participate in research studies, and actively evaluate research outputs. The original objective was to get early feedback about problems the researchers were addressing, the importance of these problems to the target users, and a sense of solutions that the target users were to adopt. This would have established a project with the active involvement of older adults or disabled users working at a policy and process level to address issues of digital inclusion.

In practice many researcher energies were evaluation-driven. There was relatively little uptake from the researchers in terms of getting early user driven feedback at the ideas stage and even less in terms of working with the users to evaluate the research outputs. While users were briefed on study outcomes, this was not the same as actively seeking their advice about the outputs.

In looking at Section 4 of this paper, there were, however, three types of research that provided some of this feedback. The first was the SiDE Workshop. This workshop gave researchers input at early stages of their thinking. The second, co-design workshops, solicited early feedback about the design of wearables to be used in research studies [25]. These workshops, however, were very targeted at designing comfortable devices for other research studies, so didn't involve the type of co-design that typically would involve asking participants about their interest in the solutions and how the solutions fit into their lives. The third set of studies that provided some early input were the focus group studies. These, too, however, tended to stop short of asking about needs, focussing instead on asking users specific questions about the design aspects of projects underway.

7. CONCLUSIONS

Our goal with this paper has been to share our experiences in managing a large group of research participants over several years. We hope that many of the lessons learned will assist others who wish to develop user pools for extended research groups.

In particular, we highlight our experience in recruiting participants and their reasons for research participation. At least among the population we were recruiting, a main motivation related to reciprocity and contributing to scientific research.

We also note that that attention to the participants (at the time of study as well as keeping them informed) is crucial. In this regard, a User Pool manager with personal and organisational skills is essential. Face-to-face recruitment strategies were most effective compared to traditional marketing drives using the media and posters. Talking to groups and giving presentations allowed for a fuller understanding and engagement with the project principles for recruitment of a wide range of older adults. Relationship building was important in maintaining the longevity of the pool in the knowledge that recruitment was never going to be static. In terms of SiDE User Pool members' loyalty and retention, the comfort of, and sensitivity to, the needs of the user as an equal in the research process is an important and an ongoing piece of work.

We note also, however, that having such a User Pool available does not guarantee that needed participants will always be readily available. In cases where researchers required participants consistent with original recruitment criteria, the SiDE User Pool worked extremely well. As researchers wished to recruit specialised participant groups, however, the SiDE User Pool had to be expanded.

In sum, our experience with the SiDE User Pool over the past several years has been – and continues to be – very positive. It is important to keep in mind, however, that these positive experiences require time and attention.

8. ACKNOWLEDGEMENTS

We thank the members of the SiDE User Pool who gave so generously of their time and ideas. We also would like to thank Kyle Montague, Sebastian Stein, and Michael Crabb for their comments on earlier versions of this paper. This work was supported by a RCUK grant, EP/G066091/1 "RCUK Hub: Inclusion in the Digital Economy".

9. REFERENCES

[1] Beach, A. Schulz, R. Downs, J. Matthews, J. Barron, B. and Seelman, K. 2009. Disability, Age, and Informational Privacy Attitudes in Quality of Life Technology Applications: Results from a National Web Survey. *ACM Trans. Access. Comput.*2, 1 Article 5 (May 2009), 21 pages. DOI=http://doi.acm.org/10.1145/1525840.1525846

[2] Bhachu, A. S. and Hanson, V. L. 2011. Older adults and Digital Interactive Television: Use of a Wii controller. *EuroITV 2011, Lisbon, Portugal, June 29 – July 1, 2011.*

[3] Bigham, J. P. and Cavender, A. C. 2009. Evaluating existing audio CAPTCHAs and an interface optimized for non-visual use. In *Proceedings of the SIGCHI Conference on Human Factors in Computing Systems* (Boston, MA, USA, April 04-09, 2009) CHI'09. ACM, New York, NY, 1829-1838. DOI= http://doi.acm.org/10.1145/1518701.1518983

[4] Butera, K. J. 2006. Manhunt: the challenge of enticing men to participate in a study on friendship. *Qualitative Inquiry. 12, 6. 1262-1282.*

[5] Cooley, M.E. et al. 2003. Challenges of recruitment and retention in multi-site clinical research. *Cancer Nursing. 2003.* 25, 5. 376-386.

[6] Crabb, M. 2013. Human Cognitive Measurement as a Metric within Usability Studies. In *Proceedings of the SIGCHI Conference on Human Factors in Computing Systems Extended Abstracts* (Paris, France, April 27 – May 2, 2013). CHI'13. ACM, New York, NY, 2677-2682. http://doi.acm.org/10.1145/2468356.2479492

[7] Czaja, S. J. Charness, N. Fisk, A. D. Hertzog, C. Nair, S. N. and Rogers, W. 2006. Factors predicting the use of technology: Findings from the Center for Research and Education on Aging and Technology Enhancement (CREATE). *Psychology of Aging, 21, 2.* 333-352.

[8] Dee, M. 2014. Can care home buildings support health and wellbeing? How the built environment can support residents' wellbeing through better visiting times. *Scottish Care Bulletin. 54. Spring.* 2014. p.26.

[9] Dee, M. and Hanson, V.L. 2012. Tales of Technology. *Digital Futures 2012, 3rd Annual Digital Economy All Hands Conference, Aberdeen University, October 23-25.* http://www.dotrural.ac.uk/digitalfutures/sites/default/files/Tales%20MDVLHFinal.pdf.

[10] Ferres, L. Lindgaard, G. and Sumegi, L. 2010. Evaluating a tool for improving accessibility to charts and graphs. In *Proceedings of the SIGACCESS conference on Computers and Accessibility* (Orlando, Fl, October 25-27, 2010) ASSETS '10. ACM, New York, NY, 83-90. http://doi.acm.org/10.1145/2533682.2533683

[11] Forbes, P. Gibson, L. Hanson, V. L. Gregor, P. and Newell, A. G. 2009. Dundee User Centre: A space where older people and technology meet. In *Proceedings of SIGACCESS Conference on Computers and Accessibility* (Pittsburgh, PA, USA, Oct 26 -28, 2009). ASSETS'09 ACM, New York, NY, 231–232. http://doi.acm.org/10.1145/1639642.1639690

[12] Gouldner, A.W. 1960. The norm of reciprocity. *American Sociological Review 25*, 161-178.

[13] Greig, C. A. Young, A. Skelton, D.A. et al. 1994. Exercise studies with elderly volunteers. *Age & Ageing 23*, 185-189.

[14] Guo, A.W. Edwards, S.J.F. Blythe, P.T. 2010. The study of elderly drivers. *Digital Futures 2010*: Digital Economy All Hands Meeting. Nottingham, UK: University of Nottingham. https://www.horizon.ac.uk/images/stories/s19-Gao.pdf

[15] Hanson, V. L. 2010. Influencing Technology Adoption by Older Adults. *Interacting with Computers, 11.* 502–509.

[16] Heron, M. Hanson, V. L. and Ricketts, I. 2013. The ACCESS Framework: A technical framework for adaptive accessibility support. In *Proceedings of the SIGCHI Symposium on Engineering Interactive Computing Systems.* (London, UK. June 24-27, 2013). EICS '13. ACM, New York, NY, USA, 33-42. DOI= http://doi.acm.org/10.1145/2494603.2480316

[17] Heron, M. Hanson, V. L. and Ricketts, I. 2013. Open Source accessibility: advantages and limitations. *Journal of Interaction Science* 2013, 1:2. DOI=10.1186/2194-0827-1-2

[18] Lindely, S. Harper, R. and Sellen, A. 2008. Designing for elders: exploring the complexity of relationships in later life. *Proceedings of the British HCI Group Annual Conference on People and Computers: Culture, Creativity, Interaction.* (Liverpool, UK. September 1-5, 2008) Volume 1, 77-86. British Computer Society Swinton, UK. ISBN: 978-1-906124-04-5

[19] McIntyre, L. and Hanson, V. L. 2013. BESiDE – The Built Environment for Social Inclusion through the Digital Economy. *In Proceedings of the SIGCHI Conference on Human Factors in Computing Systems Extended Abstracts* (Paris, France, April 27 – May 2, 2013.) CHI'13. ACM, New York, NY. 289-294. http://doi.acm.org/10.1145/2468356.2468408

[20] Medellin-Gasque, R. Reed, C. and Hanson, V. 2013. A protocol for software-supported interaction with broadcast debates. *Digital Economy DE2013: Open Digital - The Fourth Annual Digital Economy All Hands Meeting (DE2013).* Media City UK, Salford, UK.

[21] Milligan, C. Payne, S. Bingley, A. and Cockshott, Z. 2013. Place and wellbeing: shedding light on activity interventions for older men. Ageing and Society / FirstView Article 1-26. Cambridge University Press 2013 DOI=http://dx.doi.org/10.1017/S0144686X13000494

[22] Montague, K. Hanson, V. L. and Cobley, A. 2012. Designing for individuals: Usable touch-screen interaction through Shared User Models. In *Proceedings of the SIGACCESSS Conference on Computers and Accessibility (Boulder, Colorado, USA, 2012). ASSETS'12.* ACM, New York, NY. 151-158. DOI=http://doi.acm.org/10.1145/2384916.2384943

[23] Morrison, K. Hanson, V. L. and Szymkowiak, A. 2011. A questionnaire to gauge older adults' interest in using mobile phones as memory aids. *Digital Engagement. The 2nd All Hands Meeting of the Digital Economy, 2011.* (Newcastle University, November 15-17, 2011). http://de2011.computing.dundee.ac.uk/wp-content/uploads/2011/11/A-questionnaire-to-gauge-older-adults%C3%A2%E2%82%AC%E2%84%A2-interest-in-using-mobile-phones-as-memory-aids.pdf

[24] Meurer, J. Stein, M. Randall, D. Rohde, M. and Wulf, V. 2014. Social dependency and mobile autonomy: supporting older adults' mobility with ridesharing ICT. In *Proceedings of the SIGCHI Conference on Human Factors in Computing Systems* (Toronto, Canada. April 26 – May, 2014). CHI '14. ACM, New York, NY, 1923-1932. DOI= http://doi.acm.org/10.1145/2556288.2557300

[25] Nevay, S. and Lim, C. 2014. Wearables and Wearability: Care home residents tell us about their style preferences. http://www.beside.ac.uk/news/wearables_and_wearability_c are_home_residents_tell_us_about_their_style_preferences

[26] Nind, T. Hanson, V. McKenna, S. et al. 2012. *Health Website Quality: Towards Automated Analysis.* Digital Futures 2012, 3rd Annual Digital Economy All Hands Conference. (Aberdeen University, October 23-25, 2012). *http://www.de2012.org/sites/default/files/digitalfutures2012p apers/Papers/Session4BDataMiningMachineLearning/Nind_etal_HealthWebsiteQuality.pdf*

[27] Norval, C. Arnott, J. and Hanson, V. L. 2014. What's on your mind? Investigating recommendations for inclusive social networking and older adults. In *Proceedings of the SIGCHI Conference on Human Factors in Computing Systems (Toronto, Canada. April 26 – May, 2014).* ACM, New York, NY, 3923-3932. DOI=http://doi.acm.org/10.1145/2556288.2556992

[28] Patel, M. X. Doku, V. & Tennakoon, L. 2003. Challenges in recruitment of research participants. *Advances in Psychiatric Treatment. 9, 229-238.*

[29] Petrie, H. Hamilton, F. King, N. and Pavan, P. 2006. Remote usability evaluations with disabled people. In *Proceedings of the SIGCHI Conference on Human Factors in Computing Systems (Montreal, Quebec, Canada, April 22-27, 2006). Chi'06.* ACM, New York, NY. 1133-1141. DOI=http://doi.acm.org/10.1145/1124772.1124942

[30] Sears, A. and Hanson, V. L. 2011. Representing users in accessibility research. In *Proceedings of the 2011Conference on Human Factors in Computing Systems.* (Vancouver, BC, May 7-12, 2011) ACM, New York, NY, 2235 – 2238. Reprinted in *ACM Trans. Access. Comput.4, 2, Article 7 (March 2012).* http://doi.acm.org/10.1145/2141943.2141945

Sears, A. Karat, C-M. Oseitutu, K. Karimullah, A. and Feng, J. 2001. Productivity, satisfaction, and interaction strategies of individuals with spinal cord injuries and traditional users interacting with speech recognition software. *Universal Access in the Information Society, 1,* 4–15.

[31] Smith, C. L. 2013. Factors affecting conditions of trust in participant recruiting and retention: a position paper. *LivingLab '13 Proceedings of the 2013 workshop on Living labs for information retrieval evaluation. (San Francisco, CA, USA, November 01 2013).* ACM New York, NY, 13-14. DOI=http://doi.acm.org/10.1145/2513150.2513161

[32] Stewart, C. D. Hanson, V. L. and Nind, T. J. 2013. Assisting older adults in assessing the reliability of health-related websites. In Proceedings of the SIGCHI Conference on Human Factors in Computing Systems Extended Abstracts (Paris, France, April 27 – May 2, 2013.) CHI'13. ACM, New York, NY, 2611-2616. DOI=http://doi.acm.org/10.1145/2559206.2581243

[33] Stuardi, T. Cox, H. and Torgerson, D. J. 2011. Database recruitment: a solution to poor recruitment in randomized trials? *Family Practice. 28.* 329-33.

[34] Trewin, S. John, B.E. Richards, J. T. Hanson. V. L. Sloan, D. Bellamy, R. K. E. Thomas, J. C. and Swart, C. 2012. Age-specific predictive models of human performance. In *Proceedings of the SIGCHI conference on Human Factors in Computing Systems Extended Abstracts* (Austin, Texas, USA, May 05-10, 2012). CHI '12. ACM, New York, NY, 2267-2272. http://doi.acm.org/10.1145/2212776.2223787

[35] Vargheese, J. Sripada, S. Mastoff, J. Oren, N. Schofield, P. and Hanson, V. L. 2013. Persuasive dialogue in telecare: Promoting and encouraging social interaction for older adults. In *Proceedings of the SIGCHI conference on Human Factors in Computing Systems Extended Abstracts (Paris, France, April 27 – May 2, 2013). CHI'13.* ACM, New York, NY, 877-882 DOI=http://doi.acm.org/10.1145/2468356.2468

Verification of Daily Activities of Older Adults: A Simple, Non-Intrusive, Low-Cost Approach

Loïc Caroux
Inria
Talence, France
loic.caroux@inria.fr

Charles Consel
University of Bordeaux / Inria
Talence, France
charles.consel@inria.fr

Lucile Dupuy
Inria
Talence, France
lucile.dupuy@inria.fr

Hélène Sauzéon
University of Bordeaux / Inria
Talence, France
helene.sauzeon@inria.fr

ABSTRACT

This paper presents an approach to verifying the activities of daily living of older adults at their home. We verify activities, instead of inferring them, because our monitoring approach is driven by routines, initially sketched by users in their environment. Monitoring is supported by a lightweight sensor infrastructure, comprising non-intrusive, low-cost, wireless devices. Verification is performed by applying a simple formula to sensor log data, for each activity of interest. The result value determines whether an activity has been performed.

We have conducted an experimental study to validate our approach. To do so, four participants have been monitored during five days at their home, equipped with sensors. When applied to the log data, our formulas were able to automatically verify that a list of activities were performed. They produced the same interpretations, using Signal Detection Theory, as a third party, manually analyzing the log data.

Categories and Subject Descriptors

K.4.2 [**Computers and Society**]: Social Issues—*Assistive technologies for persons with disabilities*; J.4 [**Social and Behavioral Sciences**]: Psychology

General Terms

Experimentation, Human Factors, Measurement, Performance, Verification

Keywords

Activities of Daily Living; Older Adults; Activity Recognition; Routines; Verification; Pervasive Computing; Sensors; Signal Detection Theory

1. INTRODUCTION

Activities of Daily Living (ADL) are abilities defining the functional status of an individual. Verifying what ADLs are performed by an older adult is a decisive factor to determine what kinds and what levels of assistance are needed for an individual and whether aging in place is desirable. The importance of this issue has led a number of researchers to develop a range of Ubicomp approaches that can monitor activities (e.g., [11, 17, 10]).

In this paper, we take these prior results one step further and apply them to the needs of caregiver professionals to monitor older adults at their home. Specifically, our approach relies on the following key observation: as people age their daily activities are increasingly organized according to a routine to optimize their daily functioning [3]. As a result, their activities do not need to be recognized but should rather be *verified*. Deviations are a warning sign of degradation [3].

We have developed an approach to activity verification. This approach relies on a technological infrastructure that is simple, low-cost and non-intrusive. This infrastructure was deployed in four homes of older adults of 83 years of age on average. The same set of sensors was used in the four homes and was placed at strategic locations with respect to their routines to verify the target activities. The analysis of the data collected during five weekdays show that they follow very strict routines that can easily be associated with their main activities.

The contributions of this paper are as follows.

1. An approach to activity monitoring via verification that is dedicated to older adults;

2. A lightweight sensor infrastructure for activity verification;

3. An experimental study that validate the accuracy of activity verification.

In the remainder of this paper, Section 2 relates our approach to existing works. Section 3 presents our methodology to perform activity verification. Section 4 describes an experimental setting aimed to assess our approach. In Section 5, experimental data are analyzed and demonstrate their accuracy in a natural setting. Section 6 discusses the limitations of this work and outlines its applications. Finally, Section 7 concludes.

2. RELATED WORKS

This section presents key characteristics and requirements involved in the activity monitoring of older adults.

Setting.

A lot of research has been addressing the monitoring of activities. Some works have taken place in an experimental setting: a home dedicated to experimental studies, which sometimes allow subjects to live in for a few days [14]. This experimental setting usually include cameras that allow the activities measured by sensors to be matched against the ground truth video annotations [14, 21].

In the context of older adults, an unfamiliar setting is contradictory to a reliable assessment of activities. Indeed, as demonstrated by various studies [9], as their cognitive resources decrease, older adults tend to optimize the remaining ones by increasingly organizing operations of their activities according to a strict routine. As a consequence, asking older adults to perform activities in an unfamiliar setting compromises their optimization strategies. The resulting assessment of their functional status may be unrelated to their ability to live independently [9].

In a naturalistic setting, having multiple occupants in a home has been reported as introducing sources of errors in activity monitoring, even when different types of sensors are massively populating a home [14].

Activity variabilities.

Users executing increasingly strict routines is a key observation to revisit what kind of activity monitoring is desirable. Indeed, the variabilities in realizing an activity has been a major challenge in a number of works (*e.g.,* [14, 13, 16, 11, 17, 10]). This challenge is typically addressed by spreading numerous sensors of different types and using a range of machine learning algorithms [17, 11]. But in fact, when a user follows routines, sensors could be placed at strategic locations; as well, collected data could be processed by simple algorithms because they would verify rather than infer activities.

Range of sensors.

When older adults are being monitored continuously at their home, a range of sensors cannot be utilized. Typically, RFID tags cannot be used because they require that most, if not all, strategic objects be attached a tag [14, 19]. This situation is difficult to maintain without interfering with the person's life, as new objects get introduced in the home. Body-worn sensors are also delicate to introduce in naturalistic setting because they impose constraints on the user and may not deliver accurate data [14, 4, 10]. Regarding cameras, a majority of users consider them too intrusive [4, 10] in their daily life. When we interviewed older adults about monitoring of their daily activities, they massively refused to have cameras installed at their home. Besides, as pointed out by Logan *et al.,* annotating videos is tedious and thus costly [14], preventing this approach to scale up to continuous monitoring of several participants.

When comparing various types of sensors in a naturalistic setting, Logan *et al.* reported that simple technology such as motion-based sensors are very successful in detecting activities [14]. Combined with well-identified routines, this situation can open up opportunities to use low-cost sensors.

Accuracy of activity monitoring.

Researchers have proposed various granularity at which activities can be monitored. For example, Lepri *et al.* distinguish between homogeneous and non-homogeneous activities (*e.g.,* watching TV *vs.* eating/drinking) and between an on-going activity and a completed activity [13]. For another example, Mihailidis *et al.* examine the various steps of hand-washing [16].

In fact, activities can be monitored at a variety of granularities. Not surprisingly, the finer the granularity gets, the more complex the monitoring process becomes. In the context of home-based activity monitoring of older adults, studies show that the granularity of the monitoring can be coarse-grained. More specifically, cognitive decline first impacts the instrumental ADLs (IADLs – *e.g.,* meal preparation) because they require high-level cognitive functions to initiate, plan and execute a task [9]; basic ADLs (BADL – *e.g.,* eating) are affected in later stages of cognitive decline, when older adults have supposedly been already diagnosed by clinicians.

IADLs inherently involve numerous interactions with the environment to perform the sub-tasks of a given task (*e.g.,* breakfast involves preparing coffee by opening a drawer to reach for the coffee and turning on the coffee maker) [15]. This situation allows to track the execution of sub-tasks via interactions with sensor-equipped locations of the environment.

Summary.

We have outlined the behavioral characteristics of activities performed by older adults at their home. These characteristics have allowed us to sketch requirements for home-based monitoring of activities of older adults, taking into account their activity variabilities, the sensors needed, and the accuracy of the monitoring.

3. METHODOLOGY

We now present our methodology to perform activity verification. We define what we mean by an activity and list the activities of interest that will be monitored in our study. Then, we introduce the notion of routines, which are followed by users to perform activities. Routines are analyzed to determine key actions that characterize them. Finally, these key actions are associated with sensors that measure their occurrence.

Prior to presenting the methodology, we first examine the set of sensors that are used to measure the interactions of the user with the environment.

3.1 Sensors

Our approach relies on three types of sensors that have covered our needs in practice, while keeping the approach simple, low-cost and non-intrusive. These types of sensors are motion sensors, contact sensors and smart switches. Motion sensors detect motion in a specific area by orienting them at an appropriate angle. Contact sensors detect the opening of a room/cabinet door and a drawer. Smart switches are used to measure whether a connected appliance is functioning; a threshold can be set to prevent false positive (*e.g.,* the consumption of a clock built in the appliance). These three sensing functionalities are the building blocks of our approach to monitoring activities.

3.2 Activities

The notion of activity is fundamental to our work and needs to be defined in the context of our target population: older adults. Specifically, we consider self-care activities for which individuals construct or reproduce solutions, involving manipulation of objects, situated in a specific place at home [15]. These activities are well structured [1], involving sequential steps that tend to be "compiled" by older adults as a skill [20]. Accumulated reproduction of solutions, as well as aging related loss, probably explain why older adults have preferences for routines. This phenomenon is called age-related *routinization* [3]; it precludes multiple activities to be conducted simultaneously [3].

Our notion of activity comprises three key criteria that are at the basis of our verification process

Criterion 1: An activity is situated in a room. This criterion raises a need to measure motion in a given room during the activity.

Criterion 2: To conduct an activity, the user interacts physically with the environment, following a routine. This situation requires that the expected interactions be measured.

Criterion 3: Age-related functional decline leads older adults to conduct one activity at a time. This observation suggests that, to match an activity, measures of environment interactions should only pertain to that activity. In other words, if interactions involve more than one activity, they should not be considered as forming an activity.

Our study covers both types of daily activities: basic and instrumental. We chose to study two BADLs: getting dressed and taking a shower. And, we targeted one IADL: meal preparation. The main reasons to choose these activities are as follows. First, they are among the activities that are sensitive to age-related functional decline [9], as well as routinization [2]. As a result, there is a rich collection of articles reporting on the monitoring of these activities (*e.g.,* [4, 17]). Second, they allow to exercise many dimensions of our approach, illustrating different sensing functionalities, locations, and activity requirements.

3.3 Routines

We now detail how activities are instantiated with respect to users and their environment. Our goal is to determine what environment interactions are performed by a user when conducting an activity of interest. Several methods could be used to determine these interactions. As our approach is non-intrusive, methods that could compromise privacy were excluded (e.g., passive observation of activity performance with or without camera). We use a method whereby users provide knowledge about their activity routines. Specifically, this knowledge collection is conducted at the user's home by a member of our research group, trained in ergonomics, and more specifically in activity analysis. The experimenter asks the user to sketch each activity of interest. This sketching phase reveals a list of *markers* that characterizes the activity. For example, participants are asked how they prepare breakfast in the morning. Ms. Dupont (a fictitious name) shows each drawer she opens and each appliance she uses. The experimenter asks questions as the activity is sketched, to assess the degree of certainty of the collected information. For example, "Do you make coffee every morning?", "Do you always put your coffee in this cabinet?". For each routine, a set of markers is chosen. In the case of Ms. Dupont, we assess that making a coffee is an essential part of breakfast; this is our first marker. She takes milk in her coffee; this is our second marker. She gets a clean mug from a specific cabinet; this is our third marker.

Guidelines to choose robust markers include the degree of certainty of a given environment interaction and its uniqueness (*e.g.,* coffee is only made once a day using a specific appliance). It could be argued that the more markers used to monitor an activity, the more certain one can be that this activity has been performed. However, in practice, not all markers are validated. For example, one can imagine that a clean mug may not always be in a specific cabinet; it can sometimes be taken from a dishwasher, preventing this marker to be validated.

3.4 Sensor placement

The list of markers collected in the previous stage is used to determine what sensors should be used and where they should be placed. Of course, markers and sensor placement are intimately intertwined, in that markers are not chosen independently of avail-

able sensor functionalities, and the feasibility of placing a device at the right point in the physical environment. In the case of Ms. Dupont, we use a smart switch to determine when the coffee maker is turned on. We place a contact sensor on both the fridge and a specific cabinet to determine respectively, when some item (possibly milk) is taken from the fridge and a clean mug from the cabinet.

Putting it all together. To determine that environment interactions form an activity, (1) a subset of the activity's markers need to be validated via sensors (Criterion 2), over a period of time, during which, motions are observed in a specific room (Criterion 1), with no interleaving environment interactions from another room (Criterion 3).

Let us now turn our attention to the BADLs of interest. They require coarse-grain measurements. The shower activity does not offer many alternatives, considering the available sensor functionalities: it is detected by a motion detector, oriented such that as few motions outside the shower cabin are observed. In this case, false positives can be ignored based on the duration of the detected activity.

Regarding the activity of getting dressed, based on our analyses, the key marker is getting clean clothes. This environment interaction can be detected by placing a contact sensor on the door of a strategic piece of furniture (*e.g.,* a wardrobe). However, this marker has not the uniqueness property: door opening is likely to be detected many times during the day. This situation is discussed further in Section 6.

4. DESCRIPTION OF THE EXPERIMENT

In this section, we present an experiment aimed to validate whether older adults follow strict routines in their daily activities. To do so, (1) we assess to what extent the participants of our study follow routines by administering a questionnaire; (2) we describe the data collected by our methodology and why they are relevant for our goal.

Participants	A	B	C	D	*Mean (SD)*
Age	77	77	87	93	*83.5 (7.89)*
Gender	F	F	F	F	
Education years	7	8	12	10	*9.25 (7.89)*
Family status	S	W	W	W	
MMSE [0 − 30]	28	28	26	26	*27 (1.15)*
Time-based IADL [5 − 15]	5	5	7	5	*5.5 (1.00)*
Self-reported IADL [9 − 45]	12	16	24	18	*17.5 (5.00)*
Routinization [0 − 40]	15	19	15	24	*18.25 (4.27)*

SD=Standard Deviation; F=Female; S=Single; W=Widowed. Interval notations are used for score ranges.

Figure 1: Participant profiles

4.1 Participants

To test our research assumptions, it is critical to include community-dwelling, very old adults. To do so, we have collaborated with a public home care service for older adults, and have had access to the medical file of their beneficiaries. As described in Figure 1, four participants, aged 83.5 on average (SD= 7.89) have been recruited according to specific exclusion criteria: dependency syndrome; neurological or musculoskeletal disease or systemic disorders. The main inclusion criterion was cognitive integrity with an MMSE score [8] greater than 24. According to the Helsinki declaration (WMA, 2008), approval was sought and obtained from the ethics committee of the University of Bordeaux. All participants provided a written consent form prior to the participation in our study.

We have assessed their functional status for some activities of daily living. First, we evaluated their performance in IADLs, using the time-based IADL assessment test [18]. A participant is asked to perform an activity with a time limit. If the activity is achieved without error and without exceeding the time limit, a score of 1 is given. A score of 3 means that the participant has major difficulties to perform the activity. We tested our participants on five different activities; this gave scores ranging from 5 (ideal performance) to 15 (major difficulties). In Figure 1, we observe that three of our participants obtain ideal scores (5), and one shows very minor difficulties (7). We conclude that our participants show no difficulties in performing IADLs and have a high level of autonomy.

We also asked them to self-assess their functional status, using the 9-item IADL scale [12]. For each item, the participant assesses her performance: 1 denotes no difficulties and 5 denotes major difficulties. This tool shows that we have a variety of participants in the way they see themselves performing ADLs; it ranges from 12 to 24, on a scale of 45.

Finally, we evaluated the degree of routinization of our participants using the routinization scale defined by Bouisson [5]. We observe that our participants show a variety of routinization degrees. In particular, the participants B and D are more routinized than the two others.

In summary, our participants perform well in their ADLs, although they perceive themselves as experiencing difficulties. From these data, we can expect our participants to perform their ADLs on a regular basis. The variation in the routinization degrees play a key role to assess whether our verification approach covers a wide spectrum of behaviors.

4.2 Data Collected

Logs of the sensors placed in the participants' homes have been collected for 5 weekdays. The same set of sensors has been used for all participants. However, they have not necessarily been used the same way to monitor the activities of interest. For example, participants may or may not take milk from the fridge to make breakfast, or they may use a coffee maker or a microwave to prepare a hot drink.

Sensor logs consists of the sensor identifier, a changed status, and a timestamp. The sensor identifier corresponds to a sensor type (motion detector, contact sensor and smart switch) and its location. We selected the logs pertaining to the sensors located in the rooms corresponding to the activities of interest, namely, kitchen, bedroom, and bathroom.

In Figure 2, we show the apartment of Ms. Dupont, populated with sensors corresponding to the activities of interest and related rooms. In this example, sensors in the kitchen are placed in the following way. A smart switch detects whether the coffee maker is used. Two contact sensors detect whether the cupboard or the fridge are open. Note that the same sensors may be placed differently in other participants' home. For example, the smart switch can be used to detect the usage of the microwave, and the contact sensors can be used to detect the opening of the cutlery drawer and the fridge. Again, the sensor placement is strictly dependent on the activity routines of the user.

In Figure 3, we display an example fragment of a log. This table consists of three column showing sensor types, the status and the time stamp; the room information is omitted because the fragment is limited to a sequence of events only occurring in the kitchen (similarly for the date of the time stamp). All columns are self-explanatory. Notice that the level of information delivered by mo-

Figure 2: Apartment layout of Ms. Dupont

tion sensors have been raised with a software layer. The goal is to obtain two statuses: the first time and the last time a presence is detected in a room. To do so, we need to keep a state to know whether some motion detected in a room is the first occurrence. Furthermore, the last presence is a room is determined by the first environment interaction detected in another room or by an absence of motion for a period of time. This high-level sensor is referred to as a presence detector.

5. DATA ANALYSIS

In this section, we first define a set of formulas, dedicated to daily routines, which is applied to sensor log data to determine whether specific routines are performed. These formulas are then applied to log data across the four participants over weekdays to demonstrate their accuracy.

Sensor Type	Status	Time
Presence detector	Presence	09:10:23
Contact sensor - Fridge	Open	09:13:31
Contact sensor - Fridge	Closed	09:13:34
Smart switch - Coffee maker	On	09:14:16
Contact sensor - Cupboard	Open	09:14:58
Contact sensor - Cupboard	Closed	09:15:03
Smart switch - Coffee maker	Off	09:16:38
Presence detector	Absence	09:16:47

Figure 3: Fragment of activity log of Ms. Dupont

5.1 Routine Formulas

Routine formulas leverage our notion of activity, introduced in Section 3, and the criteria associated with this notion. In particular, our routine formulas are grounded in the area of ontological activity modeling and representation (*e.g.*, [6]). Specifically, our formulas are knowledge-driven, in that they rely on the fundamental attributes of an activity. Namely,

Spatial context. This is the room (*i.e.*, the location) where the activity takes place. In our work, because sensors have a fixed location, sensed interactions are situated by definition.

Temporal context. This context comprises two dimensions: (1) the time of the day at which the activity occurs; this information is specific to each participant, and (2) a minimal duration over which the activity is supposed to be performed.

Environment interactions. There are interactions related to markers of the target activity, and associated with sensors for the purpose of our work.

Further defining our notion of a routine formula, we now examine what result it produces. A formula verifies an activity by producing a *score*, whose value ranges between 0 and 1. The value 0 means that the activity has not been performed, according to the participant's routine. The value 1 indicates that the sensed measures match the participant's routine.

To specify our first formula, let us consider on the activities of interest: getting dressed (**GD**). The time of the day at which this activity occurs is on the morning (e.g., between 6 a.m. and 11 a.m. in the present experiment), as declared by all our participants, and a marker of this activity is the action of getting clean clothes from the wardrobe, thus equipped with a contact sensor. The resulting activity-specific formula is defined as follows.

$$Sc^{GD} = T^{GD} \times M^{GD}$$

Where Sc^{GD} is the score for the activity getting dressed; T^{GD} is the time of the day, which takes value 1, if it is within the expected time frame of the day, and value 0, otherwise; and, M^{GD} is the marker of this activity, which has value 1 if the sensed interaction occurred, and value 0 otherwise. We did not consider the duration of the activity because presence can be detected in the bedroom for a number of reasons, not necessarily related to dressing, even though the wardrobe may be used.

Let us examine our second activity of interest, namely, taking a shower (**TS**). This formula is defined as follows.

$$Sc^{TS} = T^{TS} \times D^{TS}$$

The time of the day is also pertinent in this formula. Furthermore, this activity requires a minimal period of time over which this activity is performed; D^{TS} takes value 1, if this minimal duration is reached and value 0 otherwise. This duration is based on a unique marker, which corresponds to the presence detector, placed in the shower.

Lastly, we investigate the activity of preparing breakfast (**BP**). Its formula is given below.

$$Sc^{BP} = T^{BP} \times \frac{A^{BP} \times 4 + \frac{S_1^{BP} + \dots + S_n^{BP}}{n}}{5}$$

This formula reflects the constraint that breakfast preparation occurs at a specific time of the day T^{BP}. Furthermore, it accounts for the fact that this preparation often includes a major marker, corresponding to an appliance (*e.g.*, a coffee machine, a kettle) that can be monitored (A^{BP}). To account for its importance, this marker is weighted by multiplying it by 4. It is added by the rest of the markers of this activity, which are averaged (S_i^{BP}). In our experiment, these markers range from 1 to 3.

To illustrate this formula, consider Ms. Dupont's morning routine. Preparing breakfast consists of making coffee, sensed by a smart switch (a major marker) and taking a clean cup from a specific cabinet and milk from the fridge, both monitored by a contact door. As can be noted, duration is ignored in our formula because this activity consists of a few markers that are to be validated over the time of the preparation.

Note that, although conceptually grounded, in practice, the formulas that we have presented are the result of a series of refinements, driven by the analysis of the sensor-log data, collected from our participants. To assess the accuracy of our formulas, we now need to apply them to the log data, across our participants. These formulas are similarly applied for all participants. Only the markers are different between them. For example, the major marker is a smart switch dedicated to the coffee maker for Ms. Dupont. But, for another participant, the major marker may be a contact sensor linked to a specific cabinet.

5.2 Analysis

We now analyze the results of applying our routine formulas on the log data of our four participants. First, we test the accuracy of the formulas with the calculation of two specific indices: the sensitivity and the response bias indices, respectively A' and $B''D$ for non-parametric data [7]. Second, we assess our methodology to perform activity verification.

5.2.1 Sensitivity indices

Sensitivity indices are used in Signal Detection Theory to measure performance in Yes/No tasks (see Stanislaw and Todorov [22]). To do so, participants of such tasks discriminate signals (stimulus is present) and noises (stimulus is absent). In the presence of a stimulus, yes responses are correct and termed *hits*. In the absence of a stimulus, yes responses are incorrect and termed *false alarms*. Then, hit and false alarms rates are used to calculate the indices. A' measures the ability of the participant to correctly discriminate the presence or the absence of a stimulus. This index is contained between 0 (extremely low sensitivity) and 1 (extremely high sensitivity). B''_D measures the general tendency of the participant to respond yes or no. B''_D is contained between -1 (tendency to respond yes and produce false alarms) and 1 (tendency to respond no and miss stimuli).

In the present experiment, the formulas take the role usually played by human participants in Yes/No tasks. Thirty sets of sensor logs were randomly selected from the data collected at participants' homes. They covered an entire morning. Our version of the Yes/No task was conducted as follows. In a first step, we recruited a naive human observer, expert in activity analysis, to judge whether our participants perform the three activities of interest. The results of this judgment were used as a base line. Then, scores of activities were computed using our formulas, from which A' and B''_D were calculated.

Results for meal preparation showed the following values $A' = 1.00$ and $B''_D = 0.00$. That is, all the responses of the formulas were correct, according to our base line (*i.e.*, the naive observer). The formula can be considered as extremely sensitive and perfectly matches the observer in the case of the activity of meal preparation.

Results for taking a shower showed the following values $A' = 0.94$ and $B''_D = 1.00$. Most of the responses of the formula were correct. The formula can be considered as highly sensitive. The response bias index indicates that the formula is conservative (*i.e.*, our formula has a tendency to respond No). This situation means that our formula may miss stimuli.

Results for getting dressed showed the following values $A' = 0.93$ and $B''_D = 0.39$. Most of the responses of the formula were correct. The formula can be considered as highly sensitive. The response bias index indicates that the formula is slightly conservative in that it misses very few stimuli.

In summary, our formulas are accurate in that they almost always detect whether an activity of interest is present in a given log data, as compared to our naive observer.

5.2.2 Longitudinal assessment of activity verification

So far, we have demonstrated that our formulas are accurate in detecting activities for a given sensor log. However, we have not determined whether a formula would find many occurrence of an activity within a day. For example, detecting that the shower is taken is useful, but this is even more valuable if this activity is detected only once (if indeed the user does not take than more shower per day).

The goal of this section is to assess our formulas in a longitudinal manner. That is, showing how many occurrences of an activity is detected each day. To do so, we consider sensor-log data from our participants, over 5-weekday mornings (from Monday to Friday). These log data are used to invoke our formulas. For each participant's data log, the formulas are applied as many times as there presence detected in a room associated with an activity of interest. Because of this wide-range application of the formulas, a lot of the computed scores show that the activities of interest have not been performed. We investigated what would be a threshold that would allow to filter out the irrelevant scores. In fact, this threshold is obvious to set because we observed that there are no scores below 0.8. Examining the log segments corresponding to a 0.8 score, we are able to match them against the routines. This situation can be explained by the way the formulas are defined in that they always include major markers that characterize a routine. For the activity of getting dressed and taking a shower, the scores detect an activity of interest with a value equal to 1 (all criteria are met) or necessarily discard the log segment with a value equal to 0. For the activity of breakfast preparation, values of scores above the threshold are between 0.8 and 1, combining the criteria of the time of the day and the major marker of the activity.

Importantly, our strategy does not discard meaningful sequences of actions, nor does it generate spurious scores. This behavior is illustrated by our experiment. We computed how many times a score above the threshold is produced by the formulas for each participant over the five weekdays. Thereafter, these scores are called *valid scores*. The analysis of the data gathered for all of our participants showed that for the activity of breakfast preparation, the number of valid scores was 1.15 per day in average (SD = 0.49), for a total of 12.95 of computed scores in average (SD = 5.09). For the activity of taking a shower, the number of valid scores was 0.60 per day in average (SD = 0.76), for a total of 6.00 of computed scores in average (SD = 2.88). For the activity of getting dressed, the number of valid scores was 0.70 per day in average (SD = 0.86), for a total of 8.30 of computed scores in average (SD = 2.64).

The ratios of valid scores per computed scores were 0.10 in average (SD = 0.05) for the activity of breakfast preparation, 0.09 in average (SD = 0.11) for the activity of taking a shower, and 0.08 in average (SD = 0.10) for the activity of getting dressed.

We observe that our approach is reliable for breakfast preparation because this activity is mostly detected once a day for our four participants. Taking a shower exhibits the same performance, even though this activity does not occur every day. Getting dressed is

also detected. However, this activity is sometimes detected many times a day, and sometimes not detected at all.

Examing the entire sensor log of some of our participants over 4 weeks,[1] we notice that our formula for taking a shower shows a periodicity for this activity. In constrast, the activity of getting dressed does not exhibit the same results.

We display an example for one of the participants in Figure 4. In this example, the activities labelled "breakfast preparation" and "taking shower" are perfectly detected. These activities are only detected once a day. However, the "getting dressed" activity is not detected as regularly as the two others. It is not detected on Monday and Friday, while it is detected three times on Thursday. This situation could mean that on this day, the user changed her clothes several times, or that opening the wardrobe may occur for other reasons. Further investigation is needed specifically for this activity. For example, the number of sensors used in our approach may not be sufficient to detect this activity accurately. See the section 6 for discussion.

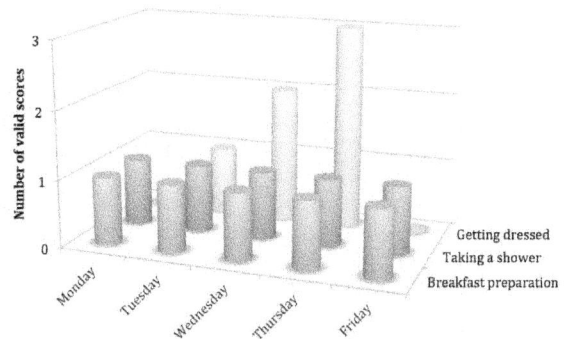

Figure 4: Longitudinal scores of a participant

6. DISCUSSION

We first discuss the limitations of our approach and then outline the main perspectives.

6.1 Limitations

Single occupant. Our approach is dedicated to monitoring a single occupant of a home. This choice stems from the fact that caregiving professionals report that when older adults live as a couple, one of them can monitor the other one that may need assistance. Therefore, we thought that our work would be more useful in the case of an older adult living alone. Furthermore, as mentioned in Section 2, experimental studies have shown that monitoring multiple occupants in a home introduce sources of errors.

Number of sensors. Our experimental study involves few sensors. This strategy is problematic for some activities such as getting dressed. Indeed, there might not be enough measures to detect a meaningful pattern. For example, opening the wardrobe may occur for a number of reasons. To recognize the activity of getting dressed, more sensors would be needed to account for other markers of this activity. For example, other doors and drawers could be used to account for additional steps of this activity.

---

[1]Unfortunately, sensor logs of participants did not cover the same number of weeks, leading us to only consider one week.

Length of the experiment. Our conclusions could also be strengthened by considering sensor data log over a longer period of time. For example, in Section 5, we noticed that the activity of taking a shower B_D'' showed that our formula tends to miss stimuli (*i.e.*, too conservative). But in fact, we applied this formula to data log, covering a longer period of time, whenever participants had been recruited earlier. With these additional data, the shower formula perfectly matches our base line. This suggests that more log data increase the confidence in our formulas to accurately verify activities with respect to Signal Detection Theory.

Assessing the accuracy of our approach. Our signal processing methodology presented in Section 5 could be strengthened by adding multiple observers. We could then compute means of their judgements and compare them to the scores of the formulas. Yet, the consistence of the comparison for a unique observer is very encouraging.

Granularity of activity monitoring. Our approach focuses on whether an activity is performed. Currently, we do not take in account in what order the steps of the activity are performed, the duration of each step, whether a step is repeated, etc. In our approach, these elements are not necessary to study the verification of activities for older adults since the objective is only to assess whether an activity is performed. However, this granularity may not match the requirements of some applications. For example, if the quality of the activity needs to be assessed, the granularity of our work is not sufficient.

6.2 Perspectives

Sample size. We are continuing to collect data from our participants and recruiting more participants. As a result, we will soon be able to further the processing of the log data to strengthen our statistical evaluation.

More activities. We are adding more activities in the participants we are monitoring. In particular, we are including all meal preparations. These additional activities will allow us to assess the scalability of our approach.

Applications. We are developing applications that can leverage the routine formulas to remind users of activities of interest. The present work is essential to assess whether activity verification is accurate enough and thus enables an application to send meaningful reminders to a user. For example, an application could be designed in case of non-detection of a routine. This situation can appear if the older adult does not perform a given activity or if he or she performs the activity, but outside of the declared parameters. Hence, such an application would detect a routine deviation. The consequence could be a message sent to the older adult and/or a caregiver that inform him or her about this deviation.

Screening. Another perspective for activity verification is screening. We plan to use our approach to analyzing the evolution of a routine (order of the steps, duration, time of the day, . . .) and the evolution of the routines with respect to each other (order of the routines, occurrences, . . .). These analyses should be useful indicators to assess the evolution of the functional status of users.

7. CONCLUSIONS

We have presented an approach dedicated to older adults aimed at verifying activities, instead of inferring them. Our approach is knowledge-based in that it relies on collecting routines that are initially sketched by users at their home. The resulting knowledge about how activities are performed by older adults is reliable be-

cause their age-related functional decline increases their degree of routinization.

Then, we have introduced markers that characterize key actions of routines and sensors that measure these actions. Based on these routines, we have defined formulas to verify whether an activity has been performed with respect to sensor log data.

We have validated our approach by conducting an experimental study addressing three daily activities and involving four participants of 83 years of age on average. This study involves a sensor infrastructure that consists of low-cost, non-intrusive, wireless devices. We have collected sensor logs from our participants' home during five weekdays. This study have showed that our formulas produce the same results as a third party, manually analyzing the log data. Using Signal Detection Theory, we also showed that our formulas are accurate and reliable. Furthermore, this approach gives a methodological support to assess the relevance of the knowledge used to define the formulas. For example, asserting that the coffee maker is a key marker of the breakfast preparation can be checked by Signal Detection Theory, and more specifically by the value of A'.

8. ACKNOWLEDGMENTS

We thank the members of the Phoenix research group at Inria for their contributions to this project. We also thank Nathalie Bier, Yves Lachapelle, and Dany Lussier-Desrochers for fruitful discussions on the topic. Our project is funded by the following partners: UDCCAS, CG33, CRA, CNSA, Chambre des métiers.

9. REFERENCES

[1] Allaire, J. C., and Marsiske, M. Well-and ill-defined measures of everyday cognition: relationship to older adults' intellectual ability and functional status. *Psychology and aging 17*, 1 (2002), 101–115.

[2] Bergua, V., and Bouisson, J. Vieillesse et routinisation: une revue de la question. *Psychologie & NeuroPsychiatrie du vieillissement 6*, 4 (2008), 235–243.

[3] Bergua, V., Bouisson, J., Dartigues, J.-F., Swendsen, J., Fabrigoule, C., Pérès, K., and Barberger-Gateau, P. Restriction in instrumental activities of daily living in older persons: Association with preferences for routines and psychological vulnerability. *The International Journal of Aging and Human Development 77*, 4 (2013), 309–329.

[4] Bharucha, A. J., Anand, V., Forlizzi, J., Dew, M. A., Reynolds III, C. F., Stevens, S., and Wactlar, H. Intelligent assistive technology applications to dementia care: current capabilities, limitations, and future challenges. *The American Journal of Geriatric Psychiatry 17*, 2 (2009), 88–104.

[5] Bouisson, J. Routinization preferences, anxiety, and depression in an elderly french sample. *Journal of Aging Studies 16*, 3 (2002), 295–302.

[6] Chen, L., Nugent, C. D., and Wang, H. A knowledge-driven approach to activity recognition in smart homes. *Knowledge and Data Engineering, IEEE Transactions on 24*, 6 (2012), 961–974.

[7] Donaldson, W. Measuring recognition memory. *Journal of Experimental Psychology: General 121*, 3 (1992), 275–277.

[8] Folstein, M. F., Folstein, S. E., and McHugh, P. R. Mini-mental state: a practical method for grading the cognitive state of patients for the clinician. *Journal of Psychiatric Research 12*, 3 (1975), 189–198.

[9] Gold, D. A. An examination of instrumental activities of daily living assessment in older adults and mild cognitive

impairment. *Journal of Clinical and Experimental Neuropsychology 34*, 1 (2012), 11–34.

[10] Hossain, M. A. Perspectives of human factors in designing elderly monitoring system. *Computers in Human Behavior 33* (2014), 63–68.

[11] Kaye, J. A., Maxwell, S. A., Mattek, N., Hayes, T. L., Dodge, H., Pavel, M., Jimison, H. B., Wild, K., Boise, L., and Zitzelberger, T. A. Intelligent systems for assessing aging changes: home-based, unobtrusive, and continuous assessment of aging. *The Journals of Gerontology Series B: Psychological Sciences and Social Sciences 66*, suppl 1 (2011), i180–i190.

[12] Lawton, M. P., Moss, M., Fulcomer, M., and Kleban, M. H. A research and service oriented multilevel assessment instrument. *Journal of Gerontology 37*, 1 (1982), 91–99.

[13] Lepri, B., Mana, N., Cappelletti, A., Pianesi, F., and Zancanaro, M. What is happening now? detection of activities of daily living from simple visual features. *Personal and Ubiquitous Computing 14*, 8 (2010), 749–766.

[14] Logan, B., Healey, J., Philipose, M., Tapia, E. M., and Intille, S. A long-term evaluation of sensing modalities for activity recognition. In *UbiComp 2007: Ubiquitous Computing*. Springer, 2007, 483–500.

[15] Marsiske, M., and Margrett, J. A. Everyday problem solving and decision making. *Handbook of the Psychology of Aging 6* (2006), 315–342.

[16] Mihailidis, A., Boger, J. N., Craig, T., and Hoey, J. The coach prompting system to assist older adults with dementia through handwashing: An efficacy study. *BMC Geriatrics 8*, 1 (2008), 28.

[17] Mokhtari, M., Aloulou, H., Tiberghien, T., Biswas, J., Racoceanu, D., and Yap, P. New trends to support independence in persons with mild dementia–a mini-review. *Gerontology 58*, 6 (2012), 554–563.

[18] Owsley, C., Sloane, M., McGwin Jr, G., and Ball, K. Timed instrumental activities of daily living tasks: Relationship to cognitive function and everyday performance assessments in older adults. *Gerontology 48*, 4 (2002), 254–265.

[19] Philipose, M., Fishkin, K. P., Perkowitz, M., Patterson, D. J., Fox, D., Kautz, H., and Hahnel, D. Inferring activities from interactions with objects. *Pervasive Computing, IEEE 3*, 4 (2004), 50–57.

[20] Salthouse, T. Consequences of age-related cognitive declines. *Annual Review of Psychology 63* (2012), 201–226.

[21] Seelye, A. M., Schmitter-Edgecombe, M., Cook, D. J., and Crandall, A. Naturalistic assessment of everyday activities and prompting technologies in mild cognitive impairment. *Journal of the International Neuropsychological Society 19*, 04 (2013), 442–452.

[22] Stanislaw, H., and Todorov, N. Calculation of signal detection theory measures. *Behavior Research Methods, Instruments, & Computers 31*, 1 (1999), 137–149.

How Companies Engage Customers Around Accessibility on Social Media

Erin Brady
Department of Computer Science, ROC HCI
University of Rochester
Rochester, New York, USA
brady@cs.rochester.edu

Jeffrey P. Bigham
HCI and LT Institutes
Carnegie Mellon University
Pittsburgh, PA, USA
jbigham@cs.cmu.edu

ABSTRACT

Social media offers a targeted way for mainstream technology companies to communicate with people with disabilities about the accessibility problems that they face. While companies have started to engage with users on social media about accessibility, they differ greatly in terms of their approach and how well they support the ways in which their users want to engage. In this paper, we describe current use patterns of six corporate accessibility teams and their users on Twitter, and present an analysis of these interactions. We find that while many users want to interact directly with companies about accessibility, companies prefer to redirect them to other channels and use Twitter for broadcast messages promoting their accessibility work instead. Our analysis demonstrates that users want to use social media to become part of the process of improving accessibility of mainstream technology, and suggests the extent to which a company is able to leverage this input depends greatly on how they choose to present themselves and interact on social media.

Categories and Subject Descriptors

K.4.2 [**Computers and Society**]: Social Issues – Assistive technologies for persons with disabilities

General Terms

Human Factors

Keywords

Social media; corporations; accessibility; Twitter

1. INTRODUCTION

Social media offers a targeted way for companies to communicate with people with disabilities about the accessibility of their products and services. This channel can be used for direct dialogues between accessibility teams and customers with disabilities that were not previously feasible. Some problems can be quickly resolved without escalation, other customer needs can be triaged

and passed on to relevant teams to address quickly, and companies can reinforce their commitment to accessibility by publicly engaging with customers around their accessibility efforts.

People are known generally to ask questions to their friends on social media [13], and prior work has explored how and when people with disabilities may want to interact with their social networks to overcome accessibility problems [1, 17]. As companies have joined social media sites such as Twitter, people with disabilities can engage them or their accessibility teams in ways that may have been difficult to do before. These accounts allow companies to advertise their efforts around accessibility, to respond to accessibility criticisms observed in broadcast social media, and even to respond to accessibility questions or criticisms on an individual level.

While companies have started to engage with users on social media about accessibility, we find that the approaches that they have taken to it differ substantially. As we think about tools that may support this sort of direct two-way interaction, it is important to understand how companies are presenting their accessibility efforts on social media now, and how customers want to engage with social media in finding support. For instance, we find that customers want to advise the companies that make the products they use of specific accessibility problems or fixes, even though most companies do not have a way to directly feed this information back to the technical teams.

In this paper, we focus our efforts primarily on Twitter[1], a broadcast social media site in which messages (tweets) can be seen by everyone by default. As a result, not only is the record of interactions available, companies may also have an extra incentive to engage with customers who raise issues about their products and services, because everyone else can see them. As Twitter content is short (140 character or less) strings of text, it is often viewed as inherently accessible, which has led to a number of accessibility-oriented web sites for interacting with Twitter, such as EasyChirp[2].

This paper contributes a characterization of the current accessibility efforts of the companies who run the 50 most popular websites. We analyze the behaviors and contents of over 200 tweets from, to, and about six corporate accessibility teams on Twitter, and describe interaction patterns from 60 conversations between accessibility teams and individual Twitter users.

2. EXAMPLE INTERACTIONS

The motivation for our research came from seeing a number of examples of people interacting with companies around accessibility. The first of these examples occurred during the 2014 Oscars season, when Deaf actress Marlee Matlin used Twitter as a venue

---

[1] http://www.twitter.com
[2] http://www.easychirp.com

to voice her complaints about the process of bringing her interpreter to a party for the awards:

> Only in Hollywood is my interpreter counted as a "guest" for a pre-Oscar party saying I can't bring anyone else. Wise up. It's called access
> – @MarleeMatlin, 2/18/2014

Less than 3 hours after her initial tweet, she updated her followers that the issue had been resolved, and thanked them for supporting her. While the resolution to her issue was not necessarily based on her tweet, it provided a compelling example of how the platform could be used to publicly call out accessibility issues.

We also saw examples of Twitter being used as a medium to request accessibility accommodations. After PBS correspondent Miles O'Brien had an arm amputated in February 2014, he turned to Twitter to update his fans and discuss his adjustment process[3]. Within a month and a half, he was also using Twitter to ask Canon for ideas on one-handed camera use:

> Hi @CanonUSA - I would love to talk with someone about possibly modifying my C-100 for easier usage with one hand. Thanks in advance.
> – @milesobrien, 3/20/2014

While Miles O'Brien's request was for preliminary information and ideas about how to accommodate one-handed use, other Twitter users are very familiar with accessibility and hope to share their expertise with others. Accessibility researcher Sina Bahram publicly tweeted the following request to Pandora Radio's Twitter account:

> .@Pandora_Radio can we please have a quick chat. A few lines of code can allow users with disabilities to use your site. #a11y
> – @SinaBahram, 1/28/2014

Despite receiving a preliminary response from the team acknowledging his request, the accessibility issues he tried to report remain unresolved[4].

After observing these examples, we wished to learn more about how Twitter could be used as a platform for discussing and improving accessibility. Are people commonly using Twitter to discuss accessibility issues and seek solutions? Are companies interacting with Twitter users and trying to engage in dialogues, or are user requests being lost in the high volume of activity on Twitter? With this paper, we hope to provide a first look into how corporations and individuals are discussing accessibility on Twitter, and what kind of interactions are taking place between them.

3. RELATED WORK

Social media sites have opened up a new channel for individuals and corporations to connect to each other. For people interested in accessibility, these channels may allow them to report accessibility issues that they've encountered in the wild, ask for help, and lend their expertise to others. In this section, we discuss how companies have begun to pay more attention to accessibility issues, how companies currently engage in social media platforms, how people use social media platforms to ask questions, and how people with disabilities use social media.

3.1 Corporations and Accessibility

In 2005, the National Federation for the Blind (NFB) reported a number of web accessibility issues on the website `target.com`

to the Target Corporation. When Target did not make any accommodations that would help screen reader users access their site, the NFB filed a lawsuit claiming that Target was violating the Americans with Disabilities Act (ADA) and California legislature governing accessibility in businesses. After Target's motion to dismiss was refused, they settled with the NFB and paid $6 million dollars to members of the class action[5].

In the years before the Target litigation, there was little improvement in the accessibility of corporate websites [11]. However, there was a marked improved in corporate website accessibility after the ruling was passed [3]. Though there is no direct evidence to indicate that this improvement in accessibility was caused by the Target case, it seems likely that many companies started to pay more attention to accessibility at this time as a strategy to avoid expensive, time-consuming litigation.

Despite improvements, accessibility problems remain widespread [11]. The reasons for these issues are complex, but many of the problems can be attributed to webmasters who, while supporting the concept of accessibility in the abstract, lack the time or knowledge of how to make their websites accessible [10].

3.2 Corporations and Social Media

Whether companies have a presence on Twitter or not, the platform is frequently home to discussions about products. 19% of tweets mention a brand or organization, and ~20% of these have either positive or negative sentiments, indicating that Twitter is a valuable platform for gauging customer sentiments or managing consumer perceptions of a brand [6].

With the discussion of brands composing such a large amount of Twitter activity, it is no surprise that many companies have joined the platform as a way to engage with consumers or lead consumer perceptions. In the popular press, the platform was heralded as an innovative way that corporations and individuals could connect with each other and form stronger, more personal relationships [8]. Two-way communication is also known to cultivate relational trust between consumers and corporations [9] and can result in positive sentiments when used while engaging with consumers [16]. Still, it does not appear that many corporations are currently taking advantage of Twitter's usefulness for two-way conversations.

In a 2010 study of dialogic communication by Fortune 500 companies on Twitter [15], 170 of the companies maintained active Twitter profiles. Of the 93 companies analyzed, 60% had responded to individuals at least once in their most recent tweets, but only 26.9% had asked follow-up questions and appeared to be engaged in active dialogue. Additionally, 30% of the companies had posed unprompted questions as a way to facilitate dialogue with consumers. However, companies were still found to be under-utilizing Twitter as a resource for dialogic communication with consumers.

Another analysis performed on non-profit organizations found a similar under-utilization of two-way communication. These non-profits primarily used Twitter as a one-way broadcast mechanism, with sending and receiving direct messages as a small percentage of their Twitter behavior [12]. The lack of two-way communication between organizations and individuals is surprising, since many individual Twitter users already take advantage of the platform to ask questions and form opinions.

3.3 Question Asking and Social Media

As social networking sites have gained traction, people have started using them to ask questions and seek out answers. In a large-scale study of Facebook users, Morris et. al found that 50% of

---

participants had asked questions on the site at least once [13]. Participants reported several motivations for asking questions on social networks, including the fact that they could target their questions to a specific audience who might be more knowledgeable about a topic than a search engine.

3.4 Social Media and Accessibility

Though social networking sites often have accessibility issues, people with disabilities are active users of the sites. In a study of blind Internet users, 92% of participants were members of social networks, with 52% using Twitter. Of these Twitter users, 40% reported asking at least 1 question a month on Twitter, and 50% said they were very or somewhat comfortable using the platform for question asking (compared to only 34% of Facebook users feeling similarly) [1]. Additionally, a recent study of blind Facebook users found that, despite the potential fears of stigmatization, people with visual impairments frequently talked about issues related to disabilities on their social networks [17]. These previous works indicate that social networking sites may be appropriate venues for people with disabilities to voice accessibility concerns and try to search for solutions.

4. CORPORATE ACCESSIBILITY ONLINE

To gauge the importance and visibility of corporate accessibility efforts, we first conducted a search for various markers of accessibility efforts from popular companies on the web.

4.1 Methodology

We chose as a sample the Alexa Top 50 companies in the United States[6]. We chose these companies since they are the most 'popular' sites on the web (based on a proprietary metric of users and pageviews) and represent a diverse group of companies (including technology companies, social media sites, banks, etc.)

The markers of accessibility efforts that we searched for were: *accessibility policies* where companies elaborate on their commitment to accessibility, as suggested in [11], *promotional materials* such as websites or blogs about the company's accessibility efforts, *customer service* for accessibility-specific requests, *contact information* including email addresses or phone numbers, and *social media presence* on Facebook or Twitter.

In order to find these markers, we searched with a standard search engine for each companies' name and a combination of accessibility-specific search terms (eg. "accessibility policy", "section 508"). We also manually browsed each site, examining the contact, support, and frequently asked question pages and the sitemaps for relevant information, or searching the help pages for accessibility-specific terms (eg. "accessibility", "screen reader"). We located Facebook and Twitter accounts both through the contact information on the websites and through manual search on the sites themselves.

4.2 Results

We categorized the accessibility markers that we found into *static* resources, which users could access for information, and *interactive* resources, where users could talk to people and voice concerns or complaints.

4.2.1 Static Accessibility Markers

We found that 8 of the companies had explicit accessibility policies, detailing their commitment to accessibility, and 3 others fell under the corporate umbrella of those 8 (eg. Youtube being owned

---

[6]http://www.alexa.com/topsites/countries/US, retrieved in April 2014

by Google, and thus subject to their policies). These policies often laid out guidelines supporting the use of assistive devices (such as screen readers), preventing discrimination on the basis of disability status, and requiring that the company have a policy for dealing with accessibility complaints.

Of the companies with accessibility policies, four were financial institutions or payment processors (Paypal, Bank of America, Chase Bank, and Wells Fargo Bank). This may indicate that these companies have better consumer-related policies in general due to their physical presences, or that there exists increased legislation over financial institutions that requires accessibility policies.

12 companies had specific portions of their websites dedicated to either talking about their accessibility teams or describing how to use their products with assistive technologies. Two of the companies had blogs specifically devoted to accessibility issues.

4.2.2 Interactive Accessibility Markers

Nearly half of the companies had some sort of customer service presence online - either contact information or live chat with customer service representatives, or online forms where users could submit feedback. For accessibility related issues, though, only 7 companies had specific venues for accessibility feedback (either a separate customer service site, or the ability to categorize feedback as accessibility-related). 4 of the companies had a specific email address where users could send accessibility concerns, and 5 had specific phone numbers or TTY contact information.

Few accessibility teams had presences on social networking sites. Six teams had Twitter accounts, and three were present on Facebook - two with organizational "pages" that users could follow, and one as a "person" that users would need to friend in order to get updates.

5. METHODOLOGY

Since more corporations had accessibility Twitter accounts than Facebook pages, we chose to focus on Twitter to learn more about corporate accessibility outreach on social media. The six companies which had Twitter accounts for their accessibility teams were Google (@googleaccess), Facebook (@fbaccess), Twitter (@a11yteam), Microsoft (@MSFTEnable), PayPal (@PayPallInclusive), and Wordpress (@wpaccessibility).

After explaining features of the Twitter platform, we present an analysis of the accessibility teams, discussing their behaviors and dialogic features when tweeting on the platform, and the content of their tweets.

5.1 Twitter

Twitter is a social microblogging platform that allows users to post messages ("tweets") up to 140 characters in length. Each user can write tweets of their own, or read tweets in their homepage feed, which collects the tweets of users they follow. Twitter users can follow other users to see their statuses in their feed, and can be followed by other users, but these relationships are not reciprocal by default.

We refer to regular tweets as *public tweets*. Tweets can *mention* other users by including their username prefaced with an '@' symbol. If a tweet begins with the '@' symbol, it becomes a *directed message* which is only visible in the homepage feed to users who follow both the tweeter and the user the message was sent to. Users can also privately message each other if both users follow the other. We refer to this as *private messaging*, and it is not included in our analysis.

Tweets can use *hashtags*, words prefaced by a '#' symbol, to denote important keywords. Clicking on a hashtag leads to a stream of all tweets which have also used that hashtag, allowing users to find more about topics of interest from people who they don't follow. Users can also share other's tweets by *retweeting*, either through formal retweeting (where the shared status appears in your followers feeds as if they followed its' author) or informal retweeting (where the user copy and pastes the status as their own tweet, preceeded by 'RT @[username]').

5.2 Twitter Behaviors

We base our analysis of Twitter behaviors primarily on Lovejoy et. al's analysis of Twitter behaviors of non-profit organizations [12]. This work provides a framework for analysing how organizations use Twitter to engage with stakeholders, and how effective they are at utilizing the two-way communication mechanisms of the platform. With the exception of mentions, which were not discussed in Lovejoy et. al's work, all of the justifications provided build upon their framework. The behavioral features analysed include *tweeting activity*, *features of the Twitter platform*, and *engagement with other users*.

We examined *tweeting activity* in order to discuss how active and responsive an organization appears. Organizations which tweet infrequently may not be gaining the awareness they desire from the Twitter platform, as their rare tweets will be buried in a users' feed and possibly missed. However, organizations which tweet excessively may alienate users for appearing spammy. The ratio of public statuses to public messages can provide insight into the perceived responsiveness of the Twitter account.

Features of the platform include the ability to add hyperlinks, which can provide information beyond the 140 limit, and hashtags, which allow tweets to be searched by keywords. Both of these features enhance the static text of the tweets, and allow interested readers to learn more about the specific tweet or related subjects.

Engagement with other users can allow organizations to build communities and spread information amongst their followers. By following users who have followed or interacted with their accounts, organizations appear interested in the users and may create mutual ties. Similarly, retweeting content from other users or mentioning users in tweets shows engagement with those users and can help information disseminate between diverse groups.

We also looked for dialogic features of the tweets sent. Dialogic communication refers to communication that, according to Kent and Taylor, involves "any negotiated exchange of ideas and opinions" between two actors [7]. In addition to measuring public messages as described above, we also manually examined tweets to find discussion prompts posed by the accessibility teams, where followers are asked an open question and can respond with their answer or opinion.

5.3 Content

While behavioral features provide some quantitative insight into the types of communication happening among accessibility teams and individual Twitter users, they do not provide much information about the content of these interactions. In order to learn more about the content of the communications, we performed an open coding analysis on all tweets retrieved by the search API when searching for each corporate accessibility Twitter handle. These search results include tweets both from and to the corporate handles, but are subject to the limitations discussed in section 5.4.

A sample of the tweets were coded and grouped into concepts, with a focus on interaction between the team and users, and direct requests asked by the users to the team. A complete round of coding was performed on the tweets, and codes and concepts were refined. The data was then re-coded with the newly developed codes.

A complete description of these codes is shown in Table 1, with frequencies of tweets both to and from the accessibility team in the sample from the month of April. Tweets could be classified with multiple codes, so totals may sum to more than 100%. The basic categories were *promotional*, *questions and criticisms*, *responses*, and *conversational*.

Promotional tweets primarily served to draw awareness to the accessibility team, through talking about the team and its' members, recommending the team's Twitter handle to other users to follow or include in discussion, and promoting accessibility efforts within the team or highlighting efforts and discussions that the team found interesting.

Questions and criticisms were tweets where users asked for more details about accessibility efforts from the team, or criticised a perceived lack of accessibility in their products. These questions could range from general inquiries about the company's accessibility efforts, requests for tutorials or instructions on how to complete a certain task, or questions about the technical details of a problem or solution.

Responses are tweets addressing questions or criticisms addressed to the team, whether the response comes directly from the team or from another Twitter user. These tweets could include instructions on how to access something with a screen reader, an acknowledgement that a problem exists or of a solution/forthcoming solution, or suggestions of other accessibility products that could be useful.

Conversational tweets encompass the remaining tweets to and from the accessibility teams and Twitter users. These tweets may reflect structural features of the Twitter platform (retweets, continuations of tweets that exceed 140 characters) or tweets with little informational content, such as greetings, redirection to other websites or resources, or any other tweets which fell outside of the previous categories.

5.4 Limitations

This work was limited by the access that we had to tweets from Twitter. Specifically, the tweets that we analyzed represented a sample of those that match a specific search term that we provided. Without access to Twitter's Firehose[7], which is both expensive and requires significant computational resources, we were unable to collect all the relevant tweets for each of our queries. Since these accessibility-related queries make up a small percentage of Twitter data, it is likely according to [14] that our samples may not properly represent the full data available on Twitter. Despite this, we have no reason to believe that the sample provided was biased in a way that would have meaningfully changed our results, and we think that our work provides a valuable first look into how Twitter is being used by some people for accessibility requests.

6. ACCESSIBILITY TEAMS ON TWITTER

Our first analysis focused on the six corporate accessibility teams on Twitter. In Table 2, we present basic information about each team's activity on Twitter since their first tweet on the platform. We also provide quantitative numbers for all tweets from each team during the month of April. In the sections below, we describe the behaviors of the teams and a content analysis of some of their tweets.

6.1 Behaviors

A behavioral analysis was performed on all 184 tweets from the six accessibility teams during the month of April 2014.

---

[7]Firehose access is available from gnip.com or datasift.com

Tweet Categorizations			To Team	From Team	Conversations
Promotional			52%	66%	33%
P1	Team & members	Discussing the team or members	14%	13%	40%
P2	Recommendation	Recommending the team's handle to others	14%	0%	10%
P3	News/outreach	Sharing promotional materials or insights	71%	87%	50%
Questions and Criticisms			15%	1%	80%
Q1	Technical question	Questions about the technical implementation of a product	23%	0%	23%
Q2	Need instructions	Asking for help with the team's product	14%	0%	6%
Q3	Problem or request	Reporting an accessibility problem or requesting a fix	23%	100%	45%
Q4	Suggestion	Suggesting a new product or feature	5%	0%	6%
Q5	Criticism	Critiquing a specific product, the company, or the team	23%	0%	13%
Q6	Additional details	Adding information to a previous question or critique	14%	0%	6%
Responses			5%	23%	68%
A1	Instructions	Providing how-to information or instructions	0%	29%	12%
A2	Acknowledgement	Acknowledging a question, request, or criticism	0%	10%	34%
A3	Resolution	Fixing a problem or addressing a criticism	14%	13%	2%
A4	Follow-up	Asking for clarification or more information	14%	6%	20%
A5	Details	Providing details about the resolution of an issue	14%	13%	0%
A6	Outside scope	Saying an issue cannot be resolved	0%	6%	2%
A7	Forthcoming fixes	Telling users to wait for a resolution	43%	13%	7%
A8	Suggestions	Suggesting a solution or accessibility tool	14%	10%	22%
Conversational			29%	10%	38%
O1	Conversational	Thanks, conversation, instructions on how to contact team	38%	54%	100%
O2	Other	Any other tweets that were not categorized	14%	0%	0%
O3	Continuation	Continuation of a previous tweet, eg. "... (2/2)"	2%	15%	0%
O4	Share me	A request for someone to share or retweet information	5%	0%	0%
O5	Retweet only	A retweet of someone's information, prefaced by "RT"	40%	31%	0%

Table 1: Categories and sub-categories identified in tweets involving accessibility teams on Twitter. The percentages for categories represent the percentage of tweets sampled that could be coded into that category; percentages for sub-categories represent the percentage of tweets in that category that can be coded into that sub-category

6.1.1 Tweet Activity

The teams analyzed had varying levels of activity. Hughes [5] used 1 tweet per week as a metric of *active* or *inactive* users, while Lovejoy [12] suggested 3 tweets per week as a standard for *active* or *inactive* organizations. By this standard, 4 of the 6 teams analyzed were *active* during the month of April (@a11yteam, @mstfenable, @paypalinclusive, and @wpaccessibility).

We also examined the ratio of public tweets and public message from the teams. Of the 5 teams who tweeted during April, only 1 had more directed messages than public statuses (@a11yteam, with 8x as many directed messages as public statuses). The other 4 had more public statuses than directed messages, with ratios ranging from 1.8x to 6.7x more public statuses (mean 3.35x).

6.1.2 Platform Features

All teams who tweeted during April used hyperlinks in at least 1 public tweet. There were 54 tweets containing hyperlinks total, nearly all in public statuses - only 4 were tweeted in directed messages. Similar behavior was exhibited in hashtag use, with all teams tweeting at least once with a hashtag and 77 total tweets with hashtag use, but only 5 direct message tweets with hashtags.

6.1.3 User Engagement

All of the teams studied were followed by far more Twitter users than they followed, with averages of 4881 followers and 85 users followed. Retweeting behaviors were very team dependent, with 3 of the teams who tweeted in April retweeting never or only once, and the other two teams (@paypalinclusive and @wpaccessibility) both having retweets as nearly 35% of their activity.

Mentioning behaviors also depended on the team. @fbaccess

and @a11yteam engaged in very little mentioning (0% and 11% of their overall tweets). The other three teams were actively mentioning others users, with between a quarter and a third of their tweets mentioning a username (excluding retweets and public messages).

Dialogic prompts accounted for a low percentage of total tweets. Prompts accounted for 12% for @msftenable, the team with the highest frequency of prompts, since they often asked discussional questions to their followers:

> Question for our followers: What are your experiences using the power of the community to help support kids w/disabilities? #MSFTAbility
> – @msftenable, 4/24/2014

While these questions were intended to prompt discussion, they did not receive many responses (7 of the 11 prompts asked by the teams were responded to, with 1 or 2 responses each) and the teams rarely followed up to create a dialogue (only 2 of the users were responded to by the teams).

6.1.4 Results

High levels of activity for most of the accessibility teams indicate that they are actively engaged in the platform. However, since many of the accounts communicated mostly through public statuses instead of directed messages, the accounts may be perceived more as promotional, broadcasting tweets to large groups, than as personal and responsive.

Heavy use of hyperlinks and hashtags indicate that many teams see Twitter as a valuable opportunity to grow their network, either by recruiting new followers through hashtags or directing current ones to outside resources with hyperlinks. The limited use of hash-

Corporate Accessibility Team Twitter Accounts

	Google	Facebook	Twitter	Microsoft/Live.com	PayPal/Ebay	WordPress
Twitter Handle	@googleaccess	@fbaccess	@a11yteam	@MSFTEnable	@PayPalInclusive	@wpaccessibility
First Tweet	Nov 1, 2010	Jan 30, 2013	Aug 5, 2013	Jan 9, 2012	Oct 3, 2012	Feb 10, 2013
Total Tweets	259	198	118	645	1153	610
Followers	17900+	2639	1557	5767	910	516
Following	29	84	0	290	80	29
Corporate Accessibility Team Behaviors in April 2014						
Tweets Total	0	6	18	68	70	22
Public statuses	n/a	4	2	50	40	9
@-messages	n/a	2	16	17	6	5
Retweets	n/a	0	0	1	24	8
Tweets with #hashtags	n/a	3	1	46	20	7
Tweets with links	n/a	3	1	27	17	6
Tweets with @-mentions	n/a	0	2	23	18	8
Tweets with prompts	n/a	0	1	8	2	
Sampled User Behaviors in April 2014						
Tweets Sampled	11	9	16	43	26	16
Public statuses	5	4	6	24	13	8
@-messages	6	4	10	16	6	7
Retweets	0	1	0	3	7	1
Tweets with #hashtags	0	0	0	2	1	0
Tweets with links	7	3	1	21	14	9

Table 2: Data about the 6 accessibility-related Twitter accounts from the Alexa Top 50 companies, retrieved in May 2014. For users, retweets are only tweets prefaced by "RT"

tags and hyperlinks in directed messages may reveal that the accessibility teams don't view two-way communication as an appropriate venue for self-promotion, but instead are trying to have more personal interactions with consumers.

Teams showed varying levels of user engagement. None of the teams followed many other users, which may make the teams appear disinterested in content from other users. However, some of the teams were actively involved in retweeting and mentioning other users, so the sense of community might not have suffered too greatly.

6.2 Content

A content analysis was performed on a sample of 108 tweets from the companies during the month of April 2014. The results of the content analysis are shown in Table 1. The majority of tweets originating from the accessibility teams were *promotional* in nature (66%). This fits with the literature showing that most corporate Twitter accounts are not using the platform for its' two-directional communication mechanism, but as a way to promote themselves and control the nature of discussion about their products. Teams had various types of promotional tweets, including updates from the team, release announcements for products, and special events:

> Hey, the new iOS app for PayPal by PayPal, an eBay Company, is out w/ #a11y improvements. Give it a go!
> https://appsto.re/us/1Rb6q.i
> – @PayPalInclusive 4/30/2014

The majority of tweets that were *responses* were simple instructions or how-tos (29%), letting users know how to complete a task or use a feature:

> @samanthaash1993 Hi, you can 1. Double-tap & HOLD your finger on the screen (wait for sound) 2. While holding slide left to launch menu...
> @samanthaash1993 ...to archive the message. We are

looking into making this experience better.
> –@fbaccess, 4/28/2014

Other responses gave more technical details about reported problems or acknowledged existing issues:

> @zkline This problem was unique to @nvaccess; works in all other SR+browser combos (except WindowEyes + IE). Let us know if we missed one.
> –@a11yteam, 4/24/2014

The presence of these tweets show that, despite the limitations on the length of tweets, Twitter can be an effective public way to provide customer service and deal with bug reports. However, this type of interaction currently makes up a relatively small portion of the accessibility teams' overall activity.

7. USERS AND ACCESSIBILITY TEAMS

We also analyzed the users on Twitter who were tweeting about the accessibility teams. We analyzed a sample of 121 tweets sent during April 2014 which were directed to or mentioned one of the accessibility teams.

7.1 Behaviors

Due to the limitations on our sampling method (as discussed in section 5.4), we cannot draw any conclusions from the total number of tweets observed directed at each team. However, we can still analyze some features of user behaviors, in order to learn more about what users want and expect from corporate accessibility teams.

Unlike with the sample of accessibility teams, the range of ratios of public tweets to public messages was much more constrained for individuals, with an average ratio of 1.2x as many public tweets as public messages (min 0.6x, max 2.17x). While this may be due to the sample provided by Twitter, it may also reflect that individual users are more interested in their own personal communications with each accessibility team than being involved in larger conversations.

Hashtag use was limited in tweets from individuals, indicating that individual users were less interested in reaching out to others with similar interests. However, many used hyperlinks to refer to external materials.

7.2 Content

The results of the content analysis of the sample from April are shown in Table 1. Many tweets about the accessibility teams were *promotional*, sharing interesting accessible products coming from the companies or promoting articles or content created by the team:

> A computer experience customizable to each unique individual #Evolve via @MSFTEnable #a11y
> http://www.youtube.com/watch?v=yklvejTgXHY...
> −@dolphinvp, 4/3/2014

These tweets were interesting, as they came from external sources but served to promote the accessibility team by describing them as curators or creators of interesting content. This also explains the high amount of hyperlinks in tweets mentioning the accessibility teams, as users were tagging the teams when distributing external content the team had created or shared.

Questions and criticisms made up a portion of the tweets about accessibility teams (15%). Types were varied based on the user asking and the team they were directed to, ranging from simple questions to critiques:

> So, what's the gist of Windows 8.1 update 1 on phones? Does it have a screen reader or not? CC @MSFTEnable
> −@MarcoInEnglish, 4/2/2014

> Really disappointed with Google. They removed custom user styles from Chrome and removed inverted rendering in Android KitKat. @googleaccess
> −@dcmouyard, 4/27/2014

These examples show the varied ways in which users are composing tweets around corporate accessibility teams, but leave outstanding questions about the interactions between the two.

8. CONVERSATIONS BETWEEN USERS AND ACCESSIBILITY TEAMS

In addition to studying individual corporate and user tweets about accessibility, we wanted to get a better picture of the interactions between the two groups. We analysed both behavioral and content features of 60 interactions between accessibility teams and users, comprising of 208 tweets in total.

8.1 Methodology

We collected the 10 most recent interactions with unique users from April 30th, 2014 and earlier for each of the 6 teams, for a total of 60 interactions. Due to the differences in tweet frequency for the teams, the span between 10 unique interactions ranged from less than a month to over a year. For each interaction, we analyzed the initial tweet, the response from the corporation, and any followup from either the initiating user, the corporation, or other users. We examined both quantitative and qualitative features of these tweets.

The quantitative features we analyzed included the number of participants in the conversation, number of messages exchanged, and length between the beginning and end of the conversation, similar to the analysis performed in [4]. We also manually coded conversations for coherence (if the conversation veered from one topic to another) and content (based on the codes in section 5.3).

8.2 Behaviors

8.2.1 Conversation Initiation

The majority of conversations were initiated by a user and directed to the team (54/60). Most of these conversations (34) were started with a user tweeting the team (half publicly messaged, half with the user mentioning the team). The others were initiated when a user responded to a public status by the team (15), or when a user tweeted something indirectly about the team and then another Twitter user mentioned the team in a response (5).

Only 6 of the conversations were initiated by the team, with half as responses to tweets by users and half as unprompted public messages or mentions of other users.

8.2.2 Conversation Features

Most conversations were personal, with only 2 (45) or 3 (13) active participants in the conversation, and short, with only 2 (23) or 3 (14) messages exchanged. The most active conversational participants in any interaction was 5, with an average of 2.30 participants (median 2). The most messages exchanged in a conversation was 9, with an average of 3.47 messages per conversation (median 3).

8.2.3 Conversation Content and Coherence

Conversations were categorized using the same categories described in section 5.3, and results are presented in Table 1. Each conversation was coded for any behavior shown in any of its' tweets, so totals exceed 100%.

Unsurprisingly, most of the conversations involved questions (80%) and responses (68%). Nearly half of the questions asked were to report problems and request solutions to accessibility issues. Responses were generally helpful, suggesting solutions (22%) or providing instructions (12%), or acknowledged the users' issue without providing a direct solution (34%), but rarely provided concrete resolutions (2%) or promises of forthcoming solutions (7%).

Almost all of the conversations (54) were coherent, and the topic of discussion stayed the same throughout the interaction. In all 6 conversations that lacked coherence, the reason was another user coming into the discussion later and interjecting a bug report of their own:

> @googleaccess I'm having an event for people with disabilities. Could you provide info I could give to people regarding accessibility?
> – @wctllc, 9/20/2012

> @wctllc check out http://www.google.com/accessibility for more info on accessibility in Google products
> – @googleaccess, 9/21/2012

> @googleaccess is google dox fairly usable, or do we still have some work i am a college student and would like to try
> – @paras12, 9/24/2012

These interjections may indicate that users think they will have trouble attracting the attention of the team, and thus they try to join into an ongoing conversation rather than initiating a new conversation. It is evident, however, from the conversations started from unprompted public messages, that these users may have been able to successfully initiate a new conversation and receive a response.

9. DISCUSSION

In this paper, we have explored how companies are engaging with accessibility on social media, and how users are interacting with those digital presences.

For the most part, we found that neither corporations or users are taking full advantage of the two-way communication channel afforded by Twitter. While some people are asking accessibility questions, and some teams are using the platform to respond, most interactions around the accessibility teams are promotional in nature. However, the popularity of retweets and mentions indicates that a community of people and corporations interested in accessibility is being formed on Twitter and may encourage more dialogue in the future.

Some of the emergent behaviors we observed may indicate opportunities for corporate accessibility teams to form stronger bonds with customers. For example, while many teams redirected users with accessibility requests to external resources, others took the information received from Twitter users and filed the bug reports directly. This helpfulness might engender positive feelings towards the company, and ensures that the team does not miss a bug if users are unwilling or unable to file a bug report on an external site.

The public nature of conversations on Twitter may also influence what kind of interactions corporations are willing to engage in. If teams can provide positive responses to user requests, they may be more likely to engage with users so they can build trust and appear responsive. If a team is unable or unwilling to assist a user, however, they may not want to reject them publicly on Twitter and be subject to criticism.

Future work could leverage some of the behaviors we observed to help solve accessibility issues. Highly technical users on Twitter who make suggestions to accessibility teams (as in Table 5.3, A8) could donate their expertise to crowdsource accessibility fixes that developers may not know about. Even just interacting with these users could help promote awareness of accessibility issues for corporations by giving them exposure to the users' perspective [2].

10. CONCLUSION

Companies are increasingly using social media for the purpose of promoting their accessibility efforts and engaging with customers who care about or experience problems with accessibility. Our investigation suggests that while users are interested in finding solutions to their own accessibility problems on Twitter, companies seem more inclined to use it as a means to broadcast messages about their activities related to accessibility, and neither group is utilizing two-way communication to its full potential. Users interacting with corporate accessibility teams may offer companies a way to connect with an important stakeholder group, both to improve the users' experience with the company's products and to leverage the unique expertise that these stakeholders stand to bring to the company. Adjusting to these trends may require new technology to be developed that would support these kinds of interactions and/or new processes to be incorporated in companies to allow them to fully leverage the users that want to engage with them.

11. ACKNOWLEDGMENTS

We would like to Jennison Asuncion and Sina Bahram for their valuable insights during this work. This work has been supported by an Alfred P. Sloan Foundation Fellowship and National Science Foundation Awards #IIS-1149709 and #IIS-1116051.

12. REFERENCES

[1] E. L. Brady, Y. Zhong, M. R. Morris, and J. P. Bigham. Investigating the appropriateness of social network question asking as a resource for blind users. In *Proceedings of the 2013 Conference on Computer Supported Cooperative Work*, CSCW '13, pages 1225–1236, 2013.

[2] E. Fischer and A. R. Reuber. Social interaction via new social media:(how) can interactions on twitter affect effectual thinking and behavior? *Journal of business venturing*, 26(1):1–18, 2011.

[3] J. Frank. Web accessibility for the blind: Corporate social responsibility or litigation avoidance? In *Hawaii International Conference on System Sciences, Proceedings of the 41st Annual*, pages 284–284. IEEE, 2008.

[4] C. Honey and S. C. Herring. Beyond microblogging: Conversation and collaboration via twitter. In *System Sciences, 2009. HICSS'09. 42nd Hawaii International Conference on*, pages 1–10. IEEE, 2009.

[5] A. L. Hughes and L. Palen. Twitter adoption and use in mass convergence and emergency events. *International Journal of Emergency Management*, 6(3):248–260, 2009.

[6] B. J. Jansen, M. Zhang, K. Sobel, and A. Chowdury. Twitter power: Tweets as electronic word of mouth. *Journal of the American society for information science and technology*, 60(11):2169–2188, 2009.

[7] M. L. Kent and M. Taylor. Building dialogic relationships through the world wide web. *Public relations review*, 24(3):321–334, 1998.

[8] R. King. How companies use twitter to bolster their brands. Bloomberg BusinessWeek, September 2008. http://www.businessweek.com/stories/2008-09-06/how-companies-use-twitter-to-bolster-their-brandsbusinessweek-business-news-stock-market-and-financial-advice.

[9] M. Knight and S. Carpenter. Optimal matching model of social support: An examination of how national product and service companies use twitter to respond to consumers. *Southwestern Mass Communication Journal*, 27(2), 2012.

[10] J. Lazar, A. Dudley-Sponaugle, and K.-D. Greenidge. Improving web accessibility: a study of webmaster perceptions. *Computers in Human Behavior*.

[11] E. T. Loiacono, N. C. Romano Jr, and S. McCoy. The state of corporate website accessibility. *Communications of the ACM*, 52(9):128–132, 2009.

[12] K. Lovejoy, R. D. Waters, and G. D. Saxton. Engaging stakeholders through twitter: How nonprofit organizations are getting more out of 140 characters or less. *Public Relations Review*, 38(2):313–318, 2012.

[13] M. R. Morris, J. Teevan, and K. Panovich. What do people ask their social networks, and why?: A survey study of status message q&a behavior. In *Proceedings of the SIGCHI Conference on Human Factors in Computing Systems*, CHI '10, pages 1739–1748, 2010.

[14] F. Morstatter, J. Pfeffer, H. Liu, and K. M. Carley. Is the sample good enough? comparing data from twitter's streaming api with twitter's firehose. *Proceedings of ICWSM*, 2013.

[15] S. Rybalko and T. Seltzer. Dialogic communication in 140 characters or less: How fortune 500 companies engage stakeholders using twitter. *Public Relations Review*, 36(4):336–341, 2010.

[16] S. Wigley and B. K. Lewis. Rules of engagement: Practice what you tweet. *Public Relations Review*.

[17] S. Wu and L. A. Adamic. Visually impaired users on an online social network. In *Proceedings of the 32nd annual ACM conference on Human factors in computing systems*, pages 3133–3142. ACM, 2014.

Buildings and Users with Visual Impairment: Uncovering Factors for Accessibility using BIT-Kit

Lesley J Mcintyre[1], Vicki L. Hanson[1]

[1]School of Computing
University of Dundee
Dundee, DD1 4HN, Scotland
lesleymcintyre@computing.dundee.ac.uk

[2]Golisano College of Computing and Information
Sciences, Rochester Institute of Technology20 Lomb
Memorial DriveRochester, NY USA 14623
vlh@acm.org

ABSTRACT

In this paper, we report on the experiences of visually impaired users in navigating buildings. We focus on an investigation of the way-finding experiences by 10 participants with varying levels of visual ability, as they undertook a way-finding task in an unfamiliar public building. Through applying the BIT-Kit framework in this preliminary user study, we were able to uncover 54 enabling and disabling interactions within the case study building. While this building adhered to building legislation, our findings identified a number of accessibility problems including, issues associated with using doors, hazards caused by building finishes, and difficulty in knowing what to do in the case of an emergency evacuation. This user study has demonstrated a disparity between design guidance and the accessibility needs of building users. It has uncovered evidence to enable architects to begin to design for the real needs of users who have a range of visual impairment. Furthermore, it has instigated discussion of how BIT-Kit's evidence could be incorporated into digital modeling tools currently used in architectural practice.

Categories and Subject Descriptors

J.5 [Arts and Humanities] Architecture; K.4.2 [**Computers and Society**] Social issues – *Assistive technologies for persons with disabilities.*

Keywords

Accessibility; architecture; buildings; visual impairment; way-finding; methods

1. INTRODUCTION

Architectural design is failing to meet the needs of many end users, particularly those who experience an impairment or disability. We are all aware, for example, of building requirements for wheelchair users and guidelines for Braille in buildings. In many cases, however, implementations of such designs fail to achieve the stated goal. From an architectural perspective, this is due to a lack of method in gathering evidence to understand the accessibility of buildings by the people who use them.

The built environment is the context for human activity. However, buildings that have failed to include the needs of users in the design process are often not fully accessible. The result is a building whereby the user experiences exclusion and disablement, and the client experiences costly, inconvenient accessibility interventions. A particular issue is the lack of design evidence in relation to what enables and disables people with visual impairment as they undertake the task of way-finding in buildings [2, 18].

The built environment is failing to support people who have a form of visual loss. Described as an *'assault course'*, the building *'poses the most serious threat to independence and full social integration'* [3]. Goldsmith [10] recognizes this as a form of *'Architectural Disablement'*.

Previous approaches in relation to understanding this problem area have focused developing models or theoretical structures of way-finding. However, the detail and real-world evidence of what enables and disables people with visual impairment is missing. Furthermore, methods to gather this evidence are lacking. Current guidance and legislation fail to provide designers with user-evidence that is transferable into accessible design practice [19]. Graphical representations (such as space syntax models), concentrate on modelling the spatial layout and environmental performance of places in relation to crowd flow, as opposed to individual's experience. Similarly, when adopting qualitative methods, the users 'voice' often becomes lost as the individual's perspective and tacit experience are diluted when converted into legislation, guidelines and access checklists. Popular strategies of utilising 'specialists' and simulating impairment are also frequently adopted, yet flawed in reliability [6].

The issues with accessibility in the built environment bear a striking resemblance to issues with technology accessibility. While numerous guidelines exist for accessible development (IBM), in many cases technologies that are fully compliant still fail to meet the needs of disabled users [21].

We describe BIT-Kit, a user-focused evidence-gathering tool, composed of semi-structured interview, observation of buildings in use, and user's interaction trace. This combination of methods is proposed to complement and strengthen the weaknesses of a single method approach. Our goal with this work is to consider the experiences of visually impaired users as they navigate buildings, determining if and when the built environment – built to meet building codes for accessibility – actually meets their needs.

In comparison to previous approaches, BIT-Kit allows built environment professionals to identify the location and reason behind enabling and disabling interactions within the building. Furthermore, to have impact in the accessibility of both new buildings and retrofit projects, there is potential for BIT-Kit's evidence to be embedded in the digital modeling tools (e.g. BIM, CAD and Sketch-up), currently used in architectural practice.

2. RELATED WORKS

We discuss the existing approaches to understand interactions by people with visual impairment as they undertake the task of way-finding within the built environment. Although this work parallels what architects consider when designing homes for people with dementia, [24], literature assessing the impact the built environment has on people with visual impairment is limited.

Previous works have identified that the built environment is failing to support people who have a form of visual loss [3] however they give no evidence based on the needs of building users with visual impairment. The task of way-finding within a public building is raised as a particular problem [2] because most designers give way-finding low priority, seeing it as a hindrance to good design or a problem to be solved with signage [5].

There is a lack of contemporary research within the profession to enable architects to mitigate problems and enhance solutions. Furthermore, research has tended to concentrate on cognitive mapping abilities of people with visual impairment [16] as opposed to capturing actual evidence of experience associated with using a building (e.g. accessibility issues experienced when trying to find the restroom or opening a fire-safety door).

Way-finding is the process of getting from A to B. It is user orientated and is the cognitive, behavioral and strategic task of planning movement [2]. It is a process composed of four sub-tasks: 1.Orientation, 2.Choosing and planning the route, 3. Keeping on the right track - Navigation, and finally 4. Discovering (and stopping at) the destination [7, 8]. It is knowing what direction and course of action is needed to reach a destination [2, 7, 11]. It is a form of goal-directed movement [2]. An un-successful way-finding task can leave a person 'lost' or disorientated in their surroundings [11].

It is a complex set of cognitive, behavioral and physical processes which are widely debated across disciplines. Familiarity of routes, building type, type of way-finding, information availability and its synthesis, individual's abilities and cognitive processes are all factors impacting on and influencing way-finding.

The psychologists' view that Cognitive Mapping is the process which enables way-finding by the 'product' of the cognitive map [7, 8] is put into practice by researchers such as Lynch [17] who has investigated ways that people structure their cognitive maps. However, this process of cognitive mapping is doubted by researchers, such as [2, 15], who argue that the skill to way-find is not acknowledged. Instead, Arthur and Passini [2] Information Processing Model puts the importance on the informative aspects of way-finding.

Whilst Lynch [17] claimed that *'Nothing is experienced by itself, but always in relation to its surroundings, the sequences of events leading up to it, the memory of past experiences.'* Brambring [13] and Harper and Green [12] fail to take this into account. Their models focus on an individual journey undertaken by a blind person however do not consider the impact these journeys have on the ability to learn or remember routes. They also fail to consider the complicated varying experiences and spectrum of visual loss.

There is a lack of a way-finding model, which incorporates all types of visual ability that is based on both experience and is in relation to a real-world setting [16]. Strategies of utilizing 'specialists' and simulating impairment are frequently adopted in architecture practice and education as a way to understand users needs [1, 22]. However, users need to be represented in accessibility research in order for inclusive design to have a positive impact on people's lives [23].

Quantitative algorithmic techniques such as work carried out by Space Syntax [14], has provided tools for architects to simulate the effects and impact of decisions on the relationships between people and the built environment. They are usually presented as digital representations of physical space in the format of site plans overlaid with matrixes' of flow patterns. These allow architects to quickly read and understand the simulations of user behavior in relation to the context of a specific setting. However, these algorithms are abstract and reductive representations of generic users. They fail to capture the diversity of the population and lack the detailed understanding of the individual and their needs. Overall, this is a recognized failing of the quantitative methods in general.

3. BIT-KIT: THE BACKGROUND

There are few evidence-based studies of way-finding in a building. Furthermore, there are no studies of real-life experiences of way-finding undertaken by real-life participants with a range of visual ability. This is a significant gap in architectural knowledge.

To address this gap, we applied both algorithmic techniques and qualitative interview-based analyses to understand how people with visual impairments use buildings. There was an absence of a single methodology that would fully meet the needs of this type of investigation. Therefore, a theoretical foundation was created from the established approaches of Grounded Theory [9] and Case Study [25], in addition to methods currently adopted in architecture (e.g. analysis of floor plans).

There was also lack of a single method that would let us gain insight into the accessibility challenges encountered by people in buildings. Limitations of previous work caused by, a lack of user experience [17], a use of method which either lacked qualities [14] or quantities [2], and a concentration on the extreme edges of impairment or disability (e.g. studies only involving legally people [12, 13]), were several of the factors that influenced the core elements of BIT-Kit.

3.1 BIT-KIT: The FRAMEWORK

We propose BIT-Kit, the Building Interactions Tool-kit [20], to facilitate the gathering of evidence of how buildings impact (both good and bad) on the accessibility of users. BIT-Kit comprises a mixed-method approach, incorporating semi-structured interview, observation of buildings in use and traces of users interactions.

This combination of methods provides detailed traces of user interactions, evidence and understanding of the disabling and enabling elements of a building.

3.1.1 Interviews

Interviews are used to gain qualitative insight into both past and present experiences of using and interacting with buildings. Beginning as unstructured interviews, to remain as open as possible, the interview becomes a planned approach that utilizes an initial framework of topics focused on the overall research question or hypothesis.

ID	Age	Gender	Aid	Self-definition and Age of VI	Mobility Training
P1 'Alfie'	55	Male	Symbol Cane *"I never leave the house without someone else with me"*	*"I am in total darkness all the time. I can see nothing." (50)*	No
P2 'Katie'	50	Female	Guide Dog *"We go everywhere together."*	*"Totally Blind. I have no useful sight at all when I am out and about." (21)*	Yes
P3 'James'	60	Male	Roller Cane	*"Registered Blind"(Since Birth)*	Yes
P4 'Evie'	65	Female	Sliding Cane	*"I have degenerative sight- loss, Peripheral vision only, sensitive to light and have double vision"(50)*	Yes
P5 'Lily'	30	Female	White Cane	Degenerative sight-loss. *"I can only see things that are really close to my face"* (13)	Yes
P6 'Adam'	20	Male	No Mobility Aid, wears prescription lenses	Degenerative sight-loss. *"no working iris, sensitive to light and registered partially sighted"* (Since Birth)	No
'Emma'	23	Female	Long Cane *"the occasional borrowed elbow of a friend"*	No vision in left eye and *'about 10-15% of vision in my right eye"(4)*	No
P8 'Jack'	21	Male	Corrective Lenses, Wheelchair and Mobility Assistant	*"I can only see straight ahead."* No peripheral vision. *(Since Birth)*	No
P9 'Grace'	40	Female	No Mobility Aid, Prescriptive Lenses	*"I am either short or long sighted – I can't remember" (Recently)*	No
P10 'Ben'	24	Male	No Aid	*"no visual loss"*	No

Table 1 Participant Profiles

The framework of topics evolves through each interview to become a semi-structured interview. Data, recorded on a Dictaphone, is downloaded, transcribed and coded using qualitative analysis software (such as Atlas.ti). This approach enables rich narrative and insight to be gained in relation to users experiences of buildings.

3.1.2 Traces of Users' interactions

User's movements through a building, or interaction with a specific element of architecture are plotted on floor plans of the building. Patterns, individual behaviors and spatial information in context, can be understood through these traces. In addition these interaction traces can convey evidence back to built environment professionals.

3.1.3 Observations of buildings in use

Within BIT-Kit, participants undertake an observed task or interaction with a building to enable understanding of the building being used. By employing this method we can define the events that are actually happening and assess how the person is being impacted by the building (i.e. positive or negative experiences). It is also possible to identify how other situational variables, such as other people or temporary changes within the building impact on experience. Through the use of observations we are able to gather the contextual information in regards to what is happening.

4. USER STUDY

The objective of this user study was to apply the BIT-Kit approach to a real world scenario. We investigated the enabling and disabling experiences of 10 participants with varying levels of visual ability, as they undertook a way-finding task in an unfamiliar public building [18].

4.1 Participants

Ten participants (5 male and 5 female, ages 20 to 70), who had a range of visual impairment (in addition to other disabilities), were recruited to take part in the Way-finding Scenario, following ethical approval from the University of Dundee. Table 1 provides an overview to the participants. The group as a whole is representative of a range of visual impairment.

4.2 Equipment and Software

A Dictaphone was used to record the interviews and a Panasonic SDT-S7 Digital Camera was used to record a video of the participant's way-finding journeys.

Qualitative Data Analysis & Research Software, ATLAS.ti was used to analyze the interview data. Timeline-based video editing software, Adobe Premier Pro was used in observations of the way-finding journeys. Adobe Premier Pro and Computer Aided Design software, AutoCAD (Version 17.0) were used together in order to plot and analyze users interaction trace from the film footage.

4.3 Procedure

The Way-finding Scenario comprised three sequential phases. The user study was designed to evaluate both the pre-existing memories of way-finding in a building and the experience of a way-finding task within a public building.

4.3.1 Phase 1: A Chat-Way-finding in Buildings.

Purposeful conversation [4] was adopted as an unobtrusive way to initially gather narrative of general way-finding topics and experiences of participants' way-finding in buildings. The purposeful conversation was a planned approach, which utilized an initial framework of topics that evolved throughout each way-finding scenario to become semi-structured interviews.

In remaining open, these interviews were focused to uncover insight into the participant demographic information and includes details of; their self-definition of their visual impairment, when their visual loss occurred, the types of way-finding aids they currently used and if they had ever undertaken orientation and mobility training.

Recorded by Dictaphone and later transcribed, all interviews went through a process of coding using the constant comparison technique of Grounded Theory [9]. The data open-coded to produce an initial code list, which through iteration was developed until the analysis reached theoretical saturation, with respect to the amount of data. Relationships were established between the categories identified in the open coding through axial coding. The data was selectively coded in terms of core and subcategories from the initial and axial list.

4.3.2 Phase 2: The Way-finding Task.
Immediately following Phase 1, participants took part in a way-finding task within the way-finding setting during the building's regular opening times. They were asked to find their way from a starting point (the boundary wall of the building) to a destination point (an office within the building) and were not provided with any directional guidance.

Each Participant was asked to undertake the task as they normally would when visiting an unfamiliar building (i.e. if they normally asked at the reception for directions then they should ask the receptionist in this building for directions). The way-finding task was not run on a timed basis. Participants carried a small digital video recorder that captured their 'way-finding encounters'.

This quantitative data was transcribed onto floor plans of the building and became the participants 'Way-finding Trace' (Figure 1) still images were also captured and aided in building understanding of what was actually happening at specific points in the building.

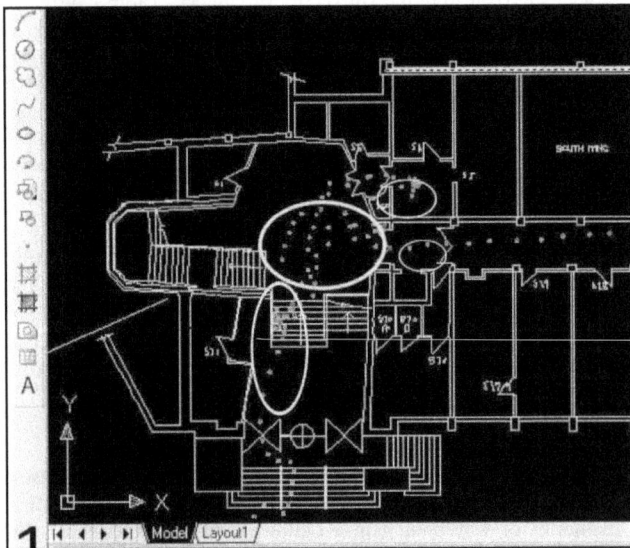

Figure 1 Way-finding Trace

4.3.2.1 The Building
The building selected for the way-finding scenario was a large, semi-public building that was fully compliant with building legislation. The selection of the building was based on a number of logistical factors (e.g. regular opening times), the complexity of the building and architectural elements available (e.g. stairs, number of floors) and the ability to gain access to the floor plans for data recording and analysis.

4.3.3 Phase 3: Observations/ Reflection Interviews.
Observations and Reflection Interviews in relation to Phase 2 were implemented immediately following the way-finding task. Purposeful conversation, which developed into a semi-structured interview, was utilised again to focus on participants' experiences of way-finding in a specific building. It was found that participants' memories of previous way-finding experiences were activated by events that happened during Phase 2 and they also talked about these. The researcher undertook observations of the way-finding task using the video camera footage. From this footage the entirety of each participant's way-finding journey could be understood in relation to the contextual, social and temporal elements of the building.

5. DATA ANALYSIS AND RESULTS
The BIT-Kit approach has uncovered 54 enabling and disabling experiences. Coined Hotspots, these are the encounters and interactions (positive and negative) that impacted on a person's experience of way-finding. In this paper we present several findings that provide insight into the types of insight extracted from employing this user-based approach.

5.1 Results
Using BIT-Kit within this case study has uncovered both qualitative and quantitative evidence of what enables and disables the task of way-finding by people with visual impairment. Through analysis of data it emerged that there were key events and occurrences, 'hotspots', which occurred within a way-finding journey and impacted on a way-finders experience of using the building. They were spatial conditions, social interactions, or temporal events. Hotspots were positive experiences such as using ground textures to find the front door of a building or being able to break a journey to find the toilets. Hotspots were also negative experiences such as not being able to understand or use way-finding signage or not being able to find and follow a route through a building because of a change of use or extension. The hotspots uncovered were the evidence to understand the impact the building had on the people using it.

Figure 1 illustrates data of a physical way-finding trace of a participant walking through and interacting with a building (each second in time is represented as a dot on the floor plan). The clusters of dots highlight a hotspot of movement – a key area of interest or critical significance – when all movement has slowed down or stopped altogether. This highlights to us that something has happened within this specific area of the building in response to either physical impediment or decision-based change in trajectory. Data collected from interviews, conversations and observations will illuminate whether hotspots are positive or negative and the underlying reason(s) for it occurring in the specific location of the building.

5.2 BIT-KIT, data analysis and 'Hotspots'
The challenge, when working with this data set, was the synthesis of different types of data (i.e. interview, floor plans, still images and film footage, illustrated in figure 2). Once this was achieved, there were different ways to identify hot spots. Each method used within BIT-Kit has uncovered hot spots, both individually and through data fusion (across 2 or more Phases).

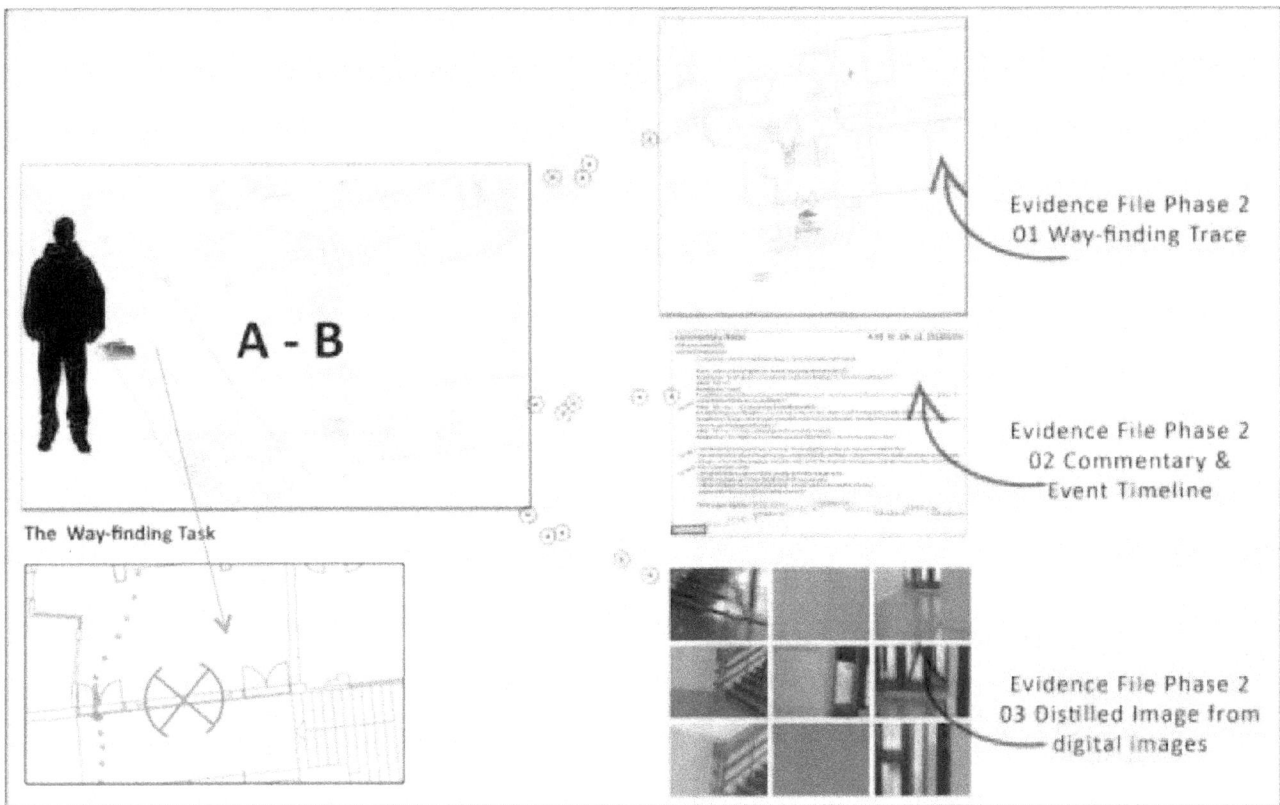

Figure 2: Quantifiable Trace Hotspots and Observations

5.2.1 Memories of Hotspots

Memories of past way-finding experiences through a building, specifically talked about in Phase 1, were identified and extracted as quotes when the participants referred to way-finding being hindered or enhanced by an event in a building. This type of hot spot is exemplified by Katie's experience of a glass staircase (Figure 3), which was encountered in a different building from the case-study setting. She explained,

'He (her guide-dog) won't go up stairs if they are open in any way or if they are made of glass. He can't see where to put his feet, so he just refuses.'

"He (guide-dog) won't go up stairs if they are open in any way or if they are made of glass. He can't see where to put his feet, so he just refuses'

Figure 3 Memories of Hotspots in other Buildings

Another example of this type of memory-based hotspot is identified in participant's experiences of knowing what to do in the case of an emergency. James, Alfie and Jack stated they would always have to rely on someone else to help them in an emergency.

Jack explained, *'I have never been put in the real life situation of there being a fire. I don't know how good I would be at figuring it out. [...] my assistant is with me. I will be ok.'*

Evie described a situation when she was in hospital and there was a fire that caused all the doors to lock. She explained the *'mass panic'* that ensued, due to occupants being unaware the doors would lock in event of an emergency, *'we could smell the smoke and everything. [...] It was really stressful and very scary.'*

Lily identified that she was not able to read fire-exit signage because of the colors green and white. She also highlighted a need to be told what to do in the case of emergency as soon as she entered a building and explained, *'Normally in case of an emergency they say "follow the emergency signs" - but [...] I can't see them. I just say "so where would they be exactly?"'*

She continued, *'Green signs with white writing are the worst colors for me. They should tell you what to do as soon as you walk in. Like they do on a plane – the safety demonstration.'*

Katie described her sense of distress and frustration of being instructed to wait in a refuge area – her fear being, *'in a large building over several floors - will I be left here?'*

She added, *'Disabled people who are mobile shouldn't have to be crowded in to refuge areas if they are capable of using stairs. I have the "D label" so I am told to go there.'*

5.2.2 Quantifiable Trace Hotspots and Observations

Within the Way-finding Trace, hotspots can be identified by occurrences such as, a clustering effect within a way-finding trace, a way-finding trace slowing in pace, a way-finding trace quickening in pace, or an interesting way-finding trace (Figure 4).

These experiences were not always described by participants during Phase 3, however they can be found in the trace and observed in the film footage. In these instances the hot spots can be understood in relation to the building elements.

Extra detail, such as situational factors (e.g. building materials or colours), temporal elements (e.g. reflective glare or temporary signage) and social interactions (e.g. input from other people) can also be understood and analyzed from the observations (figure 2).

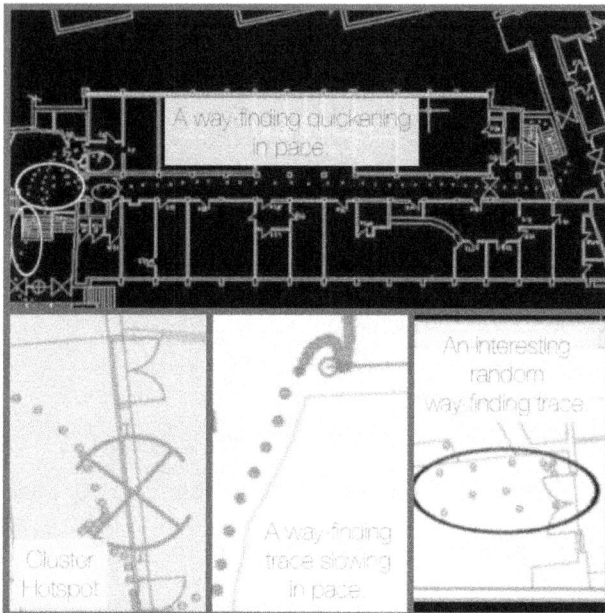

Figure 4: Finding Hotspots in the Trace

5.2.3 Experienced Hotspots not evident in the Trace

Not all hotspots were identifiable from the trace and this was evident when participants reflected on hotspots that occurred within Phase 3. For instance, Ben had a positive experience during the Way-finding Journey, which was the result of him deciding to not follow a physical path that lead to the entrance of the building. Instead, he selected his route based on a decision that it was a *'short-cut'* and explained,

'It was the shortest way to the steps. There was a path, but there were no cars so I went for it'.

However in contrast, Katie's encounter of walking through the car-park to get to the building entrance was a negative experience (Figure 5) as she struggled to find a path to the entrance. She stated,

'For a blind person, you are asking them to find their way through an open space, a nightmare, and worse still, to find their way around parked cars and moving parking cars, worse nightmare. There is a good chance of getting lost. So a different surface for a pathway through, or around the car park, should be designed in.'

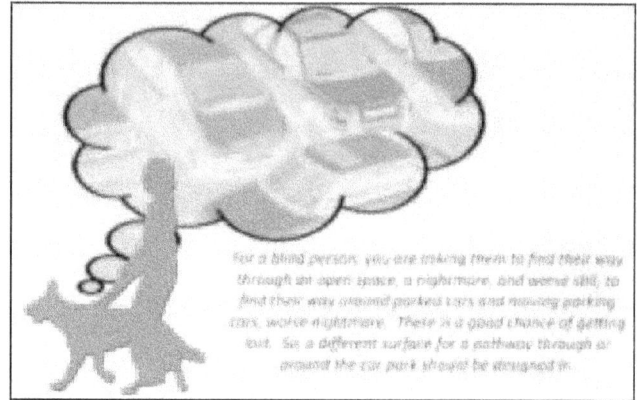

Figure 5: Experienced Hotspots not evident in the Trace.

5.2.4 Hotspots: Trace and Memories

Participant's experience of way-finding through the building in Phase 2 prompted insight into memories of hotspots experienced in other buildings. Adam, Grace, Ben and Emma all paused several times throughout their Way-finding Journeys to rest when looking through windows and over balconies. James reflected, *"I love all the different smells in a new building and I can always sniff out a good cup of coffee and cake".* He said, *"These are the wee delights I find when I am out and about."*

5.2.5 Hotspots: Trace and Reflection

Way-finding reflection and way-finding trace (Phase 2 and 3) began to give extra insight about the hotspot experienced. Figure 6 illustrates Becky's hotspot that was encountered during the way-finding task (identifiable by the clustering and doubling up of trace) and her reflection of the experience that corridors help her to way-find. She stated,

'When you are in a corridor, and you have got definition at the sides and back it is far easier to feel safe and it is easier to concentrate and figure out "right how do I start to get from A to B to C to D?"'

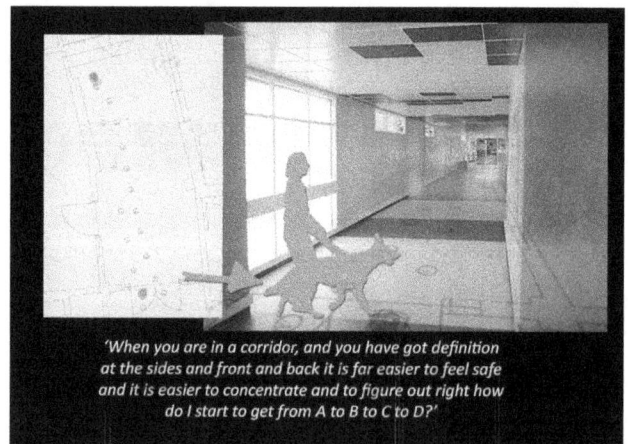

Figure 6: Trace and Reflection Hotspot

5.2.6 Hotspots: Trace, Memories and Reflection

When data-fusion occurred between all 3 Phases, this resulted in a particularly generalized finding. In James' example (Figure 7) he talked about revolving doors in Phase 1, experienced a revolving door in Phase 2 and then talked about that experience in Phase 3. He explained: *'I hate revolving doors. I have got my hand stuck in one before. I cannot see the best place to put my hand or which way to push. I can't see if someone else is coming out and if they are pushing the door. That makes me nervous. I normally try to avoid revolving doors.'*

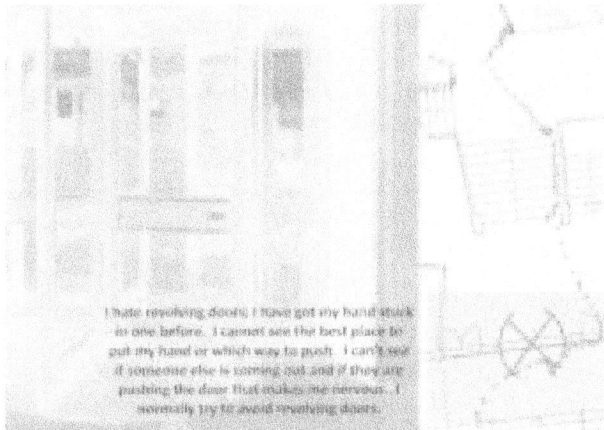

Figure 7: Data fusion across all 3 Phases

6. DISCUSSION: BIT-KIT AND HOTSPOTS

BIT-Kit is a tool that gathers evidence to assess the impact the built environment has on people. It takes steps towards uncovering evidence as to how buildings impact on the wellbeing, mobility and independence of the people who inhabit and use them.

Although only several examples can be evidenced here, each of the hotspots can be understood in relation to the type of interaction, architectural context, spatial conditions, temporal conditions, social constraints and impact of elements of architecture (micro and macro conditions). Through uncovering the hotspots, the application of BIT-Kit was successful in uncovering evidence to assess the impact the building has on way-finders who have a range of visual impairment.

In relation to factors of accessibility in the built environment, we have exposed an obvious gap in the guidance available to architects. Buildings deemed to adhere to code and regulations are still, to varying degrees, creating exclusion for building users.

In relation to the case study, which investigated a real-world problem, BIT-Kit methods were successful in presenting novel, architectural-relevant data. The successes of BIT-Kit are that methods can be developed in direct response to an architectural case study and research problem. The multi-method approach enabled weaknesses of using one method to be mitigated. For example, understanding of way-finding trace hotspots could be gained through phases of purposeful conversations. The study also uncovered the holistic impact (positive and negative hotspots) a building has on people and the underlying reason(s) for hotspots occurring in specific locations of buildings. Used in different buildings (e.g. transport hub, cultural building or medical setting) BIT-Kit has the potential to uncover more hotspots in order to identify common problems that emerge due to lack of proper accessibility features.

Several of the findings gathered from using BIT-Kit validate specific elements of current building guidance; others differ and contest current guidance whilst some take understanding further. An important aspect of these findings is that they provide the context of the hotspot as opposed to specifying prescript 'rules'. This contrasts from current guidance as it puts the designer in the role of creating a context specific solution to the hotspot, in relation to the building.

A limitation of BIT-Kit methodology can only be applied when a building has been constructed and is inhabited by people, and not in the design stage of a new building. In future work BIT-Kit's evidence could be incorporated into digital modeling tools currently used in architecture. The combination of floor plans and context related quotes allow architecturally relevant evidence to be presented to stakeholders. Through exploring the virtual floor plans, they would be able to query points of interest to gain a deeper understanding of the accessible and inaccessible interactions. Further research is beginning to explore the need for such a tool [19].

Way-finders find it difficult to give an accurate account of their way-finding experiences [2, 11, 17]. Although BIT-Kit includes methods to dilute this limitation it needs to be acknowledged that some way-finding experiences could have been missed, or misinterpreted. In addition, the findings evidenced from the case study building may not, in their entirety, be applied to other buildings. The way-finding task limits the interactions compared to the architect's complete building floor plan. Further studies in relation to this limitation, performed in a number of different buildings in order to identify common problems that emerge due to lack of proper accessibility features is needed for more generalizable data.

The major limitation of BIT-Kit is the time and skill it takes to collect, transcribe and analyse the different types of data. If BIT-Kit, in its current form, were to be adopted in architectural practice it would prove to be costly. However, in progressing BIT-Kit further within a new project BESiDE [19] (The Built Environment for Social Inclusion through the Digital Economy) it is an objective that this limitation will be addressed and certain elements, such as analyzing the conversations and plotting the interaction trace, will become automated.

6.1 Developing BIT-Kit: What's next?

We are currently developing the methods of BIT-Kit within a new project, BESiDE [19]. BESiDE is a multi-disciplinary research project that investigates themes of ageing, wellbeing, and digital technologies within the context of built environment design. Undertaken with care home and architectural design partners, BESiDE's research analyses the holistic design insight gained from evaluating the physical environment coupled with older people's experience of their surroundings.

Through the development of a dialogue tool, indoor location sensors and sensors measuring physical activity, BIT-Kit is being utilized to gain evidence of how the built environment can facilitate physical ability and wellbeing in older people's care homes. The BESiDE project investigates how older people are currently marginalized from society via the built environment. As the project progresses it will go further by identifying where digital technologies have the potential to improve the hotspots uncovered within the context of older people' care environments.

7. CONCLUSIONS

Architecture is described as a process of "learning by doing" (Lawson, 2006). Architects work from a conceptual level 'on the drawing board', to the real-life construction of buildings. However, within architectural discourse the gathering and analysing of evidence to understand the impact of accessibility in buildings is scarce. This type of analysis is vital as building users are still experiencing disabling interactions within buildings.

The Building Interactions Toolkit (BIT-Kit) is a method that builds evidence to understand the link between buildings and the independence and mobility of the people who use them. In comparison to previous approaches, BIT-Kit allows built environment professionals to identify the location and reason behind enabling and disabling interactions within the building.

BIT-Kit has been introduced and evaluated through a case study of way-finding task in a public building by persons with visual impairment [18]. In applying a mixed-method approach of purposeful conversation, observation and building interaction data, BIT-Kit has been found to be successful in uncovering 54 'hotspots' of way-finding in a building by people with visual impairment. The evidence gathered from the way-finding scenarios, direct from the user, has illustrated novel insight into human interaction with buildings. This evidence, along with the potential of future evidence from using BIT-Kit, in different buildings experienced by different types of users, provides unique insight for architects for the future of accessible building design.

BIT-Kit is currently being developed in the BESiDE project where limitations are being addressed, collating data will be automated and new hotspots will be identified. Future research will investigate how BIT-Kit's evidence could be incorporated into the design process. A way forward is that architectural and design practitioners are empowered, through digital software 'on the drawing board', to better-understand factors of accessibility in buildings, before they are constructed. A second opportunity lies in considering the role of technology in mitigating exclusion, and enhancing accessibility, within the built environment.

8. ACKNOWLEDGMENTS

We would like to thank our research participants who gave so generously of their time for this work. This work was supported by a RCUK grant, EP/G066091/1 "RCUK Hub: Inclusion in the Digital Economy" and by RCUK grant, EP/K037293/1 "BESiDE – The Built Environment for Social Inclusion in the Digital Economy"

9. REFERENCES

[1] Capability simulators: Physical simulators: 2010. http://www.edc.eng.cam.ac.uk/betterdesign/knowledge/evaltools/evaltools3.html. Accessed: 2010-07.

[2] Arthur, P. and Passini, R. 1992. *Wayfinding : people, signs, and architecture*. McGraw-Hill Ryerson.

[3] Barker, P.J., Barrick, J., Wilson, R.Royal National Institute for the Blind, 1995. *Building sight : a handbook of building and interior design solutions to include the needs of visually impaired people*. HMSO in association with the Royal National Institute for the Blind.

[4] Burgess, R.G. 1982. *Field research : a sourcebook and field manual*. G. Allen & Unwin.

[5] Carpman, J.R. and Grant, M.A. 2002.

[6] Davis, C. and Lifchez, R. 1987. An Open Letter to Architects. *Rethinking Architecture: Design Students and Physically Disabled People*. R. Lifchez, ed. University of California Press. 35–52.

[7] Downs, R.M. and Stea, D. 1973. Cognitive Maps and Spatial Behavior:Process and Products. *Image and environment*.

Cognitive mapping and spatial behavior. R.M. Downs and D. Stea, eds. Aldine Publishing Company. 8–26.

[8] Downs, R.M. and Stea, D. 1977. *Maps in minds : reflections on cognitive mapping*. Harper & Row.

[9] Glaser, B.G. 1968. *The discovery of grounded theory : strategies for qualitative research*. Weidenfeld & Nicolson.

[10] Goldsmith, S. 2012. *Designing for the Disabled: The New Paradigm*. Routledge.

[11] Golledge, R.G. 1999. Human Way-finding and Cognitive Maps. *Wayfinding behavior : cognitive mapping and other spatial processes*. R.G. Golledge, ed. Johns Hopkins University Press. 5–45.

[12] Harper, S. and Green, P. 2000. A Travel Flow and Mobility Framework for Visually Impaired Travellers. (Germany, 2000), 289–296.

[13] Hersh, M.A. and Johnson, M.A. 2008. *Assistive Technology for Visually Impaired and Blind People*. Springer.

[14] Hillier, B. 1996. *Space is the machine*. Space Sytax.

[15] Ingold, T. 2000. *The perception of the environment : essays in livelihood, dwelling and skill*. Routledge.

[16] Kitchin, R.M. 1997. Techniques to collect and analyse the cognitive map knowledge of persons with visual impairment or blindness: issues of validity. *Journal of Visual Impairment and Blindness*. 91, 4 (1997).

[17] Lynch, K. 1960. *The image of the city*. MIT Press.

[18] Mcintyre, L. 2011. *The Way-finding Journey within a large public building: A user-centred study of the holistic way-finding experience across a range of visual ability*. University of Dundee.

[19] Mcintyre, L. and Hanson, V.L. 2013. BESIDE: the built environment for social inclusion in the digital economy. *CHI EA "13: CHI "13 Extended Abstracts on Human Factors in Computing Systems*. (Apr. 2013).

[20] McIntyre, L.J. A Case Study of adopting BIT-Kit: A Method Uncovering the Impact Buildings have on People.(London).

[21] Power, C., Freire, A., Petrie, H. and Swallow, D. 2012. Guidelines are only half of the story: accessibility problems encountered by blind users on the web. (May 2012).

[22] Rousek, J.B., Koneczny, S. and Hallbeck, M.S. 2009. Simulating Visual Impairment to Detect Hospital Wayfinding Difficulties. *Human Factors and Ergonomics Society Annual Meeting Proceedings*. 53 (2009), 531–535.

[23] Sears, A. and Hanson, V.L. 2012. Representing users in accessibility research. *ACM Transactions on Accessible Computing (TACCESS)*. 4, 2 (Mar. 2012), 7–6.

[24] Van Hoof, J., Kort, H. and Van Waarde, H. 2010. Environmental interventions and the design of homes for older adults with dementia: an overview. *... and other dementias*. (2010).

[25] Yin, R.K. 2003. *Applications of case study research*. Sage Publications.

From Screen Reading to Aural Glancing: Towards Instant Access to Key Page Sections

Prathik Gadde and Davide Bolchini
Indiana University School of Informatics and Computing - Indianapolis
535 West Michigan Street, Indianapolis, Indiana 46202
[pgadde, dbolchin]@iupui.edu

ABSTRACT

Whereas glancing at a web page is crucial for navigation, screen readers force users to listen to content serially. This hampers efficient browsing of complex pages and maintains an accessibility divide between sighted and screen-reader users. To address this problem, we adopt a three-pronged strategy: (1) in a user study, we identified key page-level navigation problems that screen-reader users face while browsing a complex site; (2) through a crowd-sourcing system, we prioritized the most relevant sections of different page types necessary to support basic tasks; (3) we introduced DASX, a navigation approach that augments the ability of screen-reader users to "aurally glance" at a complex page by accessing at any time the most relevant page sections. In a preliminary evaluation, DASX markedly reduced the gap in page navigation efficiency between screen-reader and sighted users. Our contribution provides the groundwork for rethinking access strategies that strongly tie aural navigation to user's tasks.

Categories and Subject Descriptors

H.5.2 [**Information Interfaces and Presentation**]: User Interfaces – *Interaction styles;* K.4.2 [Computers and Society]: Social Issues – *Assistive technologies for person with disabilities.*

Keywords

Web navigation; voice browsing; fast browsing; direct web access; eCommerce web applications; blind users; screen-reader users.

1. INTRODUCTION

On Amazon.com, a screen-reader user wants to buy a new laptop with good customer reviews. After sifting through the search results, the user clicks on a laptop to know more. After double-checking the product details, the user looks for customer reviews. To do so, the user is forced to listen carefully to at least four page sections following the product details (e.g., "customers who bought this item also bought," "frequently bought together"). If the reviews section is missed, all previous sections need to be re-listened to. Finally, upon deciding to buy the laptop, the user goes back to the very top of the page to add the item to the cart.

This scenario highlights two main problems surrounding screen-reader navigation in large, complex websites. First, *it is difficult to quickly identify the available sections of a page.* Whereas a page visually communicates extensive information at once, including content, overall semantics, orientation cues, and navigation

possibilities, the linear reading strategies of screen readers make such multidimensional communication difficult or even impossible. What could be the aural equivalent to the fundamental act of "glancing at a page"? Second, even when users know the relevant page sections, there is currently no efficient navigation mechanism *to access that section quickly* besides trying to search for a keyword that matches the content. Screen-reader users rely on a few workarounds to break this rigidly serial reading mode. "Skip to main content," "list of links" on the page, or "searching" for a word, are examples of attempts to support direct access. Yet, because screen readers are agnostic with respect to the different structures of web pages, these strategies often fall short. For example, whereas "skip to main content" avoids the need to listen to repeating navigation headings, it can also cause serious navigation problems, such as skipping *sort* and *filter options* during search.

In this paper, we propose to augment screen reading with a novel navigation approach: instead of being forced to listen to page items serially, screen-reader users can quickly browse a selection of highly-relevant page sections through always available, dialogically-inspired commands, activated via keystrokes or voice. For example, let us imagine a user in the "product detail" page asking *What's there?* and instantly being able to access the five most important sections of that page (out of the over 30 available), including the customer reviews, which can then be selected with minimal effort. Our contribution is threefold:

- A formative user study (Section 3) with eight blind and visually impaired (BVI) and four sighted users investigated and compared web navigation experience and strategies in a complex site. We uncovered basic problems, at the page level, that account for the large amount of time and mechanical effort necessary for screen-reader users to complete even simple tasks.

- Through a custom-developed crowd-ranking system, we identified and prioritized the most important page sections for key shopping tasks (Section 4). We showed that the page sections considered relevant to the task at hand are often very difficult for screen-reader users to access.

- We introduce DASX (Section 5), a navigation approach that empowers screen-reader users to access directly the most important sections of a page. We exemplify our approach for shopping sites; in an analytical evaluation of an expert user's task performance, DASX not only accelerated screen-reader navigation but also greatly reduced keyboard usage and link clicking.

By contributing a deeper understanding of strategies for accessible, aural glancing, our work paves the way for augmenting the ability of screen-reader users to quickly get a sense of what's available on the page and accelerate access to relevant portions. Our approach can be also extended to mobile accessibility.

2. RELATED WORK

Because of its broad adoption, screen-reader navigation receives much attention from the accessibility research community. Specifically, our work joins forces with efforts aimed at *overcoming the serial nature* of screen-reader browsing during the *page-level* navigation of large, information-intensive websites.

The Web Content Accessibility Guidelines has recognized the importance of quickly targeting key page sections in large websites during screen-reader navigation [22]. Whereas Guidelines 1.3 and 2.4 emphasize the importance of presenting multiple access structures to the content, Guideline 2.4.1 specifically dictates providing mechanisms to bypass blocks of repeating content over multiple pages. Such seminal effort spurred the adoption of the "skip to content" link on many sites. This is an important first step towards more efficient page navigation for screen-reader users, but it assumes that a generic content section (however is defined) is always the primary target of interest for the user. Yet users might need direct access to different sections based on the nature of the page at hand (e.g., list page, home, product page, or order page).

Fundamental work focused on developing techniques to reduce the complexity of web pages to enhance accessibility. For example, important and highly-novel accessibility solutions have been developed by partitioning pages [7][15], extracting content based on the visual design [6], directly navigating from a page to the relevant content in the target page [3], annotate webpages with structural and navigational ontologies to enhance mobility support [21], refactoring content to make it more suitable for aural consumption [12], and thematically organizing content for fast screen-reader navigation [13]. While most of these contributions operate on the content structure of the site to make it more accessible, they can be complemented by new ways of accelerating access to the pages as they are, thus rethinking aural access without adapting the application itself.

To bridge the divide between screen-reader users and sighted users, other important research provided users with the ability to get notified about page updates that could be otherwise easily missed [4], automate repetitive tasks like bill payments [14], and provide an additional layer of "whispered" suggestions while browsing [23]. Recent work has also contributed techniques to support non-visual skimming of the content [1]. With this technique, screen-reader users can access automatic summaries of online articles to read content much faster. We argue that accessible skimming can be complemented by aural glancing, i.e. the ability to make sense of the most important sections of a complex page (which includes different types of content) and quickly access them on-demand.

To support faster screen-reader navigation, prior work has also focused on identifying and validating aural strategies to accelerate *inter-page navigation* of large collections, including bypassing lists with guided tours [10][20] and back navigation shortcuts [18]. This body of work can be extended with solutions that tackle the basic problem of having to serially navigate a large amount of *page-level sections* to make sense of the content available and immediately target relevant segments on-demand.

Generations of advanced aural browsers and strategies have also been explored in the past two decades. Examples include PWWebSpeak [9], IBM Home Page Reader [2], Emacs W3 [17], Pipebeach [5], Conversa [11], and TeleBrowse [16]. Unlike screen readers, which read out the web content serially, these browsers simplified access strategies by providing users with the ability to customize a web page based on different features. With the growth of the web, these solutions face new problems stemming from the growing complexity of today's highly-interactive and information-overloaded web applications.

By recognizing the potential of voice access to support more dialogic, direct browsing of page content, the Voice Browser Working Group has also developed and standardized several technologies [19]. Further, browsers like Opera offer voice-controlled navigation that supports basic operations, such as *opening new tabs, closing tabs, reloading documents, and going to the previous page* [24]. While these functions are key to inter-application navigation, they do not provide techniques for efficient page-level navigation in complex sites.

3. FIELD STUDY

3.1 Purpose and Participants

The goal of our formative user study was twofold: (1) to uncover and characterize page-level navigation behavior, issues, and strategies of screen-reader users while browsing a large website like Amazon.com for basic shopping tasks; and (2) to gauge, both qualitatively and quantitatively, the navigation performance gap between screen-readers and sighted users.

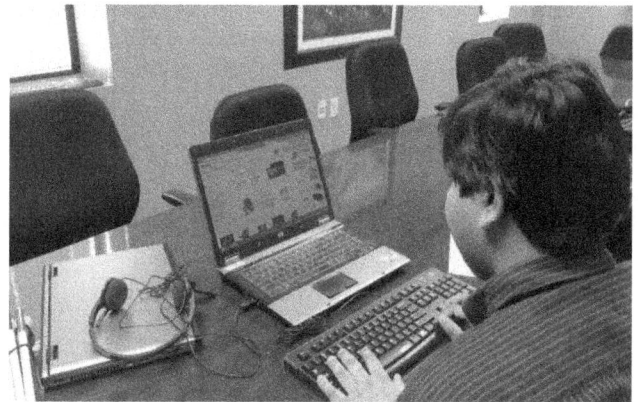

Figure 1. Screen-reader users performed basic tasks on Amazon.com and discussed their page-level navigation experience.

We conducted semi-structured interviews with screen-reader users and performed contextual observations of navigation behavior (Figure 1) with a focus on the following questions:

- What are the major obstacles for efficient intra-page navigation in large, information-intensive sites?

- To which extent does the linear navigation mechanics of screen readers slow down access for BVI users?

- How does the structure of different page types impact navigation needs and behavior?

For the purpose of this exploratory study, we selected Amazon.com because it exhibits a level of page density and complexity that is increasingly adopted by most eCommerce sites. We recruited eight BVI (aged 24-62; 5 male, 3 female) and four sighted (aged 22-26; 4 male) participants from a large Midwestern US city. All BVI participants were expert screen-reader users with at least four years of experience.

3.2 Procedure and Setting

After a brief introductory session about the study, all participants were invited to perform a training task, which enabled them to refresh their memory of using Amazon.com. Then they performed two test tasks. All sessions were organized as semi-structured interviews with the observer asking questions on critical incidents

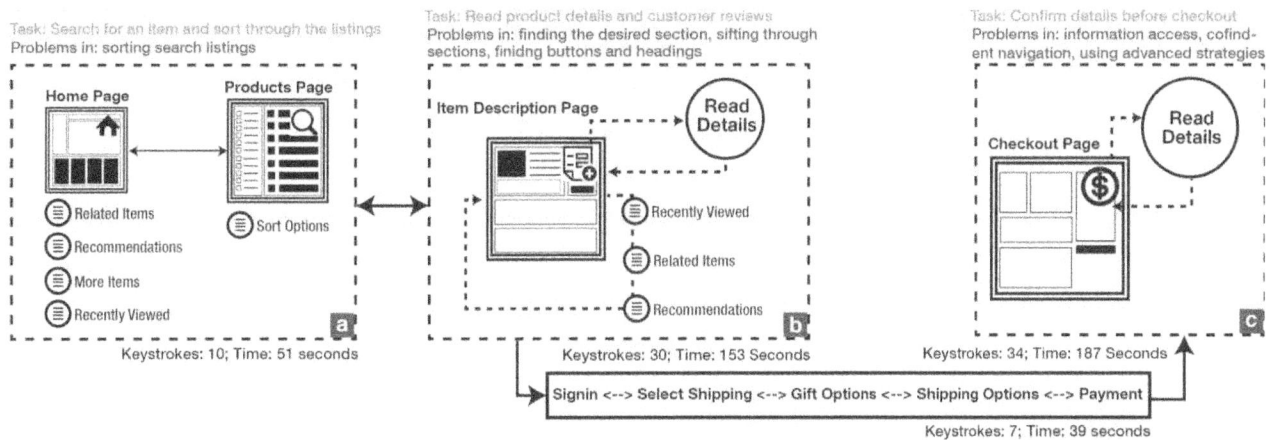

Figure 2. Users encountered problems in three key navigation contexts: (a) Moving from the home to the search results and efficiently sifting through them; (b) Browsing product details and reviews while bombarded by additional page sections; (c) Trying to quickly and frequently double-checking order details before making a confident purchase decision.

and stopping points during navigation. Participants were instructed to think aloud while performing the following two tasks, which sampled the depth and breadth of the website:

Task 1: Search and Compare. *You would like to buy a Dell laptop with at least a 500 GB hard drive, i5 processor, and 6 GB RAM. Your budget is $800. Find and compare at least three models. Select the laptop that best meets the above-mentioned criteria. Be prepared to justify the selected model.*

Task 2: Select and Checkout Review. *Your friend's birthday is coming up and you would like to give her an Amazon gift card. Without using the "search," purchase a $50 gift card. Select mail as the delivery method and add it to the cart. Proceed to checkout until you reach the screen with a "place your order" button. Double-check your order, shipping, and payment details.*

To make the participants comfortable while performing the tasks, we let them choose the study location. Ten of 12 sessions were conducted either at the participant's workplace or home. The remaining two sessions were conducted in our lab. All participants performed the training and the tasks on a laptop (minimum PC requirements: 1 GB RAM, Core 2 Duo Processor, 650 MB HDD, MS Windows XP or later) with the JAWS 15.0 screen reader and a browser of their choice. For approximately two hours of participation, each participant received a $20 gift card.

3.3 Data Collection and Analysis

We used *uLoglite* [30] to record the participants' keystrokes and time spent on each page, and we audio-recorded all sessions for transcription and analysis. The recorded audio files of the sessions were manually examined and annotated to identify explanations for the navigation problems encountered and salient instances of user's behavior. *uLoglite* recordings were examined to collect the following performance measures: user actions (including keystrokes for screen-reader users and scrolling and clicks for sighted users); time spent on each page and overall time on task. Because we adopted a thinking-aloud protocol, the time spent answering questions was removed from the time on task during data analysis. To gain further insights into the qualitative feedback, we also abstracted the low-level mechanics of the page browsing to a higher-level model that highlights the navigation contexts associated to most issues emerged (Figure 2).

4. Findings

Overall, we identified major page-level navigation issues for screen-reader users that revolve around seven main themes:

(1) Even simple pages, by structure, pose navigation problems;
(2) Rigid access to different page types hampers navigation;
(3) Fear of missing crucial information forces unnecessary mechanical and cognitive effort;
(4) Little tolerance of navigation mistakes demands careful attention and line-to-line reading;
(5) Difficulty to distinguish sections and overloaded pages obstruct access to the key section;
(6) Shortcuts like 'Skip to Content' are not always optimal;
(7) Difficulty in re-finding information forces users to remember details and unnecessarily overloads short term memory;

The rest of this section elaborates on each theme.

4.1 Even Simple Pages Obstruct Navigation

Surprisingly, all screen-reader users had more troubles navigating through the checkout page than all other pages, even though the checkout page has far fewer sections and exhibits a much simpler layout. When asked about the reason for this, participants pointed out that it was very difficult to understand how the page sections were organized. This hindered their ability to quickly identify crucial information to review their order (making sure they have all and only the right products in the cart). One participant said:

> *[P1] "I don't want to order without knowing what is there in my cart. This page is completely different from the other pages and I couldn't find what is there in my cart. After I finished everything, to sit in the checkout page and not finding the information I am ordering is frustrating."*

By examining the user performance measures, we noticed that it took more steps and time for screen-reader users to navigate through a simpler page, by structure, than a relatively complex page. While browsing through a complex *item description* page, using advanced features, screen-reader users were able to quickly achieve their information needs (Actions: 28, Time on task: 142 s). However, when navigating a simpler *checkout* page they found it extremely difficult to find information they wanted (Actions: 34, Time on task: 187 seconds).

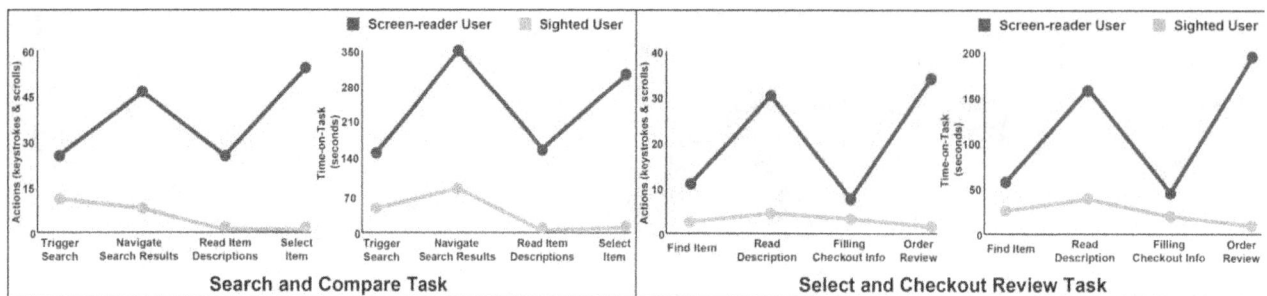

Figure 3: Navigation efficiency divide between sighted and BVI: screen-readers require users longer and more mechanical actions to complete most basic web tasks.

While navigating through the checkout page, screen-reader users who wanted to find out what was just added to the cart tried different advanced features like section skipping, JAWS find, and navigation by heading before resorting to the serial navigation through every single page element. These navigation problems emerging from the participants' experience suggest that crucial details of the page content are very difficult to access even in a simple page structure.

4.2 Rigid Access to Different Page Types

While commenting on the difficulties encountered, participants expressed concern about the fact that, although different pages exhibit a different structure, the way screen readers operate is too rigid and does not account for the flexibility needed in certain navigation contexts. One participant said:

> [P4] "I have to navigate through different pages using the same approach. There are some pages like this [checkout page] that can be cut short [in presenting the content]. Unfortunately, we don't have any sophisticated options."

Whereas a quick scroll and glance helps sighted users identify the context and important page sections to easily advance through them, screen readers are agnostic of the page type the user is browsing (e.g., a list page, a product detail page or an order review page), thus hampering an efficient navigation. In fact, participants voiced concerns about the consistent linear strategy of the screen readers and expressed the need for screen reader to somehow operate differently based on different page types.

4.3 Fear of Missing Crucial Information

> [P2] "I fear that I might lose out important information on this page."

Comments of this nature emerged frequently during the thinking aloud observation with participants. Especially when dealing with product orders and transactions, participants spent much longer time in navigating back and forth among sections and paid extra attention to the page details for the fear of either missing important information or engaging a link that might end in an unwanted action.

As shown in Figure 3, there is a large divide between the sighted and screen-reader users in terms of the actions made and time on task, especially on the item description and checkout pages. These are the two pages on which users must decide to pick a product of interest and double-check its details before placing their order, respectively. Whereas sighted users found no problem in quickly glancing through the page and double-check crucial information such as the product specification, screen-reader users spent more time going back and forth through the page elements to double-check the details.

Without the opportunity to aurally master "at a glance" the main purpose and content of the page, users are left searching and re-searching for page elements to make sure that important information are not missed.

4.4 Little Tolerance of Navigation Mistakes

Across all sessions, we observed that the screen readers offer little support to recover from a mistake. If a user mistakenly skips an important section, the whole process of scanning through the sections must be carefully repeated. For example, a participant looking for customer reviews used heading navigation to quickly look through the long list of sections on the item description page. In his first attempt, he passed the reviews section but did not realize it, and moved on to the end of the page. Once he realized that he was too far along and that he might have missed the reviews, he resorted to keying up and down each single page section until he re-found the reviews. Even for this basic task, recovering from this mistake slowed him down and required much longer and more effort than necessary.

This pattern is not just confined to user-made errors, but it can also result from labeling mismatch, excessive page content, and even the faulty interpretation of a screen reader. For example, when a participant wanted to find the product description on the checkout page, he unsuccessfully used *JAWS find* to match the information, because there is no such heading on that page. Then he used heading navigation and eventually landed on the order summary. It took awhile for him to reorient and start reading through each line on that page.

Whereas sighted users continuous monitored the overall page composition to locate the sought-after information, the screen reader impeded BVI users to exit the serial stream of links and page segments to quickly re-locate missed information from a higher-level perspective.

4.5 Blurred Sections and Overloaded Pages

> [P4] "All the content around the main content is confusing. When JAWS reads the recommended products before reading out the full details of the product, I feel I am lost. I am not even sure about the title of the product I am in."

Shopping websites features more and more often several *non-primary* sections, like *customers who bought this item also bought, frequently bought together, special offers and promotion*. In our study, we noticed that this ancillary content, although important for the site owners to promote up-selling and cross-selling, often confuses screen-reader users, because it makes it difficult to identify and access the most basic, fundamental functions of the page (*Add to Cart*). With no efficient way to work around such overload of information, users often got confused and made unnecessary steps.

We also observed that non-optimal organization of heading levels confused screen-reader users, causing a perception of *section blurring*: screen-reader users often found it difficult to *distinguish* between the available page sections and their current position on the page, thus forcing them to arrow down to each line of the content to serially scan the page.

Overall, overloaded pages and confusing section boundaries often led users to the most comfortable but inefficient mode of reading each page element, a strategy that causes unnecessary mechanical and cognitive effort for long and information-rich pages.

4.6 'Skipping Content' Not Always Optimal

Screen reader users can rely on a *"Skip to content"* link available on many websites to skip main navigation headings and menus and go directly to the main content section of a page. However, it can also cause serious navigation problems, such as the following critical incident observed in our user study:

A search string *'Dell Laptop'* on Amazon yielded *2346 results*. Amazon offers a *powerful faceted search* on the left-hand navigation panel. On the one hand, by using this function, our *sighted users quickly filtered the results down to six laptops* and accessed the product detail page in *three clicks*. However, *BVI users* did not realize the existence of the faceted search section because they "skipped" top the main content of the page. There is currently no option for the screen-reader user to facilitate the discovery of this very important function for basic search tasks.

4.7 Overloading Short-Term Memory

When asked to double-check the product details on the checkout page, a participant was able to recall them from the memory. He said:

> [P5] *"It is easier for me to remember such details than trying to find them with a screen reader."*

We observed that participants often employed external aides to save the details they need for easy re-finding at a later point in time. For example, when asked to compare different models of laptops and select one they liked, users browsed through the search results and copied the links of the products they liked in a separate file, along with a summary of product descriptions. Later in the tasks, when it was time to finalize their purchasing decision, they went back to the notepad to compare their findings and select one from there.

This behavior suggests that providing more immediate access to important details would reduce the mechanical and cognitive load now necessary to retain content details in short-term memory.

4.8 Preferences for Page-level Voice Access

At the end of the study, we asked participants to gauge their willingness to accept voice input as a modality facilitating a direct access structure. BVI users who were already accustomed to using Siri [25] or Talkback [26] on their smartphones reported feeling comfortable using voice provided the technology works as intended.

> [P7] *"I feel very comfortable using voice navigation. I always use Siri on my iPhone."*

Participants, however, expressed concern about using voice commands in public places especially when dealing with confidential details (purchasing details) or out of respect for privacy. A participant expressed his inclination toward direct access structures with no preference for the input modality, *"I am less concerned about the mode of input. I look forward to options*

to navigate through different sections quickly." Participants proposed alternative access structures like predefined key combinations to help during technological failures and for use in noisy environments:

> [P6] *"I would love to have some key combinations [shortcuts] also for voice commands. This will give me a chance to use them when I don't want to use voice commands or just in case when the technology doesn't work."*

Participants expressed interest in working with a system that can be controlled with a very small set of short voice commands (easy to remember) as an additional option to support more direct navigation across page sections.

In sum, the results of our formative study provide ample evidence of the need for having more direct access to highly-relevant page sections to accelerate navigation for screen-reader users.

5. CROWD RANKING PAGE SECTIONS

How can a group of "important" page sections be determined, given the variety and richness of modern websites? It is clear that section relevance is tied to the main user's task supported by the purpose of a page. For example, search-filtering options may still be available on the product detail page, but they are not directly supporting the main purpose of the page (browsing product-related information). Because of the complexity of the page structure of large websites, it is essential to collect reliable data from users to identify the most important sections of a preliminary set of recurring page types based on common navigation tasks.

Prioritizing relevant page sections for common tasks can inform strategies to make highly-relevant sections quickly available on-demand. To this end, we designed and executed a crowdsourcing study to elicit an appropriate task-based ranking of the sections of *four page types* on Amazon.com: *home, search results, product details, and checkout pages*. For this study, we developed a custom, crowd-based section ranking system that allows crowd workers to quickly rank order different page section via drag and drop in the context of assigned navigation tasks.

5.1 Participants

We recruited 100 participants through Amazon Mechanical Turk (AMT) [27]. To maximize the internal validity of the results, we restricted the pool of crowd workers to US residents with at least 95% acceptance rate for the Human Intelligence Tasks (HIT) completed. To ensure quality of the rankings, we tracked the time users spent on each page and the number of scrolls for each HIT. HITs with valid comments and at least 20 minutes elapsed time were accepted. In some cases when we could not decide based on the above criteria, we used the scrolling count as an extra measure to accept a HIT. We only accepted data from 40 of 95 HITs that complied with our quality guidelines. For an average 30 minutes of participation, each participant received a $3 payment through AMT platform.

5.2 Procedure and Apparatus

The HIT asked participants to rank 60 sections (including content and navigation elements) spread over nine different page instances based on their importance in helping with the purchasing decision and the checkout process. The assigned shopping tasks – properly split in sub-tasks and contextually presented across the page instances – were the same as the search, compare and checkout tasks used in the formative study. For each ranking, participants were asked also to provide page-level comment to justify their preferences. On average, it took 30 seconds to rank each section (~30 min for the overall HIT).

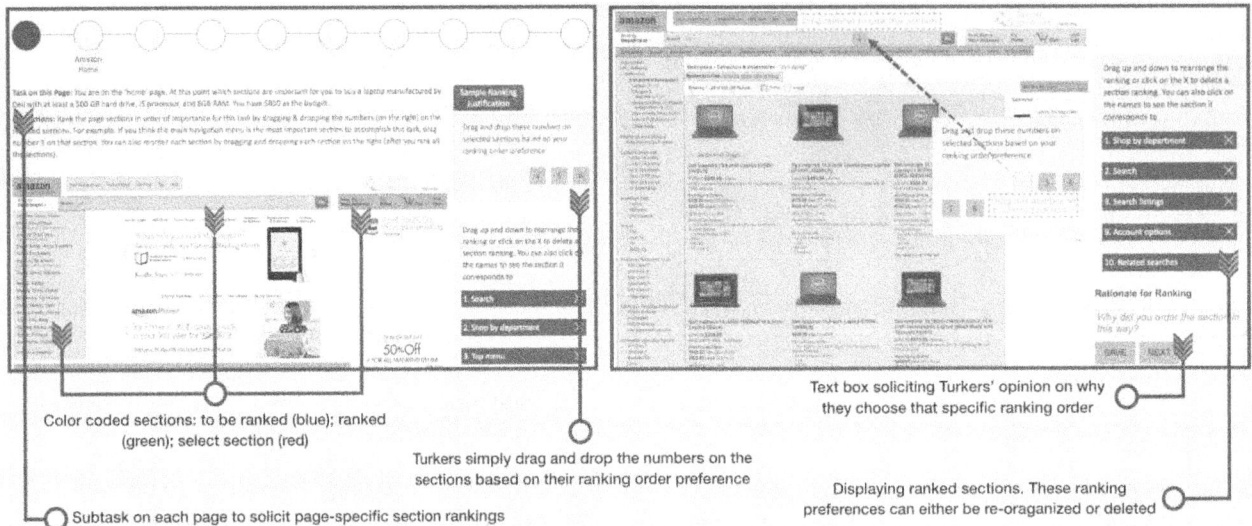

Figure 4. Our crowd-ranking system elicited from users the prioritized importance of different page sections for a common shopping task across nine instances of five different page types.

5.2.1 Custom Crowd-Ranking System

We developed a web-based interactive system [27] to facilitate this ranking process. The system (Figure 4) provides to participants a flow of screenshots simulating the navigation steps of Amazon.com. In the context of an assigned shopping task, the system enabled participants to drag and drop the rank numbers onto a matching section on the web page based on their preference. Participants could change or re-arrange the ranking as many times as they wish before submitting. At the end of the study, we gave them a reference code for validating completion and approving payment.

5.3 Analysis and Results

We calculated the mode of each ranked section in the nine different page types. Because of the rank-order nature of the collected data, we considered the mode as the most measure to determine the level of importance of a given section.

Section	Mean	Median	Mode	Our Rank
Search Listings	1.52	1	1	1
Sorting Options	3.10	2	3	2
Comment: I can drill down all the details to find my specific laptop, and then find everything I need on the first result page; all other options are not as important as this one.				
Shop by Department	3.82	3	3	3

Figure 5. When two sections in a page scored the same mode, we used mean, median, and user's comments to settle discrepancies

Figure 6 shows the *top-five ranked sections* for each of the four page types studied. We compared this ranking to the actual position of the page section in the linear reading strategy currently available via JAWS, based on input and manual calculation from one expert screen-reader user. The difference between the two rankings indicates that sections that users deemed most crucial for their task (and should, therefore, be immediately available) are inefficient to access (require several keystrokes) for expert screen-reader users. This gap can be even wider for non-expert users.

For example, in the *checkout* page, the shipping speed was considered among the five most important sections by our crowd

participants, and it is also very easy to spot for sighted users at a glance. However, to get to the shipping speed, an expert screen-reader user must execute 22 keystrokes.

Page Type	Crowd-based ranking (most important sections first)	No. of screen-reader actions (Keystrokes)
Home	Search	1
	Shop by Department	5
	Top Menu	9
	Account Options	4
	Recommended Sections	4
Search Results	Search Listings	2
	Sorting Options	11
	Shop by Department	5
	Search	1
	Item Menu	18
Item Description	Item Summary	3
	Product Information	8
	Customer Reviews	11
	Customer Questions	12
	Cart Options	6
Added to Cart	Product Summary	2
	Checkout Options	1
	Customers Also Bought	4
	Financing	10
	Recommended Sections	6
Checkout	Shipping Address	7
	Order Summary	1
	Product Summary	7
	Payment Method	12
	Shipping Speed	22

Figure 6. The serial navigation paradigm of screen readers buries highly-important sections necessary to complete common web tasks.

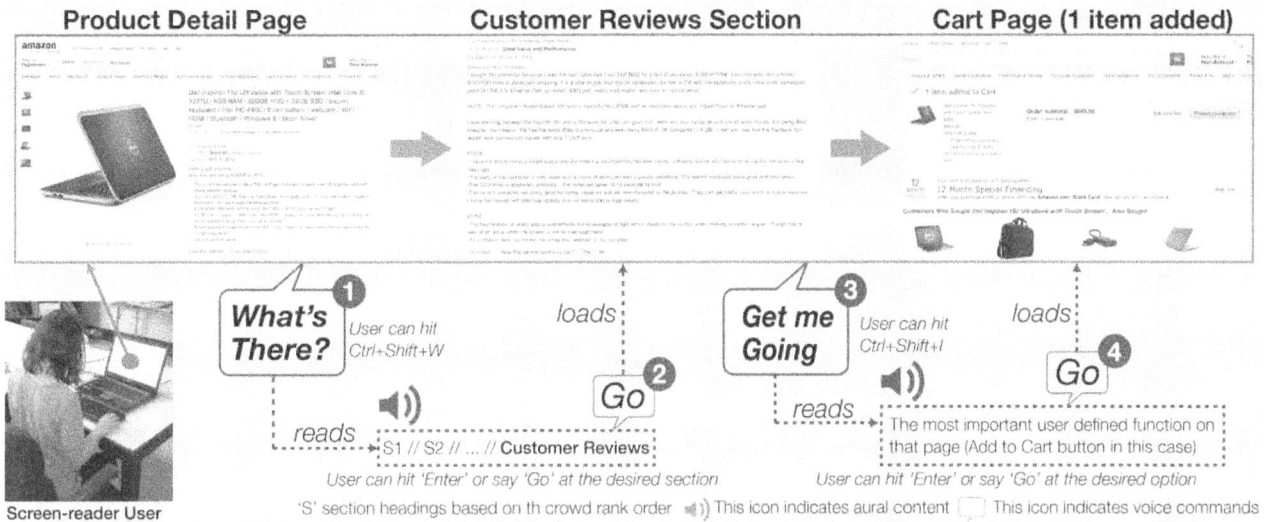

Figure 6. Through simple commands, DASX foregrounds on-demand manageable groups of key sections for different page types. By freeing users from serially listening to page content, DASX has the potential to reduce mechanical effort and access time to target relevant content.

6. AURAL GLANCING WITH DASX

Based on the results of our studies, we envision a *Dialogic Augmentation of the Screen-reader Experience (DASX)*, a novel navigation approach for instant, on-demand access to relevant sections. With DASX, screen-reader users can rely on a simple, high-level vocabulary of commands (via *key combinations* or *voice commands*) to "aurally glance" at a page by quickly invoking and browsing the most important sections available. This will enables user to bypass the heavy keyboard usage and segments scanning typical of screen-reader interaction. DASX is based on the following set of commands:

- **What's there** *(Ctrl+Shift+W)*: *Reads the top-priority, five main sections of the page* (see ranking in Figure 6).
- **More on this page** *(Ctrl+Shift+W)*: *Reads the other sections of the page.*
- **Get me going** *(Ctrl+Shift+I)*: *Reads the one, most important function on the page (e.g., "Add to Cart" for shopping site, or it goes to the product page of the first item in a list)*
- **Go** *(Enter)*: *Loads the desired option*

By augmenting, rather than replacing, screen-reader access, DASX foregrounds the five most relevant sections of a given page type (Figure 6) and makes them available to screen-reader users on-demand when they invoke a simple "What's There" command. The user may choose one of the five sections with "Enter" or "Go," or proceed to the next five by invoking "More on this page." Once the user decides to move on with an option s/he can say *Go* or hit *Enter* to load that section directly. The foreseen advantage for the user is the ability to efficiently get an overall sense of the content available (and purpose of the page) without being forced to arrow down through the detailed page segment. It is worth noticing that because DASX groups and makes available key page sections in collections of five, users do not risk missing other peripheral or ancillary content, accessible in subsequent section groups via "More on this Page."

To mitigate information overload, with a simple command "Get Me Going," DASX provides screen-reader users the ability to *activate at any time* the one, most important operation in a given page. For example, in the product detail page, "Get Me Going"

would activate the "Add to Cart" button; in the search results page, "Get Me Going" would activate the product detail page of the first product in the list.

To quantify and assess the potential advantage of DASX in bridging the gap between sighted and screen-reader users, we conducted a preliminary, *analytical evaluation* of an expert user's task performance on DASX using KLM-GOMS [8].

In terms of evaluation parameters, keyboard and voice were selected as input modalities. Display and audio were selected as output modalities. We added *wait times* (5 s) for each step to account for the lag time a real system might encounter. All other operators were kept standard. We set the aural output at 350 words per minute, as this was the most common consumption rate of screen-reader users we observed in our formative study. To ensure comparable results we used the same tasks used during our formative study on *item description* and *checkout* pages. The sequence of steps followed is listed below.

Step 1: Launch DASX, which is manifested as a browser plug-in

Step 2: Access important sections with *What's there?*

Step 3: Select a section of interest with *Go*

Step 4: Repeat steps 2 and 3 until the target information is reached

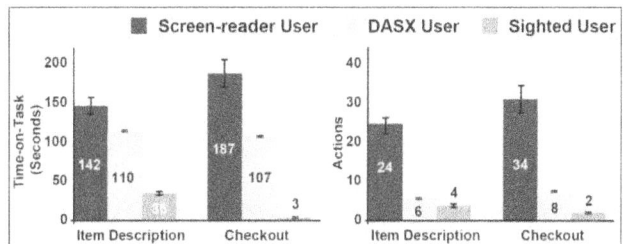

Figure 7. Expert performance suggests that DASX shortens the gap in page navigation efficiency between sighted and screen-reader users.

DASX drastically reduced the time and steps required on both *item description* and *checkout pages* as compared with the serial access of existing screen readers. With DASX, the time screen-reader users spent reviewing the order on the checkout page fell 43%. It fell only 23% on the item description page, because even with DASX screen-reader users need to listen to and attend to product description and customer reviews. DASX not only decreased the number of actions required by screen-reader users by 75% on the item description page and by 69% on the checkout page but also brought their performance much closer to that of sighted users (Figure 7).

In absolute task performance measures for the "item description" and "checkout" pages, expert users with DASX require 6 and 8 keystrokes, which are very close to the 4 and 2 required by sighted users not using screen readers. This performance is in stark contrast with the 24 and 34 keystrokes currently necessary by screen-reader users to access the most important page sections. Such preliminary results are encouraging and confirm the potential for supporting a form of "aural glancing" to make sense of the page sections available.

7. CONCLUSIONS AND FUTURE WORK

The serial nature of screen-reader navigation can be complemented by an accessible form of "aurally glancing" that enables BVI to quickly identify and access key sections on demand at any time. In this paper, we presented a formative study with BVI and sighted users that uncovered and characterized basic page-level navigation problems while completing basic shopping tasks. Based on these findings, we presented a crowd-ranking system and study that elicited users' task-based preferences for the most important sections of recurrent page types. With these results, we presented and preliminarily validated DASX, a navigation approach that empowers screen-reader users to access directly the most important sections of a page via a set of high-level, always available commands. By supporting a form of aural glancing, the main contribution of our approach is to suggest strategies to drastically reduce the mechanical effort of screen-reader users in navigating complex site pages, thus shrinking the gap between sighted and BVI users in performing common tasks.

Our future work pursues two main paths. First, we are conducting participatory design sessions with expert screen-reader users and BVI rehabilitation instructors at BOSMA enterprises [29] to further validate our crowd-ranked sections and expand the DASX vocabulary. Second, we are developing DASX as a suite of accessible browser plug-ins that receive ranked sections data from two sources: (a) an extended crowd-ranking system that can streamline the labeling process for any website; b) web designers who can directly flag (in HTML and CSS) highly-relevant sections of the page at design time.

8. ACKNOWLEDGMENTS

We thank BOSMA enterprises and all study participants for their time and contribution; J. George-Palilonis, A. Voida, and S. Voida for their feedback on the paper; C. Meyer and C. Johnson for their help in executing the studies. This research is based upon work supported by NSF grant IIS-1018054, an NSF REU supplement, and a Google Faculty Research Award.

9. REFERENCES

[1] Ahmed, F., Borodin, Y., Soviak, A., Islam, M., Ramakrishnan, I. V., & Hedgpeth, T. (2012). Accessible skimming: faster screen reading of web pages. In *Proc. of the 25th annual ACM symposium on User interface software and technology* (pp. 367-378). ACM.

[2] Asakawa, C., & Itoh, T. (1998). User interface of a home page reader. In *Proc. of the third international ACM conference on Assistive technologies* (pp. 149-156). ACM.

[3] Borodin, Y., Bigham, J. P., Stent, A., & Ramakrishnan, I. V. (2008). Towards one world web with HearSay3. In *Proc. of International Cross-Disciplinary Conference on Web Accessibility* (p. 128–129).

[4] Borodin, Y., Bigham, J. P., Raman, R., & Ramakrishnan, I. V. (2008). What's new?: making web page updates accessible. In *Proc. of the 10th international ACM SIGACCESS conference on Computers and accessibility* (pp. 145-152). ACM.

[5] Bjurstrom, H., Granberg, C., Hogberg, J., Johannsen, B., & Mcglashan, S. (2003). *U.S. Patent No. 6,594,348*. Washington, DC: U.S. Patent and Trademark Office.

[6] Cai, D., Yu, S., Wen, J. R., & Ma, W. Y. (2003a). Extracting content structure for web pages based on visual representation. In *Web Technologies and Applications*, 406-417.

[7] Cai, D., Yu, S., Wen, J. R., & Ma, W. Y. (2003b). *VIPS: a vision-based page segmentation algorithm*, 28. Microsoft tech report, MSR-TR-2003-79.

[8] Card, S., Moran, T., & Newell, A. (1983). The psychology of human-computer interaction. Hillsdale, NJ: Lawrence Erlbaum Associates.

[9] De Witt, J. C., & Hakkinen, M. T. (1998). Surfing the Web with pwWebSpeak. In *Proc. of the Technology and Persons with Disabilities Conference*.

[10] Gadde, P., & Bolchini, D. (2013). WebNexter: dynamic guided tours for screen readers. In *Proc. of the adjunct publication of the 26th annual ACM symposium on User interface software and technology* (pp. 85-86). ACM.

[11] Hanson, V. L., Richards, J. T., & Lee, C. C. (2007). Web access for older adults: voice browsing?. In *Universal Access in Human Computer Interaction. Coping with Diversity* (pp. 904-913). Springer.

[12] Harper, S., & Bechhofer, S. (2007). SADIe: Structural semantics for accessibility and device independence. ACM Transactions on Computer-Human Interaction (TOCHI), 14(2), 10.

[13] Islam, M. A., Ahmed, F., Borodin, Y., & Ramakrishnan, I. V. (2012). Thematic organization of web content for distraction-free text-to-speech narration. In *Proc. of the 14th international ACM SIGACCESS conference on Computers and accessibility* (pp. 17-24).

[14] Islam, M. A., Ahmed, F., Borodin, Y., Mahmud, J., & Ramakrishnan, I. V., (2010). Improving Accessibility of Transaction-Centric Web Objects. SDM'10.

[15] Kohlschütter, C., & Nejdl, W. (2008). A densitometric approach to web page segmentation. *In Proc. of the 17th ACM conference on Information and knowledge management*, 1173-1182.

[16] Poon, J., & Nunn, C. (2001). Browsing the Web from a Speech-based Interface. In *Proc. of INTERACT* (pp. 302-309).

[17] Raman, T. V. (2008). Specialized browsers. In *Web Accessibility* (pp. 195-213). Springer London.

[18] Rohani Ghahari, R., Ferati, M., Yang, T., & Bolchini, D. (2012, October). Back navigation shortcuts for screen reader users. In *Proc. of the 14th international ACM SIGACCESS conference on Computers and accessibility* (pp. 1-8). ACM.

[19] The Voice Browser Working Group. (2014). Retrieved from http://www.w3.org/Voice/

[20] Yang, T., Gadde, P., Morse, R., & Bolchini, D. (2013). Bypassing lists: accelerating screen-reader fact-finding with guided tours. In *Proc. of the 15th International ACM SIGACCESS Conference on Computers and Accessibility* (p. 7). ACM.

[21] Yesilada, Y., Harper, S., Goble, C., & Stevens, R. (2004). Screen readers cannot see. In Web Engineering (pp. 445-458). Springer.

[22] Web Content Accessibility Guidelines (WCAG) 2.0. (2008). Retrieved from http://www.w3.org/TR/WCAG20

[23] Zhu, S., Sato, D., Takagi, H., & Asakawa, C. (2010). Sasayaki: an augmented voice-based web browsing experience. In *Proc. of the 12th international ACM SIGACCESS conference on Computers and accessibility* (pp. 279-280). ACM

[24] http://www.opera.com/help/tutorials/voice/using

[25] http://www.apple.com/ios/siri/

[26] http://developer.android.com/design/patterns/accessibility.html

[27] https://www.mturk.com/mturk

[28] Crowd-ranking site: http://tinyurl.com/crowdranking Source Code: http://tinyurl.com/codeassets14

[29] http://www.bosma.org

[30] http://www.noldus.com/ulog/feature

Tactile Graphics with a Voice: Using QR Codes to Access Text in Tactile Graphics

Catherine M. Baker, Lauren R. Milne, Jeffrey Scofield, Cynthia L. Bennett, Richard E. Ladner
Computer Science & Engineering
University of Washington Box 352350
Seattle, WA 98195-2350
{cmbaker, milnel2, jeffsco, bennec3, ladner}@cs.washington.edu

ABSTRACT

Textbook figures are often converted into a tactile format for access by blind students. These figures are not truly accessible unless the text within the figures is also made accessible. A common solution to access text in a tactile image is to use embossed Braille. We have developed an alternative to Braille that uses QR codes for students who want tactile graphics, but prefer the text in figures be spoken, rather than in Braille. Tactile Graphics with a Voice (TGV) allows text within tactile graphics to be accessible by using a talking QR code reader app on a smartphone. To evaluate TGV, we performed a longitudinal study where ten blind and low vision participants were asked to complete tasks using three alternative picture taking guidance techniques: 1) no guidance, 2) verbal guidance, and 3) finger pointing guidance. Our results show that TGV is an effective way to access text in tactile graphics, especially for those blind users who are not fluent in Braille. In addition, guidance preferences varied with each of the guidance techniques being preferred by at least one participant.

Categories and Subject Descriptors

H.5.2. User Interfaces.

General Terms

Design, Human Factors

Keywords

Access technology; blind; camera; non-visual feedback; visually impaired; tactile graphics; QR codes.

1. INTRODUCTION

From pictures of plant cells to diagrams of parabolas, images are an integral part of most textbooks, and frequently convey information that cannot be understood from text alone. Therefore, these images and the text contained within them should be

ASSETS '14, October 20 - 22 2014, Rochester, NY, USA
Copyright 2014 ACM 978-1-4503-2720-6/14/10...$15.00
http://dx.doi.org/10.1145/2661334.2661366

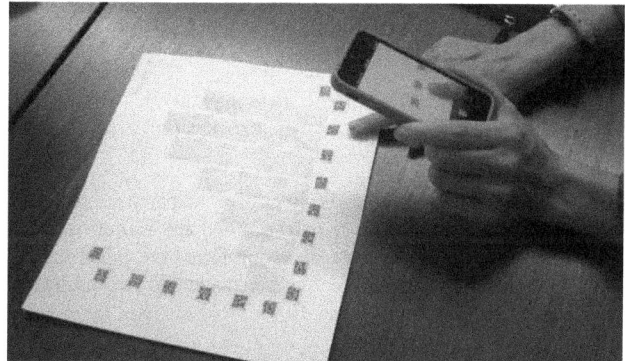

Figure 1. The Tactile Graphics with a Voice system in use. The subject is using the finger pointing mode to select which QR code to scan.

accessible to all students, thus there is a need to create alternative access methods for people with disabilities. The common solution when making a textbook accessible for blind students is to create tactile representations of the images, or tactile graphics. Tactile graphics can be low fidelity by using spaghetti glued on poster board to a high fidelity graphic printed on an embossing printer. Studies have shown that tactile graphics are valuable for conveying graphical information [8]. In a survey of 24 teachers that worked with visually impaired children, all indicated that there were situations where tactile graphics were important for and effective at teaching a lesson [20]. Teachers also indicated that the ability to explore graphics, discover the information, and answer questions about the information independently was a fundamental part of the learning process [19, 20].

The text in tactile graphics is typically represented using embossed Braille. However, a 2009 report by the National Federation of the Blind states that less than forty percent of the functionally blind population in the United States is fluent in Braille [14]. Therefore tactile graphics with Braille labels are not accessible to a significant number of blind people.

There have been a few solutions to this problem presented by the access technology community. Examples include a system where an overlaid tactile graphic on a tablet gives audio feedback when touched [11] and a talking pen to explore a tactile graphic [12]. However, these solutions require using specialized devices, which can be expensive.

We present a new system for embedding and accessing text in tactile graphics using QR codes, which are small codes that directly encode textual information (Figure 1). QR codes can be read by a smartphone and can easily be created by anyone with access to a computer. We created a smartphone application for blind users called Tactile Graphics with a Voice (TGV) that scans

QR codes and provides feedback to help users aim the smartphone camera. We conducted interviews and surveys with people who are blind or low vision to design the application and determine what types of non-visual feedback are most helpful to aim the smartphone. In addition, we developed a finger pointing method to help determine which QR code should be read when there are multiple QR codes in the camera view.

We evaluated our application in a longitudinal study and found that people who are blind or low vision were able to successfully answer questions about tactile graphics by scanning QR codes. Key findings from the study are listed below.

1. Four of our participants were able to correctly answer questions about the images using the QR codes, but were not able to use the Braille equivalents as they were not fluent in Braille.

2. Participants fluent in Braille spent an equivalent amount of time on tasks and had similar accuracy for both the QR codes and Braille equivalents.

3. Preferences varied greatly among participants as to what kind of feedback from the smartphone application is most helpful. Four of our participants preferred the Silent mode, four preferred the Finger Pointing mode and two preferred the Verbal mode.

Our contributions are:

1. The development of Tactile Graphics with a Voice (TGV), a system to access text on tactile graphics using QR codes and a smartphone application.

2. The findings from our study, which show that blind and low vision users support having a variety of non-visual feedback mechanisms to help aim a camera.

2. RELATED WORK

We discuss prior work related to three areas of our system: (i) methods to embed textual information on tactile graphics, (ii) methods to access the information and (iii) use of the finger pointing technique as a means to select which information to be read aloud.

2.1 Accessing Textual Information on Tactile Graphics

Braille labels on educational tactile graphics present difficulties for both students and teachers. Sheppard and Aldrich [1,20] found that both students and teachers had difficulties with Braille labels on tactile graphics in the classroom. Teachers, in particular, had issues placing the labels without text overlapping the figure. Students struggled with the meaning of a label when it stretched across the entire graphic.

Despite the issues with using only Braille for accessing text, there is little work in the HCI literature using alternative methods. There has been some progress made in the access technology community. Touch Graphics has developed the Talking Tactile Tablet (TTT) [11], a touch-sensitive table on which a user can place a tactile graphic and hear audio information upon touch.. However, this method requires a large touch sensitive surface (~12×15 inches, 6.5 pounds) and has to be connected to a computer via USB which contains the information for the tactile graphic to be explored. Touch Graphics also created the Talking Tactile Pen (TTP)[12], which allows blind users to access

information on custom tactile graphics tagged with a proprietary code. The pen contains a small camera used to photograph the proprietary codes. When the pen contacts a tagged area, it reads aloud the corresponding file stored on the pen. Despite the pen's portability in comparison to the TTT, it is a specialized device, and is only useful on properly tagged tactile graphics that have their information stored on the pen. TGV is a solution that attempts to solve the same problem by using non-proprietary codes and a non-specialized, portable, mainstream device like the smartphone.

Voiceye codes are also being used to encode text on graphics[7]. While not used on tactile graphics, they are used in South Korea to make government forms accessible. These are similar to QR codes, but may contain more information for a given area. Users scan these codes with a smartphone application and the corresponding text appears for reading aloud or visual magnification. However, users are not given feedback to assist in scanning the code and the codes must be created with expensive proprietary software. TGV provides a major benefit over current approaches because QR codes can be freely created.

2.2 Camera Use by Blind People

TGV requires the use of a smartphone camera, because it enables the use of QR codes. While aiming the smartphone is a challenging task for blind people, there are research efforts in the accessibility community to tackle this problem. Bigham et al. created an application called VizWiz::LocateIt [2], which allows blind users to locate objects using the camera on their smartphone. VizWiz::LocateIt uses crowdsourcing to identify the object in the photo and computer vision techniques to provide audio feedback about the proximity to the object. Our application uses similar audio feedback to guide users to the QR code, but does not rely on crowdsourcing, thus providing quicker feedback.

Using computer vision techniques exclusively with a smartphone camera may enhance camera feedback. Jayant et al. created EasySnap [9], a camera application that assists users in taking pictures by providing audio feedback. EasySnap uses computer vision to locate people or objects in the viewfinder and relays information their location and their size in proportion to the viewfinder. They followed with another application, PortraitFramer, which incorporates features of EasySnap and uses haptic feedback communicate where in the viewfinder the people or objects are located. They found that it took little training for users to take better pictures. A similar feature has been built into the camera application on recent versions of iOS [6]. When text-to-speech is enabled, the camera application provides feedback about faces, such as "face at top of screen," to guide users in taking portraits. Our application also incorporates audio feedback, but because users are using their sense of touch to explore a tactile graphic, we decided not to use haptic feedback to avoid cognitive overload.

TGV utilizes audio feedback, but there are diverse options, such as tone and speech. Vasquez et al. [22] were interested in learning what type of audio feedback was preferred among blind people using a camera. They considered speech, tone, and no feedback. People strongly preferred speech feedback and found it easier to use than either silent or tone feedback. As a result, we use speech feedback in TGV as opposed to tone.

The majority of the camera applications mentioned above were focused on taking a quality picture of a person or a physical object. Another related space is in technology that allow blind users to scan barcodes, which are similar to QR codes. The majority of commercial applications, such as the i.d. mate[1] or Digit-Eyes,[2] do not provide feedback. However, Tekin *et al.* [21] experimented with different feedback modalities to help blind users scan barcodes on products. They used both verbal feedback and sonification, but their application was evaluated by a single user. TGV distinguishes itself in two ways: 1) our QR codes are labels that can be located by touch and 2) multiple QR codes can be close together.

2.3 Finger Pointing

Because textbook images may have multiple text labels in close proximity of one another, the use of a finger may help select the preferred QR code when multiple codes are in the viewfinder. Thus, we present related work on the practicality of finger pointing as a method to select a preferred QR code.

There are numerous projects that use finger pointing to identify an object or information of interest. One example is the EyeRing [13], a camera worn on the finger that reads information aloud based on where the finger is pointing. Similarly, OrCam,[3] also uses finger pointing for people who are low vision. The OrCam is a wearable camera that uses computer vision to identify objects in which a user is pointing and reads aloud information about that object. The manufacturers envision that OrCam can recognize faces, places, objects, and text.

Kane *et al.* developed Access Lens [10], a way for people who are blind or low vision to access documents. This system uses a camera connected to a computer to read aloud the text on documents. Users can point to any element on the document to hear the associated information. This system brings promise to the accessibility of printed documents and demonstrates that finger pointing is an easy way for blind users to control what information they hear. However, Access Lens is not portable. In TGV, we capitalize on finger pointing as a simple means of selecting the information the user wants to hear.

3. FORMATIVE STUDIES

In order to determine the feasibility of substituting QR codes for text labels on tactile graphics, we conducted a survey and follow-up interviews with people who are blind or low vision. We were motivated to learn about the current use of tactile graphics and cameras, and whether people would take interest in using QR codes as labels on tactile graphics.

The online survey was distributed to blind and low vision mailing lists and inquired about their use of Braille, tactile graphics, and camera applications on the smartphone. Twenty-two people completed our survey, where fifteen of our respondents were blind and seven were low vision. There were 12 female and 10 males with an average age of 38.18 (SD=13.46). All of our respondents had taken some college courses, and nine respondents had a graduate degree. Sixteen respondents knew Grade 2 Braille, while only 3 respondents had little to no knowledge of Braille. All but one of the respondents owned a smartphone.

We conducted follow-up interviews with ten of the survey respondents, 6 of them female. We selected a diverse subset of those who indicated they would be willing to be interviewed on

the survey. The interviews provided more detail about their survey responses and provided feedback about our proposed system, TGV. The participants' ages ranged from 21 to 67 with an average of 37.6 (SD=13.95). Five participants identified as blind and five as low vision. Five used Braille at work, three knew Braille but did not use it often, and two participants had little familiarity with Braille. Eight participants used tactile graphics in their education and work.

We found that many of our respondents frequently used cameras, especially on smartphones, and were interested in using tactile graphics with QR code labels. Seven of the ten participants reacted positively to replacing Braille with QR codes. One participant noted: *"You can fit a lot more information on a QR code than on a Braille label,"* a sentiment shared by five of our participants.

In addition, many of our survey respondents were familiar with using the camera on their smartphone, and thus have completed similar tasks to scanning QR codes. Fifteen respondents used an application that required the camera on a daily to weekly basis.

We learned that people found non-visual feedback for aiming the camera to be helpful. Just over half the respondents used an application that gave them feedback to help aim the camera. The majority of those respondents indicated that the feedback was helpful, with only one respondent mentioning that he had received feedback that was not helpful as it was unclear what it meant.

In our follow-up interviews, we investigated preferences for feedback modalities on a smartphone camera application: verbal, tonal, haptic, and no feedback. While the participants had a variety of preferences, we found that most participants preferred having the option of a quiet mode. Participants wanted a quiet mode because they felt that expert users needed less feedback, and they would not want to disturb others such as during a meeting.

4. TACTILE GRAPHICS WITH A VOICE (TGV)

TGV is composed of tactile graphics with QR code labels and a smartphone application. The application provides multiple non-visual feedback modalities, and allows the user to select which QR code they want to scan.

4.1 Tactile Graphics with QR Codes

The creation of tactile graphics for TGV requires a similar amount of work as traditional tactile graphics. Traditionally, converting a textbook graphic into a tactile graphics is a labor-intensive process. First, the text must be removed from the graphic. In addition, some extra processing may be needed to make the image understandable in a tactile form. Once the text is removed, it needs to be translated into Braille and be placed back on the image in similar location to the original text. Instead of generating Braille, TGV generates a QR code from text using a free online generator. Because the embosser we used to create the tactile graphics cannot print ink, we printed QR codes on a separate sheet of paper and glued them onto the graphic (See Figure 2 for examples). It was not necessary to mark the QR codes with an embossed symbol because the height difference of the QR codes was sufficient to be felt. If you have an embosser capable of both embossing Braille and printing ink, the only difference from the traditional process is that you would place the QR code labels (with accompanying tactile markers) on the graphic in place of the Braille labels.

---

[1] http://www.envisionamerica.com/products/idmate/

[2] http://www.digit-eyes.com/

[3] http://www.orcam.com

4.2 Smartphone Application

We created an accessible application for iOS that allows a blind or low vision user to scan a QR code easily, even if there are multiple QR codes close together. The smartphone application is built on top of the ZXing software[4] for scanning QR codes. This software identifies QR codes by looking for an area of black and white variation. We added verbal feedback to help users scan QR codes, as well as the option to use finger pointing to allow the selection of a QR code when many are visible in the viewfinder.

Based on our survey and interviews, we integrated feedback for aiming the camera. In addition, we determined that it was important to have a feedback mode and a silent mode. Because the participants' preferences on feedback modalities varied, we used verbal feedback, based on prior work [22] and that most of our interview respondents indicated that verbal feedback was the easiest to learn.

We presented short clear verbal feedback to assist a user in moving the phone. We based the feedback on the screen location of the QR code, based on related work [22]. For instance, if a participant holds a smartphone in a non-traditional way (e.g. sideways), they will still hear relevant feedback because the navigational instructions to a QR code are based on the current phone orientation.

When multiple QR codes are visible, it is necessary to determine which QR code should be scanned. Therefore, we implemented finger pointing as a method to distinguish which label should be scanned. The selected QR code is the one with the shortest distance to the users' finger. To prevent the application from scanning the incorrect QR code, we set a maximum distance in which a finger can choose a QR code to scan. Unlike Kane, *et al.* [10], which selects the information at the tip of the finger, our application selects the QR code that is closest to any part of the finger. As a result, users needed to be aware of their hand placement to ensure a false positive does not occur.

We identify the finger with color based skin detection [4,16,17]. Because of the constrained black and white environment of tactile graphics, we can identify a painted fingernail by looking for colored pixels and group them as part of the finger.

4.3 Feedback Modalities

Because feedback and finger pointing are not appropriate in every situation, we created three modes for the application: Silent, Verbal, and Finger Pointing.

4.3.1 Silent

Silent mode gives no feedback to help aim the camera. If multiple QR codes are visible in the viewfinder, the application does not scan. When it has successfully scanned a QR code, it chimes and then reads the scan aloud.

4.3.2 Verbal

Verbal mode provides spoken feedback to help aim the camera. If multiple QR codes are visible in the viewfinder, the application speaks this information and does not scan. When the application has successfully scanned a QR code, it chimes and then reads the scan aloud.

4.3.3 Finger Pointing

Finger Pointing mode provides spoken feedback to help aim the camera. The application needs to detect the finger in order to scan. If the finger is not detected, the application speaks this information and does not scan. If multiple QR codes are visible, the application will scan as long as the finger is detected. When the application has successfully scanned a QR code, it chimes and then reads the scan aloud.

5. LONGITUDINAL STUDY

To evaluate the efficacy of TGV, we conducted a six-session longitudinal study with ten blind and low vision participants. Participants answered questions using TGV with the three modes of feedback (Silent, Verbal and Finger Pointing). In the last session, we had participants who knew Braille complete the same tasks using tactile graphics with Braille labels.

5.1 Participants

We conducted the study with ten participants (four male, six female), with ages ranging from 30 to 54 years, and an average age of 41.9 ($SD = 8.1$). Five had college degrees, three had some college education, and two had a high school education. Four participants identified as low vision and the remaining six identified as blind. Six participants completed the Braille portion of the study, while four were not Braille literate or were not confident in their Braille skills. Overall, participants did not have much experience with tactile graphics, with five never using them, three rarely using them, one using them once per month, and one using them once per week. Nine participants had smartphones; seven had iPhones and two had Androids. Our smartphone users had used camera applications for varying frequencies: two used them daily, two weekly, two monthly, and three rarely used their smartphone cameras. Finally, eight participants had no experience scanning QR codes with their smartphones and two had some experience.

5.2 Apparatus

The TGV application was ran on an iPod Touch 4th generation and an iPhone 5, each running iOS 6. Each participant used the same device for all six sessions. The tactile graphics were printed on standard 11x11.5 inch Braille paper and embossed with a Tiger embosser[5]. QR codes were printed on standard printer paper and cut and pasted onto the tactile graphics in the appropriate places. Braille labels were embossed directly on the graphic using Nemeth code, the type of Braille usually found in math textbooks. Numbers in Nemeth code and Grade 1 and 2 Braille are similar; in Nemeth code the dots are shifted down a row [15].

5.3 Procedure

We had each participant complete six sessions over a two week period. We wanted participants to interact with the application over time to emulate a real-world situation, such as using the application to complete schoolwork.

During the first session, we collected demographic information from the participants, and taught participants how to use the three modes of the TGV application (Silent, Verbal and Finger Pointing). We explained how each mode worked and provided basic information about using the application, such as the suggested scanning height and where the camera was physically

---

[4] http://code.google.com/p/zxing/

[5] http://www.viewplus.com/

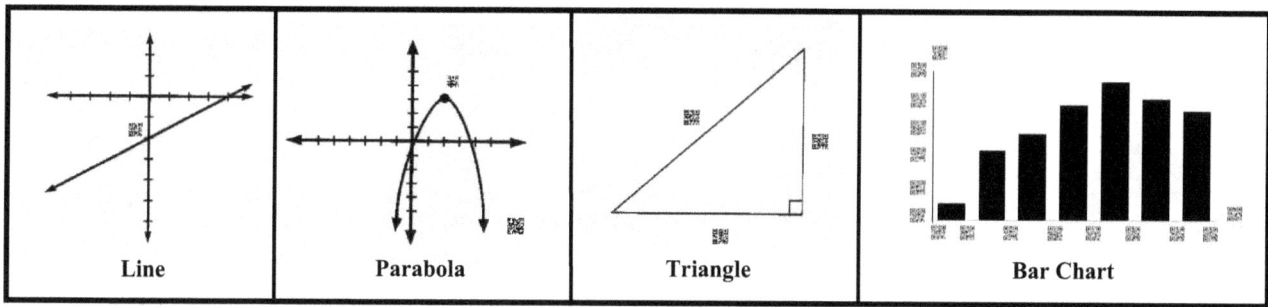

Figure 2. This is an example of each of the tasks that the participants completed. The first task is to find the y-intercept of a line. The second task is to find the (x,y)-coordinates of the vertex of a parabola. The third task is to find the length of the hypotenuse of a right triangle. The fourth task is to find the range of the tallest bar on the bar chart. In each session, participants used similar graphics, but with different labels (i.e. the parabola might be the opposite direction and have a different vertex).

located on the device. Participants had a chance to practice scanning a QR code with each mode.

During each session, participants completed a total of twelve tasks by using each mode of TGV (Silent, Verbal and Finger Pointing) on the following four tasks (Figure 2):

1. *Line.* The first task was to find the y-intercept on a line graph. The graphics always had one QR code representing the value of the intercept.
2. *Parabola.* The next task was to find the (x.y)-coordinates of a parabola vertex. The graphics used in this task always had two QR codes, one for the coordinates of the vertex and one for the equation of the parabola.
3. *Triangle.* The third task was to find the length of the hypotenuse of a right triangle. The graphics in this task always had three QR codes, as the lengths of all sides were labeled.
4. *Bar Chart.* The final task was to find the left and right values on the x-axis of the tallest bar in a bar chart. For this task, the bar chart had seven bars, and there was a QR code marking the bounds of each bar on the x-axis and each tick mark on the y-axis as well as axes labels.

The images for each task were based on images taken from a precalculus textbook [5]. At the beginning of each task, a tactile graphic was placed in front of the participant, and they were instructed to begin. The task ended when the participant responded with their answer. A researcher recorded the task completion time and their answer. We video recorded participants to validate this data. For the first three tasks (Line, Parabola, and Triangle), participants can only receive 0 or 100% accuracy. On the final task (Bar Chart) task, participants can also receive 50% accuracy, as that task required finding both the left and right values of a range. Participants were not told whether or not their answers were correct to mimic a testing situation. We randomized the order of modes used in each session but kept the order of tasks consistent: Line, Parabola, Triangle, and Bar Chart. At the end of each session, we conducted a survey to gauge the participants' preferences for the feedback modes.

In the last session, participants who were proficient in Braille attempted to complete the same tasks using Braille labels in lieu of the QR codes. We choose to have the comparison to Braille only in the last session for two reasons. The first is that participants were already familiar with Braille so we felt that they did not need the time to learn it. By completing the sessions with TGV, they would be familiar with the tasks by the sixth session, making the comparison from TGV to Braille more equal. The

second is we wanted to limit the length of the sessions to prevent fatigue. As some of our participants were Braille-literate, but not familiar with Nemeth code, we explained the difference between Nemeth and Braille to those participants.

5.4 Design and Analysis

The study was a 6×3 within-subjects design with factors for *Session* and *Mode*. The levels of *Session* were (1-6); the levels for *Mode* were (Silent, Verbal, Finger Pointing). Each participant completed a total of 72 trials, for a total of 720 trials with the smartphone, and six participants additionally performed 4 trials with Braille at the end of the session. The other four participants were not comfortable enough with Braille to attempt those tasks. We measured completion time and accuracy for each task. If participants took longer than 180 seconds to complete a task, we stopped them and recorded that they had timed-out on the task. Participants were still allowed to submit an answer if they timed-out on the task.

While analyzing completion time for a task, we used a mixed-effects model analysis of variance with fixed effects of *Session* and *Mode*, with *Participant* modeled as a random effect. For accuracy and preference data, we looked at the descriptive statistics.

6. RESULTS

6.1 Accuracy

The accuracy for each task did not vary across the different modes (Silent mode: 88%, Verbal mode: 88%, Finger Pointing mode: 89%).While there was no significant difference in the accuracy between the first and last session, we found that accuracy tended improve in the last session (Figure 3). In addition, we saw that the accuracy tended to be lower on the bar chart task (Table 1). We hypothesize this was the case because this task had the most QR codes closest together.

Table 1. The table shows the average accuracy across all sessions for each mode and each task.

	Silent	**Verbal**	**Finger Pointing**
Line	97%	97%	93%
Parabola	93%	95%	95%
Triangle	88%	88%	90%
Bar Chart	73%	70%	79%
All Tasks	88%	88%	89%

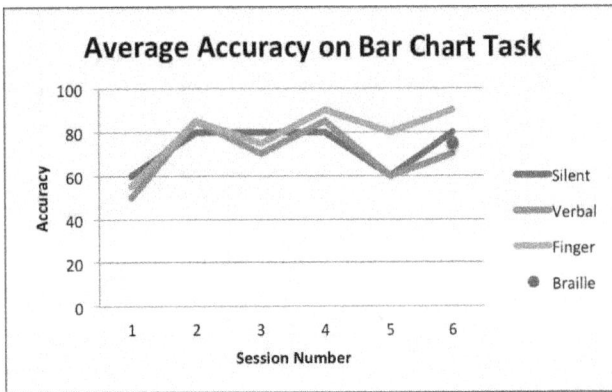

Figure 3. A comparison of the average accuracy for the Bar Chart task across the six sessions for the three modes (n=10) and Braille (n=6) on the last session. Participants were asked to find the range of the tallest bar and their answer could be 0, 50 or 100% correct.

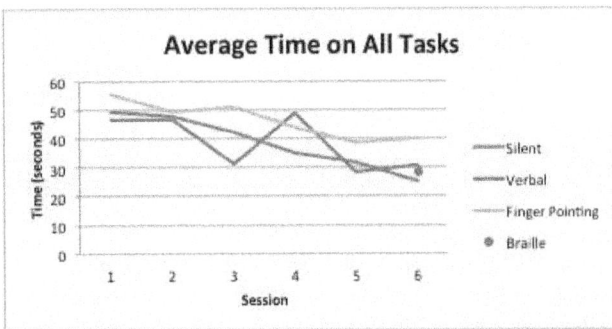

Figure 4. A comparison of the average time it took for each participant to give the answer for a task for the three modes (n=10) across the six sessions as well as for Braille (n=6) on the final session.

6.2 Time

If participants reached 180 seconds without answering the question and completing the task, this was counted as a time-out, and the time is not included in the average or the statistical analysis. Out of 720 tasks, the total number of tasks that timed out was 41, or 5.7%, and almost half of those time-outs (19) occurred in the first session. Additionally, over half of the time-outs (21) occurred during the difficult Bar Chart task. The time-outs occurred in all the modes, with 16 time-outs occurring in the Finger Pointing mode, 16 occurring in the Silent mode, and 9 occurring in the Verbal mode.

With time-outs removed, the average QR code task completion time for all sessions and all modes was 40.9 seconds (SD =36.3). However, the participants were faster in the sixth session than the first (see Figure 4) and the effect of *Session* on time was statistically significant ($F_{5, 640}$=2.268, p<.05). In session six, the average Silent mode completion time was 25.3 seconds (SD=18.7), Verbal mode completion time was 30.5 seconds (SD=29.8) and Finger Pointing mode completion time was 40.3 seconds (SD=29.4). The effect of *Mode* on time was not statistically significant ($F_{2, 640}$=0.619, p=.5391), though it is observed that Finger Pointing mode took more time than the Verbal and Silent modes.

6.3 Feedback Modality Preference

At the end of each session, we asked each participant to indicate their feedback modality preference by ranking the different modes. In addition, each participant to rated how much they liked using each mode on a 7-point Likert scale, where a rating of 1 meant that the participant liked the mode and a 7 meant they did not like it at all. Like our survey and interview, we found a wide range of preferences.

Despite the wide range of preferences, we found that Verbal mode received an average rating of 2.87 (SD=1.57), Finger Pointing mode received an average rating of 3.63 (SD=1.71) and Silent mode received an average rating of 3.98 (SD=2.11). However, the ranking of each method varied strongly between participants and over time. In the final session of the study, four out of ten participants ranked Silent mode as their favorite mode, four ranked the Finger Pointing mode as their favorite and two ranked the Verbal mode as their favorite.

Participants that preferred the Finger Pointing mode generally thought it was more accurate. Participant 1 stated:

I like the concept of the finger pointing. I feel more confident that since it looks for a finger it's getting the right QR code if you have multiple on the same page.

People who did not like the Finger Pointing mode thought it was difficult to use. Participant 3 stated that "I haven't been able to see my finger point in years, so knowing where my finger is isn't useful," but thought that it might be useful for others:

I did like that you're - that it's trying to branch out and give people options for identifying things like with a finger. It's a pretty neat touch. I like that. I could see that turning into something useful. I think my preference was still for just taking it with a simple picture with the camera

Participants that preferred the Silent mode were fatigued of audio feedback, as participant 3 said, *"To be honest, I use screen readers every day and I am so sick of electronic noise."*

Participants disliked Silent mode because they felt that they needed feedback to know what was happening in the application. In the words of Participant 1: "the lack of feedback makes it harder to use because you don't know whether it sees a QR code," and Participant 9: "I still prefer having more versus less feedback."

Participants that preferred the Verbal mode liked it because it provided feedback, but was less of a cognitive load than Finger Pointing. In the words of Participant 9: "the other thing I like about Verbal mode is that every time I hear a zero I think so I need to move it a little bit," as opposed to the Finger Pointing mode, which:

Presents more issues to deal with you already have to deal with how many labels are here and then I got this finger issue this finger needs to be there, but it can't be too close [and] it can't be too far away.

7. COMPARISON TO BRAILLE

While our system was designed primarily for blind users who are unable to read Braille, there are benefits for people who are Braille-literate as well.

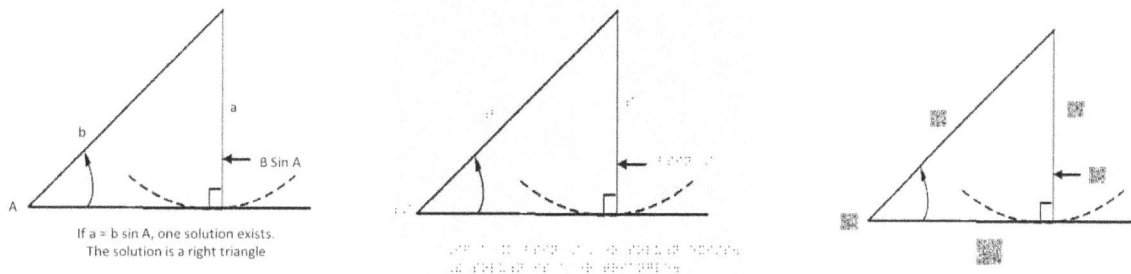

Figure 5. A comparison of the same image which is similar to one from a precalculus textbook [5] in its original form, tactile graphic form with the labels in Braille and tactile graphic form with labels as QR codes. The bottom text is a good example where the QR codes can be smaller than the equivalent Braille text.

7.1 Difficulties in Creating Tactile Graphics with Braille labels

To assess the difficulties in producing tactile graphics, we spoke with three tactile graphics experts. All three had extensive experience in creating tactile graphics and had encountered a variety of problems with the creation of tactile graphics.

From our expert interviews, one common problem was how to place Braille labels on tactile graphics. Because of the limits of human tactile perception, Braille cannot be resized to fit into a small area [3]. This means that labels with a large amount of text have to be moved. One technique for mitigating this problem is to create a key and legend. A short code is placed on the graphic where the label should be and the corresponding label is placed on a separate page. One of the experts estimated that the key and legend system is necessary for a quarter to a third of all the images he produces. Another tactile graphics expert mentioned that three quarters of tactile graphics require an explanation in order for them to be understood, and the explanation would not fit on the original graphic, requiring a second page.

7.2 Size of Braille vs QR Codes

We did a size comparison between Braille and QR code labels and found that the QR codes are able to encode 45% more text in the same amount (Figure 5). This calculation was completed by looking at 82 images from a pre-calculus textbook [5]. We calculated the estimated size of the Braille label using: the product of the number of characters in the text and the size of a Braille cell, which is the standard size of all Braille characters [3]. While many math symbols require multiple Braille characters, our conversion from text to Braille provides a good approximation. Unlike Braille, which has a standard size, QR codes vary in size based on the amount of text they encode and the distance from which they are meant to be scanned. By assuming a scan distance of six inches, we calculated the size of a QR code label based solely on the number of characters it encoded [18]. We found that the average QR code label size is 225 mm^2 and the average Braille label size is 327 mm^2.

7.3 Study

The main goal of the study was to determine if the TGV system was a feasible solution to making labels accessible to those who did not know Braille, and we feel our study demonstrates this fact. Below, we will explain the results from our comparison to Braille in the last session of our longitudinal study that was done with the 6 participants that did know Braille.

7.3.1 Accuracy

Across all participants, the average accuracy for TGV using any mode was higher than the average accuracy using Braille (Silent mode: 88%, Verbal mode: 88%, Finger Pointing mode: 89%, Braille: 77%). For the bar chart task, the TGV accuracies are similar to the average accuracy for Braille (Figure 3). While this finding goes against our hypothesis, this finding is likely due to two reasons. First, the Braille tasks the labels were written in Nemeth code. Even though we explained the how to read Nemeth-coded numbers, some participants made mistakes. Second, some of the Braille-literate participants indicated that they were out of practice reading Braille.

7.3.2 Time

The average completion time with the Braille graphics was 28.6 seconds (SD=19.0). This was faster than the average time of TGV with all of the different modes. However, after the participants learned to use the application, the times were similar. This can be seen in Figure 4, where the dot representing the Braille mode was faster than Verbal and Finger Pointing modes but slower than Silent mode in session 6.

7.3.3 Preference

Four of the six participants who used the Braille labels on the graphics stated that was their favorite. One reason was because of ease of use, as P6 stated that (with Braille): "it's already there and you can just read it." Additionally, people were more comfortable with Braille and thought it was more accurate. In the words of P4: "I'm very comfortable with Braille. It feels more reliable."

The other two participants who preferred TGV to Braille, did not feel comfortable with their Braille literacy skills. In the words of P1:

I guess if you're reading a textbook in Braille you're probably up on your Braille so you wouldn't need a smartphone or anything to access that,

and P5 said that:

I wish I had learned Braille when I was in school because that might that may have made a world of difference and I would be a lot more successful than I am right now so I do I really enjoy the Braille a lot.

8. DISCUSSION

Errors on the first three tasks (Line, Parabola, and Triangle) were a result of misidentifying which label to scan or timing out. In contrast, with the Bar Chart, errors occurred when a participant attempted to scan the correct QR code, but really scanned a different QR code. This issue occurred because of the small distances between the labels on the axes. Participants developed strategies to avoid this problem in later sessions, such as covering the neighboring QR codes. This technique helped increase the accuracy for all three modes from 55% (SD=35) for the first session to 80% (SD=30) for the last session. Figure 3 displays the changes in accuracy across the sessions by mode.

Although Finger Pointing mode was the most accurate, many participants had difficulty using the mode. If users put their finger too close to the QR code, it would not recognize the QR code. There needs to be a small gap between the finger and the QR code for both the finger and QR code to be recognized. This caused difficulties because participants did not realize that their fingers were obscuring the QR code. P2 expressed frustration:

With the pointing with the finger it kept not registering cause either my finger wasn't in the right spot or it kept picking up the wrong one somehow.

We believe this is the main reason that Finger Pointing took significantly longer than the other modes and lead to more time-outs.

9. FUTURE WORK

One opportunity for improvement is to make Finger Pointing mode easier to use. To avoid obscuring the QR code with a finger, adding tactile markers at an appropriate distance from the QR codes could make it easier for people to determine where to place their finger. Additionally, we could try using another pointer, such as a sticky note, to indicate which QR code should be selected.

The longitudinal study allowed us to assess the feasibility of TGV in a controlled setting. We look forward to see how TGV would be used in the wild. In particular, we plan to conduct a field study on the use of TGV in an educational setting.

10. ACKNOWLEDGEMENTS

This material is based upon work supported by the National Science Foundation Graduate Research Fellowship under Grant Nos. DGE-0718124 and DGE-1256082 and National Science Foundation Grant No. IIS-1116051. This work was supported by the U.S. Department of Education, Office of Special Education Programs (Cooperative Agreement #H327B100001). Opinions expressed herein are those of the authors and do not necessarily represent the position of the U.S. Department of Education.

11. REFERENCES

1. Aldrich, F.K. and Sheppard, L. Tactile Graphics in school education: perspectives from pupils. In *British Journal of Visual Impairment 19* (2), 69-73.

2. Bigham, J., Jayant, C., Miller, A. White, B., and Yeh, T. VizWiz::LocateIt – Enabling Blind People to Locate Objects in Their Environment. In *Proc. CVAVI 2010*, 65-72.

3. Braille Layout and Dimensions. http://dots.physics.orst.edu/gs_layout.html.

4. Elgammal, A., Muang, C., and Hu, D.. Skin detection-a short tutorial. *Encyclopedia of Biometrics*. 2009.

5. Gordon-Holliday, B., Yunker, L.E., Vannatta, G. and Crosswhite, F.J. *Advanced Mathematical Concepts, Precalculus with Applications*. Glencoe/McGraw-Hill, 1999.

6. Goransson, D. New VoiceOver Features in iOS 5. Access Lab. http://axslab.com/articles/new-voiceover-features-in-ios5.

7. Holton, B. Voiceye: A Breakthrough in Document Access. AFB AccessWorld Magazine 14, 6 (2013).

8. Jayant, C., et. al. Automated tactile graphics translation: in the field. In *Proc. ASSETS 2007*, ACM Press (2007), 75-82.

9. Jayant, C., Ji, H., White, S. and Bigham, J. Supporting blind photography. In *Proc. ASSETS 2011*, ACM Press (2011), 1-8.

10. Kane, S. K., Frey , B., and Wobbrock, J.O. Access lens: a gesture-based screen reader for real-world documents. In *Proc. CHI 2013*, ACM Press (2013), 347-350.

11. Landau, S., Holborow, R. and Jane, E. The Use of the Talking Tactile Tablet for Delivery of Standardized Tests. In *Proc. CSUN 2004*.

12. Landau, S. and Neile, J. Talking Tactile Apps for the Pulse Pen: STEM Binder. CSUN 2010 https://docs.google.com/presentation/d/1Ylscpk6QKX7Y5WCW3CFnhZDJJIL4X5ki8gHdcJvBp70/present#slide=id.i0

13. Nanayakkara, S., Shilkrot, R., Peen Yeo, K., and Maes, P. EyeRing: a finger-worn input device for seamless interactions with our surroundings. In *Proc. AH 2013*. ACM Press (2013), 13-20.

14. National Federation of the Blind Jernigan Institute. 2009. The Braille Literacy Crisis in America: Facing the Truth, Reversing the Trend, Empowering the Blind. https://www.nfb.org.

15. Nemeth Braille. http://www.braillebug.org/nemeth_braille.asp

16. Phung, S.L., Bouzerdoum, A. and Chai, D. Skin segmentation using color pixel classification: analysis and comparison *IEEE Transactions Pattern Analysis and Machine Intelligence, 27* (1), 148-154.

17. Phung, S.L.; Bouzerdoum, A.; Chai, D., Skin segmentation using color and edge information, In *Proc. of Seventh International Symposium on Signal Processing and Its Applications, 1*, (2003), 525-528.

18. QR Code Minimum Size. http://www.qrstuff.com/blog/2011/11/23/qr-code-minimum-size.

19. Rule, A.C., Stefanich, G.P., Boody, R.M. and Peiffer, B. Impact of Adaptive Materials on Teachers and their Students with Visual Impairments in Secondary Science and Mathematics Classes. In *International Journal of Science Education. 33* (6), 865-887.

20. Sheppard, L. and Aldrich, F.K. Tactile graphics in school education: perspectives from teachers. In *British Journal of Visual Impairment19* (3), 93-97.

21. Tekin, E. and Coughlan, J. A mobile phone application enabling visually impaired users to find and read product barcodes. In *Proc. Computers Helping People with Special Needs 2010*. 290-295.

22. Vázquez, M., and Steinfeld, A. Helping visually impaired users properly aim a camera. In *Proc. ASSETS 2012*. ACM Press (2012), 1-8.

Evaluating the Accessibility of Line Graphs through Textual Summaries for Visually Impaired Users

Priscilla Moraes, Gabriel Sina, Kathleen McCoy and Sandra Carberry
Department of Computer and Information Sciences
University of Delaware, Newark, Delaware, USA
[pmoraes | gsina | mccoy | carberry]@udel.edu

ABSTRACT

This paper presents the methodology for generating textual summaries of line graphs in the SIGHT (*Summarizing Information GrapHics Textually*) system and the evaluation of line graph summaries produced by SIGHT. The system is designed to deliver the high-level knowledge conveyed by informational graphics present in online popular media articles (newspaper and magazines) to individuals who do not have visual access to the image. It works by producing and delivering a concise summary of the graph's content including the most important visual features present in the graphic. The system is briefly described; the evaluation compares the utility of the generated textual summaries to visually viewing the graphic in order to answer important questions about the line graph.

Categories and Subject Descriptors

H.5.2 [**Information Interfaces and Presentation**]: User Interfaces; K.4.2 [**Social Issues**]: Assistive technologies for persons with disabilities.

General Terms

Algorithms; Measurement; Experimentation; Human Factors.

Keywords

Accessibility; information graphics; visual impairments; natural language generation.

1. INTRODUCTION

Having access to information graphics available online remains a challenge for those who cannot visually perceive them. Such media is commonly used to deliver data that can be more easily understood through graphics rather than tables with numbers or plain text. Because such graphics often lack appropriate alternative text (Alt-text), visually impaired users usually miss the information provided by such graphics since the content delivered by them is commonly not repeated in the article's text [1]. In the cases where the user relies on screen readers to access the content of articles from popular media, the absence of a reasonable Alt-text ignores their right to access that information.

With the goal of providing access to these graphics, the SIGHT system focuses on identifying the high-level message along with notable visual features present in graphics and conveys them

through English textual summaries. This effort consists of diverse phases and requires numerous computational tasks in order to achieve its goal.

One example of an informational graphic that was collected from popular media is presented in Figure 1. This line graph ostensibly conveys that there was a change in the trend of Durango sales, rising from 1997 until 1999 and then falling through 2006. The caption of the graphic and the annotations on the endpoints draw attention to the declining portion of the trend, making the declining portion of the trend notable. The SIGHT system works by identifying the main message along with notable visual features present in the graphic to decide on the appropriate content for a summary that will coherently and concisely deliver the most important knowledge provided by the graphic.

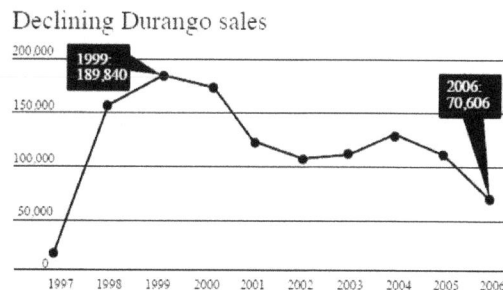

Figure 1: A line graph collected from *The News Journal*.

In this paper, we present the methodology for generating textual summaries of line graphs in the SIGHT system and present the evaluation of the generated textual summary with visually impaired users that demonstrates the system's success. The main focus of the work described here is to evaluate how useful the summaries generated by SIGHT for line graphs from popular media are in delivering the most important knowledge conveyed by the graphic. We performed a task-based evaluation and the details of it can be found in Section 5.

This paper presents related work in the area of graph accessibility in Section 2. Section 3 presents the architecture of the system, explaining the modules and their functionalities. Section 4 details the Generation Module of the system. Section 5 describes the experiment performed with visually impaired users and Section 6 considers the results. Considerations and conclusion can be found in Section 7 and Section 8 delineates our future work.

1.1 Contributions

An important contribution of this paper is the evaluation of the natural language generated summaries with visually impaired users. The focus of the evaluation was to ensure that our system was presenting the most important information in an understandable fashion. We therefore compare the ability of visually impaired users to answer important questions about the graphic to that of sighted people viewing the graphic. Our question collection methodology and novel use of a control group to fairly assess results can be generalized to the assessment of other accessibility evaluations. The detailed explanation of the experiment is a considerable addition to the field of evaluation of accessibility development.

Aside from the evaluation, the version of the SIGHT system described in this paper contributes to the field of accessibility over the previous version of SIGHT [2] in three ways: (1) the SIGHT system was extended in order to generate summaries of line graphs so that visually impaired users have access to usually neglected sources of information. (2) The processing in the system has been transferred to the cloud. Users of the system will no longer need to install the complete system on their local machines in order to have access to its functionalities. Instead, a plugin is the only tool needed to be installed on the user end, increasing the reachability of and, consequently, the accessibility to the features of the system. (3) The generation of English language textual summaries takes into account the reading level of the article on which the line graph appears in order to define the syntactical complexity of the sentences and the set of lexical items (words) to be used in the generated summary [3]. This grants access not only to people at different reading levels but also to people with learning disabilities, who might choose to read articles written at a reading level accessible to them.

2. RELATED WORK

Approaches for evaluating applications and tools that are developed for visually impaired users have been presented in the field. Rello [4] presents the evaluation of the CASSA. The study is performed with users with and without dyslexia in order to evaluate a list of synonyms that are offered to the user aiming to make the text more understandable. Evaluation of an interface that allows users with visual disabilities to browse the Web using speech is presented in [5]. The study provided participants with tasks using speech commands such as "click the search button" that were executed by the system. The experiment has generated a new dialog corpus for non-visual web access based on dialog.

A varied set of alternatives to providing access to graphics for blind and visually impaired users has been investigated. Four main categories of research exist that focus on providing alternative access to graphics. One of them is through the use sonification [6-10]. Solutions using haptic devices and raised paper are presented by [11-16]. Another methodology, proposed by [17], provides navigation schemes that work using exploratory, guided and summarization strategies in order to help visually impaired users to better comprehend Microsoft Excel™ charts.

Another option for providing access to graphics for visually impaired users motivates the research that has been performed on the generation of graphics from input data. Goncu and Marriott [18] developed a tool that automatically generates tactile versions of bar and pie charts from input data present in textbooks. The work presented by Yu et al. [19] allows blind users to create virtual graphs through the use of a low-cost haptic device. Those devices create a graphic from available information and allow the user to explore it through touch. The GraSSML approach, proposed by Fredj and Duce [20], intends to improve the accessibility of diagrams by making their structural and semantic information available at the creation stage. It captures the information contained in the diagram and allows the generation of different ways of representing it (through text, graphic, speech, etc.).

Although these previous efforts demonstrated the usefulness of their overall approach, they are not addressing the problem of making graphics that are already available in online popular media accessible to visually impaired users.

Other researchers have worked on generating textual summaries of graphics through natural language interfaces. Their approaches either construct a description of the diagram by providing its labels, axes ranges, and data sets values [21], or by providing a summary of the graphic.

The work that is closest to our approach is presented by [22] which generates a textual summary of an excel chart. In this case, the summary for each kind of chart (e.g., line graph, pie chart) follows a specific template. The main difference between the iGRAPH project and SIGHT is that our work intends to dynamically assess the intended message of the graphic and convey it along with its outstanding visual features, so the summaries for graphics containing different communicative signals will likely vary substantially in their contents. A comprehensive evaluation of the iGRAPH system is presented in [23].

Drawing an overall comparison of our system with other approaches, we can state that: (1) our system intends to provide access to the high-level message conveyed by graphics present in multimodal documents from popular media, in contrast with systems that enable the user to explore scientific graphics in detail. (2) Our work requires neither special equipment nor skills on the part of the user. (3) It also does not require high cognitive load since users do not need to make a visual representation of the graphic in their minds.

3. SYSTEM ARCHITECTURE

The previous version of the system had a Browser Helper Object installed on the user's machine, along with the whole system running locally, developed for Internet Explorer™ (IE). The version presented in this paper features a plugin developed for Google Chrome™ (to be extended to other browsers) that is installed on the user's machine and that connects to a server running the system in the cloud. The user no longer needs to have the complete system installed and running on her/his local machine. This feature allows users to only download and install a plugin that is responsible for detecting the graphic image in the webpage and sending it (along with the article's text) to the server, which will in turn process the image, the text, generate the line graph summary and return it to the client.

The extraction of the graphics features into an xml file is performed by the Visual Extraction Module (VEM). This module, however, has some limitations on the set of fonts and file types it can process. For this reason, some of the graphics in the corpus are tested for further phases of the generation system using a hand-created XML representation of the graphic that includes coordinates of connected line segments, annotations, captions, axis labels, etc. (similar to the file that is the output of the VEM). After the XML representation of the graphic is obtained, the VEM sends it to the Intention Recognition Module (IRM).

This module is in charge of identifying the intended message conveyed by the graphic. IRMs have been developed for simple bar charts [24], line graphs [25] and grouped bar charts [26] in the context of SIGHT. The focus of this paper is on the generation of line graph summaries, so we briefly summarize the IRM for this type of graphic. The possible categories of intended message for line graphs, described in detail by [25] are:

Rising Trend (RT) / Falling Trend (FT) / Stable Trend (ST) / Big Fall (BF) / Big Jump (BJ) / Change Trend (CHT) / Change Trend and Return (CTR) / Change Trend on the Last Segment (CTLS) / Contrasting Segment Change Trend (CSCT) / Point Correlation (PC)

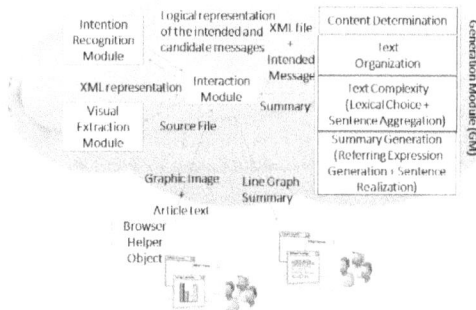

Figure 2: Current architecture of the SIGHT system.

Very briefly, the system developed by Wu employs a graph segmentation module, described in [27], that, given the representation of the line as a set of small line segments from the visual extraction module, segments the line graph into visually distinguishable trends. For example, the line graph in Figure 3 would be divided into two segments, one from 1900 to 1930 and a second segment from 1930 to 2003 (showed on red).

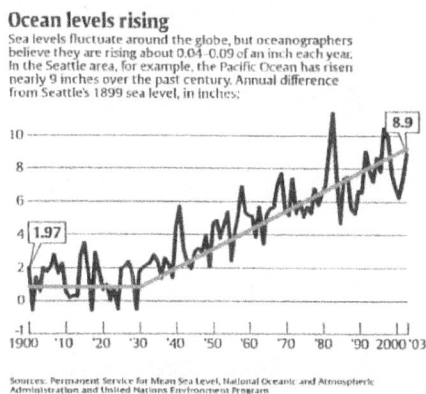

Figure 3: An example of a line graph from online popular media.

The IRM then uses a Bayesian Network tool that, based on these segments, suggests candidate messages, each consisting of one of the above categories along with instantiations of the category parameters. These suggestions, along with communicative signals extracted from the graphic (such as the word "rising" in the title), are entered into a Bayesian Network that assigns probabilities to each of the candidates and selects the most highly rated candidate as the high-level message that the graph designer intended to convey. However, some non-trivial probability may be assigned to candidate messages other than the one identified as the graphic's intended message. For the graphic in Figure 1, for example, the IRM recognizes the intended message as a Change Trend (CHT) – a rising trend followed by a falling trend. However, due to the annotations on the end points of the falling trend segment in the graph and the word "declining" in the title, the IRM also notes the possibility that the intended message could be just the Falling Trend (FT) and assigns a non-trivial probability to that message category.

Upon recognition of the intended message and candidate messages with non-trivial probabilities, the IM sends the logical representation of it, along with the XML representation of the graphic, to the generation module. For the graphic in Figure 1, the logical representation of the two candidate messages with non-trivial probabilities are CHT(rising, 1997, 1999, falling, 1999, 2003, 0.783603) and FT(falling, 1999, 2003, 0.204046), with the last values being the probability of being the intended message of the line graph. Then, the Generation Module (GM) starts the process of generating the summary of the line graph. The sub modules of the GM are the Content Determination, Text Organization, Text Complexity and Summary Generation. The GM is described in the next section.

4. THE GENERATION MODULE FOR LINE GRAPHS

This section explains the sub modules of the GM of the SIGHT system. This module outputs a line graph summary that captures the knowledge conveyed by the graphic as deemed important by the system.

4.1 Content Determination

Natural Language Generation (NLG) systems that convert data into text (Data-to-Text) usually have as their first phase the determination (or selection) of the data to be converted into text. In the case of the GM of the SIGHT system, this phase is especially critical since the final output is a summary of the line graph, meaning that not everything that could be said will be part of the summary.

In this context, determining the most important things to be said about a line graph defines this phase of the system. The first step in this process is to identify the possible pieces of information humans notice the most when looking at line graphs. For this task, a human subject experiment was performed aiming to gather the set of important pieces of line graphs users mention when describing it. The experiment is described in detail in [28] and [29]. Briefly, it presented participants with line graphs and a sentence conveying their identified intended messages. Then, it asked participants to provide additional information on what they thought were important features of the graphic. From the results, we were able to determine (1) what features of the graph were discussed and (2) how important these features were. A set of seventeen features were identified. Features such as the maximum and minimum values of the line graph, slope of the trends, fluctuation of the data values, among others, were discussed.

We hypothesized that whether or not a feature was presented depended on their strength and what other features were present. Therefore, we followed [30] and used a centrality-based algorithm based on PageRank [31] for content selection. In ur work, the initial configuration of the graph differs significantly from [30]. For line graphs, the initial importance of a proposition is based on the frequencies with which they were mentioned in the experiments mentioned previously along with assessed calculations of their prominence. For some features, such as volatility and steepness, initial values may be incremented based on how prominently they appear in the graph. The PageRank network is constructed such that nodes represent propositions and edges represent the semantic relationship between them. The semantic relationships can be of attraction, when a proposition complements or augments the information of another proposition (maximum value and minimum value) or of repellence when the information provided by two propositions is redundant (the absolute value of change in a trend and the rate of change in a trend).

After the network is set up, the algorithm runs to convergence and the top proposition is selected. Weights of edges connecting the selected node to other nodes are updated based on their relationships, allowing the algorithm to smartly select propositions that go together and, at the same time, avoid the inclusion of repetitive information. This process is repeated until a stopping criterion is met. The set of selected propositions is then forwarded to the Text Organization sub module, which is responsible for organizing the discourse.

4.2 Text Organization

The phase of organization is mainly responsible for assuring coherence on the summary. Due to this, the organization of line graph summaries is not a straightforward task. Line graphs may convey single or multiple trends.

Additionally, line graphs have a continuous nature; they usually convey information about an entity's behavior over a period. Each trend in a line graph has its own characteristics (steepness, annotations, volatility) that may or may not be selected for inclusion in the summary. Based on the selected content, one trend might carry more importance than another might. This complicates the organization process.

In order to be able to organize the text such that the final summary reflects the most important information about the line graph, we decided to take into consideration the outstanding visual features of the graphic when making decisions about what to say first. The overall organization of the summary is such that:

☐ Basic information about the overall graph comprises the first set of sentence(s) – in this group we include the graph type, its volatility, its intended message, and the entity being represented in the graphic.

☐ The second group contains sentences conveying details about the particular trends of the graphic and their characteristics that are deemed important such as initial and end values and dates of the trends, their slopes, their volatilities, and their change in values. It is in this group of sentences that the importance of an outstanding trend might change the text ordering.

☐ The last set of sentences concludes the summary by going back to the overall graphic and delivering its computational information (e.g., overall change in behavior, overall rate of increase/decrease, overall time span).

The organization of the second group is dependent on what has been deemed important. The system can order propositions based on (1) importance of a trend or (2) presence of features that can be compared across trends.

4.3 Text Complexity

For this phase, two major tasks are performed. The first is the choice of lexical items to be used in order to describe the features of line graphs. The fluctuation on the data values, for example, can be described using the lexical item *volatility* or the expression *ups and downs*. The second task is determining the amount of aggregation applied to the propositions in order to construct more complex sentences.

One goal of our work is the generation of summaries that are appropriate for the user's reading level (which we presume to be the level of the article) and that fit coherently with the text of that article. Thus when generating the initial summaries of line graphs, our system makes different lexical choices (such as *volatility* versus *ups and downs*). It then creates different text plans for each group of grade levels (each group consists of two or more grade levels starting at the 5th grade) and applies the appropriate one depending upon the assessed reading level of the text in the article containing the graphic [3]. For the evaluation presented on this work, summaries of line graphs were generated on the same reading level as the articles in which the graphs appear. The goal here is the evaluation of the effectiveness of the generated summaries regardless of reading level. [3] presents the evaluation of the generation of summaries at different reading levels.

For each group of grade levels, we define a text plan that increases the sentence syntactic structure complexity as the grade gets higher. We define a text plan for summaries that can range between grades 5 (inclusive) and 7 (exclusive), another text plan for grades between 7 (inclusive) and 9 (exclusive), a third text plan for grades 9 (inclusive) and 11 (exclusive), a fourth for 11 (inclusive) and 13 (exclusive) and, finally, one for grades greater than or equal to 13 (college level).

As mentioned in Section 4.2, the organization phase divides the set of propositions produced by the content selection module into three groups. Thus, from the set of selected propositions, the text plan of a given group defines rules on Noun Phrase (NP) density and lexical choice. When describing an entity, attributes of this entity can be added to the NP as modifiers using either adjectives e.g., "a steep rising trend", conjunctions e.g., "the rising trend is steep and volatile" or relative clauses e.g., "a rising trend, which is steep". When the modifier of an NP is a Verb Phrase (VP), it is combined using a relative clause e.g., "the line graph, which presents the Seattle's ocean levels..." VPs can be modified by adverbs e.g., "the falling trend is very steep". The text plans apply rules within sets of propositions that are grouped hierarchically. Within these major groups, propositions can only be aggregated if they belong to the same entity. Details on the aggregation, pronominalization and lexical choice phases of the system can be found in [3].

4.4 Summary Generation

Finally, referring expressions are pronominalized in order to avoid repetition. The following examples show before and after pronominalization of the referring expressions is performed on the summary of the line graph in Figure 4 (referring expressions and pronouns are shown in bold):

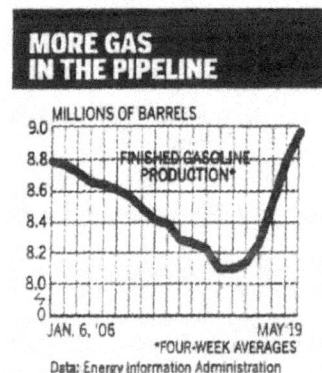

Figure 4: Example of a line graph from popular media.

Before: *The image shows a line graph, which presents the number of finished gasoline production, in millions of barrels. The line graph shows a changing trend that consists of a falling trend from 1/6/2005 to 12/16/2005 followed by a rising trend through 5/19/2006. The line graph has a maximum value of 8.97 million barrels occurring at 5/19/2006. The line graph has a minimum value of 8.09 million barrels occurring at 12/16/2005.*

After: *The image shows a line graph, which presents the number of finished gasoline production, in millions of barrels. The line* *graph shows a changing trend that consists of a falling trend from 1/6/2005 to 12/16/2005 followed by a rising trend through 5/19/2006. **It** has a maximum value of 8.97 million barrels occurring at 5/19/2006. **It** has a minimum value of 8.09 million barrels occurring at 12/16/2005.*

The last step on generating the summaries is realization. We currently use the FUF/SURGE [32] surface realizer to create the sentence templates and to realize them.

5. EXPERIMENT

For the purpose of evaluating the usefulness of the generated summaries, we performed a task-based evaluation with people with visual impairments. We decided to evaluate the system by testing if visually impaired users would be able to answer important questions regarding the high-level knowledge conveyed by the graphic by having access to the summaries, and to compare their performance to that of sighted users viewing the graphic.

The experiment was composed of three phases. The first phase was concerned with the collection of questions to be asked to the visually impaired users. The first phase was subdivided into three sub-phases. For the first sub-phase, we asked sighted users to provide us with questions that a person would be able to answer by just glancing at the graphic because the goal of the system is to initially provide a summary that will suffice for users who are reading a multimodal document containing graphics but who are not interested in analyzing the graphic in detail. The second sub-phase was the filtering of relevant questions. For this sub-phase, we asked another participant, who did not take part in the first sub-phase, to filter the questions such that questions that required world knowledge or inference, and those where answering required a careful examination of the graphic would not be included.

The participant had knowledge about Natural Language Processing but not about this project. After the questions were filtered, the set of questions to be used was restricted so that a question would only be included in the second phase if at least two of the participants posited that question. From the resulting set of questions we could find questions that were worded differently but meant the same thing. Since some questions were asked in a clearer way than others, we asked the participant who filtered them in the first sub-phase to choose a clear way to state the question.

The second phase was the evaluation with visually impaired readers, where we provided them with the summaries and asked the questions collected during the first phase. The last phase was the collection of control answers. Sighted participants were recruited and provided with the graphic images and the same questions that were asked to the blind users. All the phases are described in detail next.

5.1 Phase 1: Collection

5.1.1 Collecting Questions from Sighted Users

For this phase we recruited freshmen college students from various majors to provide us with questions that a person would be able to answer by just glancing at the graphic. Thirty-four students participated in this phase. This task was interspersed with another task, which provided data for another project. Since the second task is not relevant here, instructions for it were suppressed. The instructions on this phase of the task were the following:

1. This package contains a set of trials, each consisting of a graph and a task. For each graph you will be asked to either: A) Answer questions related to it. B) Provide questions about it.

2. For the graphs which we ask you to provide questions about, we ask you to think of a question that a person would be able to answer by just taking a quick look at it. The question should be able to be answered by the high level knowledge the graphic conveys (without the need for calculations or detailed examination).

For the trials in which we asked them to provide us with questions, we gave them a line graph and asked for two questions given the instructions above. Eleven different line graphs were used in this phase. Figure 5 shows three examples of graphics that were used. The graphics conveyed different intended messages and had different sets of visual features. A total of 216 questions were collected from 34 participants, an average of about 19 questions per graphic.

5.1.2 Question Filtering

A participant with knowledge of Natural Language Processing was recruited for the second sub-phase, which was concerned with filtering questions that were appropriate to be asked given the graphic and the instructions provided to the participants.

One of the exclusion criteria was the need for world knowledge in order to answer the questions. Examples of questions that were left out of the ones used in the next phase of the experiment were:

Why has there been growth in bottled water? *(Referring to the leftmost graphic shown in* Figure 5*);*

How does this inverse relationship impact society? *(Referring to the graphic in the rightmost position of* Figure 5*);*

Do you think this percent change is similar to other sea levels in other parts of the world? *(Referring to the graphic in the rightmost position of* Figure 5*).*

Since such questions cannot be answered by just having access to the information conveyed in the graphic, they were eliminated by the participant performing the filtering. Examples of questions that required a detailed examination of the graphic and that were left out by the participant filtering them are:

What was the amount spent on bottled water in 2004? *(Referring to the leftmost graphic shown in* Figure 5*);*

What is the lowest percentage of his approval rating? *(Referring to the graphic in the rightmost position of* Figure 5*);*

What year had the highest sea level, in inches, in Seattle? *(Referring to the graphic in the rightmost position of Figure 5).*

Another criterion for exclusion was the need for detailed examination or complex calculation needed from the reader in order to answer the question. It should be noted that questions that still required some quick calculations were left in by the participant performing the filtering. Examples of such questions are:

From 01 to 05 bottled water sales have grown by how much? *(Referring to the leftmost graphic in* Figure 5*);*

From 1900 to 2003, what is the total difference between sea levels in inches? *(Referring to the graphic in the rightmost position of* Figure 5*).*

5.1.3 Choosing/Rewording Unclear Questions

After filtering the initial set of questions, a total of 125 questions that were considered appropriate by the participant were grouped by meaning. Questions that were worded differently but meant the same thing were grouped so that we could assess the agreement between participants on which questions they thought reflected the knowledge one could acquire from the graphic. Only questions that had been provided by at least two participants were used. Since some questions (in the same group of meaning) were worded better than others and therefore were clearer, we asked the participant who filtered the question to either choose one question of each meaning group (the one that was clearer) or, if none was clear enough, we asked the participant to rewrite it such that the person reading the questions would not need access to the graphic in order to understand it. This was needed because we could find some questions that, given that the image was provided to the participants, made references to the graphic or to the context of the previous question they provided, making the question unclear if standing alone in a different scenario. After filtering and choosing/rewriting the appropriate questions, we had a total of twenty-one questions about nine different graphics. Those

questions were used for the following phases of the experiment: assessing the usefulness of the summaries with visually impaired users and collecting control answers from sighted users who would answer the questions having access to the graphic image.

5.2 Phase 2: Evaluation of the Summaries with Visually Impaired Users

For this phase we recruited four blind users with the help of the Delaware Association for the Blind. Given a line graph, the participant would have access to the summary generated by the system and would be asked one to three questions about the graphic. Navigation instructions were provided before the participants started listening to the task instructions.

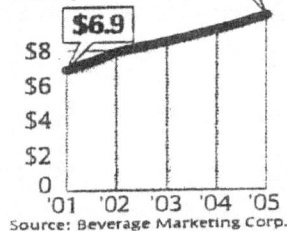

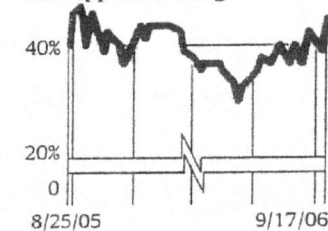

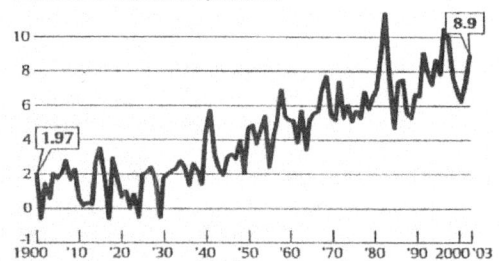

Figure 5: Example of line graphs used in the first phase of the experiment.

From demographic information collected, we assessed that all four participants have been using the Internet for reading news for more than seven years and all of them use screen readers as their main reading tool (options were braille, screen magnifier, screen reader, or other). All of them had some college education (two of them had some graduate education, one of them had a Master's degree) and all of them were native English speakers.

For this phase we collected answers for all 36 trials given (no trial was left untaken). The results and comments provided by the participants on this phase were analyzed by comparing with the control answers provided by sighted users during phase 3 of the experiment, described in the next section.

5.3 Phase 3: Collection of Control Answers from Sighted Users

In order to assess how useful the summaries generated by our system were, we designed a last phase that was meant to collect answers from sighted users viewing the graphic image to the same questions being asked to the visually impaired users. For this phase, 24 freshmen college students from various majors were recruited. The participants for this phase could not have participated in any of the previous phases of the experiment. As in the first phase, a divergent task was mixed amongst the trials in order to avoid task fatigue. The instructions for this phase were:

1. Same from Phase 1.

2. For the graphics about which we ask you to answer questions, please study the graphic such that you may be able to answer the questions about it. You will then be asked to answer one to three questions about the graphic. You may not understand some questions or feel that they cannot be easily answered with the graphic. At the end of each question, you will have a space to make

comments on it. Please let us know anything about the question you could not understand. The question might ask you to calculate something. You may use a calculator, if you wish, or just give an approximate answer. ATTENTION! While answering a question about a graphic you can go back to the image or just provide the closest answer you can remember. If you choose to go back, please let us know you did so in the space designated for it. In the cases where you do go back to the graphic, we ask you to estimate how difficult the question was to answer even with the graphic.

Even though participants were told they could go back to the graph if they needed to, we were able to see from the results, described in the next section, that most of the questions that one is able to answer by just glancing at the graphic did not cause them to go back to the image; only the ones that require a more detail examination did.

6. EVALUATION RESULTS

As described in the previous section, the four visually impaired experiment participants received a package with nine trials. Each trial had a line graph summary and one to three questions that they were asked.

Table 1 and Table 2 show the total number of questions answered (in multiples of four for sight-impaired users and multiples of nine for sighted users, respectively) and the number of answers. Analyzing those numbers we notice that line graphs L17 and L26 have considerably lower scores in the correct answers column. For these two line graphs we noticed that, during Phase 3, sighted users answering the questions for these two graphics often went back to the image to search for the answers (16 out of 27 went back to the image for the line graph L17). The questions, followed by the answers, for this line graph were: *Question 1: How many pension plans were defined in 1985? **Answer: 114,396** / Question 2: How many more pension plans were defined in 1985 than in 2004?*

Answer: 83,158 / Question 3: What is the percent decline of pension plans from 1985 to 2004? Answer: Approximately 73%

Even though 3 out of 4 visually impaired users decided to listen to the summary more than once, they still had difficulties memorizing the answers to the questions listed above. Line graph L26 had 2 questions and the summary did not provide the answer for one of them. The questions for this graph were: *Question 1: What is the difference in consumer confidence in May of 2005 and May of 2006? Answer: 0.1 / Question 2: Which month had the lowest consumer confidence in 2005 and 2006? Answer: October 2005*

The average percent of correct answers from the visually impaired users was 75%, while the average percentage of correct answers from sighted users was 80.87%. From instances where sighted users got the answers wrong, we noticed that most of the time the questions asked for specific numbers for which they preferred to guess the answer instead of going back to the graphic image (they chose to answer the questions from the memory they had attained from their first look at the graphic). For some questions where blind users performed better than sighted, we could see from the sighted users' comments that they thought the questions were hard and/or the information was not easily accessible. For example, there were cases where the question asked for maximum or minimum values and those were not annotated, making an interpolation be needed, whereas the system provided that in some of the summaries.

From the comments provided by the blind participants, we could see that individual preferences were stated (one participant declared that he would prefer the summary to have less information than what was provided, allowing the user to ask for more if he/she preferred). This consideration is aligned with our intention of providing follow-up responses as described in future work. Most of the comments provided by the blind participants stated that the summaries were clear and concise. The participants, in general, appreciated the clarity with which the information was delivered to them.

7. CONCLUSION

This paper has presented the methodology of the SIGHT system and an evaluation of the generated summaries for line graphs The results show that the system successfully provides the information needed by visually impaired users in order for them to be able to answer questions about the graphic. The system generates a summary that aims to deliver the most important information conveyed by the graphic. The summaries are adapted to the reading level of the articles in which the graphics appear, granting access to users at different reading levels. This paper also describes the implementation of a more accessible version of the system on which the users only need to install a web browser plugin, instead of the complete system, in order to have access to its capabilities. We envision that in the future SIGHT might be used for generating Alt-text for informational graphics.

8. FUTURE WORK

Our plans for future work on the context of the SIGHT system is the extension of the generation module to allow the user to access follow-up information on the graphic. Since the initial summary only delivers the most important information (intended message + outstanding visual features), follow-up responses will be able to deliver in depth information based upon request from the user. Summaries of grouped bar charts is also a planned extension to the system. Grouped bar charts have tridimensional features, making discourse planning even more challenging.

Table 1: Phase 2 Experiment results - test with visually impaired participants (Correct in %).

Graph	# of questions answered	# of wrong or incomplete answers	Correct answers
L3	4	0	100
L6	12	2	83.3
L17	12	9	25
L18	8	2	75
L21	8	1	87.5
L26	8	5	37.5
L28	12	0	100
L89	8	1	87.5
L95	8	0	100

Table 2: Phase 3 Experiment results - control answers collected from sighted users (Correct in %).

Graph	# of questions answered	# of wrong or incomplete answers	Correct answers
L3	9	0	100
L6	23	4	82.6
L17	27	6	77.7
L18	17	4	76.4
L21	19	2	89.4
L26	15	6	60
L28	29	5	82.7
L89	20	2	90
L95	19	0	100

9. ACKNOWLEDGMENTS

Our thanks to the Delaware Association for the Blind for helping us recruiting subjects for our experiment and to the Coordenação de Aperfeiçoamento de Pessoal de Nível Superior from Brazil - CAPES (*in Portuguese*) for supporting Gabriel Sina.

10. REFERENCES

[1] S. Carberry, S. Elzer, and S. Demir, "Information graphics: an untapped resource for digital libraries," in *Proceedings of the 29th annual international ACM SIGIR conference on Research and development in information retrieval*, New York, NY, USA, 2006, pp. 581-588.

[2] S. Demir, S. Carberry, and K. F. McCoy, "Generating textual summaries of bar charts," in *Proceedings of the Fifth International Natural Language Generation Conference*, Stroudsburg, PA, USA, 2008, pp. 7-15.

[3] P. Moraes, K. McCoy, and S. Carberry, "Adapting Graph Summaries to the Users' Reading Levels," in *Proceedings of the 8th International Natural Language Generation Conference*, 2014, p. Accepted for publication.

[4] L. Rello and R. Baeza-Yates, "Evaluation of DysWebxia: A Reading App Designed for People with Dyslexia," in *Proceedings of the 11th Web for All Conference*, New York, NY, USA, 2014, pp. 10:1-10:10.

[5] V. Ashok, Y. Borodin, S. Stoyanchev, Y. Puzis, and I. V. Ramakrishnan, "Wizard-of-Oz Evaluation of Speech-driven

Web Browsing Interface for People with Vision Impairments," in *Proceedings of the 11th Web for All Conference*, New York, NY, USA, 2014, pp. 12:1-12:9.

[6] J. L. Alty and D. Rigas, "Exploring the use of structured musical stimuli to communicate simple diagrams: the role of context," *Int. J. Hum.-Comput. Stud.*, vol. 62, pp. 21-40, January 2005.

[7] L. M. Brown and S. A. Brewster, "Drawing by ear: interpreting sonified line graphs," in *In Proceedings of ICAD 2003*, 2003, pp. 152-156.

[8] R. F. Cohen and R. Yu, "PLUMB: Displaying Graphs to the Blind Using an Active Auditory Interface," in *Proceedings of the 7th international ACM SIGACCESS Conference on Computers and Accessibility (ASSETS 05*, 2005, pp. 182-183.

[9] J. H. Flowers and T. A. Hauer, "Musical versus visual graphs: Cross-modal equivalence in perception of time series data," *Human Factors*, pp. 553-569, 1995.

[10] D. K. McGookin and S. A. Brewster, "SoundBar: exploiting multiple views in multimodal graph browsing," in *Proceedings of the 4th Nordic conference on Human-computer interaction: changing roles*, New York, NY, USA, 2006, pp. 145-154.

[11] S. Wall and S. Brewster, "Feeling What You Hear: Tactile Feedback for Navigation of Audio Graphs," in *Proceedings of the SIGCHI Conference on Human Factors in Computing Systems*, New York, NY, USA, 2006, pp. 1123-1132.

[12] R. Ramloll, W. Yu, S. A. Brewster, B. Riedel, A. M. Burton, and G. Dimigen, "Constructive sonified haptic line graphs for the blind student: First steps," in *Fourth International Conference on Assistive Technologies*, 2000, pp. 31-41.

[13] W. Yu and S. Brewster, "Comparing two haptic interfaces for multimodal graph rendering," in *Haptic Interfaces for Virtual Environment and Teleoperator Systems, 2002. HAPTICS 2002. Proceedings. 10th Symposium on*, 2002, pp. 3-9.

[14] W. Yu, R. Ramloll, and S. A. Brewster, "Haptic Graphs for Blind Computer Users," in *Proceedings of the First International Workshop on Haptic Human-Computer Interaction*, London, UK, UK, 2001, pp. 41-51.

[15] A. R. Kennel, "Audiograf: a diagram-reader for the blind," in *Proceedings of the second annual ACM conference on Assistive technologies*, New York, NY, USA, 1996, pp. 51-56.

[16] S. E. Krufka and K. E. Barner, "A user study on tactile graphic generation methods," *Behaviour \& Information Technology*, vol. 25, pp. 297-311, 2006.

[17] I. A. Doush, E. Pontelli, D. Simon, and O. Ma, "Making Microsoft Excel Accessible: Multimodal Presentation of Charts," in *Proceedings of the Eleventh International ACM SIGACCESS Conference on Computers and Accessibility - ASSETS 2009*, Pittsburgh, PA, 2009.

[18] C. Goncu and K. Marriott, "Tactile chart generation tool," in *Proceedings of the 10th international ACM SIGACCESS conference on Computers and accessibility*, New York, NY, USA, 2008, pp. 255-256.

[19] W. Yu, K. Kangas, and S. Brewster, "Web-based haptic applications for blind people to create virtual graphs," in

Haptic Interfaces for Virtual Environment and Teleoperator Systems, 2003. HAPTICS 2003. Proceedings. 11th Symposium on, 2003, pp. 318-325.

[20] Z. B. Fredj and D. A. Duce, "GraSSML: accessible smart schematic diagrams for all," *Universal Access in the Information Society*, vol. 6, pp. 233-247, 2007.

[21] M. Kurze, "TDraw: a computer-based tactile drawing tool for blind people," in *Proceedings of the second annual ACM conference on Assistive technologies*, 1996, pp. 131-138.

[22] L. Ferres, P. Verkhogliad, G. Lindgaard, L. Boucher, A. Chretien, and M. Lachance, "Improving Accessibility to Statistical Graphs: the inspectGraph System," in *Proceedings of the Ninth International ACM SIGACCESS Conference on Computers and Accessibility (ASSETS)*, 2007.

[23] L. Ferres, G. Lindgaard, L. Sumegi, and B. Tsuji, "Evaluating a Tool for Improving Accessibility to Charts and Graphs," *ACM Trans. Comput.-Hum. Interact.*, vol. 20, pp. 28:1-28:32, November 2013.

[24] S. Elzer, N. Green, S. Carberry, and J. Hoffman, "A Model of Perceptual Task Effort for Bar Charts and its Role in Recognizing Intention," *International Journal on User Modeling and User-Adapted Interaction*, vol. 16, pp. 1-30, 2006.

[25] P. Wu, S. Carberry, S. Elzer, and D. Chester, "Recognizing the intended message of line graphs," in *Proceedings of the 6th international conference on Diagrammatic representation and inference*, Berlin, Heidelberg, 2010, pp. 220-234.

[26] R. Burns, S. Carberry, and S. Elzer, "Visual and spatial factors in a bayesian reasoning framework for the recognition of intended messages in grouped bar charts," in *Proceedings of the AAAI Workshop on Visual Representations and Reasoning*, 2010, pp. 6-13.

[27] P. Wu, S. Carberry, and S. Elzer, "Segmenting Line Graphs into Trends," in *Proceedings of the Twelfth International Conference on Artificial Intelligence*, 2010, pp. 697-703.

[28] C. Greenbacker, S. Carberry, and K. McCoy, "A Corpus of Human-written Summaries of Line Graphs," in *Proceedings of the UCNLG+Eval: Language Generation and Evaluation Workshop*, Edinburgh, Scotland, 2011, pp. 23-27.

[29] P. S. Moraes, S. Carberry, and K. McCoy, "Providing access to the high-level content of line graphs from online popular media," in *Proceedings of the 10th International Cross-Disciplinary Conference on Web Accessibility*, Rio de Janeiro, Brazil, 2013, pp. 11:1-11:10.

[30] S. Demir, S. Carberry, and K. F. McCoy, "A discourse-aware graph-based content-selection framework," in *Proceedings of the 6th International Natural Language Generation Conference*, Stroudsburg, PA, USA, 2010, pp. 17-25.

[31] L. Page, S. Brin, R. Motwani, and T. Winograd, "The PageRank Citation Ranking: Bringing Order to the Web," Stanford InfoLab, Technical Report 1999-66, November 1999.

[32] M. Elhadad and J. Robin, "SURGE: a comprehensive plug-in syntactic realization component for text generation," *Computational Linguistics*, 1999.

Including Blind People in Computing Through Access to Graphs

Suzanne Balik, Sean Mealin, Matthias Stallmann, Robert Rodman, Michelle Glatz, and Veronica Sigler

Dept. of Computer Science
North Carolina State University
Raleigh, NC 27695-8206

{spbalik, spmealin, mfms, rodman, mlglatz, vjsigler} @ncsu.edu

ABSTRACT

Our goal in creating the Graph SKetching tool, GSK, was to provide blind screen reader users with a means to create and access graphs as node-link diagrams and share them with sighted people in real-time. Through this effort, we hoped to better include blind people in computing and other STEM disciplines in which graphs are important. GSK proved very effective for one blind computer science student in courses that involved graphs and graph structures such as automata, decision trees, and resource-allocation diagrams. In order to determine how well GSK works for other blind people, we carried out a user study with ten blind participants. We report on the results of the user study, which demonstrates the efficacy of GSK for the examination, navigation, and creation of graphs by blind users. Based on the study results, we improved the efficiency of GSK for blind users. We plan more enhancements to help meet the need for accessible graph tools as articulated by the blind community.

Categories and Subject Descriptors

H.5.2 [**Information Interfaces and Presentation**]: User Interfaces; K.4.2 [**Computers and Society**]: Social Issues – *assistive technologies for persons with disabilities;* K.3.2 [**Computers and Education**]: Computer and Information Science Education; G.2.2 [**Discrete Mathematics**]: Graph Theory.

General Terms

Human Factors.

Keywords

GSK; Universal Design; Accessibility.

1. INTRODUCTION

Combinatorial graphs, often conveyed as node-link diagrams, are very important in the field of computing as well as in other STEM disciplines. To be successful in these disciplines, it is important that blind students and professionals be able to create and access graphs and share them with sighted colleagues. Others have

created graph applications intended specifically for blind people. AudioGraf was an early attempt to make graph-like diagrams accessible via a touch panel and auditory display [13]. The Kevin system aimed to make data flow diagrams accessible to blind students and engineers [3]. Kekulé was created to enable blind students to examine the structure of chemical molecules [4] and PLUMB was developed to help them comprehend graphs and data structures [6]. The TeDUB project strived to make existing Unified Modeling Language (UML) and other diagrams accessible to blind people [14]. While the Deep View graph application allowed for collaboration between blind and sighted users, each used a separate interface [17]. We created the Graph SKetching tool, GSK, to adhere to universal design principles by including both blind and sighted users in the same interface [2, 5]. Although the sonification and tactile/haptic feedback approaches employed by others [8, 9, 22] may aid blind users in comprehending the spatial layout of a graph, we wanted to create a simple, portable graph application with no need for specialized hardware devices. Thus, we designed GSK to allow blind and sighted users to employ interaction mechanisms that are standard for them (keyboard, mouse, monitor, screen reader).

The second author, who is a blind computer science student, successfully used GSK in his automata theory, operating systems, software engineering, and artificial intelligence courses to work with graphs, both alone and in conjunction with sighted instructors. It is not surprising that, as a co-creator of GSK, he found the tool intuitive and useful. We wanted to determine how well GSK would work for other blind students and recent graduates. We therefore carried out a user study in which blind participants used GSK and Microsoft Excel, as a control, to examine and navigate graphs. They also used GSK to create several graphs. This paper provides information about the study, its participants and results, as well as improvements made to GSK that increase its efficiency for blind users.

2. OVERVIEW OF GSK

The GSK interface provides two different views of the same graph. Connection View, as shown in Figures 1 and 3, displays a graph as a node-link diagram. In this view, blind users navigate the graph via the keyboard – each time a node or edge receives focus, information about the node/edge is displayed in the status bar and voiced by the screen reader. Grid View allows blind (and sighted) users to create new nodes in the preferred layout. Sighted users may also use the mouse in Connection View to create new nodes. More information about the GSK interface may be found in our previous paper [2] and on our website, go.ncsu.edu/gsk, where GSK may be downloaded as well.

3. USER STUDY

Each of the ten user study sessions spanned five hours and consisted of three individual studies, each of which took about an hour. In the first two studies, participants *examined* and *navigated* graphs using GSK and Microsoft Excel. We chose Excel as a control because it is a standard means of representing tabular data that is in common use by both blind and sighted people. In the third study, participants used GSK to *create* graphs. Complete study details may be found in [1].

We conducted the user study on a Windows computer running the Vista Operating System. Participants used the keyboard and version 10.0 of the JAWS screen reader to interact with GSK and Microsoft Excel 2007. Because GSK is a Java application using Swing components, we installed the Java Access Bridge, which facilitates communication between the screen reader and the Java Virtual Machine. Our use of Java 6 (6u21) necessitated this installation. The Java Access Bridge is now included with Java 7 Update 6 (7u6) and later.

Table 1. Participant Characteristics

Participant	JAWS Rate	Excel Use	Graph Familiarity 1 (Low) – 5 (High)
P1/P1R	125	5-10 yrs	4
P2	115	2-3 yrs	1
P3	123	> 10 yrs	5
P4	80	5-10 yrs	5
P5	29	2-3 yrs	2
P6	113	3-5 yrs	4
P7	73	2-3 yrs	1
P8	74	< 1yr	3
P9	131	3-5 yrs	5

3.1 Participants

Obtaining a large number of blind participants was difficult due to their relatively low representation in the general population [11]. Nine different blind screen reader users participated individually in the study. All participants were novice GSK users with no prior exposure to the program, except for participant P1/P1R, who repeated the study with an improved version of GSK. Though our sample was small, the first eight study participants demonstrated the effectiveness of GSK for completing a number of graph-related tasks. They also provided us with enough information to make improvements that allowed the ninth and repeating participant to use GSK more efficiently. Each person received an honorarium for participating in the study. Prior to beginning the study, we obtained Institutional Review Board (IRB) approval from our university.

In order to maintain confidentiality with such a small group, we provide most information about the participants in aggregate form and provide individual information that may have an impact on the study results in Table 1. The participants (4 male, 5 female) ranged in age from 14 to 30 and consisted of 3 secondary students, 3 undergraduate students, 2 college graduates, and 1 graduate student. All but two participants had been legally blind

since birth; the other two became blind before the age of 5. All were experienced computer users and most were experienced JAWS users. Some participants used a very fast JAWS speech rate, which is unintelligible to most people, while others used a much slower rate.

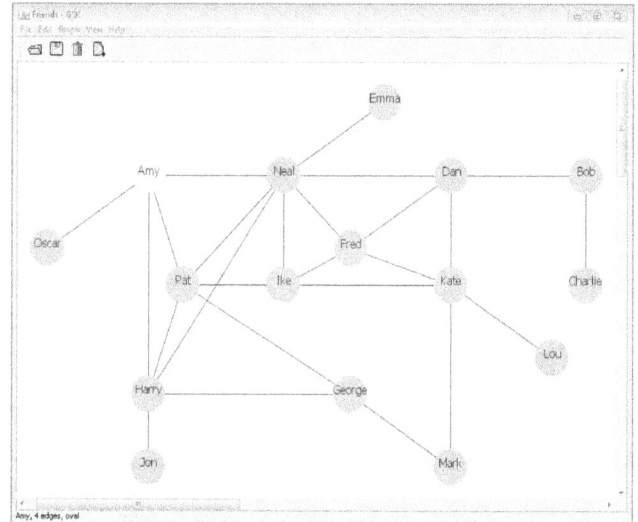

Figure 1. GSK Friends Graph

Figure 2. Excel Friends Graph

3.2 Graph Examination Study

For the graph examination study, we used a friends graph that was based on the Acquaintance graph in an undergraduate discrete mathematics textbook [20]. Each node in the Friends graph represents a person with undirected edges joining people who are friends. We found that all participants, regardless of their background and degree of familiarity with graphs, could relate to this simple example. A friends graph rendered using GSK is shown in Figure 1. The same graph represented as an Excel table is shown in Figure 2. Each row of the Excel table contains a person's name followed by the person's number of friends followed by the names of the friends. We created six versions of the Friends graph with different edges, each of which contained

16 nodes and 25 edges. All graphs used the same set of person names for the nodes, one for each letter of the alphabet – Amy, Bob, Charlie, ..., Pat. We randomly assigned node names to each GSK graph. We then created a random pairing of those names that we used to label the nodes in the corresponding Excel graph. We configured the Excel tables so that the JAWS screen reader would read the row (person's) name when navigating from cell to cell and turned off the reading of cell coordinates, e.g., A1, to eliminate confusion.

The participants were first trained to use GSK and Excel to examine a friends graph and given time to practice answering each of the four types of questions listed below. The questions correspond to graph theory concepts without being explicit. Each participant was asked one question of each of the four types for each of the six graphs using both GSK and Excel for a total of 48 trials. For each question/graph pair, we were careful to use corresponding GSK/Excel nodes. The participant response times and answers for each trial were recorded. Examples of each question type are given below.

Q1: *How many friends does Amy have?* (Node degree)

Q2: *Is Bob a friend of Dan?* (Adjacent node)

Q3: *Who is a friend of both Charlie and Dan?* (Path of length 2)

Q4: *Name two friends of Kate who are also friends with each other.* (Clique of size 3)

3.3 Graph Navigation Study

For the graph navigation study, we used a town graph in which places are connected by one-way roads (labeled directed edges). Again, this simple example was understandable by all participants. Figures 3 and 4 contain town graphs rendered in GSK and Excel respectively. Each row of the Excel table contains the name of a place followed by the number of roads leaving the place followed by each road and its destination, e.g., "Oak to Library."

We created six versions of the Town graph with different edges, each of which contained 12 nodes and 24 edges. All graphs used the same places and set of road names, one for each letter of the alphabet – Apple, Birch, Cherry, ..., X-ray. We randomly assigned node names to each GSK graph. We then created a random pairing of those names that we used to label the nodes in the corresponding Excel graph. We configured the Excel tables

so that the JAWS screen reader would read the row (place) name when navigating from cell to cell and turned off the reading of cell coordinates.

Participants were first trained to use GSK and Excel to navigate a town graph and given time to practice answering the navigation question listed below. Each participant was asked one question for each of the six graphs using both GSK and Excel for a total of 12 trials. Their response times and answers for each trial were recorded. An example of a navigation question is given below.

N: *Starting at the Park, take Birch, King, Pine. Where do you end up?*

3.4 Graph Creation Study

During the graph creation study, participants were taught to use GSK to create undirected graphs. They were then asked to create the four graphs listed below. The first two graphs were presented to them in tactile form and the last two were described for them. The time taken to create each graph was recorded.

G1: *Graph with 3 nodes and 3 edges laid out as an equilateral triangle.*

G2: *Graph with 4 nodes and 4 edges laid out as a square with one diagonal and a missing side.*

G3: *Graph with 4 nodes that are all connected to each other.*

G4: *Graph with 5 nodes and 5 edges.*

4. ANALYSIS AND RESULTS

4.1 Examination and Navigation Studies

All participants were able to use Excel and GSK to answer the examination and navigation questions in a timely and accurate manner. The mean response time ranged from 2 to 17 seconds for the relatively straightforward questions, Q1 and Q2, and from 10 to 55 seconds for the much more difficult questions, Q3 and Q4. The mean response times for the navigation question, N, fell between these two ranges with times ranging from 7 to 33 seconds. The overall accuracy rate was very high (99.3% using GSK, 97.6% with Excel). When calculating the mean response times, we omitted the response time for any question answered incorrectly from both the Excel and GSK calculations. The bar charts in Figures 5 – 9 provide comparisons of the Excel/GSK participant response times for each question.

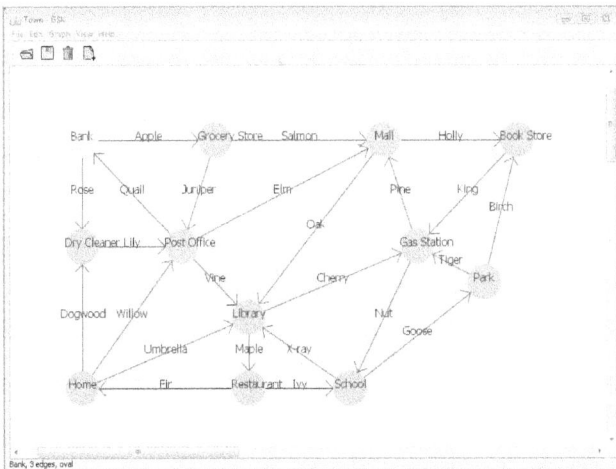

Figure 3. GSK Town Graph

	A	B	C	D	E
1	Bank	2	Apple to Grocery Store	Rose to Dry Cleaner	
2	Book Store	1	King to Gas Station		
3	Dry Cleaner	1	Lily to Post Office		
4	Gas Station	2	Nut to School	Pine to Mall	
5	Grocery Store	2	Salmon to Mall	Juniper to Post Office	
6	Home	3	Umbrella to Library	Willow to Post Office	Dogwood to Dry Cleaner
7	Library	2	Maple to Restaurant	Cherry to Gas Station	
8	Mall	2	Holly to Book Store	Oak to Library	
9	Park	2	Tiger to Gas Station	Birch to Book Store	
10	Post Office	3	Quail to Bank	Elm to Mall	Vine to Library
11	Restaurant	2	Fir to Home	Ivy to School	
12	School	2	X-ray to Library	Goose to Park	

Figure 4. Excel Town Graph

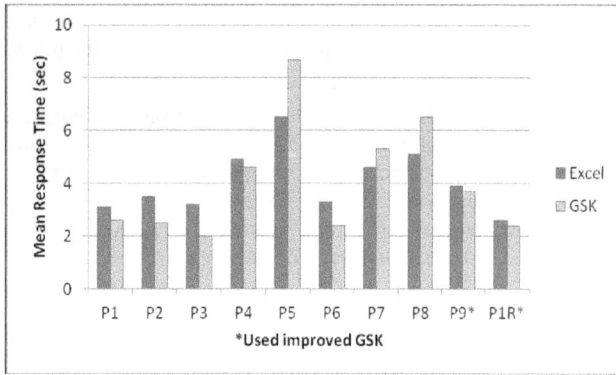

Figure 5. Examination Study Q1

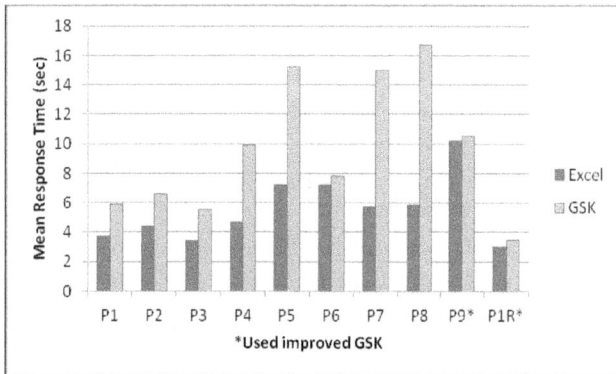

Figure 6. Examination Study Q2

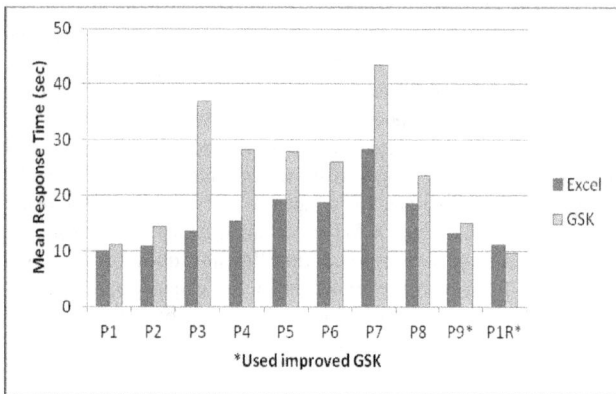

Figure 7. Examination Study Q3

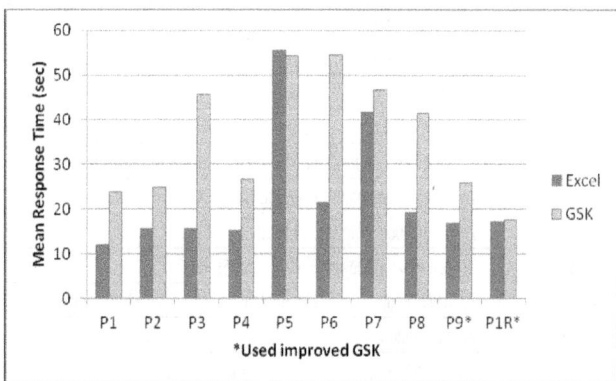

Figure 8. Examination Study Q4

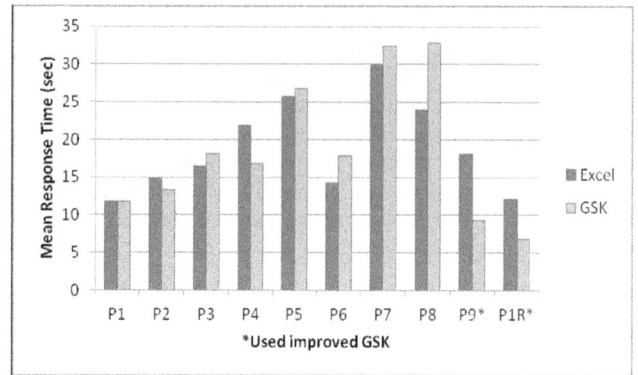

Figure 9. Navigation Study N

4.2 Creation Study

The participants were also successful in creating graphs using GSK. Participant P1, who had had no prior GSK experience, rendered all four creation study graphs perfectly, as shown in Figure 10, in less than 10 minutes. Figure 11 provides the response times for all study participants, who created the four graphs in total times ranging from 5 to 25 minutes.

To quantify the quality of the graphs, we awarded 1 point for each of the following items for each graph for a total of 5 points per graph:

a. Correct number of nodes

b. Correct number of edges

c. Correct edges

d. Correct/acceptable layout

   ▪ *Does the layout of G1 and G2 match that of the tactile graphs presented to the participant?*

   ▪ *Is the layout of G3 and G4 acceptable (reasonably proportioned, etc.)?*

e. Visually accessible (viewable by a sighted person)

   ▪ *Is there enough contrast between the foreground and background colors so that the node labels are visible?*

   ▪ *Are the nodes far enough apart so that the edges joining them are visible?*

   ▪ *Are individual edges visible (or are several nodes laid out in a line so as to render the edges between them indistinguishable)?*

Table 2 provides the individual graph scores and the total score for each participant. The average total score for the participants was 16.6 out of a possible 20. Most of the graphs (82.5%) were accurate in that they contained the correct number of nodes/edges and the correct edges. While we did not direct the participants to create visually accessible graphs, most of the graphs (70%) were viewable by a sighted person. Those that were not could easily be made so in the case of collaboration between a blind and sighted person. However, if a blind person were creating a graph to export as an image and include in a document, a visually inaccessible graph would be problematic. Detecting and reporting visual accessibility problems as well as options to automatically improve graph layouts are potential areas for future work.

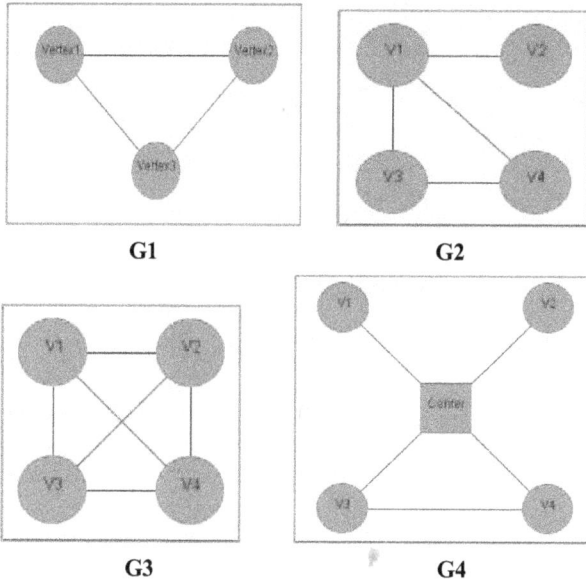

Figure 10. Creation Study graphs as rendered by P1

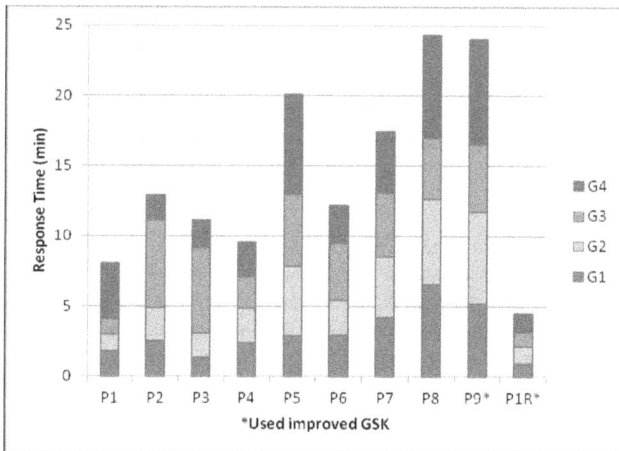

Figure 11. Creation Study

Table 2. Creation Study Scores (total(abcde) – see Sec 4.2)

	G1	G2	G3	G4	Total
P1	5(11111)	5(11111)	5(11111)	5(11111)	20
P2	4(11110)	5(11111)	5(11111)	5(11111)	19
P3	4(11110)	4(11110)	3(11100)	4(11110)	15
P4	5(11111)	5(11111)	5(11111)	5(11111)	20
P5	4(11101)	3(10011)	5(11111)	5(11111)	17
P6	5(11111)	5(11111)	5(11111)	5(11111)	20
P7	2(10001)	3(11001)	5(11111)	0(00000)	10
P8	2(10001)	3(10011)	4(11110)	5(11111)	14
P9	5(11111)	5(11111)	3(11100)	4(11110)	17
P1R	4(11011)	4(11110)	3(11100)	3(11100)	14

4.3 GSK vs. Excel

We had planned to do ten user studies, but after the first eight studies, the trends in terms of efficiency were clear. At that point we decided to analyze the data and attempt to improve the efficiency of GSK for the remaining two participants.

As appropriate for our within-subject design, we first calculated the difference between the Excel and GSK mean response times for each question for each of the first eight participants. We then analyzed the results using the Wilcoxon Signed-Rank Test rather than a paired t-test due to the non-normality of the differences. We found no significant difference between the Excel and GSK mean response times for questions Q1 and N. However, we found that the response times for Excel were significantly lower for Q2 ($p = .005$), Q3 ($p = .005$), and Q4 ($p = .001$).

These results are not surprising considering that most participants had had several years experience using Excel and no prior GSK experience. In addition, navigating the Excel tables required only the use of the arrow keys, which are located in close proximity on the keyboard. On the other hand, in addition to the arrow and escape keys needed to navigate the GSK graph, the CTRL+J ("jump to node") key combination followed by first letter navigation was used to place focus on a specific node; with more practice, these key combinations and sequences would likely become automatic. A number of participants remarked that the studies gave an advantage to Excel for two reasons. First, in the Excel Friends graph, the alphabetical listing of people, one for each letter of the alphabet, made it very easy to take shortcuts when navigating the table. Second, in the Excel Town graph, only the outgoing edges for each place were listed, whereas navigating the GSK Town graph required examining both incoming and outgoing edges.

4.4 GSK Improvements

To make GSK more efficient for blind users, we added an *advanced verbosity level* and *edge filtering,* and *simplified the edge navigation* as described in the following subsections. Participant P9 used the improved version of GSK and participant P1R repeated the study using the improved GSK. These participants used the *simplified edge navigation* throughout the user study and the *advanced verbosity level* for questions Q3, Q4, and N. They also used *edge filtering* for question N.

As shown in Figures 5 – 9 and Table 3, there was a marked improvement in their GSK response times as compared to Excel. In particular, the addition of edge filtering allowed these last two participants to answer the navigation question with GSK in about half the Excel time. We attribute the decrease in quality of the graphs created by P1R using the improved GSK, as shown in Table 2, to focusing on speed rather than attention to detail.

Table 3. Mean Response Time (sec)

Question	Original GSK (P1-P8)			Improved GSK (P9-P1R)		
	Excel	GSK	Diff	Excel	GSK	Diff
Q1	4.28	4.32	-0.04	3.25	3.05	0.20
Q2	5.26	10.32	-5.06	6.60	7.00	-0.40
Q3	16.81	26.42	-9.61	12.20	12.35	-0.15
Q4	24.60	39.79	-15.19	17.10	21.70	-4.60
N	19.84	21.24	-1.4	15.10	8.15	6.95

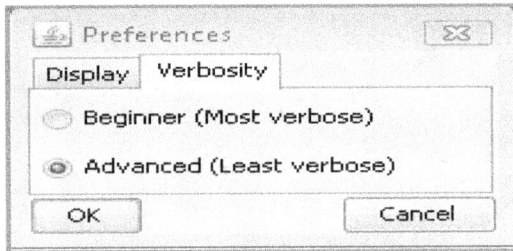

Figure 12. Verbosity Level Dialog

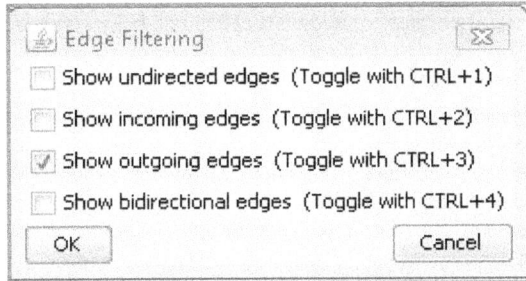

Figure 13. Edge Filtering Dialog

4.4.1 Beginner and Advanced Verbosity Levels

While the auditory cues heard by participants when using GSK provided more contextual detail than the Excel cues, they were quite verbose and often the most important information came last. For example, the auditory cues for a friends graph node and a town graph edge are "oval Amy, 4 edges" and "Outgoing edge Pine to oval Mall." Stefik, et al., recommend that auditory cues be short, "browsable," and give the most important information first [21]. We therefore decided to provide users with Beginner and Advanced Verbosity levels as shown in Figure 12. The Beginner level provides the more verbose auditory cues as described above. Using the Advanced level, the same cues are rendered as "Amy, 4 edges, oval" and "Pine, Mall, Outgoing, oval," thus allowing screen reader users to more quickly access the necessary information.

4.4.2 Edge Filtering

During the navigation study, only the outgoing edges for a node were important, but participants had to examine both the incoming and outgoing edges for each place. We added an Edge Filtering dialog, as shown in Figure 13, that allows users to select the type(s) of edges (undirected, incoming, outgoing, bidirectional) that receive focus during keyboard navigation with the left/right arrow keys. In this way, it is possible to navigate a graph using only the type(s) of edges that make sense for the problem at hand.

4.4.3 Simplified Edge Navigation

In the original GSK interface, the left arrow key placed focus on the selected node's "first" edge and the right arrow key was then used to navigate to its other edges. Likewise, the right arrow key placed focus on a node's "last" edge and the left arrow key was used to navigate to the other edges. We realized that this "context switch" was inefficient and simplified the navigation scheme by eliminating it. In the improved GSK, whenever focus is on a node, subsequent presses of the left arrow key moves focus from edge to edge as does the right arrow key, but in the opposite direction.

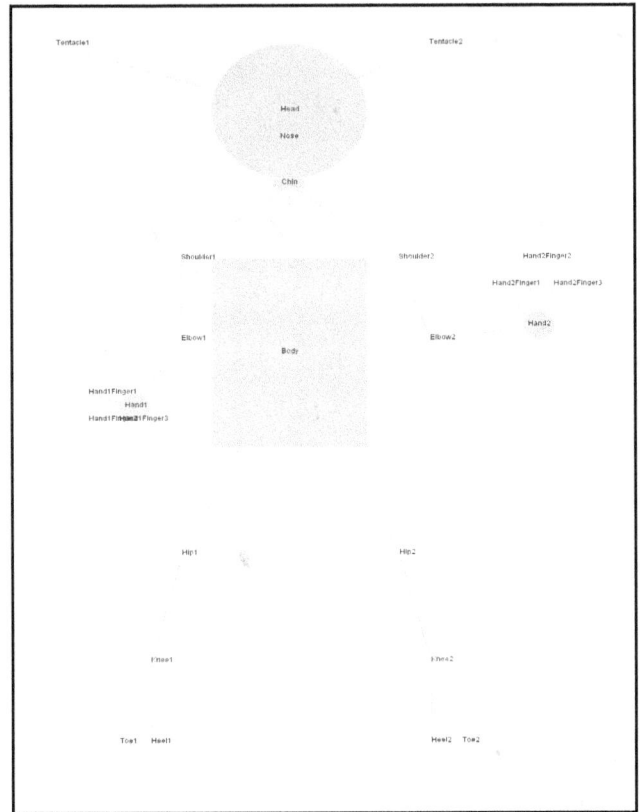

Figure 14. Alien created by a blind user with GSK

5. CONCLUSIONS AND FUTURE WORK

Through our user study, we found that GSK was effective in allowing blind users to examine, navigate, and create graphs in a reasonable amount of time. In the first two studies, we controlled for memory by having participants use a different graph for each question. In normal situations, blind users would typically work with the same graph and be able to build up a mental model of the graph. The second author has found that using GSK helps him more easily memorize which nodes are adjacent to one another and this would likely extend to other blind users as well.

We believe GSK has the potential to be very helpful to blind people for creating and working with graphs and other two-dimensional diagrams. Immediately after the user study, one blind participant used GSK to create the drawing of an alien shown in Figure 14. His sighted friend has since used GSK to create Dungeons and Dragons maps to share with him. Listed below are comments from the user study participants:

GSK has an advantage over Excel in that it is good for showing connections, especially involving towns, buildings, walls and infrastructures. I like how I can follow a path from one place to another and keep following the path.

I started to take an easy gen ed math course and switched to a different course because most of the course centered around graph theory. If I had stayed in that course, this program (GSK) would have helped me.

It's easier to edit your work (using GSK) than using a raised line drawing kit and make revisions or minor changes. You can save your work and make multiple copies for classmates and professors.

I can now make graphs that are attractive and presentable.

It makes me a lot more hopeful about producing combinatorial graphs in a visually appealing manner.

Using GSK to represent and work with graphs has advantages over Excel in that it is easier to connect things, if you are a visual learner. GSK is more fun, like "connect the dots," while Excel is just a list.

GSK also helps meet the need for accessible graph tools that has been articulated by the blind programming community [16]. Our introduction of GSK to the program-1: Visually Impaired discussion list in response to a request for accessible mind-mapping tools was met with interest by blind users around the world [18, 19]. One blind analyst/programmer commented, "My initial thoughts about how this tool might help me is in my communication with sighted co-workers. I can see it would be a very good tool for me to make graphs for them to view or print and for them to generate in a form I can then explore." [19]

We hope GSK will serve as a useful tool for both blind and sighted users alike and one that allows them to collaborate more easily. To that end, we plan to investigate the appeal of GSK for sighted users and make any necessary improvements. Based on the results of our user study and suggestions by blind users, we are also considering the following enhancements to GSK:

Graph Checker Creating visually accessible and appealing graphs could be facilitated by a Graph Checker option that lists potential problems with the visual layout of a graph -- node labels that are indistinguishable from the node color or that extend beyond the node itself, isolated nodes, excessive numbers of edge crossings, poorly proportioned layouts, etc. A user could then choose to automatically correct some or all of the problems, perhaps through the incorporation of graph drawing algorithms.

Annotation Capability The ability to annotate nodes or subgraphs, mark a node as the home or root node, and mark nodes as having been visited may be helpful for examining and navigating graphs.

Professional Presentation GSK is intended as a simple graph sketching tool in which the user controls the layout. Improved layout and/or presentation could potentially by obtained by use the Graphvis – GraphVisualization Software [7, 10] or another professional tool. By exporting a GSK graph in the tool format, the tool could then be used to create an improved visual representation.

Graph Examination Graphs created by inaccessible tools could be converted into GSK format, which would allow blind users to examine them.

Extension to Other Domains Currently GSK allows users to draw undirected and directed graphs with self-loops and/or single edges between nodes. Available nodes shapes include rectangles, ovals, and those pertaining to automata theory (state, start state, accepting state, accepting start state). Extending GSK to other domains by including entity relationship diagrams, UML class and other diagrams, resource-allocation graphs, etc., as well as providing additional general node shapes would allow it to serve more purposes.

Tactile Representation By leveraging techniques employed by the Tactile Graphics Assistant (TGA) [12, 15], Braille-labeled textured graphs could be created and output to a Braille embosser, thus providing tactile representations of graphs.

6. ACKNOWLEDGMENTS

We would like to thank Dr. Richard Ladner for the AccessComputing mini-grant that supported this work via NSF Award #CNS-1042260.

7. REFERENCES

[1] Balik, S.P. 2014. *Combinatorial Graph Creation and Navigation for Blind People.* Ph.D. Thesis, North Carolina State University, Raleigh, North Carolina. Retrieved July 3, 2014 from http://www.lib.ncsu.edu/resolver/1840.16/9504

[2] Balik, S.P., Mealin, S.P., Stallmann, M. F. and Rodman, R.D. 2013. GSK: universally accessible graph sketching. In *Proceeding of the 44th ACM technical symposium on Computer science education* (SIGCSE '13). ACM, New York, NY, USA, 221-226. DOI=10.1145/2445196.2445266 http://doi.acm.org/10.1145/2445196.2445266

[3] Blenkhorn, P. and Evans, D. G. 1998. Using speech and touch to enable blind people to access schematic diagrams. *J. Netw. Comput. Appl.* 21, 1 (January 1998), 17-29. DOI=10.1006/jnca.1998.0060 http://dx.doi.org/10.1006/jnca.1998.0060

[4] Brown, A., Pettifer, S. and Stevens, R. 2003. Evaluation of a non-visual molecule browser. In *Proceedings of the 6th international ACM SIGACCESS conference on Computers and accessibility* (Assets '04). ACM, New York, NY, USA, 40-47. DOI=10.1145/1028630.1028639 http://doi.acm.org/10.1145/1028630.1028639

[5] Burgstahler, S., and Cory, R. (2008). *Universal design in higher education: From principles to practice.* Cambridge, Mass: Harvard Education Press.

[6] Calder, M., Cohen, R. F., Lanzoni, J. and Xu, Y. 2006. PLUMB: an interface for users who are blind to display, create, and modify graphs. In *Proceedings of the 8th international ACM SIGACCESS conference on Computers and accessibility* (Assets '06). ACM, New York, NY, USA, 263-264. DOI=10.1145/1168987.1169046 http://doi.acm.org/10.1145/1168987.1169046

[7] Ganser, E.R. and North, S.C. 2000. An open graph visualization system and its applications to software engineering. *Softw. Pract. Exper.* 30, 11 (September 2000), 1203-1233. DOI=10.1002/1097-024X(200009)30:11<1203::AID-SPE338>3.3.CO;2-E http://dx.doi.org/10.1002/1097-024X(200009)30:11<1203::AID-SPE338>3.3.CO;2-E

[8] Giudice, N.A., Palani, H. P., Brenner, E., and Kramer, K. M. 2012. Learning non-visual graphical information using a touch-based vibro-audio interface. In *Proceedings of the 14th international ACM SIGACCESS conference on Computers and accessibility* (ASSETS '12). ACM, New

York, NY, USA, 103-110. DOI=10.1145/2384916.2384935
http://doi.acm.org/10.1145/2384916.2384935

[9] Goncu, C. and Marriott, K. 2011. GraVVITAS: generic multi-touch presentation of accessible graphics. In *Proceedings of the 13th IFIP TC 13 international conference on Human-computer interaction - Volume Part I* (INTERACT'11), Pedro Campos, Nuno Nunes, Nicholas Graham, Joaquim Jorge, and Philippe Palanque (Eds.), Vol. Part I. Springer-Verlag, Berlin, Heidelberg, 30-48.

[10] Graphvis – graph visualization software. Retrieved September 28, 2013 from http://www.graphviz.org/

[11] Jay, C., Lunn, D. and Michailidou, E. (2008). End user evaluations. In Simon Harper and Yeliz Yesilada, editors, *Web accessibility: a foundation for research*. Springer, London, UK, 107-126.

[12] Jayant, C., Renzelmann, M., Wen, D., Krisnandi, S., Ladner, R., and Comden, D. 2007. Automated tactile graphics translation: in the field. In *Proceedings of the 9th international ACM SIGACCESS conference on Computers and accessibility* (Assets '07). ACM, New York, NY, USA, 75-82. DOI=10.1145/1296843.1296858
http://doi.acm.org/10.1145/1296843.1296858

[13] Kennel, A. R. 1996. Audiograf: a diagram-reader for the blind. In *Proceedings of the second annual ACM conference on Assistive technologies* (Assets '96). ACM, New York, NY, USA, 51-56. DOI=10.1145/228347.228357
http://doi.acm.org/10.1145/228347.228357

[14] King, A., Blenkhorn, P., Crombie, D., Dijkstra, S., Evans, D.G., and Wood, J. Presenting UML Software Engineering Diagrams to Blind People. In *Proceedings of ICCHP*. 2004, 522-529.

[15] Ladner, R.E, Ivory, M.Y., Rao, R., Burgstahler, S., Comden, D., Hahn, S., Renzelmann, M., Krisnandi, S., Ramasamy, M., Slabosky, B., Martin, A., Lacenski, A., Olsen, S., and Groce, D. 2005. Automating tactile graphics translation. In *Proceedings of the 7th international ACM SIGACCESS conference on Computers and accessibility* (Assets '05). ACM, New York, NY, USA, 150-157. DOI=10.1145/1090785.1090814
http://doi.acm.org/10.1145/1090785.1090814

[16] Mailing list archive for programmingblind. Retrieved March 21, 2014 from http://www.freelists.org/archive/programmingblind/

[17] Miller, D. 2009. *Can we work together?* Ph.D. Thesis, University of North Carolina at Chapel Hill, Chapel Hill, North Carolina. Retrieved November 9, 2012 from http://search.lib.unc.edu/search?R=UNCb5970444

[18] Program-l: V.I. programmers discussion list. Retrieved March 21, 2014 from http://www.freelists.org/list/program-l

[19] Ray, M. [program-l] mind-mapping tools. Personal communication, 2013.

[20] Rosen, K.H. (2002). *Discrete mathematics and its applications*, 5th edition. McGraw-Hill Higher Education, New York, N.Y, USA, 541.

[21] Stefik, A.M., Hundhausen, C. and Smith, D.. 2011. On the design of an educational infrastructure for the blind and visually impaired in computer science. In *Proceedings of the 42nd ACM technical symposium on Computer science education* (SIGCSE '11). ACM, New York, NY, USA, 571-576. DOI=10.1145/1953163.1953323
http://doi.acm.org/10.1145/1953163.1953323

[22] Walker, B.N. and Mauney, L.M. 2010. Universal Design of Auditory Graphs: A Comparison of Sonification Mappings for Visually Impaired and Sighted Listeners. *ACM Trans. Access. Comput.* 2, 3, Article 12 (March 2010), 16 pages. DOI=10.1145/1714458.1714459
http://doi.acm.org/10.1145/1714458.1714459

Usability Issues with 3D User Interfaces for Adolescents with High Functioning Autism

Chao Mei
Department of Computer Science
University of Texas at San Antonio
One UTSA Circle
San Antonio, TX, USA 78249-0667
+1 (210) 872-8618
meichaomc@gmail.com

Lee Mason
Interdisciplinary Learning & Teaching
University of Texas at San Antonio
One UTSA Circle
San Antonio, TX, USA 78249-0667
+1 (210) 458-4524
lee.mason@utsa.edu

John Quarles
Department of Computer Science
University of Texas at San Antonio
One UTSA Circle
San Antonio, TX, USA 78249-0667
+1 (210) 458-7433
jpq@cs.utsa.edu

ABSTRACT

Most literature on the usability of 3D user interfaces (3DUI) in ASD therapy consists of a series of case studies based on games for rehabilitation. These games have been largely successful. However, it is difficult to generalize the results of these specific case studies. The usability of atomic 3DUI interactions (e.g., rotation, translation) with respect to adolescents with ASD has not yet been evaluated. Adolescents with ASD often have enhanced spatial cognitive abilities and less efficient hand-eye coordination. Our main research question is "Do adolescents with ASD perform 3DUI tasks differently than typically developed adolescents and if so, why?" To address this question, we present a matched pair user study including adolescents without ASD (i.e. as controls) paired with adolescents who had a high ASD severity score, but were still considered high functioning. Our results give insight into the usability of 3DUI for adolescents with ASD and provide generalizable guidelines for future 3DUI applications for children with autism.

Categories and Subject Descriptors

H.5.2 [**Information Interfaces and Presentation**]: User Interfaces – *Input devices and strategies, Evaluation/methodology.*

General Terms

Experimentation, Human Factors.

Keywords

3D User Interfaces; Autism Spectrum Disorder; User Studies.

1. INTRODUCTION

Autism spectrum disorder (ASD) is a neurodevelopmental disorder marked by impaired social communication and social interaction accompanied by atypical patterns of behavior and interest [1]. According to the Centers for Disease Control and Prevention (CDC), the prevalence of ASD in the United State has

grown from 1 case per 150 children to 1 case per 68 children from the year 2000 to 2010. Researchers have started to spend efforts on understanding, identifying and treating ASD. As part of this effort, Virtual Reality (VR) research has shown potential benefits, such as improving the activities of daily living (e.g., crossing the street in a 3D virtual city [12]). In the past, VR technology was associated with a very high price due to the expensive devices. For example, a 3D immersive display such as Head Mount Display (HMD) could cost twenty thousand dollars; optical tracking systems like Vicon cost one hundred thousand dollars. This constrained the application of VR technology to ASD therapy in rehabilitation clinics. Today, however, off the shelf and low cost VR devices are becoming more common and are affordable enough for many users to have VR systems in their homes. HMDs, like the Oculus Rift, only cost several hundred dollars; motion-tracking systems, such as Razer Hydra or Microsoft Kinect, cost no more than 150 dollars. Although VR technologies are becoming more affordable for the general use of VR applications, their usability and accessibility problems for the ASD population still remain to be formally evaluated and addressed.

In this paper, we focus on one particular aspect of VR systems, 3D User Interfaces (3DUI). Most literature on the usability of 3DUI applications in autism therapy consists of a series of case studies based on games for rehabilitation. These games have been largely successful [5, 12, 16]. For example, children with ASD improved their road safety skills after practicing with a unique driving VR game [5]. However, due to the specificity of ASD therapy games, it is difficult to generalize results to future 3DUI applications for children with ASD. The general usability of atomic 3DUI interactions (e.g., rotation, translation) with respect to adolescents with or without ASD has not yet been evaluated. Therefore we aim to investigate this issue and provide guidelines to make the 3DUI and VR based ASD intervention applications more accessible and beneficial in therapy.

Specifically, our main research question is "Do adolescents with ASD perform 3DUI tasks differently than typically developed (TD) adolescents and if so, why?" To address this question, we present a matched pair user study including adolescents without autism (i.e. as controls) paired with adolescents who had a high ASD severity score, but were still considered as high functioning (i.e., with an IQ equal or above average). Specifically, we investigate how children with autism perform basic 3DUI interaction tasks, such as rotation and translation. Our study consists of two simple tasks: 1) rotating a virtual object and making it face the same perspective as the target object, and 2) in a similar environment, translating a virtual object to the same relative position as the target object in its 3D space. The accuracy and task finishing time were recorded as the performance measurements. We also assessed their spatial abilities through written tests (i.e., Embedded Figures [24], Mental Rotation [3, 21]). We conducted the study with off-the-shelf 3DUI gaming devices instead of lab devices to make the study results more applicable to future at-home use cases, such as ASD therapy and 3D games. Based on these results we give insight from the usability and accessibility of 3DUIs for children with ASD, and suggest generalizable guidelines for future design of 3DUI applications for this population.

2. BACKGROUND
2.1 3D User Interfaces

For TD adults, atomic 3D user interface tasks, such as translation and rotation, have been extensively studied. The results of these studies can help with improving the design of 3D User Interfaces for general users in terms of usability, i.e., efficiency and ease of use. Some of this research focused on how the input devices could influence the usability. For example, Zhai et al. [25] reported an object orienting test in 3D space. In this test, users were equipped with different 6 degrees of freedom (6-DOF) input devices that enabled the freedom of inputting rotation and translation over all three axes in 3D space. Subjects with a finger ball as input device performed better than the users equipped with an electronic glove as input device. The finger ball is primarily controlled by the muscles and joints in the fingers, wrist, elbow, and shoulder. When using the glove, all translation and rotation operations are carried out by the user's shoulder, elbow and wrist. The improvement of performance was due to the fine, smaller muscle groups and joints in finger ball input. Hinckley et al. [13] discussed the effects the input device's shape had over the performance of 3D object rotation tasks, and suggested the device should afford some tactile feedback. Ware et al. [22] reported how end-to-end latency would affect the efficiency of 3D interaction.

3D interaction techniques have been developed to enable more effective methods of interaction. For instance, Poupyrev et al. [19] used non-isomorphic 3D rotational techniques, which changed the mapping from input device to output display (e.g. when the user rotates 30 degree with the controller in real world, a rotation of more than 30 degree may occur on the virtual object on screen) and made the performance 13% faster. Bowman et al [7] evaluated the advantages of a hybrid interaction technique combining other techniques such as non-isomorphic translation (translation with amplified scale), arm-extension, etc. LaViola et al. [17] further suggested that a scaling factor of 3 is the preferable amplification coefficient in a surround screen. From input device to various interaction techniques, 3DUI interaction has been studied in detail for general adult users. Unfortunately, however, there are minimal such studies conducted with ASD populations.

2.2 ASD spatial cognition

The ability of spatial cognition may influence the task performance with 3D user interfaces. This hypothesis is motivated by the literature with respect to typically developed adults. According to [18] [6], through the process of spatial cognition, typically developed adults can effectively combine visuospatial elements, perform and simulate mental transformations and effectively engage in spatial reasoning and problem solving. According to Hinckley et al. [13], the ability of subjects to process spatial information does have an impact on the 3DUI performance. For example, superior ability of spatial cognition could potentially lead to a better performance on 3D tasks.

There is literature showing that the some children with ASD have superior abilities in spatial cognition, compared to children with typical development. Empirical evidence, such as preserved or superior visual spatial abilities [18], superior recognition memory of topographical landmarks [6] and the ability to detect minimal positional changes in the environment [23], have been shown for the ASD population. These results suggest that visuospatial abilities are sometimes enhanced among persons with ASD. In addition, Caron et al. [8] performed a systematic assessment and found that individuals with high functioning autism showed superior performance in tasks involving maps, superior accuracy in ability to recall a path with graphic cues, and shorter learning times in a map learning task. In [20], the authors reported superiority of persons with ASD in visual search tasks. Intuitively, the ASD population may potentially benefit from such superior abilities, which could also improve their task performance with 3D user interfaces.

On the other hand, Falter et al. [11] have also shown that children with ASD performed worse on targeting tasks (target stimuli appearing on the screen in 2D space by moving the mouse cursor) than typically-developing children. In addition, the performance of 3D interface interaction is also related to subject's hand-eye coordination [17]. The ASD population has shown less efficient eye-hand coordination in visual detection tasks [10]. These facts may negatively affect their interactions with 3DUI. However, we could still expect the ASD group to excel in 3D tasks, since inferior performances in 2D tasks may be compensated by superior spatial abilities when conducting 3D tasks. Thus, it is unclear whether ASD populations' 3DUI performance will be influenced more substantially by spatial abilities or deficits in hand-eye-coordination. This remains an open question, which we aim to address in our study.

2.3 VR systems for ASD treatment

Although it is difficult to find basic 3DUI studies on atomic interactions (e.g., translation, rotation) conducted with the ASD population, there are several related studies such as [4] using a Virtual Reality (VR) Environment to help or study ASD populations with respect to specific high level tasks. For example, Josman et al. [16] suggest VR may be used for safely teaching children with ASD street-crossing skills due to its fidelity to real life simulations. These works employed VR mostly due to their ability to simulate real world scenarios in a carefully controlled and safe environment, as well as controlled stimuli presentation, objectivity and consistency, and gaming factors to motivate for task completion [4]. Most of these systems employed 3D user interfaces. Bian et al. [5] described a driving simulator which conducted driver training for children with ASD in a 3D virtual city. Bekeal et al. [4] studied children with autism's responses to facial expressions by presenting different facial expressions through a 3D virtual human. Although these systems were successful, the studies of basic 3D interaction should also be conducted on the ASD population in order to further improve and guide the development of more usable VR autism therapy systems.

3. OUR PROPOSED CONTRIBUTIONS

The literature that focuses on the basic atomic 3DUI interactions is mostly focused on typically developed adult users. Thus it is unknown how persons with ASD interact with 3DUIs. The main goal of our research is to find out the main factors of 3DUIs that have an impact on usability for adolescents with ASD. Specifically, this research provides:

- Quantitative and qualitative analyses of how ASD affects adolescents performing atomic 3DUI interaction tasks.

- Insights into the usability and accessibility of 3DUI for adolescents with ASD, with respect to the role of spatial ability and hand-eye coordination.

- Generalizable guidelines for designing future 3DUI applications for adolescents with ASD.

4. STUDY DESIGN

Our study (UTSA IRB# 14-003) had two main goals: 1) investigating the performance of adolescents with ASD in basic 3D interaction tasks, such as rotation and translation, and 2) understanding how ASD children perform these tasks differently than typically developing children as a control group. We conducted a matched pair user study including TD participants paired with participants who scored greater than 71 in an autism severity test (GARS-3).

Figure 1. Example of the rotation task.

Figure 2. Example of the translation task.

We designed the present experiment after the experiments by LaViola et al. [11], which investigated 3DUI usability on TD adults. Specifically, the tasks of our study included: 1. Rotating the virtual object shown on the left side of a screen to make its perspective match the target object that is shown on the right side of the screen. 2. Translating the virtual object on the left side of a screen to make its position match the target object that is shown on the right side of the screen. The system computed and logged participants' performance data (e.g., orientation error, time). We used a 3d model of a house as the virtual object to be controlled.

The target is the identical model but shown in different orientation. Figures 1 and 2 show the examples of rotation and translation tasks respectively.

Participants could rotate/translate the virtual house by holding down a button and rotating/translating the controller. Thus, ratcheting interaction, a standard approach to 3D object manipulation, was enabled. Specifically, by releasing the button participants could adjust the controller's orientation without influence on the virtual house, and then continue controlling the virtual house by holding the button again. Ratcheting was important because participants may reach the physical limit of their hand and wrist while conducting rotation/translation.

Because isomorphic rotation is the most natural type of rotation in terms of interaction in the physical world [17], we used only isomorphic mappings. E.g., when the user rotated the controller 30 degrees, a rotation of exactly 30 degrees occurred on the virtual object on screen.

To enable isomorphic translation, we set the translation scale according to the actual size of the screen. E.g., when the user moved the controller to the right by 3 inches, the virtual object was translated to the right by 3 inches on the screen. Thus, the coordinate systems of the real world and the virtual world were consistent.

4.1 Hypotheses

Previous studies on adolescents with ASD have yielded conflicting results on spatial abilities and in hand-eye coordination. Falter et al. [11] showed that a group with ASD performed better overall in the mental rotation tasks as compared to a typically developed group. It was also reported that adolescents with ASD showed worse performance on hand-eye coordination tasks than typically developing adolescents [10]. These factors could potentially have confounded influences on 3DUI performance.

However, there is no previous work that has investigated how persons with ASD perform basic interactions with 3DUI. Intuitively, although persons with ASD have worse hand-eye coordination, it could potentially be compensated by their superior spatial ability, if such ability is present. On the other hand, we know that in typically developed persons, increased spatial ability often translates to increased performance with 3DUI [9].

Specifically, our null hypotheses were:

$H0_1$: There will be no differences in 3DUI performance for TD and ASD populations.

$H0_2$: In 3DUI rotation and translation tasks, similar to TD users, ASD users' spatial abilities will correlate to task performance and interaction efficiency.

4.2 Participants

20 participants were recruited with the help of local support groups, research institutes and non-profit ASD support organization from the state of Texas, with ages ranging from 9 to 18 years. We recruited participants at adolescent ages since adolescence is an important time to develop life skills (e.g. driving, cooking) that can be potentially trained with 3DUI. 10 participants had been diagnosed with ASD, and they all had GARS-3 scores of greater than 71. To eliminate the gender influence as a variable and the great gender disparity incidence

rate of autism between male and female, in this current study, we did not recruit any female participants with ASD. The other 10 participants in the control group were typically developed male adolescents, who were each matched with an ASD subject based on age (+ or − 1 year). All participants reported some prior experience and familiarity playing video games, but none of them had prior experience of using 6 Degrees of Freedom (DOF) 3DUI input devices.

To be included in the study, participants with ASD had to score greater than 71 in the Gilliam Autism Rating Scale-3 (GARS-3) test. The GARS-3 [15] is used in identifying and estimating the severity of autism in participants. GARS-3 is based on the Diagnostic and Statistical Manual of Mental Disorders, 5th Edition (DSM-5) [2]. The American Psychological Association (APA) has adopted these criteria for ASD diagnoses. The GARS-3 consists of 56 questions that describe the characteristic behaviors of persons with autism. In this research, GARS-3 standard scores were used to group the participants. From their reports and our observation, these participants did not have any other disability that would limit understanding of or performance of the study tasks.

4.3 The Study Environment

The study was conducted in an indoor lab. We tried to avoid as much distraction as possible by providing each individual a quiet environment, where only the experimenter, the participant, and the participant's guardian were present. The virtual objects were shown on a 17' laptop screen. The participants sat behind a table as they manipulated the input devices.

4.4 Equipment

In the study, users interacted with the virtual objects through a magnetic motion sensing system - Razer Hydra. It provides 6 degree of freedom (6-DOF) tracking (i.e., position and orientation). By manipulating the controller, users move virtual objects and view the real time movements on the laptop screen. We employed the off-shelf device Razer Hydra instead of a higher-end tracking system for several reasons. First, the Hydra effectively provides the accuracy down to a millimeter and a millidegree. The latency of the system is also imperceptibly low. Most importantly, we aimed to use a system that could actually exist in a user's home. An off the shelf product like Razer Hydra is much more likely to be used in the home, based on price, and ease of installation, calibration, and application. Therefore, study results based on the Razer Hydra are more generalizable to home use and therapy. Figure 3 shows a user operating the controller.

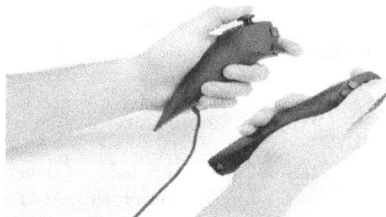

Figure 3. Razer Hydra Controller.

4.5 Procedure

The study evaluated the performance of ASD participants interacting with 3DUIs. Participants performed two types of tasks:

1) rotation and 2) translation. They were asked to finish the tasks by controlling (rotating in first session, translating in second session) the virtual object shown on the left side of a screen to make it match the target object that is shown on the right side of the screen (e.g., see Figures 1 and 2). We told each participant that both time and accuracy of their performance were equally important. We used a 3d model of a house as the virtual object to be controlled since it is a familiar object that could be seen in daily life and has sufficient depth cues to perform the tasks. The target is the identical model but shown in either a different orientation or position.

Each session (rotating or translating) included 20 trials. In each trial, the orientation or position of both the target object and the object controlled by the users were randomly generated but constant across all users. The order of the trials presented to each participant was also randomly generated in order to avoid ordering confounds in the study. Before each session, participants practiced with sample questions till they felt comfortable with the controller. The setting of the rotation task was similar to [17], since this design has been shown to effectively evaluate the performance of a general group of TD people. We extended this study to the ASD population, and further extended the investigation by including a translation task in order to more broadly investigate this population's performance with 3DUIs.

After 3D interaction sessions, the spatial ability of the participant was assessed by mental rotation [3] and embedded figure [14] tests. There are 20 and 35 questions in the mental rotation and embedded figures tests, respectively. We asked the participant to write down answers on an answer sheet in order to avoid including the computer operation time into the problem solving. Lastly, a short interview was performed with each participant. The total duration of the study was about one and a half hours per participant, including study and break time.

4.6 Measurements

4.6.1 Demographics

Age: Age of the participant (year), range 9 -18

GARS-3 score (ASD group only): ASD severity score, range 0-174

4.6.2 Spatial Ability

We assessed the spatial abilities of the two groups by comparing them on the Embedded Figures scores and Mental Rotation scores.

Embedded Figures (EF) test score: Range 0-35

Mental Rotation (MR) test score: Range 0-20

Time for EF test: Time spend on solving 35 embedded figures multiple-choice questions.

Time for MR test: Time spend on solving 20 mental rotation multiple choice questions

4.6.3 Task Performance

Time: Time spent on solving the rotation/translation question (sec.)

Rotation error is the final difference of the quaternion of the left and right virtual objects (degree)

Translation error is the location distance of the left and right virtual objects.

Number of Operations: The number of button presses was logged to determine how many independent translation/rotation changes were made.

Average Operation Time: Average time elapsed while a button was held down (sec.)

Total Operation time: Total time holding down the button (sec.)

Total Idle time: The amount of time that no buttons were pressed (sec.)

Total Translation distances and average translation speed: The summation of the input device's location change of each frame (in virtual coordinate), the speed was calculated by dividing the distance by the *operation time*.

Total Rotation angle and average rotation speed: The summation of the device's Euler angle change of each frame on each axis (in degree). The speed was calculated by dividing the angle by the *operation time*.

In order to look into their task performance, on each of the questions, we first compared the Translation and Rotation error and the total time spent solving the problem. Since some questions may have been more difficult than others, we also compared the *number of operations* and *average operation time* between the groups. Additionally, in order to address the differences we found, we also compared the *idle time* and *total operation time* for each question. For each of the questions that yielded significant differences on any of the above data, we took steps to investigate the likely causes for the differences, such as the *total rotation angle, average rotation speed, total translation distance, and average translation speed*.

4.6.4 Post-test interview:
At the end of the study, the participant was given a short interview regarding their experience of interacting with the 3DUI. The interview consisted of open-ended questions:

1. What is the strategy you used to complete the rotation and translation task?

2. Would you perform better if you were actually manipulating a real object rather than a virtual object?

5. RESULTS
Analysis justification: We performed paired-T tests to compare the ASD and TD groups' numerical data (e.g., task performance metrics), using Bonferroni correction where appropriate. When significant differences were found, we performed Pearson correlations to investigate the relationship between of spatial ability and task performance.

5.1 Rotation Task
For the measurement of time, we found significant differences on questions nos. 10, 13 and 15. As shown in Table 1, the participants with ASD spent significantly ($p < 0.05$) more time on each of these three questions than the TD participants. Figure 4 shows the distribution of the time performance of these three questions for the two groups.

Table 1. Significant differences between ASD and TD on time in the rotation task.

Question	Mean	Cohen's d	t	df	Sig. (2-tailed)
10-ASD	26.65				
10-TD	15.72	0.89	2.83	9	0.019
13-ASD	33.42				
13-TD	16.32	1.19	3.78	9	0.004
15-ASD	20.96				
15-TD	13.24	0.73	2.33	9	0.044

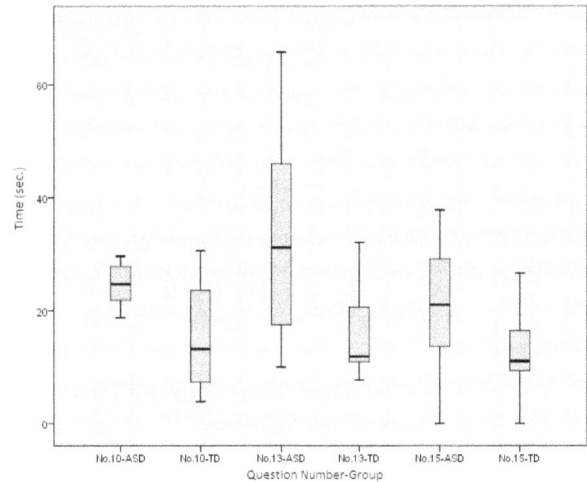

Figure 4. The distributions of the time performance across groups on rotation questions 10, 13 and 15.

To better understand how users divided their time during the tasks, we split time performance into two parts (i.e., total operation time and total idle time). We analyzed these two measurements and found ASD group displayed significantly longer total idle time on question no. 13 ($p < 0.05$), and significantly longer total operation time on question nos. 6, 10, 13 and 15 ($p < 0.05$).

On each of the rotation questions, the number of button presses and the average operation time were also tested. For the average operation time, we did not find any significant differences. However, on questions 4 and 10, the number of operations for participants in the ASD group (mean = 9.5, 8.8) was significantly more ($p < 0.05$) than participants in the TD group (mean = 5.4, 5.8).

For the questions in which we found significant differences from the above tests, we also analyzed total translation distances, average translation speed, total rotation angle and average rotation speed. On question 13, the rotation speed around the Z-axis was significantly lower for the ASD group ($p < 0.05$). For a clear view of the significant differences found in the rotation tasks, see Table 2.

We did not find any significant differences in rotation error between ASD and TD groups.

Table 2. Rotation tasks that yielded significant differences between TD and ASD groups.

	4	6	10	13	15
Longer Time-ASD			✔	✔	✔
Longer Total Idle Time-ASD				✔	
Longer Total Operation Time-ASD		✔	✔	✔	✔
Higher Number of Operations-ASD	✔		✔		
Lower Rotation Speed-ASD				✔	

5.2 Translation Task

For time performances, we found significant differences on question nos. 4 and 11. As shown in Table 3, the duration of time that participants in the ASD group spent on each of the 2 questions were significantly greater (p < 0.05) than participants in the TD group. Figure 5 shows the distribution of the time performance on the two questions across groups. We split the translation time performance into total operation time and total idle time to better understand how participant divided their time. On translation questions, we found a significant difference in time performance; The ASD group spent significantly more time (p < 0.05) for both total idle time and total operation time as compared to the TD group.

Table 3. Significant differences between ASD and TD on time in the translation tasks.

Question	Mean	Cohen's d	t	df	Sig. (2-tailed)
4-ASD	16.23				
4-TD	7.48	1.0737226	3.395	9	0.008
11-ASD	16.43				
11-TD	5.5	1.213441	3.837	9	0.004

The number of operations and the average operation time spent on each question were also analyzed. On question nos. 1, 5, 8 and 14, the number of operations for participants in the ASD group was significantly higher (p < 0.05) than the number for participants in the TD group.

Surprisingly, for the average operation time we found significantly shorter times for the ASD group on only one of the questions: 12. The mean value for ASD and TD groups were 4.2 and 7.2, respectively.

In addition, we found significant differences on translation question 11. Interestingly, the total rotated angle on each of the axes was significantly greater for the ASD group, even though the translation task required no rotation to complete it. For a clear view of those significant differences found in translation tasks, see Table 4.

For translation error, we did not find significant differences between the two groups.

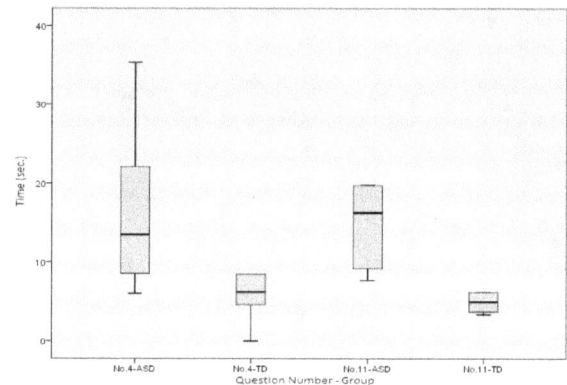

Figure 5. The distributions of the time performance across groups on translation questions 10, 13 and 15.

Table 4. Translation tasks that were found with significant differences.

	1	4	5	8	11	12	14
Longer Time-ASD		✔			✔		
Longer Total Idle Time-ASD		✔			✔		
Longer Total Operation Time-ASD		✔			✔		
Higher Number of Operations-ASD	✔		✔	✔			✔
Shorter Average Operation Time -ASD						✔	
Greater Total Rotation Angle-ASD					✔		

5.3 Correlations between Spatial Ability and Task Performance

We assessed the spatial abilities of the two groups by comparing them on the embedded figures test scores and mental rotation scores. There were no significant differences between groups on the mental rotation score and time, or embedded figure score and time. Moreover, spatial ability had no significant correlations with the GARS-3 scores (ASD group only) and age.

To further understand the role of spatial cognition in 3DUI, we performed Pearson correlations between the spatial ability scores, and each of the task performance measurements within each group. Specifically, we investigated correlations of performance on questions that had significant differences between the groups (see sections 5.1 and 5.2).

In both groups, we found strong negative correlations between spatial ability scores (i.e., mental rotation score/embedded figure score) and the error made in rotation and translation tasks.

Surprisingly, there were some correlations that appeared to be consistently different between the ASD and TD group on each of the questions. Specifically, the TD group demonstrated a strong negative correlation between spatial ability scores and the average operation times. Further, the TD group showed a strong negative correlation between the spatial ability scores and translation speed. However, in the ASD group, no such correlations were found.

Table 5. Correlations (EF or MR scores and performance metrics) that are consistently different between ASD and TD.

	Avg. operation time	Translation distance	Translation speed	Rotation speed
Rotation Task No.	4 **6 10** 13 **15**		**4 6 10 13** 15	
Translation Task No.		5 **8** 11 **12 14**		**1** 4 8 **11 14**

Note. The question numbers in **underlined bold** were significantly different between the two groups.

In the translation question set, on almost all the questions, the TD group showed a strong negative correlation between spatial ability scores and the translation distance. They also had and a strong negative correlation between spatial ability scores and rotation speed. Once again, in the ASD group, we found no significant correlations between performance and spatial ability scores. Table 5 shows the significant correlations ($p < 0.05$) with corresponding questions numbers found in the TD group but missing in the ASD group. The correlations that were significantly different across the two groups were determined by Fishers r to z test.

5.4 Post-interview

At the end of the study, we performed a short interview. Contrary to the much of quantitative data, both groups generally had similar responses.

Q1. *What is the strategy you use to complete the rotation and translation task?*

Almost all participants said that they continuously looked left and right to compare the manipulated pose with the target pose. One participant in the ASD group said, "I remember the target object sides in mind, and make comparison." Popular strategies for the rotation task mentioned by both groups included comparing the faces and comparing the shadows. Popular strategies for the translation task mentioned by both groups included looking at the scale of the virtual object (depth perception) and looking at the relative position to the question numbers on top of screens.

Q2: *Would you perform better if you were actually manipulating a real object rather than a virtual object?*

To this question, eight participants in ASD group said yes and two said no, while in TD group six said yes, three said no, and one said it depends on the type of task. In both groups, the main reason provided by the participants who said yes is that real objects are easier to control. Some of them indicated the 3DUI control was "weird" or "tricky". For those whose answer was no, the main reason provided was based on the idea that ratcheting would be missing in real world. One participant in the TD group indicated that "rotation would be more easier [*sic*] in reality but translation would be the same."

6. Discussion

Results suggest that: 1) Participants with ASD performed some 3DUI tasks less efficiently than TD participants, and 2) spatial ability seems to have less influence on 3DUI performance for users with ASD than for TD users. Thus, our null hypotheses must be rejected. Rather than the influence of spatial ability as indicated by [14], the primary difficulties with 3DUI that occur in the ASD population were more likely due to deficits in hand-eye coordination.

On the rotation tasks, the ASD group made more adjustments to the position of the object than the TD group on some questions. We hypothesize that the participants with ASD could not efficiently rotate the virtual object to the position that they intended because of deficits in hand-eye coordination. For example, on rotation question 13, the ASD group showed significantly lower rotation speed, indicating that they needed to slow down in order to effectively control the hand rotation. Although participants with ASD demonstrated the ability to successfully complete the tasks, it is likely that they would often over rotate or slow down rotations to increase accuracy.

Further, participants with ASD occasionally performed unnecessary movements, which also indicated deficits in hand-eye coordination. For example, on translation question 11, the ASD group showed significantly greater rotation angle, which is intuitively unnecessary in a translation task.

In contrast, on the translation tasks, the TD group 's spatial ability had a strong negative correlation to rotation speed and translation distance. This means the higher the participant's spatial ability, the less likely they were to conduct unnecessary operations. Thus, the TD group was more efficient in finishing translation tasks. However, in the ASD group, no such strong correlation was found. Similarly, the TD group's spatial ability showed a strong negative correlation with translation speed in rotation tasks. No such correlation was shown in the ASD group. In addition, 8 out of 10 participants in the ASD group expressed that they had some difficulties with the interface. All this evidence has shown that the ASD group's spatial ability had minimal impact on operation efficiency. Rather, their hand-eye coordination may have a greater influence on their performance.

Interestingly, there were only certain questions that seemed to give persons with ASD significant difficulty (e.g., rotation question 13 as seen in figure 1). For the rotation questions, we expect that questions 10, 13 and 15 are more difficult because in these questions, we found that the starting orientation of the house was significantly more offset from the target orientation. It may have also been more difficult to match due to fewer cues that aligned in the starting orientation, especially with respect to the long and wide sides. We noticed that some participants in the ASD group tried to initially match the controller's starting orientation to the long and wide side of the virtual house. On these three questions, if the user matched the starting controller orientation to that of the house, it put their wrist closer to the physical limit. This likely made manipulating the control much more difficult.

Results suggest that, the translation questions 4 and 11 were more difficult for the ASD group. More than other questions, the virtual houses in these two questions were already mostly aligned on the X- and Y-axes, leaving most of the work on the Z-axis. Due to a lack of stereo cues, participants relied on comparing the scale of the two houses. Participants had to precisely scale the houses over a small distance, which likely magnified the hand-eye coordination issues for the group with ASD.

There were several measurements we did not take in the current study, such as a baseline measurement of hand-eye coordination ability. Moreover, although all participants reported to be familiar with video games, we did not ask them specifically about their frequency of play. We plan to take these data in future studies and look into their correlations with other performance measurements.

7. Conclusions and Future Work

We presented a matched pair study that investigated atomic 3D interactions on adolescents with ASD. We recruited typically developed participants as controls, who had the same age and gender to participants with ASD. Each participant performed a series of basic 3D rotation and translation matching tasks. In tasks that drew more attention to precision (e.g., translation on the z axis) and tasks in which the interface was more ergonomically limiting (e.g., rotation tasks when trying to align the controller with the virtual object), the ASD group demonstrated significantly longer performance times and less efficient control than the TD group. Results suggest that the ASD group's deficits in hand-eye coordination may have influenced their 3DUI performance more than their spatial ability did.

As a guideline to effectively realize the benefits of 3DUIs for this population, interface designers should consider that users with ASD may need additional cues and assistive technologies to aid them with hand-eye coordination. Thus, in the future, we plan to investigate the 3D interaction techniques that could compensate for the deficits in hand-eye coordination of users with ASD, such as a non-isomorphic approach. This approach could beneficial for users with ASD to counteract deficits in hand-eye coordination, but it has yet to be studied with this population. In addition, we also plan to research how hand-eye coordination can play a role in other 3DUI and VR applications for persons with ASD, such as training activities of daily living and social skills.

8. ACKNOWLEDGMENTS

We would like to thank the participants and the local support groups involved. This work was in part supported by the National Science Foundation (IIS-1153229 and IIS-1218283).

9. REFERENCES

[1] AHRQ, 2013. Autism Spectrum Disorder—An Update.

[2] A. P. Association, 2013. diagnostic criteria of Diagnostic and Statistical Manual of Mental Disorders–Fifth Edition

[3] B. Bartlett, E. Albiero, and D. Rousseau, 2014. Mental Rotation Test.

[4] E. Bekele, Z. Zheng, A. Swanson, J. Crittendon, Z. Warren, and N. Sarkar, 2013. Understanding How Adolescents with Autism Respond to Facial Expressions in Virtual Reality Environments, *Visualization and Computer Graphics, IEEE Transactions on,* vol. 19, no. 4, 711-720.

[5] D. Bian, J. W. Wade, L. Zhang, E. Bekele, A. Swanson, J. A. Crittendon, M. Sarkar, Z. Warren, and N. Sarkar, 2013. A Novel Virtual Reality Driving Environment for Autism Intervention, *Universal Access in Human-Computer Interaction. User and Context Diversity,* 474-483.

[6] R. J. R. Blair, et al, 2002. Fractionation of visual memory: agency detection and its impairment in autism, *Neuropsychologia,* vol. 40, no. 1, 108-118.

[7] D. A. Bowman, and L. F. Hodges, 1997. An evaluation of techniques for grabbing and manipulating remote objects in immersive virtual environments, In *Proceedings of the 1997 symposium on Interactive 3D graphics,*(NY, USA, 1997).

[8] M.-J. Caron, L. Mottron, C. Rainville, and S. Chouinard, 2004. Do high functioning persons with autism present superior spatial abilities?, *Neuropsychologia,* vol. 42, no. 4, 467-481.

[9] A. Cockburn, 2004. Revisiting 2D vs 3D implications on spatial memory, In *Proceedings of the Fifth conference on Australasian user interface,*(Darlinghurst, Australia, 2004).

[10] A. Crippa, M. Molteni, S. Forti, and P. Perego, 2013. Eye-Hand Coordination in Children with High Functioning Autism and Asperger's Disorder Using a Gap-Overlap Paradigm, *Journal of autism and developmental disorders,* vol. 43, no. 4, 841-850.

[11] C. M. Falter, K. C. Plaisted, and G. Davis, 2008. Visuo-spatial Processing in Autism—Testing the Predictions of Extreme Male Brain Theory, *J Autism Dev Disord,* vol. 2008, no. 38.

[12] T. R. Goldsmith, 2008. Using Virtual Reality Enhanced Behavioral Skills Training to Teach Street-crossing Skills to Children and Adolescents with Autism Sectrum Disorders, *Doctoral dissertation, Western Michigan University.*

[13] K. Hinckley, et al. , 1997. Usability analysis of 3D rotation techniques, In *Proceedings of the 10th annual ACM symposium on User interface software and technology,*(Banff, AB, Canada, 1997).

[14] IndiaBix, Embedded Images.

[15] G. JE, 2013. Gilliam Autism Rating Scale 3rd Edition.

[16] N. Josman, H. M. Ben-Chaim, S. Friedrich, and P. L. Weiss, 2008. Effectiveness of virtual reality for teaching street-crossing skills to children and adolescents with autism, *International Journal on Disability and Human Development,* vol. 7, no. 1, 49-56.

[17] J. LaViola, and M. Katzourin, 2007. An exploration of non-isomorphic 3d rotation in surround screen virtual environments, In *IEEE Symposium on the 3D User Interfaces, 2007.* ,(North Carolina, USA, 2007).

[18] N. J. Minshew, G. Goldstein, and D. J. Siegel, 1997. Neuropsychologic functioning in autism: Profile of a complex information processing disorder, *Journal of the International Neuropsychological Society* vol. 3, no. 04, 303-316.

[19] I. Poupyrev, S. Weghorst, and S. Fels, 2000. Non-isomorphic 3D rotational techniques, In *Proceedings of the SIGCHI conference on Human factors in computing systems* 540-547,(The Hague, The Netherlands, 2000).

[20] B. K. Robert M. Joseph, 1 Christine Connolly,1 Jeremy M., and W. a. T. S. Horowitz2, 2009. Why is visual search superior in autism spectrum disorder?, *Developmental science,* vol. 12, no. 6, 1083-1096.

[21] R. N. Shepard, and J. Metzler, 1971. Mental rotation of three-dimensional objects, *The Philosophy of Mind: Classical Problems/contemporary Issues,* vol. 1992, 701-703.

[22] C. Ware, and R. Balakrishnan, 1994. Reaching for objects in VR displays: lag and frame rate, *ACM Transactions on Computer-Human Interaction (TOCHI)* 331-356.

[23] L. Wing, 1976. Diagnosis, clinical description and prognosis, *Early Childhood Autism,* 15-48.

[24] H. A. WITKIN, 1950. Individual Differences in Easy of Perception of Embedded Figures, *Journal of Personality,* vol. 19, no. 1, 1-15.

[25] S. Zhai, P. Milgram, and W. Buxton, 1996. The influence of muscle groups on performance of multiple degree-of-freedom input, In *Proceedings of the ACM SIGCHI conference on Human factors in computing systems,*(Vancouver, British Columbia, Canada, 1996).

ABC and 3D: Opportunities and Obstacles to 3D Printing in Special Education Environments

Erin Buehler[1], Shaun K. Kane[1,2], Amy Hurst[1]

[1]University of Maryland, Baltimore County
Information Systems Department
{eri4, amyhurst}@umbc.edu

[2]University of Colorado Boulder
Department of Computer Science
shaun.kane@colorado.edu

ABSTRACT

Consumer-grade digital fabrication such as 3D printing is on the rise, and we believe it can be leveraged to great benefit in the arena of special education. Although 3D printing is beginning to infiltrate mainstream education, little to no research has explored 3D printing in the context of students with special support needs. We present a formative study exploring the use of 3D printing at three locations serving populations with varying ability, including individuals with cognitive, motor, and visual impairments. We found that 3D design and printing performs three functions in special education: developing 3D design and printing skills encourages STEM engagement; 3D printing can support the creation of educational aids for providing accessible curriculum content; and 3D printing can be used to create custom adaptive devices. In addition to providing opportunities to students, faculty, and caregivers in their efforts to integrate 3D printing in special education settings, our investigation also revealed several concerns and challenges. We present our investigation at three diverse sites as a case study of 3D printing in the realm of special education, discuss obstacles to efficient 3D printing in this context, and offer suggestions for designers and technologists.

Categories and Subject Descriptors

K.4.2 [**Computers and Society**]: Social Issues – *assistive technologies for persons with disabilities.*

Keywords

3D Printing; Assistive Technology; Children; Cognitive Impairment; Digital Fabrication; Developmental Disability; Rapid Prototyping; Special Education; Visual Impairment

INTRODUCTION

Three-dimensional (3D) printers are a promising technology gaining acceptance in mainstream education as a means to engage students with hands-on interactions [15]. However, little has been published on the role of this technology in special education. We feel this technology can contribute to special education through 1) supporting STEM (Science, Technology, Engineering, and Math) engagement in a historically underserved population; 2) creating curricular materials; and 3) creating assistive technology (AT).

3D printing technology can offer students a powerful tool for creativity and exploration, as well as an engaging introduction to STEM topics. For example, students can print simple machines to

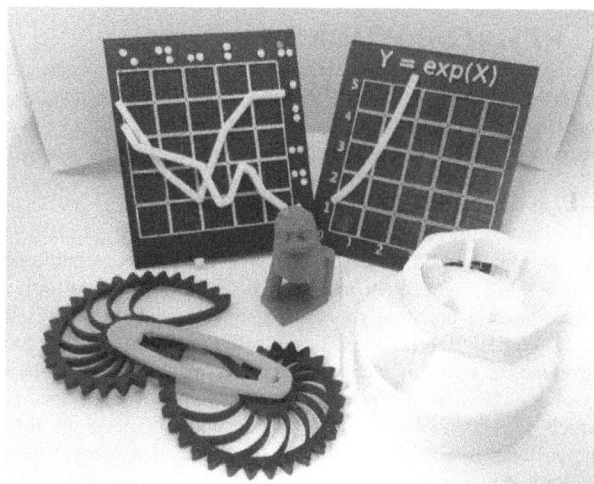

Figure 1. Examples of 3D printed objects to support special education. Pictured: tactile graphics for students with visual impairments, a small sculpture and moving nautilus gear for hands-on engagement, and two assistive devices including an easy-grip bottle opener and a pillbox.

help visualize elementary concepts in physics and engineering or design their own small-scale buildings as part of an architecture lesson. The search for ways to increase participation in science and engineering is a universal struggle, but it is particularly important for students with disabilities, as they are severely underrepresented in these disciplines [17].

Customized learning aids in the classroom and individualized assistive technology are both possibilities for 3D printing in special education. In the classroom, for example, a history teacher could download an open source model of a pharaoh's tomb and have a durable plastic diorama, which would be content-specific and could be handled, helping students with visual impairments as well as tactile learners. In the case of assistive devices, a therapist could use a 3D printer to create a custom tablet mount for a wheelchair, tailoring the design to both the tablet case and the individual student's chair, circumventing purchasing processes and exorbitant costs. In order to achieve these goals, special education institutions must first gain access to 3D printing technology. We will discuss how these tools require skill, time, and other resources to operate.

To understand how special education institutions are currently using 3D printing technologies, we studied three organizations providing special education and technology access services. We observed a classroom and conducted interviews with teachers, therapists, administrators, and technical experts. We worked with two schools that support middle- and high school-aged children, one focused on students with cognitive impairments and the other on students with vision impairments. Our third site was the technology division of a national organization offering training and support to blind individuals. Our analysis revealed insights into the current uses of 3D printing in special education and how we can better support its use.

In this paper we first summarize existing research on 3D printing in education, DIY accessibility, and learning. We describe our investigation into the current use and practices of 3D printing at three sites, and present each investigation site as a case study. We discuss the opportunities and challenges involved in efficiently implementing this technology for special education use, and offer suggestions for future designers and technologists in this space.

1. RELATED WORK

Our research builds on existing explorations of making in children's education, Do-It-Yourself (DIY) assistive technology, and Universal Design for Learning. We briefly describe relevant work from these topics to help frame our research goals below.

1.1 Education and Making

With the rise in personal fabrication there has been an increased interest in how children can interact with fabrication technologies. Encouraging engagement in STEM fields is a prevalent topic in education and one that researchers in our field are addressing using digital fabrication. Leduc-Mills and Eisenberg have developed a series of technologies and conducted workshops on involving children in 3D design. They developed the UCube [12], which is a tangible interface for designing objects in three-dimensional space. Researchers have conducted workshops to explore the implications of making in the classroom as a reinvention of constructionist learning and discussed the accessibility of tools for children in mainstream contexts [1, 10, 11]. Posch and Fitzpatrick also conducted an extensive series of workshop studies exploring children's expectations and outcomes when using 3D design tools [18]. These workshops used open source tools and personalized take-home projects, finding that, "An especially crucial factor for the children's sense of satisfaction appeared to be the technical challenge and mastery of the task and the personal engagement associated with the result." Additionally, we are starting to see books published on the topic of making and DIY skill building for children [9, 13]. Again, these focus on constructionist learning and STEM engagement.

Our study supports and extends this work by furthering the understanding of educator perspectives on making in the classroom, as well as examining the needs of students with disabilities both in terms of value gained from making and their access to this new wave of digital fabrication.

1.2 Making and Assistive Technology

DIY fabrication addresses two important issues in assistive technology—cost and customization. Financial costs of the device and assessment can be astronomical for the average user. Proper fit and personalization are key issues in AT abandonment. With 3D printing, end-users can create their own custom designs at reduced cost [7]. Brown and Hurst's VizTouch software creates 3D printable tactile mathematical graphics for use in accessible education and business [2]. Finally, Hurst and Kane [6] offer example tools designed to make DIY more accessible to a variety of populations, including encouraging children in STEM topics [8].

Creating assistive technology for children raises additional challenges that must be addressed before children will adopt these technologies. Several of these challenges are highlighted in the works of Dawe [4] and Copley and Ziviani [3], in which barriers to adoption are identified with respect not only to AT devices, but also the people and environments surrounding young users. The exploration of Hayes et al. [5] into visual support for children with autism uncovered other key factors related to children and AT. Children change and outgrow devices very quickly, which can lead to problems when being fitted for custom ordered devices or prolonged waiting times on generic items. Another aspect of AT adoption versus abandonment is the perception of others. Children are susceptible to popular opinion and the sense of belonging, making the stigma around AT a serious issue.

We investigate how 3D printing can address these concerns in the context of special education, providing inexpensive and customized solutions for young students.

1.3 Universal Design for Learning

Universal Design for Learning (UDL) research has explored the use of tangible learning aids for students with varying abilities. UDL is an extension of universal design for accessibility applied to education. UDL follows three guiding principles: 1) flexible methods of presentation; 2) flexible methods of expression and apprenticeship; and 3) flexible options for engagement [19]. By offering educators a way to create their own 3D printed objects, they can in turn offer multimodal interactions for their students. The benefits lie in presentation of information and demonstrating knowledge gained. A student with a visual impairment may gain access to graphical information tactilely or a student with a cognitive impairment might demonstrate math skills by manipulating objects rather than writing out equations. When discussing multimodal interactions, the concept of tangibles is a natural connection. Manches and O'Malley provide an extensive review on the topic of tangibles and manipulatives in education and how to support these interactions [16].

Our research examines the potential for 3D printers to assist with the creation of educational aids, adaptive devices in support of learning, and manipulatives – physical objects designed to promote comprehension through interaction.

2. METHODS

Our investigation set out to gain an understanding of how 3D printing can support special education and therapy. We conducted interviews and observations at three diverse sites: Site A, a special education school serving students with cognitive impairments and multiple disabilities; Site B, a school serving students with visual impairments; and Site C, the technology services department of a national organization working with blind individuals. We conducted long-term classroom observations and a series of interviews with staff, instructors, and therapists.

2.1 Classroom Observations

We conducted observations at Site A for 6 months while attending 6 sections of an information technology class each week. This course's curriculum teaches computer skills, ranging from office productivity to computer hardware and networking. The instructors and administrators of this school were also interested in incorporating 3D printing into the curriculum. In order to remove obstacles for them to get the printer up and running, our research group provided the classroom with a 3D printer, supplies, and technical support. Our goal was to gather real world stories about 3D printing in the classroom and remove obstacles that might prevent them from utilizing this technology.

	Instructors	Administrators	OTs	AT Specialists
Site A	3	3	2	2
Site B	1	1	0	0
Site C	0	0	0	1

Table 1. Number of stakeholders listed by type and location.

Class sections contained between 3 and 13 students, 2 instructors, and 1 to 4 student aides, and lasted 45 minutes. Students were grouped by their experience and support needs from instructors. Thus, students with more experience and lower support needs were placed together and students with less experience and greater support needs were grouped. We took detailed notes on classroom activities and artifacts such as instruction worksheets, student 3D design files, and 3D printed objects.

2.2 Interviews with Faculty and Staff

Based on our observations and experiences from working closely with Site A, we defined a set of stakeholders (**Table 1**) we perceived would be relevant to the introduction of 3D printing in special education. These stakeholders included faculty, staff, and administrators. The stakeholders at Sites A and B give support to students and represent important perspectives in the delivery of curriculum and assistive technology to students in multiple educational settings. At Site C, we spoke with a technology coordinator who provides information on assistive technology related to vision impairments to organizations and end-users.

We recruited participants through email, explaining our research interests and inviting faculty and/or staff to participate. We conducted 13 interviews across 3 sites. (**Table 1**) We conducted individual semi-structured interviews lasting 30-60 minutes, and all interviews but one were conducted in person and on-site. These interviews occurred after we began our observations at Site A and were guided by those observations. The interviews were structured around the following themes: software and hardware challenges, student engagement with 3D printing, printer maintenance, safety, intellectual property rights, and time committed to 3D printer use.

We demonstrated 3D-printed objects in the interviews to illustrate the capabilities of current printers (**Figure 1**). These objects included 3D-printed tactile graphics, small models, and working gears. Interview questions and prompts were designed to elicit discussion and further insight on observed themes, but also served to reveal new issues not previously identified. The questions were tailored for the role of the interview participant. An example question for a technology instructor: "How do you manage student expectations?" Questions for technical experts, as another example, sought to uncover the realities of the technology in practical use. For non-technical instructors and therapists, questions posed were designed to illicit perceptions of and uses for 3D printers in their unique environments.

2.3 Co-Design with Occupational Therapists

A development stemming from our observations and other interactions at Site A led to a long-term co-design partnership with some of the occupational therapists (OTs) on site. Together we worked on an assistive device project that went through several iterations of prototyping and evaluation (See Section 5.3).

MakerBot Replicator 2X (Site A and C)

Approx. Release Price: *US$2,199* Print Speed: *80-100mm/sec* Build Volume: *28.5x15x15.5cm* Print Cost: *$0.01/cc* Material: *ABS or PLA plastic, 2 color*	

ZPrinter® 450 (Site B)

Approx. Release Price: *US$40,000* Print Speed: *23mm/hour* Build Volume: *20x25x20cm* Print Cost: *$0.20/cc* Material: *Resin composite powder, multicolor*	

Cubex Duo (Site C)

Approx. Release Price: *US$2,999* Print Speed: *15mm/sec* Build Volume: *23x26.5x24cm* Print Cost: *$0.01/cc* Material: *ABS or PLA plastic, 2 color*	

Table 2. Specifications for the printers used at our sites.

3. ANALYSIS AND FINDINGS

We transcribed and hand coded observations from field notes. This process entailed two coding passes noting high-level themes associated with the expectations, goals, use, and challenges related to 3D printing. From this coding, certain themes and stakeholders emerged. These topics were then used to inform a collection of semi-structured interview questions to further explore the issues associated with 3D printing in education. Interviews were also transcribed, hand-coded, and finally examined using affinity diagramming. The richness of data gathered from Site A enabled us to split this location into findings that applied in the classroom and findings that applied to therapeutic services on the campus. We describe our findings by site in the following sections, and address common themes and challenges in Section 7.

4. SITE A (CLASSROOM): SPECIAL EDUCATION SCHOOL

Site A is a special education school that caters to students with moderate to severe cognitive disabilities and, in some cases, multiple disabilities. Students are referred to this school from public schools if the student demonstrates a need for additional support services. We looked specifically at a single classroom teaching technology literacy skills.

4.1 3D Printing and Design Resources

This site used a MakerBot Replicator 2x, on loan from our lab for the duration of the study. These printers produce objects by additive manufacturing, heating plastic (ABS or PLA) filament. The filament is fed by a stepper motor into a nozzle that extrudes melted plastic onto a heated build plate in progressive layers. The primary design software being used at Site A was Tinkercad[1], a web-based 3D design tool that is free to use and is designed to

---

[1] http://www.tinkercad.com/.

Figure 2. On the left, two items selected, downloaded, and printed by students for a fundraiser (a bracelet and a cube toy). On the right, two examples of student-designed dog figurines.

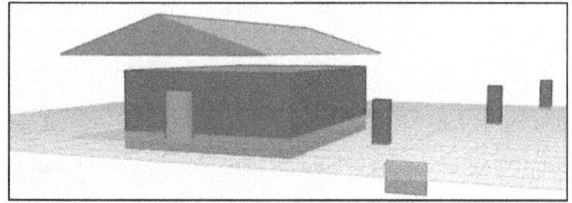

Figure 3. An example of an unprintable design. This house has a floating roof and is situated below the virtual print bed. Created by a student at site A.

support novice users. We suggested this software for its volume of tutorial materials, as well as for its novice-friendly user interface.

4.2 Primary Users

The instructors introduced the students to the concept of 3D printing by showing videos on 3D printing and giving live printing demonstrations in the classroom. The instructors encouraged students to explore existing 3D designs available for viewing, customizing, and downloading from Thingiverse[2], a 3D printing community that encourages sharing of printable designs. Students selected designs they wanted to see printed before moving on to experimenting with their own designs.

The instructors were the most frequent users of the printer, and performed maintenance and troubleshooting tasks, such as starting and stopping prints, filament changes, and printer calibration. We helped instructors when problems arose they could not resolve, as they had no prior experience with 3D printers before our study.

4.3 Use of 3D Printing

Students were given access to Tinkercad and, after completing the web site's tutorials (3 class periods for some students, more for others), students were encouraged to create their own designs for printing. However, limited curriculum time and difficulty mastering tools prevented most students from finishing custom designs. Instead, students commonly looked for designs from open-source sites to print or modify.

During our observations, the printer was frequently used to produce items for a school fundraiser. The students at this site are encouraged to engage in entrepreneurial activities like creating goods or providing services, and the faculty felt the 3D printer was ideally suited to this exercise. Students selected designs from Thingiverse and the technology instructors printed these designs to sell at a student-run sales event. These objects were chosen because they were perceived as having universal appeal, and would sell at the event. The instructor chose to sell existing designs rather than student designs because they felt the students had not yet mastered the design software.

4.4 Objectives and Obstacles

The ultimate hope at this site is for students to be autonomous in their ability to design and print objects. Instructors would like to see students use the printer more for fundraiser sales or as a type of in-house manufacturing for curriculum aids for teachers outside of the technology classroom. Ideally, other instructors could request a model or other tactile manipulative be designed and printed by the students, similar to a classroom-based engineering firm. The instructors felt this type of experience would provide both STEM engagement and empowerment for their students; however, the progress for these goals has been slow.

Even though Tinkercad is designed for novices, we observed the students experience several challenges using this software to design new models. Examples include difficulty manipulating camera angle, moving objects instead of adjusting view, confusion about which handles changed scale, rotation, and position of objects, and difficulty selecting multiple objects. These challenges were particularly characteristic of students needing high support. Students could become frustrated and distracted by the interface and their interest in completing a design appeared to diminish.

In addition to having difficulty using the software, some students had difficulty understanding the physical capabilities of the printer and its materials with respect to their own design concepts. If an object is not positioned on the building plane, this can cause complications during the printing stages either with software being able to prepare the file for the printer or resulting in a failed print. The ability to perceive designs on three planes (x, y, and z) challenged students with high support needs. This resulted in students creating designs that were not seated correctly on the build platform or designs that included object overhangs or details beyond the current capabilities of the printer (Figure 4).

5. SITE A (THERAPISTS): SPECIAL EDUCATION SCHOOL

We found that other support staff at Site A were also interested in the 3D printer and this section describes how OTs wanted to use this technology.

5.1 Printing Resources

Once we introduced the OTs to the 3D printer and explained its capabilities, they saw many opportunities for the technology in their work. We assisted therapists in the design and printing of a 3D object as a prototype for an AT design to encourage the therapists' exploration of this technology.

The therapists had access to the same MakerBot Replicator 2x in the instructional classroom, but none of them chose to use the device directly due to time constraints and training needs. Instead, we worked closely with them on the design and manufacturing of custom objects. This group was interested in scanning physical models made from clay, so we provided a MakerBot Digitizer[3] (a 3D scanner that combines images of a physical object and converts this to a closed 3D object for printing). We refined and modified these models using a combination of open-source software, including Tinkercad, MeshMixer[4], and Autodesk 123D[5].

---

[2] http://www.thingiverse.com/.

[3] http://store.makerbot.com/digitizer/.

[4] http://www.meshmixer.com/.

[5] http://www.123dapp.com/design/.

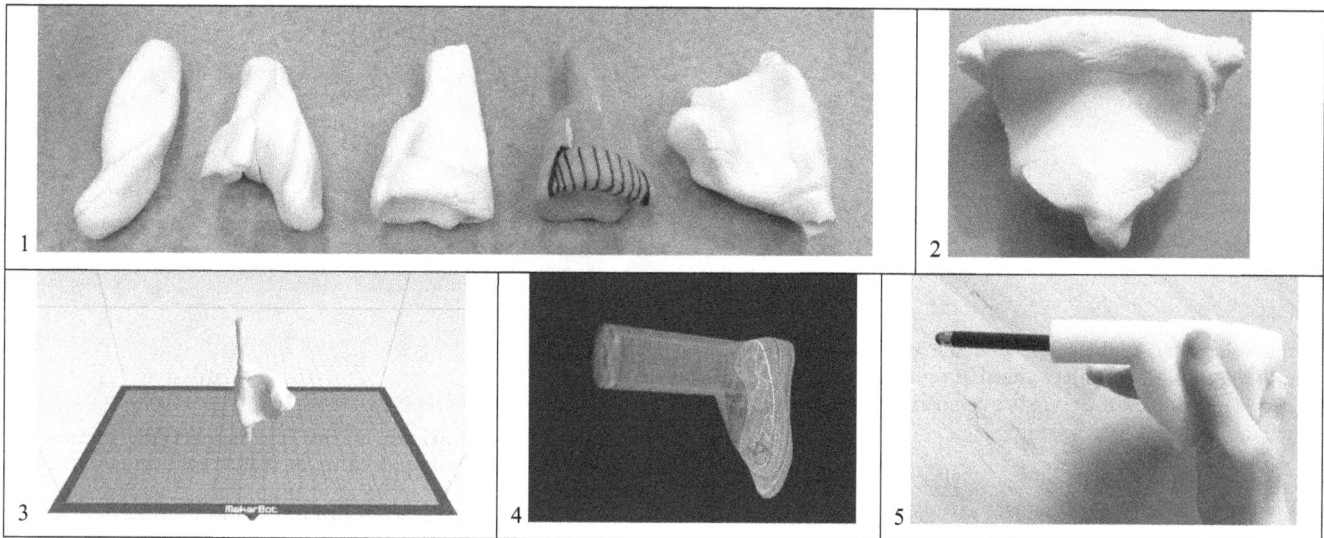

Table 3. The adaptive stylus grip went through several iterations of design. Pictured: 1) initial air-dry clay models of the student's grip, 2) the final low-fi clay design; 3) scanning the clay model with the Digitizer, 4) designing an extension to accommodate a new stylus, and 5) final 3D-printed grip design with stylus inserted.

5.2 Primary Users

The OTs at Site A provide therapy to a diverse student population. Sessions last for the duration of a class period (45 minutes) and often incorporate skills practice or other specialized therapeutic routines for students. The therapists did not feel they had the time or skills to commit to working with the printer directly, but described their existing practices for modifying AT devices or creating new ones mostly through the use of quick-fix supplies like velcro, tape, string, paper, cardboard, and so on. We felt we could translate these practices to low-fi prototyping and assisted two OTs with the technology to create a final product.

5.3 Use of 3D Printing

At Site A, we collaborated on a 3D-printed assistive technology project with two of the school's OTs. We saw this case study as an opportunity to find out what these therapists could be doing with the printer, if given the right resources. The goal was to create a unique stylus grip for a student with a limited grasp. The OTs had previously tested over $150 worth of assistive and mainstream off-the-shelf stylus and stylus-like products, but found no satisfactory solution.

Prior to our design activity, the student was using the eraser tip of a pencil combined with a soft gel grip, but this did not meet the exact needs of the student and sometimes caused discomfort or fatigue. In order to create a custom device, we agreed it would be best to create a new design shaped to fit the student's hand and that the device could be 3D printed.

This grip was designed through 3 iterative rapid prototyping sessions. The OTs created initial prototypes using lightweight, air-dry clay to create a base model of the student's grip, which was then 3D-scanned by the researchers using the Digitizer. Adjustments were made to the design to accommodate a basic stylus and the design was printed using a Replicator 2X located in our lab. The plastic prototype was delivered to the OTs, who conducted test sessions with the student. During testing, concerns were raised about the hardness of the plastic. Our lab coated the grip in a rubberizing aerosol spray to soften the texture and improve grasping. Both the new texture and the bright color

(picked by the student) were well received. Prompted by the purchase of a new, more responsive stylus, we modified the original design and printed a new grip.

5.4 Objectives and Obstacles

Therapists from Site A were excited at the prospects of 3D printing and were considering other individualized devices to create in future. However, they currently see the task of 3D design and printing to be someone else's work, and see themselves as consumers of that work. For these participants, 3D printing is largely meeting their expectations because the design and test print processes are being obscured from them.

The OTs were interested in learning how to design and create 3D prints, but were concerned about the required time commitments and learning curve to learn the software. *"I wasn't sure how much was involved in the [design and printing] process, it seemed like a lot of work." (OT, Site A)*. Each therapist works with multiple students and has limited time with each student. Their interest was piqued by the prospects of the 3D scanner used in the grip project, but because the grip needed to be altered to correctly hold the stylus the OTs again perceived the time to design and implement these modifications as outside of their capacity.

SITE B: PRIVATE SCHOOL FOR BLIND AND VISION IMPAIRED STUDENTS

Site B is a private organization that provides programs and resources for students who are blind or vision impaired between the ages of 3 and 21. Some students have multiple disabilities. The 3D printer at this site is located in a technology classroom.

5.5 Printing Resources

The 3D-printer at this site is a ZPrinter® 450 resin composite machine. This printer and most of its materials were donated to the school at no cost. Resin composite printers have a slightly different printing method from the printers discussed so far. Layers are created by sealing together resin powder with a binding agent, enabling for higher resolution, full color prints. (**Table 2**).

Figure 4. Example objects printed at Site B. On the left is a math manipulative project aimed at creating a tactile Cartesian grid. On the right is a decorative snowman figurine designed by students.

For designing, Site B used Rhinoceros 3D[6], which includes both a mouse-driven interface with more advanced tools than those found in Tinkercad, as well as a command-line driven design mode, where students can supply programming commands to draw shapes. Rhinoceros is a tool designed for experts with a very different learning curve from open source tools like Tinkercad and high costs ($1,695). This software was chosen for both its robustness and supporting tutorial materials.

5.6 Primary Users

At the time of the study, the technology instructor had been the primary user of this printer, owing to a need to gain familiarity with the software and incorporate the printer into future curriculum. A small group of students have tried the printer and software as part of an extra-curricular activity by completing small tutorials (provided with the software) similar to the snowman pictured in Figure 4. The instructor has plans to create and implement lessons for the students in his class in the future.

5.7 Use of 3D Printing

Example designs from Site B include a snowman figurine and a geometry manipulative (Figure 4), both created with Rhinoceros 3D. The technology instructor at Site B received a request to create a geometry manipulative that would allow visually impaired students to tactilely interact with their math curriculum. Three students in the technology class created the snowman figurines while learning the software.

5.8 Objectives and Obstacles

Similar to Site A, this site's goal is to teach students enough skills for them to become independent 3D designers, and the instructor had concerns about the students' ability to master the modeling software. Specifically, that the planned 3D modeling curriculum might prove a challenge for the vision impaired and blind students. The instructor anticipated struggles to fully grasping command-line based design and issues relating to the build plate and design symmetry (Figure 3). The printer at this site required very delicate calibration including tasks that bordered on the impossible for students, such as using a mirror to make adjustments to components underneath and/or deep inside the machine.

Figure 5. Models printed at Site C to support information access for visually impaired users. Pictured: a planet, the Sphinx, the Chrysler building, a DNA helix, & a landmass.

Another goal at this site was to provide tactile graphics and other manipulatives to students and teachers. Unfortunately, the durability of prints made by this type of 3D printer was an issue, as objects that come from this printer may not be strong enough to endure extensive handling. The resin composite prints are very fragile when they first come out of the print bed. Thick or large objects are often heavy and can easily break during the final stages of vacuuming off excess powder before applying a final coat of resin for strength. Additionally, after constant handling, prints can still crumble or crack and gluing them back together is not always successful. This is a serious issue for a population that relies heavily on touch and needs durable prints.

6. SITE C: TECHNOLOGY CENTER

Site C is the technology center within a national organization that provides advocacy and training for the blind. At this location, we interviewed an assistive technology expert about their exploration and promotion of 3D printing as a tool for tactile graphics and an opportunity to support alternative access to educational materials, such as hand-held models.

6.1 Printing Resources

Site C currently employs two plastic extrusion printers, a MakerBot Replicator and a Cubex Duo (Table 2). While other sites focused primarily on the cost or convenience of a 3D printer when deciding on which model to acquire, this site also focused on customer support. The technology expert from this site pointed out that many consumer-grade printer manufacturers are small companies with limited technical support, static F.A.Q.s, or forums that aren't always accessible; having a live person to call up and ask for troubleshooting assistance makes a difference.

This site uses open source software wherever possible, including Tinkercad and 123D Design. Other resources, such as Thingivese.com and GrabCAD[7] (an open engineering group offering free tools and model-sharing communities) are used to find existing models.

6.2 Primary User

At Site C, we spoke with a technology expert who provides information about and training on assistive technology tools related to visual impairment. This expert is the primary user for this site's two 3D printers and is self-taught in CAD design and

---

[6] http://www.rhino3d.com/

[7] http://grabcad.com/.

3D printing. As part of a small department serving a large population, this participant leverages 3D printing only when other options are not practical and is the sole user at this site.

6.3 Use of 3D Printing

The printers at this site are used for demonstrations, training, and support material for events put on by the organization. When individuals or groups contact Site C for information on 3D printing, the technical expert can provide the seeker with information on types of printers, hardware costs, software suggestions, and ideas on how 3D printers can be used to support visual impairment. This primarily includes tactile graphics and models to support access to information. Due to time and ability constraints, printed designs are roughly an 80-20 split between open source designs and creating novel designs. **Figure 5** illustrates some of the models that have been printed at this site.

6.4 Objectives and Obstacles

This site's current goals for the 3D printer are to create tactile graphics and handheld models and to provide information for other individuals or organizations that would like to know more about using 3D printing in support of visual impairments. However, our participant mentioned the tedious and time-consuming task of mastering CAD. They also described serious issues regarding support for users.

"For something that's supposed to be consumer-grade, that's just not workable. Their support is good, but some things I have to wait three days for a response!" (Tech. Expert, Site C) Other possibilities, such as 3D scanners, are perceived as promising ideas, but likely not as practical as advertised. *"I've very wary because I feel like so much of it is marketed as 'oh it will scan and you'll get a print-ready model' and I'm very skeptical of that." (Tech. Expert, Site C)*

7. DISCUSSION

These four case studies reveal that there is support and interest in using 3D printing in special education and therapy. Through this work we identified several recommendations for 3D hardware and software for schools and therapists.

7.1 3D Printer Accessibility Requirements

We believe it is important that the 3D printer be considered as an assistive technology in the special education classroom and not simply another piece of technology. We make the following recommendations specific to this cause.

7.1.1 Provide Accessible Feedback

One significant obstacle we observed for novices learning to use this technology was developing an accurate mental model of the printer. Common problems included not understanding why prints failed, the limits of a given printer's capabilities, and the relationships between troubleshooting techniques and the problems they are intended to solve. As we move toward a future where students with diverse abilities use these printers, it is important to provide accessible feedback about when the printer is working and when there are problems.

7.1.2 Printer Safety

3D printers can be dangerous when misused. While we didn't see specific concerns from any of our stakeholders about the safety of these machines for students, it should be considered for future audiences. All of the 3D printers our participants interacted with had enclosed all hot and/or moving parts, so they would be difficult to touch while the printer was on. Additionally, students

at these sites are monitored very closely, and the administrators felt that it was the teacher's responsibility to keep students safe.

7.1.3 Offer Appropriate Customer Support

Given that 3D printing is not yet as robust as other consumer technology, it is important to provide consumers with appropriate support. While this is true for all end users, it is particularly true for assistive technologies where end users are accustomed to having access to experts, technical support, and repairs. This was made clear to us in our interview at Site C, where purchasing decisions were informed based on available support.

7.2 3D Modeling Accessibility Requirements

7.2.1 Make Accessible Software

As 3D printing becomes more common, 3D modeling software must be accessible. Specifically, this software must support screen readers, switch input, and other common computer access customizations. According to our participant at Site C, there is currently no open source 3D modeling software that is accessible to a screen reader. The accessibility of these tools should also be considered for end users who have difficulty remembering complex task sequences or have limited short-term memory.

7.2.2 Consider the Learning Curve

It would also be prudent to explicitly design 3D modeling software to support a range of expertise and support the transition from novice to expert performance. While many of our participants were excited to use 3D printing, most found the current 3D modeling software intimidating. For these users, novice tools don't provide enough control, but expert tools come at too high of a cost in terms of outright expense, learning, and time investment. Adding optional features to support novices such as detecting unprintable designs and integrating tutorials into the modeling software might assist users when they are struggling.

7.2.3 Encourage Sharing of Existing Models

Not all end users want to create custom designs, and it is often enough to make minor tweaks to existing object models. Faculty who were not directly involved in teaching technical topics felt they would be more comfortable using a catalog of existing items, similar to Thingiverse.com, rather than learning CAD. This concept was echoed by administrators at Site A, who felt that a central repository of tools, designs, and support would be the best fit for the teaching faculty not currently involved with the 3D printer. Several participants wanted curriculum support, such as miniature models or student-tailored objects that could be selected from a list and printed on demand.

7.2.4 Support Editing Existing Models

A mix of existing tools or minor modifications to existing tools may be enough to support some of the stakeholders discussed in this paper. While we are starting to see customizable 3D models (such as Customizer on Thingiverse), these tools are limited. 3D scanning physical objects may offer an easier way to create custom designs, however many current 3D scanners have low resolution or require complex cleanup to make a printable model.

7.3 Recommendations for Special Education and Accessibility Organizations

We saw a range of exposure, comprehension, and skills related to 3D printing that impacts decisions about choosing appropriate tools. To accommodate this, we recommend carefully surveying the skills and application goals of users before choosing a printer.

7.3.1 Budget Time for Training

Participants with 3D printing experience expressed concerns about the time necessary to train themselves, other staff, or students to create novel 3D designs. They feared mastering these tools would take days, weeks, or even months. This is concerning given that our participants consider learning 3D printing as "extracurricular" and not what they were explicitly hired to do.

7.3.2 Consider Printer Reliability and Maintenance

As is a common complaint with the recent 3D printing boom, there are serious setbacks in the consistency and quality of printer performance [14]. These shortcomings include maintenance, troubleshooting, and unanticipated poor quality print outcomes.

These issues are crucial for accessibility and education applications. For example, when making custom fitted assistive devices, precision is key to successfully replicating details or measurements. When teaching 3D design and prototyping to students in special education, consistency and reliability impact the learning experience. Students with visual or cognitive impairments may already endure obstacles to accessing the design end of 3D printing; adding the complexity of unreliable print output is an additional discouraging factor.

7.3.3 Develop a Plan to Share Resources Equally

The placement of a 3D printer in a school is important and impacts who will use it. We believe that since the 3D printer at Site A was physically located in the technology classroom, the therapists were more hesitant to use it than if it had been placed in their space. As the market of consumer 3D printers under $500 continues to grow, it may make sense for educators to invest in multiple inexpensive printers rather than one high-end printer.

7.4 Recommendations for Therapists

7.4.1 3D Printing Custom Fit Objects is Possible

Our design sessions with Site A's OTs demonstrated how 3D printing can provide cost effective and highly individualized assistive technology solutions, although extensive help is currently required. If we can empower these therapists to design and prototype solutions on their own, they can utilize in-house 3D printing to overcome several challenges in assistive technology such as limited availability, high costs, and poor fit.

7.4.2 Budget Extra Time for Iteration and Fitting

While it is possible to create custom accessibility solutions, the time between iterations from design to prototype can be slow. Even though it only took two hours to 3D print the custom stylus grip discussed earlier, the development took longer than expected. The ultimate limiting factor on this project was access to the student, who was only available for testing during short therapy sessions. We believe this process could be faster if the end user were able to be more involved in the design process.

8. CONCLUSIONS AND FUTURE WORK

Our study has identified benefits of 3D printing in special education environments, and it has uncovered several obstacles to adoption. In the future, we will continue to work with a wider range of instructors in non-technical fields, and work directly with students. Our future work will continue to track the progress of 3D printing at these sites.

Three-dimensional printing can promote STEM engagement in children with varying abilities, provide tactile access to information and educational content, and encourage DIY and in-house assistive device design. To encourage the adoption of this technology in special education, we have identified barriers and points of consideration for 3D printer manufacturers, 3D modeling software developers, special education institutes and accessibility organizations, and therapists.

9. ACKNOWLEDGEMENTS

We thank the schools and institutes involved, as well as all of our individual participants and our lab interns, Ben Gershowitz and Joshua Dutterer. This material is based on work supported by the National Science Foundation under Grant No. EEEC-0540865.

10. REFERENCES

[1] Blikstein, P. and Krannich, D. 2013. The Makers' Movement and FabLabs in Education: Experiences, Technologies, and Research. IDC (2013), 613–616.

[2] Brown, C. and Hurst, A. 2012. VizTouch: Automatically Generated Tactile Visualizations of Coordinate Spaces. TEI (2012), 131–138.

[3] Copley, J. and Ziviani, J. 2004. Barriers to the Use of Assistive Technology for Children with Multiple Disabilities. Occupational Therapy International. 11, 4, 229–243.

[4] Dawe, M. 2006. Desperately Seeking Simplicity: How Young Adults with Cognitive Disabilities and Their Families Adopt Assistive Technologies. CHI (2006), 1143–1152.

[5] Hayes, G.R., Hirano, S., Marcu, G., Monibi, M., Nguyen, D., and Yeganyan, M. 2010. Interactive Visual Supports for Children with Autism. Personal and Ubiquitous Computing. 14, 7 (Apr. 2010), 663–680.

[6] Hurst, A. and Kane, S. 2013. Making "Making" Accessible. IDC (2013), 635–638.

[7] Hurst, A. and Tobias, J. 2011. Empowering Individuals with Do-It-Yourself Assistive Technology. ASSETS(2011),11-18.

[8] Kane, S.K. and Bigham, J.P. 2014. Tracking @ stemxcomet: Teaching Programming to Blind Students via 3D Printing, Crisis Management, and Twitter. SIGCSE (2014), 247–252.

[9] Kemp, A. 2013. The Makerspace Workbench: Tools, Technologies, and Techniques for Making. Maker Media.

[10] Krannich, D., Robben, B., and Wilske, S. 2012. Digital Fabrication for Educational Contexts. IDC (2012), 375–376.

[11] Leduc-Mills, B. Dec, J., and Schimmel, J. 2013. Evaluating Accessibility in Fabrication Tools for Children. IDC (2013), 617–620.

[12] Leduc-mills, B. and Eisenberg, M. 2011. The UCube: A Child-Friendly Device for Introductory Three-Dimensional Design. IDC (2011), 72–80.

[13] Libow Martinez, S. and Stager, G. 2013. Invent to Learn: Making, Tinkering, and Engineering in the Classroom. Constructing Modern Knowledge Press.

[14] Lutz, R. 2013. Workshop: Enhancing Information Technology Education (ITE) with the Use of 3D Printer Technology. SIGITE (2013), 157–158.

[15] Maker Education Initiative: 2014. www.makered.org. Accessed: 2014-02-09.

[16] Manches, A. and O'Malley, C. 2011. Tangibles for Learning: A Representational Analysis of Physical Manipulation. Personal and Ubiquitous Computing. 16, 4, 405–419.

[17 National Science Foundation 2013. Women, Minorities, and Persons with Disabilities in Science and Engineering: Special Report NSF 13-304.

[18] Posch, I. and Fitzpatrick, G. 2011. First Steps in the FabLab: Experiences Engaging Children. OzCHI (2011), 497–500.

[19] Rose, D., Meyer, A., and Strangman, N. 2002. Teaching Every Student in the Digital Age: Universal Design for Learning. Association for Supervision & Curriculum Development.

Design of and Subjective Response to On-body Input for People With Visual Impairments

Uran Oh[1] and Leah Findlater[2]
Inclusive Design Lab | HCIL
[1] Department of Computer Science
[2] College of Information Studies
University of Maryland, College Park
uranoh@cs.umd.edu, leahkf@umd.edu

ABSTRACT

For users with visual impairments, who do not necessarily need the visual display of a mobile device, non-visual on-body interaction (*e.g.*, *Imaginary Interfaces*) could provide accessible input in a mobile context. Such interaction provides the potential advantages of an always-available input surface, and increased tactile and proprioceptive feedback compared to a smooth touchscreen. To investigate preferences for and design of accessible on-body interaction, we conducted a study with 12 visually impaired participants. Participants evaluated five locations for on-body input and compared on-phone to on-hand interaction with one versus two hands. Our findings show that the least preferred areas were the face/neck and the forearm, while locations on the hands were considered to be more discreet and natural. The findings also suggest that participants may prioritize social acceptability over ease of use and physical comfort when assessing the feasibility of input at different locations of the body. Finally, tradeoffs were seen in preferences for touchscreen versus on-body input, with on-body input considered useful for contexts where one hand is busy (*e.g.*, holding a cane or dog leash). We provide implications for the design of accessible on-body input.

Categories and Subject Descriptors

H.5.2. [User Interfaces]: Input devices and strategies; H.5.m. [Information Interfaces and Presentation (e.g., HCI)]: Miscellaneous; K.4.2. [Social Issues]: Assistive technologies for persons with disabilities.

Keywords

visual impairments; mobile; gestural interfaces; on-body input; eyes-free interaction; design recommendations.

1. INTRODUCTION

On-body input such as that found in SixthSense [21], OmniTouch [14], Imaginary Phone [7], and others [3,12,14] allows users to employ their own body as an input surface with the support of a wearable camera or other sensors. Such techniques could provide new means of mobile interaction for people with disabilities, yet little work has explored this potential. For users with visual impairments, who do not necessarily need the visual display of a phone, non-visual on-body input is particularly compelling (*e.g.*, *Imaginary Interfaces* [6,7,29]).

ASSETS '14, October 20 - 22 2014, Rochester, NY, USA
Copyright 2014 ACM 978-1-4503-2720-6/14/10...$15.00.
http://dx.doi.org/10.1145/2661334.2661376

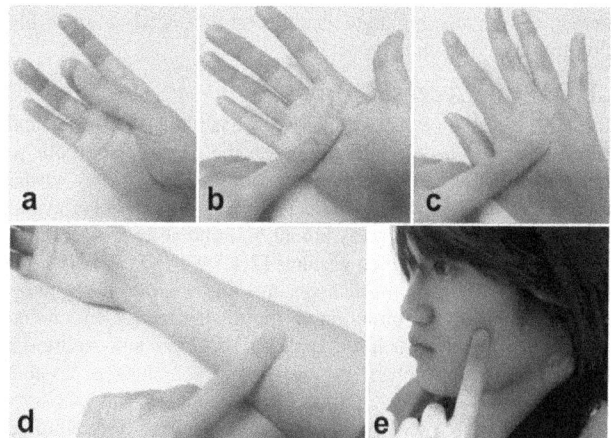

Figure 1. The five on-body input locations explored in our study: (a) same hand, (b) other hand-palm, (c) other hand-back, (d) forearm, and (e) neck and face area.

While advances in mobile screenreaders (*e.g.*, iOS VoiceOver) have led to the adoption of conventional smartphones by people with visual impairments [32], basic tasks can still be time consuming. As an *alternative* or *complementary* means of mobile interaction, on-body input including taps or swipes on the hand has the potential to provide efficient, always-available interaction. On-body input also provides increased tactile and proprioceptive feedback compared to the smooth screen of a smartphone [8], which could be particularly useful for non-visual interaction.

To investigate the design of and subjective response to on-body interaction for people with visual impairments, we conducted a lab study with 12 participants. Our first goal was to answer questions such as what locations and gestures are preferred (*e.g.*, touchscreen-style, location-specific), and what factors affect these preferences. Our second goal was to compare subjective responses to on-body input versus mobile touchscreen input. Toward the first goal, we adapted a method employed by Weigel *et al.* [33] to examine gesture preferences at five on-body locations (Figure 1) and to evaluate these locations on factors such as social acceptability, comfort, and ease of use. Toward the second goal, we implemented an on-hand sensing system that controls the VoiceOver software on an Apple iOS device and asked participants to complete basic mobile tasks with both on-hand input and a touchscreen smartphone.

Our findings show that the least preferred areas for on-body input were the face and neck, and the forearm; in contrast, locations on the hands were considered to be more discreet and natural. The results also suggest that participants may be prioritizing social acceptability over ease of use and physical comfort when assessing the feasibility of input at different locations of the body.

Finally, tradeoffs were seen in preferences for touchscreen versus on-body input, with on-body input considered useful for contexts where one hand is busy (*e.g.*, holding a cane or dog leash). The contributions of this paper are: (1) investigation of the potential of on-body input for people with visual impairments—the first in-depth study at this intersection; (2) characterization of preferences for different on-body input locations and one- versus two-handed use; (3) an exploratory, subjective comparison of on-body versus touchscreen input; and (4) design implications for accessible on-body interaction.

2. RELATED WORK

Our research builds on work in mobile accessibility and on-body interaction. We also highlight findings on the social acceptability of wearable devices more generally.

2.1 Mobile Accessibility

Mobile devices can make people with disabilities feel safer and make it easier to access information on the go [10]. Solutions to improve touchscreen accessibility for people with visual impairments have included both hardware or physical overlays to provide enhanced tactile cues [16,20,31], and software solutions that incorporate touchscreen gestures [2,4,5,9]. *Slide Rule* [9], for example, combines multi-touch gestures and audio to allow users to navigate through information on the touchscreen. Commercial accessibility features such as Apple's *VoiceOver* and Android's *TalkBack* provide built-in software that combines accessible gestures and auditory output. While these software-only techniques can be widely disseminated, they provide limited tactile feedback due to the flat input surface of the touchscreen. Ultimately, our goal is to combine on-body input—with its additional tactile and proprioceptive characteristics [8]—with audio interfaces as an alternate means of mobile interaction.

2.2 On-body (Skin-based) Interaction

Many on-body (skin-based) interaction methods have been proposed, primarily combining gestures sensed by camera [3] or acoustically [12] and a small visual display projected on the user's hand or arm [12,13,14,21,30] or on a wristwatch [18]. More closely inspiring our work is on-body interaction that exploits the user's tactile and proprioceptive senses without employing visual displays [3,7,17], allowing for eyes-free interaction. Gustafson *et al.*'s [6] *Imaginary Interfaces* provide spatial, non-visual interaction, where the user points one hand to or near the non-dominant hand. *Imaginary Phone*, for example, mimicked the layout of a smartphone for non-visual interaction on the user's hand, allowing the user to transfer existing spatial knowledge of the interface layout to their hand [7]. A recent study of the tactile and proprioceptive characteristics of palm-based imaginary interfaces showed that while sighted users primarily relied on vision to accurately target on their hand, a palm-based interface was still usable for eyes-free input [8]. That work also included an exploratory evaluation with one blind participant who reacted positively to the palm-based interaction—further motivating our study. To our knowledge, however, no larger evaluation has explored on-body interaction for visually impaired users.

Our study also builds on recent work by Weigel *et al.* [33], who investigated skin input modalities and preferred locations with sighted users. When asked to create their own on-body gestures, participants in Weigel *et al.*'s study primarily used conventional multi-touch gestures, and preferred to use the forearm and the hand over a location on the upper limb. The first of our two study tasks borrows heavily from Weigel *et al.*'s method, adapting it for users with visual impairments.

2.3 Eyes-free Wearable Devices

Beyond on-body interaction, a number of wearable input devices have been proposed that support *eyes-free* interaction. Aimed at users with visual impairments, *EyeRing* [22] is a finger-mounted camera that supports activities such as reading text and detecting color/currency. Ye *et al.* [37] explored projected impacts of a wristband input device by people with visual impairments, identifying potential for increased inclusion in social contexts and ability to access information on the go. In terms of mainstream use (*i.e.*, not focused on accessibility), several projects have proposed hand-worn or wrist-worn devices. A few examples supporting eyes-free interaction include a haptic wristwatch [26, 27], a finger-mounted camera that supports touch input on arbitrary surfaces [36], and ring-based devices such as *Nenya* [1] and *Magic Ring* [15]. While these projects did not focus on improving mobile accessibility, they offer varying degrees of applicability for accessible input. Devices that interfere with tactile perception (*e.g.,* [36]) could be problematic, whereas ring-based interaction (*e.g.,* [1]) would allow fingertips to remain free.

2.4 Social Acceptability of Wearable Input

Although not focused on wearable devices, Shinohara and Wobbrock [28] found that social stigma and misperceptions of assistive technology can impact how people with disabilities adopt devices. More recently, Ye *et al.* [37] showed that the majority of participants with visual impairments were interested in trying wearable input devices. Most work on social acceptability of wearable input, however, has looked at users without disabilities, comparing input at different on-body locations [11,25] or of different gestures [26,27]. One study on a novel textile input technique, for example, found that the upper arm was the best location for balancing orientation, ease of use, and social acceptance [22], which contrasts findings for on-body (skin) input [33]. From an observer rather than wearer point of view, Profita *et al.* [25] found that wrist and forearm locations are most popular for wearable input across both Korean and American cultures. Finally, Rico *et al.* [27] examined social acceptance of device-specific and body-specific gestures, finding participants' willingness to perform a particular gesture was significantly impacted by location and audience. We borrow from their method to examine similar questions with users with visual impairments.

3. METHOD

To investigate the design of on-body interaction for people with visual impairments and the potential impacts of such interaction, we conducted a lab-based study that included two tasks. The first task collected subjective assessments of five locations for on-body input, and the second task compared on-body versus touchscreen phone input using one or two hands.

3.1 Participants

Twelve participants (6 male, 6 female) were recruited via campus e-mail lists and local organizations that serve people with visual impairments. The average age was 44.3 ($SD = 12.9$, range 23–62). Nine participants were totally blind; six were born blind while the rest became blind later in life (years post onset: $M = 22.8$, $SD = 14.4$, range 3–42). Three participants had low vision, respectively: 20/200 for both eyes, none for left eye and 20/200 for right eye, and 20/3000. All but two participants were right-handed. While nine participants used touchscreen phones on a regular basis, the remaining three had feature phones. Participants reported using their phone at least once every few hours, with the exception of one participant who used it once a day. Participants were compensated for their time and transportation.

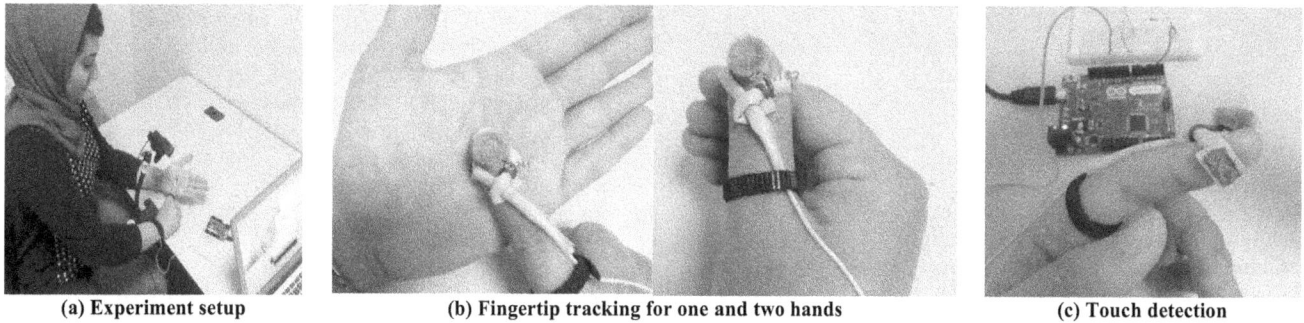

(a) Experiment setup   (b) Fingertip tracking for one and two hands   (c) Touch detection

Figure 2. On-hand sensing system used in Task 2. Participants wore a lightweight ring that included a color marker (tracked by a camera) and a capacitive touch sensor. The ring could be placed so as not to cover the fingertip.

3.2 Apparatus

To avoid limiting participants' on-body gesture creation process, no sensing technology was used for the first task, as was done by Weigel *et al.* [33] and is common more broadly with a user-defined gesture approach [34]. For the second task, we built a system that senses on-hand input to control the VoiceOver screenreading software on an Apple iOS device (Figure 2). The system could recognize four gestures: *double tap*, *left-to-right-swipe*, *right-to-left swipe* and *long tap*. These gestures were used as direct replacements for the same VoiceOver gestures, with the exception of a long press to replace the home button.

While we ultimately want to support on-hand input without instrumenting the fingers, participants wore a lightweight ring for tracking. The ring included a color marker on the top and a capacitive touch sensor made of conductive fabric on the bottom (shielded from the gesturing finger itself by non-conductive tape). To prevent tangling, thin Velcro straps held the wires around the gesturing finger and the wrist.

The system additionally consisted of a computer vision module to track *x,y* finger location, and a touch-detection module. For the computer vision module, which tracked the color marker on the participant's gesturing finger, we used a Logitech Webcam C930e and custom software running on a laptop with an Intel Core i5 processor. The custom touch-detection module ran on an Arduino Leonardo board and used the *SoftwareSerial* and *CapSense* libraries to detect capacitive input. The laptop communicated timestamped finger locations to the Arduino software, which combined them with the touch state to classify the user's gestures. Finally, the Arduino converted the sensed gestures to VoiceOver keyboard shortcuts and sent them via Bluetooth to an iPhone 4S. The participant could control VoiceOver by touching their hand.

3.3 Procedure

The procedure was designed to fit in a single two-hour session consisting of two tasks and questionnaires.

3.3.1 Task 1: Location Preference for On-body Input

Inspired by user-defined gesture protocols where users create gestures that can be analyzed to determine guessability and preferences [33][34], participants first created gestures for five mobile actions at each of five different on-body locations. Participants were allowed to use any number of fingers including their thumb, and they were asked to perform on-body gestures with their dominant hand only. They were asked to think aloud while doing so. The locations, as shown in Figure 1, were: *same hand, other hand-palm, other hand-back, forearm,* and *neck and face* area including the ears. These locations overlap with Weigel *et al.* [33], but we focused on those where the skin would likely be exposed, adding *same hand* and *neck and face* in the process.

Our participants performed five mobile actions, which were chosen to cover a range of common mobile tasks: (1) *previous*: moving to the previous item in a list, (2) *next*: moving to the next item in a list, (3) *open*: opening a selected item, (4) *home screen*: returning to the home screen, and (5) *e-mail*: creating a shortcut gesture to open an e-mail app. The on-body locations were presented in random order to each participant, and the mobile actions were further presented in random order for each location.

After creating gestures for all five on-body locations, participants evaluated each location in terms of ease of use, physical comfort, and social acceptance. We also asked about participants' openness to performing a gesture at each location in the following contexts:

- **Place:** private (*e.g.*, home), crowded public (*e.g.*, public transit, restaurant), non-crowded public (*e.g.*, library), workplace.
- **Audience:** alone, partner, friends, family, colleagues, strangers.
- **Physical constraints:**
  - *Pose*: seated, standing, walking
  - *Available hands*: both hands free, one hand busy (*e.g.*, holding a cane or a dog leash)
- ***Input***: handwriting, keyboard, number pad, sketching, and touchpad (from Weigel *et al.* [33]).

3.3.2 Task 2: Phone vs. On-hand Input

Task 2 compared smartphone input to on-hand input with one or two hands (Figure 3). The task was set up as a 2x2 within-subjects design, with factors of *device* (touchscreen phone *vs.* on-body) and *hand count* (one *vs.* two). Input in all conditions controlled the VoiceOver screenreader on an iPhone 4S, which allows for eyes-free interaction; for participants with low vision the screen curtain functionality was enabled so that the screen itself was blank. The order of presentation for the four conditions was counterbalanced using a balanced Latin square and participants were randomly assigned to orders.

Each of the four conditions in Task 2 began with brief training on basic VoiceOver gestures: horizontal flick to navigate left and right, double tap to open/activate selection, and pressing the home button (or, for on-hand input, a long press) to return to the home

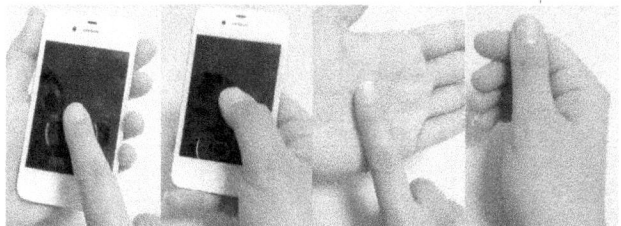

Figure 3. The four input methods used for Task 2, from left to right: two-handed phone, one-handed phone, two-handed on-body, one-handed on-body.

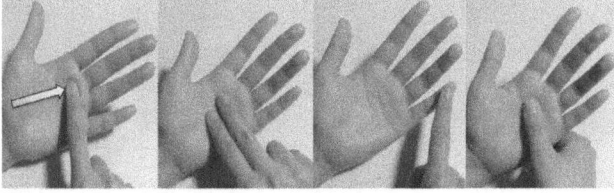

Figure 4. Participants created distinct gestures by varying (left to right): the basic gesture itself, number of fingers, landmarks used, or the gesturing finger (*e.g.*, thumb or index).

screen. These gestures were selected because they allow users to perform a range of activities on the phone like reading through e-mail and texts, and browsing a webpage. Participants then performed the same set of basic tasks per condition, including navigating through apps and information within an app, opening apps, and returning to the home screen. The task set took approximately five minutes for each condition, including training. Feedback questions were asked after each condition.

3.4 Data Analysis

Because the work is exploratory, we did not have specific hypotheses. For subjective ratings, we specify which statistical tests we used throughout the Results section. In general, however, because the normality assumption of parametric tests may not hold for the 5-point rating scale data that we collected, we used non-parametric tests: Friedman tests, repeated measures ANOVAs with Aligned Rank Transform (ART) [35] and, for pairwise comparisons, Wilcoxon signed ranks tests. Bonferroni adjustments were used to protect against Type I error for all posthoc pairwise comparisons. For qualitative data, observation notes on gesture characteristics were recorded during the sessions and later categorized. We also conducted a qualitative analysis of the think-aloud data and other participant comments.

4. FINDINGS

Our findings cover gesture creation strategies, location preferences for on-body input, and subjective tradeoffs between touchscreen phone and on-body input.

4.1 Task 1: Gesture Creation Strategies

During the Task 1 gesture creation process, we collected 300 gestures (5 gestures x 5 locations x 12 participants). For all participants across all body locations, *directional swipe* was the most commonly used gesture for navigating to a *previous* or *next* item. For the other mobile actions, however, participants created a wider variety of gestures.

Participants used the four following strategies to create their on-body gestures (Figure 4): varying a common touchscreen gesture (*e.g.*, swipe, single tap, double tap), varying the number of fingers (*e.g.,* one *vs.* two), using specific body landmarks (*e.g.*, pointing to a fingertip *vs.* palm), and varying which fingers were used (*e.g.*,

	Strategy, varying:			
	Basic gesture	Number of fingers	Specific fingers	Specific landmarks
Same hand	10	7	4	10
Other hand-palm	12	7	3	7
Other hand-back	12	9	3	7
Forearm	12	9	1	4
Face and neck	12	6	4	11

Table 1. Number of participants who used a given strategy to create distinct gestures at each on-body location (*N*=12). Multiple strategies could be used for each location.

index *vs.* middle). Table 1 shows the number of participants who used each strategy while creating a set of gestures at each on-body location. All participants employed more than one common touchscreen gesture at each location (*i.e.*, varying the "basic gesture" in Table 1), except for with the *same hand* location, where two participants used only variations of a single tap gesture. The least frequent strategy was to vary which fingers were used; only six participants created distinct gestures by switching their fingers.

4.2 Task 1: On-body Location Preference

The location of a gesture on the body had an impact on the reported ease of use, physical comfort, and social acceptability of that gesture. Overall, of the five locations, participants most preferred *other hand-palm*. We also report on predicted use under physical constraints and for specific tasks.

4.2.1 Ease of Use

Figure 5 shows the rating scale results for ease of use, comfort, and social acceptability. The *other hand-palm* location received the highest average rating at 4.8, while the *same hand* received the lowest rating at 3.2. A Friedman test showed there was a significant effect of on-body location on ease of use ($\chi^2_{(4,N=12)}$ = 10.46, $p = .033$). After a Bonferroni adjustment, no posthoc pairwise comparisons with Wilcoxon signed-rank tests were significant. When participants were asked to choose both the easiest and most difficult locations to use, *other hand-palm* was selected as easiest by 5 participants, followed by *other hand-back* (3 participants). The most common reasons for choosing locations on the other hand were that it was natural, offered a relatively wide input space compared to *same hand*, and that it was similar to using a mobile phone. For example: *"I can use my palm as a touchpad. It has enough space to perform any gesture."* (P11). In contrast, eight participants chose the *same hand* as the most difficult location to use, mostly because they found the interaction unfamiliar, for example: *"I'm not used to it. It's different."* (P4).

4.2.2 Physical Comfort

In terms of physical comfort, participants were again positive about *other hand-palm* and *other hand-back*, giving them mean ratings of 4.5 and 4.4 out of 5, respectively; see Figure 5. As with ease of use, the *same hand* was perceived to be least comfortable, at 3.2. A Friedman test showed that the impact of location on physical comfort was statistically significant ($\chi^2_{(4,N=12)}$ = 10.24, $p = .037$). After a Bonferroni adjustment, no posthoc pairwise comparisons were significant.

In terms of the single most comfortable location, *other hand-palm* received the highest number of votes (7/12). For least

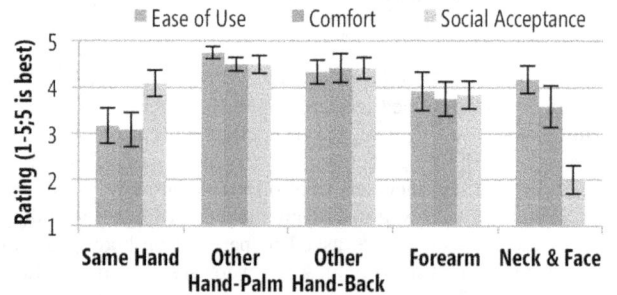

Figure 5. Average ratings for ease of use, comfort, and social acceptance for the on-body locations; 5-point scale, 1-*least*, 5-*most*. Error bars are *standard error*. Locations on the *other hand* (both palm and back) consistently fared well.

comfortable, six participants chose *face and neck* and five chose *same hand*. The most common reasons for finding the face and neck to be uncomfortable were that it is relatively far from where hands natural rest, and that it is curved; three participants preferred flat surfaces for performing gestures. For *same hand*, participants were concerned they would be limited in the number of gestures they could comfortably perform, for example: *"You don't have the freedom to move around. The movements and gestures would be limited"* (P12).

4.2.3 Social Acceptance

For social acceptance, *other hand-palm* and *other hand-back* again fared well, receiving the highest ratings at 4.6 and 4.4 out of 5, respectively; *face and neck* was considered to be unacceptable (Figure 5). A Friedman test showed that there was a statistically significant impact of location on social acceptability ($\chi^2_{(4,N=12)} = 30.31$, $p < .001$); again, due to the Bonferroni adjustment, no posthoc pairwise comparisons were significant.

Other hand-palm was selected as the single most socially acceptable location by 8 participants, who appreciated that it allows for discreet use thanks to its similarity with everyday activities, for example: *"It doesn't draw a lot of attention"* (P2). Not surprisingly, all participants considered the *face and neck* to be the least socially acceptable, most commonly because it attracts too much attention, or interferes with other activities. For example, P1 said: *"You would be considered as rude or have bad manners [if gesturing on face] during conversations."*

We further investigated social acceptability in terms of place of use and audience (Tables 2 and 3). All three hand input locations had high acceptance rates regardless of place—private, crowded public, non-crowded public, and workplace; across the four places their average acceptance rates ranged 85–96%. The *forearm* had a somewhat lower acceptance rate ($M = 71\%$), while the *face and neck* was generally unacceptable except in private. In terms of audience—alone, partner, friends, family, colleagues, and strangers—again, the *neck and face* had a much lower acceptance rate than other on-body locations. It was also interesting to note that *forearm* was again considered to be not as acceptable as the hand locations. One participant even said, while scrubbing his forearm: *"They may say I might have fleas"* (P12).

	Private	Crowded Public	Non-crowded Public	Workplace	Acceptance Rate (%) (SD)
Same hand	12	9	11	9	85.5 (12.5)
Other hand-palm	12	10	12	12	95.8 (8.3)
Other hand-back	11	8	12	10	85.4 (14.2)
Forearm	11	6	9	8	70.8 (17.3)
Face, neck	9	1	4	3	35.4 (28.4)

Table 2. Number of participants who would perform on-body gestures in different contexts, with average acceptance rates across contexts (N=12).

	Alone	Partner	Friends	Family	Colleagues	Strangers	Acceptance rate (%) (SD)
Same hand	12	11	12	12	10	8	90.3 (13.4)
Other hand-palm	12	12	12	12	12	10	97.2 (6.8)
Other hand-back	12	12	12	11	11	9	93.1 (9.74)
Forearm	11	10	9	9	7	5	70.8 (18.1)
Face, neck	9	8	6	8	3	1	48.6 (26.6)

Table 3. Number of participants who would perform on-body gestures in front of different audiences, with average acceptance rates across audiences (N=12).

4.2.4 Physical Constraints

We expected that pose (seated, standing, or walking) and whether one hand is holding a cane or dog leash would be critical factors affecting on-body input for people with visual impairments. Table 4 shows the number of participants who were willing to perform gestures at each on-body location under these physical constraints. With two hands free, the majority of participants were willing to perform gestures at all on-body locations, whether seated, standing, or walking. For one hand holding a cane or leash, however, only the *same hand* location was popular, with 9 participants willing to use *same hand* whether they were seated, standing, or walking. For two hands free, the responses suggest that participants may be less likely to want to make on-body gestures while walking than seated or standing, although further work is needed to confirm this possibility.

	Two-hands Free			One-hand Busy			Acceptance rate (%) M (SD)
	Seated	Standing	Walking	Seated	Standing	Walking	
Same hand	11	10	9	9	9	9	79.2 (7.0)
Other hand-palm	12	12	8	2	3	3	55.6 (38.6)
Other hand-back	11	12	8	3	5	5	61.1 (30.1)
Forearm	10	9	7	1	3	3	45.8 (30.6)
Face, neck	10	8	6	6	4	4	52.8 (19.5)

Table 4. Number of participants who would perform on-body gestures under different physical constraints, with average acceptance rates across constraints (N=12).

4.2.5 Input Type

To understand how participants would want to use each on-body location, we asked about five input types previously evaluated with sighted users by Weigel *et al.* [33]; see Table 5. *Other hand-palm* was seen as particularly flexible for supporting a range of input types. It was the most popular for handwriting, keyboard, number pad, and sketching, and was tied with *other hand-back* for touchpad-style input (*e.g.*, taps, swipes). *Same hand* and *face and neck* were the least likely to be used; for example, no one was willing to use the *same hand* as a keyboard.

	Hand-writing	Keyboard	Number pad	Sketching	Touchpad	Acceptance rate (%) M(SD)
Same hand	2	0	5	2	7	26.7 (23.1)
Other hand-palm	9	6	10	7	11	71.7 (17.3)
Other hand-back	7	4	8	5	11	58.3 (22.8)
Forearm	6	5	7	6	9	55.0 (12.6)
Face, neck	0	2	3	1	7	21.7 (22.5)

Table 5. Number of participants who would perform different types of input at each on-body location, with average acceptance rates across types of input (N=12).

4.2.6 Overall Preference

In terms of overall preference, and in line with the results above, the majority of participants favored *other hand-palm* (8 responses). *Same hand* and *other hand-back* also received two votes each. The *face and neck* was the least preferred location by 10 participants, while *same hand* received two votes. This overwhelming selection of *face and neck* as least preferred is particularly interesting given that its raw scores on ease of use and physical comfort were higher than *same hand* (Figure 5). This result suggests that the social unacceptability of *face and neck* overrode ease and comfort concerns.

4.3 Task 2: Touchscreen *vs.* On-hand Input

For Task 2, recall that participants performed the same input tasks on a smartphone as well as on their body. Overall, subjective preference for phone versus on-hand input depended on whether both hands were available.

4.3.1 Overall Preference and Perceived Trade-Offs

The majority of the participants preferred the two-handed on-phone condition (8 responses); three preferred one-handed on-hand input, while one preferred two-handed on hand input. The least preferred condition was one-hand with the phone (8 responses). Below, we summarize participants' perceived advantages/disadvantages for touchscreen *vs.* on-hand input.

While conventional touchscreen input (two-handed) was overall the most preferred, perhaps due to its familiarity, participants valued the advantages of on-hand interaction as well. A primary reason was that it allowed the phone to be safely stowed away, for example: *"You don't have to take out iPhone, you don't have to worry about getting it wet"* (P8). Some participants also commented that eliminating the need for the screen positively impacted ease of access and efficiency. For example, P9 said: *"You can just go right to your hand, you don't have to take the phone out. It could eliminate the screen."* Related, P7 commented on the aesthetic feel of the on-hand interaction, saying that it feels better not to have to interact with a piece of metal or glass.

All participants appreciated one-handed input for mobile computing because it can be important to have a hand free. For one-handed use, the on-hand input won out over the phone. One hand made it difficult to hold the phone and control it at the same time. P6, for example, commented that there was increased risk of dropping the phone, while P3 said: *"[It's] very uncomfortable, certain gestures can be mistaken for other gestures."* In comparison, two-handed use was considered easier, more accurate, and more stable. Four participants also noted that two hands allows for a greater variety of gestures. For example: *"It's easier because I have a free hand to maneuver the phone... do whatever you want to gesture"* (P11).

In general, all 12 participants felt it would be difficult to use their phone with both hands at times, particularly when they are walking. For example, P11 said: *"I have to stop walking and do the gestures and continue walking, or I have to wait until I get to the place where I can use it."* However, only six participants expressed the same concern with two-handed on-hand input. At the same time, even on-hand input with one hand was not always considered to be good, with five participants commenting on physical limitations of using the thumb for input with the one-handed use case. Two participants did not wish to interact with their phone at all when walking because of safety.

4.3.2 Ease of Use, Comfort, and Social Acceptability

Ratings on ease of use, comfort, and social acceptance are shown in Figure 6. To assess the effect of *device* and *hand count* on ease of use ratings, we ran a two-way repeated measures ANOVA with ART. The interaction effect between input methods (on-phone, on-hand) and number of hands was statistically significant ($F_{1,11} = 37.66$, $p < .001$, $\eta^2 = .77$). Posthoc pairwise comparisons using Wilcoxon signed rank tests showed that the phone was easier than the hand for two-handed use ($Z = -2.31$, $p = .021$). The opposite was true for one-handed use, with on-hand input being easier than the phone ($Z = -2.36$, $p = .018$). There was also a significant main effect of hand count ($F_{1,11} = 16.01$, $p = .002$, $\eta^2 = .59$) but the main effect for device was not significant.

Physical comfort ratings mirrored the ease of use results. A two-way repeated measures ANOVA with ART revealed a statistically significant interaction effect between input location and hand

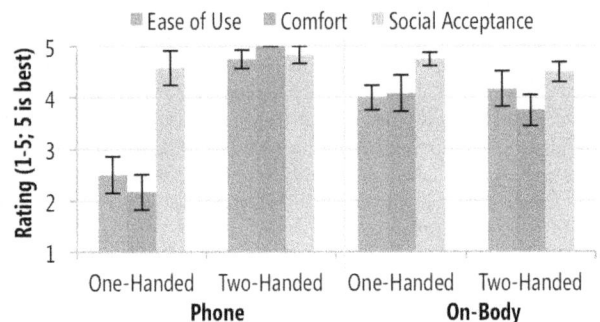

Figure 6. Average ratings for ease of use, comfort, and social acceptance for Task 2; 5-point scale, 1-*least*, 5-*most*. Error bars are *standard error*.

	Two-hands Free			One-hand Busy			Acceptance rate (%) *M (SD)*
	Seated	Standing	Walking	Seated	Standing	Walking	
Phone One	6	6	6	6	6	6	50.0 (0.0)
Phone Two	12	12	8	1	2	2	51.4 (43.0)
Hand One	11	11	10	10	11	11	88.9 (4.3)
Hand Two	10	9	5	0	0	0	33.3 (39.1)

Table 6. Number of participants who would use on-body input under different physical constraints, with mean acceptance rates across constraints (*N*=12).

count ($F_{1,11} = 63.15$, $p < .001$, $\eta^2 = .852$). Again, posthoc pairwise comparisons using Wilcoxon signed rank tests showed that participants felt more physically comfortable using two hands on the phone ($Z = -2.77$, $p = .006$), but that on-hand interaction was more comfortable for one-handed use ($Z = -3.07$, $p = .002$). There was no statistically significant main effect of input method, however, there was a main effect of number of hands ($F_{1,11} = 49.65$, $p < .001$, $\eta^2 = .82$).

Social acceptance ratings were high across all four conditions, ranging on average from 4.5 to 4.8 out of 5. A two-way repeated measures ANOVA with ART revealed no significant main or interaction effects of device and hand count on these ratings. While we asked about use of the input methods in different places and in front of different audiences as with Task 1, no clear trends emerged based on either contextual factor.

Table 6 shows the popularity of the four input conditions under different physical constraints—that is, seated, standing, or walking, and two hands free versus one holding a cane or dog leash. These results again reflect the tradeoffs between on-hand and phone input when only one hand is free. While the two-handed input conditions were both popular when two hands are free and the participant is seated or standing, these numbers quickly drop off for walking, and drop even further when only one hand is available. One-handed on-hand input, however, was perceived to be the most versatile, with 10 or 11 participants out of 12 willing to use it regardless of the physical constraints.

5. DISCUSSION

Based on findings from the study, we provide design implications for accessible on-body interaction for people with visual impairments, and reflect on our findings.

5.1 Design Implications

Dominance of hands. When combining results from both tasks, the hand-based locations (same hand, and other hand palm and back) were better received by participants than the forearm or face and neck areas. Participants appreciated, among other factors, the discreet and natural aspects of hand-based interaction compared to the relatively socially unacceptable forearm or face/neck input. We thus recommend supporting body input on the hand for people with visual impairments. This finding contrasts Weigel *et al.*'s [33] study with non-visually impaired users, which found the forearm to be the easiest and most comfortable location to use, although the palm also performed well.

Providing complementary input techniques. The preference for touchscreen input when two hands are available and on-body input when one hand is available suggests that on-body input should be used as a *complement* to the phone itself. A downside of one-handed on-body input as identified by some participants is that it does not offer the same kind of input flexibility as other locations. Even so, as a complementary form of input, it could be used to support a specific set of tasks more easily and quickly than pulling out and using a phone (*e.g.*, controlling navigation instructions, notifications, and audio).

Considering physical constraints. Relatedly, blind mobile phone users often have one hand busy with a cane or dog leash. Support for one-handed input is thus critical for supporting accessible information access on the go, a need that came out in participant comments. An issue that two participants commented on was that they hold their cane with their dominant hand, which was the same hand we had tested in our study. A system to support people with visual impairments would need to either allow for input on the same hand while also holding the cane or would need to easily support switching control to the non-dominant hand temporarily.

Creating gesture sets. Based on the user-defined gestures created in Task 1, we recommend that designers primarily utilize the basic gestures now well-established with modern touchscreens (*e.g.*, tap *vs.* swipe) for common on-body interactions. Varying the number of fingers and using specific landmarks on the body can broaden the set of distinguishable gestures. Landmarks, in particular, such as pointing to different parts of the hand, may be useful for rapid mode switching or to respond to a notification (as is done in *Imaginary Phone* [7]). These findings confirm Rico *et al.*'s [27] recommendation to create gestural interfaces that are similar to existing interfaces, and provide further support for an approach like *Imaginary Phone*, which transfers the standard phone interface to the palm. Finally, participants rarely varied their gesturing finger (*e.g.*, index *vs.* thumb), a finding that also mirrors touchscreen input preferences by sighted users [34].

Social acceptability. As with mainstream wearable research (*e.g.*, [37]), social acceptability plays an important role for on-body input for people with visual impairments. Our Task 1 findings suggest that participants prioritized social acceptability over ease of use and physical comfort by choosing the face and neck location as least *preferred* even while input on one hand was considered relatively hard to use and uncomfortable. Thus, participants preferred input locations that were discreet. This finding is in direct conflict with the dominant interaction model for Google Glass, so it will be interesting to see how heads-up display input evolves over the next few years.

5.2 Reflections and Future Work

As the first work on on-body interaction for people with visual impairments, our study was purposely exploratory, focusing on subjective responses rather than input performance. It will be important for future work to quantitatively assess performance of on-body input for people with visual impairments (*e.g.*, pointing accuracy, gesturing accuracy). A comparison to touchscreens, similar to Gustafson *et al.*'s study with sighted users [7], would

characterize the degree to which the increased proprioception of on-body pointing can aid users with visual impairments. We hypothesize that there will be a larger benefit here than for sighted users, which Gustafson *et al.* have already shown.

Participants' preferences changed between Task 1 and Task 2, from being largely positive about two-handed on-body input to more negative. This change highlights the importance of having users interact with working systems rather than assigning too much weight to subjective responses collected in the largely imaginary scenarios that the user-defined gestures method traditionally employs (*e.g.* [33,34]). Directly comparing on-body input to a touchscreen on the phone provided additional insight.

Our study identifies potential advantages of on-body input, even compared to the ubiquitous smartphone. One question, however, is how feasible it is to support on-body input for people with visual impairments. Sensing systems to date, including our own, have primarily used depth and color cameras [3,7,13,14,21]. The camera itself would need to be mounted on the body, perhaps as a pendant or on a pair of glasses. Ensuring the hands are in the camera frame could be an issue for eyes-free use although the appropriate lens would mitigate this problem. We did not encounter such framing issues in our study, but this could be because the camera was in a fixed location. Alternatively, tangible wearable devices should be further explored as a means of always-available input for this population (*e.g.* [37]).

In terms of limitations, the primary shortcoming is the disparity in how familiar participants were with touchscreens versus on-body input in Task 2, likely leading to a bias toward the touchscreen input; a multi-session study with more in-depth tasks with the interactive system could partly address this issue. Additionally, while on-body input is meant to support mobile information access, we conducted the study in a controlled lab setting and participants were seated while using the system. Different contexts of use may impact participants' reactions to the input. Finally, while most past work on wearable and on-body input has focused on sighted users, we did not include sighted users in our study. A direct comparison would be useful to understand the differences between sighted and visually impaired users' needs.

6. CONCLUSION

We conducted an exploratory study with 12 participants with visual impairments to better understand how to design accessible on-body input and to identify potential impacts of such input compared to touchscreen mobile devices. Finally, tradeoffs were seen in preferences for touchscreen versus on-body input, with on-body input considered useful for contexts where one hand is busy (*e.g.*, holding a cane or dog leash)—such as when the user is holding a cane or dog leash. The results also suggest that participants may be prioritizing social acceptability over ease of use and physical comfort when assessing the feasibility of input at different locations of the body. As such, the least preferred areas were the face and neck, and the forearm; in contrast, locations on the hands were considered to be more discreet and natural. Finally, we provided implications to inform the design of future accessible on-body input systems.

7. ACKNOWLEDGMENTS

We thank our participants, Nancy Pack, and the Maryland State Library for the Blind and Physically Handicapped. This work was funded by Nokia.

8. REFERENCES

[1] Ashbrook, D., Baudisch, P., & White, S. (2011). Nenya: subtle and eyes-free mobile input with a magnetically-tracked finger ring. *Proc. CHI'11*, 2043-2046.

[2] Bonner, M., Brudvik, J., Abowd, G., and Edwards, W.K. (2010). No-Look Notes: accessible eyes-free multi-touch text entry. *Proc. Pervasive '10*, 409-427.

[3] Dezfuli, N., Khalilbeigi, M., Huber, J., Müller, F., and Mühlhäuser, M. (2012). PalmRC: imaginary palm-based remote control for eyes-free television interaction. *Proc. EuroiTV*, 27-34.

[4] Frey, B., Southern, C., and Romero, M. (2011). Brailletouch: mobile texting for the visually impaired. *Proc. HCI International*, 19-25.

[5] Guerreiro, T., Lagoá, P., Nicolau, H., Gonçalves, D., Jorge, J. A. (2008). From tapping to touching: Making touchscreens accessible to blind users. *IEEE MultiMedia*, 48-50.

[6] Gustafson, S., Bierwirth, D., and Baudisch, P. (2010), Imaginary Interfaces: Spatial Interaction with Empty Hands and Without Visual Feedback. *Proc. UIST'10*. 3-12.

[7] Gustafson, S., Holz, C., & Baudisch, P. (2011). Imaginary phone: learning imaginary interfaces by transferring spatial memory from a familiar device. *Proceedings of the 24th annual ACM symposium on User interface software and technology*, 283-292.

[8] Gustafson, S. G., Rabe, B., and Baudisch, P. M. (2013). Understanding palm-based imaginary interfaces: the role of visual and tactile cues when browsing. *Proc. SIGCHI*, 889-898.

[9] Kane, S. K., Bigham, J. P., Wobbrock, J. O. (2008). Slide rule: making mobile touchscreens accessible to blind people using multi-touch interaction techniques. *Proc. ASSETS '08*, 73-80.

[10] Kane, S.K., Jayant, C., Wobbrock, J.O., & Ladner, R.E. (2009) Freedom to roam: a study of mobile device adoption and accessibility for people with visual and motor disabilities. *Proc. ASSETS'09*, 115–122.

[11] Karrer, T., Wittenhagen, M., Lichtschlag, L., Heller, F., and Borchers, J. (2011). Pinstripe: eyes-free continous input on interactive clothing. *Proc. CHI'11*, 1313-1322

[12] Harrison, C., Tan, D. and Morris, D. (2010). Skinput: appropriating the body as an input surface. *Proc. CHI'10*, 453-462.

[13] Harrison, C., Benko, H., and Wilson, A. (2011). OmniTouch: wearable multitouch interaction everywhere. *Proc. UIST'11*, 441-450.

[14] Harrison, C., Ramamurthy, S. and Hudson, S. E. (2012). On-body interaction: armed and dangerous. *Proc. TEI '12*. 69-76.

[15] Jing, L., Zhou, Y., Cheng, Z., & Huang, T. (2012). Magic Ring: a finger-worn device for multiple appliances control using static finger gestures. *Sensors'12*(5), 5775-5790.

[16] Landau, S. and Wells, L. (2003). Merging tactile sensory input and audio data by means of the Talking Tactile Tablet. *Proc. Eurohaptics '03*, 414-418.

[17] Lin, S. Y., Su, Z. H., Cheng, K. Y., Liang, R. H., Kuo, T. H. and Chen, B. Y. (2011). PUB - Point Upon Body: exploring eyes-free interactions and methods on an arm. *Proc. UIST'11*, 481-488.

[18] Loclair, C., Gustafson, S., & Baudisch, P. (2010). PinchWatch: a wearable device for one-handed microinteractions. *Proc. MobileHCI'10 workshop on Emsembles of on-body devices*, 4 pages.

[19] Malhotra, Y. and Galletta, D. (1999). Extending the technology acceptance model to account for social influence: theoretical bases and empirical validation. *Proc. HICSS*, 1006

[20] McGookin, D., Brewster, S. and Jiang, W.W. (2008) Investigating touchscreen accessibility for people with visual impairments. *Proc. NordiCHI'08*, 298-307.

[21] Mistry, P., Maes, P., and Chang, L. (2009). WUW - wear Ur world: a wearable gestural interface. *Proc. CHI'09 Extended Abstracts*, 4111-4116.

[22] Nanayakkara, S., Shilkrot, R., Yeo, K.P., & Maes, P. (2013) EyeRing : A Finger-Worn Input Device for Seamless Interactions with our Surroundings. *Proc. Augmented Human International Conference 2013*, 13–20.

[23] Pasquero, J., Stobbe, S.J., & Stonehouse, N. (2011). A haptic wristwatch for eyes-free interactions. *Proc. CHI'11*, 3257-3266.

[24] Perrault, S.T. & Guiard, Y. (2013) WatchIt : Simple Gestures and Eyes-free Interaction for Wristwatches and Bracelets. *Proc. CHI'13*, 1451–1460.

[25] Profita, H., Clawson, J., Gilliland, S., et al. (2013). Don't mind me touching my wrist: a case study of interacting with on-body technology in public. *Proc. ISWC'13*, 89–96.

[26] Rico, J. and Brewster, S. (2009). Gestures all around us: user differences in social acceptability perceptions of feature based interfaces. *MobileHCI'09*, No. 64.

[27] Rico, J. & Brewster, S. (2010). Usable gestures for mobile interfaces: evaluating social acceptability. *Proc. CHI'10*, 54-67.

[28] Shinohara, K. & Wobbrock, J.O. (2011). In the shadow of misperception : assistive technology use and social interactions. *Proc. CHI'11*, 705–714.

[29] Steins, C., Gustafson, S., Holz, C., & Baudisch, P. (2013). Imaginary Devices: Gesture-Based Interaction Mimicking Traditional Input Devices. *Proc. MobileHCI'13*, 123-126

[30] Tamaki, E., Miyaki, T. and Rekimoto, J. (2009). Brainy Hand: an earworn hand gesture interaction device. *Proc. CHI'09 Extended Abstracts*, 4255–4260

[31] Vanderheiden, G.C. (1996). Use of audio-haptic interface techniques to allow nonvisual access to touchscreen appliances, *Human Factors and Ergonomics Society Annual Meeting Proceedings*, 40, 1266.

[32] WebAIM. Screen Reader User Survey # 4 Results. 2012. http://webaim.org/projects/screenreadersurvey4/#demographics

[33] Weigel, M., Mehta, V. and Steimle, J. (2014). More Than Touch: Understanding How People Use Skin as an Input Surface for Mobile Computing, *Proc. CHI'14*, 179-188

[34] Wobbrock, J. O., Morris, M. R., and Wilson, A. D. (2009). User-defined gestures for surface computing. *Proc. CHI'09*, 1083-1092.

[35] Wobbrock, J., Findlater, L., Gergle, D., & Higgins, J. (2011). The aligned rank transform for nonparametric factorial analyses using only anova procedures. *Proc. CHI'11*, 143-146.

[36] Yang, X., Grossman, T., Wigdor, D., & Fitzmaurice, G. (2012). Magic Finger: always-available input through finger instrumentation. *Proc. UIST'12*, 147-156.

[37] Ye. H., Malu, M., Oh, U. Findlater, L. (2014). Current and Future Mobile and Wearable Device Use by People With Visual Impairments. *Proc. CHI'14*, 3123-3132.

Motor-Impaired Touchscreen Interactions in the Wild

Kyle Montague[1], Hugo Nicolau[1], Vicki L. Hanson[1, 2]

[1]School of Computing
University of Dundee
Dundee, DD1 4HN, Scotland
{kylemontague, hugonicolau}@computing.dundee.ac.uk

[2]Golisano College of Computing and Information Sciences
Rochester Institute of Technology, 20 Lomb Memorial
DriveRochester, NY USA 14623
vlh@acm.org

ABSTRACT

Touchscreens are pervasive in mainstream technologies; they offer novel user interfaces and exciting gestural interactions. However, to interpret and distinguish between the vast ranges of gestural inputs, the devices require users to consistently perform interactions inline with the predefined location, movement and timing parameters of the gesture recognizers. For people with variable motor abilities, particularly hand tremors, performing these input gestures can be extremely challenging and impose limitations on the possible interactions the user can make with the device. In this paper, we examine touchscreen performance and interaction behaviors of motor-impaired users on mobile devices. The primary goal of this work is to measure and understand the variance of touchscreen interaction performances by people with motor-impairments. We conducted a four-week in-the-wild user study with nine participants using a mobile touchscreen device. A Sudoku stimulus application measured their interaction performance abilities during this time. Our results show that not only does interaction performance vary significantly between users, but also that an individual's interaction abilities are significantly different between device sessions. Finally, we propose and evaluate the effect of novel tap gesture recognizers to accommodate for individual variances in touchscreen interactions.

Categories and Subject Descriptors

H.5.2 **Information Interfaces and Presentation**: User Interfaces – *Input devices and strategies.* K.4.2 **Computers and Society**: Social Issues – *Assistive technologies for persons with disabilities.*

General Terms

Measurement, Design, Experimentation, Human Factors.

Keywords

Touchscreen; Motor-Impaired; In-the-Wild; User Models.

1. INTRODUCTION

Touchscreen devices have become the norm for mobile technologies, with smartphones and tablets among the most popular. Companies are increasingly delivering their services and products via touchscreen technologies, meaning that those unable to access them are being excluded and missing out on the

advantages that these devices can offer. Touchscreens use gesture recognizers to interpret and respond to a wide variety of touch-based inputs. However, in order to accurately interpret and respond, the gesture recognizers rely on the user being able to consistently perform the touch actions as they have been defined by the device manufacturer and/or application developer.

Previous work investigating mouse interactions by people with motor-impairments demonstrated that consistent performance of interactions was not always possible as abilities were highly variable and erratic [6]. While works have investigated touchscreen interactions by people with motor-impairments, they have relied on a single session laboratory user study design, producing snapshot measurements of touchscreen performances, It is therefore not understood how variable motor abilities impact touchscreen interaction performance over time.

To address this knowledge gap, we conducted a four-week in-the-wild user study, involving nine participants with motor-impairments, to understand their interaction behaviors and measure performance abilities across multiple sessions. To the best of our knowledge, this is the first study of its kind, and offers new insights into the variable performance of touchscreen interactions by people with motor-impairments. The user study applied a novel approach, measuring user abilities of touchscreen interactions from typical device interactions with a Sudoku game. This approach allowed data collection to occur without the need for calibration tasks, and enabled greater number of collection periods than conventional laboratory studies. Using this approach, we ensure that our measurements reflect the true nature of variance associated with motor-impairments, and refrain from simply gathering a snapshot of the individual's abilities.

Our results demonstrate that not only do individuals with motor-impairments vary significantly on tap gesture performance and interaction behaviors, but also that the individual's performance varies significantly between interaction sessions. Based on these findings, we proposed novel methods to individually tailor the tap gesture recognizers to the ever-changing abilities of users. Finally, through simulations of novel tap gesture recognizers, we were able to achieve a recognition accuracy of 97%, significantly greater than the device default recognizer, thus improving touchscreen performance for individuals with variable motor abilities.

2. RELATED WORK

We discuss the existing approaches to understand and support interactions by people with motor-impairments, and strategies to conduct longitudinal in-the-wild user studies.

2.1 Motor-Impairments and Touchscreens

In recent years, there have been a number of user studies investigating interaction by motor-impaired users of touchscreen technologies. These efforts, aimed at improving accessibility, speed, and accuracy of user interactions. Particularly, authors have proposed novel techniques for user input during text entry

Table 1 Participant profile; study id, participant age and gender, prior experience with touchscreen devices, specific impairment and current accommodations to deal with symptoms. Deep Brain Stimulation (DBS)

ID	Age	Gender	Touchscreen Exp.	Impairment	Current Accommodations
P1	55	Female	Self-service machines	Parkinson's Disease, slight hand tremors	Regular medication to suppress symptoms
P2	59	Male	Tried iPod touch before.	Spinal injury, muscle spasms, hand tremors, Sensitive to light	Regular medication to suppress symptoms
P3	57	Male	Self-service machines	Parkinson's disease, hand tremors	Regular medication to suppress symptoms
P4	73	Female	Tried iPod touch before.	Myalgic Encephalomyelitis. Muscle spasms in arms and hands.	Medication to suppress mobility symptoms, not cognitive
P5	63	Male	None	Parkinson's disease, hand tremors	Regular medication to suppress symptoms
P6	21	Female	Tried iPod touch before.	Essential tremor	Medication when symptoms increase
P7	65	Female	Tried iPod touch before.	Parkinson's disease	Medication. During the study underwent DBS surgery
P8	75	Male	Has an iPod Touch	Parkinson's disease, hand tremors	Medication when symptoms increase
P9	74	Female	Tried iPod touch before.	Essential tremor	Regular medication to suppress symptoms

tasks, and recommendations for screen layouts, target sizes, and interactions styles [3, 10, 14, 13].

Guerreiro et al., [3] measured the performance abilities of tetraplegic people using tasks of common touchscreen interactions. The stimulus application included gestures such as tapping, directional swipes, swipes crossing targets, and swipes exiting the screen. The results showed that the optimal interaction method was tapping with target sizes of at least 12mm. Later Wacharamanotham et al., [14] compared tapping with Swabbing, an alternative input method of target selection for people with tremors, and found that Swabbing was able to reduce target selection error rates.

Nicolau and Jorge [10] investigated text-entry on virtual keyboards by elderly users. They reported a strong correlation between error rates and users' tremors. Furthermore, they demonstrate that applying personal touch offset models to users' inputs could significantly reduce error rates.

While these works have investigated the interaction characteristics and abilities of motor-impaired users, the laboratory study designs meant that the measurements were obtained from a single session. Therefore, it is unknown if the participants performances would remain consistent when measured for longer periods of time, or if their abilities would be subject to high variable and erratic change, as observed by Hurst et al. [6], with mouse interactions.

2.2 In-the-Wild Studies

Laboratory-based evaluations allow researchers to control for external factors that can influence participant interaction performance. Typically, these studies tailor situations to remove distraction and interruption, thus ensuring users' attention on the task and relative precision in interaction accuracy. While highly controlled laboratory experiments provide clean measurements with minimal errors, interaction behaviors captured within natural settings differ from those captured within the laboratory [2]. Additionally, laboratory-based evaluations impose time restrictions on user studies. Characteristically lasting no more than an hour at a time, they restrict the potential for capturing the performance changes that naturally occur throughout daily usage as a result of fatigue or situational constraints. During the

Dynamic Keyboard evaluations participants were asked to provide typing samples at various points throughout the day to begin to understand these changes, their findings revealed that typing performances could vary erratically, gradually or for some users remain constant [11].

Hurst et al. [6] conducted in-the-wild user evaluations to investigate the pointing performance of individuals with motor impairments in natural usage conditions. The initial phase of the evaluation required participants to complete baseline calibrations using the IDA [8] software suite, based on Fitts' Law clicking tasks. Beyond this initial phase, participants were free to login to the system and play games, or use other applications such as word processing. Using application interaction models, the authors were able to infer user intent from the mouse input, allowing measurements of overlapping button clicks, slips, accidental clicks, direction changes and excess distance travelled similar to the type of measurements possible within the controlled laboratory setting [7]. Hurst et al. [6] reported that participant performance was highly variable both between and within sessions, further supporting Trewin's early findings that individuals' performance can fluctuate due to medication, progression of a disease, or as a symptom of impairment [12]. Hurst et al. [6] argue that user evaluations with less control and constraints can help to reduce the risk of fatigue and stress by allowing participants to dictate their own break and interaction schedules.

3. USER STUDY

The purpose of this study was to capture in-the-wild touchscreen performance of motor-impaired participants in order to understand how individuals' abilities may vary over time.

3.1 Participants

Nine participants with motor-impairments, four male and five female, took part in the four-week in-the-wild user study. They were recruited through local Parkinson's UK support groups. Ages ranged from 21 to 75 (M=60, SD=17) years old. Table 1 provides details of the participants' individual abilities and medical conditions.

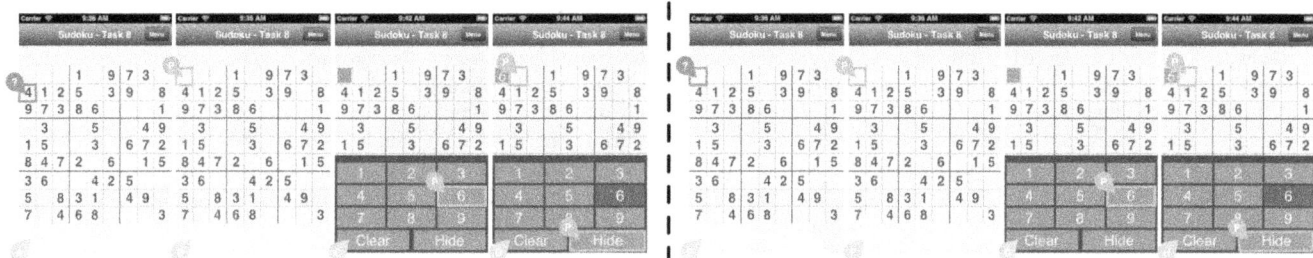

Figure 1 The Sudoku Game model refining the target intent for a wrong target error (left) and refining the gesture type of an unrecognized gesture error (right).

3.2 Apparatus

The high-level structure of the apparatus mirrors that of an earlier laboratory evaluation [9], whereby the participants were provided with a 4th Generation iPod touch device, preloaded with the stimulus application to be used in-the-wild. The Sudoku stimulus was designed to mirror typical interactions of mainstream touchscreen applications, and was embedded with the SUM framework, a data collection framework to capture the participants' interactions. The mobile device was connected to the university server via the participants' home WiFi connection, allowing the application to transmit the interaction data throughout the four-week in-situ study. The SUM framework enabled the collection of the following touch interaction features:

Touch Location (X, Y): represents the horizontal and vertical location of the user's finger when it is lifted from the screen. These locations are absolute values measured in relation to the physical screen dimensions.

Touch Offset (X, Y): captures the user's *x* or *y* offset between the touch begin (finger down) and end (lifting the finger off) states.

Touch Duration: captures the time duration between the first and final state of a touch gesture.

Absolute Touch Movement: measures the total Euclidean distance between all of the touch states of a gesture.

Straight-line Touch Movement: measures the Euclidean distance between the first and last touch states of a gesture, the combines touch x and y offset.

Relative Touch Movement: calculated as the ratio of *straight-line movement* to *absolute movement* to measure the amount of additional or unintentional movement within the gesture.

Movement Direction Changes (X, Y): measures the number of direction changes within the horizontal or vertical axis during the touch movement states.

Target Offset (X, Y): captures the user's *x* or *y* offsets from the center of the target interacted with during the touch gesture.

3.3 Experimental Application: Sudoku

This study aimed to understand the touchscreen interaction abilities of people with motor impairments; therefore, the application performed no interface adaptations or personalization. We used custom gesture recognizers to record all of the application interactions, they relied on the behaviors of the device's default recognizers to interpret and respond to the participants' inputs. A Sudoku game was selected as the stimulus application due to the appeal of mobile gaming; its logical gameplay strategy required that participants enter particular values for each cell to solve the puzzle; and roughly 40-70 precise tapping interactions could be captured from playing a single game. Furthermore, the design of the Sudoku board meant that the tapping interactions would occur throughout all of the screen

locations, giving an understanding of the participants interactions across the entire screen. Participants could interact with Sudoku application in the following modes. *New game,* this mode would ask the player to select a difficult setting depending on their skill level, and then a new Sudoku puzzle would be generated and displayed on screen. *Task game,* from which they could select one of the 14 predefined puzzles.

To interact, players had to tap on an empty cell to select it for editing, then enter the desired number using the onscreen number pad as illustrated in Figure 1. When the correct value was entered for a cell, the player could either select another cell to edit, or tap the *Hide* button to remove the number pad and reveal the entire board again. Alternatively, if a number were incorrectly entered, the selected cell would highlight this error by making the cell background *red*. Players could resolve errors by either entering another number, or by tapping the *Clear* button to remove the cell value. To complete the game the players had to solve the puzzle and enter the correct value into each of the empty board cells.

3.3.1 Touch Intent Discrimination

Within controlled laboratory user studies, it is relatively straightforward to establish a user's intended actions. Typically the design of the study is such that users have a clear goal, thus error identification is easy. For example, their brief would be to tap the onscreen targets as quickly as they can with their dominant hand. The resulting dataset would contain user touch information where the intended gesture and target are known. However, when conducting in-situ user studies it is unreasonable to assume that each user interaction carries intent, or that the device correctly interpreted the user's intentions. Therefore, it is vital to apply methods to discriminate between actions with and without intent. We leverage the logical gameplay strategy of Sudoku to aid this discrimination of the touch data.

Extract Intent from Sudoku Interactions. To successfully complete a Sudoku puzzle, the player must correctly position the numbers 1-9 into each empty cell, ensuring that no column, row or 3x3 block contains duplicate numbers. Since there is only one correct number per cell, once an empty cell has been selected we can infer the correct target for that cell. Therefore, we can discriminate between interactions that are accurate and intended, and those that are not, in the following way using our Sudoku *Game Model.*

Wrong Target. One possible scenario for intent correction is when the participant taps a target that does not respond to the tap gesture, implying that a nearby target would have been the intended target. The *Game Model* captures such scenarios in the following way, illustrated in Figure 1 (left). The participant taps the cell containing the number '4', which is not an interactive object and therefore no interaction feedback is provided. However, SUM records the tap gesture marking this object as the target. The participant next taps a nearby empty cell target that is interactive. This was potentially the intended target for the previous interaction, however there is still uncertainty. The next probable moves are either tapping the 'hide' button to remove the number pad, signifying that the user is happy with their number selection. Alternatively, they may tap a new cell and enter the next number. If either of these possible interactions occur then the game model marks the cell (B) as complete and the number '6' as committed. At this point the intended target for the original tap gesture (A) is refined to the empty cell above (B), moreover the other tap gestures are confirmed as intended tap gestures and targets.

Unrecognized gesture. Another common interaction error occurs when the participant performs a touch gesture that is unrecognized by the device. Possible reasons for a gesture being unrecognized is due to timing or movement values outside of the acceptable parameters for the tap gesture. The following example details how the Sudoku game modeler handles unrecognized gesture errors, to refine user intent, illustrated in Figure 1 (right).

The participant attempts to perform a tap gesture in the empty cell (E), but the tap duration exceeds the maximum duration parameter of the tap gesture recognizer. No interaction feedback is provided to the participant, but the gesture is captured and recorded by the SUM framework as an unrecognized gesture. Next, the participant repeats the action (F), this time it is recognized by the device and the cell receives the tap gesture. The scenario then plays out as detailed above for the *Wrong Target*. The Sudoku modeler can then refine the gesture type of the original interaction (E) from being an unrecognized gesture to being an intended tap gesture.

Unrecognized gesture and wrong target. As the name suggests, this error occurs when the participant performs a gesture that is unrecognized with a target that is not interactive. While it would be possible to use the steps detailed above to attempt to refine and correct the intent for these interactions, it was decided not to infer intent for these interactions due to the compound errors.

3.3.2 Validating The Sudoku Game Model

Participants were asked to complete data copying tasks during the study. Using the *task* game mode, they could complete one of the 14 predefined Sudoku puzzles using the solution sheets provided by the researchers. The predefined puzzles and solution sheets meant that the participants could copy the correct values for each cell without having to solve the puzzle themselves. Thus, any incorrect values entered were the result of an interaction error, such as tapping the wrong target. Leveraging the task sheets, we were able to obtain refined measurements for the participants' intended actions. When comparing the agreement between the intent classifications from the Sudoku Game Model with the copy task data, we found that the results were statistically similar, kappa $\kappa=.896$, $z=-1.524$, $p=.127$.

3.4 Procedure

At the beginning of the user study, the participants met for an initial training session and informal discussion with the researchers. This initial session took roughly 30-minutes to introduce the purpose of the study and to provide basic training of the stimulus application. Participants P1, P3, P5 had never used smartphone touchscreen devices before, and were provided further training on the basic device functionality and controls within this session. Once the participants felt confident enough to operate the device and the application on their own, the researcher entered the unique login details for that participant and activated the data

collection capabilities. Participants were provided with printed copies of the Sudoku solutions for the task puzzles, and encouraged to complete a number of the Sudoku task puzzles during the four-week study. Finally, the participants were provided with information to assist in connecting the devices to their home Wi-Fi network to ensure that the captured interaction data could be synchronized with the data collection server.

It was vital that the devices were able to regularly communicate with the data collection servers to return interaction logs, which allowed the researchers to verify that the devices were operating as intended. Additionally, participants were asked to keep a brief diary of their experience for the duration of the study. This was aimed at supporting the interpretation of the interactions, in particular providing a better understanding of extreme outliers in user performance. Since the system automatically recorded timestamps for all interactions, participants were only encouraged to take note of the unusual or out of the ordinary behaviors, such as feeling poorly or experiencing extreme symptoms.

4. RESULTS

Our goal was to understand how people with variable motor abilities interact with touchscreen devices in-the-wild. Firstly, we summarize the dataset of captured touchscreen interactions, and the extracted intent measurements. Then we describe the interaction performance abilities and relate them to the touch features and the accuracy of the device tap gesture recognizer.

4.1 Dataset Summary

Using the Sudoku application embedded with the SUM framework, a dataset containing over 244 interaction sessions, consisting of 23,474 touchscreen gesture interactions (taps, swipes and unrecognized gestures) was collected from the nine participants throughout the four week in-situ user study, show in Table 2. We breakdown and summarize the recorded touch gestures during the user evaluation in Table 3. 17,092 (72.8% of all touchscreen inputs) gestures were assigned user intent and target classifications using the Sudoku game model. These classified instances are used to test the classification accuracy of the device gesture recognizer

Table 2 Summary of participant gestures captured from the Sudoku application during the in-situ user study

Participant	Taps	Swipes	Unrecognised
P1	4275	43	1726
P2	2491	97	1053
P3	1094	22	491
P4	2529	25	86
P5	3467	13	37
P6	489	6	26
P7	3547	9	445
P8	250	5	15
P9	1026	19	173
Total	19182	239	4053

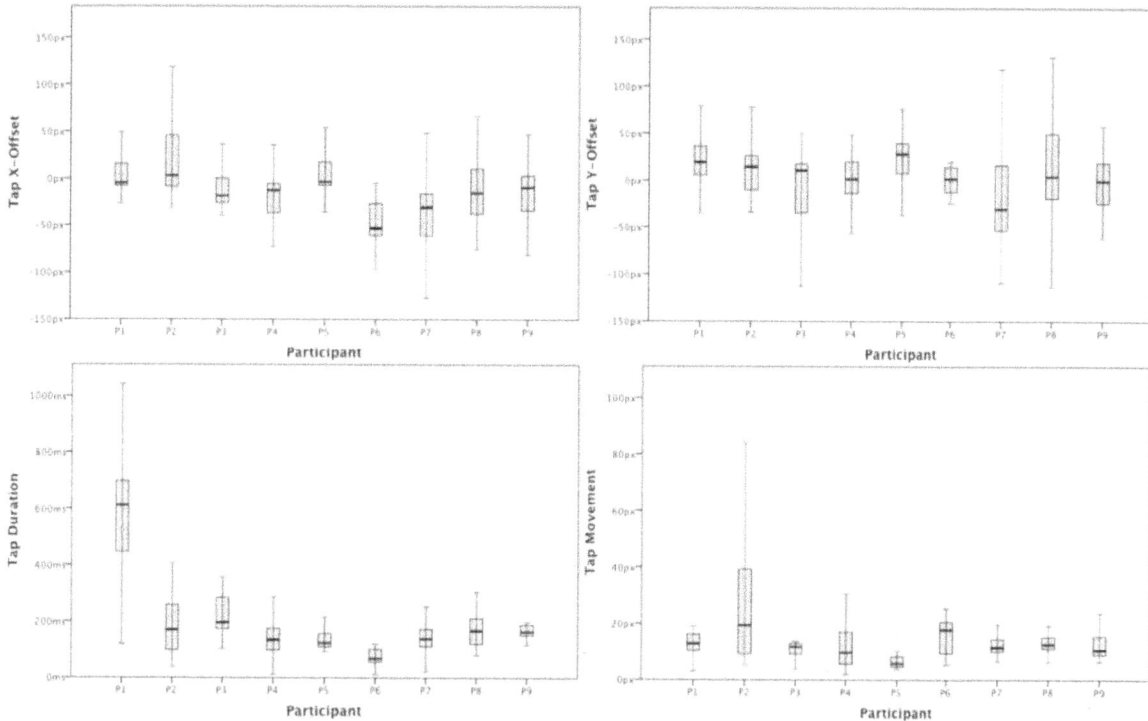

Figure 2 Boxplots of the overall tap x-offset, y-offset, duration and movement of each participant.

Table 3 Summarizes the 17,092 touchscreen gestures with intent measurements, showing the number of gestures that were recognized or unrecognized, and whether or not they were associated with the correct target. Overall, the default tap gesture recognizer was able to classify the users' input with 82.9% accuracy. The breakdown shows that 769 (39.9% of all 1928 unrecognized gestures) were in fact intended tap gestures on the correct target, however, the participants were unable to perform the tap gesture in line with the device tap gesture recognizer timing and or movement parameters. Furthermore, 2140 (14.1% of the 15,154 successful tap gestures) were recognized as the wrong target. These types of errors can be caused by involuntary movement when performing the tap gesture, or difficulties with target acquisition.

Table 3 Breakdown of recognized gestures (from default recognizers) and the resulting intent measurements using the Sudoku Game model

	Unrecognised	*Recognised*	
Correct	769	13014	**13783**
Incorrect	1159	2140	**3299**
	1928	**15154**	

4.2 Touchscreen Performance

We can see from the recognized tap gestures and corresponding intent measurements, that the participants were experiencing errors due to the selection of wrong targets and because of difficulties adhering to the fixed timing and movement constraints of the recognizers. However, it is unclear if these errors could be resolved by simply applying new fixed values for touch offsets, timing and movement parameters specific to this population, or is touchscreen performance dependent on an individual's abilities.

To answer this question Kruskal-Wallis tests were run to determine if there were differences in touch interaction characteristics between participants. We found that touch interaction characteristics were statistically significantly different between participants for, touch x-offset $\chi^2(8)=87.393$, $p<.001$; touch y-offset $\chi^2(8)=39.116$, $p<.001$; duration $\chi^2(8)=126.987$, $p<.001$; and movement $\chi^2(8)=91.970$, $p<.001$, shown in Figure 2. Our results suggest that x-offset, y-offset, duration and movement are the factors that were affecting touchscreen performance.

Our primary goal of this study was to identify how touchscreen performance behaves across time; *do performance abilities differ between sessions?* We applied Kruskal-Wallis tests to individuals' interaction characteristics to identify differences between sessions. We found that the these touch interaction characteristics were also statistically significantly different between interaction sessions for participants *P2, P3, P4* and *P7*, $(p<.001)$. No significant differences were observed in touch movement of tap gestures for participants *P1, P5* and *P8* between sessions, $(p>.05)$. However, the touch x and y-offsets were statistically significantly different between sessions, $(p<.001)$. Statistical differences in tap duration and movement only, were observed between sessions for participants *P6 and P9* $(p<.001)$.

Figure 3 illustrates the individual participant's daily average x-offset behaviors when performing tap gestures. It is clear from these figures and the aforementioned results that for most participants these interaction characteristics vary dramatically and erratically between sessions, making it unrealistic to predict a users current abilities based on previous sessions alone.

5. DISCUSSION

Our goal was to investigate the touchscreen performance abilities of people with motor impairments to understand the barriers to access these technologies. We collected interaction data from a four-week in-the-wild study with nine participants on a set of

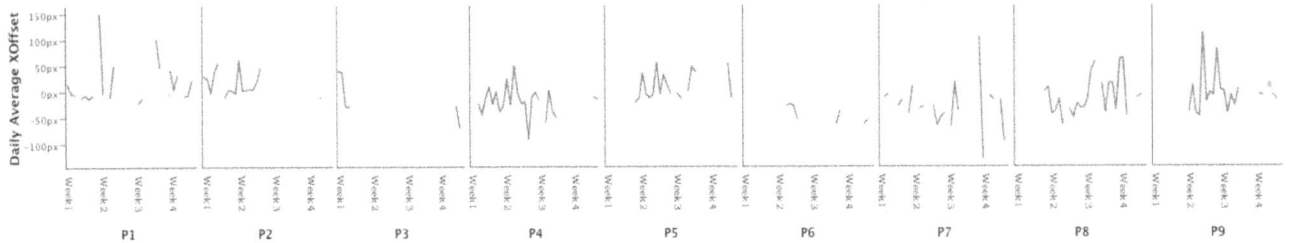

Figure 3 Line graphs showing the daily average tap x-offset of each participant.

eight touch features. Although we only collect data from a single application and analyze only the tap gesture recognizer, results show that performance widely varies between users. Moreover, we show that an individual's touch behaviors also vary between sessions, resulting in serious implications for the design of future gesture recognizers. In fact, the device's default tap recognizer was unable to deal with users' varying abilities and misinterpreted almost one in five interactions. Therefore, alternative gesture recognition methods would be required to accommodate these variances in performance, such as personalized touch models.

We can see from the gesture recognizer breakdown (Table 3) that 73.5% of the tap recognizer errors were due to the wrong target being selected, thus related to users' accuracy when tapping. A common strategy to improve accuracy when tapping targets on touchscreens, is to use touch offset models that can correct for the offsets of users' input, by shifting the intended touch x, y location a fixed amount. However, this strategy assumes that the user input is consistently offset thereafter; otherwise, this touch offset would need to be continually recalculated.

6. SESSION SPECIFIC MODELS

To mitigate the between session differences of user performance, we propose a novel approach leveraging measurements of the initial session interactions to predict current performance abilities of the user and adapt the tap gesture recognizer to match those abilities, by using probabilistic distribution functions to parameterize the tap gesture recognizer success criteria.

6.1 Probabilistic Gesture Recognition

Currently within mobile touchscreen interactions, the method of classifying *tap* gestures is the use of the x, y location (either touch begin, or touch end); and fixed movement threshold (movement between the touch begin and end states). However, we opted to use tap gesture recognizers that are not defined by fixed parameter boundaries. Instead, our tap recognizers use statistical probability to account for the variations in gesture performance between instances. The tap recognizers used in this evaluation applied Gaussian functions to define the attributes for gesture classification. Gaussian functions allow the tap recognizers to perform classifications based on probability of an action given a series of parameters, as opposed to relying on definitive parameters. For example, Gaussian functions are capable of resolving common touch offset errors whereby the touch occludes two or more possible targets. The target with the highest probability is suggested as the intended target. Similarly, they can account for variances within user performance, such as timing, rather than using a fixed maximum value to threshold all touches above this. The Gaussian function would simply return a lower probability. If the probability of the touch being intended were greater than the probability of it being unintended, then the tap would be recognized. However, the traditional fixed threshold

model would not be recognized if the touch were even 1ms over the threshold tap duration.

We defined the parameters of the tap gesture recognizer using example data of successful, intended tap gestures from our participants to obtain the mean (μ) and standard deviation (σ) values required by the probability density functions. The features included were: *x, y* location, *duration* and *movement*. In addition, the models also parameterized the *x, y* offset. Typically the x, y offset is handled by touch offset models defined on a per-device nature, shifting the user's touch input location by a fixed Euclidean vector. Previous studies have proposed user specific touch offsets models, reporting significant improvements in the precision of touch input [1, 4, 5, 15]. However, these works were not evaluated with motor-impaired users, spanning several sessions and long periods. Our results demonstrated that user performance varies significantly between sessions for people with motor-impairments. Therefore, we propose applying touch models that are specific to the abilities of the user on a per session basis.

6.2 Classifying Session Performances

Session features, based on the touch features of the gesture recognizers, were used to measure the variances of user interaction across sessions and cluster the individual sessions based on performance abilities. To ensure the sessions were clustered independent of any stereotypical groups, the features were selected based on the low-level touch interactions. Each session feature captures the mean and standard deviation of the corresponding touch feature, and are grouped by the gesture type they represent, e.g. *Tap* or *Swipe*.

The session features were then normalized using the standard score formula to aid the distance measurement process. The similarity of two sessions is based on the Euclidean distances of each normalized session feature, as shown in Equation 1.

Equation 1 Session distance formula; where F^x_i represents the feature value of the current session, F^s_i is the feature value of the comparison session.

$$d = \sum_{i=0}^{n} \left| F_i^x - F_i^s \right|$$

6.3 Evaluation of Touch Models

The purpose of this evaluation is to simulate the effects of applying our touch models and tap gesture recognizers on the Sudoku gameplay. We used the interaction data collected within the in-situ user study for both the training and testing data, it is possible to simulate the behavior of the tap gesture recognizer and measure the classification accuracy against the extracted user intention values. Our simulations explored the effect of the model subject, by using data from an *individual* user vs. a *group* model,

128

built using data from all other participants excluding the current user. Furthermore, we explored the effect of *user specific* vs. *session specific models*; these are user specific models built each session to accommodate for the user's current performance abilities.

6.3.1 Training and Testing Data

Testing Data: each simulation required 200 tap gesture instances with intent measurements. These tap gestures were sourced from the user's touchscreen interactions within the Sudoku application. Touch gestures were selected randomly from any of the user's Sudoku sessions whereby the gestures had an associated intent measurement.

Training Data: depending on the selection method of the user model condition, training data was defined as 300 touch gesture instances. For the *user specific* models, data was randomly selected from all available sessions. However, for *session specific* models, we defined a subset of sessions with similar interaction behaviors to the users current abilities, based of their session distances, from which the training data were selected. In both methods, the available sessions were subset by the subject condition of the model, i.e. *individual* contained only data from the current user. Furthermore, to ensure that the training data used to build the touch models was also not being used to evaluate the model's accuracy, the 200 testing instances were selected first, and excluded from the available dataset of training data.

6.3.2 Validation Method

Baseline performance scores were obtained for the device default configuration by measuring the number of recognized user interactions that match the previously extracted touch intent values. Each model was then scored against these baseline measurements, values greater than zero determined that user models correctly recognized more instances of user intent. In order to reduce the variability of the user model performance measurements, 30-fold cross-validation was applied to each model evaluation. Sessions were excluded if fewer than 10 touchscreen interactions were captured. Likewise, any model dataset that did not meet the required number of training (n=300) and testing (n=200) instances was excluded from the evaluation.

6.3.3 User Specific vs. Session Specific

A Kruskal-Wallis test was used to determine whether there were differences in the accuracy of the gesture recognizers between the *baseline* (*Mdn* = 85%), *user specific* (*Mdn* =79.7%), and *session specific* (*Mdn* = 95.1%) touch model conditions. Tap gesture recognizer accuracy showed a statistically significant difference between the touch models, $\chi^2(2) = 18.763, p <.001$. Pairwise comparisons were performed with a Bonferroni correction ($p<.0167$) for multiple comparisons and Post-hoc analysis revealed statistically significant differences in tap gesture recognizer accuracy between the *session specific* and *baseline* ($p=.006$), and *session specific* and *user specific* ($p<.001$) touch model conditions, but not between the *baseline* and *user specific* ($p = .118$). These results suggest that the *session specific* models have an effect on the performance of the tap gesture recognizers. Specifically, these results demonstrate that *session specific* user models can improve the touch recognition accuracy of touchscreen devices for individuals with motor-impairments, as illustrated in Figure 4.

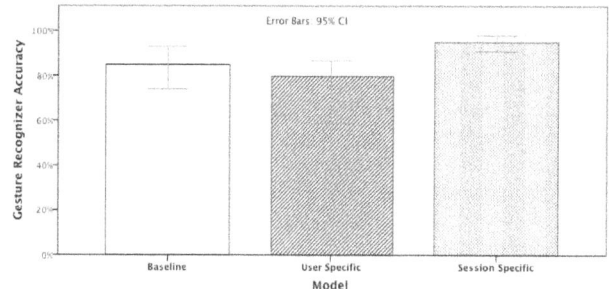

Figure 4 Classification accuracy of gesture recognizers for touch model conditions

6.3.4 Group vs. Individual Models

Mann-Whitney U tests were run to determine whether there were differences in tap gesture recognizer classification accuracy between the *Group* and *Individual* subject conditions. The median classification accuracy were not statistically significant between the stereotypical and individual user models for the *user specific*, U=48, z=1.156, p=.211 or *session specific*, U=19, z=-1.640, p=.101 models, illustrated in Figure 5. These results suggest that the subject of the dataset does not affect the accuracy of our touch models, therefore permitting the creation of touch models from the interactions of other users. However, we have found that when applying the session similarity measurements it is actually more beneficial to share data between users, with the results increasing from the *session specific individual* (*Mdn*=93.6%) to *group* (*Mdn*=97%) models. In contrast, the *user specific group* (*Mdn*=59%) decrease in accuracy from the *individual* (*Mdn*=82.6%). This shows that contemporary *user specific group* models cannot outperform *individual* models. However, by leveraging the similarity of sessions between users the *session specific* models can take advantage of larger interaction datasets to locate data that closely matches the user's current behaviors and abilities to define tap gesture recognizers that can improve the recognition accuracy of their interactions.

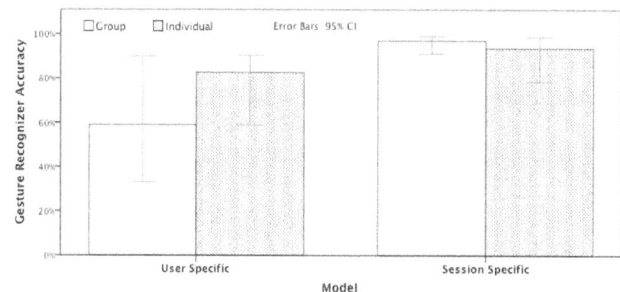

Figure 5 Classification accuracy of tap gesture recognizers for touch models by subject condition

Our results demonstrate that touch gesture recognizers using personalized user models can outperform the classification accuracy of the device default gesture recognizers. However, the *user specific* models relied on random selection of training data producing highly variable results that would not consistently improve touch recognition accuracy. Using the *session specific* models to create personalized tap gesture recognizers resulted in a more consistent performance, with significantly better recognition accuracy. Furthermore, the subject of the training data had no significant effect on the recognizer accuracy. This result was true for both *user specific* and *session specific* models. Moreover, the *session specific* models achieved higher levels of accuracy with the group condition than with the individual's own data.

7. CONCLUSIONS

We conducted a four-week in-the-wild investigation into the mobile touchscreen interaction performances of nine users with motor-impairments. We believe this study to be the first of its kind. Measurements of participants' touchscreen abilities were captured from the 23,474 touchscreen interactions made within our Sudoku stimulus application. Leveraging the logical strategy used to solve the Sudoku puzzles allowed us to obtained refined intent classifications for the captured interactions, thus removing the need for participant to complete semantically meaningless calibration tasks. Analysis of this dataset revealed that 39.9% of the unrecognized gestures were intentional taps on the correct targets, which were misclassified by device's default gesture recognizer due to the interactions exceeding timing and movement parameters. Similarly, 14.1% of recognized taps were associated with the wrong target, leading to the participants experiencing unintended actions.

Our results showed that touchscreen interaction characteristics varied significantly not only between participants, but also for the participants' own sessions. Based on these findings, we introduced and evaluated *session specific* gesture recognizers that accommodate for the variances of individuals' touchscreen performances by leveraging measurements from their current abilities. Participants' sessions were clustered using their interaction characteristics, allowing new models to be constructed from session data that closely matches the individuals' performance abilities at that point in time. Applying *session specific* gesture recognizers, we were able to achieve 95.1% recognition accuracy, significantly outperforming the device default recognizer. Finally, we investigated the effect of producing models from both the group and the individual's data only. While *session specific* models using an individual's data provided 93.6% accuracy, the models trained using data from the other participants was able to achieve 97% accuracy. These results have demonstrated that by sharing interaction data between users and accounting for their variable abilities, we can improve touchscreen performance for individuals with motor-impairments.

8. ACKNOWLEDGMENTS

Support for this project was provided by RCUK Digital Economy Research Hub EP/G066019/1 – SIDE: Social Inclusion through the Digital Economy. We thank our participants who provided so many insights and Marianne Dee who helped us locate participants for the research.

9. REFERENCES

[1] Buschek, D., Rogers, S. and Murray-Smith, R. 2013. User-specific touch models in a cross-device context. In *Proceedings of the 15th international conference on Human-computer interaction with mobile devices and services* (MobileHCI '13). ACM, New York, NY,USA,382-391

[2] Chapuis, O., Blanch, R. and Beaudouin-Lafon, M. (2007). Fitts' law in the wild: A field study of aimed movements. LRI Technical Repport Number 1480 (December 2007). Orsay, France: Universite de Paris Sud.

[3] Guerreiro, T., Nicolau, H., Jorge, J. and Gonçalves, D. 2010. Towards accessible touch interfaces. In *Proceedings of the 12th international ACM SIGACCESS conference on Computers and accessibility* (ASSETS '10). ACM, New York, NY, USA, 19-26.

[4] Henze, N., Rukzio, E. and Boll, S. 2012. Observational and experimental investigation of typing behaviour using virtual keyboards for mobile devices. In *Proceedings of the SIGCHI Conference on Human Factors in Computing Systems* (CHI '12). ACM, New York, NY, USA, 2659-2668.

[5] Holz, C. and Baudisch, P. 2011. Understanding touch. In *Proceedings of the SIGCHI Conference on Human Factors in Computing Systems* (CHI '11). ACM, New York, NY, USA, 2501-2510.

[6] Hurst, A., Mankoff, J. and Hudson, S.E. 2008. Understanding pointing problems in real world computing environments. In *Proceedings of the 10th international ACM SIGACCESS conference on Computers and accessibility* (Assets '08).ACM, New York, NY,USA,43-50.

[7] Hurst, A., Trewin, S., Hudson, S.E. and Mankoff, J. 2008. Automatically detecting pointing performance. In *Proceedings of the 13th international conference on Intelligent user interfaces* (IUI '08). ACM, New York, NY, USA, 11-19.

[8] Koester, H.H., LoPresti, E. and Simpson, R.C. 2005. Toward Goldilocks' pointing device: determining a "just right" gain setting for users with physical impairments. In *Proceedings of the 7th international ACM SIGACCESS conference on Computers and accessibility* (Assets '05). ACM, New York, NY, USA, 84-89.

[9] Montague, K., Hanson, V.L. and Cobley, A. 2012. Designing for individuals: usable touch-screen interaction through shared user models. In *Proceedings of the 14th international ACM SIGACCESS conference on Computers and accessibility* (ASSETS '12). ACM, New York, NY, USA, 151-158.

[10] Nicolau, H. and Jorge, J. 2012. Elderly text-entry performance on touchscreens. In *Proceedings of the 14th international ACM SIGACCESS conference on Computers and accessibility* (ASSETS '12). ACM, New York, NY, USA, 127-134.

[11] Trewin, S. 2003. Automating accessibility: the dynamic keyboard. In *Proceedings of the 6th international ACM SIGACCESS conference on Computers and accessibility* (Assets '04). ACM, New York, NY, USA, 71-78.

[12] Trewin, S., Keates, S. and Moffatt, K. 2006. Developing steady clicks:: a method of cursor assistance for people with motor impairments. In *Proceedings of the 8th international ACM SIGACCESS conference on Computers and accessibility* (Assets '06). ACM, New York, NY, USA, 26-33.

[13] Trewin, S., Swart, C. and Pettick, D. 2013. Physical accessibility of touchscreen smartphones. *the 15th International ACM SIGACCESS Conference.*(2013), 19–8.

[14] Wacharamanotham, C., Hurtmanns, J., Mertens, A., Kronenbuerger, M., Schlick, C. and Borchers, J. 2011. Evaluating swabbing: a touchscreen input method for elderly users with tremor. (New York, NY, USA, May 2011), 623.

[15] Weir, D., Rogers, S., Murray-Smith, R. and Löchtefeld, M. 2012. A user-specific machine learning approach for improving touch accuracy on mobile devices. In *Proceedings of the 25th annual ACM symposium on User interface software and technology* (UIST '12). ACM, New York, NY, USA, 465-476.

Designing a Text Entry Multimodal Keypad for Blind Users of Touchscreen Mobile Phones

Maria Claudia Buzzi[1], Marina Buzzi[1], Barbara Leporini[2], Amaury Trujillo[1]
[1] IIT-CNR; [2] ISTI-CNR
Via Moruzzi
Pisa, Italy
{claudia.buzzi, marina.buzzi, amaury.trujillo}@iit.cnr.it; barbara.leporini@isti.cnr.it

ABSTRACT

In this report, we share our experience and observations on the challenges blind people face with text entry on touch-based mobile phones, particularly from the perspective of one of the authors, who is blind. To better understand these issues we developed and tested *Multimodal Text Input Touchscreen Keypad* (MTITK), an audio-tactile text entry prototype based on multitap, which relies on a telephone keypad layout organized into five key groups with distinct audio-tactile feedback. Users explore the screen to identify the current selected key, tap to enter text, and gesture to edit it, while receiving the corresponding voice, audio, and tactile feedback; no additional equipment is necessary in our software-only approach. We implemented a prototype on Android and tested its usability with visually impaired participants; they welcomed its multimodality and the familiar layout, but also expressed the need to increase vibration pattern differentiation and refine the character selection mechanism.

Categories and Subject Descriptors

H.5.2. [**Information Interfaces and Presentation**]: User Interfaces – *input devices and strategies*; K.4.2. [**Computers and Society**]: Social Issues – *assistive technologies for persons with disabilities*.

Keywords

Accessibility, blindness, text entry, mobile devices, multimodal interfaces

1. INTRODUCTION

Smartphones are everywhere in our society: we use them not only to communicate with others, but also to entertain ourselves and organize our daily lives. However, the transition from hardware keys to virtual keys on a touchscreen has made their use more difficult for people who are unable to see. Cost is another detrimental factor for blind users, both for the smartphone itself and the need for additional costly equipment. For instance, external Braille keyboards are expensive and cumbersome to transport [6]. Moreover, despite the awareness of more accessible devices, some blind users prefer to buy cheaper options [7]. Even if costs were low, some users would not want to be dependent on additional physical objects in order to use their cellphones [8].

To tackle these difficulties, mobile manufacturers have incorporated accessibility suits into their products, mainly based on voice interaction, such as Apple's VoiceOver or Android's TalkBack. Still, voice interaction has its complications: it is not always accurate, it is difficult to use in noisy environments [10], and can be undesirable due to privacy or etiquette concerns [7]. Despite voice interaction flaws, mobile text entry through automatic speech recognition (ASR) and Text To Speech (TTS), remains the mode preferred by blind users [1], but it can raise privacy issues. Thus, an alternative text-entry method is worthy of investigation.

2. A PERSONAL PERSPECTIVE

This research was inspired by a previous study on haptic differentiation of user interface (UI) elements on mobile touchscreens [2], and by the personal experience of one the authors, who is blind. She uses two smartphones on a daily basis: a Nokia N95 and an iPhone 4S. The Nokia N95, released in 2007, has a slider form factor with a physical number keypad, it runs Symbian OS (v. 9.2), and the author uses TALKS as screen reader, a third party solution sold by Nuance. The iPhone 4S, released in 2011, is a touchscreen phone with no physical keyboard, and runs iOS (v. 7.1) which includes the VoiceOver screen reader. Each phone is used for a different set of tasks. In the past, she had used Nokia phones with Symbian, but it should be noted that this mobile platform was discontinued in 2011 due to a remarkable loss of market share. The author also occasionally uses an iPod Touch and an iPad, but she finds the latter cumbersome because of its larger size. In addition, she has briefly tested both Windows and Android phones, but still considers the iOS platform more accessible.

The older phone model, Nokia N95, is mostly used for traditional cellphone functionality: short text messages and voice calls. Thanks to the Nokia N95 physical keypad and the memorization of its character mapping, the author is able to type messages and dial numbers (if not present in the contacts list) more easily and comfortably than with the iPhone 4S. Besides, audio feedback without earphones is also more comfortable with the Nokia N95 especially when editing in a noisy situations. The iPhone 4S has the speakers on the bottom, so she has to hold the phone horizontally and bring its bottom side closer to her ear, which is impractical and awkward to do. In addition, the author experiences a longer battery life on the Nokia N95, due in part to a smaller screen size and lack of mobile Internet access. For these reasons, she feels more confident using the Nokia N95 as the main means of mobile communication, especially in case of emergency.

The newer iPhone 4S is used as a more portable alternative to a laptop for information and entertainment: news and ePub books reading through TTS, as well as music, audio and video podcast listening. However, the author does not like and avoids browsing the Web with VoiceOver, as she feels overwhelmed by too much feedback on page structure and navigation. Although she has some issues with text input, she also uses her iPhone 4S to communicate via online social networks, instant messaging, and especially e-mail. Because she finds the Nokia N95 more comfortable for making and receiving calls, she rarely uses her iPhone 4S for these tasks although it can be carried out in a more usable way. For example, when using an automated service over the phone, it is difficult for her to type the desired option unless she uses earphones or the speakerphone, since the phone's proximity sensor disables the screen while the device is held close to the ear. Another issue she has with the iPhone 4S, for privacy reasons, is the automatic voice announcement of the caller's identity on incoming calls.

For text input on the iPhone 4S, the author mostly uses the virtual QWERTY keyboard. She only uses Siri's speech recognition to write when she is alone and in a quiet environment. Although the author thinks that Siri's speech recognition is fairly accurate, she still has to resort to the virtual keyboard to correct and edit the inserted text. After having briefly used iOS 7 new character drawing method, the author thinks it is promising but cumbersome since some characters (e.g., letters *a* and *d*) are difficult to draw accurately enough to be recognized easily. She also likes this method's use of gestures to edit text —two-finger swipe to the right for space and two-finger swipe to the left to delete the last character for instance— and would like to use specific gestures for different text granularity, such as word or phrase deletion.

Regarding the author's use of the iOS virtual keyboard, despite being her most used text input method she has several issues with character insertion and text editing. For instance, she has accuracy problems when inserting characters while traveling by train or car given the small size of the keys, as a slight finger movement may cause the insertion of an unwanted character. Moreover, the use of the phone in horizontal mode for a modest increase in the size of the keys is not much better. Another difficulty with insertion arises from the similar sounds of adjacent letters, such as *m* and *n*; although iOS offers a phonetic pronunciation —such as Alpha, Bravo and Charlie for letters A, B and C— the author find its use impractical in the long run. She would also like to have direct access to frequently used punctuation marks (comma, period, question mark), and avoid changing the keyboard's set of characters to enter them.

Text editing with the virtual keyboard presents even more challenges. For instance, text deletion with the delete key only allows one to cancel one character at a time, and she needs to pay attention when pressing this key several times to delete more than one character. Text navigation and revision at the word and phrase level is also difficult: first, she has to explore and find the given text field, then she has to move the text cursor to the desired position, next she has to return to the virtual keyboard and find the desired key. Sometimes she prefers to clear the text field and rewrite the text from the beginning rather than editing it. Finally, the author would also like a gesture to activate the field's main actions (e.g., go, search, send and next), instead of having to search for the specific key or risk pressing it by accident.

To study additional details on blind user interaction, and collect other elements for better understanding of sightless text-entry via touchscreen, we developed the MTITK prototype, a software-only approach for multimodal text entry for blind users -- which is modeled following the standard multitap text entry system of telephone keypads.

3. MOBILE TEXT ENTRY ACCESSIBILITY

Before the advent of touchscreen smartphones, people mainly used their phones to communicate via phone calls or short text messages (SMS) using multitap on physical keys. Blind users adapted earlier cellphones in three ways: using special purpose devices, through accessible features in commodity cellphones, or without any assisting technology. Accessible mobile text entry development focused on Braille-based alternatives, word prediction, and the use of screen reader software [4].Today, touchscreen smart devices are ubiquitous, but the inherent accessibility issues with such interfaces have made their adoption by blind users difficult [5]. They have a smooth surface, which offers no distinction between display space and controls. Prior approaches regarding the use of touchscreen by blind users can be classified into three general categories: software-only, hardware-only and hybrid approaches [8].

Software-only approaches, such as TalkBack and VoiceOver, do not modify the device's hardware but adapt the underlying software. They can greatly increase accessibility but are limited to the specific device's hardware features. Hardware-only approaches do not modify the underlying software; they rely on placing physical tools between the screen and the user. For instance, special plastic cases or screen overlays can delimit screen borders; however, smartphones are not aware of such overlays and do not adapt to their presence or absence [4, 8]. Hybrid solutions combine custom software and hardware. For example Touchplates [8] are low-cost plastic overlays that interact with the underlying device software. Different overlays are available for varying interaction needs (e.g., keyboards, keypads, geographical maps), making it a flexible solution. Still, users would need to carry different overlays with them, which can be impractical.

Since MTITK mobile text entry approach is software-only, in the following we focus and expand on this sub-category.

3.1 Software-only Mobile Text Entry Approaches

Several software-only approaches for mobile eyes-free text entry on touchscreen have been proposed, and we can group them as follows: multitouch character encoding, character drawing, and constructive methods.

3.1.1 Multitouch Character Encoding

This approach relies on coded forms of characters, based on the number of fingers (pointers) the user has on the screen in a given moment. The most common encoding in use is Braille, in which a rectangular cell with six dots with a binary state (raised or not), offers 64 (2^6) possible patterns. For example, BrailleTouch is a mobile text entry solution which works on phone-size devices using both hands [13]; it was tested and well received by proficient Braille participants. A non-Braille example is DigiTaps [1], which uses encoding based on four gestures and minimal audio feedback, but it is limited to number entry only. These solutions rely on learning coded forms for every supported character, which could be a demanding cognitive task for users. Besides, despite knowledge of the encoded Braille alphabet, blind people may have low confidence in writing or reading it [4].

3.1.2 Character Drawing

In this approach, each character is input through the use of a pointer (finger or stylus), with which users draw directly on the screen. For instance, one study [14] tested eyes-free shorthand handwriting based on *Graffiti,* a commercial recognition system by Palm Inc. However, none of the participants were blind. Also, beginning with iOS 7, Apple offers a new accessibility feature for text entry called *Handwriting*, but we could not find any related formal study at the moment of writing. Even though research confirms that blind users are able to draw and make gestures on touchscreens [9], it is very difficult for them to learn and use handwriting [13].

3.1.3 Constructive Methods

In this kind of method users perform several actions to insert a character; multitap is the most famous example for mobile phones. Qwerty keyboard exploration, through touch and TTS feedback, is also a widely-used constructive text entry approach for the blind, as it is included by default in VoiceOver and TalkBack. Nevertheless, it is time-consuming and is considered to be of low usability [10]. TypeInBraille [11] is both a constructive and a multitouch character encoding method. It uses a three-step process to enter Braille characters, with four gestures for each row in a Braille cell. It is intended to be easy to learn, but it requires more actions to enter text compared to similar solutions. Another example, included in the commercial accessible suit Mobile Speak, features a touch entry mode based on the standard keypad and multitap [3]. It uses taps, gestures and a physical command key. Because of the lack of feedback before input and TTS based input confirmation, users need to memorize not only the keypad character assignment and ordering, but also the arrangement of keys; this requires several trial sessions of and is error-prone.

4. MULTIMODAL TEXT INPUT TOUCHSCREEN KEYPAD

MTITK originated from the idea of defining UI areas through haptic feedback in touchscreen cellphones using their integrated motor [2], and from the problems the blind author has with text entry on these devices, mainly in noisy environments.

4.1 Layout and Key Groups

MTITK layout is based on the common 12-button (4×3 grid) telephone layout. It is defined by the International Telecommunications Union (ITU-T E.161), and recommended by the International Organization for Standardization (ISO 9995-8). The names and characters used to identify keys on the keypad (from left to right and top to bottom) are: *one* (1), *two* (2), *three* (3), *four* (4), *five* (5), *six* (6), *seven* (7), *eight* (8), *nine* (9), *star* (*), *zero* (0) and *pound* (#).

We classified the keys into five groups, each with a distinct audio-tactile feedback, so as to identify a particular key based on its feedback and relative position to other keys or to the screen. We started by categorizing the keys into two subsets: the first comprises the odd and even numeric keys (from *one* to *nine*); the second subset is the bottom row (*star*, *zero* and *pound* keys). Each subset is further divided differently. The first subset of keys is grouped based on compass points: cardinal points (keys *two*, *four*, *six* and *eight*), intercardinal points (keys *one*, *three*, *seven* and *nine*), and a center (key *five*). The bottom row subset is grouped based on key identification characters: zero (homonymous key) and symbols (keys *star* and *pound*). With this classification, illustrated in Fig. 1, no keys with the same audio-tactile feedback are next to each other.

4.2 Character Ordering, Assignment and Insertion

The keypad character ordering and assignment used in MTITK is based on the standard for the 12-key telephone keypad of the European Telecommunications Standards Institute (ETSI ES 202 130). At the time of writing, we only support the required character repertoire and essential letters for English, French, Italian and Spanish. All the letters are assigned to keys *two* to *nine*. The assignment of special characters is not indicated in the standard, so we distributed them among keys *one*, *star*, *zero* and *pound*. Only the *new line* character is inserted through a gesture.

MTITK also has a two-state (*down* and *up*) shift status, controlled with a set of gestures, which toggles the set of characters available. If the shift status is *down*, letters will be lower case, and a subset of special characters will be available. Otherwise, letters will be upper case, and a different subset of special characters will be available. The space and numeric characters are selectable at the same amount of taps on both *down* and *up* shift statuses.

Character insertion is a two-step process. First the user explores the keypad with one finger (the primary pointer); audio-tactile feedback will be provided according to the key group of the active key (i.e., the key currently under the primary pointer). Once the desired key is active, without raising or changing the active key, the user taps the required number of times anywhere on the screen to select the given character, and finally, the device will announce the entered character name through TTS and a short vibration will confirm character insertion.

4.3 Gestures and Additional Actions

Additional gestures – simple continuous strokes drawn on the UI – allow the user to perform text editing (change shift status and delete or read text), and insert the new line character, or the current text field command (e.g., search, send, and go). When a gesture is recognized by the application and executable within the current editor context, the user is notified through a short vibration pattern (that is the same for all gestures) and the corresponding TTS feedback (e.g., "deleted all text"). We based the gestures we used on those used by TalkBack's default settings, which consist of single right-angled swipes. However, we also extended and attached granularity semantics to changes in direction or shape of gestures. For instance, a swipe left deletes the last character, a swipe left then up deletes the last word, a swipe left then down deletes the last phrase, and a swipe left then down then right clears the text field. Another example are the gestures for the shift status: a chevron for shift up and a chevron inverted for shift down, both made from left to right.

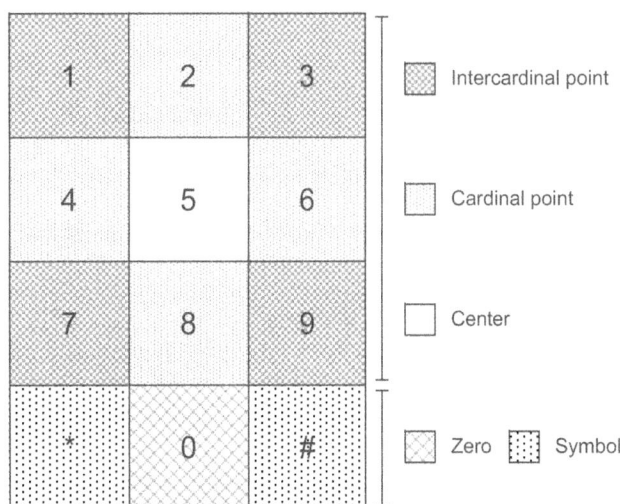

Fig. 1. Keypad layout and key groups

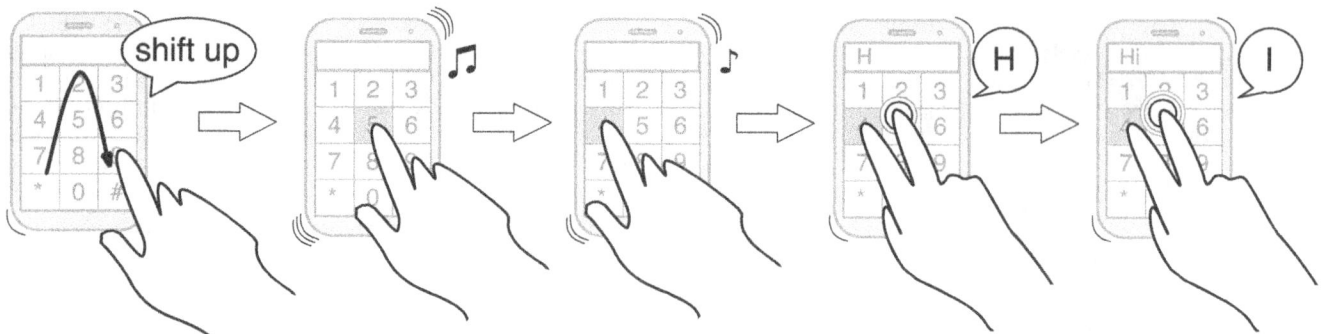

Fig. 2: An example of how a user can enter the word "HI" in MTITK.

4.4 Multimodal Interaction

MTITK has four interaction modes: finger multi-touch via the screen for input, speech, audio, and tactile vibrations for output and feedback. Speech is used for character names upon insertion; on deletion or reading of the last inserted character, word, sentence or all of the text; and on the field command name. Audio-tactile feedback is used cross-modally (both modes convey the same meaning) for the exploration and identification of the keys. In all of the previous cases, a short vibration pattern confirms the recognition and execution of the given action. Figure 2 illustrates how this multimodal approach can be used to enter text accurately. Moreover, it would be possible to locate keys in noisy environments using primarily haptic feedback, even when the audio (including speech) is not clearly heard.

5. PROTOTYPE IMPLEMENTATION

To test the use of MTITK as well as identify its usability issues, we designed and developed an initial prototype. It was implemented in Android; in order to ease development regarding the application programming interface (API) and new accessibility features, the minimum supported Android version is 4.2 (API level 17). For speech synthesis, we used Google TTS. During development and testing, we used three Android touchscreen smartphone models: Galaxy Nexus, Nexus 4 and Nexus 5. All of them have a slate form factor and share similar physical specifications. For gesture recognition we used the Android Gesture package, which offers similarity comparison of a given gesture and a gesture reference library based on their respective Euclidean and Cosine distances.

6. USABILITY TESTING

6.1 Preliminary Assessment

In an early assessment of MTITK, two blind participants, one female (the blind co-author) and one male, evaluated our initial prototype through a usability test. Both participants are proficient users of electronic devices, including computers and smartphones (both of them use iPhones). During the test we used the think-aloud protocol, in which the participants expressed their thoughts while freely using the interface or performing specific tasks.

First, we explained the scope of MTITK, its features and how to use it. Then we handed both participants our development devices (Galaxy Nexus and Nexus 4) and asked them to freely explore the keypad's interface. Once they became familiar with the layout, the distinct keypad groups and audio-tactile feedback, we finally asked them to perform specific text entry tasks (e.g., write capital letters, read the last character, delete the last entered word), in both a quiet and a noisy environment (we asked three people to have a normal conversation around them). At that point, we also

observed the way the participants held the devices, how they drew the gestures and which fingers they used for character insertion.

MTITK was well received by both participants. They could accurately identify keys through audio-tactile feedback, even in the noisy environment. They also appreciated the use of the standard keypad layout. We noted that the participant author with the secondary cellphone (with physical keys) was better at remembering character assignment and ordering. Both participants held the device in one hand and used the other (dominant) hand, for text entry. In the beginning, participants used their index finger for keypad exploration and the middle finger for tapping. Later they also used the middle finger for exploration and the index and ring fingers for tapping. We also noticed some difficulties performing gestures with steep angles, as the participants were more likely to draw rounded strokes.

6.2 Pilot Test

Based on previous observations and the feedback received from the participants during the preliminary assessment of MTTIK, we improved the prototype, mainly increasing the input and feedback timings. We then proceeded to carry out an informal pilot test, with a larger, heterogeneous group of participants. We first asked them to complete a questionnaire about their use of mobile touchscreen devices and how they perform text entry on them. Then we demonstrated MTITK and asked them to test it.

6.2.1 Participants

Fourteen visually impaired participants were recruited from three different local centers for blind and low-vision individuals. The group was composed of 6 females and 8 males, with ages ranging from 26 to 70 years (median age 44 years); 3 of the participants had severe low vision, 3 were blind from birth, 3 blind from adolescence, and 5 became blind as adults. Participants have been compensated with a flash memory card.

6.2.2 Touchscreen mobile use and text entry

All of the participants have frequently used mobile phones with a physical keypad, and most of them use this kind of mobile phone exclusively or in combination with touch-based devices. With the exception of one participant, all of them have used touchscreen phones, of which four use these devices exclusively. Almost all of participants reported they remembered the standard letter mapping of 12-key phone keypad fairly well, one reported recalling it quite well, and another one reported remembering more or less.

Most of the participants who have touchscreen phones frequently or always use the virtual QWERTY keyboard. Few participants use command and text dictation (e.g., Siri for iOS); most of them never or rarely use this feature. Only one of the participants frequently uses an alternate text entry method, based on Braille.

We asked the participants about the level of difficulty they experience while performing certain text entry tasks on the QWERTY virtual keyboard (Table 1). It should be noted that two of the participants answered "I don't know" in all of the tasks: one of them does not use this virtual keyboard; the other had not used a touch-based phone before. The two top difficult tasks, as reported by the participants, are the deletion of one or more words and the placement of the cursor. We also noticed that a considerable number of participants did not know how to select text or use autocomplete on their touch-based mobile devices.

Table 1. Number of participants by self-reported difficulty level on text entry and editing tasks on the QWERTY virtual keyboard. Scale: VE (Very easy), EA (Easy), NE (Neutral), DI (Difficult), VD (Very difficult) and DK (I don't know)

Task	VE	EA	NE	DI	VD	DK
Identify keys	4	5	1	1	1	2
Autocomplete	1	1	4	1	0	7
Delete last character	5	5	2	0	0	2
Delete one or more words	2	1	0	5	4	2
Place the cursor	1	2	2	4	3	2
Select text	1	0	0	2	2	9
Read inserted text	6	4	1	1	0	2

6.2.3 Procedure

We followed a procedure similar to the one used in the initial assessment, in which we explained the scope of MTITK, its features, and how to use it. In this test we used three Nexus 5 mobile phones with Android 4.4 as operating system. This multitouch model features a capacitive screen of 4.95 inches and weighs 130g. It has only three physical buttons: the power button on the upper right side, and volume up and down on the upper left side. No tactile boundaries were used to delimit the display area on the front of the devices. All voice feedback was given using Google TTS, Italian language pack.

In the first phase of the test, we asked the participants to freely explore the prototype's layout, the different pattern vibrations and audio feedback for each group of keys, to practice the letter mapping, and the gestures for editing actions. Next, we asked the participants to perform three tasks: write a common four-letter word, write a word with all the vowels, and compose a telephone number (using the numeric input of MTITK). The tasks were performed with vocal feedback alone, and with vocal and haptic feedback, in both a noisy and a quiet environment. We used the think-aloud protocol during the test in a quiet environment; for the noisy environment we asked them to give us feedback after task completion. In both cases, we observed participants' actions while they performed each of the tasks.

6.2.4 Results

Reception of the prototype varied from mixed to positive. All of the participants preferred both voice and haptic feedback compared to voice feedback alone. However, in the case of noisy environments, half of the users expressed difficulty in correctly identifying the keys based on haptic feedback; the other half of the participants could identify the different vibration patterns after using the prototype for a few minutes, but needed to focus more on exploration of the keypad.

Most of the participants welcomed the use of the familiar keypad layout. However, in the beginning some of the users had difficulty correctly remembering standard keypad letter mapping, although most of them had previously reported a good recall of it. Likewise, part of the group had difficulty remembering the editing gestures they had practiced in the first phase of the test. Also, when trying to enter text some participants instinctively lifted their finger from the screen and proceeded to tap the keys as they are used to doing on a physical keypad. As with the preliminary test, we observed difficulty in performing certain gesture figures, especially those with right and steep angles. We noticed that the age from which the participant has been visually impaired seems to affect form of gestures; people blind from an early age appeared to have more difficulty.

Nearly all of the participants liked the idea of using the mobile phone vibration motor to identify areas of the keypad UI, but expressed that it should be easier to differentiate the current vibration patterns. In addition, they also expressed their interest in using MTITK as an alternate text entry method for a more private and discrete interaction in scenarios where using dictation or TTS would be inconvenient. Furthermore, MTITK was most appreciated for composing telephone numbers in a noisy environment. Being a simpler task than letter entry, the participants indicated they could correctly identify the key number based on the haptic feedback and position of their finger on the touchscreen.

7. OBSERVATIONS AND LESSONS LEARNED

Despite the ongoing development and early stage of MTITK, we share the following observations and lessons learned so far during its design, implementation and testing.

- Among the participants, iOS is by far the most popular mobile platform. Of the 16 participants, only one does not regularly use a touchscreen device, 11 use an iPhone, and 4 use an Android phone. Further, 8 participants also use other mobile touchscreen devices, such as music players (mainly iPod) and tablets (mostly iPad). The main reason for the preference of iOS, as explained by the participants, is the considerable set of accessible features on the built-in screen reader VoiceOver, although significant issues have been identified regarding its usability [10]. While both VoiceOver and TalkBack were initially released in 2009 for their respective mobile platforms, VoiceOver is based on its desktop counterpart, released almost a decade ago; consequently, it has a bigger and more mature set of features than TalkBack.

- Due to the open nature of Android it is possible to change or extend many of its system-wise features, such as input method editors and TTS engines, whether with third-party solutions or customized alternatives. Only a more limited customization of these features is possible in iOS, if at all. Moreover, the core Android platform and TalkBack are open source, so it is possible to have a finer degree of customization and understanding of the software. We chose Android over iOS because of this openness and the possibility of developing software on multiple platforms, as well as the usually lower cost of the devices. Nonetheless, the Android platform is much more fragmented than iOS. Several manufacturers make a plethora of models, with different form factors, electronic components and features. This can hinder the implementation and testing of a unified user experience of publicly released software. In addition, as pointed out earlier, iOS is the most popular choice for an accessible experience on mobile touchscreen devices at the moment. Still, we think Android is more suited for academic research and development on mobile device accessibility software.

- Individual attributes and abilities have a significant impact on learning different text entry methods and on their performance [12], but so do previous experiences and technical aptitudes of users. Both participants in our preliminary test were technologically experienced and proficient, as they aimed to better understand the devices they use. Although we obtained valuable feedback from these participants, we also overlooked the different needs and aptitudes of less experienced users. For instance, during the pilot test less experienced participants had more difficulty remembering the keypad character mapping, performing gestures and remembering the editing commands. When designing for universal access, it is crucial to have early feedback of both proficient and novice users.

- For the preliminary design of UIs, we suggest wireframing with engraved and high reliefs. An expensive embossing printer is not necessary since these wireframes can be made on plastic, cardboard or other cheap material, with silicone glue or wax sticks. It is a convenient and timesaving way to explain the layout, disposition and functioning of UI elements or other graphical elements to blind or visually impaired people and obtain their feedback. Another option is to use cut cardboard, as we did in our pilot test, in order to have a complementary representation (besides verbal) of the shape of the gestures.

- A substantial proportion of visually impaired mobile phones users do not know all of the accessibility features of their devices. For instance, some participants talking among themselves realized they did not know a given gesture, feature, or option of their phones. Moreover, after the pilot test one of the participants asked the authors for help configuring and understanding his Android device, as he realized he only knew and used its basic accessibility functions.

- Awareness of existing solutions and current studies on accessibility motivates visually impaired people to adopt new technology. Several participants acquired their touchscreen phones after participating in a previous study. Some of them, after our pilot test, expressed an interest in upgrading their touchscreen mobile phones or acquiring one for the first time.

8. CONCLUSION

In this report, we have described the challenges that visually impaired people face in touch-based mobile text entry, and we have shared our experience while developing and studying a multimodal software-only solution to overcome these challenges. We have described our approach, the ideas received, and possible improvements. In addition to continuing our study, we think there is still much work to do on the use of multitouch gestures by blind people on handheld devices, based on our usability tests and available literature. For this reason, in future work we will also study how visually impaired people perform gestures on mobile touchscreen phones. In spite of the early stage of the project, we hope the lessons and observations we presented will be helpful to other researchers and entities interested in improving touch-based mobile devices for the visually impaired.

9. REFERENCES

[1] Azenkot, S. and Lee, N.B. Exploring the Use of Speech Input by Blind People on Mobile Devices. In Proc. 15th International ACM SIGACCESS Conference on Computers and Accessibility, ACM (2013), 11:11-11:18.

[2] Buzzi, M.C., Buzzi, M., Leporini, B., and Paratore, M.T., 2013. Vibro-Tactile Enrichment Improves Blind User Interaction with Mobile Touchscreens. In Human-Computer Interaction--Interact 2013 Springer, 641-648.

[3] Code Factory, 2012. Mobile Speak and Mobile Magnifier for Symbian/S60 Phones Code Factory, S.L, 08221 Terrassa (Barcelona).

[4] Guerreiro, T., 2012. User-Sensitive Mobile Interfaces: Accounting for Individual Differences amongst the Blind IST - Technical University of Lisbon, R. Alves Redol, 9, 1000-029, Lisboa, Portugal.

[5] Guerreiro, T., Jorge, J., and Gonçalves, D., 2011. Exploring the Non-Visual Acquisition of Targets on Touch Phones and Tablets.

[6] Guerreiro, T., Lagoá, P., Nicolau, H., Santana, P., and Jorge, J. Mobile text-entry models for people with disabilities. In Proc. 15th European conference on Cognitive ergonomics, (2008), 39.

[7] Kane, S.K., Jayant, C., Wobbrock, J.O., and Ladner, R.E. Freedom to roam: a study of mobile device adoption and accessibility for people with visual and motor disabilities. In Proc. 11th international ACM SIGACCESS, (2009).

[8] Kane, S.K., Morris, M.R., and Wobbrock, J.O. Touchplates: low-cost tactile overlays for visually impaired touch screen users. In Proc. 15th International ACM SIGACCESS, (2013), 22.

[9] Kane, S.K., Wobbrock, J.O., and Ladner, R.E. Usable gestures for blind people: understanding preference and performance. In Proc. SIGCHI Conference, (2011).

[10] Leporini, B., Buzzi, M.C., and Buzzi, M. Interacting with mobile devices via VoiceOver: usability and accessibility issues. In Proc. 24th Australian Computer-Human Interaction Conference, (2012), 339-348.

[11] Mascetti, S., Bernareggi, C., and Belotti, M. TypeInBraille: a braille-based typing application for touchscreen devices. In Proc. 13th international ACM SIGACCESS, (2011).

[12] Oliveira, J., Guerreiro, T., Nicolau, H., Jorge, J., and Gonçalves, D. Blind People and Mobile Touch-based Text-entry: Acknowledging the Need for Different Flavors. In Proc. 13th International ACM SIGACCESS Conference on Computers and Accessibility, ACM (2011), 179-186.

[13] Plimmer, B., Crossan, A., Brewster, S.A., and Blagojevic, R. Multimodal collaborative handwriting training for visually-impaired people. In Proc. SIGCHI Conference, (2008), 393-402.

[14] Tinwala, H. and MacKenzie, I.S. Eyes-free text entry on a touchscreen phone. In Proc. Science and Technology for Humanity (TIC-STH), IEEE (2009), 83-88.

BraillePlay: Educational Smartphone Games
for Blind Children

Lauren R. Milne[1], Cynthia L. Bennett[1], Shiri Azenkot[2], Richard E. Ladner[1]

[1]Computer Science and Engineering
University of Washington Box 352350
Seattle, WA 98195-2350
{milnel2, bennec3, ladner}@cs.washington.edu

[2]Jacobs Technion-Cornell Institute
Cornell Tech
111 8th Ave #302, New York, NY 10011
shiri.azenkot@cornell.edu

ABSTRACT

There are many educational smartphone games for children, but few are accessible to blind children. We present BraillePlay, a suite of accessible games for smartphones that teach Braille character encodings to promote Braille literacy. The BraillePlay games are based on VBraille, a method for displaying Braille characters on a smartphone. BraillePlay includes four games of varying levels of difficulty: VBReader and VBWriter simulate Braille flashcards, and VBHangman and VBGhost incorporate Braille character identification and recall into word games. We evaluated BraillePlay with a longitudinal study in the wild with eight blind children. Through logged usage data and extensive interviews, we found that all but one participant were able to play the games independently and found them enjoyable. We also found evidence that some children learned Braille concepts. We distill implications for the design of games for blind children and discuss lessons learned.

Categories and Subject Descriptors

H.5.2 [Information Interfaces and Presentation] User Interfaces-Haptic I/O. K.3.0 [Computers and Education]. K.4.2 [Computers and Society]: Social Issues-assistive technologies for persons with disabilities.

General Terms

Human Factors, Design, Experimentation.

Keywords

Accessibility; educational games; blind; children.

1. INTRODUCTION

Smartphones offer an appealing and increasingly popular platform for educational games for children. Digital games in general have been shown to be effective learning tools [12,33]. Smartphones in particular offer advantages over traditional computers because they are mobile (people can use them anywhere) and have additional sensors (*e.g.*, a touchscreen and a vibration motor). Many children already use smartphones on a regular basis [12], and educational smartphone games have generated substantial interest in industry and academia. There are currently 65,000 education applications in the Apple AppStore [6], many of which

Figure 1. The VBraille interface for "reading" and "writing" Braille characters (left) and a menu from the VBHangman game that is based on the word game Hangman (right).

are games targeted towards children [18].

While smartphone games have the potential to significantly impact children's education, they are largely inaccessible to blind children. Smartphones are generally accessible to blind people with built-in screen readers such as iOS's VoiceOver [5] and Android's TalkBack [4]. These screen readers work well with text-based interfaces that use standard UI widgets. Games, by contrast, usually have custom widgets with images rather than text. Moreover, they commonly require users to hit visual targets under time constraints, making them inaccessible. Blind children are thus unable to participate in and benefit from these promising educational tools.

In this paper, we present *BraillePlay*, a suite of educational smartphone games for blind children. Our goal was to design games that (1) were accessible and engaging to blind children and (2) promoted Braille concepts. We focused on Braille because in recent years there has been a sharp decline in Braille literacy. According to the National Federation of the Blind, only 10 percent of blind children in the US are learning Braille despite the fact that Braille literacy has been strongly linked with a higher education level, a better chance of employment, and a higher income for blind adults [29]. We designed our games for children who are 5 years old or older, so they can learn Braille concepts at the same age that their sighted peers are learning to read.

ASSETS '14, October 20–22, 2014, Rochester, NY, USA.
Copyright 2014 ACM 978-1-4503-2720-6/14/10...$15.00.
http://dx.doi.org/10.1145/2661334.2661377

The BraillePlay suite includes four applications that use the VBraille interface [19, 28] through which the user can identify (*i.e.*, "read") and enter (*i.e.*, "write") Braille characters (see Figure 1). The BraillePlay games help children learn and memorize Braille character encodings, which is a critical aspect of learning how to read Braille. Two of the games simulate Braille flashcards, testing children's ability to identify and enter characters while the other two incorporate the VBraille interface into word games. The games have speech output with high-contrast but minimal graphics, large print, and gestures that follow accessible design guidelines [20, 21].

To evaluate our games, we conducted a longitudinal study in the wild with eight blind children (ages 5 – 8). We asked participants to play instrumented versions of the games at least four times a week for four weeks. Throughout the study, we surveyed and interviewed participants and their parents. We found that most participants were able to play the games independently with minimal training. Several of the children found the games enjoyable and were motivated to play them for long periods of time, and several of the parents felt that the games helped their children learn Braille.

In summary, our contributions include:

   i.   The BraillePlay games, a set of free iOS[1] and Android[2] applications that are available online, as well as the code for the games, which is available in our online repository[3].

   ii.   Empirical findings from our longitudinal study that show how children interacted with the games.

   iii.   Design implications for accessible smartphone games for children.

   iv.   A discussion of lessons learned that provide guidance for researchers interested in conducting studies with children in the wild.

2. RELATED WORK

To our knowledge, BraillePlay games are the first educational smartphone games for blind children. The design of the VBGhost game was first presented in a poster [28], but the current paper describes all the games in detail and the longitudinal study. Our work draws from prior work on (1) representing Braille on smartphones, (2) educational games for sighted children, and (3) accessible games.

2.1 Representing Braille on Smartphones

Since BraillePlay teaches Braille concepts, we discuss several approaches to representing Braille on smartphones. People commonly read Braille on specialized devices called Braille displays [2] that display a row of characters at once. However, Braille displays cost hundreds or thousands of dollars.

BraillePlay games use Jayant *et al.*'s VBraille [19], a method of reading characters on a smartphone with no visual or audio output. VBraille displays one character on the screen at a time. The screen is divided into 3 rows and 2 columns like a Braille cell

[1]https://itunes.apple.com/us/artist/mobile-accessibility/id692203637

[2]https://play.google.com/store/apps/developer?id=Mobile+Accessibility

[3]https://code.google.com/p/mobileaccessibility/

and the phone vibrates when the user touches regions that correspond to the raised dots in the current character. Jayant *et al.* argue that VBraille can be a useful output method for deaf-blind mobile device users, since VBraille only provides haptic feedback. When using VBraille in our games, we added speech output that tells the user which dot she is touching. We also created a VBraille interface for entering characters, where the user double taps regions of the screen to raise the corresponding dots. Al-Qudah *et al.* [1] also present a method where characters are output through haptic feedback only. They use a vibration pattern for each character that is based on its Braille representation.

There has also been much work on Braille-based methods for input on a smartphone. BrailleTouch [14], Perkinput [10], and TypeInBraille [25] use multi-touch input to enter characters. These methods are likely to be difficult for young children who are not as coordinated or dexterous as adults. BrailleType [30,31] is similar to the VBraille input method we use in BraillePlay. Unlike VBraille, BrailleType users single tap the regions of the screen to raise dots. BrailleType is likely to be faster than VBraille but also more error-prone, especially for children who are learning Braille.

2.2 Accessible Digital Games

Researchers have created recreational digital games for traditional computers as well as various other hardware platforms [7, 8, 11, 16, 27, 34, 37]. McElligott *et al.* [26] conducted co-design with blind children and developed several computer games with audio feedback. They emphasized the importance of using existing, mainstream platforms and designing games that can be played autonomously and cooperatively. Researchers in the TiM project [7, 11] also designed accessible games that used audio feedback, but they required speakers for surround-sound and tactile overlays for a computer screen. Some researchers have laid out guidelines in building accessible games for blind games [3, 9, 15, 26, 32]. These guidelines have inspired us to use a universal design approach to the games by providing both audio output, and visual output with contrast for low-vision users.

There are a few accessible games designed for smartphones. Both Tapbeats [22], and the Audio Flashlight [36] use the audio interface of the smartphone to be accessible to blind people. Neither game is designed for children or for educational purposes.

2.3 Educational Games

There is a body of literature enumerating the potential benefits of using digital games for education [12,13,33]. Games can be valuable learning tools because they are engaging and motivate users to improve their gameplay skills. However, it is difficult to isolate the learning effects of games, and there is little direct evidence in the literature that games teach certain concepts [13], and results have been mixed in studies measuring the empirical evidence of learning using educational games [17,23].

There are few educational games designed for blind people. Song *et al.* [35] developed two audio-based learning games on TeacherMate, an inexpensive mobile device designed for people in developing countries. They found that children enjoyed playing their games individually and in groups, working together on challenging parts of the game. Sánchez *et al.* [34] also developed an accessible game on a custom hardware platform called MOVA3D, which teaches children orientation and mobility skills.

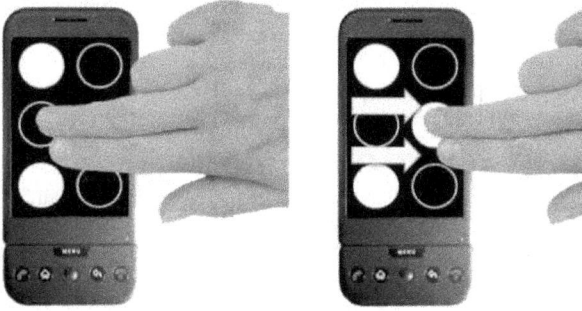

Figure 2. A two-finger swipe to the right allows users to submit a character entered in VBWriter or move to the letter input screen in VBReader.

3. BRAILLEPLAY GAMES

3.1 Design Principles

We designed the BraillePlay games to be (1) educational, (2) accessible, (3) accommodate a variety of skill levels, and (4) available for mainstream devices.

Educational. We created games to promote Braille literacy, which is in rapid decline despite the fact that it is important for success in both school and the workplace [29]. Early exposure to Braille concepts is crucial for blind children [24]. Just like their sighted peers, blind children must begin learning reading and writing concepts in preschool, and there are a variety of games and avenues to aid with this. To read Braille, children must both know the Braille dot patterns and be able to discern these dot patterns tactilely. Because it can be difficult and frustrating for children to discern the patterns using the small standard Braille cell, the Braille alphabet is often taught using over-sized stand-ins including plastic eggs in egg cartons and tennis balls in muffin tins [24].

The VBraille interface differs from standard Braille in two ways: it is much larger, and it uses vibration instead of raised bumps to represent the characters. Because of these differences, it cannot help children develop the tactile sensitivity needed to read a standard Braille cell. However, VBraille can help children learn Braille encodings, a critical component of learning how to read. Teachers already use large representations of Braille characters that they make out of egg cartons and muffin tins.

Accessible. To be accessible, the games had to be (1) age appropriate for children aged 5 years old and older and (2) accessible for people who are sighted, low-vision, and blind.

To accommodate the developing motor skills of young children, we used simple gestures such as single and double taps and swipes (Figure 2). When possible, we gave users the ability to use either the smartphone's keypad or a touchscreen gesture to complete an action. For example, users can either double tap on the touchscreen or use numbers 1-6 on the keypad to raise or lower dots in VBWriter. We chose a large representation of Braille so that young children could easily distinguish between dots in nearby rows or columns. We also used a representation that has the same spatial layout as a Braille cell, as opposed to a purely temporal representation like the one developed by Al-Qudah et al. [1], making it easier for young children to make the connection to Braille characters. Additionally, our games do not rely on timing. Instead they are self-paced, and children can hear

information about the state of the game as many times as they want.

To ensure the games were accessible for people with all levels of vision, we used high contrast and large fonts as well as audio and haptic feedback. We also relied on simple gestures and VoiceOver-like interaction techniques with menus (single tap to hear an option and double tap to select it) in line with earlier accessibility work [20, 21]

Accommodate Different Skill Levels. We wanted to design games that worked for children 5 years old and older and accommodated varying levels of Braille, vocabulary, and spelling skills. We thus created simple flashcard games (VBReader and VBWriter) for people just learning Grade 1 Braille characters, and more complex word games (VBHangman and VBGhost), which require a larger vocabulary and spelling ability. We hoped that children would begin using VBReader and VBWriter and be motivated to "graduate" to the more complex word games.

Available on Mainstream Devices. Finally, we wanted to design games that could be played using a mainstream device instead of specialized assistive technology. As smartphones become increasingly pervasive in our culture, the ability to use a smartphone is, in itself, a crucial skill. It is therefore important that blind children gain exposure and experience using smartphones just like their sighted peers.

3.2 Description of Games

We designed four BraillePlay games: VBReader, VBWriter, VBHangman and VBGhost. All four games are available for the Android platform (1176 downloads from the Play Store from August 2013 to August 2014), and VBReader, VBWriter and VBGhost are available on the iOS platform (4,471 downloads from the App Store from August 2013 to August 2014). There are minor differences between the two platforms, and in this paper, we describe the Android versions, since those were the games used in the longitudinal study.

VBReader. VBReader is a simple flashcard game in which a user identifies VBraille characters. A VBraille character is presented on the screen. When the user determines which character is presented, she uses a two-finger swipe to the right (Figure 2) or presses the trackball to load the character entry screen. Using the menu button, the user can choose between three options to enter a character: (1) a Qwerty keyboard, which presents a Qwerty keyboard in landscape orientation, which can be navigated with a VoiceOver-like gestures, (2) a two-column alphabetical keyboard, navigated in the same way, or (3) a tapping progression through the alphabet, in which a user can cycle through the alphabet with a single tap to move to the next letter and a double tap to select a letter. After the user selects a letter, the application tells the user whether the input was correct or not and presents a new VBraille letter. If the user exits the application, VBReader tells the user how many characters were identified correctly out of the total number: "You entered 5 out of 10 characters correctly!"

VBWriter. VBWriter is another simple flashcard game in which a single character is spoken aloud ("Enter A as in Alpha"), and the user must input that character using the VBraille interface. The user can press the menu button to hear the letter again. After raising the desired dots in the VBraille screen, the user can submit the character with a two-finger swipe to the right or a tap on the trackball. If the character was entered correctly, the application congratulates the user and presents anther character. If the letter was not entered correctly, the application tells the user what letter was entered and displays the correct letter on the VBraille interface. When the user exits the game, VBWriter announces the number of correctly entered characters out of the total number attempted.

VBHangman. VBHangman is based on the word game Hangman. In Hangman, the user must determine what a word is, given the length of the word and a limited number of guesses as to which letters are in the word. With each guess, the user is told whether the letter is in the word, and, if it is, where the letter is in the word. For example, if the word was "banana" and a user guessed the letter "A," she would be told "blank-A-blank-A-blank-A." Hangman is typically played between two people.

In VBHangman, the user plays against the "computer." At the start of a game, the user chooses the length of the word she would like to play using a menu. The smartphone randomly selects a word of that length, then displays the main menu (Figure 1). In the main menu, the user can choose to hear (1) the word so far ("blank-A-blank-A-blank-A"), (2) the number of trials left ("You have four trials left"), (3) the letters guessed so far ("Letters guessed: 'A' as in alpha, 'C' as in Charlie"), or (4) the instructions for the game. The menu also includes an option to enter another letter. The user enters letters through the VBraille interface, and uses a two-finger swipe to the right to submit her guess. She is given a chance to verify her guess: "You entered the letter 'B' as in bravo, swipe right with two fingers if that is correct." After each guess, the game will tell her if the letter is in the word: "Good guess, 'B' is in the word. The word so far is 'B-A-blank-A-blank-A.'" If the user successfully completes the word, the game will congratulate her and read the completed word aloud. If the user uses up all her guesses and does not correctly identify the word, the game informs her that she has lost and tells her what the word was.

VBGhost. VBGhost [28] is a slightly more complicated game, based on the word game Ghost, in which users take turns adding letters onto a word fragment. If a user adds a letter that spells out a complete word then she loses (*e.g.*, if the current word fragment is "gam," the user will lose if she adds the letter "e" because she will spell "game"). A user also loses if she adds a letter to the word fragment that makes the word fragment invalid (*e.g.*, if she adds the letter "z" to the word fragment "gam," "gamz" is no longer the start to any word).

In VBGhost, the user indicates whether she wants to play the game against the smartphone or against a co-located friend. If she plays against the smartphone, the user is taken to the VBraille screen where she can enter the first letter of the game. After entering a letter, the user swipes with two fingers to the right, and the game tells her (1) if she entered a non-alphabetic character (she is presented with a blank VBraille screen again), (2) if the letter creates an invalid word fragment or completes a word: "I am sorry, you lost, "gamz" is an invalid word fragment" (she is then presented with the main menu screen), or (3) if the letter is a valid play. If the letter is a valid play (part of a valid word fragment), the smartphone selects a letter to add to the word fragment (the smartphone will sometimes complete a word and therefore lose at this point). If the smartphone loses the game by completing a word, it informs the user of her victory and takes her to the main menu screen. Otherwise, the phone adds a letter onto the word fragment, and the user can read the letter using the VBraille interface.

In the multi-player mode, users pass the smartphone back and forth to enter letters. After one user adds a letter to the word fragment, the other user can chose to (1) enter her own letter, (2) listen to the word fragment so far or (3) challenge the previous

letter entered by her opponent as either completing a word or creating an invalid word fragment. The smartphone checks whether the challenge is correct and announces which user won based on the outcome of the challenge. We chose to include a more complex, multi-player game in the suite of BraillePlay games to facilitate collaborative learning.

4. EVALUATION

To evaluate BraillePlay, we conducted a longitudinal study with eight blind children and their parents over a four-week period. Participants were recruited from across the United States and Panama. We chose to perform a longitudinal study in the wild because we wanted to observe gameplay patterns over time that reflected natural use. We conducted the study remotely because there are few blind children locally that were willing to participate in the study.

We sought to answer three research questions:

1. Are BraillePlay games *accessible* to blind children?

2. Are BraillePlay games *engaging* for blind children?

3. Are BraillePlay games *effective* teaching tools?

4.1 Method

4.1.1 Participants

We recruited eight sets of participants (children and parents) for this study from around the United States and Panama (Table 1) through email lists related to raising and caring for blind children. We required that the children (1) be between the ages of 5 and 13 and (2) they identify as either blind or low-vision. The mean age of the child participants was 6 years old (age range was 5 to 8). There was a wide range in the children's knowledge of Braille, as some children were learning how to read single letters, while others were learning Grade 2 contractions. Participants were compensated with a $50 Amazon gift card.

Table 1. Participants in Longitudinal Study

ID	Age	Gender	Degree of Vision	Braille Knowledge	Note
P1	6	F	Light perception	Grade 1	-
P2	6	F	Low-vision	Some contractions	-
P3	5	F	No functional vision	Some letters	-
P4	6	M	No functional vision	Some letters	Language delays
P5	8	M	Light perception	Some contractions	-
P6	7	F	Light perception	Some letters	English as a second language
P7	7	F	No functional vision	Some letters	Cerebral palsy
P8	6	M	Low-vision	Some letters	Language and motor delays

4.1.2 Apparatus

We used 5 Android G1 phones with three games: VBReader, VBWriter and VBHangman (Figure 1). We did not include VBGhost because of the age range and literacy level of our participants: most participants were learning individual letters and had not progressed yet to spelling words. We included VBHangman for the participants with higher literacy skills, but the mechanics of VBGhost seemed too complex for our participants. We installed two versions of each game: one for the parent and one for the child, because we wanted to have one instrumented version that the children played exclusively ("child version") and one version that the parents could use to become familiar with the games ("parent version"). The parent and child versions of the games were identical, except that the child versions were instrumented, and the parent versions were labeled as such (*e.g.*, "Parent VBReader" vs. "VBReader"). Logged information from the child version was sent to the researchers' server when the phone was connected to the Internet and saved to a log file on the phone otherwise.

4.1.3 Procedure

Throughout the study, we conducted a preliminary survey, weekly semi-structured interviews, and a final exit interview and survey with each set of participants. The preliminary survey included questions about demographic information about the child along with information about the child's vision, siblings, and Braille knowledge. Each family was then sent a phone as described above. We instructed the families to take a few days to become familiar with the applications and the phones, using the parent version of the applications. After the orientation period, we conducted 30-minute training sessions over a video-conferencing system with each family to answer questions. The participants were then instructed to play the games for 30-minute sessions four times a week for four consecutive weeks. We encouraged families to maintain a weekly average of two hours of gameplay, but were flexible in how they did this due to differing attention spans and schedules. Because of the varying developmental stages and experience with Braille, we did not define how much we wanted the participants to play each game, and, instead, hoped each participant would play the games best suited to their ability and preference. At the end of the study, we conducted a final set of 30-minute semi-structured interviews with the parents and children.

4.1.4 Design and Analysis

We transcribed and coded the interviews and preliminary surveys. For the quantitative data, we explored two measures: accuracy and time to enter each letter. For both VBReader and VBWriter, accuracy for each letter was binary: either the user entered the letter correctly or not. To measure the length of time to enter each letter, we measured the period of time between the time the letter was presented to the user (either loaded onto the VBraille interface for VBReader or spoken aloud in VBWriter) until the time the user double-swiped to submit a character in VBWriter or selected an answer from the menu in VBReader. For analysis, we excluded extreme outliers.

Our analysis did not include entry times and accuracy measures from VBHangman. We could not compute accuracy rates because there was no way to determine what letter the user *intended* to enter in VBHangman. We had no reliable measure of entry time because the time spent in the character entry screen included the time spent *thinking* about what letter to enter.

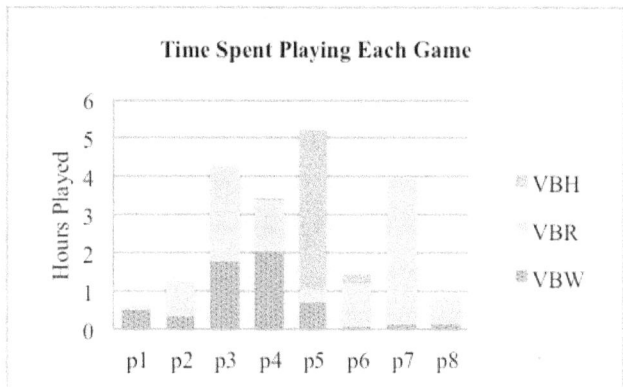

Figure 3. Time spent by participants playing VBHangman (VBH), VBReader (VBR), and VBWriter (VBW).

4.2 Results

4.2.1 Gameplay Patterns

The children collectively played the games for 21 hours (Figure 3), in which they read over 360 letters in VBReader and entered over 598 letters in VBWriter. The total time a child spent playing the games ranged from 37 minutes to 5 hours and 12 minutes (Figure 3).

Entry time and accuracy varied widely for the children (Figure 4). We could not find any visible trends in the data. We believe the variability is likely due to the differing ages, skill levels, abilities, and knowledge of Braille of the children, as well as differences in the amount of parental supervision children received while playing the games.

P4 (age 6) achieved the highest accuracy rates, entering characters correctly 96% of the time with VBReader and 90% with VBWriter. P4 did not play VBHangman. Interestingly, P4 also had the longest average entry rates on both VBReader and VBWriter, with an average of 63.3 seconds to identify a character on VBReader and 67.6 seconds to enter a character on VBWriter. P6 (age 7) achieve the lowest accuracy rates, with an average accuracy of 11% on VBReader and 8% on VBWriter. She took on average of 18.6 seconds to identify letters on VBReader and 12.6 seconds to enter letters on VBWriter. Her parent explained that she had difficulty understanding the screen reader since she was learning English as a second language.

P5 (age 8) was the only child who played VBHangman consistently. He was the oldest child in the study and had relatively advanced Braille skills.

4.2.2 Interviews and Observations

With the exception of P8 who had difficulty playing the games due to motor impairments, parents and children were enthusiastic about the games in the initial and exit interviews. In the preliminary surveys, we found a strong desire for and interest in accessible smartphone games. Five out of eight children either had their own smart device (either an iPod Touch or an iPad) or used their parent's smartphone to play games, listen to music, or listen to audiobooks. Three of those five parents mentioned (unprompted) that they had not found any accessible Braille applications. Four parents said that they had difficulty motivating their child to learn Braille concepts, signaling a need for fun Braille-based games.

From the exit interviews with the children, we found that most of the children were able to interact autonomously and enjoyed playing with the BraillePlay games. Seven children were able to

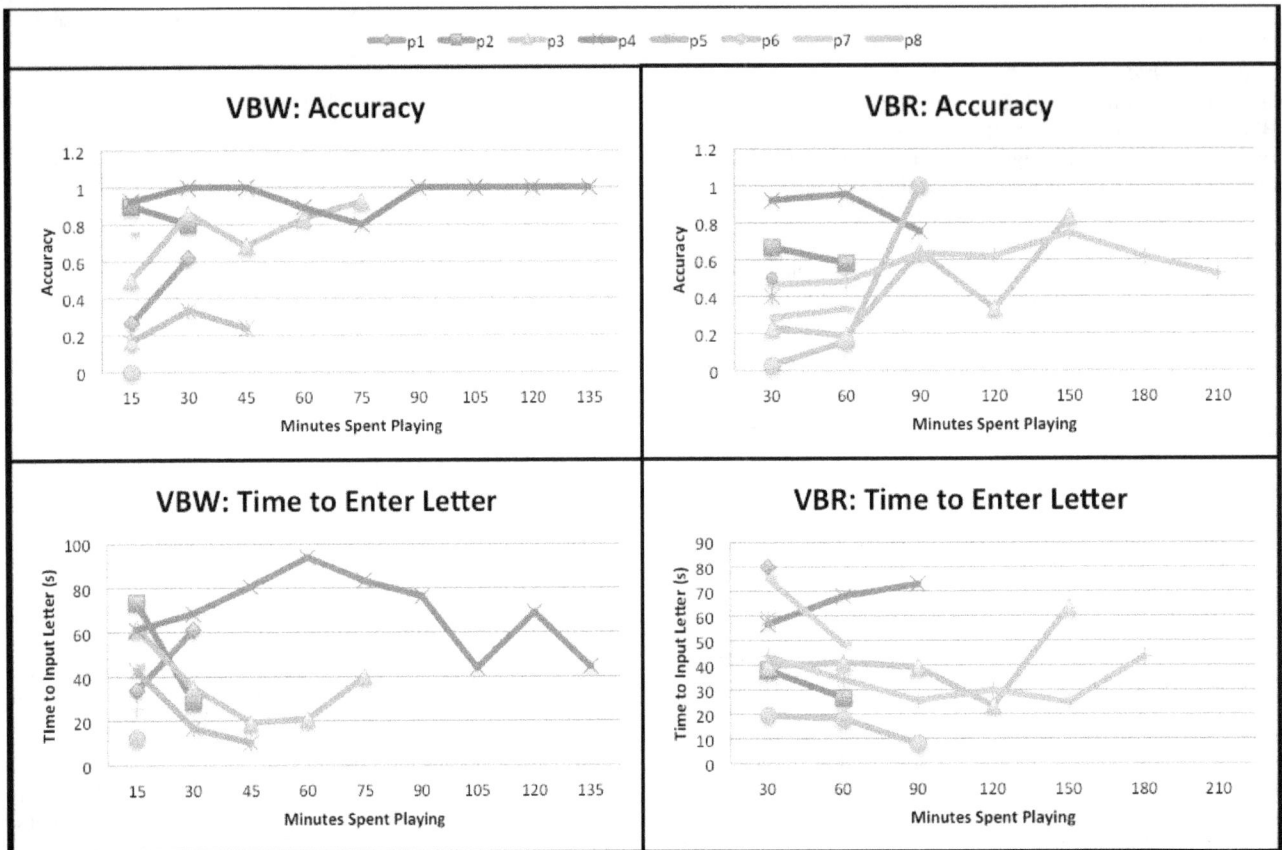

Figure 4. Gameplay patterns for all participants in the study. The top two plots show accuracy rates for participants over time for VBWriter (left) and VBReader (right). Bottom two plots show the average time to enter a letter for VBWriter (left) and VBReader (right). Accuracy rates and letter entry are computed for every 15 minutes of gameplay for VBWriter (VBW) and 30 minutes for VBReader (VBR). There is high variability and no visible trends.

play the games by themselves, while P8 needed assistance because of motor impairments. P1 – P7 reported that they had no problems holding the phone, using buttons or exploring the screen with one finger. However, three participants reported having some difficulty with the two-finger swipe, indicating that multi-touch gestures may not be suitable for children. Most importantly, all seven children (except for P8) reported liking the games.

Interestingly, we found slightly different results from the interviews with the parents: only six parents felt that their child was able to consistently play the games without help after the first few sessions of the study. P1's parent reported that her child had "problems getting the double tap to work" and the "reading with one finger on the screen was too confusing," although P1 reported that she was able to play the games autonomously.

We also found evidence that some children were able to learn Braille concepts with the Braille games. Three children thought that the games helped them learn Braille letters. Additionally, three parents reported that the games helped their child improve his or her ability to read and write Braille letters. P5's parent elaborated:

It helped him to remember that there are six dots in a cell as opposed to a whole shape and to remember which dots made up the letters. I think he loved having something on the phone that he could do in Braille.

Three parents reported that they were not sure if the games helped their children in their current stage in development, but thought it would help their child at some point. The parent of P3 said,

I'm not sure if it helped her specifically... it was an exciting app for me as a parent...I think at some point in her development, it could help a lot.

The parents of the two participants (P1 and P8) who did not think the BraillePlay games were or would be helpful stated that they had difficulty getting their children to play the games. The parent of P1 said, "No, she didn't play them enough." Figures 3 and 4 show that P1 spent little time playing the games.

4.3 Discussion

4.3.1 Research Questions

Using both the gameplay patterns and information from the interviews, we were able to answer our three research questions:

Are BraillePlay games *accessible* to blind children? For the most part, we found that the children were able to play the games autonomously. P8 had difficulty navigating the games due to a motor impairment. P1 had trouble understanding the vibration output of the phone and performing some of the more complex gestures such as the double tap or two-finger swipe. In the exit interviews, all the parents thought that their children were able to understand the concept of the vibrating dots representing the raised dots of a Braille cell. We found that only one child regularly played VBHangman; in our interviews with the parents, it appeared that this was because the children were not yet fluent enough in Braille to spell out words and were instead focused on learning the Braille character patterns.

Are BraillePlay games *engaging* for blind children? We found that most of the children enjoyed playing the BraillePlay games, but they did not play them for as long as we had hoped. The children each played the games for an average of 2.6 hours over the course of the study; this is significantly lower than the encouraged 8 hours. Interest in the games dwindled at the end of the study for many of the children, indicating that we did not design the games to have the optimal balance of challenge and success needed for game flow [33]. This is likely because two of the three games used in the study were the simple flashcard games. The only child that consistently played VBHangman was the oldest child in the study (P5) and also logged the most total hours playing the games (Figure 3). Using the VBraille interface to build more difficult word games or include contractions in the future might lead to more engaging games. Although we did not include VBGhost in the study, P5 expressed interest in playing more word games and might have enjoyed the more difficult game. Our results are similar to findings from prior work. A study with sighted children playing a literacy game over a period of two weeks found that children only played for 10 minutes at a time and interest dwindled after a few days of playing [12]. In future studies, we recommend a shorter playing period and a wider variety of games.

Are BraillePlay games *effective* teaching tools? Evidence from the final interviews with parents and children suggests that some of the children learned from the games, but these findings are only preliminary. In general, it is difficult to evaluate learning, and similar studies on educational games often have mixed results when trying to show evidence of learning [13, 17, 18, 23, 32].

The BraillePlay games seem best suited for slightly older children than most of our participants (7 - 8 years old). The three sets of parents who thought the games helped their child learn Braille concepts were the parents of P5, P6 and P7, the oldest children in the study. Interestingly, we found that the BraillePlay games helped some of the parents learn Braille. Of the six parents who played the games with their child, four said that they learned Braille characters from the games (the other two already knew all of the characters).

4.3.2 Design Implications
We distill implications for the design of educational games for blind children.

Design for collaborative play: We found that many of the participants engaged in collaborative play with their sighted siblings and parents during the study. Games should be designed for collaborative play to engage children and allow their parents and sighted peers to also learn Braille concepts and identify with blind children.

Design for blind, low-vision, and sighted children: Parents of children with low-vision in the study suggested using more exciting graphics. Games should be designed for children with all degrees of vision. This will both encourage sighted siblings and peers to play and make the games more appealing for children with some functional vision.

Design for developing motor skills: We found that many of the children had difficulty using multi-finger gestures, such as a two-finger swipe (used to submit letters), so applications for games should include single finger gestures.

4.3.3 Lessons Learned
In conducting a four-week longitudinal study in the wild with children over a large geographic area, we learned a number of lessons that will help others in the community conduct similar studies.

We found the amount of time children played the games varied wildly week to week and that 30-minute-long sessions for young children was too long. This was similar to what Chiong *et al.* [12] reported with their study of literacy games for sighted children. They found that children were only able to play mobile games for 10 minutes at a time. Instead, we recommend that researchers ask participants to do a larger number of short sessions throughout a week and have bi-weekly planned video conferencing sessions scheduled with the children to watch them interact with the games.

We also recommend that researchers studying educational games either make games complex enough to have novelty throughout the study or make different games available at different times throughout the study to aid in analysis and to mitigate some of the loss of interest in the games at the end of the study. In order to accommodate the varying ages and levels of ability of our participants, we allowed them to choose which games to play and when. This extra freedom let us know which games different children found most enjoyable, but it made data analysis difficult, as children could play one game exclusively at the beginning of the study and another at the end, making it harder to pick out trends over time. This may indicate that educational games should constantly introduce novelty if developers want them to be played for long periods of time.

5. FUTURE WORK AND CONCLUSION
Our results show that there is a compelling need and desire for educational games for blind children: both parents and children were excited about the BraillePlay games, and many participants mentioned that they were not aware of any accessible Braille-based games for the smartphone. Our longitudinal study indicates that you can create accessible ways to interact with Braille characters on a touchscreen, and that this interface can be used and understood by children. Although most of the children reported that they enjoyed playing the games, we found it was difficult to make games that continued to engage children over a four-week period. However, many additional word games can be developed with the VBraille interface, maintaining children's interest as they continue to improve their Braille skills. Our work demonstrates that there is great potential for fun and educational games for blind children on mainstream devices.

6. ACKNOWLEDGMENTS

We thank Aric Hunter, Janet Hollier, Chandrika Jayant, and William Johnson. This work was supported by the U.S. Department of Education, Office of Special Education Programs (Cooperative Agreement #H327A100014). Opinions expressed herein are those of the authors and do not necessarily represent the position of the U.S. Department of Education.

7. REFERENCES

1. Al-Qudah, Z., Doush, I. A., Alkhateeb, F., Al Maghayreh, E. and Al-Khalelle, O. 2014. Utilizing Mobile Devices' Tactile Feedback for Presenting Braille Characters: An Optimized Approach for Fast Reading and Long Battery Life. *Interacting with Computers* 26, 1, 63-74.
2. American Foundation for the Blind, "Refreshable Braille Display." http://www.afb.org/ProdBrowseCatResults.asp?CatID=43
3. Andresen, G. 2002. Playing by ear: Creating blind-accessible games. *Gamasutra Article*.
4. Android. 2014. Accessibility. http://developer.android.com/design/patterns/accessibility.html Accessed May 8, 2014.

5. Apple. 2014. iOS: A wide range of features for a wide range of needs. https://www.apple.com/accessibility/ios/ Accessed May 8, 2014.

6. Apple. 2014. iPad in Education. https://www.apple.com/education/ipad/apps-books-and-more/ Accessed May 8, 2014.

7. Archambault, D., Olivier, D. 2005. How to Make Games for Visually Impaired Children. In *Proc. ACE '05*. ACM, New York, NY. 450-453.

8. Archambault, D., Ossmann, R., Gaudy T. and Miesenberger, K. 2007. Computer games and visually impaired people. *Upgrade*, 8, 2, 43-53.

9. Atkinson, M. T., Gucukoglu, S., Machin, C., and Lawrence, A. 2006. Making the mainstream accessible: redefining the game. In *Proc. '06 ACM SIGGRAPH symposium on Videogames*. ACM, New York, NY. 21-28.

10. Azenkot, S., Wobbrock, J., Prasain, S. and Ladner, R. 2012. Input finger detection for nonvisual touch screen text entry in Perkinput. In *Proc. GI '12*. Canadian Information Processing Society, Toronto, Ont., Canada, 121-129.

11. Buaud, A. Svensson, H., Archambault, D. and Burger, D. 2002. Multimedia Games for Visually Impaired Children. In *Proc. ICCHP '02*. Springer Berlin Heidelberg, London, UK, UK, 173-180.

12. Chiong, C., and Shuler, C. 2010. Learning: Is there an app for that. *Investigations of young children's usage and learning with mobile devices and apps.* New York, The Joan Ganz Cooney Center at Sesame Workshop.

13. Eagle, M. 2009. Level up: a frame work for the design and evaluation of educational games. In *Proc. FDG '09*. ACM, New York, NY, USA, 339-341

14. Frey, B., Southern, C., Romero, M. 2011. BrailleTouch: Mobile Texting for the Visually Impaired. In *Proc. UAHCI '11*. Springer Berlin Heidelberg, 19-25.

15. Grammenos, D. 2009. Designing Universally Accessible Games. *Computers in Entertainment* (CIE), 7, 1. ACM, New York, NY, 8.

16. Grammenos, D., *et al*. 2006. Access invaders: Developing a universally accessible action game. *Computers Helping People with Special Needs*. Springer Berlin Heidelberg. 388-395.

17. Harpstead, E., Myers, B. A., and Aleven, V. 2013. In search of learning: facilitating data analysis in educational games. In *Proc. CHI '13*, ACM, New York, NY, 79–88.

18. Hoffman, T. 2013. Can Smartphones Makes Kids Smarter? Education.com http://www.education.com/magazine/article/smartphones-kids/. Accessed May 8, 2014.

19. Jayant, C., Acuario, C., Johnson, W., Hollier, J. and Ladner, R. 2010. V-braille: haptic braille perception using a touch-screen and vibration on mobile phones. In *Proc. ASSETS '10*. ACM, New York, NY, 295-296.

20. Kane, S.K., Bigham, J.P., and Wobbrock, J. O. 2008. Slide rule: making mobile touch screens accessible to blind people using multi-touch interaction techniques. In *Proc. ASSETS '10*. ACM, New York, NY, 73-80.

21. Kane, S. Wobbrock, J. O. and Ladner, R.E. 2011. Usable gestures for blind people: understanding preference and performance. In *Proc. CHI '11*. ACM, New York, NY, 413-422.

22. Kim, J. and Ricaurte, J. 2011. TapBeats: accessible and mobile casual gaming. In *Proc. ASSETS '11*. ACM, New York, NY, 285-286.

23. Linehan, C., Kirman, B., Lawson, S., and Chan, G. 2011. Practical, appropriate, empirically-validated guidelines for designing educational games. In Proc. CHI '11, ACM, New York, NY, 1979–1988.

24. Mangold, S. and Olsen, M. 1981. Guidelines and Games for Teaching Efficient Braille Reading. AFB Press.

25. Mascetti, S. Bernaregii, C., and Belotti, M. 2011. TypeInBraille: a braille-based typing application for touchscreen devices. In *Proc. ASSETS '11*. ACM, New York, NY.

26. McElligott, J. van Leeuwen, L. 2004. Designing Sounds Tools and Toys for Blind and Visually Impaired Children. In *Proc. IDC 2004*. ACM, New York, NY, 65-72.

27. Miller, D., Parecki, A., and Douglas, S. 2007. Finger dance: a sound game for blind people. In *Proc. ASSETS '07*. ACM, New York, NY, USA, 253-254.

28. Milne, L., Bennett, C. and Ladner, L. 2013. VBGhost: a braille-based educational smartphone game for children. In *Proc. ASSETS '15*. ACM, New York, NY, 75-76.

29. National Federation of the Blind Jernigan Institute. 2009. The Braille Literacy Crisis in America: Facing the Truth, Reversing the Trend, Empowering the Blind. https://www.nfb.org.

30. Oliveria, J. Guerreiro, T., Nicolau, H., Jorge, J. and Gonçalves, D. 2011. BrailleType: Unleashing Braille over touch screen mobile phones. In *Proc. INTERACT '11*. Springer Berlin Heidelberg, 100-107.

31. Oliveria, J. Guerreiro, T., Nicolau, H., Jorge, J. and Gonçalves, D. 2011. Blind people and mobile touch-based entry: acknowledging the need for different flavors. In *Proc. ASSETS '11*. ACM, New York, NY, 179-186.

32. Ossmann, R., and Miesenberger, K. 2006. Guidelines for the development of accessible computer games. *Computers Helping People with Special Needs*. Springer Berlin Heidelberg. 403-406.

33. Prensky, M. 2005. Computer games and learning: Digital game-based learning. *Handbook of computer game studies*, *18*, 97-122.

34. Sánchez, J., Sáenz, M. and Ripoll, M. 2009. Usability of a multimodal video game to improve navigation skills for blind children. In *Proc. ASSETS '09*. ACM, New York, NY, 35-42.

35. Song, D., Karimi, A. Kim, P. 2011. Toward designing mobile games for visually impaired children. *In e-Education, Entertainment and e-Management (ICEEE), 2011 International Conference on*. IEEE, 234-238.

36. Valente, L., Sieckenius de Souza, C. and Feijo, B. 2008. An exploratory study on non-visual mobile phone interfaces for games. In *Proc. IHC '08* (Porto Alegre, Brazil, October 21-24, 2008).

37. Yuan, B. and Folmer, E. 2008. Blind hero: enabling guitar hero for the visually impaired. In Proc. ASSETS '08. ACM, New York, NY

Tablet-Based Activity Schedule for Children with Autism in Mainstream Environment

Charles Fage
Inria Bordeaux Sud-Ouest
Talence, France
charles.fage@inria.fr

Léonard Pommereau
Inria Bordeaux Sud-Ouest
Talence, France
leonard.pommereau@inria.fr

Charles Consel
Inria Bordeaux Sud-Ouest
Talence, France
charles.consel@inria.fr

Émilie Balland
Inria Bordeaux Sud-Ouest
Talence, France
emilie.balland@inria.fr

Hélène Sauzéon
Inria Bordeaux Sud-Ouest
Talence, France
helene.sauzeon@inria.fr

ABSTRACT

Including children with Autism Spectrum Disorders (ASD) in mainstreamed environments creates a need for new interventions whose efficacy must be assessed in situ.

This paper presents a tablet-based application for activity schedules that has been designed following a participatory design approach involving mainstream teachers, special-education teachers and school aides. This applications addresses two domains of activities: classroom routines and verbal communications.

We assessed the efficiency of our application with a study involving 10 children with ASD in mainstream inclusion (5 children are equipped and 5 are not equipped). We show that (1) the use of the application is rapidly self-initiated (after two months for almost all the participants) and that (2) the tablet-supported routines are differently executed over time according to the activity domain conditions. Importantly, compared to the control children, the equipped children exhibited more classroom and com munication routines correctly performed after three month of intervention.

Categories and Subject Descriptors

K.4.2 [**Computers and Society**]: Social Issues- Assistive technologies for persons with disabilities; K.3.1 [**Computers and Education**]: Computer Uses in Education

Keywords

Autism; tablet application; activity schedules; participatory design; educative inclusion in mainstreamed environment; idiosyncratic multimedia contents.

1. INTRODUCTION

There is growing evidence that educational inclusion produces a positive effect on children with Autism Spectrum Disorders (ASD) [15]. Yet, inclusive education of these students is often hampered by the misgivings of school staff that presumes negative outcomes on classroom functioning if the student is not autonomous enough to perform a range of tasks [11]. Specifically, children with ASD may need help to manage daily routines, make transitions between activities and engage in social interactions [5]. If these special needs are not addressed, they can result in interruptions during class that decrease learning opportunities, not only for the student with ASD, but also for all the students [20].

Activity schedules are an efficient method to enable children with ASD to be more autonomous [16, 17, 19]. An activity schedule is based on picture and/or text sequences decomposing tasks or activities into successive steps [19]. By following such schedules, users can achieve tasks, using paper-based supports [16] and multitouch tablets [3, 13]. Hence, activity schedule is a promising assistive method, especially when it is realized on a tablet, because of the documented preference of ASD children for this device [22, 23].

Surprisingly, the use of computer-based activity schedules in school settings is only proposed for special classrooms, not in mainstreamed classrooms. This situation may stem from the complexity of specifying tasks that need support in general classroom, compared to special classroom. For instance, contrary to special education settings, inclusive education in a secondary school entails frequent changes in terms of classrooms, teachers, and classmates. Furthermore, in mainstreamed environments, the expectations of teacher may not be as personalized as in a special classroom. For instance, a pedagogical focus on a single task or a limited set of tasks is possible in a protected class, whereas a wide panel of tasks is implicitly expected as being correctly performed in mainstreamed setting.

In this paper, our contributions are as follows:

1) the creation of a tablet-based application, named *Classroom Schedule+ (CS+)*, that implements activity schedules. This application has been designed following a participatory design approach involving mainstream teachers, special-education teachers and schools aids. In doing so, we identified activities that must be supported in general classrooms for students with ASD, and we collected the requirements needed for a computer-based activity-schedule system. *CS+* supports two domains of classroom activities for which mainstream teachers have given priority: classroom routines and verbal communication.

2) the deployment of this application in general inclusive classrooms in a user study. We demonstrated the efficiency of our application with 10 students between the ages of 13 and 17 that were in an inclusion program for the first time at a secondary school (one hour per week accompanied by a school aide). Specifically, five students with moderate ASD were equipped with CS+ (ASD experimental group), while five others students with moderate ASD were not equipped (ASD control group).

2. RELATED WORK

Assistive technologies in school context.

Several computer-based intervention tools have been developed to support inclusion in mainstreamed environments. For example, Escobedo et al. provide a smartphone-based tool for practicing social skills during breaks, using an augmented reality approach [7]. For another example, a task manager, hosted by a smartphone, has been used by young adults with ASD studying at the university [9].

Activity schedules in school context.

Recently, activity schedules principles have been explored as underpinnings of the design of assistive technology for ASD children. Specifically, paper-based activity schedules supports are mostly practiced by special education teachers with children with ASD; these supports mostly consist of line drawings or photographs with Velcro© on the back [17]. However, they include limitations for school aides or teachers, such as time to create them and difficulties to record data for tracking student progress [13]. Consequently, activity schedules can be considerably improved when they are based on a multitouch tablet [3, 13]. Hirano et al. developed vSked, an interactive activity scheduling for use in special education classroom [13]. The vSked system was designed to include the benefits of traditional activity schedules (*e.g.,* transitioning between activities, independently engaging in classroom tasks) as well as new functionalities such as dynamic task creation and real-time usage tracking. Cihak et al. supported students with ASD to initiate a general classroom task (*e.g.,* writing, reading or listening), not to follow a sequence of activities [3]. The authors use photos showed to the student, self-modelling task engagement to support the initiation of a classroom task. These photos were inserted into a PowerPoint© presentation on a handheld computer.

Therefore, to the best of our knowledge, there is no study assessing the use of activity schedules to support inclusion of children with ASD in general classrooms. Although their effectiveness has been demonstrated in special education classrooms.

General principles to develop interactive technologies for children with ASD.

Prevalently, the research on the design of interactive technologies for children with ASD recommends simplicity, predictability, and clear mappings between actions [12, 14]. Because individuals with ASD tend to process visual information more effectively than auditory information, existing intervention approaches should use visual supports [12, 13, 14]. Since Autism is considered as a spectrum, the severity of the difficulties encountered is extremely variable between children. Assistive technologies must be flexible enough to support each child uniquely, now and as (s)he develops [12]. Distractive stimuli should be avoided. More precisely, they should be mistake-free to reduce frustration (*e.g.,* no error messages, no wrong answers) [14]. These well-known general principles ensure the usefulness and usability of the interactive technologies for children [12, 13, 14]. However, these principles are not enough to ensure that the technology is usable in mainstreamed environments. Indeed, these environments consist of a variety of people, often unaware of the specificities and needs of children with ASD.

Participatory design approach.

Participatory design method elicits a great interest in the area of assistive technologies [6] by relying on the active involvement of end-users and the stakeholders to identify needs and constraints. It has been extensively used in the design of technologies for children with ASD [2, 8], notably in the vSked system to identify needs and constraints of special education classrooms [13]. To the best of our knowledge, such approach has not conducted to analyze the needs of students with ASD in the context of their first inclusion in mainstream classrooms. Yet, a participatory approach could allow to identify which activities need support for children with ASD when they are included for the first time in mainstreamed classrooms.

Aim of this paper.

We have conducted a participatory design approach to developing an application that provides activity schedules to support children with ASD during their inclusion in mainstreamed classrooms. We have assessed the application's effectiveness with children with ASD at secondary school.

3. DESIGNING ACTIVITY SCHEDULES

Let us now develop design principles dedicated to making the usage of activity schedules possible in general education classrooms.

3.1 3.1 Design Principles

Requirements related to the implicit and explicit rules of general classrooms functioning have been highlighted by the school staff and often in agreement with the litterature. Practically, we worked with 3 special education teachers and 5 school aides; all of them have at least 5 years of experience with children with autism. We also worked with a dozen of teachers who had previously received children with disabilities in their classroom. Research team included psychologists, computer scientists and cognitive scientists. We conducted interviews that resulted in five main principles to be taken into account in the design of our tablet-based activity schedules application.

Activity schedules must promote reading skills.

Reading skills is a pervasive need in the school setting. Consequently, supporting this skill in any activity at school fits the school learning objectives. To support this, visual double-coding (*i.e.,* pictorial and textual) has been applied for each step in the sequence of our activity schedules application. Text and visual information are coupled to give children who cannot read the opportunity to associate words to pictures.

Sequences must be short.

Classroom instructional flow is critical for some children, especially with ASD. School staff were unanimous on the fact that the intervention had to be as short as possible, to prevent the child from losing track of what is going on in the classroom. Thus, to support inclusion of students with ASD, an activity schedule must be as short as possible (*i.e.,* decomposed into few steps). This principle is consistent with general requirements to create activity schedules [19].

Pictures and sentences must be concrete and idiosyncratic.

Each step in the sequence of our activity schedule includes a picture and a sentence. School staff was unanimous on the fact that pictures and sentences must be idiosyncratic (*i.e.,* specific to a person). Furthermore, because of the complexity of multiple concurrent behavioral requirements in an academic setting (*e.g.,* waiting at the door with classmates, waiting for an approval of the teacher, *etc.*), the use of self-modeled pictures, similar to those proposed by Cihak *et al.*. [3], is recommended. For instance, to support a classroom behavior (*e.g.,* to raise hand), students self-modeled pictures should be use (see Figure 1).

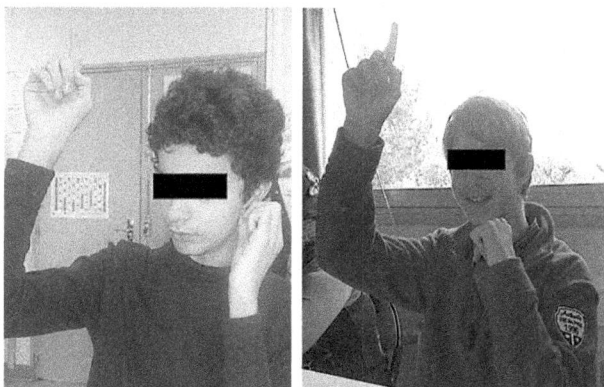

Figure 1: Self-modeled pictures of the same action.

Progress status.

To help students better manage their time, it is important to give them an indication of their progress in activity schedules. Furthermore, the use of visual timers leads to reducing anxiety - particularly present in mainstreamed classrooms. In doing so, the reduction of maladaptive behaviors may be achieved.

Activity schedules must not use the auditory channel.

The intervention inside the classroom must exclude audio materials. First, they would require the use of headphones that would cause a sensory exclusion, precluding the child from participating to the class. Second, headphones would stigmatize the child in front of others students because the use of technology for inclusion must be as unobtrusive as possible.

3.2 3.2. Identification of classroom activities

Given these principles, we worked with all stakeholders to list activities of interest in inclusive education classrooms. This step was then followed by a selection of the critical activities that required assistive support.

General listing.

We first listed general classroom activities involved in inclusion education with a participatory approach. These activities do not concern academic activities but classroom functioning involving students. Indeed, our technological support is not a pedagogical tool to improve student learning performance, but to guarantee typical classroom functioning. Mainstream teachers, special-education teachers and schools aides have participated to propose general classroom activities to list. For instance, few general classroom activities proposed are : Going into classroom; Answering to classmate; Following explanations or complex directives; Answering questions about a text which comes from it being read *etc.*. A total of 27 general classroom activities have been proposed by these stakeholders.

Priority selection.

The second step was to select critical activities to be supported in this large selection. Such activities were required not to bring the student with ASD to disturb classroom functioning. Indeed, some activities create critical disruptions, and the school staff is frequently forced to suspend the inclusion of the student with ASD and to re-place him in special education classrooms for the end of the class [11]. Furthermore, to create activity schedules properly, we also selected activities with a clear beginning and end [19]. These critical activities can be respectively regrouped in two general domains: classroom routines and verbal communication (see Table 1).

3.3 3.3. Sequencing

Each activity of the two domains has been decomposed into sequences thanks to methods described in McClannahan and Krantz (1999) [19]. Furthermore, authors specified some requirements to follow to create an activity schedule: it must be easy to manipulate, includes at least one social initiation when possible, finishes with reinforcement (*e.g.,* "Finished!") *etc.* [19].

Each classroom activity involves a sequence of steps. We have developed one activity in each domain to show examples. For all verbal communication activities, several choices are possible. For example, in the activity "talking to teacher", 3 choices are proposed: make a comment; ask for an explanation or ask to repeat. These tasks are meant

Classroom Routines	Verbal Communication
Listening and taking notes	Answering the teacher
Going to classroom	Answering a classmate
Leaving the classroom	Talking to teacher
Taking out school supplies	Talking to classmate
Using calendar	

Table 1: The two domains of classroom activities.

to bring children with ASD to be aware of the goal of their communication. Here is an example of one of them (see Table 2).

Ask to repeat
Raise your finger
Wait for the professor to interrogate you
Say: "Could you repeat please ?"
Finished!

Table 2: Example of the "talking to teacher" activity

4. APPLICATION DESCRIPTION

Our activity-schedule system runs on a touchscreen tablet. This platform enables rich visual supports and allows the application to be used in any environment. Furthermore, tablets do not carry any stigma as they are increasingly used as portable gaming platforms. Their effectiveness to support intervention has already been demonstrated with children with ASD [7, 13, 14].

Although each student is responsible for her tablet, the school aide can initiate its use. Specifically, she monitors the child and the class flow of activities to determine whether an activity schedule becomes pertinent. When such a situation occurs, she launches the appropriate activity schedule or invites the child to do so thanks to a list of activity schedules is proposed on the top left corner of the screen. Each activity schedule is represented by a text (title) and a little picture (thumbnail). After a while, the school aide only makes sure that the child initiates the use of tablet and the selection of the appropriate activity schedule.

The selection of an activity schedule consists of three stages: (1) the domain of activities, (2) the activity, and (3) the task to be accomplished. These stages are intended to structure the way the child should proceed with the execution of an activity, given that planning (*i.e.*, the activity steps) has been externalized with the tablet. Let us examine in detail each stage. In the first stage, the user chooses between two activity domains: classroom routines and verbal communications (see Figure 2). In the second stage, a list of activities is displayed (top left part of the screen). Notice that in case of verbal communications, these activities are split into two categories: answering and talking. The third stage proposes one of more tasks that address situations within the activity.

Once the activity schedule is in use by the child, the school aide solely supervises the process. The child is guided through each step of the activity via pictures annotated with instructions. This guiding process is idiosyncratic in that it consists of pictures of the child performing the required steps. An arrow on each side of the screen allows the child to navigate through the steps. Furthermore, a progression bar enables the child to visualize where she is in the activity steps.

5. EVALUATION

Participants.

Our study took place in special education classrooms in secondary schools. A total of 10 students between the ages of 13 and 17 were included in our study. Five of them were

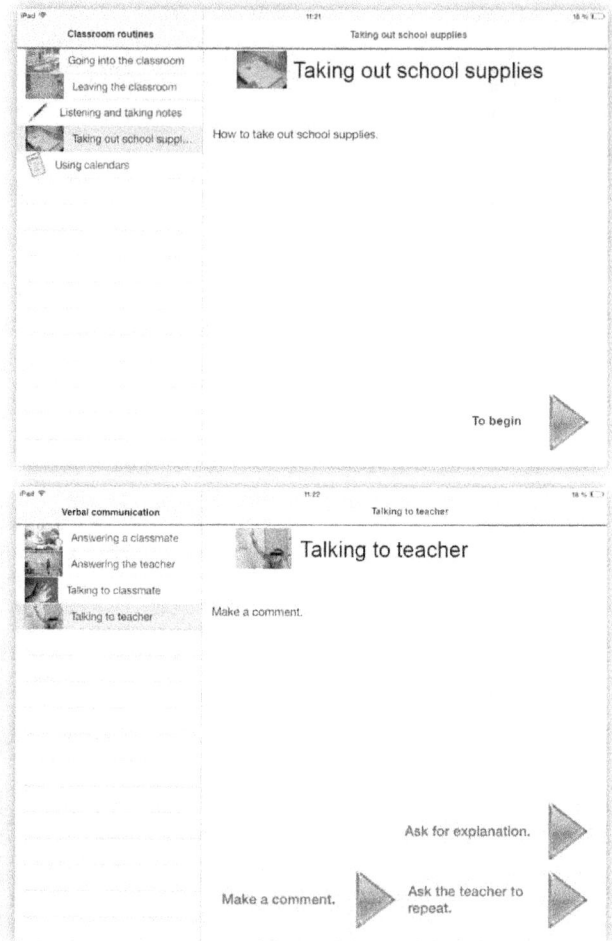

Figure 2: The selection of an activity schedule.

children with ASD equipped with $CS+$ (five boys), five others were children with ASD non-equipped (four boys and one girl). The two groups were matched by chronological age ($m_{Equipped} = 15.00$; SD=1.22; $m_{Non-equipped} = 14.60$; SD=1.14; $p > 700$) and intellectual functioning (according to the IQs estimated from abbreviated WISC-IV [10]; $m_{Equipped} = 74.00$; SD=29.83; $m_{Non-equipped} = 66.50$; SD=26.72; $p > .600$). The group comparisons were tested using a non-parametric test (Mann-Whitney U). Neuropediatricians examined all the children, and the ASD diagnosis was performed according to the criteria of the DSM-IV [1] and with respect to the "Autism Diagnostic Interview-Revised" scale [18]. To assess the severity of social impairment in the school setting, the teacher of each special education classroom initially completed the French version of the Social Responsiveness Scale (SRS) [4]. Concretely, the SRS provides a quantitative score for social impairment in a natural setting. The two groups of children with ASD had similar school-related social impairment (*i.e.*, $m_{Equipped} = 79.80$; SD=37.42; $m_{Non-equipped} = 86.80$; SD=30.51; $p > .700$). As recommended by the Helsinki convention, both parental informed consent and children's assent were obtained before participation. Also, the ethics committee of our university approved the experimental protocol, prior to recruiting participants.

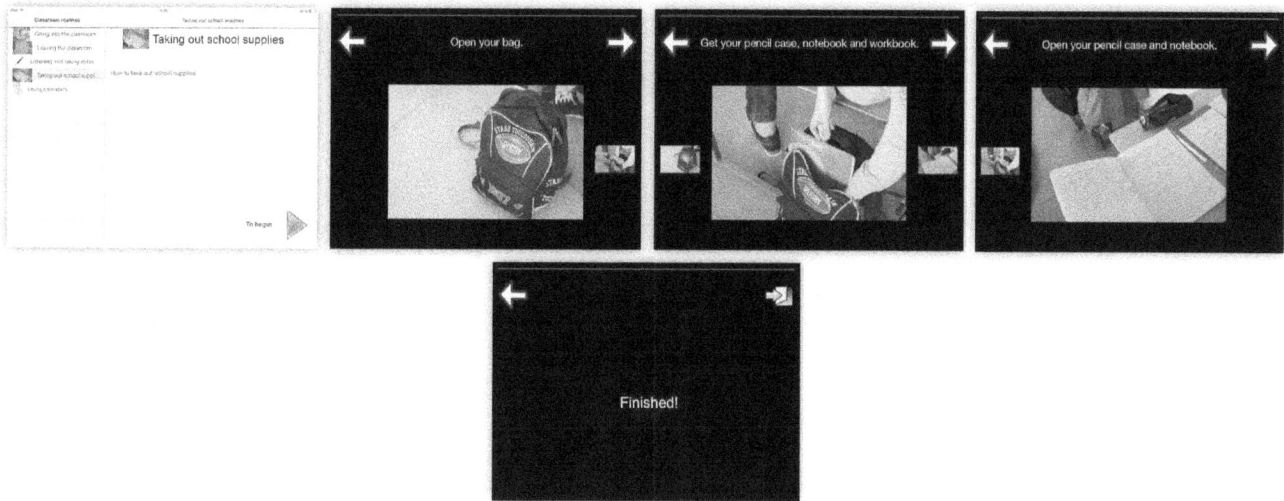

Figure 3: Each steps of the "Taking out school supplies" activity.

Materials and instruments.

Besides supporting inclusion of children with ASD in general classrooms, our application collects data regarding its usage (*i.e.*, number of uses in the inclusion class by type of activities). These data are complemented by a behavioral measurement addressing efficacy and usage of $CS+$ (see Figure 4).

Classroom Schedule+ efficacy

We have built a specific questionnaire to measure how each task of two activity domains is performed. Each step of each task is assessed by the school aide as follows: the behavior is "unobservable", "not done", "done when requested, with help or badly" or "done autonomously". The scoring is set out as follows: "unobservable" / "not done" are scored 0; "done when requested, with help or badly" is scored 1; "done autonomously" is scored 2. With this, each activity is scored according to its steps. To analyse results, we first put scores of activities into a percentage format as follows: if each step of the activity is scored 2, the percentage of this activity is 100. In this case, the child is able to realize the activity autonomously. Second, we average percentages of activities related to a given domain, a percentage on classroom routines and verbal communication, for each child.

Classroom Schedule+ usage

This part of assessment included school aide observations about the $CS+$ usage by each child and log data extracted from our application.

- Autonomous usage: at the end of each month of intervention, the school aide was asked to indicate whether the child used the application in full autonomy and in an adequate manner (scored 1) or whether (s)he had needed help to use it (scored 0).

- Number of routines activated: from the log data, the number of routines activated during the classroom inclusion period is collected (*i.e.*, for each classroom inclusion during one month period).

Procedure.

Prior to our intervention, we held a meeting with the inclusion teachers, the special education teacher, the school aides, the parents, and the children. The goal was to give them an overview of our procedure (see Figure 4), to explain the importance of using our application on a regular basis, and to answer all their questions. We also gave a demonstration of our tool, explaining its functioning. At the baseline assessment session, the special education teacher of the children with ASD completed a demographic information form and the SRS scale. The children completed the abbreviated WISC-IV. The participants were then observed during their inclusion in the classroom (French, mathematics, history, geography, or biology) for two weeks. In the context of our intervention, each participant attended a new class where new situations could occur. It was a one-hour class that occurred once a week during a period of three months. A school aide accompanied each child during inclusion. Each school aide was trained to support students with ASD. In addition, they were told how to use $CS+$ to play the role of social support during inclusion. During each class in inclusion, the school aide completed a specific questionnaire to collect the activity observations for each child (that are equipped). All post-intervention measures were completed within two weeks after the end of the three-month intervention. All interviews were conducted at school or at home.

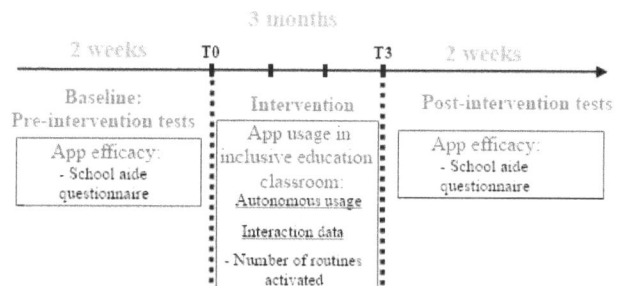

Figure 4: An overview of our procedures

Design and statistical treatments.

For efficacy measure, a mixed factorial design is implemented with two within factors and one between factor. The within factors were activity domain, which had two levels (Classroom vs. Communication) and Time, which had two levels (pre- and post-intervention). The between factor was Group, and it had two levels (Equipped and Non-equipped). For the autonomous use measure, the Friedman test is used with the Time factor (after one month, two months, and after three months of intervention) as the independent variable. For the log data from $CS+$, the factorial design included only within factors with: activity domain, which had two levels (Classroom vs. Verbal communication) and Time, which had two levels (after one month and after three months of intervention). All the dependent measures were numeric. All the pairwise comparisons were carried out with non-parametric procedures as recommended for small-size samples with non-normal distributions, notably the Mann-Whitney U (between-factor) or the Wilcoxon (within-factor) test. We used SPSS 19.

Results.

Overall, the results support the efficacy of $CS+$ in showing that both classroom and verbal communication routines performed in general education classrooms were significantly more enhanced for the ASD children equipped compared to those not equipped. Note that the pre-post progress were higher in classroom routine domain than in the verbal communication domain for all the children. In addition, the observation from the school aide indicated that the children reached a autonomous $CS+$ usage from the second month of use. Finally, log data indicated that the use of $CS+$ was high and unchanged across time for activity schedules within the verbal communication domain. By contrast, within classroom routines domain, the use of $CS+$ was high only during the first month of classroom inclusion and was considerably decreased in the third month of use.

Classroom Schedule+ Efficacy (see Figure 5). The ANOVA revealed significant effects for Activity domain [$F(1,8) = 62.74; p < .0001$] and Time factor [$F(1,16) = 32.50; p < .001$] on the routines correctly performed in classroom. The interaction effect including Time and Activity domains was also significant [$F(1,8) = 14.47; p < .01$] and showed that the performance increase with time was higher on verbal communication than on the classroom routine domain for both conditions of ASD children. Importantly, the interaction between Group and Time factors stated that the performance increase with time was significant for children with $CS+$ ($z = -2.80; p < .01$) whereas this is not obtained for children not equipped ($z = -1.35; p > .100$).

Classroom Schedule+ usage in inclusive education classroom

- Autonomous usage measure: the time factor effect was significant [$\chi^2 = 6.50; p < 04$]: a mostly autonomous usage of our application reached by the children after two months ($M_{after\ one\ month} = 0.20$; SD=0.44; $M_{after\ two\ months} = 0.80$; SD=0.44; $M_{after\ three\ months} = 1.00$; SD=0.00).

- For the number of routines activated: the ANOVA revealed a main effect of time factor [$F(1,4) = 12, 24; p < .04$] indicating that the number of activated routines decrease with time. Also, although the interaction effect (Time * Activity domain) did not reach the significance ($p > .05$), the post-hoc comparisons indicated that the use of $CS+$ did not differ significantly for

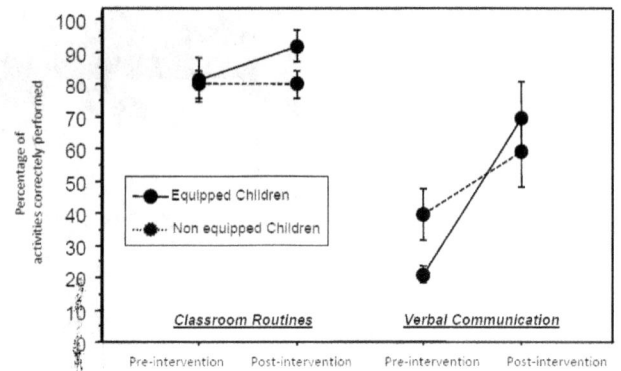

Figure 5: Percentage of activities correctly performed on classroom according to activity domain and group condition.

classroom routines and verbal communication condition during the first month ($z = -0.36; p > .700$), while its use for classroom routine domain was lower than for verbal communication domain during the third month period ($z = -2.02; p < .04$) (see Figure 6).

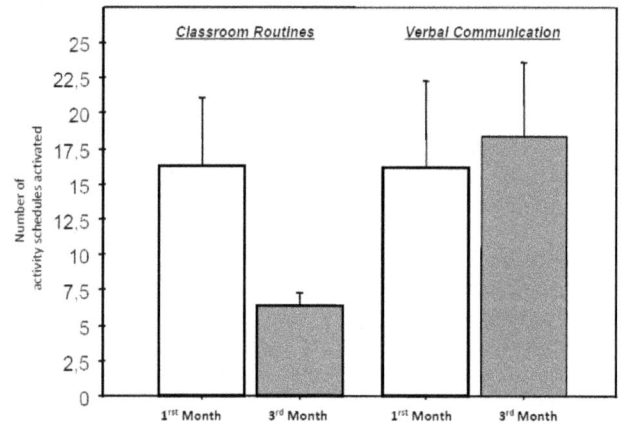

Figure 6: Number of routines activated as a function of activity domains and intervention duration

6. DISCUSSION

To the best of our knowledge, there is no study assessing a technological device for activity schedules to support children with ASD in mainstreamed school environments. Additionally, we found no study addressing the activity schedules with idiosyncratic contents to provide assistive support for first-time inclusion of ASD children in general education classroom. The results presented here provide insights on these issues.

Efficient and autonomous use in mainstreamed environments.

Our empirical results demonstrate that $CS+$ provides children with ASD with a relevant task-management support in mainstreamed environments, such as a classroom. Importantly, the socio-adaptive routines in class were greatly enhanced for equipped children with ASD, despite the short intervention time (*i.e.*, only three months). We also observe high usability of our application (*i.e.*, independent use after the 2nd month). The limited-steps interaction within one activity schedule and only two user-pointing inputs (forward and backward arrows) allow children to quickly and easily follow the critical steps of each routine for a short time. As a result, interface organization, interaction duration as well as idiosyncratic contents probably maximize the device's adoption while ensuring a child's effective presence in the classroom.

Relevance of flexible visual supports for activity schedules in school settings.

Interestingly, for all the children (equipped or not), the pre-post progress was higher in the classroom routine domain (with nearly perfect execution) than in the verbal communication domain ($\approx 70\%$ correctly performed). A related result comes from the log data. Indeed, we reported a decreased use of $CS+$ in time for classroom routines contrasting with a high and constant use of $CS+$ for verbal communication domain. This usage discrepancy is probably due to differences in socio-cognitive demands of to-be-performed tasks into the two domains. So, the more a child becomes proficient in an activity domain, the more (s)he performs the domain-related tasks autonomously, and the less (s)he uses the corresponding contents of $CS+$. This means that the child is able to select the contents of $CS+$ appropriately with respect to her own progress and needs: probably, classroom routines meet a child's needs related to the start of classroom inclusion, while verbal communication routines are persistent needs for classroom life of children with ASD. Note that $CS+$ is built as a learning and assistive device with flexible contents, so when a routine is acquired by child, stakeholders can create new adapted ones. This is possible thanks to the independent management of interface and contents in $CS+$. Indeed, routines (texts, pictures and step numbers) can be changed while the interface skin remains the same, which is desirable for children with ASD [12, 14].

Relevance of idiosyncratic and concrete contents for activity schedule in school settings.

Both efficacy and quick autonomous usage of $CS+$ may result from the superiority of idiosyncratic visual supports over general-purpose ones [21]. In light of the diversity and complexity of tasks having to be resolved in a school setting (*e.g.*, waiting at the door with classmates, waiting for an approval of the teacher, *etc.*), the use of self-modeled pictures provides illustrations of the particular child in context. This is in favor of imitative behaviors [3]. In this experiment, we included children with IQs around 70, thus, such idiosyncratic visual supports probably meet their concrete reasoning abilities well.

Collaborative evaluation induces technology acceptance.

The collaborative nature of our intervention allowed our tool to be pervasively accepted by all stakeholders of the child's mainstreamed environment. Teachers, especially, played a major role in facilitating the application usage inside their classroom. For instance, they encouraged children to use our application with sentences like "you should have a look at your tablet".

Limitations and Future Work.

Regarding the participating children, their number did not reach a sufficient sample size for statistically conclusive results, even though the use of non-parametric statistical tests has been respected. Also, the participating children did not cover the spectrum of intellectual functioning. Consequently, it remains to be shown that our results carry over to children with ASD that are on the higher end of the spectrum of intellectual functioning. To further explore our research avenue, an interesting direction would be to add a set of routines that covers all the aspects of task-management for supporting the participation of children with ASD in mainstreamed school settings. For instance, applications designed to manage tasks may be helpful for self-initiating adaptive behaviors in other school settings (such as canteen, schoolyard, school bus, *etc.*).

7. CONCLUSION

This paper presents a tablet application (*Classroom Schedule+*) supporting task-management skills of children with ASD in mainstreamed environments. This application has been used by five children with ASD during their inclusion in secondary schools. All children successfully adopted our application and have exhibited increased socio-adaptive behaviors in classroom. With a participatory design approach, we identified critical activities for ASD children and design principles that allowed *Classroom Schedule+* to be infused in a mainstreamed environment: the general education classroom. With a similar approach, other applications could be implemented to offer more adaptability to closely match the needs of children with ASD for school and other mainstreamed settings.

8. REFERENCES

[1] Association, A. P. *Diagnostic and statistical manual of mental disorders: DSM-IV-TR®*. American Psychiatric Pub, 2000.

[2] Benton, L., Johnson, H., Ashwin, E., Brosnan, M., and Grawemeyer, B. Developing ideas: Supporting children with autism within a participatory design team. In *Proceedings of the SIGCHI conference on Human factors in computing systems*, ACM (2012), 2599–2608.

[3] Cihak, D. F., Wright, R., and Ayres, K. M. Use of self-modeling static-picture prompts via a handheld computer to facilitate self-monitoring in the general education classroom. *Education and Training in Developmental Disabilities 45*, 1 (2010), 136.

[4] Constantino, J. N., Davis, S. A., Todd, R. D., Schindler, M. K., Gross, M. M., Brophy, S. L., Metzger, L. M., Shoushtari, C. S., Splinter, R., and Reich, W. Validation of a brief quantitative measure of autistic traits: comparison of the social responsiveness scale with the autism diagnostic interview-revised. *Journal of autism and developmental disorders 33*, 4 (2003), 427–433.

[5] Cramer, M., Hirano, S. H., Tentori, M., Yeganyan, M. T., and Hayes, G. R. Classroom-based assistive technology: collective use of interactive visual schedules by students with autism. In *CHI* (2011), 1–10.

[6] Druin, A. The role of children in the design of new technology. *Behaviour and information technology 21*, 1 (2002), 1–25.

[7] Escobedo, L., Nguyen, D. H., Boyd, L., Hirano, S., Rangel, A., Garcia-Rosas, D., Tentori, M., and Hayes, G. Mosoco: a mobile assistive tool to support children with autism practicing social skills in real-life situations. In *Proceedings of the 2012 ACM annual conference on Human Factors in Computing Systems*, ACM (2012), 2589–2598.

[8] Frauenberger, C., Good, J., and Keay-Bright, W. Designing technology for children with special needs: bridging perspectives through participatory design. *CoDesign 7*, 1 (2011), 1–28.

[9] Gentry, T., Wallace, J., Kvarfordt, C., and Lynch, K. B. Personal digital assistants as cognitive aids for high school students with autism: results of a community-based trial. *Journal of Vocational Rehabilitation 32*, 2 (2010), 101–107.

[10] Grégoire, J. *L'évaluation clinique de l'intelligence de l'enfant: Théorie et pratique du WISC-III*, vol. 229. Editions Mardaga, 2000.

[11] Harrower, J. K., and Dunlap, G. Including children with autism in general education classrooms a review of effective strategies. *Behavior Modification 25*, 5 (2001), 762–784.

[12] Hayes, G. R., Hirano, S., Marcu, G., Monibi, M., Nguyen, D. H., and Yeganyan, M. Interactive visual supports for children with autism. *Personal and ubiquitous computing 14*, 7 (2010), 663–680.

[13] Hirano, S. H., Yeganyan, M. T., Marcu, G., Nguyen, D. H., Boyd, L. A., and Hayes, G. R. vsked: evaluation of a system to support classroom activities for children with autism. In *Proceedings of the SIGCHI Conference on Human Factors in Computing Systems*, ACM (2010), 1633–1642.

[14] Hourcade, J. P., Williams, S. R., Miller, E. A., Huebner, K. E., and Liang, L. J. Evaluation of tablet apps to encourage social interaction in children with autism spectrum disorders. In *Proceedings of the 2013 ACM annual conference on Human factors in computing systems*, ACM (2013), 3197–3206.

[15] Hunt, P., and McDonnell, J. Inclusive education. *Handbook on developmental disabilities* (2007), 269–291.

[16] Koyama, T., and Wang, H.-T. Use of activity schedule to promote independent performance of individuals with autism and other intellectual disabilities: A review. *Research in developmental disabilities 32*, 6 (2011), 2235–2242.

[17] Lequia, J., Machalicek, W., and Rispoli, M. J. Effects of activity schedules on challenging behavior exhibited in children with autism spectrum disorders: A systematic review. *Research in Autism Spectrum Disorders 6*, 1 (2012), 480–492.

[18] Lord, C., Rutter, M., and Le Couteur, A. Autism diagnostic interview-revised: a revised version of a diagnostic interview for caregivers of individuals with possible pervasive developmental disorders. *Journal of autism and developmental disorders 24*, 5 (1994), 659–685.

[19] McClannahan, L., and Krantz, P. Activity schedules for children with autism: Teaching independent behavior. *Woodbine House* (1999).

[20] McCurdy, E. E., and Cole, C. L. Use of a peer support intervention for promoting academic engagement of students with autism in general education settings. *Journal of autism and developmental disorders* (2013), 1–11.

[21] Park, J. H., Abirached, B., and Zhang, Y. A framework for designing assistive technologies for teaching children with asds emotions. In *CHI'12 Extended Abstracts on Human Factors in Computing Systems*, ACM (2012), 2423–2428.

[22] Sampath, H., Indurkhya, B., and Sivaswamy, J. A communication system on smart phones and tablets for non-verbal children with autism. In *Computers Helping People with Special Needs*. Springer, 2012, 323–330.

[23] Tentori, M., and Hayes, G. R. Designing for interaction immediacy to enhance social skills of children with autism. In *Proceedings of the 12th ACM international conference on Ubiquitous computing*, ACM (2010), 51–60.

A Computer-Based Method to Improve the Spelling of Children with Dyslexia

Luz Rello
Clara Bayarri
Cookie Cloud
Barcelona, Spain
luz,clara@cookie-cloud.com

Yolanda Otal
Centre Creix
Barcelona, Spain
otal@creixbcn.com

Martin Pielot
Telefonica Research
Barcelona, Spain
martin.pielot@telefonica.com

ABSTRACT

In this paper we present a method which aims to improve the spelling of children with dyslexia through playful and targeted exercises. In contrast to previous approaches, our method does not use correct words or positive examples to follow, but presents the child a misspelled word as an exercise to solve. We created these training exercises on the basis of the linguistic knowledge extracted from the errors found in texts written by children with dyslexia. To test the effectiveness of this method in Spanish, we integrated the exercises in a game for iPad, *DysEggxia* (*Piruletras* in Spanish), and carried out a within-subject experiment. During eight weeks, 48 children played either *DysEggxia* or *Word Search*, which is another word game. We conducted tests and questionnaires at the beginning of the study, after four weeks when the games were switched, and at the end of the study. The children who played *DysEggxia* for four weeks in a row had significantly less writing errors in the tests that after playing *Word Search* for the same time. This provides evidence that error-based exercises presented in a tablet help children with dyslexia improve their spelling skills.

Keywords

Dyslexia; Literacy; Serious Game; Spelling; Written Errors

Categories and Subject Descriptors

K.4.2 [**Computers and Society**]: Social Issues—*Assistive technologies for persons with disabilities*; K.3 [**Computers in Education**]: Computer Uses in Education—*Computer-assisted instruction*.

1. INTRODUCTION

Worldwide, around 15-20% of the population has a language based learning disability [13]. Likely, 70-80% of them have dyslexia [13], a neurological learning disability which impairs a person's ability to read and write. Overcoming dyslexia means a great effort for children and requires doing

regular language exercises [11]. Traditionally, these exercises are done using pen and paper. More recently, it was shown that computer games are a convenient medium to provide exercises in an engaging way to significantly improve the reading performance of children with dyslexia [19, 25]. Regarding writing, there are some technologies to support writing such as spellcheckers and word prediction software for people with dyslexia. However, it has not been shown that these tools improve spelling skills.

In this paper we present the first computer-based approach to improve the spelling skills for people with dyslexia. Since, the writing errors of people with dyslexia are related to the types of difficulties that they have [40], we use real errors found in texts written by children with dyslexia to create training exercises. The exercises were integrated in a game, called *DysEggxia* (*Piruletras* in Spanish), that shows the player an incorrect word that has to be corrected. Since dyslexic readers cannot consciously see errors in words [1, 31], our hypothesis is that children could learn how to identify typical dyslexic errors and, therefore, develop compensating strategies to write better.

To evaluate our method we conducted an eight-week experiment with 48 children with dyslexia. We compared the evolution of reading and spelling skills using *DysEggxia* and a baseline condition, *Word Search*, another word-exercise game for iPad. After playing *DysEggxia* for four weeks, children made significantly less writing errors compared to the ones that played the control condition game. Our results provide evidence that exercises on the basis of errors allow children with dyslexia to improve their spelling skills.

Next, we describe related work, the design of our method and our hypotheses followed by the evaluation. Later, we present and discuss the results and we draw the conclusions.

2. DYSLEXIA

Dyslexia is a specific learning disability with neurological origin. It is characterized by difficulties with accurate and/or fluent word recognition and by poor spelling and decoding abilities. Secondary consequences may include problems in reading comprehension and reduced reading experience that can impede growth of vocabulary and background knowledge [23]. Dyslexia is frequent. From 10 to 17.5% of the population in the U.S.A. [12] and from 8.6% [14] to 11.8% [3] of the Spanish speaking population have this disability.

Since literacy acquisition is essential for all aspects of learning, high rates of academic failure are associated with dyslexia when it is not diagnosed and treated correctly [9].

Actually, the most frequent way to detect a child with dyslexia is by her or his low performance at school [3]. For instance, in Spain, approximately four out of six cases of school failure are related to a language based learning disability [7].[1]

3. RELATED WORK

We divide the related work in assistive technologies to support dyslexia and technologies for treating dyslexia.

3.1 Assistive Technologies for Dyslexia

3.1.1 Reading

Previous work has shown that specific text presentations can make text easier to read [10, 18]. Santana *et al.* [39] developed *Firefixia*, a tool that allows readers with dyslexia to customize websites to improve readability. They tested *Firefixia* with four users and found that readers with dyslexia appreciate customization. Dickinson *et al.* [5] asked 12 students with dyslexia to test different colors, sizes, spacings, column widths, and letter highlighting to improve the subjective readability of MS Word documents integrated in *SeeWord* sorfware. The results were tested by seven people with dyslexia, which reported a subjective increase in readability. *Text4All* [41] for websites, the Android *IDEAL eBook reader* [15], and the iOS *DysWebxia Reader* [34] are text customization tools developed on the basis of previous research using eye-tracking with people with dyslexia [36]. Also, the multimodal *MultiReader* was designed on the basis of user studies for readers with dyslexia as well as blind, partially sighted, and deaf people [29].

3.1.2 Writing

Previous work has also explored how to help writing. For example, tailoring spellcheckers to detect typical errors committed by people with dyslexia [17, 21, 28]. These adaptations include the detection of real-word errors, such as *witch instead of *which* or boundary errors, such as *miss spelled* instead of *misspelled*.[2] In addition, Khakhar and Madhvanath [16] describe *JollyMate*, a tool that provides handwritten character recognition to detect miswritten characters.

We believe that these assistive technologies could make reading and writing easier, however, it has not been shown that they improve literacy skills.

3.2 Technologies for Treating Dyslexia

3.2.1 Action Games

Franceschini *et al.* [8] investigated whether computer action games help children with dyslexia to improve their ability of decoding words. In a between-group experiment with 20 children, they observed that 10 children playing action games for 9 sessions (80 min each) improved their reading skills significantly more than the control group that played non-action games. They claim that action games improve

the children's spatial and temporal attention, which is essential for decoding words.

3.2.2 Serious Games to Identify Dyslexia

Lyytinen *et al.* [25] created the computer game *Literate*, later called *GraphoGame* [24],[3] which was developed to identify children at risk of having dyslexia before school age in Finland. Its exercises are aimed towards the connection of graphemes (letters) and phonemes (sounds) to improve reading. They conducted two user studies with 12 and 41 children between 6 and 7 years old with very promising results. Children who used *Literate* improved their accuracy in grapheme-phoneme connections, reading words, and naming phonemes after playing for less than 4 hours. These results show that linguistic-based exercises can support the improvement of reading.

3.2.3 Computer-Assisted Reading Interventions

Kyle *et al.* [19] compared two computer-assisted reading interventions for English inspired by the Finnish *GraphoGame*: *GG Rime* and *GG Phoneme*. In both games, the goal is to train grapheme-phoneme connections. The player hears either sounds or words and has to match them to visual targets (letters and sequences of letters) displayed on the screen. *GG Rime* includes rhyming word families to reinforce grapheme-phoneme connections. They conducted a user study with 31 children of 6 and 7 years old. They were divided in three groups of 11, 10, and 10 students which were exposed to *GG Rime*, *GG Phoneme*, and no treatment, respectively, for 5 sessions (10-15 minutes each) per week during 12 weeks. While the results show that both games may benefit decoding abilities, no significant effects were found, probably due to an insufficient number of participants or not enough training time.

3.3 What is Missing?

A technology to train and improve spelling skills of people with dyslexia because: (1) previous studies for treating dyslexia were more focused on the development of reading skills such as grapheme-phoneme connections or the improvement of attention abilities in relationship with reading acquisition; and (2) to the best of our knowledge there are no scientific reports on any assistive or treating technology which improves writing acquisition in children with dyslexia.

4. GAME DESIGN

DysEggxia is a game to support the spelling acquisition of children with dyslexia through the realization of exercises.[4] The goal of the exercises is to produce correct words. These were designed on the basis of the linguistic analysis of errors written by children with dyslexia.

We chose to use a touch interface as input media for the game instead of handwriting, because it allows to isolate the writing problems that are caused by dyslexia and not by dysgraphia [38].[5]

---

[1]The percentage of school failure is calculated by the number or students who drop school before finishing secondary education (high school). While the average of school failure in the European Union is around 15%, Spain has around 25-30% of school failure, 31% in 2010 [6].

[2]Examples with errors are preceded by an asterisk "*". We use the standard linguistic conventions: '<>' for graphemes, '/ /' for phonemes and '[ ]' for allophones.

---

[3]https://graphogame.com/

[4]*DysEggxia* was demoed at ASSETS'12 [35].

[5]Dysgraphia is a writing disorder associated with the motor skills involved in handwriting, sequencing, and orthographic coding. It is comorbid with dyslexia. Comorbidity indicates a medical condition, existing simultaneously, but independently, with another condition [27].

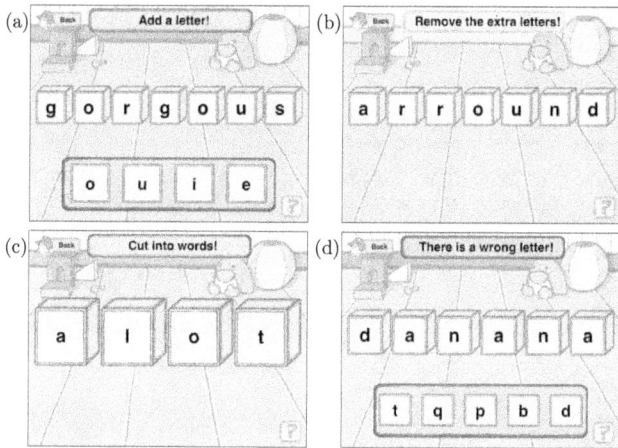

Figure 1: *DysEggxia* exercises of (a) *add a letter*, (b) *remove a letter*, (c) *cut into words*, and (d) *change a letter*.

4.1 The Knowledge of Dyslexic Errors

We decided to use errors written by people with dyslexia as the starting point because they can be used as a source of knowledge. Writing errors of people with dyslexia are not only different from regular spelling errors [28], but are also related to the difficulties that they have [40]. Their written errors have been used for various purposes such as studying dyslexia [22], diagnosing dyslexia [42], or for accessibility related purposes such as developing spellcheckers [28].

At the same time, one of the main challenges that people with dyslexia face is that they do not consciously detect errors while reading [1, 31]. By presenting children with exercises derived by typical dyslexic errors, we aim to stimulate the strategies needed for detecting writing errors and solve them.

4.2 Content Design

The game contains 5,000 exercises, 2,500 for English and 2,500 for Spanish. In order to create the exercises, we applied linguistic knowledge and natural language processing techniques. First, we analyzed the errors of two corpora composed of texts written by children with dyslexia in English [28] (2,654 errors) and Spanish (1,171 errors) [33], finding:

(a) *insertion* of letters, *arround (around)*;

(b) *omission* of letters, *emty (empty)*;

(c) *substitution* of letters, *scholl (school)*;

(d) *transposition* of letters, *littel (little)*;

(e) *word boundary errors* such as split words, *mis understanding (misunderstanding)*, and run-ons, *alot (a lot)*; and

(f) *morphology errors* such as using wrong suffixes or prefixes, *warnment (warning)*.

As a result of this analysis, we extracted a set of linguistics patterns that occur in the errors. Then, we used these patterns to design the exercises, following the next four steps.

(1) **Exercises.** The game presents six types of word exercises according to the six kinds of errors that appear in the analyzed texts: *add a letter*; *remove a letter*, *change a letter*, *put the letters in order*, *split into*

words, and *choose the correct word ending*. One example for each case can be found in Figures 1 and 2 (right). For instance, since *alot (a lot)* is a recurrent word run-on error, there is a split exercise for this case, as shown in Figure 1 (c).

(2) **Modification of the Target Words.** For the exercises that are not derived directly from the incorrect words in the corpora, we apply the linguistic patterns extracted from the errors to the most frequent words. This way, we cover frequent words that might not appear in our corpora. For instance, when the sound /ə/ (schwa) is represented by the diphthong <ou> (*tremendous*) and the triphthong <eou> (*gorgeous* or *courageous*), these two groups of letters are frequently mistaken between themselves or by other letters such as <uo, u, euo>. We use these error patterns and apply it to other target words with the same linguistic features, to create new exercises, see Figure 1 (a).

(3) **Selection of the Distractors.** We selected distractors for each exercise word. Distractors are incorrect options in a multiple-choice answer, which resemble the correct option to 'distract' the player [26]. For instance, similar letters representing similar sounds, such as the occlusive consonants [d,b,p,g,t], tend to induce more errors, so we use them as distractors, as in Figure 1 (d).

(4) **Difficulty Levels.** The game has five difficulty levels: *Initial, Easy, Medium, Hard,* and *Expert*. The levels of the exercises were designed by considering the difficulties of people with dyslexia [10]. They have more difficulties with less frequent and longer words, phonetically and orthographically similar words, and words with complex morphology. Hence, in higher difficulty levels, the target word is less frequent, longer, has a more complex morphology, and has a higher phonetic and orthographic similarity with other words.[6]

4.3 Implementation

The application was done in Objective-C by using the Model-View-Controller pattern and a high level abstraction to make it easily portable from iOS[7] to Android[8] and later to any other platform as needed.

4.4 Interface Design

Since text presentation has a significant effect on reading performance of dyslexic readers, the interface of *DysEggxia* implements the guidelines that – according to the latest findings in accessibility research [10, 18, 36] – ensures best on-screen text readability for this target group. Text is presented in black on creme background, using *Helvetica* [32] and a minimum font size of 18 points [37].

To ensure usability and user engagement, we iterated the application in a series of pilot tests with 12 children, using

---

[6]We computed the phonetic and orthographic similarity of the words taking into consideration their number of neighbors in each language. That is, words with the same length as the target word which differ in only one letter. That is, Hamming distance one.

[7]Search 'Dyseggxia' in Apple's App Store and 'Piruletras' for its Spanish version.

[8]http://dyseggxia.com/download

the think-aloud method. For instance, we replaced the written explanations of the exercises by animations and symbols, so no reading is required. Also, to increase long-term engagement, we added in-game achievements by solving different challenges: a penguin appears, grows, and wins prizes. The achievements can be shared via the iOS' Game Center.

5. EVALUATION

To study the effect of doing error-based exercises on the spelling skills in Spanish, we conducted an experiment in a primary school. For eight weeks, 48 children had to play *DysEggxia* or *Word Search*, a word-puzzle game which served as a control condition. Using a within-subject design, we compared the evolution of their reading and writing performance as well as their subjective perceptions.

We raise the following hypotheses:

- **H.1** Doing exercises based on dyslexic errors helps children with dyslexia to improve their spelling skills.

- **H.2** Doing exercises based on dyslexic errors helps children with dyslexia to improve their reading skills.

- **H.3** Doing exercises based on dyslexic errors rises the subjective perception of reading and spelling skills of children with dyslexia.

5.1 Participants

A first group of 54 potential participants with literacy difficulties was selected by their school teachers at School Lestonnac Barcelona. Then, to find out which children had dyslexia, this group was filtered using a standard test, *TALE* [42], to diagnose dyslexia in Spanish. *TALE* analyzes both reading and writing skills. On the basis of the *TALE* scores, we selected 48 participants (29 girls and 19 boys). All of them were diagnosed with dyslexia, with ages ranging from 6 to 11 years ($\bar{x}= 8.79$, $s = 1.44$). Using the *TALE* scores, we split them into two age groups of the same size according to their literacy skills, which coincidentally matched perfectly with their school year. All but two participants had Spanish as their native language and five of the participants had attention-deficit hyperactivity disorder which is comorbid with dyslexia. All the children had experience playing computer games; 44 of them regularly played games on mobile devices at home.

5.2 Design

The game played served as *independent variable* with two conditions. In the experimental condition, the children played *DysEggxia* while *Word Search*[9] served as control condition. Word Search is another game for iPad where the player has to find and mark words hidden in a matrix of letters (Figure 2, left). We chose *Word Search* as a baseline because it was the most similar game to *DysEggxia* (see Figure 2, left) that we found in the Apple's App Store. It even shares many words used in our exercises and both games offered engaging elements, such as the possibility of accumulating points while playing. Hence, we are able to isolate, whether observed effects are caused due to the specific design of the exercises of *DysEggxia*, or simply by playing word-based games on an iPad.

We did not use other specific games for treating dyslexia such as *GraphoGame* because their goal is the phonological

[9]Search 'Word Search' ('Sopa de Letras' in Spanish) in Apple's App Store.

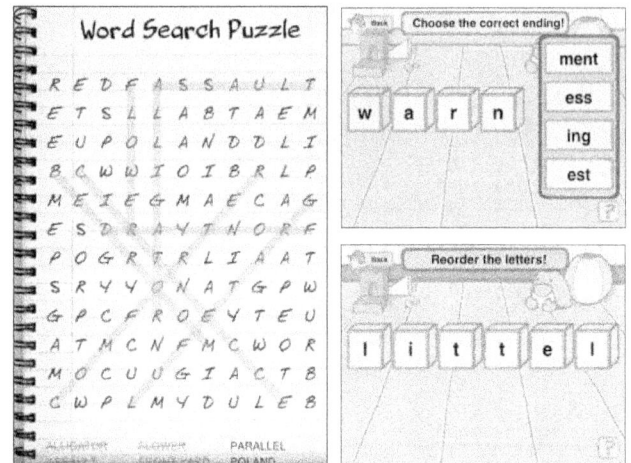

Figure 2: *Word Search* **(left) and** *DysEggxia* **(right).**

acquisition in the early stages of the language acquisition while *DysEggxia* aims at writing skills of older children. Besides, we could not find such specific games for Spanish. We did not implement a similar game to *DysEggxia* containing exercises based on other types of errors because dyslexic spelling errors overlap with regular spelling errors [40].

We used a within-subject design, that is, each participant contributed to both conditions. We divided each age group into two test groups, called A and B. To avoid biases from individual differences, test groups were balanced in terms of reading and writing level, age, and gender. A pre-test was administrated to all the children. Then, group A started by playing *DysEggxia* while Group B used *Word Search*. After four weeks (12 sessions of 20 minutes each), the first post-test was administrated and the groups switched the games. The length of the second period was the same as the first and thus both groups were exposed to both games for the same amount of time. After the second phase the participants undertook the last post-test. We used this design to cancel out sequence effects.

5.3 Dependent Measures

For quantifying writing and reading performance, we used four *dependent measures* extracted from the tests. Then, to collect the subjective perceptions of the participants we used subjective ratings extracted from questionnaires.

As *writing error* we counted the types of writing errors presented in Section 4.2. If a word contained more than one error, they were counted individually. For instance, **litel (little)* has two errors. We used the Levenshtein distance[10] to compute the number of errors. As Pedler [28], we use Damerau's variant [4] where a transposition error counts as a single error. Word boundary and morphology errors counted also as one error even if several letters or words are involved in the error. The number of writing errors depend on the length of the text, this is why we do not directly report the plain number of writing errors. Hence, we compute the following dependent variables:

[10]The minimum number of single-character edits (insertion, deletion, substitution) required to change the wrong word into the correct word [20].

Writing | *Rate of Words with Errors.* The number of words with at least one writing error divided by the total number of words.

Writing | *Rate of Errors per Word.* An incorrect word can have more than one writing error, **probley (probably)*. Therefore, we also compute the average rate of errors per word. We define it as the number of writing errors divided by the number of total words.

Writing | *Rate of Errors per Wrong Word.* This measure reports the sum of all errors divided by the number of words with at least one error. That is, it measures the severity of the incorrectness of a wrong word.

Reading | *Rate of Errors per Word.* We define it as the number of aloud reading errors divided by the number of total words. We take into account the same types of errors as before. In the same way, omitted and added words counted as one error.

Subjective Reading and Writing Skills. Subjective reading and writing skills are measured by self-report questionnaires. On a 5-point Likert scale, the participants had to rate how well they think they can read and write. The scores range from 1 = *Very bad* to 5 = *Very good*.

5.4 Materials

All the participants took three tests –one pre-test and two post-tests– to measure the development of reading and writing skills during the experiment.

(a) **Test Structure.** Each test was composed of two parts: a dictation (writing task) and a part to read out loud (reading task). Each of the tasks contained two sentences and a list of eight words. While two sentences and eight words may appear little, the pedagogues insisted limiting the tests to this size to make them comparable to the ones that they do in class. Even if the games use only single words, we include both sentences and single words in the tests because single words are processed differently when they are used individually than when they are inserted into sentences [30]. By using both the list and the text, we can test whether the exercises based on single words can also impact at the sentence level.

(b) **Word Content.** For the experiment, we created three texts for the writing test and three texts for the reading test. To ensure that the participants did not just remember words from previous tests, the lexical words used in the texts were different, with the exception of functional words (prepositions, conjunctions, pronouns, and articles), such as *at, in,* or *the.* Each test contained twelve words that appeared in the *DysEggxia* exercises. For the rest of the test, we used words that appear in the children's school textbooks.

5.5 Procedure

To motivate the children to give their best, we introduced the study as a contest. We announced prizes, to be awarded in a ceremony at the end of the study, for the players who reached the highest scores summing the points of both games.

First, we administered a questionnaire to collect demographic information: age, gender, school year, their native languages, and their habits of playing games in mobile devices. Then, we conducted the reading and writing pre-tests

Figure 3: Experimental sessions (left and centre) and reading test (right). Photos included with the parents' permission.

prior to exposing the children to any of the conditions and issued the subjective-skills questionnaires.

Recall that in Phase 1, Group A played *DysEggxia* and Group B played *Word Search*. We sent a letter to the parents, asking them to make sure that the children did not play the games at home. After 12 sessions/4 weeks, Phase 1 ended with the first post-test (Figure 3, right). This test comprised the reading and writing tests and the subjective-skills questionnaire and allowed us to compute how much the children had improved in either of the conditions.

In Phase 2, the conditions were reversed: for another 12 sessions / 4 weeks, Group A played *Word Search* and Group B played *DysEggxia*. The phase was concluded by the second post-test, containing the reading and writing tests and a subjective-skills questionnaire, which allowed us to compute the level of improvement for each child in this phase.

The sessions were conducted at School Lestonnac Barcelona. During lunch breaks the children went into a quiet classroom, where they played the game that they were assigned to for 20 minutes (Figure 3, left and centre). While doing the exercises, one psychologist and one pedagogue constantly supervised the children. If a child got stuck in an exercise, they helped to avoid frustration (Figure 3, centre). Finally, all children were gathered in a big classroom to celebrate the end of the contest. The winners of each age group were awarded with a diploma. All children received a token gift for their participation, namely crayons and a small toy.

6. RESULTS

In the first step we cleaned up the data. We had to omit the data of five children. One child refused to take part in the tests. One child had played *DysEggxia* while she should have played *Word Search*, which violates the assumptions of the experimental design. Another child had not been schooled until the age of 5 and her general skills turned out not to be comparable with the rest of her group. Two children could not attend all of the tests due to illness, and hence did not contribute to all conditions equally. Thus, our quantitative results reflect the data of the remaining 43 children.

In order to isolate the effect of the two conditions, *DysEggxia* and *Word Search*, we computed for each child how the values in all dependent variables evolved during the two phases, *i.e.* between tests 1 and 2, and tests 2 and 3. Combined, this provides one value per participant per condition, that is 86 data points for each dependent variable. To test for significant effects, we used paired t-tests for parametric data and Wilcoxon-Signed-Rank tests for non-parametric data. We used Shapiro-Wilk tests to determine whether each

Dependent Variable	DysEggxia			Word Search			Significance
	Pre	Post	Change (SD)	Pre	Post	Change (SD)	
Writing / Words With Errors	28.9%	23.9%	-5.0 (17.3) pp	28.2%	25.9%	-2.3 (15.6) pp	$p = 0.355$
Writing / Errors per Word	0.360	0.288	-0.072 (0.242)	0.325	0.355	+0.030 (0.223)	$p = 0.029$
Writing / Errors per Incorrect Word	1.178	1.007	-0.171 (0.559)	1.080	1.244	+0.164 (0.487)	$p = 0.011$
Reading / Errors per Word	0.117	0.106	-0.011 (0.093)	0.129	0.114	-0.015 (0.136)	$p = 0.410$
Subjective Writing Skills	3.395	3.721	+0.326 (1.190)	3.326	3.581	+0.256 (0.978)	$p = 0.426$
Subjective Reading Skills	3.488	3.933	+0.445 (1.099)	3.535	3.767	+0.233 (0.922)	$p = 0.176$

Table 1: The numbers show mean across all children by condition (pp = percentage points).

variable was normally distributed, hence parametric data, or not. Table 1 summarises scores for all dependent variables.

Practicing with *DysEggxia* significantly decreased the number of errors that the children made in the writing tests. There was a significant effect on the number of *errors per word* ($T = 629.5$, $p = 0.029$, $r = 0.292$) and on *errors per incorrect word* ($T = 607$, $p = 0.011$, $r = 0.353$). There was no significant effect on *words with errors* ($t(42) = 0.935$, $p = 0.355$). This means that due to playing *DysEggxia*, there were less overall errors. The results are not conclusive whether this causes children also to write more words without any error.

There was no significant effect on the number of reading errors ($T = 427.0$, $p = 0.41$). This means that *DysEggxia* did not have a significant effect on improving reading errors in this experiment.

In addition, we did not find a significant effect on the subjective writing skills ($T = 226.0$, $p = 0.426$), nor on the subjective reading skills ($T = 211.5$, $p = 0.176$). Hence, we are not able to tell whether exercising with *DysEggxia* affected the subjective reading and writing skills.

7. DISCUSSION

When playing *DysEggxia* children improved their spelling significantly compared to playing *Word Search*. Hence, we accept **H.1** *Doing exercises based on dyslexic errors helps children with dyslexia to improve their spelling skills.* We found a significant reduction of errors after playing *DysEggxia* compared to the control condition. The *rate of errors per word* decreased by 20%, that is, significantly less overall errors ($p = 0.029$). In particular, wrong words contained less errors, e.g. **acer* instead of **azer* (*'to do'*), the correct word being *hacer* ($p = 0.011$), with a 14.5% decrease. The results are inconclusive whether this will lead to less wrong words, in spite of having a decrease of 17.3% for this variable.

We reject hypothesis **H.2** *Doing exercises based on dyslexic errors helps children with dyslexia to improve their reading skills*, as we found no significant effects on the improvement of the rate of reading errors, although there was a 9.4% decrease. There are three possible reasons. First, the exercises were specifically designed to train spelling skills, since they were based on writing errors. Also, we used animations and symbols instead of text to present the instructions of the game. Hence, *DysEggxia* requires very little reading beyond the exercise words. Second, our game did not include reinforcement exercises that targeted the development of reading skills. For instance, we did not include

exercises to reinforce the grapheme-phoneme connections, such as *Literate* [25] does, which leads to an improvement in reading words. Finally, *DysEggxia* does not have the characteristics of computer action games which were shown to improve the children's attention and hence their skills in decoding words [8].

We reject hypothesis **H.3** *Doing exercises based on dyslexic errors rises the subjective perception of reading and spelling skills of children with dyslexia*, as no significant change in the subjective ratings was observed. This can be explained with the reduced ability of people with dyslexia to identify whether a word is correct or not [1, 31]. There are a number of studies which confirm that the reading performance of people with dyslexia does not correlate with their subjective perception of this performance. For instance, in a study using eye-tracking, the textual layout which lead to the fastest reading speed among people with dyslexia was chosen as the subjective best layout by only half of the participants [36]. This is one of the reasons of why dyslexia is called a *hidden disability* [23], because, as mentioned above, people with dyslexia cannot perceive whether they are reading and/or writing correctly. Also, we did not disclose the results of the tests during the experiment, so the children had no indications on whether they were improving or not.

Limitations. Our study has two main limitations. First, our current results are valid only for Spanish. Nonetheless, *DysEggxia* also has exercises in English, which are designed with the same criteria as the Spanish exercises. However, English and Spanish have different orthographies, and manifestations of dyslexia depend on the language orthography, in particular with regard to their grade of consistency and regularity [2]. English has an opaque –or deep– orthography, *i.e.* the relationships between letters and sounds are inconsistent (compare *vase* with *base*). Opaque languages present a greater challenge to beginners than languages with transparent –or shallow– orthography, *i.e.* consistent mapping between letters and sounds, such as Spanish. Therefore, an additional study would be needed to extend the results to English.

Second, we did not introduce a third condition, in which the children did not play any word game. Hence, we cannot isolate, to what extent simply playing an iPad word related game already has positive effects with respect to how much a child learns in the same period of time without playing The reason for not including this condition is because we did not want to frustrate children by leaving them out of the competition for weeks, and make them lose their engagement. Nevertheless, by selecting another word game as baseline, the identified effects can be clearly attributed to *DysEggxia*'s specific design, which is the cause-and-effect relationship we primarily wished to establish.

8. CONCLUSIONS

We presented a method to train and improve the spelling skills of children with dyslexia. In contrast to previous work, the exercises are based on common errors by children with dyslexia and are presented on a tablet game. Our results show that our method integrated in the game *DysEggxia* has an impact in improving writing skills better than doing word games with correct words.

Our game has shown effectiveness and benefits for Spanish early-writers. It provides exercises in English and Spanish, which are, after Mandarin Chinese, the second and third most spoken languages in the world. Also, it is a simple, cost-efficient way of helping children with dyslexia to improve their spelling skills. Indeed, the iOS version app has been installed more than 17,000 times since its release in June 2012. So far, three schools that support children with dyslexia[11] have adopted *DysEggxia* into their curriculum. Currently, we are working on the adaptation of the game to Catalan and German languages.

Future work also needs to study additional strategies, such as the reinforcement of grapheme-to-phonemes transformations, to not only train writing but also reading skills. We plan to research the effect of different strategies to tailor the exercises on the basis of the child's performance.

9. ACKNOWLEDGEMENTS

We thank the psychologist Catín Sintes and the pedagogue Jéssica Leal for supervising all the sessions in the school. We thank Azuki Gòrriz for the beautiful design of the graphics used in *DysEggxia*. We acknowledge Col·legi Lestonnac Barcelona for their collaboration in the study. We also thank Nancy Crushen White for her feedback during the first phase of development of the app. Finally, we specially thank Ricardo Baeza-Yates for his invaluable support during all the development process of *DysEggxia* and this article.

10. REFERENCES

[1] M. Bruck. The word recognition and spelling of dyslexic children. *Reading Research Quarterly*, pages 51–69, 1988.

[2] N. Brunswick. Unimpaired reading development and dyslexia across different languages. In S. McDougall and P. de Mornay Davies, editors, *Reading and dyslexia in different orthographies*, pages 131–154. Psychology Press, Hove, 2010.

[3] M. S. Carrillo, J. Alegría, P. Miranda, and S. Pérez. Evaluación de la dislexia en la escuela primaria: Prevalencia en español (Evaluation of dyslexia in primary school: The prevalence in Spanish). *Escritos de Psicología (Psychology Writings)*, 4(2):35–44, 2011.

[4] F. Damerau. A technique for computer detection and correction of spelling errors. *Communications of the A.C.M.*, 7:171–176, 1964.

[5] A. Dickinson, P. Gregor, and A. Newell. Ongoing investigation of the ways in which some of the problems encountered by some dyslexics can be alleviated using computer techniques. In *Proc. ASSETS'02*, Edinburgh, Scotland, July 2002.

[6] M. F. Enguita, L. M. Martínez, and J. R. Gómez. *Fracaso y abandono escolar en España (School Failure in Spain)*. Obra Social, Fundación la Caixa, 2010.

[7] FEDIS. Presidente de la FEDIS asiste a las jornadas de león (the president of fedis (Spanish Federation of Dyslexia) attends León's symposium, Januray 2008. http://actualidadfedis.blogspot.com.es/.

[8] S. Franceschini, S. Gori, M. Ruffino, S. Viola, M. Molteni, and A. Facoetti. Action video games make dyslexic children read better. *Current Biology*, 2013.

[9] J. D. Gabrieli. Dyslexia: a new synergy between education and cognitive neuroscience. *Science*, 325(5938):280–283, 2009.

[10] P. Gregor and A. F. Newell. An empirical investigation of ways in which some of the problems encountered by some dyslexics may be alleviated using computer techniques. In *Proc. ASSETS'00*, ASSETS 2000, pages 85–91, New York, NY, USA, 2000. ACM.

[11] B. Hornsby. *Overcoming dyslexia*. Martin Dunitz, London, 1986.

[12] Interagency Commission on Learning Disabilities. *Learning Disabilities: A Report to the U.S. Congress*. Government Printing Office, Washington DC, U.S., 1987.

[13] International Dyslexia Association. Frequently Asked Questions About Dyslexia, 2011. http://www.interdys.org/.

[14] J. E. Jiménez, R. Guzmán, C. Rodríguez, and C. Artiles. Prevalencia de las dificultades específicas de aprendizaje: La dislexia en español (the prevalence of specific learning difficulties: Dyslexia in Spanish). *Anales de Psicología (Annals of Psychology)*, 25(1):78–85, 2009.

[15] G. Kanvinde, L. Rello, and R. Baeza-Yates. IDEAL: a dyslexic-friendly e-book reader (poster). In *Proc. ASSETS'12*, pages 205–206, Boulder, USA, October 2012. ACM Press.

[16] J. Khakhar and S. Madhvanath. Jollymate: Assistive technology for young children with dyslexia. In *Proceedings of the 2010 12th International Conference on Frontiers in Handwriting Recognition*, ICFHR '10, pages 576–580, Washington, DC, USA, 2010. IEEE Computer Society.

[17] T. Korhonen. Adaptive spell checker for dyslexic writers. In *Proceedings of the 11th international conference on Computers Helping People with Special Needs*, ICCHP '08, pages 733–741, Berlin, Heidelberg, 2008. Springer-Verlag.

[18] S. Kurniawan and G. Conroy. Comparing comprehension speed and accuracy of online information in students with and without dyslexia. *Advances in Universal Web Design and Evaluation: Research, Trends and Opportunities, Idea Group Publishing, Hershey, PA*, pages 257–70, 2006.

[19] F. Kyle, J. Kujala, U. Richardson, H. Lyytinen, and U. Goswami. Assessing the effectiveness of two theoretically motivated computer-assisted reading

---

[11] *Centro Creix Barcelona*: www.creix.com/Barcelona
Centro Coddia: www.coddia.com and
Uditta: http://www.uditta.com/

interventions in the united kingdom: GG rime and GG phoneme. *Reading Research Quarterly*, 48(1):61–76, 2013.

[20] V. Levenshtein. Binary codes capable of correcting spurious insertions and deletions of ones. *Problems of Information Transmission*, 1:8–17, 1965.

[21] A. Q. Li, L. Sbattella, and R. Tedesco. Polispell: an adaptive spellchecker and predictor for people with dyslexia. In *User Modeling, Adaptation, and Personalization*, pages 302–309. Springer, 2013.

[22] S. Lindgrén and M. Laine. Multilingual dyslexia in university students: Reading and writing patterns in three languages. *Clinical Linguistics & Phonetics*, 25(9):753–766, 2011.

[23] G. Lyon, S. Shaywitz, and B. Shaywitz. A definition of dyslexia. *Annals of Dyslexia*, 53(1):1–14, 2003.

[24] H. Lyytinen, J. Erskine, J. Kujala, E. Ojanen, and U. Richardson. In search of a science-based application: A learning tool for reading acquisition. *Scandinavian journal of psychology*, 50(6):668–675, 2009.

[25] H. Lyytinen, M. Ronimus, A. Alanko, A.-M. Poikkeus, and M. Taanila. Early identification of dyslexia and the use of computer game-based practice to support reading acquisition. *Nordic Psychology*, 59(2):109, 2007.

[26] R. Mitkov, L. A. Ha, A. Varga, and L. Rello. Semantic similarity of distractors in multiple-choice tests: extrinsic evaluation. In *Proc. EACL Workshop GeMS '09*, pages 49–56. Association for Computational Linguistics, 2009.

[27] R. Nicolson and A. Fawcett. Dyslexia, dysgraphia, procedural learning and the cerebellum. *Cortex*, 47(1):117–127, 2011.

[28] J. Pedler. *Computer Correction of Real-word Spelling Errors in Dyslexic Text*. PhD thesis, Birkbeck College, London University, 2007.

[29] H. Petrie and J. Engelen. Multireader: a multimodal, multimedia reading system for all readers, including print disabled readers. *Assistive Technology: Added Value to the Quality of Life*, pages 61–69, 2001.

[30] S. Pinker. *Language Learnability and Language Development*. Harvard University Press, 2009.

[31] L. Rello and R. Baeza-Yates. Lexical quality as a proxy for web text understandability (poster). In *Proc. WWW '12*, pages 591–592, Lyon, France, 2012.

[32] L. Rello and R. Baeza-Yates. Good fonts for dyslexia. In *Proc. ASSETS'13*, Bellevue, Washington, USA, 2013. ACM.

[33] L. Rello, R. Baeza-Yates, and J. Llisterri. Dyslist: An annotated resource of dyslexic errors. In *Proc. LREC'14*, pages 26–31, Reykjavik, Iceland, May 2014.

[34] L. Rello, R. Baeza-Yates, H. Saggion, C. Bayarri, and S. D. J. Barbosa. An iOS reader for people with dyslexia (demo). In *Proc. ASSETS'13*, Bellevue, Washington, USA, 2013. ACM.

[35] L. Rello, C. Bayarri, and A. Gorriz. What is wrong with this word? Dyseggxia: a game for children with dyslexia (demo). In *Proc. ASSETS'12*, pages 219–220, Boulder, USA, October 2012. ACM Press.

[36] L. Rello, G. Kanvinde, and R. Baeza-Yates. Layout guidelines for web text and a web service to improve accessibility for dyslexics. In *Proc. W4A '12*, Lyon, France, 2012. ACM Press.

[37] L. Rello, M. Pielot, M. C. Marcos, and R. Carlini. Size matters (spacing not): 18 points for a dyslexic-friendly Wikipedia. In *Proc. W4A '13*, Rio de Janeiro, Brazil, 2013.

[38] C. Romani, J. Ward, and A. Olson. Developmental surface dysgraphia: What is the underlying cognitive impairment? *The Quarterly Journal of Experimental Psychology*, 52(1):97–128, 1999.

[39] V. F. Santana, R. Oliveira, L. Almeida, and M. Ito. Firefixia: An accessibility web browser customization toolbar for people with dyslexia. In *Proc. W4A '13*, Rio de Janeiro, Brazil, 2013.

[40] C. Sterling, M. Farmer, B. Riddick, S. Morgan, and C. Matthews. Adult dyslexic writing. *Dyslexia*, 4(1):1–15, 1998.

[41] V. Topac. The development of a text customization tool for existing web sites. In *Text Customization for Readability Symposium*, November 2012.

[42] J. Toro and M. Cervera. *TALE: Test de Análisis de Lectoescritura (Test of Reading and Writing Analysis)*. Visor, Madrid, Spain, 1984.

Design and Evaluation of a Networked Game to Support Social Connection of Youth with Cerebral Palsy

Hamilton A. Hernandez[1], Mallory Ketcheson[1], Adrian Schneider[1], Zi Ye[1], Darcy Fehlings[2,3],
Lauren Switzer[2], Virginia Wright[2], Shelly K. Bursick[1], Chad Richards[1] and

T.C. Nicholas Graham[1]

[1]School of Computing
Queen's University
Kingston, ON, Canada

[2]Bloorview Research Institute, Holland
Bloorview Kids Rehabilitation Hospital
Toronto, ON, Canada

[3]Department of Paediatrics
University of Toronto
Toronto, ON, Canada

(hamilton, ketchesn, aljs, zi, graham)@cs.queensu.ca, (shelly.bursick,
chad.richards)@queensu.ca, (dfehlings, lswitzer, vwright)@hollandbloorview.ca

ABSTRACT

Youth with cerebral palsy (CP) can experience social isolation, in part due to mobility limitations associated with CP. We show that networked video games can provide a venue for social interaction from the home. We address the question of how to design networked games that enhance social play among people with motor disabilities. We present Liberi, a networked game custom-designed for youth with CP. Liberi is designed to allow frictionless group formation, to balance for differences in player abilities, and to support a variety of play styles. A ten-week home-based study with ten participants showed the game to be effective in fostering social interaction among youth with CP.

Categories and Subject Descriptors

H.5.2 [Information Interfaces And Presentation]: User Interfaces - User-centered design; K.4.2 [Computers And Society]: Social Issues - Assistive technologies for persons with disabilities;

General Terms

Measurement, Design, Experimentation, Human Factors.

Keywords

Cerebral Palsy, Video Game Design, Game Accessibility

1. INTRODUCTION

Cerebral palsy (CP) is a group of disorders that affects the development of motor function [11]. Youth with CP who require a mobility aid to walk (those classified at level III of the Gross Motor Function Classification Scale - GMFCS) have decreased opportunities to participate in social activities with peers, in part due to special needs in transportation, accessible facilities, and coordination of assistive services [7].

Networked video games represent a promising approach to allow youth with CP to interact with peers from the comfort of their homes. Video games can provide a common activity for players, forming a basis for social interaction. In networked games,

players may compete against other human contestants, work cooperatively to achieve a common goal, or simply get together with others to chat [2].

The social benefits of commercial video games may not be available to youth with significant motor disabilities such as those associated with CP. Fast-paced video games that are typically popular among young people need to be designed specifically around the abilities of people with CP [5]. Since most of the interactions with the game and the other players happen in a virtual world, the computer can mediate these interactions, reducing the challenges of having a physical disability. Indeed, the virtual world can offer novel experiences that individuals with physical disabilities are not able to realize in "real-life" [13].

In this paper, we address two questions about the design of effective networked games for people with motor disabilities:

1. How should a networked game be designed to enhance social play among people with physical disabilities such as those associated with CP? and

2. How effective can such a game be in practice in promoting social engagement?

To answer these questions, we have developed Liberi, a networked game custom-designed for youth with CP. Liberi illustrates three high-level design principles for games supporting social interaction among people with motor disabilities:

- *Frictionless group formation:* It should be easy for players to join up with others for play sessions within the virtual world.

- *Dynamic balancing for player ability:* People of different physical ability levels should be able to play together.

- *Varied play styles:* The game should offer a wide range of game styles to support different preferences and abilities.

We evaluated Liberi as a means of fostering social interaction in youth with CP through a longitudinal study where ten participants, divided into successive cohorts of six and four participants, played the game from home for ten weeks. Our results were encouraging, showing that a networked video game based on our design principles can provide a social platform for youth with CP. Participants expressed high enthusiasm for being able to play with others. For example, "P5 was pretty quiet and just focused on playing the games. However, when P4 joined, he was very excited [and] said 'Yay! I don't have to play alone anymore.'" As we shall see, participants were inclusive, picking mini-games that the whole group could play, and were creative, adapting mini-games to the abilities of the current group.

This paper is organized as follows. First, we review related work on the use of video games to foster social interactions among people with physical disabilities and discuss barriers to group play in existing games. We then describe our Liberi game, and review the principles underlying its design. We describe our in-home study with ten youths with CP, and then discuss lessons for designers of social video games for youth with motor disabilities.

2. BACKGROUND

Participation in social activities helps in forming friendships, developing concept of self, and determining a sense of meaning in life [7]. Youth with cerebral palsy (CP) have been reported to have fewer social experiences with peers than youth without disabilities [7]. People with other physical disabilities can have similarly reduced social interaction [6].

Multiplayer video games can foster connections with family members, friends and others. Social interaction around these games can take place in co-located facilities or over a network, bringing physically separated people together [10]. Networked games have particular promise for people with special needs who are confined to their homes or care centres. People with physical disabilities have expressed that online video games offer them the possibility of reaching out to people in situations that would otherwise be difficult, helping the development of meaningful relationships and building a community outside the home [6].

Even within commercial networked games, there can be unintended barriers to group play, and this could partially explain reports that players of World of Warcraft spend as little as 25%-30% of their time playing with others [2].

Establishing player groups

Players may have difficulty meeting others within a virtual world. Players may be spread over a large virtual geography, requiring them to travel for a long time before being able to group for a shared activity [2]. Once players have arrived in the same location, they must formally band together as a group. This typically requires them to use a cluttered graphical user interface (GUI) to specify the group's membership and parameters. Networked games typically offer complex user interfaces for initiating or carrying on social interactions [1], which people with limited manual ability may find difficult to use [3]. Additionally, over 83% of children with CP present seriously affected visual-spatial processing abilities [9]. This can make it difficult to effectively navigate virtual worlds based on complex visual cues or to successfully find places or persons.

Differences in players' abilities

Players of commercial networked games can be hesitant to admit new players to their group, sometimes because advanced players see no benefit in cooperating with lower level players [2].

In many games, playing in groups requires strong manual ability and visual motor integration, both limited in children with CP. Multiplayer games can require players to quickly perform actions to effectively defend or attack during a competition or a group battle. Limitations in manual ability of children with CP can make it difficult to use common control schemes that involve pressing different buttons in rapid succession, using multiple buttons at a time, or selecting a specific button at exactly the right time [5]. Hand movements of children with CP are typically slower and less efficient than those of their typically developing peers [12], making it difficult for them to quickly react to time sensitive game events. These differences in ability may combine with existing groups' reticence to include new players, forming a barrier to establishing social ties.

2.1 Possible Solutions

Commercial networked games have experimented with strategies to encourage people to group. These include offering different in-game roles for the players to choose from [2], steering players towards social gathering points in the virtual world [1], giving players down-time in the game to be social with others [8], allowing players to show off their achievements [2], implementing social gestures for avatars [1], and providing matchmaking tools. These solutions may help foster social interactions, but even successful games implementing these solutions have been inconsistent at cultivating group play. For example, even though there can be thousands of people playing World of Warcraft at the same time using the same server, people tend to play alone [2]. Ultima Online offered towns with taverns where players could meet and socialize, but these spaces were almost always empty [1].

The existing literature shows promise for networked games to foster social interaction among youth with motor disabilities such as CP. However, we are the first, to our knowledge, to study how games themselves can be designed to enhance social interaction among youth with CP. In the following section, we describe the design of our game, Liberi, showing how we addressed these challenges to social interaction. In sections 4 and 5, we discuss the results of a study of the use of Liberi in ten peoples' homes.

3. DESIGN OF LIBERI

Liberi is a networked, cycling-based game designed to allow youth with motor disabilities to socialize with friends while participating in physical activity. Liberi is designed around the abilities of youth with GMFCS Level III CP. Liberi is played using a stationary recumbent bicycle specially designed for people with physical disabilities [4] and a traditional Logitech wireless game controller. Players pedal to move their avatars, aim using a joystick and invoke game actions with a single button.

Liberi was designed by a multidisciplinary team including youth with CP using a participatory and iterative design approach [5]. The team held seven design and evaluation meetings over a period of a year, learning about the youths' physical abilities, gaming experience, and game feature preferences.

The game takes place in a persistent world that allows a small group of players to meet up and play together. A central plaza gives access to six mini-games and various shops where players can purchase rewards gained from long-term play, such as avatar upgrades, costumes, weapons or a pet dragon. The mini-games embody a range of collaborative and competitive gameplay styles, and can be played in groups or "solo" with artificial intelligence "bots". Liberi provides a voice chat system that allows players to invite each other to the different mini-games, coordinate cooperative play, cheer or playfully gibe each other, or simply chat.

To support social interaction in Liberi, we followed three high-level design principles: support frictionless group formation, so that players can easily get together in a play session; balance for player ability, so that players of differing physical abilities can easily play together; and support a variety of play styles, to engage players of different physical abilities and preferences. We now review in detail how the game was designed to address these goals. In sections 4 and 5, we present our experience in deploying this gaming system in the homes of youth with CP.

3.1 Designing for Frictionless Group Formation

As discussed in section 2, players of online games often spend little time playing with others. One of the barriers to group play is the difficulty in forming groups: in finding others to play with,

Figure 1: One player stands on the launch pad to Dozo Quest. Players' stickers are enlarged to the sides of the image.

and in navigating complicated interfaces to form an in-game group. We designed Liberi to minimize these difficulties. Specific design decisions included automatic grouping, automatic establishment of voice communication, on-screen presence indicators, easily joinable activities, and short travel times within the virtual world.

Automatic grouping

Unlike traditional online games, players do not perform an explicit action to specify which other players they wish to play with. To enter a mini-game, players stand on a launch pad (Figure 1). When one of the players presses the action button on their game controller, all the players standing on the launch pad are taken into the minigame. This action implicitly forms a group for the purpose of playing that game; there is no process of requesting or granting access to a group or of specifying group membership. Players need only stand on the launch pad and press the button. Figure 1 shows a player (on the right) using the launch pad to enter the Dozo Quest mini-game.

Automatic voice communication

Most networked games support voice communication between groups of players. In most games, communication is started manually, with a user interface that allows the specification of who will take part in the voice session. The fact that some players are able to talk by voice and others (not in the session) cannot forms a barrier to grouping. In Liberi, all players are equipped with a headset and are automatically placed in the same voice channel as soon as they log in. The immediate establishment of a voice link to other players makes it easy to determine which other players are in the game, and to negotiate a group activity.

The decision to include all players in a global voice chat has the disadvantage of limiting the number of players in the game; we have found that up to eight players work well in a voice chat.

On-screen presence indicators

One of the most basic challenges in forming a group is locating other players within the virtual world. To supplement voice chat as a way of locating others, we provided visual presence indicators in the form of avatar "stickers". These consist of miniature pictures of the other players that appear on the borders of the screen. The stickers are positioned to indicate the direction in which the other players can be found. Figure 1 shows two stickers indicating that there is a player out of view to the east, and another player reachable through the portal on the left.

Easily joinable activities

In many online games, once the game has started, it can be difficult for others to join. As discussed, in Liberi, players can join an ongoing mini-game by standing on its launch pad and pressing the action button. The mini-games are designed to accommodate late-comers. For example, in the Pogi Pong team-based hockey-style game, new players are assigned to whatever side currently has fewer players. In the Wiskin Defence mini-game, the new

player joins the group of defending players, and the game difficulty increases to account for the additional player's firepower.

Short travel times

One of the major barriers to grouping in virtual world games can be the size of the world and the time required to travel across it. Liberi has a varied virtual world in which players can travel between zones as varied as jungle, desert, space and an underwater world. However, Liberi was designed to allow players to congregate quickly to allow them to play together, with a goal that players can travel to any other zone within one minute.

3.2 Balancing for Player Ability

To ensure the game was accessible for players with GMFCS level III CP, Liberi was designed using the following principles: simplify level geometry, simplify level flow, reduce consequences of errors, and limit available actions [5]. The physical abilities of individuals within the GMFCS level III classification can vary a great deal, and so it was important to ensure that the games allow people with different abilities to play together.

Balance for ability level

Liberi's mini-games were designed to allow people of differing ability to play together, in order to avoid segregating players based on skill, limiting opportunities for social interaction. In Liberi, players move by pedaling a bicycle. To eliminate differences in avatar speed due to differing gross motor function, all avatars move at the same speed rather than mapping a higher pedaling cadence to faster avatar movements. Keeping all avatars at the same speed helps to shrink the disparity in the outcomes of mini-games where speed is important, such as the Gekku Race racing game, or the Biri Brawl fighting game; and additionally, it allows players to stay together more easily as they travel around the island as a group.

Group goals instead of individual goals

It can be difficult for players with differing abilities to play in a group because the players with lower skills can feel a sense of defeat if their ability to win or to contribute to the team is much lower than the others; conversely, players with stronger skills may become frustrated if another player is not keeping up. Several of the games adopted a single group goal in order to mask differences in ability. For example, in the Bobo Ranch round up game, players work as a team to move sheep to a barn. When this goal is completed, all of the players receive the same reward for completing the objective. By hiding differences in ability, we eliminate a source of friction between players.

3.3 Supporting a Variety of Play Styles

Liberi was designed to support a variety of play styles, with the goal of satisfying individual preferences and differences in physical ability. The mini-games include competitive, collaborative and team-based styles. One of Hanarra's Laws describes how over time players who stick with a game will be those who enjoy the style of the game offered [8]. By providing a variety of play styles, we can satisfy individual players' personal preferences. Additionally, mini-games require different fine motor skills, helping players with differing manual abilities to find a game they are all able to play. Games can also be played solo, where computer controlled "bots" fill in other player slots.

There are six mini-games in total, ranging over a single player platform game, a competitive racing game, a cooperative zombie defense game, a team-based space hockey game, a brawler fighting game and a cooperative round-up game. We describe three mini-games in detail, and briefly describe the others.

Figure 2: Three players compete in Gekku Race.

3.3.1 Gekku Race

In Gekku Race (Figure 2), players are "gekku" lizards racing to be the first to reach the top of a wall. Gekkus can slow their opponents either by spitting cashews or by breathing fire. Once one gekku reaches the top, the game ends, and all of the gekkus slide back to their starting position for another round.

Gekku Race is a competitive racing game that allows players' avatars to directly interact through breathing fire and spitting cashews. This encourages social interaction by allowing players to react to others' actions towards them. A good dodge or well-timed hit can provoke verbal interactions between players. Players can gibe or cheer each other on during the game. Outside the game, players can discuss strategies of when to attack others, which attacks they like best and recall interesting interactions between their avatars during gameplay. The racetrack is short, requiring about 45 seconds to complete, allowing players to quickly join in an ongoing competition.

3.3.2 Dozo Quest

In Dozo Quest (Figure 3), players maneuver a spiky ball by rolling and dashing through a desert maze. Within the maze lie a variety of enemies, obstacles, traps and loot. Players can choose to jump over enemies or attack them. At the end of the game, players must defeat a powerful boss either alone or in a group.

Dozo Quest can be played as a single-player or group game. A group of players can traverse the maze together, collecting loot and killing enemies along the way. Barriers increase in strength when more players join, making it difficult to reach a new section without working together. Once players reach the end of the game, they are faced with a large "boss" fight. The large boss (Muferoth) also increases in strength based on the number of players that are in the game. The increase in difficulty encourages players to discuss how best to attack and defeat Muferoth. This is an example of a dynamic difficulty adjustment algorithm, used to balance mini-games for varying numbers of players.

A key aspect of Dozo Quest that encourages group interaction is that players can join in at any time. A new player is placed at the beginning of the maze and can catch up to the others. Being able to join an existing game at any time removes the need for players to wait for others to finish the game, making it easy for an individual to join the group.

3.3.3 Wiskin Defence

In Wiskin Defence (Figure 4), the wiskins are small cute penguin-like creatures sitting in a nest in the centre of the game arena. Zombies of varying types emerge from the sides of the arena and travel inward. If a zombie reaches the nest, a wiskin is eliminated. The job of the players is to defend the wiskins by killing the zombies before they can reach the centre. Players choose, purchase, and upgrade weapons at the shops in the central plaza.

Since different weapons vary in effectiveness against the different types of zombies, success is far more likely when players coordinate their movements and attacks to keep the monsters at

Figure 3: Players team up to destroy a barrier in Dozo Quest.

bay. This cooperation mainly manifests in two ways. Most commonly, players will simply ask for help from others when they are being overwhelmed. Alternatively, a player can take a commanding role and direct the movements of others, coordinating the overall defense of the wiskins. Another form of social interaction stems from discussion about the effectiveness of personal preferences for different types of weapons, allowing players to learn more about weapons they haven't used.

3.3.4 Other Mini-Games

In *Bobo Ranch*, a co-operative round up game, the players are tasked with lassoing and dragging rebel bobos (flying sheep) back home to their barn. The game ends when all bobos are home. Bobos are easier to move when lassoed by multiple players at once, encouraging cooperative play.

Biri Brawl is a competitive brawl fighting game. A biri is a jellyfish with a fist inside it. Players punch other biris (both bots and other players) to accumulate points. A defeated biri can join the battle again after a short time.

In *Pogi Pong,* players take the form of space hedgehogs. Players are split into two teams competing to knock a star into the opposing team's goal. The team that scores the most goals wins.

4. STUDY

To evaluate the design principles underlying Liberi, we conducted a ten-week trial where ten youths with CP played the game from home. We have previously reported an evaluation of the game in terms of playability and fun [4,5]; in this paper, we report the results of a second, larger study where we focused on the effectiveness of the game in fostering social interaction.

We recruited ten participants, four of whom had participated in previous design sessions. Three of our participants were female and seven were male. The mean age was 15.2, ranging from 12 to 18. Seven had spastic diplegia (lower limbs are affected) and three had spastic triplegia (lower limbs and one arm are affected). Nine were at GMFCS level III, where the main form of mobility is with the use of a walker, and one was at GMFCS level IV, where a manual wheelchair is required. All participants were able to communicate verbally without problems. A minority of participants had existing social connections through attendance in sporting groups such as sledge hockey. The majority of the participants had experience with commercial game consoles such as Nintendo Wii, PlayStation 3 and Xbox 360.

Figure 4: Three players play Wiskin Defence.

A research assistant set up an exergaming station in the home of each participant. This featured a custom-designed recumbent bike [4], a 23" screen all-in-one computer running the Liberi game, a wireless game controller, a wireless headset and a wireless heart rate monitor. Due to limited numbers of these special-purpose stations, the participants were divided into two successive cohorts, one with six participants and one with four. The game server was open six days a week for a 1.5 hour session. By opening the server for 1.5 hours instead of 24 hours a day, we intended to increase the opportunity for the participants to meet others online. Participants were free to determine when (and whether) they wanted to play within these periods; however, they were encouraged to play at least 3 times a week, summing up at least 90 minutes a week, and were limited to 60 minutes of play per day.

The game created log files when a participant joined the server. For each second they played, the game recorded the time, the mini-game or shop the participant was in, any in-game events, how many others were in that mini-game, and input from the game controller. This data allowed us to extract information about what games participants played, and who they played with.

A "game monitor" research assistant observed each game session during the trial using an administrator tool that showed the locations and activities of the participants' avatars. The game monitors were included in the open voice chat and were instructed to only interact with the participants in case of technical issues or inappropriate behavior. After each session, the game monitor wrote a report to record activities and interactions between participants. The monitors produced 119 reports, 6 per week over 20 weeks, minus one statutory holiday.

At the end of the study, participants completed a custom-designed Likert-scale questionnaire focused on their experience with the games followed by a short semi-structured interview.

To keep the novelty of the games high, we introduced the games progressively, starting with Gekku Race and Dozo Quest, and adding a new game every two weeks. The order was: Biri Brawl, Wiskin Defence, Pogi Pong, and Bobo Ranch.

A private Facebook group for the study was created. Seven of the ten participants joined the group. The game monitors posted video tutorials of upcoming games. Participants were encouraged to use the group to set up days to meet online and play together.

5. RESULTS

We found that Liberi met its design goals of enabling social interaction among youth with CP, while providing low barriers to forming and playing in groups. Our sources of evidence are data collected from the questionnaires, interviews, game session reports and the Facebook group, as well as quantitative information extracted from the log files recorded by the game. As we will see, this data indicates that, at least for this set of participants, Liberi was a highly effective platform for fostering social interaction. This allows us to conclude that when the games are designed correctly, networked gaming has great potential as a social outlet for people with motor disabilities.

We begin by giving a high level overview of the degree to which our participants chose to interact socially and the forms that this interaction took. We then tie these observations to an analysis of the effectiveness of our three design principles of frictionless group formation, balancing for ability, and supporting a variety of play styles.

5.1 Social Interaction Fostered by Liberi

Liberi successfully provided a platform for social interaction that inspired high engagement among our participants. On average,

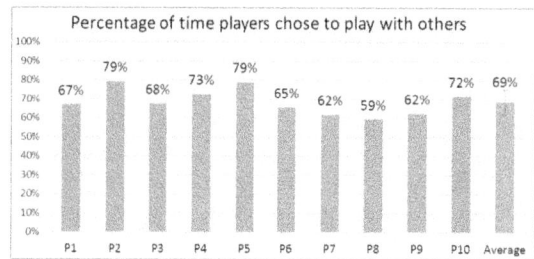

Figure 5: All players chose to play with others the majority of the time they could (average: 69% of the time).

each participant played a total of 1,659 minutes over the 10 weeks (SD: 609), or an average of 2¾ hours/week. Participants played with others 69% of the time that other people were online. Figure 5 shows that all participants spent the majority of time playing with others when at least one other person was available to play. The 31% of the time played alone includes time travelling to meet others and time spent shopping, as well as solo play.

The large percentage of time that players chose to spend with each other indicates that they highly valued group interaction. This high participation in group play also suggests that our design decisions about frictionless group formation and balancing for player ability were effective.

Participants' preference for group play is shown by differences in the length of daily gaming sessions when there were others online versus when participants were alone. We ran a two-sample t-test assuming unequal variances comparing participants' session length when online with others (M: 50.2, SD: 19.8) versus when they were alone (M: 37.1, SD: 19.4) and found that players stayed online longer when other players were online with them (t(62) = 10.87, p < 0.01). On average, sessions were approximately 13 minutes longer when players were able to play with others.

Game session reports describe players joining the server and, if others were not online, leaving the game soon after. This behavior suggests players were largely interested in playing the games together. A discussion with a participant recounts: "P10 said that Friday's session went well and that the only reason he left 20 minutes into the session is because no one else was on." To avoid playing alone, players would often use the voice chat to arrange times to meet online and play together in future sessions. One game session report explains: "When P5 had to leave, they decided to plan their next meeting on Facebook."

We also received an encouraging response from one of the participants' parents that highlights the social facet of the gaming experience for the participants and their families. One month after the study finished, we received an email from the participant's father highlighting the physical, social and entertainment benefits his child experienced during the study. He hoped to reach out to the other participants and their parents to create a community in which the youths with disabilities could continue socializing and playing networked games together.

Players used voice chat to coordinate their activities in the game, including deciding what mini-game to play, discussing strategy, and explaining gameplay. A game session report shows an example of such interaction: "When P9 came on, P10 asked him to play Wiskin Defense. P9 agreed. While P10 was waiting for P9 he played some Gekku Race. When they were playing Wiskins, P10 told P9 to buy ice gems to complement his fire gems. P10 vocally coordinate[d] P9's and his own movements to clear the fire and ice resistant zombies. After a few games, P10 suggested that they try the newly released game, Pogi Pong. Since P9 had not played Pogi Pong before, P10 offered to explain the rules of the game."

Social exchanges extended beyond gameplay. For example, one game session report states: "In between games of Wiskin Defense, these two participants talked about their mutual friends, the weather and school." Players used headsets to socialize even when playing different minigames. One monitor reported: "P1 wanted to play Wiskin Defence and P3 wanted to play Dozo Quest again. So they ended up separating but they did not stop talking. P1 was talking about strategies to beat the game and P3 participated in the conversation too. P3 got intrigued and wanted to play Wiskin Defence with P1. Although they did not get very far, they had a lot of fun!" The experience of hearing players in other games talking and having fun brought P3 and P1 together in the game where they could virtually interact.

One repeated form of social interaction was that some players took on the role of a coach. One excerpt from a game session report describes: "P2 taught P1 how to buy and place the dragon egg, and P1 taught P3 how to do the same. Although P3 did not pick up the instructions right away, P1 was patient to teach P3 again until she finally understood." This coaching behavior was not always welcome; from another report: "P1 is most active with his microphone and takes the 'team captain' role and orders P7 and P9 around. I can tell P7 and P9 get annoyed by P10 sometimes and they simply don't listen to him. However, with each passing wave, they get more excited and I believe P10 plays a huge role as a morale booster."

We were interested in whether players grouped in an inclusive way, or tended to form exclusive collections of friends who preferred to play together. Player log data showed that participants played with whoever was online, rather than forming cliques. Figure 6 presents the number of minutes the players in group 1 spent playing with the other participants in the group. Participants played with all others. Game monitors did not see incidences of exclusion of players.

Seven of the ten participants possessed Facebook accounts and were therefore able to participate in the study's Facebook group. All seven stated that this group was helpful for communicating with the other players. All seven considered it useful for arranging times to play together, with five of the seven saying it was as valuable as or more valuable than communication during the game sessions themselves. Five of the seven directly stated that access to the group encouraged them to play. The two cohorts used the Facebook group differently. In the first cohort, only two participants posted to the group, once each, at the beginning of the study. Nevertheless, the four first-group participants with accounts reported Facebook as being useful, and we see evidence from the game session reports that they were using Facebook to coordinate in ways we could not see, likely through direct messaging. In contrast, the second cohort made extensive use of the Facebook group by posting to the group's "wall". These observations led us to conclude that social media in the game is useful in coordinating game meeting times and that its use can differ greatly depending on the people involved.

To summarize, we saw strong engagement from participants in the

game. Participants preferred to play with others, as evidenced by their playing together when possible and playing longer sessions when with others. There is evidence that a component of this preference was the social interaction afforded by group play, as seen by players' engagement in discussions beyond the gaming context, the social interaction even when not playing together, the adoption of the coaching role, and the contact from parents highlighting the positive social interaction in the study.

5.2 Frictionless Group Formation

As we have discussed, virtual world games often have structural barriers to forming groups with other players, and these barriers have the potential to be particularly severe for people with motor disabilities. As we have seen, participants in our study played with others most of the time that it was possible. This indicates that the mechanisms for finding others to play with and for establishing groups were effective. We describe now the most important design decisions for this: automatic voice communication, on-screen presence indicators and automatic grouping.

Automatic voice communication

Participants used voice communication frequently to locate each other in the virtual world. One game session report mentions that: "Sometimes the players will want to join a game together, but are all sort of heading in random directions, so they'll stop and coordinate."

A second common use of voice chat was to negotiate what game to play when participants wanted to play different games. The voice chat allowed players to communicate their preferences. An example from one game session report stated: "P4 asked P5 and P3 what game they wanted to play together. After a few seconds of discussion, they decided to play Wiskin Defense."

On-screen presence indicators

While the effectiveness of the on-screen presence indicators of Figure 1 was not formally tested, there are indications that they helped participants find others to play with. For example, during a technical outage of the voice chat tool, players were able to find each other despite not being able to speak; the players must have been able to follow the avatar "stickers" to locate each other.

Automatic grouping

The high frequency with which participants grouped when others were available to play indicates that the automatic grouping feature was effective.

Interestingly, the ease of forming groups led players to treat them fluidly. We frequently saw players disband from the group, play something else for a while, and then re-join the game they had left in progress. The reason reported by game monitors for this behaviour was often that players wanted to play different games but still wanted to retain contact with the others. The following excerpt from a game session report highlights the ease with which players were able to change the group formations throughout a single session: "As time passed, P1 wanted to play Wiskin Defense and P3 wanted to play Dozo Quest again. So they ended up separating but they did not stop talking."

5.3 Balancing for Ability

We found that players experienced few difficulties in group play despite significant differences in physical abilities. Evidence of this is that all the players played with at least one more player the majority of the time when others were available (as was shown in Figure 6). Two interesting features of group play have significant consequences to game designers: first, players exhibited a preference toward cooperative play as a way of reducing the impact of different ability levels; and second, our dynamic difficulty algorithms negatively impacted accessibility.

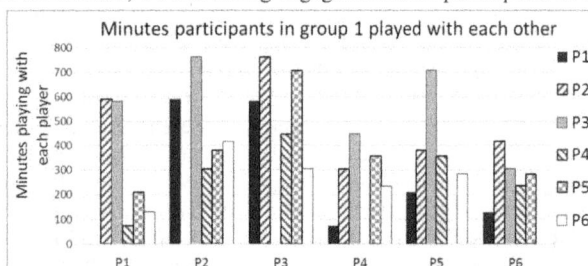

Figure 6: Players tended to play with whoever was online.

Cooperative play

Several of Liberi's mini-games allow cooperative gameplay, where the group has a common goal. As discussed in section 3.2, cooperative games help balance for players of different ability by allowing them to contribute towards the group's goal at whatever level they are capable of. For example, in Wiskin Defense, the players defend the wiskins from zombie invaders as a group; in Dozo Quest, players defeat the enemy "Muferoth" as a group. When well designed, in a cooperative game, it is not obvious which members of the group contributed most to the game's goal.

As evidence that this approach was successful, participants expressed a strong preference for cooperative group play versus competitive or solo play. During the interviews, when asked whether they preferred to play competitively with others, cooperatively with others, or alone, seven specified cooperative play, two specified competitive play, and one did not provide a clear preference. The game logs support this stated preference; Figure 7 shows that the cooperative Wiskin Defense game was the most played game by groups (and also the most popular game overall.) As an example, the game monitors reported that Wiskin Defense was particularly difficult for P3 (she had difficulty hitting the zombies). But she enjoyed playing it when others were online because she was able to interact with the other players while they held the zombies back. Here, the inability of P3 to contribute to the game was masked by the contributions of the others.

An interesting behavior was observed in the competitive Biri Brawl game. Biri Brawl is designed as a brawling game where all players fight for themselves. Computer-controlled "bots" are added in as enemies. In one session, instead of playing competitively, the players created an alliance and teamed up on the biri bots. Again, this compensated for the difficulties that one participant experienced playing the game. A monitor reported: "P3 said that 'it was intense,' and it looked like she was having a lot of fun even though she was not excellent at the game."

Challenges with dynamic difficulty adjustment

Since players are able to easily join and leave games, it was important that the difficulty of the games be dynamically adjusted for a varying number of players. To accomplish this goal, Liberi uses an adaptive balancing method where the games become more difficult as the number of players increases. For example, in Wiskin Defense, as more players join, zombies' strength increases and zombies attack from more than one direction.

We found that there is a risk in using this technique when designing a game for players with different physical abilities. If a player who finds the game difficult to play joins, the increased difficulty may make the game too difficult for the group. We witnessed this problem in Wiskin Defense with P3, who, as discussed earlier, had difficulty timing attacks on the zombies. Playing Wiskin Defense in a group of two was not a problem for any pair of participants, except for pairs including P3. In this case, the difficulty of the game increased at an interval greater than she and the other player were able to compensate for together. This situation is described in the following excerpt from a game session report: "P2 kept telling P3 to wait for him to finish

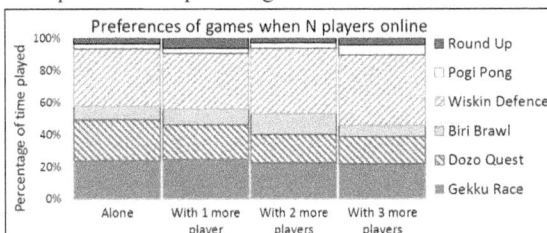

Figure 7: Preferred games based on number of players online.

Wiskins and then they would play together [Gekku Race]. He was hesitant about her joining him because then the zombies would come from both sides and he was not going to be able to help her." This situation highlights the importance of carefully scaling for all player abilities as well as the importance of removing in-game barriers for players with differing abilities in order to foster social interactions. In the case of P3, her inability to successfully perform all in-game actions meant she had to wait for P2 to finish before they could play together.

5.4 Supporting a Variety of Play Styles

Liberi's mini-games support a range of play styles, including cooperative, competitive, team-based competitive, and solo play. While participants favoured cooperative play, there is evidence that they nonetheless valued having a variety of play styles available. To the question: "Which game did you like playing the most with the others?," eight participants specified Wiskin Defense, two preferred Bobo Ranch, and one listed Gekku Race (one participant chose two games). To the question: "Which one was your favorite game?," seven participants answered Wiskin Defense, two specified Gekku Race, and one preferred Biri Brawl. Figure 7 shows that the competitive Gekku Race and Biri Brawl games were heavily played. This indicates that despite the general preference toward cooperative games, it is important to support a range of game styles both to satisfy individual players' preferences and to provide a varied experience.

Players proved adept at negotiating among preferences within groups. For example: "There were times P2, P1 and P5 wanted to play different games, but they were able to discuss and to choose the games they would enjoy the most together." The variety in game choices allowed fluctuating groups to satisfy different participants' preferences. The negotiation with other players was itself a form of social interaction, helping participants to become familiar with each other.

Having a variety of games provided viable game options to players with different abilities. Earlier, we described that P3 had difficulties playing Wiskin Defense and that in one instance, the other player online agreed to change games after finishing the game in progress. P3 played Gekku Race while she waited for P2 to finish with Wiskin Defense. Despite being a competitive game, Gekku Race was a better choice for this group.

6. DISCUSSION

The social aspects of Liberi are especially important for children with physical disabilities, providing opportunities to socialize, particularly for those for whom leaving the house is difficult. Vital to this goal is the ability for players to interact and communicate, which Liberi delivers through its connected voice chat, supplemented by social media access in the form of a Facebook group. The voice chat proved to be an important component of the game, with players grouping less with others or sometimes outright leaving the game if this communication was interrupted. Players also played less when others were unavailable to interact with, meaning it was important that they be able to find times when other players were also online. The participants reported both the voice chat and the Facebook group to be useful in coordinating play times, to ensure they had others to play with.

Liberi is designed to have frictionless grouping mechanics, enabling players to play whichever games they like with any of the other players. Since players cannot be separated by ability without restricting grouping, the game is limited in how it can account for variations in physical ability among the players. This can occasionally cause problems, such as seen above when P2 was reluctant to play Wiskin Defense with P3 because he knew the game would become harder. However, we found that players performed their own balancing by negotiating which games to play together, avoiding games that were difficult for individuals in the group. In general, the participants were inclusive, working to find a way for all members of the group to play together. This is indicative of the development of strong social links between players. It is interesting that players were able to organically compensate for the imperfections we have identified in our dynamic difficulty adjustment algorithms, changing games when the group composition rendered a game too difficult.

Oral communication is key to fostering social interaction. We found that in addition to the voice chat aiding engagement in gameplay, the game served as a seed for conversation. Often in the game session reports, we see that players began the session speaking mostly about issues related to the game, but then as they play, they begin discussing topics unrelated to Liberi. The game provides a ready-made topic for conversation, which then leads to interaction over broader topics. While further study is required, this aspect of the game indicates that Liberi is likely a better forum for social interaction than a simple chat room would be.

In terms of quantitative analysis of Liberi as a social platform, we saw that a large percentage of the time when it was possible, players actively played together. This result suggests that the aspects of Liberi designed to facilitate frictionless group formation—a small easily traversable world, immediate joining of games already in progress, and the simple non-exclusive group formation mechanic—are in fact successful.

A matter for further study is the general preference players have for cooperative games. This was seen in that 7 of the 10 players expressed a preference for cooperative play, the most popular game was the cooperative Wiskin Defense, and players transformed the competitive Biri Brawl game into a team game. A version of Biri Brawl in which players are teamed against the bots by default might prove more popular with players.

7. LESSONS FOR DESIGNERS

To summarize, we list the strategies used when designing Liberi that allowed strong social interaction among youth with CP, in hope that they will be helpful for designers of online games to promote social interaction among people with motor disabilities.

1. *Design for frictionless group formation*
   - Allow automatic grouping of players
   - Automatically establish a voice chat among all players
   - Provide clear on-screen indicators of the players presence
   - Make game activities easily joinable, and
   - Avoid virtual world designs that require long travel times.
2. *Balance for player ability*
   - Balance the mapping of player abilities to movement in the game, and
   - Provide a common group goal to mask the differences in players' abilities
3. *Support a variety of play styles*
   - Provide enough games to support individual preferences as well as differences in ability.

8. CONCLUSION

In this paper, we have shown that it is possible to create a networked video game that allows youth with CP to be socially active from the comfort of their homes.

We have identified barriers in existing online games that might prevent people with physical disabilities from socializing with others, and have described how our Liberi game helps to overcome these barriers. We discussed the effectiveness of

Liberi's design through quantitative and qualitative data collected over a ten-week home-based study. To conclude, we provided a practical set of design strategies used for the design of our game, which we believe might be useful for designers of networked games that allow social interactions not only among youths with CP, but also among people with other physical disabilities.

Acknowledgments

We gratefully acknowledge the support of the GRAND and NeuroDevNet Networks of Centres of Excellence and of CIHR and NSERC through the Collaborative Health Research program.

9. REFERENCES

1. Ducheneaut, N., Moore, R.J., and Nickell, E. Designing for sociability in massively multiplayer games: an examination of the "third places" of SWG. *Other Players*, (2004), 1–14.
2. Ducheneaut, N., Yee, N., Nickell, E., and Moore, R. Alone together?: exploring the social dynamics of massively multiplayer online games. *Proceedings of CHI'06*, (2006), 407–416.
3. Eliasson, A.C., Krumlinde-Sundholm, L., Rösblad, B., et al. The Manual Ability Classification System (MACS) for children with cerebral palsy: scale development and evidence of validity and reliability. *Developmental Medicine and Child Neurology 48*, 7 (2006), 549–54.
4. Hernandez, H.A., Graham, T.C.N., Fehlings, D., et al. Design of an exergaming station for children with cerebral palsy. *Proceedings of CHI'12*, ACM (2012), 2619–2628.
5. Hernandez, H.A., Ye, Z., Graham, T.C.N., Fehlings, D., and Switzer, L. Designing action-based exergames for children with cerebral palsy. *Proceedings of CHI'13*, ACM (2013), 1261–1270.
6. Kalning, K. For disabled, video games can be a lifesaver. *MSNBC*, 2009. http://www.nbcnews.com/id/30116040/ns/technology_and_science-games/t/disabled-video-games-can-be-lifesaver.
7. Kang, L.-J., Palisano, R.J., Orlin, M.N., Chiarello, L.A., King, G.A., and Polansky, M. Determinants of social participation--with friends and others who are not family members--for youths with cerebral palsy. *Physical therapy 90*, 12 (2010), 1743–1757.
8. Koster, R. The Laws of Online World Design. http://www.raphkoster.com/gaming/laws.shtml.
9. Kozeis, N., Anogeianaki, A., Mitova, D.T., Anogianakis, G., Mitov, T., and Klisarova, A. Visual function and visual perception in cerebral palsied children. *Ophthalmic & physiological optics : the journal of the British College of Ophthalmic Opticians (Optometrists) 27*, 1 (2007), 44–53.
10. Mueller, F. and Agamanolis, S. Exertion interfaces: sports over a distance for social bonding and fun. *Proceedings of CHI'03*, ACM (2003), 561–568.
11. Rosenbaum, P., Paneth, N., Leviton, A., et al. A report: the definition and classification of cerebral palsy April 2006. *Developmental Medicine and Child Neurology Supplement*, (2007), 8–14.
12. Saavedra, S., Joshi, A., Woollacott, M., and van Donkelaar, P. Eye hand coordination in children with cerebral palsy. *Experimental Brain Research. Experimentelle Hirnforschung. Expérimentation cérébrale 192*, 2 (2009), 155–165.
13. Yuan, B., Folmer, E., and Harris, F.C. Game accessibility: a survey. *Universal Access in the Information Society 10*, 1 (2010), 81–100.

Text-to-Speeches: Evaluating the Perception of Concurrent Speech by Blind People

João Guerreiro, Daniel Gonçalves
Instituto Superior Técnico, Universidade de Lisboa / INESC-ID
Rua Alves Redol 9, 1000-029, Lisboa, Portugal
joao.p.guerreiro@ist.utl.pt, daniel.goncalves@inesc-id.pt

ABSTRACT

Over the years, screen readers have been an essential tool for assisting blind users in accessing digital information. Yet, its sequential nature undermines blind people's ability to efficiently find relevant information, despite the browsing strategies they have developed. We propose taking advantage of the *Cocktail Party Effect*, which states that people are able to focus on a single speech source among several conversations, but still identify relevant content in the background. Therefore, oppositely to one sequential speech channel, we hypothesize that blind people can leverage concurrent speech channels to quickly get the gist of digital information. In this paper, we present an experiment with 23 participants, which aims to understand blind people's ability to search for relevant content listening to two, three or four concurrent speech channels. Our results suggest that it is easy to identify the relevant source with two and three concurrent talkers. Moreover, both two and three sources may be used to understand the relevant source content depending on the task intelligibility demands and user characteristics.

Categories and Subject Descriptors

H.5. [**Information Interfaces and Presentation (e.g. HCI)**]: Multimedia Information Systems – Audio Input/Output.

Keywords

Cocktail party effect; Screen reader; blind; visually impaired; skimming; scanning; concurrent speech.

1. INTRODUCTION

Screen readers have a central role in providing access to digital information to visually impaired users. Making this information accessible is crucial and has been the object of intensive research (e.g. [5]). A different challenge arises from the need to process potentially useful (and accessible) information more efficiently. Sighted users are able to quickly sift through a document or web page by looking through visually prominent content or diagonal reading. These skills enable to get a general idea of the content – *skimming* – or to find specific information – *scanning* [1].

Although blind people lack this visual ability, they have

developed browsing strategies [7, 29, 30], such as navigating through headings and increasing the speech rate, which help them to mitigate this limitation. Nevertheless, comparisons between sighted and blind users browsing the web highlight significant differences in prejudice of the latter [6, 26]. Unlike the visual presentation on screen that depicts a lot of information at a time, screen readers rely on a sequential channel that impairs a quick overview of the content.

The sequential characteristic of screen readers, however, does not take advantage of the human ability to process concurrent, parallel, speech channels. The *Cocktail Party Effect* states the human ability to focus the attention on a single talker among several conversations and background noise [12]. Moreover, one may detect interesting content in the background (e.g. own name or favourite subject) and shift the attention to another talker.

In addition, there is evidence that our brain's ability to segregate simultaneous speech depends on characteristics such as the number of concurrent talkers [10], their differences in spatial locations [9, 10], or voice characteristics [10, 14, 28], among others. In fact, a good configuration of these characteristics enhances the speech intelligibility for both selective [10, 14] and divided attention [24, 27] tasks. In the former, one focuses the attention on a specific talker, whilst in the latter the attention is divided amongst several speech sources. It is important to note that most experiments that focus on speech use small phrases, wherein the participants have to identify all words. We believe that with longer sentences people will be able to achieve a basic understanding of the text, and therefore perform scanning and/or skimming tasks more efficiently. This hypothesis is supported by Cherry's [12] pioneer study, which reported one's ability to perceive an entire *cliché* by hearing just a few words.

A central tenet of our approach relies on the fact that blind people have enhanced capabilities to segregate speech signals [19]. This fact is due to the process of *Neuro-Plasticity*. In the particular case of blindness, it states that a blind person's brain is reorganized so part of their visual cortex is used in auditory processing [11]. Harper highlighted such advantage [18] when suggesting the use of simultaneous audio sources to convey web information faster to visually impaired users.

In this paper, we argue that screen reader users can leverage the *Cocktail Party Effect* to scan for relevant information more efficiently. As a use case scenario, while exploring news sites one may be targeting specific subjects to pay further attention to. Instead of listening to all headings sequentially, one could listen to two or three simultaneously to detect the relevant ones. We believe that the use of concurrent speech enables blind people to listen to several unrelated information items (e.g. articles in news sites, search results and social media posts), get the gist of the information and identify the ones that deserve further attention.

We present an experiment with 23 visually impaired people that aims to evaluate the perception of concurrent speech whilst scanning for relevant information. In particular, we address the following questions: 1) How many voices can blind users listen to, and still be able to identify the one with relevant content? 2) And to keep track of its content? 3) Do differences in voice characteristics enhance both identification and selective attention?

Our results suggest that the identification of the relevant source is a straightforward task when listening to two simultaneous talkers and most participants were still able to identify it with three talkers. Moreover, both two and three simultaneous sources may be used to understand the relevant source's content depending on speech intelligibility demands and user characteristics.

2. RELATED WORK

The related work reviewed in this section is three-fold: first, we look into the research and techniques that aim to accelerate blind people's textual scanning; second, we provide a background on speech segregation using multiple sound sources; third, we present example applications that make use of simultaneous speech feedback.

2.1 Fast-Reading Techniques

Screen reader users develop several browsing strategies in order to overcome accessibility and usability limitations. For instance, web users may re-check their actions, increase the speech rate or navigate through HTML heading elements to obtain an overview of the website [7, 29]. These strategies may indeed help them browse more efficiently. For instance, a proper use of *Heading* elements can significantly speed up web browsing, particularly for scanning tasks [26, 30]. Yet, information overload remains a heavy load, as *"the biggest problem in non-visual browsing remains the speed of information processing"* [7].

A frequent approach to surpass this challenge is summarization (e.g. [1, 17]. Yet, other approaches are needed to, by themselves, or together with current browsing techniques, accelerate blind people's information processing.

2.2 Cocktail Party Effect

The *Cocktail Party Effect* states the human ability to focus the attention on a single talker among several conversations and background noise [12]. Moreover, one may detect interesting content in the background (e.g. own name or favourite subject) and shift the attention to another talker.

Several researchers investigated how concurrent speech intelligibility can be maximized. Although intelligibility decreases with the increase of competing talkers, the separation of speech signals between ears (dichotic speech) outperforms the use of mixed signals (monaural speech) [12] and is only surpassed by spatial audio [10]. In fact, the use of spatial audio is also valuable in divided attention tasks, where people have to pay attention to two speech signals [24, 27]. Regarding voice characteristics, Brungart, Darwin and colleagues [10, 14] showed the advantage in using different gender talkers, as it makes use of the human brain's ability to segregate sound frequencies [8]. Moreover, alike the use of increasing speech rates with practice, there is also evidence that even short-term training improves sound segregation and identification [2].

The increasing use of speech and sound in the interaction with computers may leverage this phenomenon to provide information more efficiently and/or effectively. Actually, blind people, in particular early-blind, are more capable to discriminate speech than sighted people are, due to the process of *neuro-plasticity* [19]. It states that areas of the brain that are not used (in this case, the visual cortex) are reorganized for different purposes [11].

2.3 Simultaneous Sound Applications

The insights provided by the aforementioned experiments led to applications that try to take advantage of concurrent speech to present larger amounts of information more efficiently. Sasayaki [22] provides the output of a standard auditory browser, augmented with a *whispering* voice channel used, for example, to locate the screen reader position in the web page or providing important contextual information. Other authors introduced spatial audio to map [13, 16] the current position in a web page, while a different voice provided other information.

Another example is Clique [20], which places 4 assistants with distinct voices around the user in a virtual sound space. Therein, each assistant has a role involving tasks or events (e.g. email, calendar and browser activity) and is able to use conversation features such as referencing, pacing and turn taking.

AudioStreamer [23] uses 3 speech sources from audio news programs in the frontal horizontal plane (1 ahead and others 60 degrees on both sides) and enhances the signal of the one that is the current focus of interest. To select the current focus it captures the gesture of turning the face to the sound's direction. Similarly, Sodnik and colleagues [25] present different files (two or three) in different spatial locations. Participants were able to keep track of two simultaneous files; yet, when three were presented, they were only able to focus in a single file.

Aoki and colleagues [3] presented a social audio space supporting multiple simultaneous conversations. They monitored the participants' behaviour to identify conversational floors as they emerge and to modify the audio delivered to each participant enhancing the signals of interest. SpeechSkimmer [4] tries to present recorded speech faster by presenting the most important segments to an ear and the discarded material to the other.

These applications are valuable contributions for their scenarios and tasks; yet, there are no guarantees that they are suitable when *scanning* for relevant content. We intend to leverage the knowledge of the previous section and assess if similar conclusions can be drawn to the use of longer sentences, when *scanning* for relevant information.

3. TEXT-TO-SPEECHES

Our main goal was to evaluate the perception of concurrent speech by blind people, in order to leverage this ability to accelerate their access to information. In this section, we describe the framework, Text-to-Speeches, which enabled such evaluation.

Text-to-Speeches is able to position several pre-recorded audio files in a 3D space simultaneously. We built a java framework on top of Paul Lamb's 3D Sound System[1], using the LightWeight Java Game Library (LWJGL[2]) binding of OpenAL Soft 1.15.1[3]. This setting supports the use of digital filters called Head Related Transfer Functions (HRTFs), which simulate the acoustic cues used for spatial localization [32]. The HRTFs are based on

---

[1] http://www.paulscode.com/forum/index.php?topic=4.0

[2] http://lwjgl.org/

[3] http://kcat.strangesoft.net/openal.html

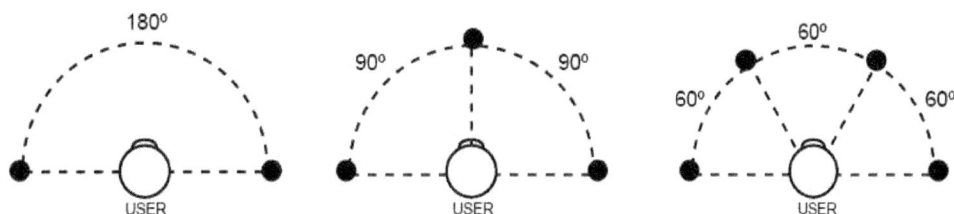

Figure 1. The sound source spatial positioning, in the user's frontal horizontal plane, for two, three and four talkers.

measurements influenced by the listener's head and ears. Alike most experiments (e.g. [10, 24]) and for simplicity purposes, we used non-individualized measurements from a KEMAR manikin (in this case, from MIT[4]).

Current Text-to-Speech software demands a unique, sequential auditory channel. Therefore, we pre-recorded all sentences to *.wav* files, using *DIXI* [21], a TTS developed by *INESC-ID's Spoken Language Systems Laboratory*[5] and now commercialized by *Voice Interaction*[6] (Vicente's voice – male). These audio files are then placed at different positions in the 3D audio space.

To guarantee different, controlled voices we manipulated our original voice's pitch (Glottal Pulse Rate - GPR) and formant frequencies (Vocal Tract Length – VTL), using the Praat software[7] the same way Darwin did [14]. Furthermore, we assured that all voices had the same mean intensity.

4. EVALUATION

The main purpose of this experiment was to investigate blind people's ability to cope with simultaneous speech, to perform fast-reading tasks such as scanning for relevant information items. In detail, we intend to answer the following research questions: 1) How many voices can blind users listen to, and still be able to identify the one with relevant content? 2) And to keep track of its content? 3) Do differences in voice characteristics enhance both identification and selective attention?

4.1 Methodology

In this experiment, the multi-talker environment was set-up based on previous work, in which the *Cocktail Party Effect* was investigated. In addition, in this experiment, all sound sources are equally important as all of them may have the information one is searching for. Hence, the selected configurations were designed to not overbalance any of the sources. For instance, we decided not to use a different onset time and volume for each voice, as it would benefit some voices over others. In what follows, we describe our setting regarding the number of talkers, their spatial location and voice characteristics.

4.1.1 Number of Talkers and their Location

Our main research questions focus in the number of simultaneous talkers that a blind user can listen to, and still identify and understand the content of the relevant one. The related work identified a constant decrease in performance as the number of talkers increase, whereas results are nearly 50% of success with

four speech sources [10]. Although these results focus on different tasks, they were a good indicator for the number of sources we should consider. We have decided to conduct the experiment with two, three and four simultaneous talkers.

The sound sources locations took inspiration from several experiments that use equally spaced positions in the frontal horizontal plane (e.g. [9, 15]). Although other spatial configurations were proposed and provided better results overall, they ended up sacrificing specific locations that dropped their results significantly [9]. Figure 1 shows our spatial setting. The sound sources are separated by 180°, 90° and 60°, for two, three and four talkers, respectively.

4.1.2 Voice Characteristics

Most experiments on simultaneous speech segregation focus on pitch variations. Yet, the best results are achieved when varying the two main characteristics that influence male and female voices - the pitch (GPR) and formant frequencies (VTL) [10, 14].

We wanted to validate these differences for longer speech signals. We resorted to a single voice whose characteristics were manipulated to obtain different voices. Similarly to Vestergaard and colleagues [28], this central voice (an androgynous talker), was obtained by manipulating a male's voice. Such variations enabled us to measure the effects of pitch and formant frequencies together while excluding other factors such as intonation or prosody. Moreover, this option favored a consistent variation towards both male and female talkers, rather than the predominance of one gender in the experiments. The analysis of previous research resulted in three conditions:

1. **Same Voice.** In this baseline condition, all talkers have the same central voice previously mentioned. This voice has a mean pitch of 155Hz and VTL of 147mm.

2. **Large Separation.** This condition aimed at the larger known separation that could still provide an improvement in performance, for both pitch and VTL variations [14]. In this condition, each voice differs from the subsequent in a distance of 7.4 semitones (a ratio of 1.53) in pitch, and a 0.88 ratio in VTL. For instance, with two voices, the mean pitch values were approximately 125.6 and 192.2 Hz, while with three voices they were 155 (the central voice), 237.2 and 100.8 Hz. The central, androgynous voice was manipulated to obtain all the others. This rather large separation between voices, when resorting to four talkers, results in voices similar to Darwin's *super male* and *super female*, which deviate from normal human voices [14].

3. **Small Separation.** This condition has half the variation (3.7 semitones in pitch and a 0.945 ratio in VTL) than the previous condition. This option guaranteed the use of human-like

---

4 http://sound.media.mit.edu/resources/KEMAR.html

5 http://www.l2f.inesc-id.pt/

6 http://www.voiceinteraction.eu/

7 http://www.fon.hum.uva.nl/praat/

voices for all talkers (including with 4). Moreover, these values are very close to the larger separation in Vestergaard's study [28]

4.2 Task and Dataset
Daily, people search for information among search engine results, posts, tweets, mail messages or news. Therein, lies a decision of which pieces of information are relevant and deserve further attention. We centered our task in this frequent need: *Relevance Scanning*. Among some distractors, the participants have to identify the relevant message and try to understand its content.

In this experiment, the dataset consists in 103 news snippets from a Portuguese news site. The snippets contain only raw text and have consistent sizes, so that all sources stop emitting the information about the same time.

The 103 snippets were randomly selected and held the following constraints: contained only Portuguese words, correctly pronounced by the TTS; all resulting audio files have durations between 10 and 11 seconds; and we changed names, places and any other element that could benefit the previous knowledge of particular news or subjects. Moreover, the sentences were chosen randomly such that none was presented twice per participant.

The task consisted in finding the relevant source among the presented snippets at each trial (there could be 2, 3 or 4 simultaneous sources) and try to understand its content. Before the trial, the researcher provides a set of cues (consistent across participants), which work as a hint, to simulate the search for relevant information.

4.3 Procedure
The experiment comprised two phases that were conducted in the same session: one to assess the participants' profiles and a second to investigate the perception of concurrent speech. It was conducted in a training centre for blind and visually-impaired people. The characterization session took approximately 15 minutes and included an oral questionnaire about demographic data and screen reader usage and a working memory assessment. To measure the working memory, the subtest *Digit Span* of the revised *Wechsler Adult Intelligence Scale* (WAIS-R) was used [31]. In a first phase, the participant must repeat increasingly long series of digits presented orally, and on a second stage, repeat additional sets of numbers but backwards. Such tasks allow the calculation of a grade to the participant's working memory.

At the beginning of the evaluation phase, participants were told that the overall purpose of the experiment was to investigate the perception of concurrent speech for its potential use in future technologic solutions. We then explained the experimental setup and adjusted the headphones' volume to a level comfortable for each participant, using two trials with a single speech signal.

The evaluation consisted in one practice trial and six test trials for each possible number of talkers (2, 3 and 4 talkers) and had a fixed ascending order. We based this decision on our objective to investigate the maximum number of simultaneous talkers, instead of a fair comparison between them. This option takes advantage of the previous trials, with fewer talkers, as practice. Moreover, we did not complete the condition with four talkers, to avoid participants' fatigue and/or frustration, when the participant missed more than half the questions with three talkers; or when s/he was not able to identify the first 3 with four talkers. Fifteen participants completed the condition with four talkers.

The six trials followed a randomized order and consisted in two trials for each voice characteristics condition (same voice, large and small separation). We assured that both the voice (except in *same voice* condition) and the location of the relevant source were different for those two repeated trials.

Each trial consisted on the following five phases:

1. **Hint given by the researcher.** The researcher gives a hint about which news/sentence the participant should pay attention. This hint consists of the three most important and defining words in the beginning of the sentence (in the first five words, excluding prepositions and connectors). It enabled the participants to understand the sentence subject and provided a clear distinction between news.. This procedure is similar to the one performed in [10, 14], but they use only one word due to their smaller sentences (5 words).

2. **Play simultaneous speech.** The simultaneous sentences started to play at the exact same time. The participant tries to identify the relevant sentence and understand as much content as possible.

3. **Participant's Report.** Participants report the content of the relevant sentence. They are encouraged to reveal everything they heard and remember, using the same or different words. Related experiments [10, 14] ask participants to report the exact same words. Herein, we want to understand if people can get the gist of the information, independently of the words perceived.

4. **Question.** The researcher asks a question about the relevant sentence, only if the participant did not refer the answer in the previous report. This question is used to help recalling some of the previously heard content. All sentences have a pre-defined question whose answer is not in the first three seconds nor in the final two seconds.

5. **Identification.** The researcher asks whether the participant was able to identify the relevant source and to describe which of them it was. Participants could use the location, voice or every other way to describe the sound source. We intended to assess the easiest way to define a specific sound source.

After the 6 trials per number of talkers, we asked for participants' feedback. The evaluation procedure took on average 45 minutes.

4.4 Apparatus
The Text-To-Speeches framework, previously described in Section 3, was used in the experiment. Participants used *AKG K540* Headphones that were connected to an Audio Interface – *Saffire Focusrite PRO 40* – to enhance audio quality. The researcher controlled the experiment through a Java application. The researcher registered the participants' answers and sound was recorded during the whole session for further analysis.

4.5 Participants
Twenty-three (23) visually impaired participants, 17 male and 6 female, took part in the experiment. Their ages ranged from 22 to 62 (M=40.74, SD=12.36) years old. Nine (9) participants had a congenital visual impairment or their onset age preceded the 18 years old (6 of them are fully blind), while 14 had later onset ages (11 fully blind). They were recruited from a training centre for visually impaired people. No participant reporteded having severe hearing impairments and only 2 reported low experience with screen readers.

4.6 Design and Analysis

We resorted to a 3x3x2 within-subjects design where participants tested each combination of *Number of Sources* level (2,3, or 4) and Source Separation (small, medium and large) two times. Furthermore, in each of these two repetitions, the frequency of the voice and the location of the relevant news item within the number of available sources was randomized. This design resulted in 366 trials, whereas 15 participants completed all conditions (18 trials) whilst the remaining 8 didn't complete the condition with 4 voices (12 trials). We performed Shapiro-Wilkinson tests of the observed values for our continuous dependent variables (relevant source identification error rate, description completeness). These showed to be not normally distributed; we applied non-parametric statistical tests to assess differences (Friedman test was used to compare 3 groups while Wilcoxon signed rank tests were used to perform post-hoc comparisons between pairs of samples (Bonferroni corrections were applied). Spearman test was used to assess correlations of non-normal data or ordinal data.

5. RESULTS

Our goal was to understand how blind people cope with simultaneous information items in a *Relevance Scanning* task. In this evaluation, we analyze blind people's ability to identify the item of interest and to focus their attention on it. Moreover, we compare voice conditions and the effect of working memory.

5.1 Identification

After each trial, participants were asked to identify which sound source contained the relevant sentence. In 366 trials, participants were able to identify the correct speech source in 301 of them (82%). In detail, participants mentioned the source location in 298 trials, whilst the talker's voice was mentioned in 16 trials.

Figure 2 presents the success rate in the identification of the audio source. It shows that voice variations alone did not affect the identification of the relevant source (p>0.05 for all comparisons within each set of sound sources – two, three and four). This can be explained by the length of our sentences (nearly 10 seconds), which provide more time to explore the audio space.

In contrast, the number of sources has a significant effect on sound source identification, mainly between two and four talkers (p<0.001 for all comparisons between each set of sound sources – two, three and four that match the identical voice separation). Moreover, results also differ when comparing between two and

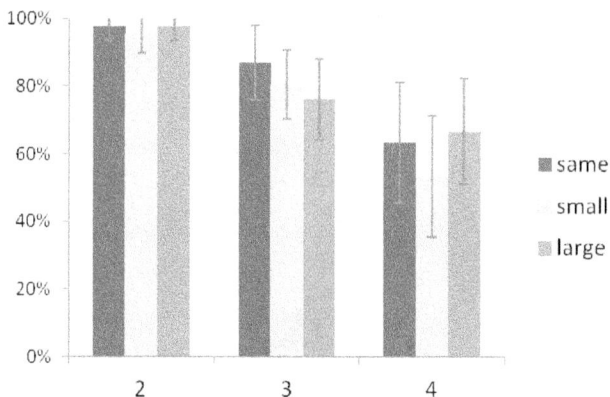

Figure 3. The success rate (y-axis) for correct answers to the pre-determined question, per voice characteristics and number of sources.

three sources, mostly in the large separation condition (p<0.01); however, the conditions with the same voice (p=0.096) and with small separations (p=0.035) also suggest an effect of the number of talkers from two to three. The difference between three and four talkers is also clear for both the same voice (p<0.01) and small separation (p<0.01) conditions. Still, there is not a significant difference in the large separation condition (p=0.132). A deeper insight on this matter is provided by the participants' comments: even though very high-pitched or deep voices are somehow annoying, they are easier to distinguish in the midst of several other voices.

These results show that users are able to identify the relevant source when there are two simultaneous talkers. In fact, 20 (from 23) participants were able to identify the relevant source in all six trials. Moreover, eight participants were able to keep this record with three simultaneous talkers, whilst seven missed only one trial. On the other hand, with four talkers no participant indentified the relevant source in the six trials (three were able to identify it in five trials).

5.2 Intelligibility and Report

To assess speech intelligibility we relied on two methods: first, participants reported everything they recalled about the relevant sentence; then, we asked them a specific question about it (if they have not answered it already). An analysis to the questions' correctness supports the decreasing tendency of speech intelligibility when the number of talkers increases (Figure 3).

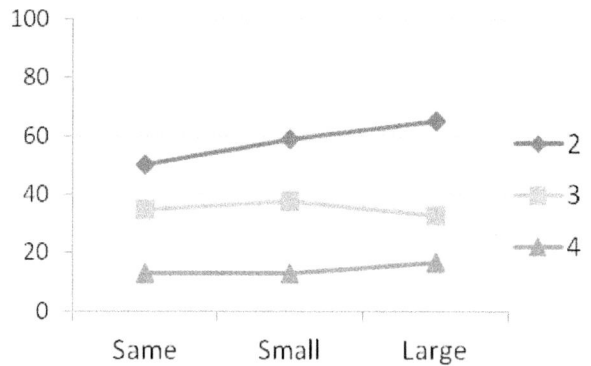

Figure 2. The success rate (y-axis) for the identification of the relevant audio source, per number of sources and voice conditions. Error bars denote 95% confidence intervals

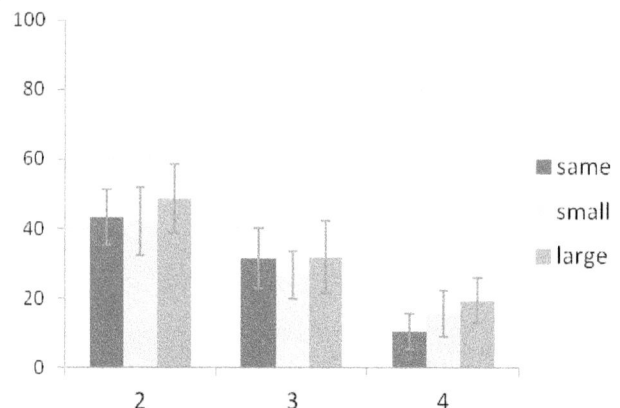

Figure 4. Average completeness (y-axis) of user descriptions – how much was reported - per number of sources and voice condition. Error bars denote 95% confidence intervals.

Table 1. *Spearman's rho correlation* between digit span scores and sentence completeness for each condition.

		2-large	2-same	2-small	3-large	3-same	3-small	4-large	4-same	4-small
Digit span	rho	0.482	0.349	0.761	0.633	0.559	0.447	-0.111	0.118	0.339
	Sig.	**0.031**	0.132	**0.000**	**0.003**	**0.010**	**0.048**	0.719	0.701	0.257
	N	20	20	20	20	20	20	13	13	13

Moreover, it seems to indicate an advantage for larger voice separations when listening to two concurrent talkers. Specifically, 65% of the answers were correct when listening to two talkers in the *large* condition (76% if we consider incomplete answers). Furthermore, these differences in the number of talkers seem to be consistent among users as seven participants were able to answer correctly to at least five trials with two talkers, but none of them achieved that result with three or four talkers. Although this measure provides us some indicators, it cannot be used to assess the intelligibility of the entire sentence. It might be the case that the participants missed, or forgot, that specific part.

The completeness of a participant's description derives from the percentage of relevant content (of the target sentence) that s/he reported (Figure 4 presents the average completeness). To measure their descriptions' completeness, we considered all verbs, nouns, adjectives and adverbs in the sentence. To establish a percentage for each description, we accounted those that were reported, either using or not the exact same words. These elements varied between 14 and 20 in the 103 news. A Friedman test for each number of talkers condition showed no effect of voice characteristics in the sentence reports. Yet, the number of sources had a significant role in speech intelligibility in almost every comparison within voice characteristics (p<0.01). The exceptions lie between three and four talkers, for both *large* and *small* conditions (p=0.041 and p=0.026, respectively), which also suggest a minor effect of the number of sources.

An average of the six trials for each talker condition shows that seven participants reported more than half sentence content when listening to two talkers, whilst three of them were able to keep that result with three talkers. If we consider an understanding of a quarter of the sentence, the numbers rise to eighteen and twelve participants for two and three talkers, respectively.

Although being a cognitively demanding task, these results suggest that the use of simultaneous speech depends on the ratio of information that needs to be processed. Moreover, the user's cognitive abilities are also crucial to assess the usage of multiple talkers. Table 1 presents the Spearman's rho correlation between

Digit Span scores and sentence completeness for each condition. It shows medium to large correlations between digit span and all the conditions with two and three talkers, suggesting that the participants were able to hear the sentences, but meanwhile forgot the content. In fact, to recall what they had been listening to, was referred as the main challenge by most participants, for two and three talkers. Yet, an accurate identification could allow the user to select or go back to the relevant item for further analysis. Moreover, participants reported that it was easier to recall information about sentences that they were genuinely interested.

5.3 Relevant Talker's Position and Voice

The positions for each number of talker's conditions were fixed and established beforehand. Still, the relevant snippet could vary among them. Figure 5 shows the average report completeness for each location depending on the number of talkers. The results are very similar with two talkers, but with three talkers, the differences are larger. The lower score for the frontal position (23.8%, in comparison to 30.7% and 35.2% for left and right, respectively) is supported by ten participants' comment, which mentioned that it was more difficult to listen to the frontal voice. One participant stated, *"When I want to focus my attention on a lateral source I shut down the other ear and therefore I'm able to focus my attention on the ear of interest. However, for the frontal voice I cannot shut down any of the ears or I would listen to that lateral voice more clearly... so I really have to listen to the 3 sources, which augments the confusion"*. With four talkers, the lateral left position held the best results. Users commented that the lateral audio sources were best perceived than the diagonal ones; however, we found no explanations for the differences between left and right positions (24% and 11%, respectively).

The variations of the relevant talker's voice ended up not having a noticeable effect. The only exception is with four talkers, where the high-pitched voice held better results (26.7%) in comparison to the others (from 10.4% to 15,4% for the androgynous and woman's voices, respectively). One participant noted that *"the high-pitched voice is irritating, but actually it is easier to distinguish it in the midst of several talkers"*.

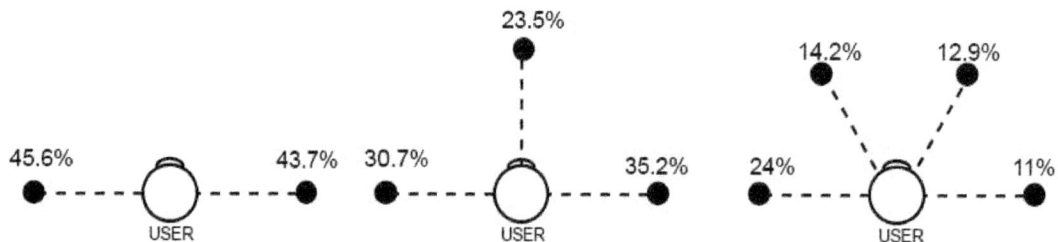

Figure 5. Average report completeness for each location, depending on the number of talkers.

5.4 Early and Late Blind Participants

The eight participants that were unable to complete the condition with four talkers were either late blind or had partial sight. Although this result suggests an effect of *neuro-plasticity* for early blind (congenital and onset prior to 18 years) participants, a Mann-Whitney U test revealed no significant differences in sentence completeness (neither source identification) between late and early blind participants, in all conditions. In contrast, a significant difference in a *two-talker* condition (*small* separation) was observed between early fully blind (six participants) and late or partially sighted participants. However, further research would be needed in order to understand the effects of onset age and residual vision, in this particular task.

6. DISCUSSION

After analyzing all data, we are now able to address the research goals by revisiting the aforementioned questions.

Two and three concurrent talkers enable identification. Results show that blind people are able to identify the relevant snippet when listening to two simultaneous talkers (Figure 2). In fact, 20 of 23 participants had a 100% success rate. Despite the fact that the identification rate reduces with three talkers, some users are still able to identify the relevant snippet. In particular, 15 participants identified the relevant snippet in at least five of the six trials. These results support the usage of concurrent speech (two to three talkers) in tasks that require the selection of an item of interest. Articles from news sites, search results or news feed posts are good examples, as users may *scan* through the content to select the ones that deserve further attention.

Identification through location. Location was by far the preferred attribute to describe the relevant snippet. This finding can be leveraged for interaction purposes, for instance to select or to increase one source's volume. It was previously done with head movements [13], but can also be applied to the usage of gestures in touch screens, specific keys in keyboards, among others.

Use two or three talkers depending on intelligibility demands. The report task is demanding by itself and is aggravated by the presence of another talker, since intelligibility is clearly influenced by the number of simultaneous talkers. The decision to use two or three talkers should take in consideration the intelligibility demands. The use of three talkers may be used when one needs to obtain solely the gist of the sentence. To cite one example, one participant suggested the use of *"three talkers in search engines, as the relevant result is usually among the first three"*. In cases where the intelligibility demands are greater, the option should go to two talkers. Actually, one participant stated: *"I usually listen to two news channels simultaneously (in the television and computer) and I am able to focus the attention on one of them when I identify relevant content."* These results show that not only concurrent speech can be used to identify the relevant content, but also to understand its content.

Working memory plays an important role. *Digit Span* scores are highly correlated to the amount of information reported after a trial. Moreover, several users pointed out the difficulty to recall what they had just heard. These scores should be used to determine the tasks that support the use of multiple sources. People with lower digit span scores can only take advantage of simultaneous speech in tasks where the intelligibility demands are lower. In contrast, people with higher scores may perform (more) demanding tasks with both two and three talkers. Moreover, our results showed that identification and intelligibility can be attained with two or three sources, whilst this was done as the user's main task. The high correlations with digit span scores suggest that this could be harder to accomplish in more demanding settings (e.g. a blind person walking in the street).

Voice differences are not crucial, but preferred. Apart from very specific situations, voice differences did not provide an advantage neither for speech identification nor to intelligibility. Although the related work shows that using different frequencies enhance speech segregation, it also shows that each attribute provide a greater effect when varied alone [10]. Herein, the use of different spatial locations seems to suffice for the task addressed. Nevertheless, the participants felt more confident when the voices were different. In detail, 16 participants preferred listening to different voices, while only two preferred the same voice. One participant stated, *"It is better to use different voices, because it requires less effort to follow the same sentence. This is particularly useful when listening to three or four talkers."*

7. CONCLUSIONS

Previous research concerning the *Cocktail Party Effect* supports the perception of simultaneous speech sources. We intended to leverage this knowledge and assess if similar conclusions could be drawn to the use of longer sentences in scanning tasks. Likewise the related work, in this experiment we found that both identification of the relevant source and speech intelligibility decrease with an increasing number of concurrent talkers. Our results show that identification of the relevant source is a straightforward task when listening to two talkers, and for most participants, it was also easy to identify with three. Moreover, both two and three simultaneous sources may be used to understand the relevant source's content depending on speech intelligibility demands and user characteristics (working memory). Unlike the related work, differences in voice characteristics did not provide a greater effect in neither speech identification nor intelligibility. However, participants preferred and felt more confident with the use of concurrent talkers with different voices.

Similar to the use of faster speech rates, simultaneous speech segregation can benefit from practice [2]. This experiment comprised a unique session with approximately 45 minutes. We believe that the frequent use of simultaneous speech will improve both speech identification and intelligibility scores. Moreover, these were one-shot trials, wherein participants' were not able to return to the relevant content. In realistic settings, interaction solutions should provide easy access to recently explored content. From this experiment, we have learned that the sound source location is the best mechanism to identify and therefore interact with such a concurrent sound source system.

A limitation of this experiment regards the number of relevant sources, which are restricted to one. Furthermore, some participants noted that the subject of the news influence their ability to recall and report what they have heard. In fact, in realist scenarios users would be focusing their attention on their favorite subjects, and therefore would be able to recall more information. In addition, in future interfaces if we prime the user with pre-defined subject locations, we can take advantage of *apriori* expectations [10]. For instance, one could listen to sports content always on the right side, whilst economics on the left.

We provided useful guidelines to the use of concurrent speech in fast-exploration tasks. In future work, we aim to explore interaction mechanisms to cope with the additional demands. Moreover, results suggested a slight advantage for early-blind participants. Still, further research is needed in order to assess the effect of *neuro-plasticity* in this *Relevance Scanning* task.

8. ACKNOWLEDGMENTS

We thank the *Fundação Raquel e Martin Sain,* Carlos Bastardo and all participants in this experiment. We also thank both Voice Interaction and INESC ID's Spoken Language Systems Laboratory. Work supported by national funds through *Fundação para a Ciência e Tecnologia,* under project PEst-OE/EEI/LA0021/2013.

9. REFERENCES

[1] Ahmed, F. et al 2012. Why Read if You Can Skim : Towards Enabling Faster Screen Reading. *In proc. of W4A.*

[2] Alain, C. 2007. Breaking the wave: effects of attention and learning on concurrent sound perception. Hearing research, 229(1), 225-236.

[3] Aoki, Paul M., et al. 2003 The mad hatter's cocktail party: a social mobile audio space supporting multiple simultaneous conversations. Proceedings of CHI, ACM.

[4] Arons, B. 1997. SpeechSkimmer : A System for Interactively Skimming Recorded Speech. ACM TOCHI – Special issue on speech as data, 4(1):3-38.

[5] Asakawa, C., & Takagi, H. 2008. Transcoding. In Web Accessibility (pp. 231-260). Springer London.

[6] Bigham, J. P. et al 2007. WebinSitu: a comparative analysis of blind and sighted browsing behavior. In Proc. of ASSETS (pp. 51-58). ACM.

[7] Borodin, Y. et al. 2010 More than meets the eye: a survey of screen-reader browsing strategies. In Proc. of the 2010 W4A.

[8] Bregman, A. S. 1994 Auditory scene analysis: The perceptual organization of sound. MIT press.

[9] Brungart, D. S., and Simpson, B. D. 2005. Optimizing the spatial configuration of a seven-talker speech display. *ACM Transactions on Applied Perception* (TAP), 2(4), 430-436.

[10] Brungart, D. S., & Simpson, B. D. (2005). Improving multitalker speech communication with advanced audio displays. Air Force Research Lab Wright Patterson AFN OH.

[11] Burton, H. 2003. Visual cortex activity in early and late blind people. The *Journal of neuroscience*, 23(10), 4005-4011.

[12] Cherry, E. C. 1953. Some experiments on the recognition of speech, with one and with two ears. The *Journal of the acoustical society of America*, 25(5), 975-979.

[13] Crispien, K.et al 1996. A 3D-Auditory Environment for Hierarchical Navigation in Non-visual Interaction. Proceedings of ICAD.

[14] Darwin, C. J., Brungart, D. S., and Simpson, B. D. 2003. Effects of fundamental frequency and vocal-tract length changes on attention to one of two simultaneous talkers. The Journal of the Acoustical Society of America, 114, 2913.

[15] Drullman, R. and Bronkhorst, A. 2000. Multichannel speech intelligibility and talker recognition using monaural, binaural, and three-dimensional auditory presentation. The Journal of the Acoustical Society of America.

[16] Goose, S., & Möller, C. 1999. A 3D audio only interactive Web browser: using spatialization to convey hypermedia document structure. In Proc. the ACM international conference on Multimedia (Part 1) (pp. 363-371). ACM.

[17] Harper, S., and Patel, N. 2005. Gist summaries for visually impaired surfers. In Proc of ASSETS (pp. 90-97).

[18] Harper, S. (2012). Deep Accessibility: Adapting Interfaces to Suit Our Senses. Invited Talk - University of Lisbon. [online] Available at: http://www.slideshare.net/simon-harper/adapting-sensory-interfaces.

[19] Hugdahl, K.et al. 2004. Blind individuals show enhanced perceptual and attentional sensitivity for identification of speech sounds. Cognitive brain research, 19(1), 28-32.

[20] Parente, P. (2006) .Clique: a conversant, task-based audio display for GUI applications. ACM SIGACCESS Accessibility and Computing 84: 34-37.

[21] Paulo, Sérgio, et al. 2008, DIXI–a generic text-to-speech system for European Portuguese. Computational Processing of the Portuguese Language. Springer Berlin Heidelberg.

[22] Sato, D. et al. 2011. Sasayaki: augmented voice web browsing experience. In Proc of CHI , ACM.

[23] Schmandt, C. and Mullins, A. 1995. AudioStreamer: exploiting simultaneity for listening. Conference companion on Human factors in Computing Systems, pages 218-219.

[24] Shinn-Cunningham, B. G., & Ihlefeld, A. 2004. Selective and Divided Attention: Extracting Information from Simultaneous Sound Sources. In ICAD.

[25] Sodnik, J. et al. 2010 Enhanced synthesized text reader for visually impaired users. Advances in Computer-Human Interactions

[26] Takagi, H. et al. 2007. Analysis of navigability of Web applications for improving blind usability. ACM Transactions on Computer-Human Interaction, 14(3):13{es.

[27] Vazquez-Alvarez, Y., & Brewster, S. A. 2011. Eyes-free multitasking: the effect of cognitive load on mobile spatial audio interfaces. In Proceedings of CHI (pp. 2173-2176).

[28] Vestergaard, M. D. et al. 2009. The interaction of vocal characteristics and audibility in the recognition of concurrent syllablesa).The Journal of the Acoustical Society of America, 125(2), 1114-1124.

[29] Vigo, M., & Harper, S. (2013). Coping tactics employed by visually disabled users on the web. International Journal of Human-Computer Studies, 71(11), 1013-1025

[30] Watanabe, T. 2007. Experimental Evaluation of Usability and Accessibility of Heading Elements Components of Web Accessibility. Disability & Rehabilitation: Assistive Technology, pages 1-8.

[31] Wechsler, D. 1981. WAIS-R manual: Wechsler adult intelligence scale-revised. Psychological Corporation.

[32] Wenzel, E. M. et al (1993). Localization using non-individualized head related transfer functions. The Journal of the Acoustical Society of America, 94(1), 111-123.

Analyzing the Intelligibility of Real-Time Mobile Sign Language Video Transmitted Below Recommended Standards

Jessica J. Tran[1], Ben Flowers[1], Eve A. Riskin[1], Richard E. Ladner[2], Jacob O. Wobbrock[3]

[1]Electrical Engineering	[2]Computer Science & Engineering	[3]The Information School
DUB Group	DUB Group	DUB Group
University of Washington	University of Washington	University of Washington
Seattle, WA 98195 USA	Seattle, WA 98195 USA	Seattle, WA 98195 USA
{jjtran, blow, riskin}@uw.edu	ladner@cs.washington.edu	wobbrock@uw.edu

ABSTRACT

Mobile sign language video communication has the potential to be more accessible and affordable if the current recommended video transmission standard of 25 frames per second at 100 kilobits per second (kbps) as prescribed in the International Telecommunication Standardization Sector (ITU-T) Q.26/16 were relaxed. To investigate sign language video intelligibility at lower settings, we conducted a laboratory study, where fluent ASL signers in pairs held real-time free-form conversations over an experimental smartphone app transmitting real-time video at 5 fps/25 kbps, 10 fps/50 kbps, 15 fps/75 kbps, and 30 fps/150 kbps, settings well below the ITU-T standard that save both bandwidth and battery life. The aim of the laboratory study was to investigate how fluent ASL signers adapt to the lower video transmission rates, and to identify a lower threshold at which intelligible real-time conversations could be held. We gathered both subjective and objective measures from participants and calculated battery life drain. As expected, reducing the frame rate/bit rate monotonically extended the battery life. We discovered all participants were successful in holding intelligible conversations across all frame rates/bit rates. Participants did perceive the lower quality of video transmitted at 5 fps/25 kbps and felt that they were signing more slowly to compensate; however, participants' rate of fingerspelling did not actually decrease. This and other findings support our recommendation that intelligible mobile sign language conversations can occur at frame rates as low as 10 fps/50 kbps while optimizing resource consumption, video intelligibility, and user preferences.

Categories and Subject Descriptors

K.4.2. [**Social Issues**]: Assistive technologies for persons with disabilities; H.5.1 [**Information Interfaces and Presentation**]: Multimedia Information Systems – Video.

General Terms

Performance; Experimentation; Human Factors.

Keywords

Intelligibility; comprehension; American Sign Language; bit rate; frame rate; video compression; laboratory study; Deaf community.

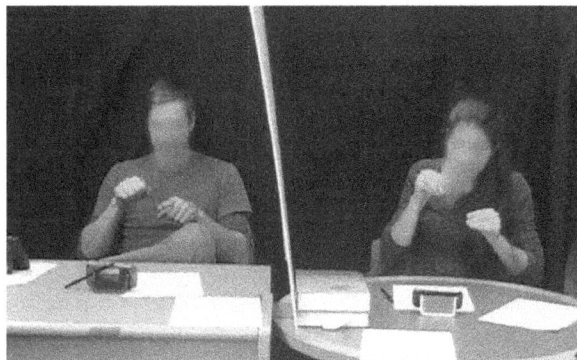

Figure 1: Two study participants holding an intelligible sign language conversation over an experimental smartphone application transmitting video at frame rates and bit rates well below industry recommended rates.

1. INTRODUCTION

Smartphones are rapidly changing the way people communicate and receive information, with over 1.9 billion smartphone users worldwide at the end of 2013 [34]. The growth of smartphone users has led to video being the fastest growing contributor to mobile data traffic [34]. Streaming video providers like YouTube, Hulu, and Netflix contribute to mobile video traffic by consuming 51% of all network traffic. Mobile video telephony is also contributing to the acceleration of video data consumption with the numerous available mobile video chat applications like Skype, Facetime, and Google Hangouts. In 2010, Skype received 7 million downloads onto Apple's iPhone alone [25]. Figure 1 is an example of two people signing over a mobile device.

Often, high fidelity video quality with little-to-no delay is a priority for mobile video telephony; however, this performance usually comes at the cost of high bandwidth consumption. Apple's Facetime app provides high quality video over Wi-Fi or cellular networks with an average bandwidth consumption of 5 MB of data per minute [11]. The high data rate cost of using FaceTime over limited data plans can quickly become expensive [6]. Other mobile video chat apps, like Skype, transmit video at lower dynamic transmission rates ranging from 40-450 kilobits per second (kbps) depending on network traffic [10]. Video intelligibility is sacrificed when relying on the available network bandwidth to regulate video transmission rates.

Deaf and hard-of-hearing people benefit from advancements in mobile video communication because it facilitates sign language communication. American Sign Language (ASL) is a visual language with its own grammar and syntax unique from any spoken languages. Intelligible video content is required for successful sign language conversations; therefore, the International Telecommunication Standardization Sector (ITU-T) Q.26/16 recommends at least 25 frames per second (fps) and 100 kbps for sign language video transmission [24]. However, total network bandwidth is limited and network congestion can lead to unintelligible content due to delayed and dropped video. U.S. cellular networks do not provide unlimited data plans and may throttle back network speeds for high data rate consumers [33].

We conducted a laboratory study in which pairs of fluent ASL signers held free-form conversations over an experimental smartphone app transmitting real-time video at 5 fps/25 kbps, 10 fps/50 kbps, 15 fps/75 kbps, and 30 fps/150 kbps, well below the ITU-T standard, for the purpose of saving bandwidth and battery life. The objectives of this study were: (1) to identify the minimum video quality settings allowable for intelligible sign language communication; (2) to learn what adaptation techniques participants use to compensate for the lowered transmission rates; (3) to objectively measure user perceived intelligibility of video content used in mobile sign language conversations; and (4) to quantify how much battery life is extended. We gathered both subjective and objective measures from participants and measured battery life drain. As expected, reducing the frame rate/bit rate monotonically extended the battery life. Video transmitted at 5 fps/25 kbps averaged 264 minutes of battery life, while video at 30 fps/150 kbps averaged 209 minutes of battery life. Subjective results revealed video transmitting at 5 fps/25 kbps had the most negative impact on perceived video quality ($\chi^2_{3,N=20}$=11.01, p<.05), fingerspelling ($\chi^2_{3,N=19}$=8.11, p<.05), and how often a participant needed to guess what the other signer was signing ($\chi^2_{3,N=20}$=29.75, p<.0001). However, frame rate/bit rate was not found to significantly impact perceived video intelligibility ($\chi^2_{3,N=20}$=5.08, $n.s.$).

Participants were successful in holding intelligible conversations across all frame rates/bit rates. All participants did perceive the lower quality of video transmitted at 5 fps/25 kbps and perceived they were signing more slowly to compensate; however, participants' rate of fingerspelling did not significantly decrease. Exit interviews revealed four recurring themes when it came to signing on mobile devices: (1) there was noticeable lower quality of video transmitted at 5 fps/25 kbps; (2) desire for larger screens; (3) different adaptation techniques were used to compensate for lower video quality; and (4) comparison of video quality used in the experimental app to commercially available apps. These and other findings compel our recommendation that mobile video software used by deaf people should support frame rates as low as 10 fps /50 kbps.

2. RELATED WORK

2.1 Bandwidth Requirements

The bandwidth requirements for transmission of sign language have been under consideration since the early 1990s. Sperling [28] investigated the ability for deaf people to transcribe ASL and fingerspelling from reduced television displays at bandwidths of 86 kHz, 21 kHz, 4.4 kHz, and 1.1 kHz. Intelligibility was found to drop to 90% at 21 kHz and to 10% at 4.4 kHz. Fingerspelling intelligibility was found to be more sensitive to bandwidth reduction, with intelligibility dropping to only 70% at 21 kHz.

Sosnowski and Hsing [27] evaluated moving images, finding that reducing the frame rate from 30 to 15 fps only produced slightly less intelligible video; however, video displayed below 15 fps resulted in intelligibility dropping dramatically. Harkins et al. [14] compared the outline of signers to a videotaped control, which

consisted of the video transmitted at the original recording rate and found that video shown below 10 fps resulted in poor intelligibility. Ultimately, these prior works suggest that frame rates between 15-30 fps are the recommended rates at which video should be transmitted to maintain intelligibility. Our work will demonstrate that intelligible sign language conversations can occur below 15 fps.

Manoranjan and Robinson [19] investigated a method to reduce bandwidth consumption by transmitting binary sketches of cartoon signers. They implemented their video processing technique on a computer that simulated the bandwidth used over telephone lines. In a laboratory study with two total participants, participant 1 signed a sentence and participant 2 wrote down what he viewed. Participants evaluated four picture sizes of video displayed at 80×60, 160×120, 120×160, and 320×240 pixels/frame with video transmitted at 8 fps. The computer simulated transmission rates at 33.5 kbps for phone lines and 100 Mbps for the LAN data rate. Participants were unable to complete the task at 320×240 pixels/frame because of the low number of bits allocated per pixel. At such a low frame rate, participants preferred to view the binary sketches of the signer at the 80×60 pixels/frame resolution. A major limitation of this prior work was the small sample size of 2 total participants, which made results hard to generalize to mobile video communication. Our laboratory study uses up-to-date technology with more participants to produce more generalizable recommendations for mobile video communication.

2.2 Prior Laboratory Studies

2.2.1 MobileASL Project

MobileASL, an experimental smartphone application running on the Windows Mobile 6 platform, was created in 2008 and provides two-way, real-time sign language video at very low bandwidth: 30 kilobits per second at 8-12 frames per second. Prior research evaluated intelligibility of pre-recorded ASL video and reducing the power consumption of MobileASL through various techniques.

Cavender et al. [5] conducted a laboratory study evaluating perceived video intelligibility of pre-recorded ASL videos transmitted at two frame rates (10 and 15 fps), three bit rates (15, 20, and 25 kbps), and three region-of-interest (ROI) encoding levels (0, -6, and -12 ROI). They discovered a frame rate preference of 10 fps for viewing ASL video at a fixed bit rate.

Cherniavsky et al. [9] conducted a laboratory study where participants in pairs were observed signing over MobileASL with an algorithm that lowered the frame rate to 1 fps during not-signing sections of a conversation. They found that applying that algorithm led to degradation in video quality, which resulted in respondents having to guess more frequently during conversations. Overall, participants expressed that having the power saving algorithm applied during their conversations did not deter their potential adoption of MobileASL for mainstream mobile video communication.

These previous studies demonstrate the potential lower limits in which intelligible mobile sign language video communication can occur. Our new laboratory study is different from prior work because we investigate intelligibility of *real-time* conversations held over smartphones with video transmitted at higher frame rates and bit rates than were explored in prior work.

2.2.2 Sign Language Learning and Comprehension

Sign language learning is more nuanced than holding sign language conversations because linguistic accuracy is more important. Therefore, the effect of frame rate reduction on sign language learning has been extensively researched [7, 16, 18, 29]. Johnson and Caird [18] investigated whether perceptual ASL learning was affected by video transmitted at 1, 5, 15, and 30 fps. In a discrimination task, participants made a *yes-no* decision about whether the displayed sign and the English word shown matched. They found that frame rates as low as 1 fps and 5 fps were sufficient for novice ASL learners to recognize learned ASL gestures. Although this work demonstrates the potential lower limits at which video can be transmitted, this work did not evaluate conversational sign language, which we evaluate in our laboratory study.

Sperling *et al.* [29] investigated sign recognition when ASL video was transmitted at 10, 15, and 30 fps displayed at 96×64, 48×32, and 24×16 spatial resolutions. They found that common isolated ASL signs shown at 96×64 pixels at 15 fps and 30 fps did not have a noticeable effect on intelligibility, but signs at 10 fps did. While prior work showed that lower frame rates can impact isolated sign recognition, these results may not hold true for mobile sign language video conversations. Our work goes beyond sign recognition and investigates video intelligibility to support two-way conversations.

3. Laboratory Study

Up until now, we have conducted web-based studies [30, 31] evaluating perceived video intelligibility of pre-recorded conversational sign language videos transmitted at frame rates, bit rates, and spatial resolutions lower than the recommended ITU-T standard. Findings from our prior work have suggested an "intelligibility ceiling effect" [32], where increasing the frame rate above 10 fps and bit rate above 60 kbps does not significantly improve perceived video intelligibility.

In a continued effort to reduce total bandwidth consumption and extend battery life for mobile sign language video telephony, we conducted a laboratory study, where fluent ASL signers in pairs held free-form conversations over an experimental smartphone app transmitting real-time video at 5 fps/25 kbps, 10 fps/50 kbps, 15 fps/75 kbps, and 30 fps/150 kbps. The objectives of this study were: (1) to identify the minimum video quality settings allowable for intelligible sign language communication; (2) to learn what adaptation techniques participants use to compensate for the lowered transmission rates; (3) to objectively measure user perceived intelligibility of video content used in mobile sign language conversations; and (4) to quantify how much battery life is extended. Results from the laboratory study also demonstrate that intelligible conversations can occur at transmission rates lower than the ITU-T standard.

3.1 Technology Used

3.1.1 Mobile Phone

The Samsung Galaxy S3 smartphone was used to run an open source video chat software app called IMSDroid[1], whose encoder was modified to transmit video at 5, 10, 15, and 30 fps. The bit rate averaged 5 kb/frame, resulting in the bit rate increasing as the frame rate increased, namely 25, 50, 75, and 150 kbps, respectively. The spatial resolution of the video transmitted was held constant at 320×240 pixels and displayed horizontally on the

phone to maximize the screen size. Prior to the selection of the Samsung Galaxy S3 phone, the Sprint EVO, Samsung Galaxy S2, Samsung Galaxy S4, HTC One, and Google Nexus Phone 4 were investigated as alternatives, but each of these phones' encoders failed to allow for the lowered frame rates. Only the Samsung Galaxy S3 encoder was compatible with the IMSDroid frame rate modifications and thus, the Galaxy S3 was selected for the laboratory study.

3.1.2 IMSDroid

IMSDroid is an open source video conferencing application running on Doubango [17], a 3GPP IMS/LTE (IP Multimedia Subsystem) framework for embedded systems. IMSDroid is a Java-based front-end to Doubango, which is open source VoIP client that references implementation to the Doubango framework. IMSDroid has a GUI interface allowing for both audio and video calls with the robustness of selecting different video encoder. Doubango is the backend framework running 3GPP IMS/LTE which can run many different types of protocols like SIP/SDP, HTTP/HTTPS, and DNS. In this study, the Session Initiation Protocol (SIP) was selected for the VoIP.

3.1.3 Asterisk Server

An Asterisk [2] server was set up as the communication server for the laboratory study. Asterisk is an open source framework that supports the server side of facilitating Voice over Internet Protocol (VoIP) video communication, where we used the Session Initiation Protocol. A specific configuration file was modified to regulate the bit rate at which video was transmitted, specifically averaging 5 kb/frame. Asterisk uses User Datagram Protocol, which is suitable for fast efficient transmission of data for video conversations.

3.1.4 Unobtrusive Logging

Network traces were conducted on the Asterisk server monitoring the frame rate and bit rate at which video was transmitted for each video call. The battery drain of each phone was also unobtrusively logged on the mobile device using an open source mobile application called AndroSensor [1]. AndroSensor logged the battery life percentage every 30 seconds.

3.2 Participants

Social media and email listservs were used to recruit fluent ASL signers to participate in the study. Participant inclusion criteria included: (1) deaf and/or hard-of-hearing people for whom ASL is the primary language; (2) hearing people who fluently sign ASL (over 5 years of signing experience); and (3) people 18 years old or older. Participants received a $25 gift card upon completing the 75-minute laboratory study. Those who responded to the e-mail were either paired with a random person to sign with or brought a friend fluent in ASL. Demographic questions asked in the laboratory study (described below) were used to further ensure language fluency.

The laboratory study had 20 participants (11 women), all of whom fluently signed ASL. Their age ranged from 26-74 years old (median=48.5 years, SD=13.5 years). Of the 20 participants, 18 were deaf (2 of 18 wore hearing aids) and 2 were Children of Deaf Adults with full hearing. Eight participants were randomly assigned to their signing partner (4 sessions) and the other participants were paired with a friend (6 sessions). Thirteen participants indicated that ASL was their daily language, and the number of years they had spoken ASL ranged from 26-74 years (mean=47 years, SD=13 years). All but one participant owned a smartphone and everyone had sent text messages; 19 participants indicated they use video chat; and 17 use video relay services.

---

[1] http://doubango.org/. Accessed on May 9, 2012.

3.3 Study Design

3.3.1 Apparatus

Participants sat on the same side of a table with a black drape behind them. They were separated by a board. Two phones were propped up with a business card holder and placed, one each in front of the participants. Participants were told to adjust the location of the phone for comfortable conversation. Figure 2 is a photo of the experimental setup.

3.3.2 Conversation Task

Participants were instructed to hold five, 5-minute free-form conversations over the provided smartphones. The first conversation was a practice round for participants to familiarize themselves with the phone and available signing space. Participants were instructed to talk about whatever they liked, but for each subsequent conversation, they were asked to discuss a different topic than the conversation before. After each session, participants filled out a paper questionnaire, described below. All participants were video recorded during the study. The smartphone did not record conversations. A randomized Latin Square was used to assign the order in which video frame rate was used on IMSDroid. Participants were not told how the video quality was altered, only that they were using different versions of the smartphone app. A certified ASL interpreter was present during all study sessions and facilitated communication between the study participants and the first author, who conducted the studies.

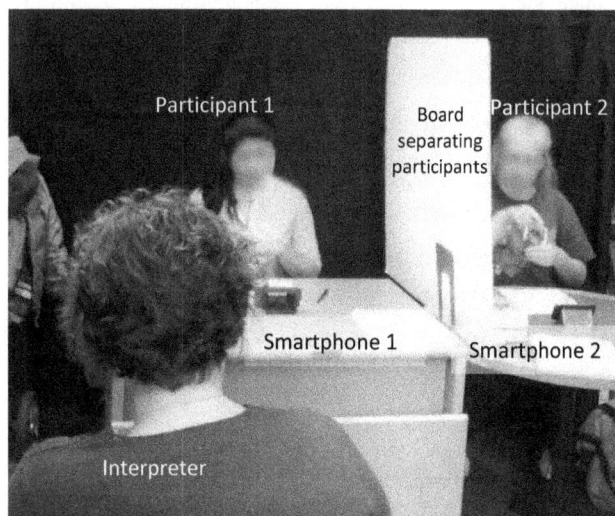

Figure 2: Experimental setup with two participants separated by a board. A certified ASL interpreter was always present.

3.3.3 Subjective Measures

Participants were asked to fill out a subjective questionnaire after each 5-minute conversation. The questions are listed below and respondents circled the response that best answered the question.

- Question 1: How easy was it to understand the video?
  (7-point Likert scale ranging from very easy to very difficult)

- Question 2: Rate the video quality for sign language.
  (7-point Likert scale ranging from excellent to poor)

- Question 3: Rate the video quality for fingerspelling.
  (7-point Likert scale ranging from excellent to poor)

- Question 4: Rate the video quality for lip reading.
  (7-point Likert scale ranging from excellent to poor);

- Question 5: During the conversation, indicate how often you had to guess what the other signer was signing.
  (0% never, 25% sometimes, but not often, 50% half the time; 75% most of the time, and 100% all of the time).

After all trials were completed, participants filled out a demographic questionnaire which included questions such as, "how long have you been signing ASL?'; "what language do you prefer to sign with family?"; and, "do you own a smartphone?" Lastly, participants were asked exit interview questions regarding their overall experience while signing over the different frame rates and bit rates. Examples of questions asked included, "did you notice changes in video quality?"; "at any time were you frustrated with the video quality provided?"; and, "would you use the lower video quality if you knew you could save battery life?"

3.3.4 Objective Measures

A conversation with low intelligibility may contain a lot of requests for repetitions, called "repair requests" [35], which may include signing "what?" or "again" and "conversational breakdowns," where a signer may sign the equivalent of, "I didn't understand what you said." Also, the rate of signing may decrease with the lowered frame rate/bit rate. Therefore, we analyzed the rate of fingerspelling. Fingerspelling occurs when a signer spells out the name of something, which is usually for titles, proper names, and technical words. Signs that are lexicalized "loan signs," which are common words that have become the stylized fingerspelling, are not counted in our fingerspelling measure.

The objective measures were the number of repair requests, average number of turns associated with repair requests, number of conversational breakdowns, and speed of fingerspelling. These measures were calculated from the videotaped sessions with the assistance of a certified ASL interpreter. For each repair request, the number of turns was counted until the concept was understood. Conversational breakdowns were counted as the number of times the participant signed the equivalent of "I can't see you" due to the video being blurry, choppy, or frozen. An unresolved repair request was also counted as a conversational breakdown. Finally, the speed of fingerspelling was measured as the time it took to sign each letter of the word, divided by the number of characters in that word, producing the characters per second.

4. RESULTS

4.1 Perceived Intelligibility

Nonparametric analyses were used to analyze each question, which captured responses on 7-point Likert scales. Since data gathered were ordinal and dichotomous responses, a Friedman test [13] was used to analyze the main effect of frame rate/bit rate for each question. Separate pairwise Wilcoxon tests [36] with Holm's Sequential Bonferroni procedure [15] were performed to investigate the effect of frame rate/bit rate. Results will be reported for each question.

Question 1 asked participants to rate how easy it was to understand the video from 7-very easy to 1-very difficult. The Friedman test did not indicate a significant main effect of frame rate on perceived video intelligibility ($\chi^2_{3,N=20}=5.08$, *n.s.*).

Question 2 asked participants to rate the video quality for sign language communication from 7-excellent to 1-poor. The Friedman test indicated a significant main effect of frame rate on perceived video quality ($\chi^2_{3,N=20}=11.01$, *p*<.05). Wilcoxon tests with Holm's Sequential Bonferroni procedure were performed to identify the effect of frame rate on perceived video quality.

Increasing the frame rate from 5 fps/25 kbps vs. 10 fps/50 kbps, 15 fps/75 kbps, and 30 fps/150 kbps, respectively, was found to increase perceived video quality ($\chi^2_{3,N=20}$=46.5, p<.05). However, comparing perceived video quality between 10 fps/50 kbps, 15 fps/75 kbps, and 30 fps/150 kbps was not found to significantly increase perceived video quality ($\chi^2_{3,N=20}$=9.0, $n.s.$).

Question 3 asked participants to rate the video quality for fingerspelling from 7-excellent to 1-poor. The Friedman test indicated a significant main effect of frame rate on perceived video quality for fingerspelling ($\chi^2_{3,N=19}$=8.11, p<.05). Wilcoxon tests with Bonferroni procedure were performed to identify the effect of frame rate on perceived video quality for fingerspelling. Increasing the frame rate from 5 fps/25 kbps vs. 10 fps/50 kbps, 15 fps/75 kbps, and 30 fps/150 kbps, respectively, was found to increase perceived video quality ($\chi^2_{3,N=20}$=35.5, p<.05). However, comparing perceived video quality between 10 fps/50 kbps vs. 15 fps/75 kbps vs. 30 fps/150 kbps was not found to significantly increase perceived video quality for fingerspelling ($\chi^2_{3,N=20}$=10.0, $n.s.$).

Only half of the participants indicated that they lip read during signing. Therefore, analysis for question 4, which asked participants to rate the perceived video quality for lip reading from 7-excellent to 1-poor, was performed for 10 participants. The Friedman test did not indicate a significant main effect of frame rate on perceived video intelligibility for lip reading ($\chi^2_{3,N=10}$=2.92, $n.s.$).

Question 5 asked participants to rate how often they had to guess what the signer was signing during their conversation (0% never, 25% sometimes, but not often, 50% half the time; 75% most of the time, and 100% all of the time). The Friedman test indicated a significant main effect of frame rate on the rate at which participants had to guess what their signing partner was signing ($\chi^2_{3,N=20}$=29.75, p<.0001). Wilcoxon tests with Bonferroni procedure were performed to identify the effect of frame rate on participants guessing what the other signer was signing. Increasing the frame rate from 5 fps/25 kbps vs. 10 fps/50 kbps, 15 fps/75 kbps, and 30 fps/150 kbps, respectively, was found to decrease how often a participant had to guess what the other signer was signing ($\chi^2_{3,N=20}$=52.5, p<.001). However, comparing how often a signer had to guess what their partner was signing for video transmitted between 10 fps/50 kbps vs. 15 fps/75 kbps vs. 30 fps/150 kbps was not found to significantly reduce how often they guessed what the other person was signing ($\chi^2_{3,N=20}$=6.0, $n.s.$).

4.2 Objective Measures

All sessions were video recorded to be objectively analyzed in post-analysis with a certified ASL interpreter. Each conversation was analyzed to identify and count instances of (1) repair requests during a conversation; (2) conversational breakdowns; and (3) speed of fingerspelling (reported as characters per second - 1). Examples of repair requests include instances when a signer signs the equivalent of "what?" or "again."

A Friedman test was performed for each objective measure to determine how varying the frame rate affected it. Frame rate was found to significantly impact the number of repair requests ($\chi^2_{3,N=10}$=11.0, p<.05) and the number of conversation breakdowns made during a conversation ($\chi^2_{3,N=10}$19.8, p<.001); however, varying the frame rate was not found to statistically significantly impact the speed of fingerspelling ($\chi^2_{3,N=10}$=2.48,

$n.s.$). Table 1 lists the number of instances of fingerspelling and the average characters signed per second at each frame rate. As Table 1 demonstrates, the average number of characters per second did not change as the frame rate increased, even though participants perceived changes in video quality. Perhaps, participants adapted quickly to the temporal video quality or used alternative methods, which are discussed further below.

Table 1: Count of the number of fingerspelled words and the average, max, min, and standard deviation of the number of characters signed per second.

frame rate/bit rate (fps/kbps)	5/25	10/50	15/75	30/150
Total count of finger spelled words (over all sessions)	153	191	166	180
average characters/sec	4.08	4.16	4.03	4.29
SD of characters/sec	1.99	2.03	1.45	1.97

Sign language conversations held over video transmitted at 5 fps/25 kbps received the most counts for both repair requests and conversational breakdowns, as expected. Video transmitted at 10 fps/50 kbps, 15 fps/75 kbps, and 30 fps/150 kbps did not have any instances of repair requests or conversational breakdowns across all sessions. Figure 3 lists the number of repair requests and conversational breakdowns that occurred for each session.

Figure 3 shows that sessions 6 and 7 received the highest counts for conversational breakdowns with 11 total breakdowns occurring in a 5 minute conversation. Participants in sessions 4, 5, 6, 7, 8, and 9 were friends while the other sessions had participants paired with strangers.

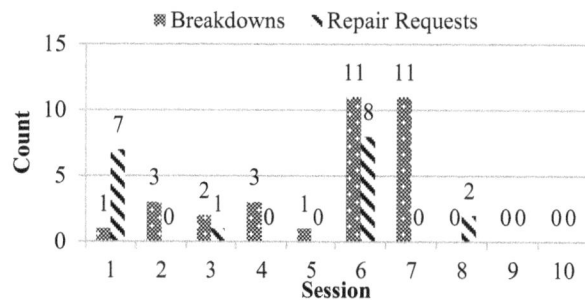

Figure 3: Count of conversational breakdowns and repair requests that occurred for each session when video was transmitted at 5 fps.

4.3 Exit Interviews

During the exit interviews, participants were asked to indicate which version of the video app they preferred use. There were four recurring themes that arose during the exit interviews, which were: (1) there was noticeable lower quality of video transmitted at 5 fps; (2) desire for larger screens; (3) different adaptation techniques were used to compensate for lower video quality; and (4) comparison of video quality used in the experimental app to commercially available apps. (Note that consent was obtained from study participants to include excerpts in publication.)

4.3.1 5 FPS Video Quality

All participants voiced their observations that video transmitted at 5 fps was noticeably more "choppy" or "frozen" than other versions of the app that they used. When asked what they liked or disliked about signing over video shown at 5 fps, many participants said they "would not want to use the video at all." P3 signed that she really could not express herself like she normally would when signing to someone in-person because of the lower video quality. P13 and P14 said they chose to have a "lighter conversation," *i.e.*, not talk about anything that required a lot of background information to be signed first. They were unsure how often they would need to repeat themselves so they wanted to keep the conversation short.

Many participants signed that they would not use mobile video communication at 5 fps, even though the video quality provided intelligible content. When asked if they would "give up" signing to each other at video transmitted at 5 fps, participants expressed that they probably would turn to texting to clarify what they wanted to say since texting is more reliable than mobile video at 5 fps. P17 and P18 said they would rather text message instead of sign over video transmitted at 5 fps. When asked why, they said because more energy was needed to repeat themselves over video, while texting required only one message. P17 did acknowledge that texting was asynchronous, but believed texting was more reliable than current mobile video apps. P18 followed up by saying she didn't use mobile video chat on her phone, so texting was her solution for mobile communication.

4.3.2 Desire for Larger Screens

During the exit interviews, many participants spoke about the form factor of the device, specifically desire for larger screen sizes. P13 and P14 made comments that they preferred to sign over a larger device with a bigger screen similar to the screens available on the iPad or Samsung Galaxy Note. P14 expressed she did not feel like she could express everything she wanted to say because of the confined signing space. Also, the angle at which video was shown made it more difficult to understand her signing partner. Mainly, the hands were closer to the screen, but the signer's head appeared to look like a "pin head" because of the camera angle. P14 also said that lip reading was hard to do because of the "pin head" appearance of her signing partner.

4.3.3 Adaptation Techniques

When participants were asked what adaptation techniques they used to compensate for the lower video quality, a majority of the participants said they deliberately fingerspelled more slowly than their regular signing speed. They also had to ask their signing partner to repeat what was signed and slow down whatever they were signing. Some participants also said doing this often disrupted what they were trying to say, which caused some frustration for both the signer and receiver. Interestingly, participants did not actually fingerspell more slowly when the frame rate varied (mean characters per second: 4.97 at 5 fps vs. 5.22 at 30 fps), as listed in Table 1, even though they were perceived to sign more slowly.

When participants were asked which version of the video app they preferred to use, many participants indicated they preferred signing over video transmitted at 15 and 30 fps; however, many participants indicated that they could not tell the difference between video transmitted at 15 fps and 30 fps. When asked if they noticed changes in video quality when video transmitted at 10 fps, participants did say it was better than video transmitted at 5 fps, but not as good as video transmitted at 15 or 30 fps.

4.3.4 Comparisons to Commercial Video Apps

In many of the laboratory sessions, participants compared the video quality they were using to commercially available apps like Skype and FaceTime. Those participants who referred to FaceTime said that FaceTime's video quality was clearer and

smoother. This particular comment was expected since FaceTime transmits video at 30 fps at 1-3 Mbps at 960×640 screen resolution [20]. In one of the sessions, P7 and P8 were signing over video transmitted at 15 fps and began to discuss how IMSDroid's video quality compared to FaceTime:

P7: How does this compare to FaceTime?

P8: FaceTime is more clear, but this is fine... your hands are a little more blurry. I understand you fine though.

P7: Am I signing too fast?

P8: No, you're signing fine.

P7: Well...I'm signing normal, just trying to test the limitations. Is the fingerspelling clear?

P8: Yeah, I can see you fine.

P7: So when I spelled 'amoeba'

P8: Yes, amoeba

P7: Did you see all the signs or did you just catch the 'b' 'a'?

P8: ...I saw the full spelling, but deaf [people] understand what you're saying anyhow. We're used to doing that.

This snippet of the conversation is an example of how people who are deaf naturally interpolate what they view to understand the overall message of a conversation. For instance, when words are fingerspelled, all the letters of the word may not have been viewed by the receiver, but the word can be discerned from the context of the conversation.

4.4 Battery Drain

The battery drain was unobtrusively logged using an open source app called AndroSensor, which ran in the background and logged the percentage battery drain every 30 seconds for each 5 minute conversation. Data were collected from the phones after each session for later analysis.

The rate at which the battery percentage depleted was calculated for each 5 minute video call. We verified that the battery drain was linear, which allowed us to use linear regression to model the data. The estimated average battery duration for each frame rate was calculated for every conversation and shown in Figure 4. As anticipated, the higher the frame rate at which video was transmitted, the higher the rate at which the battery drained. We found that the Samsung Galaxy S3 has an average battery life of 1000 minutes in standby mode and an average battery life of 750 minutes if IMSDroid was "active" but not transmitting video.

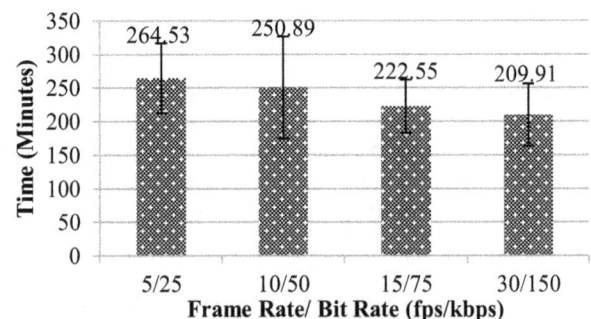

Figure 4: Estimated average battery life (in minutes) for sign language video transmitted on IMSDroid at each frame rate.

4.5 Bandwidth Consumption

Network traces were performed on the Asterisk server to monitor the average rate at which data was transmitted. Bit rate control is an active area of research [8, 12, 21, 26] and was not the focus of this study. Table 2 lists the average bit rate at which video was transmitted for each frame rate. The bit rate was controlled by the Asterisk server and the network traces confirmed that the frame rate dictated the bit rate at which video was transmitted.

Table 2: Average, min, max, and SD of the bit rate when varying the frame rate as captured by the network traces.

frame rate (fps)	target bit rate (kbps)	average bit rate (kbps)	min bit rate (kbps)	max bit rate (kbps)	SD (kbps)
5	25	23.89	20.87	32.19	3.38
10	50	50.00	39.78	67.76	8.67
15	75	73.04	64.43	91.25	8.67
30	150	129.89	114.78	147.38	9.91

5. DISCUSSION

Participants were successful at holding intelligible conversations across all frame rates. All participants did notice and complain about the lower quality of video transmitted at 5 fps; however, participants' rate of fingerspelling did not decrease, even though they perceived their signing speed to be slower. Video transmitted at 5 fps had more instances of conversational breakdowns and repair requests. Sessions 6 and 7 received the most counts for conversational breakdowns (11 instances); the frequencies at which breakdowns occurred were low across other sessions. Closer inspection of the conversations held in sessions 6 and 7, where the most breakdowns and repair requests occurred, revealed that the topic of conversation was very detailed and required more explanation. For example, P11 and P12 from session 6 were talking about a trip to Iceland. P12 asked if P11 was going to see the Aurora Borealis. It took multiple attempts by P11 asking the question to clarify what P12 was asking. The frame rate at which the video was signing was 10 fps/50 kbps. The conversational breakdown could have resulted from the conversation topic and not because of the video transmission rate.

5.1 Signing Adaptation Techniques

Signers are versatile when it comes to adapting their signing to the technology they use to communicate. The context of a conversation, signs used, loan signs (signs that represent an English word that has developed a unique movement), and fingerspelling words all assist in filling in missing information [4]. Signers may be naturally taking advantage of the "word superiority effect" where people are more successful recognizing letters presented within words that just isolated letters [3]. This may explain why the rate of fingerspelling did not vary across the frame rates.

During objective analysis of the video conversations, there were instances in which a participant would begin to finger-spell a word; however, she did not spell every letter within that word. For example, a participant was talking about the different seasons, but when she fingerspelled "season," she only signed "s" and "n" of the word. The receiver of the message was still able to infer the word. The receiver may also have been able to infer the word from the context of the message. Often the context of a conversation can aid in understanding a word that was not seen during the conversation [22].

5.2 Willingness to Use Lower Video Quality

When asked if they were willing to use a low video quality to hold conversations, all participants said they would be willing to use the mobile technology if there were a guarantee that video would be transmitted at 15 fps/75 kbps or 30 fps/150 kbps. However, video transmitted at lower frame rates would only be used for very short conversations, such as asking a quick question. When given the option between texting and mobile video chatting, participants said they always would prefer to sign over video; however, if the person they are communicating with does not sign, texting is considered necessary.

5.3 Technology Position Adjustments

Participants were allowed to adjust the mobile device to a position that felt comfortable. Some of the participants adjusted the phone to increase the angle at which it was displayed or raised the phone to increase their signing space. Figure 5(a) shows the original position of the phone placed in front of the participants. Figure 5(b) shows how a participant placed a pen behind the phone to increase the angle at which he viewed the phone. Figure 5(c) and 5(d) are two different examples of how participants requested to use stacks of books located in the room to raise the smartphone's position.

5.4 Recommendations

As anticipated, reducing the frame rate at which sign language video is transmitted increases the average battery life of IMSDroid. From the laboratory results, it is recommended that conversational video transmitted at 10 fps/50 kbps best balances resource consumption, video intelligibility, and user preferences. Transmitting video at 10 fps/50 kbps, 15 fps/75 kbps, and 30 fps/150 kbps received, on average, the same subjective responses from participants when asked to rate how easy it was to understand the video; rate the video for picture quality, fingerspelling, and lip-reading; and how often the signer had to guess what the other person was signing. While the battery life lasted the longest when video was transmitted at 5 fps/25 kbps, video transmitted at 5 fps/25 kbps also received the most counts for repair requests and conversational breakdowns. Finally, in the exit interviews, participants voiced their dissatisfaction of communicating at video transmitted at 5 fps/25 kbps because of the choppy video quality. Although some participants were able to tell that there was a difference between video transmitted at 10 fps/50 kbps vs. 15 fps/75 kbps vs. 30 fps/150 kbps in the exit interviews, both the subjective and objective results support that video transmitted at 10 fps/50 kbps is the lowest threshold at which intelligible sign language conversations can be comfortably held.

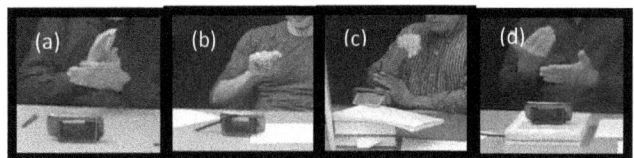

Figure 5: Four examples of how participants adjusted the phone position. (a) Original phone setup using a business card holder. (b) Phone propped up with a pen. (c) Increased height and viewing angle. (d) Increased height from table.

6. CONCLUSION AND FUTURE WORK

The ITU-T standard recommends that video should be transmitted at least at 25 fps and 100 kbps for intelligible conversations. Our laboratory study clearly demonstrates that there is a lower limit at which intelligible mobile sign language video can be transmitted. Our findings suggest that video transmitted at 10 fps with a bit rate averaging 50 kbps can facilitate intelligible sign language conversations, and can extend battery life by almost 20% compared to transmitting at 30 fps and 150 kbps.

The findings from this study provide the motivation for the creation of video technology specifically designed for use during emergencies and natural disasters, where the full cellular network infrastructure may become unavailable. In 2005, it was estimated that 50% of the total phone lines and wireless subscribers lost access to phone service for multiple days after Hurricane Katrina hit land [23]. In the laboratory study, people were still successful at holding intelligible conversations at 5 fps (averaging 23.89 kbps) even though participants did not prefer communicating at those video transmission rates. Having the capability to transmit emergency videos, even at these low transmission rates, would be useful to relay important information.

7. ACKNOWLEDGMENTS

The authors wish to thank the participants; Tobias Cullins, Coordinator of Deaf & Hard of Hearing Services; Jennifer Austin for interpreting video content; Rafael Rodriguez for the implementation of IMSDroid. Lydia Runnels from ZVRS. Samsung Research for the smartphones. This work was funded in part by Google.

8. REFERENCES

[1] AndroSensor: 2013. *http://www.fivasim.com/androsensor.html*.

[2] Asterisk: 2014. *http://www.asterisk.org/*. Accessed: 2014-01-04.

[3] Baron, J. and Thurston, I. 1973. An analysis of the world-superiority effect. *Cognitive Psychology*. 4, 2, 207–228.

[4] Battison, R. 1978. *Lexical borrowing in American Sign Language*.

[5] Cavender, A., Ladner, R. and Riskin, E. 2006. MobileASL: Intelligibility of sign language video as constrained by mobile phone technology. *Proc. ASSETS*, 71–78.

[6] Chen, B. 2013. AT&T allows FaceTime for limited data users. What about unlimited? *The New York Times*.

[7] Chen, J.Y.C. and Thropp, J.E. 2007. Review of low frame rate effects on human performance. *IEEE Trans. on Systems, Man, and Cybernetics - Part A: Systems and Humans*. 37, 6, 1063–1076.

[8] Chen, Z. and Ngan, K. 2007. Recent advances in rate control for video coding. *Signal Processing: Image Communication*. 22, 1, 19–38.

[9] Cherniavsky, N., Chon, J., Wobbrock, J.O., Ladner, R. and Riskin, E. 2007. Variable Frame Rate for Low Power Mobile Sign Language Communication. *Proc. ASSETS*, 163–170.

[10] Cicco, L., Mascolo, S. and Palmisano, V. 2008. Skype video responsiveness to bandwidth variations. *NOSSDAV*.

[11] Costs associated with using FaceTime: 2013. *http://www.ilounge.com/index.php/articles/comments/costs-associated-with-using-facetime/*.

[12] Ding, W. and Liu, B. 1996. Rate control of MPEG video coding and recording by rate-quantization modeling. *IEEE Trans. Circuits Syst. Video Technol*. 6, 1, 12–20.

[13] Friedman, M. 1937. The use of ranks to avoid the assumption of normality implicit in the analysis of variance. *Journal of the American Statistical Association*. 32, 200, 675–701.

[14] Harkins, J., Wolff, A., Korres, E., Foulds, R. and Galuska, S. 1990. Intelligibility experiments with a feature extration system designed to simulate a low-bandwidth video telephone for deaf people. *RESNA*, 92–95.

[15] Holm, S. 1979. A simple sequentially rejective multiple test procedure. *Scand J Stat*. 6, 2, 65–70.

[16] Hooper, S., Miller, C., Rose, S. and Veletsianos, G. 2007. The effects of digital video quality on learner comprehension in an American sign language assessment environment. *Sign Language Studies*. 8, 1, 42–58.

[17] IMSDroid-High Quality Video SIP/IMS client for Google Android: *http://code.google.com/p/imsdroid/*. Accessed: 2012-05-23.

[18] Johnson, B.F. and Caird, J.K. 1996. The effect of frame rate and video information redundancy on the perceptual learning of American sign language gestures.

[19] Manoranjan, M.D. and Robinson, J. a 2000. Practical low-cost visual communication using binary images for deaf sign language. *IEEE transactions on rehabilitation engineering : a publication of the IEEE Engineering in Medicine and Biology Society*. 8, 1, 81–8.

[20] Ou, G. 2010. Estimate of network bandwidth for iPhone 4 FaceTime. *Digital Society*.

[21] Reed, E. and Lim, J. 2002. Optimal multidimensional bit-rate control for video communication. *IEEE Trans. Image Process*. 11, 8, 873–885.

[22] Reicher, G. 1969. Perceptual recognition as a function of meaningfulness of stimulus material. *Experimental Psychology*. 81, 2, 275–280.

[23] Reilly, G., Jrad, A., Nagarajan, R., Brown, T. and Conrad, S. 2006. Critical infrastructure analysis of telecom for natural disaters. *Telecom. Network Strategy and Planning*, 1–6.

[24] Saks, A. and Hellström, G. 2006. Quality of conversation experience in sign language , lip - reading and text. *ITU-T Workshop on End-to-end QoE/QoS*.

[25] Skype Statistics: 2012. *http://www.statisticbrain.com/skype-statistics*.

[26] Song, H. and Kuo, C. 2001. Rate control for low-bit-rate video via variable-encoding frame rates. *IEEE Trans. Circuits Syst. Video Technol*. 11, 4, 512–521.

[27] Sosnowski, T. and Hsing, T. 1983. Toward the conveyance of deaf sign language over public telephone networks. *RESNA*.

[28] Sperling, G. 1981. Video transmission of American Sign Language and finger spelling: present and projected bandwidth requirements. *IEEE Transactions on Communications*. 29, 12, 1993–2002.

[29] Sperling, G., Landy, M., Cohen, Y. and Pavel, M. 1985. Intelligible encoding of ASL image sequences at extremely low information rates. *Computer Vision Graphics, and Image Processing*. 31, 335–391.

[30] Tran, J.J., Kim, J., Chon, J., Riskin, E., Ladner, R. and Wobbrock, J.O. 2011. Evaluating quality and comprehension of real-time sign language video on mobile phones. *Proc. ASSETS*, 115–122.

[31] Tran, J.J., Riskin, E., Ladner, R. and Wobbrock, J.O. 2013. Increasing mobile sign language video accessibility by relaxing video transmission standards. *Third Mobile Accessibility Workshop at Proc. CHI*.

[32] Tran, J.J., Rodriguez, R., Riskin, E. and Wobbrock, J.O. 2013. A web-based intelligibility evaluation of sign language videotransmitted at low frame rates and bitrates. *Proc. ASSETS*.

[33] Verizon begins throttling iPhone unlimited 3G customers who use 2GB/month | 9to5Mac | Apple Intelligence: *http://9to5mac.com/2011/09/17/verizon-begins-throttling-iphone-2gbmonth-unlimited-3g-customers/*. Accessed: 2012-01-04.

[34] Video is fastest growing mobile data traffic source: 2013. *http://www.humanipo.com/news/36341/video-is-fastest-growing-mobile-data-traffic-source/*.

[35] Watson, A. and Sasse, M.A. 1998. Measuring perceived quality of speech and video in multimedia conferencing applications. *Multimedia*, 55–60.

[36] Wilcoxon, F. 1945. Individual comparisons by ranking methods. *Biometrics Bulletin*. 1, 6, 80–83.

Enhancing Caption Accessibility Through Simultaneous Multimodal Information: Visual-Tactile Captions

Raja S. Kushalnagar, Gary W. Behm, Joseph S. Stanislow and Vasu Gupta
National Technical Institute for the Deaf
Rochester Institute of Technology
{rskics,gwbnts,jssnbs,vxg1421}@rit.edu

ABSTRACT

Captions (subtitles) for television and movies have greatly enhanced accessibility for Deaf and hard of hearing (DHH) consumers who do not understand the audio, but can otherwise follow by reading the captions. However, these captions fail to fully convey auditory information, due to *simultaneous delivery of aural and visual content*, and *lack of standardization in representing non-speech information*.

Viewers cannot simultaneously watch the movie scenes and read the visual captions; instead they have to switch between the two and inevitably lose information and context in watching the movies. In contrast, hearing viewers can simultaneously listen to the audio and watch the scenes.

Most auditory non-speech information (NSI) is not easily represented by words, e.g., the description of a ring tone, or the sound of something falling.

We enhance captions with tactile and visual-tactile feedback. For the former, we transform auditory NSI into its equivalent tactile representation and convey it simultaneously with the captions. For the latter, we visually identify the location of the NSI. This approach can benefit DHH viewers by conveying more aural content to the viewer's visual and tactile senses simultaneously than visual-only captions alone. We conducted a study, which compared DHH viewer responses between video with captions, tactile captions, and visual-tactile captions. The viewers significantly benefited from visual-tactile and tactile captions.

Categories and Subject Descriptors

H.5.1 [**Information Interfaces and Presentation**]: Multimedia Information Systems; K.4.2 [**Social Issues**]: Assistive technologies for persons with disabilities

General Terms

Human Factors, Design, Experimentation

Keywords

Aural-to-tactile information; Caption Readability; Multimodal Interfaces; Deaf and Hard of Hearing Users

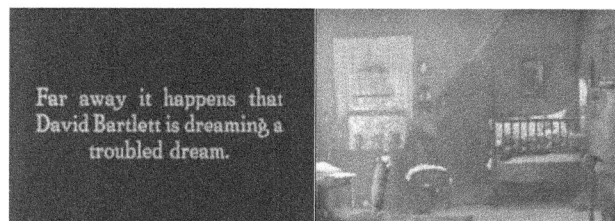

Figure 1: Intertitle-Scene temporal and spatial separation: The movie briefly narrates what will happen in the scene, and then displays the scene.

1. INTRODUCTION

In the U.S., most DHH viewers are accustomed to always available captioning for television, especially after the passage of the Americans with Disabilities Act in 1991. The advent of online entertainment has increased technical capabilities and expectations for more customizable and accessible captions. Subtle barriers remain: multiple simultaneous visuals and imprecision in translating speech and non-speech information (NSI) [14].

Interestingly, depending on the state of art in movie display technology, the amount of accessible information for DHH viewers has varied dramatically over the years. The era from 1900-1920 was a golden era for deaf and hard of hearing consumers who could watch and understand movies. During that era, all movies were exclusively visual, and therefore silent, as movie projectors in that era could not play synchronized audio. Speech and non-speech information alike was conveyed through pantomime or partially synchronized "intertitles" that were spliced between scenes; they paraphrased dialogue and other bare-bones information about the story not apparent from visual clues as shown in Figure 1. Although the intertitles effectively transformed aural to visual information, the streams were separated both spatially and temporally. Movie consumers did not complain, for they were not aware of any alternatives.

From 1927, movies could show both video and audio, which ushered in the "talkies" era and by 1929, the talkies completely supplanted the silents. Intertitling continued to be used for showing dialogue in foreign language movies. Consumers, now exposed to audio and acutely aware of the importance of audio-visual synchronization, rapidly noticed the lack of intertitling synchronization with the video and their complaints were doubtlessly heard. With this incentive solidly in place, by 1933, spatially synchronized subtitles completely replaced intertitles.

Figure 2: Caption-Scene spatial separation: The captions are shown simultaneously with the scene. But they are at the bottom of the screen, away from the main scene action. The DHH viewer's gaze path shows how the viewer reads the captions, and then scans the scene looking for the people who uttered the words that were shown in the captions.

DHH viewers mourned the loss of movie accessibility. They could foresee regaining access via yet-to-be-invented technology (captions), but they also knew captioned talkies would not be fully accessible, as shown in the quote below:

> Perhaps, in time, an invention will be perfected that will enable the deaf to hear the "talkies," or an invention which will throw the words spoken directly under the screen as well as being spoken at the same time. ... The real solution, I believe, is to have a silent theatre in every city where there are a large number of deaf people.
>
> — *Emil S. Ladner*, a deaf high school senior, in an essay that won in a nationwide competition sponsored by Atlantic Monthly in 1931 [15].

1.1 Enhancing Caption Accessibility

In this paper, we explore two simple but effective approaches to aid DHH viewers in watching movies with non-speech audio content: *tactile* captions and *visual-tactile* captions. Our experiments measure students' preference and recall of captions and associated scenes in a captioned movie by asking them to complete a preference and recall survey after using each of our two tools compared to the baseline case of regular captions.

We find that, while both approaches have a positive impact on viewer preferences and recall accuracy scores, captions with visual-tactile information is preferred over captions with tactile information, and both are preferred over captions alone. Moreover, visual-tactile enhanced captions yield significantly higher recall over the other two. We discuss the relevant design criteria based on the feedback we received from users during our iterative design process, and suggest future work that builds on these insights. In general, there is much potential in leveraging multiple sensory systems to maximize DHH viewers' information access to audiovisual movies. Combining both aural and visual information into a single visual caption channel can result in reduced understanding and scene or caption recall. We discuss the implications of converting a unimodal presentation to a bimodal one (visual/tactile).

The rest of this paper is organized as follows:

- We discuss the impact of technological evolution on movie accessibility, including modern approaches that leverage the web to enable more accessible captions in settings where they may not have previously been practical.

- We present the design of a tactile caption interface that allows viewers to *feel* simple non-speech auditory events that can occur simultaneously with captions.

- Based on the results of the tactile captioning study, we present a visual-tactile caption interface that allows viewers not only feel simple non-speech auditory events but also. Our results show that users prefer this method to pausing and perform significantly better on comprehension tests.

- We then discuss the implications of our findings, and design principles for caption presentation that we derived from the feedback of our study participants.

- We conclude with a discussion of potential future improvements to captioning that can further address the problems faced by viewers while watching movies.

2. BACKGROUND AND RELATED WORK

Aural and visual information contained in a "talkie" can be combined to a single "silent movie" with captions. Though a captioned movie is far more accessible to DHH viewers, their access is generally less than their hearing peers due to captioning interface issues.

2.1 Captioning Interface Issues

Many DHH viewers who watch captioned media deal with multiple factors such as simultaneous visuals, visual search, non-speech information, and identifying sound sources. These issues challenge viewers to watch video and read captions that convey sufficient aural information, yet remain synchronized and readable. They are also likely to miss information that requires both seeing the scene as well as reading captions. For example, some DHH viewers miss the point of visual gags or fail to identify who is talking in a group.

2.1.1 Simultaneous visuals

Viewers split their attention between the video and the captions and this reduces the amount of time they can spend on each [13]. Most DHH viewers spend a majority of their time reading the captions [9], and thus, have little time to watch the scenes as shown in Figure 2. Many DHH viewers are not fluent in English and may need extra time to read the captions. [8].This means that they often fall behind and do not catch all of the dialog. Due to the spatial separation between captions and the scene as shown in Figure 3, the viewers have to manage and split attention among the captions and scene, which remains an elusive goal. Previous studies have found that DHH students usually watch the captions most of the time and barely spend any time watching the slides or teacher.

Overall, deaf students looked at the instructor 10% of the time and on the slides 14% of the time [12], as compared to 15% and 22% reported by Marschark et al. [16], and 12% and 18% [6]. Hearing students on the other hand, have no captions to focus on, and usually spend most of their time watching the instructor or lecture visuals.

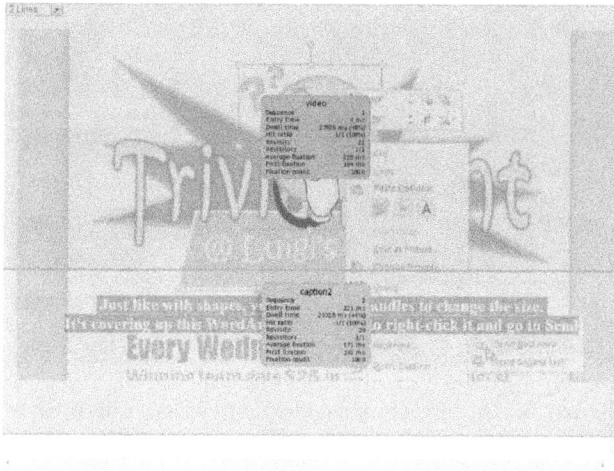

Figure 3: Caption-Scene spatial separation: The captions are shown simultaneously with the scene. The viewer has to decide which visual to focus on and read, and ignore the other one.

2.1.2 Visual Search

Deaf viewers spend lot of time searching for visuals when switching in to video, as shown in Figure 2. This wasted time in searching discourages gaze shifting. Hearing viewers do not need to look at the audio source, while deaf viewers have to actively look at the visual translation of the audio in order to understand it. This is problematic for the deaf viewer who has to switch between the lecture visual and the aural-to-visual translation, and this can significantly interfere with audiovisual perception and understanding. Video with lot of visual detail can also increase the time needed to switch between video and captions.

2.1.3 Non-speech information

It is difficult to represent all auditory information through captions. First, most NSI is not easily expressed in text, as they are perceptually meaningful, but semantically vague. These sounds are not usually part of the language. Even if these sounds are expressed as onamatoepic words, different cultures use different words to represent these sounds [19]. They do not map well to text and are often ambiguous; moreover they can also occur simultaneously with speech. In these cases, the captions usually show only the text representation of the speech and do not show the non-speech text representation. In other words, non-speech information is not easily or accurately described and be inserted into the captions.

2.1.4 Speaker Identification and NSI Localization

Where there are multiple speakers or sources of NSI, captions usually do not have the bandwidth to indicate the sound source. For instance, in Figure 2, if one of the group members speaks up, a hearing person often can recognize by the audio signature alone who spoke, while captions do not carry this information. Similarly, if a group member's phone rings, a viewer can often localize the sound and more quickly identify whose phone rang, while this information is not available to a viewer reading captions. The duration also may not be clear - for example, is the phone still ringing or did it just ring once?

2.2 Need for Improved Caption Interfaces

Modern user interfaces increasingly mirror physical and social interaction, as this leverages existing human interactive knowledge. However, the range of this interaction, such as gesture and speech is incredibly diverse and can be a barrier for users with different abilities and cultures. We explore deaf and hard of hearing consumer preferences of tactile captions that enhance auditory information, such as a phone ring.

The extra effort that has to be put into reading subtitles often diminishes the quality of visual attention on the movie and reduces total satisfaction in watching it. Yet, if viewers are unaware of alternatives, they cannot articulate or act on their issues clearly. It is our belief that simultaneous information in two modalities can be most accurately conveyed in two modalities, not necessarily the original modalities. We investigate the efficacy of transforming audio-visual movies to visual-tactile movies by inserting visual-tactile cues.

2.2.1 Tactile feedback

This approach conveys information through through vibrations to a person who can feel. Vibrotactile stimulation activates numerous mechanoreceptors in the skin, and their responses depend on the frequency, amplitude, and duration of vibration and the area of the motor on skin [10]. Vibrotactile discrimination of 0.4 to 1000 Hz is relatively poor compared with aural discrimination from 20 to 20000Hz [18]. Encoding parameters available for a vibrotactile stimulus (tactons), namely frequency, intensity, locus, and duration, and the latter two hold the most promise for encoding information in a tactile display [5]. Frequency and intensity appear to be the least exploitable dimensions, primarily because the skin is rather poor at discriminating differences in frequency [4].

Research on translating sound to vibration goes back to the earliest days of electronic devices: indeed Norbert Weiner invented a hearing glove as a sound-to-tactile prosthesis for deaf people [17]. The frequency limitations were not well understood, and there were many failed inventions from the 1920s to the 1960s that tried to translate speech to vibrations for deaf consumers, including Weiner's hearing glove.

However, there is scant prior research on combining video captions with tactile feedback for videos. One line of research has focused on simulating the hearing experience by providing a rich, whole body tactile experience. Prior research has explored sensory substitution via a tactile chair. The tactile chair provided a tactile sensory system to provide sensory substitution for music. It provided a high-resolution audio-tactile version of music to the body [2, 3]. The system uses eight separate audio-tactile channels to deliver sound to the body, and provides an opportunity to experience a broad range of musical elements as physical vibrations. The other line of research has focused on augmentation of audio or visual information with tactile information. For example, Apostolopoulos et al. [1] and Khoo et al. [11] used the vibration function of smart phones to provide tactile information in parallel with auditory information for navigation for blind and low vision users.

In terms of multimodal interfaces, tactile perception has much potential in supplementing other modalities for simple sounds, especially those that are distinguishable temporally. For instance, perception through tactile feedback nicely complements reading through visual perception.

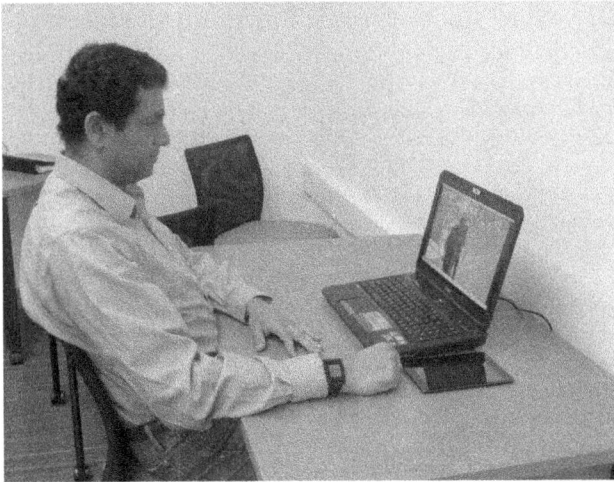

Figure 4: A DHH viewer watching a captioned video.

Figure 5: A snapshot of the captioned video at a specific moment that has NSI: (object falls). This information is conveyed through the captions alone or supplemented through tactile feedback.

First, there is high overlap between aural and tactile perception unlike aural and visual perception. Human ears and skin detect physical oscillations, while the eyes perceive electromagnetic vibrations. Second, tactile perception has much finer temporal discrimination than its visual analogue - almost a magnitude larger [7]. Third, tactile perception tends to be perceived directly and untranslated, unlike visual reading. The viewer does not have to semantically interpret the sound; instead, he or she can directly feel it.

A single non-speech sound can be captioned in multiple ways and there is no clear agreement on which one to pick. For example, a phone ringing could be represented in at least three different ways: [Phone Ringing] or as [Phone Rings Multiple Times] or [Phone rings 3 times].

3. PRELIMINARY EVALUATION

From prior studies [8, 6, 12], we know that DHH viewers spend the majority of time reading captions; for example, Jensema et. al found that viewers spent 84% on the captions and less than 16% on the scenes [9]. By contrast, hearing viewers who listen to the audio and watch the scenes spend close to 100% of the time watching the scenes. From prior observation, we note that DHH viewers struggle to identify and locate auditory cues such as a ringing phone or determining the identity of who is speaking. For many non-speech event captions, DHH viewers also spend a significant amount of time searching for the location and nature of cues. This extra searching time discourages viewers from shifting to the scene and obtaining more contextual information.

3.1 Pilot Study

We conducted a pilot study to investigate viewer recall of NSI events after they watched a captioned movie as shown in Figure 5.

3.1.1 Setup

We recruited 27 DHH participants (15 male, 12 female) from the National Technical Institute for the Deaf. The average participant age was 19.8 years old. Our participants all had prior experience with watching captioned movies from birth, reflecting the fact that they had grown up after the passage of the Americans with Disabilities Act. They sat in front of a laptop and viewed a 5 minute long captioned movie that contained exactly seven NSI events, such as phone ringing or foot stomps as shown in Figure 4. Next, they completed a survey that tested the ability to 1) recall and narrate the NSI events, and 3) to identify and describe the location of the NSI in the scene.

3.1.2 Results

The participants were asked to recall and describe all seven NSI events (NE), e.g., [object falls], that they observed in the video. For all correctly described NE, the mean and standard deviation was $\overline{NE} = 4.73, \sigma = .44$. Next, the participants were asked to describe the item that caused the NSI (NI) in each video scene when the event occurred (e.g., floor stand). For all correctly described NI, the mean and standard deviation was $\overline{NI} = 3.87, \sigma = .35$.

The lower number of correctly described NSI items in comparison with described NSI items suggests that DHH viewers miss important information by not being able to see both the item causing the NSI event and reading the captions that describe the NSI event. An approach that assists viewers in better perception of the non-speech sounds would be a logical place to start. The responses indicated that some could not associate the captions quickly with the visuals. Most likely this is due to the fact that many deaf viewers do not have 'auditory' memory, needed to associate and recognize sounds and the item causing the sound.

3.1.3 Participant Feedback

The participants stated that the captions were clear, but sometimes could not was all text. Additionally, they often did not see which item triggered the NSI until after the event.

> The movie was funny! But! Many times I could not see where the sound was coming from.

> I got a little irritated at the captions. The phone rang, but I could not tell whose phone rang.

> Some of the captions was distracting. I need time to read words like printer whirring

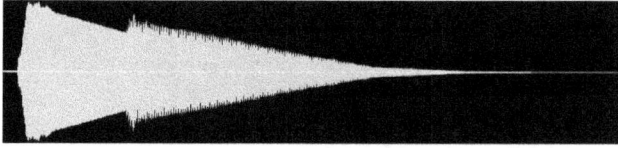

Figure 6: The sound envelope of an RIT office doorbell.

4. ITERATIVE SYSTEM DESIGN

Our goal is to develop accessible multi-modal captions that enable DHH users to better perceive, follow and manage both the auditory and visual information that is simultaneously presented, which is common in most sitcoms and movies. Adding additional NSI information along with the textual description can help DHH viewers understand the plot, especially if the NSI is semantically important. In addition to assessing the impact of tactile captions, we also assess the impact of tactile-visual captions to indicate where the sound originated and its duration.

The multi-modal captions interface should also be intuitive and customizable in order to meet the needs of the diverse population of deaf and hard of hearing consumers. The formative study identified two main issues:

1. Inability to interpret the caption words meaningfully in time, for many phrases including NSI.

2. Inability to associate scene content with the NSI caption content, and vice versa.

We investigated whether the synchronization of tactile and/or visual-tactile feedback with the captions could address both issues.

4.1 Vibration mappings

While some non-speech sounds can be represented with standardized onomatopoeic words, there are far more non-speech sounds that have no standardized print representation. For example, there is no standard way to represent many ambient noises, such as air duct or printer noises. Moreover, written representations do not show most aural properties such as loudness that can be important depending on context. For example, captions usually indicate printer noises as [printer whirring] or [printer noise]. These descriptions do not convey duration or loudness. With tactile feedback, a viewer can simultaneously watch the entire video scene including the printer whirring and feel it. If the printer noise is important to the plot, the viewer will notice and relate better to the plot.

4.2 Vibration device characteristics

Like most personal consumer devices, personal vibration information devices should be usable, accurate, durable, low-cost, highly reliable, and easily worn. For our study, we focused on usability in terms of watching captioned videos:

1. The auditory to tactile translation should convey salient information such as duration, rhythm or amplitude.

2. The captions describing the auditory event to be translated to tactile information should occur simultaneously with the tactile information.

3. The device should not feel intrusive while being used or worn.

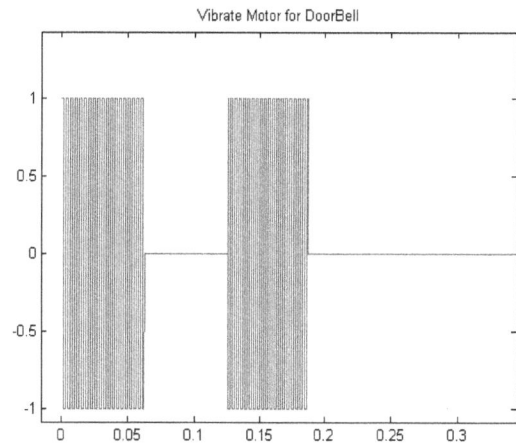

Figure 7: A vibration envelope that is temporally faithful to the sound envelope in Figure 6.

4.3 Tactile Captions

We built a library of NSI tactile events that faithfully replicated the NSI auditory temporal and amplitude changes over time. First, we implemented a program to scan the caption text for non-speech information enclosed by brackets, e.g., [phone ringing]. We analyzed the auditory envelope for that timeframe. We picked video-specific minimum amplitudes to aid in identifying the start and end times for the NSI event. As touch has excellent temporal resolution, we focused only on preserving temporal fidelity by looking and copying the peak-to-peak temporal fidelity as closely as possible. For example, in Figure 6, the doorbell sound envelope has two peaks that can be transformed into the following vibration envelope as shown in Figure 7. This tactile envelope was added into a library. When the entire video was completed, the library was transferred to the vibration microcontroller.

For viewing, users start a integrated program that displays both the video and captions. When the program detects the NSI captions, it sends the NSI description caption to the vibrator microcontroller, which looks up the matching vibration pattern in its library and runs it.

4.4 Visual-Tactile Captions

In addition to the synchronous tactile information, we added synchronous visual information overlaid on the NSI items to supplement the caption text. We created multiple parallel wavy lines over the NSI item. We extracted the NSI amplitude and automatically set its width is proportional to the auditory amplitude. We also automatically set the length of the thick wavy lines according to its duration. We overlaid these lines over the NSI item whenever the corresponding NSI caption was shown. We used a single solid and bright color to call attention to the sound, but not to convey any additional information.

4.5 System

The hardware for both the tactile and visual-tactile captions consists of a Windows 8 laptop, a mBed NXP 1768 micro-controller and a ROB-08449 vibration motor (tactor). The software is a stand-alone C# program that displays captioned multimedia and simultaneously scans the captions for

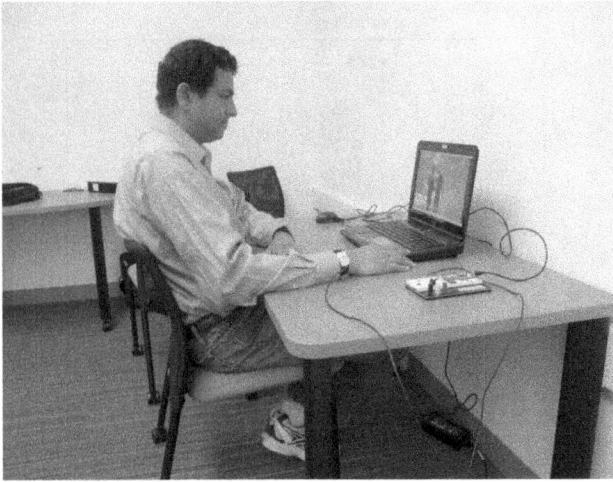

Figure 8: A DHH viewer watching a captioned video with a strapped on tactor.

(object falls)

Figure 9: A snapshot of visual-tactile enhanced captioned video at a specific moment when there is non-speech information, transmitted both through text, corresponding visual cue and temporally faithful vibration.

NSI. When NSI is detected, the program sends a trigger via bluetooth to the micro-controller. Based on the trigger command, the micro-controller selects and executes the corresponding tactile envelope from its library. The program cannot reproduce the amplitude or frequency due to the tactor's single power setting. At first, we found that the current supplied to it was too low. We then increased the current via a MOSFET to make the vibrations stronger and more easily noticeable. The microcontroller can control the vibration motor such that different kinds of vibration through varying the frequency and duration of pulses.

We developed a specific vibration envelope to mimic the feel for each NSI event. For all vibration envelopes, we preserved the amplitude in terms of temporal fidelity. That is, we carefully mapped the shape of the sound envelope amplitude to the vibration envelope amplitude as shown in Figures 6 and 7.

4.6 Experiment

To get a sense of whether or not the users benefited from tactile and/or visual-tactile captions, we conducted a study using a new video that had both kinds of captions. We recruited 21 new DHH participants (15 male, 7 female) from the National Technical Institute for the Deaf at the Rochester Institute of Technology. The average participant was 19.5 years old and all had some degree of hearing loss at birth. All participants had prior experience with watching captioned movies from birth, reflecting the fact that they had grown up with mandated universal captions required after the passage of the Americans with Disabilities Act in 1991.

4.6.1 Experiment Setup

We created a movie for this study that featured fellow peers to keep it interesting and relevant. The movie featured all deaf students, with the protoganist remembering that he has homework due, and trying to find a computer to print it before it is due in class, and with a surprising twist at the end.

We divided the movie into four equal clips, each with seven NSI events such as phone ringing or foot stomps, used by DHH people to call others via vibration instead of sound.

The first clip was set up to provide practice. That clip was divided into three sections. The first section had only captions, then the second one had tactile enhanced captions, and the third section had visual and tactile enhanced captions, as shown in Figure 9. The experiment script then presented the second, third and fourth clips in a balanced and randomized order, each of the three kinds of captioning: regular, tactile and visual-tactile enhanced, so as to avoid bias.

4.6.2 Study Setup

When participants came in for the study, we informed them that the entire session would be about 30 minutes long. They signed the consent form, and then filled out a demographics questionnaire. They were told that each clip had seven NSI events, and that they should pay attention to the NSI event and the item that triggered the event.

The participants strapped on a tactor as shown in Figure 8. They were invited to become familiar with all three kinds of captioning by watching the first clip.

Next, they viewed clips with the associated in randomized order. After viewing each clip, they completed a survey that asked them to 1) rate their satisfaction with the clarity of captions, 2) their ability to recall and narrate the NSI events, and 3) their ability to identify and describe the location of the non-speech sound in the scene at the time of the sound event. They were asked open-ended questions to solicit feedback on each kind of captions, and compensated for their participation and time.

5. RESULTS

We assessed the mean and standard deviations for all questions: Likert ratings, number of accurately described NSI, and number of accurately described NSI location and item in the scene.

For the Likert ratings, a chi-square test was used to compare the ratings for tactile and visual-tactile captions against captions. In terms of ease of use, there was no significant difference between captions ($\overline{C} = 4.2, \sigma = .4$) and tactile captions ($\overline{TC} = 4.3, \sigma = .3$), $\chi^2 = 18.44, p = .4$). However, there was a significant difference between captions ($\overline{C} = 4.2, \sigma = .4$) and visual-tactile captions ($\overline{VTC} = 4.7, \sigma = .3$), $\chi^2 = 10.87, p < .01$.

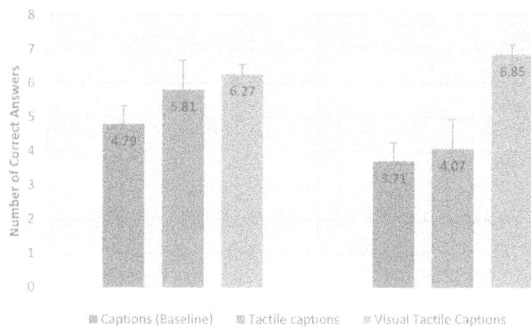

Figure 10: Left chart: Average NSI events recalled; Right chart: Average NSI locations/items recalled.

We find visual-tactile captions yielded an improvement over captions in terms of participant recall on NSI and scenes that occurred during the NSI as shown in Figure 10.

For the recall accuracy of NSI events and associated NSI location, an independent samples t-test was used to compare captions with tactile captions, and captions with visual-tactile captions. For accuracy in describing NSI events, tactile captions showed a 21.3% increase over captions, $t(40) = 2.98, p < .01$, while visual-tactile captions had a 30.90% increase over captions, $t(40) = 3.21, p < .01$.

In terms of participant accuracy in locating NSI in the corresponding scene, tactile captions yielded a 9.70% improvement over captions, $t(40) = 1.47, p < .01$, while visual-tactile captions yielded a 84.64% increase over captions, $t(40) = 6.42, p < .01$.

5.1 Participant Feedback

Overall, the participants were very positive about the enhancements to regular captions, especially the visual-tactile enhanced captions. In particular, they liked being able to quickly locate the location of the non-speech sounds. They also liked the ability to perceive a temporally faithful description of the sound. When asked to fill out the open ended answers, the participants commented:

> The strength for the tactile feedback is that I can feel the vibration very well. It is pretty strong and understandable. Also, it is like a watch so it can stay on my arm and not feel loose or will fall off of the arm.

> It was interesting to see how the tactile feedback was being use to vibrate to warn about some things like the fall. I don't mind wear that to let me know that something happen.

6. DISCUSSION

The participants liked the tactile captions more than the captions, and in turn, liked the visual-tactile captions more than either tactile captions or visual-tactile captions.

6.1 Strengths

Participants recalled significantly more NSI when they watched tactile or visual-tactile captions, as compared to watching visual captions alone. These findings are supported by participant comments. For example, one participant noted: "Tactile captions let me feel the doorbell rather than just looking at the description: "doorbell ringing"".

There was a significant increase in recall of details with visual-tactile enhanced captions as compared to the tactile enhanced captions. This aligned with the feedback by the students in the initial pilot study.

Most participants were able to adapt to both tactile and visual-tactile captions. Out of all of our participants, none of the visual-tactile caption users, and only three of the tactile caption users actually decreased their score between the baseline and trial conditions. While we had expected some level of variation in this result, this is an additional indicator that our approach is reliably beneficial to users.

6.2 Weaknesses

For regular captions, the viewers commented that they were sometimes distracting because there was not always a visual connection between the captions and the scene details. In other words, they did not have auditory memory to identify or relate to auditory suggestions in the scene. Because many of them lacked experience of understanding and interpreting environmental or non-speech sounds, they occasionally found it confusing to read the description as it was not always obvious what these relatively abstract descriptions were.

For tactile captions, the viewers commented that they were sometimes distracting because they could not identify the tactile feedback was as they were too busy reading the captions. The caption description did not always help them identify or relate to auditory events. One participant stated: "I like the vibration to get my attention, but at the same time, it was distracting when trying to watch the video."

When asked to directly compare tactile captions against visual-tactile captions, the viewers commented that the former was sometimes distracting because there was not always a visual connection between the tactile feedback and the scene details.

6.3 Conclusions

The results suggest that while tactile captions alone can make a significant difference in visualization and recall of NSI, the open ended feedback indicated that they were sometimes confused about the NSI presumably as they had no prior experience with them. On the other hand, for most viewers, the visual-tactile captions made a significant difference in the visualization and recall of NSI, and this was supported by the feedback which indicated they were able to connect unfamilar NSI information with familiar visuals. Although touch is not as information-rich as vision, we conjecture that the increased recall is due to simultaneous perception in the visual and tactile modalities.

Feedback also indicated that some preferred stronger vibrations, while others liked the weaker ones. This suggests that visual-tactile systems should have adjustable baselines to adapt to consumer preferences.

Users noted that visual cues were very helpful in guiding their attention towards immediately identifying the location and nature of the thing producing the NSI. The variable thickness that was proportional to the amplitude may have been too subtle, for none of them commented on its helpfulness.

The ability to directly perceive salient properties of auditory information via visual-tactile captions adds a new dimension to accessibility in watching multimedia and enables viewers to gain more access to multimodal information.

7. FUTURE WORK

There is great potential in maximizing the enjoyment and recall of visual-tactile captions. We will explore new methods to enhance traditional captions through visual and tactile feedback for DHH consumers, such as the issue of interference between simultaneous visual and tactile input, with the goal of maximizing information perception.

Another important limitation of captions is the fact that it strips out volume information, which is imperceptible to the caption user. Every sound becomes equally "loud" when it is transferred to the caption track. The distinction between background and foreground blurs. We will explore approaches to pass on speech loudness to viewers, possibly through programmable MOSFETS that can adjust vibration amplitude to provide more dimensions for tactile feedback.

We plan to investigate vibration properties that work best in terms of enjoyment or recall alone or in combination with visual captions. We plan to do evaluation studies in which viewers will be asked to describe what they saw and felt. We will rate these descriptions for accuracy in relation to the auditory event, such as turn-signal versus seat-belt beeps.

The current research work has laid a foundation for taking the idea behind the research to the next level. The aim is to explore more and more patterns and intensities of vibrations in order to build a continuous vibration system rather than the current discrete vibration system.

The effectiveness of visual-tactile captions suggests that presenting accessible multimodal information can increase a DHH viewer's viewing and recall ability. This has implications for all users, including blind and low vision people (BLV). They face similar problems, in that multimodal information is all conveyed over audio, i.e., the audio description plus the movie dialog. The problems are not quite identical, and future studies would tackle different issues.

8. ACKNOWLEDGMENTS

This work is supported by a grant from the National Science Foundation IIS-1218056.

9. REFERENCES

[1] I. Apostolopoulos, N. Fallah, E. Folmer, and K. E. Bekris. Integrated online localization and navigation for people with visual impairments using smart phones. *ACM Transactions on Interactive Intelligent Systems*, 3(4):1–28, Jan. 2014.

[2] A. Baijal, J. Kim, C. Branje, F. Russo, and D. I. Fels. Composing vibrotactile music: A multi-sensory experience with the emoti-chair. In *2012 IEEE Haptics Symposium (HAPTICS)*, pages 509–515. IEEE, Mar. 2012.

[3] C. Branje, M. Karam, D. Fels, and F. Russo. Enhancing entertainment through a multimodal chair interface. In *2009 IEEE Toronto International Conference Science and Technology for Humanity (TIC-STH)*, pages 636–641. IEEE, Sept. 2009.

[4] S. Brewster and L. M. Brown. Tactons: Structured Tactile Messages for Non-Visual Information Display. In *AUIC '04 Proceedings of the fifth conference on Australasian user interface*, pages 15–23, 2004.

[5] S. Brewster, F. Chohan, and L. Brown. Tactile feedback for mobile interactions. In *Proceedings of the SIGCHI conference on Human factors in computing systems - CHI '07*, page 159, New York, New York, USA, 2007. ACM Press.

[6] A. C. Cavender, J. P. Bigham, and R. E. Ladner. ClassInFocus. In *Proceedings of the 11th International ACM SIGACCESS Conference on Computers and Accessibility - ASSETS '09*, pages 67–74, New York, New York, USA, 2009. ACM Press.

[7] W. Fujisaki and S. Nishida. Audio-tactile superiority over visuo-tactile and audio-visual combinations in the temporal resolution of synchrony perception. *Experimental brain research*, 198(2-3):245–59, Sept. 2009.

[8] C. Jensema. Closed-captioned television presentation speed and vocabulary. *American Annals of the Deaf*, 141(4):284–292, 1996.

[9] C. J. Jensema, R. S. Danturthi, and R. Burch. Time spent viewing captions on television programs. *American annals of the deaf*, 145(5):464–8, Dec. 2000.

[10] L. A. Jones and N. B. Sarter. Tactile Displays: Guidance for Their Design and Application. *Human Factors: The Journal of the Human Factors and Ergonomics Society*, 50(1):90–111, Feb. 2008.

[11] W. L. Khoo, E. L. Seidel, and Z. Zhigang. *Designing a virtual environment to evaluate multimodal sensors for assisting the visually impaired*, volume 7383 of *Lecture Notes in Computer Science*. Springer Berlin Heidelberg, Berlin, Heidelberg, 2012.

[12] R. S. Kushalnagar, P. Kushalnagar, and G. Manganelli. Collaborative Gaze Cues for Deaf Students. In *Dual Eye Tracking Workshop at the Computer Supported Cooperative Work and Social Computing Conference*, Seattle, WA, Mar. 2012. ACM Press.

[13] R. S. Kushalnagar, W. S. Lasecki, and J. P. Bigham. Captions Versus Transcripts for Online Video Content. In ACM, editor, *10th International Cross-Disciplinary Conference on Web Accessibility (W4A)*, 32, pages 1–4, Rio De Janerio, Brazil, May 2013. ACM Press.

[14] R. S. Kushalnagar, W. S. Lasecki, and J. P. Bigham. Accessibility Evaluation of Classroom Captions. *ACM Transactions on Accessible Computing*, 5(3):1–24, Jan. 2014.

[15] E. S. Ladner. Silent Talkies. *American Annals of the Deaf*, 76:323–325, 1931.

[16] M. Marschark, G. Leigh, P. Sapere, D. Burnham, C. Convertino, M. Stinson, H. Knoors, M. P. J. Vervloed, and W. Noble. Benefits of sign language interpreting and text alternatives for deaf students' classroom learning. *Journal of Deaf Studies and Deaf Education*, 11(4):421–37, Jan. 2006.

[17] M. Mills. On Disability and Cybernetics: Helen Keller, Norbert Wiener, and the Hearing Glove. *differences*, 22(2-3):74–111, Dec. 2011.

[18] C. E. Sherrick, R. W. Cholewiak, and A. A. Collins. The localization of low- and high-frequency vibrotactile stimuli. *The Journal of the Acoustical Society of America*, 88(1):169–79, July 1990.

[19] S. Sundaram and S. Narayanan. Classification of sound clips by two schemes: Using onomatopoeia and semantic labels. In *2008 IEEE International Conference on Multimedia and Expo*, pages 1341–1344. IEEE, June 2008.

Age, Technology Usage, and Cognitive Characteristics in Relation to Perceived Disorientation and Reported Website Ease of Use

Michael Crabb[1]
[1]School of Computing
University of Dundee
Dundee, DD1 4HN, Scotland.

michaelcrabb@acm.org

Vicki L. Hanson [1, 2]
[2]Golisano College of Computing and Information Sciences
Rochester Institute of Technology
20 Lomb Memorial Drive
Rochester, NY USA 14623
vlh@acm.org

ABSTRACT

Comparative studies including older and younger adults are becoming more common in HCI, generally used to compare how these two different age groups will approach a task. However, it is unclear whether user 'age' is the underlying factor that differentiates between these two groups. To address this problem, an examination into the relationship between users' age, previous technology experience, and cognitive characteristics is conducted. Measures of perceived disorientation and reported ease of use are used to understand links that exist between these user characteristics and their effect on browsing experience. This is achieved through a lab-based information retrieval task, where participants visited a selection of websites in order to find answers to a series of questions and then self reported their feelings of perceived disorientation and website ease of use through a Likert-scored questionnaire.

The presented research found that age accounts for as little as 1% of user browsing experience when performing information retrieval tasks. Further, it showed that cognitive ability and previous technology experience significantly affected perceived disorientation in these searches. These results argue for the inclusion of metrics regarding cognitive ability and previous technology experience when analyzing user satisfaction and performance in Internet based-studies.

Categories and Subject Descriptors

H3.3 Information Search and Retrieval: Search Process. H.5.2. User Interfaces – Theory and methods; J.4 [Computer Applications]: Social and behavioral Sciences – Psychology.

General Terms

Measurement, Human Factors.

Keywords

Older Adults; cognitive ability; HCI; web search; search strategies.

ASSETS'14, October 20–22, 2014, Rochester, NY, USA.
Copyright © 2014 ACM 978-1-4503-2720-6/14/10...$15.00.
http://dx.doi.org/10.1145/2661334.2661356

1. INTRODUCTION

The UK Office of Communication (Ofcom) report that over 50% of adults aged 65-74 and 25% of those aged 75+ now have access to the World Wide Web [27]. With a growing number of adults using this technology comes a challenge in designing interfaces that this diverse population group can use. However, calling this cohort of users a single 'group' may cause problems - the methods and skills used by one of these users might well be completely different to that of another [16].

Differences have been found in the strategies used by older and younger adults in completing computer-based tasks [3, 7, 13]. Users' abilities can change greatly over time and these changes can differ depending on both the individual and the culture in which they live [15]. How important, then, is 'age' in determining the experiences that users' may have when searching online? Would metrics other then age perhaps provide richer information?

In this paper, we examine the use of age as a predictor of users' perceived disorientation and reported website ease of use. We report on a study in which older and younger adults participated in an information retrieval exercise to examine the perceived disorientation and reported website ease of use they experience. We then use multiple regression models to determine the suitability of users' age, cognitive characteristics, and previous technology usage in relation to these metrics. Perceived disorientation and reported website ease of use is obtained from participants through self-reported user data, relying on first hand participant information rather than inferred experience metrics that can be obtained through log-file analysis.

2. RELATED WORK

A wide body of work exists that examines the design needs of older adults. However, this can focus on a 'deficit model' attached to aging, concentrating on general declines in vision, reduction in working memory, and use of slower movements [23]. Such deficit models have been used to create 'age' based guidelines that recommend the use of bigger text, larger buttons, and simpler websites [19]. A problem exists in that 'senior-friendly' adaptions to websites assume that the changes made will then allow older adults to successfully use the Internet based on a standard set of age-based assumptions. This presents an issue, as older adults are a dynamic population with differing ability levels that can change highly between individuals.

Table 1 - Participant Internet and Cognitive Comparisons

Ability Measures	Younger Adult		Older Adult		t(18)	Age Group Comparison (α = .05)
	M	SD	M	SD		
Age	22.12	3.18	73.66	9.11	-15.26**	YA < OA
Internet Usage	48.00	10.85	29.92	12.86	3.27**	YA > OA
Internet Confidence	54.88	12.59	44.25	13.38	1.78*	YA > OA
Fluid Intelligence	23.63	2.26	18.17	2.82	4.57**	YA > OA
Processing Speed	46.63	6.04	45.08	6.94	.511	YA ≈ OA
Short Term Memory	6.88	2.94	7.25	1.91	-.547	YA ≈ OA
Long Term Memory	13.75	5.34	14.92	4.76	-.512	YA ≈ OA

One of the most common alternatives to using age as a metric is to examine previous technology usage [7]. This can be measured using a variety of methods, with the most prevalent being user self-reported information. Possible implementations involve the use of questionnaires allowing users to report on aspects relating to technology usage, experience, and comfort. When examining the relationship between technology experience and task performance, older adults with high levels of previous technology experience have shown to have higher levels of performance in data-entry, file modification, and inventory management tasks than those with low levels of previous technology experience [6].

An alternative to user age that is more related to individuals' ability could be to examine their cognitive characteristics. One area of cognitive psychology that has shown to have promise in HCI surrounds fluid intelligence - the ability of an individual to adapt to a situation based on their problem solving skills [21]. Fluid abilities include aspects such as inductive reasoning, short-term memory, speed of processing information, and problem solving abilities. The process of aging results in many changes in cognitive abilities with fluid attributes diminishing as individuals get older [20]. These changes can have a profound effect on individuals' skill in understanding new technologies, and to efficiently carry out tasks. Technology, therefore, needs to be designed to optimize a person's capabilities, while also compensating for their weaknesses [17]. Differences have been found to exist in the search strategies used by older and younger adults, with younger adults relying on system interface features when searching while older adults rely on a broad range of features [3]. It is possible, however, that these 'age' differences between older and younger adults are related to other characteristics, as clear links have been drawn between demographic data, cognitive abilities, and computer usage [7].

Fluid intelligence has been previously used to examine user task performance although the results from this have been varied [4, 31]. A decline in fluid cognitive abilities has been shown to relate to a decline in the reformulation of information retrieval requests [10] – especially important when using search functionality on websites. Combined with fluid intelligence, other cognitive factors have been successfully related to task performance including processing speed, short-term memory, and long-term memory. These factors have been used both as a combined cognitive ability scoring [4, 5] and also as individual factors in their own right [12, 24, 26, 29, 34].

In this work, the roles of age, user Internet abilities, and cognitive factors in relation to user online satisfaction levels are explored. Firstly, chronological age is analyzed to determine its relationship to user browsing experience. Internet experience and Internet confidence are then included to understand if they can account for any additional variance. Finally, users' cognitive characteristics

are included to examine the combined relationship between these factors and browsing experience. This work attempts to gain an increased understanding into the use of these Internet and cognitive based metrics when examining user browsing experience rather than user performance.

One of the most common problems faced by users when searching online it that of disorientation [25]. There are clear links between the methods used to navigate though a website and the tendency for users to lose their sense of location [33]. Many studies have tried to infer disorientation levels through the use of browser log information, rather than measuring users' feelings [1]. We use this second approach by gathering Likert scored data from participants within an information retrieval study. Sandelands and Buckner [28], among others, argue that the best method of gathering participant feelings is through quantitative responses and not qualitative work. We use this rationale to support this methodology.

3. METHODOLOGY
The main aim of this work was to consider how the inclusion of metrics other than chronological age could be used to enhance the understanding of how browsing experience can change between users when searching for information online. While previous research in this field has focused on user performance, we examined the effect that these factors have on overall browsing experience. Ethical approval for all areas of this work was obtained through a university ethics procedure.

3.1 Experimental Variables
Participant Age Group, Internet Ability (Internet Usage and Internet Experience), and Cognitive Measures (Inductive Reasoning, Perceptual Speed, Memory Span and Meaningful Memory) were used as independent metrics. Browsing Experience (Perceived disorientation and Reported Website Ease of Use) were used as dependent metrics.

3.2 Participants
Twenty participants were recruited for this study. This consisted of 12 older adults (*M* = 73.66, *SD* = 9.11, *Range* 63-90) and eight younger adults (*M* = 22.12, *SD* = 3.18, *Range* 19-29). Older adults were recruited from a pool of potential participants in the local area that had previously expressed interest in taking part in academic studies, being contacted by the user pool coordinator through either phone or e-mail. Younger adults were recruited through e-mail and university message boards and then added into the user pool database. All clarified in pre-screening that they had not taken part in any HCI research studies in the past 12 months.

Table 2 - Participant Testing Battery Information

Measure	Ability Tested	Description
Letter Sets Test [11]	Fluid Induction	Participants determine which of four letter sets is unrelated to the others
Meaningful Memory Test [2]	Long Term Memory	Participants given a list of objects to study and then asked to select similar words after a 10 minute break
Number Comparison Test [11]	Perceptual Speed	Participants required to inspect pairs of large numbers and indicate if they were the same or different
Auditory Number Span [11]	Short Term Memory	Participants were read random-number sequences and asked to repeat each sequence.
Internet Usage Questionnaire	Internet Usage	19-item questionnaire assessing participant Internet Usage
Internet Confidence Questionnaire	Internet Confidence	16-item questionnaire assessing participant Internet confidence

3.3 Materials and Equipment

Demographic Information —Demographic information including participant age, education and occupational status were collected from participants through a questionnaire.

Internet Ability—Two questionnaires examining participant Internet Ability were used. The first of these examined participant Internet *Confidence* and consisted of 16 questions. These questions asked participants their confidence in completing a number of Internet based tasks, measured on a 5-point scale (Strongly Agree, Agree, Neither Agree nor Disagree, Disagree, Strongly Disagree). The second examined participant Internet Usage and consisted of 19 questions. These questions asked participants how often they would complete a number of Internet based activities and was measured on a 7-point scale (Everyday, Several Times a week, Several Times a month, Every few months, Less Often, Never).

Cognitive Measures—Four cognitive measures were used to gather information on a subset of individuals' abilities. This consisted of the Letter Sets Test (measuring fluid induction) [11], Number Comparison Test (perceptual speed) [11], Meaningful Memory Test (long-term memory) [2], and Auditory Memory Span (memory span and working memory) [11]. Summary Information on *Internet Ability* and *Cognitive Measures* are found in Table 2.

Browsing Experience—A questionnaire based on work by Ahuja and Webster [1] was used to gather information on users Perceived Disorientation and Reported Website Ease of Use. This questionnaire was designed to measure perceived disorientation and participant reported 'website ease of use' during online tasks and has been widely used since its introduction [18, 22, 32]. This questionnaire consisted of 10 questions, measured on a 7-point scale (Strongly Disagree, Disagree, Somewhat Disagree, Neither Disagree or Agree, Somewhat Agree, Agree, Strongly Agree).

Task Question Set— 30 questions were created that prompted users to create a path through a website in order to complete an information retrieval task. These questions were created based on 30 individual websites that were selected for inclusion in this study. One question was created for each website. Twenty-five of these sites were selected from the top 100 visited websites in the UK (according to Alexa[1]), split into five categories: health, shopping, news, governmental, and banking. Five additional websites were also selected that included information on attractions in the local area. Each task required participants to visit between two and five pages on the optimum path. However, the number of pages participants would visit increased if they used an alternative route.

Experimental Equipment—The experiment ran on an apple laptop computer (Macbook Pro Mid-2010[2]), with the Google Chrome Browser being used. The laptop was placed in front of the researcher and the participant was given control through a 22" Widescreen Monitor, and a standard Microsoft Keyboard and Mouse. Monitor display was mirrored between the laptop and the additional monitor. Control of the experiment was achieved through a tablet device handled bit the researcher. This allowed the researcher to see the current question that is being asked, and additionally navigate through questions to control the flow of the study

3.4 Procedure

Participants were firstly invited to take part in a group session in order to gather data on their *demographic information, Internet Ability,* and *Cognitive Measures.* Four separate sessions were used allowing for participants to be split into smaller, more manageable groups. Younger adults were tested separately to older adults.

After completing the testing battery, participants were then invited to take part in a second individual session where they completed a number of information retrieval tasks taken from the *Task Question Set.* Once an individual question was completed, participants were given the *Browsing Experience* questionnaire to complete relating to the information retrieval task that they had just completed. Task order was randomized between participants in order to reduce ordering effects.

3.5 Analysis

An initial analysis of the two age groups (younger and older adults) showed differences between participants' Internet usage, Internet confidence, and Inductive Reasoning. No age-related differences were noticed regarding perceptual speed, memory span / working memory, or meaningful memory. This was unexpected, as previous literature has shown that these metrics deteriorate with age and differences should be seen between these two groups [20].

A possible explanation (and limitation), can be explained in the educational background of the older adults recruited for this study. 9 of the 12 (75%) older adults reported education of Bachelors

---

[1] http://www.alexa.com/topsites/countries/GB

[2] http://support.apple.com/kb/SP584

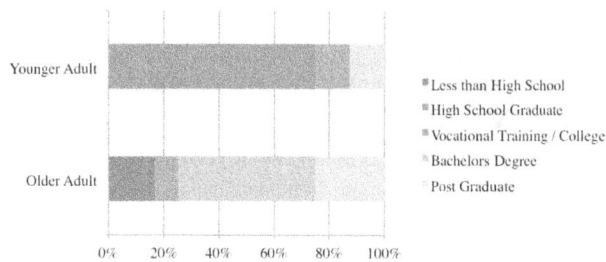

Figure 1 Participant Education Background Summary

Degree or higher, with previous literature showing a link between educational background and these characteristics. This is detailed in Figure 1.

Analyses was designed to determine the impact that Age, *Internet Ability*, and *Cognitive Measures* had on understanding the *Browsing Experience* of this population. This was done to discover if any additional variance could be uncovered by examining Internet and Cognitive factors on top of that discovered between age groups. Multiple regression was therefore used to analyse the data. Cognitive Measures, Internet Ability, and age were split into three separate models during analysis. Cognitive Measures and Internet Ability were normalised by dividing individual participant metrics by two times of the group standard deviation and age groups coded as a dummy variable (Younger Adult = 0, Older Adult = 1). This method, suggested by Gelman [14], allows for a direct comparison between scalar and binary predictors.

In Model 1 only participant age was included as a measured variable. Model 2 expanded on this by including *Internet Ability*. Model 3 contained all *Cognitive Measures* along with the metrics outlined in Models 1 and 2. The three regression models were performed consecutively, with additional metrics being added with each analysis.

Three multiple regressions were performed in total, the first focussing on participants' perceived disorientation, the second on reported website ease of use, and the third on a combined *Browsing Experience* score.

4. RESULTS

When examining the effectiveness of metrics to predict a user's disorientation and website ease of use, the results gathered indicate that age cannot be used as a metric to understand feelings of disorientation or website ease that occur when carrying out an information retrieval task. In Figure 2, Model 1 represents the variance accountable for only age. When examining the models, age cannot account for any variance present when analysing user perceived disorientation or users overall browsing experience. Age was only able to predict 1.6% of any variance when examining user feelings on a websites ease of use. As previously stated, the younger and older adult were coded as 'dummy' variables in analysis, and while using these two dichotomous groups is a limitation in this work as it may over inflate any results comparing these two groups, the results show that only a very small amount of variance regarding users browsing experience can be explained by the differences between these two age categories. This provides initial evidence to support the objectives set out in this paper – examining the extent to which age accounts for variance in user satisfaction when completing information retrieval tasks. Similar results are reported by Czaja et. al [7] who found that including age within the final step of a

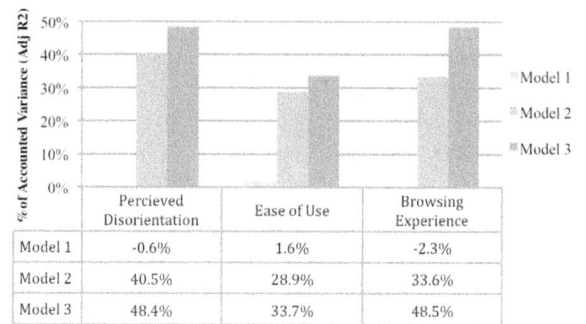

Figure 2 Regression Model Comparison Summary

regression analysis did not significantly help in predicting individuals' technology usage.

Model 2 improves on Model 1 by including participants' previous Internet usage and Internet confidence. This created a noticeable improvement in the amount of perceived disorientation accounted for between groups with this increasing to 40.5%. This indicates that it is possible to understand more about why an individual may feel lost completing information retrieval tasks by examining their previous experiences and confidence in using the Internet rather than relying on their age. Similarly, users feelings of website ease of use increased to 28.9% and their combined browsing experience increased to 33.6%. The inclusion of cognitive characteristics in Model 3 again provided an increase in the amount of variance accounted for, with perceived disorientation of participants improving a further 7.9% to reach a total of 48.4%. While the increases seen between Model 2 and Model 3 may not seem significant, the reason for this is the order in which these variables were placed into the regression. A high percentage of regression overlap appears between these variables, and therefore accounts for the small increase in accounted variance.

A summary of regression analysis participant perceived disorientation is detailed in Table 3. Age as a single factor accounted for a very small amount of variance (Adj. R^2 = -.006) with the addition of technology factors causing an increment in

Table 3 Multiple Regression Model - Perceived Disorientation

	B	SE B	β
Model 1			
Constant	1.795	.155	
Age	.189	.200	.217
Model 2			
Constant	3.276	.425	
Age	-.168	.197	-.194
Internet Usage	-.238	.202	-.272
Internet Confidence	-.552	.174	-.632**
Model 3			
Constant	4.310	1.267	
Age	-.188	.292	-.216
Internet Usage	.021	.220	.024
Internet Confidence	-.646	.177	-.740**
Fluid Induction	-.051	.242	-.059
Perceptual Speed	-.404	.170	-.462*
Short Term Memory	-.063	.190	-.072
Long Term Memory	.359	.201	.411

Note: Adj R^2 = -.006 for Step 1, Adj R^2 = .405 for Step 2 (p < .01), Adj R^2 = .484 for Step 3 (p < .05).

*p < .05, **p < .01, ***p < .001.

	B	SE B	β
Table 4 Multiple Regression Model - Ease of Use			
Model 1			
Constant	3.060	.115	
Age	-.170	.148	-.261
Model 2			
Constant	2.153	.348	
Age	.033	.161	.051
Internet Usage	.092	.165	.141
Internet Confidence	.381	.142	.583*
Model 3			
Constant	1.044	1.075	
Age	.144	.248	.221
Internet Usage	-.103	.187	-.157
Internet Confidence	.447	.151	.683*
Fluid Induction	.186	.205	.284
Perceptual Speed	.285	.144	.437
Short Term Memory	.019	.161	.029
Long Term Memory	-.260	.171	-.398

Note: Adj R^2 = .016 for Step 1, Adj R^2 = .289 for Step 2 (p < .01), Adj R^2 = .337 for Step 3 (p < .05).

*$p < .05$, ** $p < .01$, *** $p < .001$.*

	B	SE B	β
Table 5 Multiple Regression Model - Browsing Experience			
Model 1			
Constant	1.177	.123	
Age	.120	.159	.176
Model 2			
Constant	2.258	.354	
Age	-.129	.164	-.188
Internet Usage	-.134	.168	-.195
Internet Confidence	-.435	.144	-.632**
Model 3			
Constant	3.920	.998	
Age	-.281	.230	-.411
Internet Usage	.064	.173	.093
Internet Confidence	-.518	.140	-.752**
Fluid Induction	-.212	.190	-.307
Perceptual Speed	-.370	.134	-.538*
Short Term Memory	-.068	.149	-.099
Long Term Memory	.248	.158	.361

Note: Adj R^2 = -.023 for Step 1, Adj R^2 = .336 for Step 2 (p < .05), Adj R^2 = .485 for Step 3 (p < .05).

*$p < .05$, ** $p < .01$, *** $p < .001$.*

Adjusted R^2 to .405. The addition of cognitive factors increases the Adjusted R^2 by an additional .008 to .484. In this final regression, it was found that key components, which correlated with perceived disorientation, were Internet confidence and processing speed.

These results suggest that when examining the amount of disorientation that is reported by an individual when carrying out an information retrieval task similar to the ones used in this work, a large amount of variability between participants is down to their confidence in using the technology, and also their perceptual speed levels.

Summary analysis for reported website ease of use is presented in Table 4. Similar to perceived disorientation, age again accounted for a very small amount of variance (Adj R^2 = .016) with the addition of technology factors increasing Adjusted R^2 to .289. The attachment of cognitive factors increased Adjusted R^2 to .337 with Internet Confidence being the only significant factor present in the model.

This again suggests that when examining how easy users find a website to use, a large amount of variability exists due to user confidence in the technology. No significant results were found regarding user age, suggesting that the age group a user is in has very little to do with how easy or difficult they find a website to navigate around.

The final regression analysis collated the dependant measures into a single scoring, containing reported website ease of use and perceived disorientation. In this model, summarized in Table 5, age produced an Adjusted R^2 of -.023. This increased to .336 when including technology factors and again to .485 when including cognitive factors. In this final model, Internet Confidence and Processing Speed were seen to be significant factors.

Similar to a measure of only user perceived disorientation, this suggests that individuals' browsing experience is heavily influenced by their confidence in using technology, and not the overall amount of usage that they may report. Additionally, individuals' perpetual speed has shown to have an effect on the overall browsing experience, while age category does not have any effect.

5. DISCUSSION

In the analysis, the main factors that could be used to predict levels of perceived disorientation in users were their confidence in using the Internet and also their perceptual speed. Figure 3 shows coefficients (B) for reported disorientation complete with 95% confidence intervals (an increase in value of 1 from any of the given metrics leads to a related change indicated by the bars, with 'error bars' indicating confidence that 95% of results would be between the two limits). This chart indicates that higher levels of Internet confidence and processing speed lead to reductions in perceived disorientation. From this, it can be inferred that an increase in confidence in using technology has a direct correlation on feelings of low perceived disorientation when completing information retrieval tasks online, with similar results appearing with their processing speed. An interesting point to note here is that no meaningful correlation was found between the amount of previous experience that an individual has in using the World Wide Web and any feelings of perceived disorientation. Significance is placed more on the confidence in using technology.

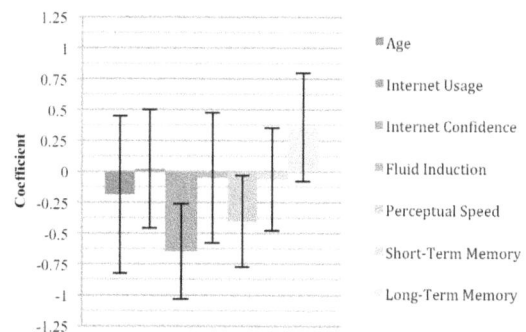

Figure 2 Coefficient for Perceived Disorientation with 95% Confidence Intervals

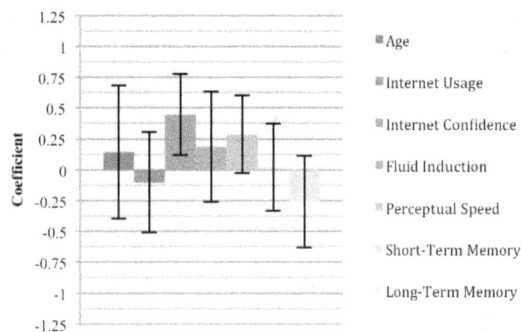

Figure 4 Coefficient for Ease of Use with 95% Confidence Intervals

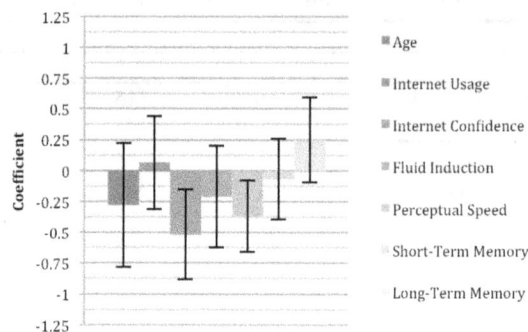

Figure 5 Coefficient for Browsing Experience with 95% Confidence Intervals

A slight difference was found when examining the reported website ease of use of participants (shown in Figure 4). It was found that only Internet confidence played a significant part in determining whether a website was easy to use when performing information retrieval tasks. All other metrics had 95% confidence intervals which spanned both sides of 0, indicating that they could not accurately determine whether they may have a positive or detrimental effect on the reported ease of use of a website.

Combining perceived disorientation and reported ease of use into one metric examining overall browsing experience creates results similar to that of perceived disorientation, with both Internet experience and perceptual speed producing significant correlations (shown in Figure 5). No other factors contributed significantly in this model. This indicates that when examining the overall browsing experience of an individual when completing information retrieval tasks, a large amount of variance can be accounted for by again focusing on the previous confidence that a user has in using the Internet, and also the mental quickness that is attached to levels of user perceptual speed.

It was found in all three of the regression models that individuals' Internet confidence can account for a large amount of the variance that is associated with the perceived disorientation, website ease of use, and overall browsing experience of individuals when completing information retrieval tasks. Additionally, it was found that individuals' perceptual speed could influence their perceived disorientation and overall browsing experience. However, in all cases, age was unable to account for any variance and could not be used to predict any aspect of users browsing experience when completing this study.

User age has a very small effect when predicting users' browsing experience. All regressions in this study reported that age could not account for a significant amount of variance that is attached to participant perceived disorientation, reported website ease of use, or overall browsing experience. As such, one of the key findings from this study, and a recommendation for future HCI work, is that age cannot be used as a grouping variable when examining the browsing experience of individuals.

Internet Confidence, rather than Usage, is important in predicting browsing experience. While the amount of usage that individuals have in using a particular technology may increase their speed at completing tasks, the finding in this work suggests that it is their *confidence* in using technology that has an impact in their overall browsing experience. It is therefore suggested that a possible method of increasing the browsing experience for users is to attempt to invoke feelings of confidence in a system or service from an early stage, in order to make users feel more comfortable in using them.

Inductive Reasoning did not show to be a predictor of Browsing Experience. A surprising outcome from this work surrounds inductive reasoning, and its inability to act as a predictor of browsing experience. A large amount of literature in the past has examined fluid intelligence as a predictor of user performance, and Inductive reasoning is one of the 3 sub-abilities in this measure. This work found that while higher levels of inductive reasoning pointed towards less participant disorientation and a higher ease of use scoring, this was not at significant levels. A possible reason for this may be down to this work using a more subjective measure of performance, and that measures such as inductive reasoning are more key in objective performance metrics such as task completion time.

Perceptual Speed showed to be a predictor of Browsing Experience. The processing speed sub-ability, perceptual speed, was successfully used as a predictor of user browsing experience. Higher levels of perceptual speed, resulted in lower levels or perceived disorientation, high levels of reported website ease of use, and higher levels of overall browsing experience. This findings suggests that the mental quickness that is associated with this ability, can be utilized in order to quickly understand links between information retrieval questions, and the possible routes through a website. However, caution must be applied, as high levels of processing speed have been shown to correlate with high education levels in an individual, and this may in turn produce a secondary effect.

6. CONCLUSIONS

This paper has provided evidence that age is not a suitable metric to distinguish between users. Factors such as previous Internet usage and cognitive abilities can illuminate more significant contributors to ease of use than age alone. The primary finding to emerge from this study is that cognitive factors can be used to account for a substantial amount of variance within both older and younger adults, with factors acting as both negative and positive influencers. While this has been examined before regarding user performance [8, 9, 30], we have shown that similar results can be obtained when using hedonic measures such as search experience. This further demonstrates the ability of cognitive metrics to provide reasoning into how users interact with technology.

We have also shown that Internet experience metrics can be used to aid in understanding user disorientation, with an emphasis placed on users' Internet confidence rather than Internet usage. Complementing this finding, we have also shown that the amount of confidence that an individual has in using the Internet results in an increase in perceived disorientation in younger adults, but a decrease in disorientation in older adults.

Additionally, we have also demonstrated that differences between older and younger adults confidence in using technology can effect their overall disorientation in different ways. Older adults with high Internet confidence showed a reduction in perceived disorientation, while younger adults with high Internet confidence showed an increase in perceived disorientation. This clearly highlights the differences in behavior between these two generations of technology users.

A key implication for research practice arising from this work surrounds the use of participant age as a grouping variable within future research studies. This work has shown that age cannot be used as a suitable metric to distinguish between individuals when examining their browsing experience, and as such, further questions must be asked regarding its usage as a suitable metric when distinguishing between individuals in both the HCI and User Experience fields. It is suggested that while age can be used to distinguish between different generational groups, and this may be beneficial in study design, analysis should consider alternative metrics such as participant confidence in using the technology or service being tested. This method may provide additional information into reasoning's surrounding the experiences of individuals before assuming that age based differences occur.

Additionally, and of importance when examining cognitive abilities, the work in this paper has shown that subjective measures, such as perceived disorientation and browsing experience, can be used as alternative measures to understand user performance rather than relying on objective measures such as task completion time. This finding may have wider implications in the user experience domain as with a move to subjective based metrics, it is possible adapt methods to allow quantitative user experience experiments similar to those used in the HCI domain in general.

It was also found that Internet confidence is a key measure in accounting for the perceived disorientation, reported website ease of use, and overall browsing experience of an individual. This has implications for future user training, as it could be viewed that a focus on increasing the confidence that individuals have in using a particular service will increase their overall experience in using it. This approach, as opposed to providing users with information on how all aspects of a system works, may provide individuals with a higher level of satisfaction, improving their experience in using a service and in turn may also increase technology retention rates.

From these results, we recommend that users' cognitive factors and Internet confidence demographics should be used within the analysis of online activities, rather than relying on user age. We have demonstrated that when examining the experiences felt by users, age is a very limited metric in terms of developing an understanding of why users are reporting feelings of disorientation and ease of use. A much greater understanding can be achieved by including cognitive factors and Internet based demographics.

7. ACKNOWLEDGMENTS

This research is support by RCUK Digital Economy Research Hub EP/G066019/1 – SIDE: Social Inclusion through the Digital Economy. The researchers would also like to thank all participants for giving up their valuable time to take part in this work.

8. REFERENCES

[1] Ahuja, J. S., & Webster, J. (2001). Perceived disorientation: an examination of a new measure to assess web design effectiveness. *Interacting with computers*, *14*(1), 15-29.

[2] Cattell, R.B. 1982. *Meaningful Memory*. Institute for Personality and Ability Testing.

[3] Chin, J., & Fu, W. T. (2010, April). Interactive effects of age and interface differences on search strategies and performance. In *Proceedings of the SIGCHI Conference on Human Factors in Computing Systems* (pp. 403-412). ACM.

[4] Chin, J., Fu, W. T., & Kannampallil, T. (2009, April). Adaptive information search: age-dependent interactions between cognitive profiles and strategies. In *Proceedings of the SIGCHI Conference on Human Factors in Computing Systems* (pp. 1683-1692). ACM.

[5] Czaja, S. J., & Lee, C. C. (2007). The impact of aging on access to technology. *Universal Access in the Information Society*, *5*(4), 341-349.

[6] Czaja, S. J., & Sharit, J. (1993). Age differences in the performance of computer-based work. *Psychology and aging*, *8*(1), 59.

[7] Czaja, S. J., Charness, N., Fisk, A. D., Hertzog, C., Nair, S. N., Rogers, W. A., & Sharit, J. (2006). Factors predicting the use of technology: findings from the Center for Research and Education on Aging and Technology Enhancement (CREATE). *Psychology and aging*, *21*(2), 333.

[8] Czaja, S. J., Sharit, J., Lee, C. C., Nair, S. N., Hernández, M. A., Arana, N., & Fu, S. H. (2013). Factors influencing use of an e-health website in a community sample of older adults. *Journal of the American Medical Informatics Association*, *20*(2), 277-284.

[9] Czaja, S. J., Sharit, J., Ownby, R., Roth, D. L., & Nair, S. (2001). Examining age differences in performance of a complex information search and retrieval task. *Psychology and aging*, *16*(4), 564.

[10] Dommes, A., Chevalier, A., & Lia, S. (2011). The role of cognitive flexibility and vocabulary abilities of younger and older users in searching for information on the web. *Applied Cognitive Psychology*, *25*(5), 717-726.

[11] Ekstrom, R.B., French, J.W., Harman, H.H. and Dermen, D. 1976. Manual for kit of factor-referenced cognitive tests. *Princeton, NJ: Educational Testing Service*. (1976).

[12] Etcheverry, I., Terrier, P., & Marquié, J. C. (2012). Are older adults less efficient in making attributions about the origin of memories for web interaction?. *Revue Européenne de Psychologie Appliquée/European Review of Applied Psychology*, *62*(2), 93-102.

[13] Fairweather, P. G. (2008, October). How older and younger adults differ in their approach to problem solving on a complex website. In *Proceedings of the 10th international ACM SIGACCESS conference on Computers and accessibility*(pp. 67-72). ACM.

[14] Gelman, A. (2008). Scaling regression inputs by dividing by two standard deviations. *Statistics in medicine*, *27*(15), 2865-2873.

[15] Gregor, P., Newell, A. F., & Zajicek, M. (2002, July). Designing for dynamic diversity: interfaces for older people. In *Proceedings of the fifth international ACM conference on Assistive technologies* (pp. 151-156). ACM.

[16] Hanson, V. L. (2009, April). Age and web access: the next generation. In*Proceedings of the 2009 International Cross-Disciplinary Conference on Web Accessibililty (W4A)* (pp. 7-15). ACM.

[17] Hart, T. A., Chaparro, B. S., & Halcomb, C. G. (2008). Evaluating websites for older adults: adherence to 'senior-friendly' guidelines and end-user performance.*Behaviour & Information Technology*, *27*(3), 191-199.

[18] Herder, E., & Juvina, I. (2004). Discovery of individual user navigation styles.

[19] Hodes, R. J., & Lindberg, D. A. (2002). Making your website senior friendly.*National Institute on Aging and the National Library of Medicine.*

[20] Horn, J. L., & Cattell, R. B. (1967). Age differences in fluid and crystallized intelligence. *Acta psychologica, 26*, 107-129.

[21] Horn, J. L., & Cattell, R. B. (1966). Refinement and test of the theory of fluid and crystallized general intelligences. *Journal of educational psychology, 57*(5), 253.

[22] Juvina, I., & Van Oostendorp, H. (2006). Individual differences and behavioral metrics involved in modeling web navigation. *Universal Access in the Information Society, 4*(3), 258-269.

[23] Kurniawan, S., & Zaphiris, P. (2005, October). Research-derived web design guidelines for older people. In *Proceedings of the 7th international ACM SIGACCESS conference on Computers and accessibility* (pp. 129-135). ACM.

[24] Laberge, J. C., & Scialfa, C. T. (2005). Predictors of Web navigation performance in a life span sample of adults. *Human Factors: The Journal of the Human Factors and Ergonomics Society, 47*(2), 289-302.

[25] McDonald, S., & Stevenson, R. J. (1998). Effects of text structure and prior knowledge of the learner on navigation in hypertext. *Human Factors: The Journal of the Human Factors and Ergonomics Society, 40*(1), 18-27.

[26] O'brien, M. A., Rogers, W. A., & Fisk, A. D. (2012). Understanding age and technology experience differences in use of prior knowledge for everyday technology interactions. *ACM Transactions on Accessible Computing (TACCESS), 4*(2), 9.

[27] Ofcom 2013. *Adults' media use and attitudes report.*

[28] Sandelancls, L. E., & Buckner, G. C. (1989). Of art and work: Aesthetic experience and the psychology of work feelings. *Research in organizational behavior, 100*, l05-l3l.

[29] Sharit, J., Hernández, M. A., Czaja, S. J., & Pirolli, P. (2008). Investigating the roles of knowledge and cognitive abilities in older adult information seeking on the web. *ACM Transactions on Computer-Human Interaction (TOCHI), 15*(1), 3.

[30] Sharit, J., Hernandez, M. A., Nair, S. N., Kuhn, T., & Czaja, S. J. (2011). Health problem solving by older persons using a complex government web site: Analysis and implications for web design. *ACM Transactions on Accessible Computing (TACCESS), 3*(3), 11.

[31] Trewin, S., Richards, J. T., Hanson, V. L., Sloan, D., John, B. E., Swart, C., & Thomas, J. C. (2012, October). Understanding the role of age and fluid intelligence in information search. In *Proceedings of the 14th international ACM SIGACCESS conference on Computers and accessibility* (pp. 119-126). ACM.

[32] Schaik, P. V., & Ling, J. (2012). An experimental analysis of experiential and cognitive variables in web navigation. *Human–Computer Interaction, 27*(3), 199-234.

[33] Webster, J., & Ahuja, J. S. (2006). Enhancing the design of web navigation systems: the influence of user disorientation on engagement and performance.*MIS Quarterly*, 661-678.

[34] Westerman, S. J., Davies, D. R., Glendon, A. I., Stammers, R. B., & Matthews, G. (1995). Age and cognitive ability as predictors of computerized information retrieval. *Behaviour & Information Technology, 14*(5), 313-326.

The Gest-Rest: A Pressure-Sensitive Chairable Input Pad for Power Wheelchair Armrests

Patrick Carrington[1], Amy Hurst[1], Shaun K. Kane[1,2]

[1] UMBC
1000 Hilltop Circle
Baltimore, MD USA 21250
{carpat1, amyhurst}@umbc.edu

[2] Department of Computer Science
University of Colorado Boulder
Boulder, CO 80309 USA
shaun.kane@colorado.edu

ABSTRACT

Interacting with touch screen-based computing devices can be difficult for individuals with mobility impairments that affect their hands, arms, neck, or head. These problems may be especially difficult for power wheelchair users, as the frame of their wheelchair may obstruct the users' range of motion and reduce their ability to reach objects in the environment. The concept of *chairable input devices* refers to input devices that are designed to fit with the form of an individual's wheelchair, much like wearable technology fits with an individual's clothing. In this paper, we introduce a new chairable input device, the Gest-Rest, which provides a pressure-sensitive input surface that fits over a standard power wheelchair armrest. The Gest-Rest enables users to perform traditional touch screen gestures, such as press and flick, as well as pressure-based gestures such as squeezing and punching. The Gest-Rest enables multiple inputs, unlike most switches, and does not substantially change the shape of the wheelchair armrest. We present a formative evaluation in which nine wheelchair users and three clinicians tested multiple gestures using the Gest-Rest prototype, and provided recommendations for integrating the Gest-Rest with computing applications. Our study showed that our motor impaired participants were each able to perform multiple gestures using the prototype, but had some difficulty with the pre-set sensitivity settings, and would thus benefit from a more robust gesture recognizer.

Categories and Subject Descriptors

K.4.2 [**Social Issues**]: Assistive technologies for persons with disabilities

General Terms

Design, Human Factors

Keywords

Power Wheelchair; Mobile Computing; Accessibility; Pressure Input; Chairable; Touch; Gesture; Input.

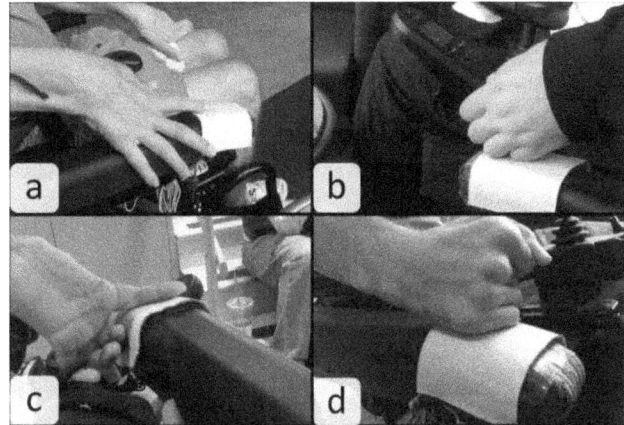

Figure 1. The Gest-Rest is a prototype, pressure sensitive interaction platform for power wheelchair users. Each image shows a power wheelchair user with a different hand pose performing a swipe gesture.

1. INTRODUCTION

Interacting with computing devices can be difficult due to mobility impairments that affect hands, arms, neck, and head of power wheelchair users. The wheelchair's frame can cause physical obstructions to the user's range of motion and their ability to reach different objects in the environment. Accessing devices can be difficult and may require assistance from others. Previous work has identified opportunities to design inputs and outputs for power wheelchair users. Many custom solutions draw unwanted attention to the individual, leading wheelchair users to choose mainstream devices, even if they do not provide appropriate accessibility features. Because touch screen devices may be difficult to hold or reach, power wheelchair users must often purchase adaptive equipment or learn workarounds in order to use their devices [1]. The concept of *chairable input devices* refers to input devices that are designed to fit with the form of an individual's wheelchair, much like wearable technology fits with an individual's clothing [3].

Building on design principles identified in our previous work [3], we present the Gest-Rest (Figure 1), a pressure sensitive input device for touch and gesture input on a wheelchair armrest. The Gest-Rest was designed for power wheelchair users to support interaction with mobile computing devices. The Gest-Rest supports traditional touch screen gestures such as tapping and swiping as well as new pressure-based gestures. Pressure provides benefits over traditional touch screen interfaces by supporting more expressive input while preserving a familiar, touch-based interaction pattern [2].

In this paper, we introduce the Gest-Rest and demonstrate its ability to capture touch and gesture input. We designed a set of 26 hand- and finger-based gestures that could be performed on an armrest, which we evaluated with nine wheelchair users and three therapists. We present our participants' preferred gestures, their suggestions for new gestures, and their ideas for applications of this technology. We also report on usability challenges encountered when using the prototype and identify next steps for bringing pressure sensitive input to power wheelchairs.

2. RELATED WORK

2.1 Switch-Based Computer Input

People with motor impairments, including power wheelchair users, commonly adopt input based on physical switches. These switches may come in a variety of sizes and materials, and may be placed in various locations, including near the user's hands, elbows, shoulders, feet, or head [5]. Because different switches may require different levels of pressure, switches must be selected to be actuated at the level of pressure appropriate to a specific user The versatility of switches allows them to be used when an individual cannot effectively interact with a keyboard, mouse, or touch screen. While there are alternative inputs, such as speech or eye gaze, the focus of this work is on physical inputs.

Typically, switches are mechanically actuated, and the simplest switches support only one function. More complex switches may provide multiple integrated controls but require the user to have greater dexterity. Switch inputs are usually mapped to a single keyboard key when connected to a PC. Because switch users are often only able to activate a small number of switches, the user interface must be designed to support a limited number of inputs. Such interfaces may use an array of switches for directional controls, or may use scanning-based input (*e.g.,* [11]*).*

Switches are a versatile form of input and can support users with various levels of ability. However, as mechanical devices, switches are often limited in their ability to support different types of input from the user. This can limit the user's ability to provide input to their computing devices. Thus, we have explored the use of variable pressure and gestures to provide more expressive input and to support multiple interactions within limited space.

2.2 Accessible Touch and Gesture

The proliferation of touch screen-based devices has provided new types of input that can support users with varying abilities. However, touch screen user interfaces present accessibility challenges for some individuals with motor impairments, as using a touch screen effectively often requires precise control of the user's hand movements.

Significant past research has explored touch screen use by individuals with motor impairments. Guerreiro et al. [10] explored touch screen use and tapping performance for people with motor impairments. Of the gestures they tested tapping was the most preferred and one of the most effective for selecting targets. Trewin *et al.* [18] evaluated the usability of multi-touch gestures on smartphone touch screens for people with mobility impairments. They found that several multi-touch gestures on mobile touch screens, especially three- and four- finger gestures, were difficult for users to perform. Time sensitive gestures were also difficult for users to perform. Anthony et al. [1] analyzed YouTube videos recorded by individuals with motor impairments in which they demonstrated their use of touch screen devices. These videos demonstrated the wide variety of hand poses and adaptive technologies used by people with motor impairments

when operating touch screen-based devices. Numerous examples in this data set involved adaptations to make the device easier to reach. Thus, in designing appropriate input for users with upper body mobility impairments it is important to design gestures that can be actuated with different hand poses, and to ensure the interaction surface is easy to reach even for users with limited mobility. Our research explores devices that can be installed within the user's reach and activated using a variety of hand movements.

Researchers have also explored alternative gestures for touch screen users with motor impairments. EdgeWrite [21] added a physical template around a touchpad, enabling users with impaired motor ability to accurately draw gestures representing letters by dragging a stylus along the physical edge of the template. Barrier Pointing [8] extended the idea of navigating along the physical edge of a device in order to accurately select menu items with a stylus. Swabbing [19] is a selection technique that makes it easier to select on-screen targets for users with tremor. While touch screen performance can be improved through alternative selection techniques, there are some aspects of the touch screen devices themselves, such as the sensitivity of capacitive touch screens and the difficulty moving and positioning touch screen devices, which may generate problems for users with motor impairments. For these reasons, we have chosen to explore alternative form factors for interactive touch-based user interfaces.

2.3 Pressure-Sensitive Input

Pressure sensitive input devices, which record both the position and force of a touch, enable an additional dimension to touch interactions without changing the size of the input device [17], Different levels of pressure can be mapped to different functions, so that pressing softly in one area can trigger a different action than pressing firmly in the same area. Mandalapu et al. [12] explored the use of touch with varying pressure as an alternative to multi-touch gestures, specifically for the task of zooming. They found that pressure input was not only a suitable alternative but it was also faster than the traditional two-finger pinch gesture. Wilson, Brewster, and Halvey [20] explored the use of one handed pressure input by adding force sensors to the back of a mobile phone. They were able to demonstrate the potential for increasing the input options provided by a single sensor by assigning functions to different levels of pressure. Rendl et al. [14] explored users' ability to accurately perform multi-touch gestures while applying different levels of pressure and found that users could accurately reproduce at two different levels of pressure (soft *vs.* hard).

Since many individuals with motor impairments have a limited range of hand motion, supporting multiple levels of pressure could enable these individuals to provide more expressive input in a small space. Furthermore, individuals with motor impairments often have reduced strength or mobility in their hands. Varying the pressure required to perform a gesture could therefore enable these users to perform more gestures correctly and perform fewer accidental gestures.

2.4 The Chair as a Command Center

Prior projects have augmented traditional office chairs with sensors to enable users to control devices by interacting with the chair. The Internet Chair [4] added orientation sensors to a chair, so that spatial audio could adapt to the user's current orientation. The ChairMouse [6] used the position and orientation of an office chair to manipulate a cursor on large display. Moving the chair would move the cursor. This technique allows the user to navigate the larger display environment more quickly by turning the chair toward the desired position on the screen. Probst *et al.* [13] explored the design and use of office chair gestures that enabled control of computer applications by moving the chair.

The SenseChair [7] was an intelligent assistive lounge chair for older adults. There are sensors embedded around the chair to allow users to explicitly interact and convey their intentions. The chair captures information about the user's behavior and responds with information via ambient displays or other notifications. The SenseChair was used to explore the idea of the chair as a "command center" for the home. Forlizzi *et al.* found that elders placed important objects around the lounge chair that they would need to interact with throughout the day. We aim to extend the idea of the chair as a "command center" to the power wheelchair, enabling users to control their environment through interactions with their wheelchair.

3. DEVELOPMENT OF THE GEST-REST

In this paper, we introduce the Gest-Rest, a prototype of a pressure-sensitive armrest for power wheelchairs (Figure 1). The Gest-Rest enables users to perform hand and finger gestures directly on the armrest of their power wheelchair. The Gest-Rest is pressure sensitive, so that gestures can react not only to the location of a touch, but pressure (*e.g.,* differentiating between a soft push and a firm punch). Furthermore, since individuals with motor impairments have varying levels of strength and control, the pressure-sensing input can be customized to the user.

The Gest-Rest is designed to be a *chairable technology* [3]. Our previous study explored desirable form factors for accessible computing devices with 13 power wheelchair users and 30 clinicians. We discussed different possible form factors for input on the power wheelchair. Participants stated that they preferred technology form factors that could be worn on the body or integrated with the wheelchair, especially the armrests. We coined the term chairable technology to describe technological devices that were integrated with a wheelchair form factor.

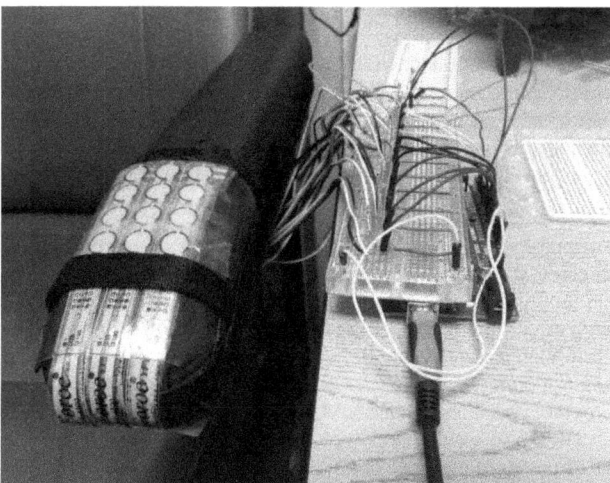

Figure 2. Prototype Hardware. 12 Flexiforce FSRs arranged in a grid attached to the wheelchair armrest. (left) The sensors are connected to an Arduino (right), which outputs information via USB. When assembled, the electronics fit under the armrest, it has been disassembled for this photo.

3.1 Hardware

The Gest-Rest consists of a pressure-sensitive overlay that can be placed on a power wheelchair armrest, where it can easily be reached; even by users with limited mobility. The Gest-Rest consists of a 3 × 4 array of FlexiForce A201 Force Sensitive Resistors (FSRs) embedded in a fabric "sleeve" (Figure 2). The sensor area measures approximately 5cm × 8cm. Each sensor is wired in parallel and connected to an analog input on an Arduino Mega ADK board through a 15K ohm resistor. The Arduino is connected to a laptop through USB. The cost of the materials for the prototype device cost around US$240. The Gest-Rest attaches to a wheelchair armrest using adhesive tape, but can be installed on most standard wheelchair armrests. We built the prototype using the armrest from an Invacare Pronto M91 power wheelchair.

3.2 Software

The Gest-Rest prototype hardware is controlled by an Arduino application. This application measures the state of each sensor and passes it to the computer via USB. We created a second application in the Processing programming language to visualize the pressure applied to each sensor and to log the sensor values and timestamp every 30ms.

While the Gest-Rest hardware could support a wide variety of motions and gestures at varying pressures, we developed a very simple recognizer for our prototype evaluation. The gesture recognizer accepts tap or press gestures, as well as directional gestures in four directions. The gesture recognizer determines which gesture has been performed by comparing the center point of the pressure at the start of the gesture to the center point at the end of the gesture. The center point is calculated using the geometric "center of mass" of the touches. This simple recognizer is not able to differentiate between a large set of gestures, but was useful in demonstrating the use of the Gest-Rest as an input device.

3.3 Gesture Set Design

The array of pressure sensors used by the Gest-Rest may enable additional gestures beyond standard touch screen gestures, such as soft and hard presses. Furthermore, the shape of the armrest may afford different gestures than a touch screen, such as squeezing the edge of the armrest. We identified a set of 21 gestures, based on existing gesture sets for touch screen devices [22], which could be used on an interactive armrest. These gestures include standard tap or press gestures and directional swipes. We tested an additional five, force-sensitive, gestures designed specifically for an armrest interface. These gestures are all location independent and may be performed anywhere on the surface. They may also be performed at varying levels of pressure.

The set was divided into three categories 1) Tap or Press Gestures, 2) Directional Gestures, and 3) Pressure-Based Gestures. We did not include multi-finger gestures in this initial set, as they are often difficult to perform for individuals with motor impairments [18], but we may include these gestures in a future version of the prototype.

3.3.1 Tap or Press Gestures

Tap or press gestures could be performed anywhere on the surface and did not require the user to move their hand once they pressed down on the surface. There were six gestures in this category.

Tap or Press. Taps and presses were treated similarly across the surface of the device. We tested *single press, double press,* and *triple press* gestures.

Press and Hold. We implemented *short, medium,* and *long press and hold* gestures with durations of one, three, and ten seconds, respectively.

3.3.2 Directional Gestures

We based these gestures on traditional directional gestures (*e.g.,* swipe and flick), but participants were able to use any part of their hand or arm to perform this gesture. These gestures could be performed in the cardinal or diagonal directions. We identified different gesture "types" based on the duration of the gesture. For directional gestures we allowed users to define the timing for each type of gesture.

Flick. This gesture was defined as a quick sharp motion in the given direction after pressing down on the surface.

Swipe. Sliding the hand or finger across the surface in the given direction.

Drag. The drag gestures were similar to slides however they were performed slower across the surface in the given directions.

3.3.3 Pressure-Based Gestures

These gestures were designed to use the pressure sensing capability of the Gest-Rest. They involved pressure applied by the whole hand, arm, or wrist. There were five gestures in this category.

Squeeze. To perform this gesture the user needed to grip the outside edges of the armrest and squeeze, then release.

Roll. To perform this gesture the user places the hand or wrist on the surface and rolling left or right then lift off.

Punch. To perform this gesture the user punched the surface.

Lift. To perform this gesture the user would just lift their hand or arm from a rest position.

Rock. This gesture was similar to the roll gesture; however, in this case, a user is expected to roll the hand or arm left and right multiple times before lifting off of the surface.

4. EVALUATING THE GEST-REST

To understand which types of gestures would work best on an interactive wheelchair armrest, we conducted a formative usability study with wheelchair users to try various gestures on the Gest-Rest. Participants were asked to use the Gest-Rest to perform the preliminary set of gestures, evaluate their ease of use, and to complete a selection task using the basic gesture recognizer.

4.1 Participants

We recruited nine power wheelchair users to participate in this study. As our prototype was designed primarily for power wheelchair users, the majority of our participants (seven of nine) were power wheelchair users. We included 2 manual wheelchair users (P5 and P8) to see whether this prototype would be useful for manual wheelchair users, who typically have greater upper body mobility. Participants were recruited from a local spinal cord injury clinic. All nine participants were male, and ranged in age from 18 to 47 (mean=28.44, SD=9).

We also recruited three clinicians: one physical therapist (PT) and two occupational therapists (OTs). Therapists did not perform the gesture evaluation task, but took part in a group interview session. We included clinicians in our evaluation because we previously observed that PTs and OTs provided feedback that complemented that of wheelchair users [3]. T1 participated in an interview alone, while T2 and T3 were interviewed together. Participant information can be found in Tables 1 and 2.

Table 1. Wheelchair users that participated in our formative usability evaluation.

PID	Age	Age/Sex	Wheelchair Type
P1	28	M	Power
P2	28	M	Power
P3	23	M	Power
P4	21	M	Power
P5	37	M	Manual
P6	47	M	Power
P7	31	M	Power
P8	23	M	Manual
P9	18	M	Power

Table 2. Therapists that participated in our group interview session.

TID	Sex	Title
T1	F	Occupational Therapist
T2	F	Physical Therapist
T3	F	Occupational Therapist

4.2 Procedure and Task Overview

We followed slightly different protocols for our wheelchair participants and our clinicians. We describe the tasks and procedures used for each user group below.

4.2.1 Procedure for Wheelchair Users

Participants first completed a brief questionnaire about their background and their use of technology. Next, participants were given a brief introduction to the Gest-Rest and were able to try it out. We attached our armrest to a stand and positioned it next to participants' wheelchairs in the position of their existing armrest. Participants performed three study tasks using the Gest-Rest prototype. The study session took approximately one hour.

Gesture Rating Task. During this task, each participant attempted each gesture in the set at least three times. For directional gestures, each gesture was performed in the four cardinal directions and one diagonal direction. After completing the gesture, the participant rated the difficulty of performing the gesture on a scale of one to five (*very easy, slightly easy, neutral, slightly difficult, very difficult*). Participants were encouraged to provide verbal explanations for their ratings. Participants first tested the press/tap and directional gestures, then tested the pressure-based gestures, but did not provide numerical ratings for the pressure-based gestures.

Because our basic gesture recognizer did not support a wide range of gestures, the gestures in this task were performed with visual feedback only (Figure 3), and did not control a user interface. Participants were given an opportunity to test the Gest-Rest interactively during the selection task.

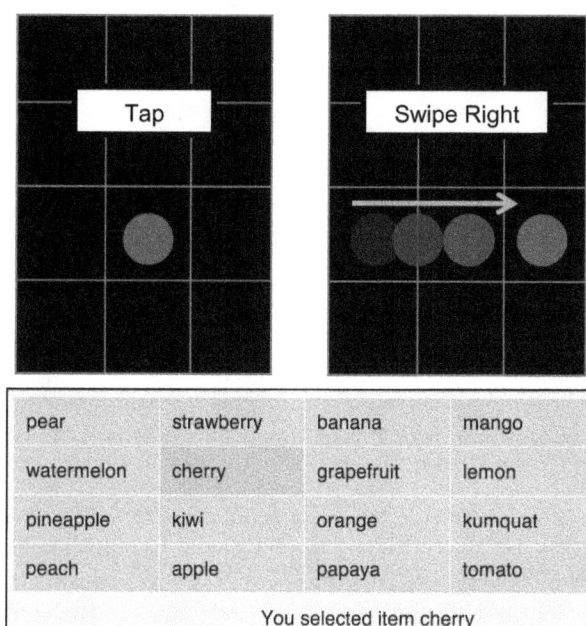

Figure 3. (Top) Representation of the visualization interface. The blue circle represents the touch point location on the sensor grid. For directional gestures, the blue circle would track across the grid. (Bottom) Menu interface for the selection task. The interface is navigated using single swipes in the four directions. An item is selected from the list by pressing.

Selection Task. Participants next tested the Gest-Rest in an interactive scenario. Participants were presented with a 2-dimensional menu interface, similar in layout to some switch-based user interfaces (Figure 3). The menu contained a list of names of fruits. Participants were asked to select a few of their favorites from the list using directional swipes (up, down, left, and right) to move and a press to select. Participants were encouraged to think aloud during this task.

Gesture Invention Task. After completing the gesture and selection task we asked participants to generate ideas for new gestures that used the Gest-Rest. Participants also provided general feedback about the design of the Gest-Rest and its potential uses for everyday computing tasks.

4.2.2 Procedure for Therapists

Therapists were first introduced to the Gest-Rest prototype and given a description of the gesture set. Therapists had an opportunity to test gestures using the prototype, but did not complete the full gesture rating activity. The therapists discussed provided feedback about various gestures in the gesture set, and discussed potential benefits and obstacles that might occur when using this device. Therapists also provided feedback about the usefulness of Gest-Rest for participants with varying levels of motor ability.

5. FINDINGS

All of our wheelchair users were able to use the Gest-Rest to perform gestures in each of the three tasks, although some participants had difficulty with specific gestures.

5.1 Gesture Feedback

Overall, manual wheelchair users rated all of the gestures as easy to perform, while power wheelchair users showed more diversity reflecting the difficulty they experienced with different gestures. We asked participants to elaborate on the difficulty ratings they assigned to each gesture in the set. Participants identified a few challenges that made some gestures more difficult to perform: identifying appropriate pressure and individual differences in ability.

Identifying appropriate pressure. The seven power wheelchair users who participated in the study all expressed uncertainty about how much pressure was needed to perform a gesture correctly. While gestures produced in the gesture task were not passed on to the gesture recognizer, participants saw the visual feedback from the sensors as visualized on the computer screen. Although the sensors could detect very light pressure, this was not always visible on the screen. Some participants were unsure whether they were pressing firmly enough for the sensors to register their contact. Although participants were told not to worry about the visual feedback and to simply perform the gestures as they normally would, some participants remained concerned. When confronted with the lack of visual feedback, some participants attempted to apply more pressure to generate the visual feedback, which was more difficult, while others simply rated the gesture as more difficult since they felt it did not register their input. We can address this concern in future prototypes by dynamically adjusting the sensitivity of the Gest-Rest, or perhaps by simply hiding the visual feedback and only providing feedback when a gesture has been completed.

Individual differences in ability. Participants who used power wheelchairs expressed particular difficulty with certain directions or the duration of gestures. For instance, P1 described that he had difficulty with gestures that required the application of a certain level of pressure over longer periods of time. P4 described having particular difficulty with gestures that were toward the left and up (forward) as these were moving further away from his body. These types of comments were common among our participants.

5.2 Selection Task Feedback

Seven of the nine participants completed the selection task. The two participants who did not complete this task (P1 and P9) needed to leave the study session early to prepare for therapy appointments or transportation. Of the seven who completed the navigation task, three found it easy to navigate and select items. Two experienced moderate difficulty (difficulty with a subset of gestures) and two found it very difficult to complete this task (not able to make desired selections).

In this task, participants relied upon the basic gesture recognizer to recognize their gestures. There were two primary difficulties encountered with the gesture recognizer. First, in some situations the participants were unable to press firmly enough to complete the gesture. Second, some participants failed to perform directional gestures correctly. Our gesture recognizer relied upon the heuristic of comparing the touch down point to the touch up point. However, some participants placed their hand on the surface, moved their hand in the direction they wished to gesture, and then rolled their hand back to the center position before lifting. In this case, our gesture recognizer incorrectly recognized a press gesture.

5.3 User-Invented Gestures

Following the selection task, participants were given an opportunity to suggest additional gestures that could be useful for an armrest touch pad. Most participants were comfortable with the gesture set we offered, and did not suggest additional gestures. However, four participants did offer additional gestures.

Edge Slide. P1 described having difficulty turning the display of his mobile devices on and off using the phone's power button, and requested a gesture on his armrest to perform that function. He suggested that sliding his hand along the edge of the Gest-Rest could toggle his phone display.

Rhythmic Tapping. P2 suggested the use of rhythmic tapping to perform different actions. He also suggested using various rhythms to authenticate his device or to input text.

Palm Swipe. P7 found it easier to use his perform gestures on the Gest-Rest using his palm than when using his finger, and suggested that this palm swiping could be an additional gesture. This was interesting since we made no specification of which part of the hand need be used to interact with the device. P7 had experience using touch screen devices, but after attempting the roll gesture thought it might be easier to use his palm to swipe instead of his fingers.

Drawing Letters. P8 suggested that he could perform actions by drawing letter shapes on the touchpad. Each letter could act as a shortcut for actions or applications. P8 was particularly interested in using these gestures for safety features, such as calling for help and sharing his location with emergency services.

5.4 Applications of the Gest-Rest

We asked participants to identify potential uses for the Gest-Rest. Power wheelchair users were especially interested in using this device as a command center to operate environmental controls (lights, fans, doors, etc.) around the home. Participants also mentioned using this device as an alternative for speech input as it would be always available to them without needing someone to set up the software.

Both of our manual wheelchair users (P5, P8) had full hand function and were able to perform all of the gestures in the set without difficulty. While they appreciated the ideas behind the prototype, they were less interested in using the device for themselves. Neither of them currently used armrests on their wheelchairs. Their reluctance may be in part due to the fact that most manual wheelchairs do not have a large armrest that could support the Gest-Rest.

5.5 Feedback on Form Factor

Participants liked that the Gest-Rest matched the shape of the armrest but wanted it to be even more closely integrated. The surface of the touchpad was raised a few millimeters above the top of the armrest, and participants preferred this to be flush with the armrest. Users suggested that, if possible, the Gest-Rest should be made out of, or covered with, the same material as the armrest itself. Since the type of armrests varied the desired material would also vary. Figure 4 shows examples of the different types of armrests our participants had. Although we only tested the prototype attached to one type of armrest, the design of the prototype allows for flexibility and the adhesive would allow the device to conform to other armrest shapes.

5.6 Feedback from Clinicians

Our clinicians had a perspective that differed from the wheelchair users themselves, as they work with a diverse range of patients and can offer more general insights pertaining to the use of the Gest-Rest by people with diverse abilities. Their feedback addressed several broader themes.

Technology benefit and injury level. We asked therapists which types of individuals might benefit most from this type of device. Therapists agreed that this device would be most useful for people with moderate spinal injuries in which they had impaired hand movement (*e.g.,* C3–C5 injuries). Individuals with less severe injuries than C3 level would likely be able to use standard touch screen devices, unassisted. Individuals with more severe injuries than C5 level would likely lack the hand function to use a gesture-sensing armrest.

Form factor and feedback. Overall, therapists were pleased with the design of the device, but suggested some improvements. In particular, therapists suggested adding feedback mechanisms into the hardware, such as visual or vibrotactile feedback. These additions could be used to provide users with feedback about whether they were performing their gestures correctly.

Two therapists suggested replacing the current surface material, a vinyl, with a material with less friction. The therapists agreed that the design of the armrest could be improved by making the pressure sensors flush with the rest of the armrest, as the raised pressure sensors could cause unwanted friction when users rested their arms on it over long periods of time. Therapists also suggested a larger touch area, and a touch area with adjustable tilt, to accommodate users with varying ranges of motion.

Therapists also suggested that the pressure-sensitive Gest-Rest could be placed at different locations on the wheelchair, such as near the elbows and shoulders. These areas may be easier to interact with for individuals with lower hand and arm function.

Suggested applications and use cases. Therapists suggested that this device would be useful for access to many remote controlled appliances around the house. One therapist suggested it as an alternative to speech software solutions to provide access to keyboard and mouse functions on a PC. Therapists appreciated that the Gest-Rest could be used in addition to the traditional wheelchair joystick, as it would enable users to perform additional functions without having to switch modes on the device.

6. DISCUSSION

6.1 Chairable Pressure-Based Gestures

Participants in our study performed a set of 26 gestures using the Gest-Rest prototype. Participants in the study were able to perform all of the finger-based gestures, but some participants had difficulty performing the pressure-based gestures such as squeeze

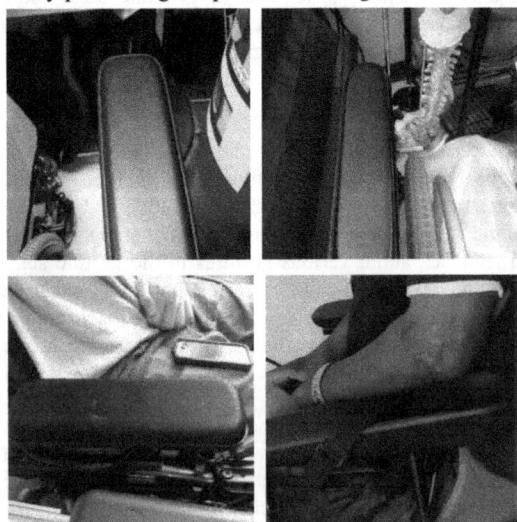

Figure 4. The length, width, and position of the armrests on our participants' current wheelchairs were diverse. The Gest-Rest could be attached to any of these armrests.

and roll. None of the power wheelchair users had the hand function to be able to squeeze the armrest. P1, P6, and P9 had difficulty performing the roll gesture because they had difficulty rotating their wrists. The punch gesture was easy to perform for all participants, but some participants were uncertain how much pressure to use. T1 and T3 noted that the downward pressure required to punch the armrest might be difficult for patients who have little muscular control in their lower arms, as they may rely upon their shoulder muscles to move their entire arm.

Our evaluation shows that pressure-based gestures could be a viable input option for many users with power wheelchairs. The ability to perform the gestures with varying levels of pressure has several benefits. The sensors are designed to measure different levels of pressure and are therefore more durable and flexible to harder presses. In contrast to other pressure-based interfaces, our aim is to utilize the different levels of pressure applied during natural interactions to understand more about how gestures might be performed by people with mobility impairments.

It is unclear how to indicate the start and end point of a directional gesture. Touch gestures on capacitive surfaces require discrete touch down and touch up interactions to start and end a gesture. With pressure gestures we have the freedom to adjust how the start and end of a gesture is performed using varying levels of pressure. Since the interface is an armrest it is important to allow the user to continue to use it normally and not as an input device. As we found from this study using a simple threshold level of pressure may not be enough to determine deliberate actions without making things more difficult for the user. We will likely need to develop a more robust gesture recognizer to support directional gestures with varying levels of pressure

6.2 From Switches to Gestures

Traditional switch interfaces can only have two states, on and off. With the Gest-Rest we can support simple state changes through taps and presses while adding the dimension of pressure. This design supports a number of advantages.

First, the Gest-Rest can support multiple interactions in a single area, even for individuals with motor impairments. Thus, a user may be able to replace two or more switches with a single pressure-sensitive Gest-Rest. This could enable a user to reclaim free space on his or her wheelchair, or to perform additional input that was not previously possible.

Second, a gesture-based input device like the Gest-Rest can enable users to perform familiar gestures on their own wheelchair. We were able to demonstrate familiar gestures that are typically performed on capacitive touch screen devices, which was appealing to both users and clinicians.

Third, our pressure-sensitive input enabled users to perform actions using multiple areas on their hands and arms. Most consumer touchscreen devices are designed to support interaction from the fingers only. Some power wheelchair users may lack fine motor control in their hands, and may be unable to perform finger-based gestures easily. To compensate, they may perform gestures using another part of their hand, such as the back or bottom of their clenched hand [1]. The Gest-Rest does not explicitly detect fingers, and instead relies only on pressure, enabling users to perform gestures with other parts of their hand or body.

Finally, using pressure as an element of input can provide advantages over other types of touch input. Users with limited strength may be unable to provide sufficient pressure to actuate a touch screen, or may be unable to lift their arm off of the touch screen. Using pressure as an element of input would enable users to actuate the screen with very little pressure, or even to perform gestures while resting their hand on the input surface, which is impossible with most current touch screen-based devices.

However, there may indeed be some drawbacks to replacing switch control with gesture control. A gesture-sensing input area may be less reliable than a simple switch. All participants in our formative user evaluation experienced some gesture recognition errors. While we were able to adjust the pressure sensitivity of the device, participants still experienced errors related to providing incorrect levels of pressure. Higher resolution sensing techniques such as those used by Rosenberg et al. for the Unmousepad [15], and Grau et al. [9], called Mechanical Force Redistribution (MFR), could be applied to our platform to improve performance. Our research confirms some of the limitations of resistive pressure sensing and highlights the need for high resolution sensing, specifically for use with wheelchair-based interactive surfaces.

7. FUTURE WORK

In the future, we intend to continue to develop the gesture recognition capabilities of the Gest-Rest. During this study we tested 26 gestures at least 3 times with nine participants, making a total of 702 attempts. We will use this data to begin creating a customizable gesture recognizer. These expressive gesture attempts can also allow us to generate user-defined gestures.

We will also explore the feasibility and acceptability of a larger sensing area and installing interaction surfaces on other parts of the body. The selected location for the prototype is just one of many possibilities. A few additional locations such as the elbow and shoulder area were suggested by participants in this study however, these do not comprise the complete list of potential locations for interaction on the wheelchair.

We would also like to explore the use of this type of interaction platform while driving a wheelchair, and for longer periods of time for everyday use situations. Participants interacted continuously with the device for approximately 45 minutes during the study; however, it is difficult to determine how this device would actually be used in everyday situations, and whether the device would interfere with other activities of daily living.

We have identified several potential applications for this device that could improve access to other computing devices; however, there may be features or use cases where this device may become inaccessible to users. More research on extended use scenarios is needed to understand and identify situations where using this device is not appropriate or inaccessible.

8. CONCLUSION

There are many opportunities to design user interfaces for people with power wheelchairs. In this paper we presented the Gest-Rest, a platform to support touch and gesture interactions on the wheelchair armrest. We explored the use of pressure-sensitive input and demonstrated its feasibility as an alternative to switch-based and multi-touch interaction for power wheelchair users. We evaluated this prototype with nine power wheelchair users and three clinicians and identified important design and interaction considerations including hardware and software requirements.

9. ACKNOWLEDGMENTS

We thank our participants, the International Center for Spinal Cord Injury at the Kennedy Krieger Institute, Caroline Galbraith, and members of the UMBC Prototyping and Design Lab. This work was partially funded by Microsoft and Nokia.

10. REFERENCES

[1] Anthony, L., Kim, Y., and Findlater, L. 2013. Analyzing user-generated YouTube videos to understand touchscreen use by people with motor impairments. In *Proceedings of the SIGCHI Conference on Human Factors in Computing Systems* (CHI '13) (pp. 1223-1232). ACM.

[2] Buxton, W., Hill, R., and Rowley, P. 1985. Issues and techniques in touch-sensitive tablet input. *ACM SIGGRAPH Computer Graphics*, 19(3), 215-224.

[3] Carrington, P., Hurst, A., and Kane, S.K. 2014. Wearables and chairables: inclusive design of mobile input and output techniques for power wheelchair users. In *Proceedings of the SIGCHI Conference on Human Factors in Computing Systems* (CHI '14) (pp.3103-3112). ACM

[4] Cohen, M. 2003. The internet chair. International Journal of Human-Computer Interaction, 15(2), 297-311.

[5] Cook, A. M., and Polgar, J. M. 2013. Cook and Hussey's assistive technologies: principles and practice. Elsevier Health Sciences.

[6] Endert, A., Fiaux, P., Chung, H., Stewart, M., Andrews, C., and North, C. 2011. ChairMouse: leveraging natural chair rotation for cursor navigation on large, high-resolution displays. In *CHI'11 Extended Abstracts on Human Factors in Computing Systems* (pp. 571-580). ACM.

[7] Forlizzi, J., DiSalvo, C., Zimmerman, J., Mutlu, B., and Hurst, A. 2005. The SenseChair: The lounge chair as an intelligent assistive device for elders. In *Proceedings of the 2005 conference on Designing for User eXperience*. AIGA: American Institute of Graphic Arts.

[8] Froehlich, J., Wobbrock, J. O., and Kane, S. K. 2007. Barrier pointing: using physical edges to assist target acquisition on mobile device touch screens. In *Proceedings of the 9th international ACM SIGACCESS conference on Computers and accessibility* (pp. 19-26). ACM.

[9] Grau, A. M., Hendee, C., Rizzo, J. R., and Perlin, K. 2014. Mechanical force redistribution: enabling seamless, large-format, high-accuracy surface interaction. In *Proceedings of the 32nd annual ACM conference on Human factors in computing systems* (pp. 4137-4146). ACM.

[10] Guerreiro, T., Nicolau, H., Jorge, J., and Gonçalves, D. 2010. Towards accessible touch interfaces. In *Proceedings of the 12th international ACM SIGACCESS conference on Computers and accessibility* (pp. 19-26). ACM.

[11] Mackenzie, I. S., and Felzer, T. 2010. SAK: Scanning ambiguous keyboard for efficient one-key text entry. *ACM Transactions on Computer-Human Interaction (TOCHI)*, 17(3).

[12] Mandalapu, D., and Subramanian, S. 2011. Exploring pressure as an alternative to multi-touch based interaction. In *Proceedings of the 3rd International Conference on Human Computer Interaction* (pp. 88-92). ACM.

[13] Probst, K., Lindlbauer, D., Haller, M., Schwartz, B., and Schrempf, A. 2014. A chair as ubiquitous input device: exploring semaphoric chair gestures for focused and peripheral interaction. In *Proceedings of the 32nd annual ACM conference on Human factors in computing systems* (pp. 4097-4106). ACM.

[14] Rendl, C., Greindl, P., Probst, K., Behrens, M., and Haller, M. 2014. Presstures: exploring pressure-sensitive multi-touch gestures on trackpads. In *Proceedings of the 32nd annual ACM conference on Human factors in computing systems* (pp. 431-434). ACM.

[15] Rosenberg, I., and Perlin, K. 2009. The UnMousePad: an interpolating multi-touch force-sensing input pad. In *ACM Transactions on Graphics (TOG)* (Vol. 28, No. 3). ACM.

[16] Roudaut, A., Lecolinet, E., and Guiard, Y. 2009. MicroRolls: expanding touch-screen input vocabulary by distinguishing rolls vs. slides of the thumb. In *Proceedings of the SIGCHI Conference on Human Factors in Computing Systems* (pp. 927-936). ACM.

[17] Stewart, C., Rohs, M., Kratz, S., and Essl, G. 2010. Characteristics of pressure-based input for mobile devices. In *Proceedings of the SIGCHI Conference on Human Factors in Computing Systems* (pp. 801-810). ACM.

[18] Trewin, S., Swart, C., and Pettick, D. 2013. Physical accessibility of touchscreen smartphones. In *Proceedings of the 15th International ACM SIGACCESS Conference on Computers and Accessibility*. ACM.

[19] Wacharamanotham, C., Hurtmanns, J., Mertens, A., Kronenbuerger, M., Schlick, C., and Borchers, J. 2011. Evaluating swabbing: a touchscreen input method for elderly users with tremor. In *Proceedings of the SIGCHI Conference on Human Factors in Computing Systems* (pp. 623-626). ACM.

[20] Wilson, G., Brewster, S., and Halvey, M. 2013. Towards utilising one-handed multi-digit pressure input. In *CHI'13 Extended Abstracts on Human Factors in Computing Systems* (pp. 1317-1322). ACM.

[21] Wobbrock, J. O., Myers, B. A., Aung, H. H., LoPresti, E. F. 2004. Text entry from power wheelchairs: EdgeWrite for joysticks and touchpads. In *ACM SIGACCESS Accessibility and Computing* (No. 77-78, pp. 110-117). ACM.

[22] Wu, M. and Balakrishnan, R. 2003. Multi-finger and whole hand gestural interaction techniques for multi-user tabletop displays. In *Proceedings of the 16th annual ACM symposium on User interface software and technology* (pp. 193-202). ACM.

Accessibility in Context: Understanding the Truly Mobile Experience of Smartphone Users with Motor Impairments

Maia Naftali and Leah Findlater
Inclusive Design Lab I HCIL
College of Information Studies
University of Maryland, College Park, MD
maia.naftali@gmail.com, leahkf@umd.edu

ABSTRACT

Lab-based studies on touchscreen use by people with motor impairments have identified both positive and negative impacts on accessibility. Little work, however, has moved beyond the lab to investigate the truly *mobile* experiences of users with motor impairments. We conducted two studies to investigate how smartphones are being used on a daily basis, what activities they enable, and what contextual challenges users are encountering. The first study was a small online survey with 16 respondents. The second study was much more in depth, including an initial interview, two weeks of diary entries, and a 3-hour contextual session that included neighborhood activities. Four expert smartphone users participated in the second study and we used a case study approach for analysis. Our findings highlight the ways in which smartphones are enabling everyday activities for people with motor impairments, particularly in overcoming physical accessibility challenges in the real world and supporting writing and reading. We also identified important situational impairments, such as the inability to retrieve the phone while in transit, and confirmed many lab-based findings in the real-world setting. We present design implications and directions for future work.

Categories and Subject Descriptors

K.4.2 [Computers and society]: Social issues—*assistive technologies for persons with disabilities*

General Terms

Design, Human Factors.

Keywords

Accessibility; mobile; assistive devices; smartphones; contextual interviews; case study.

1. INTRODUCTION

The vast majority of research on mobile accessibility for people with motor impairments has focused on controlled lab settings. These studies have shown, for example, that users with motor impairments make more errors than users without impairments [9], are slower, and—for users with *gross* motor impairments—exhibit longer dwell times [14]. Another common challenge is the difficulty of multitouch gestures [14,24]. Early solutions with PDAs and styli employed the raised bezel of the device or a physical overlay to guide the user's input [10,26], physical features that are not available on today's smartphones. More recent recommendations highlight specific target sizes for users

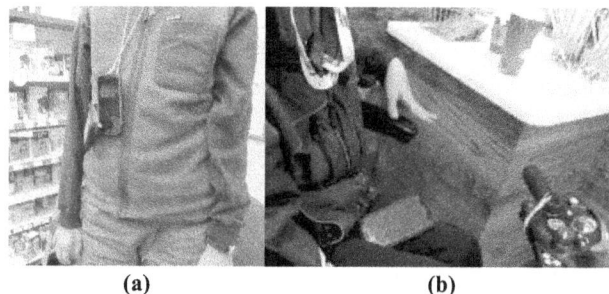

Figure 1. Two study participants in the contextual sessions: (a) phone is hanging by a lanyard around the neck, and (b) phone is on the lap.

with quadriplegia (12mm) [13], and the utility of sliding rather than tapping to reduce input errors for users with tremor [25].

Yet, little is known about the *truly mobile* experiences of smartphone and tablet users with motor impairments: How are such devices being integrated on a daily basis into activities such as communication, transit, and shopping? What challenges arise in a mobile context that affect how devices are being adopted, such as the ability to use a smartphone in a busy café or on the street? What activities have smartphones enabled that were previously difficult or even impossible? Perhaps the closest study to answering these questions comes from Kane *et al.* [15], who conducted an interview and diary study on the use of mobile devices that included eight participants with motor impairments; however, smartphones had only recently emerged and only one motor-impaired participant owned one. Their findings highlight the accessibility challenges of mobile devices (largely pre-smartphone), the impact of mobile devices on independence, and the general importance of making mainstream devices accessible. While Anthony *et al.*'s [1] more recent observational study of YouTube videos provides some insight into smartphone and tablet use by people with motor impairments, only 2% of their data included a context outside of the home, school, work, or hospital.

In this paper, we investigate smartphone use by people with motor impairments in a mobile context, primarily outside of the home, through an online survey with 16 participants and multi-method case studies with four expert smartphone users (Figure 1). Both the survey and the case studies compared use of smartphones *in* versus *out* of the home, the activities that smartphones enable, and the accessibility challenges participants encounter. The case studies further included three components: a 30-minute initial interview, a two-week diary study, and, finally, a three-hour contextual session that included neighborhood activities during which participants used the phone.

The contributions of this paper include: (1) Characterizing how smartphones are enabling everyday activities for people with motor impairments, particularly in overcoming physical accessibility challenges in the real world, and supporting writing and reading. (2) Extending work on situational impairments and people with disabilities [15] to more explicitly address the needs of people with motor impairments—for example, the at times extreme difficulty of retrieving the phone while in transit. (3) Confirming the real-world impact of challenges previously documented in the lab (e.g. [24]), particularly in acquiring small targets and inputting and correcting text. Finally, we present design implications and directions for future work. These results should be of interest to mobile application designers and accessibility researchers who wish to enhance future mobile computing for motor-impaired users.

2. RELATED WORK

We cover studies of mobile adoption and touchscreen interaction for users with motor impairments, and general findings on mobile adoption and situational impairments.

2.1 Accessibility of Touchscreen Input

Mobile devices can increase independence [15] and a sense of empowerment [1] for users with motor impairments. Anthony et al. [1] analyzed how users with physical disabilities operate and adapt mobile devices such as tablets and smartphones, finding that, despite challenges, many users were able to use mainstream touchscreen devices and considered them to be empowering. Touchscreen input also offers the advantage that it requires less strength to use compared to physical buttons [12]. At the same time, many basic touchscreen interactions have proven difficult or in some cases impossible [1,3,9,10,14,16,24,25] For instance, Guerreiro et al. [13] measured the accuracy of tapping, crossing, exiting and directional gesturing operations with users with tetraplegia, finding that targets located at the bottom of the screen and next to the preferred hand were the easiest to select. As for multi-touch gestures, Trewin et al. [24] found that users with motor impairments encountered difficulties in pinching and performing three-finger slides (confirming [1]). Finally, for some users with motor impairments touchscreens are not just difficult but impossible to use [3]. While our research focuses on more holistic questions of mobile device use and adoption, we confirm and extend several of these basic input findings outside of the lab.

2.2 Use and Adoption of Mobile Devices

While not in the context of accessibility, many studies have focused on mobile device use and information needs, including diary studies similar to our own (e.g. [5,20,23]). Sohn et al. [23], for example, found that the context of use significantly influences mobile information needs and that less essential needs are often put off until later. More closely related to our work is a study by Kane et al. [15] that included interviews and a week of diary entries by people with visual and motor impairments. Their design recommendations included the need to support accessibility of mainstream devices, the importance of configurability, and the potential for contextual adaptation; however, as mentioned in the Introduction, only one of the eight motor-impaired participants used a smartphone, which are today widely adopted and are the focus of our study. Moreover, we complement the diary and interview methods with a survey and in situ observations to provide a richer characterization of problems encountered in mobile settings. Our focus on mainstream mobile devices is also inspired by Shinohara and Wobbrock's work on stigma [22].

2.3 Situational Impairments

Situational impairments brought on by contextual factors can affect how users interact with a device, such as lighting, glare, noise, rain, weather [21]. These factors are particularly relevant with mobile computing. Research with users without motor impairments has shown that input is particularly challenging when the user is in motion, reducing input speed and increasing errors [11,16,17,18,28]. Mobile devices can also impact the user's ability to read information, with motion affecting text legibility [14] and reading comprehension [2]. For users with visual and motor impairments, Kane et al. [15] identified crowded spaces, lighting and weather, walking, and interruptions as contextual factors impacting mobile device use; however, the findings emphasized experiences of visually impaired participants, with only one explicit reference to a motor-impaired participant (blocking the sidewalk with the wheelchair when stopping to use the device). Our case studies and online survey expand on these findings by explicitly investigating situational impairments encountered by motor-impaired users.

3. ONLINE SURVEY

To compare mobile phone use trends inside versus outside of the home (i.e., when mobile), we conducted an online survey with 16 users with motor impairments.

3.1 Method

Mobile phone users with motor impairments were recruited through distribution lists, online forums, local organizations, Facebook and Twitter; as remuneration, participants could opt into a drawing for a $100 Amazon gift certificate. The survey was designed to take up to 25 minutes and included 26 open- and close-form questions. Questions covered general background (e.g., age, gender, motor impairments), type of mobile device owned, challenges found with basic touchscreen operations (e.g., text input/correction, multitouch gestures), and a comparison of device use, physical setup and challenges encountered in use at home versus around town. For these lattermost questions, we randomized whether at-home or around town was presented first.

Forty complete surveys were submitted worldwide and 23 more were partially completed. Because of regional differences, only surveys from the US were considered (31); surveys that did not indicate motor impairments or that did not include touchscreen experience were further excluded. For the 16 remaining surveys, the average completion time was 15.7 minutes ($SD = 8.6$).

3.2 Participants

Of the 16 participants, 15 owned a smartphone and one owned only a tablet. Eleven were female, and the median age range of all participants was 35–44. Respondents reported a range of diagnosed medical conditions, including cerebral palsy (8), neuropathy (4), arthritis (4), and spinal cord injury (4), and one each for muscular dystrophy, spina bifida, multiple sclerosis, and spinal muscular atrophy (note: some participants reported more than one condition). Nine participants indicated often using a wheelchair and three did so only occasionally. In addition to motor impairments, seven participants reported speech impairments, six hearing impairments, and three visual impairments. The majority reported that their motor impairment affects their use of the device either substantially (6) or to some degree (3); the remaining 7 reported very little or no impact. Of the 15 smartphone owners, most were iPhone (8) or Android (6) owners, with one Windows Phone owner, and all but two participants used their phones at least once every few hours. Among accessibility tools adopted, nine participants used speech-to-text and one used a screenreader.

3.3 Findings

Participants used their mobile devices in a variety of locations, most commonly the home (15), but also the street, car, or public

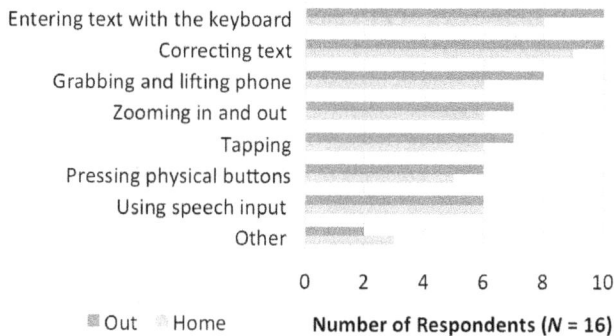

Figure 2. Number of survey respondents citing each input difficulty when using the phone at home versus out (N = 16).

transit, among others (at least 8 participants each). To get a sense of how situational impairments impact input, Figure 2 shows the relative difficulties of completing basic input tasks at home versus out. While the overall trends are similar for both contexts (*e.g.*, text entry and correction were most frequently cited as difficult), more participants reported difficulty while out than at home for all but speech input and "other". Physical position of the phone was also different in the two contexts. At home, the most commonly used positions were flat on a table (7) or lap (5), but these locations were reversed when out, where the lap was most preferred (7), followed by table (3).

In terms of application use at home versus out, participants used a wide range of applications in both contexts, such as email, SMS, games, online shopping, and personal organization tools. Similar patterns of use were found for both contexts, except for navigation and personal organization apps, which were more common when out—7 participants used while at home *vs.* 11 while out.

Although not focused on use at home versus out, we asked about three common input difficulties in general: multitouch gestures, text entry, and text correction. On a 5-point scale from very easy to very difficult, 7 out of 16 participants rated multitouch gestures as difficult or very difficult, while 7 and 10 rated text entry and correction, respectively, as difficult or very difficult.

In summary, these results provide some evidence that using the phone outside of the home increases input difficulties for people with motor impairments, a theme that we explore further in the case studies. As well, about half of the participants found text entry and multitouch difficult, which confirms past work [1,24] and highlights the need for more research in these areas to develop accessible solutions.

4. MULTI-CASE STUDY METHOD

To more deeply investigate how smartphones are used by people with motor impairments and the challenges encountered therein, we conducted a multi-case study with four expert smartphone users. The study included an initial interview, two weeks of diary entries, and a 3-hour contextual session.

4.1 Participant Recruitment

Four participants with motor impairments were recruited from Maryland, DC, and Northern Virginia from October to December 2013. We advertised the study through e-mail lists and social networks, at local events and organizations, and through direct contact. To qualify as an expert smartphone user, participants were required to have at least 18 months of smartphone experience and to use the device more than twice a week. All participants were male, aged 24–46; more details can be found in the cases themselves (Section 5). Compensation was provided.

4.2 Procedure

The study procedure consisted of three parts: an initial interview, a two-week diary study, and a three-hour contextual session.

Initial interview. The 30-minute structured interview collected information on demographics, diagnosed medical conditions, smartphone model used, frequency of smartphone use, and assistive technologies used. Interviews were conducted via phone and were audio recorded. The diary procedure was also explained.

Diary entries. Participants reported on their use of the phone once a day for two weeks: applications used, positive/negative experiences, and challenges encountered. The requirement was to complete at least 10 entries, each of which took about 10 minutes; entries could be completed at most one day late. For accessibility, participants could use a Google Form, email or voicemail, but all chose the Google Form. We sent a reminder at 7PM each day by email, SMS, or voice message, whichever mode was preferred by the participant. The diary form included the following close- and open-ended questions, with the last two questions being optional:

- *For which of the following tasks did you use your phone today?* Set list, such as "Navigation/GPS" and "Email".

- *What activities did you do outside the home today?* Set list, such as "Traveling around town" and "Shopping".

- *For what activities was the phone especially helpful today inside or outside the home?*

- *What are the worst experiences you had with the phone today?*

- *Were there other accessibility issues you encountered today not involving the phone? If so, please explain.*

- *Please share any other comments or ideas you have about your phone experience.*

Contextual session. Finally, a three-hour contextual session was scheduled with each participant. Contrasting the diary entries, this session allowed for interview and observation *in situ*, as participants completed tasks on the go. Sessions took place in public locations (*e.g.*, coffee shop, pharmacy), with the exception of one participant (discussed later). Each session consisted of:

1. *Basic smartphone actions (10 minutes).* To assess basic smartphone accessibility for each participant, we had them complete ten tasks on a Samsung Exhibit smartphone: pick the phone off a table, long swipe in any direction, horizontal and vertical swipe, short tap on a target (at center, left, and right of screen), long tap, pinch, and drag. Participants performed each action twice and could fail twice before moving on to the next action.

2. *Semi-structured interview and short demos (1.5–2 hours).* Questions covered general aspects of smartphone adoption, and expanded on points from the diary entries. The latter questions also included demonstrations by the participant of particular use scenarios and accessibility challenges.

3. *Neighborhood activities (up to 1 hour).* Up to three activities were selected based on the diary entries and in consultation with the participant about regular errands and activities outside of the home (*e.g.*, shopping, public transit). During these activities, participants demonstrated use of the phone.

For the contextual session, audio recording devices were attached to the participant and the researcher during mobile activities. Video was taken of the basic smartphone actions (to capture success/failure) and of short demos. During the neighborhood activities, video and still images were selectively taken. Written notes were taken during and after the session, particularly on physical use of phone.

4.3 Data Analysis

We analyzed the data using a case study approach [7]. The initial interviews and contextual sessions were transcribed, after which the transcripts and diary entries from the in-person sessions were qualitatively coded. We created an initial code set on a first pass of the data, and subsequently grouped codes in a hierarchy. After a second pass to refine the code set, emergent categories were selected for an axial coding analysis. From this process we identified four main themes covering 18 categories (for 80 codes in total). The themes and sample categories were *enablement* (*e.g.,* organization, transport, activities), *challenges* (*e.g.,* situational impairments, physical world, mobile input), *personalization* (*e.g.,* customization, preferences), and *wishes* (*e.g.,* mobile enhancements, physical world control).

The coding process was validated on a subset of the data using peer-review [7] with one external reviewer not on the research team. Six of the 18 categories were reviewed: three randomly selected categories (activities, organization, transport), and the three categories most relevant to our research questions (situational impairments, social acceptance, physical world control). The external reviewer read through all excerpts in these categories, and marked agreement or disagreement about whether the correct code had been applied. Finally, both coders reviewed instances of disagreement.

5. MULTI-CASE STUDY FINDINGS

We first present each case individually, focusing on physical use and the themes of enablement and situational impairments (our primary topics of investigation), followed by a cross-case analysis. For each participant, their smartphone model, physical ability to use the phone, and common information tasks are summarized in an accompanying table.

5.1 Case P1

P1, a male aged 46, has muscular dystrophy and some visual impairment; he uses a wheelchair only occasionally and owns an Android Nexus (Table 1; Figure 3). He completed 14 diary entries over 14 days. During the contextual session, he demonstrated sharing files on Dropbox, checking sports information, reading books, playing games, using SMS with voice control, and using social networks (Facebook). Neighborhood activities included a short walk to a pharmacy and a visit to a subway station.

Enablement. Using a smartphone allows P1 to take care of home activities like meal planning and laundry, to write and read more, and to access information on the go. He prepares meals by using the Kindle app to read recipes in the kitchen, and keeps track of shopping lists, to-dos and calendar entries on the phone:

"Because I have a disability I am not doing the physical work of the house. My job is meals, meals planning. Keeping a calendar straight. It would be more difficult for me to do that without the phone."

While P1 has difficulty with physical writing due to a lack of strength, he can enter text on the touchscreen for notes and other personal organization needs. The phone also allows him to read books and newspapers by enlarging text, reversing colors, or using text-to-voice (*e.g.,* Kindle or Darwin Reader apps). P1 compared the phone to printed text:

"I've already tried very, very hard to read print because there wasn't as much available and now 90%...at least 75% of all books are

Table 1. Overview of P1's phone use based on diary entries and the basic smartphone actions in the contextual session.

Smartphone: Android Nexus with magnification and text reader.
Primary uses: Communication (email, voice calls, SMS), weather reports, books, calendar and scheduling.
Position of phone: P1 manipulates the phone by holding it with his left hand on his lap. When not in use, he stores the phone in a pocket or attaches it to a neck-worn lanyard by a hook on the case.
Physical ability to use phone (10 basic actions): Grabbing and lifting the phone, and multitouch gestures (pinch) were difficult.
Activities outside of the home: Traveling around town and commuting, work, shopping and groceries, sport and social.

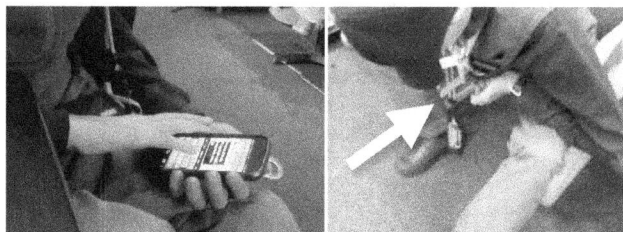

Figure 3. P1 entering text in the phone (left) and moving his phone from the pocket to his lap (right).

available in electronic format, so I actually read more now than I read four years ago ... just because of the accessibility."

Finally, mobile information helps P1 avoid physical challenges while out. For example, subway fare machines are not accessible to him, so he adds fare to his card on the mobile website. He can also check if a business is open before visiting, or perform mobile online payments. Without the phone he commented that he would need to be more cautious in preparing for activities.

Situational impairments. P1 must sit to use the phone, so he tries to complete any necessary mobile tasks before leaving. Because of the considerable effort to take out and store the phone, he typically uses it only on longer public transit rides. Among other factors, weather and clothing impact P1's ability to use the phone:

"When it is warm out I can carry it [the phone] in my shirt pocket and access it. When it is cold I have to carry it in my jacket pocket. I am afraid I will drop it. And, it is more difficult for me to access the mobile phone while wearing a jacket."

Privacy can be an issue with the text-reader mode on the phone, such as when P1 forgets to turn the sound off at work. That said, he prefers having the mode enabled rather than taking his phone out of his pocket, trading off privacy for accessibility.

Other accessibility challenges. P1 finds voice-to-text on his phone so inaccurate compared to Dragon Naturally Speaking on his desktop computer as to not be useful. Text input is also a problem, and he waits until home to compose longer messages.

5.2 Case P2

P2, a male aged 24, has had cerebral palsy since birth, affecting motor control and speech; he uses a wheelchair and owns a Samsung Galaxy S4 (Table 2; Figure 4). He completed eight diary entries over 10 days. During the contextual session he demonstrated use of the phone for personal organization with calendars and emails, web browsing, online shopping, social networks, restaurant coupons, and tourism apps to book hotels. Neighborhood activities included a walk to a mall, a visit to a pharmacy and a visit to a coffee shop.

Enablement. P2 finds the phone especially useful for working remotely because he can work any place and any time: "*I would go in my scooter, reading and working from there, so I would work whenever.*" When he was in college and working, he also sent and responded to work emails on his phone while on campus.

Mobile information also allows P2 to plan or adapt his daily activities when an incident occurs—similar to P1. One diary entry discussed a morning with inclement weather:

"*I coordinated with my co-workers and taxi driver to make sure I could safely get to work on my phone before I even got out of bed.*"

As with P1, P2 finds writing on paper to be difficult, but the phone allows him to write reminders, manage contacts, and use calendars. He makes use of these tools across devices. For instance, he mentioned that when he goes grocery shopping, he takes notes from his iPad at home, emails them, and accesses them from the phone at the store. As he commented:

"*I don't write very well. I have always used an online calendar since high school. Now, I have my Outlook connected to my Google calendar, so they are all in sync.*"

Situational impairments. Weather is the primary contextual factor affecting P2. He prefers to have his phone on his lap (Figure 4, left), which makes rain and snow problematic. During inclement weather he has to protect his phone and thus cannot take it out easily:

"*I got caught in freezing rain. I cannot easily use pockets, so I have trouble finding a place to put my phone where it won't get wet.*"

Other accessibility challenges. While P2 can operate his smartphone as-is, he reported challenges in text correction, copy-paste, multitouch gestures and plugging in the phone. Touchscreen input becomes challenging when he needs to type fast: "*With my tight schedule, trying to hurry and quickly dial into a call is frustrating because I make mistakes.*" Text correction is also difficult, particularly because the control to correct a word is so small. For long text input, P2 prefers to use other devices,

saying: "*typing a lot on my phone can get difficult so I use my laptop and iPad to type when I can.*"

5.3 Case P3

P3, a 30-year-old male with a spinal cord injury (quadriplegia with poor hand dexterity), completed 13 diary entries over 14 days; he owns an iPhone 5 (Table 3; Figure 5). The contextual session included demonstrations of operating his workstation remotely from the phone, accessing podcasts and videos, using Assistive Touch, and entering text with Siri and the iPhone keyboard. As his diary entries included few activities outside of the home and because P2 lives in a rural area, the session was adjusted to include a driving demonstration and use of GPS for navigation instead of neighborhood activities.

Enablement. One area of enablement for P3 was the support of routine tasks and personal organization at home, for which the phone provides a sort of freedom—for example, being able to create reminders whenever he needs help with housework activities like changing bed sheets. He also uses the phone to pass time during a daily two-hour physical routine:

"*Before I had the phone, I used to drag my laptop into the bathroom with me, set it up on my sink and listen to Google videos and things like that. The phone has completely replaced that.*"

As with P1 and P2, P3 uses his phone to reduce physical effort. With *Pocketcloud* he remotely controls his workstation, allowing him to manage video processing or play music from the bed or couch without having to use his wheelchair to get to his desk.

Situational impairments. While he is out, P3 sometimes has physical difficulty retrieving his phone from his bag. This can make it difficult to answer a call, for which he typically prefers to wait until later: "*I'd just wait until I have a moment where I have some quiet or peace or I can lock my wheelchair.*"

Other accessibility challenges. P3 finds it difficult to select small targets and to complete multitouch gestures. For example, he demonstrated the difficulty of tapping targets and making accidental taps in Assistive Touch. Problems with tapping small

Table 2. Overview of P2's phone use based on diary entries and the basic smartphone actions in the contextual session.

Smartphone: Samsung Galaxy S4 with no assistive technology.
Primary uses: Communication (SMS, social network services, email and voice calls), web browsing, personal organization, and mobile payments.
Position of phone: P2 operates his phone by holding it on a table or with his left hand. When he moves around, the phone is located on his lap or on his scooter table.
Physical ability to use phone (10 basic actions): P2 encountered challenges performing a one-hand multitouch gesture. To zoom in and out he used both hands for the pinch gesture, which requires to the phone to be on a table or other support.
Activities outside of home: Shopping and groceries, travelling around town and commuting, work, and social.

Table 3. Overview of P3's phone use based on diary entries and the basic smartphone actions in the contextual session.

Smartphone: Apple iPhone 5 with no assistive technology.
Primary uses: Entertainment, access to email, access to social networks, web browsing, and reading news and articles.
Position of phone: P3 prefers to hold the phone in his left hand, using a tripod stand on the case to do so in a stable manner (Figure 5). When mobile, he places the phone on his lap or in a bag.
Physical ability to use phone (10 basic actions): For pinch-to-zoom, P3 first tried with the ring and middle fingers on one hand, but had to switch to two hands when that did not work.
Activities outside of home: Visiting family and occasionally dining with friends on weekends.

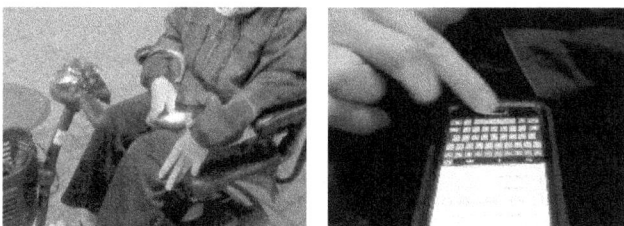

Figure 4. P2 with his phone on his lap while stationary (left), and showing challenges correcting text (right).

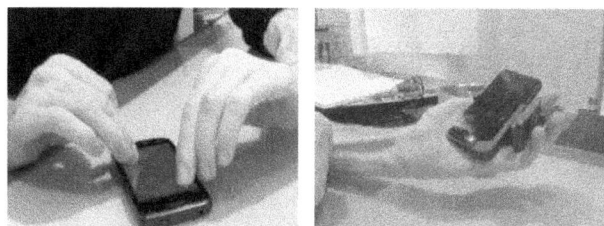

Figure 5. P3's two-handed pinch gesture (left); holding the phone by using the tripod mount on the case (right).

elements also appear when he has to correct text by placing the cursor within a block of text. As for voice-to-text, while P3 uses Siri, he finds it difficult for writing an email because he has to plan in advance exactly what to say to avoid having to correct it: *"I don't think it is natural for me to think out a whole sentence that's grammatically correct."*

5.4 Case P4

P4 is a 29-year-old male with cerebral palsy; he uses a wheelchair and owns an iPhone 5 (Table 4; Figure 6). He completed 14 diary entries over 16 days. During the contextual session he demonstrated use of his phone for checking transit information, using a calendar and email, and social networking. Neighborhood activities included visits to a mall, a pharmacy, and a coffee shop.

Enablement. The smartphone enables P4 to overcome physical world challenges, for example: *"So I mean, having the mobile access just reduces the physical effort so much."* For transit, P4 makes daily use of a mobile application to check the elevator status at subway stations. This app is critical because he can know in advance when the elevators are broken and get off at a different station to avoid delays. P4 also uses GPS navigation and maps for long trips. As he summed up regarding transportation:

"It's being able to anticipate elevator outages, and being able to plan outside your routes on public transit and being able to have weather alerts."

P4 also uses the phone to remotely control his TV and stereo speakers via voice commands, freeing him from having to use standard remote controls. The phone is also another device on which he can do online shopping and payments, which he prefers to in-person shopping—grocery store aisles, for example, can be narrow and difficult to navigate:

"Shopping online enables my independence. Shopping in the physical world, well, let's just say I'm a happy Amazon Prime customer."

The mobile device is also important for P4's work. Often when he can't commute due to inclement weather he works from home. As

Table 4. Overview of P4's phone use based on diary entries and the basic smartphone actions in the contextual session.

Smartphone: Apple iPhone 5 with Siri as an assistive technology.
Primary uses: Access to information (weather, web, news and articles), communications (SMS, phone, email and social networks), navigation, and personal organization.
Position of phone: P4 holds his phone in his right hand to use it. When he moves around, he keeps the phone in his pocket or hand.
Physical ability to use phone (10 basic smartphone actions): P4 performed all tasks successfully, although he had to use his right hand to hold the phone for the swipe gesture. He reported that he finds it difficult to select small targets and occasionally uses a stylus for text input due to hand tremors or spasms.
Activities outside of home: Traveling around town and commuting, social, work, leisure and shopping.

Figure 6. P4 in a pharmacy, stretching his arm to get items from an aisle (left); P4 holding the phone for use (right).

he reported in his diary: *"With mobile access I don't have to worry about that. I don't need to go to this inaccessible place to get my job done."* He can even work from his couch without necessarily needing to use his laptop.

Finally, P4 uses notes, reminders and calendars on his phone for personal organization. He uses reminders created with Siri on his phone and synchronized with his calendar and other devices.

Situational impairments. Few situational impairments arose in P4's case. One aspect of context that impacts P4's phone use is privacy, for which reason he doesn't use screenreaders: *"The reason I don't use VoiceOver or whatever, because I mean there's not a lot of privacy there."*

Other accessibility challenges. P4 finds touchscreen text input and correction challenging and for long emails waits until he can use speech dictation on his desktop. The 20-second dictation window that Siri allows is too short for him and impacts the type of emails he writes on the phone. He also finds small target acquisition difficult, such as selecting small areas in a file list or when correcting text. As another challenge, P4 considers size and weight when acquiring a mobile device because of the difficulty in grabbing and lifting it. For these reasons, he does not use a case or headphones.

5.5 Cross-case Analysis and Summary

Overall, mobile phones were used for a range of activities both inside and outside of the home, as participants found smartphones to be more portable than tablets or laptops. All participants reported some activities traditionally performed on their desktop computers were now being done with the phones—for example, P1's recipes or P3's entertainment. In terms of personalization, our participants had adopted no or few assistive technologies with their phones—including software and cases—confirming Trewin et al.'s [24] findings with mobile phone (primarily not smartphone) users with motor impairments. Several factors appeared to impact this low rate of adoption, including the desire to maintain portability (e.g., not adding a bulky case), limitations in some assisitive technologies (e.g., poor speech recognition), and in some cases a general lack of need.

We highlight overarching findings for the themes of enablement, situational impairments, and accessibility challenges; we also briefly discuss participants' wishes for future technologies.

Enablement. Mobile information was particularly important for mitigating physical world accessibility challenges: (1) One example is to support *transit*, where P4 checked the elevator status at subway stations and P1, P2, and P4 frequently used navigation apps, as reported in their diaries. (2) The phones also supported *remote work*, allowing for flexibility and the ability to skip the commute altogether in inclement weather. (3) *Online shopping* and mobile apps for *home banking* were found to be useful for similar reasons (P1, P2, P4); the challenges of on-site shopping were evident in the contextual sessions—navigating through aisles, carrying bags, and waiting for assistance to pay. (4) The phones were used to reduce physical effort by *controlling other devices at home*, such as P3's workstation, and P4's TV and stereo via voice commands. (5) Finally, mobile devices provided an *accessible alternative to physical writing*, allowing participants to use calendars, reminders, notes, and lists.

Situational impairments. By focusing on smartphone use and people with motor impairments specifically, we extend Kane et al.'s [29] findings, highlighting challenges due to movement, restrictive clothing, and weather. Most notably, all participants preferred to have their phones easily available (e.g., on the lap), but during inclement weather P1 and P4 stored it in a pocket and P2 and P3 stored it in a bag, making access difficult. Participants also had privacy concerns about using speakers and voice-to-text technology in public, similar to Ye *et al.*'s [27] findings with visually impaired users. However, as opposed to reducing these privacy concerns, the use of external devices such as headphones was a detriment to portability for some participants (P3, P4).

Other accessibility challenges. Despite participants being experienced smartphone users, text input, voice-to-text, and acquisition of small targets were still challenging. Participants preferred to use their desktops or tablets to write lengthy text, which reflects similar findings from non-motor-impaired users [23]. Confirming past findings on the accessibility challenges of multitouch input [1,24], only one participant was able to perform multitouch gestures with one hand during the performance tasks—two participants needed both hands and one used AssistiveTouch. Finally, we found that mobile dictation (notably Siri) was not comparable to desktop software (P1, P3, P4) and that text correction was particularly frustrating (P1, P2, P3, P4).

Wishes for future technologies. Three participants wanted more accurate voice-to-text and voice control. P2 also mentioned the need for alternatives to multitouch (*"no pinching"*). Other suggestions collected were: more accessible social apps to share images, cordless battery charging, and apps for image editing as powerful as on a desktop. P3 envisioned self-driving cars and future mobile devices integrated with our bodies, while P4 proposed to control more household devices remotely (*e.g.*, thermostat, coffee machine) using voice commands on the phone.

6. DISCUSSION

Our findings highlight both the ongoing accessibility challenges of touchscreen smartphones for users with motor impairments and the numerous ways in which these devices can be empowering. Though the sample size was small (*N*=16), the online survey results offer additional evidence to support these conclusions. We extend Kane *et al.*'s [15] and Anthony *et al.*'s [1] findings that mobile devices can be empowering for users with disabilities by characterizing new ways in which this empowerment occurs. Here, we reflect on design implications and areas for future work.

Physical world accessibility. Participants in the case studies used smartphones to mitigate accessibility challenges in the real world and to reduce physical effort—from transit planning to mobile banking to controlling household devices. Building on these trends, designers of *physical* spaces, such as transit hubs, libraries, and malls, should explicitly consider how mobile services can complement and improve physical accessibility (*e.g.*, real-time accessibility information such as crowdedness or working elevators). Likewise, our findings emphasize the potential benefits of future smarthomes, where the mobile device can control a range of household elements [8,19]. Such alternative access would allow users to select a control modality that works for their abilities, such as controlling the device directly, using the touchscreen, or using voice control.

Mobile text input. Several case study participants found mobile text input or speech dictation to be an accessible alternative to physical writing (*e.g.*, notes, calendars). At the same time, text input was remarked to be inefficient, particularly for text correction, selection and copy-pasting; the survey confirmed these findings. While accessible mobile text input has long been a research focus (*e.g.*, [6,26]), text correction has not been prioritized. To improve the accessibility of mainstream keyboards, designers could increase the size of the selection controls, use a modal approach where entering a correction mode magnifies all

text, or provide alternative, indirect controls such as sliders to manipulate the cursor. Improved mobile speech input could also address these issues in contexts where it is socially appropriate.

Situational impairments. Kane *et al.* [15] previously identified situational impairments affecting people with disabilities, but as mentioned in Related Work their focus was primarily on visual impairments. Our findings thus extend an understanding of how contextual factors impact mobile accessibility for people with motor impairments. Most notably, participants encountered serious difficulties in physically retrieving the phone for use while they were in transit. For one participant this was a problem all of the time (his phone hung on a lanyard around his neck), while for others it only became serious with restrictive clothing or in inclement weather when the phone was stowed away. Answering phone calls was also difficult on the go, with some participants choosing to postpone calls.

Potential of wearable devices. To address the situational impairments described above, mobile input could be distributed to other devices, such as small wearables (*e.g.* rings, watches), voice control, and the human body. Such devices would be always available, eliminating the cost of retrieving the device. Accessible wearable input is an emerging area of work (*e.g.*, [4,27]), and we expect to see many new solutions in the next few years.

Lab to real-world accessibility challenges. With the exception of Anthony *et al.*'s [1] study of YouTube videos, past work on touchscreen input for people with motor impairments has largely focused on lab settings. Of course, lab findings derived in controlled settings and from artificial tasks do not necessarily translate to meaningful real-world impacts. Our findings confirm, in particular, that difficulties of tapping on small targets, performing multitouch gestures, and entering text are impacting daily smartphone use even for experienced users. Moreover, by studying use in the real world, we were able to identify further challenges, such as the situational impairments described above.

7. LIMITATIONS

Case study participants were all expert smartphone users, male, 24-56, and US residents. As a result, the findings may not generalize across gender, age, culture, and technology experience. For both studies, all participants could use mobile devices, and we did not collect data from those who have more severe motor impairments. While we used multiple methods across the two studies (survey, interview, diary study, observation), overall limitations of the case studies include the small sample size and the lack of a standardized performance assessment of each user's motor abilities and ability to use the mobile device; to overcome this latter issue to some degree, we included a set of ten basic mobile phone tasks (the outcomes are listed in each participant table). Finally, the survey included only a relatively small number of participants. While it provides some evidence to complement the in-person study, the survey findings are preliminary.

8. CONCLUSION

We conducted two studies, a small online survey (*N* = 16) and a more in-depth set of case studies with four participants with motor impairments. Participants used the devices frequently and for a range of tasks. Our findings highlight the ways in which smartphones are enabling everyday activities for people with motor impairments, particularly in mitigating accessibility challenges in the physical world and in supporting accessible reading and writing. Documented challenges in touchscreen input persist, emphasizing the need for further work on making basic input accessible. We also identified situational impairments that are especially impactful for users with motor impairments. We predict that wearable devices will be a fruitful direction for addressing these challenges in the future, better supporting truly mobile access for people with motor impairments.

9. ACKNOWLEDGMENTS

We would like to thank our participants, as well as Meethu Malu for helping with the coding validation and Jon Froehlich for providing comments on a paper draft. This research was funded by the National Science Foundation under grant IIS-1350438.

10. REFERENCES

1. Anthony, L., Kim, Y., and Findlater, L. Analyzing user-generated youtube videos to understand touchscreen use by people with motor impairments. *Proc. CHI '13*, ACM Press (2013), 1223–1232.

2. Barnard, L., Yi, J.S., Jacko, J.A., and Sears, A. Capturing the effects of context on human performance in mobile computing systems. *Personal and Ubiquitous Computing 11*, 2 (2006), 81–96.

3. Biswas, P. and Langdon, P. Developing multimodal adaptation algorithm for mobility impaired users by evaluating their hand strength. *International Journal of Human-Computer Interaction 28*, 9 (2012), 576–596.

4. Carrington, P., Hurst, A., and Kane, S.K. Wearables and chairables. *Proc. CHI'14*, ACM Press (2014), 3103–3112.

5. Church, K. and Smyth, B. Understanding the intent behind mobile information needs. *Proc. IUI'09*, (2008), 247–256.

6. Condado, P. A., Godinho, R., Zacarias, M., and Lobo, F.G. EasyWrite : A touch-based entry method for mobile devices. *Proc. INTERACT 2011*, (2011), 1–8.

7. Creswell, J.W. *Qualitative inquiry and research design: Choosing among five approaches.* Sage, 2012.

8. Derthick, K., Scott, J., Villar, N., and Winkler, C. Exploring smartphone-based web user interfaces for appliances. *Proc. MobileHCI '13*, ACM Press (2013), 227.

9. Duff, S.N., Irwin, C.B., Skye, J.L., Sesto, M.E., and Wiegmann, D.A. The effect of disability and approach on touch screen performance during a number entry task. *Proc. HFES'10*, (2010), 566–570.

10. Froehlich, J., Wobbrock, J.O., and Kane, S.K. Barrier Pointing: Using Physical Edges to Assist Target Acquisition on Mobile Device Touch Screens. *Proc. ASSETS'07*, ACM Press (2007), 19–26.

11. Goel, M., Findlater, L., and Wobbrock, J.O. WalkType : Using Accelerometer Data to Accommodate Situational Impairments in Mobile Touch Screen Text Entry. *Proc. CHI'12*, ACM Press (2012), 2687–2696.

12. Guerreiro, T., Nicolau, H., Jorge, J., and Gonçalves, D. Towards accessible touch interfaces. *Proc. ASSETS '10*, ACM Press (2010), 19–26.

13. Guerreiro, T.J.V., Nicolau, H., Jorge, J., and Gonçalves, D. Assessing Mobile Touch Interfaces for Tetraplegics. *Proc. MobileHCI '10*, ACM Press (2010), 31–34.

14. Irwin, C.B. and Sesto, M.E. Performance and touch characteristics of disabled and non-disabled participants during a reciprocal tapping task using touch screen technology. *Applied Ergonomics 43*, 6 (2012), 1038–1043.

15. Kane, S.K., Jayant, C., Wobbrock, J.O., and Ladner, R.E. Freedom to Roam: A Study of Mobile Device Adoption and Accessibility for People with Visual and Motor Disabilities. *Proc. ASSETS'09*, ACM Press (2009), 115–122.

16. Lin, M., Goldman, R., Price, K.J., Sears, A., and Jacko, J. How do people tap when walking? An empirical investigation of nomadic data entry. *International Journal of Human-Computer Studies 65*, 9 (2007), 759–769.

17. MacKay, B., Dearman, D., Inkpen, K., and Watters, C. Walk 'n Scroll: a comparison of software-based navigation techniques for different levels of mobility. *Proc. MobileHCI'05*, ACM Press (2005), 183–190.

18. Mizobuchi, S., Chignell, M., and Newton, D. Mobile text entry: relationship between walking speed and text input task difficulty. *Proc. MobileHCI '05*, (2005), 122–128.

19. Nichols, J., Myers, B.A., Higgins, M., et al. Generating remote control interfaces for complex appliances. *Proc. UIST '02*, ACM Press (2002), 161.

20. Nylander, S., Lundquist, T., and Brännström, A. At home and with computer access: why and where people use cell phones to access the internet. *Proc. CHI'09*, ACM Press (2009), 1639–1642.

21. Sears, A., Lin, M., Jacko, J., and Xiao, Y. When Computers Fade: Pervasive Computing and Situationally-Induced Impairments and Disabilities. *Proc. of HCII 2003*, (2003), 1298–1302.

22. Shinohara, K. and Wobbrock, J. In the shadow of misperception: assistive technology use and social interactions. *Proc. CHI'11*, ACM Press (2011), 705–714.

23. Sohn, T., Li, K., Griswold, W., and Hollan, J. A diary study of mobile information needs. *Proceedings of the SIGCHI Conference on Human Factors in Computing Systems*, ACM Press (2008), 433–442.

24. Trewin, S., Swart, C., and Pettick, D. Physical accessibility of touchscreen smartphones. *Proc. ASSETS '13, Article 19*, ACM Press (2013), 1–8.

25. Wacharamanotham, C., Hurtmanns, J., Mertens, A., Kronenbuerger, M., Schlick, C., and Borchers, J. Evaluating swabbing : a touchscreen input method for elderly users with tremor. *Proc. CHI'11*, ACM Press (2011), 623–626.

26. Wobbrock, J.O., Myers, B.A., and Kembel, J.A. EdgeWrite: A Stylus-Based Text Entry Method Designed for High Accuracy and Stability of Motion. *Proc. UIST '03*, ACM Press (2003), 61–70.

27. Ye, H., Malu, M., and Oh, U., Findlater, L. Current and future mobile and wearable device use by people with visual impairments. *Proc. CHI'14*, ACM Press (2014), 3123–3132.

28. Yesilada, Y., Harper, S., Chen, T., and Trewin, S. Small-device users situationally impaired by input. *Computers in Human Behavior 26*, 3 (2010), 427–435.

"Just Let the Cane Hit It":
How the Blind and Sighted See Navigation Differently

Michele A. Williams[1], Caroline Galbraith[1], Shaun K. Kane[1,2], Amy Hurst[1]

[1]Information Systems Department
University of Maryland Baltimore County (UMBC)
Baltimore, MD 21250
{mawilliams, cgalb1, amyhurst} @umbc.edu

[2]Department of Computer Science
University of Colorado Boulder
Boulder, CO 80309 USA
shaun.kane@colorado.edu

ABSTRACT

Sighted people often have the best of intentions when they want to help a blind person navigate, but their well meaning is also often coupled with a lack of knowledge and understanding about how a person navigates without vision. As a result what sighted people think is the right feedback is too often the wrong feedback to give to a person with a visual impairment. Understanding how to provide feedback to blind navigators is crucial to the design of assistive technologies for navigation. In our research investigating the design of a personal pedestrian navigation device, we observed firsthand the ways that sighted people seemingly misunderstand how many blind people navigate when using a white cane mobility aid. Throughout our qualitative end user studies that included focus groups and observations (including couple-based observations with a close companion) we gathered data that explicitly shows how the language and understanding of sighted vs. blind pedestrians differs greatly and even how it can be dangerous when people interfere in the wrong way. From our findings we discuss why it is difficult for a blind person to navigate like a sighted person to ensure designers are aware of the difficulties and designing with new training in mind, not simply designing from their own point of view. We also want to encourage advocacy and empathy amongst the sighted community towards this activity of walking around independently.

Categories and Subject Descriptors

K.4.2 [Social Issues]: Assistive technologies for persons with disabilities

General Terms

Design; Human Factors

Keywords

Blind navigation; white cane; empathy

1.1 INTRODUCTION

Navigation without vision is difficult. Common successful strategies include using additional aids ranging from low-tech solutions such as a white cane to high-tech solutions such as handheld GPS devices. Our eventual research goal is to contribute to the high-tech solutions, however we are first interfacing with end users to study the current strategies, techniques, and products.

ASSETS '14, October 20 - 22 2014, Rochester, NY, USA
Copyright 2014 ACM 978-1-4503-2720-6/14/10...$15.00
http://dx.doi.org/10.1145/2661334.2661380

To help us learn about this task and avoid incorrect assumptions we conducted immersive, in-depth qualitative research for over one year and developed an understanding of navigation from the perspective of individuals with visual impairments. Our observations have revealed diverse navigation strategies directly impacting how instructions should be given to someone walking independently. We found that the strategies taught in Orientation and Mobility (O&M) training often conflict with the type of information that sighted people and/or new technology provide, which makes comprehension more difficult for the visually impaired. While we do not propose to cease innovations beyond the traditional navigation strategies, we thought it important to note the differences. Dramatically changing the way a blind person walks has serious safety implications and other implications impacting the likelihood of adoption and success, which do not seem to be currently accounted for in literature.

It's important to note that not every blind person needs a mobility aid and that not everyone obtains O&M training. However, for those that use a cane or seeing eye dog, there are certain techniques that are taught and relied upon to ensure safe travel. There are also certain non-visual cues that are universal for people with vision impairments that provide substitutions for visual cues used in navigation. Based on responses from our visually impaired participants we believe more people with vision could use a better understanding of using a different modality for receiving the same environmental feedback.

In this paper, we present our findings from several research studies that have explored how assistance from sighted people often creates complications for people with vision impairments. Through interviews and observations with independent blind travelers, we identified mismatches between information provided by sighted assistants and information needed by blind travelers. We also conducted a study in which blind participants explored a location along with a sighted companion, and found these mismatches even when the individuals knew each other. Since the majority of the participants in our study (and in the visually impaired population) were cane users, and using a cane presents a very different navigation strategy than using a seeing eye dog, we focus primarily on cane users in our findings and discussion. Based on these insights, we discuss design implications for creating automated navigation tools that provide information best suited to independent blind travelers.

2. RELATED WORK

In order to understand how best to design navigation tools to support blind travelers, our research is significantly informed by prior research in designing navigation aids for blind people. In addition, our research is also informed by prior studies examining social interactions during navigation activities.

2.1 Blind Navigation Devices

For over 40 years researchers and practitioners have been applying the latest technology trends to aiding people with vision impairments with more accurate orientation, obstacle detection and avoidance, and real-time as well as virtual wayfinding [4]. In the latest available systems, users are able to use either a handheld GPS device such as Humanware's TrekkerBreeze[1] or applications on their smartphone devices such as Google Maps[2] to hear landmarks they are passing, receive turn-by-turn directions (for walking and taking transit), and simply regain orientation in space with compass-style features. While the latest technology has presented marked improvements in the available features and streamlined hardware, there are still open challenges for technology designers to undertake. For example, there are outdoor locations not available on a GPS device for which users could still use support, such as a park or college campus. Also, commercially available indoor wayfinding applications such as Talking Signs[3] have not been widely adopted; thus, indoor navigation devices are still primarily a focus of current research but not available to users at the present. Given the continued opportunity to improve the availability of technology for visually impaired navigators, we are building upon the current research and commercial devices but also ensuring we take a user-centered design approach to address the most pressing issues in the most usable interface.

2.2 Blind Navigation Training and Strategies

In proposing an algorithm for indoor navigation, Swobodzinski and Raubal provide a comprehensive description of what is generally taught in Orientation and Mobility (O&M) training, focusing on training for people whose vision requires a mobility aid [5]. This intensive and extremely detailed training helps people learn how to use their other senses to discover information about their environment as well as walk safely. Techniques include listening for distinct environmental sounds, using the white cane to trail (glide) along a wall to walk straight and keep one's orientation, and the differences between "obstacles, hazards, clues, and landmarks" (referring to the many objects one encounters in the environment). Using the O&M training strategies, the researchers built a system specifically for blind pedestrians that chose the "optimal route by trading off distance and the number of landmarks and clues along a route". They compared their routes to those generated by algorithms assuming a sighted traveler and asserted that their distinctive approach was more appropriate and optimal. Taking into account the substantial differences between how a blind and sighted person approaches a navigation task underscores our desire to involve end users in our development process and to include many different research probes to ensure we have a full understanding of the technology needs and interface and interaction requirements.

2.3 Collaboration in Navigation

By examining how humans interact during a navigation task, we can better understand user information needs and the shortcomings of existing navigation technology. Even though navigation is an activity frequently performed within a group, there is little research exploring group interactions – whether for blind navigation or more general navigation studies. One noted exception is work by Forlizzi, et al, where they observed pairs of people navigating in a vehicle [2]. The person driving navigated with directions from a passenger (deemed the "navigator") who was able to familiarize themselves with maps and directions prior to starting the journey. They found interesting dynamics about the teamwork employed by the participants such as negotiating the optimal timing of giving out upcoming maneuvers, determining when to give solely directional cues versus more details (such as which lane to move into), and analyzing the tangential conversations they carried on outside of the navigation tasks (such as reminiscing based on passing landmarks). This study provided insights for in-car GPS devices based on the human interaction; thus, much like this study we set out to examine similar human interaction behaviors for pedestrian navigation. We conducted a similar study with blind participants and sighted companions, finding many of the same teamwork negotiations and social interactions. Following we explain the findings from this study as well as findings from single-person observations and focus group discussions related to navigation technology needs.

3. RECALLING NAVIGATION EXPERIENCES

We sought to understand the current navigation challenges experienced by people with vision impairments through several studies. Our prior work detailed findings from over-the-phone interviews conducted with 30 adults with vision impairments [6]. We added to that data with other collection methods including focus groups (which included regular diary entries) and observations of everyday navigation with a person with a vision impairment. Each study allowed an opportunity to identify, and even see firsthand, remaining challenges despite the prevalence of navigation technology. We also learned that some of these challenges stem from the environment but others from people.

3.1 Focus Groups and Observations

3.1.1 Participants

We recruited 20 participants for the focus groups and observations – 17 focus group participants and 5 observation participants (2 participants participated in both). Table 1 details their ages, genders, and visual impairments. "FG" denotes a focus group participant, "O" an observation participant, and note 2 participants conducted both studies and thus have 2 identifiers. FG5, FG15, and O3 were guide dog users; all others were cane users.

3.1.2 Methods

We convened 2 focus groups in 2 different metropolitan areas. The first group of 8 (6 female, ages 31-63) met once a month for 6 months in Washington, D.C. The second group consisted of 7 participants (4 female, ages 30-66) who met once in Atlanta. Both focus groups were led in guided discussions of past navigation training, current navigation challenges, and ideas for future navigation technology.

Participants were also asked to type "diary" entries during the month after the session(s). Diaries are a freelance journal entry related to the study, in this case related to navigation experiences or technology ideas. Diary studies provide a means for capturing anecdotes not recalled or shared during the meeting, chronicling day-of experiences, and relaying ideas upon further reflection.

---

[1] http://www.humanware.com/en-usa/home

[2] https://www.google.com/maps/preview

[3] http://www.talkingsigns.com

ID	Age / Gender	Vision Impairment	ID	Age / Gender	Vision Impairment
FG1	30/M	Glaucoma age 4; gradual vision loss; no usable vision	FG10 (O4)	58/M	RP age 27; gradual vision loss, some light perception
FG2	31/F	Legally Blind: Myopia and Nistagmus	FG11	61/F	Blind since birth
FG3	38/M	Gradual vision loss from age 5	FG12	61/M	Blind from birth, ROP
FG4	44/F	Lost vision age 31	FG13 (O5)	63/F	Blind from birth, ROP
FG5	48/M	Retinitis Pigmentosa (RP)	FG14	63/F	Lost vision age 23
FG6	48/M	PR, low day vision, no night vision	FG15	66/F	Blind from birth, ROP
FG7	51/M	Choroidermia at 12	O1	25/F	Blind since birth
FG8	57/F	Stills Disease age 5, gradual vision loss, little usable vision	O2	29/F	Low vision, requires magnification
FG9	58/F	Glaucoma age 38; low vision	O3	29/M	Blind from birth, some light perception

Observation participants were accompanied on diverse everyday tasks including running errands (using public transit), mall shopping, and commuting home during an evening rush hour. The participants chose the task for observation and were followed by one researcher for one session. The researcher asked questions during and after the observations.

3.2 Findings

The studies provided us with valuable overall navigation insights concerning a breadth of topics including what participants found useful as navigational cues, what they wanted to know about their surroundings, and obstacles they encounter. However, discussions also often led to the unexpected topic of difficulties they have with strangers as they navigate. For this paper we will focus primarily on these interactions between blind and sighted people, particularly because participants indicated they are often treated differently (and in many ways awkwardly) by sighted individuals.

3.2.1 Navigation Techniques – Actual vs. Perceived

Visually impaired individuals use many environmental characteristics to recall and confirm their path and help move along a path safely. When asked what is used to help with guidance participants would unanimously and emphatically exclaim, "Everything!" Those who have been trained to concentrate on feedback from their other available senses can detect even the smallest of features.

To expound, landmarks such as stairs and doors are often counted and used to trigger navigation cues. Tactile features such as the slope and raised bumps of a wheelchair curb cut can signal both an intersection and a step to complete along a path. And a variety of audio cues are also utilized for environmental awareness and navigation; for instance, elevators beep as they transition between floors, providing a clue as to their location.

Sometimes devices built to help supplement these navigation techniques don't quite hit the mark for users. For instance, FG11 mentioned she once used a sonar cane to help her navigate, but found it often told her about things she already knew about including when she was near a wall (which she could sense on her own). She stopped using the cane because it wasn't giving her enough valuable unknown information in relation to giving her cues of what she already knew.

More apparent than miscues in technology, however, were misconceptions by sighted people. FG1 and FG3 brought up the frequent misconception that blind navigation, like sighted navigation, is easiest in wide-open places. Visually impaired individuals actually benefit the most from navigating in areas where they have boundaries and many navigational cues such as walls. Since white cane users use the cane to connect with objects, fewer objects equates to less information about the surroundings and path.

An additional misconception that was mentioned by the participants was that they do not count paces (as many sighted people believe they do), because the size of the paces varies too much. Counting steps is also too difficult to do when walking with others and carrying on a conversation.

3.2.2 Unhelpful Assistance – Grabbing and Shouting

Participants mentioned the hazard of sighted people trying to provide unnecessary assistance to them, even though they may have good intentions. We describe several examples of sighted people grabbing people while navigating, shouting directions, and surprising someone. While the sighted person may only be trying to help, they are not always aware of the type of information that is helpful to the visually impaired person, and can often create more dangerous hazards.

One repeated encounter, particularly for the white cane users, was being grabbed or having their cane grabbed while they are walking. Our participants theorized that sighted people are often under the impression that visually impaired individuals are not suppose to run into things with their cane. FG13 noted that people would grab her before she gets on the escalator, and she needed to explain to them how dangerous that is since it could make her fall. O3 mentioned that people will often grab him to stop him from running into obstacles, for instance puddles, but that a verbal warning would be much less surprising and less dangerous. Being grabbed unexpectedly is very alarming, and as FG8 mentioned, it can result in a feeling of loss of control. As FG5 noted, "it only takes one person grabbing you to make you fall." FG13 and O3 said they actually purposefully walk very quickly and try to appear confident so that people do not try to reach out and grab them or provide well intentioned but hazardous assistance.

Another common occurrence was having directions shouted out, particularly when one is concentrating. FG10 takes the train and utilizes audio cues to know when the doors open and other boarding cues. However, he mentioned that people will often shout at him (such as, "Over here!") as he stands listening for his cues. The sighted people who see him believe that he is just standing, is lost, or requires some sort of assistance; however, when they yell at him it actually "throws him off" and distracts him from the audio cues he needs to focus on. Multiple participants from the focus groups mentioned that they found that type of distracting assistance very irritating.

An additional comment about sighted assistance was that sighted people trying to help do not always give a verbal warning. People will also not make any noise, even when a person is running into them with their cane. For example, FG10 mentioned that often he will run into people when he is waiting to pay the fare for his metro card. FG11 explained that people will try to help, but that she is unaware of the help unless she is verbally told about it. For example, phrases such as "open door on your left" are very useful to visually impaired individuals, where as if the door is held open and the visually impaired person is not aware of it, it will most likely just cause more confusion.

3.2.3 Walking With Others

Participants explained that when walking with other sighted people they prefer the "sighted guide" technique. This is when a blind person grasps the elbow/arm of a sighted person and simply uses their body movement to navigate. (This is in addition to their cane but to a lesser extent, and guide dog owners will allow their dogs to simply follow along.) This is a more relaxed way of navigating for both people because the sighted person does not have to give verbal cues for every navigation occurrence and the blind person will walk under the assumption that the sighted person will avoid any hazards in the way.

O3 and many others in our groups prefer to use this technique because it doesn't interrupt the conversation as much and is easier on the sighted companion. FG12 said he prefers it because he doesn't want his sighted companions to feel bad for providing unhelpful information and doesn't want to feel he's training his companions on what information is most helpful to speak aloud. Others in the focus group agreed they felt like not using sighted guide was putting a sense of responsibility on a sighted companion. He also emphatically proclaimed that sighted people are often very bad at deciphering left from right when giving directions, to which other focus group participants also agreed. This preference for sighted guide actually had a large impact on our second set of user studies with sighted partner navigation.

4. SIMULATING REAL NAVIGATION

Continuing our investigation into the navigation technology device needs of people with vision impairments, we conducted observations of a blind participant navigating real environments with a known sighted companion. We anticipated we would learn how to best design navigation technology for independent travelers by noting (and attempting to mimic) the successes of the same interaction between people.

4.1 Partner Observations

4.1.1 Participants

Adults with visual impairments who used a white cane or guide dog were recruited for partner observations of navigating a real world environment. We recruited participants who had undergone navigation training and were comfortable enough to conduct the study without using the "sighted guide" approach - being led by a sighted person with the use of physical touch. We asked participants to identify a close companion to act as their guide (for instance, a spouse or friend).

Table 2 details the gender, age, and relationship of the participants. 'N#' indicates the visually impaired participant, while 'C#' indicates the sighted companion. The participants varied on the onset and state of their visual impairment but all but participant N3 had no usable vision and all were white cane users. All participant pairs had some prior experience navigating together (though not always in completely unfamiliar locations).

Table 2: Partner observation participants.
N=blind participant (i.e., the navigator); C=sighted participant (i.e., the companion). *Note N1 conducted the study twice with two different companions.*

ID	Gender, Age	Vision Impairment Or Companion Relationship & Time Known
N1	36/M	RP, gradual loss age 3, most age 20
C1a	32/F	Wife, 10 years
C1b	29/F	Friend, 3 months
N2	53/F	Accident age 6, lost all vision at age 9
C2	19/F	Child, 19 years
N3	58/M	No vision left eye, poor residual right eye
C3	58/M	Friend, 30 years
N4	55/M	Glaucoma at 9, gradual loss until 18, now no vision (and hearing impaired)
C4	21/F	Volunteer, < 1 year
N5	19/F	Fully blind since 13
C5	20/F	Volunteer, 2 months
N6	32/F	ROP, light perception in right eye
C6	48/F	Friend, 6 years

4.1.2 Study Method

After considering several locations, we decided to conduct the study on our college campus (at least for the first iteration). In our prior work we identified several commonly encountered environments as well as noted differences about how to navigate in those places [6]. Our UMBC campus provided a variety of indoor and outdoor spaces in a very close proximity, which would be difficult to find in other locales. Having one location also allowed us to compare our findings across participants.

We designated four locations for participants to explore in different sections of campus: 1) a hallway art gallery, 2) a research laboratory, 3) a sculpture garden outdoor park, and 4) the bookstore and food court in a university center. The first stop simulated a gallery scenario, particularly useful for observing subjective environment descriptions as well as navigation; the second location simulated an office setting; the third highlighted navigation techniques in wooded areas (a particularly difficult terrain); and the last stop simulated a shopping experience as well as a food ordering experience. We intentionally asked participants to arrive in the morning or early afternoon while classes were in session and the food court was busy, again to simulate different environments including crowd density. Since most of these participants had not been to our campus before, it served as an unfamiliar environment for them, presenting the most extreme of navigation scenarios for which one would rely most heavily on a navigation device. Participant N1 is a student; however, he had only been a student a few months at the time of the study and was not familiar with many parts of the route.

In addition to the navigation tasks, participants engaged in three brief interviews during their tour. When participants first arrived on campus we sat them in the lobby of the nearest building to where they arrived and gave sighted companions a paper map with the buildings and suggested routes outlined. We then explained the overall structure of the study (we delayed explaining the study prior to their arrival mostly to gather pre-planning habits). The second interview was conducted in the research lab and we conducted a mini-interview of the blind participant regarding their navigation strategies and challenges as well as gathered each participant's feelings about the study thus far. We allowed participants to clarify if the navigation instructions had been helpful to receive and/or difficult to give out. If necessary, we then let the blind participant express how they would like to navigate in the second half (since usually there was some difficulty). Then participants moved through the final two destinations where they had a final interview after grabbing lunch in the university center.

4.2 Findings

Because most of our past data focused on strangers interfering with navigation, we believed our prior-relationship requirement would result in observing successful navigation strategies. However, not being able to use the sighted guide technique (that is, having the blind participant hold the sighted participant's arm) presented many more miscues than anticipated. Only one couple had ever navigated in the independent fashion we designated for the study. Thus, having to verbalize navigation cues that were typically simply inferred by their body movement brought to light many misunderstandings sighted companions had about how cane users navigate. In the end, however, blind participants were able to cope (much like they do with strangers they encounter on a regular basis) and the study resulted in an education for the companions.

4.2.1 Misunderstanding "Cues" vs. "Hazards"

Most especially during the first part of the study (before the mid-interview at the research laboratory) sighted companions attempted to have their blind partners walk the way they would typically walk, or based on their understanding of what was safe.

4.2.1.1 Walking a Straight, Wide Open Path

Much like what was found in our focus groups and observations, the sighted companions thought navigating in big open paths was the easiest navigation portion. Thus, the sighted companions often told their partners to "just go straight" in a relaxed tone of voice (and used the time to look at their maps) when really this was the most difficult task to do. It was common for the sighted participants to jokingly scold their partners for not walking straight when they began to veer, not realizing that a lack of vision nearly prevents being able to reach a destination in an undefined path without some other form of tactile or verbal feedback.

Not realizing the difficulty of the task of walking in open space, the directions then became a cyclical round of instructions similar to the following: "Go straight, no come left, too far, ugh – just walk straight!" Rather than focusing on the overall directions, companions spent a lot of time and energy trying to nudge participants into walking down the sidewalk and in open spaces in the same straight lines they usually do.

4.2.1.2 Avoiding Helpful Boundaries

Many companions thought that boundaries were hazards or didn't recognize important navigation cues. Companions also often walked on the right of their partners (away from the natural boundaries) forcing partners to negotiate avoiding the oncoming pedestrian traffic. When we suggested to C5 that she let her partner walk on the right side of the sidewalk she said she didn't want her to walk into the grass (Figure 1). She didn't initially understand that the grass (even if it was lined with bushes for a while) was actually a good cue for keeping straight and also kept her partner from having people walking towards her direct path.

Figure 1 – During the study, a sighted companion (C5) said she didn't want her partner to walk along the grass area (like as shown) because she saw it as a hazard (not a walking cue).

At a sidewalk intersection C3 wondered how his partner would "know to turn" without reading the signage indicating the building was to the right. He didn't realize that the fence and the grass line surrounding the path would indicate a curve and upcoming stairs. Later C3 wondered about a slightly angled portion of the sidewalk (somewhat like an "L" shape) and said it was a falling hazard. But N3 clarified that in the sunlight he could see the contrast of the grass and sidewalk and there's no other obstacles that he'd run into anyway (like trees) so walking into the grass wouldn't harm him.

During the walk with N4 and C4 they encountered two trucks blocking a pathway (the path doubles as a driveway for delivery trucks) (Figure 2). While C4 tried to explain how to walk down the center of the trucks, N4 used his cane to tap between the trucks to gather the width. She saw he was hitting the cars and wanted him to stop and just follow her instructions but he instinctively (and correctly) ignored her to make sure he didn't run into any obstacles as he negotiated the path. The companion jokingly scolded him for hitting the cars.

N1 explained the importance of boundaries to his second sighted companion, C1b (Figure 3): "Boundaries are very important. Because when you don't find boundaries then you lose all your direction. I don't have any sign of where I am now, what I'm doing. [C1b: "Yeah, you don't have a feedback mechanism, right?"] A very flat area with no boundaries is a place where the blind can easily lose direction."

Figure 2 – As N4 uses his cane to tap between the two trucks to understand the width of the gap, his companion (C4) laughs and admonishes him for "hitting people's cars". She didn't understand his strategy to understand his boundaries.

Figure 3 – N1 shows how he uses a grass line to walk straight.

4.2.2 Sighted People Give Wrong/Bad Directions

N3 put it rather bluntly when he said, "Never trust sighted people." While he was being sarcastic, we did notice that having vision didn't seem to help the companions give accurate directions. While we're mindful that many of the companions were experiencing an overload by having to narrate the navigation experience, there were still surprises in the miscues.

4.2.2.1 Ambiguous Phrases

The companion's directions often incorporated ambiguous phrases such as "here" or "over there" along with the companion pointing in the general direction of the target object – obviously neither of which is helpful for someone who cannot see the visual references to which the phrases apply. Companions would also mix up saying "left" when they meant "right" (and vice versa).

4.2.2.2 Timing

There was also a tendency with companions who were not used to giving verbal instructions to give directions as soon as they saw an item approaching. For example, saying, "We're coming up to some steps on the left" as soon as the sighted companion saw them would cause the blind participant to turn too early. When companions tried to compensate for this by giving distance estimates they were generally inaccurate measurement estimations and often presented with little confidence and in the form of a question, as in "In about 10, maybe 20 feet?"

4.2.2.3 Missing and Misinformation

Companions also didn't know what alerts to give participants such as warning of pending stairs and then announcing the end of the stairs. Companions eventually learned to give this warning after seeing their partners slow down and explore at the junctures. However, C5 told her partner they were done with a flight of stairs while on a long landing, but there were actually 2 more flights. This discouraged her partner (who initially thought she was kidding because she so confidently told him they were done).

While companions did their best to provide their partners with relevant information, there were instances when the most relevant information was missed or what was needed was not understood. As a detailed example, C3 spent time explaining his concern about the handrail being close to the wall (Figure 4) (as opposed to the other hand railing which was more open). Instead he needed to warn N3 that the stairs shifted from normal wide to very long and spread out (information he needed to keep from falling). The companion also allowed him to walk up the left side of the stairs, which made him vulnerable to running into people (as people tend to walk down on the left and up on the right) and then walking next to him took up the entire staircase. Overall he was trying to see things from his visually impaired friend's perspective but missed the mark.

Then, once at the top of the stairs (Figure 5), N3 asks, "What's on the left?" but C3 says, "It's just up here," and points to the destination building and then names buildings in the incorrect order (based on his orientation, not that of his partner).

Figure 4 – C3 expressed concern that the handrail was close to the brick wall, but didn't warn N3 about the unusual stair length or that he was walking on the wrong side of the stairwell for oncoming traffic.

Figure 5 – At the top of the stairs, N3 asks his companion, "What's on the left?" but their differing orientations causes the companion to give incorrect information based on his interpretation of "left" as they stand perpendicular to one another.

4.2.2.4 Speaking Their Language (Eventually)

Many of the visually impaired participants used the second interview (in the research lab) to educate their partners on what is most helpful to provide given they were not allowed to use the sighted guide technique.

N4 was the most vocal as he began his explanation as soon as we were seated. Their exchange was the most detailed in terms of how each person was feeling during the encounter:

N4: "If there's something in my way on the ground as long as it's cane level I don't mind hitting it so you don't have to worry about – go to the left a little bit – I can just let the cane hit it and go around it. But the overhead stuff is a different story. "

[He explains how he uses his cane to trail a wall and uses the grass line to stay straight.]

C4: "I don't want him to fall over a trash can or something. I know his stick will hit it but I don't want him to fall." *[After more discussion...]* "Do you want me or the stick?"

[N4 and the researchers explicitly tell her to switch her mode and don't think he's going to fall.]

C4: "I'll just tell you left, right, and forward and if you hit a wall or a foot that's on you."

[N4 tells her to clarify between saying "left" for a sharp turn vs. "veer left" for slight body adjustment.]

C4: "Okay, I'll let you be more independent."

The conversation helped them. Once they left the research laboratory C4 let N4 use the handrail to walk down the stairs (which caused N4 to walk faster than she did). C4 also delayed speaking a landmark on the path (like the stairs) until N4 was very nearby but also pointed out upcoming parts of the path (such as describing a set of steps then a landing then another set of steps). During one exchange she told him "You're gonna hit a grass line" and shifted her position to let him find it to which he responded, "Oh cool." In the final interview he explained that her change in verbal direction cues and allowing him to use the environmental cues helped make the experience much smoother and more enjoyable for him.

Aside from one pair (noted below) all of the other companion pairs had the same type of shift from the first to the second half. Not only were explicit conversations had such as that with N4 and C4, but overhearing the answers to our questions about common navigation strategies educated companions (such as learning how participants hear audio cues or use the change in floor texture to know there's a pending navigation action).

Of note was the second companion pair – the mother/daughter team. Rather than having miscues along the way or a transformation between the first and second half, they grasped the independent navigation task right away. C2 let N2 (her mom) walk independently and guide off environmental cues such as hitting a fence, retaining walls, and grass lines. In the meantime with every new environment they encountered C2 explained the surroundings as they walked. C2 only chimed in with feedback on the mobility portion of the study when it was absolutely necessary (for instance her mom had trouble finding the automatic door opener on one of the doors). When we commented about how comfortable they seemed to be at navigating in this separated manner they explained that this is how they often walk together. The mother had to be independent in order to raise her children and her children have been around an independent blind traveler all their lives so it was a natural occurrence. It was nonetheless interesting to see this type of interaction happen seamlessly and naturally.

4.2.2.5 *Coping with Sighted People*

Multiple participants mentioned during the interviews that none of the miscues experienced in our study were different from what they experience with strangers on the street (further confirming our prior findings as well). Due to the common occurrences, they've learned to cope in several ways.

N5 mentioned that she's learned to cope with the incorrect left/right directions by listening for the direction in which a person's head turns, as people tend to look in the direction they want you to go.

Not completely tuning out their other senses, during the study both N3 and N6 heard the beeping sound of the elevator and were able to gather its direction while their companions looked down the hallway or had to first turn a corner to notice it.

N3 explained that he's learned to ask 3 different people for directions before he acts on their advice because he finds people are nice and don't want to tell you "no" so they'll give some information, even if it's wrong.

Much like having to cope in real life navigation as expressed by our prior study participants, partner study participants worked well with their sighted companions to probe for the information they needed, use their own instincts to override bad instructions, and educate their companions along the way.

5. DISCUSSION

Our research probes set out to inform the design of new navigation technology for people with vision impairments by first identifying current navigation challenges then exploring possible device features. Our focus group discussions and subsequent diary entries asked participants to recall past navigation occurrences, our single-person observations allowed us to experience the scenarios firsthand, and our partner observations provided device emulation without actual device prototyping and use. Our findings not only contributed to device design considerations but, somewhat unexpectedly, also pointed to broader social implications.

Many of the design considerations that can be inferred from the findings (particularly the partner observations) are similar to any navigation device and application. These include providing optimal timing of giving directions and determining the level of detail to provide (from simply what one is passing to detailed directional cues). Note this is not dissimilar from the findings (explained in the Related Work section) for the collaborative in-car GPS navigation study of Forlizzi, *et al* [2]. However, as expressed in prior work by Swobodzinski and Raubal (also detailed in Related Work), navigation without vision has very unique attributes from navigating with vision [5]. Thus, future systems will need to continue optimizing routes and become smarter about what is considered a "boundary" (such as the wall) versus what is a "hazard" (such as a hole in the ground).

To expand further, many systems are designing for obstacle avoidance but with a view that any object is an "obstacle" and the optimal path is one that is clear and wide open throughout. While this may be an ideal scenario for swifter navigation and less cognitive load in the amount of encounters one has in a given path, this also immensely changes the structure of how a person is taught to navigate and how they "see" the world. To make the point differently, in order for a person to see their environment, their eyes hit objects with light; similarly, in order to navigate without vision, currently a white cane user (literally) hits objects with their cane (and therefore their hand, wrist, and arm). Because the sensation is different, people with vision don't necessarily realize the similarity in needing object feedback in order to map out a path, but it is actually the same concept just experienced differently. Thus, future system designs should either take into account the need for a cane to "just hit" objects or provide enough sensory information to substitute for the lack of visual stimulus.

Our open-ended discussions in the focus groups as well as observations in the wild and with partners also revealed troubling findings around the lack of knowledge about vision impairments and the subsequent interactions that range from awkward to dangerous, particularly with strangers. It appears there is opportunity for more activities to build awareness, advocacy, and empathy within the sighted community. Numerous advocacy groups make great strides in this area in their everyday endeavors but it appears more voices need to carry the message. Social media coupled with multimedia presentation seems a very promising way to reach a wider audience for a group this is large but still a minority in their respective communities. Prior work with emulation software for people with disabilities [1],[3] has also demonstrated strides in building empathy between people with diverse abilities that can lead to better communication, patience, and overall better social interactions.

6. CONCLUSION

In our research to understand the needs of people with vision impairments in regards to pedestrian navigation technology, we have uncovered many ways in which blind and sighted persons see navigation tasks very differently. Through our interviews and observations of people with vision impairments, including observations of participants with close sighted companions, we see where assistance from a sighted person can be incorrect and even interfere with safe navigation. Often sighted people are overly concerned about non-threatening hazards and fail to communicate the needed guidance information. We hope that by bringing awareness to these situations we can begin to foster education, empathy, and ultimately better communication between the two groups. We also hope the examples assist other technology designers to prevent these misunderstandings from becoming interface mishaps.

7. FUTURE WORK

Our future work includes continuing to conduct partner observations. We wish to include different environments like major cities as well as move to locations outside of our state. This will likely reveal more findings on navigation strategies such as how street crossings are negotiated. We also plan to run the study with more pairings, including with two blind participants. Through continual iterative coding we plan to identify more specific guidelines to contribute for future intelligent navigation aids that build upon the lessons learned from the current human interaction, ensuring the device sees navigation the way the user does.

8. ACKNOWLEDGMENTS

Many thanks to our participants for their valuable time and feedback. This work was supported by Toyota Motor Engineering & Manufacturing North America and in part by the National Science Foundation under grant IIS-1353312. Any opinions, findings, conclusions or recommendations expressed in this work are those of the authors and do not necessarily reflect those of the National Science Foundation.

9. REFERENCES

[1] Flatla, D. R. and Gutwin, C. "So that's what you see": building understanding with personalized simulations of colour vision deficiency. *Proceedings of ASSETS '12,* 2012. New York: ACM Press, 167–174.

[2] Forlizzi, J., Barley, W. C., and Seder, T. Where should I turn: moving from individual to collaborative navigation strategies to inform the interaction design of future navigation systems. *Proceedings of CHI '10,* 2010. New York: ACM Press, 1261–1270.

[3] Hailpern, J., Danilevsky, M., Harris, A., Karahalios, K., Dell, G., and Hengst, J. ACES: promoting empathy towards aphasia through language distortion emulation software. *Proceedings of CHI '11,* 2011. New York: ACM Press, 609–618.

[4] Roentgen, U. R., Gelderblom, G. J., Soede, M., and de Witte, L. P. Inventory of electronic mobility aids for persons with visual impairments: a literature review. *Journal of Visual Impairment & Blindness, 102* (11), 702 - 724.

[5] Swobodzinski, M. and Raubal, M. An indoor routing algorithm for the blind: development and comparison to a routing algorithm for the sighted. *International Journal of Geographical Information Science, 23* (10), 1315 - 1343.

[6] Williams, M. A., Hurst, A., and Kane, S. K. "Pray before you step out": Describing personal and situational blind navigation behaviors. *Proceedings of ASSETS '13,* 2013. New York: ACM Press, 28:1–28:8.

Path-Guided Indoor Navigation for the Visually Impaired Using Minimal Building Retrofitting

Dhruv Jain

Department of Computer Science and Engineering
Indian Institute of Technology Delhi
dhruv.cstaff@cse.iitd.ac.in

ABSTRACT

One of the common problems faced by visually impaired people is of independent path-based mobility in an unfamiliar indoor environment. Existing systems do not provide active guidance or are bulky, expensive and hence are not socially apt. In this paper, we present the design of an omnipresent cellphone based active indoor wayfinding system for the visually impaired. Our system provides step-by-step directions to the destination from any location in the building using minimal additional infrastructure. The carefully calibrated audio, vibration instructions and the small wearable device helps the user to navigate efficiently and unobtrusively. Results from a formative study with five visually impaired individuals informed the design of the system. We then deployed the system in a building and field tested it with ten visually impaired users. The comparison of the quantitative and qualitative results demonstrated that the system is useful and usable, but can still be improved.

Categories and Subject Descriptors: K.4.2 [**Computers and Society**]: Social Issues - Assistive technologies for persons with disabilities

Keywords: Visual Impairment; Indoor Navigation

1. INTRODUCTION

Navigation and wayfinding to reach a desired destination is a considerable challenge for a visually impaired person particularly in an unknown indoor environment [14]. Path finding is a composition of several cognitive processes like map building, landmark identification, obstacle avoidance and interaction with by-standers to ask directions [25, 26]. Most of the globally present signages are vision based and are inaccessible to them. Locating an accessible signage (tactile, audio) again poses a problem. Navigators currently rely on sporadic help from bystanders and use path integration to follow a given direction [25]. This causes anxiety, embarrassment and makes them reluctant to go alone in an unfamiliar building [15]. This was also corroborated in our own formative study.

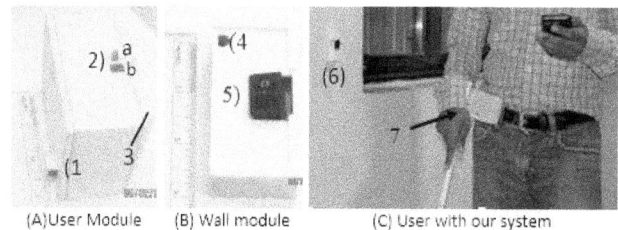

Figure 1: System prototypes. (1)IR receiver, (2a)tactile push button switch for operation, (2b)charging port and (3)belt fix, (4)IR transmitter and (5)switch, (6)wall module retrofitted in the building, (7)user module.

Existing commercial navigation systems based on GPS (eg. StreetTalk [3], Sendero [1]) have made navigation a lot easier in outdoor environments. But their major shortcoming is that they can only identify very specific landmarks encountered by the user and typically do not work indoors. Several attempts have been made to address the problem of indoor navigation for the visually impaired. However, no single solution has found wide acceptability and long term deployment for use. Most of the systems present today are either only landmark identification systems with no path-based guidance (eg. RFID [22, 13], infrared based systems [5, 32, 34]) or are inaccurate for an indoor environment (eg. dead-reckoning [17, 12, 36], Wifi [28, 31]). Few systems exist which are both omnipresent (which could localize the user accurately from any point in the building) and provide step-by-step path based wayfinding (eg. Building Navigator [18], Andha Astra [33]). These systems are bulky to carry [10] or expensive to operate [29].

In this work, we present the design and implementation of a portable and self-contained indoor navigation system which is currently deployed in a university building. Comprising of a network of wall mounted units and a user module coupled with a mobile application (Figure 1), the system downloads the map of the building, localizes the user within the building, takes the destination as input from the user, and then helps him to independently navigate to his destination using step-by-step navigational instructions. Novel features of the system are:

- Path-based navigation with active guidance for turns and *important landmarks* in the course of travel.
- Update on *position awareness* information particularly *obstacle warning instructions*.
- Update on *position correction* information in case the user deviates from the path.
- Use of *minimal additional building augmentation* while providing good accuracy.

- *Small, compact design* of user module and hence convenient to carry.

These features make the system a socially apt and efficient indoor navigation guide, thereby reducing anxiety and embarrassment in public places.

Further, we present the results and insights from a before-and-after study in which a group of 10 users participated to validate the usefulness and usability of the system and gather insights for improvements.

2. RELATED WORK

Most of the proposed wayfinding systems for visually impaired are outdoor systems which mainly use GPS for localization purposes [24, 32]. Indoor systems cannot use GPS signals, as buildings block them. To surpass this issue, researches have developed alternative localization techniques that can be distinguished into two different categories [10].

Dead-Reckoning techniques estimate the user's current localization based on a previously estimated or known location. While the user is moving, dead reckoning estimates the user's location by interpreting readings from one or more sensors that the user carries such as accelerometers, magnetometers, and gyroscopes [12, 17, 21]. The initial location is typically determined using GPS [17], RFID tags [21], or cellular phone positioning [30]. One significant benefit of this approach is the low installation cost, as it does not require physical infrastructure. The main drawback of this technique is the error accumulation over time as dead reckoning is a recursive process and each sensor has some inaccuracy.

Beacon-based approaches augment the physical space with identifiers. Such beacons can be retro-reflective digital signs detected by a camera [7, 35], infrared [5, 32, 34], RF [9], RFID tags [22, 13, 8], or ultra-sound identifiers [29]. Locating identifiers may be hard, as beacons may require line of sight or close proximity to the human. This significantly delays the user and makes him embarrassed. Other beacon-based techniques use triangulation to locate the user. For example, wireless network positioning systems [28, 31, 23] may triangulate the location of base stations using the provided signal strength or could be building signal strength maps. Wireless nodes however, often suffer from multi-path effects or interference.

The system most similar to ours is a commercial product called Talking Signs [5]. It uses a network of infrared transmitters installed on the walls or poles at tactical locations. Despite the low-cost of the IR technology, it suffers from the same limitation as other beacon-based approaches. A lot of IR modules have to be installed for precise localization and the system cannot provide path-based navigational directions. This increases cognitive load on a visually impaired user and is hazardous in case of any deviation or mistake.

Beacons are often integrated with dead-reckoning to correct the accumulated error through environmental knowledge [17], RFID tags [21], ultrasound beacons [20], and map-matching [21, 27]. Our system builds upon the beacon based Talking Signs system [5] by using infrared sensor installation at turns and important landmarks in the building to localize the user when he is near them and; augments it with selective dead-reckoning by using only the accelerometer to calculate the position in between any two infrared sensors. Thus it is omnipresent, provides step-by-step path

based guidance and topological information of the surroundings, obstacle warning instructions and corrective directions when the user gets deviated. The dead-reckoning technique significantly reduces the number of IR beacons and hence the overall system cost. Further, the system is convenient to carry, easy to learn and operate, not easily visible and can be easily mounted on existing building infrastructure.

3. SYSTEM OVERVIEW

We describe the design process using a formative study with the visually impaired persons before providing the technical description and implementation details of the system.

3.1 Design Process

We conducted a formative study to gain insights into the process of indoor wayfinding and arrive at desired specification for the proposed system. Five people (3 males and 2 females) from Delhi were recruited; ages 21-35 years, varied onset of blindness from birth to legally blind for 3 years, and varying level of blindness from partial vision to fully blind. All the participants were accessible mobile phone users with screen readers installed in them. They mostly used canes and would take help from sighted persons for finding their path since no indoor wayfinding system exist in India.

The task: Participants were asked to navigate a predefined track in two places unfamiliar to them: a 90m track in an uncrowded academic building and a 120m track in a busy shopping mall in Delhi. We assigned a common destination to each user and asked them to take their usual approach to find their way to the destination. We saw that they usually try to find signs, ask for help or resort to ad hoc approaches. The main issues observed during navigation were confusion regarding the correctness of their current course, absence of bystanders in some areas, language barriers in asking for help, unhelpful and aggressive bystanders in some cases, vulnerability to injuries during navigation and lack of confirmation upon reaching the destination.

The interview: After the study, we interviewed the participants to discuss the problems faced during independent indoor navigation in general and compiled their views for an effective technological solution. The interviews emphasized their high degree of anxiety in accessing unfamiliar locations independently. Their requirement for sighted assistance in general induces inertia towards going anywhere alone. They are frequently subjected to gaze and unwanted attention from the surrounding people. Some participants also reported getting lost and injured in cases at times.

All the participants emphasized the need and utility of an affordable navigation guide to travel independently. The key requirements articulated by the participants included:

- Audio-based guidance system which would give information about the *current location, impending turns and important landmarks to the destination* and approximate distance of each section between the turns.

- Warning about *impending obstacles* in the path of travel.

- Audio feedback to *confirm the arrival of the destination.*

- Preferably, *utilize a device an individual may already own* and be comfortable with operating the same.

These insights informed the design of our system which is presented in the following sections.

3.2 System Design

The system consists of the two major components: (1) wall modules deployed in building and, (2) user end comprising of a waist-worn device coupled with a mobile phone.

Building: The system consists of network of infrared based wall units retrofitted at specific locations in the building. We chose to use IR technology for locating the user as they are extremely accurate and inexpensive [11]. These sensors transmit the unique IR tags corresponding to their location perpendicular to the direction of motion of the user.

User end: The user end consists of two modules, a mobile phone and a user module.

Mobile phone: A primary goal of the work was to employ a device already owned by the user. Thus, we chose to use a mobile phone which is commonly used by people [16]. Furthermore, applications on new smart phones offer many functionalities and services including accessibility features like screen readers and vibration alerts.

User module: To receive the IR signal transmitted from the wall modules, we have develop a custom user module since modern day mobile phones do not have infrared components. Also, to enhance the accuracy of the system and to substantially reduce the number of wall mounted units, we decided to use the accelerometer used in high precision pedometers. It returns the number of steps traveled by the user which, when multiplied by the average step length, gives the distance traveled. The average step length is user configurable on the basis of his height. Since an accelerometer has to be worn close to the legs of the user to calculate steps, we decided to put the module near the waist. Putting the module on legs gives better accuracy but that may be inconvenient for the user. The module connects with the mobile phone over bluetooth. System prototypes are shown in Figure 1.

To provide an estimate of the number of wall units reduced by the use of accelerometer, consider the following: The maximum localization error of the system is $\pm 1.6m$ calculated via separate experiments. This accuracy is provided by a network of infrared modules situated at an interval of 3m. The use of accelerometer gives the same accuracy and path-guidance, but with increased interval between the infrared modules of 8-10m! Details on localization experiments are beyond the scope of this paper.

User interface: All the information is conveyed to the user via the Text-to-Speech (TTS) engine of the mobile application, and also displayed in a large font size to provide for someone with partial vision. Vibration alerts are used to provide continuous feedback for being on the right track.

Figure 2 shows sample screens from the mobile application interface. The text on top shows the audio message when the particular screen is activated. The screen on the right is displayed when the user is moving. The screen is divided into at most two parts so it is convenient for visually impaired person to touch and operate. Within a screen, the relative sizes of the buttons are kept according to the need. E.g., in the rightmost screen, chances are more that the user would press the 'more information' button to get the navigational instructions for travel and hence, the 'cancel travel' button is kept small. We also have a qwerty keypad based phone implementation (not shown). The texts at the bottom are example audio messages during navigation.

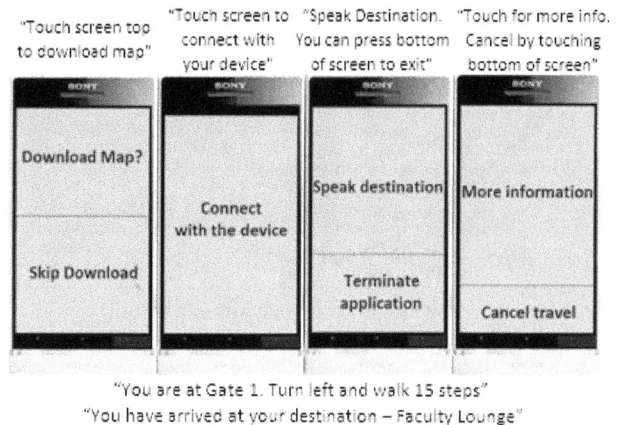

"Touch screen top to download map"   "Touch screen to connect with your device"   "Speak Destination. You can press bottom of screen to exit"   "Touch for more info. Cancel by touching bottom of screen"

"You are at Gate 1. Turn left and walk 15 steps"
"You have arrived at your destination – Faculty Lounge"

Figure 2: Sample screens from the mobile application.

Maps: The building map consists of a topological map with metric information between the waypoints, annotated with additional information about the path like obstacles. An example map file converted from a L shaped path is shown in the Figure 3. In each line, the first block represents the landmark and the other blocks represent its neighbors. Within each block, the string is the name of the landmark followed by x-coord, y-coord and the floor number.

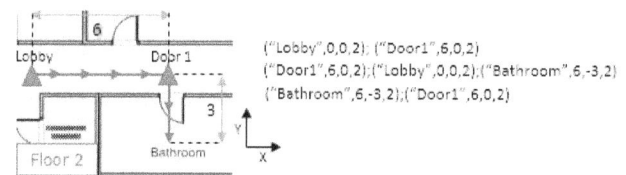

("Lobby",0,0,2); ("Door1",6,0,2)
("Door1",6,0,2);("Lobby",0,0,2);("Bathroom",6,-3,2)
("Bathroom",6,-3,2);("Door1",6,0,2)

Figure 3: An example map file converted from floor plan of a building. Red arrowed path is the navigational track.

3.3 System Usage

The basic process to use the system is shown in Figure 4. The user downloads the map of the particular building from our server. He chooses from the list of building maps stored on our server and the selected map gets downloaded in about 2 sec. He then connects the mobile application to the user module using the touch screen. After a successful connection, the user has an option of either speaking his desired destination or typing the destination using the QWERTY keypad. If a close match with a location in our database is found, the main process of the application begins.

As the user walks, the mobile application receives the current position and the number of steps data from the user module and dynamically calculates the path to the destination using the shortest path algorithm. The user is kept

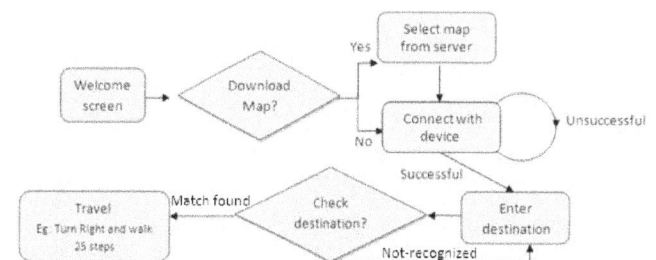

Figure 4: Flowchart of the mobile application explaining the surface working of the device.

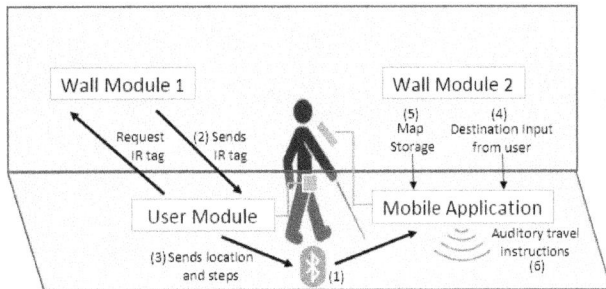

Figure 5: Background operation of the system.

informed about his current location and navigational directions to the next waypoint in the path of travel (viz. intersection, lift, destination etc.). The navigational directions include any turn to take and the number of steps to travel. Also, a warning is given if the user takes a wrong turn or deviates from the path, and the path is re-calculated from the user's current location to his destination.

3.4 System implementation

An example overview of the system is shown in Figure 5. (1) The mobile application connects to the user module through Bluetooth; (2) The wall module when requested by the user module, transmits the location specific tag. (3) IR location information and steps from the accelerometer are transfered to the mobile application. (4) The user inputs the destination to the mobile application which calculates the path of travel from the stored building map (5) and the information received from the user module (3). (6) The application then conveys the navigational directions to the user.

User module: The user module consists of an Atmega328 microcontroller, a serial RN-41 bluetooth module, a 3-axis accelerometer (ADXL345), two ST-12 IR Codec chip from Sunrom technologies [4], IR transmitter and receiver (TSOP 1738) and two Ultralife UBP001 Li-ion batteries (each 3.7 V, 900mAh) connected in series. The battery life is approx. 14 hours with the full charging time of 6-7 hours. When the battery is low, the module sends the "BATTERY LOW" signal to the mobile application through Bluetooth which informs the user. The two ST-12 IR Codec chips act as encoder and decoder for transmitting and receiving data respectively. Projected cost of the fully customized user module is < $20.

Wall module: The wall module consists of Microchip's PIC18LF4550 microcontroller with two ST-12 IR Codec chips for encoding and decoding, IR transmitter and receiver (TSOP 1738), 9V battery from Duracell and a magnetic buzzer (Piezo buzzer - B20). The PIC microcontroller runs on nano-watt technology to save power. The tag of the wall module is saved in EEPROM of the PIC microcontroller. The microcontroller operates in sleep mode to save power and wakes through the interrupt from user module to transmit data. As explained in Section 6.1, the buzzer is an add-on feature to help the user identify the exact location of his destination. A single 9V Duracell battery can run the module for 2-2.5 years with continuous operation. Cost of setup per floor in a typical building (20 wall modules) is $200.

Mobile application: The mobile application is built for Google Android based platforms. The application uses *Text-to-Speech (TTS)* API of Android to give auditory output in English language to the users. We have used *Amarino*

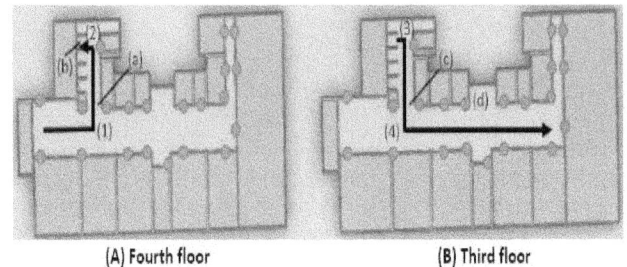

Figure 6: Track used for user trials. Starting point is on floor 4, end point is on floor 3. The dots represent the position of wall units and black arrows show the traversed path. 1,2,3 and 4 represent four turns in the path; door (a), lift (b), door (c) and wide corridor (d) are annotations. Total length of the path is 75m.

toolkit for bluetooth communication with the user module. The application uses our map file to find the shortest path to the destination using the Dijkstra's algorithm. Users can enter the destination via the QWERTY keypad and the application auto-completes the entered string if there is only one possible match. For Android phones with OS version 2.3 or above, the speech recognition feature can also be used to identify the location speech input using Google *RecognizerIntent* API but since it is rather inaccurate in interpreting regional accents, the recognized strings are further matched with our database of locations in the building.

Building maps: The floor plans of the buildings are available in the DWG format with the building authorities. With the help of any floor plan viewing software like AUTOCAD, the specific locations of the wall modules can be marked. This DWG file is then converted to coordinate format (x,y,z) in the form of a text file which forms our map file. After this one-time task, the map is uploaded to a central server from where the file can be downloaded to the user phones.

4. USER EVALUATION
4.1 Study Design

Goal: The goal of the study was to determine the efficacy of the system for enabling persons with visual impairment in the age group of 18-40 years to independently navigate in indoor environments with narrow corridors.

Experimental setup: The system was installed in 4 floors of a university building. A total of 84 wall modules (21 per floor) were deployed at an interval of about 8m (Figure 6). We conducted the user study on the third and fourth floors of the building. The walking corridor was tiled, which facilitated quantitative estimation of deviations from the path.

Participants: The study participants included 5 males and 5 females selected randomly from two NGOs (Table 1). They had basic English literacy and adequate knowledge of using a mobile phone. Individuals possessing additional impairments like locomotor or hearing problems were excluded from this study. Participants mostly used canes and would typically ask for directions from sighted individuals while navigating. Two participants were somewhat familiar with the building while the rest had no familiarity.

4.2 Methodology

The major phases of the study are outlined in Figure 7.

The user visited the experiment building 6 times over a period of about 12 days (1 visit for baseline study, 3 for train-

Table 1: Characteristics of the participants used for the study.

	User[a]	M/F	Age	Impairment	Onset Age	Familiarity with site	Phone model	Accessible?	O&M Training?
1	Amit	M	30	Full	Birth	Low	Nokia E71	Yes	No
2	Rita	F	32	Partial	Birth	Low	Samsung Pro	No	No
3	Sita	F	17	Full	Birth	Low	Nokia 101	No	No
4	Anu	F	22	Full	2.5yrs	Low	Digibee G225	No	Yes
5	Raju	M	27	Full	Birth	Medium	Huawei U8850	No	Yes
6	Neha	F	25	Full	20yrs	Low	Nokia 112	No	Yes
7	Asha	F	26	Partial	18yrs	Low	Nokia 3310	No	Yes
8	Raj	M	27	Full	Birth	High	Nokia C5	Yes	Yes
9	Anil	M	21	Full	Birth	Low	Nokia N97	Yes	Yes
10	Ali	M	21	Full	2-3yrs	Low	Nokia C5	Yes	No

[a]We replaced the names of the participants to protect their anonymity.

Figure 7: Phases of the study indicating key activities.

ing, 1 for device testing and 1 for Focus Group Discussion). The experiments were conducted in the morning time when people roamed around. The study was scheduled as follows:

Baseline Study: Before introducing the device, we asked the users for problems they face in indoor navigation. Then, they navigated between two predefined locations on the 3rd and 4th floors of the building using their usual navigation methods. For comparative analysis, volunteers gave the same instructions to reach the destination as given by our system except that all of them were given at the beginning once. Also, they could stop navigating midway and raise their hand to ask for directions if they forgot or got confused. In such a case, the volunteer correctly oriented the user from their current position and the navigational directions were repeated. If a major deviation was observed[1], reorientation was done to avoid the anxiety of getting lost.

User Training: User training involved demonstration of the system, testing the understanding by performing basic operations like opening the mobile application, entering possible destinations, wearing and operating the waist module etc. and, volunteer assisted mock navigation with the device on the training tracks containing 21 different locations.

Device Testing: The user performed device assisted navigation on the same track as used for baseline study. Randomization of the path was done by introducing artificial obstacles like boxes and bars in the path. The users had only one prior attempt at navigating on the sufficiently long track during the baseline study and there was a period greater than a week between the two tests (interspersed with periods of training, done at a separate location). The testing concluded with a qualitative interview session (and also a focus group discussion later) in which the users expressed their views on the utility, merits, demerits, ease of learning and further improvements for the device.

Pilot Study: The entire process was first piloted on Amit. During the baseline trial, he significantly deviated from the path and took a lot of time to complete. So, for the subsequent users, additional precautions were introduced like reorienting test subjects after a major deviation.

---

[1]Any deviation greater than 6m is reported as a major deviation.

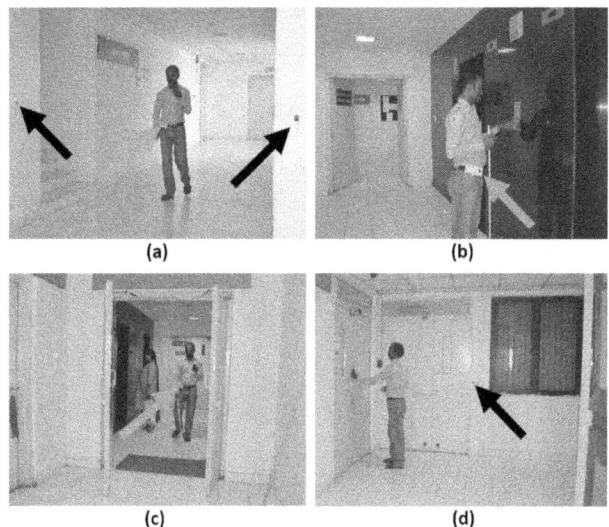

Figure 8: User reaching the destination with the aid of the system. User module (red arrow) and wall module (black-arrow). (a)Start position on floor 4, (b)waiting for lift, (c)entering floor 3, (d)final position.

5. FINDINGS

5.1 Quantitative Results

All users were able to successfully navigate to their destination using our system. Figure 8 shows some examples for one user. Significant improvements were observed in the measured parameters.

Minimal deviation: No major deviations were observed for all the participants in the study during device testing. Comparison of the results for baseline and device testing are shown in Table 2. Our system was able to successfully guide the users around turns and obstacles. However, two users were close to colliding with the half-closed door shown in Figure 8(c), indicating that information about similar structures also needs to be provided. Figure 10 shows how our system instructed the user to walk straight on a wide corridor. The trial with Neha was aborted as she became conscious of five volunteers focusing on her trial.

Reduction in help seeking events: Table 3 shows the reduction in number of times the users asked for navigational directions during device testing. The system was able to effectively guide 7 out of 9 users to the destination without any external sighted help. Sita and Raju were uncomfortable in operating the lift and volunteers had to intervene.

Table 2: Comparison of 'major deviation from the path' for baseline and device testing.

	Rita	Sita	Anu	Raju	Raj	Asha	Anil	Ali	Amit	Neha
Without system	1	2	2	3	3	2	2	3	4	3
With system	0	0	0	0	0	0	0	0	0	-

Table 3: Comparison of 'number of help seeking events' for baseline and device testing.

	Rita	Sita	Anu	Raju	Raj	Asha	Anil	Ali	Amit	Neha
Without system	3	3	4	6	4	3	2	5	3	4
With system	0	1	0	1	0	0	0	0	0	-

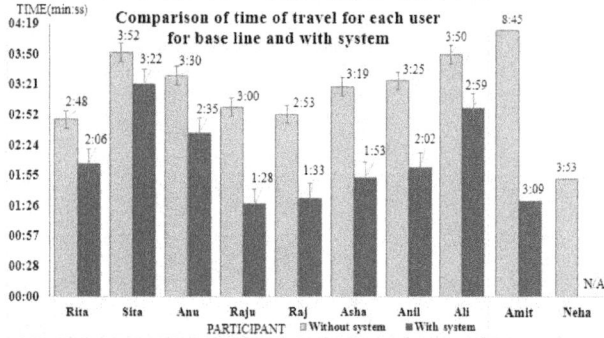

Figure 9: Graph showing the 'time of travel' for each user without and with our system. The graph for Amit and Neha is shown separately.

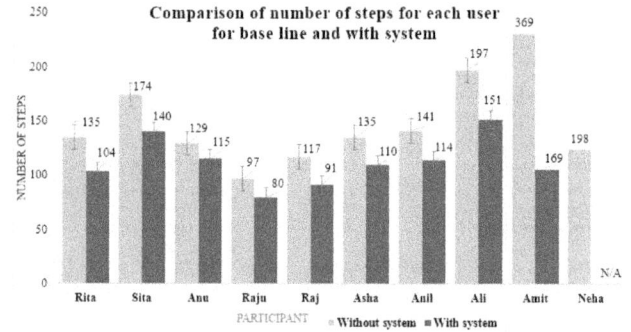

Figure 11: Graph showing the 'number of steps taken' by each user without and with our system.

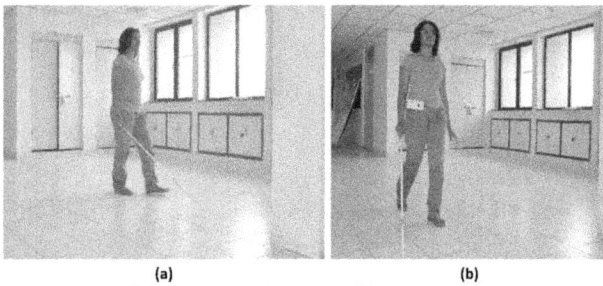

Figure 10: (a)User gets deviated while navigating without the system at position 'd', Figure 6. (b)Corrective navigation with the indoor navigation system.

Optimal time of travel: All users were able to reach the destination much faster with our system. Figure 9 plots the time taken by the users to traverse the experimental path during baseline and device testing. The pairwise t-test was significant (*two-tailed p<0.01*). The pilot participant (Amit) was not stopped by the volunteers even after he deviated beyond 6m from the ideal path.

Straight, path-directed motion: The number of steps taken by users reduced during device testing as they followed the accurate instructions of the mobile application and did not depend on exploration of the surroundings (Figure 11). Pairwise t-test yielded *two-tailed p<0.01*.

5.2 Qualitative Analysis

The majority of users expressed that indoor navigation is a day to day problem and they have to resort to a hit and trial approach for finding their way. They understood the usage of the device effectively during training and comfortably reached their destination during device testing.

Easy to wear and operate
Users mentioned that the module was easy to put on, remove and carry. They appreciated the on/off push buttons which allow them to operate the module without braille markers. The charging port was compatible with the Nokia mobile phones that they commonly use (Table 1). The texture was slightly rough for them but we explained that this was a trial prototype. There were two suggested improvements. First, they advised to reduce the dimensions (and weight) of the module to the size (and weight) of a data-card (approx. 7X3 cm). This would ease the operation further and make it less visible. Second, some users were concerned with the belt attachment. Raju was quoted as saying - *"The device should have a hook to attach it easily to any part on the body. Opening and closing of belt in public is very embarrassing and hence, not an option."* A female user Anu expressed: *"Women do not always wear jeans. They may wear skirt, sari or salwaar/kamiz (traditional Indian dresses with a long top). So, it is necessary to develop an alternate attachment."* We propose to develop a hook attachment in the future.

Two users forgot to switch-on the user module before the trial. The application successfully prompted them to turn it on. One forgot to switch-off the user module after the trial leading to power wastage. He suggested that the module should periodically vibrate when on. All users preferred the white color for the module.

Friendly application interface
Users were happy with the carefully designed stages of the mobile application and appreciated its features.

Raj: *"Since the literacy rate is quite low in developing countries, the speech input can make the device universal to work with. The application is user-friendly and the touch input is easy to learn."*

Asha: *"I have so many options to use the application. I can either listen to audio messages or use the large font to read... or can even use the screen reader to read the text."*

Average time taken to operate all the initial stages of the application was 9.5 sec (best: 7 sec, worst: 16 sec); average time spent in individual stages being 3 sec to download the map, 2.5 sec to connect with the phone and 4 sec to enter the destination. All measurements were done through visual inspection by the volunteers and are approximate.

The users preferred speech over QWERTY over touch-based input whenever there was a choice. They found it easier to directly respond to the application as it was speaking to them, hence speech input was the most preferred. The preference of QWERTY keypad input over touch is evident as all the participants owned non-touch based phones (Table 1) and consequently, it was easier for them to type. The users said that the applications in developing countries should also target non-touch based dumbphones due to low penetration of smartphones among visually impaired population, even in urban areas like Delhi.

We observed problems with speech recognition during the training. Users had different ways of pronunciation as they came from different geographical locations in India. Few uncommon locations required 2-3 repeats for some users having a peculiar accent. The android version we used does not recognizes Indian accent.

Guided, clear and audible instructions

Users appreciated that the navigational instructions were accurate and precise to not cause any cognitive overload, yet were detailed enough to create a good mental map of the environment. One contribution of our research is the conveying of selective amounts of two types of navigational information at appropriate times: landmark/topology based (eg. wide corridor, obstacles) and metric based (steps). Landmarks and turns were informed 2-3m before reaching them. To prevent information overload, automatic metric directions were only given at the start and the end of the corridor but users had an option for manually obtaining them anywhere by clicking on the 'more information' button (Figure 2). Otherwise there were vibration alerts for continuous confirmation of being on the right path. This balance of pushed and pulled information is another contribution of our research.

Amit: *"The device conveys the navigational instructions accurately and even warns me when I mistakingly take a wrong turn. Initially, I got lost and took a long time to reach the destination. When introduced to the device, I was very optimistic. I gained confidence with the system during training and was able to easily reach the destination."*

Raj: *"I can't believe that the system gives me much needed directions on how to operate the lift and open the door. I feel myself efficiently navigating as any other person around..."*

The instructions were clear and audible. Specifically, the speech-rate (120 words/min) and pitch (150 Hz) of the instructions were appropriate for all users both in crowd and solitude. Some users had trouble understanding some TTS words initially during training though they eventually got used to the application. There was no visible interference or confusion when users passed each other during training.

The application also has a user triggered exploration mode where detailed information about the surroundings is given as if one is exploring the place. For example, application would say: "On your left, there is a Saloon... On your right, there is a Nike showroom... Walk straight 55 steps to go to Washroom." We did not test this feature on our sample population during the controlled trial but when asked during F.G.D., users expressed that this option would be useful for public museums and malls. However, it is possible that too much information could ultimately become annoying [19][37]. We plan to test this in future.

Helpful features like buzzer, map download module

In our earlier studies, after reaching the vicinity of the desired destination, the users used to get confused about the exact location of the door. Thus, we have fitted the destination doors with a special user triggered buzzer module.

Neha: *"Audible Indicator (buzzer on destinations) is a great feature. This helps me not to enter the wrong room or collide with obstacles. Also, pinpointing the location of doors is easier"*

Ali inquired on how would they use the system for multiple buildings if they do not know the building name and hence could not choose the building map from the server. For this, we have developed a lab prototype for a module which shall be installed at the building entrance to transfer the map to the mobile phone via bluetooth. This also informs the user that the building contains our system.

Overall system effectiveness

Users appreciated that the system was easy to learn. Average time for learning the system was about 2.5 hrs over a span of 3 days (training stage 1: 11.2 min, 2: 23 min, 3: 112 min). Total learning time for each user is shown in Table 4. Users found our training protocol to be effective (Likert scale responses: M=4.5/5, SD=0.5) but suggested the requirement of a self-training manual for remote areas.

The anxiety of the users decreased while navigating with the aid of the system as shown in Table 4. Average confidence level on Likert scale responses was 2.3/5 (SD=0.9) for baseline and 4.2/5 (SD=0.8) for navigating with the system.

The system did not attract unwanted attention from people. There was no visible interference from by-standers during navigation. Volunteers reported that some people were even unaware of the blind user navigating close-by.

During F.G.D., 9 out of 10 users expressed their intention to buy the module for $20 if the improvements were incorporated. The mean overall satisfaction with the product was 3.6/5 (SD=1.1). One user who gave the low rating (2/5) wanted to reevaluate after the improvements.

6. DISCUSSION AND FUTURE WORK

Impact of not using the primary mobile phone: We have developed the application only for android phones and none of the users had an Android based mobile phone. The users operated the phones provided by us. This might have led to an increase in the training time. However, to have a more reliable estimate of the system learning time, we also did the first and second stages of training with an additional android phone user - Atul. He was able to learn the usage of the application relatively faster than others. However, we can not generalize the results with only one sample. Due to time constraints, Atul could not come for the entire trial.

Line-of-sight requirement: Our system uses line-of-sight communication between the user module and the wall modules. Though our IR signal is strong enough to pass through a thin cloth and has a wide receiving beam angle of about 35°, this could still pose a problem in crowded places and in cases where user is wearing a long thick top. However, we did not observe any IR signal misses during our trials. Also, infrequent IR misses are unlikely to cause system failure.

Building infrastructure requirement: Though we have substantially reduced the number of wall modules as compared to other beacon based approaches, our system still

Table 4: Total learning time (min) and comparison of the confidence level for baseline and device testing.

Parameter	Rita	Sita	Anu	Raju	Raj	Asha	Anil	Ali	Amit	Neha
Confidence w/o system	3	1	2	4	3	3	2	1	2	2
Approx. learning time	155	225	150	90	90	130	150	170	170	130
Confidence with system	4	3	5	5	5	5	3	4	4	-

requires installation of about 20 modules per floor in a typical public building. We propose to augment more dead-reckoning sensors like gyroscopes and compasses in future (eg. [10]) to further decrease the wall units to the extent of 1 or 2 per building floor while still providing path-based guidance. Further, use of small solar charging batteries which can be charged indoors (eg. [2]) would eliminate the need for replacing the batteries of wall units. These steps would reduce system maintenance and increase scalability.

Unideal bystanders: Our strategy of asking the user to raise his hand in case he feels discomfort during the trials and only then giving him directions for the path ahead, is not an idealistic portrayal of the real world situation wherein the user can ask for instructions from the bystanders only when they are present and if they are present in large numbers, as and when he wants.

Managing permissions for downloading maps: This is outside the scope of the present work and we hope to address this in future. Also, technology for creating 3D models from programs like Sketchup (eg. [10]) would make the system more scalable. The anticipation is that it will be possible to have community-based efforts for the annotation of large scale module creation for public spaces such as airports, museums, railway stations etc.

7. CONCLUSIONS

We reported the user-centric design and evaluation of a novel system which when deployed can help the blind users to effectively navigate in indoor environments. It uses minimal building retrofitting, provides step-by-step path based guidance and is socially apt. The system can also be used by people with cognitive disabilities and sighted people. Due to its low-cost implementation ($< \$20$ per user module, $\$200$ per building floor), this contribution will be particularly important in low-income regions, as well as in developing countries where about 90% of the blind people reside [6].

8. ACKNOWLEDGEMENTS

We thank Chris Schmandt, Jeffrey P. Bigham, and Shaun K. Kane for reviewing drafts of this work.

9. REFERENCES

[1] Sendero Group. www.senderogroup.com/.
[2] Solar Charger and Battery Pack from Sparkfun Electronics. www.sparkfun.com/products/11496.
[3] StreetTalk VIP. www.freedomscientific.com/products/fs/streettalk-gps-product-page.asp.
[4] Sunrom Technologies. www.sunrom.com/.
[5] Talking Signs Inc. 2000. www.ski.org/Rehab/WCrandall/introts.html, June 2007.
[6] W.H.O. Fact Sheet no. 282: VI and blindness. www.who.int/mediacentre/factsheets/fs282/en, June 2012.
[7] J. D. Anderson, D.-J. Lee, and J. K. Archibald. Embedded stereo vision system providing visual guidance to the visually impaired. In *LISA*, IEEE, 2007.
[8] S. Chumkamon, P. Tuvaphanthaphiphat, and P. Keeratiwintakorn. A blind navigation system using rfid for indoor environments. In *ECTI-CON*. IEEE, 2008.
[9] V. Coroama. The chatty environment-a world explorer for the visually impaired. In *Ubicomp*, 2003.
[10] N. Fallah, I. Apostolopoulos, K. Bekris, and E. Folmer. The user as a sensor: navigating users with visual impairments in indoor spaces using tactile landmarks. In *CHI*, 2012.
[11] N. Fallah, I. Apostolopoulos, K. Bekris, and E. Folmer. Indoor human navigation systems: A survey. *Interacting with Computers*, 2013.
[12] L. Fang, P. Antsaklis, L. Montestruque, M. McMickell, et al. Design of a wireless assisted pedestrian dead reckoning system - the navmote experience. *TIM*, 2005.
[13] A. Ganz, S. R. Gandhi, J. Schafer, T. Singh, et al. Percept: Indoor navigation for the blind and visually impaired. In *EMBC*. IEEE, 2011.
[14] R. Golledge, R. Klatzky, J. Loomis, and J. Marston. Stated preferences for components of a personal guidance system for nonvisual navigation. *JVIB*, 2004.
[15] R. G. Golledge. Geography and the disabled: a survey with special reference to vision impaired and blind populations. *Trans. Institute of British Geographers*, 1993.
[16] R. Guy and K. Truong. Crossingguard: exploring information content in navigation aids for visually impaired pedestrians. In *CHI*, 2012.
[17] T. Höllerer, D. Hallaway, N. Tinna, and S. Feiner. Steps toward accommodating variable position tracking accuracy in a mobile augmented reality system. In *AIMS*. Citeseer, 2001.
[18] A. A. Kalia, G. E. Legge, R. Roy, and A. Ogale. Assessment of indoor route-finding technology for people with visual impairment. *JVIB*, 2010.
[19] T. Kapic. Indoor navigation for visually impaired. *A project realized in collaboration with NCCR-MICS*, 2003.
[20] L. Kleeman. Optimal estimation of position and heading for mobile robots using ultrasonic beacons and dead-reckoning. In *IEEE Robotics and Automation*, May 1992.
[21] S. Koide and M. Kato. 3-d human navigation system considering various transition preferences. In *SMC*. IEEE, 2005.
[22] V. Kulyukin and C. Gharpure. Rfid in robot-assisted indoor navigation for the visually impaired. In *LIROS*. IEEE, 2004.
[23] A. M. Ladd, K. E. Bekris, A. Rudys, L. E. Kavraki, and D. S. Wallach. Robotics-based location sensing using wireless ethernet. *Wireless Networks*, 2005.
[24] J. M. Loomis, R. G. Golledge, and R. L. Klatzky. Navigation system for the blind: Auditory display modes and guidance. *Presence: Teleoperators and Virtual Environments*, 1998.
[25] J. M. Loomis, R. L. Klatzky, R. G. Golledge, et al. Navigating without vision: basic and applied research. *OVS*, 2001.
[26] K. Lynch. *The image of the city*. the MIT Press, 1960.
[27] K. Nakamura, Y. Aono, and Y. Tadokoro. A walking navigation system for the blind. *Systems and Computers in Japan*, 1997.
[28] J. Rajamäki, P. Viinikainen, and J. Tuomisto. Laureapop indoor navigation service for the visually impaired in a wlan environment. In *EHAC*. WSEAS, 2007.
[29] L. Ran, S. Helal, and S. Moore. Drishti: an integrated indoor/outdoor blind navigation system and service. In *PerCom*, 2004.
[30] G. Retscher. Pedestrian navigation systems and location-based services. In *IEEE 3G Mobile Comm. Technologies*, 2004.
[31] T. Riehle, P. Lichter, and N. Giudice. An indoor navigation system to support the visually impaired. In *EMBS*. IEEE, 2008.
[32] D. A. Ross and B. B. Blasch. Development of a wearable computer orientation system. *Personal and Ubiquitous Computing*, 2002.
[33] S. Selvi, U. Kamath, and M. Sudhin. Andha asthra-a navigation system for the visually impaired. In *MFI*. IEEE, 2008.
[34] Y. Sonnenblick. An indoor navigation system for blind individuals. In *Technology and Persons with Disabilities*, 1998.
[35] Y. Tian, X. Yang, and A. Arditi. Computer vision-based door detection for accessibility of unfamiliar environments to blind persons. In *Computers Helping People with Special Needs*. Springer, 2010.
[36] B. Tjan, P. J. Beckmann, R. Roy, N. Giudice, and G. Legge. Digital sign system for indoor wayfinding for the visually impaired. In *CVPR*. IEEE, 2005.
[37] W. R. Wiener and B. B. Blasch. *Foundations of orientation and mobility*. AFB Press, 2010.

An Accelerated Scanning Communication System with Adaptive Automatic Error Correction Mechanism

[Extended Abstract]

Hiroki Mori
Graduate School of Engineering, Utsunomiya University
7-1-2, Yoto, Utsunomiya, 321-8585 Japan
hiroki@speech-lab.org

ABSTRACT

This paper describes a novel automatic error correction method for scanning communication, whose mechanism is basically analogous to that of continuous speech recognition. It has two core components: one is the switch timing model, and the other is the statistical language model. By employing these models, the proposed system can estimate most probable sequence of input syllables for a given sequence of switch timing, with taking user characteristics into account. Thirteen subjects without disabilities and an ALS subject participated in a text input experiment using the proposed scanning communication system. For the ALS subject, the system improved the character correct rate from 77.7% to 97.7%, allowing dramatically fast input.

Categories and Subject Descriptors

K.4.2 [**Computers and Society**]: Social Issues—*Assistive technologies for persons with disabilities*

Keywords

ALS; AAC; user characteritics; language model

1. INTRODUCTION

The scanning input method is a widely used augmentative and alternative communication tool mainly for people with severe physical disabilities such as ALS. In Japan, a character matrix "Gojūon" is widely used for scanning communication. The major drawback of these systems is that it takes long time to input. One possibility to accelerate scanning communication would be dynamic rearrangement of the matrix [1]. Although this would theoretically reduce time for cursor arrival, it would cause additional mental workload to find characters from the matrix. In this paper, an alternative way to accelerate scanning communication is proposed: Just speed up the cursor, do not care about errors. The system will automatically correct the errors.

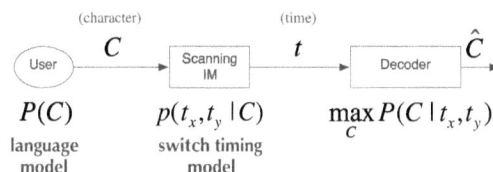

Figure 1: Diagram of the proposed algorithm.

2. ERROR CORRECTION ALGORITHM

The error correction can be realized by finding the sequence of character C that maximize the following posterior probability for a given sequence of switch timings.

$$P(C|t_x, t_y) = \frac{P(C)p(t_x, t_y|C)}{\sum_C P(C)p(t_x, t_y|C)} \quad (1)$$

Equation (1) has two major components. The first part, $P(C)$, corresponds to the prior probability of input text, generally called *language model* in the speech community. The second part, $p(t_x, t_y|C)$, is the joint probability density of switch timing for column x and row y for given character C that the user is trying to input. We call $p(t_x, t_y|C)$ the *switch timing model*. Solving Eq.(1) can be regarded as the problem of decoding from noisy channel (Fig. 1), and analogous to the framework of statistical continuous speech recognition.

It should be emphasized that the switch timing model reflects user characteristics. As shown in Sect. 3, the model can be estimated through text input experiments using the scanning input method, which we call "user enrollment."

3. SWITCH TIMING MEASUREMENT

Thirteen college students without disabilities (no experience in scanning communication systems), and a male with ALS (age 57, 10 months experience in scanning communication system, using a foot switch), participated in the experiment. They were asked to input an Aesop story "The North Wind and The Sun" (254 chars) with an experimental scanning communication system. This system has a functionality to present current sentence to input just above the character matrix. The subjects were instructed not to correct input errors due to "slips" of the cursor.

Figure 2(a) shows the switch timing distribution of a subject without disabilities at the scan period of 200 ms. Despite the very fast scan speed, the switch timing was precise

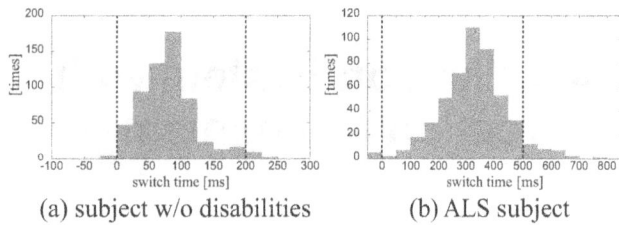

(a) subject w/o disabilities   (b) ALS subject

Figure 2: Switch timing distribution of (a) a subject without disabilities (200 ms), and (b) an ALS subject (500 ms).

for this subject (SD = 42.6 [ms]). The figure also implies that the subject is "hasty," i.e. he tended to trigger the switch at early timings (< 100 ms). Figure 2(b) shows the distribution of the ALS subject at the scan period of 500 ms. Usually he set the scan period of his scanning communication system to 1000 ms or longer for daily use. Due to muscle weakness and atrophy, the ALS subject had difficulty in operating the foot switch at precise timings. The SD was much higher (116.8 ms) than that of subjects without disabilities. The most frequent switch timings distributed around 300–400 ms after the cursor's arrival to target rows/columns. It is also understood that a considerable part of the timings exceeded 500 ms, which would cause a slip to the next row/column.

4. EXPERIMENTS AND RESULTS

Proposed algorithm was implemented in our scanning communication system. Switch timing was modeled per user with Gaussian distribution according to prior measurement (Sect. 3). For language model, character 4-gram was adopted.

Figure 3 shows the Character Correct Rate (CCR) for subjects without disabilities, for the combinations of the two speed conditions (500 ms, 300 ms) and two output decision mechanisms (without correction, with correction). "Without correction" condition corresponds to the conventional scanning communication systems, where characters at the selected rows/columns are directly generated, while "with correction" corresponds to the proposed method, where most probable sequences obtained by Eq.(1) are generated instead. CCR for each subject is plotted by '×', and the bold lines indicate the mean CCR. This figure clearly shows the effectiveness of the proposed automatic error correction method for most subjects without disabilities. Mean CCR was improved from 98.14% to 98.79%, and from 97.04% to 98.27%, for the scan period of 500 ms and 300 ms, respectively. Because 500 ms was slow enough to trigger the switch at precise timings for most subjects, baseline score was relatively high, so the error correction appeared to have no significant effect on the mean CCR. However, when the scan period was 300 ms, the error correction mechanisms successfully recovered the baseline score drop due to inaccurate switch timing. The result of a paired t-test showed the mean CCR difference is significant ($p < 0.05$). Figure 3 also suggests that the automatic error correction gave a negative effect for some subjects. They gradually became proficient in scanning communication systems through the experiments, which resulted in model mismatch of switch timing.

Table 1 shows the CCR for the ALS subject. As shown in Fig. 2(b), 500 ms was too fast for this subject to catch up the moving cursor, resulting in quite low (< 80 %) CCR when

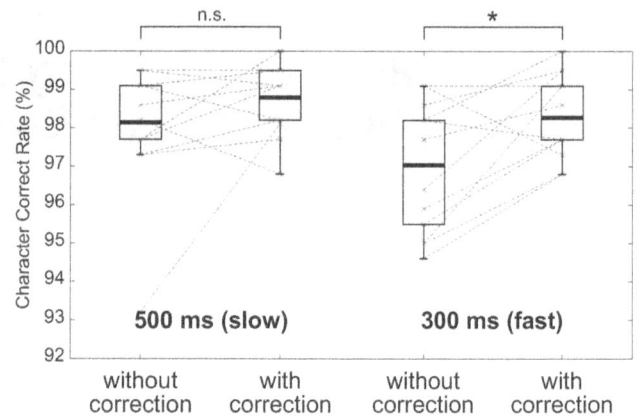

Figure 3: Character Correct Rate for subjects without disabilities, comparing without correction and with correction (*: $p < 0.05$).

Table 1: Character Correct Rate for an ALS subject.

	800 ms	500 ms
without correction	95.0%	77.7%
with correction	97.7%	97.7%

the automatic error correction was not employed. However, CCR was surprisingly improved when using the automatic error correction. The effectiveness was even clearer for the scan speed of 500 ms, where CCR of 77.7% raised to 97.7%. Because this value exceeded the one for the slower (800 ms) condition without correction, it can also be said that the proposed automatic error correction mechanism accelerated the input speed to 160% compared to the conventional scanning communication system, without sacrificing correctness.

5. CONCLUSIONS

In this paper, an error correction method was proposed, which is based on the switch timing model and language model. It was shown that proposed system improved CCR for an ALS subject from 77.7% to 97.7%, and its effectiveness was revealed.

We expect a positive side-effect of the proposed system: it tolerates *inaccurate* switch timing. In general scanning communication, user's mental workload can be high because it demands concentration on the cursor movement. The automatic error correction mechanism would relieve the pressure. This hypothesis is to be proven by mental workload measurement in the future.

6. ACKNOWLEDGMENTS

The author would like to thank Ms. Hiromi Arai for her assistance. This work was supported in part by JSPS KAKENHI Grant Number 25560279.

7. REFERENCES

[1] G. Lesher, B. Moulton, and J. D. Higginbotham. Techniques for augmenting scanning communication. *Augmentative & Alternative Communication*, 14(2):81–101, 1998.

Accessible mHealth
for Patients with Dexterity Impairments

Daihua X. Yu[1], Bambang Parmanto[1], Brad E. Dicianno[2], Valerie J. Watzlaf [1], Katherine D. Seelman[3]

[1]Department of Health Information Management, [2]Department of Physical Medicine and Rehabilitation, [3]Department of Rehabilitation Science & Technology, University of Pittsburgh
Pittsburgh, PA 15260, USA
(dxy1, parmanto, dicianno, valgeo, kds31)@pitt.edu

ABSTRACT

A novel mobile health (mHealth) system to support self-care and adherence to self-care regimens for patients with chronic disease, called iMHere (interactive mobile health and rehabilitation), has been developed at the University of Pittsburgh. However, the existing design of the iMHere system was initially not suitable for users with a myriad of dexterity impairments. The goal of this study was to design and transform an iMHere system that is usable and accessible for this particular group of users. We approached the accessibility from two essential components of user interface design and development: physical presentation and navigation. Six participants with dexterity impairments were included in this study. User satisfaction significantly improved when using revised apps (P<0.01). The importance of personalization for accessibility and the identified strategies to approach personalization for the mHealth system are discussed.

Categories and Subject Descriptors

K.4.2 [**Computers and Society**]: Social Issues—*Assistive technologies for persons with disabilities*;
H.1.2 [**Information Systems**]: User/Machine System—*Human factors*;
D.2.2 [**Software Engineering**]: Design Tools and Techniques—*User interfaces*

General Terms

Design; Experimentation; Human Factors

Keywords

Mobile health; accessibility; smartphone apps; self-care; dexterity impairments

1. INTRODUCTION

There is strong evidence to support the importance of self-management skills for improved health outcomes and independence in activities of daily living for persons with disabilities (PwDs) [1, 2], who are susceptible to secondary conditions (e.g., skin breakdown). The mHealth system that allows PwDs to be more independent in managing their conditions [3] is a new type of support for PwDs. We have developed an innovative mobile health system called iMHere aimed at empowering individuals to be more independent in managing their own health. Instead of a single app, the iMHere system consists of a suite of smartphone apps, a Web-based clinician portal, and two-way communication connecting the patients and clinicians. Five apps that comprise the iMHere gallery were released to support preventive self-care for managing medications (MyMeds), neurogenic bladder (TeleCath) and bowel (BMQs), mood (Mood) and skin breakdown (SkinCare). The skincare app includes the capability for the patient to take pictures of the skin/wound to be sent to the clinicians. Using a Web-based portal, caregivers or clinicians can monitor an individual's conditions and compliance as well as provide support.

An earlier evaluation study [4] showed the existing design of the iMHere apps was not suitable for users with dexterity impairments. The accessible design required the following changes: 1) Streamlining the procedures with in-app training; 2) Allowing participants to set their own icon/touch size in apps; 3) Binding the camera function in the skincare app to a physical button. Participants also suggested using different colors to separate apps. Some of them might be more comfortable with dark text on a white background and vice versa. Additionally, streamlining the cognitive process of tasks and reducing the layout complexity in one screen might help to improve accessibility. Providing fewer functions on a small screen might help reduce confusion about what to do next.

Although the smartphone is an ideal tool for implementing wellness programs for PwDs [5], it poses accessibility challenges: such as lack of screen space [6] and small form factors [7, 8]. Some of these accessibility issues, such as the size of text and the complexity of menus, can be mitigated with better user interface design. The goal of this study is to develop an accessible system for 4.04 million adults in the US with dexterity impairments [9].

2. METHODS

We developed a personalized and accessible profile that includes the ability for users to choose which apps they wish to use, to change the background and text color, to change the text size, and to set button size. Additional functions to simplify the navigation process and to enhance the interaction with users were also added to the profile settings. Participants from the earlier evaluation study [4] were included in a usability study afterward.

Inclusion criteria were 18–55 years of age with dexterity impairments, have the potential for skin breakdown, and using at least one medication. Exclusion criteria were severe vision, hearing, or conversation impairments.

The accessible design was focused on the two most complex apps in iMHere: MyMeds and SkinCare apps. A laboratory-setting evaluation with an in-depth interview was conducted after a one-week field trial. Six tasks were included in this lab-test: 1) scheduling a new medication alert; 2) modifying a medication reminder; 3) responding to a medication alert; 4) scheduling a skin checkup alert; 5) responding to a skincare reminder that included reporting issues; and 6) setting personalized configurations. The time to complete each task was recorded. After performing the tasks, participants were asked to complete the modified Telehealth Usability Questionnaire (TUQ) [10] to reveal their levels of satisfaction with the iMHere apps.

3. RESULTS & DISCUSSION

Six participants with dexterity impairments participated in this study including two females, and four males. Five participants had Spina Bifida; one had Spinal Cord Injury. Four of their ages ranged from 18-30 years, two from 31-55 years. Participants spent more time in seconds on the tasks for scheduling a medication (202 vs. 89, improved 44%) and reporting a new skin problem (148 vs. 61, 41%), compared to modifying a medication alert (62 vs. 19, 30%), or scheduling a skincare alert (43 vs. 16, 37%). Only one touch was required for a user to respond to a medication alert in the original app and accessible app. The main difference was that directional notes and images of the medication were presented in the accessible design. Participants were able to verify the pill or bottle with the image to assist in taking the correct medication.

When comparing the average TUQ score from this study with the earlier evaluation study, users' satisfaction improved from 5.86 (out of 7 points) with the original designed apps to 6.80 on accessible apps. Improvements were seen in the sections for "ease of use & learnability" (5.45 vs. 6.72), "interface quality" (6.1 vs. 6.96), and "reliability" (5.46 vs. 6.47). An unequal variances t-test revealed a significant difference between the mean TUQ score from the 2013 evaluation study (M=5.86, s=0.396) and this study (M=6.80, s=0.187), t(7.098)=-5.23, p=0.001, α=0.05.

A list of accessibility features was highlighted in the accessible apps. Four participants thought the ability to hide selected apps from the home screen was important. It made the system simpler and more appropriate for personal use. Three participants indicated that using customized text display size was important to improve the comfort of reading. Five participants thought the ability to set the minimum target size as their finger size was important to improve the accessibility, especially for persons with higher levels of dexterity impairments. Four participants thought a customized keypad was important to reduce the number of touches on a smartphone screen. Text guidance was implemented in the accessible design for training purposes. By using text-to-speech technology, a user was able to listen to it from the audio output. All of them liked having voice and text guidance work together.

Additionally, the concept of personalization applied to the navigation levels as well. For example, the system would check the database for personalized settings after installing our app on a smartphone. The system would lead the new user to set his/her preferences before going to the home screen (a list of apps). Four participants indicated the shortcut was important. All participants liked the ability to select their preferred background color and the color of display text, and four of them thought this feature was essential to make the apps personalized.

4. CONCLUSION

The average time to complete the tasks to schedule a new medication and to report a new skin problem was reduced by about 41% in the accessible apps. Scores from the TUQ indicated the accessible apps that were implemented in this study were viewed positively (6.80 out of 7 points, 97%). Compared to the TUQ score on the original iMHere apps from the 2013 evaluation study, users' satisfaction significantly improved by using accessible apps (p<0.01). Great improvements were highlighted in the factors of the "ease of use & learnability" (5.45 on the original iMHere design vs. 6.72 on accessible apps), "interface quality" (5.61 vs. 6.79) and "reliability" (5.46 vs. 6.47). All of the participants were satisfied and preferred to use the accessible apps and would use them again in the future. The ability to customize physical presentations and to detect shortcuts within activity flows would be the optimal solution to enhance accessibility. Categorizing UI elements, such as text and icons, into a specific group and allowing the modification of its attributes including size and color will affect user experience with mHealth apps on a small screen. Navigation, on the other hand, addresses accessibility from the efficiency perspective. A simple and straightforward user interface is important to enhance users experiences.

5. ACKNOWLEDGEMENTS

The research is supported by the National Institute of Child Health and Human Development (NICHD) (#1R21HD071810-01-A1), and the Craig H. Neilsen Foundation.

6. REFERENCES

[1] K. R. Lorig, and H. Holman. Self-management education: history, definition, outcomes, and mechanisms. *Ann Behav Med,* 26(1):1-7, August, 2003.

[2] N. M. Clark. Management of chronic disease by patients. *Annu Rev Public Health,* 24(1), pages 289-313, 2003.

[3] B. Parmanto, G. Pramana, D. X. Yu, A. D. Fairman, B. E. Dicianno, and M. P. McCue. iMHere: A Novel mHealth System for Supporting Self-Care in Management of Complex and Chronic Conditions. *JMIR mhealth and uhealth,* 1(2):e10, 2013.

[4] D. X. Yu, B. Parmanto, and B. E. Dicianno. The Accessibility Needs of Patients with Dexterity Impairments to Use mHealth Apps on Smartphone. Presented in *SDA The Disability Experience Conference,* Pittsburgh PA, 2013.

[5] H. Holman. Chronic disease—the need for a new clinical education. *JAMA,* 292(9):1057-1059, 2004.

[6] S. Brewster. Overcoming the lack of screen space on mobile computers. *Personal and Ubiquitous Computing,* 6(3):188-205, 2002.

[7] J. Abascal, and A. Civit. Mobile communication for older people: new opportunities for autonomous life. *Proceedings of the 6th ERCIM Workshop.* pages 255-268, 2000.

[8] S. K. Kane, C. Jayant, J. O. Wobbrock, and R. E. Ladner. Freedom to roam: a study of mobile device adoption and accessibility for people with visual and motor disabilities. *Proceedings of the 11th ASSETS Conference,* pages 115-122, October 2009.

[9] P. F. Adams, M. E. Martinez, and J. L. Vickerie. Summary health statistics for the US population: National Health Interview Survey, 2009. *Vital and health statistics. Data from the National Health Survey,* 10(248): 1-115, 2010.

[10] B. Parmanto, A. Saptono, G. Pramana, W. Pulantara, R. M. Schein, M. R. Schmeler, M. P. McCue, and D. M. Brienza. VISYTER: Versatile and integrated system for telerehabilitation. *Telemedicine and e-Health,* 16(9):939-944, 2010.

An Accessible Robotics Programming Environment for Visually Impaired Users

Stephanie Ludi
Department of Software Engineering
Rochester Institute of Technology
Rochester, NY USA
1.585.475.7407
salvse@rit.edu

Lindsey Ellis
School of Interactive Games and Media
Rochester Institute of Technology
Rochester, NY USA
lle6138@rit.edu

Scott Jordan
Department of Computer Science
Rochester Institute of Technology
Rochester, NY USA
saj1832@rit.edu

ABSTRACT

Despite advances in assistive technology, challenges remain in pre-college computer science outreach and university programs for visually impaired students. The use of robotics has been popular in pre-college classrooms and outreach programs, including those that serve underrepresented groups. This paper describes the specific accessibility features implemented in software that provides an accessible Lego Mindstorms NXT programming environment for teenage students who are visually impaired. JBrick is designed to support students with diverse visual acuity and who use needed assistive technology. Field tests over several days showed that JBrick has the potential to accommodate students who are visually impaired as they work together to program Lego Mindstorms NXT robots.

Categories and Subject Descriptors

H.5 [**Information Interfaces and Presentation**]: User Interfaces; K.4.2 [**Social Issues**]: Assistive tech for persons with disabilities

General Terms

Design, Experimentation, Human Factors

Keywords

Accessibility; visual impairment

1. INTRODUCTION

As robotics has become popular as a means for engaging pre-college students in computing and engineering [1, 4, 6], the need for accessibility persists. Robotics, such as Lego Mindstorms, are as appealing to students who are visually impaired as they are to sighted students [2]. The default programming software available from Lego uses icons to represent commands. This software is not accessible to visually impaired users, most notably in terms of screen reader compatibility. Whether for in-class activities or extracurricular outreach, the software needs to maximize accessibility in order to promote interest in computer science and related disciplines.

ASSETS'14, October 20–22, 2014, Rochester, NY, USA.
ACM 978-1-4503-2720-6/14/10.
http://dx.doi.org/10.1145/2661334.2661385

The goal of the JBrick project is to design accessible Lego Mindstorms programming software that can be used by those with or without sight. In the case of the ImagineIT workshops and future outreach, the target users are teens who are visually impaired. These teens are often novice programmers, as the focus of the outreach is to enable the participants to explore Computer Science via robotics, a common vehicle for engaging pre-college students [1, 3, 5]. Given that independent tool use and activity participation is needed (as opposed to reliance on a sighted person) this paper will focus on the features and design decisions that can be leveraged in other programming tools.

2. SOFTWARE DESIGN

JBrick is implemented in Java to facilitate cross-platform deployment. The NXC compiler is used so programs implemented in JBrick and BricxCC are interoperable. Standard Java libraries have been used, including the Java Accessibility libraries.

The JBrick user interface is designed to be accessible to programmers with various degrees of vision. In addition to compatibility with screen readers, refreshable braille displays, and magnification software, the user interface itself is designed to accommodate both sighted and low vision users. For the current version of JBrick, the focus is:

- Displaying or reading of code in a manner that is accurate and discernable to the user (including screen reader and refreshable braille display compatibility).

- Executing commands via keyboard or mouse.

- Locating code by line number (audio and visual).

- Providing visual and audio-based system feedback, including compilation, program download, and robot connection status.

3. EVALUATION

Ten participants with visual impairments ranging from moderate vision to completely blind used JBrick between 3-4 hours per day over the course of 4 days. The 5 males and 5 females participated in a Computer Science exploration program. Programming experience varied with only 3 having any experience (1 had enough functional vision to use the graphical Lego NXT-G software). For the purposes of the exploration workshop novice programmers were encouraged to participate. Participants worked in teams of 2-3 for the duration of the activity. Groupings were random within gender. The overview of the field test consisted of assistive technology setup, training in the NXC language and JBrick via a tutorial, and applying NXC via JBrick to solve a challenge for the duration of the activity.

Before the tutorial started, any assistive technology was configured for the participants. 2 participants used refreshable Braille displays, 6 participants used screen readers, and 3 used screen magnification software and 1 adjusted screen resolution and appearance in the Windows Display preferences. During the first day, the participants were asked to go through the NXC programming tutorial with a provided Lego robot for each team that required each participant team to add sensors as needed [3]. Display options were modified for those who needed customized views (e.g. font, cursor resizing; color adjustments).

Participant groups worked at their own pace with members of the project team floating to answer questions and offer guidance as needed (e.g. how to use the robot, add sensors). Participants entered commands, constructs, expressions, and variables throughout the tutorial, which consists of 3 sections. The programming workflow of design, implementation (including compilation and downloading), testing, and evaluation was practiced many times during the tutorial and subsequent activities. A post-activity semi-structured interview was conducted.

4. RESULTS AND DISCUSSION

The participants were asked their level of agreement that line numbering helped them locate code faster when locating compiler errors, as well as their level of agreement that the line highlighting and cursor placement had in locating code when fixing compiler errors. In terms of line numbering, the mean for blind participants is 4.4 while the mean for the visually impaired participants is 5. When looking at the responses by programming experience, the mean for the four experienced programmers is 5 while the mean for the six novice programmers is 3.67. In terms of the line highlighting/focus and cursor placement, the mean for blind participants is 3.6 while the mean for visually impaired participants is 4.2. The means for experience and novice programmers are 4.5 and 3.5 respectively. Familiarity with the keyboard had a more significant impact as there were many times when the novice programmers who are blind would add extraneous characters, thus adding to the defect correction task.

When asked the degree of confidence in following the structure of their code, blind participants have a mean of 3.8 while visually impaired participants have a mean of 4.6. In terms of programming experience, novice programmers have a mean of 3.83 while experience programmers have a mean of 4.75. The means between both pairings are similar, indicating that there are issues with navigating the code that will need further study such as using audio differences (e.g. pitch, earcons) to aid in code orientation and navigation. Observations of the blind participants, who sped up the reading of text, sometimes became lost during code orientation in terms of constructs such as if/then and repeat blocks especially when trying to fix errors. Of particular issue were nested if/then statements. Impacting the issue was that some participants were not familiar with the use of punctuation such as braces and brackets, including their location on the keyboard.

Participants were then asked to rate their level of agreement in terms of how satisfied they were in using JBrick to program their robot. The mean for blind participants is 4.0 while the mean for visually impaired participants is 4.6. The mean for novice programmers is 4.0 while the mean for experienced programmers

is 4.75. For the final statement, participants were asked to what degree they would recommend JBrick to a visually impaired friend who was interested in programming a Lego Mindstorms robot. Blind participants had a mean of 4.0 while visually impaired participants had a mean of 5. In terms of programming experience, novice programmers have a mean of 4.33 while experience programmers have a mean of 4.75. Overall the experience was positive for novice and experienced programmers, regardless of visual acuity. This is partly due to the generally open-ended nature of the activity where participants designed the robot and the program along the way, learning from mistakes and redesigning as needed. In addition, for most participants the opportunity to work with a robot was completely new. The newness of the experience may have influenced the results. Regardless, the challenges that the blind participants had using JBrick did not severely impact their impressions of the software to the extent of recommending it to a peer.

5. FUTURE WORK

Moving forward, further study is needed in order to improve the user experience for blind, novice programmers. Some issues such as screen reader skill is outside the scope of JBrick. However additional features will be explored and added in order to provide students the ability to navigate code using audio cues, as well as debugging (a tool to help work through coding and logic defects). Remaining work will be completed in order to provide Mac OSX and EV3 support.

6. ACKNOWLEDGEMENTS

JBrick is supported by the National Science Foundation (#1240809). Thanks to students who have contributed to this project, as well as the participants who have provided feedback.

7. REFERENCES

[1] Cannon, K., Panciera, K., and Papanikolopoulos, N. 2007. Second Annual Robotics Camp for Underrepresented Students. In Proceedings of the 12th Annual SIGCSE Conference on Innovation and Technology in Computer Science Education. Scotland. 14-18.

[2] Dorsey, R., Park, C. H., and Howard, A. 2014. Developing the Capabilities of Blind and Visually Impaired Youth to Build and Program Robots. *Journal on Technology and Persons with Disabilities*. 1.1 (Feb. 2014). 55-67.

[3] Ludi, S. 2014. Robotics Programming Tools for Blind Students. *Journal on Technology and Persons with Disabilities*. 1.1 (Feb. 2014). 77-89.

[4] Ludi, S, and Reichlmayr, T. 2011. The Use of Robotics to Promote Computing to Pre-College Students with Visual Impairments. *ACM Transactions on Computing Education*. 11.3 (Oct. 2011), 1-20.

[5] National Federation of the Blind. 2009. Youth Slam 2009 Homepage. Retrieved January 17, 2010, from National Federation of the Blind: http://nfbyouthslam.org/

[6] National Science Foundation. 2010. Recent Awards for the Broadening Participation in Computing Program. Retrieved January 22, 2010, from National Science Foundation: http://www.nsf.gov

Assessing Technology Use in Aphasia

Abi Roper
Language & Communication Science
and Centre for HCI Design
City University London
Northampton Square, London
+4420 7040 8198
Abi.Roper.1@city.ac.uk

Jane Marshall
Language & Communication Science
City University London
Northampton Square, London
+4420 7040 8668
J.Marshall@city.ac.uk

Stephanie Wilson
Centre for HCI Design
City University London
Northampton Square, London
+4420 7040 8152
S.M.Wilson@city.ac.uk

ABSTRACT

We report a novel and accessible questionnaire designed to examine levels of technology use in adults with severe aphasia and to assess the impact of a co-designed computer-delivered gesture therapy (GeST) on participants' wider technology use. The questionnaire is currently being used in a group study of 30 participants with severe aphasia. Early outcomes indicate that people with severe aphasia are able to use the questionnaire effectively to report levels of technology use. Data from 11 participants suggests low levels of use for many items of everyday technology prior to therapy. Presented work will further examine the effect of GeST therapy on individuals' reported technology-use and also examine correlations between questionnaire outcomes and three other factors: performance on measures of cognition; and the amount and diversity of GeST-use.

Categories and Subject Descriptors

K.4.1 [**Computers and Society**]: Public Policy Issues – Computer-related health issues.

General Terms

Experimentation, Human Factors

Keywords

Aphasia; stroke; speech and language therapy; speech and language pathology; technology questionnaire; gesture therapy

1. INTRODUCTION

Aphasia is a communication difficulty affecting one third of people who have had a stroke. It affects the ability to produce and understand spoken language and to read and write in people with previously functioning language systems. Individuals with aphasia can be affected to varying levels in each modality and although some specific facets of cognition may be affected, general intellect is typically preserved.

One implication of aphasia commonly reported by those affected is a limitation upon access to technology of varying forms. However, the precise degree of such limitations is not reported in the literature. Indeed, although standardised assessments of technology use and confidence have been implemented in the non-aphasic community - for example in the population of older

ASSETS'14, October 20–22, 2014, Rochester, NY, USA.
ACM 978-1-4503-2720-6/14/10.
http://dx.doi.org/10.1145/2661334.2661397

adults [1], the authors are aware of no such measures of technology use being used to describe the aphasic population. One potential reason for this might be the dependence within existing measures upon the relatively high level of language competence required to read and rate a series of given statements about technology.

2. AIMS OF THIS WORK

This paper aims to report a novel and accessible technology-use questionnaire that has been designed specifically for individuals with severe aphasia to capture current levels of technology use and confidence. The questionnaire is currently being used to capture changes in technology-use following exposure to a co-designed computer-delivered gesture therapy [2]. Future analysis aims to examine correlations between questionnaire outcomes and three other factors: performance on measures of cognition and the amount and diversity of GeST-use.

3. QUESTIONNAIRE

The technology-use questionnaire reported here assesses use of a series of 18 items of everyday technology (for example television, cash machine, mobile telephone). It is intended to be accessible even to people with very severe language difficulties due to aphasia. Participants are shown a picture of each technology and asked to report whether they have used this technology within the last month by pointing to the yes or no icon printed beneath the picture (figure 1). Following each response, participants are then asked to rate how confident they feel in using that piece of technology by pointing to a mark on a five-point visual rating scale, adapted - with permission - from an item within a standardised aphasia measure of self-esteem [3].

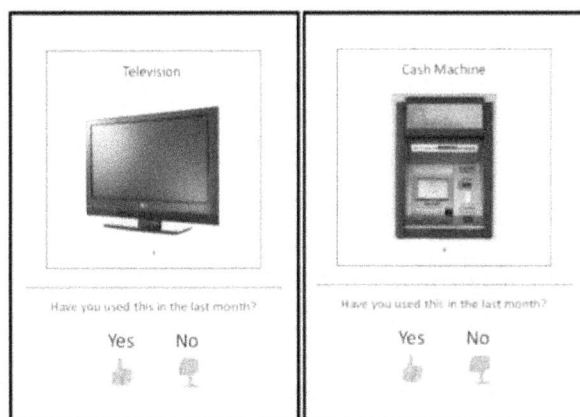

Figure 1. Example *television* and *cash machine* picture stimuli from the technology-use questionnaire.

At the end of the assessment, participants are awarded a technology usage score of up to 18 points – with one point awarded for each item of technology they report using within the last month. The inclusion of a confidence scale alongside each item also facilitates an exploration of participants' confidence in relation to the use of individual items of technology. Participants receive a score of 1 to 5 for each item with 1 being not at all confident and 5 being very confident.

4. METHODS

Within the current study, 30 participants with aphasia will receive 5 weeks of computer-delivered therapy with GeST. The technology-use questionnaire will be implemented before and after therapy. Prior to therapy, participants also complete standardised aphasia language assessments and an assessment of visuospatial ability taken from a formal test of cognition [4]. Finally, computer log data captures the time spent using GeST, the number of therapy practice sessions undertaken and the number of computer level changes demonstrated within practice.

5. PARTICIPANTS

Data collection is currently under way for 30 participants. Pre-therapy measures from the first 11 participants are reported here. (Post-therapy outcomes will be reported subsequently).

4 of 11 participants are female. The average age is 66.5 years (range 58 to 80). In formal language assessments, all participants demonstrate severe difficulties with spoken language output and varying levels of difficulty with spoken and written language comprehension. On tests of visuospatial cognition, 7 participants demonstrate severe impairment and 2 demonstrate moderate impairment.

6. RESULTS

All participants so far tested, demonstrated an ability to respond to questions regarding item use by pointing to a yes/no icon underneath a given picture. 4 participants however, were unable to provide confidence ratings for items using the 5-point scale – each indicating a lack of understanding of the scale and also of the question being asked of them.

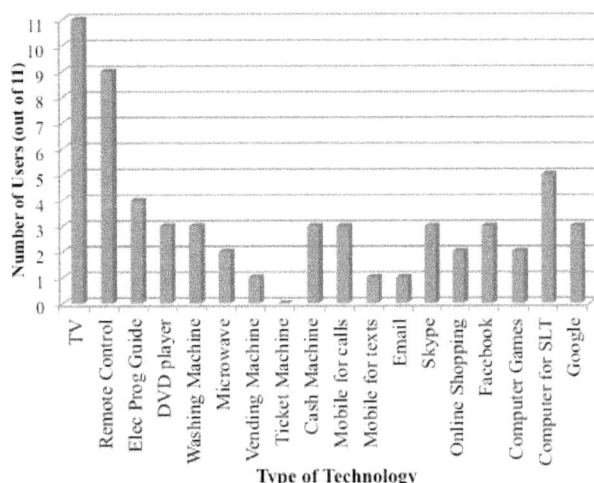

Figure 2. Pre-therapy questionnaire responses showing the number of participants (N=11) who stated that they had used a particular technology within the last month.

Usage data from an initial administration of the technology questionnaire (figure 2) indicates high levels of participant use for the items television (n=11) and television remote control (n=9) and much lower levels of use of mobile and Internet technologies (n = 1 to 3 for all mobile and internet items). Additionally, very low levels of use for basic everyday technologies such as microwaves, washing machines and cash machines / ATMs (n=3 for each) are reported.

Further analyses are ongoing and will be presented. These will include changes in technology use/confidence following GeST computer therapy and correlations between questionnaire outcomes and both visuospatial cognition and the amount and diversity of GeST-use.

7. CONCLUSIONS

This work presents a novel technology usage questionnaire developed to be accessible by people with severe aphasia. Early indications suggest that participants are able to utilise the questionnaire to provide an indication of their level of everyday technology use and that some – but not all – are able to additionally use the corresponding five-point scale to report their level of confidence in using individual items of technology.

Outcomes from initial assessment of the measure suggest a relatively low level of technology usage for adults with severe aphasia. Further analysis will enable us to ascertain whether this level can be improved through the participants' use of a co-designed, computer-delivered gesture therapy (GeST). It will additionally enable us to examine the links between technology-use and levels of visuospatial cognition in adults with severe aphasia and also the relationship between self-reported technology use and the amount and diversity of use of computer-delivered therapy. Findings will contribute to the understanding of the impact of aphasia upon technology use and may also offer insights into the wider role of language and visuospatial cognition within our understanding of the successful and confident use of everyday technology.

8. ACKNOWLEDGMENTS

This work is funded as a part of a City University London PhD scholarship for the first author. We thank the participants for their involvement in this research.

9. REFERENCES

[1] Czaja, S. J., Charness, N., Fisk, A. D., Hertzog, C., Nair, S. N., Rogers, W. A., & Sharit, J. 2006. Factors predicting the use of technology: findings from the Center for Research and Education on Aging and Technology Enhancement (CREATE). *Psychology and aging*, 21(2), 333.

[2] Galliers, J., Wilson, S., Roper, A., Cocks, N., Marshall, J., Muscroft, S., and Pring, T. 2012. Words are not enough: empowering people with aphasia in the design process. in *Proceedings of the 12th Participatory Design Conference: Research Papers – Volume 1*, (Roskilde, DK, 2012), ACM Press, 51-60.

[3] Brumfitt, S., & Sheeran, P. 1999. VASES: Visual Analogue Self-esteem Scale; User's Manual. *Winslow*.

[4] Helm-Estabrooks, Nancy. *Cognitive Linguistic Quick Test: Examiner's Manual*. Psychological Corporation, 2001.

Automatically Identifying Trouble-Indicating Speech Behaviors in Alzheimer's Disease

Frank Rudzicz[1,2], Leila Chan Currie[2], Andrew Danks[2], Tejas Mehta[2], Shunan Zhao[2]
[1] Toronto Rehabilitation Institute - University Health Network; and
[2] Department of Computer Science, University of Toronto
Toronto, Canada
{frank,leila,danks,tmehta,szhao}@cs.toronto.edu

ABSTRACT

Alzheimer's disease (AD) deteriorates executive, linguistic, and functional capacity and is rapidly becoming more prevalent. In particular, AD leads to an inability to follow simple dialogues. In this paper, we annotate two databases of dyad conversations, that include individuals with AD, with *trouble indicating behaviors* (TIBs). We then extract lexical/syntactic and acoustic features from all utterances and identify those that are most indicative of TIB (which include speech rate and utterance likelihoods in a standard language model) and classify utterances as having TIB or not with up to 79.5% accuracy. This will allow us to build automated dialogue systems and assessment tools that are sensitive to confusion in people with AD.

Categories and Subject Descriptors

Human-centered computing [**Accessibility**]: Accessibility technologies; Applied computing [**Life and medical sciences**]: Health informatics

Keywords

Trouble-indicating behavior, dementia, classification

1. INTRODUCTION

Alzheimer's disease (AD) is a progressive neuro-degenerative disease that deteriorates memory (short- and long-term), executive capacity, visual-spacial reasoning, and linguistic ability [3]. Caregivers who assist individuals with AD at home are common, but their involvement is often the precursor to long-term care [5]. As populations age, the incidence of AD will double or triple, with Medicare costs alone reaching $189 billion in the US by 2015 [1]. Given the growing need to support this population, there is an increasing interest in the design and development of technologies that support this population at home and extend one's quality of life and autonomy.

ASSETS'14, October 20–22, 2014, Rochester, NY, USA.
ACM 978-1-4503-2720-6/14/10.
http://dx.doi.org/10.1145/2661334.2661382.

We are designing intelligent dialog software that can engage in two-way communication for two purposes: a) to help guide individuals towards the completion of daily household tasks, and b) to fulfill social functions. Our goal is to encode in software the techniques used by caregivers to help their patients achieve these activities; this includes automatically identifying and recovering from breakdowns in communication. Here, we consider conversational data between patients and interviewers and develop methods of feature analysis and classification to identify confusion.

Trouble indicating behaviors (TIBs) are indications that the speaker requires aid to resolve phonological, morphological/syntactic, semantic, or discourse confusion [10]. There are 12 TIBs: **1)** neutral or non-specific requests for repetition (local), **2)** request for confirmation – repetition with reduction, **3)** request for confirmation – complete repetition, **4)** request for confirmation – repetition with elaboration, **5)** request for specific information, **6)** request for more information, **7)** correction of semantic inaccuracy, **8)** lack of uptake / lack of continuation, **9)** hypothesis formation (guessing), **10)** metalinguistic comment, e.g., *I can't remember.*, **11)** reprise / minimal dysfluency, e.g., *Eerrr, I want to – we went to the river.* , **12)** request for repetition – global, e.g., *wait – go back to the part about....*

2. EXPERIMENTS

We use the Carolina Conversations Collection (CCC) [7] and DementiaBank [2]. The CCC consists of conversations between older adults (> 60 years) and young adult interviewers. There are 31 interviewees diagnosed with AD (7 male) and 41 interviewees without AD (9 male). DementiaBank is a longitudinal collection of conversations where 196 older adults with dementia and 98 matched controls performed the 'cookie theft' picture description task with an interviewer [6] annually. Audio and textual transcriptions, annotated temporally at the utterance level, are available in each case. Here, every utterance is further annotated with TIBs by a speech-language pathologist and members of the research team.

We extract over 200 lexical/syntactic and acoustic features from these data, which cannot all be enumerated here. Instead, we use a method similar to [4] except instead of a t-test criterion, we use an analysis of variance (ANOVA) to rank features according to how well they separate classes, according to

$$F = \frac{\text{between-group variability}}{\text{within-group variability}} = \frac{\sum_i n_i (\bar{x}_i - \bar{x})^2 / (K-1)}{\sum_{ij} (x_{ij} - \bar{x}_i)^2 / (N-K)},$$

Table 1: The means (μ) and variances (σ^2) of the top 5 most relevant features to TIB discrimination, according to the ANOVA method.

Feature	No TIB μ (σ)	TIB μ (σ)
Brown bigram model (negative log-likelihood)	-11.35 (4.15)	-10.735 (2.27)
Words/minute	177.31 (1480.10)	164.47 (2244.89)
Ratio of PRP to NN+PRP	0.40 (0.127)	0.487 (0.137)
Mean 2nd MFCC	-2.62 (3.53)	-3.14 (3.33)
% of strong neutral words	0.136 (0.0731)	0.0794 (0.041)

Table 2: Accuracy of TIB identification across databases and classifiers, given either all features or the top 15 as determined by the ANOVA method.

Classifier	Features	Database CCC	Database DementiaBank
NB	Top 15	79.5%	67.0%
	All	63.1%	63.1%
SVM	Top 15	71.0%	59.2%
	All	55.7%	68.4%
Adaboost	Top 15	48.3%	65.0%
	All	26.7%	58.3%

where $K = 2$ since we are comparing TIB to non-TIB utterances, and N is total number of samples. Table 1 shows the top five most relevant features according to this method, in order: 1) the log-likelihood of the utterance given a bigram model trained with MLE on the Brown corpus; 2) words/minute; 3) the ratio of pronouns (PRP) to nouns (NN) and PRP, given the Stanford tagger [9]; 4) the mean of the 2nd Mel-frequency cepstral coefficient over the utterance; 5) the proportion of words that are strong neutral, obtained from the MPQA subjectivity lexicon [11].

We compare three binary classifiers that differentiate TIB utterances from non-TIB utterances in table 2. Specifically, we use naïve Bayes (NB) to model the likelihood of an utterance given the class with a Gaussian using maximum *a posteriori* training, a support vector machine (SVM) with the Gaussian kernel, and Adaboost, which is a common ensemble method based on iteratively building a number of decision trees to focus training on the relatively 'difficult' examples [8]. In general, results are promising except for Adaboost in the CCC database.

3. DISCUSSION

This paper presents an analysis of lexical/syntactic and acoustic features that are indicative of *trouble indicating behaviors* in the speech of individuals with AD across two popular databases. Although some of these features are expected (e.g., confusion tends to be related to slower rates of speech), others are more surprising (e.g., MFCC features generally refer to the transfer function of the vocal tract). With feature selection and simple naïve Bayes classification,

up to 79.5% of utterances can be correctly classified as having TIB or not. Future work will include refinement of classification methods and integration of this functionality into automated personal assistants for use by people with AD.

4. ACKNOWLEDGMENTS

This work is funded by the Toronto Rehabilitation Institute - University Health Network and the Natural Sciences and Engineering Research Council of Canada (RGPIN 435874).

5. REFERENCES

[1] A. J. Bharucha, V. Anand, J. Forlizzi, M. A. Dew, C. F. R. III, S. Stevens, and H. Wactlar. Intelligent assistive technology applications to dementia care: Current capabilities, limitations, and future challenges. *American Journal of Geriatric Psychiatry*, 17(2):88–104, February 2009.

[2] F. Boller and J. Becker. *DementiaBank Database Guide*. University of Pittsburgh, 2005.

[3] J. L. Cummings. Alzheimer's disease. *New England Journal of Medicine*, 351(1):56–67, 2004.

[4] K. Fraser, F. Rudzicz, and E. Rochon. Using text and acoustic features to diagnose progressive aphasia and its subtypes. In *Proceedings of Interspeech 2013*, Lyon France, August 2013.

[5] J. E. Gaugler, F. Yu, K. Krichbaum, and J. Wyman. Predictors of nursing home admission for persons with dementia. *Medical Care*, 47(2):191–198, 2009.

[6] H. Goodglass and E. Kaplan. *The Assessment of Aphasia and Related Disorders*. Philadelphia, PA: Lea and Febiger, 2nd edition, 1983.

[7] C. Pope and B. H. Davis. Finding a balance: The carolinas conversation collection. *Corpus Linguistics and Linguistic Theory*, 7(1):143–161, 2011.

[8] R. E. Schapire and Y. Singer. Improved boosting algorithms using confidence-rated predictions. In *Machine Learning*, pages 80–91, 1999.

[9] K. Toutanova, D. Klein, C. D. Manning, and Y. Singer. Feature-rich part-of-speech tagging with a cyclic dependency network. In *Proceedings of the 2003 Conference of the North American Chapter of the Association for Computational Linguistics on Human Language Technology-Volume 1*, pages 173–180. Association for Computational Linguistics, 2003.

[10] C. M. Watson. An analysis of trouble and repair in the natural conversations of people with dementia of the Alzheimer's type. *Aphasiology*, 13(3):195 – 218, 1999.

[11] T. Wilson, J. Wiebe, and P. Hoffmann. Recognizing contextual polarity in phrase-level sentiment analysis. In *Proceedings of the conference on human language technology and empirical methods in natural language processing*, pages 347–354. Association for Computational Linguistics, 2005.

A Braille Writing Training Device with Voice Feedback

Fumihito Aizawa
Electrical and Information Engineering
Graduate School of Science & Technology
University of Niigata
Niigata, Japan
f14c085d@mail.cc.niigata-u.ac.jp

Tetsuya Watanabe
Department of Biocybernetics
Faculty of Engineering
University of Niigata
Niigata, Japan
t2.nabe@eng.niigata-u.ac.jp

ABSTRACT

A device incorporating both voice feedback and tactile sensation has been developed to help blind children practice the use of a Braille stylus. A microcomputer and voice-synthesis LSI are used to give voice feedback, and a switch under each hole representing a Braille dot is used to give tactile feedback when the stylus is inserted in a hole. A switch is pressed by the user to hear the voice feedback. A one-cell prototype was used to gather feedback from potential users. Four improvements were identified from this feedback and applied to a six-cell version of the device. Testing of the six-cell device by six school children revealed that, although the device received positive scores for four aspects, further improvements are necessary.

Categories and Subject Descriptors

H.5.2 [Information Interfaces and Presentation]: User Interfaces

General Terms

Human Factors, Performance

Keywords

Braille Writing; Training Device; Voice Feedback; Blind Persons

1. INTRODUCTION

We were asked by a blind grammar school teacher to develop a device that would help blind children practice the use of a stylus for writing in Braille. The training device we developed uses an electronic circuit to create tactile sensations and voice feedback, thereby enabling user to easily confirm their actions and to enjoy using the device. We developed two versions, a one-cell prototype version and a six-cell version (where a cell, comprising six dot positions, corresponds to a character).

ASSETS '14 , Oct 20-22 2014, Rochester, NY, USA
ACM 978-1-4503-2720-6/14/10.
http://dx.doi.org/10.1145/2661334.2661390 .

2. RELATED WORK

A similar device is the "Braille Writing Tutor" [1]. Users practice writing Braille using a stylus and a slate and receive voice feedback on their actions. This device does not provide tactile sensation and requires a PC (stand-alone use is not supported).

3. DEVELOPMENT REQUIREMENTS

The teacher had three requirements for the device we were to develop.

(1) A tactile sensation should be provided when the stylus is pushed into a particular hole.

(2) Acoustic feedback should be provided immediately after a character is produced.

(3) It should be usable without a PC.

4. ONE-CELL DEVICE

4.1 System Architecture

We first developed the one-cell prototype version of a Braille writing training device. It uses an Arduino nano microcomputer and an AquesTalk pico voice-synthesis LSI to give voice feedback. The six dots comprising a cell are implemented as six holes in the top of the case, as shown in Figure 1. There is a "Braille" switch under each hole that is used to give tactile feedback when the stylus is inserted in a hole. The holes have 10-mm spacing because the switches are 10 mm × 10 mm. This is much wider than the actual spacing on a Braille writing slate. The user presses the voice switch on the top of the case to hear the voice feedback. The microcomputer is connected to the Braille switches, the voice switch, and the voice-synthesis LSI.

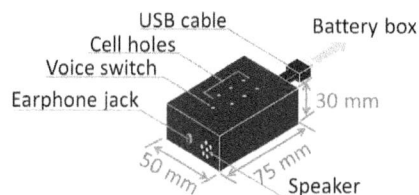

Figure 1: One-cell device.

4.2 Function

When the stylus is inserted into a hole and the switch underneath it is pressed, the user receives a tactile sensation. The microcomputer determines the state of each Braille switch and sends an appropriate signal to the voice-synthesis LSI for creating voice feedback for the character corresponding to the states of the six switches. When the user presses the voice switch, the synthesized voice feedback is created, amplified by the amplifier, and output from the speaker, and the device is reset. Since the device has only one cell, only unvoiced consonant feedback can be output (voiced consonant feedback requires two cells).

4.3 Evaluation

We exhibited our one-cell device at Sight World 2013, an exhibition for the visually impaired, and collected feedback from the visually impaired and their supporters. From their feedback, we identified four improvements to be made.

(1) Attach a plate that tactually guides the stylus to the holes.

(2) Enhance the contrast between the case and the holes.

(3) Generate a beep sound when the voice switch is pushed.

(4) Reposition the voice switch to make it easier to push.

5. SIX-CELL DEVICE

5.1 System Architecture

The system architecture of the six-cell version is basically the same as that of the one-cell device. The number of cells was increased from one to six, as shown in Figure 2, so that the user can practice writing complete words. This resulted in an increase in the number of Braille switches from 6 to 36. The microcomputer does not have enough digital I/O pins to support 36 switches, so we used a key matrix, which reduces the number of switches required.

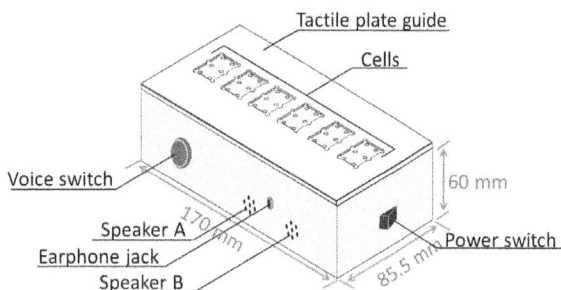

Figure 2: Six-cell device.

5.2 Improvements Made

The four identified improvements were made.

(1) A plate was attached for tactilly guiding the stylus to the holes. By following the edge of the plate, the user can haptically determine the hole positions.

(2) The color of the case was changed from black to white to make it easier for low vision users to see the holes.

(3) A beep sound is output each time a Braille switch is pressed to enable the user to quickly know whether a switch was pressed.

(4) The voice switch was enlarged and moved to the side of the case to make it easier for the user to find and push it.

5.3 Evaluation

The usability of the six-cell device was evaluated on a scale of one to five, with one being poor, by six third and fourth grade students in a school for the blind. The students used the device for two weeks and then assessed four aspects of the device; Size of device, Ease of finding holes, Comfort of pressing Braille switches, and Quality of output voice As shown in Figure 3, each aspect had an average score greater than three.

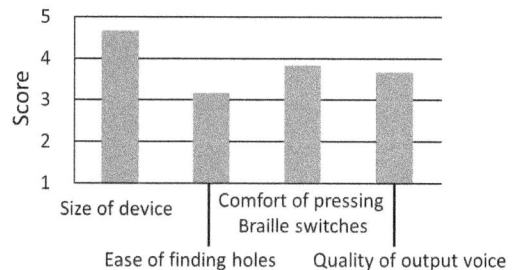

Figure 3: Evaluation result.

5.4 Discussion

The high score for device size is attributed to the device being light enough for the students to easily handle it.

The relatively low score for ease of finding holes is attributed to the gap between the holes and the plate guide, which made it difficult to remove the stylus from the holes. We need to fabricate and attach a guide that does not leave a gap.

The relatively high score for comfort of pressing Braille switches indicates that the students received a pleasurable tactile sensation when they pressed the switches. Unfortunately, this feature would be hard to implement in a device with hole spacing close to the actual spacing on a Braille writing slate due to the unavailability of small enough tactile switches.

Although the score for quality of output voice was in the positive range, comments were made that the speaking was too fast and that the volume was too low. We plan to reduce the speed and to add a volume control function.

6. CONCLUSION

Testing of our six-cell device incorporating both voice feedback and tactile sensation demonstrated that it is potentially useful for helping people learn to use a Braille stylus but that further improvements are necessary. Future work will focus on reducing the size of the device so that it is closer in size to a Braille writing slate.

7. ACKNOWLEDGMENTS

We are grateful to the teacher for motivating us to undertake this work, to the visitors at Sight World 2013 for their feedback, and to the students for their careful evaluations.

8. REFERENCES

[1] N. Kalra, T. Lauwers, D. Dewey, T. Stepleton, and M. B. Dias, Iterative Design of A Braille Writing Tutor to Combat Illiteracy, IEEE/ACM ICTD 2007, pp.2-10, 2007.

Color-via-Pattern: Distinguishing Colors of Confusion Without Affecting Perceived Brightness

Matthew Herbst
Miami University
herbstmb@MiamiOH.edu

Bo Brinkman
Miami University
Benton Hall, 205G
Oxford, OH 45056
Bo.Brinkman@MiamiOH.edu

ABSTRACT

In this poster we describe pilot work on a new visualization technique, Color-via-Pattern (CvP), to help individuals with color deficiency distinguish between colors of confusion, as well as correctly determine relative perceived brightness among all colors. Existing assistive technologies tend to distort the hue and brightness of colors. CvP is designed to address this flaw while being just as effective. Human subject testing was performed to evaluate our approach.

Categories and Subject Descriptors

D.0 [**Software**]: General. K.4.2 [**Computer and Society**]: Social Issues – *Assistive technologies for persons with disabilities.*

General Terms

Measurement, Design, Experimentation, Human Factors

Keywords

Color deficiency; colorblindness; perceived brightness

1. INTRODUCTION

Color deficiency, commonly known as colorblindness (this term is an incorrect description of most cases), is a genetic condition that affects about ten percent of men (women carry and pass, but rarely present, the condition) [1]. There have been many attempts to use mobile apps to assist color deficient individuals in identifying colors correctly. Most existing methods only attempt to help differentiate between different hues, and tend not to preserve other color features such as brightness and saturation. We set out to develop and test a new technique, CvP, which allows users to distinguish between different hues, but without significantly impacting color brightness or saturation.

2. COLOR DEFICIENCY
2.1 The Eye and Types of Color Deficiencies

Two of the primary structures within the human eye are rods, which function in low light, and cones, which function in greater light levels and detect color. Color deficiency is caused by the cone structures within the eye being impaired or not present. There are three types of cones, L (long), M (medium), and S (short), each corresponding to a respective range of wavelengths that they detect; red, green, and blue respectively. For a deeper understanding of rods and cones see [8].

ASSETS '14, Oct 20-22 2014, Rochester, NY, USA
ACM 978-1-4503-2720-6/14/10.
http://dx.doi.org/10.1145/2661334.2661383

In this poster we are concerned with two types of color deficiency, dichromacy and anomalous trichromacy. Dichromacy occurs when the individual only has two of three cones working correctly. Anomalous trichromacy occurs when one or more types of cone structures are acting irregularly, responding to a different range of color than normal.

Within dichromacy there are three major types of deficiencies; protanopia (L cone deficiency), deuteranopia (the most common sub-type, M cone deficiency), and tritanopia (S cone deficiency). These deficiencies result in color confusion, which is when two colors that look different to a person with full trichromacy look identical to a person with the deficiency. (There are similar categories for anomalous trichromacy.)

2.2 Effects on Perceived Brightness

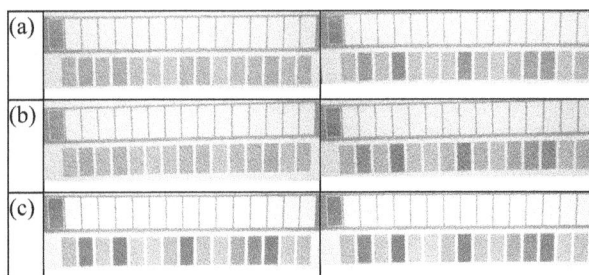

Figure 1. (a) left: Farnsworth hue test, right: deuteranopia simulation applied. (b) left: CvP applied, right: CvP followed by deuteranopia simulation. (c) left: ColorDeBlind (CDB) applied, right: CDB followed by deuteranopia simulation. Note that CDB significantly darkens the blue/turquoise colors, while the colors and brightness are mostly unchanged by CvP.

In addition to affecting the range of hues that an individual can experience, color deficiency also affects that person's ability to perceive the brightness or luminance of one color compared to another. While there exists a fair body of work [9, 10] on general formulas for calculating perceived brightness, we found little to no research on how to adapt these formulas to color deficient individuals.

3. EXISTING TECHNIQUES

There are many existing color visualization techniques for color deficient individuals. The most common technique is color shifting (see [5, 6, 7, 11]), which involves changing the hue and/or luminance of colors of confusion into a range that the individual can easily distinguish. For example, for an individual with deuteranopia, the application might change all reds to blues [7]. This allows the individual to easily distinguish red from green, but potentially creates new confusions between red and blue. In other approaches luminance is used to disambiguate, perhaps by making greens brighter and reds darker [11]. In all of these cases, however, compensating for color deficiency leads to introducing new perceptual errors.

4. COLOR-VIA-PATTERN

CvP is a new technique developed to address the problems with the previously mentioned techniques. In what follows we discuss only red-green color deficiencies, though the approach for yellow-blue deficiencies is similar.

We add a striped pattern, the strength of which is directly related to where the color falls on the continuum between red and green (see Figure 2). Strong right-to-left diagonal lines are drawn in red regions, while left-to-right lines are drawn in green regions. Neutral colors (yellow, white, gray, black, etc.) have no stripes.

Lines are made by alternately darkening and lightening the existing colors. This means that the average brightness, saturation, and hue of two side-by-side lines should be roughly the same in our altered view as in the original image.

Figure 2. Close-up of CvP striping. Yellow is neutral (no stripes), while greenish colors have left-right stripes and reddish colors have right-left stripes.

5. EXPERIMENTATION AND RESULTS

To test CvP we developed an iOS application that implemented it. We then performed human subjects testing using our app, a placebo app (no image alteration), and a popular existing application (ColorDeBlind, [2]). Both hue and brightness testing was done using each app, for a total of six tests per subject. App testing order was random. The test setup involved the subjects performing tests on a webpage (using a mouse) while looking at the webpage (being displayed on a laptop) through an iPad running our app. Eleven subjects from the Miami University community were tested, of which nine (all male) self-identified as having a color deficiency. All nine had some form of red-green color deficiency.

5.1 Test Design

To test how well the apps helped the user correctly compare different hues we administered the Farnsworth D-15 test (see [3, 5] and Figure 1). The test asks users to place fifteen colored tiles into correct hue order, with hues intentionally chosen to confuse color deficient individuals.

To test brightness we need a color deficiency test that requires subjects to rank colors by brightness, not hue. We were unable to find an existing test of this sort, so we developed our own. Taking ideas from the D-15 test, we created a test with 15 tiles; 5 shades of blue, 5 shades of green, and 5 shades of red. Users were asked to place the tiles in order by brightness. Grading was done by counting the number of pairs of tiles that were mis-ordered.

5.2 Results

Using the Mann-Whitney U-Test, we found that CvP performed as well as ColorDeBlind (CDB) in the hue test, with both apps outperforming the placebo app. On the brightness test, CvP performed significantly better than CDB in every case. However,

CvP did not perform better than the placebo app on the brightness tests. With $N = 9$, the maximum value of U is 81. A U value near 0 or 81 indicates high statistical significance; a value near 40.5 indicates low significance.

Hue	U	P	Interpretation
CvP vs Placebo	6	0.00123	CvP much better
CDB vs Placebo	6	0.00123	CDB much better
CvP vs CDB	34	0.60481	No difference

Brightness	U	P	Interpretation
CvP vs Placebo	49	0.48942	No difference
CvP vs ColorDeBlind	0	4.11E-05	CvP much better

6. TAKEAWAYS

More work needs to be done on developing algorithms and tests to measure perceived brightness for individuals with color deficiency. Looking at Figure 1, CvP still leads to an incorrect perception of brightness by individuals with color deficiencies. To correct this we need an appropriate formula for perceived brightness for such individuals. Our brightness test also needs further work. While it was sufficient to show the benefit of CvP vs. CDB, it lacks the subtlety and power of the Farnsworth test.

7. REFERENCES

[1] A.D.A.M. Medical Encyclopedia. 2011. Color Blindness. U.S. National Library of Medicine. http://www.ncbi.nlm.nih.gov/pubmedhealth/PMH0001997

[2] elektron software. 2013. ColorDeBlind. https://itunes.apple.com/us/app/colordeblind-how-color-blind/id513529073

[3] Farnsworth, D. 1947. Farnsworth Dichotomous Test for Color Blindness: Panel D-15.

[4] Flatla, D. R., & Gutwin, C. 2012. Situation-Specific Models of Color Differentiation. ACM Transactions on Accessible Computing, 4(3), 13.

[5] Flück, D. 2009. http://www.color-blindness.com/color-arrangement-test/

[6] Iaccarino, G., Malandrino, D., Del Percio, M., and Scarano, V. 2006. "Efficient edge-services for colorblind users." Proceedings of the 15th international conference on World Wide Web (WWW). Pages 919-920 ACM.

[7] Jefferson, L. and Harvey, R. 2006. "Accommodating Color Blind Computer Users." Proceedings of the 8th international ACM SIGACCESS conference on Computers and accessibility. Pages 40 – 47. ACM.

[8] Montag, E. D. Rods and Cones. http://www.cis.rit.edu/people/faculty/montag/vandplite/pages/chap_9/ch9p1.html

[9] Ridpath, C. and Chisholm, W. 2000. Techniques For Accessibility Evaluation and Repair Tools. W3C. http://www.w3.org/TR/AERT#color-contrast

[10] Stokes, M., Anderson, M., Chandrasekar, S., and Motta, R. 1996. A Standard Default Color Space for the Internet – sRGB. http://www.w3.org/Graphics/Color/sRGB

[11] Wakita, K. and Shimamura, K. 2005. "SmartColor: disambiguation framework for the colorblind." Proceedings of the 7th international ACM SIGACCESS conference on Computers and accessibility. Pages 158-165. ACM.

Designing Exergames Combining the Use of Fine and Gross Motor Exercises to Support Self-care Activities

Karina Caro, Ana I. Martínez-García, Mónica Tentori, Iván Zavala-Ibarra
Department of Computer Science, CICESE
3918, Carretera Ensenada-Tijuana, Zona Playitas, Ensenada, B.C. México, 22860
{karicaro, martinea, mtentori, izavala}@cicese.edu.mx

ABSTRACT

Motor coordination problems are common in different developmental disorders including autism and dyspraxia. Gross and fine motor coordination skills are critical to the appropriate motor coordination development that is relevant to support individuals' independence. Exergames are a good tool to help children practice motor skills as they find them engaging. In this work, we present how FroggyBobby –an exergame designed for practicing gross motor coordination skills, can be extended to combine gross and fine motor exercises for supporting children with motor problems to practice self-care activities that require motor coordination.

Categories and Subject Descriptors

K.4.2 [**Computers and Society**]: Social Issues – *Assistive technologies for persons with disabilities*; K.8.0 [**Personal Computing**]: General – *Games.*

Keywords

Exergames; game design; children; motor coordination.

1. INTRODUCTION

Different disorders are characterized by motor coordination problems including autism [5], developmental coordination disorder or dyspraxia [8], among others. The lack of motor coordination may severely limit motor skills use and age-appropriate development [8]. Motor coordination skills are commonly used as a measure of quality of life as they are critical to help individuals to be independent [9], especially when conducting the activities of daily living like self-care (e.g., get dressed and eating).

Most exergames are appropriate to help children practicing motor skills as children find them engaging [11]. Reflecting from our experiences in designing and evaluating FroggyBobby, an exergame to promote the appropriate practicing of gross motor skills [2], in this paper, we propose a set of fine-motor exercises that could be integrated to this game to help children practice self-care activities and develop age-appropriate fine-motor skills.

2. RELATED WORK

Several projects have investigated how exergames could be used for promoting physical activity (*Astrojumper* [4]), and motor rehabilitation (*Arrow Attack* [1]) in support of different

ASSETS '14, Oct 20-22 2014, Rochester, NY, USA
ACM 978-1-4503-2720-6/14/10.
http://dx.doi.org/10.1145/2661334.2661403

populations, e.g., children with cerebral palsy [6], and stroke patients [1]. These studies show that using exergames benefits physical activity, which may have an impact on health [11] and in motor skills rehabilitation [1]. However, exergames for children with motor problems and those focusing in the fine-motor skills development are scarce. In addition, there are projects of games using touch displays that can help children to practice fine motor coordination [3]. But, these projects set aside the combination of gross and fine motor coordination skills that can be exploited to support the practice of self-care activities of children with motor problems.

3. THE FROGGYBOBBY EXERGAME

We followed an iterative user-centered design methodology, to design and develop FroggyBobby, an exergame for children with motor problems where children control the tongue of a frog avatar practicing with each arm several gross motor coordination exercises [2]. The *basic gameplay* of FroggyBobby demands children to move their left or right arm up and down in a lateral or cross-lateral way. When children play FroggyBobby, they swipe their arms following a path from a start button (Figure 1a) to an end button (Figure 1b), trying to get the frog to catch as many flies as they can. FroggyBobby uses Kinect to track the user's movements for performing the motor coordination exercises and it was implementing using C# and Microsoft Kinect SDK.

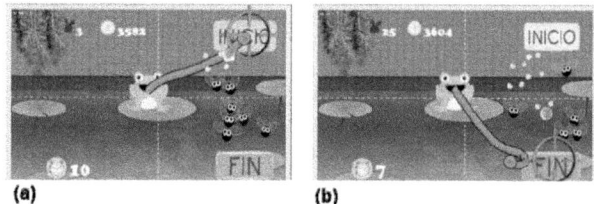

(a)   (b)
Figure 1: Screenshots of the first level of FroggyBobby.

3.1 Methods

To extend FroggyBobby and uncover the fine motor coordination activities that are relevant for children with motor problems, we carried out two participatory design sessions with three psychologist-teachers that attend children with autism presenting motor coordination problems, and one HCI expert. During the design sessions, teachers expressed the importance of combining fine and gross motor exercises, and modified the dynamics for each level and their aims. Data analysis for the results of the design sessions included the use of qualitative techniques such as open coding and affinity diagramming [10].

4. SUMMARY FINDINGS

From the results of the participatory design sessions emerge that for supporting children with motor problems in the practice of self-care activities that require motor coordination, children need to master gross motor coordination exercises. Next, they should practice fine motor coordination exercises. Finally, they should use both fine and gross exercises when conducting self-care activities. To follow this process, a set of fine motor exercises was established to support scaffolding of fine motor coordination. In addition, a set of self-care activities was designed that will promote the practicing of those newly learned motor skills.

4.1 New levels using fine motor coordination exercises

Three new levels of FroggyBobby were proposed based on the fine motor exercises that resulted from the design sessions:

- *Press*, for focusing a target: To keep the hand opened pointing towards an object and then tap it on top of the object.
- *Grip*, for preparing the fine movements: To grab objects with the open hand and then close the hand to move the objects around or catch it.
- *Fine pincer*, for performing fine pincer movements: To use the thumb and the index finger to take an object.

Three levels for each motor exercise were proposed mimicking the game dynamics already available in the original version of FroggyBobby. To prevent frustration in children, instead of catching multiple flies, children must only catch one fly. Another fly will appear after children catch the previous one.

4.2 Using coordination exercises during the practicing of self-care activities

The following informal guidelines were emerge from data analysis to support self-care activities for children with motor problems through exergames:

G1. Learn the cognitive process through gross motor exercises. The exergame should allow children solve some cognition challenges making sure they have the basic cognitive abilities to perform self-care activities (e.g., select the elements for tooth brushing). For that, children can use gross motor exercises, allowing children learn the cognitive process.

G2. Practice of self-care activities through fine motor exercises, combining tangible computing. The exergame should be combined with tangible computing [7], which allows the use of tangible objects interfaced with computers. This provides support for practicing self-care activities with real objects performing fine motor exercises.

G3. Sustained attention management. The exergame should motivate children to practice the self-care activity. Then, the exergame should allow children focus their attention on the tangible objects (e.g., show a waiting screen). Finally, the exergame should provide a strategy to link the use of tangible objects with the system.

Three mini-games were designed for FroggyBobby following these informal guidelines: tying shoelaces, tooth brushing, and selection of the appropriate serve ware for eating (Figure 2).

5. FUTURE WORK AND CONCLUSIONS

As a future work, we are planning to develop the levels for fine motor coordination exercises and one self-care mini-game. We plan to conduct a deployment of the extended version of FroggyBobby with children with motor problems and analyze if the exergame can help with the development of fine motor skills.

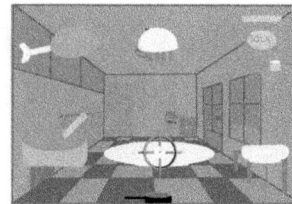

Figure 2: Screenshot of a mini-game for practicing self-care activities using gross motor exercises (informal guideline G1).

We expect FroggyBobby serves to support self-care activities of children with motor problems, supplementing current practices and therapeutic interventions of children with motor problems.

6. ACKNOWLEDGMENTS

This work is funded by the Mexican Council for Science and Technology (CONACyT) fellowship and trough Dr. Monica Tentori's Microsoft Fellowship gift.

7. REFERENCES

[1] Burke, J.W. et al. 2009. Optimising engagement for stroke rehabilitation using serious games. *The Visual Computer*. 25, 12 (Aug. 2009), 1085–1099.

[2] Caro, K. et al. 2014. FroggyBobby: an exergame to support children with motor problems practicing gross motor skills during therapeutic interventions. *Journal of Computers in Human Behavior*. (2014), Submitted.

[3] Dunne, A. et al. 2010. Upper extremity rehabilitation of children with cerebral palsy using accelerometer feedback on a multitouch display. *IEEE Engineering in Medicine and Biology Society*. (Jan. 2010), 1751–4.

[4] Finkelstein, S.L. et al. 2010. Astrojumper: Designing a Virtual Reality Exergame to Motivate Children with Autism to Exercise. *Virtual Reality Conference* (2010), 267–268.

[5] Fournier, K. a et al. 2010. Motor coordination in autism spectrum disorders: a synthesis and meta-analysis. *Journal of autism and developmental disorders*. 40, 10 (Oct. 2010), 1227–40.

[6] Hernandez, H.A. et al. 2012. Design of an Exergaming Station for Children with Cerebral Palsy. *Human Factors in Computing Systems* (Austin, Texas, USA, 2012), 2619–2628.

[7] Ishii, H. and Ullmer, B. 1997. Tangible Bits: Towards Seamless Interfaces between People , Bits and Atoms. *Proceedings of the ACM SIGCHI Conference on Human factors in computing systems* (Atlanta, Georgia, USA, 1997), 234–241.

[8] Miyahara, M. and Möbs, I. 1995. Developmental dyspraxia and developmental coordination disorder. *Neuropsychology review*. 5, 4 (Dec. 1995), 245–68.

[9] Shumway-Cook, A. and Woollacott, M.H. 2001. *Motor control: Theory and practical applications*. Lippincott Williams and Wilkins.

[10] Strauss, A. and Corbin, J. 1998. *Basics of Qualitative Research: Techniques and Procedures for developing grounded theory*. SAGE Publications.

[11] Yim, J. and Graham, T.C.N. 2007. Using Games to Increase Exercise Motivation. *Future Play* (Toronto, Canada, 2007), 166–173.

Development of Accessible Toolset to Enhance Social Interaction Opportunities for People with Cerebral Palsy in India

Manjira Sinha
Indian Institute of Technology Kharagpur
Kharagpur 721302
tirtha@cse.iitkgp.ernet.in

Tirthankar Dasgupta
Indian Institute of Technology Kharagpur
Kharagpur 721302
manjira@cse.iitkgp.ernet.in

Anupam Basu
Indian Institute of Technology Kharagpur
Kharagpur 721302
anupam@cse.iitkgp.ernet.in

ABSTRACT

In this paper we have developed a toolset that will allow people with severe spastic cerebral palsy (CP) and highly restricted motor movement skills to access popular social-networking and communication mediums like, Facebook and E-mails. To understand the requirements of the intended users we have performed a number of surveys that acted as basis of our system design. The developed tools use special access switch based scanning technique for easy navigation in different applications. We have evaluated the toolset with six target users. The preliminary results demonstrate a positive response.

Categories and Subject Descriptors

K.4.2 [**Social Issues**]: Assistive technologies for persons with disabilities. H.1.2 [**User/Machine Systems**]: Human factors.

General Terms

Design, Economics, Human Factors

Keywords

Cerebral palsy; user interactions; Facebook; e-mail client.

1. INTRODUCTION

Despite such a widespread penetration, social-networking and communication mediums like, Facebook and E-mails still remain "very difficult to access" for people with severe speech and motor impairments (SSMI) in India. This is primarily due to their inability to use standard computer peripherals like, keyboard and mouse that requires fine motor skills to operate [3]. Therefore, it is important to circumvent such problems particularly for developing countries like, India where disability issues are still not the frontrunners in popular policy making decisions and social support system for such group has not yet been effectively developed.

The aim of this work is to build assistive tools to facilitate people with severe form of SSMI to access communication portals such a Gmail, Yahoo Mail, and Facebook. The tools have been developed in constant interaction with both the target user group and their instructors.

2. PRE-DEVELOPMENT INTERACTION

We have interacted with individuals with SSMI along with their parents and instructors from Indian Institute of Cerebral Palsy(IICP), Kolkata, India. Through this process we have collected their requirement specifications, designed the interface and developed an initial prototype, and then visited them again for their input midway through the implementation process. Table 1 summarizes some of the findings. We initially tried to identify reasons behind the failure of the existing tools and technologies in penetrating the Indian population. We found that a) most of the present assistive devices need to be imported. Hence, there is an issue of lack of local support and maintenance, b)The existing systems are too costly for average Indian users. For instance, some of these systems like E-Z Keys, and Gyro-Head Mouse costs around £1495[1]. As a result of this, our target users prefers the special access switch enabled scanning techniques as, they are cheap, locally manufactured thus, readily available, require less maintenance and very much familiar in India.

Computer usage time	30-45 minutes, once a day
Mode of access	Keyboard, mouse
Problem Faced: Moving a mouse pointer requires a smooth navigating ability over a two dimensional screen; keyboards switches demand a small and specific area to be pressed, therefore shortcuts like Tab key or multiple keypress do not provide much help. Yahoo Mail accessibility features for persons with disabilities provide support for screenreader, and mouse-free control. Accessibility guidelines of Facebook added many useful features for the blind, but not with SSMI.	
Instructor assistance	strongly required
Familiarity with scanning mechanism	Comfortable with the scanning mechanism and access switches

Table 1: Summarizing the user survey

3. System Description

We have developed a customized E-mail client interface to make it more accessible to our target users. In order to keep the GUI simple, we have discarded all advance options of a standard mail client and kept the essential features like, *Inbox, compose mail* and *draft mail*. We have used Microsoft IMAP API to extract all the mails for a user. Typically, three fields were extracted from the mail server, *the senders name and mail-id, Date of delivery,* and *mail subject*. This information is presented to the user in a more lucid way so that can understand and operate. Similarly, in the *compose mail* module, a user can send a mail to any number of recipient. The composed mail is also integrated with a predictive keyboard (see Figure 1). Similarly, for accessibility of popular social networking sites like, Facebook, a specialized scanning enabled wrapper has been developed. The wrapper interface provides user options to operate a Facebook profile like, browsing posts in a wall, commenting/ liking a post, and creating or sharing of posts (see Figure 2).

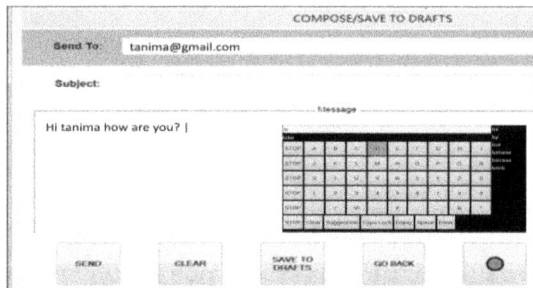

Figure 1: Illustration of the E-mail Client

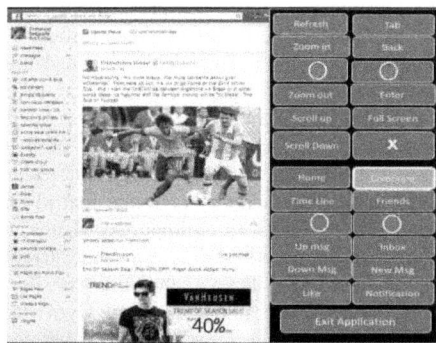

Figure 2: Accessing Facebook wall using our proposed system

4. EVALUATION OF THE SYSTEM

The browser has been deployed and field tasted with six participants[1] of age group 25 to 32. We have installed the systems at IICP Kolkata and provided a 15 day time period for the participants to get familiar with the system. We made sure that each user gets to use the system for at least 6 sessions each of about 1 hour. All the users were able navigate through the applications independently. In this duration, we determined the preferred scanning delay for each user through trials. After the familiarization period, the testing phase started.

The performance of the browser has been measured in terms of: a) *Task execution time* (TET) or the time required by a subject to accomplish a given task. We asked participants to perform 16 tasks from each application for a period of 1 month using both the conventional method T_{trad} and our new method T_{new}. Response time (RT) for both the browsers and for each user were recorded and compared (refer to Table 2 for a sample set of tasks and their RTs). We observe T_{new} is less than that of T_{trad} for all the tasks. This, to some extent, implies the effectiveness of our proposed browsing techniques. b) *Error rates analysis(ER)*: measures the number and the type of errors encountered performing a task. This was done by both manual inspection of the user's performance and by installing a key logger program. We found most of the errors occur due to: a) text entry errors (TE) b) subjects fails to press the access switch when the desired control is activated (FP) and c) subjects selects a wrong element (WE). Both of the error types are interrelated as, failing to press access switch at the

---

1 Gross Motor Functioning Classification System(GMFCS) and Manual Ability Classification System(MACS) level 5

correct time results in wrong selection of elements (see Table 4 for details). Nevertheless, as the number of evaluation session increases, the rate of making errors decreases. **c) *Overall usability score***: We asked individuals to grade both the applications according to different usability criteria like, a) the *overall impression (OI)* of the applications, b) *learnability (L)* and c) *the ease of use (EU)*. The grading has been done through a 10-point Likertscale; 10 being very satisfied and 1 being very disappointed. The results are reported in Table 3.

Task	t_{trad}	t_{new}
Go to the e-mail GUI	0	8
Log-in to either G-mail or Yahoo	160	80
Open the 5th e-mail in inbox	78	30
Compose and send mail (involves subtask like type the recipients mail id, compose the e-mail and send)	423	372
Go to the Facebook icon and click it	X	75
Scroll down page to browse posts	48	20
Like a post and share a post	X	45

Table 2: Comparing TET of t_{trad}(in msec) and t_{new}

CP	E-Mail			Facebook		
	OI	L	EU	OI	L	EU
CP1	6	7	5	8	9	9
CP2	6	8	6	8	7	9
CP3	7	7	5	9	9	9
CP4	7	7	6	10	9	9
CP5	8	7	8	8	7	7
CP6	7	8	7	7	8	7

Table 3: Usability rating of the six users based on the *Overall usability score* parameters.

Type of errors	% of Error
TE	72
FP	18
WE	10

Table 4: Error rates across classes

5. CONCLUSION

In this paper, we have developed a novel scanning based GUI to facilitate persons with SSMI to access Facebook and E-mail applications. The primary objective of the work was to enhance the experience of the focus users and the secondary goal was to provide the benefits within an affordable range. The later point is very important for the general population of a developing country like, India. Both the system requires very low price hardware and configuration support and the software was distributed free of cost. The overall system got a positive response. However, it would be premature to conclude anything concrete based only on the current experimental results. Hence, a more rigorous testing of the system different group of participants and over a larger number of sessions is required to establish a concrete claim.

ACKNOWLEDGEMENT

We are thankful to Indian Institute of Cerebral Palsy (IICP), Kolkata and the different participants to allow us to conduct our evaluation of the developed systems. We are also grateful to Dr. Shari Tarwin for providing us useful feedback about the system.

REFERENCE

[1] http://www.wordsplus.com/website/products/soft/ezkeys.htm

[2] David Beukelman and Pat Mirenda. Augmentative and alternative communication. 2005.

[3] Constantine E Steriadis and Philip Constantinou. Designing human-computer interfaces for quadriplegic people. *ACM Transactions on Computer-Human Interaction (TOCHI)*, 10(2):87–118, 2003.

Development of Tactile Graph Generation Software Using the R Statistics Software Environment

Kosuke Araki
Graduate School of Science & Technology
University of Niigata
Niigata, Japan
f13c095g@mail.cc.niigata-u.ac.jp

Tetsuya Watanabe
Department of Biocybernetics
Faculty of Engineering
University of Niigata
Niigata, Japan
t2.nabe@eng.niigata-u.ac.jp

Kazunori Minatani
National Center for University Extrance Examinations
Tokyo, Japan
minatani@rd.dnc.ac.jp

ABSTRACT

We have worked on the development of software that uses the R statistics software environment to automatically generate tactile graphs–i.e., graphs that can be read by blind people using their sense of touch. We released this software as a Web application to make it available to anyone, from anywhere. This Web application can automatically generate images for tactile graphs from numerical data in a CSV file. This report discusses the Web application's functions and operating procedures.

Categories and Subject Descriptors

H.5.2 [Information Interfaces and Presentation]: User Interfaces

General Terms

Human Factors

Keywords

Blind Persons; Tactile Graphs; R Statistical Software; Web Application

1. INTRODUCTION

Graphs are used to represent changes, trends and correlations in data. Since graphs are generally visual representations, it is difficult for blind people to use them. One way of supporting the use of graphs by blind people is to generate "tactile graphs" that can be read by the sense of touch. The task of generating tactile graphs is usually performed manually by helpers such as Braille translation volunteers and teachers at schools for the blind. Consequently, the preparation of tactile graphs can require considerable time and effort, making it impossible for blind people to obtain tactile graphs straight away. Another problem is that it is

ASSETS '14, Oct 20-22 2014, Rochester, NY, USA
ACM 978-1-4503-2720-6/14/10. .
http://dx.doi.org/10.1145/2661334.2661389.

difficult for blind people to generate tactile graphs by themselves.

Based on this state of affairs, we have worked on the development of software that makes it easy to generate several different types of tactile graph and is capable of being used by blind and sighted people alike. This software is provided as a Web application, making it easy for anyone to obtain tactile graphs. We developed it using R, which is a statistics software environment with specialized drawing functions. Tactile graphs can be generated by the simple method of microcapsule paper, which is widely used in education.

2. THE R STATISTICS SOFTWARE

R is a statistics software environment with specialized statistical analysis and drawing functions. It also includes programming functions. It is free software, and can be obtained from the Comprehensive R Archive Network (CRAN) website[1]. Since R is compatible with various operating systems, it can be used by anyone.

There were two reasons why we chose R for the development of tactile graph generation software:

(1) R is capable of changing various graph parameters, and to fine-tune settings such as the line thickness, the format of the axes, and the text font. It is therefore possible to generate tactile graphs with layouts that are suitable for reading by touch.

(2) Availability of package for the creation of Web applications. There is a package for R called Shiny that can turn R programs into Web applications.

3. TACTILE GRAPH GENERATION SOFTWARE

3.1 Overview

Our Web application software reads numerical data from a CSV file, accepts user input such as the title of the graph, and automatically generates images for tactile graphs based on this information. The resulting images are printed on microcapsule paper and passed through a heater to produce the finished tactile graphs.

3.2 Development environment

We used the Mac OS X operating system (version 10.9).

We used R (version 3.1.0) as the development language, together with the RStudio (version 0.98.507) integrated development environment (IDE). We also used the Shiny package (version 0.9.1) to convert the R program into a Web application.

3.3 Software operating method

A screenshot of the Web application is shown in Fig. 1. At the top left of the screen is a file selection button for selecting the CSV file. Below that is a set of radio buttons for changing types of the graph to be generated. These are followed by a set of textboxes for setting the graph title and the units and ranges of each axis. The graph image is displayed on the right side of the screen. This graph image immediately reflects any changes the user makes to the graph parameters. Below the graph image, there is a download button.

Users operate the Web application as follows:

(1) Select CSV file

A CSV file is selected, and the numerical data is read in by the software. At this point, a graph image of the selected data is displayed at the right side of the screen.

(2) Select graph type

The type of tactile graph is selected from the following: scatter plot, line graph, bar graph and pie chart.

(3) Select font

The style of text displayed in the graph can be selected from inked characters and Braille characters. Using inked characters, it is possible for a sighted person to operate the software while checking that there are no errors in the graph's text annotations.

(4) Select whether or not to include grid lines

The user can choose whether or not grid lines should be included in the graph.

(5) Input titles

The user enters titles for the graph and for the horizontal and vertical axes.

(6) Set y-axis range

The display range of the graph can be set by entering minimum and maximum values for the y axis. If not set, the y-axis range of the graph is set from the minimum and maximum values of the numerical data.

(7) Save the results

The tactile graph image can be saved by clicking the download button. The image is then saved as a PNG file in the user's download folder.

(8) Print and develop the image

The saved image can be printed on microcapsule paper by an ordinary printer. When passed through a heater, the black parts form raised bumps to produce the final tactile graph.

3.4 Content of tactile graphs

Fig. 2. shows an example of a tactile line graph generated using this software.

The elements of the tactile graph are the line graph itself, the graph title, the text annotation for the vertical axis, the units of the horizontal axis, the axis labels, grid lines and an exterior frame.

The characters and numbers in the graph title, axis units and axis labels are displayed in Braille, and are all oriented horizontally. The graph title is positioned at the very top of the tactile graph, and a description of the units on the

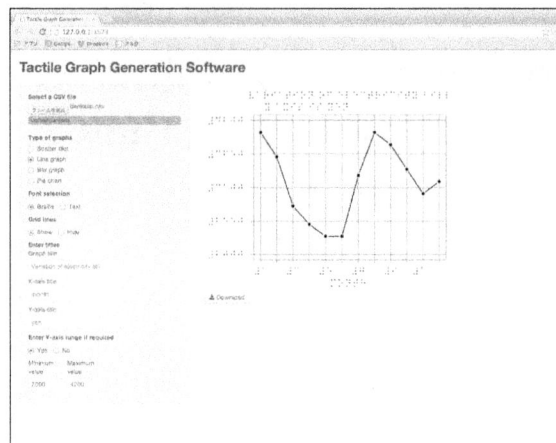

Figure 1: Screenshot of the Web application

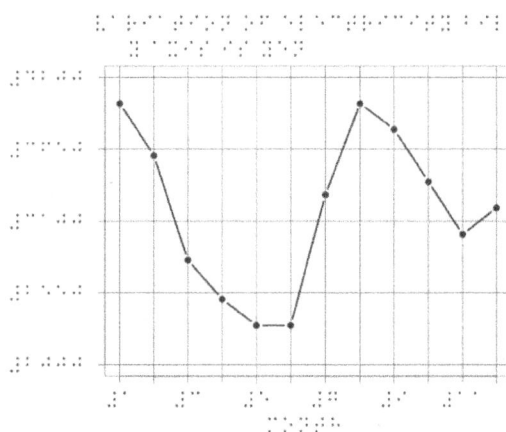

Figure 2: Example of a tactile line graph

vertical axis appears below this title. The horizontal axis units are positioned at the very bottom of the graph.

The line graph and the grid/frame lines are represented by two types of line with different line styles and thicknesses. The line graph is represented by a dot-dash line, using a 1-mm-thick solid line for the line segments, and 3-mm-diameter dots for the dots. The grid lines and frame line are represented by solid lines with a thickness of approximately 0.5 mm. The line thicknesses and dot diameters were determined according to the guidelines for tactile illustration (such as [2]).

4. FUTURE WORK

In the future, we will work on the following two issues:
(1) Increase the kinds of graph generated.
(2) User evaluation

5. REFERENCES

[1] The Comprehensive R Archive Network, http://www.cran.r-project.org/.

[2] The N.S.W. Tactual and Bold Print Mapping Committee, A Guide for the Production of Tactual and Bold Print Maps 3rd Edition, Sydney, 2006.

Digital Tools for Physically Impaired Visual Artists

Chris Creed
Digital Humanities Hub
University of Birmingham
Edgbaston, B15 2TT
+4401214149658
creedcpl@bham.ac.uk

Russell Beale
HCI Centre
University of Birmingham
Edgbaston, B15 2TT
+4401214149658
r.beale@cs.bham.ac.uk

Paula Dower
DASH
5 Belmont
Shropshire SY1 1TE
+4401743272939
paula@dasharts.org

ABSTRACT

We present work-in-progress that is exploring the potential for visual artists with physical impairments to use new non-intrusive mid-air gesturing sensors to enhance and extend their practice. We highlight the key results from an initial informal user evaluation with two disabled and two non-disabled visual artists examining use of the Leap Motion sensor as an artistic tool. Future work will explore how related technologies can be better utilized to support disabled artists in their practice.

Categories and Subject Descriptors

H.5.2 [**Information Interfaces and Presentation**]: User Interfaces - Ergonomics, Evaluation/Methodology, Input devices and strategies, Screen design, User-centred design

General Terms

Design, Human Factors

Keywords

Assistive Technologies; Digital Accessibility; Disabled Artists; Physical Impairment; Mid-Air Gesturing; Disability Arts

1. INTRODUCTION

Visual art is an activity that presents many opportunities for people with physical impairments such as providing a creative outlet, encouraging social inclusion, raising self-esteem, aiding with rehabilitation, and supporting general well-being. However, disabled artists with physical and motor impairments still have significant difficulties when working on their craft often resulting in a tedious and frustrating experience that requires huge patience and perseverance.

Perera et al. [1] observed a group of disabled artists and found that they typically used a range of assistive devices such as head wands, mouth sticks, and specially designed grips for holding devices. Whilst these tools can help make the production of artwork more accessible, they also involve repetitive unnatural movements which can result in additional issues (e.g. neck strain). The authors also observed the essential role of carers who are required for setting up canvases, paints, brushes, and any further adjustments that are required after the initial setup. This lack of

independence and reliance on support staff can be particularly frustrating for disabled artists and can hinder their creative process.

New technologies can potentially overcome some of the issues that disabled artists experience, yet little work to date has explored how digital tools can support the production of their artwork. To address this lack of work we are currently investigating the potential of mid-air gesturing using the Leap Motion sensor [2] to help visual artists with physical impairments. This sensor can detect mid-air finger gestures performed by users in a three dimensional space (e.g. swipe, grab, brushing motions). It can also detect a single physical pointer such as a brush, pencil, head wand, mouth stick, or other assistive devices.

This technology can be particularly useful for people who have difficulty in holding traditional tools and applying pressure to a canvas. Different mid-air gestures can be used to provide disabled artists with much more control over their canvas, selection of brushes and paints, and can give them access to a broad range of tools they may normally have difficulty in using. A digital application can also be designed and trained to support people with specific disabilities - for instance, the brush strokes of an artist with cerebral palsy and tremor could be dynamically smoothed out. Furthermore, this type of approach can reduce the amount of support required from carers as it provides artists with more independence.

We are aware of no existing work exploring the potential of mid-air gesturing as an assistive tool for physically impaired visual artists and as such it remains unclear how people will respond to this type of approach. How do disabled artists feel about the use of hands and fingers as a substitute for traditional tools (e.g. brushes)? Do they prefer using tangible objects such as performing painting gestures with a "physical" brush in mid-air? It is also unclear what the general interaction issues with mid-air gestures are for disabled artists and how the interface should be tailored for different types of disability. Moreover, how should the interface adapt for people with degenerative diseases (i.e. the tools required in the early stages of a condition are likely to be significantly different from later stages)?

This paper provides an overview of work in progress that is exploring the potential of mid-air interactions for disabled artists. We present the results of an evaluation of three Leap Motion applications conducted with disabled and non-disabled artists and highlight some of the key interaction issues that need to be addressed.

2. LEAP MOTION APPLICATIONS

We wanted to test a selection of Leap Motion applications that allow users to create digital art using mid-air gestures. As such, we decided to test the following three different applications available on the Leap Motion application store [3]:

Photoshop Ethereal [4]: This application allows users to interact with Photoshop using mid-air gestures and has some unique features developed specifically for the Leap Motion sensor (e.g. digital brush pressure control via mid-air gestures)

Freeform [5]: This is a 3D sculpting and modeling application that allows users to create different objects using mid-air gestures.

Leap Motion Orientation: This application is included with the sensor and provides the ability to create basic and simple brush strokes using mid-air gestures.

3. EVALUATION

We conducted an evaluation with two disabled and two non-disabled artists. One of the disabled artists has arthrogryposis and the other is in the early stages of multiple sclerosis. The session lasted three hours and started with an overview of the technology. We then tested the Leap Motion applications - the artists were asked to share their thoughts as they used the technology using a think-aloud protocol. The Leap Motion sensor was placed on a table in front of a wall where the applications were projected (Figure 1). There were several key findings:

- The hand structure of the artist with arthrogryposis resulted in multiple points being detected by the sensor (as opposed to a single finger) which created a frustrating interaction experience as the cursor would jump around the screen. A rolled up piece of paper was used as a makeshift brush which the artist could hold and use more effectively.

- Determining the firmness of stroke was problematic and it was felt that some form of calibration for setting the firmness would help. The digital canvas also had no depth or movement which felt strange to the artists (thickness of canvas has implications on the artist's strokes).

- Navigation of the (Photoshop) interface was an issue and attempting to select different tools was often frustrating due to the size of icons and attempting to perform the "click" mid-air gesture. It was also difficult for all artists to get a sense of where the brush was located on the screen (especially when starting a new session).

- Continuous line drawing and brushing was challenging - the brush would often come away from the canvas which would result in unintentional blank spaces. Painting with mid-air gestures on a digital canvas also lacked the pencil and brush reactions you would get on paper or a traditional canvas (i.e. the process of mid-air painting *felt* strange).

- One of the disabled artists found that using opacity control could simulate brushwork via the use of mid-air gesturing, but commented that it was not nearly as responsive as using a Wacom or Intous tablet.

In discussions with the artists they made several suggestions about what an application would need to make it more usable for themselves and other disabled artists:

- The interface design used in mobile and tablet drawing applications could be more appropriate for Leap Motion software as they tend to focus only on essential features and have a more simplistic and minimalistic design.

- Voice commands to set and control different tools would help to create a more fluid interaction and avoid the cost of having to navigate to specific tools with a cursor.

- Brushes and erasers need to have lots of options that are easily accessible via mid-air gesturing to create a more complete tool.

- Disabled users with physical impairments need to have a simple operating system (the Photoshop interface was too complex).

- The range of motion (brush strokes) needs to be adapted (e.g. the ability to flick paint or dabbing of a paint brush).

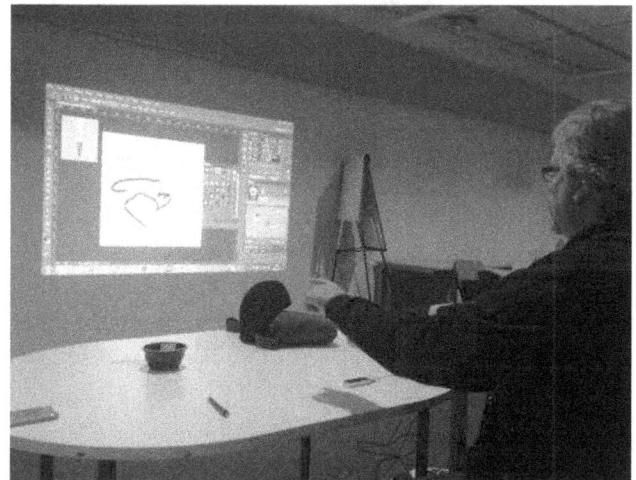

Figure 1. Disabled artist using the Photoshop Ethereal application

4. CONCLUSION

It is clear from the evaluations that the current design of the Leap Motion applications tested are not well suited for artists with physical impairments. Photoshop, for instance, had too many options and it was difficult to select different tools due to the small size of icons and difficulties in performing the appropriate selection gestures. New interface designs and specialist applications are required to help support disabled artists using mid-air gesturing tools for artistic purposes. Our work in this field is ongoing and we are currently exploring novel design approaches and developing new tools that better support disabled artists which we will evaluate in longitudinal user studies.

5. ACKNOWLEDGMENTS

This research has received support from the British Council.

6. REFERENCES

[1] Perera, D., Eales, R. J., and Blashki, K. 2009. Supporting the creative drive: investigating paralinguistic voice as a mode of interaction for artists with upper limb disabilities. *Universal Access in the Information Society*. 8, 2, 77-88.

[2] The Leap Motion Controller. https://www.leapmotion.com/

[3] Airspace Store. https://airspace.leapmotion.com/

[4] Photoshop Ethereal. http://bit.ly/1lvyN5j

[5] Freeform. http://bit.ly/1nMYmxj

Enhancing Multi-Touch Table Accessibility
for Wheelchair Users

Chris Creed
Digital Humanities Hub
University of Birmingham
Edgbaston, B15 2TT
+4401214149658
creedcpl@bham.ac.uk

Russell Beale
HCI Centre
University of Birmingham
Edgbaston, B15 2TT
+4401214149658
r.beale@cs.bham.ac.uk

ABSTRACT

Wheelchair users can find accessing digital content on large multi-touch tables particularly difficult and frustrating due to their limited reach. We present work in progress that is exploring the potential of enhancing touch table accessibility through the use of mid-air gesturing technology. An overview of an experimental prototype is provided along with the key findings from an evaluation conducted with fifteen wheelchair users at a public library and heritage centre.

Categories and Subject Descriptors

H.1.2 [**User/Machine Systems**]: Human factors. H.5.2 [**Information Interfaces and Presentation**]: User Interfaces - Ergonomics, Evaluation/Methodology, Input devices and strategies, Prototyping, User-centred design

General Terms

Design, Human Factors

Keywords

Assistive Technology; Digital Accessibility; Wheelchair Users; Physical Impairment; Mid-Air Gesturing; Multi-Touch Tables

1. INTRODUCTION

Multi-touch tables are increasingly being used in public spaces such as museums, libraries, and art galleries to provide engaging interactive experiences [1]. However, whilst touch tables are generally intuitive and easy to access for the majority of the general public, they can be particularly frustrating to use for those who have physical impairments. In particular, people in wheelchairs can have significant accessibility issues when attempting to interact with content on touch tables due to their limited reach.

One potential solution is the use of mid-air gestures to access and manipulate content that is out of reach. The recent release of affordable sensors such as the Leap Motion [2] have made it more feasible to build interactive systems that can be controlled by

body movements. Mid-air gesturing can provide several benefits in terms of enhancing touch table accessibility - for instance, the Leap Motion sensor can easily be incorporated into the border around a touch table allowing people to simply approach the table and start interacting with content (without the need of an external device). The design of a touch table application would also not need to be significantly altered to accommodate physically disabled users as a mid-air interface could enable them to easily access all features.

Related work has started to examine how users can perform mid-air gestures to interact with digital content [3]. There has also been research that has investigated the use of mid-air gesturing above a multi-touch table [4-5]. However, despite this work, there have been no research studies to date that have explored the potential for mid-air gesturing to enhance touch table accessibility for people with physical impairments. This paper therefore presents the first body of work in this area - we initially provide an overview of an experimental prototype that has been developed and then highlight the key results from an initial user evaluation with fifteen wheelchair users. We conclude with an overview of the next steps we plan to take in this project.

2. PROTOTYPE

We have developed a prototype that enables people to interact with touch table content using mid-air gestures performed over a Leap Motion sensor. In this application people can select and drag images around the table via both multi-touch and mid-air gestures. We created two different mid-air selection techniques - Thumb Trigger and Screen Tap (Figure 1). The Thumb Trigger gesture allows a user to control a cursor on the screen using a single index finger. Once the cursor is positioned over an image the user can pick it up by extending their thumb. The image can then be dragged around and dropped in a desired location by placing the thumb back in. The Screen Tap version also allows people to control the cursor with a single finger, but requires a rapid downward tap gesture to pick an object up. The user can then drag the image around and perform another downward tap to drop the image.

3. EXPERIMENT

We ran an initial user evaluation to explore the potential of the prototype to enhance accessibility for people in wheelchairs and to investigate performance and perceptions around the different selection techniques (Figure 2). This evaluation was conducted on a 55" multi-touch table installed at a public library and heritage centre. We recruited fifteen participants (three female) who are all wheelchair users. The sample had a mean age of 33.4 years ranging from 16-72. There were three conditions - Touch Only, Thumb Trigger, and Screen Tap. The experimental task involved participants having to move eight images into designated boxes along one border of the table. The first condition always involved them completing the task using touch gestures only. The researcher initially gave a demonstration of the appropriate gestures and the participants then had five minutes to complete the task. This process was then repeated for the other two mid-air conditions. When a participant had completed all three versions a semi-structured interview was conducted to explore further their perceptions of the technology. We videoed all interactions and interviews for later analysis.

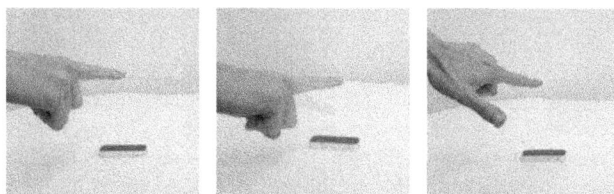

Figure 1. The mid-air gestures (from left-right: single finger cursor control, screen tap, thumb trigger)

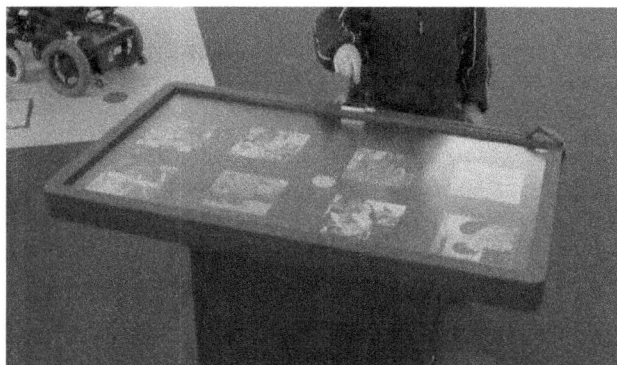

Figure 2. A participant in a manual wheelchair interacting with the table via the Leap Motion sensor

4. RESULTS

Analysis of the video footage demonstrated that users were able to manipulate content via mid-air gestures that would have normally been out of their reach (this was measured through the number of images placed in appropriate boxes and task completion times). However, there were also several interaction issues that will need to be addressed in our ongoing work:

Cursor Control: Only small finger movements were required above the Leap Motion sensor to control the cursor, but people naturally tended to make larger movements at first which moved the cursor off the screen. People also tended to move their hand out of the range of the sensor which could result in jittery cursor movements (although this became less of an issue with practice).

Thumb Trigger: Several participants had issues in manipulating the images using this gesture. This was often due to the position of the thumb which could occasionally occlude the index finger making it difficult for the sensor to see the gesture. This occlusion could sometimes result in participants unintentionally dropping images or not being able to efficiently pick up the images as expected.

Screen Tap: Participants typically had to make numerous attempts to perform this gesture before they could pick an image up (sometimes on up to twenty occasions). This was usually due to not performing the downward tap gesture quickly enough.

Spreading of Fingers: Some participants had a tendency to spread their fingers over the sensor when only a single finger was required. The application was programmed to track the nearest finger to the sensor, so when fingers were spread this could result in a jittery cursor or issues with selection gestures.

Not intuitive for first time users: During interviews several participants commented that the device would not be intuitive to use without some instruction as they would be unsure about which gestures they could perform. This raises important questions around how to subtly inform people how to use the sensor without impacting significantly on the overall design of the application.

Tiredness: A couple of participants commented on how their arm started to feel tired during the study. They had difficulty holding their arm in an "artificial" position. One participant wanted more flexibility in where the sensor could be placed (e.g. the arm of their chair might have been more comfortable).

Practice: Participants highlighted a desire to spend more time playing with the device to get used to performing the gestures. It took the majority of participants between 1-5 minutes to try and complete both the Screen Tap and Thumb Trigger tasks. However, one of the authors who has had more time to practice with the application was able to consistently complete both the Screen Tap and Thumb Trigger tasks in around 12 seconds.

5. CONCLUSION

The work completed to date has highlighted both the potential of mid-air gesturing for enhancing accessibility and some of the interaction issues that need to be resolved. We are now looking to refine the prototype in terms of adjusting cursor sensitivity, making the selection gestures easier to perform, and exploring how to subtly inform people about the gestures available with minimal instruction. We also plan to examine and compare other approaches such as simply being able to point at an object of interest to select it and then manipulate that object through a range of different mid-air gestures.

6. REFERENCES

[1] Geller, T. 2006. Interactive tabletop exhibits in museums and galleries. *Computer Graphics and Applications*. IEEE, 26, 5, 6-11.

[2] The Leap Motion Controller. https://www.leapmotion.com/

[3] Song, P. et al. 2012. A handle bar metaphor for virtual object manipulation with mid-air interaction. In *Proceedings of the SIGCHI Conference on Human Factors in Computing Systems*. ACM, 1297-1306

[4] Pyryeskin, D., Hancock, M., and Hoey, J. 2012. Comparing elicited gestures to designer-created gestures for selection above a multitouch surface. In *Proceedings of the 2012 ACM international conference on Interactive tabletops and surfaces*. ACM, 1-10.

[5] Banerjee, A. et al. 2011. Pointable: an in-air pointing technique to manipulate out-of-reach targets on tabletops. In *Proceedings of the ACM International Conference on Interactive Tabletops and Surfaces*. ACM, 11-20

Evaluating the Accessibility of Crowdsourcing Tasks on Amazon's Mechanical Turk

Rocío Calvo[1], Shaun K. Kane[2,3], Amy Hurst[3]

[1] Computer Science Department
Universidad Carlos III de Madrid
Leganés, 28911, Spain
mrcalvo@inf.uc3m.es

[2] Department of Computer Science
University of Colorado Boulder
Boulder, CO 80309 USA
shaun.kane@colorado.edu

[3] Information Systems Department
UMBC
Baltimore, MD 21250 USA
amyhurst@umbc.edu

ABSTRACT

Crowd work web sites such as Amazon Mechanical Turk enable individuals to work from home, which may be useful for people with disabilities. However, the web sites for finding and performing crowd work tasks must be accessible if people with disabilities are to use them. We performed a heuristic analysis of one crowd work site, Amazon's Mechanical Turk, using the Web Content Accessibility Guidelines 2.0. This paper presents the accessibility problems identified in our analysis and offers suggestions for making crowd work platforms more accessible.

Categories and Subject Descriptors

H.5.2. [Information Interfaces and Presentation]: User Interfaces–*evaluation/methodology;* K.4.2. [Computers and Society]: Social issues—*assistive technologies for persons with disabilities.*

Keywords

Accessibility; Evaluation; Mechanical Turk; Crowdsourcing.

1. INTRODUCTION

Gaining independence through employment is a goal of many people with disabilities [1]. For individuals who experience challenges in commuting to a workplace, working from home can provide an accessible alternative. In 2012, 24.5% of employed US citizens with disabilities completed some of their work from home [9]. Crowd work services, such as Amazon Mechanical Turk (MTurk), enable individuals to perform short, simple tasks (called Human Intelligence Tasks, or HITs) in exchange for a small payment. These sites offer new employment opportunities that may be desirable to some people with disabilities [8].

Because crowd work tasks are performed through a web interface, these web sites must be accessible if they are to be used by people with disabilities. In this paper, we describe an accessibility analysis of the current MTurk user interface. We performed a heuristic analysis of four MTurk pages and eleven popular HITs using the Web Content Accessibility Guidelines (WCAG 2.0). We summarize current accessibility problems with the current MTurk user interface and suggest ways to fix these problems.

2. RELATED WORK

The World Wide Web Consortium's WCAG 2.0 guidelines have previously been used to verify the accessibility of general web sites [3], technology company web sites [4], and e-government sites [2]. However, these guidelines have not been used to analyze crowd work sites. While using WCAG 2.0 in a heuristic evaluation provides different feedback than performing a user evaluation with people with disabilities, heuristic evaluation is commonly used to find web accessibility problems.

Other researchers have analyzed the usability of MTurk[1] tasks but have not analyzed the accessibility of MTurk's user interface. Khanna *et al.* [6] evaluated the usability of MTurk for workers with low technology literacy, and found that HITs often featured complex and confusing interfaces. Kobayashi *et al.* [7] analyzed the usability of crowd work tasks for older adults, and found that crowd work sites could be especially confusing for older adults.

3. HEURISTIC EVALUATION

In order to explore the current levels of accessibility of crowd working platforms, we conducted a heuristic accessibility analysis of MTurk's web interface, along with eleven popular HITs.

First, we analyzed MTurk web pages used to browse, search, and perform HITs: the login and general page, the list of HITs, and the account dashboard and status pages. As our exploration focused on the accessibility problems that a worker might encounter, we excluded pages from MTurk's requester interface.

Next, we chose a sample of popular HITs and evaluated them. We chose the most common HITs from the 10 most popular requesters as listed on MTurk-Tracker[2] [5] and TurkAlert[3], collected in August 2013. We excluded HITs that required workers to have prior MTurk experience, as we were interested in the experience of new workers. This resulted in eleven HITs that involved tasks such as cleaning and verifying information, transcribing audio, and extracting information from images.

3.1 Evaluation Method

Our evaluation followed the Website Accessibility Conformance Evaluation Methodology 1.0 [9] and used the AA priority level of WCAG 2.0. Our evaluation was conducted using Windows 7 operating system and Firefox 23 and Chrome 28.0.1500.95 browsers and we used the following tools to test the accessibility:

Automated analysis. We used AChecker[4], WAVE[5], and W3C's HTML[6] and CSS Validators[7] to identify structural problems.

---

[1] Amazon Mechanical Turk http://mturk.com
[2] MTurk Tracker http://mturk-tracker.com/
[3] TurkAlert http://www.turkalert.com/
[4] AChecker http://achecker.ca/

Screen reader compatibility. We tested pages by turning the monitor off and navigating using the JAWS[8] screen reader.

Reading level analysis. We used Readability Score[9] and The Readability Test[10] Tool to measure web page reading levels.

Audio analysis. Tasks were completed with the computer's audio turned off to identify inaccessible audio content.

3.2 Problems Facing Specific User Groups

Here we summarize violations of the WCAG 2.0 guidelines that may affect users with specific disabilities.

Visual disabilities: Some HITs did not use page headings (violated guideline 2.4.6 and occurred in 14 of the 16 pages; WCAG 2.4.6 | 14/16). Some pages included images without alternative text (WCAG 1.1.1 | 9/16) and unlabeled input elements (WCAG 1.3.1; 2.4.6; 3.3.2; 4.1.2 | 14/16).Others used inaccessible images to represent text (WCAG 1.4.5 | 4/16). Some pages did not provide skip links, which makes browsing the page with a screen reader difficult (WCAG 2.4.1 | 4/16). Other pages used HTML tables as page structure without proper labeling (WCAG 1.3.1| 7/16). Besides, other pages lacked sufficient metadata describing the page language, which could cause a screen reader to have difficulty pronouncing page text (WCAG 3.1.2 | 5/16).

Cognitive and reading disabilities: Our automated tools reported that the majority of pages had a Flesch-Kincaid Grade level between 3.75 and 7.85 and a Reading Ease level between 62.2 and 83.7. Only two of the HIT pages were more complex and had a higher reading difficulty. (WCAG 3.1.5 | 2/16) The pages we tested also had time limits for completion (WCAG 2.2.1 | 2/16), and used nested tables (WCAG 1.3.1| 2/16), which could make HITs more difficult for some users.

Physical disabilities: Some page elements could not be accessed through keyboard navigation (WCAG 2.1.1| 5/16), and some pages used *iframe* elements that could hide the keyboard cursor (WCAG 2.4.7 | 3/16). Some pages also had fixed time limits that could be too brief for some users (WCAG 2.2.1 | 2/16).

Auditory disabilities: Only HITs involving audio transcription tasks (3/16) presented accessibility challenges for users with auditory disabilities. No other pages included audio.

4. RECOMMENDATIONS

Based on our evaluation, we offer several recommendations for improving the accessibility of MTurk and its HITs.

Promote Accessible HITs: provide accessible templates and guidelines for requesters to create accessible HITs in order to avoid accessibility problems.

Validate and report accessibility: pages should be checked for accessibility validation errors, and these errors should be corrected. Moreover, requesters should be able to mark their HITs as being accessible, or as requiring specific abilities.

Filter by ability requirements: Users should be able to filter tasks by the abilities required to complete them. For example, a deaf or hard of hearing user should be able to easily filter out tasks which require audio. This feature would also help workers who do not wish to listen to audio when completing tasks.

Flexible time: MTurk tasks typically have a time limit for completion. Users should be able to request extra time to complete a task if they are actively working on that task.

5. CONCLUSIONS AND FUTURE WORK

Based on this analysis, workers with disabilities who want to use MTurk may face accessibility challenges when using the current interface. The majority of these challenges could be corrected by addressing known accessibility problems in the structure of the pages. However, this study also uncovered broader issues about the accessibility of crowd work tasks, including the challenge of time-limited tasks, and the prevalence of tasks that required specific visual or auditory abilities.

Our current work is limited in that it presents only an expert heuristic analysis of accessibility problems In the future, we would like to involve end users with disabilities, and representatives from job coaching organizations, to understand the frequency and severity of accessibility problems during real world use. Furthermore, we see opportunities to create tools to support the creation and validation of accessible crowdsourcing tasks.

6. ACKNOWLEDGMENTS

This work was supported by a UC3M-based grant for research mobility in national or foreign research centers.

7. REFERENCES

[1] Abberley, P. The significance of work for the citizenship of disabled people. Presented at University College Dublin, (1999), 1-18.

[2] Baowaly, M. K. and Bhuiyan, M. Accessibility analysis and evaluation of Bangladesh government websites. In *Proc. ICIEV 2012* (2012) 46–51.

[3] Costa, D., Fernandes, N., Neves, S., Duarte, C., Hijón-Neira, R.,and Carriço, L. Web accessibility in Africa: a study of three African domains. In *Proc. INTERACT '13*, (2013), 331-338.

[4] Gilbertson, T. and Machin, C..Guidelines, icons and marketable skills: an accessibility evaluation of 100 web development company homepages. In *Proc. W4A '12*, (2012), 17-20.

[5] Ipeirotis, P.G. Analyzing the Amazon Mechanical Turk Marketplace. *XRDS 17*, 2, (2010), 16-21.

[6] Khanna, S., Ratan, A., Davis, J. and Thies, W. Evaluating and improving the usability of Mechanical Turk for low-income workers in India. In *Proc. DEV '10*, (2010), 1-12.

[7] Kobayashi, M., Ishihara, T., Kosugi, A., Takagi, H., and Asakawa, C. Question-answer cards for an inclusive micro-tasking framework for the elderly. In *Proc. INTERACT '13*, (2013), 590-607.

[8] Kruse, D., Schur, L. and Ali, M. Projecting potential demand for workers with disabilities. *Monthly Labor Review,* (2010), 1-20.

[9] U.S. Department of Labor. Persons with a disability: barriers to employment, types of assistance, and other labor-related issues. U.S. Bureau of Labor Statistics News Release (2012). http://www.bls.gov/news.release/archives/dissup_04242013.pdf

[10] W3C. Website accessibility conformance evaluation methodology 1.0. http://www.w3.org/TR/WCAG-EM/

---

[5] WAVE http://wave.webaim.org/

[6] W3C HTML Validator http://validator.w3.org/

[7] CSS Validator http://jigsaw.w3.org/css-validator/

[8] JAWS http://freedomscientific.com

[9] Readability Score http://readability-score.com/

[10] The Readability Test http://www.read-able.com/

Gestures with Speech for Hand-Impaired Persons

Darren Guinness
Dept of Computer Science
Baylor University
Waco, TX 76798 USA
darren_guinness@baylor.edu

G. Michael Poor
Dept of Computer Science
Baylor University
Waco, TX 76798 USA
michael_poor@baylor.edu

Alvin Jude
Dept of Computer Science
Baylor University
Waco, TX 76798 USA
alvin_jude@baylor.edu

ABSTRACT

Mid-air hand-gestural interaction generally causes a fatigue due to implementations that require the user to hold their arm out during this interaction. Recent research has discovered a new approach to reduce fatigue related to gestural interaction, by allowing users to rest their elbow on a surface, and calibrate their interaction space from this rested position [1]. Additionally, this approach reduced stress on the hand and wrist compared to the mouse, by shifting much of the load to the forearm and shoulder muscles. In this paper we evaluated gesture and speech multimodal interaction as a form of assistive interaction for those with hand impairments. Two participants with hand impairments were recruited to perform the evaluation. We collected qualitative and quantitative data, which showed promising results in using this method for assistive interaction.

Author Keywords

Gestural Interaction; Speech-based input; Assistive interaction;

ACM Classification Keywords

K.4.2 [**Social Issues**]: Assistive technologies for persons with disabilities

1. INTRODUCTION

Our previous work attempted to solve the gestural fatigue problem known as "Gorilla Arm Syndrome," which causes arm and shoulder fatigue over prolonged periods of interaction. To reduce this fatigue, we developed the Personal Space approach to gestural interaction, which allowed the user to rest their elbow on the table during the interaction [1]. This rested gestural interaction also attempted to reduce repetitive wrist movement compared to the mouse, which has been strongly associated with hand impairments [2]. This was achieved by shifting primary motions from the wrist and hand to larger muscle groups such as the forearm and shoulder areas. Several studies were conducted using this approach and uncovered interesting results; fatigue was greatly reduced, performance degradation when switching hands was minor when compared to the touchpad and mouse, and pairing gestural cursor navigation with speech based selection yielded no significant loss in throughput.

Each result by itself was interesting, but the combination showed promise for those with hand impairments. To evaluate gestures with speech as an assistive interaction we conducted a small case study using two participants with hand impairments and the new gestural approach. Hand impairments reported were fibromyalgia, osteoarthritis, and carpal tunnel syndrome. Participants performed an experimental task designed to reflect normal computer usage using 4 different interaction styles: mouse hover, mouse click, gesture hover, gesture multimodal. Initial results were promising with both participants expressing that the reduction of wrist movement was beneficial when using the gestural multimodal interaction. Several improvements were also discovered in the study with the help of participants and a speak-aloud procedure. These findings are detailed in the evaluation section.

2. EXPERIMENT

2.1 Participants

Two participants (both female) between 50 and 65 years of age with hand impairments were recruited to participate in the study which lasted approximately 1 hour.

2.2 The Interaction

Figure 1. During calibration, the software guides users to position their hand at the 4 corners. Users can then rest their elbow on the table during the task, which reduces fatigue.

In tasks that use a mouse, a regular off-the-shelf mouse (LogitechM-U0032-O) was employed. Gesture-based navigation implemented the Personal Space approach using the Leap Motion Controller [1]. This approach allows users to define their own interaction space through a calibration step, as shown in figure 1. This step creates a quadrilateral flat plane in 3-dimensional space which is then affine-mapped to the display screen. A 2-minute training video detailing the use of gestures and the calibration was shown to the participants. Speech recognition was done with commercial software called "e-Speaking" version 4.1.1 and a pre-trained speech recognition model.

2.3 Experimental Tasks

Participants were asked to perform a point-select task over 70 randomly placed targets using each of the four different interactions: mouse hover, mouse click, gesture hover, and gesture multimodal. Index of difficulty ranged from 1-4 bits. Either the mouse or gestures was used to control the position of the cursor. Both the mouse and gesture hover tasks required participants to navigate and hover over each target for 500 milliseconds. Gesture multimodal tasks asked participants to navigate using gestures to the target and use voice commands for selection of the specified target which was either "Left-click", "Right-click", or hover. The mouse click task was used as a control in which the mouse was used for both selection and navigation.

3. EVALUATION

For the evaluation we collected both quantitative and qualitative data. We have provided throughput values in table 1 for comparison, but chose to focus on qualitative findings and suggestions to better highlight the needs of these individuals.

Participant	Mouse Hover	Mouse Clicks	Gesture Hover	Gesture Multimodal
1	3.17	3.44	2.10	2.41
2	3.91	3.96	1.97	2.38

Table 1. Throughput (bits/sec) per task

3.1 Participant 1

The first participant has fibromyalgia and osteoarthritis. Before the experiment the participant mentioned that the hand they used for cursor input alternated with pain flares. During the gestural experimental tasks, the participant tended to move her wrist. In gestural interaction, the hand is meant to stay in an open or cupped position, and the wrist is supposed to stay in a neutral straight position for both tracking and ergonomic purposes. This is detailed in the training video. When asked about this behavior she responded that it was simply a natural tendency.

This wrist movement was recorded during calibration causing the system to expect this behavior and caused further problems in the corner regions when the hand was in a neutral position. After the first gestural round the participant requested the elbow cushion which she had previously declined at the beginning.

After the experiment the participant gave some very helpful feedback. She noted that using larger muscle groups was favored over smaller muscle group interactions such as wrist movements with the mouse. The participant also noted that holding the hand in an open position caused some pain, and encouraged the use of a

brace to solve the problem. The participant also suggested that the use of the elbow cushion should be encouraged.

3.2 Participant 2

The second participant has carpal tunnel syndrome. Before the experiment she noted that she had previously used ergonomic mice for pointing, but that she had adapted to using the touchpad with her knuckles to ease pain when interacting with her personal computer. When performing the mouse click task she felt pain within less than a minute. She specifically noted that pain generally occurred during selection tasks, due to the required finger movement.

During the gestural experimental tasks, the participant again exhibited wrist movement. After the being encouraged to keep the hand in a neutral position the participant quickly adapted to the described behavior. The participant noted that fine movements took longer, and gradually got used to the interaction and relaxed her hand as the experiment went on.

When asked for feedback, the participant noted that she experienced no hand issues using the gestural interaction, and using voice commands was highly preferred to clicking.

4. DISCUSSION AND FUTURE WORKS

In this paper we evaluated the use of gesture and speech based input as an assistive technology for those with hand impairments. The interaction style proved to be feasible and has promising results, but certain design considerations should be addressed. First, keeping the hand in an open position can cause strain to those with hand impairments. Second, participants may move their wrist during the gestural tasks which can cause strain similar to that of normal mouse usage. Finally, strain can be experienced in rested gestures on the elbow. These problems will be addressed by using an ergonomic cushion, and an assistive brace to alleviate strain in the next study.

5. CONCLUSION

In this paper we evaluated gesture and speech based interaction as an assistive technology for persons with hand impairments. The evaluation demonstrated that the interaction was feasible, and uncovered improvements for the next study. We expect that this interaction style could lead to better assistive technologies for those with hand impairments

6. REFERENCES

[1] Jude, A., Poor, G. M., and Guinness, D. Personal space:User defined gesture space for gui interaction. In *CHI'14 Extended Abstracts on Human Factors in Computing Systems*, CHI EA '14, ACM (New York, NY, USA, 2014).

[2] Wieslander, G., Norbäck, D., Göthe, C. J., & Juhlin, L. Carpal tunnel syndrome (CTS) and exposure to vibration, repetitive wrist movements, and heavy manual work: a case-referent study. *British Journal of Industrial Medicine*, 46, 1 (1989), 43-47.

Implementation and Evaluation of Animation Controls Sufficient for Conveying ASL Facial Expressions

Hernisa Kacorri
The Graduate Center, CUNY
Computer Science Ph.D. Program
365 Fifth Ave, New York, NY 10016
hkacorri@gc.cuny.edu

Matt Huenerfauth
Rochester Institute of Technology (RIT)
Golisano College of Computing and Information Sciences
20 Lomb Memorial Drive, Rochester, NY 14623
matt.huenerfauth@rit.edu

ABSTRACT

Technology to automatically synthesize linguistically accurate and natural-looking animations of American Sign Language (ASL) from an easy-to-update script would make it easier to add ASL content to websites and media, thereby increasing information accessibility for many people who are deaf. We are investigating the synthesis of ASL facial expressions, which are grammatically required and essential to the meaning of sentences. To support this research, we have enhanced a virtual human character with face controls following the MPEG-4 Facial Action Parameter standard. In a user-study, we determined that these controls were sufficient for conveying understandable animations of facial expressions.

Categories and Subject Descriptors

H.5.2 [**Information Interfaces and Presentation**] User Interfaces – *evaluation/methodology*; K.4.2 [**Computers and Society**]: Social Issues – *assistive technologies for persons with disabilities.*

General Terms

Design, Experimentation, Human Factors, Measurement.

Keywords

Accessibility Technology for People who are Deaf, MPEG-4, Facial Expression, American Sign Language, Animation.

1. INTRODUCTION

There are approximately 500,000 users of ASL in the U.S. [4], and it is possible for users to have fluency in ASL but difficulty with written English because the two languages are distinct. Many signers prefer to receive information in the form of ASL. One simple method of presenting ASL content online would be to display video recordings of human signers on websites, but this approach is not ideal: the recordings are difficult to update, and there is no way to support just-in-time generation of content. Software is needed that can automatically synthesize understandable animations of a virtual human performing ASL, based on an easy-to-update script as input. This software must select the details of the movements of the virtual human character so that the animations are understandable and acceptable to users. Facial expressions and head movements are essential to the fluent performance of ASL, conveying: emotion, variations in word

ASSETS '14, Oct 20-22 2014, Rochester, NY, USA
ACM 978-1-4503-2720-6/14/10.
http://dx.doi.org/10.1145/2661334.2661387

meaning, and grammatical information during entire syntactic phrases. This paper focuses on this third use, which is necessary for expressing questions or negation. In fact, a sequence of signs performed on the hands can have different meanings, depending on the syntactic facial expression that co-occurs [5]. E.g., a declarative sentence (ASL: "JOHN LIKE PIZZA" / English: "John likes pizza.") can become a Yes-No question (English: "Does John like pizza?"), with the addition of a Yes-No Question facial expression (eyebrows raised, head tilted forward). Similarly, the addition of a Negation facial expression (left and right headshaking with some brow furrowing) during the verb phrase "LIKE PIZZA" can change the meaning of the sentence to "John doesn't like pizza." The word NOT is optional, but the facial expression is required. For interrogative questions (with a "WH" word like what, who, where), a WH-Question facial expression (head tilted forward, eyebrows furrowed) is required during the sentence, e.g., "JOHN LIKE WHAT."

There is variation in how these facial expressions are performed during a given sentence, based on the length of the phrase when the facial expression occurs, the location of particular words during the phrase (e.g., NOT, WHAT), the facial expressions that precede or follow, the overall speed of signing, and other factors. Thus, for an animation synthesis system, it is insufficient to simply play a single pre-recorded version of this facial expression whenever it is needed. For this reason, we are researching how to model the performance of facial expressions in various contexts. Other researchers are also studying synthesis of facial expressions for sign language animation, e.g., interrogative questions with co-occurrence of affect [8], using clustering techniques to produce facial expressions during specific words [7], etc.

2. IMPLEMENTATION & EVALUATION

To support this research, we had to parameterize the face of our virtual human character so that we can control it by specifying a vector of numbers. Then, a full performance is a stream of such vectors. We needed a parameterization with some properties:

- Values should be invariant across signers with different face proportions who are performing an identical facial expression so we could use recordings from multiple humans in our work.

- The parameterization must be sufficient for controlling the face of a character and should be invariant across animated characters with different facial proportions. This property would allow us to use a variety of characters in our work.

- The parameterization should be a well-documented, standard method of producing and analyzing facial movements. This property would enable our research to be useful for other researchers, using other animation platforms.

The MPEG-4 standard [3] defines a 3D model-based coding for face animation and has all the above properties. In short, a face is controlled by setting values for 68 Facial Action Parameters (FAPs), which are displacements of points shown in Fig. 1a with the displacements normalized according to scaling factors based on the proportions of the character's face. This normalization allows for a set of 68 FAPs to produce equivalent facial expression on faces of different sizes or proportions.

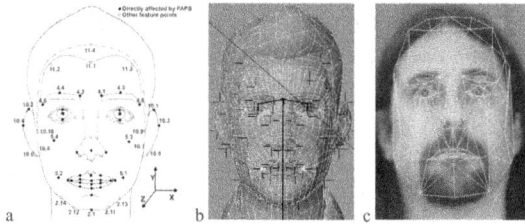

Figure 1: (a) Some MPEG-4 feature points, (b) wireframe and feature points in Max, (c) Visage tracker adaptive mask.

Our lab extended the character named Max from the open source animation platform EMBR [1] (Fig. 1b) with MPEG-4 FAPs for the upper face controlling the eyes, eyebrows, and nose. EMBR allows for head and torso movements, enables blinking as a background behavior, and has been used for creating sign language animations. As part of our enhancements to EMBR, a professional artist modified the surface mesh and constraints to cause the skin on the face to wrinkle automatically as the face controls are modified. The artist also assisted in the design of a lighting scheme for the character to highlight these wrinkles, which are essential to perception of ASL facial movements [8].

We conducted a user study, where 14 native ASL signers viewed animations of short stories and then answered comprehension questions and scalar-response questions as to whether they noticed the correct facial expression. The 18 stories included Yes-No Question, WH Question, or Negation (6 of each type), and the comprehension questions were engineered so that the correct answer depended on understanding the facial expression. We publically released these stimuli and evaluation questions for evaluating facial expression animations; details appear in [2]. In a between-subjects design, we compared two types of animations with identical hand movements but differed in their face, head, and torso movements: (a) *driven* by a recording of a human performing that type of facial expression or (b) face, head, and torso movements are static and *neutral* throughout the story. The type "b" animations therefore did not reveal any of the capabilities of the new MPEG-4 controls or skin-wrinkling of our character. Face and head movements for the *driven* animations were created using Visage Face Tracker, automatic software [6] that provides MPEG-4 compatible output. Fig. 1c illustrates the 3D mask in the tracking system that is fitted to a native signer's face. We implemented software to convert MPEG-4 data to EMBRscript, the script language supported by the EMBR platform. Example shown in Fig. 2 and at: http://latlab.cs.qc.cuny.edu/2014assets/.

Figure 2: Screenshots from a human-recording-driven and neutral version of a Yes-No Question stimulus in the study.

Fig. 3 displays the scores of the comprehension questions and the question that asked if participants noticed the correct facial expression. Medians are shown above each boxplot. There was a significant difference in the Notice scores (Mann-Whitney test used since the data was not normally distributed, p<0.00014). There was also a significant difference in the comprehension question scores (t-test, p<0.000001). Note that comprehension scores depend on the difficulty of the questions asked; so, such scores are meaningful only for comparison within a single study.

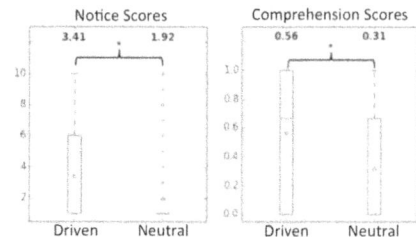

Figure 3: Notice and Comprehension scores for animations with facial expressions (Driven) and without (Neutral).

These results indicate that our new animation system is a useful platform for evaluating our on-going research on designing new methods for automatically synthesizing facial expressions of ASL. This finding is significant because it allows for research on ASL facial expression to take advantage of prior tools and research on facial animation with MPEG-4. In order to evaluate the expressivity of our character, we used human recordings in this study; however, in future work, we will be investigating learning-based models for *automatic* synthesis of ASL facial expressions.

3. ACKNOWLEDGMENTS

This material is based upon work supported by the National Science Foundation under award number 0746556 and 1065009. We thank Andy Cocksey and Alexis Heloir for their assistance.

4. REFERENCES

[1] Heloir. A, Nguyen, Q., and Kipp, M. 2011. Signing Avatars: a Feasibility Study. *2nd Int'l Workshop on Sign Language Translation and Avatar Technology (SLTAT)*.

[2] Huenerfauth, M., Kacorri, H. 2014. Release of experimental stimuli and questions for evaluating facial expressions in animations of American Sign Language. *Workshop on the Representation & Processing of Signed Languages, LREC'14*.

[3] ISO/IECIS14496-2Visual, 1999.

[4] Mitchell, R., Young, T., Bachleda, B., and Karchmer, M. 2006. How many people use ASL in the United States? Why estimates need updating. *Sign Lang Studies*, 6(3):306-335.

[5] Neidle, C., D. Kegl, D. MacLaughlin, B. Bahan, and R.G. Lee. 2000. *The syntax of ASL: functional categories and hierarchical structure*. Cambridge: MIT Press.

[6] Pejsa, T., and Pandzic, I. S. 2009. Architecture of an animation system for human characters. In. *10th Int'l Conf on Telecommunications (ConTEL)* (pp. 171-176). IEEE.

[7] Schmidt, C., Koller, O., Ney, H., Hoyoux, T., and Piater, J. 2013. Enhancing Gloss-Based Corpora with Facial Features Using Active Appearance Models. *3rd Int'l Symposium on Sign Language Translation and Avatar Technology (SLTAT)*.

[8] Wolfe, R., Cook, P., McDonald, J. C., and Schnepp, J. 2011. Linguistics as structure in computer animation: Toward a more effective synthesis of brow motion in American Sign Language. *Sign Language & Linguistics*, 14(1), 179-199.

Increasing the Bandwidth of Crowdsourced Visual Question Answering to Better Support Blind Users

Walter S. Lasecki*
Dept. of Computer Science
University of Rochester
wlasecki@cs.rochester.edu

Yu Zhong*
Dept. of Computer Science .
University of Rochester
zyu@cs.rochester.edu

Jeffrey P. Bigham
HCI and LT Institutes
Carnegie Mellon University
jbigham@cmu.edu

ABSTRACT

Many of the visual questions that blind people ask cannot be easily answered with a single image or a short response, especially when questions are of an exploratory nature, *e.g.* what is in this area, or what tools are available on this work bench? We introduce RegionSpeak to allow blind users to capture large areas of visual information, identify all of the objects within them, and explore their spatial layout with fewer interactions. RegionSpeak helps blind users capture all of the relevant visual information using an interface designed to support stitching multiple images together. We use a parallel crowdsourcing workflow that asks workers to define and describe regions of interest, allowing even complex images to be described quickly. The regions and descriptions are displayed on an auditory touchscreen interface, allowing users to know what is in a scene and how it is laid out.

Categories and Subject Descriptors

K.4.2 [**Computers and Society**]: Social Issues – Assistive technologies for persons with disabilities

Keywords

Visual question answering; Crowdsourcing

1. INTRODUCTION AND BACKGROUND

Crowdsourcing answers to visual questions can help blind and low vision users better access the world around them [1]. Prior work on systems such as VizWiz, an application that has allow thousands of blind users to take a picture, speak a question, and get an answer from groups of online workers ("the crowd") in around 30 seconds, and Chorus:View [3], a system that answers questions via streaming video and ongoing conversation between the crowd and users, have shown that crowdsourcing can effectively provide a source of answers to visual questions. In this paper, we present Region-Speak, a system that builds on the VizWiz platforms and allows blind users to more easily explore a scene by getting more information in a single interaction.

*Equal authorship, listed in alphabetical order.

ASSETS'14, October 20–22, 2014, Rochester, NY, USA.
ACM 978-1-4503-2720-6/14/10.
http://dx.doi.org/10.1145/2661334.2661407.

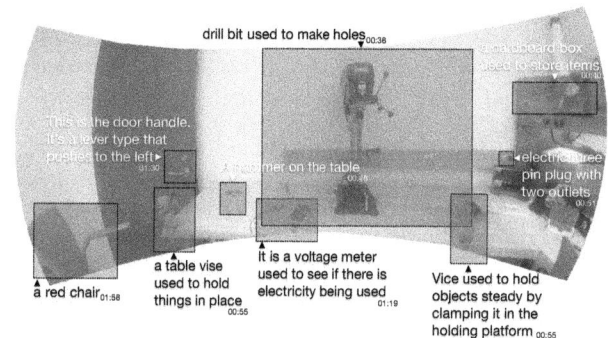

Figure 1: An image of a workbench formed by stitching images together. Important regions are identified and labeled by crowd workers within seconds so that blind users can explore the regions spatially to more easily find what they want.

VizWiz struggles with up to 18% of questions asked because the single-image, single-response model does not efficiently help users frame the information required. Chorus:View overcomes this by engaging users in *continuous* interactions with the crowd via voice and video to help reduce the overhead associated with multi-turn interaction. However, video-based approaches are expensive, more difficult to scale, and can be cumbersome for end users who must actively wait while the crowd determines a response. Our goal is to account for the large set of tasks that fall somewhere between the ideal case for single images in VizWiz, and the continuously-engaged interaction of Chorus:View.

2. IMAGE STITCHING

The first way to reduce the number of interactions needed to answer a question is to allow users to provide the crowd with more information in a single turn. We explore image stitching as a way to do this.

RegionSpeak combines an image stitching algorithm and a key frame extraction algorithm to created a panorama interface for RegionSpeak which has no restriction that needs visual inspection – users can move the camera in any direction, and the key frame extraction algorithm will detect substantial changes in view port and alert users to hold their position to capture a new image. RegionSpeak then takes a photo automatically when the view port is stabilized and gives users audio cue to move on. Users can choose to stop the process, or keep going until they hit the limit of 6 photos. The photos are then sent to our server and stitched before being sent to the crowd.

2.1 Evaluation

We conducted a study with 5 blind people to compare RegionSpeak with single picture approaches (over 28 tasks total). The study was conducted remotely from the blind participants' home using their own iPhones. Participants were paid $10 each, and consented online.

Stitching completed all three tasks within the 10 minute limit, with an average time of 141.1 seconds, while VizWiz failed 1 of the user name reading tasks, and had an average time of 250.5 seconds. This difference is significant, $t(28) = 2.29$ ($p < .01$). The average number of Q&A iterations it takes for stitching (1.79) to yield right answers is also significantly lower than VizWiz(2.79), $t(28) = 2.90$, ($p = .03$). The results confirmed with the stitching interface blind users were likely to capture more visual information in each dialog turn and save time and iterations in subsequent interactions.

In exit interviews, participants said that stitching was easy to understand, learn and use, and they preferred using a stitching interface when taking photos for all task types in our study. They wanted to continue using the stitching interface after the experiments ("*look forward to seeing it released to the general public*"). The feature participants liked most in the stitching interface was the audio guidance which allows "*easy identifying of many things*" and really helps when looking for a specific but small piece of information. It was also mentioned that the fact our stitching interface "*cleverly put different images together figures out the orientation of them*" give them more freedom of interaction.

3. REGIONSPEAK

The other way in which we can reduce the number of interactions required to answer a users question is to allow the crowd to provide more rich answers to users. We introduce RegionSpeak for this purpose. Users begin by either taking a single image or a stitched image, at which point they can set the phone down and wait for responses from the crowd. When responses arrive, RegionSpeak opens up the real time camera view port and starts aligning regions marked by the crowd in the view port using OpenTLD [2]. When a region returned from the crowd is recognized, it is added as an overlay on the camera view port and tracked in real time as the camera is being re-framed. Users can then use their finger to explore the scene, using an interface similar to Voiceover.

RegionSpeak's worker interface asks them to select an important region of the image that they will provide a label. Workers are left to select this region on their own, just as they would be left to choose what level of description to give in a typical VizWiz task. Our selection process is similar to LabelMe [4], which asked crowd workers to carefully select objects and areas in an image by outlining them, but using simple rectangles to make it easier for workers to complete the task quickly, and for end users to find the rough boundaries when scanning the screen with their finger.

3.1 Evaluation

We evaluated RegionSpeak on five images that are similar to questions frequently asked by VizWiz users: a set of five packages of food, a simple diagram on a whiteboard, a set of buttons on a microwave, a menu from a restaurant, and an outdoor scene in a commercial area.

For each of the images, we collected region tags and descriptions from five workers. We coded five features: validity, minimalism, number of objects identified, number of details given, and number of spacial cues provided. For number of objects identified and number of spacial cues, bounding boxes were counted as object identifiers (assuming they contained valid label for a portion of the image). Additional objects and details could be identified within the tag as well. The inter-rater reliability, measured using Cohen's kappa, was between 0.69 and 0.95. We also added "bound tightness" to determine how well workers selected an appropriate region for a given label. We coded all 25 marked segments with two coders. There was strong inter-rater agreement between both raters (Cohen's kappa .74).

Overall, these labels resulted in no minimal answers; an average of 5.2 distinct items marked (median 5, $\sigma = 1.64$); an average of 5.2 descriptive details (median 6, $\sigma = 2.95$); and an average of 6.2 spacial cues (median 5, $\sigma = 2.39$). Additionally, 75% of segments marked by workers were rated as being a "tight bound" on the object they were framing, 20% were considered a "loose bound", and just 5% (1 marking) was rated as an incorrect bound.

However, because the validity of tags was marked per-image, as would be the case with a single description from a worker in our baseline labeling example, just 20% of our images were rated as containing a completely valid label set, with the remaining 80% being rated partially correct. None of the label sets were entirely wrong. This highlights an important aspect of aggregating answers from the crowd: by using aggregated answers, it is more likely that *some* error is introduced, but the chance of an answer containing *entirely* errors falls similarly. In our case, "partially correct" ratings were almost always small errors in one or two labels. On average, responses took 1:05 minutes to arive.

4. CONCLUSIONS AND FUTURE WORK

Our results show that RegionSpeak's image stitching provides a faster and easier means for blind users to capture visual information, and that spatial region labeling encourages crowd workers to provide more descriptive results than traditional labeling. Our next steps are to integrate user feedback into RegionSpeak, and deploy it to the existing VizWiz platform so that users have access to these features.

RegionSpeak fills an important role between existing lightweight visual question answering tools such as VizWiz, which use a single phone image and elicit single responses from workers, and conversational approaches such as Chorus:View, which engage users in longer conversational interactions for questions that require maintaining context across multiple questions. RegionSpeak allows users to send and receive more information with the crowd in each dialogue turn, significantly reducing the number of interactions and the total time spent finding answers.

5. REFERENCES

[1] J. P. Bigham and et al. Vizwiz: Nearly real-time answers to visual questions. In *UIST 2010*.

[2] M. K. . M. J. Kalal, Z. Tracking-learning-detection. In *Pattern Analysis and Machine Intelligence*, 2012.

[3] W. S. Lasecki, P. Thiha, Y. Zhong, E. Brady, and J. P. Bigham. Answering visual questions with conversational crowd assistants. In *ASSETS 2013*.

[4] B. C. Russell, A. Torralba, K. P. Murphy, and W. T. Freeman. Labelme: A database and web-based tool for image annotation. *Int. J. Comput. Vision*.

Moving from Entrenched Structure to a Universal Design

Leyla Zhuhadar
Information Systems Department
Western Kentucky University
Leyla.Zhuhadar@wku.edu

Bryan Carson
Dept. of Library Public Services
Western Kentucky University
Bryan.Carson@wku.edu

Jerry Daday
Department of Sociology
Western Kentucky University
Jerry.Daday@wku.edu

ABSTRACT

Section 508 of the Rehabilitation Act [1] requires electronic and information technology communications to be in made available in an accessible format by alternative means perceptible by people with disabilities. These provisions apply to all entities—including colleges and universities—that receive Federal money (17 U.S.C. § 794). The Accessible Educational STEM Videos Project aims to transform learning and teaching for students with disabilities through integrating synchronized captioned educational videos into undergraduate and graduate STEM disciplines. This Universal Video Captioning (UVC) platform will serve as a repository for uploading videos and scripts. The proposed infrastructure is a web-based platform that uses the lasted WebDAV technology (Web-based Distributed Authoring and Versioning) to identify resources, users, contents, etc. It consists of three layers: i) an administrative management system; ii) a faculty/staff user interface; and iii) a transcriber user interface.

Categories and Subject Descriptors

H. INFORMATION SYSTEMS.

General Terms

Algorithms, Design, Experimentation, Human Factors.

Keywords

Universal Design; Video Captioning; Accessibility; STEM.

1. INTRODUCTION

Section 508 of the Rehabilitation Act [1] requires electronic and information technology communications to be in made available in an accessible format by alternative means perceptible by people with disabilities. These provisions apply to all entities—including colleges and universities—that receive Federal money [2]. During the last 7 years, faculty members at WKU have produced over 13,000 video lectures in the STEM disciplines. The Office of Distance Learning is working to caption these videos, a process that currently is performed semi-automatic and is extremely tedious. At this time, only 36% are currently captioned. Meanwhile, it is projected that faculty generates, on average, an addition 4,000 new video lectures by the end of each year. In 2007, we developed the first open-source closed-captioning software. It is a *Time Stamped Java program*. This program takes text transcriptions (Word documents) as an input. The application then embeds time stamps the script to generate a closed-

ASSETS'14, October 20–22, 2014, Rochester, NY, USA.
ACM 978-1-4503-2720-6/14/10.
http://dx.doi.org/10.1145/2661334.2661409

captioning file (e.g., caption.txt) that synchronizes the text with speech. This software is available at [2]. For more details, refer to section 3. However, the current workflow is extremely tedious and labor-intensive. Therefore, we propose using a Universal Video Captioning (UVC) platform to accommodate the unprecedented growth of video lectures. The proposed software platform will provide an automatic approach to embed captions into accessible STEM-related videos.

2. Project Details & Design

The process involves five transcribers who are undergraduate student do the transcription process. The process consists of downloading the video to a desktop computer, listening to the audio, and type the script. The transcribers use a "Wave Pedal" to control the audio speed (start, stop, move forward, move backward, etc.) This software is available at [2]. Students enter the starting and ending times of the lecture in HH:MM:SS format. The software works with rate of speech (1-10) using a simple algorithm. The program divides the number of vocabularies in the script over the length of the audio.

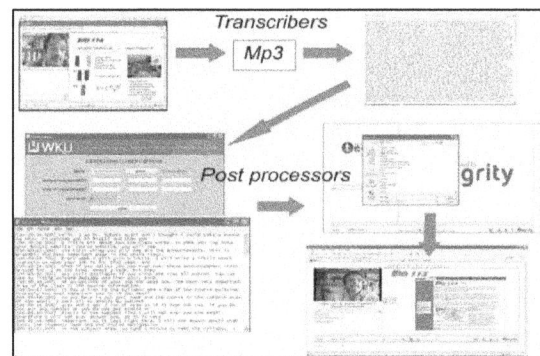

Figure 1

An example of a video lecture with embedded captions can be seen in (Figure 1).

2.1 Proposed Architecture

The purpose of our research is to establish an automatic workflow that is accessible over the web to everyone. The proposed infrastructure is a web-based platform that uses the lasted WebDAV technology (Web-based Distributed Authoring and Versioning) to identify resources, users, contents, etc. The front end will consist of Solr Search Engine, Flex, and PHP, while the back end will be MySQL Server, and Apache Tomcat Server. The platform infrastructure consists of an administrative management system, a faculty/staff user interface, a transcriber user interface, and a synchronized captioning apple.

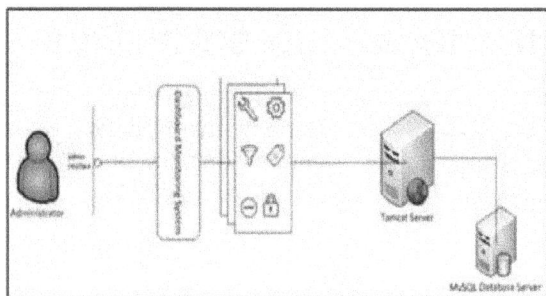

Figure 2

2.1.1 Layer1: Administrative Management Interface

The purpose of this layer (Figure 2) is to control user access, provide upload and download interfaces, maintain the database system, and troubleshooting problems. Finally, the administrative module will provide a search engine mechanism to allow searching for a specific course, faculty, video, caption, or script.

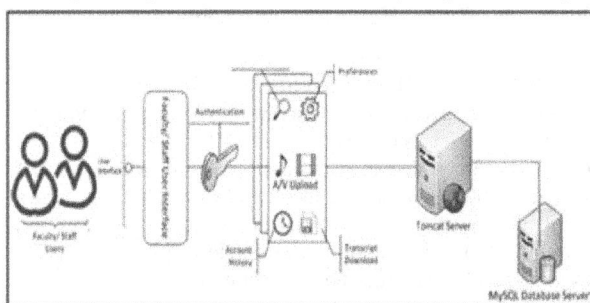

Figure 3

2.1.2 Layer2: Faculty/Staff User Interface

The Faculty/Staff User Interface module (Figure 3) will consist of the registration and login access. The uploading dashboard will allow users to upload video or audio or reference to video or audio by using WebDAV technology. A universal identifier will be associated with each resource. If the multimedia item is already located on the web, only a reference to that resource will be added to the database. The downloading dashboard will list the current status of each submitted request (download captioned video, download script, and status ("in process" or "completed")).

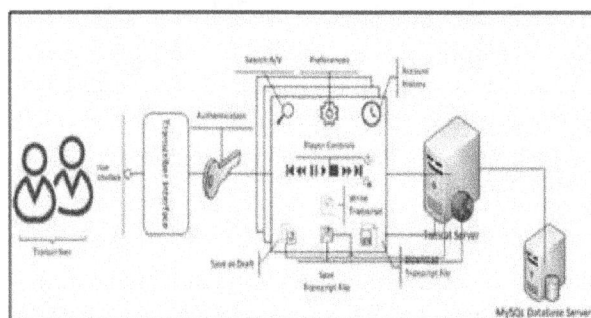

Figure 4

2.1.3 Layer3: Transcriber User Interface

The transcriber user interface (Figure 4) will provide registration and login access, as well as task management. Four dashboards are available for these users. The transcribers will receive notices of requested audio or video files that need transcription. When a transcriber receives a notice, this task will be moved to her personal interface.

2.1.4 Synchronized Captioning Applet

We noticed over the last five years that the software has three drawbacks: 1) it is not web-based and cannot be accessed in real-time over the web; 2) the accuracy of the synchronization between the audio and the script is affected negatively when there are long pauses; 3) the application only works with specific video formats. We therefore propose using an Applet embedded inside the platform, which can be accessed easily by transcribers. To improve accuracy, we propose using a segmentation process to the audio file before we add the script. We will use short-time energy (*Short_time En*) to detect long pauses in the audio. This measure can differentiate silence from speech and is calculated by the following equation [1]:

$$Short_{time}En = \sum_{-\infty}^{\infty}[x(m)w(n-m)^2] = \sum_{m=n-N+1}^{m=n} x(m)^2 \qquad (1)$$

Where $x(m)$ is audio signals, $w(m)$ is a rectangle window of length equal to N, and n is the index of the *Short_time En*. When *Short_time En* drops below a certain threshold, we consider this frame as a pause. After such a pause has been detected, we save its location. Therefore, there will be no captioning during long pauses. This process is fully automated since we are not going to make any physical changes to the original audio. The speech that is converted to equivalent text in Dashboard 2 (transcriber interface) will be selected, long pauses will be identified, text vocabularies will be divided over the length of the audio after extracting long pauses, and vocabularies will be embedded in the correct time frame with no pauses. As we know, the manual captioning is labor intensive. Therefore, this solution will have a significant impact on the system performance.

3. Conclusion and Future Work

This project will implement an innovative platform and apply statistically valid instruments to increase our understanding of the learning process for students with disabilities in STEM programs, and to collect, analyze, and share data that will reveal patterns in these students' learning behaviors. The (UVC) platform presented in this proposal is modular to provide interoperability, and will serve as a repository for uploading videos and scripts. All the building blocks of this project—literature, software, developed model, and instruments—will be made available to the public and other interested researchers online using the Creative Commons Open-source License (CC BY-NC 3.0—Creative Commons Attribution¬ Non-Commercial 3.0). Our contribution to open-source learning has the potential to provide a solution to thousands of individuals and universities who already have educational videos.

4. REFERENCES

[1] Jaeger, P. T. Assessing Section 508 compliance on federal e-government Web sites: A multi-method, user-centered evaluation of accessibility for persons with disabilities. *Government Information Quarterly*, 23, 2 2006), 169-190.

[2] Zhuhadar, L. Open-Source Closed-captioning Software: Time Stamped Java program: http://ada-wku.pbworks.com/w/page/1367266/FrontPage2007-2013.

"OK Glass?" A Preliminary Exploration of Google Glass for Persons with Upper Body Motor Impairments

Meethu Malu
Inclusive Design Lab | HCIL
Department of Computer Science
University of Maryland, College Park
meethu@cs.umd.edu

Leah Findlater
Inclusive Design Lab | HCIL
College of Information Studies
University of Maryland, College Park
leahkf@umd.edu

ABSTRACT

Head-mounted displays such as Google Glass offer potential advantages for persons with motor impairments (MI). For example, they are always available and offer relatively hands-free interaction compared to a mobile phone. Despite this potential, there is little prior work examining the accessibility of such devices. In this poster paper, we perform a preliminary assessment of the accessibility of Google Glass for users with MI and the potential impacts of a head-mounted interactive computer. Our findings show that, while the touchpad is particularly difficult to use—impossible for three participants—advantages over a phone include that it is relatively hands free, does not require looking down at the display, and cannot be easily dropped.

Categories and Subject Descriptors

K.4.2 [**Computer and Society**]: Social Issues-Assistive technologies for persons with disabilities

Keywords

Accessibility; Google Glass; motor impairments

1. INTRODUCTION

As wearable devices increasingly enter the mainstream, head-mounted displays such as Google Glass could open new means of mobile information access for users with motor impairments (MI). Such devices are always available and offer relatively hands-free interaction. In this poster, we present a study on the accessibility of and reaction to Google Glass from five participants who use wheelchairs and have upper body MI—four diagnosed with cerebral palsy and one with a spinal cord injury.

While several studies have examined the accessibility of smartphones and other mobile devices (*e.g.*, [1,2]), very little prior attention has been paid to the design of emerging wearable devices to support mobile computing. One exception comes from McNaney *et al.* [3], who explored the applicability of Google Glass for persons with Parkinson's disease. Through both a focus group and a 5-day field deployment with four participants, they found that initial reactions to Glass were promising, including providing an increased sense of independence and security. Participants could use the device, although speech input was problematic for two individuals and some participants found

ASSETS '14, Oct 20-22 2014, Rochester, NY, USA
ACM 978-1-4503-2720-6/14/10.
http://dx.doi.org/10.1145/2661334.2661400

tapping on the device's touchpad to be more difficult than swiping on it. A second exception comes from Carrington *et al.* [2], who explored the idea of input and output that employs the space around a power wheelchair. While participants in their study did not use a head-mounted display, they were introduced to the idea and several felt it would be a useful output modality, particularly if paired with a pico projector for more public information.

These previous findings [2,3] point to the potential of head-mounted displays for users with MI, yet the first study focused only on users with Parkinson's [2] and in the second study participants did not interact with the device [3]. In this poster paper, we focus on the accessibility of one head-mounted display—Google Glass—for five participants with MI. We present initial results on the accessibility challenges of Google Glass for these individuals, as well as potential impacts of accessible head-mounted displays.

2. METHOD

We recruited five participants through United Cerebral Palsy in Lanham, MD and by word-of-mouth; see Table 1. All participants were wheelchair users with upper body MI; P3 had dysarthria. The study procedure lasted up to 60 minutes and included three parts: background questionnaire (demographics and current mobile use), tasks with Google Glass, and a semi-structured interview on the experience of using the device.

Glass provides input through a touchpad on the right arm of the device that senses taps and swipes, and through voice commands. Output is through the head-mounted display that sits in front of the right eye and a bone-conduction headphone. For the Glass tasks, the researcher first demonstrated the touchpad and voice commands. The participant then completed a series of basic tasks over about 20 minutes, such as viewing activity on the timeline, looking up the weather, and taking pictures. To complete these tasks required at a minimum 8 forward swipes, 3 backward swipes, 11 downward swipes, 12 taps, and 10 voice commands. Because of accidental taps and swipes, these numbers are a lower bound. For participants who could not reach the touchpad, the researcher performed that input. Following the tasks, participants used 5-point scales to rate the physical comfort and ease of use of the touchpad and the visual display, and ease of use of the voice commands. The session concluded with open-ended questions about the potential impacts of head-mounted displays and brief feedback on design ideas for alternative forms of input beyond the built-in touchpad. Sessions were video recorded and analyzed to

ID	Age	Gender	Diagnosed Med. Condition	Mobile Device Owned
P1	46	Male	Spinal cord injury (C5)	None currently
P2	25	Female	Cerebral palsy	Smartphone (iPhone 5)
P3	53	Male	Cerebral palsy	Brick phone
P4	25	Female	Cerebral palsy	Smartphone (HTC)
P5	22	Female	Cerebral palsy	Smartphone (iPhone 5S)

Table 1. Overview of participants.

observe interaction successes and challenges, and to summarize open-ended responses.

3. FINDINGS

3.1 Basic Interaction

Table 2 shows participant ratings on ease of use and physical comfort for the touchpad, voice commands, and visual display.

3.1.1 Touchpad Input

The accessibility of the touchpad depended on each individual's abilities, with these differences reflected in Table 2's subjective ratings. P2 encountered the fewest issues, having trouble with only 7 of 61 touchpad interactions. Her most common challenges were accidentally tapping instead of swiping, and the device not responding when she swiped. P4 was also able to use the touchpad, though had difficulty in 34 of 93 interactions. By far the most common issue for P4, in 47% of problematic interactions, was that the touchpad did not respond to her input, likely because of the angle of her finger. She also had persistent trouble correctly locating the touchpad, despite intervention from the researcher. In contrast, P1 and P5 could not physically reach the touchpad at all. For P5, the location of the touchpad on the right of the device was particularly problematic because she had limited movement in her right hand; she may have been able to use it had it been on the left. Finally, P3 could reach the touchpad but physically moved the device when trying to tap and swipe, making it so he could not read the display. After a few attempts, he asked the researcher to perform the gestures.

3.1.2 Voice Commands

Of the participants only P3, who had dysarthria (slurred speech), had difficulty with the voice commands—for him the device only successfully recognized the word 'Google.' P1 and P4 expressed surprise at how well Glass recognized their voices and P4 commented that the voice recognition with her current smartphone does not always work. P2 suggested that Glass should be fully accessible by voice, and wanted voice commands like 'Go Back' or 'Home Screen' instead of swiping or tapping multiple times on the touchpad. These findings are in contrast to McNaney et al. [3], whose participants experienced more issues with voice input perhaps partly because they used Glass in a field setting.

3.1.3 Visual Display

All participants were able to read text on the display when prompted. However, P1, P3, and P5 said that looking at it strained their eyes, and P3, P4, and P5 needed the display to be frequently adjusted. P4 had problems sitting up and keeping her head upright, which affected her ability to look at the display. During the session, she asked to be strapped to her wheelchair so that she could sit up and see the display better. Participants did not complain about the font size or size of the display.

3.2 Potential Impacts of Glass

Comparing Glass to a mobile phone, three participants mentioned the touchpad on Glass as a disadvantage. Advantages, however, included, not having to look down at the display (P2, P4), keeping the hands free (P2, P4) and reducing the risk of dropping and damaging the device (P1). For example, P1 said:

> "That someone who has limited mobility could wear a technological device without fear of dropping or damaging it that seems a lot more useful than a notepad or a laptop in my aspect, in my living situation."

P2 expressed the physical ease of not having to hold her phone:

> "My hands are free. It didn't require me to pick up anything as opposed to having to pick up this [phone] and you know look down on it and you know I was looking up so I didn't have my head down."

We also asked about the ability to pay attention to surroundings while using Glass, and impacts on personal safety and independence. Three participants said that voice commands on Glass would enable independence especially in situations where they have to ask for help to type text. Only P1 expressed safety concerns about wearing the device (e.g., mugging).

At the end of the session we briefly introduced theoretical alternatives to the touchpad for controlling Glass: mid-air gestures, wearable physical buttons, and a portable touchpad. While the responses were generally positive, each participant had different yet specific places where they would like the touchpad to be located, like the armrest, joystick or tray (which mirrors Carrington et al.'s [2] findings). Participants also spoke about using body and facial movements and customized voice commands as other alternatives to the touchpad.

4. DISCUSSION AND CONCLUSION

For our five participants, Google Glass presented exciting possibilities for mobile information access but also serious accessibility challenges. The always-available, head-mounted display could allow for easy access to information on the go, without the physical requirement to hold a mobile phone. At the same time, more than half of the participants couldn't use the touchpad input. For one participant, this issue could have been mitigated had the touchpad been on the left side of the head; for others, expanded voice control or input elsewhere on the body or wheelchair (as with some of the ideas in [2]), is needed. These initial findings are the first step in a larger research project. We intend to design and evaluate more accessible alternative input methods for controlling head-mounted displays, such as mid-air gestures and wearable, tangible inputs. Ultimately, our goal is to design and assess the extent to which accessible head-mounted displays can improve independence and mobile information access for users with MI.

5. ACKNOWLEDGMENTS

We thank UCP in Lanham, MD, especially Michael McGee and Melissa Schick. This study was funded by the National Science Foundation under grant IIS-1350438.

6. REFERENCES

[1] Anthony, L., Kim, Y., Findlater, L. 2013. Analyzing user-generated YouTube videos to understand touchscreen use by people with motor impairments. Proc. CHI '13, 1223-1232.

[2] Carrington, P., Hurst, A., Kane, S.K. 2014. Wearables and chairables: inclusive design of mobile input and output techniques for power wheelchair users. Proc. CHI '14, 3103-3112.

[3] McNaney, R., Vines, J., Roggen, D., Balaam, M., Zhang, P., Poliakov, I., Olivier, P. 2014. Exploring the acceptability of Google Glass as an everyday assistive device for people with Parkinson's. Proc. CHI '14, 2551-2554.

[4] Trewin, S., Swart, C., Pettick, D. 2013. Physical accessibility of touchscreen smartphones. Proc. ASSETS '13, Article 19, 8 pages.

ID	Visual Display		Touchpad Gestures		Voice Commands
	Comfort	Ease	Comfort	Ease	Ease
P1	2	2	5	5	1
P2	1	1	1	1	1
P3	4	4	5	1	4
P4	1	2	1	2	1
P5	3	3	5	5	2

Table 2. Ease of use and physical comfort ratings for aspects of Glass interaction (1=very easy to 5=very difficult).

Older Adults Interaction with Broadcast Debates

Rolando Medellin-Gasque, Chris Reed,
Vicki Hanson
School of Computing, University of Dundee
{rmedellin,chris,vlh}@computing.dundee.ac.uk

ABSTRACT

The constant emergence and change of current technologies in the form of digital products and services can cause certain groups of the population to feel excluded. Older adults represent one such group. Our research combines computational models of argument and human-centric computing to impact the way in which older adults interact with broadcast debates. We present a preliminary user study where older adults interact with a debate and propose an application which uses speech recognition to classify spoken utterances and related them to segmented debates. Moreover, we discuss preliminary results on older adults interacting with the application in pilot experiments.

Categories and Subject Descriptors

[**Information Systems Applications**]: Collaborative and social computing systems and tools.

General Terms

Human Factors

Keywords

Speech Recognition; Broadcast Debates; Argument Representation; Argument Web

1. INTRODUCTION

Our work explores whether a common desire to interact with debates can be tapped, in conjunction with technology, with a very low barrier to entry, to both support better engagement with broadcasts debates and encourage greater use of social media. As broadcasters and governments increasingly use social media to communicate with their audience, it is worrying to note that social media use amongst

older adults[1] is still at very low levels. Older adults are not typically characterised to engage with internet technologies, however the number of adults using tablets to go online in the U.K. has almost trebled from 5% in 2012 to 17% in 2014 in the U.K. As for the usage of usage of social networking sites, in the U.S. 46% of adults online use sites such as Facebook [4]. In contrast, a large majority of the population have access to radio and/or TV (e.g., in the U.K. 74% and 90% respectively) [3]. As an indicator of participation, the 2012 televised presidential debates in the US attracted around 7.2 million *tweets* [2]. Our aim is to develop technologies with a low barrier to entry to encourage engagement with broadcast debates through social media. By doing this, we want promote engagement with digital social communities and provide a sense of empowerment by making them feel their voice is being heard.

2. PRELIMINARY USER STUDY

This study aimed to understand the way in which older adults engage with broadcast debates in order to design an application that supports interaction and motivates digital engagement with broadcast debates. We conducted a study with 15 older adults who listen to and/or watch regularly broadcast debates. In group sessions, they listened and interacted with an audio debate expressing freely their opinions. The sessions were recorded, transcribed and analysed using a qualitative data analysis software. We also conducted semi-structured interviews where they were asked about their habits while listening to broadcast debates. The remainder of this section presents our main findings.

Lack of Participation. None of the participants have ever interacted with debates in radio or TV, although all use email regularly and less than a half use social media. About a half of them reacted positively to the suggestion of software that helps them to interact in a simple way with debates.

Interacting with Debates. We were interested on how participants expressed their opinion and interact between them. The two main types of expressions to participate used were: (1) expression to agree or disagree with specific opinions or persons and (2) expressions to provide their point of view without taking a side in the debate. We were able to identify that the most common patterns to express their

---

[1]In our research we consider *older adults* as persons over 65 years old without distinguishing based on cognitive or physical conditions.

[2]http://www.digitaltrends.com/social-media/the-internets-reaction-to-last-nights-presidential-debates

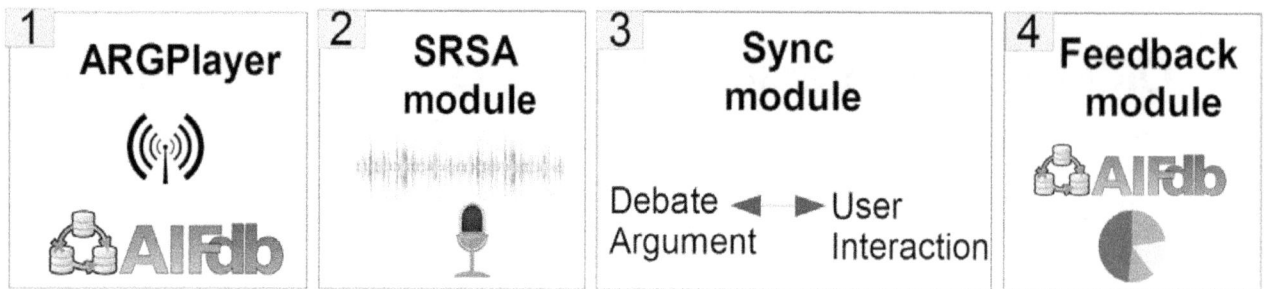

Figure 1: (1) ARGPlayer synchronises audio with AIFdb nodes, (2) Speech Recognition and Sentiment analysis (3) Synchronising the debate with the user participation, (4) Feedback to users on their participation.

opinions were the use of *Arguments from Experience* and *Arguments from Analogy*.

Software Recommendations. As a result, we developed a set of recommendations to support software interaction with debates [2]. Participants expressed their desire to use simple commands and interfaces. A participant said:

"I do not want to login and browse hundreds of menus to participate, the simpler the better."

3. A PROTOTYPE APPLICATION

The prototype relies on a speech recognition and keyword spotting interface that classifies spoken utterances that represent the sentiment related to opinions in the debate. The application is comprised of the following modules (see Figure 1):

(1) The *ARGPlayer* module synchronise the audio of a debate with segmented arguments (i.e., concise sentences that represent an argument or part of an argument from the debate) taken from AIFdb [1], a database implementation that allows the storage and retrieval of argument structures.

(2) The *Speech Recognition and Sentiment Analysis* (*SRSA*) module captures and classifies user participations at the time at which they are verbalised with no specific commands to interact with the application. By using speech recognition, we aim to provide a low barrier to entry as a way to drive greater engagement.

(3) The *Synchronisation* module creates a relation between arguments from the debate and verbalised interactions.

(4) The *Feedback* module presents to the users their participation and the "view of other listeners" (i.e., data on how other people interacted with the debate) so that they can compare their reaction with others.

4. INITIAL EXPERIMENTS

We invited seven older adults that listen regularly to debates on the TV and/or radio to interact with the prototype. In individual sessions, the users listened to debate extracts and were able express their opinion through a microphone. We also showed them, without stopping the audio, segmented arguments and graphs on the views of other listeners related to the opinions listened to encourage participation. With a questionnaire after the study, we obtained their opinion about the prototype application, and their interest to participate in broadcast debates using their phone line.

Results revealed that all participants want to know about the "views of other listeners" and that segmented arguments helped them to understand and interact better with the debate. This is an important finding because information provided by the application can be used as a tempting feature to encourage engagement and a push to in-line participation. Furthermore, we can consider this as a motivator for social media engagement.

5. CONCLUSIONS

Preliminary results suggest that participants interested in broadcasts debates could benefit from using an application to interact with segmented content. We are currently undertaking evaluations with a larger sample size and different scenarios e.g., social sessions where participants discuss briefly the topic before and after using the application, audio feedback (as opposed to visual feedback) embedded in the audio, a complementary tablet application to interact manually using the same protocol, etc. Our aim is to better understand how older adults would like to engage with broadcast debates. One limitation with our approach is that speech recognition under noisy environments and unconstrained grammars is not completely accurate and this could confuse participants if data is not handled and presented correctly. However, we believe the prototype application presents a fundamental first step to motivate older adults to engage further with debates and have the potential to be a driver for adoption of more sophisticated technologies to support better engagement with digital social communities.

Acknowledgements. This research was supported by RCUK grant EP/G066019/1 "RCUK Hub: Social Inclusion through the Digital Economy".

6. REFERENCES

[1] J. Lawrence, F. Bex, C. Reed, and M. Snaith. AIFdb: Infrastructure for the Argument Web. In *COMMA*, pages 515–516, 2012.

[2] R. Medellin-Gasque, C. Reed, and V. L. Hanson. Guidelines to support older adults interaction with broadcast debates. *AI and Society. Under Review.*

[3] Ofcom. Adults media literacy in the nations: Summary report. (July), 2011.

[4] A. Smith. Older adults and technology use. Technical report, Pew Research Center, April 2014.

Online Learning System for Teaching Basic Skills to People with Developmental Disabilities

Luke Buschmann
University of California, Santa Cruz
1156 High Street
Santa Cruz, CA 95064
lnbuschm@ucsc.edu

Lourdes Morales
University of California, Santa Cruz
1156 High Street
Santa Cruz, CA 95064
lommoral@ucsc.edu

Sri Kurniawan
University of California, Santa Cruz
1156 High Street
Santa Cruz, CA 95064
skurnia@ucsc.edu

ABSTRACT

We report an online learning system for adults with developmental disabilities (DD) developed in collaboration with Imagine!, a Colorado based organization that provides support services to people with developmental and cognitive disabilities. Our HTML5 online application includes lessons to teach adults with DD of all ages about numbers, letters and currency. We implemented the application on an iPad to take advantage of the simplicity of touch-based interactions. Our preliminary user evaluation suggests that the system is well-received by its intended users, and unlike competitor systems that teach basic skills, is not considered childish and boring.

Categories and Subject Descriptors

H.5.2. Information interfaces and presentation (e.g., HCI): User interfaces.

Keywords

Developmental disability; iPad; basic skills.

1. INTRODUCTION

People with developmental disabilities (DD) struggle through basic tasks such as recognizing numbers or colors, or using money, and require help from someone else (e.g. those in charge their care) to effectively carry out such tasks. Hence, the participation of such individuals with DD in valued/meaningful social/societal roles (e.g. adult, worker, student, citizen) is limited, and this in turn can reduce these individuals' overall life satisfaction [1, 2, 5]. In addition, this dependency on others increases the amount of care these individuals with DD need from the people in charge of their care.

Technologies such as those based on augmentative and alternative communication and audio [5] and/or video prompting [1, 2] can help support individuals with DD in academic, employment, and independent living settings [1, 2, 4, 5, 6]. This can lead these individuals to have positive expectations and outcomes regarding valued social roles, and further, it may also enable them to assume those roles [1, 5, 6].

The advent of touchscreen devices has spurred development of applications (apps) designed to teach, train, and rehabilitate users with disabilities. A review of various works dealing with the use of an iPad or iPod Touch to teach individuals with DD either 1)

ASSETS '14, October 20-22, 2014, Rochester, NY, USA.
ACM 978-1-4503-2720-6/14/10.
http://dx.doi.org/10.1145/2661334.2661391

daily living skills such as cooking and cleaning (by delivering instructional prompts through the device), or 2) how to use an iPad or iPod Touch; suggests that these devices can be viable technological aids for individuals with DD [3]. While many adults with DD require the same lessons as children, such as learning numbers, letters, and currency; the majority of apps available to teach these basic skills are geared mainly towards children, which are problematic for individuals with DD in two ways: 1) The apps usually contain loud colors, animations and distractive information and 2) The graphics design and reward system for completing tasks are child-appropriate but not necessarily motivating or appropriate for adults with DD. For example, LetterSchool[1] is a letter learning app for iPad and is geared toward 2-5 year olds (Figure 1, left). It has very busy screens with lots of color and images and motion. There is also Learning Gems – Colors N Shapes[2], which is designed for children aged 2-6 (Figure 1). The later latter is more simplistic than LetterSchool, but it is also vibrantly colored and it has a relatively busy design that is not compatible for older individuals with DD. In general and in our preliminary investigation, these apps geared toward children are not well received by adults with DD due to their childish nature.

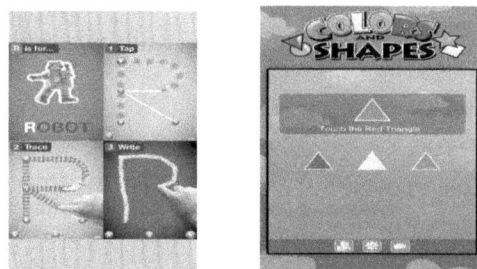

Figure 1. LetterSchool (left) and Learning Gems – Colors N Shapes (right) are two similar apps in the iTunes store

The purpose of this project is to develop and test a new method of providing lessons of basic skills to individuals with DD of all ages through an online system that works as a web-app on the iPad. This work is in collaboration with Imagine!, a not-for-profit organization based in Boulder, Colorado that provides support services to people with developmental and cognitive disabilities including autism, cerebral palsy and Down syndrome.

2. METHODS

The majority of system requirements were gathered with the help of the technical coordinator of Imagine!. We gathered requirements through ethnographic observations and interviews,

---

1 http://www.letterschool.com/

2 http://www.learninggems.com/our-apps/learning-gems-colors-n-shapes

and based on those requirements, we performed a participatory design with a group of professional caregivers and adults with DD to produce a low-fidelity prototype with the desired functionality on a whiteboard. Based on the feedback on the low-fidelity prototype and on the interviews of the group members that we conducted over the phone/Skype, we developed a high-fidelity prototype in the form of an interactive power point that mimicked a web-app that provided all the lessons. Additionally, features for securely logging user data and progress per user were also included. The typical usage scenario is for a caregiver to administer a specific app-based lesson to the person with a developmental and/or cognitive disability that they care for during a day habilitation program. We iterated over the design of this high-fidelity prototype based on the feedback we got through focus group sessions that we held over the phone with the Imagine! group. This was done until the prototype was accepted as the base of the final product. Figure 2 shows the money (left) and color (right) app-based lessons. The money lesson basically asks the user to choose a currency by tapping on the one that was spoken by a prompt. If a wrong currency is chosen, the prompt is repeated and the correct currency is highlighted yellow (seen in Figure 2). When this fails, all the other currencies disappear, leaving only the correct one. A similar scenario is followed in the color lesson (Figure 2, right).

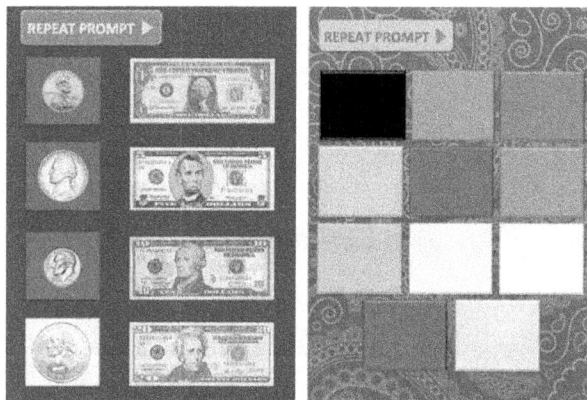

Figure 2. The money (left) and color (right) app-based lessons

Taking into account the feedback, we developed another high-fidelity prototype consisting of only three lessons (Number, Color, and Money) in the form of an actual web-app that worked on the iPad (the requirement that the system had to work on the iPad was set by the Imagine! group, since a lot of their clients' healthcare providers were starting to cover the purchase of such devices for rehabilitation therapy). Again, we iterated over design of this high-fidelity prototype based on the feedback we got through focus group sessions with the Imagine! group. Once the prototype was accepted as the base for the final product, with the help of the Imagine! group we started testing the app-based lessons with persons with developmental or cognitive disabilities at Imagine!'s care providing facilities.

The user study consisted of seven users testing each of the three reviews. They are 28 to 53 years old and a median age of 42. The feedback we sought (qualitative in nature) was mainly on the intuitiveness of the information flow and the graphics design.

3. RESULTS

The three app-based lessons were well received by users in the study. Users that reported normally using flash cards or paper to do similar lessons said that these app-based lessons were more enjoyable than the paper versions. All users reported that the questions and tasks were clear and easy to understand. All users enjoyed the default reinforcers (audio and GIF files that play when the user answers correctly), citing "[Denver] Broncos", "fun", and "telling me good job" as reasons. Constructive feedback from one user was a request for longer sessions and more pictures (reinforcers). Most users reported that the app-based lessons were easy to use and understand.

4. DISCUSSION

The user study shows promising results for the online learning system and showcases the necessity for such a system. By providing a simplistic interface with entertaining reinforcers, adults of various ages enjoyed the time spent practicing fundamentals of daily life. Future development will include increased difficulty and customized reinforcers, as well as widening the application suite to teach several more fundamentals like shapes, money addition, letters, and telling time.

5. ACKNOWLEDGMENTS

We thank the team at Imagine! Colorado for all their help.

6. REFERENCES

[1] Canella-Malone, H., Sigafoos, J., O'Reilly, M., de la Cruz, B., Edrisinha, C., and Lancioni, G. E. (2006). Comparing video prompting to video modeling for teaching daily living skills to six adults with developmental disabilities (Doctoral dissertation).

[2] Goodson, J., Sigafoos, J., O'Reilly, M., Cannella, H., and Lancioni, G. E. (2007). Evaluation of a video-based error correction procedure for teaching a domestic skill to individuals with developmental disabilities. *Research in Developmental Disabilities*, 28(5), 458-467.

[3] Kagohara, D. M., et al. (2013). Using iPods® and iPads® in teaching programs for individuals with developmental disabilities: A systematic review. *Research in developmental disabilities*, 34(1), 147-156.

[4] Lancioni, G. E., O'Reilly, M. F., Seedhouse, P., Furniss, F., and Cunha, B. (2000). Promoting independent task performance by persons with severe developmental disabilities through a new computer-aided system. *Behavior Modification*, 24(5), 700-718.

[5] Mcnaughton, D., and Bryen, D. N. (2007). AAC technologies to enhance participation and access to meaningful societal roles for adolescents and adults with developmental disabilities who require AAC. *Augmentative and Alternative Communication*, 23(3), 217-229.

[6] Wehmeyer, M. L., Palmer, S. B., Smith, S. J., Parent, W., Davies, D. K., and Stock, S. (2006). Technology use by people with intellectual and developmental disabilities to support employment activities: A single-subject design meta analysis. *Journal of Vocational Rehabilitation*, 24(2), 81-86.

Pilot Evaluation of a Path-Guided Indoor Navigation System for Visually Impaired in a Public Museum

Dhruv Jain

Indian Institute of Technology, Delhi
dhruv.cstaff@cse.iitd.ac.in

ABSTRACT

One of the common problems faced by visually impaired people is of independent path-based mobility in an unfamiliar indoor environment. Existing systems do not provide active guidance or are bulky, expensive and hence are not socially apt. Consequently, no system has found wide scale deployment in a public place. Our system is an omnipresent cellphone based indoor wayfinding system for the visually impaired. It provides step-by-step directions to the destination from any location in the building using minimal additional infrastructure. The carefully calibrated audio, vibration instructions and the small wearable device helps the user to navigate efficiently and unobtrusively. In this paper, we present the results from pilot testing of the system with one visually impaired user in a national science museum.

Categories and Subject Descriptors: K.4.2 [**Computers and Society**]: Social Issues - Assistive technologies for persons with disabilities

Keywords: Visual Impairment; Indoor Navigation

1. INTRODUCTION AND RELATED WORK

Navigation and wayfinding to reach a desired destination is a considerable challenge for a visually impaired person particularly in an unknown indoor environment. Path finding is a composition of several cognitive processes like map building, landmark identification, obstacle avoidance and interaction with by-standers to ask directions [8]. Most of the globally present signages are vision based and thus are inaccessible to them. Locating an accessible signage (tactile, audio) again poses a problem. Navigators currently rely on sporadic help from bystanders and use path integration to follow a given direction [8]. This causes anxiety, embarrassment and makes them reluctant to go alone in an unfamiliar building [6].

Existing commercial navigation systems based on GPS (eg. Sendero [2]) have made navigation a lot easier in outdoor environments. But their major shortcoming is that they can only identify very specific landmarks encountered by the user and typically do not work indoors. Several attempts have been made to address the problem of indoor navigation for the visually impaired. However, no single solution has found wide acceptability and long term deployment for use. Most

ASSETS'14, October 20–22, 2014, Rochester, NY, USA
ACM 978-1-4503-2720-6/14/10.
http://dx.doi.org/10.1145/2661334.2661405

Figure 1: User navigating with the aid of the system. User module (red arrow) and wall module (black-arrow). Left image is the start position of the exhibition.

of the systems present today are either only landmark identification systems with no path-based guidance (eg. RFID [7], infrared based systems [3]) or are inaccurate for an indoor environment (eg. dead-reckoning [5], Wifi [10]). Few systems exist which are both omnipresent (which could localize the user accurately from any point in the building) and provide step-by-step path based wayfinding. These systems are bulky to carry [4] or expensive to operate [9].

The system: We have developed a portable and self- contained indoor navigation system for the visually impaired [6]. Comprising a network of wall mounted units and a user module coupled with a mobile application (Figure 1, left image), the system downloads the map of the building, localizes the user within the building, takes the destination as input from the user, and then helps him/her to independently navigate to his destination using step-by-step navigational instructions. Earlier work field tested the deployment with 10 visually impaired users in a university building [6]. In this work, we present the qualitative results from pilot testing of the deployment in a public museum at New Delhi.

The museum: National Science Center (NSC), located in New Delhi, is part of the National Council of Science Museums, Govt. of India [1]. Inviting more than 500,000 annual visitors, it aims to popularize science among the people of India in general and among the students in particular. NSC consists of 4 floors containing 7 exhibition galleries, each build on a unique science theme, covering a total area of 6409 sq. m. There is a single navigational path which starts from the ground floor, takes the visitor up to the fourth floor using the escalator and brings him/her down to the ground floor via distributed small stairs, while covering all the galleries in between. Exhibits are either located on the narrow track connected to the main path or are spread across wide halls situated on the path.

Figure 2: Sample screens from the mobile application.

2. USER INTERFACE

Figure 2 shows sample screens from the mobile application interface for navigating in a museum. All the information is conveyed to the user via the Text-to-speech (TTS) engine of the mobile application. The screens are designed such that it is convenient for a visually impaired person to touch and operate. They also contain pictures for giving it an aesthetic look to surrounding people and in case we extend the system for sighted persons in future. All the information stored in the app database was provided by the museum authorities and mimics the information displayed on the information boards attached to the exhibit or exhibition.

On starting the application, the app logo is displayed (not shown). As the user enters an exhibition, the first screen pops up with an audio message conveying the name of the exhibition. It has a 'learn more' button and a small picture of the exhibition, both of which can be touched to know more information about the exhibition. While navigating in an exhibition, the middle screen is displayed when the user is near an exhibit. Again, the written information is spoken to the user and the 'learn more' button can be touched for a detailed description of the exhibit. The screen remains till the user is near the exhibit. The rightmost screen is the standby screen which is displayed when the user is not near any exhibit. It contains the status of the bluetooth connection with the user module and options for social networking, both of which can be accessed with a screen reader. It also conveys auditory information to navigate further which include any turn to take and the number of steps to travel. If the user deviates from the path during any stage of the application, a warning is given. Moreover, when any screen pops up, a vibration alert is also given.

3. USER EVALUATION

Study Design: The system was installed in one of the smaller exhibitions located on floor 2 of NSC called Pre-Historic Life. It consists of a narrow main track approx. 60m of length and some smaller paths originating from it and leading to the exhibits. There are 7 large and 2 small groups of exhibits on the track. A total of 16 wall modules were deployed, 7 for navigation, at an interval of about 8m and additional 9 near the exhibits for precise localization.

The male study participant was selected from a NGO in Delhi. He had basic English literacy and adequate knowledge of using a mobile phone. He was fully blind from birth and possessed no other impairment. He used cane and would typically ask for directions from sighted individuals while navigating. The participant had never visited any public museum alone and this was his first visit to NSC.

Qualitative evaluation: The participant was given a demonstration of the system, trained for approx. 45 min in a separate conference room of the museum and was brought to the entrance of the exhibition. He was told to navigate in the exhibition using his cane and the system. The participant identified and gained information about the exhibits as and when he desired. Upon satisfaction, he navigated out through the exit. The process lasted for approx. 20 min, following which a 15 min interview was taken.

The user was able to effectively understand the usage of the device and successfully navigate in the exhibition as shown in Figure 1. He eagerly expressed been able to identify majority of the exhibits and find out more information about them. However, it was difficult for him to distinguish some of the closely located exhibits. We realized that a few wall modules were located very close to each other, and since the range of the modules is large (8 m), this caused interference. We propose to decrease the range of the wall modules installed close to the exhibits using carefully designed rapid prototyped covers.

"The museum is very informative and the application instructions were appropriate to learn about the exhibits. This would be very educational for (blind) school students."

The user was happy with the carefully designed stages of the application and appreciated its features.

"The application instructed me to come back to the main track every time I deviated to closely observe an exhibit. It was easy to navigate independently within the crowd."

"I don't want to know about every exhibit... Some of them appeal to me more than others and I can choose to hear more about them by pressing 'Learn more' button..."

The instructions were clear and audible. The user was able to control the volume to suit according to the crowd. He expressed however, that controlling volume takes time and if possible, would like the application to automatically set the volume based on the surrounding noise.

4. CONCLUSIONS

In this paper, we reported the results from pilot evaluation of an unobtrusive and efficient indoor navigation system for visually impaired in a public museum in India. The results indicated that the system is usable and useful but can still be improved. Future work includes long-term deployment and field testing with more users.

5. REFERENCES

[1] National Science Center, Delhi. http://www.nscdelhi.org/.
[2] Sendero Group. http://www.senderogroup.com/.
[3] Talking Signs Inc. 2000.
http://www.ski.org/Rehab/WCrandall/introts.html, June 2007.
[4] N. Fallah, I. Apostolopoulos, K. Bekris, and E. Folmer. The user as a sensor: navigating users with visual impairments in indoor spaces using tactile landmarks. In *CHI*, 2012.
[5] T. Höllerer, D. Hallaway, N. Tinna, and S. Feiner. Steps toward accommodating variable position tracking accuracy in a mobile augmented reality system. In *AIMS*. Citeseer, 2001.
[6] D. Jain, A. Jain, R. Paul, A. Komarika, and M. Balakrishnan. A path-guided audio based indoor navigation system for persons with visual impairment. ACM ASSETS, 2013.
[7] V. Kulyukin, C. Gharpure, J. Nicholson, and S. Pavithran. Rfid in robot-assisted indoor navigation for the visually impaired. In *LIROS*. IEEE, 2004.
[8] J. M. Loomis, R. L. Klatzky, R. G. Golledge, et al. Navigating without vision: basic and applied research. *OVS*, 2001.
[9] L. Ran, S. Helal, and S. Moore. Drishti: an integrated indoor/outdoor blind navigation system and service. In *PerCom*, 2004.
[10] T. Riehle, P. Lichter, and N. Giudice. An indoor navigation system to support the visually impaired. In *EMBS*. IEEE, 2008.

Tactile Aids for Visually Impaired Graphical Design Education

Samantha McDonald, Joshua Dutterer, Ali Abdolrahmani, Shaun Kane, Amy Hurst
UMBC
1000 Hilltop Circle
Baltimore MD, 21250
{ sam30, dutter1, aliab1, skane, amyhurst } @umbc.edu

ABSTRACT

In this demonstration, we describe our exploration in making graphic design theory accessible to a visually impaired student with the use of rapid prototyping tools. We created over 10 novel aids with the use of a laser cutter and 3D printer to demonstrate tangible examples of color theory, type face, web page layouts, and web design. These tactile aids were inexpensive and fabricated in a relatively small amount of time, suggesting the feasibility of our approach. The participant's feedback concluded an increased understanding of the class material and confirmed the potential of tactile aids and rapid prototyping in an educational environment.

Categories and Subject Descriptors

K.4.2 [Social Issues]: Assistive technologies for persons with disabilities

General Terms

Design, Experimentation.

Keywords

Visual Graphics; Visually Impaired; Graphics Education, Visual Aid; Tactile Aids; 3D Printing; Rapid Prototyping

1. Introduction

Classes that focus on graphics and web design include vision based topics such as color, grid layouts, font families, font types, and alphanumeric character spacing. Traditionally, these topics are taught through visual images and examples, a technique that is not accessible to individuals with limited or no vision. This paper describes our efforts to create tangible representations of fundamental graphic design concepts using rapid prototyping tools. These instructional aids were created for a visually impaired student taking an introduction to human-centered computing class with a unit on graphic design. All designs were created and tested in a three week span. We first describe our techniques to generate these instructional aids followed by our evaluation of the experiment.

ASSETS'14, October 20–22, 2014, Rochester, NY, USA.
ACM 978-1-4503-2720-6/14/10.
http://dx.doi.org/10.1145/2661334.2661392

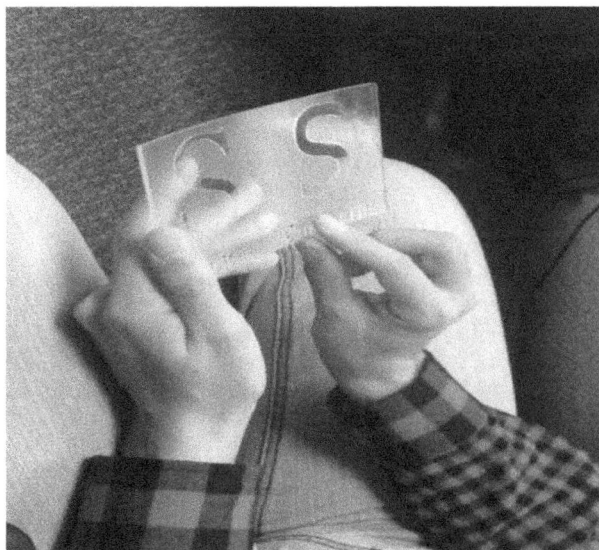

Figure 1. Participant examining the difference between serif and sans serif fonts

2. Construction

Our visual tactile aids were derived from traditional images and concepts of the student's graphic design class. We focused on one specific unit of the class with a high density of visual graphics. The class images were converted into 3D printable and laser cut designs for tactile creation. The tactile aids were fabricated from acrylic, wood, and thermoplastic elastomer filament. Each tactile created was similar if not identical to the images directly taken from the class slides. However to avoid content clutter, small changes were made to the graphics in order to minimize misdirection and an overload of class material. For example, in Figure 1 we see a tactile tool used to compare serif and sans serif fonts. The original class images provided for Figure 1 also labeled certain parts of the serif letter like counter, stroke, and ascender. These labels did not assist in the tactile comparison of serif and sans serif fonts and were removed. Other tactile tools like Figure 2 represent an example of information separation. The left image depicts a grid anatomy to display web design layout topics like column, row, and spatial zones. The tactiles created from this grid anatomy were separated into different tactile tools to minimize clutter. This method provided the student with a better understanding of broad concepts without interference of extra material.

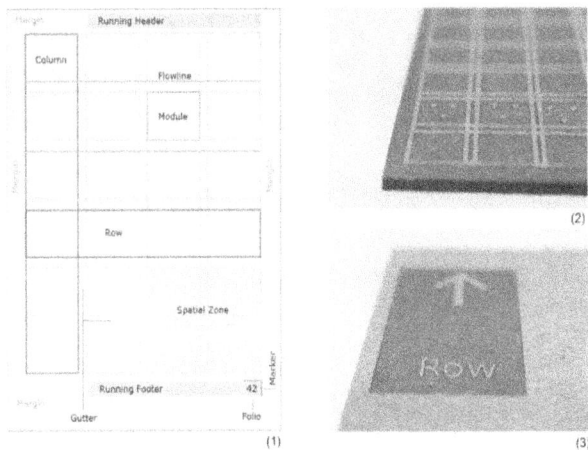

Figure 2. Left image is a Grid Anatomy Graphic taken from class slides (1). Right images depict the front (2) and back (3) of the grid anatomy based tactile tool representing a row. The arrow in image 3 directs tactile orientation.

3. Evaluation

Giving the user the ability to design and give input in their technology can improve the successfulness of the product [1]. Each design was shared with the participant in class and designated meetings in order to receive as much feedback and suggestions from the participant as possible. Originally, we described the tactile aids to the participant as he was feeling the object. After the course unit was over we provided improved tactile images to the participant. Without explanation of the image or educational purpose, we evaluated the participants understanding of the concepts represented through the tactile aids.

4. Findings

By the end of evaluations, our participant noticed an increased real time understanding of class material and increased emotional satisfaction in the material taught. The participant could follow along with the rest of the class on certain material without feeling behind or lost. Although our participant is unable to read Braille; the participant could previously read printed text and can still recognize alphanumeric letter shapes. The ability to read alphanumeric letters made it easier to explain and educate the participant on type face and font styles.

During the study, we also noticed a set of findings that could be useful for the future of tactile creation. In terms of creating raised alphanumeric characters, one issue was the shape and structure of the English letters. Some words like 'COLUMN' are much harder for our participant to read as a result of too many raised vertical lines. For examples the letters 'L','U','M', and 'N' have a total of seven vertical lines. This can cause the user to misinterpret the word as a set of vertical lines instead of a readable word. We addressed this concern by adding space between each letter and by providing larger filled letters that are easier to differentiate. Our participant also noted it was easier to read capitalized words. This could be because of the naturally increased size and spacing of capital letters. When looking at the topic of fonts, the larger and more oversized the letters, the easier it was for the participant to identify the shape.

Another finding was the type of material used. Time restraints during the rapid prototyping phase required a more flexible use of materials. The first rounds of designs were cut on standard hardwood. This later proved to be an ineffective material for tactile tools. The participant complained of finger exhaustion after using the wooden tactile for a long period of time. The wood was too grainy and eventually dulled the sensations of touch in the participant's fingers, not allowing him to differentiate the raised and unraised parts of the tactile. A switch to acrylic and 3D plastic filament soon resolved this issue.

5. Discussion

Given the diversity of student preferences and learning styles, creating a general set of tactile aids creates difficulties with a variety of needs for each student. However, simplistic computer programs and scanning techniques can make it easier for 2D visuals to be adapted and customized into 3D tactile aids at a fast rate. Future studies that can make it easier for the student and teacher to scan and print designs on their own can provide a more flexible and creative system. Combining the idea of visually impaired programming with tactile aids, future research can study a student's ability to print their own customizable tactile aids [2].

This research also addresses the field of web development. As the industry of web development and web design grows, so does the need for workers that are educated in the fields of graphics and graphic development. Making these topics more accessible and understandable to the visually impaired community is necessary in order modernize and stay up to date on necessary educational concepts.

6. Conclusion

Our research improved a single student's ability to understand graphical concepts and provided a demonstration of accessible 3D printed and laser cut designs created in fast and customizable manner. When given proper visual aids, a visually impaired student can learn and explore ideas in the topics of graphical and digital design.

7. ACKNOWLEDGMENTS

Our thanks to our participant and the University of Maryland Baltimore County Information Systems Department for providing this opportunity.

8. REFERENCES

[1] Amy Hurst and Shaun Kane. 2013. Making "Making" accessible. In Proceedings of the 12th International Conference on Interaction Design and Children (IDC '13). ACM, New York, NY, USA, 635-638.

[2] Shaun K. Kane and Jeffrey P. Bigham. 2014. Tracking @stemxcomet: teaching programming to blind students via 3D printing, crisis management, and twitter. In Proceedings of the 45th ACM technical symposium on Computer science education (SIGCSE '14). ACM, New York, NY, USA, 247-2522

Tongue-able Interfaces: Evaluating Techniques for a Camera Based Tongue Gesture Input System

Shuo Niu
Department of Computer Science
Virginia Tech
Blacksburg, VA 24061, USA
shuoniu@vt.edu

Li Liu
Department of Digital Media
Utah Valley University
Orem, UT 84058, USA
lliu@uvu.edu

D. Scott McCrickard
Department of Computer Science
Virginia Tech
Blacksburg, VA 24061 USA
mccricks@cs.vt.edu

ABSTRACT

Tongue-computer interaction techniques create a new pathway between the human and the computer, with particular utility for people with upper limb impairment. This study investigated the usability problems of camera-based tongue computer interface reflected through the user behavior and participants' feedback; specifically the exploration of referential techniques to make users aware of their tongue position and help adjust their gesture. Pros and cons of the referential strategies are discussed to foster future assistive tongue-computer interface design.

Categories and Subject Descriptors

H5.2 [**Information interfaces and presentation**]: User Interfaces - *Input devices and strategies*; K.4.2 [**Computer and Society**]: Social Issues – *assistive technologies for persons with disabilities.*

General Terms

Performance, Design, Human Factors

Keywords

Gesture; hands-free interfaces; camera; self-awareness; functional representation

1. INTRODUCTION

A great many people worldwide have limitations in the use of their hands and arms. In our previous work, a novel noncontact camera-based tongue computer interface (CBTCI) is introduced to assist people with upper limb limitation to access computers [2]. In contrast to intrusive TCIs (e.g., [4]), tongue gesture input systems provide higher degrees of motional freedom (DOF) and require minimal setup. However, there are many questions regarding potential usability of such systems. Many of these questions stem from the lack of tangible feedback found in the more intrusive physical devices. To maintain the high DOF and to reduce system fluctuation, self-awareness is considered a common strategy in gesture-based research (e.g., [5]). Presented with a

captured video window of oneself, a user can monitor motions by referring to the camera window. However, in gesture-based interaction, a user must engage in multitasking (e.g., performing the task and monitoring the camera), potentially resulting in performance degradation [1]. We hypothesize that tracking feedback of the input and monitoring the motions simultaneously requires more mental effort, resulting in more errors. From our previous study, two referential awareness techniques are captured in the CBTCI: one that uses the captured video technique and another that uses an interpreted technique. Our study investigates how two referential strategies affect self-awareness of inputs during user tongue gesture adjustment.

2. TEXT INPUT APPLICATION

The experimental task seeks to explore how the referential techniques influence the behavioral adaption in inputting text with CBTCI. The user interface is comprised of a text pad and a text area (Figure 1). The text pad included two letter keys and a word list. The letters from A to N are assigned to the left key and the rest of the letters are assigned to the right key. The left and right tongue gestures are used to choose the corresponding letter-selection keys. After the key selection sequence is finished, matched words appear vertically in the word list. We use MacKenzie's two key text-entry technique to generate the potential word list [3]. Up and down tongue gestures will be used to select a word. To confirm a word selection, the user will open his/her mouth and the selected word will appear in the text area. When any of the four tongue gestures is maintained for 1.8 seconds, the matching instruction will be executed.

3. REFERENTIAL FEEDBACK

The self-awareness strategy is presented in a different interface window (Figure 2 *left*). A mirror window showing the video stream captured by the camera is placed under the text pad. The user can watch the real-time video to get real-time feedback.

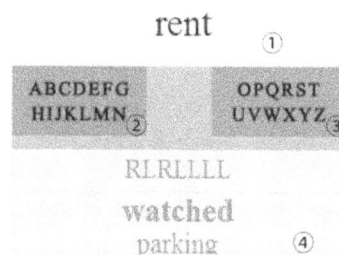

Figure 1. The text input application. The text pad locates in the middle top of the screen and the text area is full screen. ① Text area. ② Left key ③ Right key. ④ Word list.

ASSETS '14, Oct 20-22 2014, Rochester, NY, USA
ACM 978-1-4503-2720-6/14/10.
http://dx.doi.org/10.1145/2661334.2661395

To implement the functional representation in the task, four progress bars are used to indicate the time of each tongue protrusion and a gesture icon representing the current recognized tongue gesture is included in the text pad (Figure 2 *right*). The four progress bars indicate the time of corresponding directional tongue gestures. The icon between the left and right keys changes based on the tongue gesture.

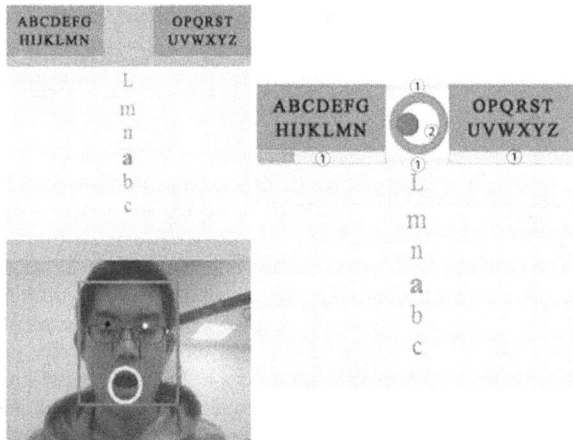

Figure 2. Referential feedback approaches. *Left:* **Self-awareness window. A "mirror" window at the bottom of the screen shows the current video frame of the user.** *Right:* **Functional representation window. At the top center, ① four progress bars reflect the time of directional tongue gestures, and ② Gesture indicator points out the current recognized tongue position.**

Three female and nine male college students (mean age=22.67, SD=3.26) participated in the experiment. Participants were randomly assigned into one of two groups (A and B). Participants from Group A used the functional representation strategy and those from Group B used self-awareness strategy. Each participant performed the task using the tongue interface with one of the referential strategy three times.

The results showed that without the referential information, participants' time to adjust their tongue (adjustment time, AT) does not differ significantly for the last baseline trials, but their time to hold the tongue position (effective time, ET) differed significantly during the trials with different referential strategies

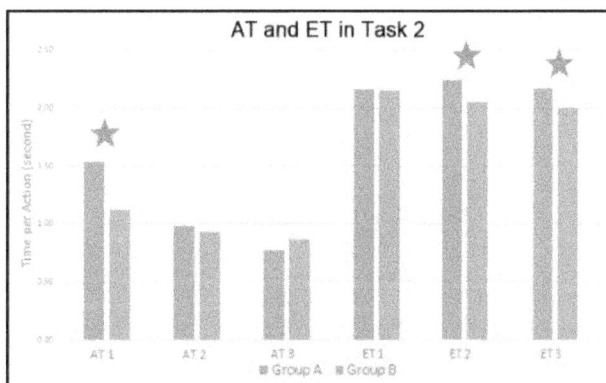

Figure 3. Adjustment time and effective time of the 3 trials in the Task 2. AT 1-3 on the left data of the three trials in Task 2, ET 1-3 on the data of three trials in Task 2. The trial marked with star has significant difference between Group A and Group B.

(Figure 3). The average ET of Group A of all three trials in Task 2 is 2.25s (SD=1.01), while with self-awareness strategy, participants in Group B achieve ET of 2.17s (SD=0.86), which is significantly less than Group A (p<0.0001). The ET values of Group B are smaller than Group A in all three trials with significant difference for the last two trials (p=0.0468 and 0.0300).

The numbers of errors in the task with referential strategy were counted in the three trials (see Table 1). The number in the table was obtained by subtracting the number of necessary actions from the total number of actions taken in the system in the corresponding trial. Unnecessary actions include misspelling, moving the words list before the letter sequence is finished, and passing the correct word and moving back. It is notable that the group with the mirror window made many more errors.

Table 1. The number of errors for different referential strategies in the task for the five participants in each of the two groups (A and B).

	A01	A03	A04	A06	A07	B01	B02	B04	B06	B07
#1	0	0	2	0	0	1	0	12	0	21
#2	0	0	0	0	0	1	11	10	8	8
#3	0	0	2	2	1	0	0	24	0	8

4. CONCLUSIONS AND FUTURE WORK

This work shows tradeoffs for tongue gestures in pointing and simple text entry tasks. Self-awareness through a video window helps the user establish and maintain the tongue gesture to an appropriate degree, but the added complexity brings more distraction than using extracted window components. Moving forward, it is important to develop and test applications that leverage these findings for people with disabilities; e.g., simple web or document browsing, SMS, and social media. As we develop and explore a broader set of applications used by larger numbers of participants, we expect to see different strategies emerge for fast, accurate, and easy gesturing using the tongue, mouth, and face—reflecting how people learn how to gesture in ways that are recognizable by the system.

5. REFERENCES

[1] Karam, M., Lee, J. C., Rose, T., Quek, F., & McCrickard, S. (2009). Comparing gesture and touch for notification system interactions. In *Proc. ACHI* 7-12.

[2] Liu, L., Niu, S., Ren, J., & Zhang, J. (2012). Tongible: a non-contact tongue-based interaction technique. In *Proc. SIGACCESS*, 233-234.

[3] MacKenzie, I. S. (2009). The one-key challenge: searching for a fast one-key text entry method. In *Proc. SIGACCESS*, 91-98.

[4] Slyper, R., Lehman, J., Forlizzi, J., & Hodgins, J. (2011). A tongue input device for creating conversations. In *Proc. UIST*, 117-126.

[5] Tu, J., Tao, H., & Huang, T. (2007). Face as mouse through visual face tracking. *Computer Vision and Image Understanding*, *108*(1-2), 35-40.

Tracking Mental Engagement:
A Tool for Young People with ADD and ADHD

Bobby Beaton, Ryan Merkel, Jayanth Prathipati, Andrew Weckstein, D. Scott McCrickard

Department of Computer Science

Virginia Tech

Blacksburg, VA 24061, USA

rbeaton,orion22,jayanth,awex,mccricks@vt.edu

ABSTRACT

This paper describes a reflective mobile application to help young people with ADD and ADHD better understand their engagement levels during their daily tasks. The mobile application, paired with an electroencephalographic (EEG) device, collects data about user-specific task engagement and pairs it with geographic and temporal data to provide insights into the degree to which a user is engaged in tasks based on time and location. The paper describes two mobile prototypes developed to investigate the problem space of contextual visualizations of engagement information, and it presents future directions for development and study.

Categories and Subject Descriptors

H5.2 [**Information interfaces and presentation**]: User Interfaces
- *Input devices and strategies*

General Terms

Design; Human Factors

Keywords

Mobile interfaces; electroencephalograph; EEG; attention; ADD; ADHD

1. INTRODUCTION

Electrophysiological measures have been used for over forty years to study brain processes in children and adults with attentional difficulties, including attention deficit disorder (ADD) and attentional deficit hyperactivity disorder (ADHD). During that time, researchers have attempted to characterize, identify, and quantify the brainwave activity patterns of people diagnosed with ADD and ADHD. Recent years has seen an increase in neurofeedback studies investigating ADHD, even being used as a supplemental tool for diagnosis (e.g., [Mazaheri et al. 2013]). This project seeks to identify tasks for which an awareness of biometric data can be of value to the user based on reflections on attention, interruption, cognitive and task performance. Building on foundational therapies, we will build an understanding of the behaviors of people who identify as attentionally deficient—those for whom awareness of biometric data may help them lead more productive and contented lives.

Many personal attentional metrics have relied primarily on

ASSETS '14, Oct 20-22 2014, Rochester, NY, USA
ACM 978-1-4503-2720-6/14/10.
http://dx.doi.org/10.1145/2661334.2661399

subjective evaluation, making it difficult to compare across other activity attention levels. New mobile and wireless EEG devices can unobtrusively collect objective user-specific task engagement throughout the day and share it wirelessly with other devices (e.g., mobile phones), providing select user populations with the opportunity to review their personal values and identify engagement trends. Our initial target user population focuses on college-age students, a demographic often on their own for the first time and prone to distractions and mental distress. We will consider those with known attentional issues (e.g., ADHD), though we will not target them exclusively.

The efforts described in this paper focus on the capture and sharing of EEG data, categorized by time and location. As one common therapy approach for young people with ADD and ADHD is to plan daily activities through a calendaring program, our capture and categorization approach holds promise in providing ways to reflect upon the day, toward

2. ENGAGEMENT MONITORING

No two brains are the same, as such EEG-derived engagement indices are useful for comparing activities by the same person, but not across people. To describe engagement activity, it is possible to show the user a relative metric, rather than an absolute number—as such supporting comparison over time through change in current engagement index above or below a baseline index. This high, neutral, low conceptualization of engagement is similar to other papers in the field that visualize engagement and arousal [McDuff et al., 2012]. A common personal engagement index uses a metric defined by Alexander Pope that derives values from EEG powers [Pope et al, 1995]. This metric is computed by obtaining EEG readings for Alpha, Beta, and Theta brainwaves and applying the following formula:

Engagement Index = Beta / (Alpha + Theta)

This engagement index is represented by a number between 0 and 1. The scale is notably unique for each person, such that if two people both have values of 0.7 for their engagement index, it does not necessarily mean that they are equally engaged. It should be noted that Pope's metric was derived with a specific activity in mind and may not be scalable to other activities.

Our belief is that engagement information displays should at minimum provide:

1. a quick reflection of user information about overall engagement trends

2. contextual information about location, time, and events (through geotagging, timestamping, and integration with calendaring programs)

3. real time as well as historic data about user engagement

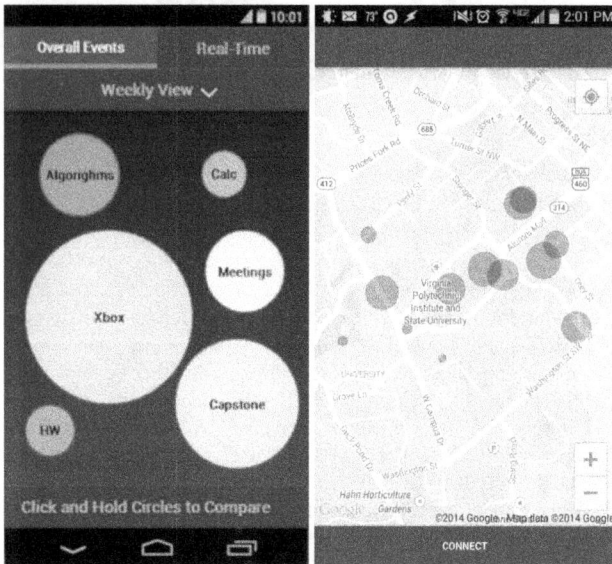

Figure 1: Example UI showing user engagement displayed by activity and mean engagement during activity (left) and GPS tag location (right).

3. PROTOTYPING A TOOL

The objective of this work is to design tools that allow the user to reflect over their personal engagement levels throughout a day, week, or month. But data-logging isn't enough. What will the user do with this data? How will they interact and interpret it? An initial design workshop focused on biometric engagement design as well as two prototyping projects have resulted in initial answers these questions. Users want to know comparative engagement values, not necessarily based around time. As an example, one of our prototypes focuses on providing a categorical view of the engagement data.

One design to support the categorical comparison scenario was a "Bubble UI". An example of this concept can be seen in Figure 1a. Users are presented with bubbles labeled with their activity (derived from calendar scraping). The size of the bubble correlates to their mean engagement score during the activity. Users can quickly determine which activities they were most and least focused in. Numerical engagement and timestamp values were available by tapping a bubble for more information. Each bubble represents an activity derived from calendar scraping. Users can filter by time using the view option at the top of the screen. The size of the bubble represents the mean user engagement level during that activity. The color fill of each bubble represents the arousal frequency during the activity.

Figure 1b shows a second prototype where user engagement information was displayed as GPS location and time. Each map node conveyed time spent in location by the dot size, and the color of the dot reflects the mean engagement of the user during

the time spent there. This prototype is under review now and will be used in an upcoming user study.

This work is part of a larger research project focused on helping people achieve temporal understanding of derived engagement through prototyping—toward knowledge that leads to improved wellbeing. It is particularly important to focus on those with attentional issues, particularly young people with ADD and ADHD Deriving engagement through a combination of unobtrusive objective (biosensed) as well as subjective (calendar scraping, self report, social media scraping) methods addresses two of the dimensions traditionally associated with engagement: user level and activity type. By asking the questions how engaged was I (corresponding to subjective and objective activity focus measurements) and what activity was I doing (corresponding to activity type) we can begin to explore the factors and trends of our attention behavior.

4. CONCLUSIONS AND FUTURE WORK

This paper introduced a tool for mobile devices and EEGs that captures and shares temporally and geo-tagged information about a user's attentional levels. It was designed with a focus on people with attentional difficulties, in particular college students with ADD and ADHD. Deployment of the tools is currently in the planning stages, toward understanding the usability and utility of the tools and visualizations that we have created.

Our ongoing and future work will examine how biometric data can be combined with other readily available information about user activity to provide a contextually connected view of the user's behavior. Our efforts at calendar scraping associates user events and deadlines with changes in biometric data, and geographical information from a mobile phone's GPS provides a continuously updated view of user location. Information from online classroom management tools like Sakai and Scholar augment these other data sources with course-related deadlines. We will investigate how objective engagement information can be used in practice, and which metrics are appropriate. Tracking tools like the Fitbit and heart rate monitor tracking devices have seen increased deployment and use in recent years, and we hope that attention-monitoring tools will yield similar benefits.

5. REFERENCES

[1] Beaton, B. (2014). Investigating mental focus using mobile devices and biometrically driven attention monitoring and reflection tools. In *Proc. HCIC*.

[2] Mazaheri, A. et al. (2013). Differential oscillatory electroencephalogram between attention-deficit/hyperactivity disorder subtypes and typically developing adolescents. *Biological Psychiatry*.

[3] McDuff, D. et al. (2012). AffectAura: An intelligent system for emotional memory. In *Proc CHI*.

[4] Merkel, R., Prathipati, J., Weckstein, A. (2014). Tracking mental engagement: Bringing context on EEG data. In *Proc VTURCS*.

[5] Pope, A.T. et al., (1995). Biocybernetic system evaluates indices of operator engagement in automated task.*Biological Psychology*.

Using Computer Vision to Access Appliance Displays

Giovanni Fusco[1], Ender Tekin[1], Richard E. Ladner[2] and James M. Coughlan[1]

[1]The Smith-Kettlewell Eye Research Institute
2318 Fillmore St.
San Francisco, CA 94115 USA
{giofusco,ender,coughlan}@ski.org

[2]University of Washington
Computer Science & Engineering, DUB Group
Seattle, WA 98195 USA
ladner@cs.washington.edu

ABSTRACT

People who are blind or visually impaired face difficulties accessing a growing array of everyday appliances, needed to perform a variety of daily activities, because they are equipped with electronic displays. We are developing a "Display Reader" smartphone app, which uses computer vision to help a user acquire a usable image of a display, to address this problem. The current prototype analyzes video from the smartphone's camera, providing real-time feedback to guide the user until a satisfactory image is acquired, based on automatic estimates of image blur and glare. Formative studies were conducted with several blind and visually impaired participants, whose feedback is guiding the development of the user interface. The prototype software has been released as a Free and Open Source (FOSS) project.

Categories and Subject Descriptors

I.5.5 [**Pattern Recognition**]: Applications: Computer Vision

General Terms

Algorithm, Performance, Experimentation, Human Factors.

Keywords

Access, blindness, low vision.

1. INTRODUCTION

People who are blind or visually impaired face severe difficulties performing a variety of daily activities due to the growing array of everyday appliances equipped with inaccessible electronic displays, often controlled with touch screens. Such appliances include microwave ovens, media players, digital blood pressure monitors, thermostats and vending machines. Available access technology to make printed documents accessible to persons with visual impairments is not equipped to handle the challenges of reading text on electronic displays, which is significantly different in appearance from printed text, and is often obscured by glare, reflections or poor contrast (Fig. 1b).

There is a small but growing body of work on computer vision-based display readers. One influential early work is Clearspeech [4], in which special markers are affixed around the borders of a display to help the system localize and read the display characters in the image. More recent work focuses on detecting and reading display text without the use of markers [6, 5]. Our current prototype uses a marker in order to provide rapid and accurate feedback to help guide the user to find the display, but we aim to eliminate the need for the marker in the future.

ASSETS '14, Oct 20-22 2014, Rochester, NY, USA
ACM 978-1-4503-2720-6/14/10.
http://dx.doi.org/10.1145/2661334.2661404

A key challenge in any camera-based system for blind or visually impaired users is that of aiming the camera properly to frame the target of interest. One such system, VizWiz [1], is a versatile tool that uses crowdsourcing to obtain descriptive information about images photographed by the user, which can include images of appliance displays. However, VizWiz has two major limitations: (a) it typically takes about 30 sec. for the user to receive feedback on an image, which is too long for some applications, and (b) it is difficult to obtain usable pictures because of frequent errors in "blur, lighting, framing, and composition" [1]. We seek to overcome both limitations in our Display Reader project.

We describe formative studies on a Display Reader prototype, which is tested with blind and low vision participants. The current phase of research focuses on a user interface (UI) that helps the user acquire one or more usable images of the desired display. The challenge of aiming the camera properly towards the display is compounded by an additional complication of LED and LCD displays: poor contrast and the presence of bright specularities (i.e., reflections from light sources). These complications make many images of displays difficult or impossible to read, even when the display is well framed in the image (e.g., as in Fig. 1b). The final stage of actually reading the display contents will be addressed in future research.

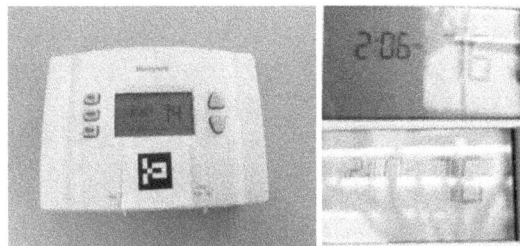

Figure 1. (a) Appliance with LCD display, with marker affixed below the display. (b) Examples of specularities (reflected glare) that severely impair visibility of display.

2. APPROACH

Our prototype consists of an Android smartphone, which is used to acquire images of the display of interest, running in conjunction with a laptop. (In the future we will port the software to the smartphone so that it runs as a self-contained app.) We affix a black-and-white fiducial paper marker [2] to each appliance, placed close to the display of interest (Fig. 1a). The marker includes a simple tactile marking to help blind users find the display; we note that it is already common practice for many people who are blind to affix tactile markings to appliances they own to help them locate and distinguish appliance buttons. Using a marker also simplifies and speeds up the process of detecting and localizing the display in the images acquired by the camera.

Rather than attempt to find and read the display "from scratch", which requires the ability to detect, localize and read arbitrary text with non-standard fonts and poor visibility, we exploit the prior knowledge of the display encoded in a *display template* that we have constructed for each appliance. The display template is a set of one or more high-quality, "clean" images of the display with annotations indicating the precise locations of display text fields. Other information, such as the locations and possible values and appearances of special symbol fields, can also be included. Such display templates may be generated by a sighted friend or a crowdsourcing process in which sighted volunteers acquire images of appliances and manually annotate them, to be shared freely on the web.

The prototype finds the marker (when visible) in each video frame, and computes a transformation between the marker in the current frame and the template to rectify (i.e., unwarp) the display, yielding a *rectified display image* (see Fig. 1b for examples).

We analyze each frame to assess its quality in two respects: the amount of blur and the severity of specularities (glare reflections) visible on the display region. Images with too much blur are rejected from further analysis. In our formative studies we found that different lighting conditions may require different thresholds for glare; we will investigate more robust methods for estimating glare in the future. Currently, our approach seeks a *single* high-quality view of the entire display, but in the future we will consider techniques for synthesizing such a view from multiple vantage points [3].

We devised a simple UI for the prototype (similar to that in [7]), using audio feedback to help guide the user until a satisfactory image is acquired. If the marker is detected and the *pose* is good (i.e., the marker and display are well centered in the camera's field of view and are at an appropriate viewing distance), and if the blur is acceptably low, then a pleasant audio tone is issued. Verbal directions ("closer," "farther") indicate that the camera is too far or too close to the display; directions ("up", "down", "left", "right") help the user center the display in the image.

Our software is a Free and Open Source (FOSS) project, available at: http://www.ski.org/Rehab/Coughlan_lab/DisplayReader/

3. FORMATIVE STUDIES

We conducted formative studies of our prototype with five volunteer participants, four of whom are blind and one of whom has low vision. The feedback from each participant was used to make improvements to the UI and computer vision algorithms. Users were usually able to acquire good images of the tested appliances, demonstrating the feasibility of our approach.

Two main themes emerged from these studies. The first is that, while most participants found it fairly straightforward to frame the display properly in the camera's field of view (with the help of a training session and the UI's real-time feedback), they found it challenging to explore a wide range of viewing angles, which may be necessary to find a glare-free view of the display. This is because exploration of viewing angles requires the user to move the smartphone to multiple locations, while rotating the camera line of sight to keep the display in the field of view. An additional complication is that the prototype has no way of knowing in advance which viewing angle is optimal, and can offer no feedback about which viewing direction the user should try next.

The other theme that emerged is the trade-off between incorporating additional feedback in the UI, which offers more information to the user, and the need for a simple UI. Towards the end of the formative study we modulated the "pleasant" audio tone in three possible variations to communicate the severity of estimated glare (low, medium and high), which appeared to improve the search process without unduly complicating the UI.

Finally, the participants offered useful feedback about how they wanted a mature Display Reader system to operate. Three participants said they would be willing to aim the camera at the display for 30 sec. to a minute to get a reading, but no longer. Two participants expressed privacy concerns about a Display Reader system that would send images to a sighted assistant in the cloud. One enthusiastic participant recommended that training videos be posted online; this recommendation is consistent with our observation that the training sessions we conducted were essential for enabling the participants to operate the prototype.

4. CONCLUSION

We have described formative studies with a prototype Display Reader, which is a smartphone app that guides the user to take a usable image of a display. These studies demonstrate the feasibility of our approach, and suggest that future research should focus on improving the UI and training procedures to help users explore a wider range of viewing angles. Other avenues of future research include: algorithms for glare detection and estimating the image contrast); automatic reading of the display contents; visual display enhancement for low vision users; and using visual features extracted from the image template to eliminate the need for the marker. We will test Display Reader on an ongoing basis with blind or visually impaired volunteers to maximize the system's effectiveness and ease of use during its development.

5. ACKNOWLEDGMENTS

Ladner was partially supported by the Intel Science and Technology Center on Pervasive Computing and NSF grant IIS-1116051; the other authors acknowledge support from NIH, grant 2 R01 EY018890-04, and the Dept. of Education, NIDRR grant H133E110004. David Vásquez provided extensive assistance with participant recruitment and experimental procedures.

6. REFERENCES

[1] Brady, E., Morris, M.R., Zhong, Y., White, S.C. & Bigham, J.P. "Visual Challenges in the Everyday Lives of Blind People." Proc. ACM SIGCHI Conference on Human Factors in Computing Systems (CHI 2013), Paris, France, 2013.

[2] Garrido-Jurado, S., Muñoz-Salinas, R., Madrid-Cuevas, F. J., & Marín-Jiménez, M. J. "Automatic generation and detection of highly reliable fiducial markers under occlusion." Pattern Recognition, 47(6), pp.2280-2292.

[3] Lee, P.S. & Ladner, R.E. "Homography-based Reflection Removal Specialized for Object Recognition on Mobile Platform." Demo in CVPR 2013.

[4] Morris, T., Blenkhorn, P., Crossey, L., Ngo, Q., Ross, M., Werner, D., Wong, C. "Clearspeech: a display reader for the visually handicapped." IEEE Trans Neural Syst. Rehab. Eng. Dec 2006, 14(4), pp.492-500.

[5] Rasines, I., Iriondo, P. and Díez, I. "Real-Time Display Recognition System for Visually Impaired." Int'l Conf. on Computers Helping People with Special Needs (ICCHP '12). Linz, Austria, July 2012.

[6] Tekin, E., Coughlan, J. & Shen, H. "Real-Time Detection and Reading of LED/LCD Displays for Visually Impaired Persons." IEEE Workshop on Applications of Computer Vision (WACV 2011). Kona, HI, Jan. 2011.

[7] Vázquez, M. & Steinfeld, A. "Helping visually impaired users properly aim a camera." Proceedings of the 14th Intl. ACM SIGACCESS Conf. on Computers and Accessibility, (ASSETS '12), Boulder, CO, 2012, pp.95-102.

Visually Impaired Orientation Techniques in Unfamiliar Indoor Environments: A User Study

Abdulrhman A. Alkhanifer
Computing and Information Science Program
Rochester Institute of Technology
Rochester, NY, USA 14623.
akhnaifer@mail.rit.edu

Stephanie Ludi
Software Engineering Department
Rochester Institute of Technology
Rochester, NY, USA 14623.
salvse@rit.edu

ABSTRACT

Individuals who are visually impaired encounter a number of challenges when attempting to orientate their own position or the position of others in relation to them within an unfamiliar indoor environment. To design an orientation assistive technology, it is crucial to understand the factors that reduce the user's sense of orientation. In this work, we discuss the disorientation factors that resulted from three user studies, which were conducted to formulate the basic requirements for an orientation assistive technology to assist visually impaired individuals in unfamiliar indoor areas. Using the feedback we elicited from one survey and two interview studies, we shed light on the factors that reduce the user's sense of orientation in unfamiliar buildings such as noise and traffic levels.

Categories and Subject Descriptors

H.5.2 **[User Interfaces]**: *User-centered design*; H.1.2 **[User/Machine Systems]**: *Human factors*; K.4.2 **[Computers and Society]** *Social issues – Assistive technologies for persons with disabilities*.

Keywords

User study; visual impairment; orientation assistive technology; and indoor navigation.

1. INTRODUCTION

Situational awareness can be explained as the user's understanding of an environment and its changing factors as well as the ability to predict future changes in the environment [4]. Developing situational awareness within environments can be challenging for individuals with visual impairments, particularly in unfamiliar environments. This challenge can be greater in unfamiliar indoor environments that are changing constantly as well as in environments where obtaining auditory and tactile cues are difficult. In our previous paper [1], we highlighted our goal of developing a user interface to support assistive technology to aid target users with the non-visual cues needed for orientation and situational awareness. Toward our goal, we have conducted three user studies to realize user needs and experiences, as well as to elicit initial requirements that can guide our design process [2]. This short paper will focus on the factors that affect the

orientation of individuals with visual impairments when orienting in unfamiliar indoor environments. Using feedback from 95 participants in three different studies, we will shed light on factors and concerns that relate to the visually impaired individual's orientation in unfamiliar indoor open spaces, such as atriums, with the long term goal of developing a system to support the users.

2. RELATED WORK

In literature, numbers of researchers have discussed issues that relate to orientation of individuals who are visually impaired, in both indoor and outdoor environments. Many works such as [3],[6] discuss such issues with a focus on eliciting requirements to build an indoor orientation aid. While such work facilitates many issues that relate to indoor orientation, none have discussed factors that affect individuals' orientation indoors. In the research highlighted in this paper, we have investigated the strategies used by individuals who are visually impaired to orient position and to gain situational awareness in any unfamiliar indoor open space. This includes developing an understanding of their location in relation to different important landmarks.

3. USER STUDIES

We performed a series of three studies, with a view to identify the appropriate cues to support situational awareness and orientation among individuals who are visually impaired. These include (1) a domain understanding study, (2) Orientation and Mobility (O&M) recommendations, and (3) a user survey. Two of our user studies – domain understanding and O&M recommendations – were presented in the form of semi-structured interviews, while the third study was a validation study in the form of an online survey. Table 1 illustrates key facts about each of our user studies. To analyze our results, we applied the following qualitative techniques: content analysis [5] and open coding method that is a part of the grounded theory method [8]. All studies received ethical approval from the university's IRB.

4. KEY FINDINGS

We have collated our studies' results due to the relevance between the three studies. Key findings from our studies relate to the disorientation factors that affect individuals with visual impairments' orientation in unfamiliar indoor environments as well as referencing landmarks.

Maintaining a good orientation in unfamiliar indoor open spaces requires the performance of orientation techniques as well as attention to certain cues in the environment. In our studies, we discussed with our participants the aspects that help individuals with visual impairments to orient themselves in unfamiliar indoor spaces. In this section, we will discuss some important aspects that were reported in our studies.

Table 1. User studies' details

No.	Study	Study's Information
1	Domain	• N= 24 • 10 males and 14 females • Mean age =49.2 y (SD = 14.8) • Criteria: Adult, VI, cane or guide-dog user
2	O&M	• N= 6 • 3 male and 3 female • Mean age= 50 y (SD= 11.9) • Criteria: Certified O&M instructor
3	Survey	• N= 65 • 31 female, 32 male, and 2 did not answer • Mean age= 53.26 y (SD=11.29) • Criteria: Adult, VI, able to walk unassisted and not hard of hearing or deaf

4.1 Disorientation factors

To understand the challenges faced in the orientation process, we used our previous interview results (studies 1 and 2) as a basis for formulating questions in our online survey (study 3). We coded the *disorientation factors* that were provided by our participants as the following:

- Noise/traffic level
- Physical barriers that block landmarks
- Unavailability of braille signs
- Lack of availability of human help
- Human interference in the discovery process
- Lack of consistent building layout
- Large and empty open spaces
- Lighting levels

Generally, the absence of information sources such as braille signs and human help can lead to disorientation. High noise caused by high pedestrian traffic or a noise source can interfere with individuals' ability to listen for auditory cues in the environment, as vital cues may be masked. Also, inconsistent atrium shapes, and embargoed reception desks behind walls can cause disorientation. The absence of landmarks in an indoor open space can also be a barrier to gaining a good orientation. Bright lights may distract low vision individuals and generate disorientation.

4.2 Referencing landmarks

To present landmark information to individuals with visual impairments, it is important to understand the way that landmarks are referenced. In our interviews, the O&M instructors indicated two types of referencing systems that can be used by the individuals with visual impairments when navigating indoors: clock-positioning and cardinal systems. O&M instructors told us that the clock-positioning system is preferred for indoor environments, as apposed to the cardinal system for outdoor environments; however, the cardinal system can be helpful in both environments. Thus, we used O&M instructors' feedback to formulate questions for our online survey participants. We asked them about their preferred method to reference landmarks while indoors. We investigated four different systems: clock positioning, angle or degree, cardinal, and relative systems. Our questions' results indicate that clock-positioning system is the preferred referencing system among our sample by 54%. In clock-positioning method, the system refers to landmarks in the clock shape.

5. CONCLUSION AND FUTURE WORK

Individuals with visual impairments face many challenges when traveling in unfamiliar indoor environments. In this work, we briefly discussed key findings that we gained from three user studies that were conducted to guide our design for a situation-awareness-based orientation assistive technology that will support individuals with visual impairments when exploring unfamiliar open indoor spaces. Our results show the disorientation factors that affect individuals with visual impairments' orientation. Paying attention to those factors when designing an assistive technology can help in enhancing users' orientation.

Our next step is to start the design process. Using Participatory Design (PD) method [7], and with help from a number of target users, we will work to evolve our elicited initial design requirements as well as users' preferences. Through that stage, we will investigate the best ways to present unfamiliar open indoor space layout information. Also, prototypes will be validated with the study's participants.

6. ACKNOWLEDGMENTS

We thank all the participants and O&M instructors who dedicated their time to contribute to this research. Also, the first author would like to thank King Saud University in Riyadh, Saudi Arabia for their provided scholarship.

7. REFERENCES

[1] Alkhanifer, A. 2014. Enhancing situational awareness of indoor orientation for the visually impaired. *ACM SIGACCESS Accessibility and Computing.* 108 (Jan. 2014), 16–19.

[2] Alkhanifer, A. and Ludi, S. 2014. Towards a Situation Awareness Design to Improve Visually Impaired Orientation in Unfamiliar Buildings: Requirements Elicitation Study. *Requirements Engineering Conference (RE), 2014 22nd IEEE International* (Karlskrona, Sweden, 2014), 23–32.

[3] Banovic, N., Franz, R.L., Truong, K.N., Mankoff, J. and Dey, A.K. 2013. Uncovering information needs for independent spatial learning for users who are visually impaired. *Proceedings of the 15th International ACM SIGACCESS Conference on Computers and Accessibility - ASSETS '13* (New York, New York, USA, 2013), 1–8.

[4] Dominguez, C. 1994. Can SA be defined? *Situation Awareness: Papers and Annotated Bibliography. Interim Report No. AL/CF-TR-1994-0085.* M. Vidulich, C. Dominguez, E. Vogel, and G. Mcmillan, eds. 5–15.

[5] Lazar, J., Feng, J.H. and Hochheiser, H. 2010. *Research Methods in Human-Computer Interaction.* Wiley Publishing.

[6] Miao, M., Spindler, M. and Weber, G. 2011. Requirements of Indoor Navigation System from Blind Users. *Information Quality in e-Health SE - 48.* A. Holzinger and K.-M. Simonic, eds. Springer Berlin Heidelberg. 673–679.

[7] Muller, M.J. 2003. Participatory design: The third space in HCI. *Human-Computer Interaction Handbook.* J. Jacko and A. Sears, eds. L. Erlbaum Associates Inc. 1051–1068.

[8] Strauss, A. and Corbin, J. 2008. Basics of Qualitative Research (3rd ed.): *Techniques and Procedures for Developing Grounded Theory.* SAGE Publications, Inc.

Web Browsing Interface for People with Severe Speech and Motor Impairment in India

Tirthankar Dasgupta
Indian Institute of Technology
Kharagpur
India
tirtha@cse.iitkgp.ernet.in

Manjira Sinha
Indian Institute of Technology
Kharagpur
India
manjira@cse.iitkgp.ernet.in

Anupam Basu
Indian Institute of Technology
Kharagpur
India
anupam@cse.iitkgp.ernet.in

ABSTRACT

We present design and development of a web browser that allow easy dissemination of information through World Wide Web for people with cerebral palsy in India. Our focus user group comprises people with severe form of spastic cerebral palsy and highly restricted motor movement skills. Throughout the development process we have interacted with the target users to understand their requirements and to get design advises. The browser is augmented with an intelligent auto-scanning mechanism through which the web contents and browser GUI controls can be accessed with less time and effort. We have field tested the browser with the target users where preliminary evaluation results suggests that the proposed browser is quite effective in terms of task execution time, cognitive effort and overall usability.

Categories and Subject Descriptors

K.4.2 [**Social Issues**]: Assistive technologies for persons with disabilities; H.1.2 [**User/Machine Systems**]: Human factors

Keywords

Web Browser; Cerebral Palsy; Web Content Scanning; India

1. INTRODUCTION

People with severe speech and motor impairment(SSMI) are, to a great extent, disconnected from the vast source of information available throughout the World Wide Web (WWW)[3]. This is primarily due to the difficulty experienced by them in communicating through traditional methods like keyboard, mouse. There is a dearth of quality accessible devices that facilitates web access for persons with dexerity and speech disability; further, they are too expensive for an average user from developing countries like India, where disability issues are still not the frontrunners in popular policy making decisions and social support system for

such group has not yet been effectively developed. Therefore, the aim of this paper is to design and develop a new web browsing interface that can be used by people with SSMI for accessing the WWW with a specific focus towards Indian context.

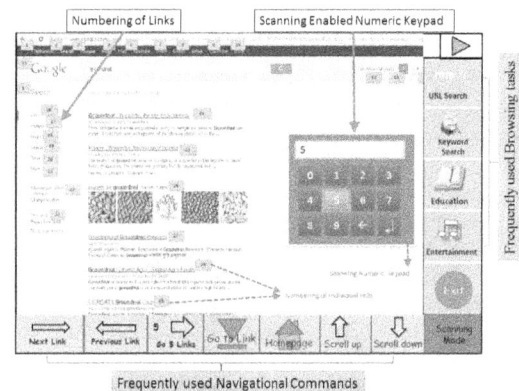

Figure 1: **Illustration of the browsing interface**

2. INTERACTING WITH THE USERS

We have interacted with individuals with SSMI along with their parents and instructors from Indian Institute of Cerebral Palsy(IICP), Kolkata, India. Through this process we have collected their requirement specifications, designed the interface and developed an initial prototype, and consulted them for further implementation;in this way the system has been finalized. We have identified the reasons behind the failure of the existing tools and technologies in penetrating the Indian population and our findings are a) most of the present devices need to be imported, hence, there is a issue of lack of local support and maintenance, b)The existing systems are too costly for average Indian users; for instance, some of these systems like, E-Z Keys [1], and Gyro-HeadMouse costs around $1495 [2]. As a result of this, our target users prefers the special access switch enabled scanning techniques as, they are cheap, locally manufactured thus, readily available, require less maintenance and very much familiar in India.

Our inquiry regarding accessibility of the browser interface revealed that almost all of the target users face difficulty in accessing web pages due to: a) unavailability of proper assistive interfaces, b)The existing tools assumes a limited ability of the user to access mouse and keyboard devices, c) practically very few web-pages are designed adhering to the accessibility guidelines, d) The keyboard shortcuts are

Tasks	t_{trad}(in sec.)	t_{new}(in sec.)
Go to the next page	24	16
Bookmark a page	44	32
Open the 7th page of bookmark	48	42
Scroll up/down the page	30	28
Open *google* & search for *bike*	180	83
Search/Play/Stop a song *anthahin*	143	23

Table 1: **Comparing TET of t_{trad}, and t_{new} for a sample set of tasks**

difficult to perform as it often require simultaneous pressing of multiple keys (Ctrl+h to open browser history), e) to select from the numerous links present in a web page one needs to keep on pressing the *tab* button until the desire link is reached, moreover, skipping a goal link by mistake requires to traverse the whole page again, this increases the chance of failure and subsequently user disappointments. In addition, almost all the existing systems suffer from the issue of portability as they are mainly developed for desktop PC and thus, cannot be mounted on a wheelchairs.

3. SYSTEM DESCRIPTION

The browser has got a number of salient features: a)The browser GUI is divided into three pannel, the browsing window, the frequently used navigational and browsing tasks (refer to Fig. 1). It is also integrated with an automatic scanning mechanism [5] for access and navigation through web pages. The system seamlessly interfaces with different types of indigenously made access switches like, burger, lip, and paddle switches b) An intelligent link parsing technique has been developed that makes reaching out to web contents like links, images and embedded videos easier. The link parser parses a given page in order to extract the hyperlinks and attaches an index number to each link. A user only needs to type the desired link number in a numeric virtual scanning keypad to access the link. Different intelligent techniques were used to identify important links. Those links are represented by less number of digits thus, requires less switch press to access. c) The browser provides two different text entry options: i) the predictive virtual scanning keyboard [4] and ii) a novel predictive icon based query entry scheme that generates search queries through the selection of multiple icons. AOL query logs were used to develop language models for prediction.

4. EVALUATION RESULTS

The browser has been deployed and field tasted with six participants[1] (of age group 25 to 32). The performance of the browser has been measured in terms of: a) *Task execution time* (TET) or the time required by a subject to accomplish a given task. We asked participants to perform 16 different browsing tasks for a period of 1 month using both the conventional Microsoft IE 6.0 web browser t_{trad} and our new web browser t_{new}. Response time(RT) for both the browsers and for each user were recorded and compared (refer to table 1). We observe t_{new} is less than that of t_{trad} for all the tasks. This, to some extent, implies the effectiveness of our proposed browsing techniques. b)*Error rates analysis*(ER): measures the number and the type of errors

---

[1]Gross Motor Functioning Classification System(GMFCS) and Manual Ability Classification System(MACS) level V

CP	CP1	CP-2	CP-3	CP-4	CP-5	CP-6
(a)	9	7	6	7	8	6
(b)	10	8	8	7	8	8
(c)	6	6	7	7	6	5
(d)	8	7	5	6	7	5
(e)	9	9	7	8	7	7

Table 2: Usability rating of participants

encountered performing a task. This was done by both manual inspection of the user's performance and by installing a key logger program. We found most of the errors occur due to: a) subjects fails to press the access switch when the desired control is activated and b) subjects selects a wrong element. Both of the error types are inter related as, failing to press access switch at the correct time results in wrong selection of elements. Nevertheless, as the number of evaluation session increases, the rate of making errors decreases. c) *Overall usability score:* We asked individuals to grade the proposed browser according to different usability criteria like, a) the overall impression of the browser, b) the link access technique, c)iconic keyboard, d) alphabetic keyboard and e)learnability. The grading has been done in 1-10 scale, 10 being excellent and 1 is poor. The results are reported in Table 2.

5. CONCLUSION

We present the development of an assistive web browsing interface for people with SSMI. The browser has a number of novel features like, access through special switches, an iconic query generation system, and an intelligent web content access techniques. Presently, the Desktop version of the browser has been evaluated by our target users. Results shows that the performance of our proposed browser is better than the existing techniques. However, it would be premature to conclude anything concrete based only on the current experimental results. Hence, a more rigorous testing of the system different group of participants and over a larger number of sessions is required to establish a concrete claim.

5.1 Acknowledgements

We are thankful to participants of Indian Institute of Cerebral Palsy(IICP), Kolkata helping us to conduct the evaluation of the system.

6. REFERENCES

[1] Ez keys from words+ inc. http://www.words-plus.com/website/products/soft/ezkeys.htm.

[2] www.advancedperipheral.com.

[3] D. Beukelman and P. Mirenda. Augmentative and alternative communication. 2005.

[4] G. Lesher, B. Moulton, and D. J. Higginbotham. Techniques for augmenting scanning communication. *Augmentative and Alternative Communication*, 14(2):81–101, 1998.

[5] C. E. Steriadis and P. Constantinou. Designing human-computer interfaces for quadriplegic people. *ACM Transactions on Computer-Human Interaction (TOCHI)*, 10(2):87–118, 2003.

AVD-LV: An Accessible Player for Captioned STEM Videos

Raja S. Kushalnagar, John J. Rivera, Warrance Yu and Daniel S. Steed
National Technical Institute for the Deaf at Rochester Institute of Technology
Rochester, NY 14623-5604
{rskics, jjr7497, wxy1697, dss1638}@rit.edu

ABSTRACT

The Americans with Disabilities Act requires online lecture creators to caption the videos for deaf and hard of hearing students, or for deaf and low vision (DLV) students who request these accommodations. While current captioned lecture video interfaces are usually accessible to deaf students, it is more challenging to provide full accessibility to DLV viewers who have restricted vision, as they cannot see both the lecture and captions simultaneously. We present an enhanced interface for YouTube lectures (Accessible View Device interface for Low Vision) that provides more accessibility for DLV viewers. This interface provides the ability to pause either the video or the captions with a single key-press, so that the viewer can follow simultaneous audio and video information. This interface is available to anyone and can be used with any captioned lecture on YouTube.

Categories and Subject Descriptors

K.4.2 [**Computers and Society**]: Social Issues – Assistive Technologies for persons with disabilities.

Keywords

Deaf, Low-vision; Online video accessibility.

1. INTRODUCTION

Closed captions translate auditory information to visual text for individuals who do not get auditory information, usually for deaf, or deaf and low-vision consumers. In the United States, about 15%, i.e., 50 million use closed captions [1]. Most US television content is required to have closed captions per the Communications and Video Act 2010. Unfortunately captioned videos are not always accessible to Deaf and Low Vision (DLV) consumers some captioned videos difficult to follow.

2. Related Work

The term 'low vision' covers a broad range of vision problems that cannot be resolved by eyeglasses or contacts. Most low vision people lack either a central high resolution focus (fovea), or a wide field of view with low resolution (peripheral vision) [6]. Low-vision aids can improve either central or peripheral vision, but negatively impact the other one. For example, magnifying devices reduce the field of view of the whole presentation, while minifying devices reduce resolution of individual visuals [2,5].

Figure 1: DLV students with limited field of views have to switch focus between the video and the captions. If important visual and aural information occur simultaneously, the student will miss the information source that they were not looking at.

3. AVD-LV

While hearing consumers can watch and listen simultaneously, the transformation of audio to text requires deaf and low-vision (DLV) viewers to watch two simultaneous visual streams: the video and the audio text [4].

The DLV viewer will miss what is happening on the video. In general, this is not a problem when there is little visual information to be processed, such as when the lecturer is simply speaking. Problems arise when there are two simultaneous visuals to read or process – such as reading the slides, in addition to reading the synchronized transcript as shown in Figure 1. This is even more hard when the video has a lot of text or the content is dense, especially STEM videos [3]. We avoid this tradeoff by not using magnification or minification. Instead, we use a visual gaze management approach. Since most low vision students do not have enough field of view to see both the video view and caption view, we support their ability to focus on one view, and pause the other view.

3.1 Browser Interface

We developed a Chrome Application that can be downloaded and used to view YouTube videos. Consumers can use the application from any computer, anytime and anywhere with minimal set up. This approach also allows us to extend the interface to adapt to multiple caption and transcript standards on the web, unlike TV captioning. Now, most closed caption interfaces for web videos fetch separate caption information and display it via a browser plugins (e.g., Flash and QuickTime) or through built-in browser video functionality. This makes it straightforward to fetch the caption file and display it either as a synchronized transcript (many lines of text that represent several seconds of audio), and as captions (1-2 lines representing 0.5 to 1 second of audio). We include the ability to show both, due to the fact that while transcripts show more information, they can be harder to read because they are further away from the video. Conversely, the captions are easier to read since they are always shown in the same spot and are closer to the video, but the displayed information is shown for a shorter amount of time.

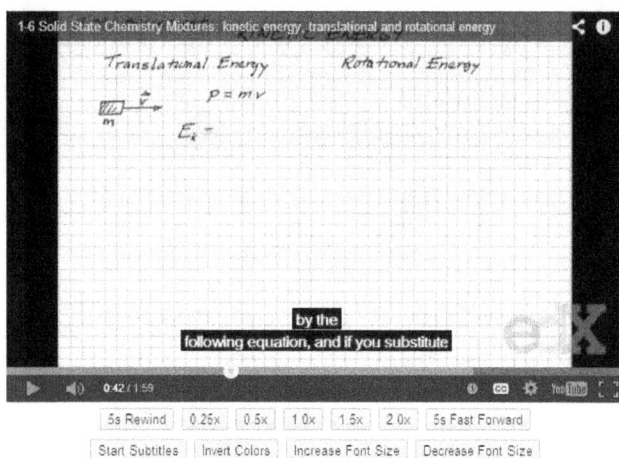

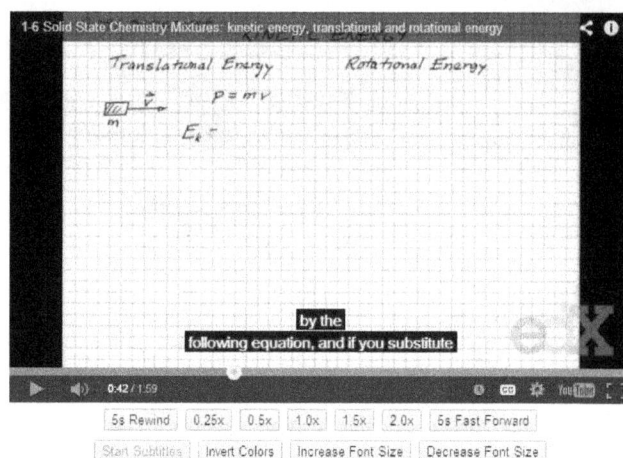

gy. Translational energy is just like what it

ie course, translational energy and rotational

1 is the idea of kinetic energy. We'll use two different ty

Figure 2: There was little new visual information, so the viewer is able to alternate between the video explanation and the captions. The viewer has not clicked on the video to pause, but should soon press pause, as the lecturer will simultaneously explain the equation while writing it on screen.

Figure 3: The viewer paused the video, in order to read the next few seconds of the transcript. Once the viewer finishes reading the transcript, the viewer resumes the video at a faster rate (e.g., 2x) to catch up with the lecture.

3.2 Enhanced Text and Video Interfaces

Since the DLV viewers alternate between reading the text and watching the video, We enhanced the interface to support DLV viewers with the following functions: 1) increase text readability through inverting colors and increasing font size through button clicks, and 2) to simultaneously display transcript and captions, and to freeze one or the other, as shown in Figure 3.

In Figure 4, the viewer has magnified the transcript text and is reading it after freezing the video by clicking on it. The click also displays a highlight on the video to support the viewer's rapid restart their watching or reading process in the video. When they resume watching the video, they can play the video at a faster rate, until the video has caught up. Another advantage of reading the transcript is that the viewer is less likely to lose context. For example, the latest line of captions may look like this:

and sugar for taste.

This would seem, from simply reading this one line, nonsensical. However, when the whole transcript line is bookmarked at the prior line, it reads as follows:

Then we add some cinnamon
and sugar for taste.

This example shows how the DLV viewer is able to switch views and use bookmarks to reduce the chance of losing context.

4. Conclusion

The AVD-LV application can support a DLV student's viewing of complex visuals as they read the aural-to-visual translation. The application allows the viewer to focus on the captions or video when there is miniscule simultaneous overlap. When the overlap is significant, the viewers are able to alternate between the views through pausing one of the views, usually the transcript.

They can bookmark before they switch, which eliminates search time and the student can rapidly switch between visuals. The student can magnify the text and adjust contrast as needed. The platform is scalable as it extends existing browser interfaces for DLV consumer's use. The larger project focuses on both deaf and low vision students. The user interface development for low vision students is an on-ongoing project with low vision students.

5. ACKNOWLEDGMENTS

This work is supported in part by NSF-IIS 1218056, and two associated REU supplements, and two University of Washington AccessComputing grants to support a REU internship and a co-op.

6. REFERENCES

1. Chao, G. *The State of Closed Captioning Services in the United States*. 2003.

2. Hayden, D.S., Zhou, L., Astrauskas, M.J., and Black, J.A. Note-taker 2.0. *Proceedings of the 12th international ACM SIGACCESS conference on Computers and accessibility - ASSETS '10*, ACM Press (2010), 131–137.

3. Kushalnagar, R.S., Lasecki, W.S., and Bigham, J.P. Captions Versus Transcripts for Online Video Content. *10th International Cross-Discliplinary Conference on Web Accessibility (W4A)*, ACM Press (2013), 1–4.

4. Kushalnagar, R.S., Lasecki, W.S., and Bigham, J.P. Accessibility Evaluation of Classroom Captions. *ACM Transactions on Accessible Computing 5*, 3 (2014), 1–24.

5. Peli, E. Vision multiplexing: an engineering approach to vision rehabilitation device development. *Optometry & Vision Science 78*, 5 (2001), 304–315.

6. Peli, E. Vision multiplexing: an optical engineering concept for low-vision aids. *Proceedings of SPIE*, SPIE (2007), 66670C.

Building Keyboard Accessible Drag and Drop

Rucha Somani[1], Jiahang Xin[2], Bijay Bhaskar Deo[3], Yun Huang[4]

School of Information Studies[1,4], LC Smith College of Engineering and Computer Science[2,3]

Syracuse University, NY

rasomani[1], jxin[2], bbdeo[3], yhuang[4]@syr.edu

ABSTRACT

Drag and Drop (DnD) web design has been widely used by E-learning systems. However, it may take a lot of effort for web developers who have limited knowledge of web accessibility to build complex keyboard accessible DnD components. In this demo, we present our conceptual design of keyboard accessible DnD, and explain how web developers can leverage the design to implement their own pages. We further discuss how to extend this design to enable different DnD scenarios.

General Terms

Web Accessibility; Software API

Keywords

Keyboard Accessible; Screen Reader; Drag and Drop.

1. INTRODUCTION

When developing an E-learning website that teaches classification of objects, e.g. animals [1], web developers often need to implement Drag and Drop (DnD) interactive components that the students can use to classify certain objects into categories. If web developers are not aware of web accessibility issues, these pages may not be accessible to students who mainly use keyboard and screen readers to navigate websites. To reduce the technical barrier of implementing complex DnD components, we developed an API that the web developers can use to create DnD environment quickly.

2. KEYBOARD ACCESSIBLE DnD

We first show one demo of a DnD design, and then explain how to leverage the design to create other DnD web products.

2.1 Demo

Figure 1 shows the demo [2] developed using our API. In this demo, users will practice picking the pink items (e.g. "January", "Sunday" etc) on the left and dropping them to the correct zones (e.g. Days and Months) on the right. Users can use keyboard to access the button and elements by pressing the tab key.

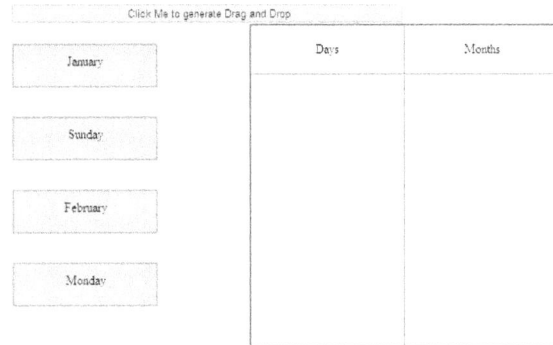

Figure 1. The demo scenario [2]

Upon clicking the "Click Me to generate Drag and Drop" button, the website pops up a window as shown in Figure 2. The texts within the window will be read by screen reader, which helps users to perform DnD tasks. At this moment, DnD is enabled and the page elements are keyboard accessible. In this demo, we install ChromeVox [4] as the screen reader.

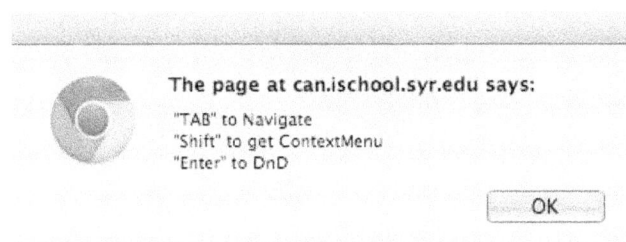

Figure 2. Pop up window

After activating the DnD function, users can traverse the drag items by using the tab key. When selecting one element, users can press the Context Menu Button to invoke the menu, as shown in Figure 3. If Context Menu button is not available, using Shift key can invoke the menu too.

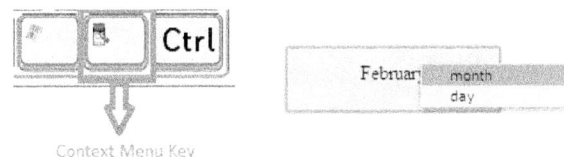

Figure 3. Context Menu Button and the Context Menu

This menu lists the zones that where the selected drag item can be dropped to, and it can be traversed using up and down arrow keys or tab key. Selecting desired value (e.g. the "month" zone in Figure 3) and pressing Enter key will drop the drag item to the drop zone. Once a correct drop is made, a confirmation message window is popped up for the user to confirm the correct action, as shown in Figure 4.

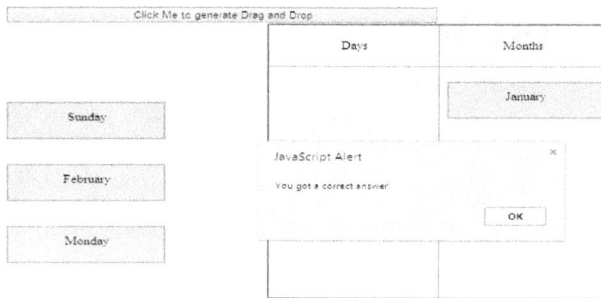

Figure 4. A correct "drag" action

2.2 Design

We developed the DnD according to WCAG guidelines, and our DnD specifications can pass the WCAG 2.0 check [3]. More specifically, we specify that all drag items should be reached by using Tab key and take the advantage of screen reader. Once screen reader reaches the bounding box of the drag items, it should read description about the entire activity and also how to use the DnD action through keyboard. Once a drag item is focused, the screen reader should read out descriptive text about the drag item. Items can be only "dragged and dropped" to the right zone. Meanwhile, to make DnD more user-friendly, any drop attempt here will receive a confirmation message regarding if this is a correct action or not.

To implement this design, web developers have to create elements to be dragged and drop zones, where the elements can be dropped. In our demo, drag items (e.g. "January") are <div> elements, and drop zones (e.g. "Days") are <th> elements within <table > tag. In fact, they can be <div> elements as well.

```
var obj= new Object();
        obj.dragId="dragitem1";   // should contain <div> id
        obj.dropTarget="drop1";  // contains <div> id of the drop zone where it's supposed to drop
        obj.tabIndex=1;  // to control navigation sequence
arrDrags[0]=obj;         //-- this item  has an object. Create such items depending on the
                         //number of drag items
```

Figure 5. Populating Drag Items

Web developers can populate the array of drag items as shown in Figure 5. The drop slots can be populated in similar fashion, with different parameters. Given space limitation, we do not show the sample code.

```
obj= new Object();
        obj.accept="#dragitem2,#dragitem4";  // Comma separated list of drag item //
                                             // <div>ids to accept.
        obj.dropId="drop1";  // ID of the <div> which is supposed to be the drop zone.
arrDrops[0]=obj;
```

Figure 6. Associating Drag Items with Drop Zones

Then web developers need to define the rules where the drag items can be dropped. Figure 6 shows one example of associating two drag items with one zone. Finally, calling a function provided by our design [5] can make the web components keyboard accessible.

Our current design allows web developers to define as many number of drag items as possible. After the developers define drag elements, they can associate the drag elements with drop zones using the function provided by us. Our program takes the configuration information, binds the elements together and makes them keyboard accessible. This helps the developer focus on defining the content of their pages, instead of worrying about the accessibility issue from end user prospective. In the meantime, the proposed solution is a Javascript/JQuery program, which provides flexibility such that the web developer has full control over how the DnD functions.

In this demo and design, we address keyboard accessibility issues. In order to support assistive technologies, web developers need to follow W3C Recommendation and implement WAI-ARIA [6] semantics in the code as well. In particular, developers should add "aria-grabbed" attribute when defining every drag item and add "aria-dropeffect" attribute when defining every drop zone, as well as make sure the values of the two attributes are set appropriately. Some examples are presented in Figure 7.

```
document.getElementById(arrDrags[i].dragId).setAttribute('aria-grabbed', 'true');
var objDI=$(options.selector);
document.getElementById(objDI.data("target")).setAttribute('aria-dropeffect','move');
```

Figure 7. Adding WAI-ARIA attributes

3. FUTURE WORK

We are extending the API to allow customization of the number of correct drop zones for a single drag item. We also plan to create a test framework for auto-checking and fixing. For example, it can detect the absence of WAI-ARIA and add corresponding attributes automatically. A conceptual design of Rich Internet Applications (RIAs) accessibility evaluation tool provided us a great source of reference [7].

4. ACKNOWLEDGMENTS

This paper is based upon work developed under a Sub-recipient Agreement that is sponsored by the US Department of Education, Award Number H33A130057. Any opinions, findings, conclusions or recommendations expressed herein are those of the author(s) and do not necessarily reflect the views of the United States Department of Education or Carnegie Mellon University.

5.REFERENCES

[1] Kids' Educational Apps
    http://www.kidseducationalapps.com/tag/drag-and-drop/

[2] Link to the Drag and Drop Demo
http://can.ischool.syr.edu/DnDAccessible/

[3] W3C recommendations of WCAG 2.0:
    http://www.w3.org/TR/WCAG20/

[4] ChromeVox Screen Reader for Chrome
    http://www.chromevox.com

[5] DnD Context Menu Function
http://can.ischool.syr.edu/DnDAccessible/common/contextMenu.js

[6] Accessible Rich Internet Applications (WAI-ARIA) 1.0, W3C Recommendation 20 March 2014.
http://www.w3.org/TR/wai-aria/

[7] Iyad Abu Doush, Faisal Alkhateeb, **The Design of RIA Accessibility Evaluation Tool.** Advances in Engineering Software 03/2013; 57:1-7

Coming to Grips:
3D Printing for Accessibility

Erin Buehler, Amy Hurst
University of Maryland, Baltimore County
Information Systems Department
{eri4, amyhurst}@umbc.edu

Megan Hofmann
Colorado State University, Fort Collins
Computer Science Department
hofmann.megan@gmail.com

ABSTRACT

In this demonstration, we discuss a case study involving a student with limited hand motor ability and the process of exploring consumer grade, Do-It-Yourself (DIY) technology in order to create a viable assistive solution. This paper extends our previous research into DIY tools in special education settings [1] and presents the development of a unique tool, GripFab, for creating 3D-printed custom handgrips. We offer a description of the design process for a handgrip, explain the motivation behind the creation of GripFab, and explain current and planned features of this tool.

Categories and Subject Descriptors

K.4.2 [**Computers and Society**]: Social Issues – *Assistive technologies for persons with disabilities*

General Terms

Design; Human Factors.

Keywords

3D Printing; Assistive Technology; Children; Digital Fabrication; Developmental Disability; Motor Impairment; Rapid Prototyping; Special Education

1. INTRODUCTION

Historically, assistive devices and custom accessibility solutions have been costly and offered little in the way of selection. With the "maker" movement, a resurgence of the Do-It-Yourself (DIY) culture, there is an opportunity to create individualized and low-cost assistive technology (AT) solutions and to empower end-users to create those solutions themselves. Our current research has explored the role of making in special education by introducing 3D printing to students with cognitive and developmental disabilities [1]. In working with students, faculty, and support staff at a special education facility, we have identified several uses for 3D printing in this setting, including Science Technology Engineering and Math (STEM) encouragement and employability skills for students, tactile objects to promote accessible education, and a means to create assistive aides and AT-friendly modifications to existing technologies. In this paper, we discuss an example of a 3D-printed assistive aide created in collaboration with occupational therapists at this site.

As part of a 6-month long study evaluating 3D printing at the investigation site, we spoke with two occupational therapists

ASSETS '14, Oct 20-22 2014, Rochester, NY, USA
ACM 978-1-4503-2720-6/14/10.
http://dx.doi.org/10.1145/2661334.2661345

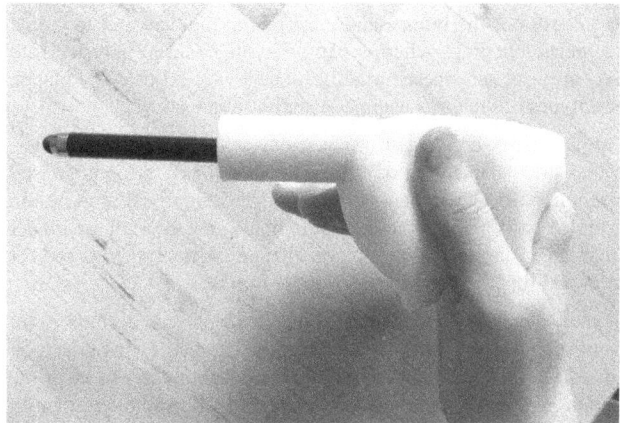

Figure 1. A custom 3D-printed grip designed to hold a stylus.

(OTs) about the accessibility needs of the students on campus. We worked with these OTs to develop a specialized stylus grip for a student with motor impairments who was not able to hold writing implements unassisted. This paper presents the design process we embarked on with the therapists, reflects on obstacles, and introduces GripFab, a simple software interface for generating specialized 3D-printable handgrips to assist in holding various objects. We believe tools like GripFab can empower persons with disabilities and other users to create functional assistive devices with entry-level DIY technologies.

2. DESIGN PROCESS

During our 6-month evaluation of a special education facility, we spent 2 months working with OTs on a project for a student with limited grasping capability that was negatively impacting the student's ability to write and use the iPad. We developed a set of requirements and conducted a series of iterative prototyping sessions to arrive at a 3D printed solution to this challenge.

2.1 Gathering Requirements

We interviewed two OTs who regularly administer therapy sessions with this student about their prior unsuccessful explorations helping this student access an iPad using off-the-shelf products. They found the cushioned pen grips and ergonomic styluses were designed to provide support and comfort to a person without a motor impairment rather than to supplement a person with reduced hand strength and a different gripping position. They also described the different methods they used to create workarounds with common crafting supplies such as tape, cardboard, and air-dry clay. These DIY solutions were not uncommon in their work, but the OTs stated that they were not durable and frequently failed after repeated handling.

2.2 Prototyping and Iteration

Based on the therapists' previous explorations with off-the-shelf solutions and crafting, we suggested utilizing 3D scanning technology to transform their ephemeral modifications into a more permanent 3D-printed object. The OTs created three air-dry clay models of the student's hand and unique grip. Two of the designs featured a cuff-like ring fitted to the student's thumb for support and the third was a small wedge intended to augment the stylus similar to a traditional soft pencil grip. We scanned all three designs with the Makerbot Digitizer. The Digitizer creates a 3D model, stored as a stereolithography (.stl) file, for use with CAD software. We then took the models and performed minimal edits to smooth out the bumps and cracks from the clay and to create geometric openings where a pen or stylus could be inserted into the grip. After these modifications, we 3D-printed plastic prototypes of the grips using a Makerbot Replicator 2x.

The therapists conducted test sessions with their student to see which grip shape worked best. The thumb-cuff designs caused discomfort for the student and the wedge design proved to be too tiring to hold, and so the therapists opted to create a new model from clay. This second model was again digitized by us, edited for form and function, and then 3D-printed for testing.

In the second evaluation, the new grip shape was deemed more comfortable (see Figure 1). Instead of using a cuff, this grip took advantage of the student's resting grasp enabling her to keep the grip in her hand without discomfort yet still allowed the student to press down firmly for writing or making selections on an iPad. This new shape was successful in the short-term, but after extended use the therapists made note of new challenges.

After building our first successful prototype, the therapists wanted to replace the generic stylus that the student had been using with a more responsive, slightly thicker one. The therapists also stated that even though the grip was comfortable, the way the stylus was held in place within the grip forced the student to stretch forward to reach her writing surface. Based on these new criteria, we modified the grip to accommodate the larger stylus and we extended the front of the grip so the stylus would protrude further forward. Instead of reverting to a new clay model, we utilized basic CAD tools to adjust the diameter and length of the stylus insertion point on the existing .stl file.

The revised grip design was 3D-printed and delivered to the therapists for testing. The final version of the grip was tested by the therapists with the student and is functioning correctly. The student now has a highly individualized grip made from a sturdy material that can be reprinted or modified with relative ease.

3. TOOL DEVELOPMENT

In evaluating the stylus grip design process, we noted that there were very few if any steps that required expert understanding of engineering or CAD tools. The biggest barrier to the OTs completing this project on their own was the time and lack of training. The therapists felt that they could master novice design software, but they simply did not have room in their schedules to learn the processes and spend extra time on the 3D model revisions that we provided for them. OTs and other faculty at the investigation site also commented that they would be keen to use a design repository similar to Thingiverse.com, but with content and privacy settings specific to their professional needs. A catalog of existing AT designs would be beneficial, but this would still leave much of the customization up to the OTs.

Based on the success and generalizability of this project, we are developing a tool to automatically generate grips similar to this one, but with an automated design process. We believe this is possible without creating a custom clay model for each person's hand because the grip prototype has been well received by a wide variety of users with diverse hand shapes and gripping abilities.

One of our design goals for this software is to obscure the complexity of the design process from therapists and even end users, so end users could potentially print their own custom grip. We have begun developing GripFab (see Figure 2), a software tool that enables the user to select a basic grip model, scale or mirror it to fit in the desired hand, and then choose from a variety of possible attachments. In our case study, for example, the therapists needed to be able to fit a different size of stylus. GripFab would provide the therapists with the ability to supply the stylus dimensions and then automatically adjust the base model of the grip to accommodate. Behind the scenes, GripFab accepts user-defined measurements and preset grip positions that it processes with OpenSCAD to generate a customized .stl file. The output file can be printed directly without editing. The program can rapidly alter a 3D model as the user presents new needs.

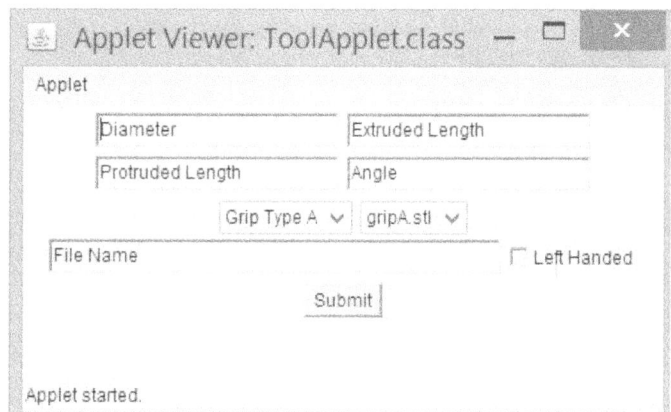

Figure 2. Screenshot of a prototype interface for GripFab.

4. CONCLUSIONS AND FUTURE WORK

We are continuing to develop GripFab and hope to test it with therapists at our original investigation site and other locations. At the time of this writing, the software offers one grip style based on our original grip project, but we intend to explore other generalizable grip postures common to hand/motor impairments. Additionally, we are expanding on the attachments that the program can generate. One example of an alternative attachment might be a grip with a slot for a fork for a modified eating apparatus. With continued testing, we would like to see end-users able to find, modify, and print an assistive grip for themselves without assistance.

5. ACKNOWLEDGMENTS

We would like to thank all of our participants. This material is based on work supported by the National Science Foundation under Grant No. EEEC-0540865.

6. REFERENCES

[1] Buehler, E., Kane, S.K., and Hurst, A. (2014). ABC and 3D: Opportunities and Obstacles to 3D Printing in Special Education Environments. (*ASSETS'14*).

Evaluation of Non-Visual Panning operations using Touch-Screen Devices

HariPrasath Palani
School of Computing and Information Science
University of Maine,
5711 Boardman Hall, Orono, Maine, USA 04469
hariprasath.palani@maine.edu

Nicholas A. Giudice
School of Computing and Information Science
University of Maine,
5711 Boardman Hall, Orono, Maine, USA 04469
nicholas.giudice@maine.edu

ABSTRACT

This paper summarizes the implementation, evaluation, and usability of non-visual panning operations for accessing graphics rendered on touch screen devices. Four novel non-visual panning techniques were implemented and experimentally evaluated on our experimental prototype, called a Vibro-Audio Interface (VAI), which provides completely non-visual access to graphical information using vibration, audio, and kinesthetic cues on a commercial touch screen device. This demonstration will provide an overview of our system's functionalities and will discuss the necessity for developing non-visual panning operations enabling visually-impaired people access to large-format graphics (such as maps and floor plans).

Categories and Subject Descriptors

H.5.2 [**User Interfaces**]: Haptic I/O, Auditory (non-speech) feedback, Evaluation/methodology; H.5.4 [**Hypertext/ Hypermedia**]: Navigation; K.4.2 [**Social Issues**]: Assistive technologies for persons with disabilities

Keywords

Accessibility (blind and visually-impaired); Assistive Technology; Touch-screens; Haptic cues; Auditory Cues; Vibro-Audio Interface; non-visual maps.

1. INTRODUCTION

An increasing amount of information content used in the workplace, educational settings, and for everyday living is presented in graphical form. However, the visual nature of this graphical material prevents numerous visually-impaired users from accessing this key information. Although several approaches have been advanced for providing non-visual access to graphical material, they are often very expensive and have not experienced broad market penetration or end-user acceptance. As this demographic is estimated to number around 285 million people worldwide [11], the need for developing devices that are both affordable and usable for accessing non-visual graphics is critical for educational, social, and vocational purposes. With the advent and proliferation of touch-screen devices (such as smartphones), several R&D projects have focused on developing touch based

accessibility solutions. Most of these solutions involve incorporation of vibro-tactile and/or auditory feedback to convey patterns on the touch-screen. However, these solutions are generally used for research purposes, meaning that they are not commercially available. Also, many of these R&D efforts emphasize technical design features and algorithms as opposed to empirical experiments and behavioral evaluations [1, 6, 8]. In addition, touch has a very coarse spatial resolution when compared to vision [2, 4], which causes restrictions in translating visual representations to tactile representations. These shortcomings have led to a huge information gap in accessing graphical information for visually-impaired persons. To bridge this gap, the tactile representation should be as functionally equivalent as possible with the visual representation by maintaining the spatial and geometric properties of the original rendering. We addressed these issues in our earlier work [1, 6] by developing and evaluating a novel touch-screen based interface called a Vibro-Audio Interface (VAI). VAI was developed based on empirical results and usability guidelines derived from human behavioral evaluations [8]. Findings from these experiments provided strong evidence that the VAI is a viable solution for accurate learning of graphical materials on touch-screen devices.

2. NON-VISUAL PANNING

One limitation of commercial touch-screen devices is their limited display size. This necessitates the use of panning operations to access large-format graphics. Use of panning is common for visually-rendered material on portable devices, or even on standard computer monitors. However, this action is not generally done with tactile graphics, which are usually rendered statically on hardcopy tactile output or fixed-format digital displays. Even with approaches that have used dynamic haptic displays and touch screens, non-visual panning has not been widely studied [7, 9, 10]. In order to access large-format graphics, it is necessary to incorporate panning operations for both visual and non-visual interfaces. The need for panning is particularly critical in tactile interfaces owing to the lower spatial resolution of touch and the limited information density of dynamic-tactile displays. For instance, consider a 7 inch touch-screen device (~170 ppi resolution). A visual interface could render ~776 vertical lines of width at 0.116 mm (width that can be perceived by the naked eye at a viewing distance of ~400 mm) on this display real estate. By contrast, the optimal line width for perceiving vibro-tactile lines on a touchscreen is 0.35inch (8.89 mm) [1, 8]. This means that for the same screen size, only 10 tactile lines could be rendered, a reduction of information of over 7 orders of magnitude. Because of this huge difference in spatial resolution, it frequently requires multiple displays of information using a non-visual interface to convey the same content of a single visual display. Thus, effectively incorporating panning operations are crucial for any touch-screen based interfaces using vibro-tactile cuing.

3. EXPERIMENTAL EVALUATION

With visual interfaces (such as Google maps), panning is a default feature and sighted users can perform panning operations in many ways, such as using drag, swipe, and other gestures. However, these techniques are almost always visually based and lead to some significant challenges when implemented in a non-visual interface. In order to conceptualize the issue, the reader is invited to try to pan a map using their map interface of choice (e.g., Google map) with their eyes closed. Once panned, the user will likely lose knowledge of their location on the map, as there is no reference between the graphical elements perceived before and after panning. By explanation, tactile perception is serially processed and has a small field of view from a given tactile sample (e.g., exploring the screen with one fingertip). By contrast, vision is highly parallel and has a large field of view (e.g., seeing the whole screen at once). As such, haptic spatial perception can be a challenging process [3, 5, 9], and unless carefully considered, incorporating additional operations such as panning will likely increase the complexity of accessing graphical materials. Based on empirical studies with the VAI [6], we identified a variety of problems that arise during haptic map learning. For instance, the smooth touch screen surface makes it difficult to stay oriented on the display while tracing graphics [6] and finger transpositions lead to misunderstanding of relationships between the graphical elements [3]. Also, finger location acts as the primary and only orienting reference on the map, which mandates the user to always remember where they are within the given graphic. Accurate orientation is a key design requirement for any tactile based non-visual interface, as it allows users to develop a reference and integrate graphical elements across time and space. This makes visual panning techniques such as swipe and drag impractical for use in tactile based non-visual interfaces as these actions cause the user to lose their reference finger location after panning. To address these problems, we developed four novel non-visual panning methods and implemented and tested them on the VAI. The panning methods involve use of either single or multi-touch actions, physical buttons (See Figure 1).

Figure 1: Sample stimuli and different panning methods on a Touch screen.

Experiments were performed on 15 sighted blindfolded participants (8 males and 7 females) between the ages of 19 and 29. Inclusion of blindfolded-sighted people is reasonable in this scenario as our focus is on testing the ability to learn and represent non-visual graphics, which are equally perceptible to both blindfolded-sighted and blind groups [6]. A total of five conditions were tested, namely, Two-finger pan, Button-touch pan, Button-Swipe pan, Grip-Tap pan and one without panning. In each condition, participants learned a corridor layout map and performed subsequent spatial testing and reconstruction tasks. The study followed a within-subject design, where a total of 10 performance measures (such as learning time, reconstruction accuracy, etc.) were measured. The performance data for each of the measures were then analyzed using repeated measures ANOVAs and paired-sample t-Tests between the conditions.

Results (see [6]) showed that incorporating panning operations that are optimized for non-visual use do not lead to any detrimental effects on the cognitive representation of the graphical material tested. Indeed, for many of the directional and reconstruction tasks, the performance accuracies with panning were found to actually be better than the control (no-pan) condition, indicating that panning may actually strengthen the learning process. Based on participants' post-test feedback, we found that there was a preference for use of the multi-touch technique to perform non-visual panning. These findings are substantial given the necessity of panning operations for access to large-format graphics on touch-based devices, especially given the lack of other solutions addressing this critical information access problem for visually-impaired people.

4. ACKNOWLEDGMENTS

We acknowledge support from NIDRR grant H133S100049 and NSF grant CHS-1425337 on this project.

5. REFERENCES

[1] Giudice, N.A., Palani H.P. et al. 2012. Learning non-visual graphical information using a touch-based vibro-audio interface. *Proceedings of the 14th international ACM SIGACCESS conference on Computers and accessibility* (New York, NY, USA, 2012), 103–110.

[2] Jones, L.A. and Lederman, S.J. 2006. *Human hand function.* Oxford University Press.

[3] Klatzky, R.L., Giudice, N.A. et al.(in press). *Touch-screen technology for the dynamic display of 2D spatial information without vision: Promise and progress.* Multisensory Research.

[4] Loomis, J.M. et al. 2012. Sensory substitution of vision: Importance of perceptual and cognitive processing. *Assistive Technology for Blindness and Low Vision*. R. Manduchi and S. Kurniawan, eds. CRC. 162–191.

[5] Loomis, J.M. et al. 1991. Similarity of Tactual and Visual Picture Recognition with Limited Field of View. *Perception.* 20 (1991), 167–177.

[6] Palani, H.P. 2013. *Making Graphical Information Accessible without Vision using Touch-Based devices.* Masters Thesis. University of Maine.

[7] Poppinga, B. et al. 2011. TouchOver Map : Audio-Tactile Exploration of Interactive Maps. *In Proceedings of the 12th international conference on Human computer interaction with mobile devices ACM, Stockholm, Sweden.* (2011), 545–550.

[8] Raja, M.K. 2011. *The development and validation of a new smartphone based non-visual spatial interface for learning indoor layouts.* Masters Thesis University of Maine.

[9] Rastogi, R. et al. 2013. Intuitive tactile zooming for graphics accessed by individuals who are blind and visually impaired. *IEEE transactions on neural systems and rehabilitation engineering : a publication of the IEEE Engineering in Medicine and Biology Society.* 21, 4 (Jul. 2013), 655–63.

[10] Su, J. et al. 2010. Timbremap: enabling the visually-impaired to use maps on touch-enabled devices. *Proceedings of the 12th international conference on Human computer interaction with mobile devices and services* (2010), 17–26.

[11] WORLD HEALTH ORGANIZATION 2011. Visual impairment and blindness Fact Sheet. *http://www.who.int/mediacentre/factsheets/fs282/en/.*

Expression: A Google Glass based Assistive Solution for Social Signal Processing

ASM Iftekhar Anam, Shahinur Alam, and Mohammed Yeasin
Department of Electrical and Computer Engineering
University of Memphis, Memphis, TN
{aanam, salam, myeasin}@memphis.edu

ABSTRACT

Assistive technology solutions can help people with disability from social isolation, depression, facilitate social interaction and enhance the quality of life. Limited access to non-verbal cues hinders the social interaction of people who are blind or visually impaired. This paper presents **Expression** — an integrated assistive solution using Google Glass. The key function of the system is to enable the user to perceive social signals during a natural face-to-face conversation. Subjective evaluation of **Expression** was performed using a five (5) point Likert Scale and was found to be excellent(4.383).

Categories and Subject Descriptors

H.5.2 [**Information Interfaces and Presentation**]: User Interfaces- *Evaluation/ methodology, User-centered design*; K.4.2 [**Computers and Society**]: Social Issues- *Assistive technologies for persons with disabilities*

General Terms

Information Interfaces and Presentation, Assistive technologies for persons with disabilities

Keywords

Wearable system; Visually Impaired; Assistive Technology; Facial and Behavioral Expression Recognition

1. INTRODUCTION

Limited or no access to nonverbal cues is a setback for people who are blind or visually impaired in understanding and managing social interactions. To facilitate social interaction, such as dyadic conversation, we propose an assistive technology solution using Google Glass. In particular, we have developed a Google Glass-based soft real-time system called **Expression**. It is designed to predict interlocutor's social signals (such as facial appearance features, behavioral expressions, and emotions) and also to provide speech feedback to the user through the ear buds.

ASSETS '14, Oct 20-22 2014, Rochester, NY, USA
ACM 978-1-4503-2720-6/14/10
http://dx.doi.org/10.1145/2661334.2661348 ...$15.00.

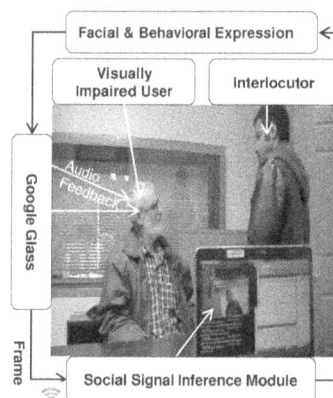

Figure 1: Expression in social interaction

A number of systems were reported in designing assistive solutions to help people who are blind and visually impaired. For example, **Dristi** [6] is a portable system designed to facilitate navigation in the indoor and outdoor environment. In [2], Krishna et al. reported a social interaction assistant to facilitate learning and recognizing faces. While these systems function well within their design constraints but are not portable and will have limited utility for everyday use.

Most closely related work to **Expression** was reported in **IMAPS** [5] — a prototype that predicts affective dimensions (valence, arousal, and dominance) in dyadic conversations. Another system called **iFEPS** [7] — is a sensory substitution system that produces auditory feedback to notify changes in facial features and expressions to the user. Both systems are implemented on a smartphone platform and have their limitations in terms of deployment (such as hanging from the neck, limited field of view, etc.). The design and implementation of the **Expression** benefited from the lessons learned in implementing both the **IMAPS** [5] and **iFEPS** [7]. A number of challenges arose due to different form factor of the Google Glass — especially the heating problem, short battery life, and bandwidth for data transmission.

2. SYSTEM DESIGN

Design and implementation of **Expression** followed the ideas from participatory design and went through a number of iterations. Figure 1 shows the system being used by a person who is blind (hence forward termed as a representative user). It consists of three main modules: (a) data communication protocol; (b) social signal inference engine; and (c) feedback system.

Data Communication Protocol: With the **Expression** application installed, it captures video stream (5 − 8 Frames per second) using the Google Glass (henceforth termed as Glass) camera and transmit it to the server. Due to limited battery life, the Glass is not suitable for continuous use in mobile applications. Moreover, the device gets overheated if the camera is used continuously. Likamawa et al. [3] investigated various use cases to quantify the power consumption and characterize temperature profile of the Glass. The alpha prototype of the **Expression** was designed only to capture and send frames to the server. That caused some delay in finding a face when the application starts. A Viola-Jones face detector [8] was incorporated to the application to address the issue. However, detecting faces in every frame significantly increased the processing time, and the device gets overheated quickly. Therefore, the face detector was used only at the start of the application to find a face and also after receiving a message of tracking failure.

Social Signal Inference Engine: This module at the server analyzes the images to detect facial features and predict nonverbal behaviors and return them to the Glass. A set of nonverbal behaviors were selected through participatory design process that are also supported by Psychology literature [1]: (a) head movements (look up/down, look left/right, tile left/right); (b) facial expressions (smile, open smile); and (c) behavioral expressions (yawn, sleepy). Face-to-face conversation data were recorded using a Glass where one of the designers acted as a user and the subjects (6 visually impaired and 14 sighted) as interlocutors. Five annotators performed frame by frame annotation of the data that were used to train the models (Fleiss' Kappa: 0.791). A rule-based classifier proposed in [5] was adopted to model the nonverbal expressions.

Feedback System: Based on a survey with the users it was concluded that speech feedback through ear-bud is the preferred mode for the **Expression**. The **Expression** does not require any training as compared to sensory substitution systems such as vOICE [4] and iFEPS [7]. The initial prototype provided continuous feedback of the spotted behavioral expressions. To avoid distraction, it was later modified to produce feedback only when there is a change in expressions. We also provide feedback to the user to move closer towards the interlocutor when the face size is smaller than 40×40.

3. EVALUATION AND DISCUSSION

Usability studies were performed with ten (10) subjects (six visually impaired and four blind-folded) to illustrate the utility of the system. The participants were asked to complete a set of usability questionnaire using a 5-point Likert scale (5 being the highest). Figure 2 shows the qualitative evaluation result. The comparatively low score of "Willing to Use" can be explained by the perceived uncertainty in social acceptance of a new device such as the Glass.

As future work, we will experiment with multi-modal feedback since one user wanted tones along with the speech feedback. According to her if she misses the speech feedback while concentrating on the conversation, tones will be helpful. We plan to increase the number of behavioral expressions and use machine learning technique to improve the robustness of the model.

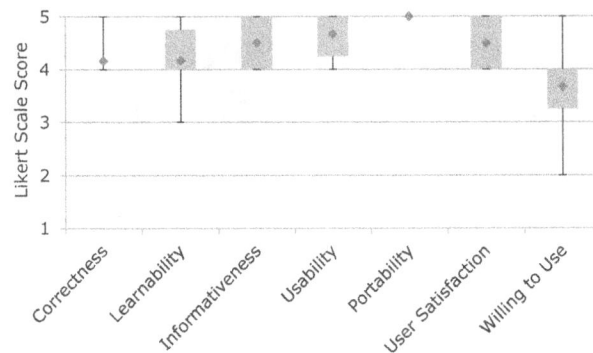

Figure 2: Qualitative Evaluation of the Expression

4. ACKNOWLEDGEMENTS

This work was partially funded by National Science Foundation (NSF–IIS-0746790), USA. Any opinions, findings, and conclusions or recommendations do not reflect the views of the funding institution.

5. REFERENCES

[1] M. Argyle, F. Alkema, and R. Gilmour. The communication of friendly and hostile attitudes by verbal and non-verbal signals. *European Journal of Social Psychology*, 1(3):385–402, 1971.

[2] S. Krishna, D. Colbry, J. Black, V. Balasubramanian, S. Panchanathan, et al. A systematic requirements analysis and development of an assistive device to enhance the social interaction of people who are blind or visually impaired. In *Workshop on Computer Vision Applications for the Visually Impaired*, 2008.

[3] R. LiKamWa, Z. Wang, A. Carroll, F. X. Lin, and L. Zhong. Draining our glass: An energy and heat characterization of google glass. *arXiv preprint arXiv:1404.1320*, 2014.

[4] P. B. Meijer. An experimental system for auditory image representations. *Biomedical Engineering, IEEE Transactions on*, 39(2):112–121, 1992.

[5] A. Rahman, M. Tanveer, A. Anam, and M. Yeasin. Imaps: A smart phone based real-time framework for prediction of affect in natural dyadic conversation. In *Visual Communications and Image Processing (VCIP), 2012 IEEE*, pages 1–6, Nov 2012.

[6] L. Ran, S. Helal, and S. Moore. Drishti: an integrated indoor/outdoor blind navigation system and service. In *Pervasive Computing and Communications, 2004. PerCom 2004. Proceedings of the Second IEEE Annual Conference on*, pages 23–30. IEEE, 2004.

[7] M. I. Tanveer, A. Anam, M. Yeasin, and M. Khan. Do you see what I see?: designing a sensory substitution device to access non-verbal modes of communication. In *Proceedings of the 15th International ACM SIGACCESS Conference on Computers and Accessibility*, page 10. ACM, 2013.

[8] P. Viola and M. J. Jones. Robust real-time face detection. *International journal of computer vision*, 57(2):137–154, 2004.

A Google Glass App to Help the Blind in Small Talk

M. Iftekhar Tanveer
ROC HCI
Computer Science
University of Rochester
itanveer@cs.rochester.edu

Mohammed E. Hoque
ROC HCI
Computer Science
University of Rochester
mehoque@cs.rochester.edu

ABSTRACT

In this paper, we present a wearable prototype that can automatically recognize affective cues such as number of people present, their age and gender distributions given an image. We customize the prototype in the context of helping people with visual impairments to better navigate social scenarios. Running an experiment to validate this technology in real life situations remains part of our future work.

Categories and Subject Descriptors

K.4.2 [**Social Issues**]: *Assistive Technologies for persons with disabilities*
H.5.1 [**Multimedia Information Systems**]: *Artificial, augmented, and virtual realities.*

General Terms

Algorithms, Design, Human Factors

Keywords

Google Glass; Face; Age; Gender; Accessibility; Blind

1. INTRODUCTION

Ever faced a situation in which you had to initiate small talk with someone you barely knew? How did you start? In a one-on-one conversation, many would commonly begin by inquiring about the weather. However, starting a conversation can be tricky when multiple people are present, as attempts to initiate small talk may be viewed as impolite or even intrusive. People with sufficient social skills are able to pick up on social cues (e.g. number of people, their age and gender distribution, choice of clothes, locations, etc.) to initiate conversation within a group. The ability to successfully launch small talk is an important social skill that may lead to meaningful discussions and new social relationships.

Now imagine someone with visual impairment initiating small talk with a random individual or a group of people. How would this impairment limit that person's social skills and his/her ability to form new relationships? In this paper, we demonstrate a wearable prototype (Google Glass) that is able to automatically sense and synthesize information about people within conversational distance using computer vision and machine learning techniques. Visually impaired individuals can take pictures of a scene by pressing a button or using the double-tap gesture. The picture is then uploaded to the cloud or to a nearby local computer to automatically analyze its content. Our current implementation of the framework allows for automated analysis of number of people present, their approximate age and gender

ASSETS '14, Oct 20-22 2014, Rochester, NY, USA
ACM 978-1-4503-2720-6/14/10.
http://dx.doi.org/10.1145/2661334.2661338

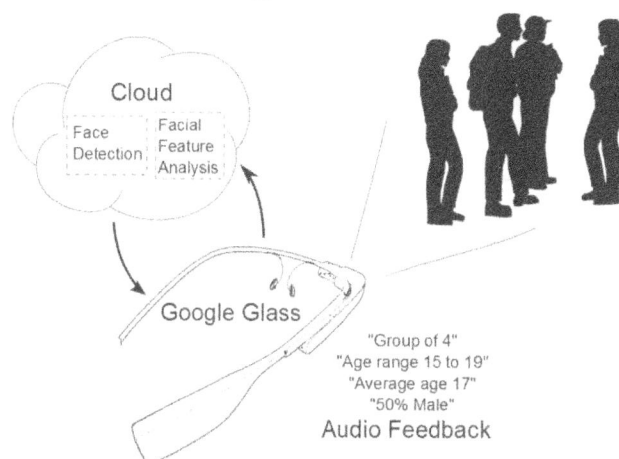

Figure 1. Main idea of the prototype: Picture taken by Google Glass is transmitted and analyzed in the cloud. The Glass gives speech feedback based on the analysis.

given an image. Our algorithm then retrieves and synthesizes the information to the user using a text-to-speech engine (Figure 1). For example, given the information that four people are present — two males and two females with respective ages 15, 17, 22, and 19, our app can synthesize the following speech feedback:

``Group of 4. Age range 15 to 22. Average age 18. 50% male''

2. RELATED WORKS

In the past, accessible technologies have often been designed as self-contained, separate devices, such as money detectors, color detectors, water level detectors, etc. As a result, users had to carry all these devices with them which limited their ubiquity and accessible functionalities. The notion of social stigma also accompanied the usage of these devices. Kane et al. [1] showed that the use of devices for a more general user group (e.g. smartphone) attracts users with reduced cost, increased mobility, improved usability, and less social stigma. As a result, we opted to use the publicly available Google Glass[1] as the medium of our prototype.

Given the difficulty of automated labeling of objects, systems such as VizWiz [2] were introduced to use crowdsourcing techniques for accurate labeling of information in an image to assist blind users. While this solution of using crowd workers to label images is effective, it has several limitations. For one, relying on a crowd worker to label an image may not consistently yield nearly real-time solutions. Also, given that the system requires competent workers who desire compensation in return for their services, large-scale deployment could be expensive. Moreover, privacy concerns may arise, given that the pictures are being shared with random Turkers. In our prototype, we addressed

---

[1] https://www.google.com/glass/start/

these limitations by relying on automated computer vision techniques.

The most relevant work on giving blind users feedback on affective cues was performed by Tanveer et al. [3], Rèhman et al. [4], and Rahman et al. [5]. Tanveer et al. [3] reported that along with facial expressions, visually impaired individuals would also benefit from information related to the identity of a person. For example, such individuals would prefer to receive information about the interlocutor's age, gender, ethnicity, and height. In our prototype, we provide feedback on the number of people present, their approximate age and gender distribution as an early proof of concept. Providing feedback on other cues (clothes, ethnicity, height etc.) remains part of our future work.

3. DESIGN CONSIDERATIONS

In the following section, we describe some design considerations and issues we faced while designing the prototype.

3.1 Vision Framework

For computer vision methods of detecting age and gender, we used a library named SHORE — Sophisticated High-speed Object Recognition Engine [6]. SHORE detects and analyzes the pictures of faces present within an image. The framework extracts features related to age and gender, for example, and provides a statistical summary of pixel intensities associated with beard, mustaches, and wrinkles on the face. A boosting algorithm [7] is used to train and use a bunch of classifiers for detecting age and gender from ground truth information based off these pictures. More details as well as limitations and benchmark performances are available in [6].

Accuracy of SHORE for detecting facial features is within the range of 92% to 94% on BioID[2] and CMU+MIT[3] databases. SHORE achieves a gender classification accuracy of 94.3% on BioID and 92.4% on FERET dataset [8]. Age recognition rate is 95.3% on JAFFE database. SHORE is also faster in comparison to its competitors. It takes only 9ms to detect a face in a 384 x 286 pixel image on an Intel Core 2 Duo 6420 CPU. As SHORE is trained on a European dataset, it is possible bias may exist on some specific cultural components. With the introduction of more datasets, this bias could be addressed in future.

3.2 Heating Issue with Google Glass

Google Glass has an inherent limitation of overheating in the case of continuous processing. As it is purposed as a low powered device, it does not have any heat dissipation mechanism. As a result, executing too many computations can render the app nonresponsive [9]. Also, overheating causes the device to become uncomfortable to use.

Due to this limitation, our framework uses a light CPU load only to establish connection with a remote computer. Once the user double taps or presses a button to take a picture, the Glass starts transmitting the image to the remote computer for further processing. The ability to process a continuous video stream may be possible in the future with further enhancement of the Google Glass framework.

---

[2] http://www.bioid.com/downloads.html

[3] http://vasc.ri.cmu.edu/idb/html/face/frontal_images/

4. FEEDBACK DESIGN

We are currently using a Text-to-Speech feedback scheme to describe the faces within the picture. Running an informed user study to iterate through possible feedbacks remains part of our future work. The feedback structure is dynamically based on the number of faces it detects. When it detects only a few faces in the picture, it describes the primary features using Android's Text-to-Speech functionality. Otherwise, when the system spots more than three faces in the input, it describes the summary statistics associated with the group.

5. FUTURE WORK

In our future study, we plan to conduct interviews with both blind and sighted people to gain a thorough understanding on the specific cues that people rely on for initiating small talk. Based on these insights, we will add more features to the prototype. Additionally, we seek to run a participatory design technique with a small focus group of blind users to design a more comprehensive feedback system. Finally, we will run a qualitative study by freely distributing the application to a community of blind people. Following this, we would collect feedback on their use.

6. CONCLUSION

This paper presents a wearable prototype that can sense and synthesize affective information about people in a group (number of people, age and gender distribution). We envision validating this prototype in the context of helping individuals with visual impairments in order to help initiate small talk and make them more comfortable in groups. In the future, we plan to expand the framework so that visually impaired individuals may navigate conversations given real time feedback.

7. REFERENCES

[1] S. Kane et al. 2009 Freedom to roam: a study of mobile device adoption and accessibility for people with visual and motor disabilities In *Proceedings of ASSETS*

[2] Bigham, J., et al. 2010 VizWiz: nearly real-time answers to visual questions." *Proceedings of the 23rd UIST.*

[3] M. Tanveer et al. 2013 Do you see what I see? Designing a sensory substitution device to access non-verbal modes of communication. In *Proceedings of ASSETS*.

[4] S. Rèhman et al. 2010 ifeeling: Vibrotactile rendering of human emotions on mobile phones. *Mobile Multimedia Processing*

[5] Rahman, AKM et al. 2012 IMAPS: A smart phone based real-time framework for prediction of affect in natural dyadic conversation. *Visual Comm. & Image Processing (VCIP)*

[6] Ruf, T. et al. 2011 Face detection with the sophisticated high-speed object recognition engine (SHORE). *Microelectronic Systems.*

[7] Freund Y et al. 1999 A Short Introduction to Boosting, In *Journal of Japanese Society for Artificial Intelligence*

[8] Phillips, P et al. 1998 The FERET database and evaluation procedure for face-recognition algorithms. *Image and vision computing* 295-306

[9] Chen et al, 2014. Towards wearable cognitive assistance. *Mobile systems, applications, and services MobiSys*

An Immersive Physical Therapy Game for Stroke Survivors

Conor Kaminer, Kevin LeBras, Jordan McCall, Tan Phan, Paul Naud, Mircea Teodorescu,
Sri Kurniawan

University of California, Santa Cruz
1156 High Street
Santa Cruz, CA 95064

[ckaminer, klebras, jmccall, tatphan, pnaud, mteodore, skurnia]@ucsc.edu

ABSTRACT
We report a system for gamifying physical therapy for stroke survivors that provides a fully immersive 3D environment. The system consists of a Kinect, an Oculus Rift immersive goggle and a pair of haptic gloves. The Kinect is used to provide bodily gesture for the game as well as to record data to allow assessment of therapy progress regarding body postures. The haptic gloves operate as a controller for the player's in-game hands as well as to record data that provides therapy progress regarding finger flexibility.

Categories and Subject Descriptors
H.5.m. Information interfaces and presentation: Miscellaneous.

Keywords
Kinect, stroke, physical therapy, virtual reality

1. INTRODUCTION
Stroke is the number one cause of adult disability. In 2013 there was over 750,000 stroke incidents [4]. For those who survive stroke, long-term disabilities can occur, varying from physical to cognitive disabilities depending on the affected areas of the brain. These disabilities are usually compounded with aging-related disabilities (a majority of stroke survivors are 60-80 years old [2]. Successful physical therapies for stroke survivors have one common characteristic: they are time intensive (they range between 5-10 hours a week for 12 weeks [1] and they start as soon as the medical condition has been stabilized (often within 24 to 48 hours after the stroke) [3]. The intensity and duration of rehabilitation makes it difficult for patients receiving outpatient therapy to follow the schedule, especially when long travel is involved, opening opportunities for remote therapy systems. In addition, because of the intense duration, abandonment due to boredom often occurs, also opening opportunities for finding more enjoyable ways for stroke rehabilitation.

We report an immersive 3D game for independent use at patient homes that present exercises in more fun way while at the same time allows recording of therapy progress.

ASSETS '14, Oct 20-22 2014, Rochester, NY, USA
ACM 978-1-4503-2720-6/14/10.
http://dx.doi.org/10.1145/2661334.2661391

2. SIMILAR SYSTEMS
There are a few recently developed systems that aim at providing remote physical therapy that are similar to our system. A project sponsored by Microsoft Research and Seoul National University called "Stroke Recovery with Kinect[1]" is an interactive rehabilitation system prototype that helps stroke patients improve their upper-limb motor functioning in the comfort of their own home. This system tracks user gestures and adjusts the difficulty of rehabilitation sessions based on their progress. They also have future plans of stroke patient interaction through social networking and also large scale data analysis of rehabilitation data trends.

One reason behind the increased interest is the prospect that therapy may be cost effectively administered in patient's own homes as an alternative to what is accepted by most professionals as the most effective treatment, Constraint-Induced Movement Therapy (CI). Ohio State University's Wexner Medical Center research team have built a model for exactly this purpose. Their prototype comes in the form of a boat rowing game that utilizes a Kinect and two gloves; one to weigh down a patients unaffected side, and the other to track movement by their affected side[2].

3. OUR SYSTEM
At the highest level our system consists of two main components; the external devices (glove, Kinect, Oculus Rift) and the game. The Kinect tracks the movement of the user's body. This allows users and stroke therapists to assess how well stroke patients can move their outer extremities. We incorporated gloves for finger motion capture and pressure sensing. Most existing systems are limited to simply tracking the entire hand as one point. Collecting detailed data on user's fingers allows us to create scenes that focus on the rehabilitation of hand motion and strength.

The gloves use bend sensors to capture the motion of the glove wearer's fingers and send a corresponding linearized value for each bend sensor to the computer using Bluetooth. The software takes this data along with Kinect and Oculus Rift input and uses these devices to power a game in the Unity3D engine that has the player do exercises and games that are inspired by physical therapy techniques. The movements to be implemented were provided to us by the physical therapist of the Cabrillo College Stroke and Disability Learning Center. The software records data regarding the users' movements from the Kinect and the gloves into a database so that it can be read and graphed using a utility

---

[1] http://research.microsoft.com/en-us/projects/stroke-recovery-with-kinect/

[2] http://www.themarysue.com/stroke-rehab-game/

developed in Python that make it easy to see and manipulate the data. Figure 1 depicts the relationship of the different components.

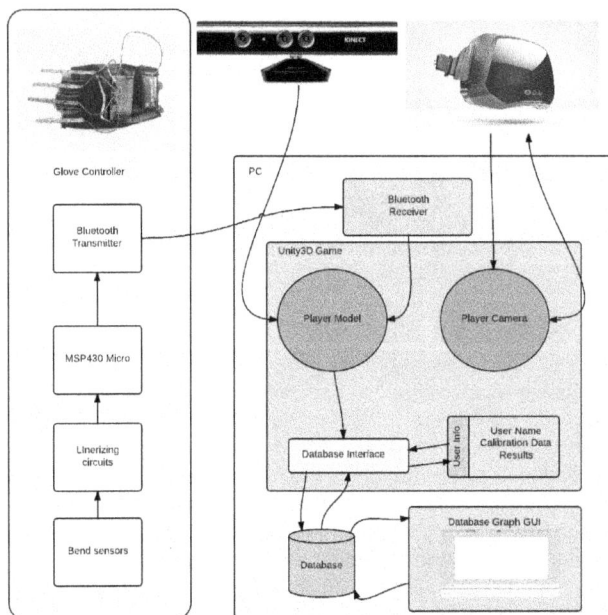

Figure 1. The components of our system

3.1 The Game

Our first exercise scene tasks the user with moving four cylinders placed around him/her into a box in front of the user. Two of the cylinders are on a shelf above the user and the other two are on a counter behind the user, providing users with a variety of reaching and grabbing activities. The scene records user position data continuously and the time it takes the user to place the objects in the box. The user is represented in-game is a virtual character who mimic's the user's movements.

Along with this scene, we have a scene which acts more as an exercise then a game. The screen gives the player instructions like "Raise right arm as high as you can" and records relevant data. In this case it would be the maximum angle of the arm from the shoulder. The idea is to show that our system can make taking goniometric measurements much easier.

To integrate the Kinect into our Unity project we are using a middleware created by the San Francisco startup, Zigfu. The Zigfu Development Kit (ZDK) for Unity3D is a wrapper that provides numerous tools for establishing communication between Microsoft's Kinect for Windows and the Unity3D game engine. The game works by leveraging the Kinect to control the in game character model's movements, the Oculus Rift as the screen as well as control the camera orientation, and the GloveReader to control the finger animations as well as the hand gestures. A script on the hand checks for collisions with cylinders and if the player is grabbing at the time of collision the cylinder's position is attached to the hand's position until the "grab" gesture is false. When this happens the cylinder falls from whatever position the hand is in at the time of the gesture change.

3.2 The Gloves

To gather data from the user's hand, we used the 2.2" flex sensor, SEN - 10264. This flex sensor behaves like a variable resistor. As the sensor is bent, the resistance across the sensor increases. We tested these sensors to observe if the resistance and angle of bend had a linear relationship. Using a goniometric protractor and a multi-meter we were able to measure the resistance of these bend sensors in 15 degree increments.

3.3 Data/Analysis

This system gathers a lot of data during the exercise. Inside Unity3D, the Kinect gives us X, Y, Z coordinates and angles of each joint on the user's body. We record these locations/angles 10 times a second to give us snapshots of the user's movement at any given time. This allows us to reconstruct the user's actions in a graphing tool that shows a skeletal outline of the user at any given time through the exercise with a slider that allows a user or therapist to move through the exercise virtually.

4. PRELIMINARY USER EVALUATION

This system had only been tested by one stroke survivor. He had stroke 4 years ago and was a musician and a music store owner prior to stroke (he still runs a music store). In general, the user was quite happy with the system and would recommend it to others but were concerned about the geekiness of the system. Some of his actual comments were: "I can see this system to be useful for those who cannot travel to Cabrillo College all the time" and "I would definitely recommend this system to the more geeky friends. I am not sure how others would react though."

5. CONCLUSION

At ASSETS we will be demonstrating the system. Our very preliminary user study shows promise and we would like to receive feedback from ASSETS attendees to improve the next generation of our system.

6. ACKNOWLEDGMENT

We thank Cabrillo College Stroke and Disability Learning Center for allowing us to demonstrate our system, Lenny Norton who provided us with the movements that needed to be implemented, and the anonymous participant for testing our system and providing us feedback for improvement.

7. REFERENCES

[1] Brindley P., Copeland M., Demain C., Martyn P. (1989). A comparison of the speech of ten chronic Broca's aphasics following intensive and nonintensive periods of therapy. Aphasiology 3, 695–707.

[2] Hickenbottom, S. L., Fendrick, A. M., Kutcher, J. S. et al. (2002). A national study of the quantity and cost of informal caregiving for the elderly with stroke. Neurology 58:1754–1759.

[3] Marshall R.C., Wertz R.T., Weiss D.G., Aten J.L., Brookshire R.H., Garcia-Bunuel L., Holland A.L., Kurtzke J.F., LaPointe L.L., Milianti F.J. (1989). Home treatment for aphasic patients by trained nonprofessionals. Journal of Speech and Hearing Disorder 54, 462–470.

[4] National Stroke Association. Stroke 101 Fact Sheet. http://www.stroke.org/site/DocServer/STROKE_101_Fact_Sheet.pdf?docID=454

Immersive Simulation of Visual Impairments Using a Wearable See-through Display

Halim Çağrı Ateş, Alexander Fiannaca, Eelke Folmer

Computer Science & Engineering - University of Nevada
{cagri, fiannaca, efolmer}@cse.unr.edu

ABSTRACT

Simulation of a visual impairment may lead to a better understanding of how individuals with visual impairments perceive the world around them and could be a useful design tool for interface designers to identify accessibility barriers. Current simulation tools, however, suffer from a number of limitations, pertaining cost, accuracy and immersion. We present a simulation tool (SIMVIZ) that mounts a wide angle camera on a head-mounted display to create a see-through stereoscopic display that simulates various types and levels of visual impairments. SIMVIZ enables quick accessibility inspections during iterative software development.

Keywords

Design Tools; Accessibility Testing; Visual Impairment; Augmented Reality; Wearable Computing; Oculus Rift.

Categories and Subject Descriptors

H.5.1 [**Multimedia Information Systems**]: Augmented Reality

1. INTRODUCTION

There are a wide range of visual impairments; each which affect remaining vision to a different extent. For example, macular degeneration blurs central vision with no effect to peripheral vision, where retinopathy and glaucoma reduce or blur peripheral vision but central vision remains. Such differences pose a significant challenge in accessibility testing. Various techniques can be used for detecting accessibility problems (see [9]). User studies can be time consuming and costly to perform in addition to the fact that it is difficult to recruit subjects covering every type of visual impairment. Guidelines and automated test tools require expertise on behalf of developers to be used and do not detect all accessibility problems [11]. Expert reviews are most effective for uncovering accessibility problems [9]. Test tools are valuable for experts and inexperienced designers, but there is currently a lack of: (1) lightweight evaluation tools that support iterative design [9] and (2) tools that can visualize the experience of users with a disability [11]. This demo presents a low-cost simulator that is built using recent advances in head-mounted display technology and which can simulate a myriad of

Figure 1: Accessibility inspection of a smart phone app using our see-through display. Designers can cycle through different types of visual impairments to quickly identify potential accessibility barriers.

visual impairments with a high degree of immersion. SIMVIZ addresses the need for more usable accessibility design tools [9, 11] by enabling quick accessibility inspections during iterative design.

2. RELATED WORK

Various simulation kits are commercially available [7, 2]. These kits typically include goggles, lenses and funnels, which –when combined– can simulate different visual impairments. Goggles are low cost, and as they cover the users field of view, they closely mimic how a visually impaired person actually sees the world. A drawback is that goggles generally allow for simulating only a few of the most common visual impairments with a fixed level. For quick evaluations, switching between impairments may be cumbersome due to the requirement of having to switch lenses and funnels. Various software based visual impairments simulators [9, 6, 1] have been developed that offer larger flexibility than goggles. They allow designers to quickly cycle through various impairments and adjust the level of impairment; however, most simulators are confined to a desktop screen. Highly immersive, realistic 3D simulations of visual impairments are possible using virtual reality environments [10, 8] but these systems are expensive and not portable.

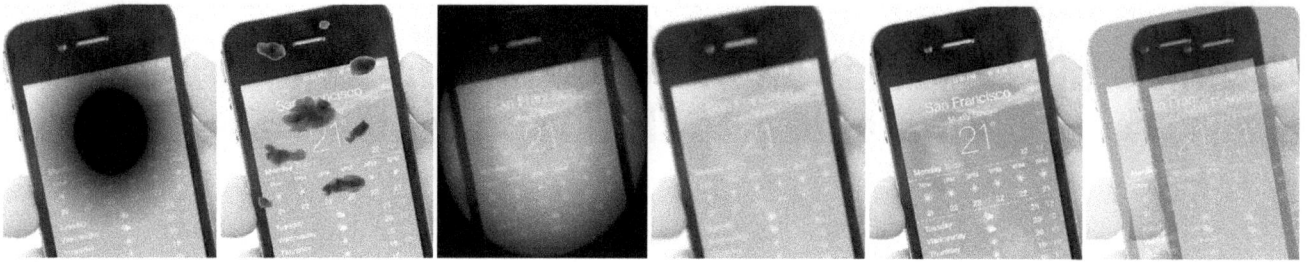

Figure 2: Visual impairments implemented in our simulator: (a) Macular Degeneration; (b) Diabetic Retinopathy; (c) Glaucoma; (d) Cataracts; (e) Protanopia; (f) Diplopia. Filters applied to a still image in VR Player for illustration purposes.

3. DESIGN OF SIMVIZ

To address the need for more usable design tools [9, 11], we developed a novel simulator (SIMVIZ) that offers the flexibility of a software simulator, the immersion and stereo vision of a VR simulator, and the ability to perform real-world accessibility inspections like goggles. We created an augmented reality see-through display by mounting a camera to a VR HMD and feeding this camera feed into the HMD. Various filters can be applied to the camera stream to simulate different visual impairments.

VR display. For our display, we used the popular Oculus Rift HMD. The Rift uses a 7" LCD display and offers a resolution of 640x800 per eye at 60Hz. The image for each eye is rendered in the panel as a barrel distorted image that is then corrected by the pincushion effect created by lenses in the headset, generating a spherical-mapped image for each eye. The depth of the lenses can be manually adjusted. Additional interchangeable lenses for dioptric correction are provided. A distinguishing feature of the Oculus Rift is its large 110° diagonal and 90° horizontal FOV which fills the users entire field of vision and creates a strong sense of immersion. The stereoscopic vision is not a 100% overlapping, mimicking human vision and makes the combined horizontal resolution greater than 640 pixels. Drift-less head tracking is implemented using 3-axis gyros, accelerometers, and magnetometers. The HMD accepts DVI and HDMI input and weighs 379 grams.

Camera. To create a realistic see-through display, we need a camera that matches the resolution (1280x800), refresh rate (60Hz) and FOV (110°) of the Oculus Rift. The camera should also be light to avoid straining the users neck. This led us to using the PlayStation 4 Camera. This motion sensing accessory features twin wide-angle cameras with an 85° FOV for each sensor and can stream two 1280x800 feeds at 60 fps. This sensor uses a USB 3.0 cable with a proprietary AUX connector, however we were able to splice a standard USB 3.0 connector to the cable. Using an adhesive the sensor was attached to the front of the Oculus Rift (see Fig 1).

Software. To render our video stream into the Oculus Rift we used VR Player [5], an open source VR media player which can play stereoscopic video files. VR Player is available on Windows and supports various projections and distortions, including the barrel distortion needed for the Oculus Rift. VR Player is able to play video streams using the VideoLan VLC media player plugin. VR Player supports various effects that can be defined using the High-level shading language (HLSL). Because a Windows driver is not available yet for the PS4 camera we used the available OSX driver [3] and connected our PS4 camera to a Macbook Pro. We connected the Oculus Rift to a high-end Desktop PC (Intel Core i7/ GeForce GTX 660). Using VLC media player, we setup a unicast stream from the Mac to the PC. We acquire a 1280x800 stream from each camera in the sensor and VLC combines this into a single 1280x800 MPEG stream using a fixed horizontal offset that

represents the distance between the lenses. On the PC we run VR Player and open the video stream from the Mac. VR's headtracking feature is disabled. We used an open source shader editor called Shazzam to create HLSL shaders for simulating different visual impairments. Shaders can be activated in VR player using a keyboard shortcut. Though the correctness of certain visual impairment simulations like colorblindness can be easily verified using an Ishihara test plate, other types of visual impairments, such as diabetic retinopathy are subject to large amounts of inter-individual variation. A visually impaired user can provide a verbal description of their specific visual impairment but they may be unable to verify the correctness of the filter as they may not be able to use the HMD. Similar to other simulation tools, we used example photos provided by the National Eye Institute [4] to implement our simulations (see Figure 2). For each simulation three levels of severity or types (colorblindness) are implemented and users can cycle through these using a keyboard shortcut.

3.1 Demo

Conference attendants can try our simulator and see the world through the eyes of someone who is visually impaired.

4. REFERENCES

[1] The braille institute: VisionSim, http://www.brailleinstitute.org/digital/mobile-applications.html.

[2] Fork in the road vision rehabilitation services, http://www.lowvisionsimulators.com.

[3] PS4 camera tools, https://github.com/ps4eye/ps4eye.

[4] National Eye Institute: Eye Health Information, https://www.nei.nih.gov/health.

[5] VR player, http://vrplayer.codeplex.com.

[6] Web based vision simulator, http://visionsimulations.com.

[7] Zimmerman low vision simulation kit, http://www.lowvisionsimulationkit.com.

[8] Jin, B., Ai, Z., and Rasmussen, M. Simulation of eye disease in virtual reality. In *Proc. of EMBS'05*, 5128–5131.

[9] Mankoff, J., Fait, H., and Juang, R. Evaluating accessibility by simulating the experiences of users with vision or motor impairments. *IBM Syst. J. 44:3*, 2005, 505–517.

[10] Maxhall, M., Backman, A., Holmlund, K., Hedman, L., Sondell, B., and Bucht, G. Participants responses to a stroke training simulator. In *Proc. of ICDVRAT'04*, 225–230.

[11] Trewin, S., Cragun, B., Swart, C., Brezin, J., and Richards, J. Accessibility challenges and tool features: An IBM web developer perspective. In *Proc. of W4A '10*, 32:1–32:10.

Legion Scribe: Real-Time Captioning by Non-Experts

Walter S. Lasecki[1], Raja Kushalnagar[2], and Jeffrey P. Bigham[3]

Computer Science, ROC HCI[1]
University of Rochester
wslasecki@cs.rochester.edu

Computer Science, NTID[2]
Rochester Institute of Technology
rskics@rit.edu

HCII[3]
Carnegie Mellon University
jbigham@cmu.edu

ABSTRACT

The promise of affordable, automatic approaches to real-time captioning imagines a future in which deaf and hard of hearing (DHH) users have immediate access to speech in the world around them my simply picking up their phone or other mobile device. While the challenges of processing highly variable natural language has prevented automated approaches from completing this task reliably enough for use in settings such as classrooms or workplaces [4], recent work in crowd-powered approaches have allowed groups of non-expert captionists to provide a similarly-flexible source of captions for DHH users. This is in contrast to current human-powered approaches, which use highly-trained professional captionists who can type up to 250 words per minute (WPM), but also can cost over $100/hr. In this paper, we describe a real-time demo of Legion:Scribe (or just "Scribe"), a crowd-powered captioning system that allows untrained participants and volunteers to provide reliable captions with less than 5 seconds of latency by computationally merging their input into a single collective answer that is more accurate and more complete than any one worker could have generated alone.

Categories and Subject Descriptors

H.5.2 [Information interfaces and presentation]: User Interfaces. - Graphical user interfaces.

General Terms

Design, Human Factors

Keywords

Captioning; speech-to-text; real-time human computation; deaf; hard of hearing; crowdsourcing

ASSETS'14, October 20–22, 2014, Rochester, NY, USA.
ACM 978-1-4503-2720-6/14/10.
http://dx.doi.org/10.1145/2661334.2661352

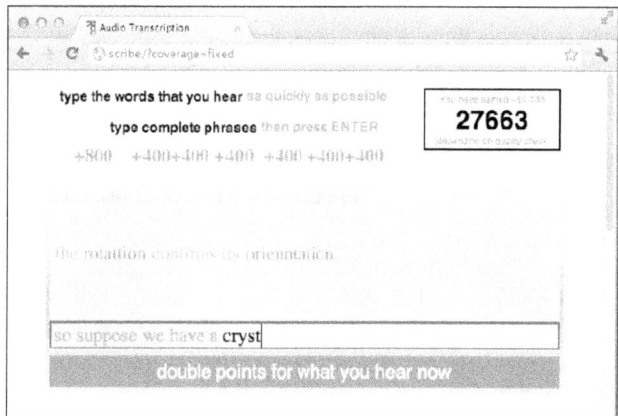

Figure 1: The worker interface encourages workers to type audio by locking in words soon after they are typed. To encourage typing specific segments, visual and audio cues are given, and the volume of the audio is reduced during off periods, while rewards are increased for on periods.

1. LEGION SCRIBE

Real-time captioning provides word-for-word transcription of spoken content with a latency of less than 5 seconds. This can provide as an access to live events for deaf and hard of hearing people, and help hearing users keep track of their place and avoid missing content they might have otherwise missed.

Currently, the only reliable solution in real-life situations with differing speaker and environments is to hire a professional stenographer who provides captions for over $100/hour or more, depending on their skill level.

Real-time captioning is difficult because even fast typists cannot type at the 250 words per minute (WPM) necessary to keep up with natural speech (stenographers train to use special keyboards and input phonemes instead of individual letters, resulting in much lower typing rate requirements). Automatic speech recognition (ASR) only captures about 40% of the speech in real settings and confuses readers by making seemingly random errors [4].

Legion:Scribe [2] allows a small group (often as low as 3-5 people) of people who can hear and type at a ordinary rate to collectively caption speech in real-time, for 20-30% the cost of an expert stenographer. Because of the relative frequency of people who know how to type at a nominal rate compared with those who are trained stenographers, Scribe presents a captioning service that can be available at a moment's notice, rather than at least 24 to 48 hours, as is the case with professionals.

Scribe can now be deployed using a server architecture that allows workers to simply connect to a web page, enter an automatically generated easy-to-remember pass phrase (e.g., "apple", or "hard hat"), and immediately be routed to an audio stream with appropriate indicators of when to type what they hear. For end-users, they simply arrive at a viewing page, enter a pass phrase, and see a display of the captions as they are entered.

By using multiple captionists, it is less likely that the system falls very far behind the speaker. This means that compared to a single stenographer, the flow of the text is more consistent. This likely helps users read content more easily, and is one reason why the captions produced by Scribe, while not perfect, can actually be preferred to professionals [4]. The interface also includes pausing and highlighting controls that allow individual readers to control how they access the captions themselves, which has been shown to help readers better follow content [1].

2. ENHANCING INDIVIDUAL ABILITIES

Scribe asks multiple people to type what they hear into the interface shown in Figure 1 and then merges the partial captions back together using a multiple sequence alignment algorithm. How many workers are required to cover everything a speaker says depends on the speaker's rate and the typing rate of the captionist. However, typically between 3 and 5 people can accomplish the task effectively.

In our experiments, we also recruited workers cheaply and on-demand from crowdsourcing marketplaces like Amazon Mechanical Turk, Mobile Works, and oDesk. These non-expert captionists can be recruited on-demand for as long or as short as the user needs, allowing the workforce used for powering these service even more flexible and available than a set of rare, highly-skilled professionals could be.

Our approach leverages both the fact that people are available on-demand, often as volunteers, as well as that by properly coordinating group work, group systems can outperform even the highest-skilled individual in the group. We have also shown that by systematically slowing down and speeding up the audio for individual workers we can improve both precision and recall by more than 10% [3]. This is the *TimeWarp* approach to real-time human computation. Our interface (Figure 1) coordinates different workers so they type different portions of the streaming audio while maintaining the context of all of the speech.

Scribe currently comes close to the performance of stenographers in terms of *coverage,* how many of the words in the ground truth appear in the final output stream, and *precision,* how many of the output words are correct. Tests have shown Scribe is currently able to reach a precision of 84.8% of that of a professional. We expect that over time Scribe will become even more competitive and might be able to even surpass the performance of stenographers in terms of both coverage and precision. Additionally, experiments with TimeWarp also indicate the potential for improvements in latency, meaning multiple workers might also be able to outperform a single expert even in terms of speed, given the right workflow.

3. DEMO

Our demo will have three components. First, our remote captionists (volunteers and students with no previous captioning training) will listen to audio and provide captionists via Scribe. Second, readers will be able to access the real-time captions generated by Scribe via both an on-screen projection, and a viewing page with playback controls that each reader can use independently. Finally, we will allow the volunteers from the audience to participate in generating captions shown in a second public display.

4. SUMMARY

We have presented Scribe, a reliable human-powered approach for providing on-demand real-time captioning at low cost. Scribe uses multiple individual captionists, each of whom type a piece of what they hear, and then stitches the partial captions back together automatically. Scribe performs competitively with current approaches, but for a fraction of the cost to operate. Our demo will allow members of the audience to both view and, if they choose, help collectively produce captions.

5. REFERENCES

[1] W. S. Lasecki, R. Kushalnagar, J. P. Bigham. Helping students keep up with real-time captions by pausing and highlighting. In Proceedings of W4A 2014. Article 39, p1-8. DOI=10.1145/2596695.2596701

[2] W. S. Lasecki, C. D. Miller, A. Sadilek, A. Abumoussa, D. Borrello, R. Kushalnagar, and J. P. Bigham. Real-time captioning by groups of non-experts. In *Proceedings of UIST 2012*. p23-33. DOI=10.1145/2380116.2380122

[3] W. S. Lasecki, C. D. Miller and J. P. Bigham. Warping Time for More Effective Real-Time Crowdsourcing. In *Proceedings of CHI 2013*. p2033-2036. DOI= 10.1145/2470654.2466269

[4] R.S. Kushalnagar, W.S. Lasecki, J.P. Bigham. Accessibility Evaluation of Classroom Captions. ACM Transactions of Accessible Computing (TACCESS). 5,3, Article 7. DOI=10.1145/2543578

littleBits go LARGE: Making Electronics More Accessible to People with Learning Disabilities

Nic Hollinworth,
Faustina Hwang
School of Systems Engineering,
University of Reading, UK
{n.d.hollinworth,
f.hwang}@reading.ac.uk

Kate Allen
Department of Art,
University of Reading, UK
k.allen@reading.ac.uk

Gosia Kwiatkowska,
Andy Minnion
The Rix Centre
University of East London, UK
{g.kwiatkowska, a.minnion)@uel.ac.uk

ABSTRACT

The "littleBits go LARGE" project extends littleBits electronic modules, an existing product that is aimed at simplifying electronics for a wide range of audiences. In this project we augment the littleBits modules to make them more accessible to people with learning disabilities. We will demonstrate how we have made the modules easier to handle and manipulate physically, and how we are augmenting the design of the modules to make their functions more obvious and understandable.

Categories and Subject Descriptors

H.5.m. Information interfaces and presentation (e.g., HCI): Miscellaneous.

General Terms

Design, Human Factors

Keywords

Sensory Objects; Learning Disabilities; Accessible Electronics.

1. INTRODUCTION

The work presented in this paper is part of a larger project titled "Interactive sensory objects developed for and by people with learning disabilities" [5] which investigates ways of helping to make museum/heritage sites more exciting and appealing to people with learning disabilities. Over the past two years, we have held a series of workshops with people with learning disabilities, engaging them as co-researchers [e.g. 1, 2] in the creation of interactive sensory objects that relate to and improve cultural understanding and experiences.

In these workshops, the co-researchers explore the senses through art-based and technology-focused activities, and look at ways to engage the senses through interactive objects. In designing the interactive elements, the co-researchers have a key role in selecting what technologies they want to use, and we aimed to facilitate this process through hands-on activities exploring 'simple' electronics. A significant challenge for our workshops was that many current electronics require a relatively high level of

ASSETS '14, Oct 20-22 2014, Rochester, NY, USA
ACM 978-1-4503-2720-6/14/10.

http://dx.doi.org/10.1145/2661334.2661341

knowledge and understanding (e.g. Arduino), as well as sensory and motor capabilities (e.g. for wiring things together), which made exploration challenging. Hence, we adopted littleBits [3], which are small electronic components which snap together with magnets.

The littleBits kits provide a relatively straightforward introduction to electronics technologies, and were used as a vehicle for exploring the potential of technology. The co-researchers were encouraged to experiment with different methods of using and triggering media using littleBits (See Figure 1), which could eventually be integrated into their own artwork. For example, different methods of triggering audio were explored, such as clapping, using a bend sensor and using a squeeze sensor. The explorations were documented using video and photographs, and we had also one-to-one interviews with participants to get a clear sense of the challenges they were having.

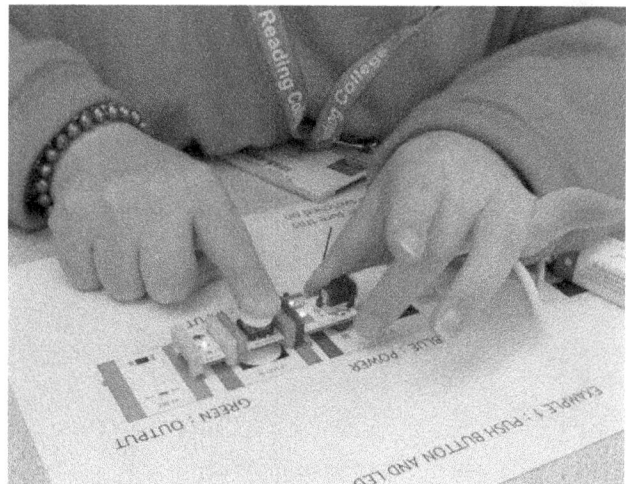

Figure 1: A co-researcher experimenting with littleBits.

2. CHALLENGES WITH LITTLEBITS

Whilst the response to using littleBits in the workshops was very positive and the co-researchers showed a lot of enthusiasm, we observed a number of challenges associated with the practical use of the kit (previously reported in [4]):

1. The littleBits components snap together via pairs of magnets on each face. Most of the bits have two faces, the input side and the output side, but it is difficult to tell which side is for which. If it is the wrong way round, then the magnets repel, and the objects will not snap together. This occurred frequently.

2. It can be difficult to tell whether the component is the right way up, as the top and bottom are similar in appearance. If the component is upside down, then you cannot connect the bits together. This also occurred frequently (see Figure 2).

3. The affordances of the bits are often unclear, so it is not always obvious what they should do or how to use them. For example, the sound trigger has a small microphone on top, which resembles a small button. This caused many people to press it, rather than talk into it or clap their hands near to it, as it is intended to be used (see Figure 3, left).

4. Whilst not a criticism of the design, the components are small, making them difficult to grasp, which can be a problem for our co-researchers many of whom have limited motor control or manual dexterity, and may cope better with handling objects which are larger.

5. The components themselves were difficult to handle, but the controls on the littleBits objects were even more difficult. Figure 3, right, shows two of the co-researchers together adjusting the potentiometer on a „pulse" component (a timed trigger). This needs to be turned using a small screwdriver with a slot size measuring about 2mm. Although the two group members shown here managed to adjust the tiny controls, this was with some difficulty and it was clear that they could benefit from larger, more robust, controls.

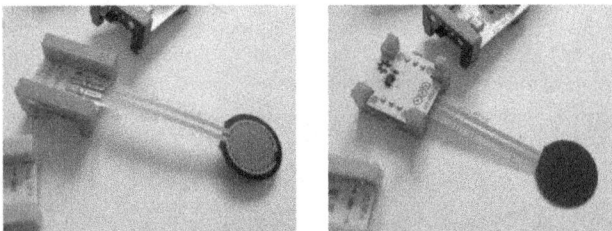

Figure 2: Modules look similar on both sides.

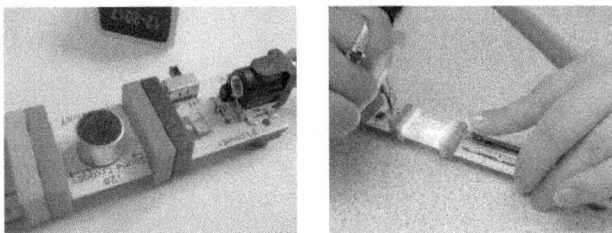

Figure 3: (left) one module resembles a button, but is in fact a microphone; (right) controls are very small and can be difficult to operate.

3. MAKING ACCESSIBLE TECHNOLOGY

As evidenced by observations of co-researchers using our modified modules, we have made significant progress with the issues in handling and assembly by designing a larger (3D printed) base [4] to which the existing littleBits modules are attached. We will demonstrate our modifications, which shows how the larger surface area of the base makes the components easier to grasp and hence pick up, and the redesigned shape clearly indicates which way around to connect the modules. The extended modules also provide a clear distinction between the top and bottom of the component, thereby assisting with assembly the components into a circuit (See Figure 4).

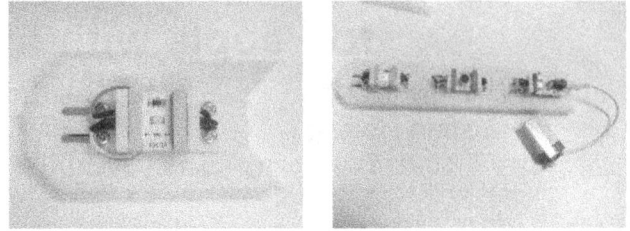

Figure 4: The augmented littleBits modules. The existing bits are attached to a larger base, which will only fit one way.

4. CONTINUING DEVELOPMENT

We are currently investigating the issues of affordances and the need for larger controls, and through participatory workshops with co-researchers we will be exploring ways of clarifying the intention of the modules, making them easier to use and more understandable. The overall aim is to develop a set of attachments that will 'snap-on' over the existing components without having to modify the original modules. For example, one idea is to make the sound trigger (see Figure 3) look more like an ear or a microphone, as a way to invite users to speak or sing into it in order to operate it. We will also demonstrate the attachments designed in these participatory workshops.

The extended littleBits components are aimed at making electronics more accessible to people with learning disabilities, so that they can explore and experience technology for themselves, and learn what it can offer. The improvements we have made in terms of accessibility widens the audience for electronics experimentation, rather than narrowing it as enabling technologies can sometimes do, and in this way, the work could bring electronics to a larger number of people. Part of littleBits" mission is to "break down the barriers between the products we consume and the things we make, to make everyone into an inventor" [3]. littleBits go LARGE extends this aim to include and empower people with learning disabilities.

5. ACKNOWLEDGMENTS

This research is funded by the Arts and Humanities Research Council (AHRC), grant AH/J004987/1. We thank Reading College and The Museum of English Rural Life at the University of Reading. littleBits is a trademark of littleBits inc.

6. REFERENCES

[1] Anthony, L., Prasad, S., Hurst, A., & Kuber, R. A. Participatory design workshop on accessible apps and games with students with learning differences. In *Proc. of ASSETS'12*, 253-254.

[2] Benton, L., Johnson, H., Ashwin, E., Brosnan, M., & Grawemeyer, B. Developing IDEAS: Supporting children with autism within a participatory design team. In *Proc. of CHI'12*, 2599-2608.

[3] http://littlebits.cc/ Last accessed on 25/06/2014

[4] Hollinworth, N., Hwang, F., Allen, K., Kwiatkowska, G.M., and Minnion, A. Making electronics more accessible to people with learning disabilities. In *CHI EA '14*,1255-1260.

[5] http://www.sensoryobjects.com/ Last accessed on 25/06/2014

M.I.D.A.S. Touch: Magnetic Interactive Device for Alternative Sight through Touch

Taylan K. Sen
ROC HCI
Computer Science
University of Rochester
tsen@cs.rochester.edu

Morgan W. Sinko
ROC HCI
Computer Science
University of Rochester
msinko@u.rochester.edu

Alex T. Wilson
ROC HCI
Computer Science
University of Rochester
awils18@u.rochester.edu

Mohammed E. Hoque
ROC HCI
Computer Science
University of Rochester
mehoque@cs.rochester.edu

ABSTRACT

This paper describes the development of a working prototype of a novel free-space haptic human-computer interface called MIDAS Touch. MIDAS Touch works by applying physical forces to a user's finger through the production of a dynamic magnetic field. The magnetic field strength is adjusted in real-time based on the user's movement of his/her finger. A user's hand/finger motion in the real world is mapped to movement of a virtual finger in a virtual world through the use of a Leap Motion 3D tracking sensor. As a person's virtual finger collides with objects in the virtual world, the magnetic field strength is varied. In this demo, we present a case of MIDAS Touch coupled to a standard PC as a computer drawing viewer and drawing application for helping individuals with visual impairment feel what they or others have drawn.

Categories and Subject Descriptors

K.4.2 [**Social Issues**]: *Assistive Technologies for persons with disabilities*

H.5.1 [**Multimedia Information Systems**]: *Artificial, augmented, and virtual realities.*

General Terms

Algorithms, Design, Human Factors

Keywords

Haptic; Magnetic; Free-Space; Finger; Drawing; Accessibility; Visually Impaired; Blind; Leap Motion

1. INTRODUCTION

Imagine a daughter wishing to share the drawing she created of her family with her father. If her father is blind, he would have no easy way to see the drawing besides relying on another person's description of what was in the art. Having to rely on another individual's sight can not only be disempowering, but for works of art, it may rob one of his/her own personal artistic interpretation. Whoever describes the drawing to the father will inadvertently add his/her own biases and interpretations in the description. Additionally, if the father wanted to share in a drawing activity with his daughter, he would have a hard time remembering exactly what he drew and where he drew things as his picture progressed. This would often result in disjointed figures in his drawing, limiting the experience with his daughter.

ASSETS '14, Oct 20-22 2014, Rochester, NY, USA
ACM 978-1-4503-2720-6/14/10.
http://dx.doi.org/10.1145/2661334.2661350

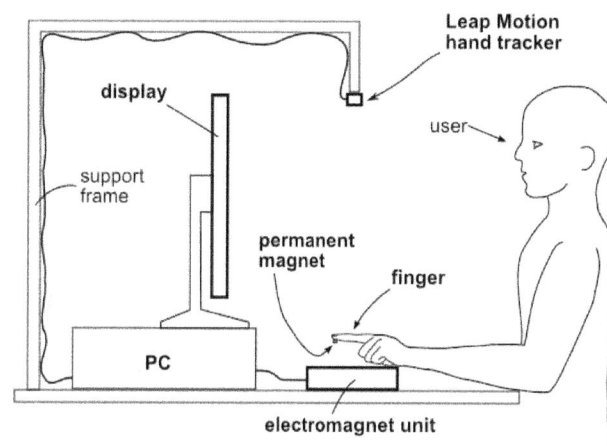

Figure 1. Side view of MIDAS Touch system.

Effective drawing typically requires either vision, or some other form of feedback to let the artist know what was drawn. Providing visually impaired individuals a physical feedback-enhanced drawing viewer and drawing application would augment their communication skills by empowering them to independently and personally perceive basic line art and create their own drawings.

As part of our demo, we have developed a computer based drawing application in which the MIDAS Touch system provides feedback for perceiving what has been drawn through physical touch. The prototype device allows a visually impaired user to control the position of a virtual pen tip by moving the position of their finger under a hand tracker sensor. As the virtual pen tip passes over a virtual drawing canvas, a haptic feedback force is applied to a user's finger whenever the virtual pen passes over a region in which a line has previously been drawn. The force is applied by attaching a permanent magnet to the user's finger, and dynamically controlling the magnetic field generated by an electromagnet. Because the electromagnet can be rapidly turned on or off, a user may perceive the lines drawn on the virtual campus by rapidly scanning his/her finger over the 2D canvas and sensing the changes in force applied by the electromagnet to their finger in much the same way a blind individual may rapidly scan his/her finger tips over a line of Braille.

1.1 Prior Work

Haptic technology has been previously used to aid the blind and visually impaired. Optical to tactile displays have been developed as early as the 1970's [1]. Sjöström, *et al.* found that users could interpret simple line drawings and diagrams by touch alone after adding textures to the drawings through the use of a force feedback stylus [2]. Another method of assisting the visually impaired to perceive their drawings involves the mechanical deformation of the drawing surface [3]. Force feedback based systems suffer from mechanical backlash which reduces fine resolution. Mechanical deformation based systems cannot be used to perceive drawings made by others. A feature unique to our drawing system for the visually impaired is that it provides a *free-space* haptic feedback, which applies a force without contacting mechanical linkages. Thus, this system does not suffer from the backlash and/or resolution issues associated with linkages.

2. DESIGN

The MIDAS Touch system includes the major components of a Leap Motion 3D hand tracker, an electromagnet unit, a computer system hosting a virtual world, and a permanent magnet to be coupled to the user's finger through either tape or a finger glove. These components work together to apply a physical force to the user's index finger as a function of the user's finger position. When the user moves his/her finger in the real world, he/she effectively moves a virtual tool, such as a virtual pen tip, in a virtual world hosted on the computer system. When the virtual pen tip is moved over virtual ink that has been drawn, a physical force is applied to the user. This force is realized when the computer system commands the electromagnet unit to turn on, which creates a magnetic field which causes a force to be applied to the permanent magnet coupled to the user's finger, creating the sensation of touch. When the user moves his/her finger such that the virtual pen tip is no longer touching a region in the virtual world which has been drawn on, the computer system commands the electromagnet to turn off. Thus, a user can literally feel what has already been drawn in the virtual world simply by scanning his/her finger back and forth and side to side.

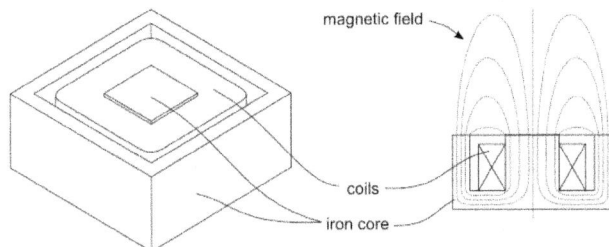

Figure 2. a) isometric view of electromagnet b) side section view of electromagnet showing magnetic flux distribution.

2.1 Hardware Implementation

The Leap Motion 3D hand tracker is a binocular infrared camera which, in our experimental testing, was capable of reliably providing multiple finger tracking over a 5cm x 5cm x 5cm volume of space at a bandwidth of 30Hz. As shown in Figure 1, we mounted the Leap Motion sensor from above the user's hand using a rigid frame. The permanent magnet coupled to the user's finger is a 1/2" x 1/2" x 1/8" neodymium magnet. The magnet is held to the user's finger either with scotch tape, or a latex glove finger. The electromagnet unit contains an electromagnet converted from a 900W transformer with an estimated turns ratio of 20:1 and an E-shaped laminated iron core. The electromagnet is oriented with the E-shaped core on its side such that the magnetic flux is directed vertically upwards from the electromagnet unit towards a potential user's finger. The electromagnet unit contains a 3KW driver coupled to a 24 volt power supply. At full power, the electromagnet is capable of applying a dynamic force of over ±250 mN. The total volume of

space where perceptible force may be applied ranges over a 3 cm x 3 cm x 1.5 cm volume. The driver is directly controlled by an Arduino Mega microcontroller board, which communicates with the computer system via a serial port. The computer system used is a Windows 7 based 1.9 GHz AMD A4 notebook computer.

2.2 Application Design

The drawing application was implemented in Python 2.7.7 using the Pygame game library. The drawing application runs as a continuous loop. As a first step, the user's finger positions are read from the Leap Motion sensor as x,y,z coordinates. A virtual pen is arranged at tip of the user's index finger. Whether the pen is "down" (i.e. in a state in which it is actively drawing) vs. "up" (i.e. the pen does not draw virtual ink, but still tracks its position for determination of haptic feedback) is controlled by the position of the user's middle finger. If a user holds his/her index finger and middle fingers apart (i.e. in the form of scissors), the virtual pen is placed in the "up" state by the application. Alternatively, when the user places his/her index and middle finger together, the software changes the pen state to the "down" (drawing) state. As the user moves his/her fingers around with the pen in the "down" state, virtual ink is drawn onto the virtual canvas. In each iteration of the software, after determining the pen location and state from the user's fingers, the software checks whether the virtual pen is over a region in which virtual ink has already been drawn more than 5 seconds ago. If the pen is over a region of drawn ink, the application sends a message over the computer's serial port to the Arduino microcontroller commanding the electromagnet to turn on. This causes a force to be applied to the user's finger, giving the user the perception of ink being present at his/her current finger position. The application repeats this loop of detecting finger position, mapping it to virtual pen position and state, determining whether to draw virtual ink, and appropriately commanding the electromagnet to turn on. As the user moves his/her hand away from a region where ink was drawn, the application senses this and commands the electromagnet to turn off, and thus removing the applied force from the user's finger.

3. CONCLUSION

In this paper we discuss our prototype for providing a visually impaired individual the ability to feel drawings that he/she create. We designed MIDAS Touch with the motivation of helping the visually impaired improve their ability to perceive and create basic drawings. We hope that this demo will serve as a proof of concept that will establish the viability of low cost electromagnet-based haptic human computer interaction devices for assisting the visually impaired to interpret drawings, draw, and more generally to improve usability of a variety of computer applications. Evaluating this framework with visually impaired individuals remains a goal of our future work.

4. REFERENCES

[1] J. Bliss, M. Katcher, C. Rogers, and R. Shepard. Optical-to-tactile image conversion for the blind. IEEE Transactions on man-machine systems, MMS-11(1), 1970.

[2] C. Sjöström, H. Danielsson, C. Magnusson, K. Rassmus-Gröhn. Phantom-based haptic line graphics for blind persons. Visual Impairment Research, 5(1), 13-33, 2003.

[3] J. Kennedy. How the Blind Draw. Scientific American, 16, 44 - 51, 2006.

Motion History to Improve Communication and Switch Access for People with Severe and Multiple Disabilities

Guang Yang, Mamoru Iwabuchi, Rumi Hirabayashi, Kenryu Nakamura
RCAST, The University of Tokyo, Tokyo, Japan
{yang, mamoru, rumi, kenryu} @bfp.rcast.u-tokyo.ac.jp

Kimihiko Taniguchi, Syoudai Sano
Takamatsu Special Education School, Kagawa, Japan
hamuossan8603@gmail.com, s_sanocch@ybb.ne.jp

Takamitsu Aoki
Inariyama Special Education School, Nagano, Japan
aokitaka@mac.com

ABSTRACT

In this study, a computer-vision based technique called Motion History that visualizes the history of movement of the user, was applied to support communication and switch access for people with severe and multiple disabilities. Seven non-speaking children with severe physical and intellectual disabilities participated in the study, and Motion History successfully helped to investigate their voluntary movement and cognition. In addition, based on the feedback comments of the study, a new system was developed, which used the built-in camera of the tablet PC to observe Motion History, and made the system easier and more mobile to use. One of the features of the system could convert the recognized body movement into a switch control, where a good switch fitting was automatically established based on the motion history.

Categories and Subject Descriptors

I.4.8 [**Image Processing and Computer Vision**]: Scene Analysis – motion;

K.4.2 [**Computers and Society**]: Social Issues – assistive technology for persons with disabilities

General Terms

Measurement, Experimentation, Human Factors

Keywords

Motion history; OAK; communication; switch access; severe and multiple disabilities

1. INTRODUCTION

Our team has developed a computer vision-based noncontact switch software called OAK (Observation and Access with Kinect) for people with severe and multiple disabilities [1, 2]. The software uses Microsoft Kinect for Windows to observe the motion of the user. One of unprecedented features of OAK is Motion History which visualizes the history of movement [1, 3].

2. MOTION HISTORY

As shown in Figure 1, Motion History is displayed in a heat map like representation and created based on the frequency of the brightness change with a six-color scale (purple, blue, green, yellow, orange, and red), which corresponds to the motion of the user, in each pixel of the captured video. The redder the color of a pixel is in the Motion History, the greater the movement was at the point during the observation. Selecting the most active region of the Motion History allows the user to create a sensitive switch, a virtual switch called "Air Switch", to activate [4]. Motion History can also provide helpful information about the cognitive state of the user by comparing the data of the situations before/after an effective interaction.

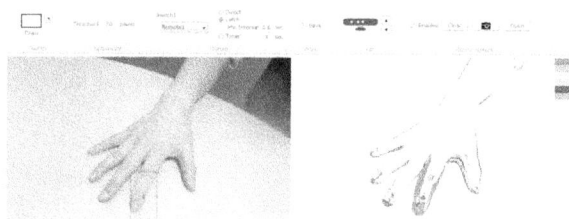

Figure 1. OAK interface displaying Motion History on the right.

3. CASE STUDIES

3.1 Method

Motion History was used to distinguish voluntary movement of seven children with both physical and intellectual disabilities. All children have had either little or very limited success in communication with others including their family members. The children's Motion History and video were taken under several different conditions, such as with/without different stimuli. The Motion History was recorded for every 5-10 seconds. The Motion History of these conditions were compared to investigate the change of the children.

3.2 Results and Discussion

Figure 2 shows the transition of the Motion History of a twelve year old boy with intellectual disability and profound paralysis due to cerebral hypoxia at birth. Before the study, the boy had only subtle movement and what his voluntary movement was unclear. It was said that the boy seemed uneasy when his classroom teacher was not with him, and had relaxed look with the teacher. However, this was only a subjective interpretation of the teacher. Moreover, it was unknown how much and often the change occurred.

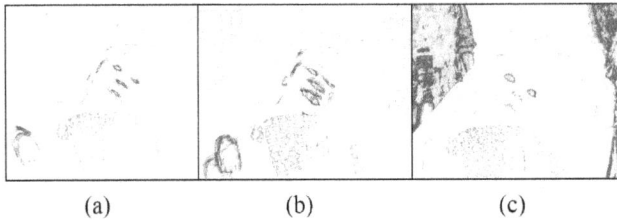

Figure 2. Motion History of the boy in the first case study. His classroom teacher stood by him in (a) and (c). The teacher was not with him in (b).

In this case study, both Fig. 2(a) and 2(c) were taken from the condition with the teacher, and 2(b) without the teacher. The teacher standing next to the boy told him she was going out of the room at the timing between Fig. 2(a) and 2(b). The teacher came back and spoke to the boy between Fig. 2(b) and 2(c).

The Motion History tells that the boy did not move very much, but blinked and slightly shook his head when the teacher stood by him in Fig. 2(a). When the teacher went out of the room, the boy shook his head more as shown in Fig. 2(b). The boy stopped shaking his head when the teacher came back to him in Fig. 2(c). His blinking was solely observed in the last picture. The Motion History showed the boy's voluntary movement of shaking his head according to the teacher's attendance, although no evidence could be seen about his uneasiness or relaxed mood here.

Figure 3 shows the Motion History recorded of another eleven year old boy with cerebral palsy and intellectual disability. No substantial success was made in communicating with the boy until this case study. It was thought that the boy enjoyed self-stimuli and often shook his body and touched his lips. His classroom teacher hoped to find a way to turn his attention from the self-stimuli to interaction with others.

The boy was lying on a mattress on the floor in the study. No intervention was applied in the condition of Fig. 3(a). There was a whisper and the fricative sound of newspaper into his ears in Fig. 3(b) and 3(c), respectively. A massager was put behind his back in Fig. 3(d).

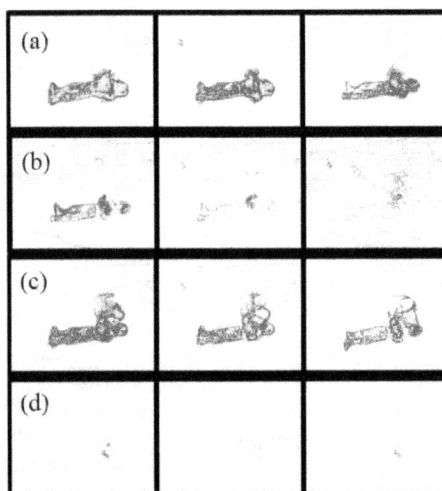

Figure 3. Motion History of the boy in the second case study. No intervention was applied in (a). There was a whisper in (b), and the fricative sound of newspaper in (c) into his ears. A massager was put behind his back in (d).

vibration was put to his back as shown in Fig. 3(b) and 3(d). In addition to these stimuli, testing with a variety of stimuli with this boy led us find several external stimuli that made the boy decrease his body movement and pay his attention.

As shown in the case studies described above, Motion History helped to visualize voluntary movement and cognition of all seven children participated, and this was possible by focusing on the changes of their movement under different conditions. This suggests us greater possibility of the use of Motion History for evidence-based interaction with people with severe and multiple disabilities in the future.

4. OAK FOR TABLET

There were several feedback comments about the system from family members and teachers of the children in the study. One of the most important requests was more convenient use of the camera. Motion History in the case studies was recorded using our switch software, OAK, which worked with Kinect for Windows. We hence developed a new OAK system that uses the built-in camera of the tablet PC instead to observe Motion History. This made the system easier and more mobile to use. The system can also convert the recognized body movement into a switch control, where a good switch fitting is automatically established based on the motion history. This system will be demonstrated at the conference.

5. CONCLUSIONS

This study used a computer-vision based technique called Motion History that visualizes the history of movement of the user. Motion History successfully helped to investigate voluntary movement and cognition of children with severe and multiple disabilities. Based on the feedback comments of the study, a new system was developed, which used the built-in camera of the tablet PC and made it easier to observe Motion History.

6. ACKNOWLEDGMENTS

This work was partly supported by a grant from the Ministry of Health, Labour and Welfare of Japan (Shogaisha Taisaku Sougo Kenkyu Jigyo) and Microsoft Japan Co., Ltd. The authors would like to show their sincere gratitude to them.

7. REFERENCES

[1] Yang, G., Iwabuchi, M., Nakamura, K, Sano, S., Taniguchi, K., and Aoki, T. 2013. Observation and potential exploration for people with severe disabilities using vision technology, Proceedings of Human Interface Symposium 2013, pp.107-110.

[2] Assist-I. 2014. Observation and Access with Kinect, http://www.assist-i.net/at/en/

[3] Bobick, A.F., and Davis, J.W. 2001. The Recognition of Human Movement Using Temporal Templates, IEEE Transactions on Pattern Analysis and Machine Intelligence, Vol. 23, No.3, pp.257-267.

[4] Yang, G., Iwabuchi, M., Nakamura, K. 2013. Automatic convenient switch fitting based on motion history for people with physical disabilities, Correspondences on Hu-man interface, Vol.15, No.11, pp.5-6.

Move&Flick: Design and Evaluation of a Single-finger and Eyes-free Kana-character Entry Method on Touch Screens

Ryosuke Aoki, Ryo Hashimoto, Akihiro Miyata, Shunichi Seko
Masahiro Watanabe, Masayuki Ihara
NTT Service Evolution Laboratories, NTT Corporation
1-1 Hikarinooka Yokosuka-shi Kanagawa Japan
{lastname.firstname}@lab.ntt.co.jp

ABSTRACT

We are aim to produce a Japanese Kana-character entry method on touch screens for visually impaired people. We propose "Move&Flick" which allows them to move a single finger in any of eight directions twice without lifting the finger to select a character and to lift the finger to decide the character. The method uses radial areas with dead zones to detect each of the eight movement directions. An experiment showed that the dead zones and voice feedback let the users acquire proper finger directions in an easy learning process. The method also has an algorithm to correctly detect a change point from the first movement direction to the second movement direction. We evaluate Move&Flick in experiments with visually impaired subjects and confirm that Move&Flick works well.

Categories and Subject Descriptors

H.5.2 [**Information Interfaces and Presentation**]: User Interfaces – *input devices and strategies*

General Terms

Design

Keywords

Text Entry Method; Visually Impaired People; Learning Process; Touch Screen; Voice Feedback; Clearance; Dead Zone

1. INTRODUCTION

Our aim is to realize Japanese Kana-character entry for visually impaired people, being encouraged to use mobile devices with flat touch screens. Combining a consonant and a vowel generally inputs a Kana-character.

Standard text entry methods such as Grid Flick [1] are installed in recent mobile devices with a touch screen for visually impaired people. However, how to select a software key in the mobile devices is different from that in general devices. When they touch a screen, a voice reader echoes the name of the software key being touched on the screen. Since they could not a target position on the screen precisely, they look for a target software key by moving their finger on the screen and listening the echoed voice for each touched key. When they find the target software key, they touch the key twice in rapid succession to select it. While they can select a software key by using this method, the motion is both physical and mental burden for the users. Since touched

ASSETS'14, October 20–22, 2014, Rochester, NY, USA.
ACM 978-1-4503-2720-6/14/10.
http://dx.doi.org/10.1145/2661334.2661347

positions are different every time, it is difficult for them to memorize finger movements like touch-typing of PC. It takes a long time for them to find the target key even if they memorize the assignment of software keyboards. Other methods [3-4] including key selection have the same problems as GridFlick [1] for visually impaired people. Since number of Kana-characters is larger than that of alphabet, it is physical burden to increase tap number to input a character such as [5].

To solve the problems, we propose Move&Flick as a Japanese text entry method [2].

2. MOVE&FLICK

Basic Move&Flick operations are shown below (see Figure 1). (STEP1) Touch an arbitrary position around the center of the screen. (STEP2) Move the single finger in any of eight directions (up, right-up, right, right-down, down, left-down, left, left-up) over a prescribed amount to select a consonant. (STEP3) Move the single finger in any of eight directions again without lifting the finger from the screen to select a vowel after STEP2. (STEP4) Lift the finger from the screen if target character is reached.

The finger motions of STEP1 and STEP2 mean Move, moving the finger from one position to another position on the screen without lifting it. The finger motion of STEP3 and STEP4 means Flick, that is, lifting the finger from the screen while moving the finger in the desired direction. STEP1 of Move&Flick shows that the burden of finding the initial position is eliminated.

It is preferable that beginners should be assisted in learning directions by the movement directions close to ideal ones. This method uses radial areas with dead zones to detect the movement direction (Figure 2). Voice feedback is muted in the dead zones and is echoed in the radial areas. The use of dead zones allows the users to acquire accurate finger.

The accuracy, with which a changing point from first movement direction to second movement direction is detected, also affects the accuracy with which the second movement direction is detected. The changing point is Point Y (see Figure 1(STEP3)). To measure the second movement direction, two points are needed. One point is Point Y. the other point is the finger release point from the screen. However, Point B, where the device detects first movement direction, doesn't coincide with Point Y. The reason is that each user moves his/her finger by different amounts with each input. The proposed algorithm shown in Figure 3 confirms whether the detected first finger movement direction and the finger motion is the same every time the finger moves over a prescribed distance that is the radius of C2 shown in Figure 3(iii).

Since the number of consonants in Japanese is over eight kinds and increasing the level of menu lead increment of errors, we handle this situation by setting a tap entry prior to STEP1. Therefore, Move&Flick offers 128 (two modes * eight directions * eight directions) inputs.

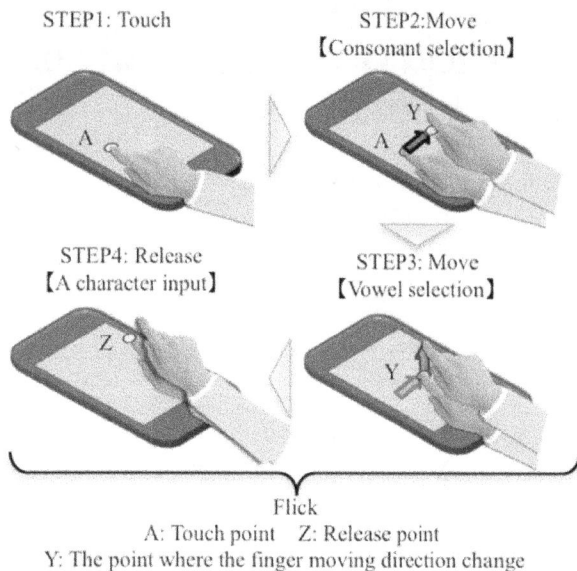

STEP1: Touch

STEP2:Move
【Consonant selection】

STEP4: Release
【A character input】

STEP3: Move
【Vowel selection】

Flick
A: Touch point   Z: Release point
Y: The point where the finger moving direction change

Figure 1. An operation sequence of Move&Flick

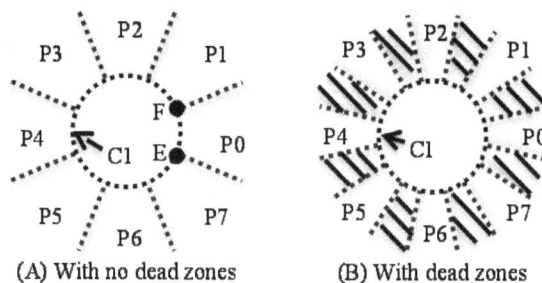

(A) With no dead zones   (B) With dead zones

Figure 2. Nine areas with dead zones to let the visually impaired acquire proper finger motion needed to select a consonant

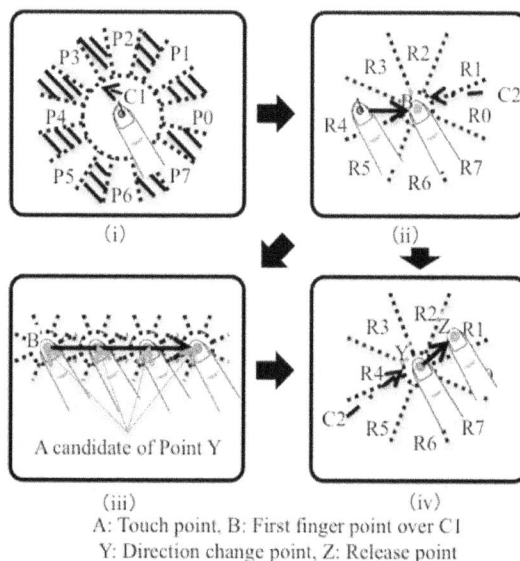

(i)   (ii)   (iii)   (iv)

A: Touch point, B: First finger point over C1
Y: Direction change point, Z: Release point

Figure 3. An algorithm to detect the changing point of finger movement direction

3. EXPERIMENT&RESULT

We conducted an experiment with 6 subjects to evaluate the performance of Move&Flick. A between-subjects design was used. The independent variables were without/with dead zones. 3 subjects frequently couldn't select target consonants in the case of no dead zones. They were confused and couldn't acquire finger movement directions. Meanwhile, other 3 subjects could acquire the finger movements in the case of dead zones and average character input speed of all subjects was 36 CPM (characters per minute). It was also confirmed that movement distance differs with each input of each person. This shows that the proposed detection algorithm is effective in catching the change point (Point Y). Interview with the 3 subjects showed that Move&Flick was acceptable for visually impaired people aspects of inputting characters without depending on voice feedback once the users learn movement directions.

4. CONCLUSION

In this paper, we proposed Move&Flick, a Kana-character entry method for the visually impaired using touch screens. Move&Flick has areas with dead zones to detect the moving directions of the finger. An experiment showed that the dead zones and voice feedback let the users acquire proper finger directions in an easy learning process. In addition, it was shown that the algorithm that can detect the change point of finger movement was effective. As result, the paper showed potential of Move&Flick.

This research and development activity is supported by Ministry of Internal Affairs and Communications in Japan Government.

5. REFERENCES

[1] Grid Flick
     http://ja.wikipedia.org/wiki/フリック入力

[2] Aoki, R., Hashimoto, R., Seko, S., Kataoka, Y., Ihara, M., Watanabe, M. and Kobayashi, T. Move&Flick: A Text Entry Method on a Touch Screen for The visually impaired, In Interaction2013, 72-79. (in Japanese)

[3] Sánchez, J. and Aguayo, F. Mobile Messenger for the Blind. In Proc. ERCIM2006, 369-385

[4] Fukatsu, Y., Shizuki, B. and Tanaka, J. No-Look Flick: Single-handed and Eyes-free Japanese Text Input System on Touch Screens of Mobile Devices. In Proc. Mobile HCI2013, 161-170.

[5] Oliveira, J., Guerreiro, T., Nicolau, H., Jorge, J., Gonçalves, D., Blind People and Mobile Touch-based Text-Entry: Acknowledging the Need for Different Flavors, In Proc. ASSET2011, 2011.

New Tools for Automating Tactile Geographic Map Translation

Nizar BOUHLEL and Anis ROJBI
University Paris 8, Laboratory CHART, team THIM, France
nizar.bouhlel@uvsq.fr, Anis.rojbi@univ-paris8.fr

ABSTRACT

We present a new software program that converts a geographic map given in a formatted image file to a tactile form suitable for blind students. The software is designed to semi-automate the translation from visual maps to tactile versions, and to help tactile graphics specialists to be faster and more efficient in producing the tactile geographic map. The developed tools cover a wide variety of image processing techniques, optical character recognition and Braille translation.

Categories and Subject Descriptors

K.4.2 [**Social Issues**]: Assistive technologies for persons with disabilities—*People with visual disabilities*

General Terms

Human Factors

Keywords

Tactile geographic map, image processing, OCR, machine learning, Braille translation, visual disability

1. INTRODUCTION

Graphical images, such as geographic maps, are prevalent in school book illustrations. However, graphical information is inaccessible for people with visual impairment or blind students. Studies have demonstrated that tactile graphics are the best modality for comprehension of graphical images [1, 7] for blind users. Usually, graphical images are converted to tactile form by tactile graphic specialists (TGS) involving non-trivial manual steps. Although there exists techniques that contribute to helping TGS in converting a graphical images into a tactile format, the procedures involved are typically time-consuming, expensive and labor-intensive. In recent years, efforts have been devoted to automate the tedious manual creation and the translation task. Image processing as edge detection and image segmentation is intensively employed on tactile graphics [8, 5]. In our study, We propose a complete application developed with Matlab to support TGS. We use advanced image processing and machine learning techniques to produce the tactile map and recognize text within the image. Two other techniques are also added: the attribution of texture for each color of the segmented image and Braille translation. The main differences with previous works are 1) the system is all included in one software program which is extremely useful in the community 2) the attribution of texture for each class of the segmented image. Texture is a key feature of graphics which is quickly grasped by tactile means due to the spatial layout. In the following sections, we introduces the proposed application and the technical choices related to this method. In the last section, we discusses future improvements to our program and the outlook for its implementation.

2. METHODS

The process of translating a visual geographic map into a tactile one takes several processing steps:(1) image acquisition and pre-processing, (2) image segmentation, (3) image simplification, (4) texture attribution, (5) optical character recognition (OCR), (6) Braille translation, (7) tactile image output. In the first step, the original geographic map is scanned and then filtered for noise removal. The second step is used to partition the image into objects or classes. The third step involves simplification using a number of image processing techniques to reduce the level of details and complexity of the original image. The next step consists of associating the color of each class or object with a distinct shape or texture. With these tools, the user can translate the image to its tactile form in ways that are similar to current manual practices.

2.1 Image processing

Several useful image processing tasks are required to simplify and reduce the level of detail and complexity of the original image. Due to the nature of the geographic map, we choose to segment image using the clustering method. Data clustering is the process of dividing data elements into classes or clusters so that items in the same class are as similar as possible, and items in different classes are as dissimilar as possible. Fuzzy C-Means [2] technique is used in our study. The number of classes is fixed by the user or the TGS to avoid a fastidious calculus to find the best numbers of classes. With the clustering method, the classified text can be removed and filled by the color of the surrounding

ASSETS'14, October 20–22, 2014, Rochester, NY, USA.
ACM 978-1-4503-2720-6/14/10.
http://dx.doi.org/10.1145/2661334.2661335.

area. Some mathematical morphology (MM) operators are used in our application, like the dilation which allows us to expand an area and erasing the surrounding areas and hiding complex border details. Another algorithm used to simplify the border region and modify the geometrical structure is the Douglas-Peucker algorithm [6]. Its purpose is, given a curve composed of line segments, to find a similar curve with fewer points. The legend is also removed and it will be used in the text processing step (OCR). The final step is very important. It makes the treated map image tactile. It consists to choose starkly contrasting textures to each area in order to clearly understood by blind students. TGS have a variety of textures to choose from to facilitate better tactile perception. They have the possibility to change the size and the shape of the pattern.

2.2 Optical character recognition: OCR

This section will outline how we will locate and recognize text characters in the image and finally translate them to Braille format. What makes our work unique is that all the OCR steps are developed in Matlab. We used a morphological operation for text localisation and a Neural Network (NN) for character recognition with post processing tasks. In our approach, we used a combination of an edge-based technique with a morphological operation for text localization [3]. Once character extraction has been completed, the next step will be feature extraction. Each character (two-dimensional image) is represented by a set of features (one-dimensional feature vector) that represent the relevant information of the character image and are used to discriminate it from the other characters. In our work, we used the zoning technique because it is simple to implement and yields satisfactory results. The extracted features are then put into the classifier for classification. The classifier searches for a resemblance between the feature extracted from the given character and the library of character models, and at the end it gives the correct character model. For our application, we used the NN [4] with Multi-layer perceptrons (MLPs) as classifier. It consists of multiple layers of neurons: one input layer, hidden layers and one output layer [4]. We first train the NN with the extracted feature vectors from the training dataset. Second, we test the NN to obtain the recognized character. After text is generated by OCR, it must be translated to Braille. This is done with Matlab. The final step is to combine the Braille, the text location and the segmented image without text into a new document suitable for the PIAF or embosser tactile image printer. This new document is composed of two pages. The first contains the texture with the Braille code and the second contains the legend described in Braille with a brief description of texture as shown in figure 1.

3. CONCLUSIONS AND DISCUSSION

In this paper we have presented new tools to automate the conversion of a visual geographic map into tactile form, and to help tactile graphics specialists be more efficient in their work. These new tools, developed exclusively with Matlab, encompass all the traditional steps: segmentation, simplification, texture attribution, OCR, and Braille translation. The development of these tools has benefited from feedback from specialists of INSHEA [1] and from volunteers. We in-

---

[1] http://www.inshea.fr

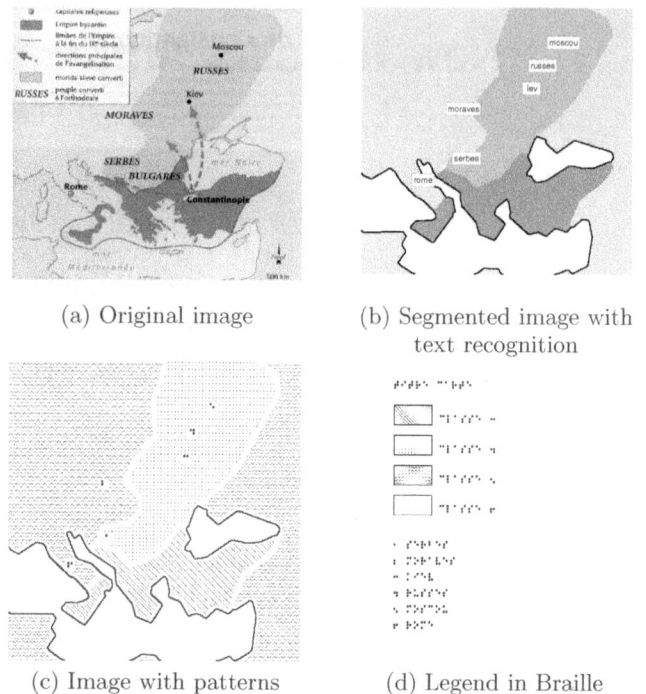

(a) Original image

(b) Segmented image with text recognition

(c) Image with patterns

(d) Legend in Braille

Figure 1: Example of transformation of a geographic map image to a tactile form at various steps of the process.

tend to expand our program to work with other kinds of images in the fields of science and art and to deal with the unique needs of each image modality. There is much research left to do concerning character extraction and recognition, especially in images containing text.

4. REFERENCES

[1] M. Batusic and F. Urban. Preparing tactile graphics for traditional braille printers with brlgrapheditor in computers helping people with special needs. *ICCHP 2002, in Computer Science*, 2398:535–536, 2002.

[2] J. C. Bezdek. *Pattern Recognition with Fuzzy Objective Function Algorithms*. ISBN 0-306-40671-3, 1981.

[3] R. Chandrasekaran. Morphology based text extraction in images. *IJCST*, 4 (2), 2011.

[4] D. Chen, J. M. Odobez, and H. Bourlard. Text detection and recognition in images and video frames. *Pattern Recognition*, (37):595–608, 2004.

[5] D. Crombie, R. Lenoir, N. McKenzie, and G. Ioannidis. The bigger picture: Automated production tools for tactile graphics. *ICCHP*, pages 713–720, 2004.

[6] D. Douglas and T. Peucker. Algorithms for the reduction of the number of points required to represent a digitized line or its caricature. *The Canadian Cartographer*, 10(2):112–122, 1973.

[7] W. Schiff and E. Foulke. *Tactual Perception*. Cambridge University Press, Cambridge, 1982.

[8] T. Way and K. Barner. Automatic visual to tactile translation, part ii: Evaluation of the tactile image creation system. *In IEEE Transactions on Rehabilitation Engineering*, pages 95–105, 1997.

OS-Level Surface Haptics for Touch-Screen Accessibility

Suhong Jin, Joe Mullenbach, Craig Shultz, J. Edward Colgate, Anne Marie Piper

Northwestern University

2145 Sheridan Road

Evanston, IL 60208

{suhongjin, mullenbach, craigdshultz}@u.northwestern.edu, {colgate, ampiper}@northwestern.edu

ABSTRACT

The TPad Tablet combines an Android tablet with a variable friction haptic touch-screen and offers many novel interaction possibilities. For example, unique textures may be associated with different user interface elements, such as text boxes and buttons. This paper presents an Android AccessibilityService that was created to give operating system-wide (OS) access to haptic effects. Prior to this work, the haptic feedback of the TPad could be controlled only from within specific applications. With the new implementation, all applications and primary user interfaces (e.g. home screen) will have access to the TPad. Rather than focus on specific elements or applications, we seek to provide a high fidelity haptic experience that elevates the TPad's accessibility to the standard of Talkback and Voiceover, Android's and Apple's accessibility programs respectively. The code for the application is available on our website.

Categories and Subject Descriptors

H.5.2 [Information Interfaces And Presentation]: User Interfaces - Haptic I/O. K.4.2 [Social Issues]: Assistive Technologies For Persons With Disabilities.

Keywords

Surface Haptics; Touchscreen; Tablet; Accessibility; Variable Friction

1. INTRODUCTION

Existing accessibility solutions such as Apple's Voiceover and Android's Talkback services rely heavily on audio cues [3, 5]. Both programs speak to the user, providing information on the current screen and any UI element that a user touches. As has been previously reported, auditory feedback may not always be the optimal solution [11]. Users may not hear well in noisy environments and headphones can limit user's awareness of obstacles in their path and surroundings. With haptic feedback, a user can quickly identify different elements on the screen [11]. To realize this vision more broadly, we implemented OS-level haptic accessibility using the TPad Tablet, a variable friction haptic surface integrated with a 7-inch Android tablet shown in Figure 1 [8, 12]. Different than vibration feedback that is most common in mobile devices today, the TPad surface is driven ultrasonically to reduce friction between the surface and the fingertip. This creates a slippery feeling that is felt only when the fingertip slides across the

ASSETS'14, October 20–22, 2014, Rochester, NY, USA.

ACM 978-1-4503-2720-6/14/10.

http://dx.doi.org/10.1145/2661334.2661343

screen, and not on the hand that is holding the device. Past versions of the TPad Tablet software allowed haptic feedback to be accessed through specific applications that called TPad methods. In this project, an operating system-level interface to haptic functionality was created through Android's AccessibilityService.

2. Background

In recent years, several attempts have been made to improve touch-screen accessibility for people with vision impairments. Touchplates [10] gave users different acrylic overlays, including a

Figure 1: TPad in use on the home screen

QWERTY keyboard and a numeric keypad to provide tactile feedback during typing. Other overlays include a map, mouse, and a menu bar. While a useful solution, the user is constrained to a physical haptic guide, limiting its flexibility and requiring them to manage physical plates in addition to their device. Haptic rendering of images has also been researched to allow devices to provide haptic feedback on 2d images [6, 9]. By analyzing the colors of the images, various textures were mapped to the image. Electrovibration haptic feedback has also been used in a mobile, visuo-tactile sensory device for the visually impaired [1]. The device has an attached webcam used to explore the user's surroundings and identify an object of interest. The object is displayed on a screen at which point a finger can be swept across the screen, in essence feeling the object.

Other techniques focus on novel gesture-based input to improve accessibility of number entry (e.g. DigiTaps [11]). In this system, the user performs a unique combination of swipes and taps to input a specific digit. The system provides haptic feedback to notify the user that the gesture was received and correctly interpreted. Audio feedback is also optionally available.

3. Implementation

In the present work, rather than focus on specific elements or applications, we seek to provide high fidelity haptic experience that increases accessibility across the entire device, much as Talkback and Voiceover do for audio. We use a time based friction modulation method to create distinct "texture tones", single-frequency amplitude modulated variable friction waveforms, for different icons and elements on the screen. This method of variable friction rendering has been used in previous studies, and was found to have a range of expressive capabilities, interpreted by users as a physical texture, as a sensation, or as an action [7].

3.1 AccessibilityService

An AccessibilityService is a background service that can be installed on an Android device and turned on through the Accessibility section of the settings of the smart device [2]. Talkback is one example of an AccessibilityService [5]. The AccessibilityService detects when the user interface's state changes. When the user puts his or her finger down on the screen (Figure 1), the service alerts the system of the touch interaction. If the user enters a view (for example, a button) the service also detects that change. As the users explores different UI elements, any changes are sent to the service to be handled.

3.2 Integrating the TPad

The TPad communicates with Android applications through IOIO libraries [4]. The IOIO libraries specific to Android applications have been modified to generate a custom library. When a developer creates an Android application, he or she adds this custom library to use the TPad-specific methods. For the AccessibilityService, a IOIO class that worked with services, instead of applications was created. The front-end TPadAccessibilityService class utilizes this new IOIO class to access the TPad.

3.3 Handling AccessibilityEvents

All AccessibilityService classes require an onAccessiblityEvent method. This method is called when an AccessibilityEvent is triggered. The TPadAccessibilityService focuses primarily on two AccessibilityEvents. The VIEW_HOVER_ENTER event occurs when a user slides his or her finger over a UI element, while VIEW_HOVER_EXIT is triggered when exiting a UI element. When the user's finger moves to a UI element, the TPad sends a texture tone while exiting the element turns the TPad off. Information about the UI element examined can be retrieved through AccessibilityRecords [2]. For example, the service can retrieve the contentDescription tag of elements, a concept Android documentation has stressed when implementing accessibility for applications. In the current implementation of the service, a look-up table of a few popular applications is searched with the UI element's currentDescription, though this could easily be expanded and customized to cover all applications. If the string is in the table, a unique texture is generated. Otherwise, the service checks the view's properties (editable, checkable, clickable, etc.). Each of these different properties have different texture tones to distinguish them from each other.

4. Advantages of AccessibilityService

With an operating system-level implementation of the TPad, Android application developers need not add TPad-specific code. The AccessibilityService automatically generates TPad texture tones through the service. However, developers can still add additional haptic feedback by implementing TPad methods within their application. Using the AccessibilityService also allows the TPad to work on the home screen, and other native applications. The AccessibilityService can also allow Android developers to customize a texture tone for a given element in their application. The developer can pass a Bundle with the properties of a TPad texture (floats for frequency and amplitude and an integer for wave type). The AccessibilityService can retrieve the Bundle through the AccessibilityRecord and generate the custom texture.

The ability to generate specific textures based on whether a view is editable, checkable, clickable, etc. elevates the TPad Tablet's accessibility toward the standard of Voiceover & Talkback. A user can be on any screen in the smart device, whether it is the home screen, the browser, or a specific application, and detect buttons, checkmarks, and edit boxes not just with audio and vibrational feedback from Voiceover & Talkback, but also with variable friction surface haptic feedback from the TPad.

5. Conclusion

Android's AccessibilityService has been used to give developers operating system-wide access to haptic feedback via the TPad. This makes the TPad available not just in specific applications, but in the home screen and other native application pages and should pave the way to broader and more diverse uses of surface haptic technology. The code is open-source and available for download [12].

6. ACKNOWLEDGMENTS

This work was supported by NSF Grant 0964075, McCormick School of Engineering, and the Segal Design Institute. Thanks also to the open-source IOIO project [4]. Special thanks to the many contributors to The TPad Tablet Project [12].

7. REFERENCES

[1] Ali Israr, Olivier Bau, Seung-Chan Kim, and Ivan Poupyrev. 2012. Tactile feedback on flat surfaces for the visually impaired. New York, NY, USA, 1571-1576.

[2] Android Accessibility. http://developer.android.com/guide/topics/ui/accessibility/index.html. Acc. June 17, 2014.

[3] Apple Inc., iPhone Accessibility. http://www.apple.com/accessibility/ios/. Acc. June 16, 2014.

[4] Ben-Tsvi, Y. IOIO Documentation. https://github.com/ytai/ioio/wiki. Acc. June 17, 2014.

[5] Google, Android Accessibility Help Center. http://www.support.google.com/talkback/. Acc. June 16, 2014.

[6] Jialu Li, Aiguo Song, and Xiaorui Zhang. 2010. Image-based haptic texture rendering. New York, NY.

[7] Joe Mullenbach, Craig Shultz, J. Edward Colgate, Anne Marie Piper. 2014. Exploring Affective Communication Through Variable-Friction Surface Haptics. (CHI '14). New York, NY.

[8] Joe Mullenbach, Craig Shultz, Anne Marie Piper, Michael Peshkin, and J. Edward Colgate. 2013. Surface haptic interactions with a TPad tablet. (UIST '13 Adjunct). New York, NY.

[9] Seung-Chan Kim, Ki-Uk Kyung, Dong-Soo Kwon. 2011. Haptic annotation for an interactive image. New York, NY.

[10] Shaun K. Kane, Meredith Ringel Morris, and Jacob O. Wobbrock. 2013. Touchplates: low-cost tactile overlays for visually impaired touch screen users. New York, NY.

[11] Shiri Azenkot, Cynthia L. Bennett, and Richard E. Ladner. 2013. DigiTaps: eyes-free number entry on touchscreens with minimal audio feedback. New York, NY.

[12] TPad Tablet Project. http://www.tpadtablet.org. Acc. June 17, 2014

Real-Time Caption Challenge: C-Print

Michael Stinson, Pamela Francis, Lisa Elliot and Donna Easton
National Technical Institute for the Deaf
Rochester Institute of Technology, Rochester, NY 14523
(msserd, lbenrd, pggncp)@rit.edu

ABSTRACT

This poster/demonstration session showcases C-Print, a typing-based transcription system. This form of real-time captioning will be provided for approximately one half day during the ASSETS 2014 Conference and will be part of a real-time caption challenge. The C-Print system requires a trained transcriptionist who uses computerized abbreviations and condensing strategies to produce the text display of spoken information. This spoken information appears as text on a computer or mobile device for viewing by the consumer approximately two seconds later.

Keywords

Accessibility; captioning; deaf; hard of hearing

1. INTRODUCTION

This poster/demonstration session will showcase a form of real-time captioning: C-Print, a typing-based transcription system. This form of real-time captioning will be provided for approximately one half day during the ASSETS 2014 Conference and will be part of the real-time caption challenge that Raja Kushalnagar is organizing.

When deaf or hard of hearing (D/HH) individuals participate in classes, meetings, etc. with hearing individuals, they often have difficulty understanding the speaker and other participants. Access services help D/HH individuals understand the participants who speak. One reason that providing appropriate access services is difficult is that different D/HH individuals have different communication needs. One D/HH individual may use sign language and use an interpreter for communication access. Other individuals may rely on speech-reading and a hearing aid or cochlear implant and know little sign language. Another challenge is the setting: D/HH individual's communication access needs may be different for a history class and for a business meeting.

Real-time captioning, also called speech-to-text, is one way to provide communication access for D/HH individuals. Other options for communication access are sign language interpreting and note taking. The captioning option recognizes the importance of printed information for D/HH people. These individuals often send text messages; read captions on television, etc.

In C-Print real-time captioning, a service provider who is often in the classroom or other setting with the D/HH individual (s) produces text as it is being spoken by a speaker (teacher, etc.) and displays it on a device so that the D/HH individual can understand what is happening in the class, meeting, etc. The C-Print captioning technology is used to produce a text display of spoken information for individuals who are deaf or hard of hearing (or other individuals who may have difficulty understanding speech).

For the past 25 years, a group of researchers and developers in the National Technical Institute for the Deaf (NTID), a college at the Rochester Institute of Technology (RIT), has been developing the C-Print real-time captioning system.

2. C-PRINT CAPTIONING TECHNOLOGY AND SERVICE

This poster/demonstration describes the C-Print technology and highlights a recent development, C-Print Mobile, which is currently being evaluated with National Science Foundation funding. Figure 1 provides a schematic of how C-Print works.

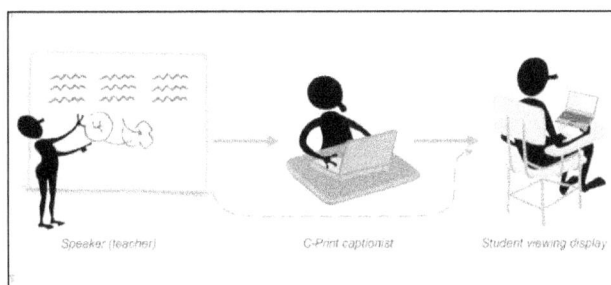

Figure 1. How C-Print Real-Time Captioning Works

The C-Print system requires a trained transcriptionist who uses computerized abbreviations and condensing strategies to produce the text display of spoken information. Approximately two seconds later, the spoken information is displayed on a computer or mobile device. The content can be saved and distributed as a transcript afterward. C-Print is a keyboard-based system. (It uses a standard keyboard.) To increase typing speed, the provider of C-Print services, called a "captionist," uses a computerized word-abbreviation system. C-Print abbreviations are primarily based on phonetic rules. The examples here demonstrate how the abbreviations typed in the C-Print software expand into the information displayed.

A captionist types:
"wlkm to t nxl tknkl nsttt f t deaf"

The information displayed:
"Welcome to the National Technical Institute for the Deaf"

The C-Print service may also be provided remotely. If a captionist is located remotely, the captionist hears the spoken information via a phone or VoIP service and the information is transmitted via Wi-Fi or mobile data service so the student can view the information in class.

The C-Print system enables a captionist to produce a display of text that is a thorough and complete translation, or paraphrase, of the spoken English content. Although C-Print sometimes does not provide word-for-word transcription because it cannot keep up with the speed of speech (variable, but often approximately 150 words per minute), the system does capture virtually all of the meaning of the lecture.

2.1 Benefits

C-Print helps facilitate communication by aiding access to and understanding of spoken communication. The words in the C-Print display remain on the computer screen for enough time for an individual to comprehend and consider them. In contrast, with a sign language interpreter, individuals only see the words for a fraction of a second. In addition, captions are visually accessible: This means that the captionist arranges the information in a visually informative way. For example, in certain situations the captionist may highlight, bold, or use numbers.

C-Print provides a succinct delivery of spoken information. The C-Print captionist produces text that states information concisely. The text includes all the meaning, but does not include redundancies. Stating information concisely means that the C-Print transcript, or C-Print notes, will be shorter and easier to study than a verbatim transcript.

C-Print provides a record for review after a class, meeting. etc. The stored text, or C-Print notes, is a valuable study tool. The similarity between the text that an individual sees during the class, meeting, etc. and the text one uses to study afterwards helps one relate the information to the class, etc.

C-Print may also help improve a D/HH or other individual's language use. The C-Print captionist produces a display of the written language that provides repeated exposure to a model of the language. Another benefit of C-Print is that D/HH and other users can view the spoken information from a remote location; they do not need to be in the class or meeting room.

2.2 Training of Providers of C-Print Captioning

The C-Print captionist is trained to include all information being said in producing the text display. One cannot just go into the classroom and provide C-Print services; training in provision of C-Print services is necessary. On average, learning the abbreviation system requires about 50 hours of training. In this training, the captionist learns abbreviations for words in order to increase typing speed by 50% and to reduce strain on wrists and hands. The trainee learns a set of rules for abbreviating; the trainee does not memorize individual abbreviations for the words. Additional parts of the training include condensing spoken information, the provider's role, formatting text, and preparing notes for distribution. Providers must sometimes eliminate a few of the spoken words, such as very repetitious material. Training for C-Print providers is online, and it is desirable to have a mentor, such as a person who is already a provider of C-Print services. Mentoring may be by phone or online, as well as in person. After enrolling in the training, a person has a year to complete it. More than 2000 individuals have completed or are undergoing C-Print training.

3. C-PRINT MOBILE

The new C-Print Mobile app allows users to view captioning in a variety of settings; for example, in traditional classrooms, labs, and meetings. Users can also use the Mobile app to view captioning in remote settings, such as a classroom field trip. C-Print Mobile was developed partly to incorporate advances in technology, such as wide use of iPads, other tablet devices, and Smart phones, and also to enable C-Print to effectively meet D/HH communication access needs in situations where it has not been possible to effectively provide services with standard laptops. For example in laboratory settings, lab tables often have considerable paraphernalia and a laptop for viewing captions takes up too much table space. In addition, students often need to move around a lab when carrying out an experiment, go up to the instructor, etc., and it is cumbersome to carry and read an open laptop while moving around the laboratory.

C-Print Mobile has been developed in part with NSF support (Award 0726591) and is being evaluated in laboratory contexts at RIT and 3 other postsecondary institutions (Award 1032033). In July 2013 the app for viewing C-Print real-time captions on mobile devices was released to the general public as a free download from the Apple iTunes and Google Play stores. Figure 2 show C-Print being displayed on a standard iPad and a mini iPad.

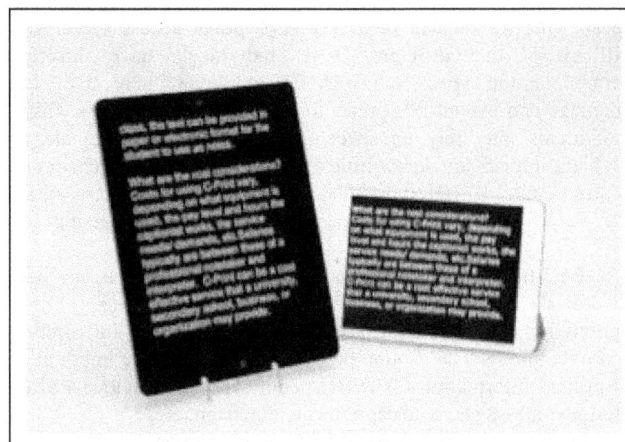

Figure 2. C-Print display on a standard iPad and a mini iPad.

4. ACKNOWLEDGEMENTS

The work reported in this paper has been supported in part by NSF awards HRD-072659 and HRD-0726591

SpeechOmeter: Heads-up Monitoring to Improve Speech Clarity

Mansoor Pervaiz
Northeastern University
360 Huntington Ave.
Boston, MA 02115, USA
mansoor@ccs.neu.edu

Rupal Patel
Northeastern University
360 Huntington Ave.
Boston, MA 02115, USA
r.patel@neu.edu

ABSTRACT

Individuals with neuromotor speech disorders due to conditions such as Multiple Sclerosis, Parkinson Disease and Cerebral Palsy have soft and slurred speech. These individuals receive speech training to increase vocal loudness and to speak slowly and clearly. Although successful in clinical settings, generalizability of these techniques to daily conversation requires technological innovation. To address this issue we designed SpeechOmeter, a Google Glass application that provides unobtrusive real-time visual feedback on vocal loudness relative to the ambient noise level. The system also provides clinicians with treatment adherence and performance statistics in order to further personalize speech training regimes. In a longitudinal usability study 12 individuals with MS increased vocal loudness when provided with feedback. A live demonstration of SpeechOmeter will enable attendees to experience the system.

Categories and Subject Descriptors

K.4 [**Computers and Society**]: Social Issues—*Assistive technologies for persons with disabilities*; H.5 [**Information Interfaces and Presentation**]: User Interfaces—*Screen design*

General Terms

Design, Human Factors

Keywords

Assistive communication, speech therapy, visual feedback, speech clarity, speech prosthesis

1. INTRODUCTION

Dysarthria is a speech impairment that accompanies neuromotor disorders such as Multiple Sclerosis, Parkinson Disease and Cerebral Palsy, which results in a soft, breathy, fluctuating voice and imprecise articulation that hinders clarity and restricts interpersonal interactions [1].

ASSETS'14, October 20–22, 2014, Rochester, NY, USA.
ACM 978-1-4503-2720-6/14/10.
http://dx.doi.org/10.1145/2661334.2661339

There are two main intervention strategies used by clinicians to improve speech intelligibility: 1) reduced speaking rate [8] and 2) increased vocal loudness [7]. Lee Silverman Voice Treatment (LSVT), which focuses on increased loudness improves speech clarity for individuals with Parkinson's disease (PD) [5] and has also shows promise for individuals with Multiple Sclerosis [6], Cerebral Palsy [2] and Down syndrome [4]. Adherence and generalizability are limited by three main issues: 1) the lack of qualified clinicians limits access to the treatment to fewer than 5% of the effected population [3], 2) LSVT requires speaking at maximum effort at all times which may not be appropriate in all situations and may result in vocal fatigue and 3) clients require frequent reminders and cues to implement the strategies. To build upon empirical evidence that increased vocal loudness improves speech clarity and yet to address these concerns, we sought to design a novel heads-up interface that provides users with visual biofeedback cues as to their own vocal loudness while engaged in daily conversation.

2. SPEECHOMETER

SpeechOmeter provides visual cues to vocal loudness relative to the ambient noise level for speech monitoring and improved treatment adherence. The user's vocal loudness is measured and shown on a head-up display in a relatively unobtrusive manner and in real-time to encourage users to speak atleast upto 5 decibels (dB) louder than the ambient noise level. This threshold was selected based on post-LSVT treatment increases noted among participants in previous studies [5]. The interface provides users with frequent feedback to calibrate their speaking volume relative to the ambient environment rather than a static level that may be too fatiguing. The system also maintains usage and performance history and shares it with the user and clinician. The clinician can thereby customize an individual's treatment plan accordingly.

The SpeechOmeter application consists of two parts: a mobile phone module and a Google Glass module. The phone module, records the ambient noise signal (sampling at 8kHz with 16 bit quantization), computes the dB value over a 20-millisecond window, and sends it to the Glass module over bluetooth. The Glass module, records user's voice signal (sampling at 8kHz with 16 bit quantization), computes a dB value over a 20-millisecond window, subtracts the ambient noise dB received from the phone module and provides visual feedback based on the difference of the two dB values.

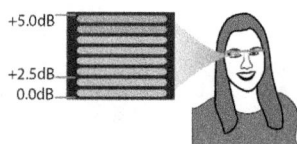

Figure 1: Illustration of SpeechOmeter system vocal loudness feedback

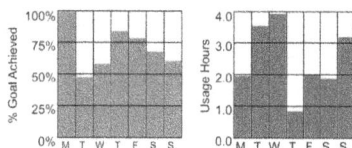

Figure 2: Sample performance (left) and adherence (right) graphs

Table 1: Preliminary data

Speakers	No Feedback(dB)	Feedback(dB)	dB increase
1	67.98	75.26	7.28
2	69.62	77.11	7.49
3	65.23	75.56	10.33
4	70.09	74.30	4.21
5	71.04	74.78	3.74
6	79.91	81.74	1.83
7	80.13	82.95	2.82
8	78.12	79.88	1.76
9	77.89	80.79	2.90
Avg	77.89	77.93	4.52

SpeechOmeter provides visual feedback in a relatively unobtrusive manner (Figure 1) to allow for monitoring visual cues in one's peripheral vision a consideration that accommodates for focal vision deficits. The target loudness range of 5dB has been segmented into eight bars such that when a user speaks > 5 dB above the ambient level, all bars turn green. However, the distribution of loudness is not linear. The lower two bars depict half of the target range (0 to 2.5 dB above the ambient noise) and the upper 6 bars represent the remaining half of the target dB (2.6 to 5dB+ above the ambient noise).

The system provides performance and adherence statistics that can be computed over a few minutes to a full week (Figure 2). The performance graph indicates the percentage of time a user was able to maintain the target volume while speaking, and the adherence graph shows number of hours an individual used the system every day. While the graphs only display information for past seven days, prior history can be viewed by downloading data from the Glass device.

3. PRELIMINARY RESULTS

To evaluate the efficacy of SpeechOmeter on a target population, we conducted a longitudinal usability study at an assisted living facility that serves individuals with MS. 12 participants were enrolled in our 6 week long study. Preliminary analysis of data, from nine participants, (Table 1) indicates that the average loudness change of 4.52 dB in the feedback condition is comparable to the average 4.68 dB increase achieved [5] using conventional clinician-based intervention. Participants with loudness under 70 dB in no-feedback condition increased their loudness by more than 7 dB in feedback condition.

4. SUMMARY

The SpeechOmeter addresses shortcomings of conventional speech treatment by providing users with: 1) visual feedback about vocal loudness on a heads-up display in the absence of clinician cues; 2) an adaptive interface that considers the ambient noise to minimize fatigue while optimizing speech clarity and 3) performance and adherence statistics to help customize intervention. The system has the potential to extend clinician mediated training to daily conversations to track user adherence and performance for customized intervention. We envision the next iteration of SpeechOmeter will include feedback on speech rate to further improve speech intelligibility.

5. ACKNOWLEDGMENT

We thank residents of The Boston Home and their speech therapist (Alex Burnham) for their participation and are grateful to Emily Vishnja, Fallon Cassidy, and Kevin Jiang for their contribution to the design of the SpeechOmeter.

6. REFERENCES

[1] P.-A. Bringfelt, L. Hartelius, and B. Runmarker. Communication Problems in Multiple Sclerosis: 9-Year Follow-Up. *International Journal of MS Care*, 8(4):130–140, July 2006.

[2] C. M. Fox and C. A. Boliek. Intensive voice treatment (LSVT LOUD) for children with spastic cerebral palsy and dysarthria. *Journal of Speech, Language, and Hearing Research*, 55(3):930–945, 2012.

[3] L. Hartelius and P. Svensson. Speech and swallowing symptoms associated with Parkinson's disease and multiple sclerosis: a survey. *Folia Phoniatrica et Logopaedica*, 46(1):9–17, 1994.

[4] J. Petska, A. Halpern, L. Ramig, and T. Robinson. Lsvt and children with down syndrome: A pilot study. In *Conference on Motor Speech, Austin, TX*, 2006.

[5] L. O. Ramig, S. Countryman, C. O'Brien, M. Hoehn, and L. Thompson. Intensive speech treatment for patients with Parkinson's disease: short-and long-term comparison of two techniques. *Neurology*, 47(6):1496–1504, Dec. 1996.

[6] S. Sapir, A. A. Pawlas, L. O. Ramig, E. Seeley, C. Fox, and J. Corboy. Effects of intensive phonatory-respiratory treatment (LSVT) on voice in two individuals with multiple sclerosis. *Journal of Medical Speech-Language Pathology*, 9(2):141–151, 2001.

[7] N. P. Solomon, A. S. McKee, and S. Garcia-Barry. Intensive voice treatment and respiration treatment for hypokinetic-spastic dysarthria after traumatic brain injury. *American Journal of Speech-Language Pathology*, 10(1):51–64, 2001.

[8] K. M. Yorkston, M. Hakel, D. R. Beukelman, and S. Fager. Evidence for effectiveness of treatment of loudness, rate, or prosody in dysarthria: a systematic review. *Journal of Medical Speech-Language Pathology*, 15(2):XI–XXXVI, 2007.

Tactile Graphics with a Voice Demonstration

Catherine M. Baker, Lauren R. Milne, Jeffrey Scofield, Cynthia L. Bennett, Richard E. Ladner

Computer Science & Engineering
University of Washington Box 352350
Seattle, WA 98195-2350
{cmbaker, milnel2, jeffsco, bennec3, ladner}@cs.washington.edu

ABSTRACT

Textbook images are converted into tactile graphics to be made accessible to blind and low vision students. The text labels on these graphics are an important part of the image and must be made accessible as well. The graphics usually have the labels embossed in Braille. However, there are some blind and low vision students who cannot read Braille and need to be able to access the labels in a different manner. We present Tactile Graphics with a Voice, a system that encodes the labels in QR codes, which can be read aloud using the application, TGV, we developed. TGV provides feedback to support the user in scanning the QR code and allows the user to select which QR code to scan when multiple are close together.

Categories and Subject Descriptors

H.5.2. User Interfaces

General Terms

Design, Human Factors

Keywords

Access technology; blind; camera; non-visual feedback; visually impaired; tactile graphics; QR codes.

1. INTRODUCTION

From parabolas to diagrams of a cell, STEM textbooks are filled with images and these images are an essential part of the learning experience. Many of the images in textbooks contain important information that cannot be conveyed by text alone; therefore it is important to make sure that these images are accessible to all students.

A current solution to make these images accessible to those who are blind or low vision is to create a tactile representation of the image called a tactile graphic. Tactile graphics can range from low fidelity versions made out of craft materials to high fidelity versions which are embossed on paper. The labels for these graphics are generally placed on the tactile graphic in Braille. While Braille is a great access method for those who know it, a report from the National Federation of the Blind [4] indicated that

ASSETS '14, Oct 20-22 2014, Rochester, NY, USA
ACM 978-1-4503-2720-6/14/10.
http://dx.doi.org/10.1145/2661334.2661349

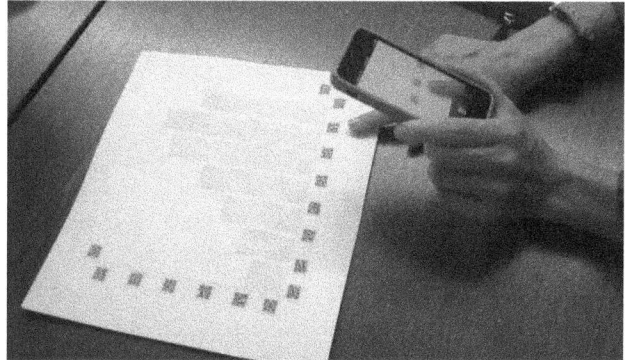

Figure 1. The Tactile Graphics with a Voice system in use. The subject is using the finger pointing mode to select which QR code to scan.

only 40% of the functionally blind population actually knows Braille. Many who are become blind late in life do not know Braille. This enforces the need for there to be a way for those who don't know Braille to access the text labels.

We present Tactile Graphics with a Voice, a system that makes the labels on tactile graphics accessible to blind and low vision users who do not know Braille. For more information on the design and evaluation of the system, please see our full paper in this conference [1].

2. TACTILE GRAPHICS WITH A VOICE

Tactile Graphics with a Voice consists of two parts. The graphics, which have been embossed with text labels transformed into QR codes (see Figure 1) and the accessible smartphone application, TGV, which helps the users scan the QR codes.

2.1 Creating the Graphics

The graphics needed for Tactile Graphics with a Voice can be created with few changes to the normal process to create tactile graphics. In general, to create tactile graphics there are three main steps: 1) Remove the text and do any processing to the image needed to transform it into a tactile format, 2) translate the text into Braille, and 3) place the Braille onto the image in the same or a nearby location as the original text. Our process only changes steps 2 and 3. To translate the text into a QR code you can use any free QR code generator. As most embossers do not have the ability to both emboss and print ink, we printed the QR codes on separate adhesive backed paper to cut and place on the embossed image. The labels can be easily located tactilely. Figure 2 shows the difference between a tactile graphic that has Braille and a tactile graphic with QR codes.

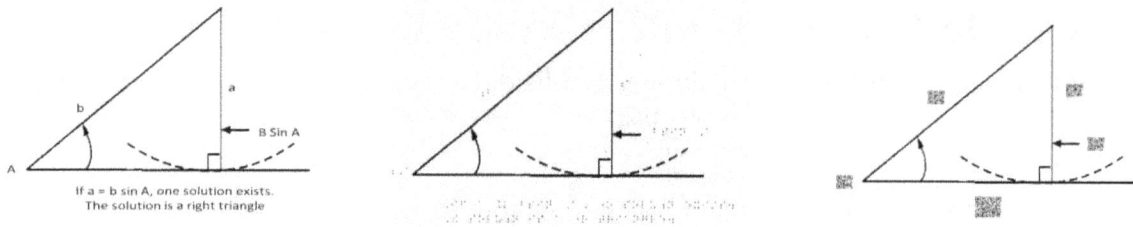

Figure 2. A comparison of the same image from a precalculus textbook [3] in its original form, tactile graphic form with the labels in Braille and tactile graphic form with labels as QR codes.

2.2 TGV Smartphone Application

TGV enables a blind or low vision user to easily scan the QR codes. TGV was built on top of the ZXing[1] software. This code looks for areas of black and white variation to determine where the QR codes are. We added a mode that allows the user to select between multiple QR codes and provides feedback to help the user scan the QR code.

2.2.1 Handling Multiple QR Codes

As we looked at the images in the textbooks, it was clear that there would be cases where there are multiple QR codes close together. When ZXing views multiple QR codes, it is not consistent on which one is scanned. We developed two modes to handle multiple QR codes being in view.

The first mode was to not scan anytime there were multiple QR codes visible. This would make the user responsible for isolating the QR code. In our user studies, we found that participants would isolate the QR code either by moving the phone closer to the graphic or by covering up the neighboring QR codes with their fingers.

The other mode was finger pointing. This mode works by scanning the QR code that is closest to the finger. We used skin detection techniques similar to those found in the literature to train TGV to identify the finger [2,5,6]. Due to the black and white nature of the graphics and QR codes, we were able to train our finger detection algorithm to detect more than just skin. We can also detect many different colors of nail polish.

As the code may recognize the presence of some, but not all, QR codes, we added a constraint to the finger pointing mode to require the finger to be within a certain number of pixels to the QR code. This will prevent the code from scanning the second closest QR code erroneously when the closest QR code is not detected.

2.2.2 Feedback

As aiming the camera can be a challenge for blind and low vision users, TGV integrated an option for auditory feedback to help aim the smartphone toward a QR code. A second option was to have no such auditory feedback. We felt it was important to leave the feedback as an option as interview participants indicated that there were situations where a quiet mode would be preferred.

The feedback we employed was based off results from Vázquez, et al. [7] who found that directives can be confusing as the orientation of the phone changes. As we understand that our users will not always hold the phone in the same way, the feedback indicated the location of the QR codes on the screen with the phrases "Top," "Bottom," "Left," and "Right."

TGV provides different types of feedback when multiple QR codes are visible depending on whether or not finger pointing mode is enabled. If it is enabled, feedback is given about the presence of a finger. If it does not detect a finger, it cannot scan so it says, "No Finger." If finger pointing mode is not enabled, it will say how many QR codes it detects.

3. CONCLUSION

Making textbook images accessible is an important problem in providing equal access to the materials for students with disabilities. Tactile Graphics with a Voice provides a new way to access the text for users who do not know Braille. The system encodes the labels in QR codes which can be scanned and read aloud with TGV.

4. ACKNOWLEDGEMENTS

This material is based upon work supported by the NSF Graduate Research Fellowship under Grant Nos. DGE-0718124 and DGE-1256082 and NSF Grant No. IIS-1116051. This work was supported by the U.S. Department of Education, Office of Special Education Programs (Cooperative Agreement #H327B100001). Opinions expressed herein are those of the authors and do not necessarily represent the position of the U.S. Department of Education or NSF.

5. REFERENCES

1. Baker, C.M., Milne, L. R., Scofield, J., Bennett, C. L, Ladner, R.E. Tactile Graphics with a Voice: Using QR Codes to Access Text in Tactile Graphics. In *Proc. ASSETS 2014*. ACM Press (2014).

2. Elgammal, A., Muang, C., and Hu, D.. Skin detection-a short tutorial. *Encyclopedia of Biometrics*. 2009.

3. Gordon-Holliday, B., Yunker, L.E., Vannatta, G. and Crosswhite, F.J. *Advanced Mathematical Concepts, Precalculus with Applications*. Glencoe/McGraw-Hill, 1999.

4. National Federation of the Blind Jernigan Institute. 2009. The Braille Literacy Crisis in America: Facing the Truth, Reversing the Trend, Empowering the Blind. https://www.nfb.org.

5. Phung, S.L., Bouzerdoum, A. and Chai, D. Skin segmentation using color pixel classification: analysis and comparison *IEEE Transactions Pattern Analysis and Machine Intelligence, 27* (1), 148-154.

6. Phung, S.L.; Bouzerdoum, A.; Chai, D., Skin segmentation using color and edge information, In *Proc. of Seventh International Symposium on Signal Processing and Its Applications, 1*, (2003), 525-528.

7. Vázquez, M., and Steinfeld, A. Helping visually impaired users properly aim a camera. In *Proc. ASSETS 2012*. ACM Press (2012), 1-8.

---

[1] http://code.google.com/p/zxing/

Headlock: a Wearable Navigation Aid that Helps Blind Cane Users Traverse Large Open Spaces

Alexander Fiannaca, Ilias Apostolopoulous, Eelke Folmer

Computer Science & Engineering - University of Nevada
{fiannaca, ilapost, efolmer}@cse.unr.edu

ABSTRACT

Traversing large open spaces is a challenging task for blind cane users, as such spaces are often devoid of tactile features that can be followed. Consequently, in such spaces cane users may veer from their intended paths. Wearable devices have great potential for assistive applications for users who are blind as they typically feature a camera and support hands and eye free interaction. We present HEAD-LOCK, a navigation aid for an optical head-mounted display that helps blind users traverse large open spaces by letting them lock onto a salient landmark across the space, such as a door, and then providing audio feedback to guide the user towards the landmark. HEADLOCK consists of interface modes for discovering landmarks, guiding a user towards a landmark, and recovering from an error state if a landmark is lost. HEADLOCK is designed with two forms of audio feedback: sonification and text-to-speech.

Categories and Subject Descriptors

K.4.2 [**Social Issues**]: Assistive technology

Keywords

Wearable computing, visual impairment, head-mounted display, veering, mobility, navigation, sonification.

1. INTRODUCTION

Vision plays a dominant role in spatial perception [5], the human ability to sense the size, shape, movement, and orientation of objects or people in space. Spatial perception is an essential skill for efficiently navigating spaces, i.e., navigating without running into obstacles or veering from an intended path. Navigating spaces is quite a challenge for users who are blind as they largely have to rely on their hands and ears for spatial perception. Consequently, in complex or loosely structured spaces (e.g. large open spaces like building foyers), blind people often rely on sighted people to describe spaces for them or to help them navigate spaces. This dependency on others reduces their mobility [8].

ASSETS'14, October 20–22, 2014, Rochester, NY, USA.
ACM 978-1-4503-2720-6/14/10.
http://dx.doi.org/10.1145/2661334.2661344.

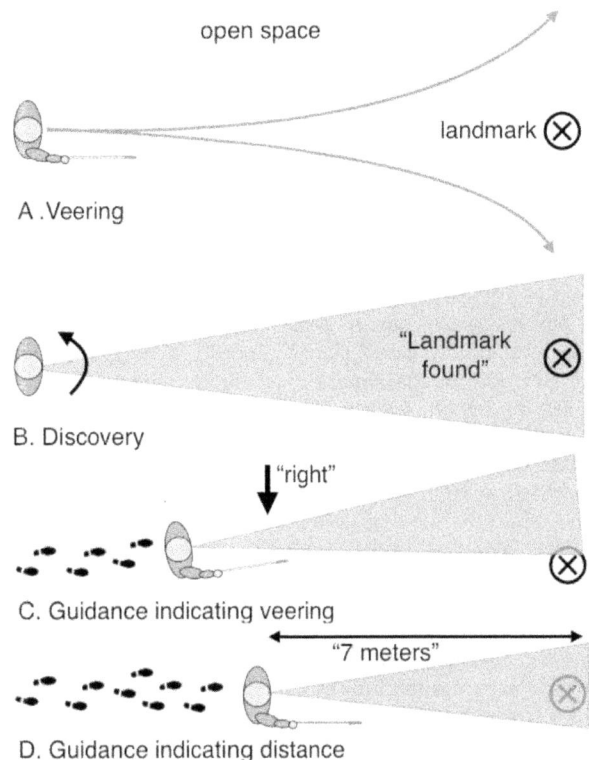

Figure 1: (a) Without any tactile features to follow in an open space, cane users may start to veer from their intended path to a landmark. (b) Users scan the space for landmarks and select a target landmark. (c) Audio feedback is provided to correct for veering while the user navigates to the landmark. (d) Updated distance information is provided while approaching the landmark.

Related Work. A series of wearable solutions [3, 6, 10] have been developed to aid in blind navigation. Each of these techniques either require a priori knowledge in the form of environment maps, require prohibitively expensive instrumentation setups, or require large-scale augmentation of the navigable environment with beacons. Additionally, several smartphone-base approaches [9, 1] have been developed to utilize computer vision to aid in blind navigation. These approaches suffer from the fact that it is challenging for blind users to aim smartphone cameras without being able to see the viewfinder [7].

2. HEADLOCK

Within the context of the challenges associated with navigation for blind individuals in large open spaces, we identified two primary issues which this project addresses:

○ **Veering.** Traversing large open spaces is a challenge for cane users, as either there aren't any tactile features to be followed or the distance between landmarks is large, which cause users to veer (see Fig 1:a).

○ **Handsfree.** Because cane users already use one hand to hold a cane, it is desirable to leave the other hand free to allow for identification of landmarks (doors, elevators, railings) and to allow for interaction with the environment (e.g., open doors, press a button, hold handrail).

To address these issues, we developed HEADLOCK, a navigation app for optical head-mounted displays (OHMD). For the current implementation, the Google Glass OHMD was selected [2]. A benefit of using an OHMD is that the camera is closely aligned with the user's field of view (FOV), giving the user an accurate indication of the direction in which the camera is aimed, which helps with orientation. Additionally, OHMDs are non-obtrusive, an important factor, as a recent study shows blind users prefer "small, easily accessible, and discreet" forms of wearables [4]. HEADLOCK allows users to remotely sense the presence of a landmark, and then lock onto this landmark to efficiently navigate towards it while minimizing veering. Similar to Manduchi [9], HEADLOCK distinguishes a *discovery* and a *guidance* mode.

Discovery. Computer vision is employed to parse the video stream from the OHMD's camera allowing users to scan a space by moving their head horizontally in order to detect salient landmarks (see Fig 1:b). In the case of the current implementation, a simple color blob detection algorithm is employed for detecting doorways; however, this algorithm could easily be replaced with any number of more advanced vision algorithms for detecting a range of landmarks. Particular landmarks may have a known size, which allows HEADLOCK to also acquire an estimate of the distance to the landmark. Once the desired landmark has been found, the user instructs HEADLOCK to lock onto this landmark, at which point HEADLOCK transitions to the guidance phase (see Fig 2).

Guidance. The goal of the guidance mode is to provide feedback so that the user navigates efficiently to the landmark. To detect veering, we track the position of the landmark relative to the center of the camera's FOV. When it diverges from the center by a certain threshold, feedback is provided to indicate the direction and magnitude of the error allowing the user to correct their course (see Fig 1:c). To convey progress, distance information is provided while the user navigates towards the landmark (see Fig 1:d). Upon reaching a landmark, the navigation task is considered complete and feedback is provided accordingly (see Fig 2).

Error Recovery. In the case HEADLOCK loses visual track of the target landmark, we inform the user of this event and indicate the direction in which the user should turn to bring the landmark back into view. The discovery mode is automatically restarted, allowing for a landmark to be relocated quickly.

Feedback. The system provides feedback to the user either in the form of sonification or text-to-speech. For sonification, HEADLOCK uses different pitches of beeps with

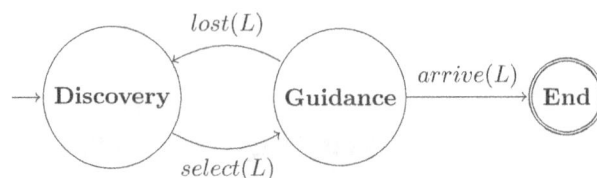

Figure 2: Finite State Machine describing the different modes and transitions between modes with landmark L.

varying durations of silence between equal length beeps to convey information such as the presence or absence of a target landmark, the user's distance to the target landmark, and the direction in which a user needs to make a correction in order to stay on the path to the target landmark. For text-to-speech, the system conveys the same information using simple cues such as "door present", "50%", and "left" or "right", respectively.

3. DEMO

Conference attendants will be able to explore examples of:
1. HEADLOCK 's discovery and guidance modes;
2. Sonification and Text-to-Speech feedback; and
3. Error recovery during use of HEADLOCK.

4. REFERENCES

[1] J. Bigham, C. Jayant, A. Miller, B. White, and T. Yeh. Vizwiz::locateit - enabling blind people to locate objects in their environment. In *Proc. of CVPRW'10*, pages 65–72.

[2] Google glass, http://www.google.com/glass/start/.

[3] S. Ertan, C. Lee, A. Willets, H. Tan, and A. Pentland. A wearable haptic navigation guidance system. In *Proc. of ISWC'98*, pages 164–165.

[4] H. Ye, M. Malu, U. Oh, and L. Findlater. Current and future mobile and wearable device use by people with visual impairments. In *Proc. of CHI'14*. To Appear.

[5] T. Ghirardelli and A. Scharine. *Helmet-mounted displays: Sensation, perception and cognition issues*, Auditory-Visual Interactions, pages 599–618. US Army Aeromedical Research Lab, 2009.

[6] A. Hub, J. Diepstraten, and T. Ertl. Design and development of an indoor navigation and object identification system for the blind. In *Proc. of ASSETS '04*, pages 147–152.

[7] C. Jayant, H. Ji, S. White, and J. P. Bigham. Supporting blind photography. In *Proc. of ASSETS '11*, pages 203–210.

[8] G. Kempen, J. Ballemans, A. Ranchor, G. van Rens, and G. Zijlstra. The impact of low vision on activities of daily living, symptoms of depression, feelings of anxiety and social support in community-living older adults seeking vision rehabilitation services. *Qual Life Res*, Nov 2011.

[9] R. Manduchi. Mobile vision as assistive technology for the blind: An experimental study. In *Proc. of ICCHP '13*, 2012. pages 9–16.

[10] D. A. Ross and B. B. Blasch. Development of a wearable computer orientation system. *Personal Ubiquitous Comput.*, 6(1):49–63, 2002.

Accessible Web Chat Interface

Valentyn Melnyk[1,2]

[1]Dept of Computer Science
Stony Brook University
Stony Brook, NY, USA

[2]Charmtech Labs LLC
CEWIT, 1500 Stony Brook Rd.
Stony Brook, NY, USA

ABSTRACT

Screen readers generally do not recognize widgets that dynamically appear on the screen; as a result, blind users cannot benefit from the convenience of using them. This work describes the development of accessible web chats, a pervasive "go-to" tool in web applications for real-time communication. The results of a user study with 18 blind screen-reader users are presented to demonstrate the utility of the accessible web chat interface.

Categories and Subject Descriptors

H.5.2 [**Information Interfaces And Presentation**]: User Interfaces – *interaction styles, natural language.*

General Terms

Experimentation, Human Factors, Languages.

Keywords

Accessible Web Widget

1. INTRODUCTION

A *web widget* is a "discrete user interface object with which the user can interact". Web development libraries and toolkits (e.g., [7, 8, 12]) are providing an ever growing number of ready-to-use web widgets that can be further customized by web developers to fit the needs of individual web sites. Unfortunately, the diversity of the libraries and a lack of standardization and enforcement of W3C specifications have proven to be an insurmountable problem for blind users.

For web browsing, blind people employ screen readers (*e.g.*, JAWS, VoiceOver), Unfortunately, screen readers do not recognize widgets that dynamically appear on the screen, so the user has no easy way to find them; at best, a dynamically appearing widget will be "navigable," meaning that it can be found and narrated by the screen reader, but without giving any indication as to what kind of widget it is.

To make web applications with dynamic content such as widgets more accessible, web developers have to follow Accessible Rich Internet Applications (ARIA) specifications [13]. For instance, ARIA allows developers to mark up live regions where the content may update, specify the importance of those updates, and provide simple roles such as "progressmeter." Unfortunately, web developers do not follow ARIA specifications consistently, and ARIA does not have predefined roles for complex widgets such as date picker. So the problem of making widgets accessible remains.

As an illustration of the principles and process of designing accessible widgets, in this paper we describe the development of an ARIA-independent accessible interface to web chats widgets. These chat widgets are pervasive in web applications these days and is a "go to" tool for real-time communication with family, acquaintances, customer support, service providers, etc. To demonstrate the feasibility of the approach, we present the results of an evaluation of the interface with 18 screen-reader users and report on the accuracy of web chat identification in the wild.

The deficiency of screen readers in handling the problem with dynamic widgets is well documented [1-4, 6, 9]. To overcome this issue with screen readers, researchers have proposed several approaches for making dynamic widgets accessible, starting with recognition of these widgets within web applications [1, 2, 5], followed by improving the accessibility of individual components within each of these widgets [6, 9]. But the main drawback of all these approaches is their inability to handle all kinds of widgets.

2. CHAT WIDGET INTERFACE

There are three major facets to making widgets accessible with a screen reader: (i) detecting the widget in the web page when they dynamically appear; (ii) identifying, i.e. classifying the widget type (such as a web chat widget, a calendar widget, etc.); (iii) designing an accessible user interface for real-time interaction with the widget.

In our prior work, we have proposed solutions to the first two problems. In [3] we described Dynamo, a unified approach to handling content changes in web pages that is agnostic of the technical methods used to update the pages. Locating widgets is essentially the problem of detecting content changes in a web page. Regarding the identification problem, in an upcoming paper we describe a scalable machine learning approach for classification of *dynamic* widgets [10], where we demonstrated high accuracy in identifying popular dynamic widgets such as date pickers, popup menus, suggestion lists, and HTML alert windows. Here we discuss the development of the third component, namely the interface and put all of the pieces together to create an accessible web chat system.

The interface was enabled using the Screen Reader, developed using the Capti Narrator platform [11]. Capti Screen Reader supports all the standard keyboard shortcuts as are used by common Windows screen readers JAWS and NVDA.

The visual user interface of a typical chat widget has three main components, in top-down order: (a) *title*: usually the name of the correspondent, (b) *history*: the conversation history of chat messages, with the most recent message at the bottom, and (c) *message box*: the input textbox used to send new messages. .

3. USER STUDY

To evaluate the interfaces, we recruited 18 blind screen-reader users for a controlled laboratory study. Gender representation was approximately equal.

The experimental setup included the following two conditions:

Condition A (the baseline) loosely emulated typical behavior of the screen reader with an ARIA [13] enabled chat app. Although the baseline interface uses two TTS channels, pressing any shortcut (including typing in the message box) interrupts and canceled any speech output by both the primary and the secondary TTS (which is identical to having a single audio channel). If the participant stopped typing and a new message arrived, the participant would hear the new message content. All canceled messages could always be reviewed by visiting the history component of the chat window.

Condition B offered an advanced chat interface: the Ctrl key toggled (paused or resumed) the primary TTS output used by the screen reader, while the Alt key toggled the secondary TTS output used by the incoming messages. Pressing any other shortcut canceled only the primary TTS output. In this scenario, the participant was able to take advantage of the cocktail party effect of listening to two streams of audio information simultaneously. If attention was required the participant could selectively pause either of the two audio streams, and listen to the other stream.

In both conditions the participants were always notified of arrival of new messages with a distinct earcon, even if the voicing of the corresponding messages was canceled or paused to minimize the chance of a message being lost.

The experiment required that users perform the following 4 tasks.

- Task 1a: *Weather and News*
  The participant has to chat with two people *Anna* and *Bob* (the experimenter plays the role of both Anna and Bob) at the same time. The conversation with Anna is about weather and the conversation with Bob is about the latest news.
- Task 1b: *Trip details and Meeting plan*
  As in Task 1a, the participant has to simultaneously chat with both Anna and Bob (roles played by the experimenter). The conversation with Anna is about the participant's trip to New York for the user study and the conversation with Bob is about setting up a meeting.
- Task 2a: Book a flight
  The participant has to chat with a travel agent (role played by experimenter) to book a flight.
- Task 2b: Book a hotel room
  The participant has to chat with a travel agent (role played by experimenter) to book a hotel room.

At the end of the study, we administered a questionnaire to get subjective feedback. In general, Condition B was preferred over Condition A. Furthermore it is safe to conclude that the participants enjoyed the web chat interfaces (especially Condition B) and that the interface enhances their experience with several web applications (email, social networks, etc.) that provide facilities for chatting.

4. CONCLUSION AND FUTURE WORK

In the future, we plan to explore accessible interfaces for other kinds of widgets and use the experience and insights gained to formulate a framework for designing generic fit-all interfaces.

Acknowledgements

This work was developed under a grant from the Department of Education, NIDRR grant number H133S130028. However, contents do not represent the policy of the Department of Education, and you should not assume endorsement by the Federal Government.

5. REFERENCES

[1] Bezemer, C.-P., A. Mesbah, and A.v. Deursen, *Automated security testing of web widget interactions*, in *Proceedings of the the 7th joint meeting of the European software engineering conference and the ACM SIGSOFT symposium on The foundations of software engineering*. 2009, ACM: Amsterdam, The Netherlands. p. 81-90.

[2] Bolin, M., M. Webber, P. Rha, T. Wilson, and R.C. Miller, *Automation and customization of rendered web pages*, in *Proceedings of the 18th annual ACM symposium on User interface software and technology*. 2005, ACM: Seattle, WA, USA. p. 163-172.

[3] Borodin, Y., J.P. Bigham, R. Raman, and I.V. Ramakrishnan, *What's new?: making web page updates accessible*, in *Proceedings of the 10th International ACM SIGACCESS Conference on Computers and Accessibility*. 2008, ACM: Halifax, Nova Scotia, Canada.

[4] Brown, A., C. Jay, A.Q. Chen, and S. Harper, *The uptake of Web 2.0 technologies, and its impact on visually disabled users*. Univers. Access Inf. Soc., 2012. **11**(2): p. 185-199.

[5] Brown, A., C. Jay, and S. Harper, *Audio access to calendars*, in *Proceedings of the 2010 International Cross Disciplinary Conference on Web Accessibility (W4A)*. 2010, ACM: Raleigh, North Carolina. p. 1-10.

[6] Chen, C.L. and T.V. Raman, *AxsJAX: a talking translation bot using Google IM: bringing Web-2.0 applications to life*, in *Proceedings of the 2008 International Cross-Disciplinary Conference on Web Accessibility (W4A)*. 2008, ACM: Beijing, China.

[7] DevExpress. *DevExpress Widget Library*. 2014 [cited 2014]; Available from: https://www.devexpress.com.

[8] Google. *Google Web Toolkit*. 2014 [cited 2014]; Available from: http://gwt-ext.com/demo/.

[9] Jay, C., A.J. Brown, and S. Harper, *Internal evaluation of the SASWAT audio browser: method, results and experimental materials*. 2010, The University of Manchester.

[10] Melnyk, V., V. Ashok, Y. Puzis, A. Soviak, and Y. Borodin, *Widget Classification with Applications to Web Accessibility*, in *to appear in Proceedings of the 2014 International Conference on Web Engineering*. 2014.

[11] Puzis, Y., Y. Borodin, R. Puzis, and I.V. Ramakrishnan, *Predictive Web Automation Assistant for People with Vision Impairments*, in *To appear in proceedings of the 22th international conference on world wide web*. 2013, ACM: Rio de Janeiro, Brazil.

[12] Telerik. *Telerik Widget Library*. 2014 [cited 2014]; Available from: http://www.telerik.com.

[13] WAI-ARIA. *W3C Accessible Rich Internet Applications*. 2013 [cited 2013]; Available from: http://www.w3.org/TR/wai-aria.

Capti-Speak: A Speech-Enabled Accessible Web Interface

Vikas Ashok

vganjiguntea@cs.stonybrook.edu

Department of Computer Science
Stony Brook University
Stony Brook, NY, 11794, USA

Charmtech Labs LLC,
CEWIT, 1500 Stony Brook Rd,
Stony Brook, NY, 11794, USA

ABSTRACT

People with severe vision impairments generally interact with web pages via screen readers that provide keyboard shortcuts for navigating through the content. However, this traditional press-and-listen mode of interaction has several drawbacks, notably: time wasted listening to irrelevant content, extensive use of the keyboard to navigate the content, and the need to remember numerous keyboard shortcuts and browsing strategies. Augmenting traditional screen reading with a speech interface has the potential to alleviate many of the above limitations. This work describes Capti-Speak, an accessible web-browsing interface that supports both speech commands and standard screen-reader shortcuts. A user study with a dozen blind participants showed that Capti-Speak was significantly more usable and efficient compared to the conventional screen readers, especially for ad-hoc browsing, searching, and navigating to the content of interest.

Categories and Subject Descriptors

H.5.2 [**Information Interfaces and Presentation**]: User Interfaces; H.5.4 [**Information Interfaces and Presentation**]: Hypertext/Hypermedia – *navigation*

General Terms

Human Factors, Experimentation, Design.

Keywords

Web Accessibility; Blind Users; Low-Vision users; Web Browser; Screen Reader; Non-Visual; Audio Interface.

1. INTRODUCTION

Web has become the "go-to utility" for participating in our globally connected digital society. However, as it evolved from text-based web pages to interactive web applications, the Web has become less accessible for people with vision impairments. Blind users typically interact with web browsers using screen readers. The standard (keyboard) press-and-listen mode of interaction with screen readers has several notable drawbacks: excessive use of shortcuts for doing simple browsing tasks, need to remember an assortment of shortcuts and browsing strategies, and listen to reams of irrelevant content while navigating the webpage.

Augmenting screen readers with speech interface has potential to

ASSETS '14, Oct 20-22 2014, Rochester, NY, USA
ACM 978-1-4503-2720-6/14/10.
http://dx.doi.org/10.1145/2661334.2661416

alleviate the problems listed above. For example, to search and navigate to some ad-hoc content of interest on any web page, it is easier for the blind users to issue a single speech command (e.g., "go to search results") as opposed to using a sequence of several shortcuts while listening to irrelevant content along the way. Other examples include clicking on select links and buttons by specifying associated properties (e.g., "click on link about admission"), filling form fields, etc. I have developed Capti-Speak, a speech-augmented screen reader for the Web built on top of Capti Narrator platform [4]. Capti-Speak supports all standard screen-reader shortcuts in addition to speech commands.

I conducted a user study with a dozen blind participants to evaluate Capti-Speak. The study showed that, despite the presence of speech recognition errors by ASR (Automatic Speech Recognition), the participants rated Capti-Speak to be significantly more usable and efficient compared to the conventional keyboard-operated screen-reading interface, especially for ad-hoc browsing, searching, and navigating to the content of interest.

2. RELATED WORK

Talking to web browsers is not a new idea. For example, House et al. [6] proposed a modified version of the NCSA Mosaic system [1] that was capable of translating very basic spoken user commands (e.g. opening URLs, new windows, etc.) to browsing actions. Capti-Speak, on the other hand, supports commands for interacting with the webpage itself: navigating to the content of interest, searching for content is present on a web page, acting on buttons and links, filling forms, etc.

Several commercial voice activated personal assistants are now available (e.g., Apple's Siri [7], Samsung's S Voice [2], Google Now [5]). In addition to searching restaurants, movies, etc., these assistants are capable of satisfying simple requests associated with routine tasks such as reminders, alarms, notes, etc. Although these assistants can be very handy for people with vision impairments, these tools cannot operate with a web browser and hence cannot be used alongside a screen reader to perform basic operations (e.g., searching, navigating, clicking, etc.) in a web page. On the contrary, the voice assistant provided by Capti-Speak is implemented as an extension to the Capti screen-reading framework, thereby making it usable within a web browser.

3. CAPTI-SPEAK

Capti-Speak was built on top of the Capti web browsing application [4], which has a standard screen-reader interface (akin to JAWS). Capti-Speak extends this screen-reader interface by providing an additional shortcut to input speech commands. Capti-Speak (Figure 1) consists of a screen reader "Capti-Narrator", a speech recognizer and a speech command processor.

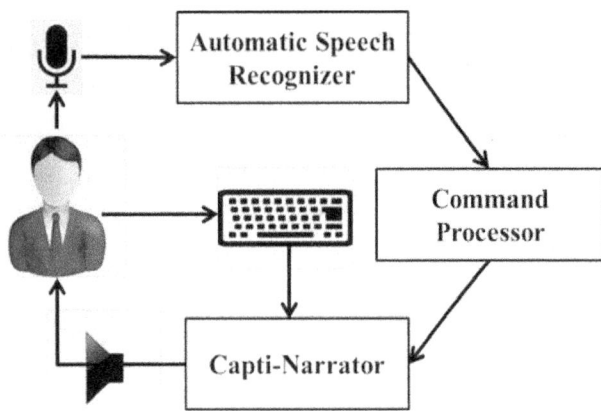

Figure 1. Capti-Speak Architecture

3.1 Capti-Narrator

Capti-Narrator supports all the standard keyboard shortcuts, and adds an additional shortcut for activating the microphone. The recorded audio is then sent to the Automatic Speech Recognizer (ASR) module for speech-to-text conversion. Capti-Narrator uses Text-to-Speech (TTS) synthesizer to narrate the result of every speech-command execution as instructed by the Command Processor. I used the Microsoft Windows built-in TTS with voice "Anna" speaking at the "Normal" speech rate, which is about 120 words per minute.

3.2 Automatic Speech Recognizer

I enlisted the assistance of publicly available Google ASR web service for speech-to-text conversion. The received text from the web service is passed on to the command processor for interpretation and subsequent execution. I observed latency of 1-2 seconds between the transfer of the recorded speech command to the Google ASR web service and the receipt of text response. The accuracy of speech recognition, i.e. the percentage of speech commands correctly translated to text was 72.1%.

3.3 Command Processor

The command processor interprets the speech command by determining its type. I used the types 'Command-Task' (e.g. click, select, edit, etc.) and 'Command-Navigation' (e.g. go to, next, previous, top, etc.) listed in the dialogue act scheme [3] that was designed specifically for non-visual web browsing. To determine the type of command, I used a decision-tree based classifier trained on the non-visual dialogue corpus [3]. The command-processor then uses an appropriate command-execution template listed under the identified command-type, to fulfill the user request. The template library also included execution plans for all commands that represented standard key-board shortcuts.

4. EVALUATION

4.1 Methodology

Capti-Speak was evaluated in a user study with a dozen visually impaired screen-reader users performing tasks on web pages with and without Capti-Speak. Gender representation was equal.

The participants were asked to perform 4 different kinds of browsing tasks on different websites, (1) Shopping, (2) University Admission, (3) Advertisement, (4) Email. The participants had to perform these tasks under 2 conditions: (1) with Capti-Speak, and (2) without Capti-Speak. Each condition was evaluated with 2 consecutive tasks. The order of conditions, tasks and task-to-condition assignment was randomized for each participant to minimize the impact of the learning effect. For each task, the completion time was recorded and for each condition, questions concerning usability were administered at the end of the experiment to obtain subjective feedback.

4.2 Preliminary Results

4.2.1 Task Completion Times

Participants were found to be nearly 1.5 times faster with Capti-Speak compared to that without Capti-Speak, with respect to task completion time. As future work, I plan on conducting a comprehensive user study with a more detailed objective analysis.

4.2.2 Usability

The post experiment questionnaire indicated that the participants preferred Capti-Speak over a standard screen reader for performing tasks on the web. The participants also indicated that Capti-Speak was much more usable than a standard screen reader. A more detailed subjective analysis is scope of future work.

5. CONCLUSION

In this research work, I presented Capti-Speak, a speech-augmented Screen Reader for web browsing, capable of interpreting spoken commands and performing browsing actions on behalf of the user. A study with a dozen blind subjects showed that Capti-Speak was significantly more efficient and usable compared to the traditional keyboard-based screen reader. In the future I plan on improving the robustness of Capti-Speak in order to be more tolerant to speech recognition errors.

6. ACKNOWLEDGEMENTS

Research reported in this publication was supported by the National Eye Institute of the National Institutes of Health under award number 1R43EY21962-1A1.

7. REFERENCES

[1] Andreessen, M., *NCSA Mosaic technical summary*. National Center for Supercomputing Applications, 1993. **605**.

[2] Android, *S Voice*. 2012.

[3] Ashok, V., Y. Borodin, S. Stoyanchev, and I.V. Ramakrishnan, *Dialogue Act Modeling for Non-Visual Web Access*, in *to appear in the 15th Annual SIGdial Meeting on Discourse and Dialogue, SIGDIAL*. 2014: Philadelphia, PA, USA.

[4] Borodin, Y., Y. Puzis, A. Soviak, J. Bouker, B. Feng, R. Sicoli, A. Melnyk, V. Melnyk, V. Ashok, G. Dausch, and I.V. Ramakrishnan, *Listen to everything you want to read with Capti narrator*, in *Proceedings of the 11th Web for All Conference*. 2014, ACM: Seoul, Korea. p. 1-2.

[5] Google. *Google Now*. 2012; Available from: http://www.google.com/landing/now/#utm_source=google&utm_medium=sem&utm_campaign=GoogleNow.

[6] House, D., D. Novick, M. Fanty, and J. Walpole, *Spoken-Language Access to Multimedia (SLAM): Masters Thesis*.

[7] Siri. *The Personal Assistant on Your Phone*. 2013 [cited 2013]; Available from: http://siri.com/.

Does It Look Beautiful? Communicating Aesthetic Information about Artwork to the Visually Impaired

Caroline Galbraith

University of Maryland, Baltimore County

Cgalb1@umbc.edu

ABSTRACT

'A picture says a thousand words' is a fitting phrase to express the difficulty in communicating visual information to a sighted individual. But what happens when the person the artwork is being described to doesn't have any vision? What features of the artwork enhance their comprehension of the aesthetics, and what details are excluded from the description? This paper will explore the ways in which artwork is described to visually impaired individuals, and the details the visually impaired express interest in knowing about the artwork. Specifically, we focus on the value of drawing from shared experiences and prompts. These findings are based on observational data that was gathered from a study involving a visually impaired participant and a sighted companion exploring a gallery of artwork together and conversing about the artwork.

Categories and Subject Descriptors

K.4.2 [**Social Issues**]: Assistive technologies for persons with disabilities

Keywords

Visual impairments; accessible information; communication; visual art

1. INTRODUCTION

Being able to describe visual art effectively to visually impaired individuals is important for many reasons. For instance it can play a vital role in social interaction by being a topic of conversation and enabling them to experience a part of life they may miss if they were once sighted. Application of effective strategies for communicating aesthetic information can also beneficially apply to other mediums of information, thus making a variety of things more accessible to the visually impaired.

As a portion of a study based on blind navigation, visually impaired individuals and sighted companions explored an art gallery on the University of Maryland, Baltimore County campus. The observations from this led to findings concerning what the visually impaired participant wanted to know about the aesthetics of the artwork, the circumstances that prompted their

ASSETS '14 October 20-22, 2014, Rochester, NY, USA.

ACM 978-1-4503-2720-6/14/10

http://dx.doi.org/10.1145/2661334.2661411

Figure 1: After his sighted companion stops to look at a series of pictures, P1 asks her "Are they are beautiful?" She responds "no, not really", and the participant and companion move on to the other artwork. This is one example suggesting that the interest of a visually impaired individual in a particular art piece is prompted by the opinions and interest of others.

interest in a particular art piece, and the manner in which the complex visual information was described to the visually impaired participant.

2. RELATED WORK

Prior work concerning communicating visual information involves developing systems to convey visual information more effectively by utilizing other mediums such as audio and tactile cues, such as Hribar [2], and Wall [4]. By incorporating audio and tactile cues into communicating visual information, results showed that visual information could be more effectively shared. The topic was also explored by researches interested in conveying data information to visually impaired users, Such as Goncu [1], who focused on 2 dimensional graphics, and McGookin[3], who focused on communicating data from tables and graphs. These authors prompt the necessity and importance of the ability to convey graphic and aesthetic information to the visually impaired, and emphasize the necessity of having alternative methods to communicate such information. Through knowledge and exploration of effective communication methods, visually impaired individuals can be empowered by more accessible information.

3. PARTNER STUDY

This research was conducted as a portion of a partner study concerning how the visually impaired navigate with a sighted companion. The study involved navigating to various places on a university campus. The study had six pairs of participants, with a total of six locations to navigate to. The present research focuses on analysis of conversation within an art gallery displaying student work.

Through this study many results supporting better understanding of visually impaired tendencies and common misconceptions were found. Williams [5] discusses the many misconceptions sighted people often have about blind navigation. This prompted analysis of other communication tendencies that could be observed in the study.

4. FINDINGS

4.1 Drawing on Shared Experience

A frequently utilized method for describing something visual is to reference another item that has similar visual attributes. This was commonly observed during the partner study, and varied based on the familiarity between the companions. If the companions were less familiar with each other they had a tendency to reference shared knowledge items, which were items that they had not necessarily interacted with in each other's company, but both knew about. For example, a Rubik's cube, that was referenced to describe a piece of artwork by fifth participant's sighted companion.

With the companions that were more familiar with each other, the tendency to describe artwork through shared memories was observed, for example saying a piece is similar to a piece of art the sighted companion had made when they were a child. The sighted companion of participant 3 described a piece of artwork made with Styrofoam and hanging from the ceiling as "I remember when I made this in third grade...It's the little balls you stick the little picks in to get them to stick together. Remember I made that in third grade?" By referencing a shared memory the visually impaired participant was able to better understand the aesthetics of the artwork.

The descriptions of the artwork tended to incorporate more objective language, and involve information about the medium utilized to create the artwork, as well as the color, size, or shape. The visually impaired participant would occasionally ask more subjective questions concerning the aesthetics of an art piece. When this did occur, trends were noticed concerning actions by the sighted participant suggest that the actions prompted the visually impaired participant's interest.

4.2 Interest Prompts

The next finding comes from the circumstances that prompt the visually impaired participant to express interest in the aesthetics of a particular piece of artwork when they are surrounded by numerous pieces of art. The observations of the companions showed trends in expressing interest in an art piece when the sighted companion also showed interest in a an art piece, and likewise for situations when the sighted companions expressed disinterest in an art piece. An example of this would be when the participant one started expressing interest and asking for additional visual information in response to the companion commenting that she though the art piece was nice. The blind participant even touched the art piece to gain even more understanding of it, and wanted to know if she was touching the one her companion thought was nice.

The opposite occurred when the sighted companion of participant one said that the artwork was not really beautiful, as described in Figure 1. The companions continued navigating down the hall after, and the blind participant did not ask any more questions about the art piece. This is another example suggests that the interest of a visually impaired individual in a particular art piece is prompted by the opinions and interest of their sighted companions.

5. CONCLUSION AND FUTURE WORK

References to shared knowledge were often made for the purposes of describing aesthetic features to individuals with visual impairments in the observational partner study. Since a visually impaired individual requires more detailed information about visual artwork, referencing shared knowledge and assigning multiple qualities or features to the art piece is an effective way to communicate multiple qualities at once.

Increased interest in aesthetic information from the blind participants occurred when they believed that the art piece was pleasing to their sighted companion. This indicates that while the visually impaired frequently desire objective descriptions in order to understand the features of the artwork, they are interested in art pieces that their sighted companion expresses a subjective opinion about.

These findings about describing aesthetic features of artwork can be useful in providing more comprehensive descriptions to the visually impaired, and thus make information about the aesthetics of artwork more accessible to them. Future work could include exploring recommendation systems for describing aesthetic information

6. ACKNOWLEDGEMENTS

I thank my study participants, the prototyping and design lab at UMBC and my mentors Amy Hurst an. Shaun Kane. This work was partially funded by Toyota Engineering and Manufacturing North America.

7. REFERENCES

[1]   Goncu , Cagatay and Marriott Kim. 2011. GraVVITAS: generic multi-touch presentation of accessible graphics. *Proceedings of the 13th IFIP TC 13 international conference on Human-computer interaction - Volume Part I* (INTERACT'11), Pedro Campos, Nuno Nunes, Nicholas Graham, Joaquim Jorge, and Philippe Palanque (Eds.), Vol. Part I. Springer-Verlag, Berlin, Heidelberg, 30-48.

[2]   Hribar, Victoria E. and Pawluk, Dianne T.V. 2011. A tactile-thermal display for haptic exploration of virtual paintings. In Proceedings of the ACM SIGACCESS Conference on Computers and Accessibility (ASSETS '11). ACM, New York, NY, USA, 221-222.

[3]   McGookin, David, Robertson, Euan and Brewster, Stephen 2010. Clutching at straws: using tangible interaction to provide non-visual access to graphs. In Proceedings of the ACM SICHI Conference on Human Factors in Computing Systems (CHI '10). ACM, New York, NY, USA, 1715-1724

[4]   Wall, Steven and Stephen A. Brewster. 2006. Tac-tiles: multimodal pie charts for visually impaired users. In NordiCHI '06), ACM,9-18

[5]   Williams, Michele. 2014. "Just let the cane hit it": How the blind and Sighted see Navigation Differently. In Proceedings of the ACM SIGACCESS Conference on Computers and Accessibility (ASSETS '14) ACM,

Improving Programming Interfaces For People With Limited Mobility Using Voice Recognition

Xiomara Figueroa Fontánez
University of Puerto Rico
xiomara.figueroa2@upr.edu

Patricia Ordóñez Franco
University of Puerto Rico
patricia.ordonez@upr.edu

ABSTRACT

Programing is an arduous task for individuals with motor impairments who rely on independent tools to interact with their digital environment. Providing a bimodal Integrated Development Environment is key to tackling a program's complex syntax and to improving the programming interface. This project is an effort to facilitate the interaction between programmers with motor impairments in their hands and Integrated Development Environment (IDE's) through the interaction of modified versions of open source assistive technology software. We are working on the prototype for a specific user, who is a computer scientist with spinal muscular atrophy (SMA) that can no longer physically attend classes and can only type with one finger. The user is a crucial part of this project providing invaluable input into the design of the interface.

Categories and Subject Descriptors

H.5.2 [Information Interfaces and Presentation]: User Interfaces - Input devices and strategies, Voice I/O.; K.4.2 [Computers and society]: Social issues - assistive technologies for persons with disabilities.

General Terms

Performance, Design; Experimentation; HCI; Languages

Keywords

Programming; voice recognition; SIMON; open source

1. INTRODUCTION

One way to introduce the amount of typing while programming is to use speech recognition. Speech interfaces may help reduce the onset of repetitive strain injuries among computer programmers, and at the same time, increase access for those who have motor

ASSETS'14, October 20–22, 2014, Rochester, NY, USA.
ACM 978-1-4503-2720-6/14/10.
http://dx.doi.org/10.1145/2661334.2661417

impairments in their hands. Many programmers who are physically disabled are already bootstrapping voice recognition into existing programming environments [2]. However, speech does not map well onto the available applications and programming tasks [1]. Voice recognition software for programming is very uncommon, yet necessary. Programming itself has a structures format that can be incorporated into an IDE that may enhance speed of code production with fewer keystrokes and navigation through the display.

2. PREVIOUS WORK

Some forms of assistive technology challenge our expectations of technology enhance performance because of their complexity. While there is software for speech recognition available that is utilized by programmers, most is designed to use a standard vocabulary of spoken or written language and is not for programming languages or coding itself [1]. Current products are time-consuming making users do software customizations for programming use [4]. As an assistive technology, several advantages of word prediction allow for increasing text entry rate, minimizing keystrokes for individuals with motor limitations, enabling people with learning or cognitive disabilities to more quickly recollect and retrieve words, and reducing spelling errors. Still, many word prediction applications are limited because they are dependent on specific operating systems or text editors for functionality [3].

3. METHODOLOGY

This project is developing through the integration of modified versions of an open source speech recognition software called Simon. In contrast to existing commercial software for speech recognition, Simon provides pre-trained speech models, an interface to create language and acoustic models from scratch. One scenario makes up one complete use case of Simon. To control Firefox, for example, the user just installs the Firefox scenario. In other words, scenarios tell Simon what words and phrases to listen for and what to do when they are recognized. In previous work, Simon was integrated with the Gedit text editor of Gnome through its Assistive Technology Service Provider Interface, and there has also been previous work with training Vi for programming using voice recognition [2]. Simon let us create scenarios to carry out and control various tasks on our computers by voice commands. With these existing tools in Simon we created two types of scenarios to control both the IDE we want to use and the programming language in which we want to program. So far we have created scenarios for Simon that allow us to control different IDE's such as Netbeans, Sublime, Gedit and others. We have also created model scenarios for programming in different programming languages such as C++, Python and Java.

There exist a need to create a structure for the existing commands in order to create templates efficiently and perform auto completion when creating scenarios that are specifically for programming. Ideally, voice commands should be easy to remember, efficient and effective. While facilitating and reducing keystrokes, Simon's speech recognition mode can perform any task available to it through the IDE taking advantage of convenient features of the IDE such as word completion, word prediction, embedded application commands (open, close, save), or grammar specific commands (comment, collapse, expand). Such functionality reduces stress on extremities by relying on voice commands.

The interface should be easy to learn, preferably using spoken constructs that the programmer already knows. But, would all programmers naturally speak the same language when they verbalize their program? This question was answered by Andrew Begel and his team in [1]. They conducted an experiment in which participants read a one-page pre-existing Java program out loud. They found that there exist a common vernacular among programmers for speaking programs independent of their diverse educational training. This finding may enable us to create a spoken programming language which will work for most programmers. Most people would find the idea of using the same type of text editor to write a memo and edit a photo to be a strange one. Similarly, we shouldn't expect that adding a few voice commands to a primarily keyboard-driven editor will produce an excellent voice-driven editor.

4.FUTURE WORK
As part of this project, we will be developing a platform to maintain a dynamic language model that would support free dictation (variable names, for example). Addressing this objective will require a lot of careful planning. There are many very specific issues to address, and it should be approached as creating a radically new programming environment, taking advantage of the existing tools for programming but having in mind that is has to satisfy specific needs. Because the target is to program by voice

recognition, the future work would be in the way of a whole new kind of activity, a new kind of input.

5.CONCLUSION
Assistive Technology provides people with disabilities the means to perform many activities with minimal or no assistance. People with limited access to their keyboard may benefit from speech recognition technology. Automatic speech recognition systems can be enormously beneficial for people with physical disabilities, having a potential to provide a fast and easy-to-use interfaces for computer access and control of the home environment, for example. Our work can give the, the flexibility to obtain the same accessibility as everyone else in front of the computer. Also, in the process of creating this tool, others can benefit from it such as like programmers suffering with carpal tunnel and other similar conditions. We are also contributing to an open source project, which allows for innovative ideas to be worked on by the community of programmers, as the project becomes more accessible to all potential user.

6.ACKNOWLEDGMENTS
Our thanks to Peter Grasch, lead programmers for Simon, for his assistance during this process.

7.REFERENCES

[1] Begel, A. and Graham, S. L., "An Assessment of a Speech-Based Programming Environment", In Visual Languages and Human-Centric Computing (VL/HCC"06), pp. 116-120, 2006

[2] Xan Lee, 2013, Using Voice to Code Faster that Keyboard, (accessed May 1, 2014) from, http://ergoemacs.org/emacs/using_voice_to_code.html

[3] Disables programmers need help finding a code editor. (n.d) Channel 9. Retrieved March 23, 2014, from http://channel9.msdn.com/Forums/CoffeeHouse/569583-Disabled-programmers-need-help-finding-a-code-editor

[4] Dragon Naturallyspeaking Professional, Speech Recognition Software for the financial Services Industry, Nuance Communications Inc, 2011.

Introducing Web Accessibility to Localization Students: Implications for a Universal Web

Silvia Rodríguez Vázquez

Cod.eX Research Group
TIM/FTI - University of Geneva
40, Bd. du Pont d'Arve - CH-1211 Geneva 4 - Switzerland
Silvia.Rodriguez@unige.ch

ABSTRACT

The importance of web accessibility has spread throughout close technical disciplines, leading to new forms of collaboration between that area of study and other related fields, such as internationalization and web localization. Recent investigations have illustrated that web accessibility experts support the involvement of localization professionals in the achievement of a more accessible web for all, especially in the case of the multilingual web. However, most training institutions do not teach yet the basic technical competence on the matter. Within such research framework, over the last two years, a series of seminars on web accessibility have been taught both for undergraduate and graduate translation students at two European universities. The relevance of acquiring web accessibility knowledge and know-how was generally welcomed by all participants, who showed a high level of interest and motivation. Data gathered up to date have helped to develop a better informed theoretical framework about the participation of localizers in the web development cycle and their contribution to a universal web.

Categories and Subject Descriptors

K.7.1 [**The Computing profession**]: Occupations; K.7.4 [**The Computing profession**]: Professional Ethics – *Codes of good practice;* J.5 [**Arts and Humanities**]: Language Translation.

General Terms

Performance; Human Factors; Languages.

Keywords

Localization Training; Multilingual Web; Web Accessibility.

1. INTRODUCTION

Web localization, understood by scholars as a complex communicative, cognitive, textual and technological process by which interactive digital texts are modified to be used in different linguistic and sociocultural contexts, is guided by the expectations of the target audience and the specifications requested by initiators [4]. Similarly, accessibility is not an intrinsic characteristic of a digital resource, but is determined by political, social and other contextual factors, as well as technical aspects

[1]. The overlap between both areas and their shared interests towards the goal of an inclusive, accessible and universal web have been already brought to the forefront in previous research [2,4], but little or no adjustments have been made to localization curricula in order to integrate core skills acquisition related to web accessibility implementation. This paper provides insight into the extent of the success of introducing web accessibility to localization students and puts forward potential implications of an inter-professional teamwork approach to achieve the goal of a universal web.

2. BACKGROUND AND MOTIVATION

While the first web content accessibility guidelines (WCAG) reach their fifteen anniversary, compliance continues to be lower than expected [3]. Researchers in the field have pointed to the lack of awareness about accessibility issues by those responsible for websites as one of the main reasons for this failure (*ibid*). In the particular case of multilingual websites, localizers are considered as key actors within the product life-cycle. This follows from the multi-faceted nature of their profession, which requires not only traditional translation competences, but also an in-depth set of technological and management skills, including knowledge of main web authoring tools and mark-up languages such as HTML and XML [4]. With this in mind, we carried out a survey targeting web accessibility experts with the aim of clarifying localizer's expected commitment towards accessibility. Findings suggested that the achievement of an accessible multilingual web is a group effort and localization practitioners should be involved in it [7,8]. In the light of the conclusions drawn from that study, we argue that training on web accessibility is needed both at undergraduate and graduate levels to increase awareness and understanding of accessibility issues among the next generation localization community. We therefore designed and implemented a series of seminars for localization students as an initial pilot study, in order to measure the potential impact on a long term basis.

3. OBSERVATIONAL STUDY

Due to space constraints, the present paper mainly focus on general observations inferred from two out of the six seminars organized until present: one held at the University of Salamanca, Spain, in November 2012, and another one at the University of Geneva, Switzerland, in June 2013.

3.1 Students' Profile

Eleven undergraduate translation students (aged between 20 and 23, $\bar{x} = 21$, $sd = 0.33$; 3 male, 8 female) participated in the web accessibility module at the University of Salamanca. All students were Spanish native speakers and most of them ($N=7$ out of 11)

were in their 4th year. None had previous knowledge on the subject. In Geneva, 25 students pursuing a Master's in Translation took part in the seminar (aged between 21 and 43, $\bar{x}$ = 26, sd = 1; 6 male, 19 female). Fifteen students were in their 1st year of MA and 10 in their 2nd year. 68% of them were French native speakers and only three knew the basic web accessibility principles.

3.2 Seminars Setup and Outcome

Seminars were taught within the frame of the Localization and Project Management course at both Universities, with the approval of the corresponding lecturers. At the moment of the seminars, students had already acquired basic knowledge on web and software technology. The training included theoretical presentations and accessibility-oriented localization exercises, preceded and followed by task-related questionnaires. The author prepared introductory materials on web accessibility main concepts and best practices, as per WCAG 2.0. There were three hours allocated for the seminar in Geneva and six for Salamanca's, where we devoted the last two hours to discuss about web accessibility evaluation, repair and guidance tools that could prove useful in their future career.

3.2.1 Main Remarks from Labs

During the accessibility seminar at Salamanca, students were asked to localize a non-accessible English simple website into an accessible Spanish website, paying special attention at forms, tables and graphics, as well as textual content. They had one week to submit a final report on the task, describing steps followed and tools used. The evaluation of the exercises showed that students had managed to obtain a higher degree of accessibility, both in the source and in the target web product. The author observed a responsive use of HTML, but less effort was devoted to language-related aspects: translatable content remained unchanged in English, some readability problems were not solved and text alternatives for images were often inappropriate.

In the second seminar, held in Geneva, we placed more emphasis on showing how to find the balance between new technical aspects learned and the students' extensive linguistic background. At the beginning of the lab, participants were presented with the same website as in the previous seminar, but without CSS and images. This was followed by a 45min lecture, after which they were asked to perform the same localization task, this time founded on the complete site. Students' responses to the post-task questionnaire indicated that 88% of the participants had not recognized alt image or summary table attributes' values as such before the web accessibility presentation, thus not suggesting pertinent translation proposals. Also, 76% of the students reported that they would have liked to apply more changes as regards layout and textual content in the target website, in order to render it more accessible than the source. The latter suggests that localizers with web accessibility knowledge could potentially report to developers or clients problems found and solved them in the multilingual version of the site.

3.3 Students Feedback

Upon completion of each seminar, students replied to a general questionnaire about their advocacy for accessibility as future localizers. Interestingly, 80% felt accountable for the accessibility degree achieved in the target product and expressed their willingness to be more involved in the web development cycle. Most participants also highlighted the need to work as a team

together with web developers and other actors in the web production chain, echoing W3C WAI [5] message, with a view to work more effectively and prevent unnecessary redesign efforts at later stages.

4. RESEARCH INDICATORS AND FUTURE AVENUES

Although web accessibility modules have not been fully integrated in the translation and localization curriculum, as it has been already done in computer science-related courses [9], students have demonstrated interest in and commitment towards accessibility and the larger goal of a universal web, and have acknowledged the need to receive a complete training to perform localization tasks professionally, with web accessibility in mind. Web accessibility best practices were taken into account for the course final projects, which shows a high degree of acceptability of the topic. Our modules have also contributed to raise awareness at a faculty and university scale, notably among webmasters. Finally, observations made have also guided further work on the author's doctoral thesis, currently in progress. Difficulties undergone by students to improve textual accessibility and text alternatives adequacy have fed back into the current development of an accessibility-oriented controlled language (CL) tool [8] that will be evaluated in a large-scale experiment in November 2014.

5. REFERENCES

[1] Cooper, M., Sloan, D., Kelly, B. and Lewthwaite, S. 2012. A Challenge to Web Accessibility Metrics and Guidelines: Putting People and Processes First. In *Proceedings W4A 2012*, Lyon, France, April 2012.

[2] Gutiérrez, E. and Martínez, L. 2010. Localisation and Web Accessibility. In *Tradumàtica*, 8(1), 383-388.

[3] Hanson, V.L. and Richards, J.T. 2013. Progress on Website Accessibility? In ACM *Transactions on the Web*, 7(1), 2:1-2:30.

[4] Jiménez-Crespo, M.A. 2013. Translation and Web Localization. New York: Routledge.

[5] Lawton Henry, S., Abou-Zahra, S. and Brewer, J. 2014. The Role of Accessibility in a Universal Web. In *Proceedings W4A 2014*, Seoul, Republic of Korea, April 2014.

[6] Rodríguez Vázquez, S. and Bolfing, A. 2013. Multilingual Website Assessment for Accessibility: a Survey on Current Practices. In *Proceedings ASSETS 2013*, Bellevue, WA, USA, October 2013.

[7] Rodríguez Vázquez, S. 2013. Towards Defining the Role of Localization Professionals in the Achievement of Multilingual Web Accessibility. In *Tradumàtica*, 11(1), 383-388.

[8] Rodríguez Vázquez, S., Bolfing, A. and Bouillon, P. 2014. Applying Accessibility-Oriented Controlled Language (CL) Rules to Improve Appropriateness of Text Alternatives for Images: an Exploratory Study. In Proceedings *LREC 2014*, Reykjavik, Iceland, May 2014.

[9] Waller, A., Hanson, V.L. and Sloan, D. 2009. Including Accessibility Within and Beyond Undergraduate Computing Courses. In *Proceedings ASSETS 2009*, Pittsburgh, Pennsylvania, USA, October 2009.

Strategies: An Inclusive Authentication Framework

Natã Barbosa
Syracuse University
School of Information Studies
nmbarbos@syr.edu

ABSTRACT

This paper briefly describes a proposed interaction workflow that is currently being developed as part of a research effort towards providing better solutions for accessible authentication, strongly guided by contextual inquiry and evidence-based guidelines. The approach described herein is being developed and tested to be foundations for tests and findings of the research, consequently evolving along the research progress towards providing a scalable, deployable, secure, usable for everyone, and last, but not least, privacy preserving platform for web authentication.

Categories and Subject Descriptors

D.4.6 [**Security and Protection**]: Security and Protection – *Access Controls, Authentication, and Verification*

General Terms

Human Factors, Authentication

Keywords

Authentication; Contextual Inquiry; Disability; Privacy

1. INTRODUCTION

The interaction workflow proposed in this framework is aiming to reduce the difficulties that people with disabilities currently face when authenticating to several web pages and web services. By focusing heavily on improving the user experience of web authentication, the hopes over the outcomes of the work under way are that of solving user experience problems while providing a secure and scalable mechanism that can be deployed by websites around the world, towards easing the process of authentication.

Specific goals of this project include, but are not limited to (1) design accessible authentication that is secure, fast and usable for everyone; (2) design new authentication mechanisms that are privacy-preserving (i.e., service providers do not know what disability condition a user has); and (3) evaluate these new mechanisms with users with disabilities in longitudinal field trials.

The framework is being designed from the beginning to be extensible, meaning that it will allow for new strategies to be implemented for catering certain types of disabilities. The main characteristics of said interaction workflow are: (1) the gap between the user disability and the task of authentication is filled/eased with a suitable mechanism of communication between the browser (most likely a JavaScript Application Programming Interface) and the user, such suitable mechanism is to be

ASSETS '14, Oct 20-22 2014, Rochester, NY, USA

ACM 978-1-4503-2720-6/14/10.

http://dx.doi.org/10.1145/2661334.2661413

compatible with the user's disability (perhaps machine learning can be implemented in order to guess the first-time suitable mechanism); (2) once the initial Device-API pairing is successfully completed, the user is no longer required to type passwords. Instead, they make use of a broader range of authentication possibilities that are available through mobile devices (e.g. accelerometer, microphone, camera, gyroscope, GPS) to prove identity to the phone. The user is then able to communicate seamlessly with the mechanism once the suitable mechanism has been successfully identified (3) the web application server knows nothing about this process, the process is triggered by a script included into a webpage; (4) suitable mechanism of communication between human and computer must be able to address user's disability; (5) user authentication to the mobile device should make use of one or combined biometrics and/or other factors (e.g. location) from mobile device resources (e.g. voice, face, gesture, gait).

2. INTERACTION WORKFLOW

2.1 First-Time Authentication

The following steps describe the process of having a user authenticate the first time using the proposed workflow. (1) the JavaScript API requests user approval to have a device (e.g. smartphone) start the authentication process. A unique token is sent to the user using a suitable mechanism that the user can understand (suitable mechanism can be guessed by machine learning/usage profile at the first time?); (2) user passes on the token to user's phone (or phone can detect the user token through a suitable mechanism); (3) phone asks for user credentials; (4) user enters credentials on the phone; (5) user submits form with credentials; (6) credentials are stored locally on the phone (local storage) for subsequent authentication; (7) form fields are filled based on credentials entered on the phone. The suitable mechanisms not defined in the interaction workflow should (1) be able to communicate with the user; and (2) allow for user input that can prove for identity. The suitable mechanism should take user's disability into account.

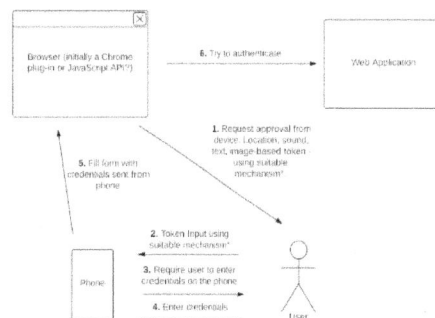

Figure 1. First Time Authentication

2.2 Subsequent Authentication

After previously having sent credentials through the aforementioned workflow, the process for authentication is almost the same, except for the fact that the user is no longer required to enter credentials on the phone if the credentials are the same as the ones used at first time authentication (i.e. the password has not changed), according to the workflow in Figure 2.

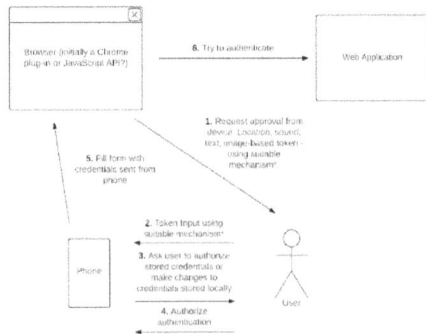

Figure 2. Subsequent Authentication

3. USER SCENARIO AND STRATEGIES

A user with low vision accesses the Facebook login page. A script on the page tells the user that they can use their phone to authenticate. This message/token is sent through a visual message that is readable by the screen reader or by playing a sound. The user picks up his smartphone and enters the token or makes the phone listen to the token. The smartphone lets the user know that the token is valid and shows the form to enter credentials on smartphone's screen. The user types credentials and authenticates to his Facebook profile. The next day, the user goes through the same one-time token validation process, except that they no longer need to enter their credentials as they are now stored on the phone. The phone asks the user if they want to use stored credentials or enter new credentials (in case a password has been changed). The user authorizes stored credentials to be sent or enters new credentials and authenticates to his Facebook profile. It is also important to remember that the token is not used for authentication purposes, but it is used for establishing communication. Once a token is used (i.e. communication is established), that token can no longer be used for starting the process of authentication. The user scenario described above implements some of the potential strategies that can be plugged into the framework, but it is important to highlight that the main advantage of this framework is that it can accommodate different strategies for addressing different disabilities. In the scenario above, the user with low vision could simply scan the token through QR code on the screen, or make the phone listen to the one-time token generated by the web page through the phone's microphone. In order for the user to authenticate to the phone in any subsequent authentication, they could simply shake their phone in a certain way, allowing for the smartphone to authenticate the user based on phone's motion or even speak a passphrase that would allow their phone to send their credentials over the network, instead of having to type passwords. Smartphones provide a broad range of interaction that can be used to prove for one's identity, and the purpose of using smartphone is to allow for developers to implement different strategies that can be used given the hardware available (e.g. GPS, gyroscope, accelerometer, camera, microphone).

4. EARLY IMPLEMENTATION

At the time of this writing, the framework is implemented under a minimum systems architecture scheme that will allow the

interaction workflow to be tested. The framework will support authentication using both smartphones and phones that are not smartphones, here called "Dumbphones". The architecture proposed in this document is being developed to be foundations of the framework that is subject of this paper and is further described in Figure 3.

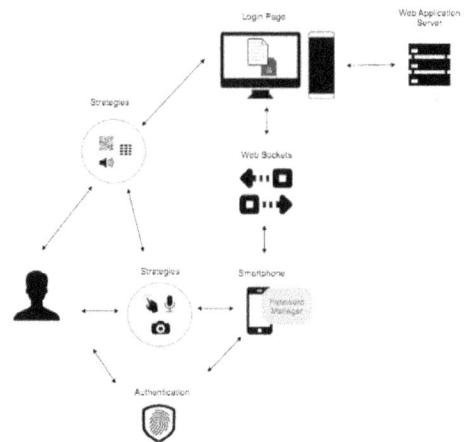

Figure 3. Framework Architecture – Using Smartphones

For "Dumbphones" the process is slightly different because resources on the phone are limited (i.e. no internet, no local storage). However, the same strategies approach can be used to establish communication with the web sockets server (e.g. SMS server to get and send token to web sockets server).

5. ONGOING WORK

The current status of the architecture uses the user's smartphone as a password manager. The implementation is being developed to accommodate different strategies of communication with the user. For example, in the current implementation, it is possible to inform the token to the user through text, sound, and QR code. The underlying infrastructure will allow for different strategies of communication to be easily integrated, as different disabilities will require different approaches. The framework is already foundations for executing early user testing so that assumptions can be validated and uncertainties eliminated. In the future, insights might also allow for implementation such that no credentials will be required (i.e. new ways to prove one's identity can be used on the web). Early user interviews have provided insights to support "dumbphones". This is only the beginning of tapping into the potential of an approach that can accommodate several communication and user interaction needs through the use of different strategies.

6. ACKNOWLEDGMENTS

I thank the guidance of my faculty advisor Dr. Yang Wang as well as the discussion with and feedback from Bryan Dosono, Jordan Hayes, Tarun Rajput, Huichuan Xia, Dr. Kevin Du, and Dr. Joon Park. I am also grateful to the support from the School of Information Studies at Syracuse University. This paper is based upon work developed under a Sub-recipient Agreement that is sponsored by the US Department of Education, Award Number H33A130057. Any opinions, findings, conclusions or recommendations expressed herein are those of the author(s) and do not necessarily reflect the views of the United States Department of Education or Carnegie Mellon University

VisAural: A Wearable Sound-Localisation Device for People with Impaired Hearing

Benjamin M. Gorman
University of Dundee
Dundee, Scotland
b.gorman@dundee.ac.uk

ABSTRACT

Although our sense of hearing, smell, and vision allow us to perceive things at a distance, the detection of many day-to-day events relies exclusively on our hearing. For example, finding a ringing phone lost in a sofa, hearing a child cry in another room, and use of a car alarm to locate a vehicle in a car park. However, individuals with total or partial hearing loss have difficulty detecting the audible signals in these situations. We have developed VisAural, a system that converts audible signals into visual cues. Using an array of head-mounted microphones, VisAural detects the direction of a sound, and places LEDs at the periphery of the user's visual field to guide them to the source of the sound. We tested VisAural with nine people with hearing impairments and found that this approach holds great promise but needs to be made more responsive before it can be truly helpful.

Categories and Subject Descriptors

K.4.2 [**Social Issues**]: Assistive technologies for persons with disabilities

Keywords

Hearing impairments; Sound localisation

1. INTRODUCTION

For many people, the ability to hear allows them to detect everyday events such as a misplaced phone ringing, or a baby crying. But for almost 17% of the UK population who have a hearing impairment [6], audible signals used to detect these events are not available. Hearing aids have been developed to help overcome challenges of general deafness, but uptake is low (only 14%)[6], and it has been demonstrated that they do not preserve spatial information, impeding sound localisation [2]. The Positional Ripples Display [4] partially addresses this problem, but requires knowledge of the deployment location and is therefore not easily adaptable. Similar work on developing a peripheral display of sound was undertaken in 2007 [1], however this solution was not portable.

These pieces of work demonstrate the capability to aid individuals through visualisation of audio; and both underline the value of using abstract visualisations to do so.

To address these problems, we have developed a wearable device that detects sounds in any environment, converting sound information into directional visual cues to inform the user of the direction of sounds. By using the visual cues from our device, people with hearing impairments should be able to interactively identify the location of sounds in their environment. The visual system is a suitable alternative to the auditory system as localising sounds typically uses visual search. Furthermore, out of all our senses, vision is the most synonymous with hearing; both are used to construct spatial understanding of our environment, both enable sensing at a distance, and it is arguable that they are the two dominant means by which humans develop an understanding of the world. A similar device to our system was developed [5], but this work focussed purely on the engineering task of creating the device, not on evaluating its effectiveness for helping people with hearing impairment.

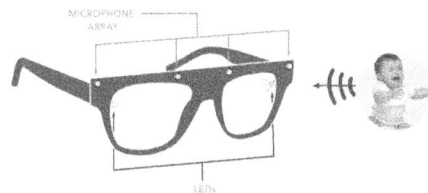

Figure 1: Device detects the baby's cry to the left of the user, lighting an LED in their left peripheral vision - signalling the sound is to their left.

2. VISAURAL

For input, VisAural uses an array of microphones mounted on a pair of eyeglasses (Figure 2). For output, LEDs are fixed on the left and right of the eyeglass frame (Figure 1) . Signals from the microphones are processed through a unit comprised of modified commodity hardware and a laptop computer. Sound is sampled from each of the four microphones and stored in a buffer every 0.2 seconds. The data is checked to ensure it has values above the microphone array's noise threshold to determine that there is a loud enough sound present. Using a delay-and-sum beamforming algorithm [3], the delay between each microphone and a common reference point (midpoint of array) is computed for each potential angle a sound can arrive from. In order to reduce computation, the system only checks for sounds arriving from either the left or the right at 15°, 30°, 45°, 60°, 90°. The resulting delay relates to how much longer it takes for a sound to arrive to the reference point versus the adjacent microphone. Each signal is delayed by the number of samples required and summed together. This results in 10 signals (five angles each on the left and the right), one for each potential direction. These signals are compared and the signal with the largest gain is taken to represent the direction of the sound.

When no sound is detected, both LEDs are off. If the loudest post-threshold sound is detected on the left side of the head, then the left LED is activated, signalling the user to turn towards the left. If the loudest sound is detected on the right, then the right LED is activated. When the left and right have roughly equal volumes, both LEDs activate telling the user that the origin of the sound lies within their visual field. In this manner, the user will be able to "hone in" on the source of the sound.

Figure 2: Prototype with microphone array at centre of a pair of eyeglasses and peripheral LEDs connected to an Arduino.

3. EVALUATION

To assess VisAural, we recruited nine participants (avg. 39.6 years, six male) who self-reported some degree of hearing impairment. We recorded their sound localisation performance (error rates and response times) both with and without VisAural and gathered their subjective impressions through loosely-structured interviews once the evaluation was completed. The study was composed of two parts. The first was to assess the hearing ability of each participant through an online audiometry tone test (ATT)[7], in which the participant's ability to hear different frequencies between 250Hz and 8kHz at different volume levels was measured. Any participant with any responses above 40 dBHL (indicating at least mild hearing loss) was included in the study. Any participant who did not meet this condition continued in the study but their data was not included in the analysis.

The second part of the study was a sound localisation task. Participants sat, surrounded by 6 evenly-spaced speakers in a semi-circular arrangement. Each participant had to localise 54 sounds. Each sound had three components: frequency (low, medium, high), volume level (low, medium, high) and a speaker number (1-6). The order of the sounds were randomised at the beginning of the study. The participant began the task by pressing the spacebar key, after which the first sound would play. The participant was instructed to press a number on a keypad relating to the speaker which they believed the sound originated from. After the participant had pressed the keypad there was a brief delay after which the next sound would play. This would repeat until all sounds had been played. This task was completed once with no assistance and once whilst wearing the prototype, and was counterbalanced between participants.

4. RESULTS & DISCUSSION

Through analysis of the evaluation data, no quantitative difference between participants' performance with or without the use of our prototype was found (see Figure 3). The response time for VisAural (5.8s) was significantly slower

than the response time with no device (3.3s; paired t-test, $p < 0.01$) (see Figure 4).

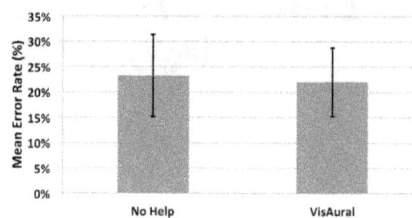

Figure 3: Mean error rates with and without assistance ($\pm$ s.e.).

During follow up questions, we first found that participants were very enthusiastic about using their visual system to aid the task of sound localisation, with one participant noting that use of the system, "could become second nature". Second we found that the system needs to be faster at notifying the user of sound direction. This could be caused due to processing of the microphone array input. This delay may affect completion time (see Figure 4) and could affect error rates as one participant stated that the "Ambiguity [caused by the delay] overruled the device". Third, in order for both LEDs to light at once, indicating that the sound is directly in front of the user, the sound source needs a direct line of sight to the device. This turned out to be a key interaction element for participants but with one reporting that it was "Difficult to get both lights to appear", we determine that this field of notification needs improved. As a result of these findings, we are now working to reduce the response time of the prototype, as well as exploring the potential of more expressive visual cues.

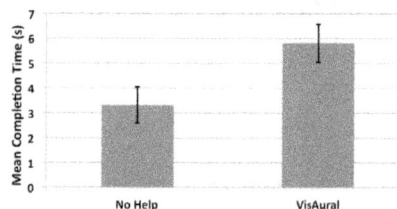

Figure 4: Mean completion time with and without assistance ($\pm$ s.e.).

5. REFERENCES

[1] J. Azar, H. Saleh, and M. Al-Alaoui. Sound visualization for the hearing impaired. *iJET*, 2007.

[2] S. Gatehouse, G. Naylor, and C. Elberling. Benefits from hearing aids in relation to the interaction between the user and the environment. *Int. J. Audiol.*, (42):S77–S85, 2003.

[3] A. Greensted. Microphone arrays beamforming. http://www.labbookpages.co.uk/audio/beamforming/fractionalDelay.html.

[4] F. Ho-Ching, J. Mankoff, and J. A. Landay. Can you see what I hear? The design and evaluation of a peripheral sound display for the deaf. *CHI'03, 161–68*.

[5] K.-W. Kim, J.-W. Choi, and Y.-H. Kim. An assistive device for direction estimation of a sound source. *Assist. Technol.*, (25):216–221, 2013.

[6] A. on Hearing Loss. Facts and figures on deafness and tinnitus. http://www.actiononhearingloss.org.uk/.

[7] S. Pigeon. Online audiogram and hearing test. http://myhearingtest.net/.

Web Accessibility Evaluation with the Crowd: Using Glance to Rapidly Code User Testing Video

Mitchell Gordon
University of Rochester
Rochester, NY 14627
m.gordon@rochester.edu

ABSTRACT

Evaluating the results of user accessibility testing on the web can take a significant amount of time, training, and effort. Some of this work can be offloaded to others through coding video data from user tests to systematically extract meaning from subtle human actions and emotions. However, traditional video coding methods can take a considerable amount of time. We have created Glance, a tool that uses the crowd to allow researchers to rapidly query, sample, and analyze large video datasets for behavioral events that are hard to detect automatically. In this abstract, we discuss how Glance can be used to quickly code video of users with special needs interacting with a website by coding for whether or not websites conform with accessibility guidelines, in order to evaluate how accessible a website is and where potential problems lie.

Categories and Subject Descriptors

K.4.2 [**Social Issues**]: Assistive technologies for persons with disabilities; H.5.m [**Information Interfaces and Presentation**]: Misc.

General Terms

User studies, Experimentation, Human Factors.

Keywords

Accessibility, video, data analysis, crowdsourcing

1. INTRODUCTION

User testing is considered an important part of web accessibility evaluation. In the W3C's Website Accessibility Conformance Evaluation Methodology draft, they recommend involving people with disabilities as part of the evaluation methodology. The W3C also published Web Content Accessibility Guidelines (WCAG 2), which help identify the types of important questions to ask when evaluating website accessibility.

ASSETS'14, October 20–22, 2014, Rochester, NY, USA.
ACM 978-1-4503-2720-6/14/10.
http://dx.doi.org/10.1145/2661334.2661412.

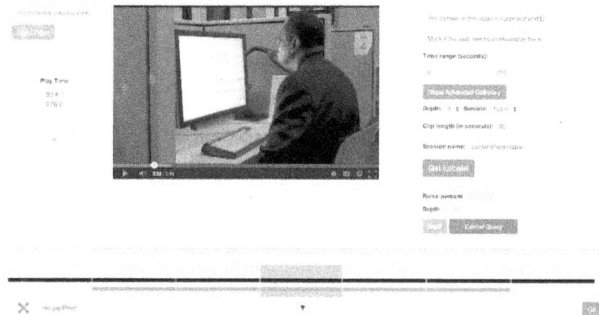

Figure 1: The Glance user interface. Glance can code events in user testing video quickly and accurately. When a usability question is asked, small clips from the video are sent to crowd workers who label events in parallel. The judgements are then quickly merged together and displayed. In this example, we use Glance to determine if and when a disabled user encountered unpredictable content.

However, involving people with disabilities directly in the evaluation process may require both time and training, which developers frequently lack [6]. While testing can be performed remotely, the nature of self-reports mean that the data collected may be limited when compared to in-person studies [7]. In addition to user testing, automated testing is also commonly used to evaluate the accessibility of a website [7]. This type of testing is significantly easier to run, quicker, less costly to evaluate than user testing, and often consists of simply entering a website URL and receiving a list of possible accessibility issues. Though not evaluated in the context of accessibility, the crowd-powered system PatFinder is able to use video of users performing tasks to identify higher-level interaction patterns, which describe how to complete tasks such as 'buying a book about HCI.' [4] However, automated techniques have not previously been able to evaluate subtle human actions and emotions that can result from users during user testing [7].

This submission introduces the use of Glance, a crowd-powered video coding tool [5], as a way to code video recordings of user testing and significantly decrease the time and cost associated with evaluating the results of a user test.

2. VIDEO CODING

Behavioral video coding allows researchers in the social sciences to study human interactions [2]. In HCI, researchers often use video coding to discover how users interact with technology [3], and to help better explain those interactions [2].

Video coding is important because it provides a systematic measure of behavior. However, it is commonly considered a very time-consuming process, with some researchers claiming that it can take 5-10x longer than the play time of the video itself [1]. Additionally, video coding requires a significant amount of overhead. In order to perform video coding on data, researchers must develop a reliable coding scheme, acquire and train coders, and check for inter-rater reliability. All these factors combined means that performing video coding to evaluate user tests has previously had a very high barrier to entry.

3. GLANCE

Previously, we have presented Glance, a system that allows researchers to analyze and code events in large video datasets by segmenting videos and then parallelizing the video coding process across a crowd of online workers (Figure 1) [5]. This approach significantly reduces the amount of time required to gather information from video data, and allows video to be coded in a fraction of the actual play time, depending on the size of the available crowd. To ensure accuracy, Glance can distribute the same video segments to multiple unique workers, and then calculate the variance to provide quick feedback. Glance provides a front-end interface for analysts to enter natural-language queries and to visualize coding results as they arrive.

Coding video with Glance to evaluate the results from user studies can significantly reduce the amount of time and effort required to obtain actionable information from user tests using the power of the crowd. Additionally, the time, cost, and effort savings that Glance affords makes the use of video coding to evaluate user tests feasible for a larger number of web developers.

We can use the WCAG 2 guidelines, created by the W3C, to determine what to code video of user studies for. For example, some questions we might ask are "did the user encounter this type of problem: no caption or other alternative provided for multimedia" or "did the user encounter unreadable or difficult to understand text?". By using sighted crowd workers as video coders, we are able to identify problems which may not be identified through remote self-reported accessibility evaluations [7] without requiring developers to take time from the development process to conduct usability testing themselves.

4. EVALUATION AND RESULTS

To evaluate Glance's ability to code video of accessibility user testing and return reliable results, we ran a feasibility experiment using Glance's "gist" mode, which asks workers to simply mark if any instance of the event occurs within a small clip, rather than asking them to mark the exact range in which it occurs. We believe that gist mode is appropriate for this scenario because determining, for example, exactly what time a user starts and stops being confused is highly subjective and may require additional context that only the web developer is able to provide.

Our evaluation used a video of a user test that consisted of multiple visually-impaired users both using a website on a desktop computer and providing verbal feedback. We coded for the WCAG 2 guideline "make content appear and operate in predictable ways" (though slightly re-worded to help the crowd better understand what to code for). This small evaluation consisted of 20 Mechanical Turk workers coding a three and a half minute video. The crowd correctly coded clips with a precision of 80% and recall of 100%. These scores are comparable to the scores obtained from Glance's initial evaluation, showing that video coding of accessibility user tests is no less accurate than other anticipated uses of Glance.

5. FUTURE WORK

We would like to expand our evaluation to include a larger variety of user study videos and code them for all WCAG 2 guidelines, as well as other sets of accessibility guidelines.

We also believe that, in addition to website user test evaluations, Glance has many possible applications within accessibility. These are limited only by what types of videos can be created and by what types of events can be accurately coded for. Some of these possibilities include:

- Visually-impaired users taking a panoramic video with their phone and asking a question about it.
- Disabled users can upload a video of their interaction with a website or app that is not accessible. If they were not able to completed a desired action in the inaccessible app, they could ask a question to help figure out where in the process of using the app they went wrong.

6. REFERENCES

[1] *Handbook of Research Methods in Social and Personality Psychology*. Cambridge University Press, 2000.

[2] R. Bakeman and J. M. G. PhD. *Observing Interaction: An Introduction to Sequential Analysis*. Cambridge University Press, 1997.

[3] B. Jordan and A. Henderson. Interaction analysis: Foundations and practice. *The Journal of the Learning Sciences*, 4(1):pp. 39–103, 1995.

[4] W. Lasecki, T. Lau, G. He, and J. Bigham. Crowd-based recognition of web interaction patterns. In *Adjunct Proceedings of the 25th Annual ACM Symposium on User Interface Software and Technology*, UIST Adjunct Proceedings '12, pages 99–100, New York, NY, USA, 2012. ACM.

[5] W. S. Lasecki, M. Gordon, D. Koutra, M. Jung, S. P. Dow, and J. P. Bigham. Glance: Rapidly coding behavioral video with the crowd. UIST 2014, New York, NY, USA, 2014. ACM.

[6] J. Lazar, A. Dudley-Sponaugle, and K.-D. Greenidge. Improving web accessibility: a study of webmaster perceptions. *Computers in Human Behavior*, 20(2):269–288, 2004.

[7] J. Mankoff, H. Fait, and T. Tran. Is your web page accessible?: A comparative study of methods for assessing web page accessibility for the blind. CHI '05, pages 41–50, New York, NY, USA, 2005. ACM.

AccessBraille: Tablet-based Braille Entry

Stephanie Ludi
Department of Software Engineering
Rochester Institute of Technology
Rochester, NY USA
1.585.475.7407
salvse@rit.edu

Michael Timbrook
Department of Software Engineering
Rochester Institute of Technology
Rochester, NY USA
mpt2360@rit.edu

Piper Chester
Department of Software Engineering
Rochester Institute of Technology
Rochester, NY USA
pwc1203@rit.edu

ABSTRACT

This paper outlines the development of the AccessBraille framework, an iOS framework designed to provide a Braille keyboard to an iOS application. The proof-of-concept app developed with this framework is presented as an example of how the framework can be utilized, demonstrating its use across multiple contexts where Braille entry is used. The AccessBraille keyboard framework provides a natural way for blind users to enter US Type 1 or Type 2 Braille text into an app. The keyboard allows for users to customize finger placement for comfort and hand size.

Categories and Subject Descriptors

H.5 [**Information Interfaces and Presentation**]: User Interfaces; K.4.2 [**Social Issues**]: Assistive tech for persons with disabilities

General Terms

Design, Human Factors

Keywords

Accessibility; braille; tablet; visual impairment

1. INTRODUCTION

On mobile devices, text entry is primarily accomplished by tapping on virtual keys displayed on the screen. Over time various styles of keyboards have been developed on the Android and iOS platform, including efforts to support users with disabilities [3, 4]. In this paper, we describe the design of the AccessBraille keyboard. The AccessBraille keyboard enables users who are blind to enter text via Braille directly onto an iPad's screen. The keyboard framework is designed to enable consistency in Braille entry within and potentially across iOS apps.

The iOS platform already has several built-in accessibility features such as the VoiceOver screen reader, color inversion, and toggle labels [1]. With VoiceOver, the user can tap on a button and VoiceOver will state what the item is (the label for the item). Braille support exists for third party refreshable Braille displays.

The AccessBraille keyboard is used as part of an iOS app, providing different modes to interactively practice Braille. The project is designed around educational word-based games for

ASSETS'14, October 20–22, 2014, Rochester, NY, USA.
ACM 978-1-4503-2720-6/14/10.
http://dx.doi.org/10.1145/2661334.2661421

children in K-12 who have not mastered the (US) Grade 1 or the Grade 2 Braille system. The project goal is to be a tool for students who are visually impaired to practice the Braille. Many Braille typing machines are cumbersome and/or expensive, with limited portability and access issues for those with limited. The AccessBraille keyboard (as part of the app) is intended to be portable and useful in terms of learning Braille and as a Braille writer.

2. RELATED WORK

Much of the current work in enabling Braille entry has focused on the tactile keyboard, often involving a new screen material or an overlay for the screen. This work is a different approach than the AccessBraille keyboard framework, which can be used on existing iPad hardware. Other keyboards are intended to be adaptive in order to predict text entry [3]. While many such keyboards are useful to users, they do not serve well as a means for Braille entry or instruction where practice is important. In 2011, a student project used an approach whereby each of the user's fingers are within a circle that in turn is used to enter Braille on an Android device [2]. Such a system may be an option on the Android platform, though our user testing showed that there are user interaction issues with the approach when the keyboard is integrated into a realistic workflow (context of tasks).

In terms of the AccessBraille app itself, work is limited. Current apps tend to serve as translators to/from text (VisualBraille, BrailleWriter) and teach the alphabet for sighted users (PocketBraille, BrailleNow). The primary users for these types of apps are sighted users not individuals (much less children) who need to learn Braille in order to be fully literate. The Braille Input Editor and most other Braille editors use predefined Braille keys, which is inadequate for smaller hands. Given the project goal and approach to achieving it, the current options are lacking.

3. SOFTWARE DESIGN

The scope of this paper will discuss the AccessBraille in the context of the BrailleWriter part of the app. The goal is to provide a means for the user to enter Braille in a natural, yet flexible manner that can accommodate different finger spacing. This is akin to how the user would set their fingers when using a manual Braille entry device such as a Perkins Brailler.

To initialize the keyboard, the user must swipe 6 fingers (three on each hand) upwards on the screen (see Figure 1). This will present the 6 columns where each corresponds to one of the six dots that comprise a Braille character (or a grouping of characters in the case of Grade 2). The column is aligned under each of the six fingers even if the fingers are right next to each other. The columns are numbered the same as standard braille keyboards: starting from the left side of the screen the columns is numbered,

3-2-1 and 4-5-6. Throughout this paper, these columns will be known as 3-C, 2-C, 1-C, etc. Based on a Perkins mechanical Brailler. The developers intended 1-C to be the location where users would place the index finger of their left hand, 2-C would be for the middle finger, and 3-C the ring finger. 4-C is where users would put their right index finger, 5-C their middle, and 6-C their ring. The six collumns can be set as close or far apart as the user desires. Initial testing showed that some users wish to have their fingers right next to each other.

By typing in the same manner as the letters of Grade 1 braille the user is able to enter text. E.g., by pressing 1-C, the user will type an 'a'. The letter 'a' will be printed in a rectangular view behind the typing columns as well as be read aloud. When a word is completed, the word is spoken via the build-in iOS voice.

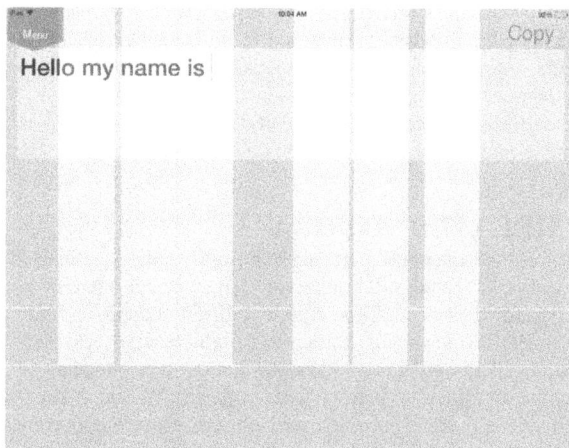

Fig. 1. Screenshot showing the redesigned Braille keyboard using columns The collumns are labeled (left to right) 3-C, 2-C, and 1-C, 4-C, 5-C and 6-C. Note that columns 2-C and 1-C (left hand) are very close together.

The shift, backspace and enter functionality of the keyboard is activated outside of the columns. The space on the left is referred to as 7-C and on the right 8-C, this is how 8 dot Braille's denote these extra keys. When originally implementing these functions, backspace was 8-C and 7-C toggled shift and caps lock. Enter was not a feature yet. After spending some time using a Focus Blue 40 this functionality was deemed, non-standard and the team went ahead to implement this in the same way as the Perkins Brailler.

Audio feedback is also critical to the keyboard. Each typed letter is spoken as is each work when the space is pressed. When the keyboard is initiated a sound is heard that sounds like a series of notes increasing in pitch (signifying movement upward). When the keyboard is exited or stopped, a series of tones is played that decreases in pitch (signifying movement downward).

The development of the AccessBraille keyboard framework transcends the app itself. In particular the keyboard framework was designed for use in other apps in order to promote a consistent user experience in Braille entry on the iOS platform. Developers can easily integrate the keyboard as an option for a variety of iPad applications such as productivity or communication apps. Facilitating a build-in Braille keyboard will provide an opportunity for the blind to use Braille among their apps, which will promote literacy as well as efficiency in entering text.

4. FUTURE WORK

While we have gathered initial results from users, we will continue to gather feedback after the app is deployed. As part of the ongoing feedback, user reviews and an embedded link to a satisfaction survey will be used as a mechanism to gather feedback for future releases. For example, expanding a feature to copy and paste material to other apps (e.g. email client or text message apps) will be assessed.

5. ACKNOWLEDGEMENTS

AccessBraille is supported by seed funding from RIT.

6. REFERENCES

[1] Apple Developer Center. Understanding Accessibility on iOS; Available:
https://developer.apple.com/library/ios/documentation/UserExperience/Conceptual/iPhoneAccessibility/Accessibility_on_iPhone/Accessibility_on_iPhone.html#//apple_ref/doc/uid/TP40008785-CH100-SW1

[2] Belezina, J. "Student-made tablet app may make dedicated Braille writers obsolete". Gizmag. Available:
http://www.gizmag.com/touchscreen-braille-writer/20118/

[3] Cheng, L., Liang, H., Wu, C., and Chen, M. 2013. iGrasp: grasp-based adaptive key-board for mobile devices. In Proceedings of the SIGCHI Conference on Human Factors in Computing Systems (CHI '13). ACM, New York, NY, USA, 3037-3046. DOI=10.1145/2470654.2481422
http://doi.acm.org/10.1145/2470654.2481422

[4] Dale, O., and Schulz, T. 2012. Easier mobile phone input using the jusfone keyboard. In Proceedings of the 13th international conference on Computers Helping People with Special Needs - Volume Part II (ICCHP'12), Klaus Miesenberger, Arthur Karshmer, Petr Penaz, and Wolfgang Zagler (Eds.), Vol. Part II. Springer-Verlag, Berlin, Heidelberg, 439-446. DOI=10.1007/978-3-642-31534-3_65
http://dx.doi.org/10.1007/978-3-

DigitCHAT: Enabling AAC Input at Conversational Speed

Karl Wiegand
Northeastern University
360 Huntington Ave
Boston, MA 02115, USA
wiegand@ccs.neu.edu

Rupal Patel
Northeastern University
360 Huntington Ave
Boston, MA 02115, USA
r.patel@neu.edu

ABSTRACT

Augmentative and alternative communication (AAC) systems are used by many different types of people. While almost all AAC users have speech impairments that preclude the use of verbal communication, they may also have varying levels of vision or motor impairments, perhaps due to age or the particular nature of their disorder. Speed, expressiveness, and ease of communication are key factors in choosing an appropriate system; however, there are social considerations that are often overlooked. AAC systems are increasingly being used on mobile devices with smaller screens, in part because ambulatory AAC users may feel uncomfortable carrying around large or unusual machines. DigitCHAT is a prototype AAC system designed for fast and expressive communication by literate AAC users with minimal upper limb motor impairments. DigitCHAT's interface was designed to be used discretely on a mobile phone and supports continuous motion input using a small set of visually separated buttons.

Categories and Subject Descriptors

H.5.2 [**User Interfaces**]: Graphical User Interfaces; K.4.2 [**Social Issues**]: Assistive Technologies for Persons with Disabilities

General Terms

Design, Human Factors

Keywords

AAC, Continuous Motion, Mobile

1. MOTIVATION

People who use augmentative and alternative communication (AAC) systems often have speech impairments severe enough to prevent the use of verbal communication [1]. Depending upon the nature of their disorders, many AAC

ASSETS'14, October 20–22, 2014, Rochester, NY, USA.
ACM 978-1-4503-2720-6/14/10.
http://dx.doi.org/10.1145/2661334.2661422.

users may have accompanying motor impairments, such as tremors or reduced mobility of their hands and arms [2]. They may also have vision impairments that make it difficult to see small font sizes. AAC systems that operate on small mobile devices often use on-screen keyboards that were not designed for people with bigger hands or people with upper limb motor impairments. These keyboards usually occupy less than half of the available screen real estate and have small buttons that are positioned adjacent to each other. Many elderly users, much less users with diagnosed motor or vision impairments, have difficulty with these keyboards because of the button and font sizes [4]. Additionally, these systems tend to focus on the creation and use of stored utterances instead of real-time composition, unnecessarily reducing the flexibility of conversation. The current work aims to address the need for an AAC system that can be used at conversational speeds on a small-screen mobile device by ambulatory users with mild upper limb motor impairments. Although intended for AAC users, this prototype system also has potential for non-AAC users who may be temporarily unable to use their voices.

2. APPROACH

DigitCHAT enables rapid, face-to-face communication via small touch-screen devices, such as mobile phones. The system uses large buttons to assist users who may have difficulty making precise movements. Buttons are visually separated to maximize visibility when a user naturally obscures part of the screen by touching it. The interface is organized as a telephone number pad, resulting in higher lexical ambiguity compared to commercial systems like Swype or SwiftKey; however, this design provides familiarity, especially for older users, and reduces the time required to learn the layout.

To further increase communication speed and assist users with upper limb motor impairments, DigitCHAT supports two types of input: mixed and continuous. In mixed mode, users can provide a combination of discrete taps or noncontiguous path segments to specify the desired word. At any given time, the most likely word is displayed at the top of the screen, and can be selected by tapping it or ending a path on it. In continuous mode, users draw a single line through all desired buttons. As the user's finger or stylus moves over the screen, the most likely word is displayed at the top of the screen. When the user disconnects from the screen's surface, the most likely unigram is spoken aloud immediately. Users can cancel the current path, without speaking the displayed word, by ending on the Stop or Cancel sign. With many current AAC systems, listeners must

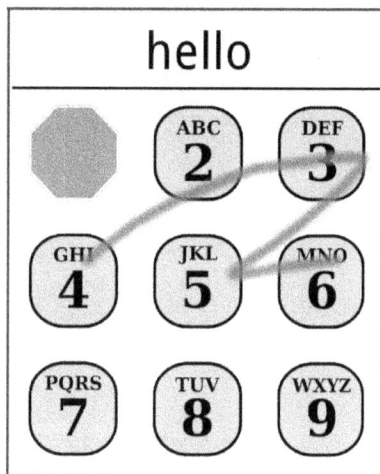

Figure 1: Example input path for the word "hello."

Figure 2: Example input path for the word "today."

wait while the user composes a complete utterance [3, 6]. This waiting period places increased pressure on the AAC user to generate utterances as quickly as possible, creating uncomfortable silences and often encouraging the use of telegraphic utterances. By automatically speaking each word as it is completed, DigitCHAT can significantly reduce these gaps and facilitate conversational turn-taking.

DigitCHAT uses a predetermined vocabulary and dictionary-based implementation with unigram statistics based on the Crowdsourced AAC-Like Corpus [5]. Every word in the dictionary is converted into a physical path traversing a standard telephone number pad. The width of this path is incrementally varied up to the size of a standard button and ordered collisions are recorded as possible sequences that a user might take to specify a given word. These paths are then reverse-indexed, so that DigitCHAT can look up the user's provided path and retrieve the set of words, with unigram probabilities, that the path could indicate.

Words that share the same sequence of buttons are sometimes called "textonyms." For example, the words "bat" and "cat" are textonyms because they are both specified with the discrete numeric sequence 2-8 or the continuous motion sequence 2-5-8. DigitCHAT implements two approaches to resolving textonyms. In the first approach, the most likely textonym is displayed and users can scribble over the last button in their numeric sequence to rotate through possible textonyms. Users can disconnect from the screen to speak the displayed word aloud or end their scribbling on the Stop sign to cancel the utterance. In the second approach, DigitCHAT implements basic learning and remembers the user's preferred textonyms for any given path.

3. FEEDBACK AND FUTURE WORK

We have made DigitCHAT freely available for Android devices on the Google Play Store in order to gauge interest and elicit feedback. Thus far, DigitCHAT has undergone two design and development iterations based on suggestions from users in the target population. In addition to informal feedback from ad-hoc testers, we have received narrative emails from three users and are preparing for a formal study with participants at a clinical facility that serves individuals with chronic neuromotor disorders. A common request, which has

since been implemented, was to allow cancellation in order to prevent unexpected or undesirable words from being spoken. We have created several user-configurable options, such as the movement threshold for textonym rotation, but it may be possible to implement a learning algorithm to discover the ideal values for these settings automatically. While the current version of DigitCHAT relies primarily on unigram statistics, we intend to look at potential improvements from using skip-grams or implementing phrasal prediction. We are also experimenting with different methods to efficiently add and remove words from the dictionary to allow for full vocabulary customization.

4. REFERENCES

[1] J. Higginbotham, H. Shane, S. Russell, and K. Caves. Access to AAC: Present, past, and future. *Augmentative and Alternative Communication*, 23(3):243–257, Jan. 2007.

[2] J. Light, D. Beukelman, and J. Reichle. *Communicative competence for individuals who use AAC: From research to effective practice*. Paul H. Brookes Publishing Co., 2003.

[3] J. Light and K. Drager. AAC technologies for young children with complex communication needs: State of the science and future research directions. *Augmentative and alternative communication*, 23(3):204–216, 2007.

[4] H. Nicolau and J. Jorge. Elderly text-entry performance on touchscreens. In *Proceedings of the 14th International ACM SIGACCESS Conference on Computers and Accessibility*, ASSETS '12, pages 127–134, New York, NY, USA, 2012. ACM.

[5] K. Vertanen and P. O. Kristensson. The imagination of crowds: Conversational AAC language modeling using crowdsourcing and large data sources. In *Proceedings of the Conference on Empirical Methods in Natural Language Processing (EMNLP)*, pages 700–711. ACL, 2011.

[6] B. Wisenburn and J. J. Higginbotham. An AAC application using speaking partner speech recognition to automatically produce contextually relevant utterances: objective results. *Augmentative and alternative communication*, 24(2):100–109, 2008.

Explorations on Breathing Based Text Input for Mobile Devices

Jackson Feijó Filho
Nokia Technology Institute
Av. Torquato Tapajós, 7200 - Col.
Terra Nova. Manaus-AM Brasil.
69093-415
+55 92 8134 0134
jackson.feijo@indt.org.br

Thiago Valle
Nokia Technology Institute
Av. Torquato Tapajós, 7200 - Col.
Terra Nova. Manaus-AM Brasil.
69093-415
+55 92 8109 0999
thiago.valle@indt.org.br

Wilson Prata
Nokia Technology Institute
Av. Torquato Tapajós, 7200 - Col.
Terra Nova. Manaus-AM Brasil.
69093-415
+55 92 8805 1071
wilson.prata@indt.org.br

ABSTRACT

This work proposes progresses on the use of a breathing based text input software for mobile as an alternative interaction technology for people with motor disabilities. It attempts to explore the processing of the audio from the microphone in mobile phones to select characters from dynamically generated keyboard. A proof of concept of this work is demonstrated by the implementation and experimentation of a mobile application prototype that enables users to perform text entry through "puffing" interaction.

Categories and Subject Descriptors

H.1.2 [**User/Machine Systems**], K.4.2 [**Social Issues**]: Assistive technologies for persons with disabilities, Handicapped persons/special needs.

General Terms

Algorithms, Performance, Design, Experimentation, Human Factors, Languages.

Keywords

Breathing; Alternative HCI; Text Input, Mobile; Accessibility.

1. INTRODUCTION

Assistive technologies have been researched and developed as an important part of the field of human–computer interaction. Various forms of assistance have been created for technology users with particular disabilities that reduce their capabilities to perform text input on some devices. Several alternative user interfaces for users with motor disabilities have been developed and reported. Typically, these solutions include methods that implement speech recognition techniques, eye-trackers and sip-and-puff controllers. Speech recognition software is well documented to be particularly useful for textual input aid, while additional devices are usually employed as pointing devices, allowing the control of e.g. the mouse pointer [2].

ASSETS '14, Oct 20-22 2014, Rochester, NY, USA
ACM 978-1-4503-2720-6/14/10.
http://dx.doi.org/10.1145/2661334.2661425.

This work will initially debate on the disadvantages of these solutions, compare this proposal to related work, followed by the advocacy of the present solution and explanation of its functioning. A specific part of the paper will emphasize the progress of this exploration, compared to the work in [7].

In the end, experimentation will state this as a valuable alternative to a hands-free and silent textual input for mobiles phones.

2. THE PROBLEM SPACE

Textual input and other interaction between people with motor disabilities and their mobile phones have challenged the academy and industry to develop alternative software and hardware solutions. These solutions will not rely on any manual interaction e.g. keystroking, screen-touching. Text input through other physiological signals [1][4] is often considered. Speech recognition is also a solution used by the targeted audience [7].

3. RELATED WORK

3.1 PuffText

It attempts to detect three distinct events based on 'puffing': a single short puff, a double short puff and a long puff. The single short puff stops the spinning keyboard, zooming the character positioned under the cursor. A second short puff selects the character and adds it to the text box. If the user does not puff the second time, shortly after the first, the keyboard starts spinning again. A long puff will change keyboards from letters to numbers/punctuation/special characters [7].

4. PROGRESSES ON PUFFTEXT

Several usability and performance tests were conducted after the implementation of [7]. The experiments were reproduced with the new software, proving the enhancements to be efficient and more user-friendly.

4.1 User interface redesign

Usability studies were conducted in the context of a usability laboratory containing 7 cameras and 9 microphones, capturing reactions of the test subjects using PuffText. The experiment described in detail in [7] was performed in 8 rounds, over the period of 6 months. Each round consisted in recruiting at least 6 distinct subjects, being 3 disabled and 3 able-bodied. The disability on the test subjects made them unable to handle a mobile device manually.

Some of the subjects reported having difficulties to understand the "dial" metaphor of the spinning keyboard. Some also mentioned that the circle disposition of the characters made it difficult to perceive sequence.

Ambient noise and microphone gain visual feedback also lacked in [7]. Subjects reported to be difficult to remember the strength they should puff – decreasing memorability and learnability of the interface. Subjects have reported that it was difficult to prevent false-positives in noisy spaces and mentioned that a visual feedback of sound levels would benefit overall usability.

To improve keyboard sequence understanding and provide visual feedback from the sound level of ambient noise and puff strength, we implemented the interface shown in Figure 3.

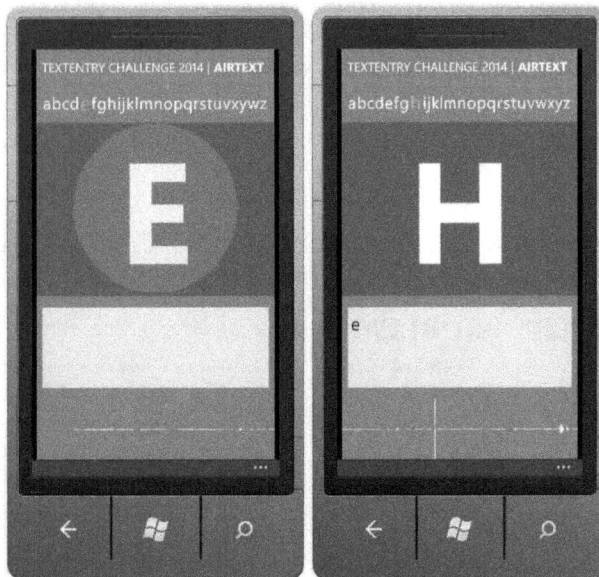

Figure 3 – Screenshots of the application. On (a) the character "E" is being selected. The interface shows a circle highlight to provide clear visual feedback of the selection. At the bottom, a wave form representation is being displayed to inform user of ambient noise and in (b) we can see the sound level peak that caused the character "e" to be selected.

4.2 Interaction design restructuring

Using only short and long puffs simplified the interaction, increasing learnability, memorability and overall performance. Short puffs are used to select character. Longs puffs delete entire words.

5. EXPERIMENT

As described in sections 4.1 and 4.2 continuous experiments from [7] promoted various improvements in the user interface and interaction design of the present solution. As soon as we reached the current implementation, additional 10 rounds of tests were conducted.

Each round consisted in one trying to perform the task of inputting a given text of 20 words.

Some text entry features, such as text prediction are being tested, for preliminary evaluation simplification.

The first 2 rounds were meant to be purely instructional. After that, 6 rounds of entering text using the present solution were timed. Three able-bodied and three disabled, high school students of 15~18 years old, were tested.

The disabled group represented two types of disabilities: having no arms (birth defects) or lack of motor dexterity (due to accidents). The three subjects in this group are unable to handgrip a mobile phone manually.

The users were instructed to keep the distance of approximately 20, 30 and 50 centimeters during the first three rounds of tests. These different distances were meant to evaluate:

- Puff accuracy at distance
- Background noise immunity
- Shortness of breath due to application usage

6. RESULTS

A proof-of-concept application was developed to perform tests in order to support the argument of this work. The mobile application is able to provide a way for users to perform text input in a hands-free, speech-free solution. This alternative approach is software based, meaning it will not require extra hardware to function. It also presents itself as a somewhat discreet and private application, as it implies minimum representation (just breath) of whatever is being inputted, to the periphery auditory.

The final average typing rates for the current solution with this study group and given text was 5.8 words per minute. Compare to [6] were a Morse code typist makes 12.6 and a Mouth stick (hardware based) input solution gives 7.88 words per minute. The WPM was measured through logging character/timestamp in a text file on the phone and performing post-test calculation.

However, differently from [7], the present solution provided visual feedback of the sound levels.

7. REFERENCES

[1] Arroyo-Palacios, J., Romano, D.M., Exploring the use of a respiratory-computer interface for game interaction. ICE-GIC 2009, London, UK (2009) 154-159.

[2] Sibert L.E., Jacob R.J.K., Evaluation of eye gaze interaction. Proceedings of CHI 2000 Conference on Human Factorsin Computing Systems. ACM Press (2000), The Hague, pp 281–288.

[3] Patel, S., Abowd, G., BLUI: Low-cost Localized Blowable User Interfaces. Proceedings of the 20th annual ACM symposium,(2007).

[4] Jones, M., Grogg, K., Anschutz, J., Fierman, R. A Sip-and-Puff Wireless Remote Control for the Apple iPod. Assistive Technology: The Official Journal of RESNA,Volume 20, Issue 2, 107-110, (2008)

[5] Sporka AJ, Kurniawan SH, Slavík P - Whistling user interface (U3I). The 8th ERCIM International Workshop "User Interfaces For All", Vienna, Austria, (2004)

[6] Simon Levine, John Gauger, Lisa Bowersand Karen Khan,comparison of Mouthstick and Morse code text inputs. Augmentative and Alternative Communication 1986, Vol. 2, No. 2 , Pages 51-55 (1986)

[7] Feijó Filho, J., Prata, W., Valle, T. PuffText: a voiceless and touchless text entry solution for mobile phones. Proceeding ASSETS '13 Proceedings of the 15th International ACM SIGACCESS Conference on Computers and Accessibility Article No. 63. ACM New York, NY, USA 2013

KeyGlasses: Semi-transparent Keys on Soft Keyboard

Mathieu Raynal
IRIT - ELIPSE Team
University of Toulouse
31062 Toulouse, cedex 9, FRANCE
mathieu.raynal@irit.fr

ABSTRACT

This paper presents the KeyGlass system: a text entry system with dynamic addition of characters based on the previously entered ones. This system is optimized by the use of a prediction algorithm based on a lexicographic tree and bigrams.

Categories and Subject Descriptors

H.5.2 [**User Interfaces**]: Input devices and strategies

General Terms

Algorithms

Keywords

soft keyboard, character prediction

1. INTRODUCTION

Currently, the keys and characters of the most commonly used soft keyboards are laid out similarly to the physical AZERTY or QWERTY keyboards (depending on culture). This arrangement has the advantage of being known to everyone. However, the major drawback lies in the distance of the most frequently used characters, which is not an issue for physical keyboards given the use of different fingers. On the other side, the use of a single pointer to select characters implies moving it between each character to enter. The distance of the most frequently used characters causes an increase of the distance with the pointer, which results in a decrease of the text entry speed for the user, but also motor or eye fatigue [7].

To minimize travelled distances, two main approaches were studied:

- First, to match the different characters on the keyboard to bring the characters which frequently follow each other closer. Keyboards have been generated either intuitively (eg Fitaly or OPTI keyboards[3]) or

from optimization algorithms (such as the GAG keyboard[6]);

- Second, the use of a word prediction system. One of the most classic use of a prediction system is to provide a set of the most probable words from the beginning of the user input. If one of the proposed words is the desired one, the user can then validate this word instead of continuing inputting via the keyboard. This reduces the number of characters to be entered. Several systems have been proposed on this principle like [1].

Both methods have advantages, but also disadvantages: in the first case, no matter the layout, some characters will still be distant on the keyboard. For the second proposal, the position of the word list prediction may not be optimal: it may be placed on one side of the keyboard, as for KeyStrokes or cover a part of the keyboard as proposed in the POBox system [4].

In order to reduce the movement of the pointing device, we propose a system between the two main lines of research described above: the KeyGlass system offers the most likely characters near the last entered.

2. KEYGLASS SYSTEM

2.1 Principle

Keyglass is a system that provides the user with additional characters throughout the text input. These characters are dynamically added near the last entered character. Proposed characters after each typed character are those most likely to succeed it. The objective was to minimize the distances traveled by the pointer. The text entry speed is not necessarily improved due to visual search time on new keys. To increase the probability of reducing the distances, the system also works recursively: after each new inputted character, either on a fixed key or dynamically added key, new characters are available around the last typed character (see Figure 1). However minimizing the dsplacement length reduces motor fatigue.

As the semi-transparent toolbox near the pointer proposed in the *toolglasses* [2], we chose to display additional characters on semi-transparent round keys (see figure 1). We preferred to use semi-transparency to give the user an overview of the keyboard, and so never overlapping a character by displaying another that would be positioned above. The character selection is done by clicking on the key re-

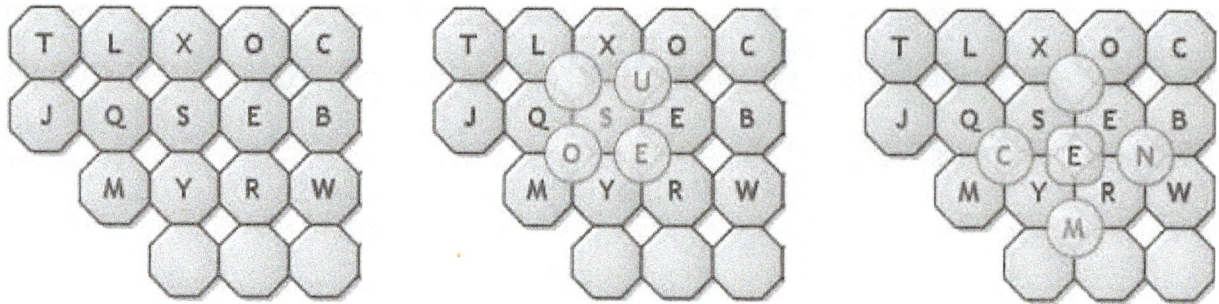

Figure 1: Left: part of the keyboard layout; middle: the KeyGlasses proposed after entering the 's'; Right: the KeyGlasses appearing after entering the 'e' which was placed on a KeyGlass.

gardless of whether this character is associated with a fixed key or with a KeyGlass.

2.2 System architecture

2.2.1 A modular system

We designed the system in a modular way in order to be able to change each part independently. Our system is split into three parts:

- **The fixed layout of the soft keyboard:** it concerns all the keys that will not move during the text input. Associated characters with these keys are also fixed. This set of keys / characters is described in an XML format. We chose an XML language because it allows to easily change the characteristics of the basic keyboard. We can change the shape, position, color of a key and its associated character. This fixed layout is thus completely independent of KeyGlasses that can be added on top;

- **The prediction system:** it receives the characters entered by the user. From these characters, it returns a ranking of characters that have the highest probability of being typed;

- **The display manager:** it manages the display of the KeyGlasses above the fixed keyboard. It handles the KeyGlasses' positions, their shape and color. For each keyglass, it associates one of the highest ranked character with the additional key.

2.2.2 Operating Mode

Figure 2 shows the operating principle of the KeyGlass system. The numbers on the arrows describe the order of transmission of messages between the different modules.

1. When a character is entered, it is sent to the prediction system. At the same time, the pointer coordinates are sent to the display manager.

2. The prediction system calculates the probability of each character following the last one received. It then ranks these characters in ascending order according to their probability of appearing, before sending this classification to the display manager.

3. Finally, the display manager, after determining the KeyGlasses positions, affects each character on a Key-Glass and returns the information to the soft keyboard that displays them.

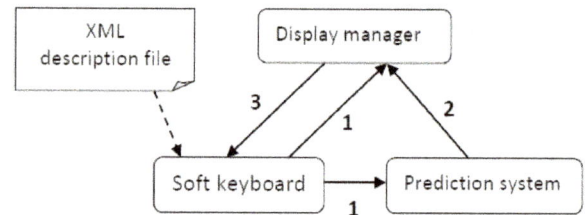

Figure 2: Architecture of KeyGlass system

Once the KeyGlasses are displayed above the soft keyboard, they are considered by the system as belonging to the soft keyboard. Thus, as we mentioned in Section 2.1, this process can operate recursively. Pressing a KeyGlass to enter a character leads exactly to the same process that we have described above.

2.2.3 Communication protocol

We used the IVY bus for communication between the different modules. To facilitate the replacement of a module with another one, we defined a communication protocol. Thus, each module knows exactly what it can receive and / or send. Replacing a module with another is easy: the new module must be connected to the IVY bus and follow the communication protocol.

To be compatible with the E-ASSISTE platform [5], this communication protocol uses the same protocol than E-ASSISTE. The various messages respecting this protocol can also be collected by the E-ASSISTE platform and enable analysis of user input and functioning of KeyGlass system.

3. REFERENCES

[1] C. Beck, G. Seisenbacher, G. Edelmayer, and W. Zagler. First user test results with the predictive typing system fasty. In *9th ICCHP : Computer Helping People with Special Needs*, pages 813–819, 2004.

[2] E. Bier, M. Stone, K. Pier, W. Buxton, and T. DeRose. Toolglass and magic lenses: the see-through interface. In *Proc. of SIGGRAPH'93*, pages 73–80. ACM Press, 1993.

[3] I. MacKenzie and S. Zhang. The design and evaluation of a high-performance soft keyboard. In *Proc. of CHI'99*, pages 25–31. ACM Press, 1999.

[4] T. Masui. An efficient text input method for pen-based computers. In *Proc. of CHI'98*, pages 328–335. ACM Press/Addison-Wesley Publishing Co., 1998.

[5] M. Raynal, S. Maubert, N. Vigouroux, F. Vella, and L. Magnien. E-assiste: A platform allowing evaluation of text input system. In *Proc. of UAHCI'05*. Lawrence Erlabaum Associates (LEA), 2005.

[6] M. Raynal and N. Vigouroux. Genetic algorithm to generate optimized soft keyboard. In *CHI '05 extended abstracts*, pages 1729–1732. ACM Press, 2005.

[7] F. Vella, N. Vigouroux, and P. Truillet. Sokeyto: a design and simulation environment of software keyboards. In A. Pruski and H. Knops, editors, *8th European conference for the advancement of assistive technology in europe*, pages 723–727. IOS Press, 2005.

Phoneme-based Predictive Text Entry Interface

Ha Trinh
Northeastern University

hatrinh@ccs.neu.edu

Annalu Waller
University of Dundee

awaller@computing.dundee.ac.uk

Keith Vertanen
Montana Tech

kvertanen@mtech.edu

Per Ola Kristensson
University of St Andrews

pok@st-andrews.ac.uk

Vicki L. Hanson
Rochester Institute of Technology

vlhics@rit.edu

ABSTRACT

Phoneme-based text entry provides an alternative typing method for nonspeaking individuals who often experience difficulties in orthographic spelling. In this paper, we investigate the application of rate enhancement strategies to improve the user performance of phoneme-based text entry systems. We have developed a phoneme-based predictive typing system, which employs statistical language modeling techniques to dynamically reduce the phoneme search space and offer accurate word predictions. Results of a case study with a nonspeaking participant demonstrated that our rate enhancement strategies led to improved text entry speed and error rates.

Categories and Subject Descriptors

K.4.2 [**Computers and Society**]: Social Issues – *assistive technologies for persons with disabilities.*

General Terms

Performance, Design, Human Factors.

Keywords

Phoneme-based text entry; prediction; speech impairments.

1. INTRODUCTION

It is well documented that people with severe speech impairments often face challenges in literacy acquisition [4]. Without literacy skills, they are unable to effectively use conventional orthographic-based text entry approaches. In addition, speech impairments are often accompanied by reduced motor control, which restricts the affected individuals from accessing traditional input methods such as full-sized keyboards.

Previous research has proposed phoneme-based text entry as an alternative typing approach for people with spelling difficulties [3]. By combining sequences of phonemes (i.e. speech sounds), spoken or written words can be created without knowledge of orthographic spelling. Existing phoneme-based systems,

ASSETS'14, October 20–22 2014, Rochester, NY, USA.
ACM 978-1-4503-2720-6/14/10.
http://dx.doi.org/10.1145/2661334.2661424

however, suffer from a number of usability issues, including poor entry rate, difficult access methods to select phonemes, and high learning demands [1].

We began to address this issue in our previous work on applying prediction methods to phoneme entry [5]. We developed the iSCAN system [5], which provides two rate enhancement strategies: *dynamic phoneme layout* and *word auto-completion*. iSCAN dynamically rearranges the phoneme layout to allow for faster access to the most probable next phonemes. The word auto-completion offers a single word prediction based on the current phoneme prefix and prior words. Results of our evaluations evidenced the effectiveness of our predictive strategies [5]. However, we also identified the need to provide enhanced support during the phoneme search process and to improve the hit rate of word predictions.

In our current work, we have refined iSCAN to develop iSCAN-2. iSCAN-2 increases the hit rate of the word predictions by offering a *5-word prediction menu* that is seamlessly integrated into the phoneme layout. In addition to the *dynamic phoneme layout*, the system offers a *phoneme set reduction* feature that dynamically narrows down the phoneme search space.

2. iSCAN-2 DESIGN
2.1 Phoneme Entry Method

Implemented as an iPad application, iSCAN-2 provides access to 42 spoken phonemes from the Jolly Phonics literacy program [2] using a two-layer pie menu interface specifically designed for users with limited dexterity. The phonemes are classified into 7 groups and mapped onto 7 directions on the front layer of the pie menu (Figure 1a). Phoneme with the highest probability of entry in each group (as estimated from a 6-gram phoneme language model) is chosen as the representative of the group and displayed on the front layer. Selecting a phoneme group on the front layer switches the pie menu to the phoneme layer, which displays all phonemes within the group (Figure 1b).

The phoneme entry consists of three steps: (1) selecting the correct phoneme group from the front layer; (2) navigating within the phoneme layer to search for the intended phoneme; (3) moving back to the center circle to confirm the selection.

2.2 Rate Enhancement Strategies
2.2.1 5-Word Prediction Pie Menu

Once the user has selected a phoneme and moved back to the center circle, the pie menu switches to the prediction layer displaying up to 5 most probable words (Figure 1c). The word probabilities are estimated from a 3-gram word language model, taking into account the current phoneme prefix and up to two

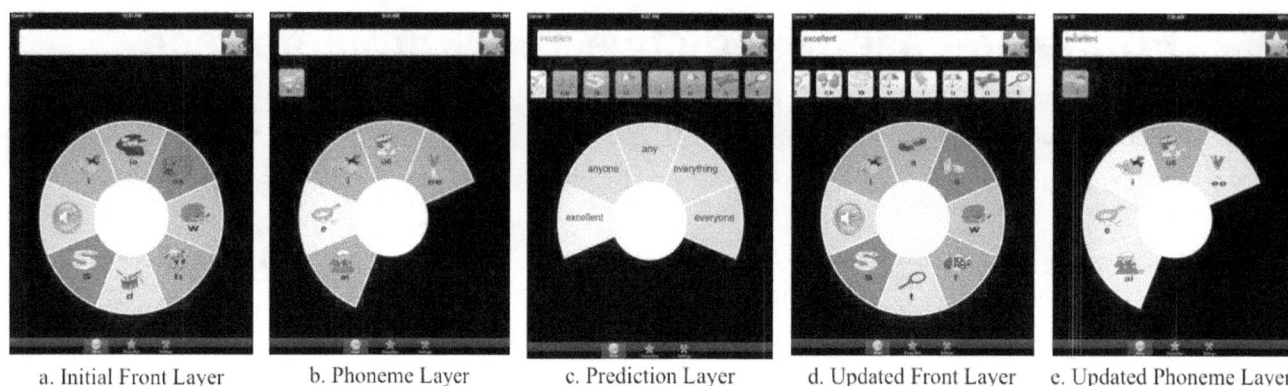

| a. Initial Front Layer | b. Phoneme Layer | c. Prediction Layer | d. Updated Front Layer | e. Updated Phoneme Layer |

Figure 1. Five stages of the pie menu in the process of creating the word *"excellent"*

prior words. The user navigates the prediction layer to identify the target word, then moving back to the center circle to confirm the selection and switch back to the front layer. If the target word has not appeared on the prediction menu, the user can touch an empty area (i.e. the black area) to escape from the prediction layer and continue entering the next phonemes. Auditory feedback is provided throughout the navigation process to aid users with limited reading skills.

2.2.2 Dynamic Phoneme Layout

After each phoneme or word selection, the system recalculates the probability of entry of each phoneme and rearranges the phoneme layout accordingly. The most probable next phoneme in each group becomes its new representative and appears on the front layer of the pie menu (see Figure 1d). The remaining phonemes in the group are reordered so that phonemes with higher probabilities are closer to the representative phoneme and hence require fewer movements to navigate to from the representative phoneme.

2.2.3 Dynamic Phoneme Set Reduction

After each phoneme selection, the system greys out any phonemes *not* in the most 20 probable next phonemes as determined by the 6-gram phoneme language model and a pronunciation dictionary. For example, in Figure 1e, three phonemes in the "Wide Mouth" phoneme group have been greyed out. If all phonemes from a group are eliminated, that group will be greyed out from the front layer. This provides additional visual cues for a more guided phoneme search. Our theoretical evaluation showed that the dynamically reduced 20-phoneme set achieved a very high average hit rate of 97.2%.

3. FORMATIVE EVALUATION

We report results of a case study with a nonspeaking adult, comparing the usability of three versions of our phoneme-based text entry interface: *non-predictive* (i.e. all the rate enhancement features are turned off), *iSCAN* (with dynamic phoneme layout and word auto-completion), and *iSCAN-2*.

3.1 Participant

Our participant is a 41-year-old male adult who has cerebral palsy and limited literacy as measured by our pre-study literacy tests. The participant had used our previous iSCAN system for four months prior to this study.

3.2 Procedure

The study consisted of four sessions, including one training session on iSCAN-2 and three testing sessions. In each testing

session, the participant was asked to transcribe 10 randomly generated phrases as quickly and accurately as possible. The participant used iSCAN in Session 2, followed by the non-predictive version in Session 3 and iSCAN-2 in Session 4.

3.3 Results and Discussion

We measured the participant's entry rates in words per minute (WPM). His text entry accuracy was measured as word error rate (WER). The results were: *non-predictive* (1.14 WPM, 50% WER), *iSCAN* (2.54 WPM, 19.26% WER), *iSCAN-2* (4.19 WPM, 0% WER).

The participant expressed a strong preference for the 5-word prediction over the word auto-completion in iSCAN. Even with limited reading skills, he showed very little problems selecting desired words from the menu with support of the auditory feedback. This suggests that, for users who rely heavily on the predictions, it is crucial to maintain high prediction accuracy even at the cost of the physical and cognitive workload required to scan a multi-word menu. However, the presentation of the prediction results should be carefully designed to minimize such workload and facilitate the scanning process.

4. CONCLUSION

We present the development and formative evaluation of a phoneme-based predictive text entry system. While our system was specifically designed for nonspeaking individuals, it could potentially be applicable to a wider population who experience spelling difficulties.

5. REFERENCES

[1] Goodenough-Trepagnier, C., Prather, P. Communication systems for the nonvocal based on frequent phoneme sequences. *Journal of Speech and Hearing Research*, 24. 322-329.

[2] Lloyd, S.M. *The Phonics Handbook*. Jolly Learning Ltd., Chigwell, 1998.

[3] Schroeder, J.E. Improved spelling for persons with learning disabilities. in *20th International Conference on Technology and Persons with Disabilities*, (California, USA, 2005).

[4] Smith, M. *Literacy and augmentative and alternative communication*. Elsevier Academic Press, 2005.

[5] Trinh, H., Waller, A., Vertanen, K., Kristensson, P. O., Hanson, V. L. iSCAN: A phoneme-based predictive communication aid for nonspeaking individuals. in *ASSETS'12*, (Colorado, USA, 2012).

Speech Dasher: A Demonstration of Text Input using Speech and Approximate Pointing

Keith Vertanen
Montana Tech
Butte, Montana, USA
kvertanen@mtech.edu

David J.C. MacKay
Cambridge University Engineering Department
Cambridge, UK
djcm1@cam.ac.uk

ABSTRACT

Speech Dasher is a novel text entry interface in which users first speak their desired text and then use the zooming interface Dasher to confirm and correct the recognition result. After several hours of practice, users wrote using Speech Dasher at 40 (corrected) words per minute. They did this using only speech and the direction of their gaze (obtained via an eye tracker). Despite an initial recognition word error rate of 22%, users corrected virtually all recognition errors.

Categories and Subject Descriptors

K.4.2 [**Computers and Society**]: Social Issues - assistive technologies for persons with disabilities.

Keywords

Speech recognition, eye tracking, error correction

1. INTRODUCTION

While people can dictate text to a computer quickly, correcting speech recognition errors can substantially reduce entry rates. Corrections can be made via speech, but recognizers tend to make similar mistakes when the same text is spoken during a correction attempt. Using other input modalities for correction such as a keyboard and a mouse can help avoid a frustrating cascade of errors. But such modalities often require precise motor control that some users lack.

Dasher [4] is a text entry interface in which users write by navigating a world of nested boxes (Figure 1). Each box is labeled with a letter and a box's size is proportional to the letter's probability under a language model. Letters appear in alphabetical order from top to bottom. Users control Dasher using some type of pointing device (e.g. a mouse, stylus, or eye-tracker). Crucially, Dasher works well even when a user's pointing accuracy is poor. Currently Dasher is one of the fastest ways to enter text using an eye tracker [1].

In Speech Dasher, users first speak their desired text to a speech recognizer. Dasher's probability model is modified to predict not only the recognizer's best hypothesis but also its competing alternatives. Here we focus on the performance of Speech Dasher when driven using an eye tracker. Our presentation here is necessarily brief. For further details about the interface, model and evaluation, see [2, 3].

ASSETS'14, October 20–22, 2014, Rochester, NY, USA.
ACM 978-1-4503-2720-6/14/10.
http://dx.doi.org/10.1145/2661334.2661420.

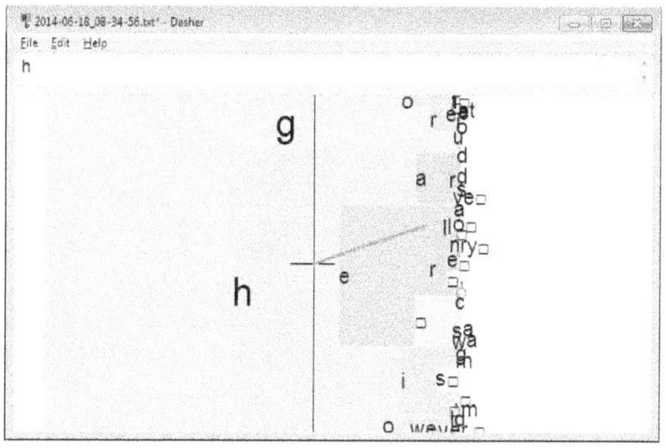

Figure 1: The Dasher interface. The user has currently written "h". The red line shows the direction a user would point in order to write "hello".

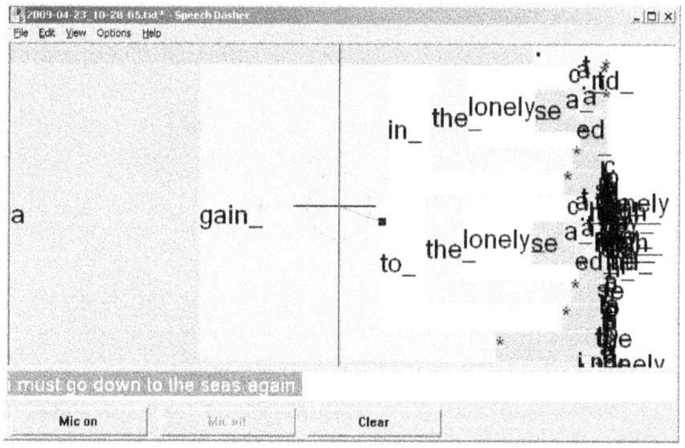

Figure 2: The Speech Dasher interface. The user is midway through the sentence "I must go down to the seas again to the lonely sea and the sky". The user must now choose between the word "in" or "to".

2. INTERFACE AND MODEL

In Speech Dasher, users first speak their intended text and then navigate using Dasher to confirm and correct the recognition result (Figure 2). *Primary predictions* are the words that Speech Dasher thinks are most probable at the current location. Primary predictions appear in alphabetical order and are always big and easy to navigate to. In Figure 2, the words "in" and "to" are the current primary predictions.

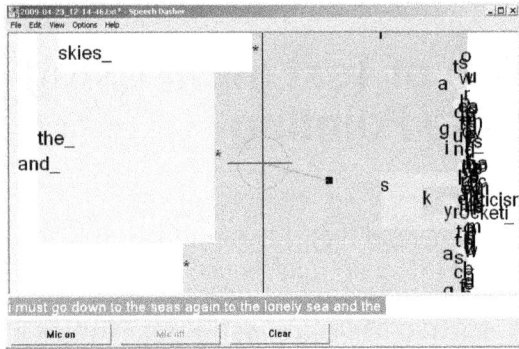

Figure 3: The user wants to write "sky" but the primary prediction was "skies". The escape box allows "sky" to be spelled using information from the recognition result and from a letter language model.

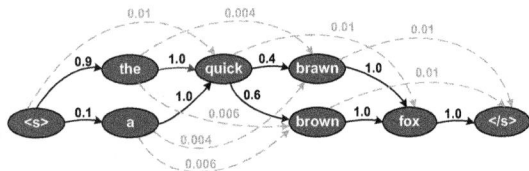

Figure 4: Lattice after the new edges in red were added to cover all one-word insertion errors.

The recognizer may also have a set of less probable word predictions. These *secondary predictions* appear below the primary predictions inside the *escape box*. The escape box is a red asterisk box appearing at word boundaries. Inside the escape box, the model offers the secondary word predictions as well as all the other letters of the alphabet (Figure 3). This makes it possible to write any word, regardless of whether it was predicted by the speech recognizer or not.

The backbone of Speech Dasher's probability model is the word lattice obtained from the speech recognizer for a given utterance. A lattice is graph containing the word hypotheses explored during the recognizer's search including acoustic and language model scores. We prune the lattice to remove unlikely hypotheses. We also convert the lattice scores to posterior probabilities. Finally we add edges that skip over words in order to cover all one-word insertion errors (Figure 4). The probability of skip edges was set to a constant multiplied by the probabilities of the skipped edges.

Each box in Dasher needs a probability distribution over all letters (including space). This is done by finding the set of lattice paths consistent with the current symbol history. Given the lattice in Figure 4, if the symbol history is "the_quick_br", there is one path to "brawn" and one path to "brown". Given these paths, the model predicts that the next symbol would be either "a" or "o". A letter's probability is based on the total penalties incurred by its path.

A sequence of letters may not be in the lattice, for example if the user spells out a word using the escape box. After completing the out-of-lattice word, Speech Dasher tries to get the user back on track somewhere in the lattice. We assume the recognizer has made a deletion or substitution error somewhere. We initiate a new search, allowing paths to make one error (Figure 5). Paths incur different penalties for using a deletion error or a substitution error. If no paths are found using one error, two errors are used, and so on. Using the paths allowed to make one or more errors, we calculate the probability distribution over all letters.

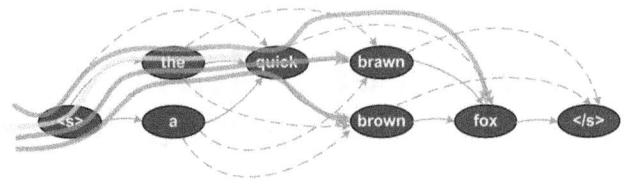

Figure 5: The user has written "the_quiet_". A substitution at "quick" allows the red paths to reach "brawn" and "brown" and the blue path to reach "fox". An insertion before "quick" allows the green path to reach "quick". Currently we would predict the letters "b", "f" and "q".

3. FORMATIVE USER STUDY

We conducted a longitudinal study with three users we anticipated would have different levels of recognition accuracy due to their accent. The user denoted US1 was American, UK1 (the second author) was British, and DE1 was German.

Users completed 6–8 training sessions followed by 3 test sessions. In each session, users wrote newswire sentences for 15 minutes using normal Dasher or Speech Dasher. After a break, they wrote for 15 minutes in the other condition. The order of conditions was swapped between sessions. We used a Tobii P10 eye tracker calibrated at the start of each session. We give results on the final 3 test sessions.

Users' initial recognition results had a word error rate (WER) of 22%. The WER varied significantly between users: 7.8% for US1, 12.4% for UK1, and 46.7% for DE1. In both conditions, we measured the error rate of the user's final text. Users left few errors uncorrected. The final WER was 1.3% in Dasher and 1.8% in Speech Dasher.

Users' average entry rate was 20 wpm in Dasher and 40 wpm in Speech Dasher. In Speech Dasher, users showed a wide range of entry rates, presumably due to their differing recognition error rates: US1 54 wpm, UK1 42 wpm, and DE1 23 wpm. On sentences with at least one recognition error, users still wrote at 30 wpm in Speech Dasher.

4. CONCLUSIONS

While our user study was small and used able-bodied users, preliminary results show Speech Dasher may be a promising input method for people who want to dictate text via speech but cannot use a conventional keyboard and mouse for correction. After four hours of practice, users were able to write nearly error-free at 40 wpm despite an initial speech-recognition error rate of 22%.

5. REFERENCES

[1] D. Rough, K. Vertanen, and P. O. Kristensson. An evaluation of Dasher with a high-performance language model as a gaze communication method. In *Proc. AVI*, May 2014.

[2] K. Vertanen. *Efficient Correction Interfaces for Speech Recognition*. PhD thesis, University of Cambridge, Cambridge, UK, April 2009.

[3] K. Vertanen and D. J. C. MacKay. Speech Dasher: Fast writing using speech and gaze. In *Proc. CHI*, pages 595–598, April 2010.

[4] D. J. Ward, A. F. Blackwell, and D. J. C. MacKay. Dasher - a data entry interface using continuous gestures and language models. In *Proc. UIST*, pages 129–137, 2000.

Text Entry by Raising the Eyebrow with *HaMCoS*

[Demo Proposal]

Torsten Felzer
Inst. for Mechatronic Systems
Techn. Universität Darmstadt
Petersenstr. 30, D-64287 Darmstadt, Germany
felzer@ims.tu-darmstadt.de

Stephan Rinderknecht
Inst. for Mechatronic Systems
Techn. Universität Darmstadt
Petersenstr. 30, D-64287 Darmstadt, Germany
rinderknecht@ims.tu-darmstadt.de

ABSTRACT

This demo actually showcases not one but four different text entry methods for persons with very severe physical disabilities. All four rely on the same kind of input signals: tiny contractions of the brow muscle which are captured using electromechanical coupling. The input device involves a piezoelectric element which is attached to the user's forehead and kept in place with the help of an elastic sports headband. The switch-like signals are used in combination with the *HaMCoS* system – which allows to fully emulate a two-button mouse – and various auxiliary applications to enter text. This proposal talks about the input hardware in more detail and describes the text entry ideas shown in the demo.

Categories and Subject Descriptors

H.5.2 [**Information Interfaces and Presentation**]: User Interfaces—*Input devices and strategies*; K.4.2 [**Computers and Society**]: Social Issues—*Assistive technologies for persons with disabilities*

General Terms

Human Factors

Keywords

Human-computer interaction, intentional muscle contractions, keyboard replacement, mouse emulator, word prediction, ambiguous keyboard

1. INTRODUCTION

Certain progressive diseases end in a so-called "locked-in" state, where communication with the outside world using physical abilities is nearly impossible. The only exception is sometimes retained physical control over a single muscle, for example, a facial muscle. The system featured in this demo – depicted in Figure 1 – tries to provide a communication channel for members of that user group.

ASSETS'14, October 20–22, 2014, Rochester, NY, USA.
ACM 978-1-4503-2720-6/14/10.
http://dx.doi.org/10.1145/2661334.2661418.

Figure 1: Usage of *HaMCos* and *StartScreen* for launching framework applications.

2. INPUT HARDWARE

The "HAnds-free Mouse COntrol System" (*HaMCoS*) relies on tiny intentional contractions of an arbitrary muscle as input signals. They are detected with the help of a very sensitive piezoelectric element attached to that muscle. To illustrate the idea, a headband has been designed to capture the activity of the brow muscle. The resulting sensor only requires frowning, that is, extremely little physical effort.

3. TARGET SOFTWARE

The raw input signals are translated into two related contraction events: single contractions (plain, isolated input signals) or double contractions (a series of two input signals in quick succession). To realize movements of the mouse pointer, *HaMCoS* reacts to those events by following transitions in a *finite state machine* (FSM) with five states.

The initial state (active at program start) corresponds to a halted mouse pointer, that is, nothing moves. In the other four states, the mouse pointer is displaced repeatedly into one of the four cardinal directions. To set the mouse pointer in motion, the user generates a double contraction, which activates the "Left" state at that point. Subsequently, single contractions cycle through the four moving states, and a double contraction halts the mouse pointer and emulates a click at the current position. After a double contraction, the user actually first selects a click type by active scanning.

The effect is complete mouse emulation, and the auxiliary software described below relies on that to allow text entry.

3.1 On-Screen Keyboard

The most straightforward idea to realize text entry using mouse pointer movements is implemented in the *MouseEditor* [3]. This framework application consists of an on-screen keyboard with large buttons for all characters (which are entered by clicking on the corresponding button). It also offers word completion and everything one would expect from an editor program, including a movable text cursor, as well as CUT and PASTE.

3.2 Character Coding

A common technique for text entry involves encoding the selectable characters with certain patterns and reproducing those to enter them. One example is Morse code where each character is associated with a unique sequence of dots and dashes. The *LURDWriter* [2] leverages that idea and combines it with *HaMCoS* – which coincides with horizontal or vertical (but not diagonal) mouse pointer movement.

Placing the mouse pointer repeatedly in the center of an input square, setting it in motion, and sending it "Left", "Up", "Right", "Down", results in a sequence of edges of the square crossed (intersected) in each round. Distinguishing between valid and invalid sequences, and setting certain rules to restrict valid ones, particularly with respect to sequence length, finally defines a code with a limited number of elements which are easy to enter with *HaMCoS*.

Each code element is assigned to a selectable character which may be a letter, a digit, a special character (e.g., punctuation), or BACKSPACE. The associations for the letter characters are loosely based on Morse code (in terms of the time needed to produce the corresponding sequence).

3.3 Subset Scanning

To select one option among a set of options (in the context of text entry, the term "option" typically refers to a character) with the help of scanning, the set is split into several, usually disjoint subsets, which are linearly scanned (i.e., cyclically highlighted until the user generates an input signal). The corresponding subset is spit again, and the process is repeated until a subset with only one element is selected. The subsets in the same scan cycle often have an equal number of elements (e.g., in row-column scanning), but this is not necessarily so.

In *Scan_LURD* [4], the choice of subsets leans against the associations between characters and code sequences in the *LURDWriter*. Therefore, it is not surprising that the entry rates reported for the two framework applications is similar. However, the *LURDWriter* requires its user to learn a whole new way of entering text, whereas *Scan_LURD* is much more intuitive.

Scanning does not rely on actual mouse pointer movement. The application just "listens" to the plain input signals captured by *HaMCoS*.

3.4 Scanning Ambiguous Keyboard

Qanti [1] is an implementation of a scanning ambiguous keyboard [5], allowing efficient text entry with only a single input signal. It basically consists of two sets of virtual keys. Initially, four keys are scanned linearly. The first three of them are ambiguous keys, representing roughly one third of the characters of the alphabet each.

Table 1: Framework Applications

Application	Principle	Introduced At	Entry Rate
MouseEditor	On-Screen Keyboard	CWUAAT 2006	1.2 wpm
LURDWriter	Character Coding	ASSETS 2006	1.8 wpm
Scan_LURD	Subset Scanning	Telehealth/AT 2008	2.0 wpm
Qanti	Scan. Amb. Keyboard	ICCHP 2010	2.5 wpm

Entering a word is T9-like, that is, the user enters a sequence of characters by successively generating an input signal while the virtual key corresponding to the character to be entered is highlighted. As the user enters a sequence, the program looks for matches or extensions in an internal dictionary and displays them on the virtual keys belonging to the second set mentioned above.

Once the desired word is in the list, the user can switch over to the second set by selecting the fourth key in the first set. The second set allows to select the desired candidate using row-column scanning. Waiting for one cycle after the last character selection calls up a menu (instead of the candidate list) upon selection of the fourth "linear key", which offers many helpful features (e.g., error correction or a full-blown scanning keyboard for out-of-dictionary words).

4. CONCLUSION

HaMCoS is an assistive system for persons who cannot use their hands. It allows mouse control by frowning, and auxiliary software employs this to offer hands-free text entry.

Table 1 summarizes the framework applications presented in the demo. The mentioned entry rates were achieved in various user trials with the single same participant, reported in the conference papers cited in this proposal.

5. ACKNOWLEDGMENTS

This work is partially supported by DFG grant FE 936/6-1 "EFFENDI – EFficient and Fast text ENtry for persons with motor Disabilities of neuromuscular orIgin".

6. REFERENCES

[1] T. Felzer, I. S. MacKenzie, P. Beckerle, and S. Rinderknecht. Qanti: A software tool for quick ambiguous non-standard text input. In *Proc. ICCHP 2010*, pages 128–135. Springer Heidelberg, 2010.

[2] T. Felzer and R. Nordmann. Alternative text entry using different input methods. In *Proc. ASSETS 2006*, pages 10–17. ACM Press, 2006.

[3] T. Felzer and R. Nordmann. Speeding up hands-free text entry. In *Proc. CWUAAT'06*, pages 27–36. Cambridge University Press, 2006.

[4] T. Felzer, B. Strah, and R. Nordmann. Automatic and self-paced scanning for alternative text entry. In *Proc. IASTED Telehealth/AT 2008*, pages 1–6, 2008.

[5] I. S. MacKenzie and T. Felzer. SAK: Scanning Ambiguous Keyboard for efficient one-key text entry. *ACM Trans. Comp.-Human Int.*, 17(3):11:1–39, 2010.

Text Entry Using a Compact Keypad with *OSDS*

[Demo Proposal]

Torsten Felzer
Inst. for Mechatronic Systems
Techn. Universität Darmstadt
Petersenstr. 30, D-64287 Darmstadt, Germany
felzer@ims.tu-darmstadt.de

Stephan Rinderknecht
Inst. for Mechatronic Systems
Techn. Universität Darmstadt
Petersenstr. 30, D-64287 Darmstadt, Germany
rinderknecht@ims.tu-darmstadt.de

ABSTRACT

This demo is about *OSDS*, a very powerful tool allowing computer users who cannot use a standard keyboard to replace that with a compact number-pad-like device, the so-called *DualPad*. The idea is to offer efficient text entry *despite* the smaller number of keys. The tool basically implements two input methods: One involving the selection of row and column of a character in a two-dimensional virtual keyboard and the other one using an ambiguous keyboard with dictionary-based disambiguation. A special focus is on its applicability to "real-world" use.

Categories and Subject Descriptors

H.5.2 [**Information Interfaces and Presentation**]: User Interfaces—*Input devices and strategies*; K.4.2 [**Computers and Society**]: Social Issues—*Assistive technologies for persons with disabilities*

General Terms

Human Factors

Keywords

Human-computer interaction, keyboard replacement, mouse emulator, word prediction, ambiguous keyboard, neuromuscular disease

1. INTRODUCTION

Using a standard full-size keyboard for computer operation is cumbersome for many persons with neuromuscular diseases although mostly being physically able to do so because of the "travel" distances between consecutive keys, especially if the keys are far apart. All keys have to be aimed at carefully (still resulting in many typos), so text entry usually requires constant repositioning of the hands, thus being terribly slow. The demo presents a replacement solution involving a compact keypad (see Figure 1), which has been identified as the perfect alternative for that user group [2].

ASSETS'14, October 20–22, 2014, Rochester, NY, USA.
ACM 978-1-4503-2720-6/14/10.
http://dx.doi.org/10.1145/2661334.2661419.

Figure 1: **Usage of the *DualPad* and the newest version of *OSDS*.**

2. INPUT HARDWARE

The input hardware of the presented system is extremely inexpensive: it simply consists of an off-the-shelf 19-key numeric keypad (only 18 keys – all but NumLock – are used), equipped with keytop stickers symbolizing the functionality of each key. The advantage of this device, which replaces also a two-button mouse, is its form factor: the rotated keypad is held firmly with two hands, and its overall size makes every key reachable with the thumbs *without* repositioning; however, since every individual key roughly has normal size, it is not hard to hit the right (i.e., the intended) one.

3. TARGET SOFTWARE

"OnScreenDualScribe" (*OSDS*) is a Windows® software built around the *DualPad* detailed above. Its goal is to map every key found on a regular keyboard to a key (or sequence of keys) on the small keypad, without causing too much overhead (thereby providing a viable alternative). The idea is to intercept physical keystrokes of the user on the *DualPad* and to translate them into emulated virtual keystrokes; as a result, the software acts as an "on-screen" interface between the user and the currently active window.

Computer operation consists of a number of activities; text entry is one, mouse control another, and system configuration, for example, a third. *OSDS* offers one or more program modes for many of these activity groups. There are two modes, implementing two different methods, for text entry. They are explained in the following.

3.1 Virtual Keyboard

The basic text entry method in *OSDS* is somehow similar to row-column scanning: selectable characters are arranged in a two-dimensional grid and entered by selection of row and column. Instead of scanning, two or more keystrokes are required – that is why it is called *Dual Mode*.

To help save keystrokes, *OSDS* suggests completions of the current word prefix. Candidates are taken from a frequency-ordered dictionary with 100k entries.

3.2 Ambiguous Keyboard

The keys of an ambiguous keyboard represent more than one character each. An example is the numeric phone keypad, where the keys "2" to "9" are assigned three or four characters each.

Ambiguous Mode of *OSDS*, which is inspired by the proof-of-concept implementations in [5], offers six ambiguous keys covering all 26 letters of the alphabet. In analogy to T9 (for entering SMS messages), the user composes key sequences, and the program checks the same dictionary as before for matches or extensions. If there are more than one suitable candidates, the user chooses from a frequency-ordered list.

This mode is so efficient that it ultimately requires on average *less than* one keystroke per letter.

3.3 Ten Other Program Modes

In addition to text entry, *OSDS* offers a lot of functionality for specific tasks, which makes it a valuable assistant for computer operation. For example, it can check the spelling of words, update the dictionary, or emulate special keystrokes like function keys.

Besides, it has a mode for defining and sending arbitrary keystroke sequences (i.e., macros) and one to configure typematic delay and repeat. As another mode gives access to the text cursor, CUT, and PASTE, editing a text is *not* limited to deleting the character entered last (a shortcoming of many assistive text entry solutions).

Certain computing tasks, such as activating a different window, usually require a pointing device. As there are three modes completely replacing a two-button mouse each (following different approaches), there is no need to drop the *DualPad* in order to switch to another device.

4. "REAL-WORLD" USE

The tool was originally developed for a certain someone who needed an efficient and effortless alternative to the regular keyboard, as he had growing motor problems due to a progressive neuromuscular disease. He gradually switched to the new input method as the program gained maturity and participated in various user studies evaluating *OSDS* and its preliminary versions.

The direct predecessor of *OSDS* is called *DualScribe*. At first, he used an initial variant which was optimized for a game controller and did not have an ambiguous keyboard mode yet [4] to start practicing with *Dual Mode*.

When *DualScribe* was finished [1], he used that (and its more efficient *Ambiguous Mode*) for composing longer texts or emails. However, as the output only appeared in a dedicated editor window, the texts always had to be copied and pasted into the email client, for example, at the end, which was not terribly practical.

Table 1: Practice Effect

	February 2011	November 2011	January 2014
Software Version	*DualScribe* ver. 0.99	*DualScribe* ver. 1.0	*OSDS* ver. 2.0
Input Method	*Dual Mode*	*Ambiguous Mode*	*Ambiguous Mode*
Reported At	ASSETS 2011	ICCHP 2012	ICCHP 2014
Entry Rate	2.2 wpm	4.1 wpm	6.6 wpm

OSDS finally meets all his interaction needs. The tool is practically usable and he does not need any other input device any more. A recent experiment with version 2.0 [3] showed that practicing with the tool makes him faster and faster. This effect, which further emphasizes the tool's practical usability, is summarized in Table 1.

5. CONCLUSION

OSDS is a powerful tool allowing to replace the standard input devices for computer operation – full-size keyboard and mouse – with a single number pad-like device, the *DualPad*, which is held firmly and securely in both hands, and operated with the thumbs only. The left and right edges of the input device (which is rotated by 90 degrees, counter-clockwise) serve as a guide, empowering the user to control the device with a maximum of confidence and reliability.

The demo shows how the tool, which is in daily practical use, can be employed to efficiently enter text with less keys than characters.

6. ACKNOWLEDGMENTS

This work is partially supported by DFG grant FE 936/6-1 "EFFENDI – EFficient and Fast text ENtry for persons with motor Disabilities of neuromuscular orIgin".

7. REFERENCES

[1] T. Felzer, I. S. MacKenzie, and S. Rinderknecht. DualScribe: A keyboard replacement for those with Friedreich's Ataxia and related diseases. In *Proc. ICCHP 2012*, pages 431–438, Springer Heidelberg, 2012.

[2] T. Felzer, I. S. MacKenzie, and S. Rinderknecht. OnScreenDualScribe: A computer operation tool for users with a neuromuscular disease. In *Proc. HCI International 2013, UAHCI/HCII 2013, Part I, LNCS 8009*, pages 474–483. Springer Heidelberg, 2013.

[3] T. Felzer, I. S. MacKenzie, and S. Rinderknecht. Applying small-keyboard computer control to the real world. In *Proc. ICCHP 2014*, Springer Heidelberg (in press), 2014.

[4] T. Felzer and S. Rinderknecht. Using a game controller for text entry to address abilities and disabilities specific to persons with neuromuscular diseases. In *Proc. ASSETS 2011*, pages 299–300, ACM Press, 2011.

[5] I. S. MacKenzie and T. Felzer. SAK: Scanning Ambiguous Keyboard for efficient one-key text entry. *ACM Trans. Comp.-Human Int.*, 17(3):11:1–39, 2010.

Text Entry Using Single-Channel Analog Puff Input

Adam J Sporka
Department of Computer Graphics and Interaction
Faculty of Electrical Engineering, Czech Technical University in Prague
Karlovo nam. 13, 12135 Praha 2, Czech Republic
sporkaa@fel.cvut.cz

ABSTRACT

The purpose of this prototype is to demonstrate a use of puff input for text entry. The entry method is based on hierarchical scanning-like selection of characters located in a static table organized according too the letter frequency. The cursor is moved in a way similar to operating a claw crane machine with two buttons. To move the cursor to the target position the user needs to produce two puffs, the first selects the column, and the second selects the row.With a brief training the method is capable of entry rate of 5 WPM.

Categories and Subject Descriptors

H.5.2 [**Information interfaces and presentation**]: User Interfaces – Input devices and strategies;

General Terms

Design, Experimentation, Human Factors.

Keywords

Assistive technology, text input, analog input, sip-and-puff, MIDI.

1. BACKGROUND

The sip-and-puff techniques are well-known approaches to input by people with motor disabilities in assistive technology. Frequently they are used for applications such as wheelchair control.

The use of breath detection via acoustic interfaces has been reported by Al-Hashimi [1] who created an interactive environment for collaborative visual expression, and recently also by Filho at al. [2] who implemented a simple text entry method based on detection of discrete control signals.

2. DESIGN AND IMPLEMENTATION

AKAI EWI USB is a MIDI controller emulating the interface of woodwind instruments. The device quantifies the amount of airflow on the scale from 0 (no flow) to 127 (maximum) and provides this information to the host application via MIDI interface in real time (controller CC2) at interactive rates required in professional music performances. We repurposed this device as a puff pressure sensor.

The prototype consists of a simple application for Microsoft Windows 7, implemented by the author, and an AKAI EWI USB with appropriate drivers installed on the host system.

The characters were arranged in a 2D on-screen keyboard as shown in Fig. 1. The layout reflects the frequency of the English letters in a common text corpora as reported by Lewand [3]. The character layout is static.

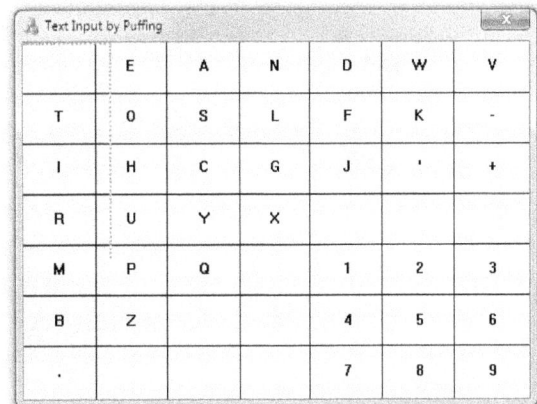

Figure 1: Screenshot of the User Interface. The trace of the cursor illustrates the process of selecting letter P.

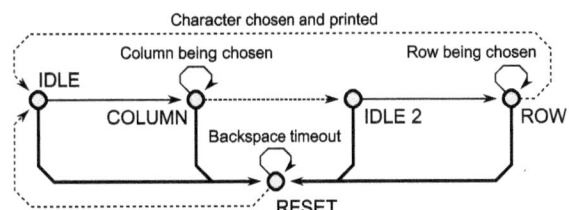

Figure 2: Function of the input technique. Dashed lines – no flow; solid lines – flow between 1 and 126 on the CC2 MIDI event scale; thick lines – maximum air flow (CC2 = 127).

A simple 2D scanning-like approach was employed. The function of the method is shown in Fig. 2. A letter is selected by placing the cursor over the desired character.

The cursor is moved in a way similar to operating a claw crane machine with two buttons. To move the cursor to the target position the user needs to produce two puffs, the first selects the column, and the second selects the row. The cursor moves until the airflow is interrupted. While the cursor is moving, it is possible to adjust the speed by modifying the intensity of the airflow. Upon the end of the second puff the application emulates a keystroke.

Maximum air flow is interpreted as the request to cancel the current selection. This is useful for the case when the user overshoots the target since the direction cannot be changed. A backspace is triggered if the flow is maintained for at least .5 seconds. A brief informal test revealed that 1 character out of 10 was entered incorrectly and the entry rate of this method was about 25 characters (5 words) per minute.

3. ACKNOWLEDGMENTS

This study has been partially supported by project TextAble (H12070; Ministry of Education, Youth and Sports of the Czech Republic.)

4. REFERENCES

[1] S. Al-Hashimi. Blowtter: A voice-controlled plotter. In *Proceedings of HCI 2006 Engage, The 20th BCS HCI Group conference in co-operation with ACM, vol. 2, London, England*, pages 41–44, September 2006.

[2] J. F. Filho, T. Valle, and W. Prata. Pufftext: A voiceless and touchless text entry solution for mobile phones. In *Proceedings of the 15th International ACM SIGACCESS Conference on Computers and Accessibility*, ASSETS '13, pages 63:1–63:2, New York, NY, USA, 2013. ACM.

[3] R. Lewand. *Cryptological mathematics*. The Mathematical Association of America, 2000.

Text Entry via Discrete and Analog Myoelectric Signals

Adam J. Sporka, Antonin Posusta, Ondrej Polacek, Tomas Flek, Jakub Otahal
Department of Computer Graphics and Interaction
Faculty of Electrical Engineering, Czech Technical University in Prague
Karlovo nam. 13, 12135 Praha 2, Czech Republic
sporkaa@fel.cvut.cz

ABSTRACT

The purpose of this prototype is to demonstrate the feasibility of text entry via detection of the surface myoelectric signals on user's body. Our system is capable to detect the movement of two fingers and the entire palm. The detector produces discrete signals as well as continuous quantifications of the exerted force. Two mappings of the signals on text entry were implemented, Scanning LetterWise and 2-FOCL, in two modes, discrete and continuous.

Categories and Subject Descriptors

H.5.2 [**Information interfaces and presentation**]: User Interfaces
– Input devices and strategies;

General Terms

Design, Experimentation, Human Factors.

Keywords

Assistive technology, text input, analog input, electromyography, biosignals.

1. INTRODUCTION

Electromyography is a set of techniques of detection the electric signals emitted by the muscles during their contraction. Surface electromyogram (sEMG) is the electrical representation of the muscular contraction. sEMG is the sum of signals emitted by the motor units, which are muscle fibers innervated by the single motoneurons. Using the sEMG, it is possible to quantify the muscle contractions.

Our system is intended for people with a disability of upper extremities who have not lost the ability to control the muscles in them. This demonstration is based on our previous article [3].

2. HARDWARE

We have implemented a portable measurement device with a USB driver. The device was able to capture the EMG signals from the user and recognize and report the movement of two fingers (typically the index finger and the little finger) and the palm.

ASSETS'14, October 20–22, 2014, Rochester, NY, USA.
ACM 978-1-4503-2720-6/14/10.
http://dx.doi.org/10.1145/2661334.2661426

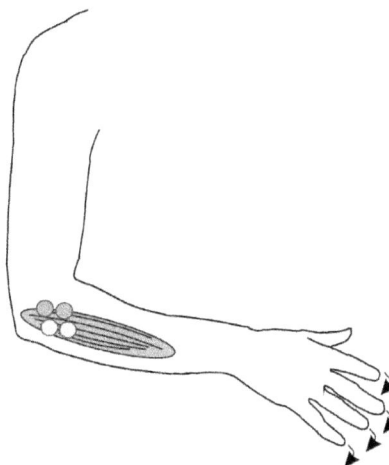

Figure 1: Placement of the electrodes

We used standard ECG type electrodes (self-adhesive Ag/AgCl) for the acquisition of the signal placed above extensor muscles on the forearm (extensor carpi ulnaris and extensor digitorum). The acquisition is performed also using our custom-made device consisting of an analog part [2] (with amplifiers and filters) and a digitizing circuit (with ARM microprocessor) which is connected to the computer over USB.

We implemented two versions of the muscle activation recognition algorithm, one allowing a discrete classification of presence of finger movement, another allowing a quantification of the movement of the entire hand.

3. TEXT ENTRY METHODS

We present three methods. Two are based on binary detection of activity ("muscle active" / "muscle inactive"). The third one is utilizing the analog output from our system, quantifying the amount of activity of the muscle.

3.1 2-FOCL

A text entry method called LetterWise was described by MacKenzie at al. [1]. In this methods, groups of 3 or 4 letters are shown on a 3×3 matrix, similar to MutliTap, a method used on 12-button mobile phones. The LetterWise method, however, uses prediction and with each entered letter, the letters in each group are reordered according to the current probability. With the direct selection used in the method, this technique results in decreased number of keystrokes needed to enter a text. See Fig. 3. We modified this

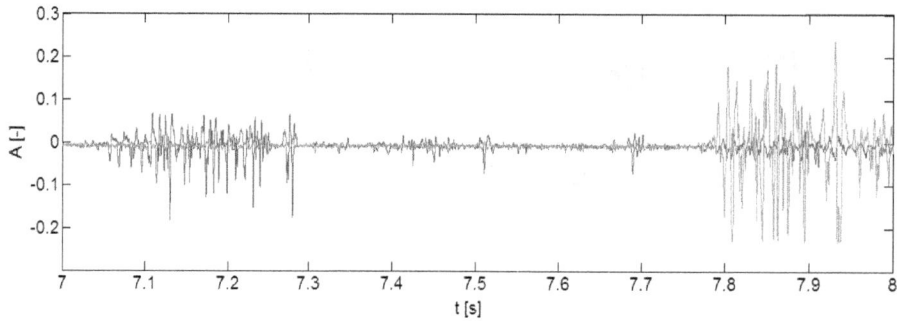

Figure 2: Myoelectric signals detected while extending two fingers - middle finger and small finger, one after another. Blue – channel 1, red – channel 2.

method so that it supports 2-key input, as shown in Fig. 4. Each "key" is mapped to a separate EMG sensor.

3.2 Scanning Letterwise Method

This method was based on the LetterWise method. Three scan selections were required to enter a character: First, the row of groups was selected, then the group, and then the character in the group. The scanning was self-paced by one finger while selection was performed by the other finger. The user could backtrack the last selection (or delete the last character) by raising the whole hand. The user interface is show in Fig. 5.

3.3 Analog input

The characters to select are organized in a matrix of n rows and m columns. The user first determines from which row the selection should be done by activating the Sensor 1 (binary interaction). Sensor 2 is reporting an analog value enabling a rapid selection of 1-of-m. Sensor 1 is then activated again to confirm the selection. The first row requires no activation of Sensor 1, the second row requires one activation, the third row two activations etc. The layout of the characters in the matrix therefore corresponds to the frequency of letters in the English alphabet so that the most frequent characters can be entered by the least amount of effort.

4. CONCLUSION

This prototype demonstrates the feasibility of text entry via detection of user's surface myoelectric signals using standard ECG electrodes. Three methods of mapping of EMG on text input input were implemented.

5. ACKNOWLEDGMENTS

This study has been partially supported by project TextAble (LH12070; Ministry of Education, Youth and Sports of the Czech Republic.)

6. REFERENCES

[1] I. S. MacKenzie, H. Kober, D. Smith, T. Jones, and E. Skepner. LetterWise: prefix-based disambiguation for mobile text input. In *Proceedings of the 14th annual ACM symposium on User interface software and technology*, UIST '01, pages 111–120, New York, NY, USA, 2001. ACM.

[2] A. Pošusta and J. Otáhal. Recording and conditioning of surface emg signal for decomposition. *Bulletin of Applied Mechanics*, 8(30), 2012.

[3] A. J. Sporka, A. Posusta, O. Polacek, T. Flek, and J. Otahal. Text entry methods controlled by myoelectric signals. *Bulletin of Applied Mechanics*, (In print).

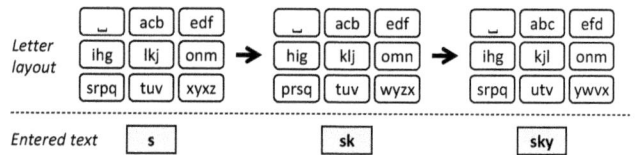

Figure 3: Typing "sky" with the LetterWise method. The example illustrates use of a dynamic layout. Note the shifting position of letters on individual keys with each entered character.

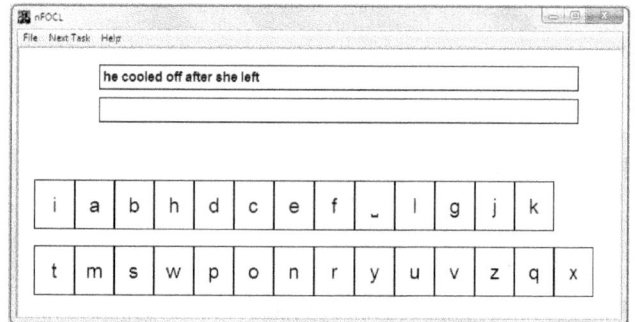

Figure 4: Stimulus for the 2-FOCL condition.

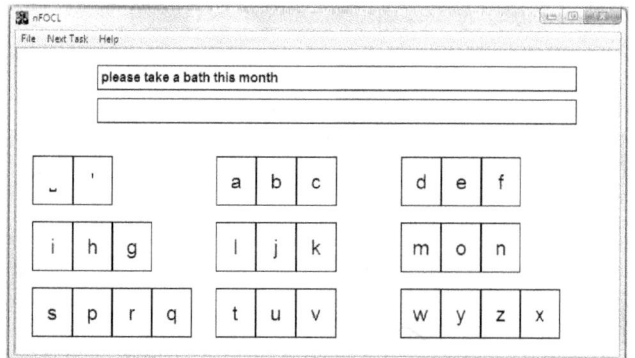

Figure 5: Stimulus for the Scanning LetterWise condition.

Author Index